Disney's Christmas Classics

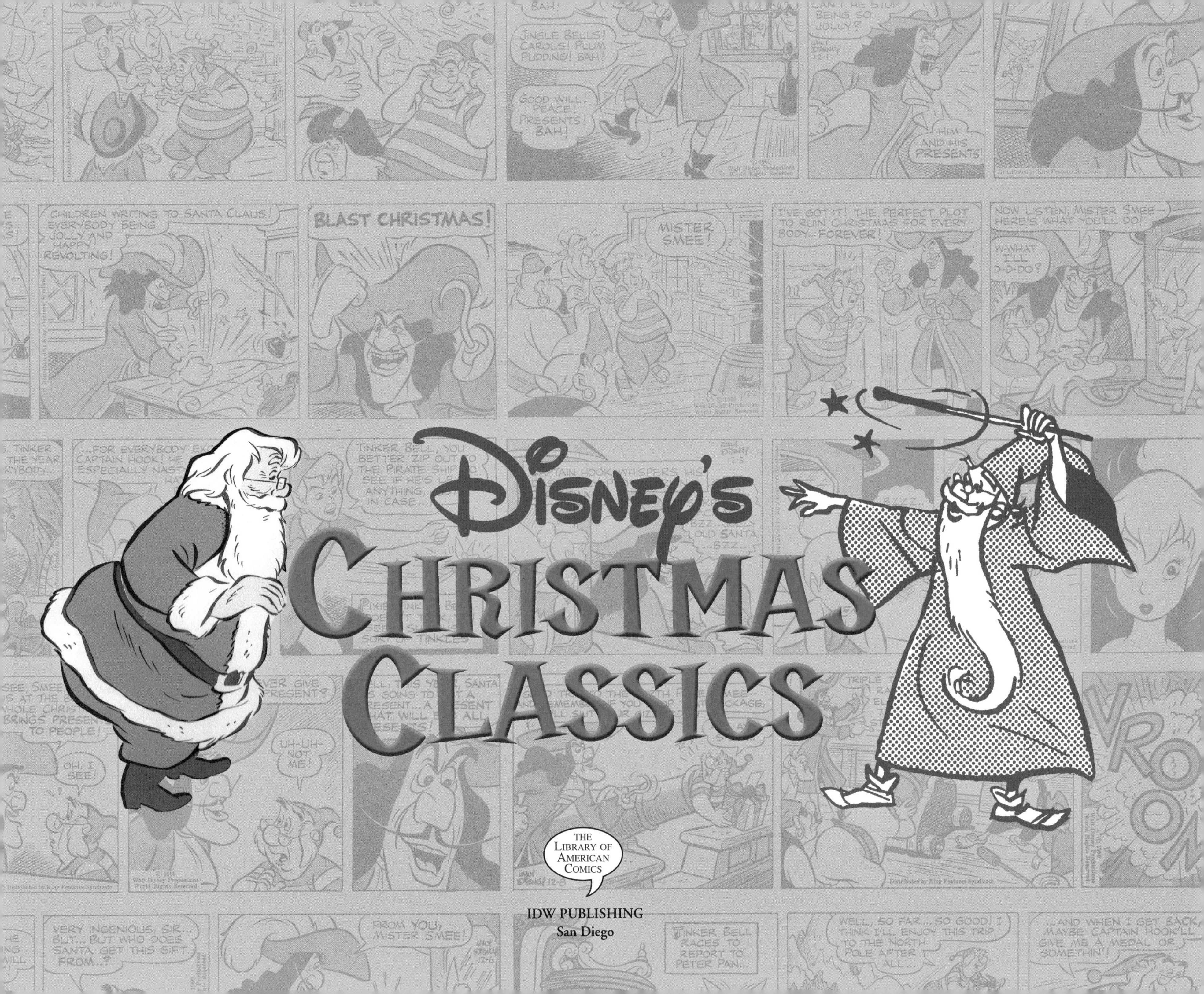
JINGLE BELLS! CAROLS! PLUM PUDDING! BAH!
GOOD WILL! PEACE! PRESENTS! BAH!
BEING SO JOLLY?
HIM AND HIS PRESENTS!
CHILDREN WRITING TO SANTA CLAUS! EVERYBODY BEING JOLLY AND HAPPY! REVOLTING!
BLAST CHRISTMAS!
MISTER SMEE!
I'VE GOT IT! THE PERFECT PLOT TO RUIN CHRISTMAS FOR EVERY-BODY... FOREVER!
NOW LISTEN, MISTER SMEE-- HERE'S WHAT YOU'LL DO!
W-WHAT I'LL D-D-DO?
UH-UH-NOT ME!
OH, I SEE!
VERY INGENIOUS, SIR... BUT... BUT WHO DOES SANTA GET THIS GIFT FROM..?
FROM YOU, MISTER SMEE!
TINKER BELL RACES TO REPORT TO PETER PAN...
WELL, SO FAR... SO GOOD! I THINK I'LL ENJOY THIS TRIP TO THE NORTH POLE AFTER ALL...
...AND WHEN I GET BACK, MAYBE CAPTAIN HOOK'LL GIVE ME A MEDAL OR SOMETHIN'!

Disney's Christmas Classics

THE LIBRARY OF AMERICAN COMICS

IDW PUBLISHING
San Diego

THE LIBRARY OF AMERICAN COMICS

EDITOR/CO-DESIGNER DEAN MULLANEY

ASSOCIATE EDITOR BRUCE CANWELL

ART DIRECTOR/CO-DESIGNER LORRAINE TURNER

CONSULTING EDITOR DAVID GERSTEIN

INTRODUCTION ALBERTO BECATTINI PUBLISHED BY TED ADAMS

RESTORATION ASSISTANTS DALE CRAIN and JOSEPH KETELS

ISBN: 978-1-68405-006-2

First Printing, September 2017

Published by:
IDW Publishing
a Division of Idea and Design Works, LLC
2765 Truxtun Road, San Diego CA 92106
www.idwpublishing.com
LibraryofAmericanComics.com

Ted Adams, Chief Executive Officer/Publisher
Greg Goldstein, Chief Operating Officer/President
Robbie Robbins, EVP/Sr. Graphic Artist
Chris Ryall, Chief Creative Officer
David Hedgecock, Editor-in-Chief
Matthew Ruzicka, CPA, Chief Financial Officer
Laurie Windrow, Senior VP of Sales and Marketing
Lorelei Bunjes, VP of Digital Services
Jerry Bennington, VP of New Product Development

Distributed to the book trade by Penguin Random House
Distributed to the comic book trade by Diamond Book Distributors

Special thanks to: Alberto Becattini, David Gerstein, Joakim Gunnarsson, Niels Houlberg Hansen, Thomas Jensen, Jim Korkis, Rolf Lindby, Jeffrey Lindenblatt, Fredrik Strömberg, and Steve Geppi at Diamond International Galleries; Becky Cline, Kevin Kern, and Joanna Pratt at the Walt Disney Archives; and Holly Brobst at the Walt Disney Archives Photo Library.

Additional thanks to Chris Cerasi, Justin Eisinger, and Alonzo Simon.

RIGHT: Part of the brochure King Features sent to newspaper editors to help sell the new *Disney Christmas Story* in 1960.

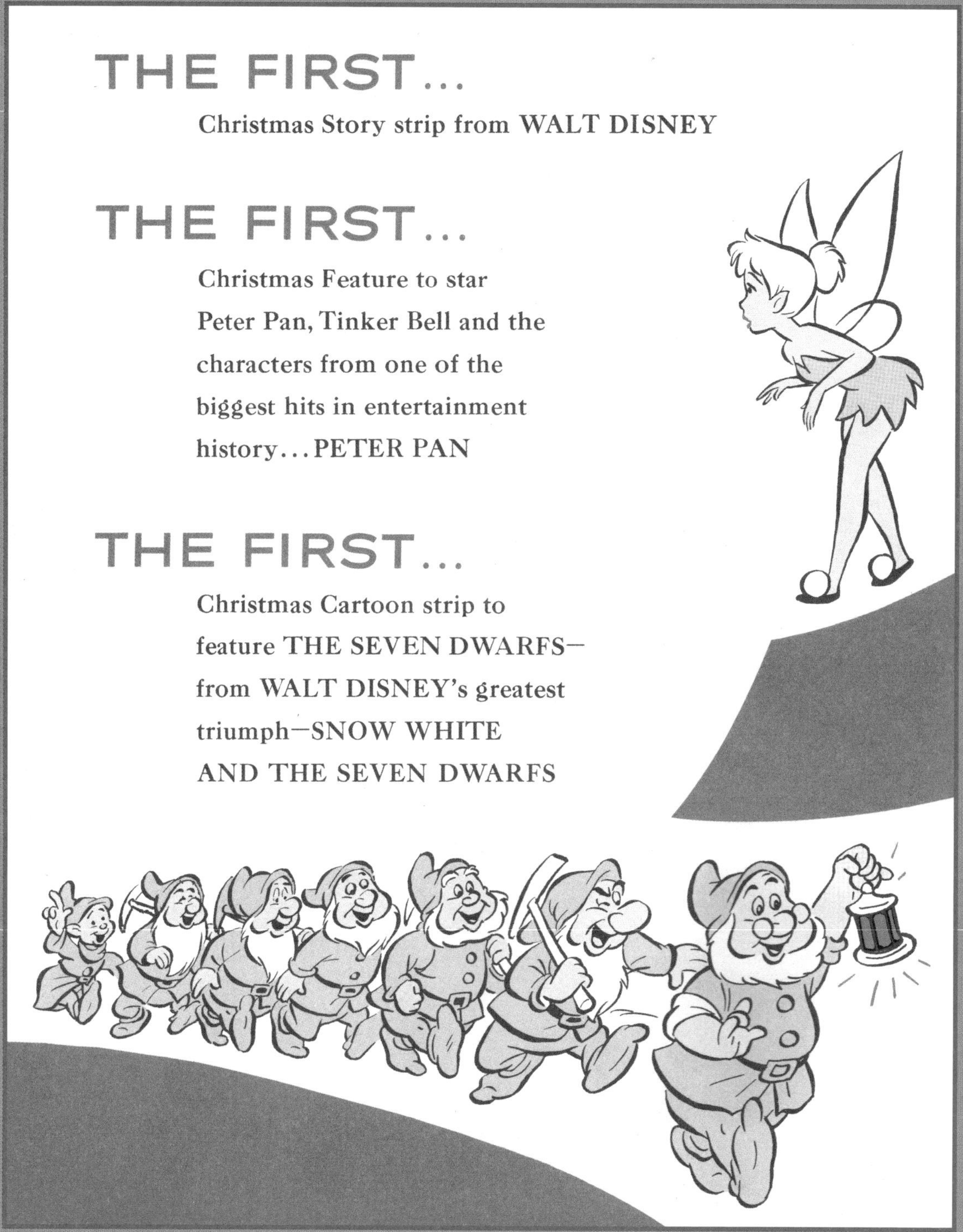
THE FIRST...
Christmas Story strip from WALT DISNEY
THE FIRST...
Christmas Feature to star Peter Pan, Tinker Bell and the characters from one of the biggest hits in entertainment history... PETER PAN
THE FIRST...
Christmas Cartoon strip to feature THE SEVEN DWARFS—from WALT DISNEY's greatest triumph—SNOW WHITE AND THE SEVEN DWARFS

PUBLISHER'S NOTE: These comic strips were created in an earlier time and may contain cartoon violence and occasional historically-dated content, such as gags about smoking, drinking, gunplay, and racial stereotypes. Needless to say, the characters in these stories wouldn't mix it up with these elements today; we include them here with the understanding that they reflect a bygone era. Enjoy the show!

MERRY CHRISTMAS, DISNEY STYLE

by ALBERTO BECATTINI

November, 1960 brought something new to the range of newspaper comic strips produced by the Walt Disney Studio. Frank Reilly, who had been the managing editor and administrator of Disney's Comic Strip Department since 1946, thought that the time was ripe for Disney to send Christmas greetings to millions of readers by means of an annual newspaper strip. He pitched the concept to King Features Syndicate, which had distributed the Disney strips since their inception in January, 1930.

King Features had once produced its own non-Disney annual Christmas strips, from 1935 until 1940, and in 1936 another syndicate, NEA, had started a long tradition of Christmas strips which would last until 2010. (Coincidentally, eleven of the NEA strips were drawn by Walt Scott, who had been a Disney story sketch artist and animator from 1938-41.) King's comics editor, Sylvan Byck, heartily approved of the proposal, realizing that the syndicate could exploit the Disney characters' popularity during the key holiday shopping season.

The characters in each story would be drawn primarily from the animated features. Disney and King did not want Mickey Mouse or Donald Duck, who had their own daily and Sunday newspaper strips, to also appear in the special Christmas continuities. In addition, Frank Reilly had been adapting scores of animated features for the *Walt Disney's Treasury of Classic Tales* Sunday series since 1952, which had made him familiar with all of the the studio's characters.

Each annual tale was to last three to four-and-a-half weeks, usually ending on Christmas Eve. (The longest story appeared in 1964, with a total of twenty-eight strips; the shortest in 1971, with just seventeen strips.)

The first sequence—which debuted on November 28, 1960—was entitled *Peter Pan's Christmas Story*, featuring characters from the 1952 animated movie. Initially set in Never Land, the story saw Captain Hook trying to sabotage Christmas with a "gift bomb." Santa Claus, also known as Kris Kringle, first appeared in the series on December 19, 1960, four days before Peter Pan intervened to foil Captain Hook's evil plan. The Seven Dwarfs also featured in the strip, their diamond mine and house having been relocated to the North Pole, which gave Mr. Smee, pretending he was Bashful, an excuse to deliver the ticking parcel to Santa. The artwork was provided by Manuel Gonzales, who had been the Sunday *Mickey Mouse* artist since 1938. In the final strip, dated December 24, 1960, readers saw Santa in his flying sleigh, sending a "Merry Christmas to all," which would later change to "A Merry Christmas to one and all." The strip was a huge success, running in more than four hundred U.S. newspapers, as well as in other countries such as Finland, Italy, France, and Poland. The stories were also reformatted in comic book form and published around the world.

The "Disney-villain-wants-to-spoil-Christmas" formula was regularly repeated, with inventive variations, in subsequent continuities. Classic animation villains would join forces to face their respective traditional adversaries who, in turn, joined together. Drawn by Chuck Fuson (with an assist by Floyd Gottfredson), 1961's *Pinocchio's Christmas Story* was a short, alternate version of the classic 1940 feature, with Stromboli's puppets (including Pinocchio himself) eventually set free by the Blue Fairy.

Sleeping Beauty's Christmas Story in 1962 was the first Christmas continuity drawn by John Ushler, who had recently taken over art chores on the *Treasury of Classic Tales* and *Uncle Remus and His Tales of B'rer Rabbit* weekly series. In addition to the classic characters from the 1959 movie, the sequence featured Professor Ludwig Von Drake, the Austrian-born duck genius who had recently become popular as a co-host (with Walt Disney himself) on the *Walt Disney's Wonderful World of Color* TV show and was also regularly featuring in the *Donald Duck* newspaper strip. Von Drake was one of the few Disney standard characters to feature in the Christmas series. In the strip, which took place three years after the facts related in *Sleeping*

Beauty, Von Drake travelled through time and space to wake Princess Aurora from another sleeping spell cast upon her by Maleficent, who was surprisingly still alive and evil, although she had been fatally pierced by Prince Phillip's sword while in black dragon guise in the animated feature.

The 1963 entry, *The Three Little Pigs' Christmas Story*, was the first of three continuities that fully benefited from Floyd Gottfredson's immense talent. Gottfredson pencilled, inked, and lettered it, drawing the Big Bad Wolf and the Pigs, as well as Santa Claus and his wife Kristina (who made her debut in the series, totalling ten appearances through 1987). The Li'l Bad Wolf, Zeke Wolf's son, who had been a mainstay in comic books since 1945, also made his first appearance in a Disney newspaper strip.

Cinderella's Christmas Party followed in 1964, with Gottfredson leaving the inking chores to Manuel Gonzales. 1965's *Bambi's Christmas Adventure* was instead drawn by Guillermo (Bill) Cardoso, who was concurrently drawing Disney comic book stories, but Gottfredson's touch-ups are detectable in various spots, mainly in Santa's and Kristina's faces and the Wolf that attacks Bambi and his friends, Flower and Thumper.

Better known as a realistic artist who had drawn, among other things, a *Mary Poppins* comic book adaptation, Mike Arens did the artwork for the next two years. *Snow White's Christmas Surprise* in 1966 featured an odd bunch of monkey "diamerald" miners exploited by an evil witch doctor in Africa. It was significant, as it was the last in the series to include the "Walt Disney" signature. That was, in fact, the saddest of Disney Christmases, as Walt passed away on December 15, 1966.

Dumbo and the Christmas Mystery in 1967 featured the flying elephant alongside the Seven Dwarfs against a brand-new villainous and witchy team made up of Maleficent and Mad Madam Mim. Mim was the crazy sorceress from *The Sword in the Stone* (1963). Arens drew Santa Claus and other human characters in his own style here, while he had somewhat stuck to Gottfredson's model in the previous story.

1968's *Santa Claus in Never Land* saw the return of the *Peter Pan* cast and was the first *Disney Christmas Story* pencilled not by an artist from the Comic Strip Department, but from the Animation Department: Cliff Nordberg, who was a Disney animator from 1938 to 1979 and had the theatrical *Peter Pan* among his credits.

James Swain, who pencilled 1969's *The Quest for Christmas*, went from being an inbetweener to an animation editor at Disney from 1952 to 1971. Both Nordberg's and Swain's pencils were inked by Manuel Gonzales, to keep the Disney style consistent.

Tom McKimson had been a Disney animator as early as 1928-31 and an art director at Western Printing from 1947-72, but had not drawn the Disney characters in comics for over thirty years when he turned in quite a good job with Dumbo and the Seven Dwarfs in 1974's *Santa's Crucial Christmas*.

In 1976's *Captain Hook's Christmas Caper*, animator Lorna Smith (a.k.a. Lorna Cook, a.k.a. Lorna Pomeroy-Cook) drew an unprecedented villainous trio made up of the *Peter Pan* pirate captain, J. Worthington Foulfellow (a.k.a. Honest John), and The Big Bad Wolf, as they faced the "good guy" team-up of Santa, the Seven Dwarfs, Pinocchio, and Merlin the Magician and his owl Archimedes, among others!

John Ushler drew another four *Disney Christmas Story* sequences in 1970, 1972, 1973, and 1975. *Santa's Christmas Crisis* (1970) is notable in that its protagonist was one of Maleficent's Goons, touched and redeemed by the Christmas Spirit.

In 1971's *The Christmas Conspiracy*, Mike Arens drew the *Cinderella* mice alongside the Beagle Boys, whose only prior newspaper strip appearances had been in two *Donald Duck* Sunday pages. For their Christmas stint they wore numbers "367," "368," and "369," which had little to do with the "1-6-7" combination conceived by their creator, Carl Barks.

1975's *Santa and the Pirates* was the last *Disney Christmas Story* written by Frank Reilly, who retired on October 1st that year. The writing was then entrusted to veteran animation and comic book scribe Carl Fallberg, who was also tackling the *Treasury of Classic Tales* adaptations. Unlike Reilly, who provided written scripts for his artists, Fallberg was accustomed to creating his stories in storyboard form, giving the artist a graphic guideline which a typescript alone could not provide. The second sequence he wrote, 1977's *No Puppets for Christmas*, was drawn by former animator and then current Comic Strip Department staffer Willie Ito, who would also pencil the 1983-85 stories.

The pencil art on the 1978-82 continuities was done by another veteran, the ever-reliable Tony Strobl. With inking by Larry Mayer, Mike Royer, and Steve Steere, Strobl did an excellent job, starting with 1978's *The Day Christmas Was Banned*, which featured almost the entire *Robin Hood* cast, plus Dumbo and Mr. Stork. Also remarkable was

RIGHT: Frank Reilly and Floyd Gottfredson at the Disney Studio Comic Strip Department in 1967.

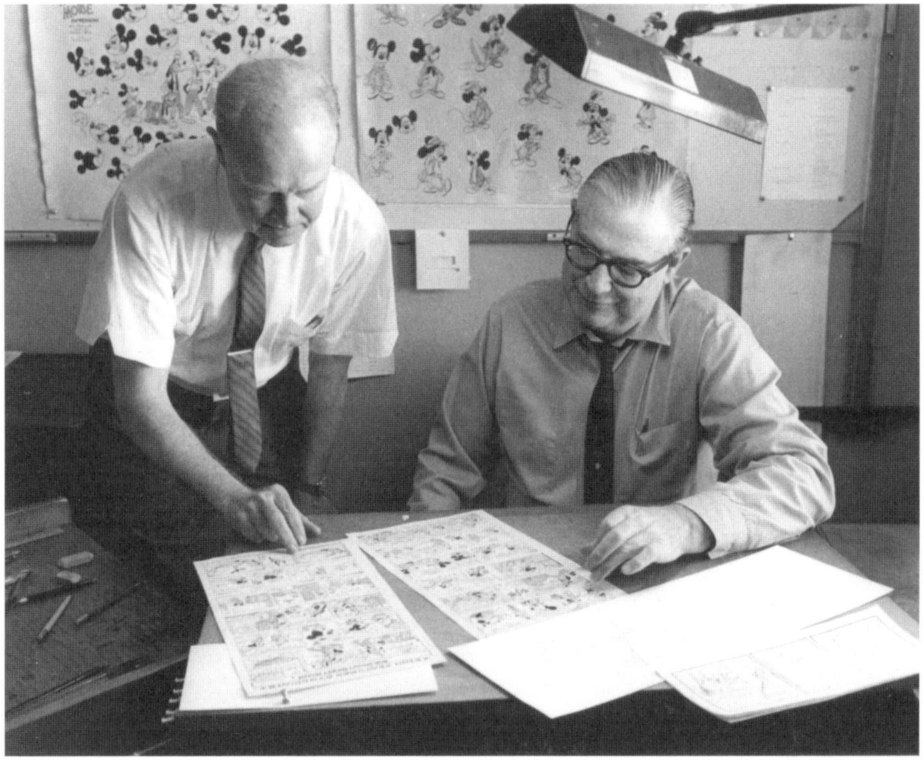

1979's *Madam Mim's Christmas Grudge*, which featured a replica of Mim's memorable wizards' duel with Merlin, sixteen years after *The Sword in the Stone.*

By 1985 the *Disney Christmas Story* had a new, more contemporary look. Floyd Norman, who had joined the Disney Studio as an inbetweener in 1956 and had been writing the *Mickey Mouse* newspaper strip since 1984, assumed the scripting chores on the Christmas strip. He reminisced in a December 17, 2012 blog entry entitled "The Disney Holiday Stories" on *MrFun—The Official, Informative and Pointless Blog of Floyd Norman*:

> After reading several stories by my predecessors, I couldn't help but be somewhat bothered by the approach the writers took. Usually, the stories blended Disney characters from several shorts and feature films…Mickey and Pluto didn't fit in the same world as Dumbo, and the Seven Dwarfs certainly didn't mix well with Jaq and Gus from *Cinderella.* I decided if I was going to write a holiday story, the characters used would have to be consistent. That means they would have to be from the same world, even if that world was a Disney one.

Following this principle, in 1985 Norman brought back the characters from *101 Dalmatians* writing (in rough sketch form) *Cruella's Very Furry Christmas*, which was drawn by Willie Ito with inking and lettering by Mike Royer. Norman continued his explanation:

> The first story I penned featured Pongo and Perdita from the Disney film *101 Dalmatians.* As you can imagine, it was Cruella De Vil who wanted to screw up the holiday, and she enlisted her inept henchmen, the two men known as the Baduns, to help her ruin Christmas for the family. As you might expect, the Dalmatian puppies save the day, and the family enjoys a merry holiday.

Children's book illustrator Keith Moseley pencilled 1987's *Snow White's Sinister Christmas Gift*, which was written by Carl Fallberg and inked by Bill Langley, who headed Disney's Comic Strip Department in the late '80s. That was to be the last *Disney Christmas Story.* Disney and King Features cancelled both the Christmas strips and *Treasury of Classic Tales* in 1987.

• • • • •

Five years went by before Disney and the syndicate decided to revive their Christmas strip. King Features's comics editor, Jay Kennedy, agreed that the new series, called *Disney Holiday Story*, should focus on recent Disney animated feature films, although offering original tales that would take place somewhere during the movie's timespan.

The new creative team was comprised of Floyd Norman and veteran artist Richard Thomas "Sparky" Moore, whose long career with Disney included drawing comic books, as well as such newspaper strips as *Scamp*, *Winnie the Pooh*, and *Treasury of Classic Tales.* The new series began with *Beauty and the Beast—A Christmas Story*, which appeared from

Monday, November 30 until Friday, December 25, 1992—a year after the *Beauty and the Beast* movie had first been released in November, 1991. Disney Licensed Publishing editor Karen Kreider reportedly collaborated on the plot.

The four-week duration that characterized the first *Disney Holiday Story* was also kept for the four stories that followed. *Aladdin* was first released in U.S. theaters on November 25, 1992, and the Christmas strip it inspired appeared a year later. (Dealing with Christmas themes in Aladdin's world was not an easy task, but Floyd Norman managed to do it.) Sparky Moore—who had drawn the comic book adaptation of *The Lion King* that appeared concurrently with the movie's release in June, 1994—tackled the Christmas continuity five months later. The newspaper version featured young Simba, his father Mufasa, the evil Scar, Banzai, Ed and Shenzi the hyenas, Rafiki the baboon, and Zazu the hornbill. *Pocahontas* was first seen in U.S. cinemas in June, 1995 and the corresponding Christmas strip premiered five months later. Likewise, *The Hunchback of Notre Dame*'s movie debut took place in June, 1996, over five months before the first strip of a Christmas story starring Quasimodo appeared on December 2nd. Floyd Norman recalled:

> This time around, my story was based on the wonderful characters from Disney's *The Hunchback of Notre Dame*. It was one of those rare times when the Disney property fit the subject matter perfectly. After all, our story takes place in a huge church. What better place for a Christmas story, you might ask? However, it gets even better. I had also worked on the Disney movie in the nineties.

For the last *Disney Holiday Story*, which ran from December 1-27, 1997, the comics editors must have decided that year's feature—*Hercules*, set in ancient Greece—had little to do with Christmas, so opted instead for the watery world of *The Little Mermaid*. The animated movie inspired by Hans Christian Andersen's tale was re-released in U.S. theaters in November, 1997, eight years after its original 1989 release. In the newspaper strip, the evil octopus witch Ursula obviously tried to spoil the underwater Christmas celebration planned by Ariel and her friends.

• • • • •

A collection of the *Disney Christmas Story* and *Disney Holiday Story* strips is a godsend for Disney fans, collectors, and scholars. No other Disney strip has ever featured such a variety of characters, let alone so many together in one story…nor has any Disney strip ever allowed readers to get acquainted with the styles of so many talented artists. The stories may appear linear and even naïve, but it is precisely this simplicity that makes these yarns so delightful and enjoyable. By interweaving so many everlasting icons of a magical world, the tales allow readers to keep their sense of wonder intact and, like Peter Pan, never truly grow up.

DON'T MISS THE GREATEST ALL STAR CHRISTMAS STORY EVER...
© 1960 Walt Disney Productions World Rights Reserved
WALT DISNEY
Starring PETER PAN and TINKER BELL
CHRISTMAS, BAH! JINGLE BELLS! CAROLS! BAH!
Distributed by King Features Syndicate.
MISTER SMEE...
...CAPTAIN HOOK and
HEIGH-HO-HEIGH-HO!
...THE SEVEN DWARFS
(from SNOW WHITE and the SEVEN DWARFS..)
..and SANTA CLAUS himself
They're all in PETER PAN'S CHRISTMAS STORY by America's Master Storyteller WALT DISNEY
STARTING MONDAY

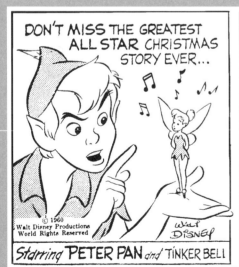

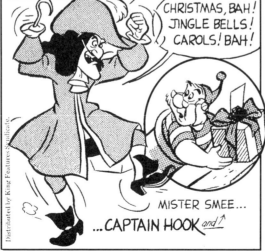

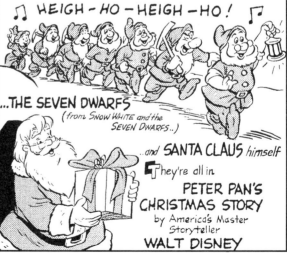

ABOVE: Teaser strip published in newspapers on Saturday, November 26, 1960. The artwork was cribbed from various panels by Manuel Gonzales.

TABLE OF CONTENTS

1960

PETER PAN'S CHRISTMAS STORY

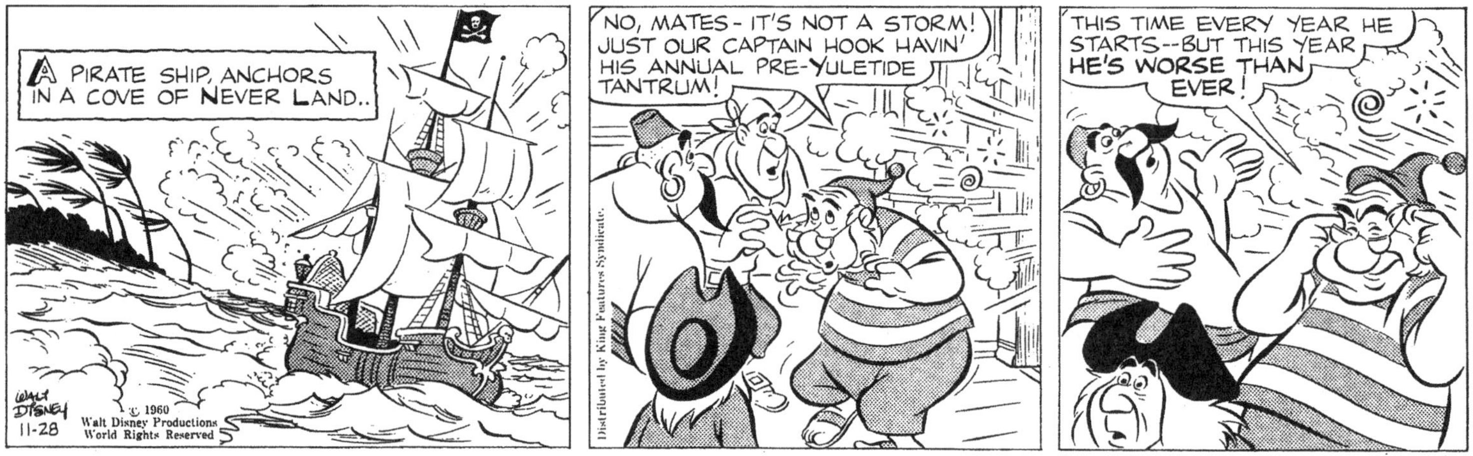

A PIRATE SHIP, ANCHORS IN A COVE OF NEVER LAND..
WALT DISNEY 11-28
© 1960 Walt Disney Productions World Rights Reserved
NO, MATES - IT'S NOT A STORM! JUST OUR CAPTAIN HOOK HAVIN' HIS ANNUAL PRE-YULETIDE TANTRUM!
Distributed by King Features Syndicate.
THIS TIME EVERY YEAR HE STARTS--BUT THIS YEAR HE'S WORSE THAN EVER!

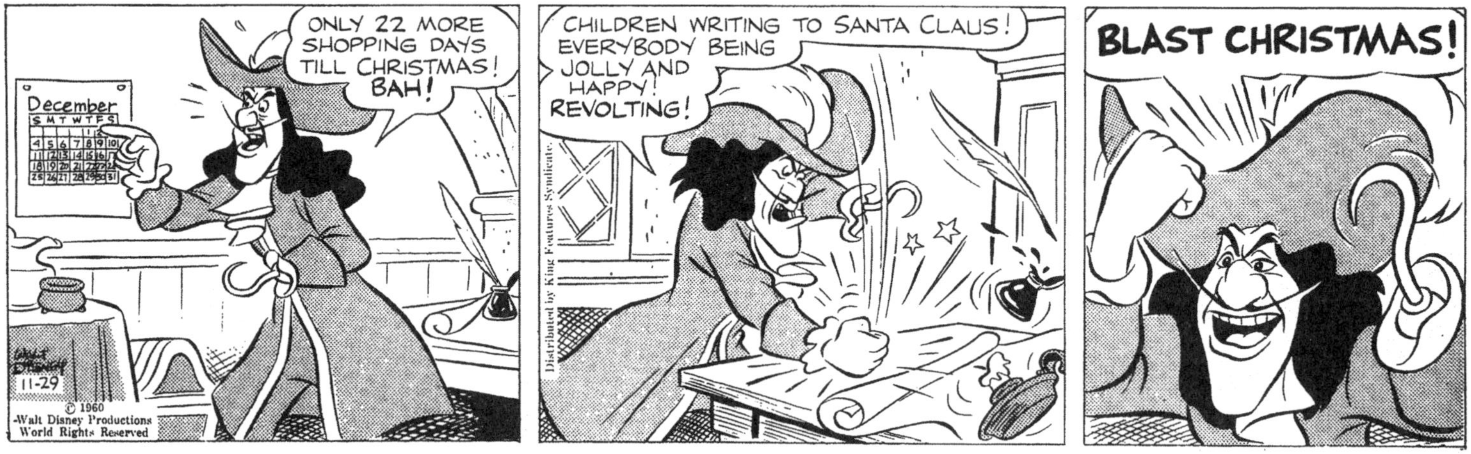

December
ONLY 22 MORE SHOPPING DAYS TILL CHRISTMAS! BAH!
WALT DISNEY 11-29
© 1960 Walt Disney Productions World Rights Reserved
CHILDREN WRITING TO SANTA CLAUS! EVERYBODY BEING JOLLY AND HAPPY! REVOLTING!
Distributed by King Features Syndicate.
BLAST CHRISTMAS!

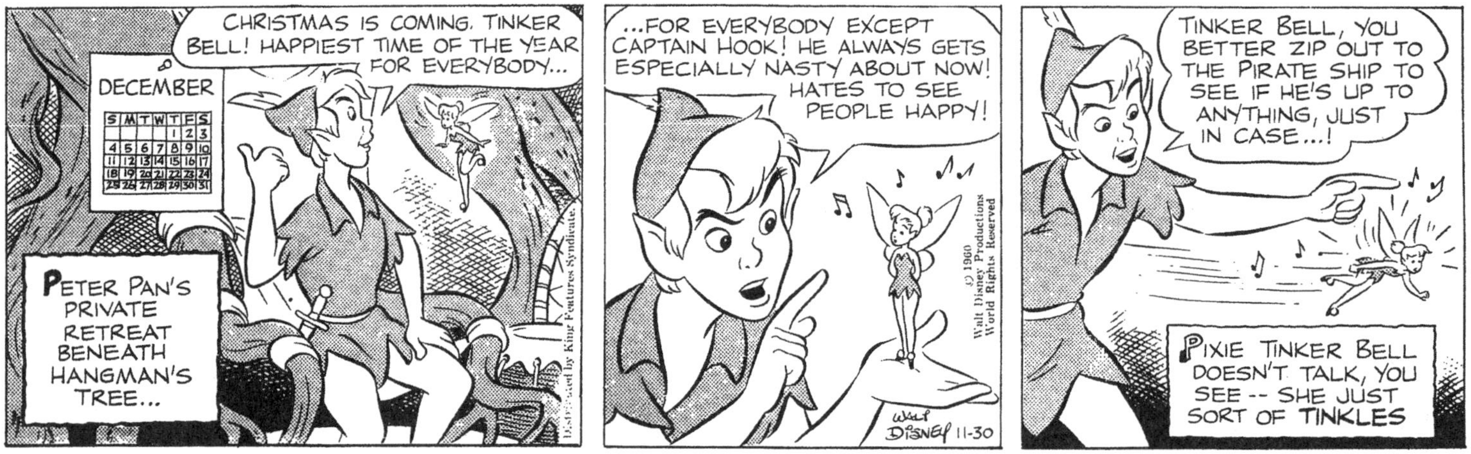

CHRISTMAS IS COMING, TINKER BELL! HAPPIEST TIME OF THE YEAR FOR EVERYBODY...
DECEMBER
PETER PAN'S PRIVATE RETREAT BENEATH HANGMAN'S TREE...
Distributed by King Features Syndicate.
...FOR EVERYBODY EXCEPT CAPTAIN HOOK! HE ALWAYS GETS ESPECIALLY NASTY ABOUT NOW! HATES TO SEE PEOPLE HAPPY!
© 1960 Walt Disney Productions World Rights Reserved
WALT DISNEY 11-30
TINKER BELL, YOU BETTER ZIP OUT TO THE PIRATE SHIP TO SEE IF HE'S UP TO ANYTHING, JUST IN CASE...!
PIXIE TINKER BELL DOESN'T TALK, YOU SEE -- SHE JUST SORT OF TINKLES

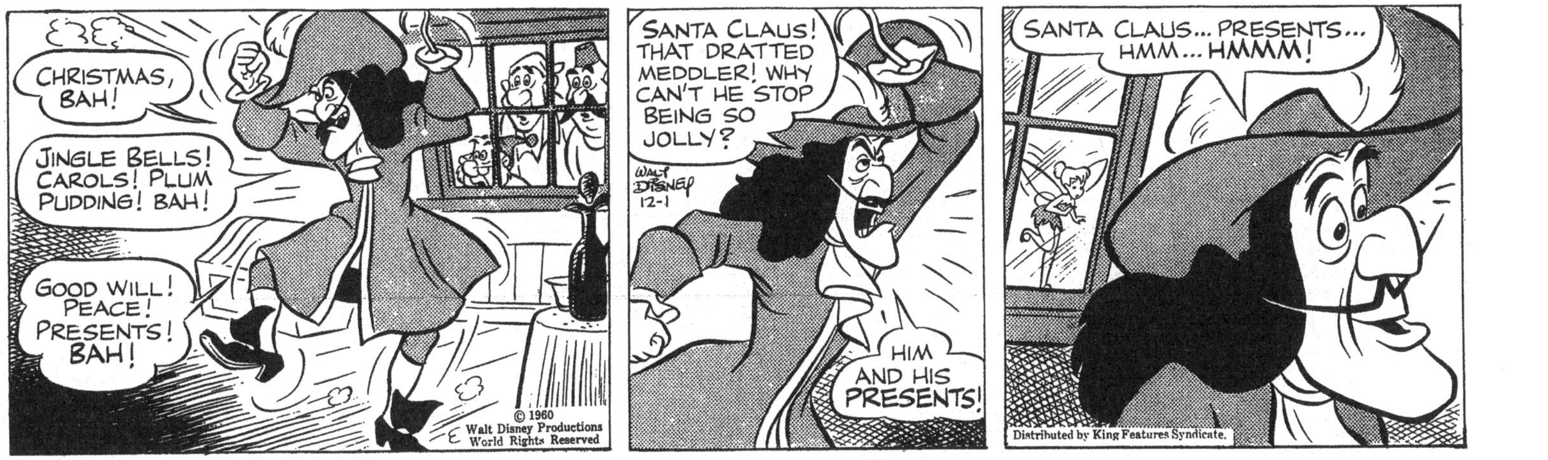
CHRISTMAS, BAH!
JINGLE BELLS! CAROLS! PLUM PUDDING! BAH!
GOOD WILL! PEACE! PRESENTS! BAH!
© 1960 Walt Disney Productions World Rights Reserved
SANTA CLAUS! THAT DRATTED MEDDLER! WHY CAN'T HE STOP BEING SO JOLLY?
WALT DISNEY 12-1
HIM AND HIS PRESENTS!
SANTA CLAUS... PRESENTS... HMM... HMMM!
Distributed by King Features Syndicate.

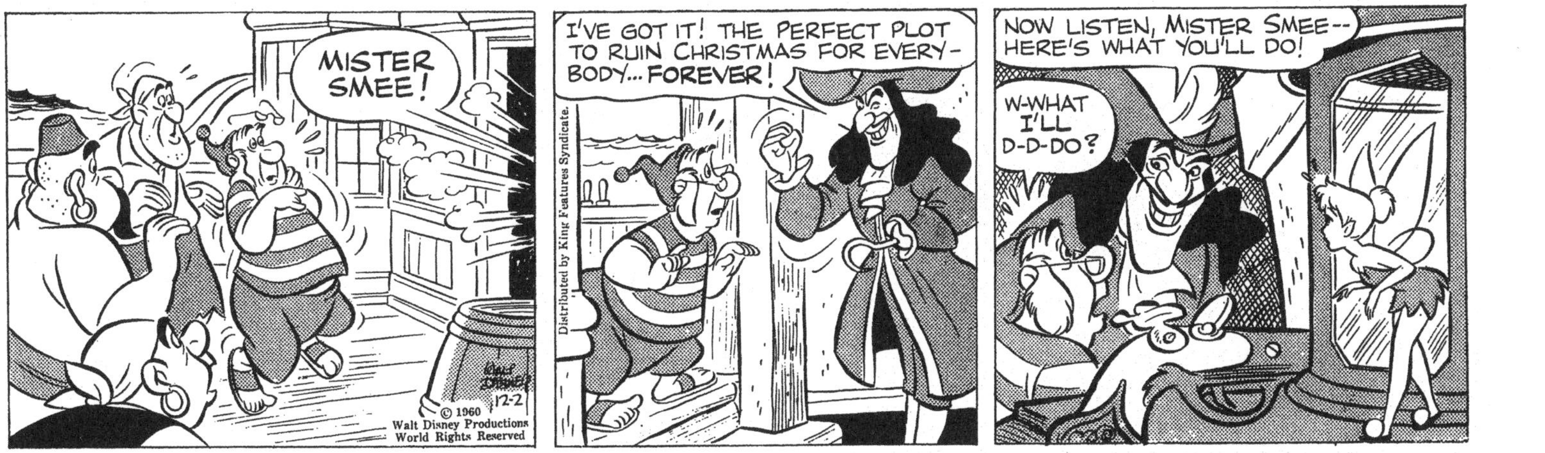
MISTER SMEE!
WALT DISNEY 12-2
© 1960 Walt Disney Productions World Rights Reserved
Distributed by King Features Syndicate.
I'VE GOT IT! THE PERFECT PLOT TO RUIN CHRISTMAS FOR EVERYBODY... FOREVER!
NOW LISTEN, MISTER SMEE-- HERE'S WHAT YOU'LL DO!
W-WHAT I'LL D-D-DO?

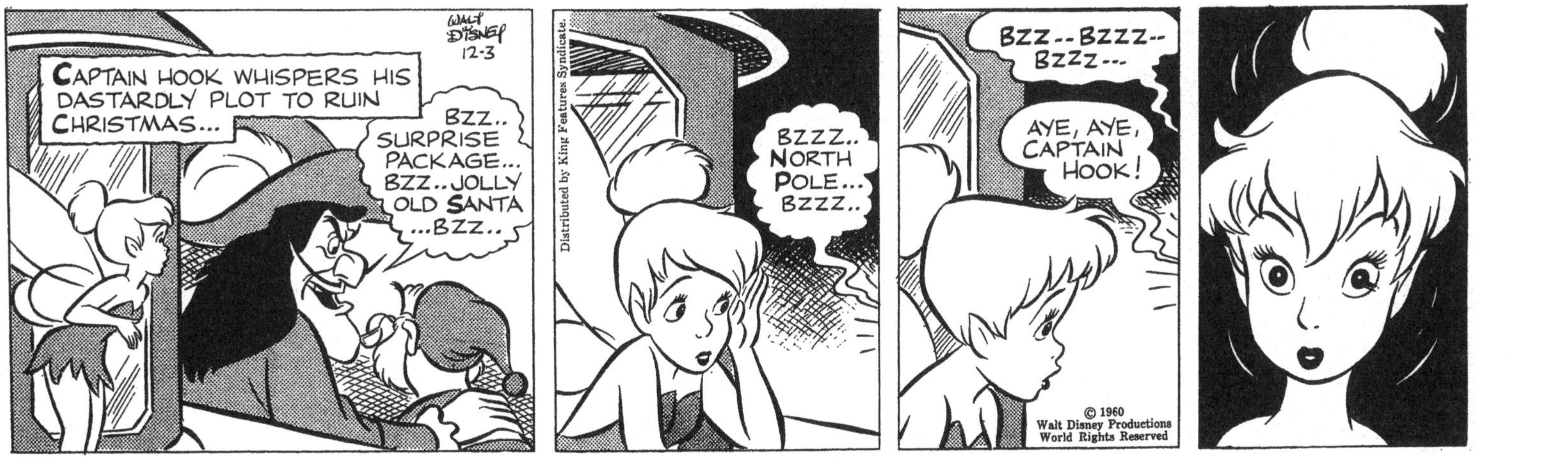
WALT DISNEY 12-3
CAPTAIN HOOK WHISPERS HIS DASTARDLY PLOT TO RUIN CHRISTMAS...
BZZ.. SURPRISE PACKAGE... BZZ.. JOLLY OLD SANTA ...BZZ..
Distributed by King Features Syndicate.
BZZZ.. NORTH POLE... BZZZ..
BZZ--BZZZ-- BZZZ---
AYE, AYE, CAPTAIN HOOK!
© 1960 Walt Disney Productions World Rights Reserved

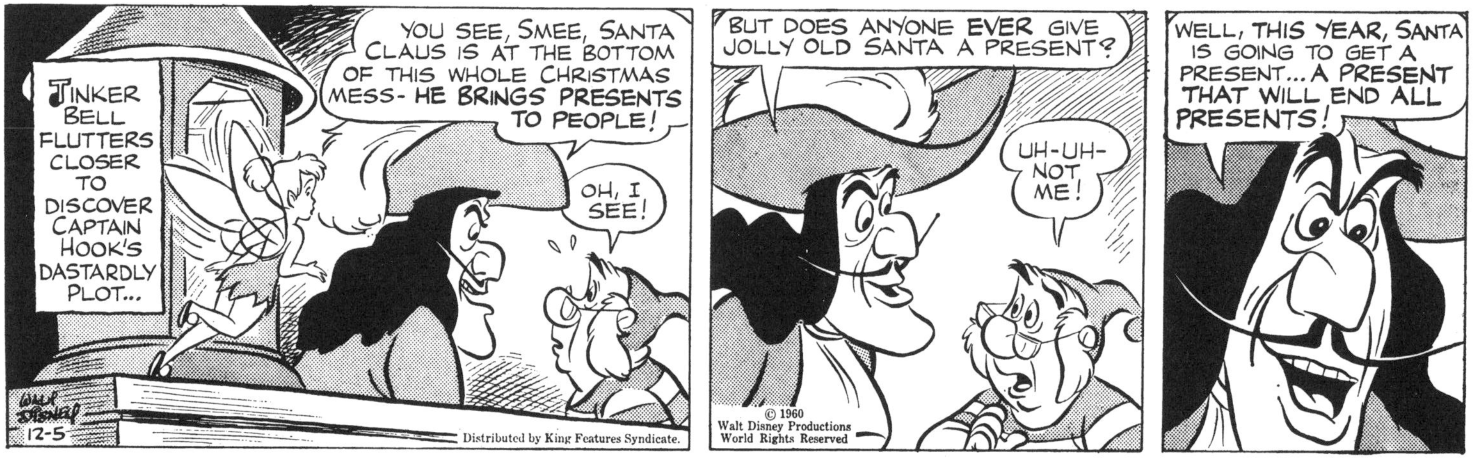
TINKER BELL FLUTTERS CLOSER TO DISCOVER CAPTAIN HOOK'S DASTARDLY PLOT...
YOU SEE, SMEE, SANTA CLAUS IS AT THE BOTTOM OF THIS WHOLE CHRISTMAS MESS- HE BRINGS PRESENTS TO PEOPLE!
OH, I SEE!
WALT DISNEY
12-5
Distributed by King Features Syndicate.
BUT DOES ANYONE EVER GIVE JOLLY OLD SANTA A PRESENT?
UH-UH- NOT ME!
© 1960 Walt Disney Productions World Rights Reserved
WELL, THIS YEAR, SANTA IS GOING TO GET A PRESENT... A PRESENT THAT WILL END ALL PRESENTS!

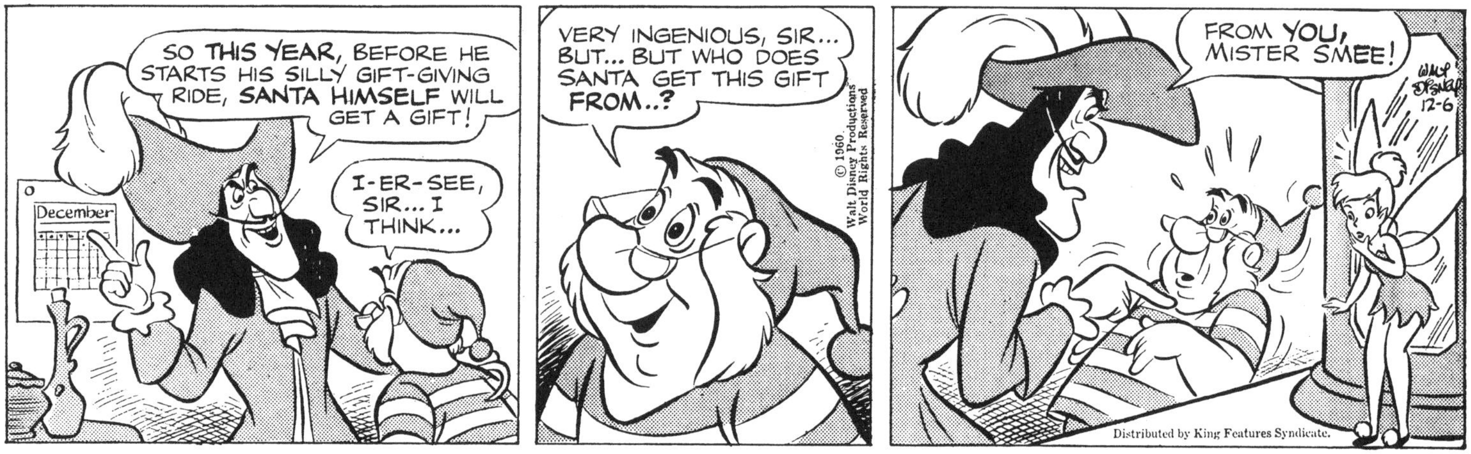
SO THIS YEAR, BEFORE HE STARTS HIS SILLY GIFT-GIVING RIDE, SANTA HIMSELF WILL GET A GIFT!
December
I-ER-SEE, SIR... I THINK...
VERY INGENIOUS, SIR... BUT... BUT WHO DOES SANTA GET THIS GIFT FROM..?
© 1960 Walt Disney Productions World Rights Reserved
FROM YOU, MISTER SMEE!
WALT DISNEY
12-6
Distributed by King Features Syndicate.

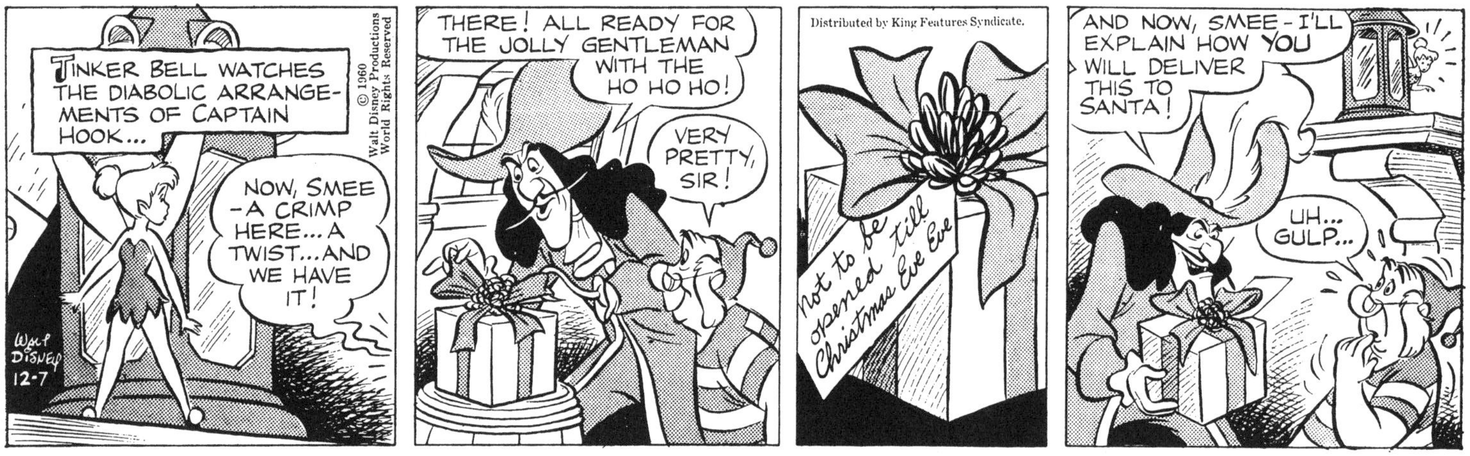
TINKER BELL WATCHES THE DIABOLIC ARRANGEMENTS OF CAPTAIN HOOK...
NOW, SMEE -A CRIMP HERE... A TWIST... AND WE HAVE IT!
© 1960 Walt Disney Productions World Rights Reserved
WALT DISNEY
12-7
THERE! ALL READY FOR THE JOLLY GENTLEMAN WITH THE HO HO HO!
VERY PRETTY, SIR!
Distributed by King Features Syndicate.
not to be opened till Christmas Eve Eve
AND NOW, SMEE - I'LL EXPLAIN HOW YOU WILL DELIVER THIS TO SANTA!
UH... GULP...

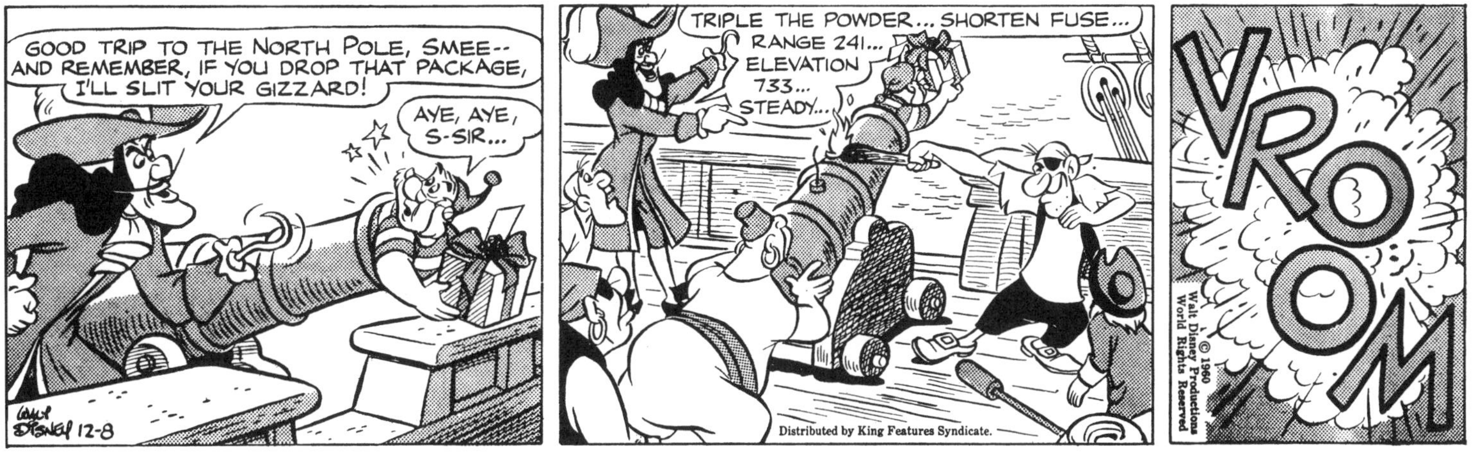
GOOD TRIP TO THE NORTH POLE, SMEE-- AND REMEMBER, IF YOU DROP THAT PACKAGE, I'LL SLIT YOUR GIZZARD!
AYE, AYE, S-SIR...
WALT DISNEY 12-8
TRIPLE THE POWDER... SHORTEN FUSE...
RANGE 241... ELEVATION 733... STEADY...
Distributed by King Features Syndicate.
VROOM
© 1960 Walt Disney Productions World Rights Reserved

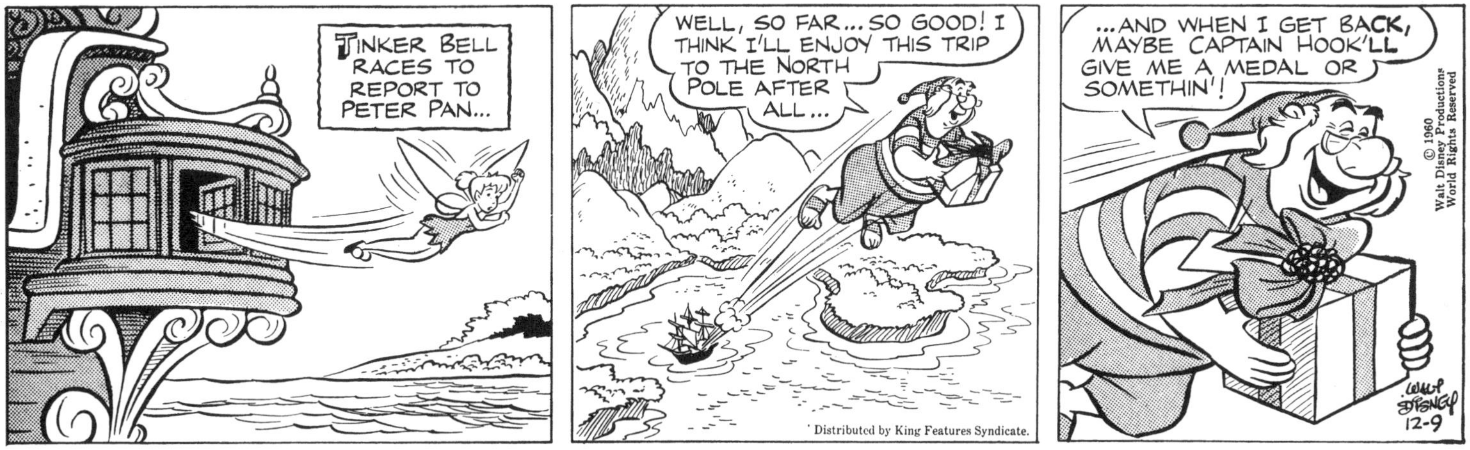
TINKER BELL RACES TO REPORT TO PETER PAN...
WELL, SO FAR... SO GOOD! I THINK I'LL ENJOY THIS TRIP TO THE NORTH POLE AFTER ALL...
Distributed by King Features Syndicate.
...AND WHEN I GET BACK, MAYBE CAPTAIN HOOK'LL GIVE ME A MEDAL OR SOMETHIN'!
© 1960 Walt Disney Productions World Rights Reserved
WALT DISNEY 12-9

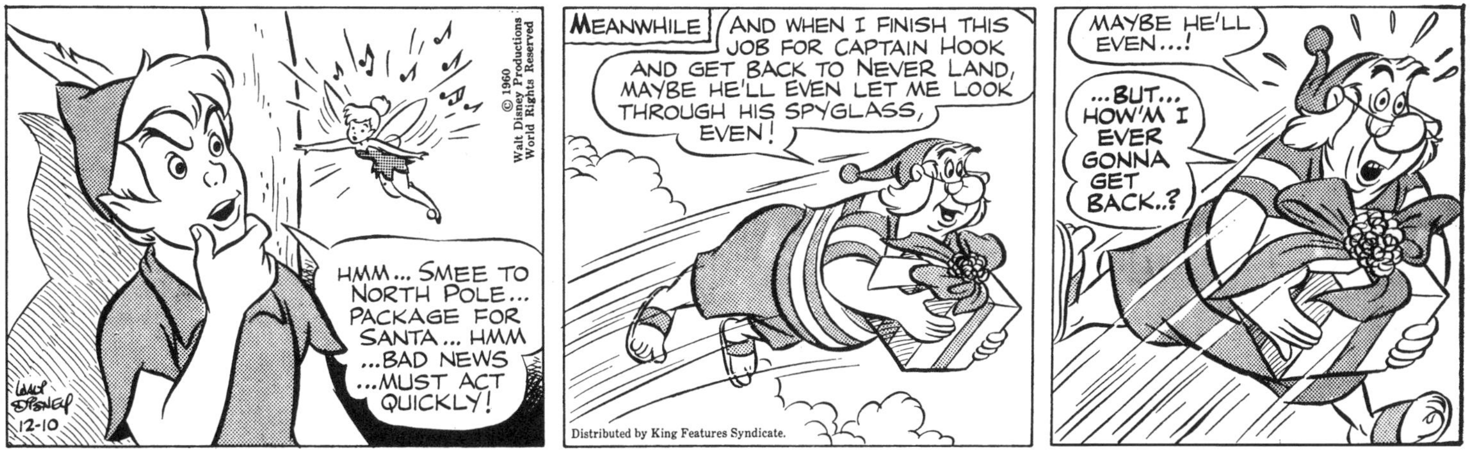
© 1960 Walt Disney Productions World Rights Reserved
HMM... SMEE TO NORTH POLE... PACKAGE FOR SANTA... HMM ...BAD NEWS ...MUST ACT QUICKLY!
WALT DISNEY 12-10
MEANWHILE
AND WHEN I FINISH THIS JOB FOR CAPTAIN HOOK AND GET BACK TO NEVER LAND, MAYBE HE'LL EVEN LET ME LOOK THROUGH HIS SPYGLASS, EVEN!
Distributed by King Features Syndicate.
MAYBE HE'LL EVEN...!
...BUT... HOW'M I EVER GONNA GET BACK..?

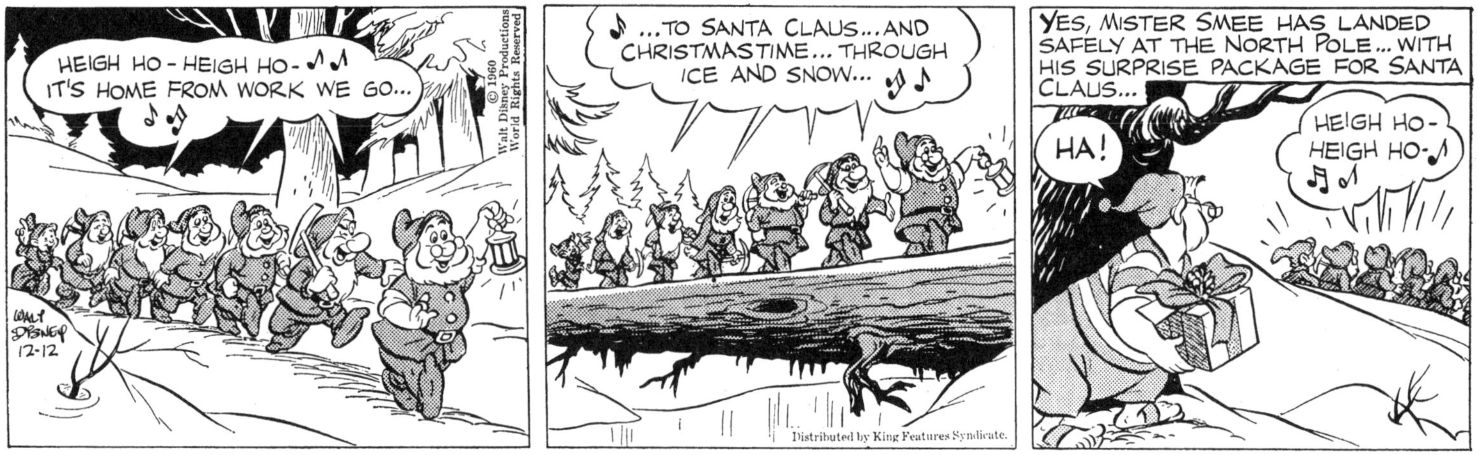
HEIGH HO - HEIGH HO -
IT'S HOME FROM WORK WE GO...
© 1960 Walt Disney Productions World Rights Reserved
WALT DISNEY 12-12
...TO SANTA CLAUS... AND CHRISTMASTIME... THROUGH ICE AND SNOW...
Distributed by King Features Syndicate.
YES, MISTER SMEE HAS LANDED SAFELY AT THE NORTH POLE... WITH HIS SURPRISE PACKAGE FOR SANTA CLAUS...
HA!
HEIGH HO-
HEIGH HO-

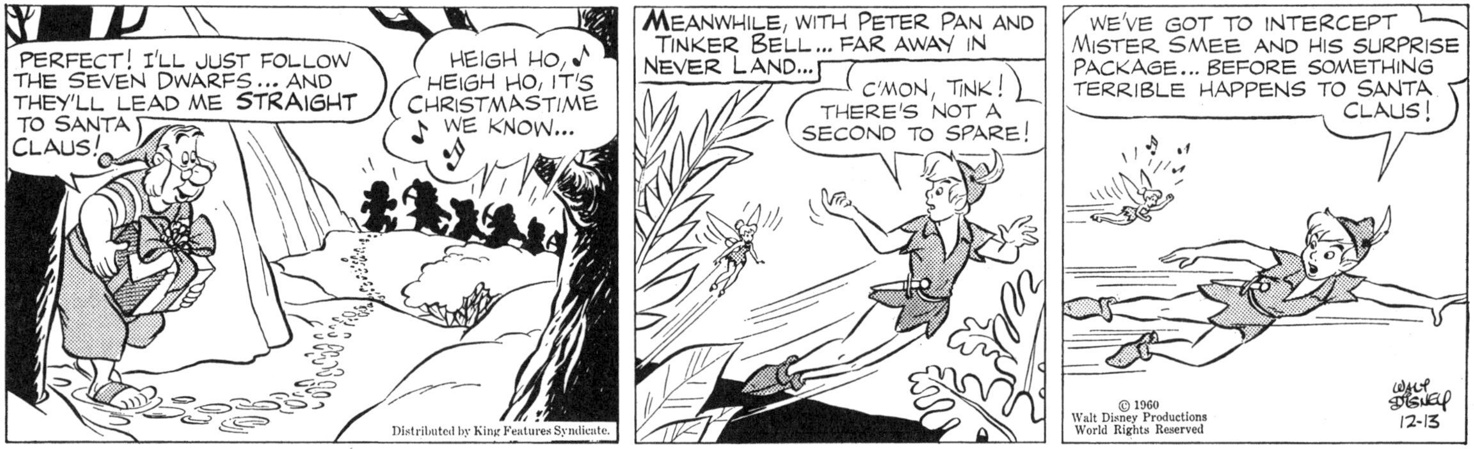
PERFECT! I'LL JUST FOLLOW THE SEVEN DWARFS... AND THEY'LL LEAD ME STRAIGHT TO SANTA CLAUS!
HEIGH HO, HEIGH HO, IT'S CHRISTMASTIME WE KNOW...
Distributed by King Features Syndicate.
MEANWHILE, WITH PETER PAN AND TINKER BELL... FAR AWAY IN NEVER LAND...
C'MON, TINK! THERE'S NOT A SECOND TO SPARE!
WE'VE GOT TO INTERCEPT MISTER SMEE AND HIS SURPRISE PACKAGE... BEFORE SOMETHING TERRIBLE HAPPENS TO SANTA CLAUS!
© 1960 Walt Disney Productions World Rights Reserved
WALT DISNEY 12-13

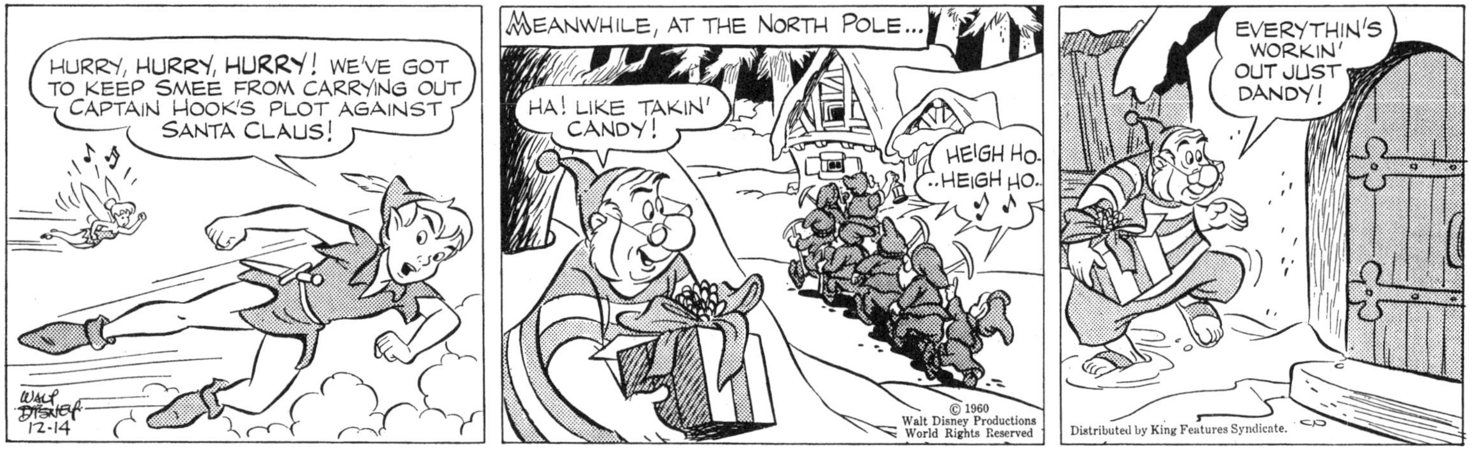
HURRY, HURRY, HURRY! WE'VE GOT TO KEEP SMEE FROM CARRYING OUT CAPTAIN HOOK'S PLOT AGAINST SANTA CLAUS!
WALT DISNEY 12-14
MEANWHILE, AT THE NORTH POLE...
HA! LIKE TAKIN' CANDY!
HEIGH HO- ..HEIGH HO..
© 1960 Walt Disney Productions World Rights Reserved
EVERYTHIN'S WORKIN' OUT JUST DANDY!
Distributed by King Features Syndicate.

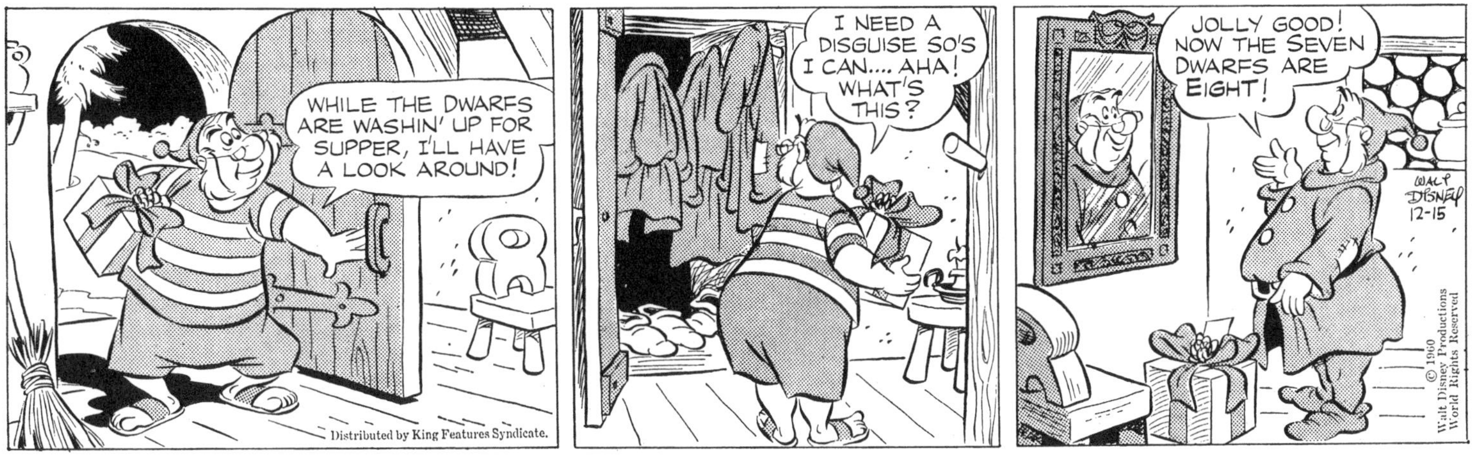
WHILE THE DWARFS ARE WASHIN' UP FOR SUPPER, I'LL HAVE A LOOK AROUND!
Distributed by King Features Syndicate.
I NEED A DISGUISE SO'S I CAN.... AHA! WHAT'S THIS?
JOLLY GOOD! NOW THE SEVEN DWARFS ARE EIGHT!
WALT DISNEY 12-15
© 1960 Walt Disney Productions World Rights Reserved

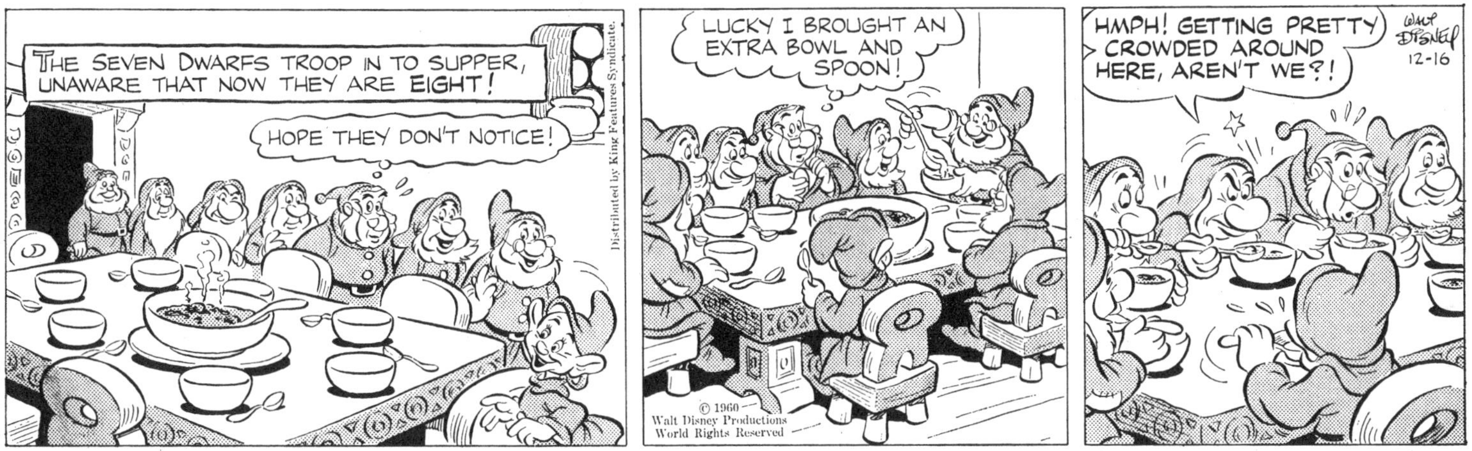
THE SEVEN DWARFS TROOP IN TO SUPPER, UNAWARE THAT NOW THEY ARE EIGHT!
HOPE THEY DON'T NOTICE!
Distributed by King Features Syndicate.
LUCKY I BROUGHT AN EXTRA BOWL AND SPOON!
© 1960 Walt Disney Productions World Rights Reserved
HMPH! GETTING PRETTY CROWDED AROUND HERE, AREN'T WE?!
WALT DISNEY 12-16

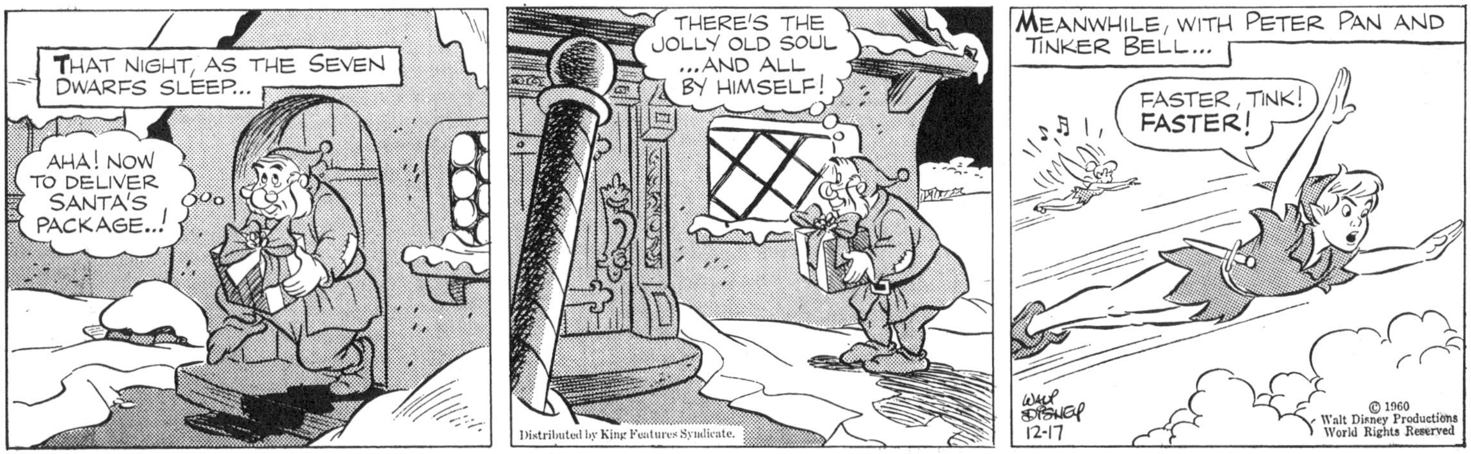
THAT NIGHT, AS THE SEVEN DWARFS SLEEP...
AHA! NOW TO DELIVER SANTA'S PACKAGE..!
THERE'S THE JOLLY OLD SOUL ...AND ALL BY HIMSELF!
Distributed by King Features Syndicate.
MEANWHILE, WITH PETER PAN AND TINKER BELL...
FASTER, TINK! FASTER!
WALT DISNEY 12-17
© 1960 Walt Disney Productions World Rights Reserved

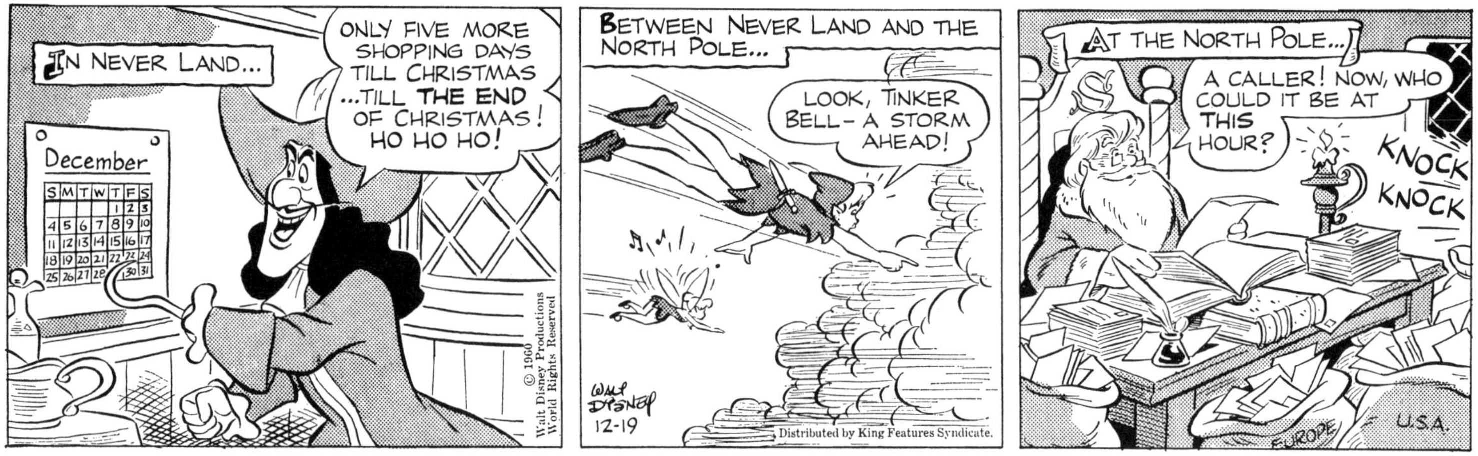
IN NEVER LAND...
December
ONLY FIVE MORE SHOPPING DAYS TILL CHRISTMAS ...TILL THE END OF CHRISTMAS! HO HO HO!
© 1960 Walt Disney Productions World Rights Reserved
BETWEEN NEVER LAND AND THE NORTH POLE...
LOOK, TINKER BELL- A STORM AHEAD!
WALT DISNEY 12-19
Distributed by King Features Syndicate.
AT THE NORTH POLE...
A CALLER! NOW, WHO COULD IT BE AT THIS HOUR?
KNOCK KNOCK
EUROPE
U.S.A.

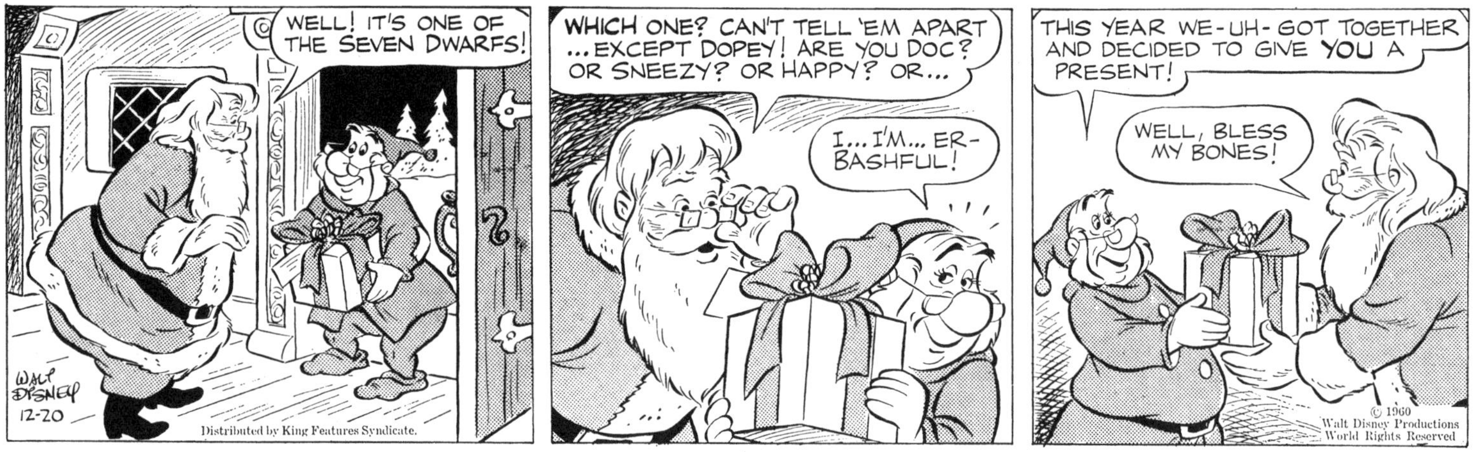
WELL! IT'S ONE OF THE SEVEN DWARFS!
WALT DISNEY 12-20
Distributed by King Features Syndicate.
WHICH ONE? CAN'T TELL 'EM APART ...EXCEPT DOPEY! ARE YOU DOC? OR SNEEZY? OR HAPPY? OR...
I... I'M... ER- BASHFUL!
THIS YEAR WE-UH- GOT TOGETHER AND DECIDED TO GIVE YOU A PRESENT!
WELL, BLESS MY BONES!
© 1960 Walt Disney Productions World Rights Reserved

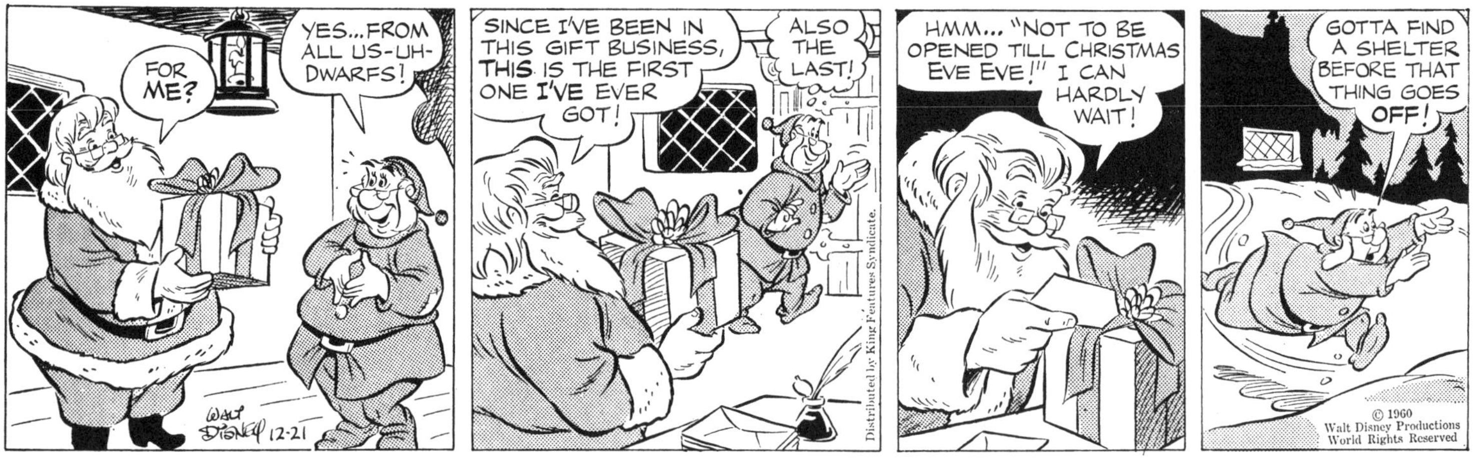
FOR ME?
YES...FROM ALL US-UH- DWARFS!
WALT DISNEY 12-21
SINCE I'VE BEEN IN THIS GIFT BUSINESS, THIS IS THE FIRST ONE I'VE EVER GOT!
ALSO THE LAST!
Distributed by King Features Syndicate.
HMM... "NOT TO BE OPENED TILL CHRISTMAS EVE EVE!" I CAN HARDLY WAIT!
GOTTA FIND A SHELTER BEFORE THAT THING GOES OFF!
© 1960 Walt Disney Productions World Rights Reserved

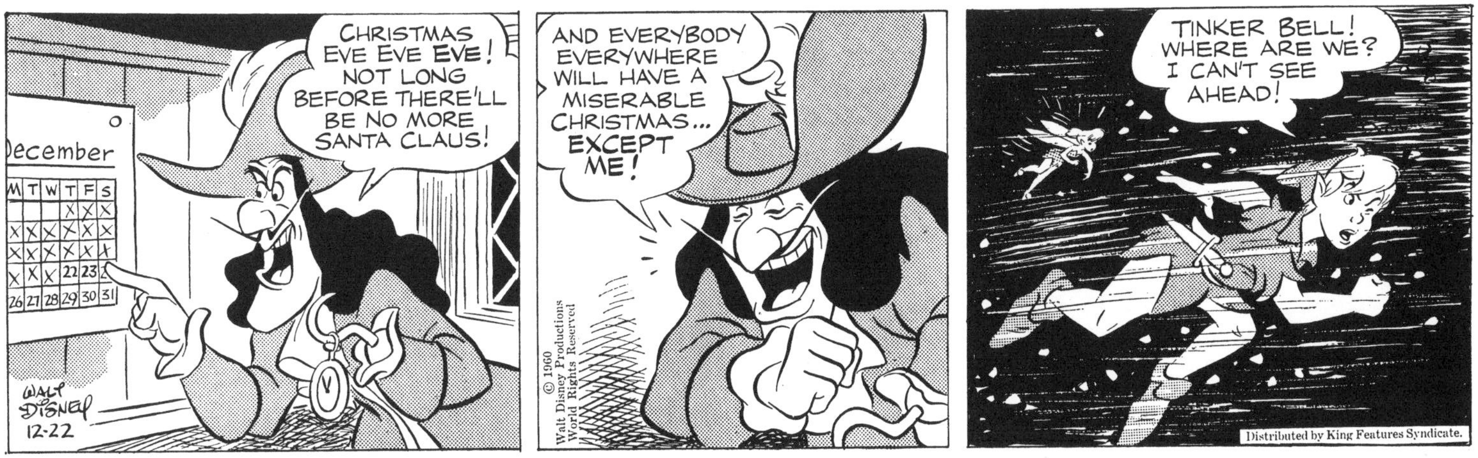
December
CHRISTMAS EVE EVE EVE! NOT LONG BEFORE THERE'LL BE NO MORE SANTA CLAUS!
WALT DISNEY 12-22
AND EVERYBODY EVERYWHERE WILL HAVE A MISERABLE CHRISTMAS... EXCEPT ME!
© 1960 Walt Disney Productions World Rights Reserved
TINKER BELL! WHERE ARE WE? I CAN'T SEE AHEAD!
Distributed by King Features Syndicate.

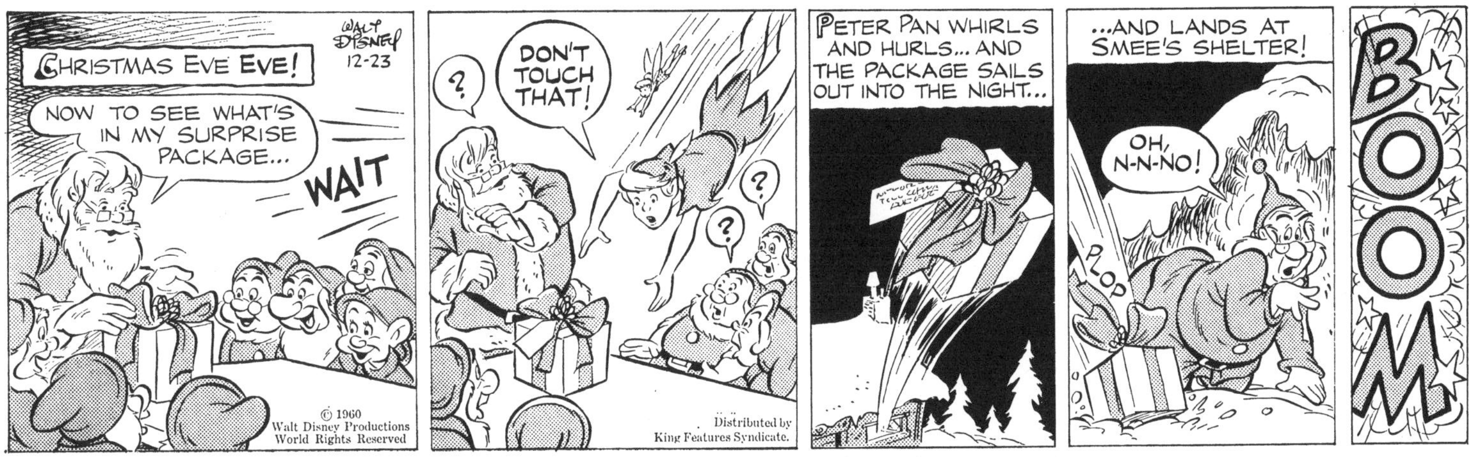
CHRISTMAS EVE EVE!
WALT DISNEY 12-23
NOW TO SEE WHAT'S IN MY SURPRISE PACKAGE...
WAIT
© 1960 Walt Disney Productions World Rights Reserved
?
DON'T TOUCH THAT!
?
?
Distributed by King Features Syndicate.
PETER PAN WHIRLS AND HURLS... AND THE PACKAGE SAILS OUT INTO THE NIGHT...
...AND LANDS AT SMEE'S SHELTER!
OH, N-N-NO!
PLOP
BOOM

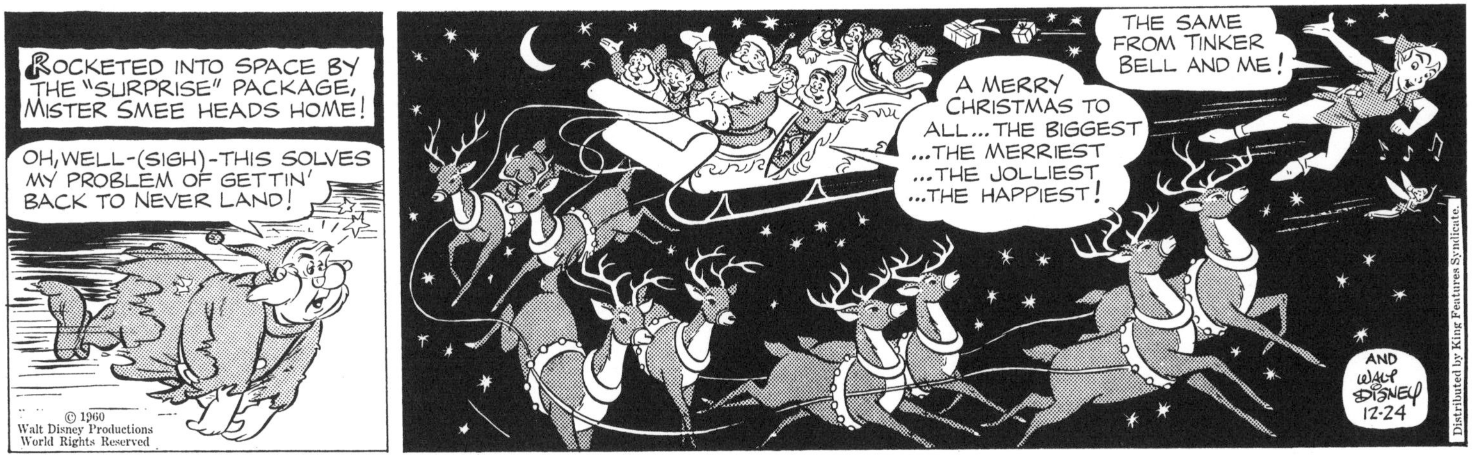
ROCKETED INTO SPACE BY THE "SURPRISE" PACKAGE, MISTER SMEE HEADS HOME!
OH, WELL-(SIGH)-THIS SOLVES MY PROBLEM OF GETTIN' BACK TO NEVER LAND!
© 1960 Walt Disney Productions World Rights Reserved
A MERRY CHRISTMAS TO ALL... THE BIGGEST ...THE MERRIEST ...THE JOLLIEST ...THE HAPPIEST!
THE SAME FROM TINKER BELL AND ME!
AND WALT DISNEY 12-24
Distributed by King Features Syndicate.

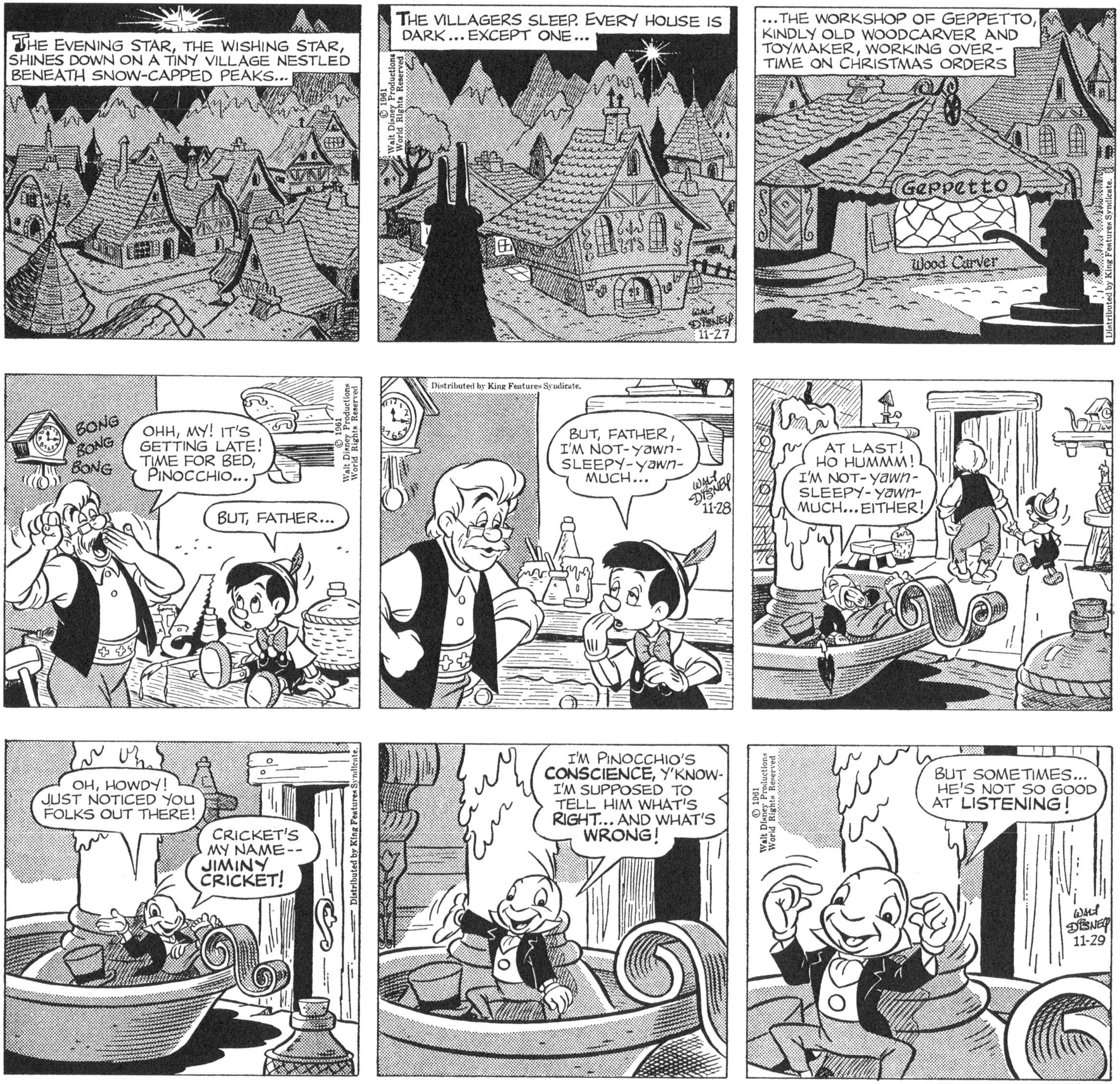
THE EVENING STAR, THE WISHING STAR, SHINES DOWN ON A TINY VILLAGE NESTLED BENEATH SNOW-CAPPED PEAKS...
THE VILLAGERS SLEEP. EVERY HOUSE IS DARK... EXCEPT ONE...
© 1961 Walt Disney Productions World Rights Reserved
WALT DISNEY 11-27
...THE WORKSHOP OF GEPPETTO, KINDLY OLD WOODCARVER AND TOYMAKER, WORKING OVER-TIME ON CHRISTMAS ORDERS
Geppetto
Wood Carver
Distributed by King Features Syndicate.
BONG BONG BONG
OHH, MY! IT'S GETTING LATE! TIME FOR BED, PINOCCHIO...
BUT, FATHER...
© 1961 Walt Disney Productions World Rights Reserved
Distributed by King Features Syndicate.
BUT, FATHER, I'M NOT-yawn-SLEEPY-yawn-MUCH...
WALT DISNEY 11-28
AT LAST! HO HUMMM! I'M NOT-yawn-SLEEPY-yawn-MUCH... EITHER!
OH, HOWDY! JUST NOTICED YOU FOLKS OUT THERE!
CRICKET'S MY NAME-- JIMINY CRICKET!
Distributed by King Features Syndicate.
I'M PINOCCHIO'S CONSCIENCE, Y'KNOW-I'M SUPPOSED TO TELL HIM WHAT'S RIGHT... AND WHAT'S WRONG!
© 1961 Walt Disney Productions World Rights Reserved
BUT SOMETIMES... HE'S NOT SO GOOD AT LISTENING!
WALT DISNEY 11-29

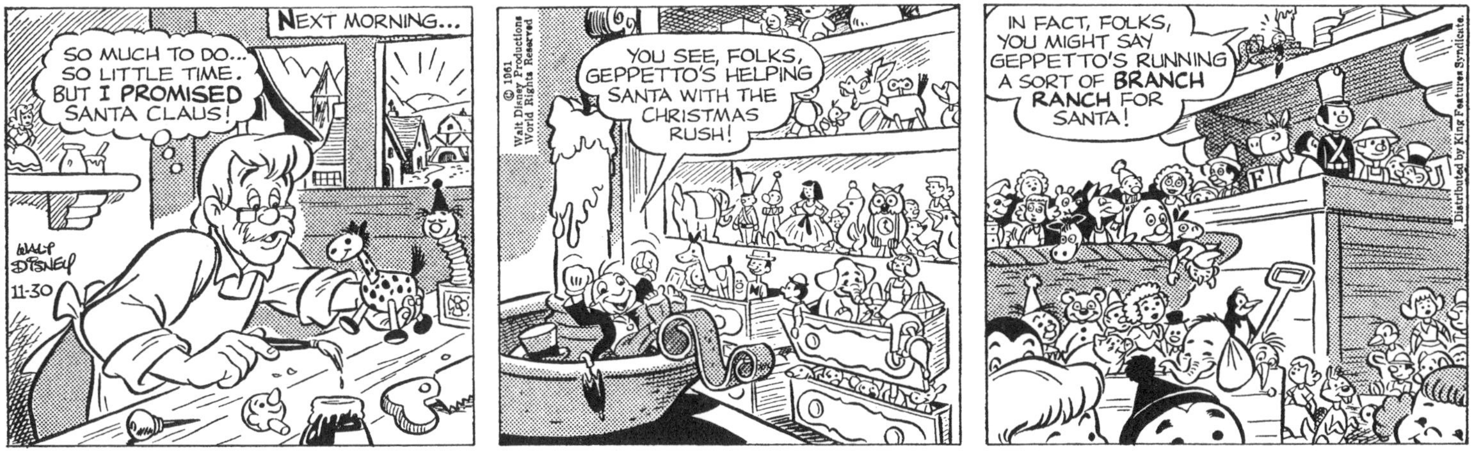
NEXT MORNING...
SO MUCH TO DO... SO LITTLE TIME. BUT I PROMISED SANTA CLAUS!
WALT DISNEY
11-30
© 1961 Walt Disney Productions World Rights Reserved
YOU SEE, FOLKS, GEPPETTO'S HELPING SANTA WITH THE CHRISTMAS RUSH!
IN FACT, FOLKS, YOU MIGHT SAY GEPPETTO'S RUNNING A SORT OF BRANCH RANCH FOR SANTA!
Distributed by King Features Syndicate.

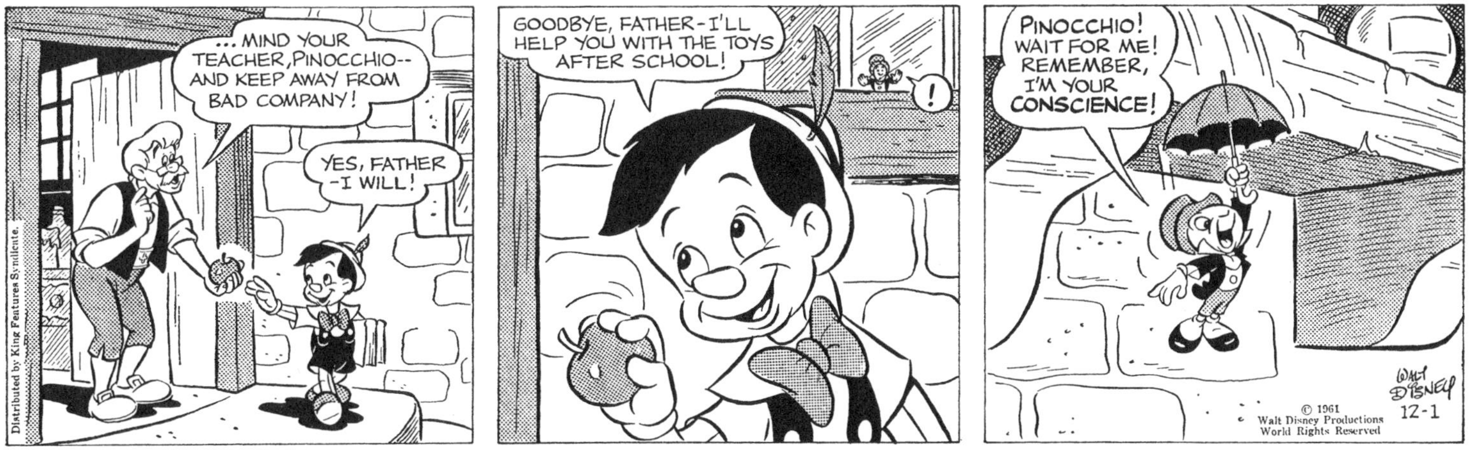
...MIND YOUR TEACHER, PINOCCHIO-- AND KEEP AWAY FROM BAD COMPANY!
YES, FATHER -I WILL!
Distributed by King Features Syndicate.
GOODBYE, FATHER-I'LL HELP YOU WITH THE TOYS AFTER SCHOOL!
!
PINOCCHIO! WAIT FOR ME! REMEMBER, I'M YOUR CONSCIENCE!
WALT DISNEY
12-1
© 1961 Walt Disney Productions World Rights Reserved

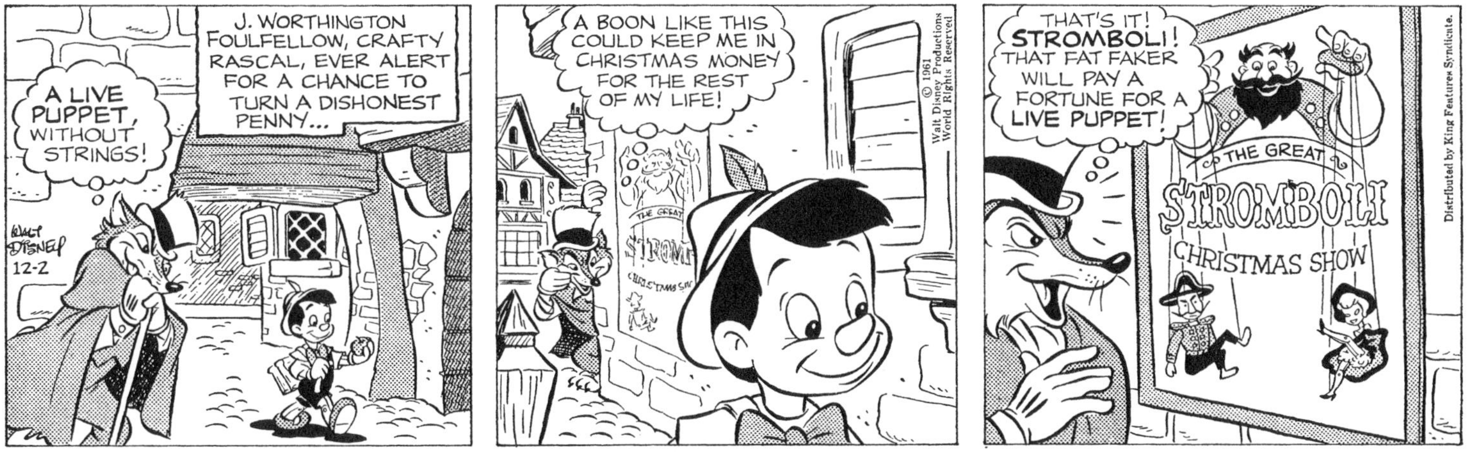
J. WORTHINGTON FOULFELLOW, CRAFTY RASCAL, EVER ALERT FOR A CHANCE TO TURN A DISHONEST PENNY...
A LIVE PUPPET, WITHOUT STRINGS!
WALT DISNEY
12-2
A BOON LIKE THIS COULD KEEP ME IN CHRISTMAS MONEY FOR THE REST OF MY LIFE!
© 1961 Walt Disney Productions World Rights Reserved
THAT'S IT! STROMBOLI! THAT FAT FAKER WILL PAY A FORTUNE FOR A LIVE PUPPET!
THE GREAT
STROMBOLI
CHRISTMAS SHOW
Distributed by King Features Syndicate.

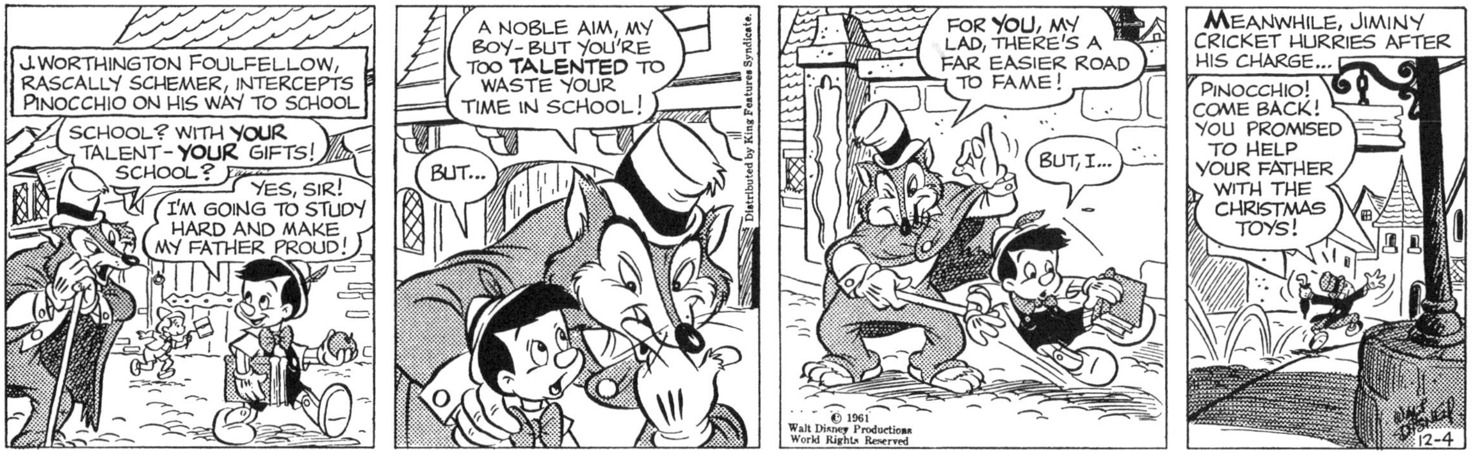
J. WORTHINGTON FOULFELLOW, RASCALLY SCHEMER, INTERCEPTS PINOCCHIO ON HIS WAY TO SCHOOL
SCHOOL? WITH YOUR TALENT- YOUR GIFTS! SCHOOL?
YES, SIR! I'M GOING TO STUDY HARD AND MAKE MY FATHER PROUD!
A NOBLE AIM, MY BOY- BUT YOU'RE TOO TALENTED TO WASTE YOUR TIME IN SCHOOL!
BUT...
Distributed by King Features Syndicate.
FOR YOU, MY LAD, THERE'S A FAR EASIER ROAD TO FAME!
BUT, I...
© 1961 Walt Disney Productions World Rights Reserved
MEANWHILE, JIMINY CRICKET HURRIES AFTER HIS CHARGE...
PINOCCHIO! COME BACK! YOU PROMISED TO HELP YOUR FATHER WITH THE CHRISTMAS TOYS!
WALT DISNEY
12-4

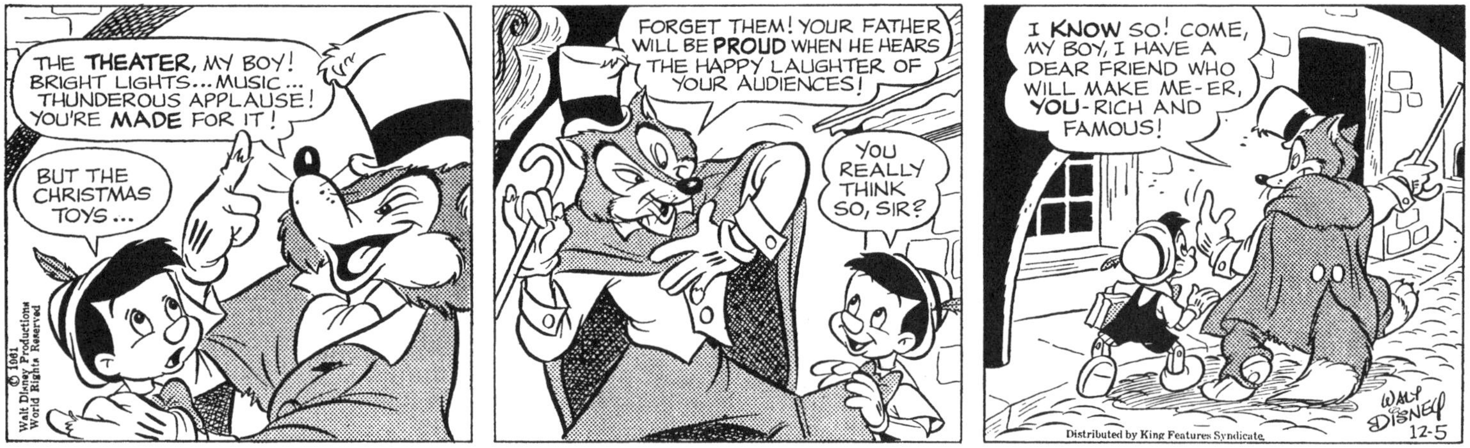
THE THEATER, MY BOY! BRIGHT LIGHTS... MUSIC... THUNDEROUS APPLAUSE! YOU'RE MADE FOR IT!
BUT THE CHRISTMAS TOYS...
© 1961 Walt Disney Productions World Rights Reserved
FORGET THEM! YOUR FATHER WILL BE PROUD WHEN HE HEARS THE HAPPY LAUGHTER OF YOUR AUDIENCES!
YOU REALLY THINK SO, SIR?
I KNOW SO! COME, MY BOY, I HAVE A DEAR FRIEND WHO WILL MAKE ME-ER, YOU-RICH AND FAMOUS!
Distributed by King Features Syndicate.
WALT DISNEY
12-5

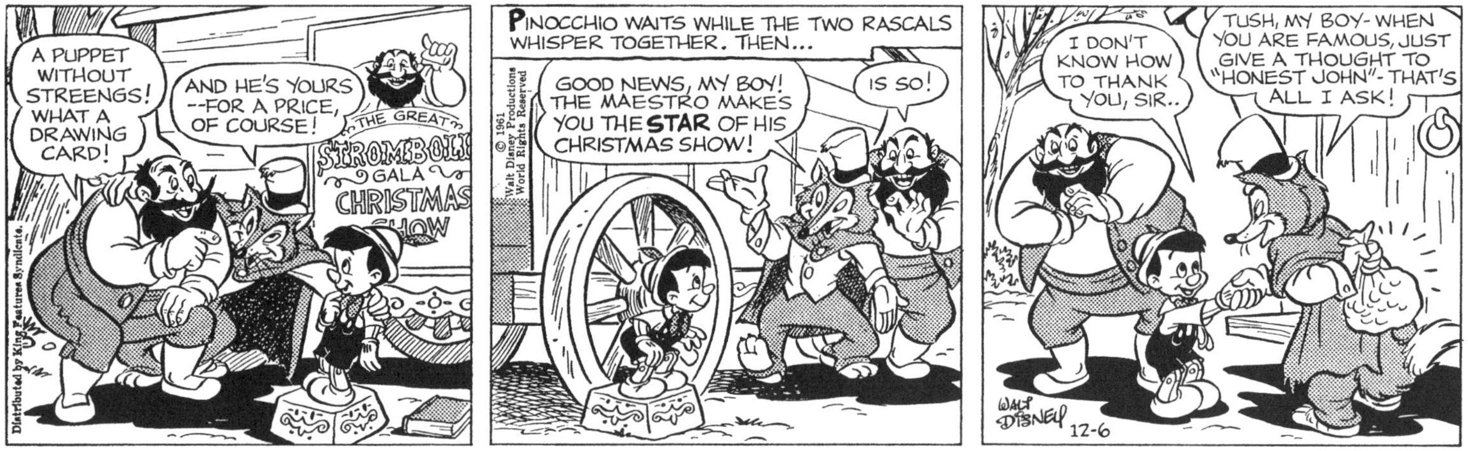
A PUPPET WITHOUT STREENGS! WHAT A DRAWING CARD!
AND HE'S YOURS --FOR A PRICE, OF COURSE!
THE GREAT STROMBOLI GALA CHRISTMAS SHOW
Distributed by King Features Syndicate.
PINOCCHIO WAITS WHILE THE TWO RASCALS WHISPER TOGETHER. THEN...
© 1961 Walt Disney Productions World Rights Reserved
GOOD NEWS, MY BOY! THE MAESTRO MAKES YOU THE STAR OF HIS CHRISTMAS SHOW!
IS SO!
I DON'T KNOW HOW TO THANK YOU, SIR..
TUSH, MY BOY- WHEN YOU ARE FAMOUS, JUST GIVE A THOUGHT TO "HONEST JOHN"- THAT'S ALL I ASK!
WALT DISNEY
12-6

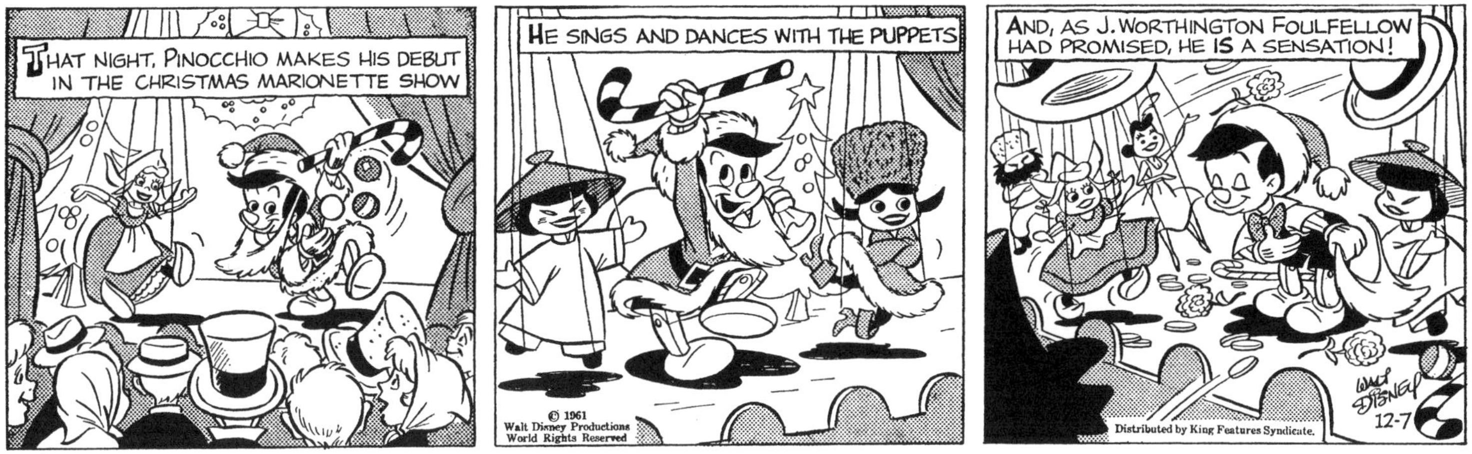
THAT NIGHT, PINOCCHIO MAKES HIS DEBUT IN THE CHRISTMAS MARIONETTE SHOW
HE SINGS AND DANCES WITH THE PUPPETS
© 1961 Walt Disney Productions World Rights Reserved
AND, AS J. WORTHINGTON FOULFELLOW HAD PROMISED, HE IS A SENSATION!
Distributed by King Features Syndicate.
WALT DISNEY
12-7

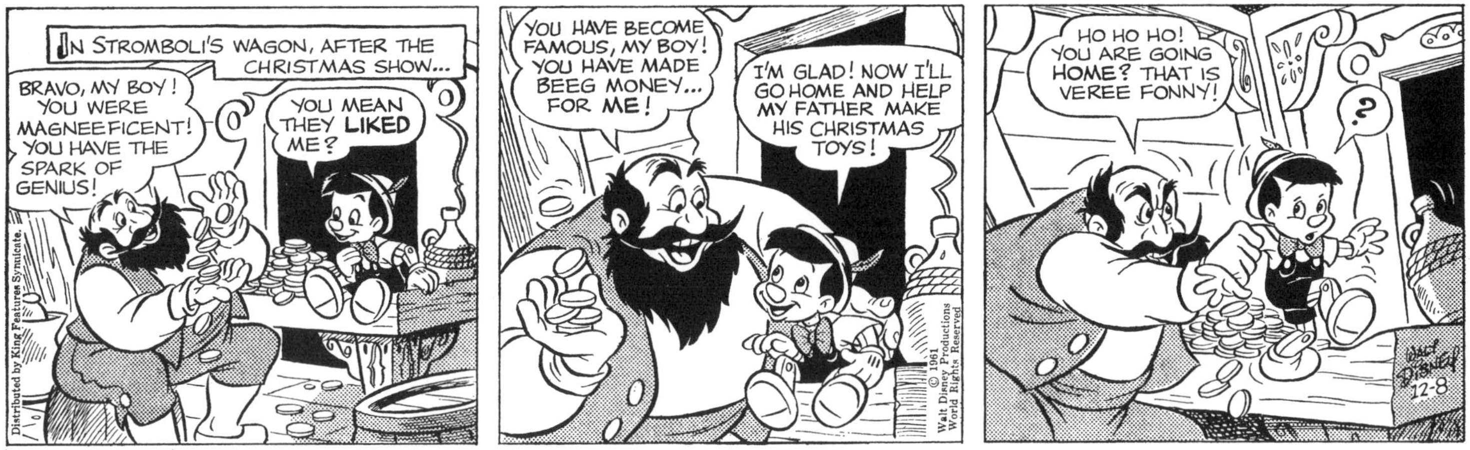
IN STROMBOLI'S WAGON, AFTER THE CHRISTMAS SHOW...
BRAVO, MY BOY! YOU WERE MAGNEEFICENT! YOU HAVE THE SPARK OF GENIUS!
YOU MEAN THEY LIKED ME?
Distributed by King Features Syndicate.
YOU HAVE BECOME FAMOUS, MY BOY! YOU HAVE MADE BEEG MONEY... FOR ME!
I'M GLAD! NOW I'LL GO HOME AND HELP MY FATHER MAKE HIS CHRISTMAS TOYS!
© 1961 Walt Disney Productions World Rights Reserved
HO HO HO! YOU ARE GOING HOME? THAT IS VEREE FONNY!
?
WALT DISNEY
12-8

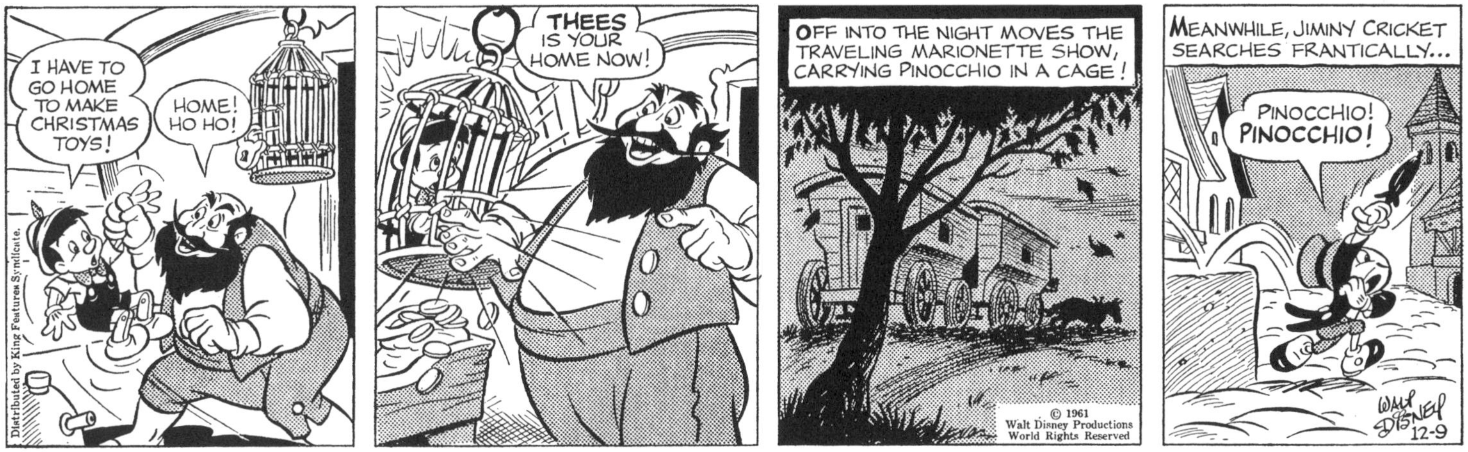
I HAVE TO GO HOME TO MAKE CHRISTMAS TOYS!
HOME! HO HO!
Distributed by King Features Syndicate.
THEES IS YOUR HOME NOW!
OFF INTO THE NIGHT MOVES THE TRAVELING MARIONETTE SHOW, CARRYING PINOCCHIO IN A CAGE!
© 1961 Walt Disney Productions World Rights Reserved
MEANWHILE, JIMINY CRICKET SEARCHES FRANTICALLY...
PINOCCHIO! PINOCCHIO!
WALT DISNEY
12-9

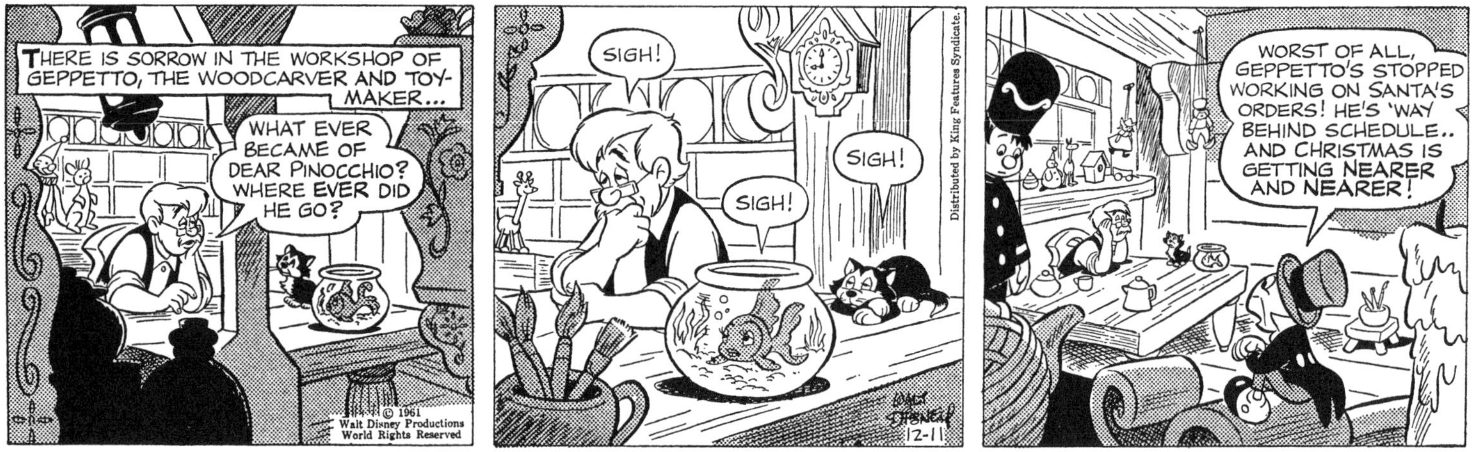
THERE IS SORROW IN THE WORKSHOP OF GEPPETTO, THE WOODCARVER AND TOY-MAKER...
WHAT EVER BECAME OF DEAR PINOCCHIO? WHERE EVER DID HE GO?
© 1961 Walt Disney Productions World Rights Reserved
SIGH!
SIGH!
SIGH!
WALT DISNEY 12-11
Distributed by King Features Syndicate.
WORST OF ALL, GEPPETTO'S STOPPED WORKING ON SANTA'S ORDERS! HE'S 'WAY BEHIND SCHEDULE.. AND CHRISTMAS IS GETTING NEARER AND NEARER!

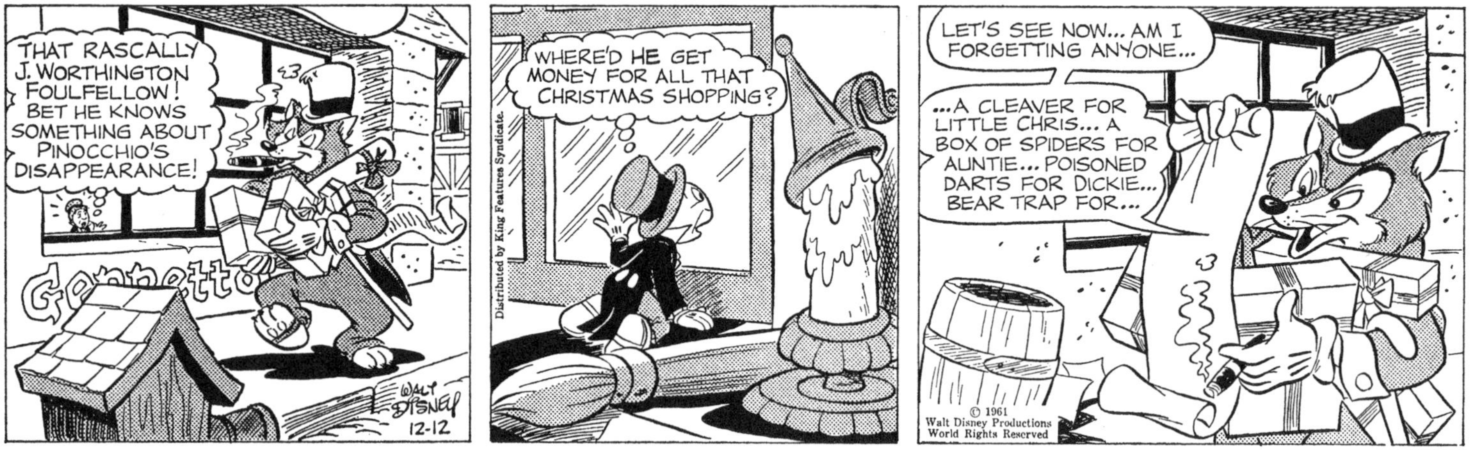
THAT RASCALLY J. WORTHINGTON FOULFELLOW! BET HE KNOWS SOMETHING ABOUT PINOCCHIO'S DISAPPEARANCE!
Geppetto
WALT DISNEY 12-12
Distributed by King Features Syndicate.
WHERE'D HE GET MONEY FOR ALL THAT CHRISTMAS SHOPPING?
LET'S SEE NOW... AM I FORGETTING ANYONE...
...A CLEAVER FOR LITTLE CHRIS... A BOX OF SPIDERS FOR AUNTIE... POISONED DARTS FOR DICKIE... BEAR TRAP FOR...
© 1961 Walt Disney Productions World Rights Reserved

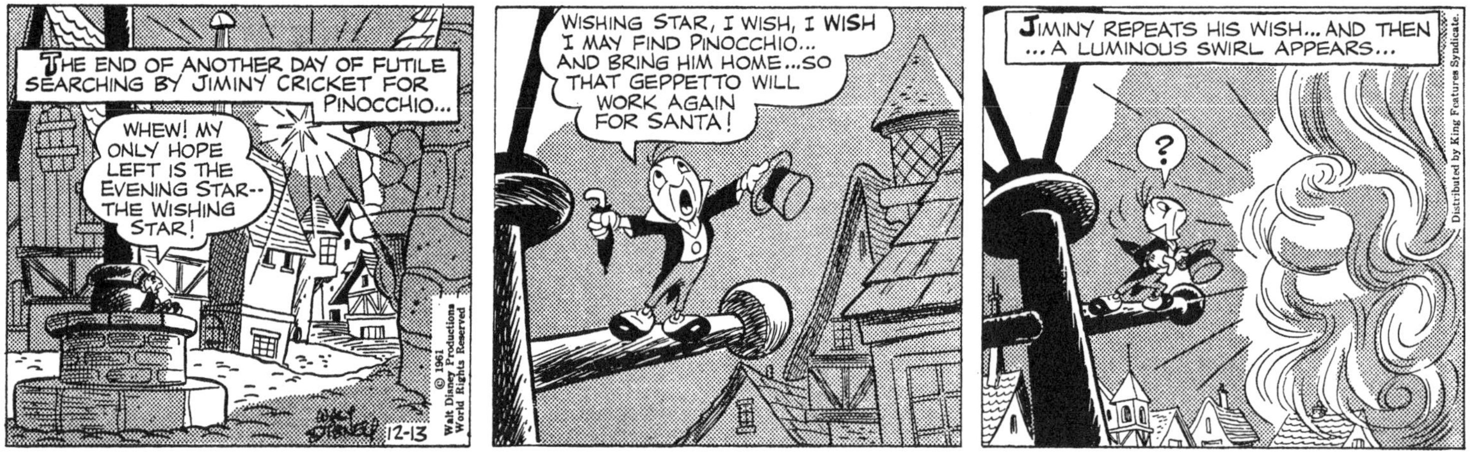
THE END OF ANOTHER DAY OF FUTILE SEARCHING BY JIMINY CRICKET FOR PINOCCHIO...
WHEW! MY ONLY HOPE LEFT IS THE EVENING STAR-- THE WISHING STAR!
© 1961 Walt Disney Productions World Rights Reserved
WALT DISNEY 12-13
WISHING STAR, I WISH, I WISH I MAY FIND PINOCCHIO... AND BRING HIM HOME...SO THAT GEPPETTO WILL WORK AGAIN FOR SANTA!
JIMINY REPEATS HIS WISH...AND THEN ...A LUMINOUS SWIRL APPEARS...
?
Distributed by King Features Syndicate.

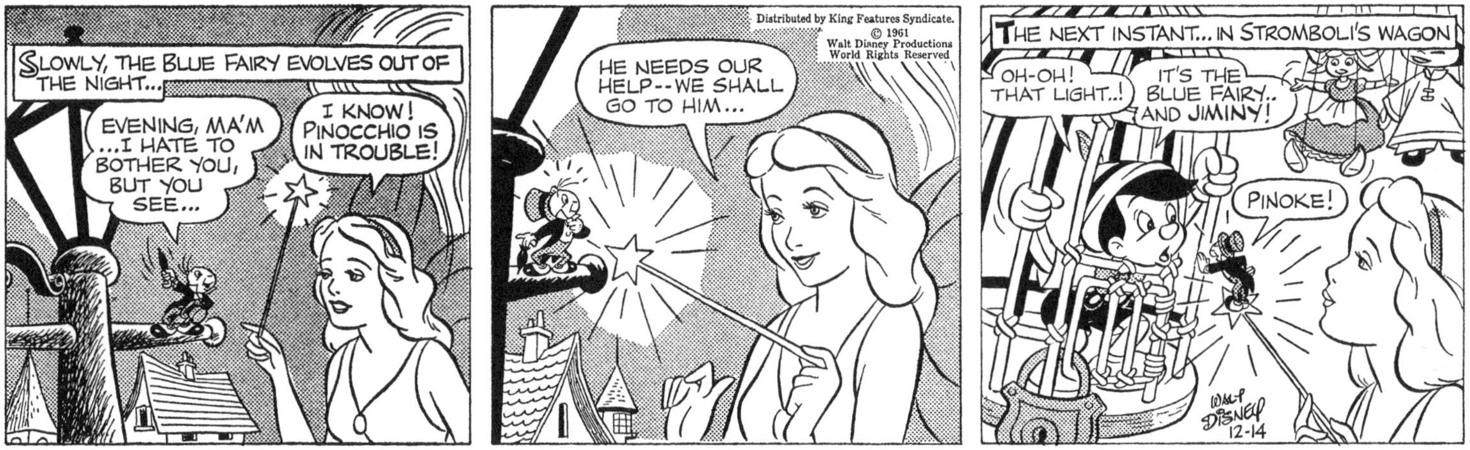
SLOWLY, THE BLUE FAIRY EVOLVES OUT OF THE NIGHT...
EVENING, MA'M ...I HATE TO BOTHER YOU, BUT YOU SEE...
I KNOW! PINOCCHIO IS IN TROUBLE!
Distributed by King Features Syndicate. © 1961 Walt Disney Productions World Rights Reserved
HE NEEDS OUR HELP--WE SHALL GO TO HIM...
THE NEXT INSTANT... IN STROMBOLI'S WAGON
OH-OH! THAT LIGHT..!
IT'S THE BLUE FAIRY.. AND JIMINY!
PINOKE!
WALT DISNEY 12-14

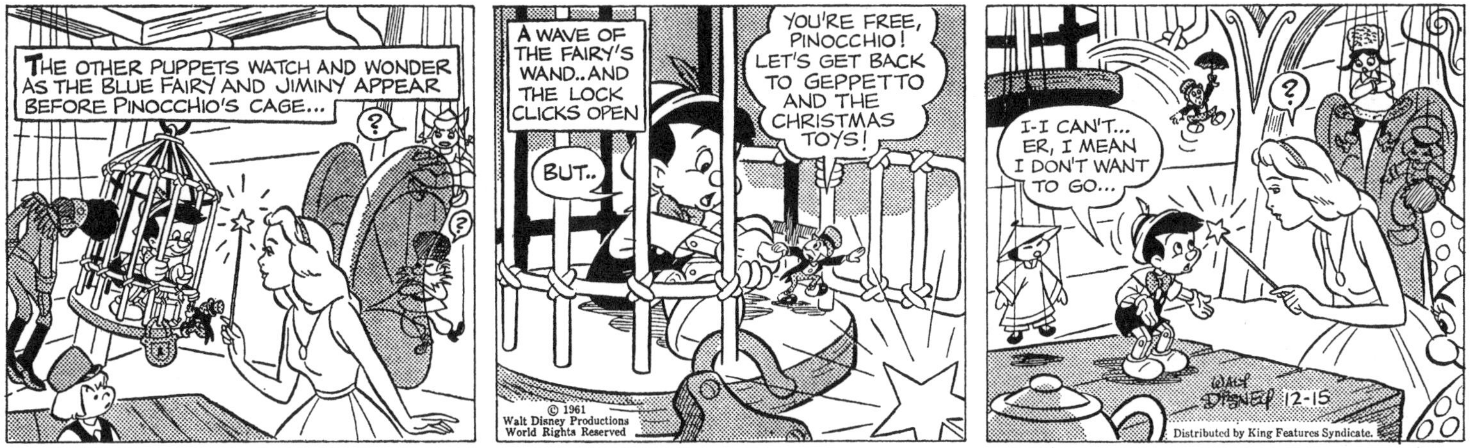
THE OTHER PUPPETS WATCH AND WONDER AS THE BLUE FAIRY AND JIMINY APPEAR BEFORE PINOCCHIO'S CAGE...
?
?
A WAVE OF THE FAIRY'S WAND..AND THE LOCK CLICKS OPEN
YOU'RE FREE, PINOCCHIO! LET'S GET BACK TO GEPPETTO AND THE CHRISTMAS TOYS!
BUT..
© 1961 Walt Disney Productions World Rights Reserved
?
I-I CAN'T... ER, I MEAN I DON'T WANT TO GO...
WALT DISNEY 12-15
Distributed by King Features Syndicate.

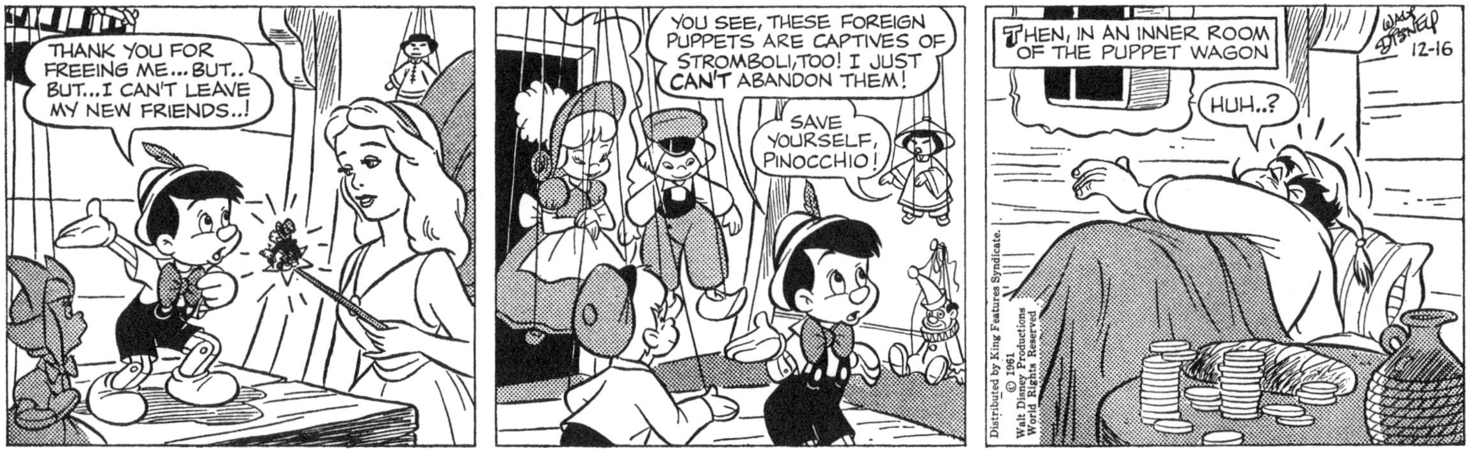
THANK YOU FOR FREEING ME... BUT.. BUT...I CAN'T LEAVE MY NEW FRIENDS..!
YOU SEE, THESE FOREIGN PUPPETS ARE CAPTIVES OF STROMBOLI,TOO! I JUST CAN'T ABANDON THEM!
SAVE YOURSELF, PINOCCHIO!
Distributed by King Features Syndicate. © 1961 Walt Disney Productions World Rights Reserved
THEN, IN AN INNER ROOM OF THE PUPPET WAGON
WALT DISNEY 12-16
HUH..?

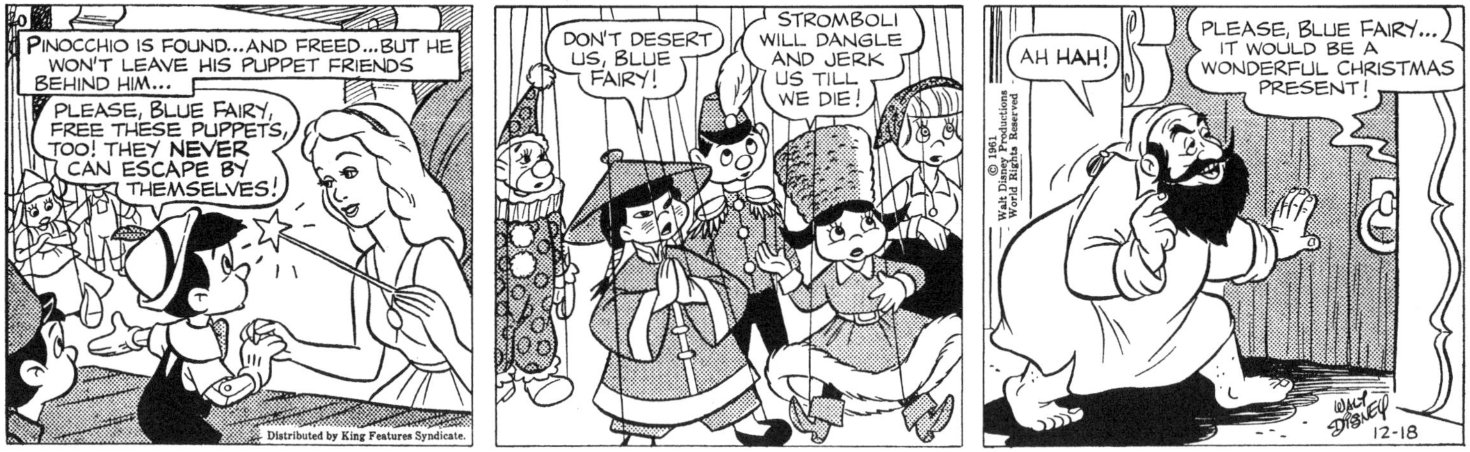
PINOCCHIO IS FOUND...AND FREED...BUT HE WON'T LEAVE HIS PUPPET FRIENDS BEHIND HIM...
PLEASE, BLUE FAIRY, FREE THESE PUPPETS, TOO! THEY NEVER CAN ESCAPE BY THEMSELVES!
Distributed by King Features Syndicate.
DON'T DESERT US, BLUE FAIRY!
STROMBOLI WILL DANGLE AND JERK US TILL WE DIE!
© 1961 Walt Disney Productions World Rights Reserved
AH HAH!
PLEASE, BLUE FAIRY... IT WOULD BE A WONDERFUL CHRISTMAS PRESENT!
WALT DISNEY
12-18

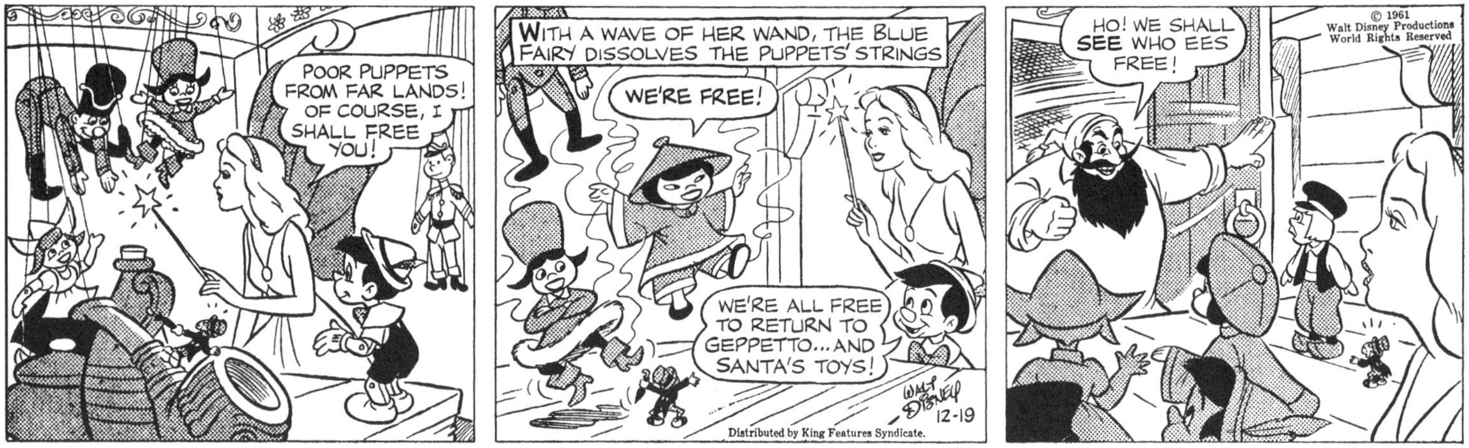
POOR PUPPETS FROM FAR LANDS! OF COURSE, I SHALL FREE YOU!
WITH A WAVE OF HER WAND, THE BLUE FAIRY DISSOLVES THE PUPPETS' STRINGS
WE'RE FREE!
WE'RE ALL FREE TO RETURN TO GEPPETTO...AND SANTA'S TOYS!
WALT DISNEY
12-19
Distributed by King Features Syndicate.
© 1961 Walt Disney Productions World Rights Reserved
HO! WE SHALL SEE WHO EES FREE!

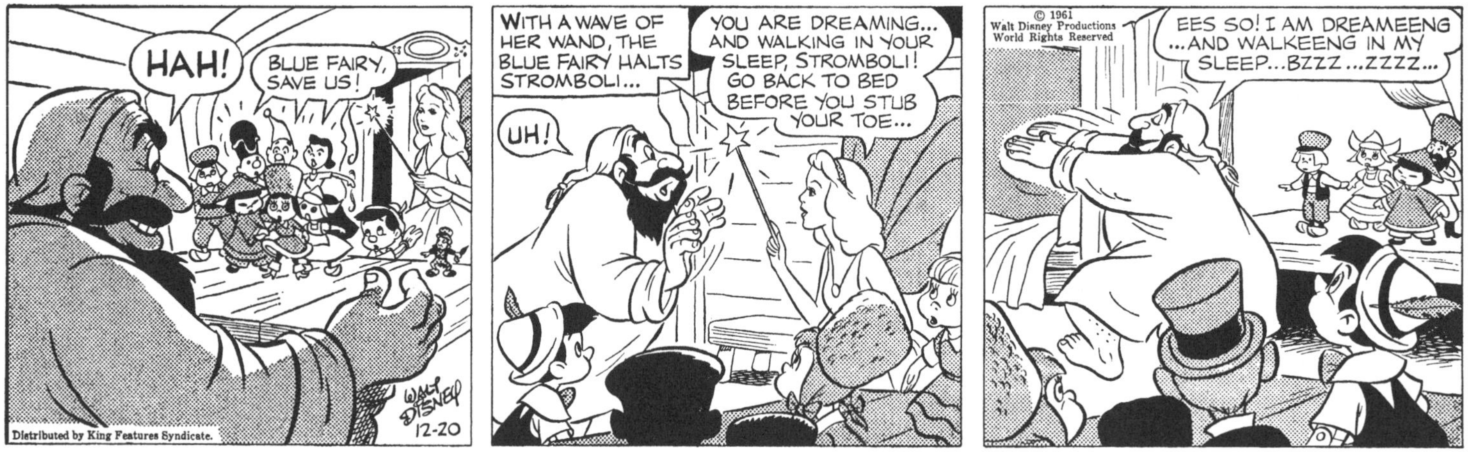
HAH!
BLUE FAIRY, SAVE US!
WALT DISNEY
12-20
Distributed by King Features Syndicate.
WITH A WAVE OF HER WAND, THE BLUE FAIRY HALTS STROMBOLI...
YOU ARE DREAMING... AND WALKING IN YOUR SLEEP, STROMBOLI! GO BACK TO BED BEFORE YOU STUB YOUR TOE...
UH!
© 1961 Walt Disney Productions World Rights Reserved
EES SO! I AM DREAMEENG ...AND WALKEENG IN MY SLEEP...BZZZ...ZZZZ...

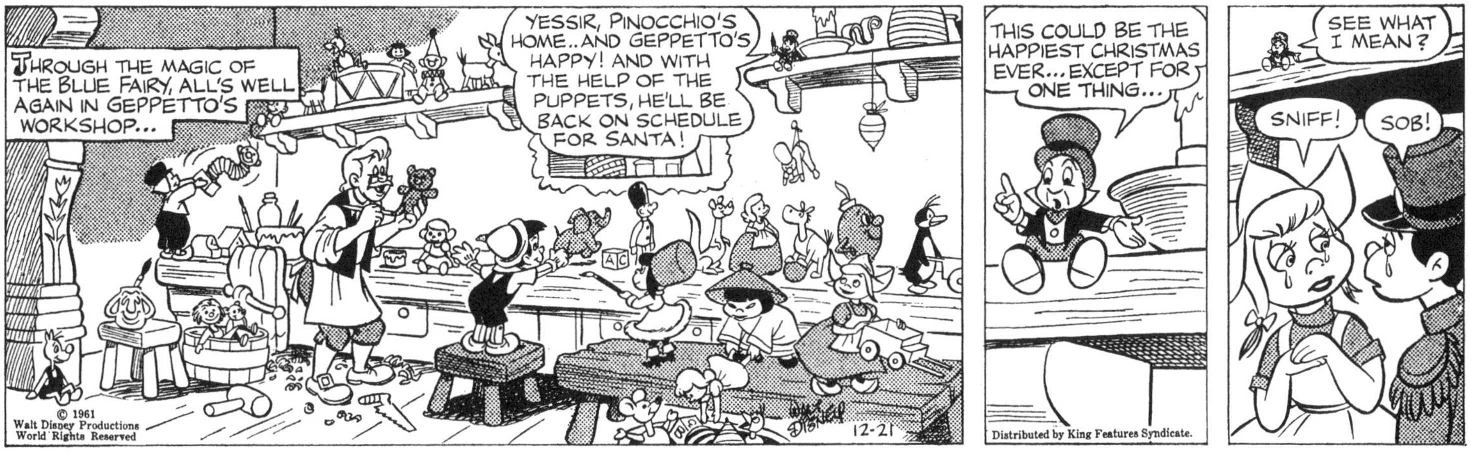
THROUGH THE MAGIC OF THE BLUE FAIRY, ALL'S WELL AGAIN IN GEPPETTO'S WORKSHOP...
YESSIR, PINOCCHIO'S HOME..AND GEPPETTO'S HAPPY! AND WITH THE HELP OF THE PUPPETS, HE'LL BE BACK ON SCHEDULE FOR SANTA!
© 1961 Walt Disney Productions World Rights Reserved
12-21
THIS COULD BE THE HAPPIEST CHRISTMAS EVER... EXCEPT FOR ONE THING...
Distributed by King Features Syndicate.
SEE WHAT I MEAN?
SNIFF!
SOB!

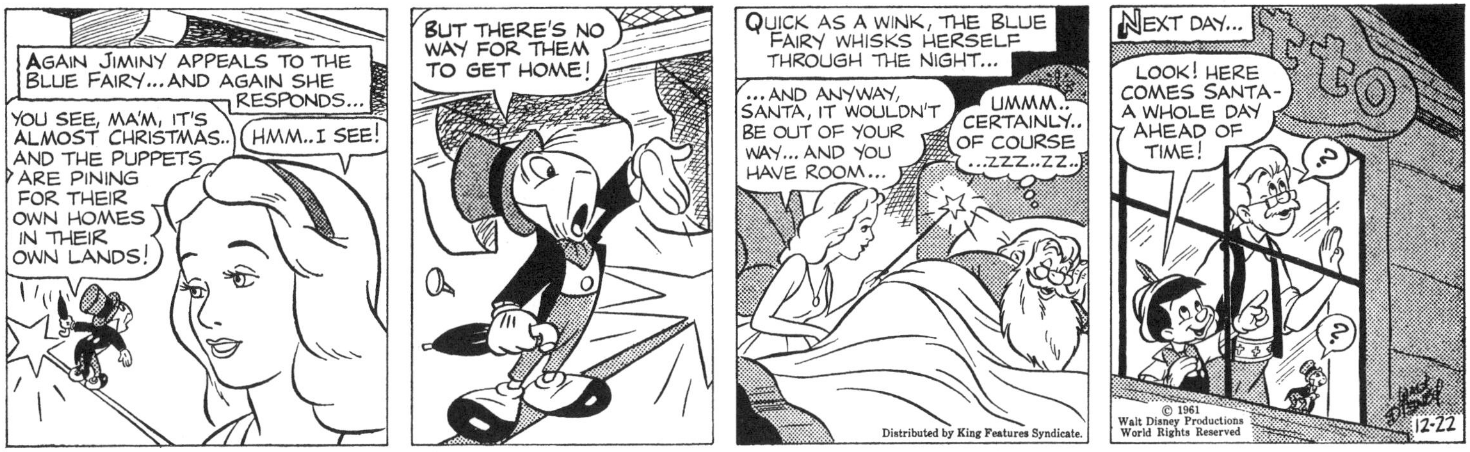
AGAIN JIMINY APPEALS TO THE BLUE FAIRY... AND AGAIN SHE RESPONDS...
YOU SEE, MA'M, IT'S ALMOST CHRISTMAS.. AND THE PUPPETS ARE PINING FOR THEIR OWN HOMES IN THEIR OWN LANDS!
HMM..I SEE!
BUT THERE'S NO WAY FOR THEM TO GET HOME!
QUICK AS A WINK, THE BLUE FAIRY WHISKS HERSELF THROUGH THE NIGHT...
...AND ANYWAY, SANTA, IT WOULDN'T BE OUT OF YOUR WAY... AND YOU HAVE ROOM...
UMMM.. CERTAINLY.. OF COURSE ...ZZZ..ZZ..
Distributed by King Features Syndicate.
NEXT DAY...
LOOK! HERE COMES SANTA - A WHOLE DAY AHEAD OF TIME!
?
?
© 1961 Walt Disney Productions World Rights Reserved
12-22

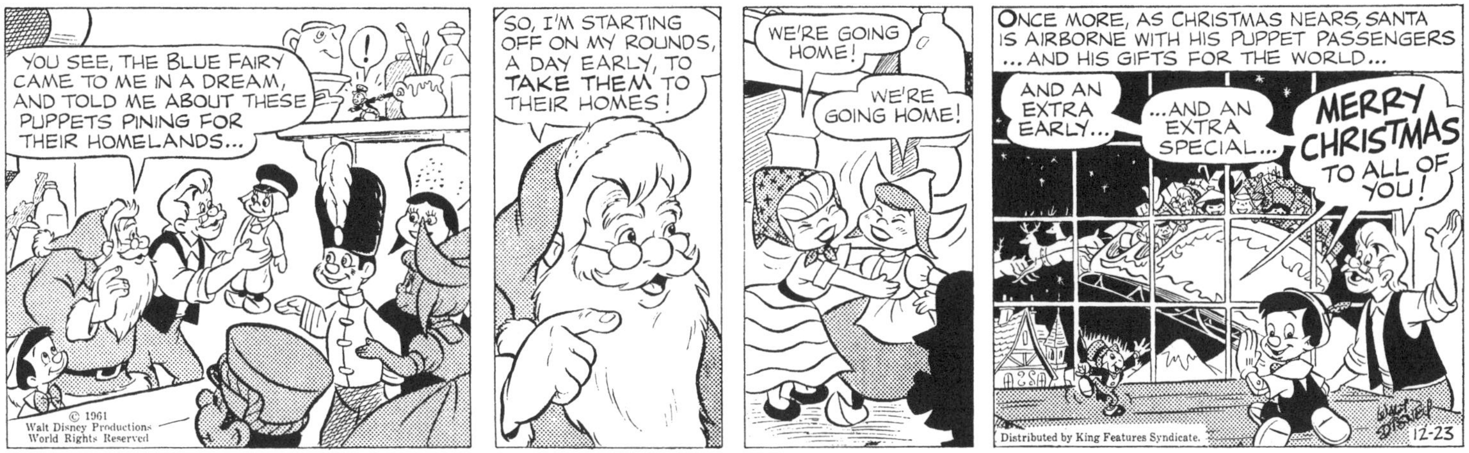
YOU SEE, THE BLUE FAIRY CAME TO ME IN A DREAM, AND TOLD ME ABOUT THESE PUPPETS PINING FOR THEIR HOMELANDS...
!
© 1961 Walt Disney Productions World Rights Reserved
SO, I'M STARTING OFF ON MY ROUNDS, A DAY EARLY, TO TAKE THEM TO THEIR HOMES!
WE'RE GOING HOME!
WE'RE GOING HOME!
ONCE MORE, AS CHRISTMAS NEARS, SANTA IS AIRBORNE WITH HIS PUPPET PASSENGERS ...AND HIS GIFTS FOR THE WORLD...
AND AN EXTRA EARLY...
...AND AN EXTRA SPECIAL...
MERRY CHRISTMAS TO ALL OF YOU!
Distributed by King Features Syndicate.
12-23

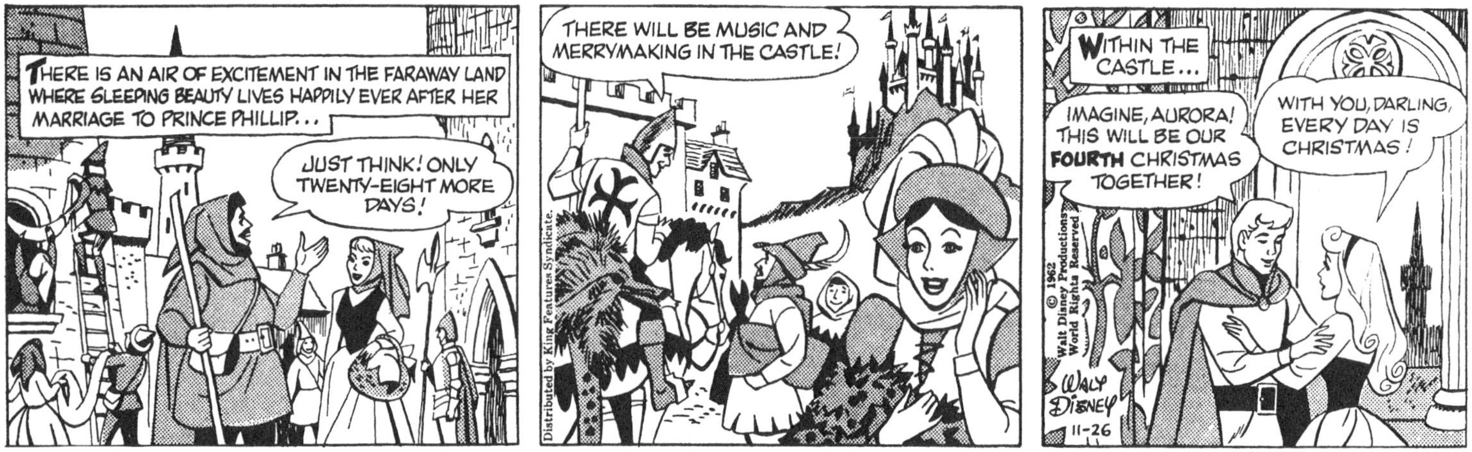
THERE IS AN AIR OF EXCITEMENT IN THE FARAWAY LAND WHERE SLEEPING BEAUTY LIVES HAPPILY EVER AFTER HER MARRIAGE TO PRINCE PHILLIP...
JUST THINK! ONLY TWENTY-EIGHT MORE DAYS!
Distributed by King Features Syndicate.
THERE WILL BE MUSIC AND MERRYMAKING IN THE CASTLE!
WITHIN THE CASTLE...
IMAGINE, AURORA! THIS WILL BE OUR FOURTH CHRISTMAS TOGETHER!
WITH YOU, DARLING, EVERY DAY IS CHRISTMAS!
© 1962 Walt Disney Productions World Rights Reserved
WALT DISNEY
11-26

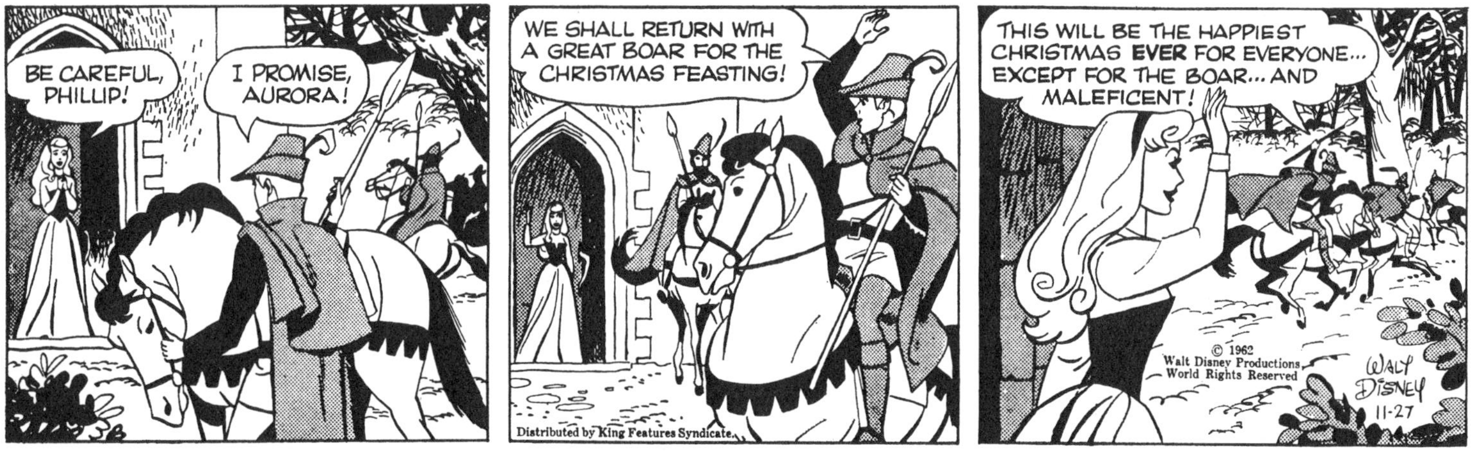
BE CAREFUL, PHILLIP!
I PROMISE, AURORA!
WE SHALL RETURN WITH A GREAT BOAR FOR THE CHRISTMAS FEASTING!
Distributed by King Features Syndicate.
THIS WILL BE THE HAPPIEST CHRISTMAS EVER FOR EVERYONE... EXCEPT FOR THE BOAR... AND MALEFICENT!
© 1962 Walt Disney Productions World Rights Reserved
WALT DISNEY
11-27

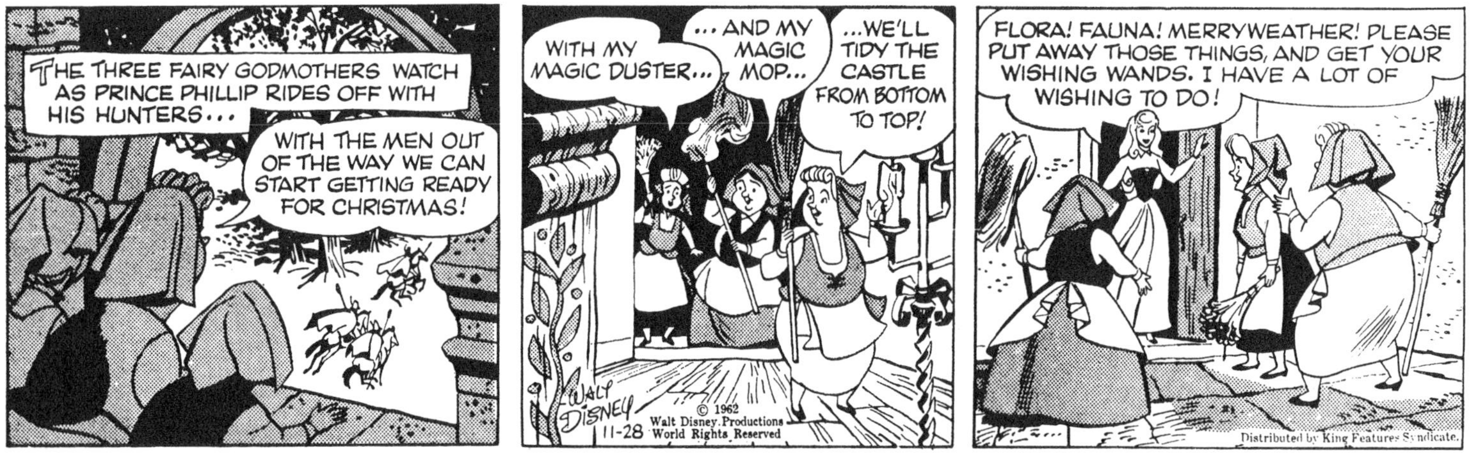
THE THREE FAIRY GODMOTHERS WATCH AS PRINCE PHILLIP RIDES OFF WITH HIS HUNTERS...
WITH THE MEN OUT OF THE WAY WE CAN START GETTING READY FOR CHRISTMAS!
WITH MY MAGIC DUSTER...
...AND MY MAGIC MOP...
...WE'LL TIDY THE CASTLE FROM BOTTOM TO TOP!
WALT DISNEY
11-28
© 1962 Walt Disney Productions World Rights Reserved
FLORA! FAUNA! MERRYWEATHER! PLEASE PUT AWAY THOSE THINGS, AND GET YOUR WISHING WANDS. I HAVE A LOT OF WISHING TO DO!
Distributed by King Features Syndicate.

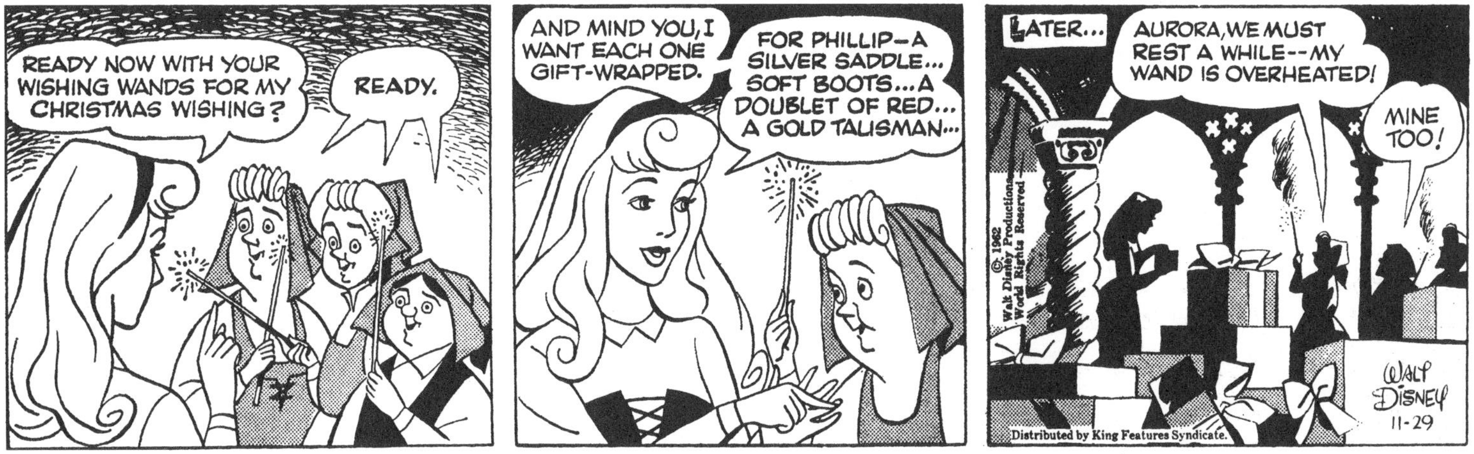
READY NOW WITH YOUR WISHING WANDS FOR MY CHRISTMAS WISHING?
READY.
AND MIND YOU, I WANT EACH ONE GIFT-WRAPPED.
FOR PHILLIP—A SILVER SADDLE... SOFT BOOTS...A DOUBLET OF RED... A GOLD TALISMAN...
LATER...
AURORA, WE MUST REST A WHILE--MY WAND IS OVERHEATED!
MINE TOO!
© 1962 Walt Disney Productions World Rights Reserved
WALT DISNEY 11-29
Distributed by King Features Syndicate.

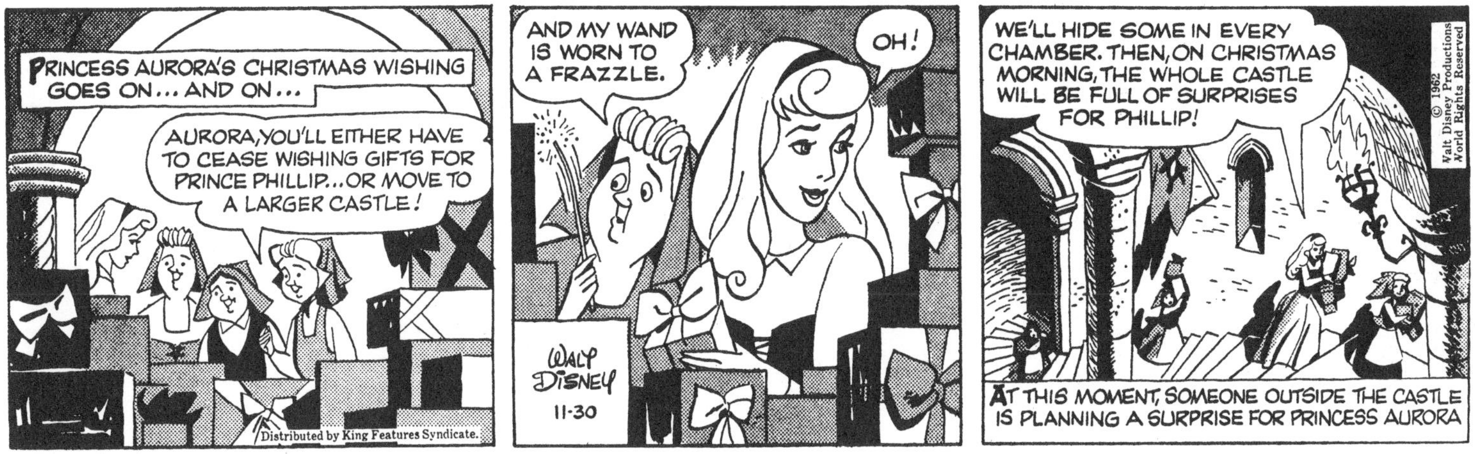
PRINCESS AURORA'S CHRISTMAS WISHING GOES ON... AND ON...
AURORA, YOU'LL EITHER HAVE TO CEASE WISHING GIFTS FOR PRINCE PHILLIP...OR MOVE TO A LARGER CASTLE!
Distributed by King Features Syndicate.
AND MY WAND IS WORN TO A FRAZZLE.
OH!
WALT DISNEY 11-30
WE'LL HIDE SOME IN EVERY CHAMBER. THEN, ON CHRISTMAS MORNING, THE WHOLE CASTLE WILL BE FULL OF SURPRISES FOR PHILLIP!
© 1962 Walt Disney Productions World Rights Reserved
AT THIS MOMENT, SOMEONE OUTSIDE THE CASTLE IS PLANNING A SURPRISE FOR PRINCESS AURORA

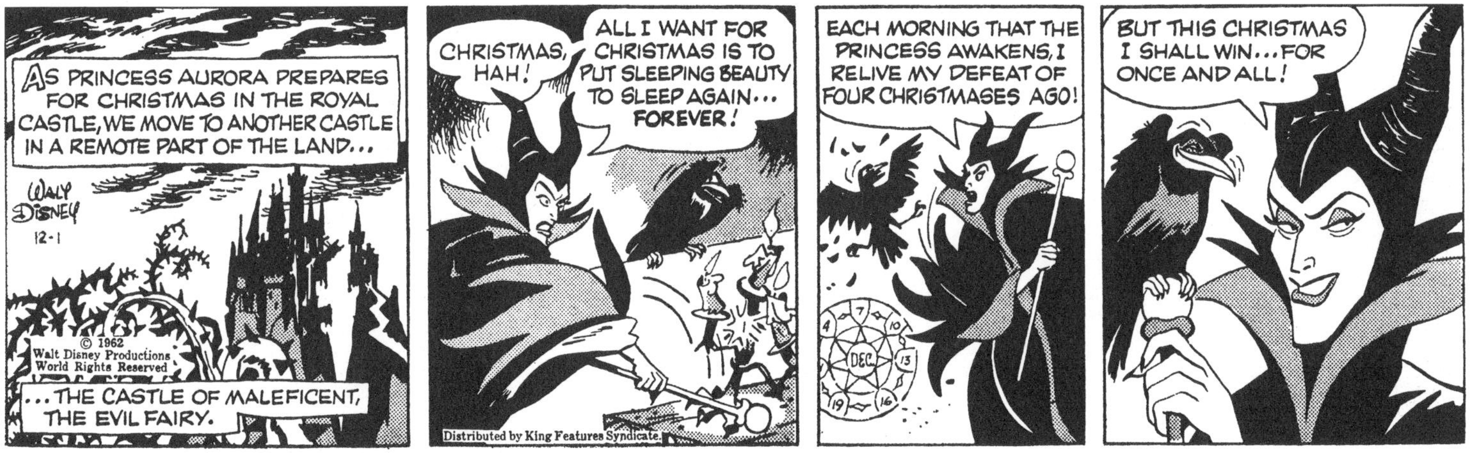
AS PRINCESS AURORA PREPARES FOR CHRISTMAS IN THE ROYAL CASTLE, WE MOVE TO ANOTHER CASTLE IN A REMOTE PART OF THE LAND...
WALT DISNEY 12-1
© 1962 Walt Disney Productions World Rights Reserved
...THE CASTLE OF MALEFICENT, THE EVIL FAIRY.
CHRISTMAS, HAH!
ALL I WANT FOR CHRISTMAS IS TO PUT SLEEPING BEAUTY TO SLEEP AGAIN... FOREVER!
Distributed by King Features Syndicate.
EACH MORNING THAT THE PRINCESS AWAKENS, I RELIVE MY DEFEAT OF FOUR CHRISTMASES AGO!
DEC
BUT THIS CHRISTMAS I SHALL WIN...FOR ONCE AND ALL!

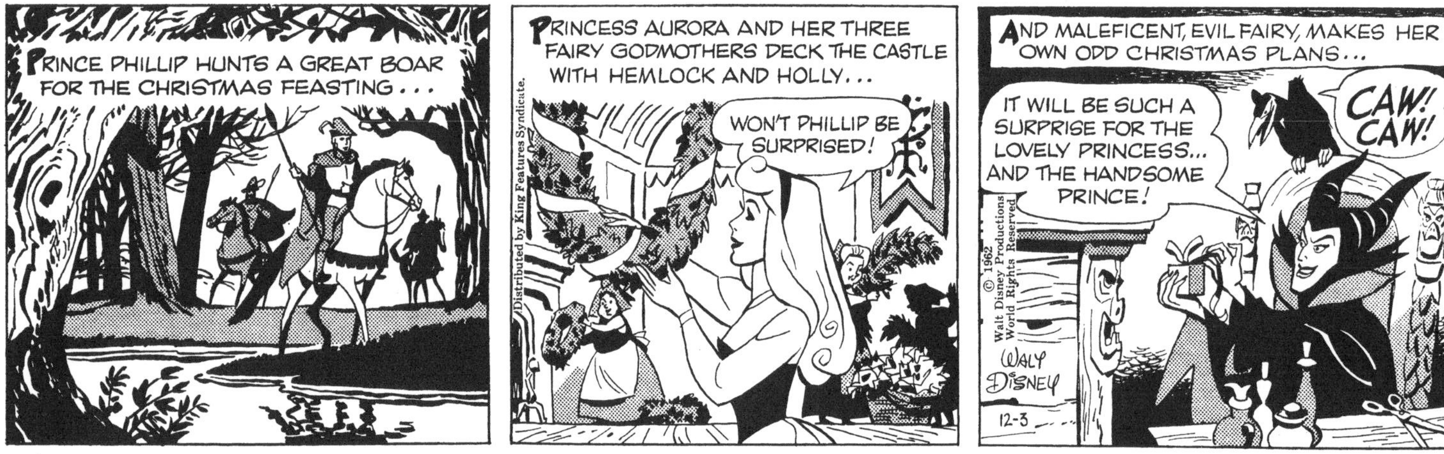
PRINCE PHILLIP HUNTS A GREAT BOAR FOR THE CHRISTMAS FEASTING . . .
PRINCESS AURORA AND HER THREE FAIRY GODMOTHERS DECK THE CASTLE WITH HEMLOCK AND HOLLY . . .
WON'T PHILLIP BE SURPRISED!
Distributed by King Features Syndicate.
AND MALEFICENT, EVIL FAIRY, MAKES HER OWN ODD CHRISTMAS PLANS . . .
IT WILL BE SUCH A SURPRISE FOR THE LOVELY PRINCESS... AND THE HANDSOME PRINCE!
CAW! CAW!
© 1962 Walt Disney Productions World Rights Reserved
WALT DISNEY
12-3

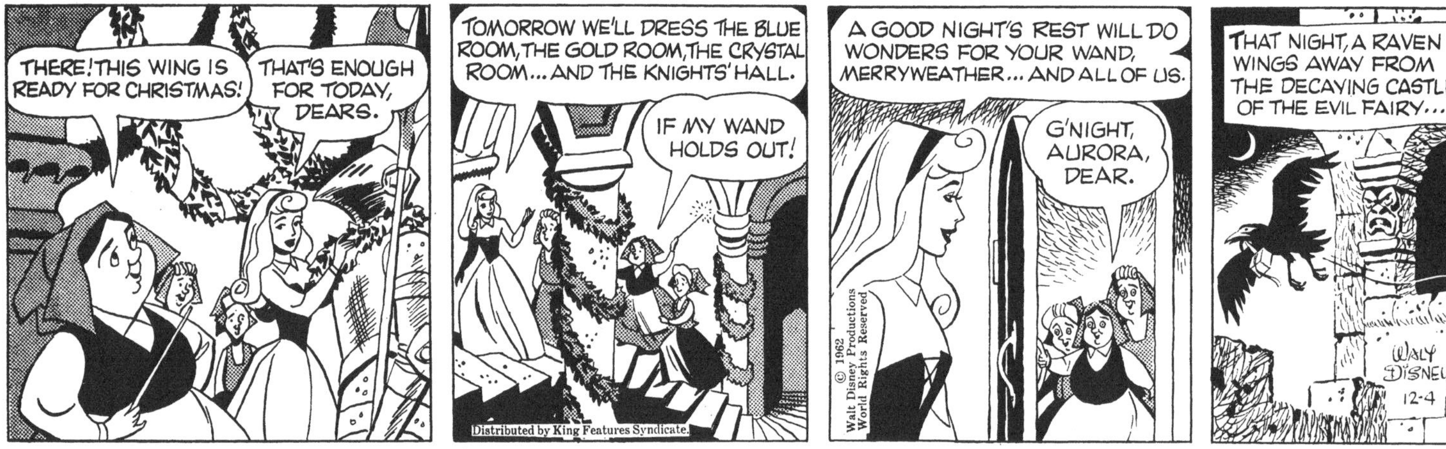
THERE! THIS WING IS READY FOR CHRISTMAS!
THAT'S ENOUGH FOR TODAY, DEARS.
TOMORROW WE'LL DRESS THE BLUE ROOM, THE GOLD ROOM, THE CRYSTAL ROOM ... AND THE KNIGHTS' HALL.
IF MY WAND HOLDS OUT!
Distributed by King Features Syndicate.
A GOOD NIGHT'S REST WILL DO WONDERS FOR YOUR WAND, MERRYWEATHER ... AND ALL OF US.
G'NIGHT, AURORA, DEAR.
© 1962 Walt Disney Productions World Rights Reserved
THAT NIGHT, A RAVEN WINGS AWAY FROM THE DECAYING CASTLE OF THE EVIL FAIRY...
WALT DISNEY
12-4

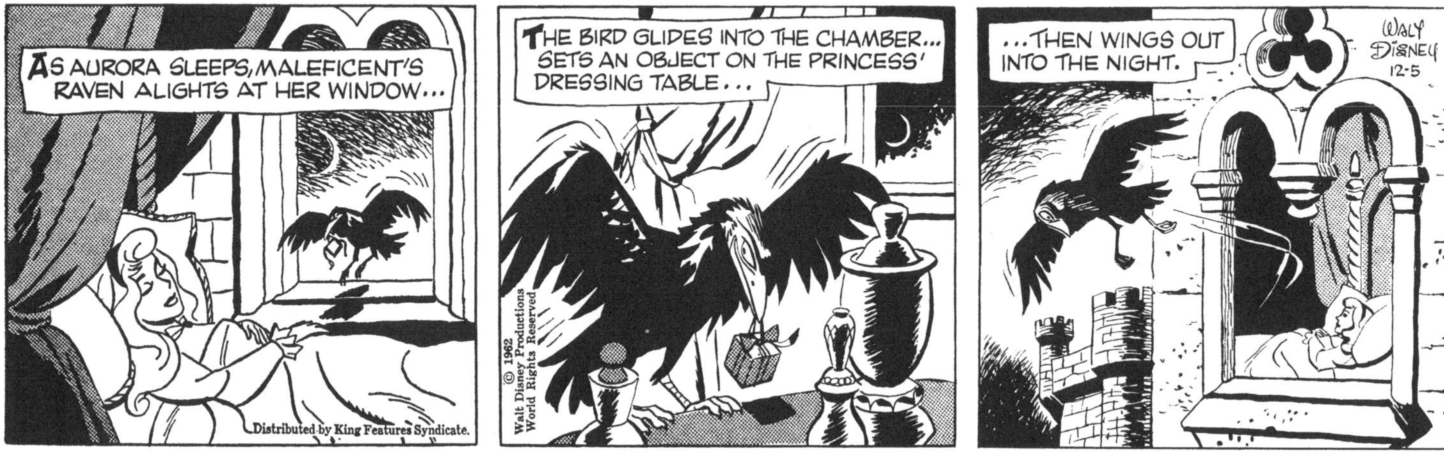
AS AURORA SLEEPS, MALEFICENT'S RAVEN ALIGHTS AT HER WINDOW...
Distributed by King Features Syndicate.
THE BIRD GLIDES INTO THE CHAMBER... SETS AN OBJECT ON THE PRINCESS' DRESSING TABLE . . .
© 1962 Walt Disney Productions World Rights Reserved
. . . THEN WINGS OUT INTO THE NIGHT.
WALT DISNEY
12-5

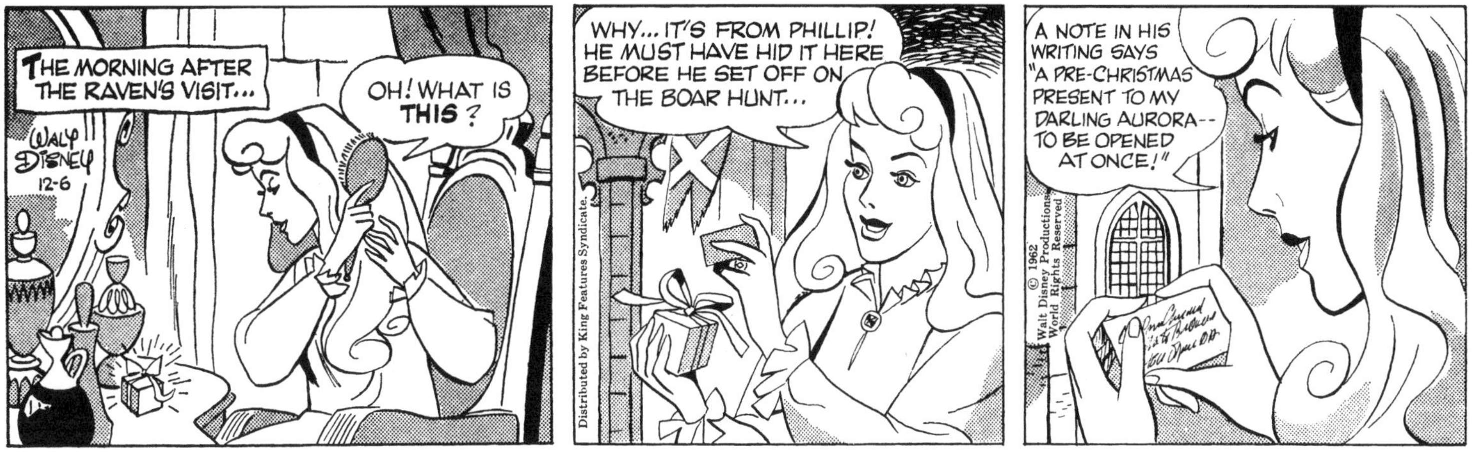
THE MORNING AFTER THE RAVEN'S VISIT...
OH! WHAT IS **THIS**?
WALT DISNEY 12-6
WHY... IT'S FROM PHILLIP! HE MUST HAVE HID IT HERE BEFORE HE SET OFF ON THE BOAR HUNT...
Distributed by King Features Syndicate.
A NOTE IN HIS WRITING SAYS "A PRE-CHRISTMAS PRESENT TO MY DARLING AURORA-- TO BE OPENED AT ONCE!"
© 1962 Walt Disney Productions World Rights Reserved

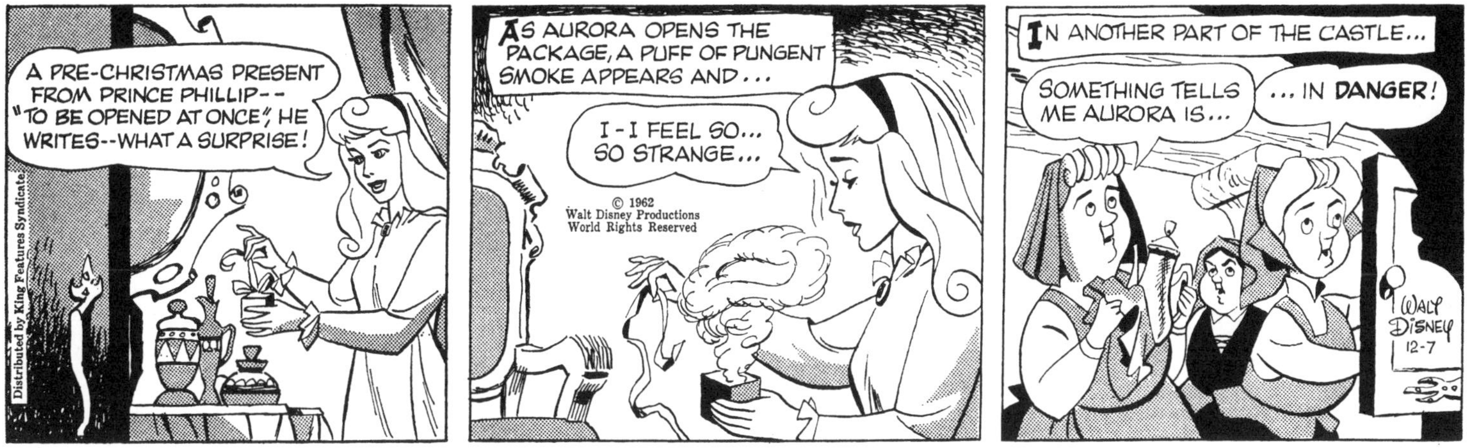
A PRE-CHRISTMAS PRESENT FROM PRINCE PHILLIP-- "TO BE OPENED AT ONCE", HE WRITES--WHAT A SURPRISE!
Distributed by King Features Syndicate.
AS AURORA OPENS THE PACKAGE, A PUFF OF PUNGENT SMOKE APPEARS AND...
I-I FEEL SO... SO STRANGE...
© 1962 Walt Disney Productions World Rights Reserved
IN ANOTHER PART OF THE CASTLE...
SOMETHING TELLS ME AURORA IS...
... IN **DANGER**!
WALT DISNEY 12-7

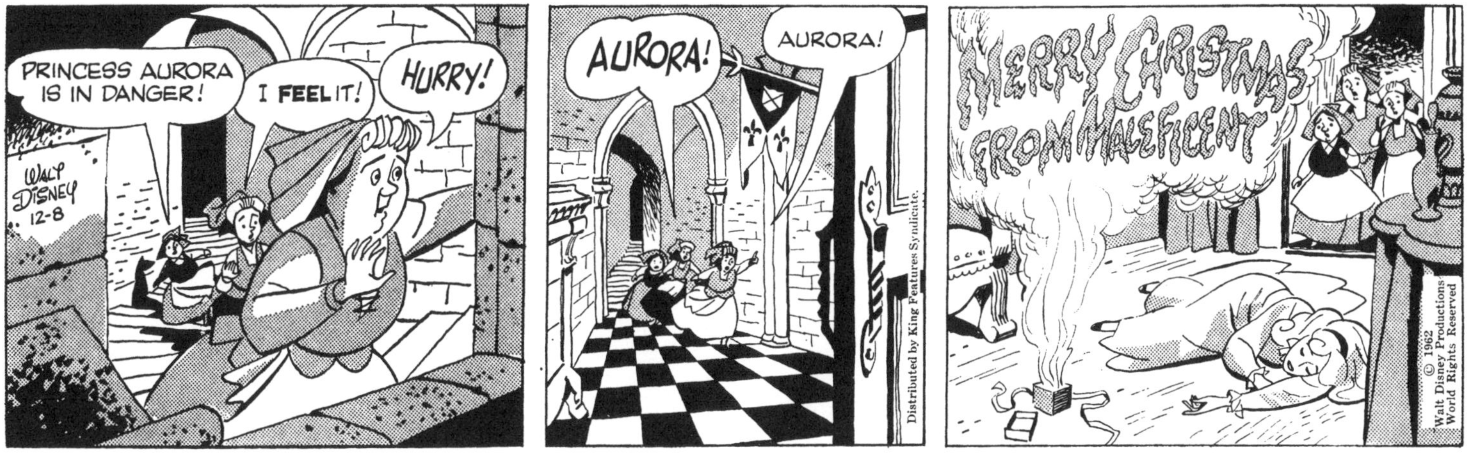
PRINCESS AURORA IS IN DANGER!
I **FEEL** IT!
HURRY!
WALT DISNEY 12-8
AURORA!
AURORA!
Distributed by King Features Syndicate.
MERRY CHRISTMAS FROM MALEFICENT
© 1962 Walt Disney Productions World Rights Reserved

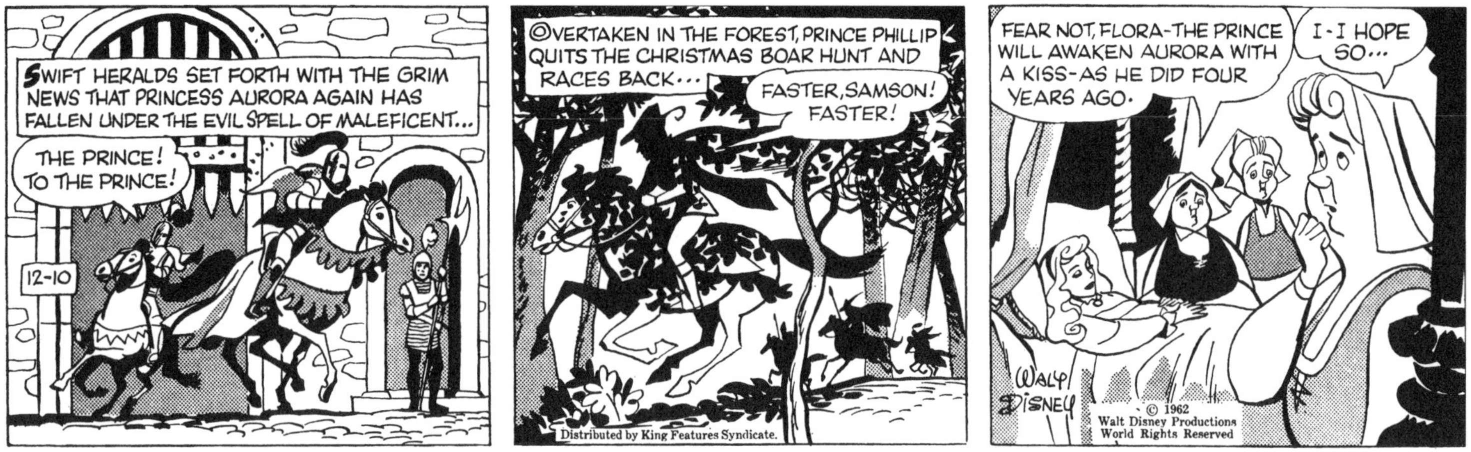
SWIFT HERALDS SET FORTH WITH THE GRIM NEWS THAT PRINCESS AURORA AGAIN HAS FALLEN UNDER THE EVIL SPELL OF MALEFICENT...
THE PRINCE! TO THE PRINCE!
12-10
OVERTAKEN IN THE FOREST, PRINCE PHILLIP QUITS THE CHRISTMAS BOAR HUNT AND RACES BACK...
FASTER, SAMSON! FASTER!
Distributed by King Features Syndicate.
FEAR NOT, FLORA-THE PRINCE WILL AWAKEN AURORA WITH A KISS-AS HE DID FOUR YEARS AGO.
I-I HOPE SO...
WALT DISNEY
© 1962 Walt Disney Productions World Rights Reserved

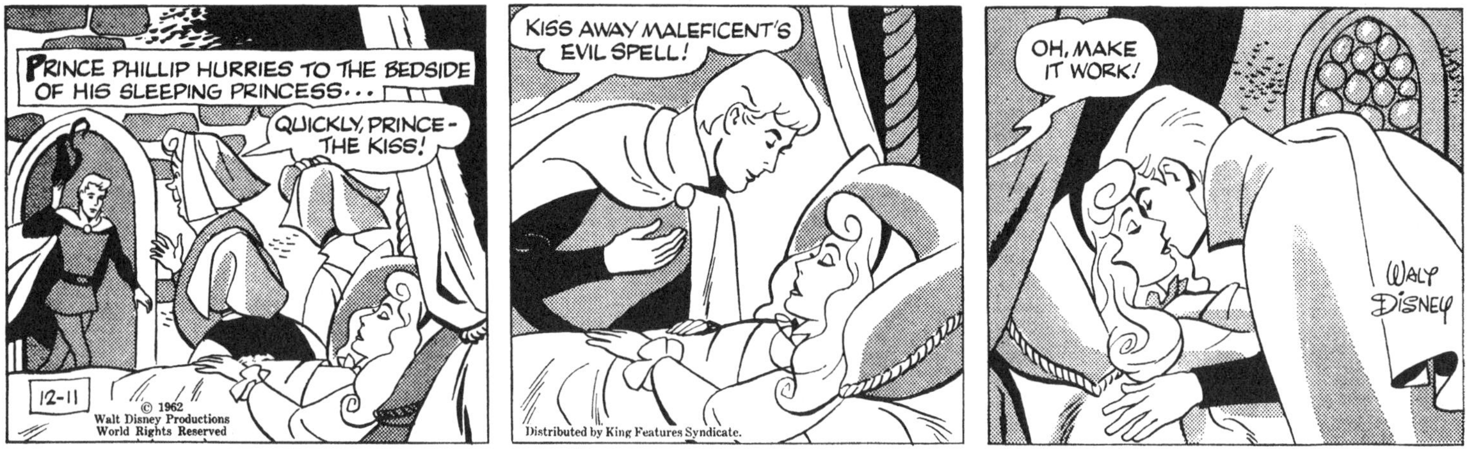
PRINCE PHILLIP HURRIES TO THE BEDSIDE OF HIS SLEEPING PRINCESS...
QUICKLY, PRINCE-THE KISS!
12-11
© 1962 Walt Disney Productions World Rights Reserved
KISS AWAY MALEFICENT'S EVIL SPELL!
Distributed by King Features Syndicate.
OH, MAKE IT WORK!
WALT DISNEY

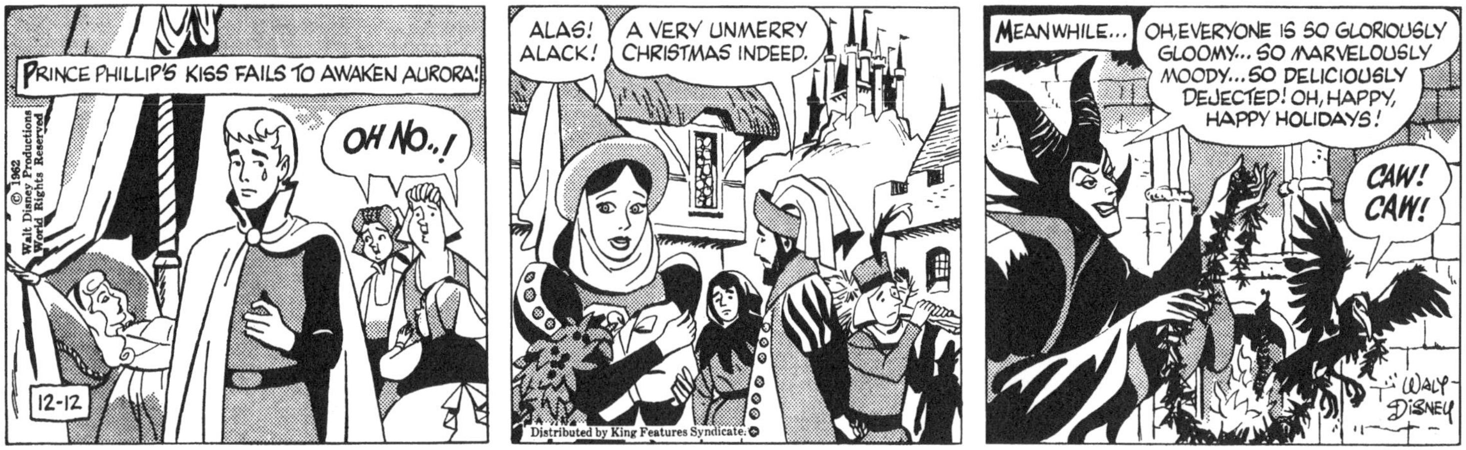
PRINCE PHILLIP'S KISS FAILS TO AWAKEN AURORA!
OH NO..!
© 1962 Walt Disney Productions World Rights Reserved
12-12
ALAS! ALACK!
A VERY UNMERRY CHRISTMAS INDEED.
Distributed by King Features Syndicate.
MEANWHILE...
OH, EVERYONE IS SO GLORIOUSLY GLOOMY... SO MARVELOUSLY MOODY... SO DELICIOUSLY DEJECTED! OH, HAPPY, HAPPY HOLIDAYS!
CAW! CAW!
WALT DISNEY

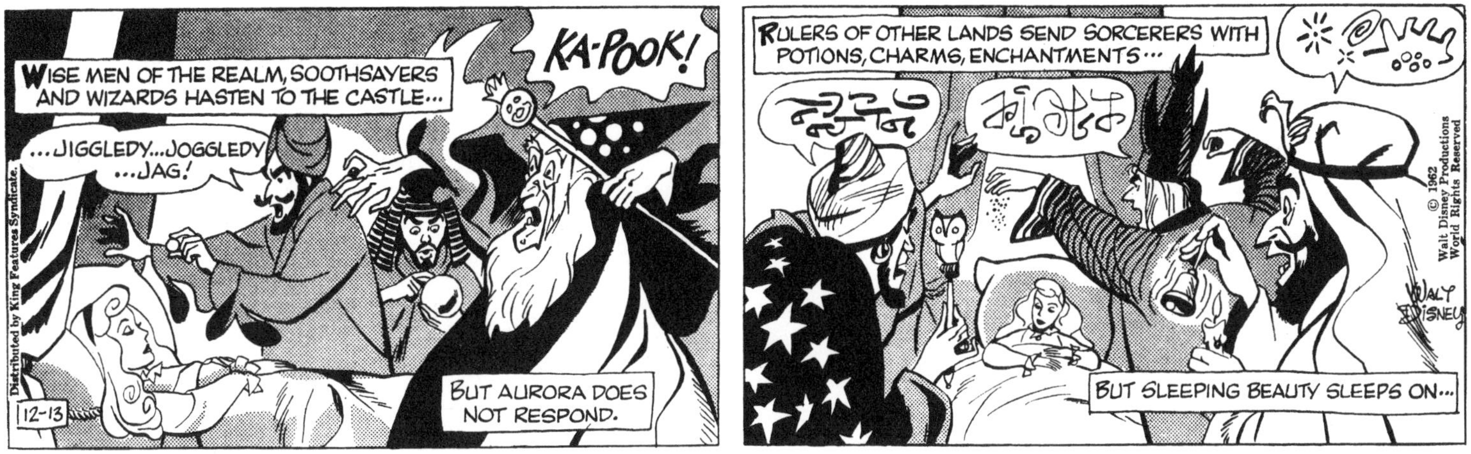
KA-POOK!
WISE MEN OF THE REALM, SOOTHSAYERS AND WIZARDS HASTEN TO THE CASTLE...
...JIGGLEDY...JOGGLEDY ...JAG!
BUT AURORA DOES NOT RESPOND.
12-13
Distributed by King Features Syndicate.
RULERS OF OTHER LANDS SEND SORCERERS WITH POTIONS, CHARMS, ENCHANTMENTS...
BUT SLEEPING BEAUTY SLEEPS ON...
© 1962 Walt Disney Productions World Rights Reserved
WALT DISNEY

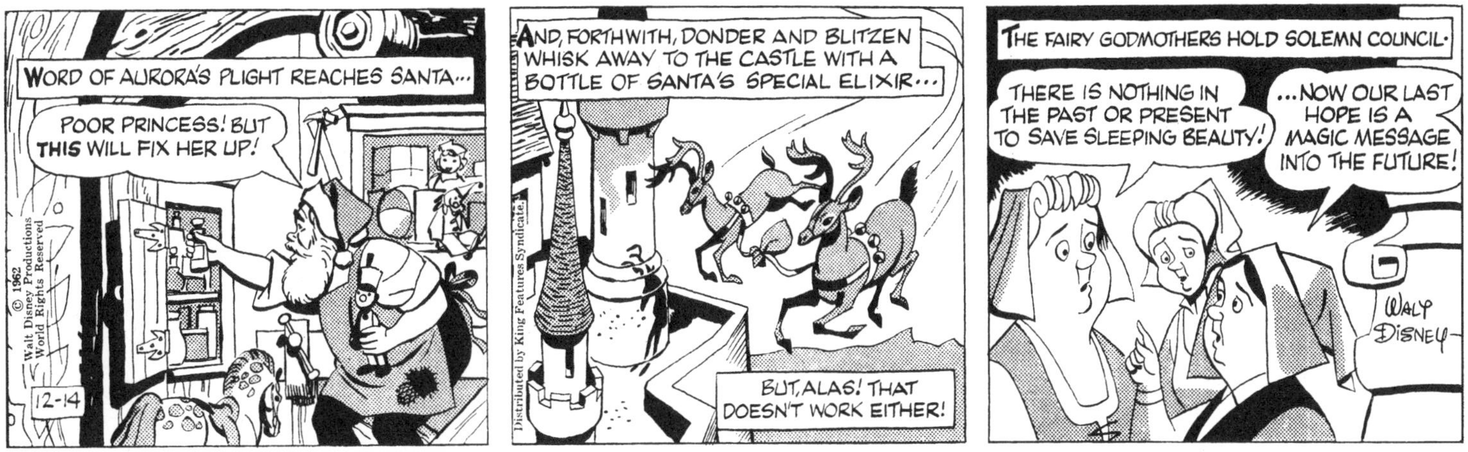
WORD OF AURORA'S PLIGHT REACHES SANTA...
POOR PRINCESS! BUT THIS WILL FIX HER UP!
© 1962 Walt Disney Productions World Rights Reserved
12-14
AND, FORTHWITH, DONDER AND BLITZEN WHISK AWAY TO THE CASTLE WITH A BOTTLE OF SANTA'S SPECIAL ELIXIR...
BUT, ALAS! THAT DOESN'T WORK EITHER!
Distributed by King Features Syndicate.
THE FAIRY GODMOTHERS HOLD SOLEMN COUNCIL.
THERE IS NOTHING IN THE PAST OR PRESENT TO SAVE SLEEPING BEAUTY!
...NOW OUR LAST HOPE IS A MAGIC MESSAGE INTO THE FUTURE!
WALT DISNEY

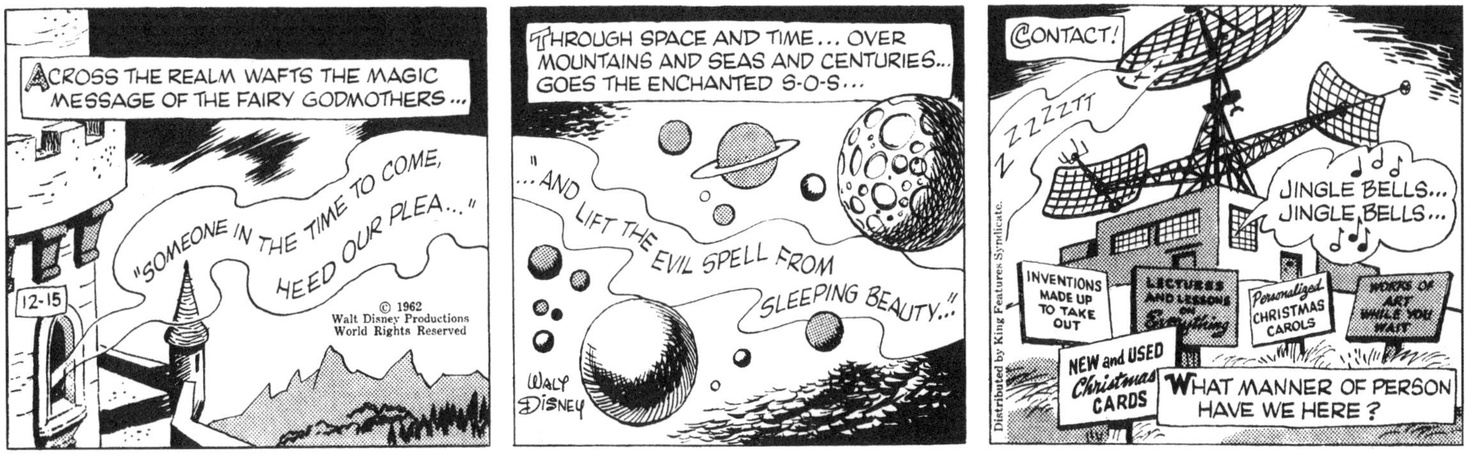
ACROSS THE REALM WAFTS THE MAGIC MESSAGE OF THE FAIRY GODMOTHERS...
"SOMEONE IN THE TIME TO COME, HEED OUR PLEA..."
12-15
© 1962 Walt Disney Productions World Rights Reserved
THROUGH SPACE AND TIME... OVER MOUNTAINS AND SEAS AND CENTURIES... GOES THE ENCHANTED S-O-S...
"...AND LIFT THE EVIL SPELL FROM SLEEPING BEAUTY..!"
WALT DISNEY
CONTACT!
ZZZZZTT
JINGLE BELLS... JINGLE BELLS...
INVENTIONS MADE UP TO TAKE OUT
LECTURES AND LESSONS ON Everything
Personalized CHRISTMAS CAROLS
WORKS OF ART WHILE YOU WAIT
NEW and USED Christmas CARDS
WHAT MANNER OF PERSON HAVE WE HERE?
Distributed by King Features Syndicate.

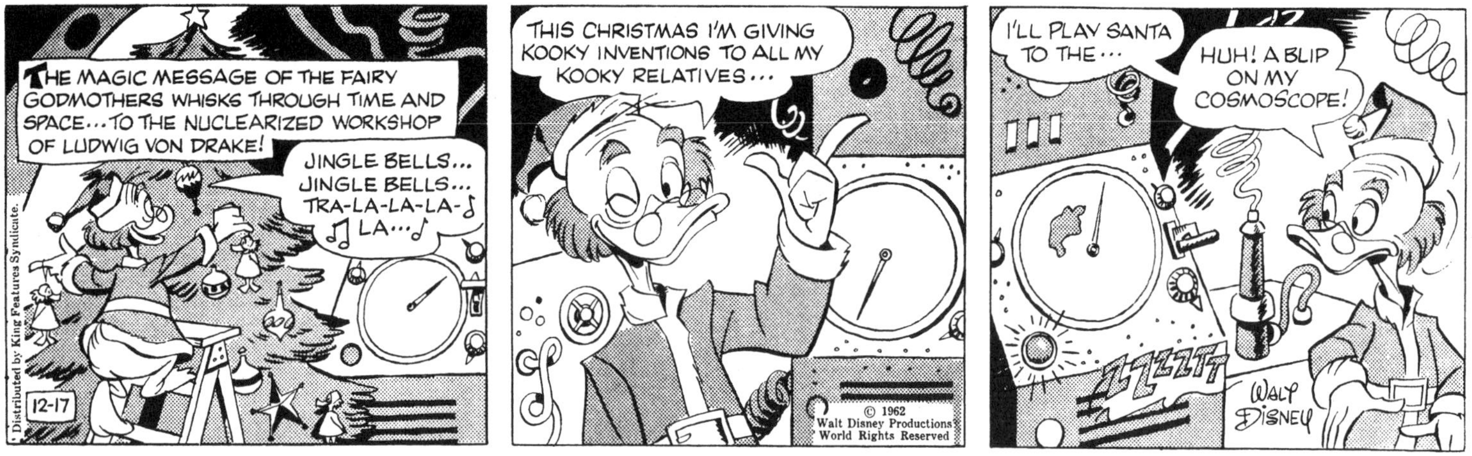
THE MAGIC MESSAGE OF THE FAIRY GODMOTHERS WHISKS THROUGH TIME AND SPACE...TO THE NUCLEARIZED WORKSHOP OF LUDWIG VON DRAKE!
JINGLE BELLS... JINGLE BELLS... TRA-LA-LA-LA- LA...
Distributed by King Features Syndicate.
12-17
THIS CHRISTMAS I'M GIVING KOOKY INVENTIONS TO ALL MY KOOKY RELATIVES...
© 1962 Walt Disney Productions World Rights Reserved
I'LL PLAY SANTA TO THE...
HUH! A BLIP ON MY COSMOSCOPE!
ZZZZTT
WALT DISNEY

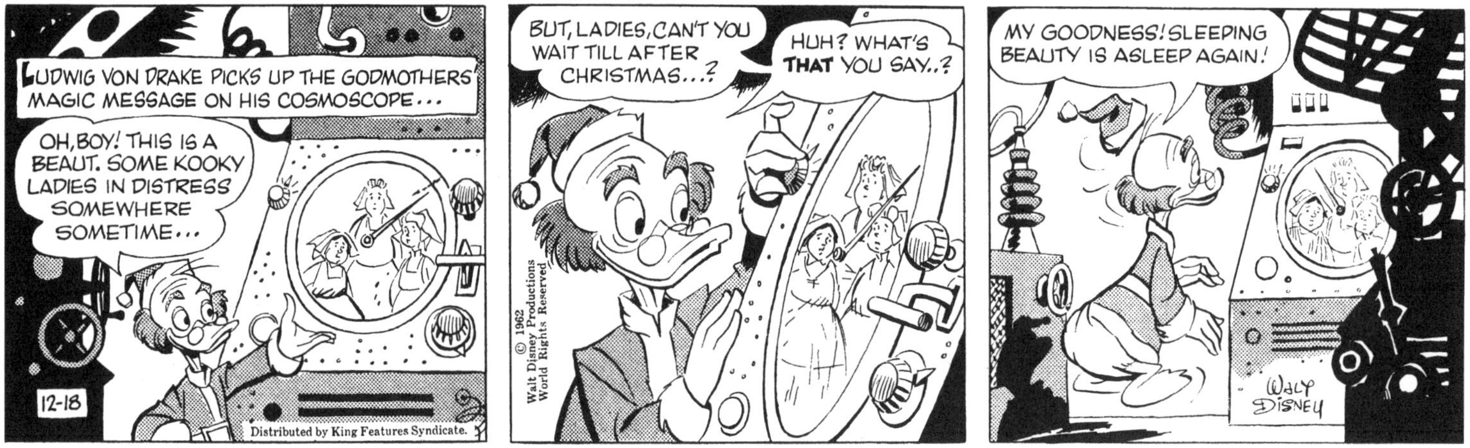
LUDWIG VON DRAKE PICKS UP THE GODMOTHERS' MAGIC MESSAGE ON HIS COSMOSCOPE...
OH, BOY! THIS IS A BEAUT. SOME KOOKY LADIES IN DISTRESS SOMEWHERE SOMETIME...
12-18
Distributed by King Features Syndicate.
BUT, LADIES, CAN'T YOU WAIT TILL AFTER CHRISTMAS...?
HUH? WHAT'S THAT YOU SAY..?
© 1962 Walt Disney Productions World Rights Reserved
MY GOODNESS! SLEEPING BEAUTY IS ASLEEP AGAIN!
WALT DISNEY

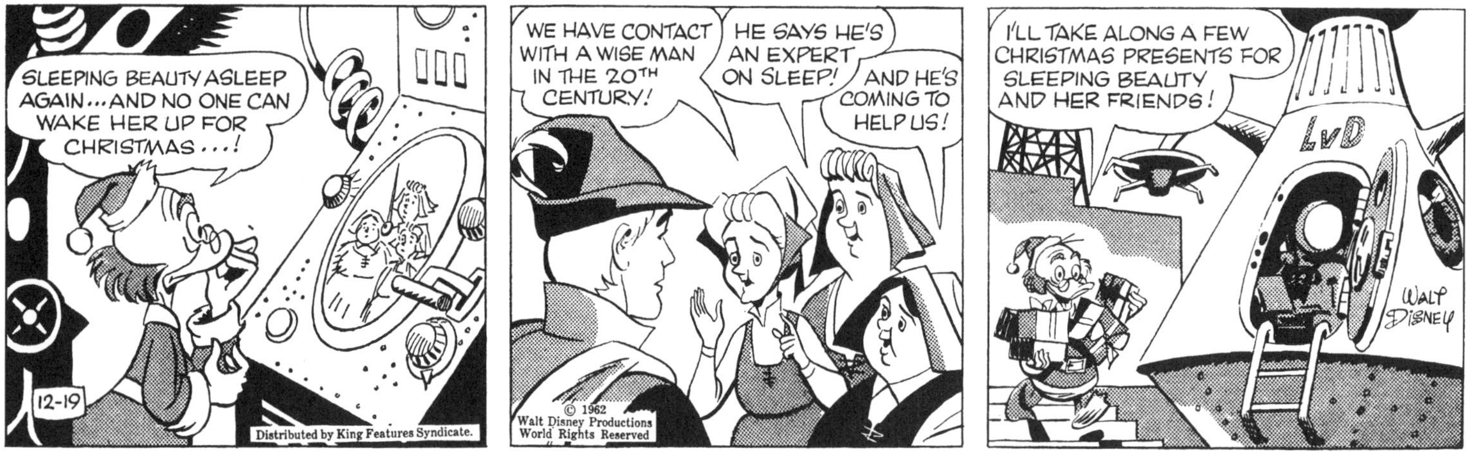
SLEEPING BEAUTY ASLEEP AGAIN...AND NO ONE CAN WAKE HER UP FOR CHRISTMAS...!
12-19
Distributed by King Features Syndicate.
WE HAVE CONTACT WITH A WISE MAN IN THE 20TH CENTURY!
HE SAYS HE'S AN EXPERT ON SLEEP!
AND HE'S COMING TO HELP US!
© 1962 Walt Disney Productions World Rights Reserved
I'LL TAKE ALONG A FEW CHRISTMAS PRESENTS FOR SLEEPING BEAUTY AND HER FRIENDS!
LvD
WALT DISNEY

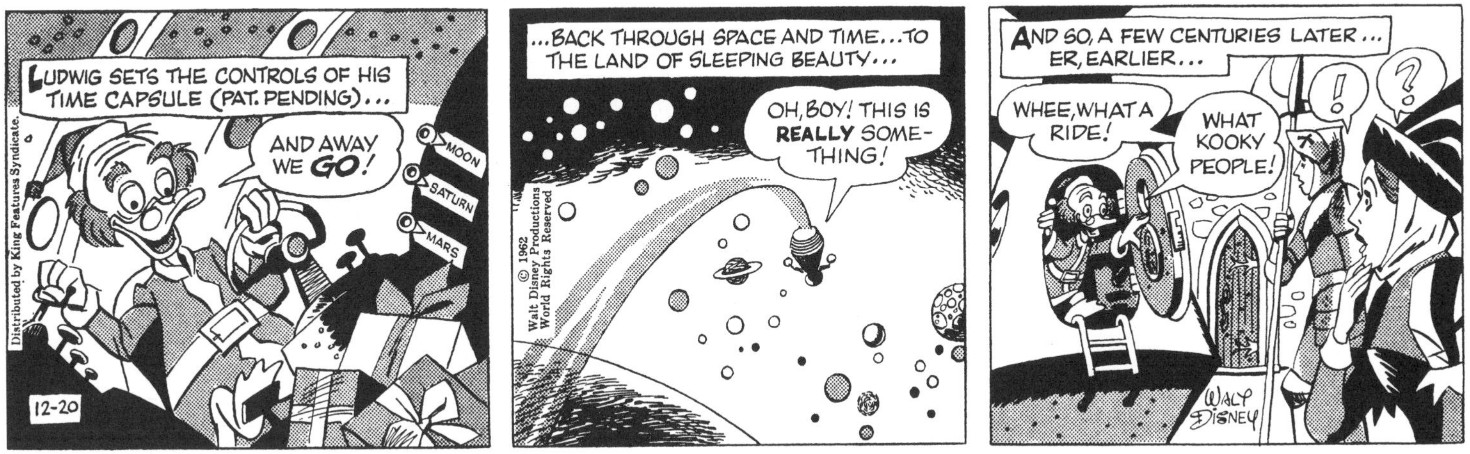

LUDWIG SETS THE CONTROLS OF HIS TIME CAPSULE (PAT. PENDING)...
AND AWAY WE GO!
MOON
SATURN
MARS
12-20
Distributed by King Features Syndicate.
...BACK THROUGH SPACE AND TIME...TO THE LAND OF SLEEPING BEAUTY...
OH, BOY! THIS IS REALLY SOMETHING!
© 1962 Walt Disney Productions World Rights Reserved
AND SO, A FEW CENTURIES LATER... ER, EARLIER...
WHEE, WHAT A RIDE!
WHAT KOOKY PEOPLE!
!
?
WALT DISNEY

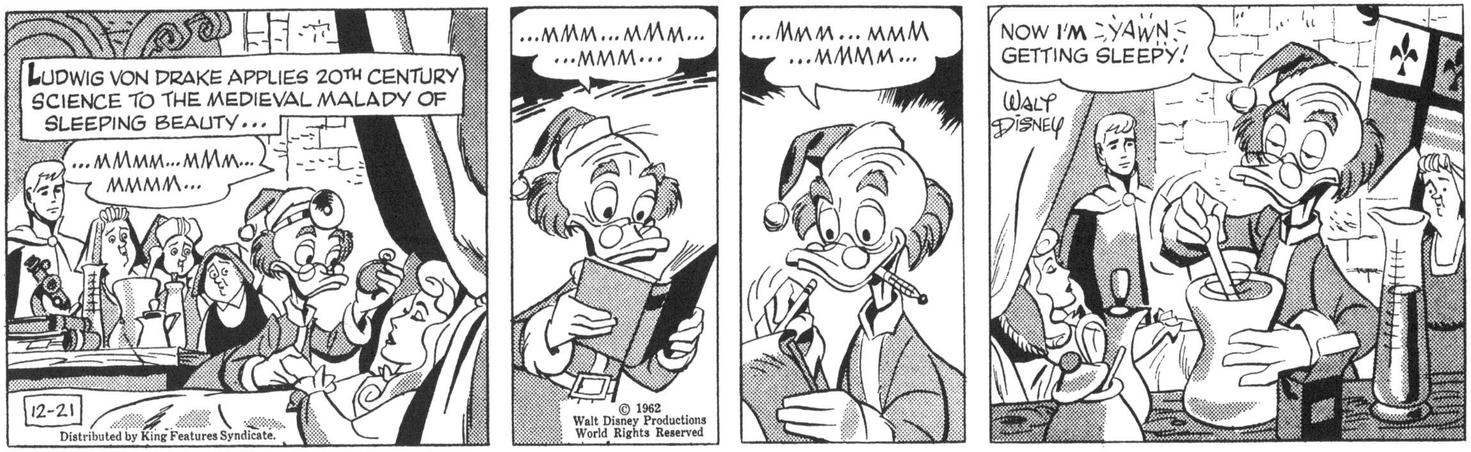

LUDWIG VON DRAKE APPLIES 20TH CENTURY SCIENCE TO THE MEDIEVAL MALADY OF SLEEPING BEAUTY...
...MMMM...MMM... MMMM...
12-21
Distributed by King Features Syndicate.
...MMM...MMM... ...MMM...
© 1962 Walt Disney Productions World Rights Reserved
...MMM... MMM ...MMMM...
NOW I'M -YAWN- GETTING SLEEPY!
WALT DISNEY

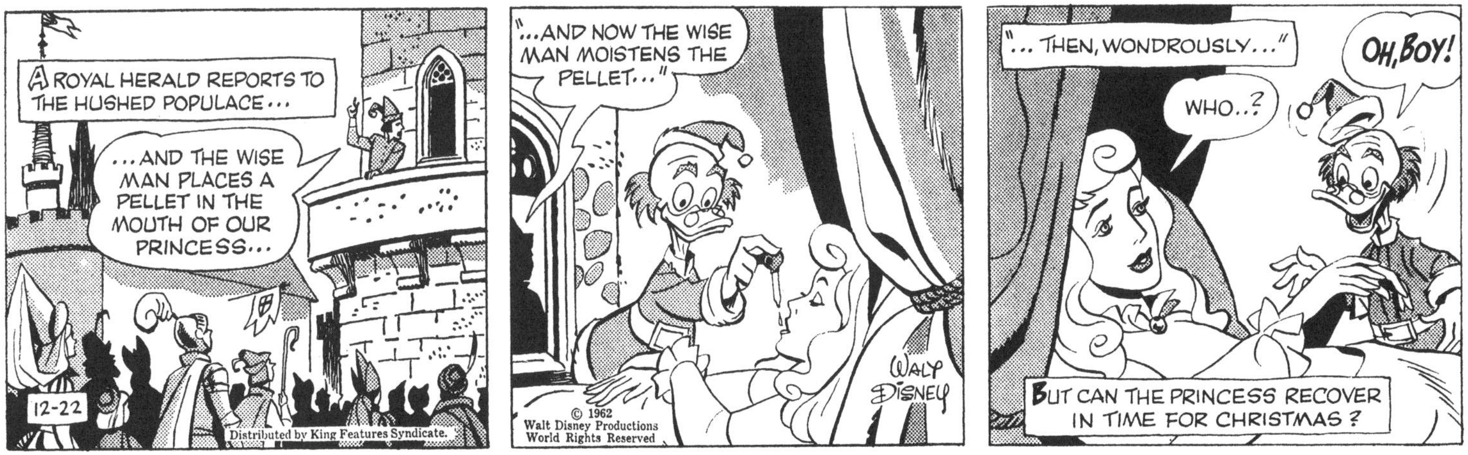

A ROYAL HERALD REPORTS TO THE HUSHED POPULACE...
...AND THE WISE MAN PLACES A PELLET IN THE MOUTH OF OUR PRINCESS...
12-22
Distributed by King Features Syndicate.
"...AND NOW THE WISE MAN MOISTENS THE PELLET..."
© 1962 Walt Disney Productions World Rights Reserved
WALT DISNEY
"... THEN, WONDROUSLY..."
OH, BOY!
WHO..?
BUT CAN THE PRINCESS RECOVER IN TIME FOR CHRISTMAS?

BONG BONG
BONG
THE BELLS OF THE REALM PEAL CHRISTMAS MELODIES AS THE PRINCESS BIDS LUDWIG FOND FAREWELL...
WISE MAN, HOW CAN WE EVER THANK YOU- SMACK
BONG
J-JUST... DON'T STOP...
BONG
12-24
Distributed by King Features Syndicate.
OH, IF ONLY I DIDN'T HAVE TO GET BACK FOR MY OWN KOOKY CHRISTMAS PARTY...!
SOON, LUDWIG SETS HIS TIME CAPSULE FOR THE RETURN TO THE PRESENT...
WANT TO KNOW HOW I WOKE HER UP?
I GAVE HER A SLEEPING PILL UPSIDE DOWN... AND IT WORKED IN REVERSE!
© 1962 Walt Disney Productions World Rights Reserved
AS HE WHIZZES HOME THROUGH TIME AND SPACE, LUDWIG HAS HIS OWN MAGIC MESSAGE...
MERRY CHRISTMAS
TO EVERYBODY... EVERYWHERE!
WALT DISNEY

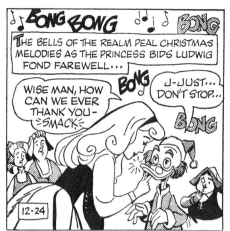

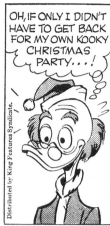

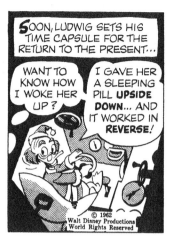

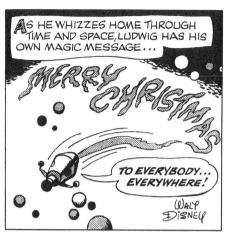

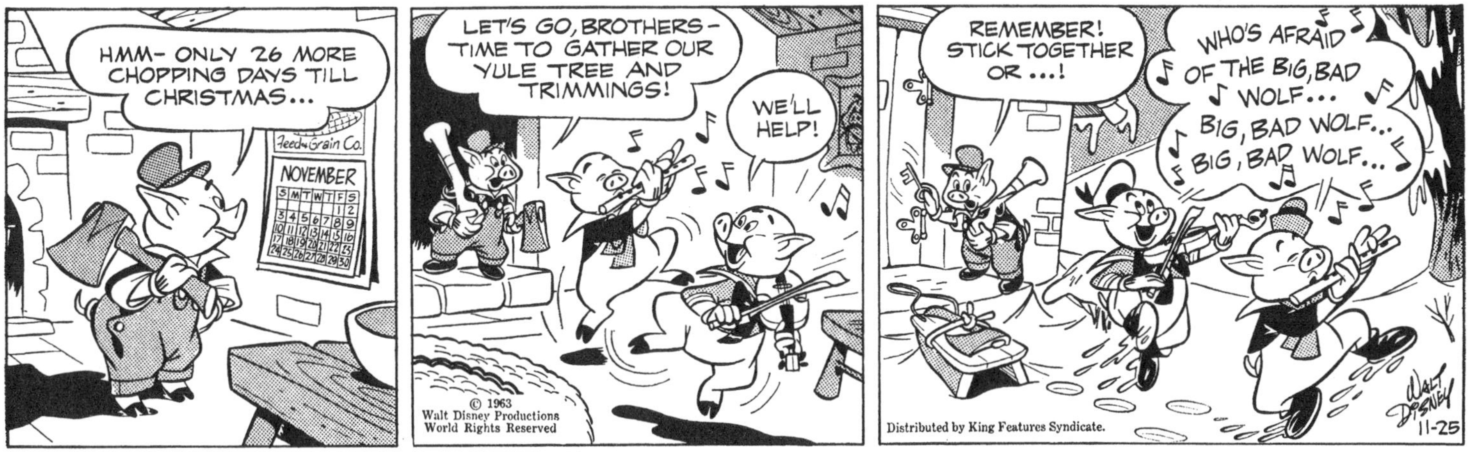
HMM- ONLY 26 MORE CHOPPING DAYS TILL CHRISTMAS...
Feed & Grain Co.
NOVEMBER
LET'S GO, BROTHERS- TIME TO GATHER OUR YULE TREE AND TRIMMINGS!
WE'LL HELP!
© 1963 Walt Disney Productions World Rights Reserved
REMEMBER! STICK TOGETHER OR ...!
WHO'S AFRAID OF THE BIG, BAD WOLF... BIG, BAD WOLF... BIG, BAD WOLF...
Distributed by King Features Syndicate.
WALT DISNEY 11-25

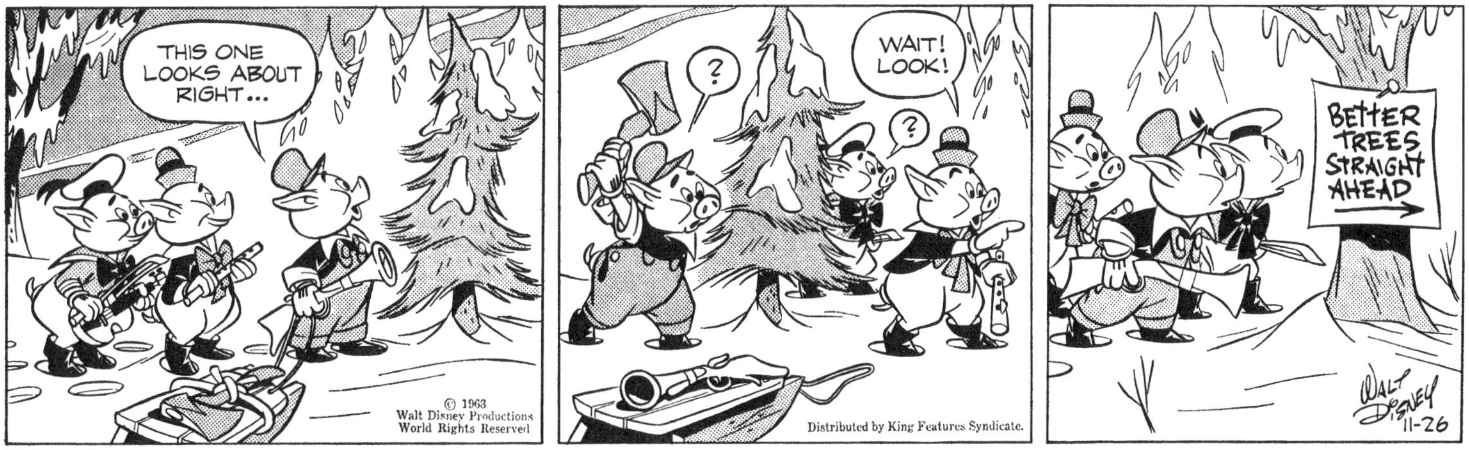
THIS ONE LOOKS ABOUT RIGHT...
© 1963 Walt Disney Productions World Rights Reserved
?
WAIT! LOOK!
?
Distributed by King Features Syndicate.
BETTER TREES STRAIGHT AHEAD
WALT DISNEY 11-26

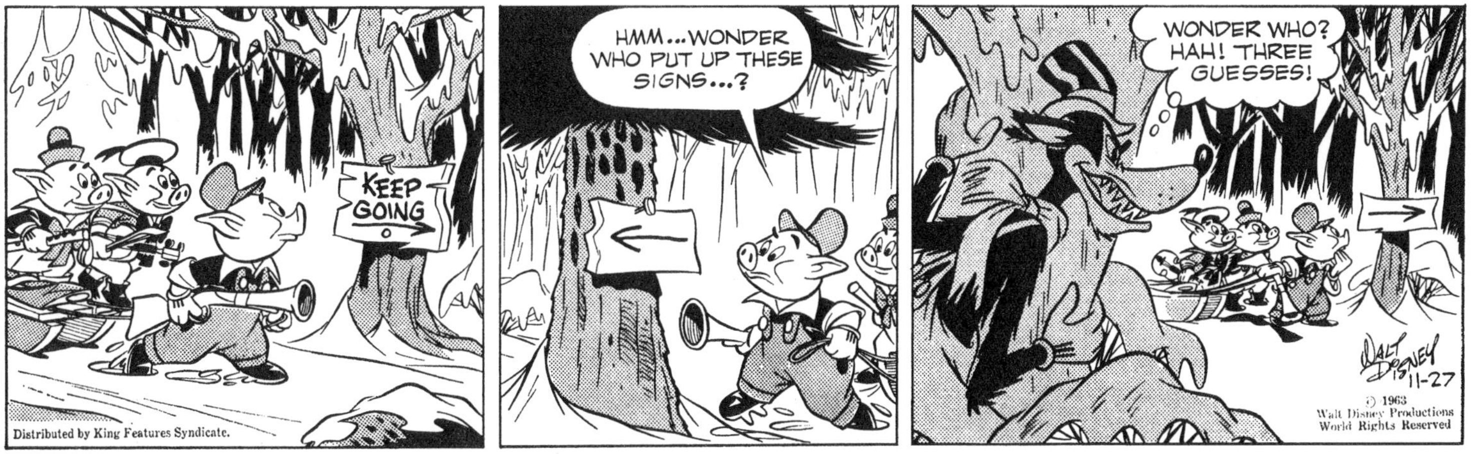
KEEP GOING
Distributed by King Features Syndicate.
HMM...WONDER WHO PUT UP THESE SIGNS...?
WONDER WHO? HAH! THREE GUESSES!
WALT DISNEY 11-27
© 1963 Walt Disney Productions World Rights Reserved

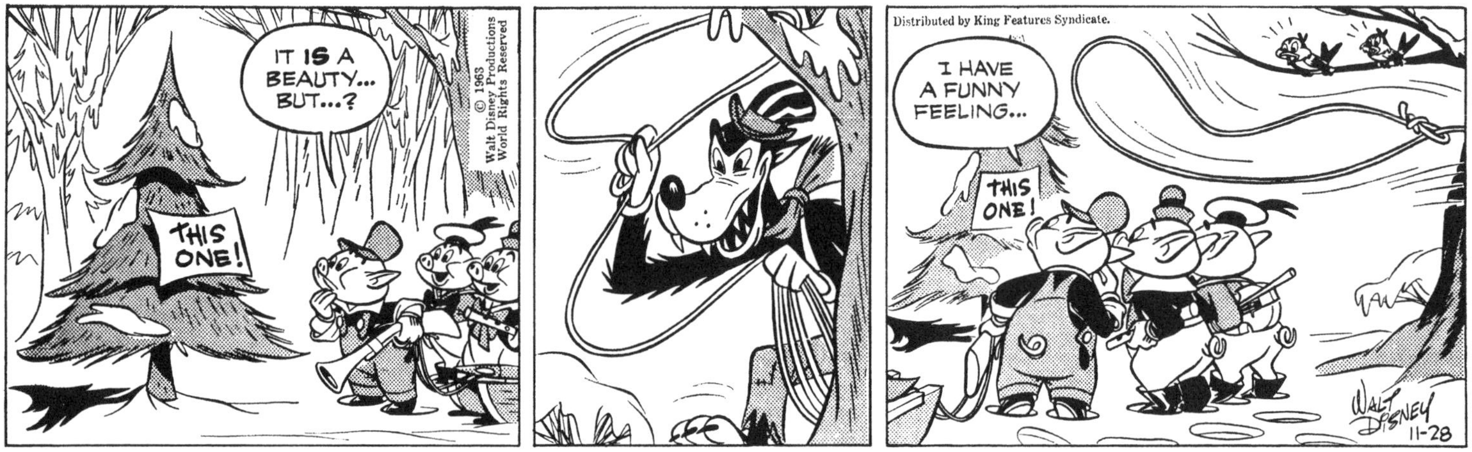
IT IS A BEAUTY... BUT...?
THIS ONE!
© 1963 Walt Disney Productions World Rights Reserved
Distributed by King Features Syndicate.
I HAVE A FUNNY FEELING...
THIS ONE!
WALT DISNEY 11-28

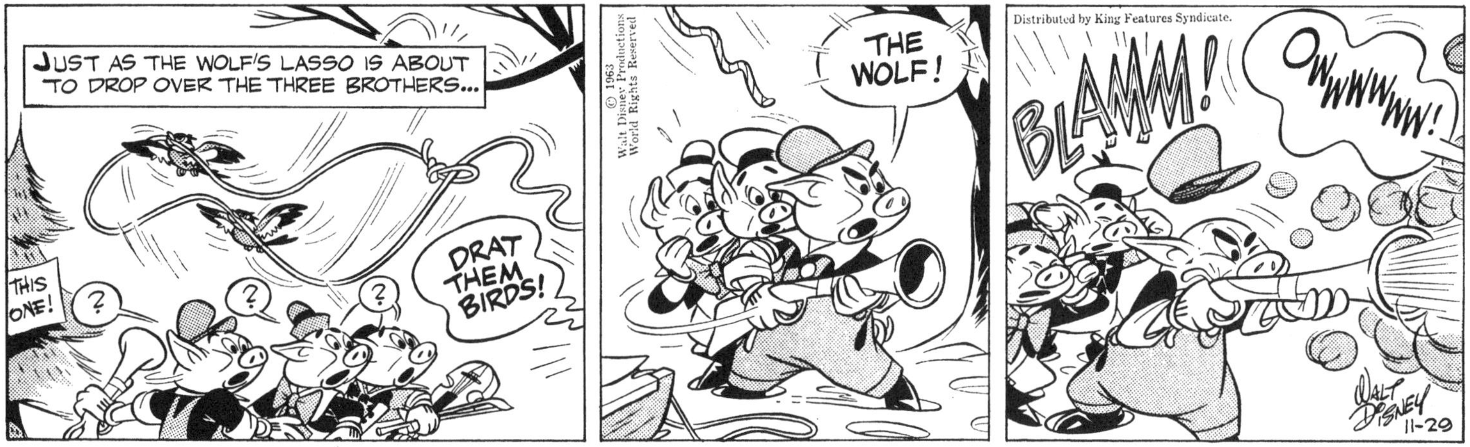
JUST AS THE WOLF'S LASSO IS ABOUT TO DROP OVER THE THREE BROTHERS...
THIS ONE!
?
?
?
DRAT THEM BIRDS!
© 1963 Walt Disney Productions World Rights Reserved
THE WOLF!
Distributed by King Features Syndicate.
BLAMM!
OWWWWWW!
WALT DISNEY 11-29

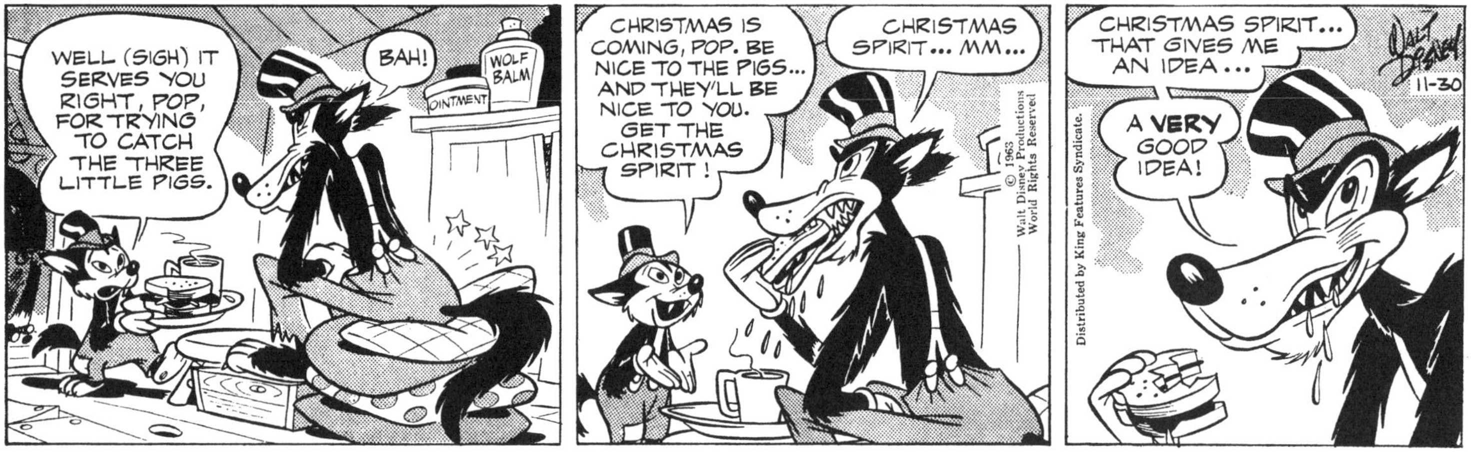
WELL (SIGH) IT SERVES YOU RIGHT, POP, FOR TRYING TO CATCH THE THREE LITTLE PIGS.
BAH!
OINTMENT
WOLF BALM
CHRISTMAS IS COMING, POP. BE NICE TO THE PIGS... AND THEY'LL BE NICE TO YOU. GET THE CHRISTMAS SPIRIT!
CHRISTMAS SPIRIT... MM...
© 1963 Walt Disney Productions World Rights Reserved
Distributed by King Features Syndicate.
CHRISTMAS SPIRIT... THAT GIVES ME AN IDEA...
A VERY GOOD IDEA!
WALT DISNEY 11-30

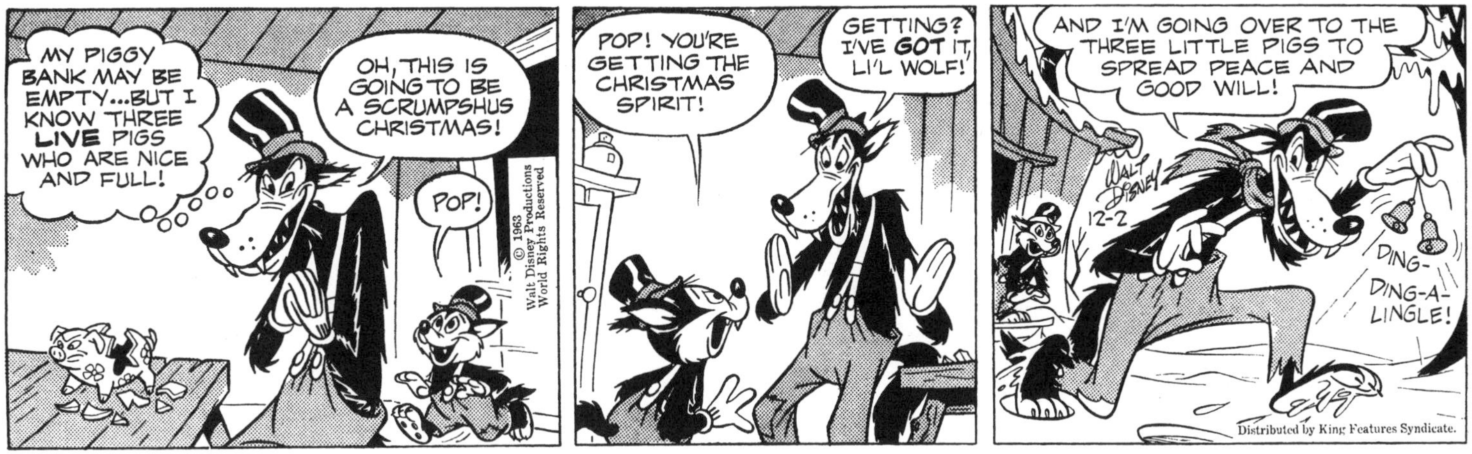
MY PIGGY BANK MAY BE EMPTY...BUT I KNOW THREE **LIVE** PIGS WHO ARE NICE AND FULL!
OH, THIS IS GOING TO BE A SCRUMPSHUS CHRISTMAS!
POP!
© 1963 Walt Disney Productions World Rights Reserved
POP! YOU'RE GETTING THE CHRISTMAS SPIRIT!
GETTING? I'VE **GOT** IT, LI'L WOLF!
AND I'M GOING OVER TO THE THREE LITTLE PIGS TO SPREAD PEACE AND GOOD WILL!
WALT DISNEY
12-2
DING-DING-A-LINGLE!
Distributed by King Features Syndicate.

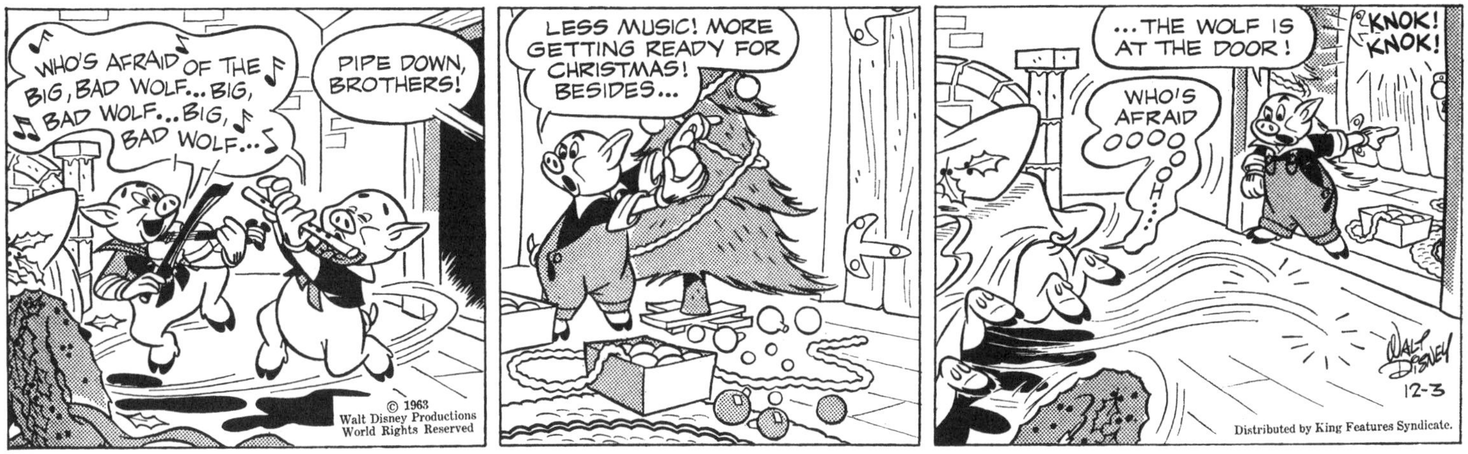
WHO'S AFRAID OF THE BIG, BAD WOLF...BIG, BAD WOLF...BIG, BAD WOLF...
PIPE DOWN, BROTHERS!
© 1963 Walt Disney Productions World Rights Reserved
LESS MUSIC! MORE GETTING READY FOR CHRISTMAS! BESIDES...
...THE WOLF IS AT THE DOOR!
KNOK! KNOK!
WHO'S AFRAID OOOOOH...
WALT DISNEY
12-3
Distributed by King Features Syndicate.

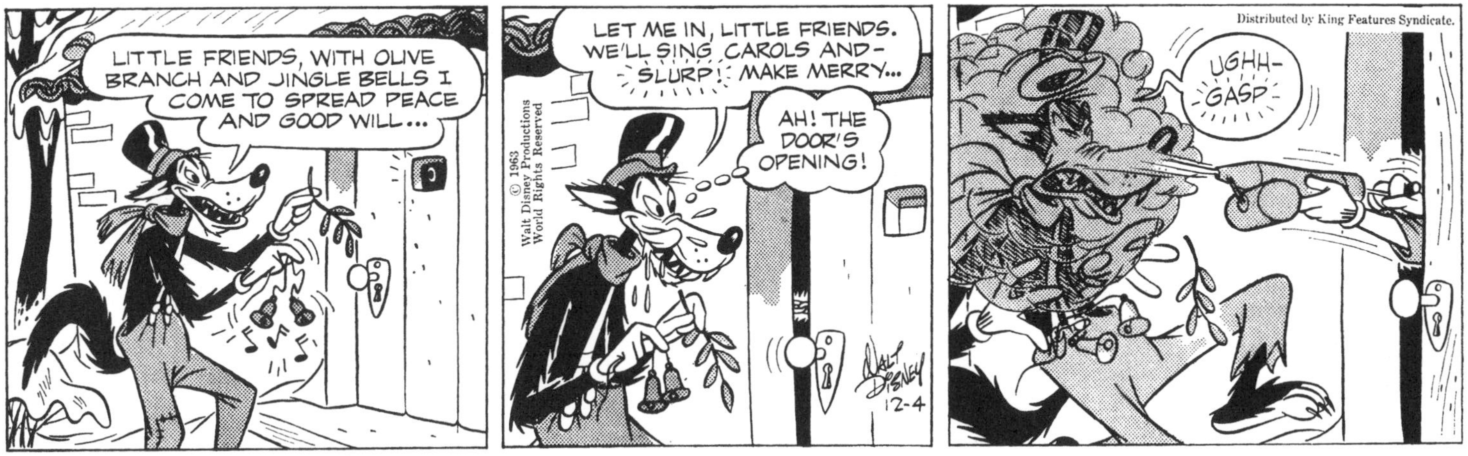
LITTLE FRIENDS, WITH OLIVE BRANCH AND JINGLE BELLS I COME TO SPREAD PEACE AND GOOD WILL...
© 1963 Walt Disney Productions World Rights Reserved
LET ME IN, LITTLE FRIENDS. WE'LL SING CAROLS AND-SLURP!- MAKE MERRY...
AH! THE DOOR'S OPENING!
WALT DISNEY
12-4
Distributed by King Features Syndicate.
UGHH-GASP

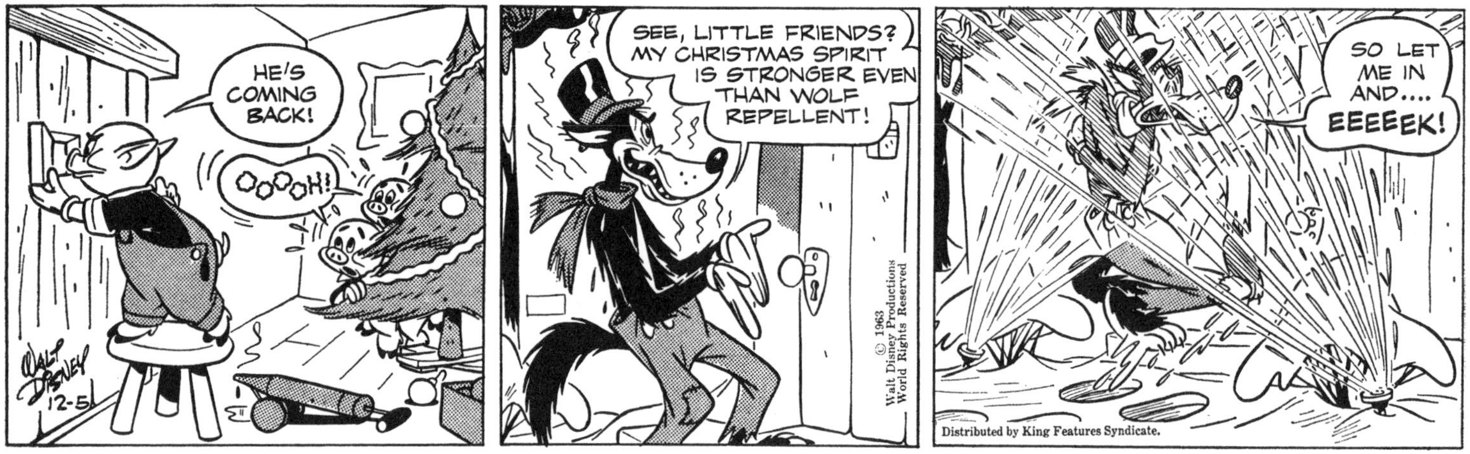
HE'S COMING BACK!
OOOOH!
WALT DISNEY 12-5
SEE, LITTLE FRIENDS? MY CHRISTMAS SPIRIT IS STRONGER EVEN THAN WOLF REPELLENT!
© 1963 Walt Disney Productions World Rights Reserved
SO LET ME IN AND.... EEEEEK!
Distributed by King Features Syndicate.

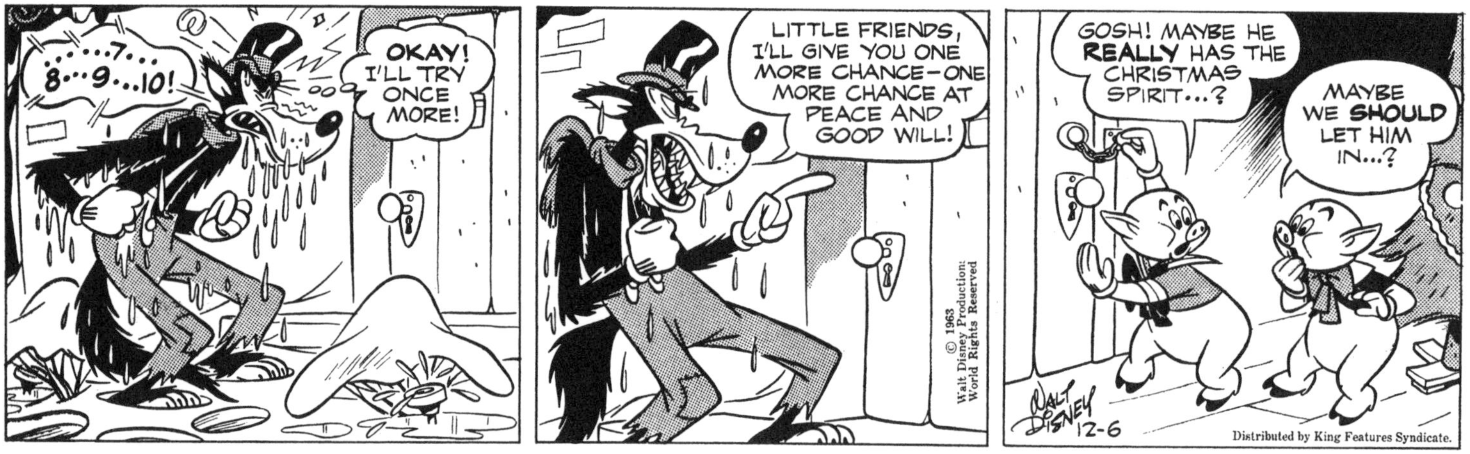
...7... 8...9...10!
OKAY! I'LL TRY ONCE MORE!
LITTLE FRIENDS, I'LL GIVE YOU ONE MORE CHANCE—ONE MORE CHANCE AT PEACE AND GOOD WILL!
© 1963 Walt Disney Productions World Rights Reserved
GOSH! MAYBE HE **REALLY** HAS THE CHRISTMAS SPIRIT...?
MAYBE WE **SHOULD** LET HIM IN...?
WALT DISNEY 12-6
Distributed by King Features Syndicate.

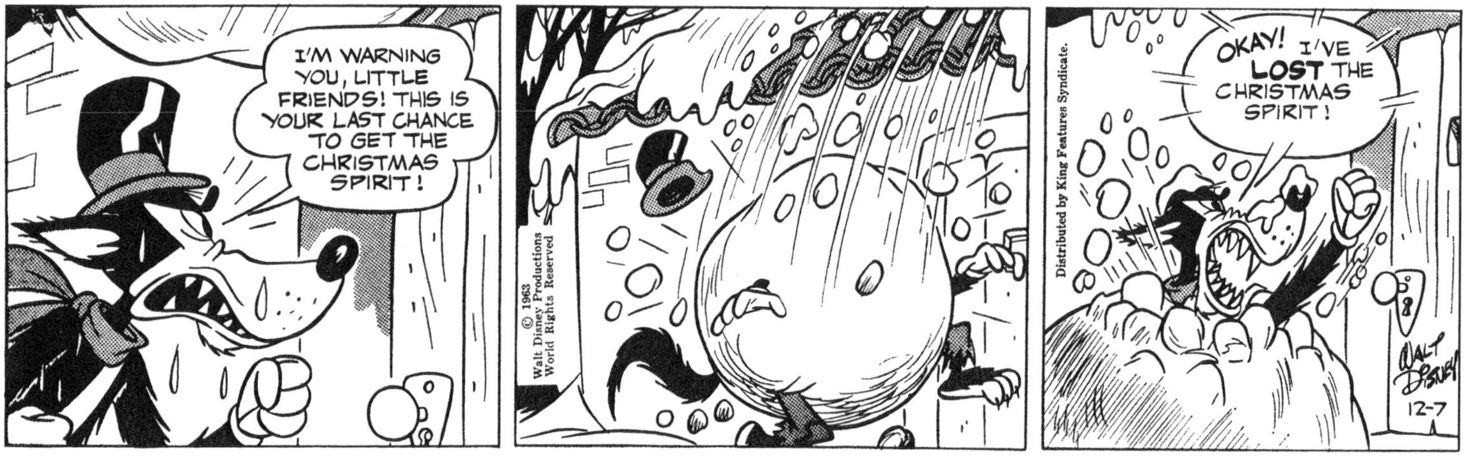
I'M WARNING YOU, LITTLE FRIENDS! THIS IS YOUR LAST CHANCE TO GET THE CHRISTMAS SPIRIT!
© 1963 Walt Disney Productions World Rights Reserved
Distributed by King Features Syndicate.
OKAY! I'VE **LOST** THE CHRISTMAS SPIRIT!
WALT DISNEY 12-7

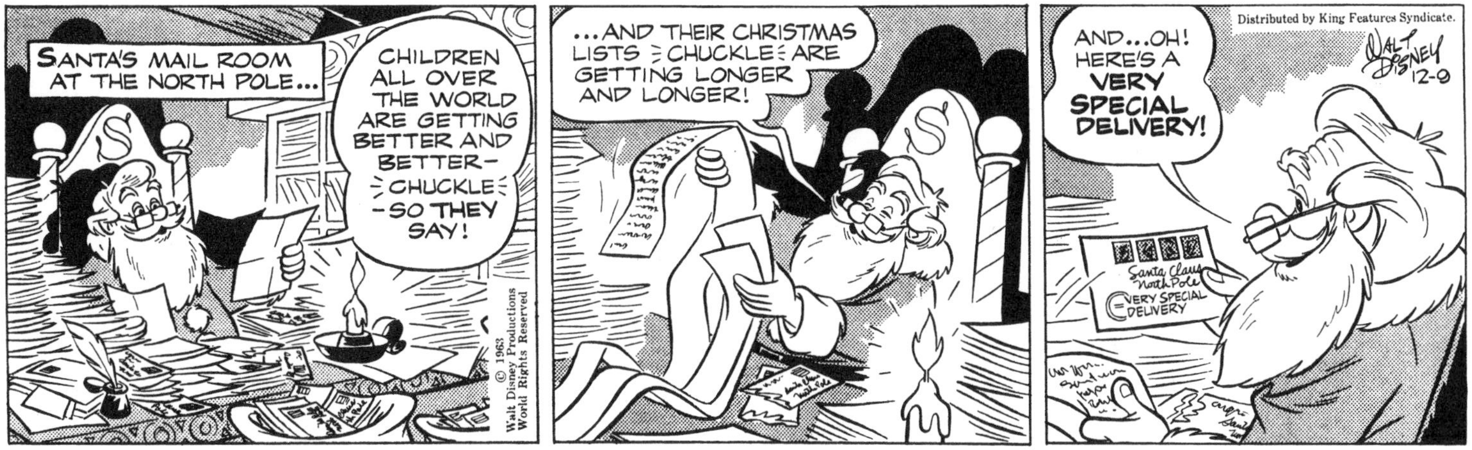
SANTA'S MAIL ROOM AT THE NORTH POLE...
CHILDREN ALL OVER THE WORLD ARE GETTING BETTER AND BETTER– CHUCKLE –SO THEY SAY!
© 1963 Walt Disney Productions World Rights Reserved
...AND THEIR CHRISTMAS LISTS CHUCKLE ARE GETTING LONGER AND LONGER!
Distributed by King Features Syndicate.
WALT DISNEY 12-9
AND...OH! HERE'S A VERY SPECIAL DELIVERY!
Santa Claus North Pole
VERY SPECIAL DELIVERY

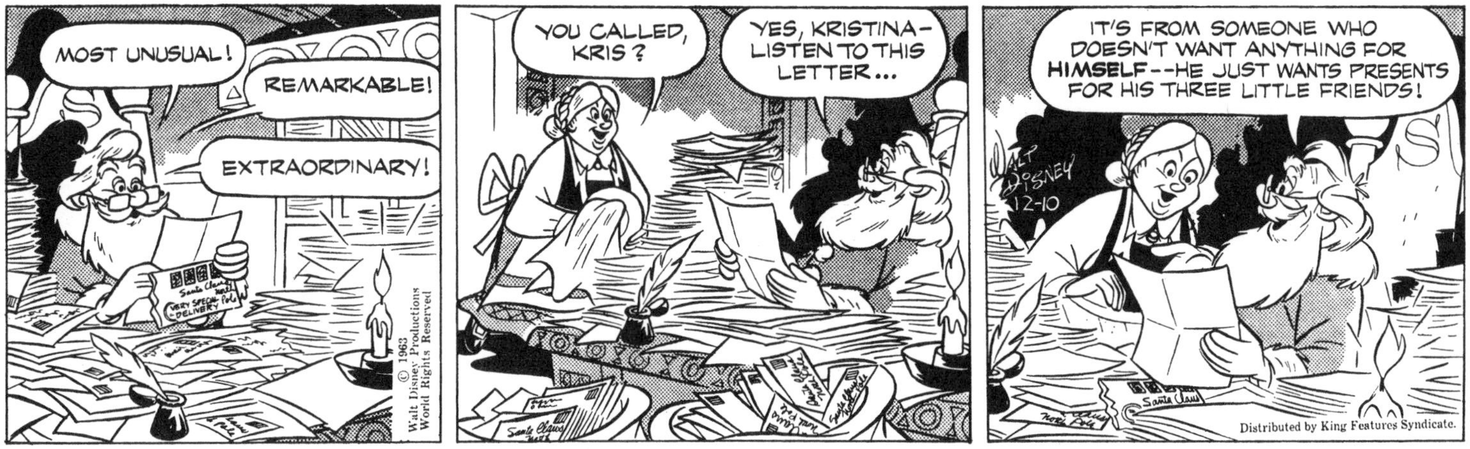
MOST UNUSUAL!
REMARKABLE!
EXTRAORDINARY!
© 1963 Walt Disney Productions World Rights Reserved
YOU CALLED, KRIS?
YES, KRISTINA– LISTEN TO THIS LETTER...
IT'S FROM SOMEONE WHO DOESN'T WANT ANYTHING FOR HIMSELF--HE JUST WANTS PRESENTS FOR HIS THREE LITTLE FRIENDS!
WALT DISNEY 12-10
Distributed by King Features Syndicate.

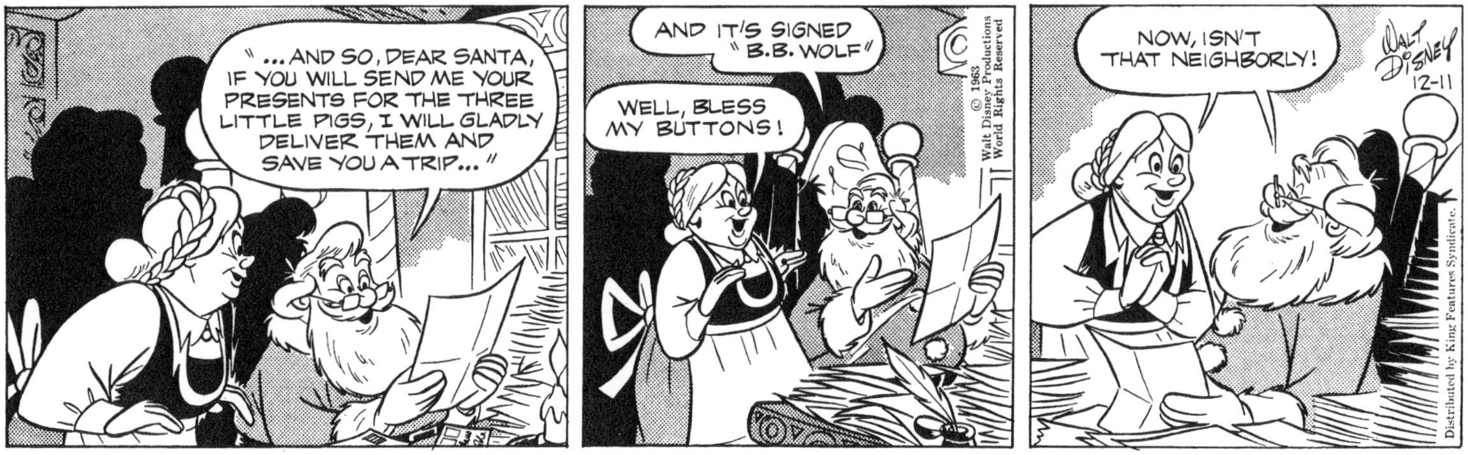
"...AND SO, DEAR SANTA, IF YOU WILL SEND ME YOUR PRESENTS FOR THE THREE LITTLE PIGS, I WILL GLADLY DELIVER THEM AND SAVE YOU A TRIP..."
AND IT'S SIGNED "B.B. WOLF"
WELL, BLESS MY BUTTONS!
© 1963 Walt Disney Productions World Rights Reserved
NOW, ISN'T THAT NEIGHBORLY!
WALT DISNEY 12-11
Distributed by King Features Syndicate.

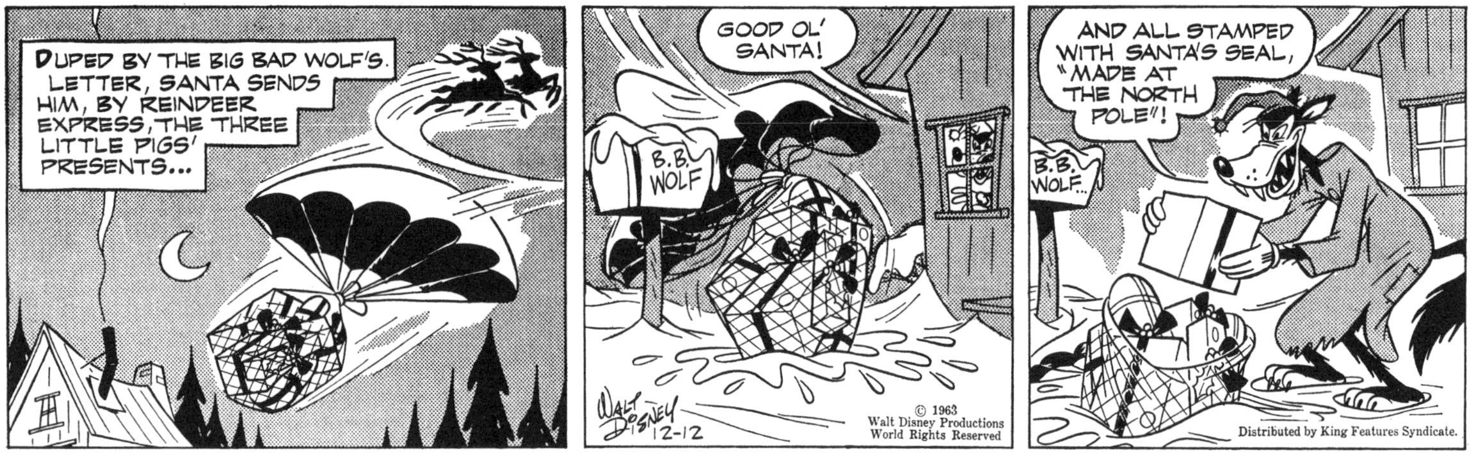
DUPED BY THE BIG BAD WOLF'S LETTER, SANTA SENDS HIM, BY REINDEER EXPRESS, THE THREE LITTLE PIGS' PRESENTS...
GOOD OL' SANTA!
B.B. WOLF
WALT DISNEY 12-12
© 1963 Walt Disney Productions World Rights Reserved
AND ALL STAMPED WITH SANTA'S SEAL, "MADE AT THE NORTH POLE"!
B.B. WOLF...
Distributed by King Features Syndicate.

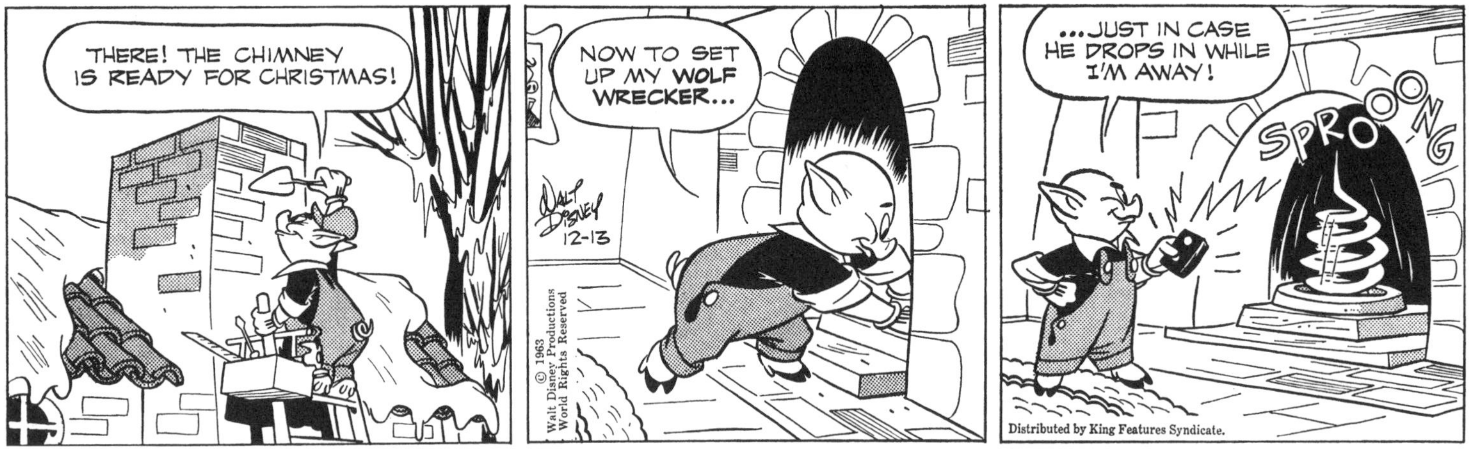
THERE! THE CHIMNEY IS READY FOR CHRISTMAS!
NOW TO SET UP MY WOLF WRECKER...
WALT DISNEY 12-13
© 1963 Walt Disney Productions World Rights Reserved
...JUST IN CASE HE DROPS IN WHILE I'M AWAY!
SPROOONG
Distributed by King Features Syndicate.

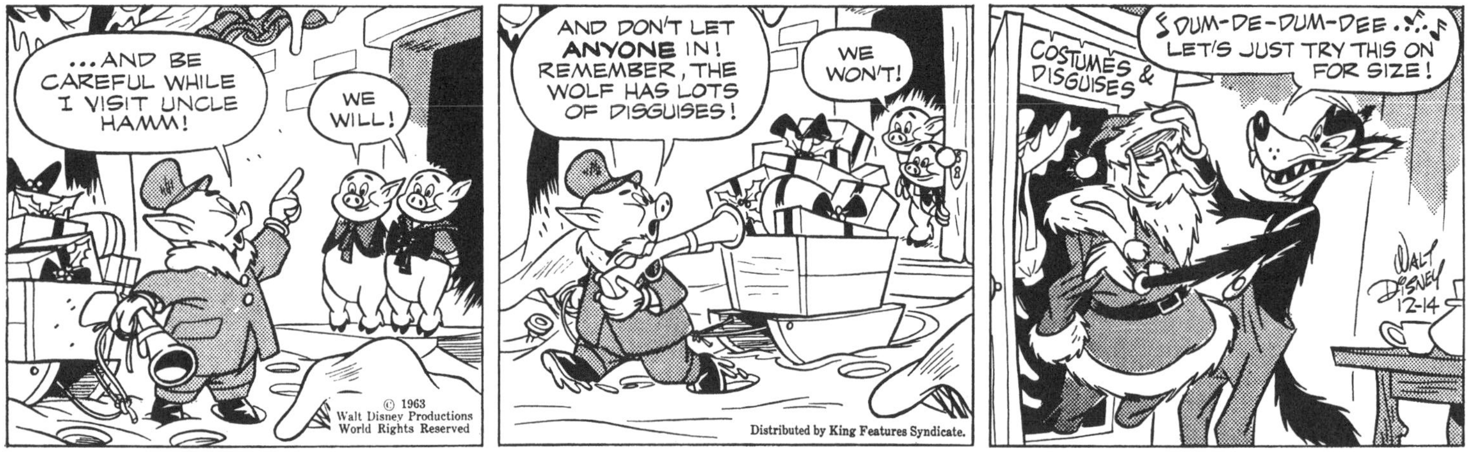
...AND BE CAREFUL WHILE I VISIT UNCLE HAMM!
WE WILL!
© 1963 Walt Disney Productions World Rights Reserved
AND DON'T LET ANYONE IN! REMEMBER, THE WOLF HAS LOTS OF DISGUISES!
WE WON'T!
Distributed by King Features Syndicate.
DUM-DE-DUM-DEE... LET'S JUST TRY THIS ON FOR SIZE!
COSTUMES & DISGUISES
WALT DISNEY 12-14

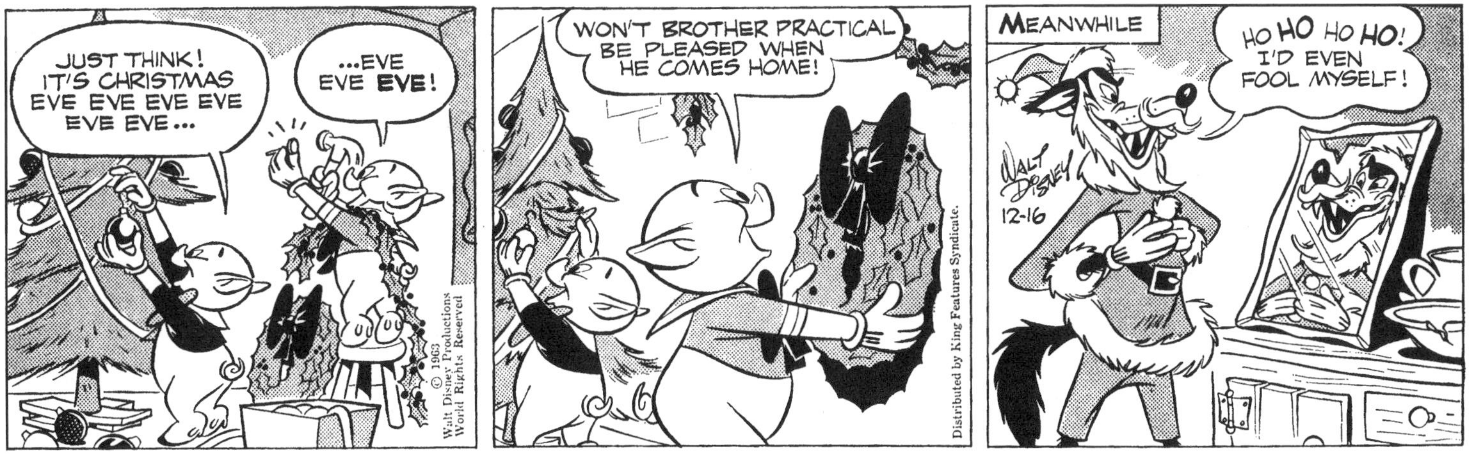
JUST THINK! IT'S CHRISTMAS EVE EVE EVE EVE EVE EVE...
...EVE EVE **EVE**!
© 1963 Walt Disney Productions World Rights Reserved
WON'T BROTHER PRACTICAL BE PLEASED WHEN HE COMES HOME!
Distributed by King Features Syndicate.
MEANWHILE
HO **HO** HO **HO**! I'D EVEN FOOL MYSELF!
WALT DISNEY 12-16

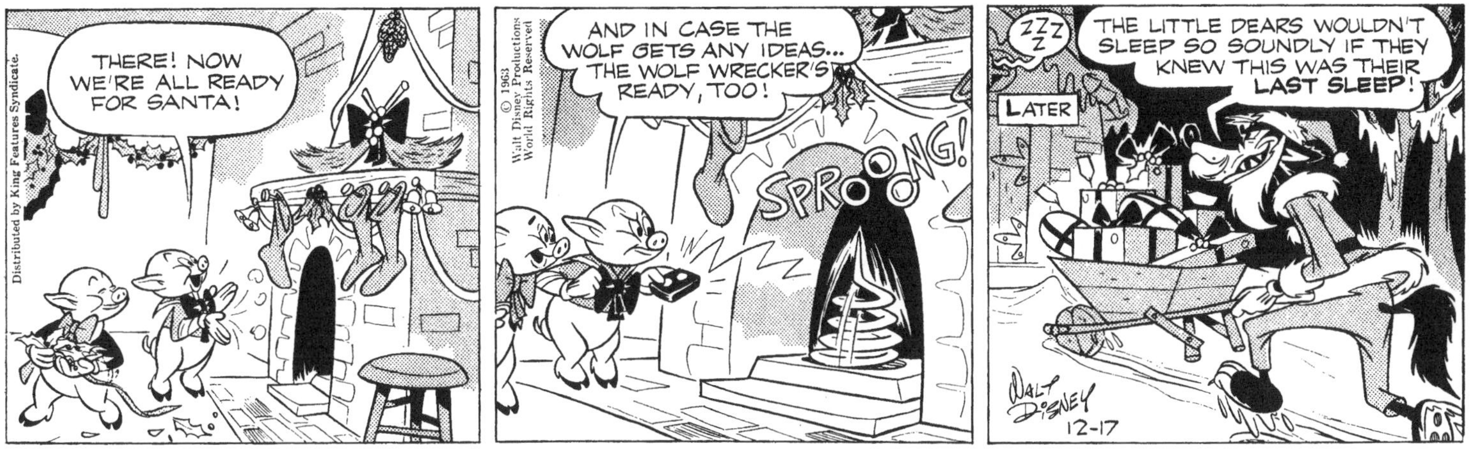
Distributed by King Features Syndicate.
THERE! NOW WE'RE ALL READY FOR SANTA!
© 1963 Walt Disney Productions World Rights Reserved
AND IN CASE THE WOLF GETS ANY IDEAS... THE WOLF WRECKER'S READY, TOO!
SPROOONG!
ZZZ Z
LATER
THE LITTLE DEARS WOULDN'T SLEEP SO SOUNDLY IF THEY KNEW THIS WAS THEIR **LAST SLEEP**!
WALT DISNEY 12-17

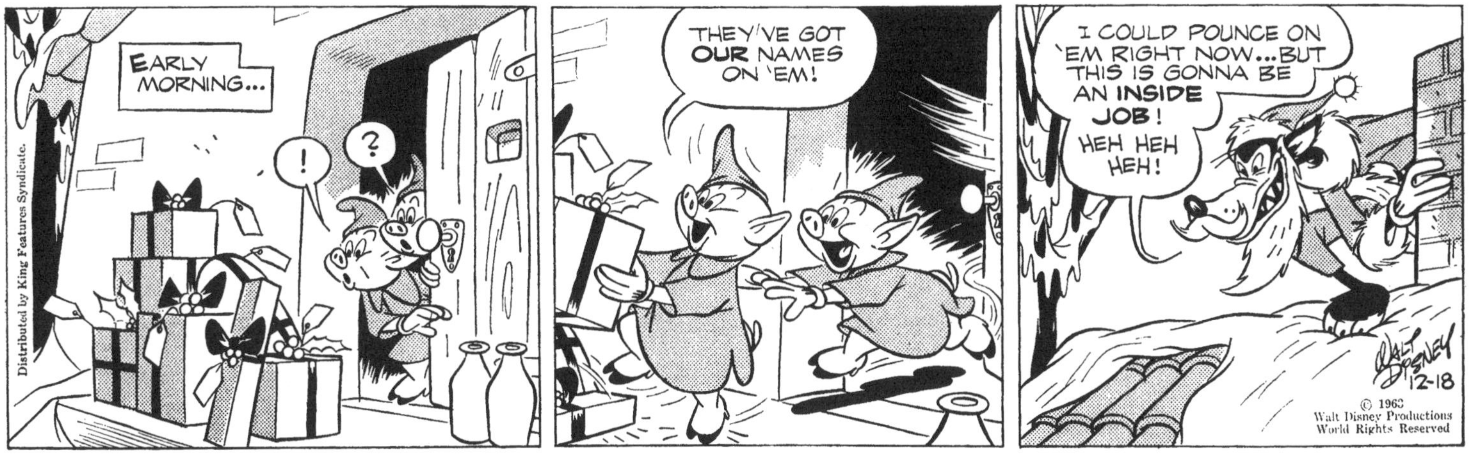
Distributed by King Features Syndicate.
EARLY MORNING...
!
?
THEY'VE GOT **OUR** NAMES ON 'EM!
I COULD POUNCE ON 'EM RIGHT NOW...BUT THIS IS GONNA BE AN **INSIDE JOB**!
HEH HEH HEH!
WALT DISNEY 12-18
© 1963 Walt Disney Productions World Rights Reserved

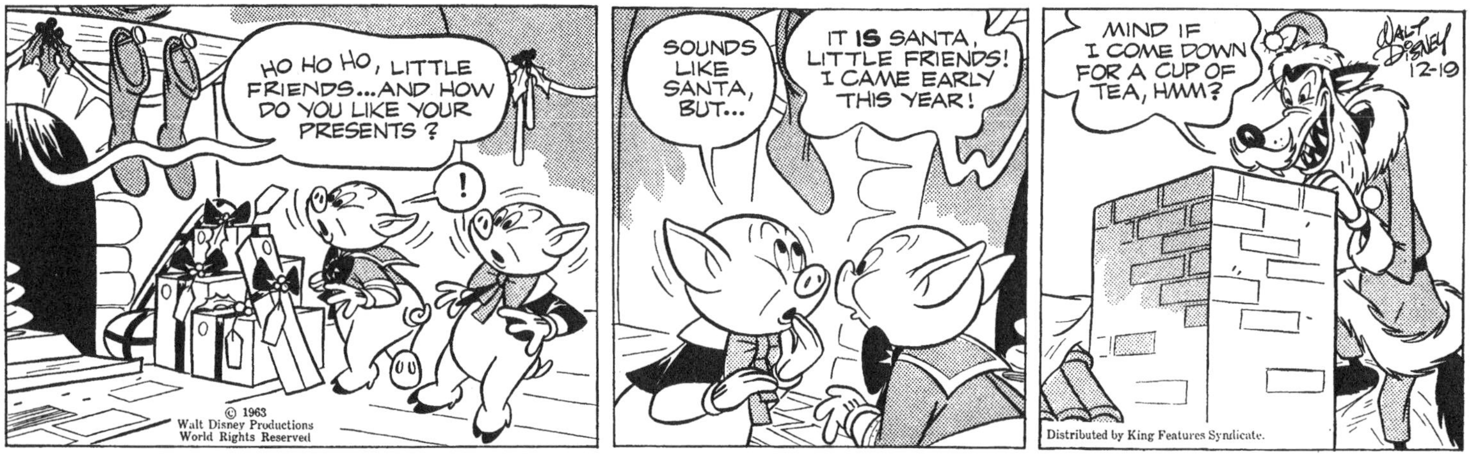
HO HO HO, LITTLE FRIENDS...AND HOW DO YOU LIKE YOUR PRESENTS ?
!
© 1963 Walt Disney Productions World Rights Reserved
SOUNDS LIKE SANTA, BUT...
IT IS SANTA, LITTLE FRIENDS! I CAME EARLY THIS YEAR!
MIND IF I COME DOWN FOR A CUP OF TEA, HMM?
WALT DISNEY 12-19
Distributed by King Features Syndicate.

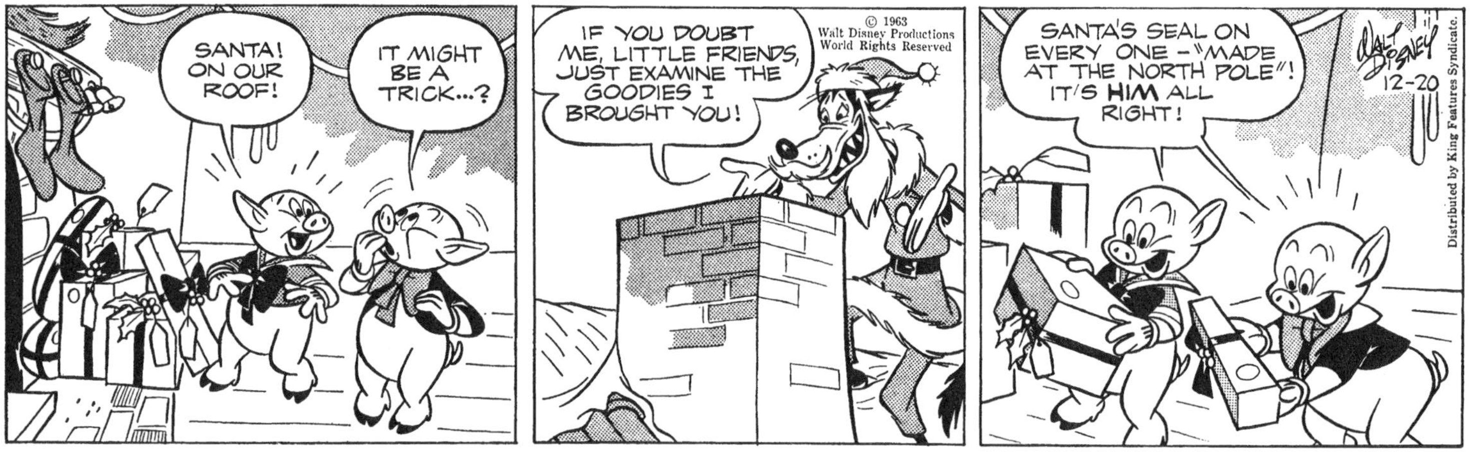
SANTA! ON OUR ROOF!
IT MIGHT BE A TRICK...?
IF YOU DOUBT ME, LITTLE FRIENDS, JUST EXAMINE THE GOODIES I BROUGHT YOU!
© 1963 Walt Disney Productions World Rights Reserved
SANTA'S SEAL ON EVERY ONE - "MADE AT THE NORTH POLE"! IT'S HIM ALL RIGHT!
WALT DISNEY 12-20
Distributed by King Features Syndicate.

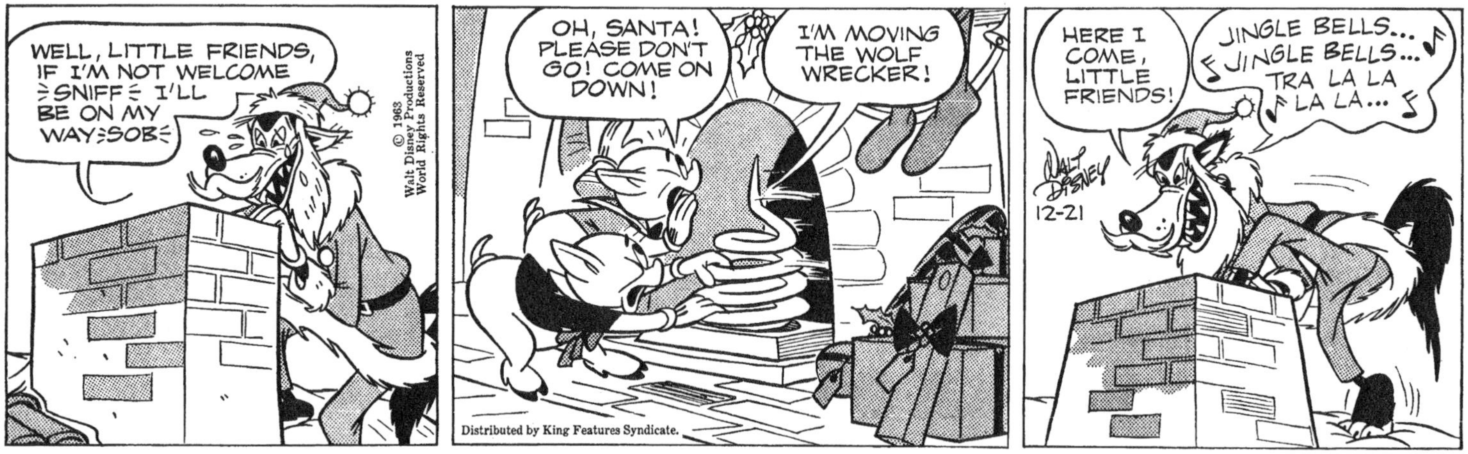
WELL, LITTLE FRIENDS, IF I'M NOT WELCOME SNIFF I'LL BE ON MY WAY SOB
© 1963 Walt Disney Productions World Rights Reserved
OH, SANTA! PLEASE DON'T GO! COME ON DOWN!
I'M MOVING THE WOLF WRECKER!
Distributed by King Features Syndicate.
HERE I COME, LITTLE FRIENDS!
JINGLE BELLS... JINGLE BELLS... TRA LA LA LA LA...
WALT DISNEY 12-21

THE PRACTICAL PIG RETURNS HOME JUST AS THE WOLF STARTS DOWN THE CHIMNEY...
...TRA LALA LA LA...
!
© 1963 Walt Disney Productions World Rights Reserved
Distributed by King Features Syndicate.
BUT IT'S THE WOLF WHO IS SURPRISED!
EEEEEEE!
HA!
SLAMM!
JUST AS I FIGURED!
SNAP!
WALT DISNEY 12-23

IT'S THE NIGHT BEFORE CHRISTMAS... AND ALL THROUGH THE HOUSE... EVERYONE'S STIRRING ...EXCEPT THE WOLF .....
READY FOR THE COUNTDOWN ...THREE ...TWO ...ONE!...
JUICE
FRUIT
© 1963 Walt Disney Productions World Rights Reserved
MERRY CHRISTMAS, EVERYBODY...EVERYWHERE!
JUICE
FRUIT
WALT DISNEY 12-24
Distributed by King Features Syndicate.

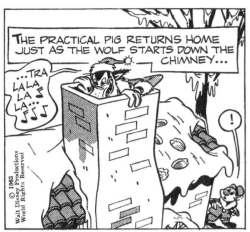

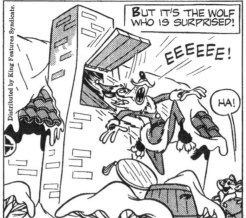

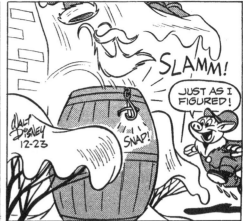

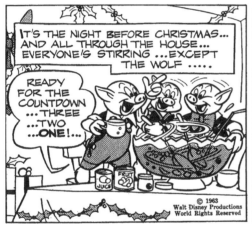

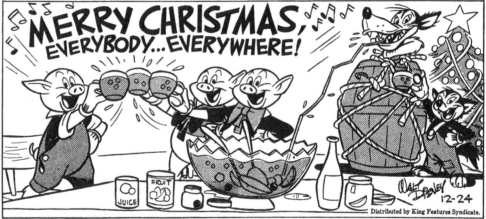

CINDERELLA'S CHRISTMAS PARTY

1964

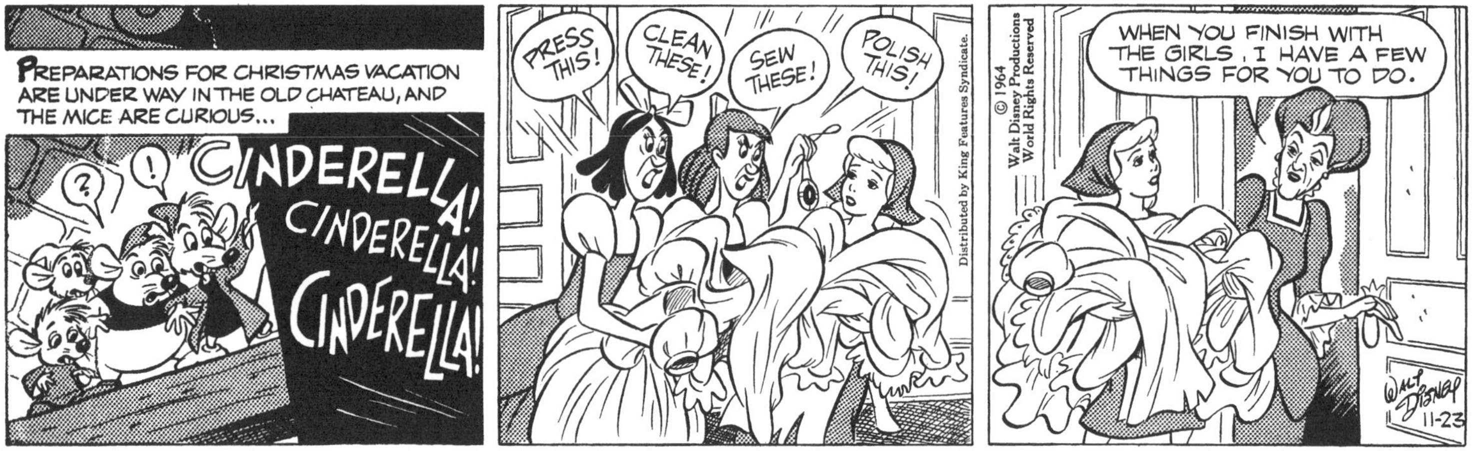
PREPARATIONS FOR CHRISTMAS VACATION ARE UNDER WAY IN THE OLD CHATEAU, AND THE MICE ARE CURIOUS...
?
!
CINDERELLA! CINDERELLA! CINDERELLA!
PRESS THIS!
CLEAN THESE!
SEW THESE!
POLISH THIS!
Distributed by King Features Syndicate.
© 1964 Walt Disney Productions World Rights Reserved
WHEN YOU FINISH WITH THE GIRLS, I HAVE A FEW THINGS FOR YOU TO DO.
WALT DISNEY 11-23

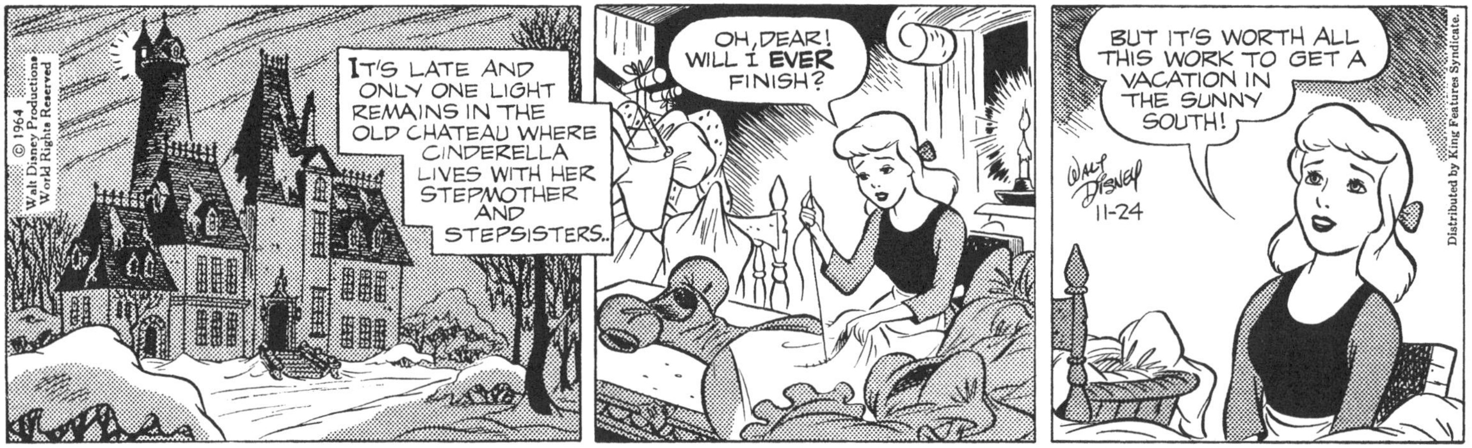
© 1964 Walt Disney Productions World Rights Reserved
IT'S LATE AND ONLY ONE LIGHT REMAINS IN THE OLD CHATEAU WHERE CINDERELLA LIVES WITH HER STEPMOTHER AND STEPSISTERS..
OH, DEAR! WILL I EVER FINISH?
BUT IT'S WORTH ALL THIS WORK TO GET A VACATION IN THE SUNNY SOUTH!
WALT DISNEY 11-24
Distributed by King Features Syndicate.

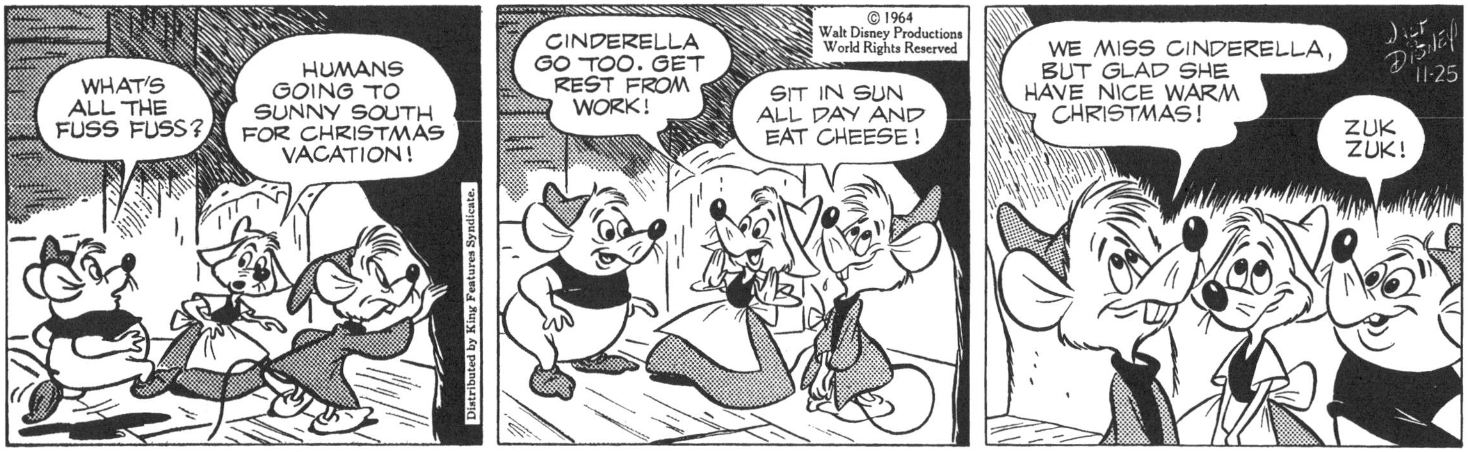
WHAT'S ALL THE FUSS FUSS?
HUMANS GOING TO SUNNY SOUTH FOR CHRISTMAS VACATION!
Distributed by King Features Syndicate.
© 1964 Walt Disney Productions World Rights Reserved
CINDERELLA GO TOO. GET REST FROM WORK!
SIT IN SUN ALL DAY AND EAT CHEESE!
WALT DISNEY 11-25
WE MISS CINDERELLA, BUT GLAD SHE HAVE NICE WARM CHRISTMAS!
ZUK ZUK!

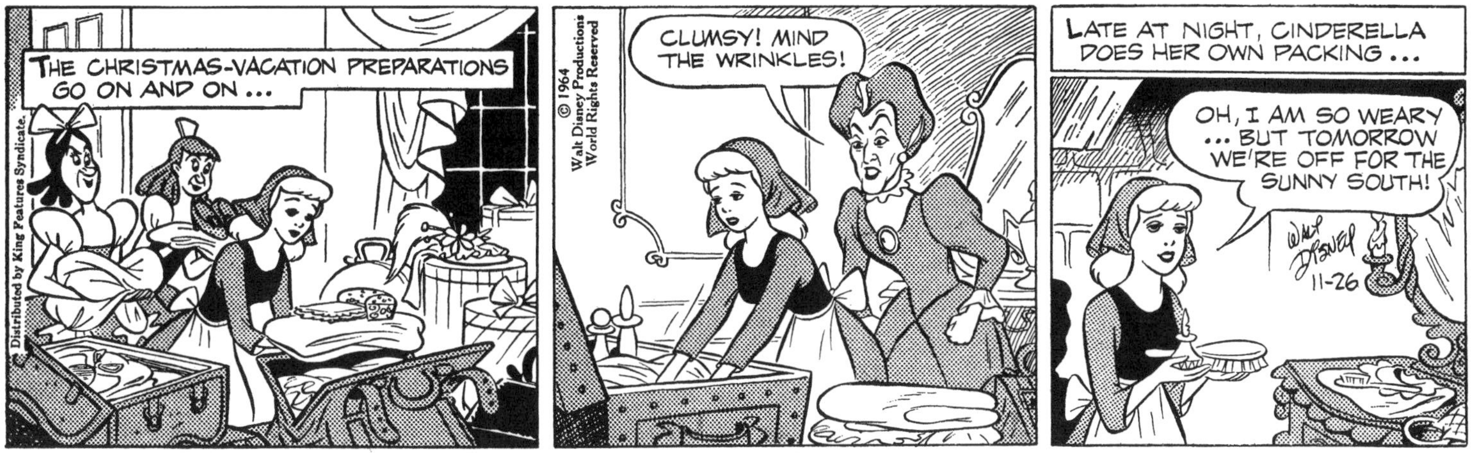
THE CHRISTMAS-VACATION PREPARATIONS GO ON AND ON ...
Distributed by King Features Syndicate.
© 1964 Walt Disney Productions World Rights Reserved
CLUMSY! MIND THE WRINKLES!
LATE AT NIGHT, CINDERELLA DOES HER OWN PACKING ...
OH, I AM SO WEARY ... BUT TOMORROW WE'RE OFF FOR THE SUNNY SOUTH!
WALT DISNEY
11-26

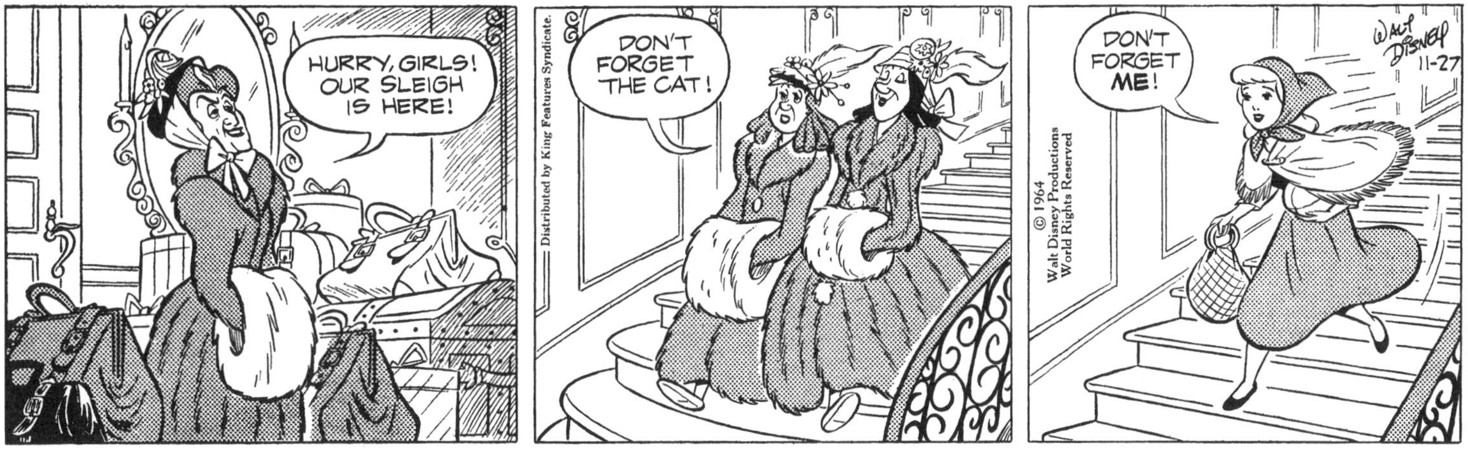
HURRY, GIRLS! OUR SLEIGH IS HERE!
Distributed by King Features Syndicate.
DON'T FORGET THE CAT!
© 1964 Walt Disney Productions World Rights Reserved
DON'T FORGET ME!
WALT DISNEY
11-27

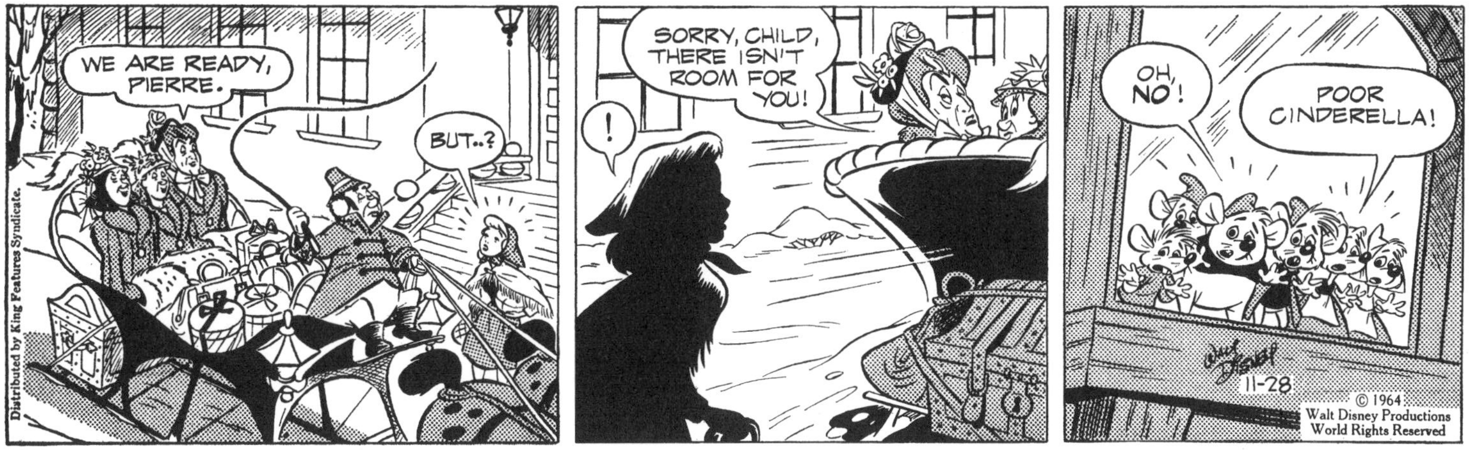
Distributed by King Features Syndicate.
WE ARE READY, PIERRE.
BUT..?
SORRY, CHILD, THERE ISN'T ROOM FOR YOU!
!
OH, NO!
POOR CINDERELLA!
WALT DISNEY
11-28
© 1964 Walt Disney Productions World Rights Reserved

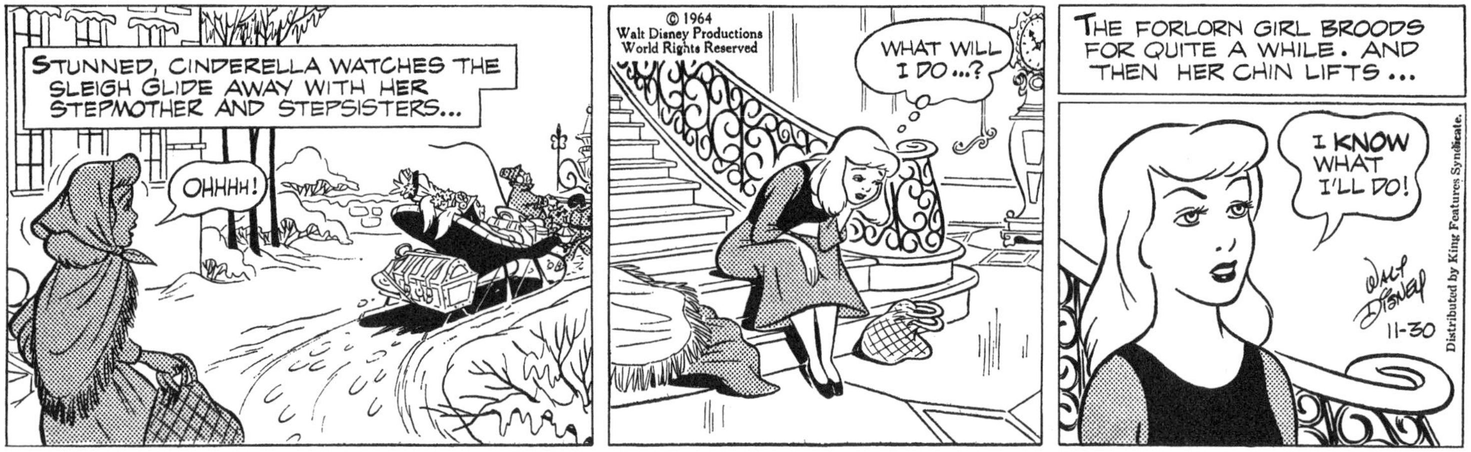
STUNNED, CINDERELLA WATCHES THE SLEIGH GLIDE AWAY WITH HER STEPMOTHER AND STEPSISTERS...
OHHHH!
© 1964 Walt Disney Productions World Rights Reserved
WHAT WILL I DO...?
THE FORLORN GIRL BROODS FOR QUITE A WHILE. AND THEN HER CHIN LIFTS...
I KNOW WHAT I'LL DO!
WALT DISNEY
11-30
Distributed by King Features Syndicate.

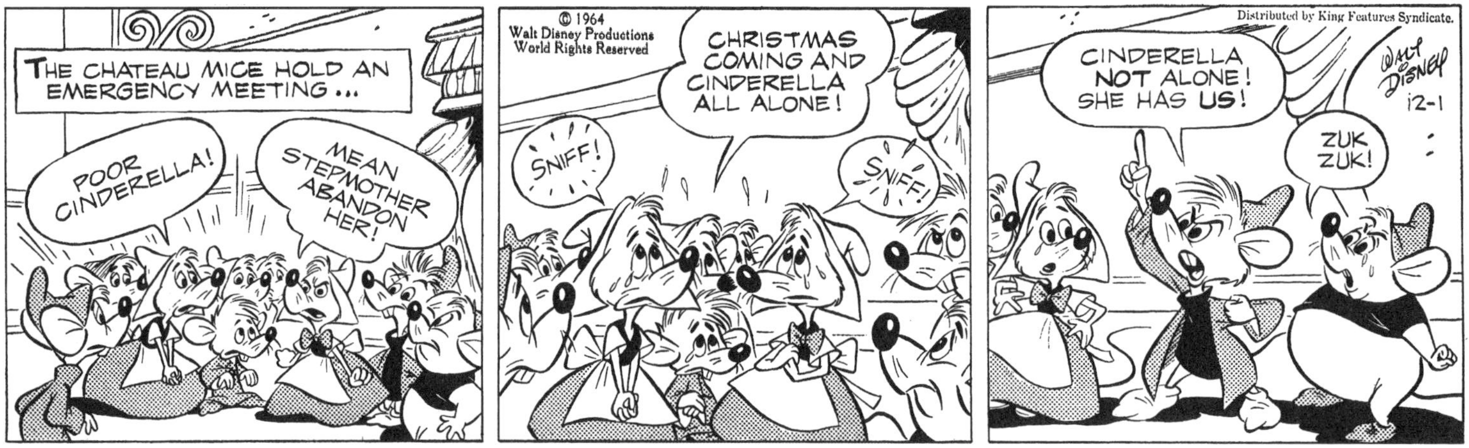
THE CHATEAU MICE HOLD AN EMERGENCY MEETING...
POOR CINDERELLA!
MEAN STEPMOTHER ABANDON HER!
© 1964 Walt Disney Productions World Rights Reserved
CHRISTMAS COMING AND CINDERELLA ALL ALONE!
SNIFF!
SNIFF!
Distributed by King Features Syndicate.
CINDERELLA NOT ALONE! SHE HAS US!
WALT DISNEY
12-1
ZUK ZUK!

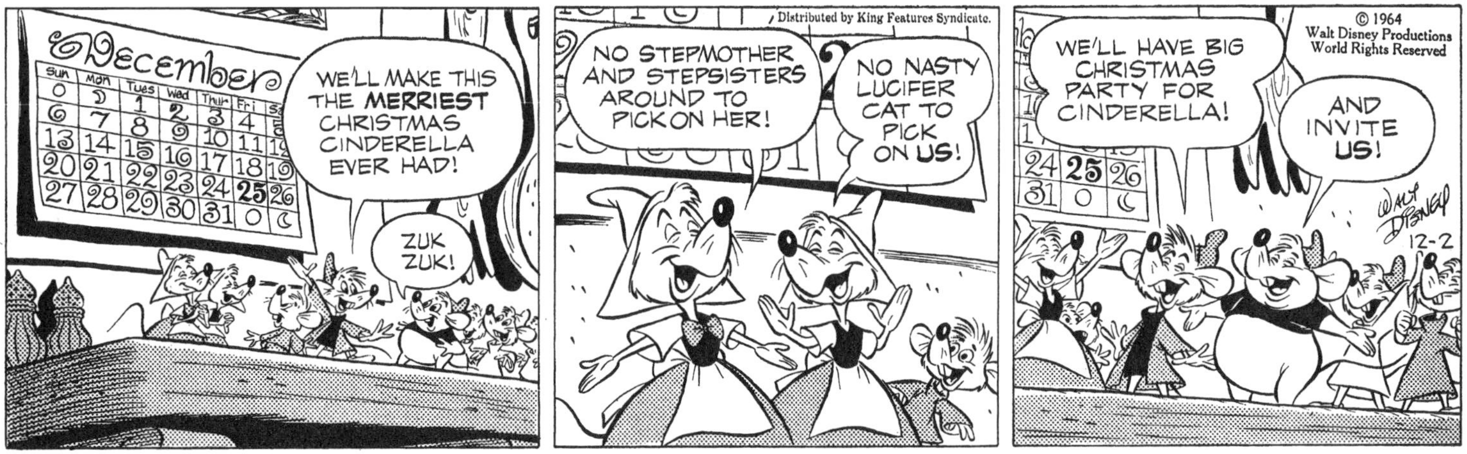
December
Sun Mon Tues Wed Thur Fri Sat
WE'LL MAKE THIS THE MERRIEST CHRISTMAS CINDERELLA EVER HAD!
ZUK ZUK!
Distributed by King Features Syndicate.
NO STEPMOTHER AND STEPSISTERS AROUND TO PICK ON HER!
NO NASTY LUCIFER CAT TO PICK ON US!
© 1964 Walt Disney Productions World Rights Reserved
WE'LL HAVE BIG CHRISTMAS PARTY FOR CINDERELLA!
AND INVITE US!
WALT DISNEY
12-2

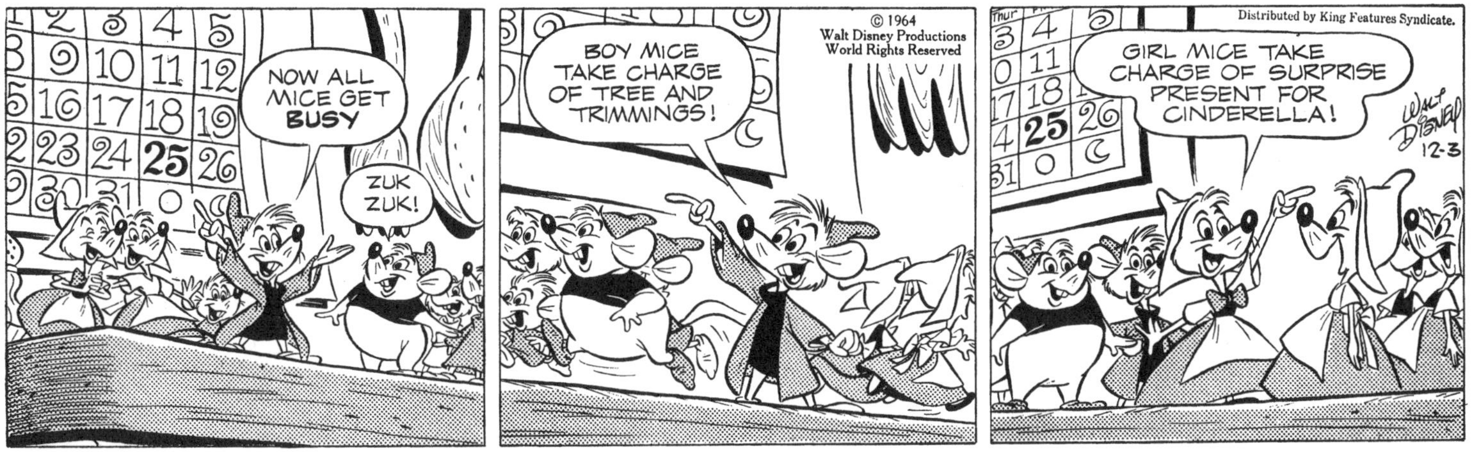
NOW ALL MICE GET BUSY
ZUK ZUK!
© 1964 Walt Disney Productions World Rights Reserved
BOY MICE TAKE CHARGE OF TREE AND TRIMMINGS!
Distributed by King Features Syndicate.
GIRL MICE TAKE CHARGE OF SURPRISE PRESENT FOR CINDERELLA!
WALT DISNEY 12-3

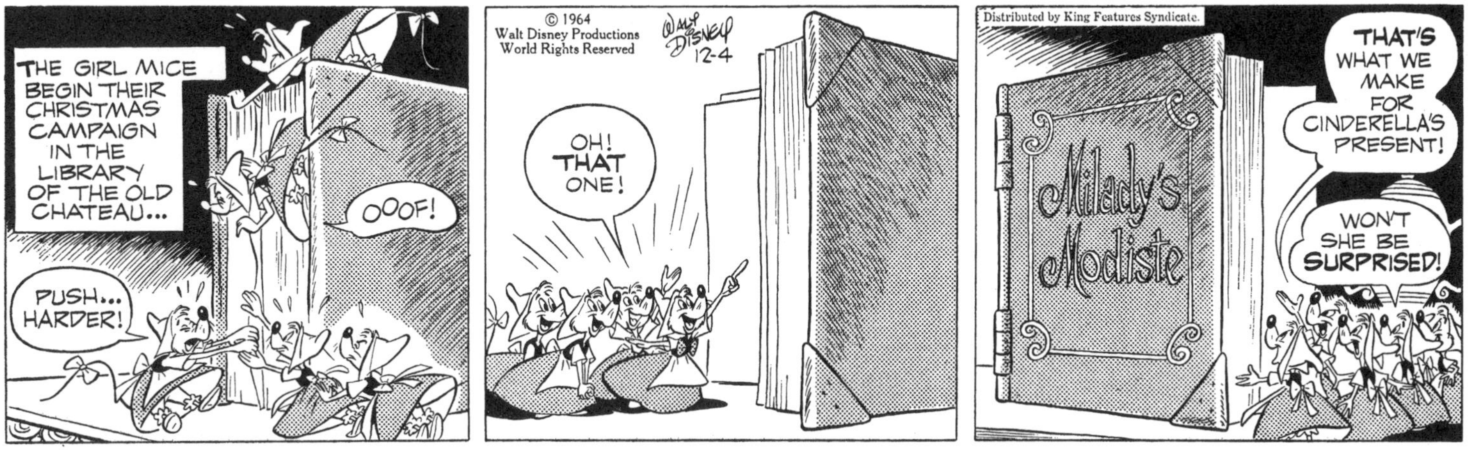
THE GIRL MICE BEGIN THEIR CHRISTMAS CAMPAIGN IN THE LIBRARY OF THE OLD CHATEAU...
OOOF!
PUSH... HARDER!
© 1964 Walt Disney Productions World Rights Reserved
WALT DISNEY 12-4
OH! THAT ONE!
Distributed by King Features Syndicate.
Milady's Modiste
THAT'S WHAT WE MAKE FOR CINDERELLA'S PRESENT!
WON'T SHE BE SURPRISED!

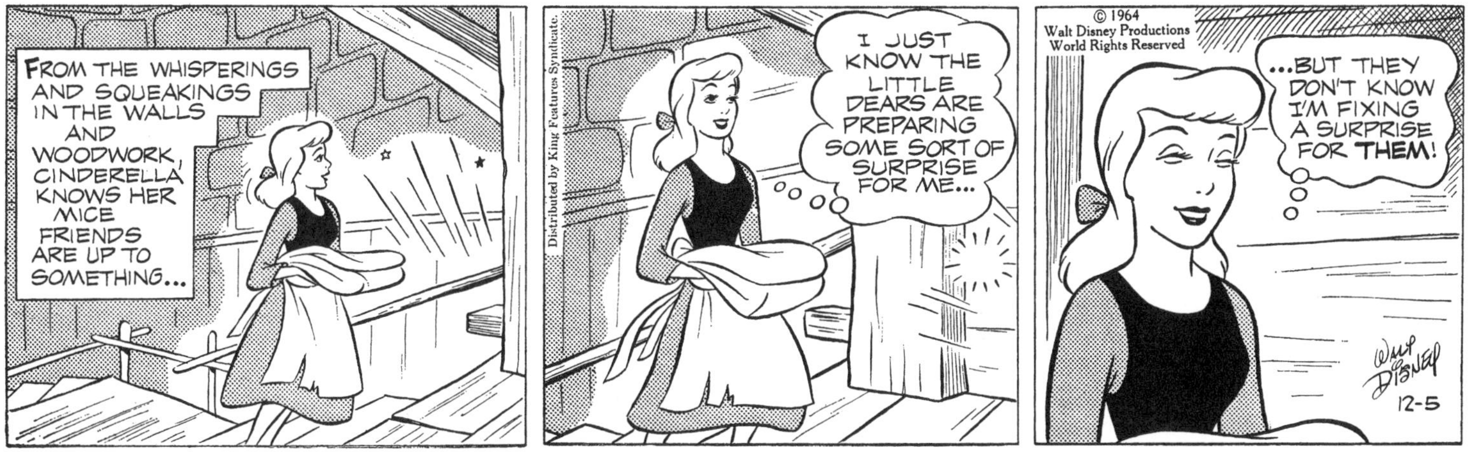
FROM THE WHISPERINGS AND SQUEAKINGS IN THE WALLS AND WOODWORK, CINDERELLA KNOWS HER MICE FRIENDS ARE UP TO SOMETHING...
Distributed by King Features Syndicate.
I JUST KNOW THE LITTLE DEARS ARE PREPARING SOME SORT OF SURPRISE FOR ME...
© 1964 Walt Disney Productions World Rights Reserved
...BUT THEY DON'T KNOW I'M FIXING A SURPRISE FOR THEM!
WALT DISNEY 12-5

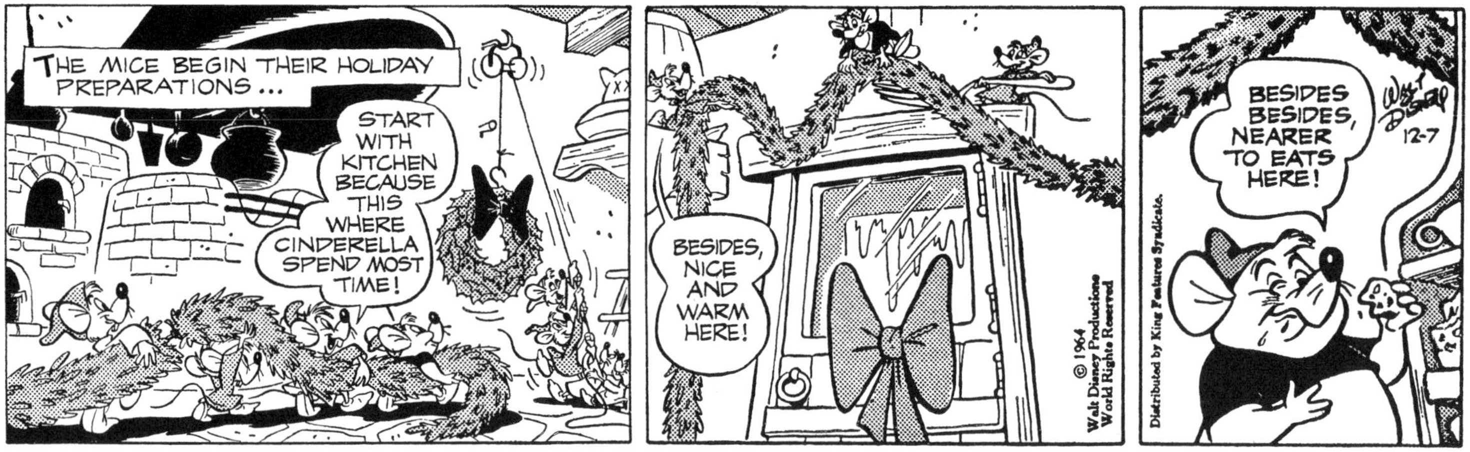
THE MICE BEGIN THEIR HOLIDAY PREPARATIONS...
START WITH KITCHEN BECAUSE THIS WHERE CINDERELLA SPEND MOST TIME!
BESIDES, NICE AND WARM HERE!
© 1964 Walt Disney Productions World Rights Reserved
BESIDES BESIDES, NEARER TO EATS HERE!
WALT DISNEY 12-7
Distributed by King Features Syndicate.

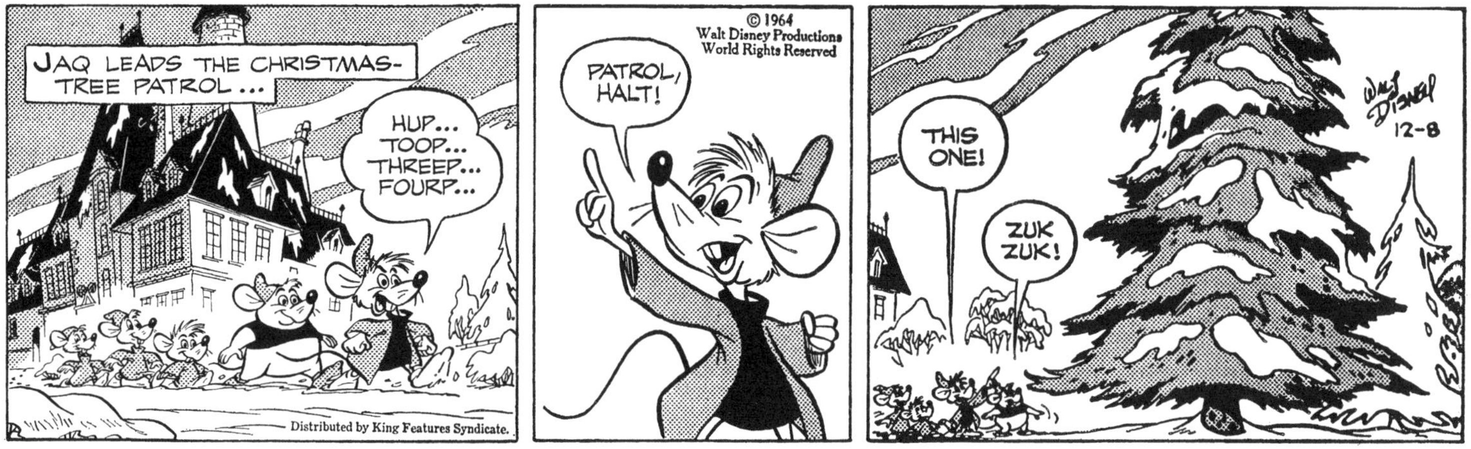
JAQ LEADS THE CHRISTMAS-TREE PATROL...
HUP... TOOP... THREEP... FOURP...
Distributed by King Features Syndicate.
© 1964 Walt Disney Productions World Rights Reserved
PATROL, HALT!
THIS ONE!
ZUK ZUK!
WALT DISNEY 12-8

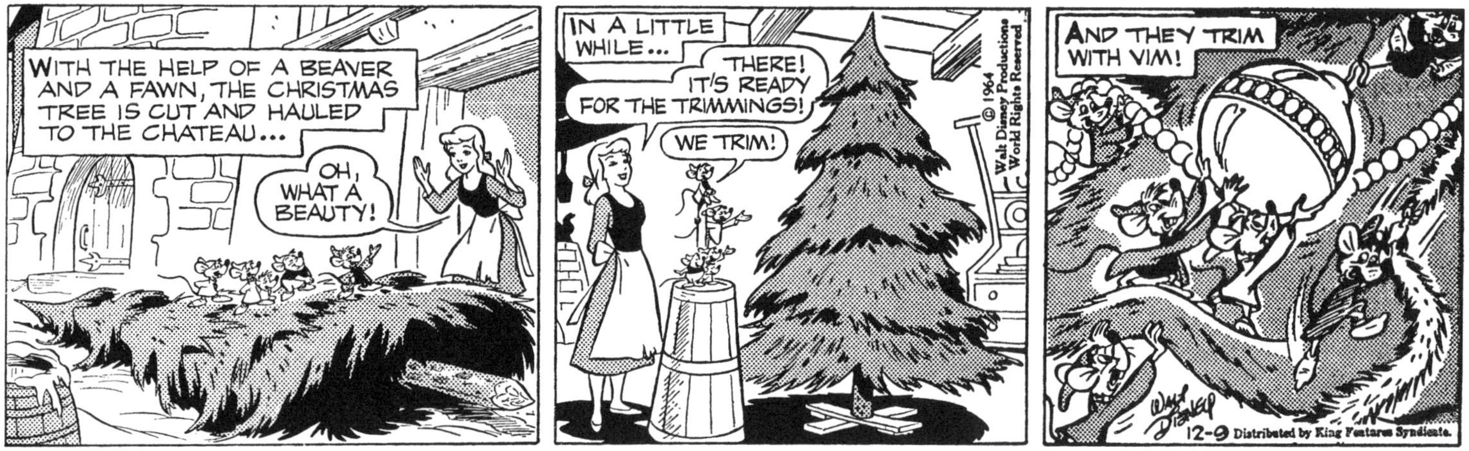
WITH THE HELP OF A BEAVER AND A FAWN, THE CHRISTMAS TREE IS CUT AND HAULED TO THE CHATEAU...
OH, WHAT A BEAUTY!
IN A LITTLE WHILE...
THERE! IT'S READY FOR THE TRIMMINGS!
WE TRIM!
© 1964 Walt Disney Productions World Rights Reserved
AND THEY TRIM WITH VIM!
WALT DISNEY 12-9 Distributed by King Features Syndicate.

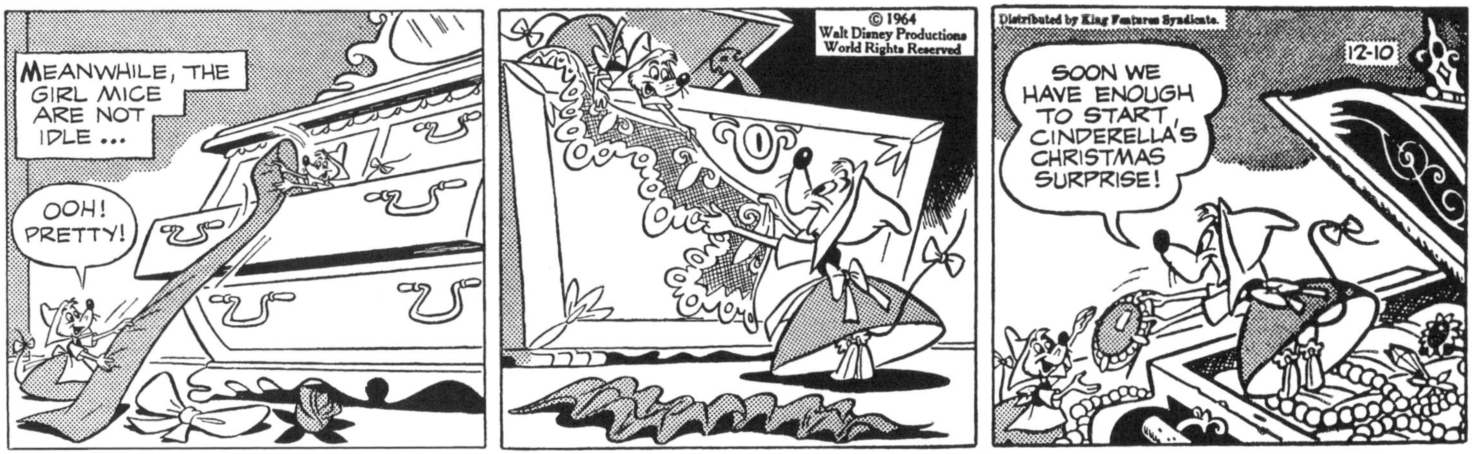
MEANWHILE, THE GIRL MICE ARE NOT IDLE ...
OOH! PRETTY!
© 1964 Walt Disney Productions World Rights Reserved
Distributed by King Features Syndicate.
12-10
SOON WE HAVE ENOUGH TO START CINDERELLA'S CHRISTMAS SURPRISE!

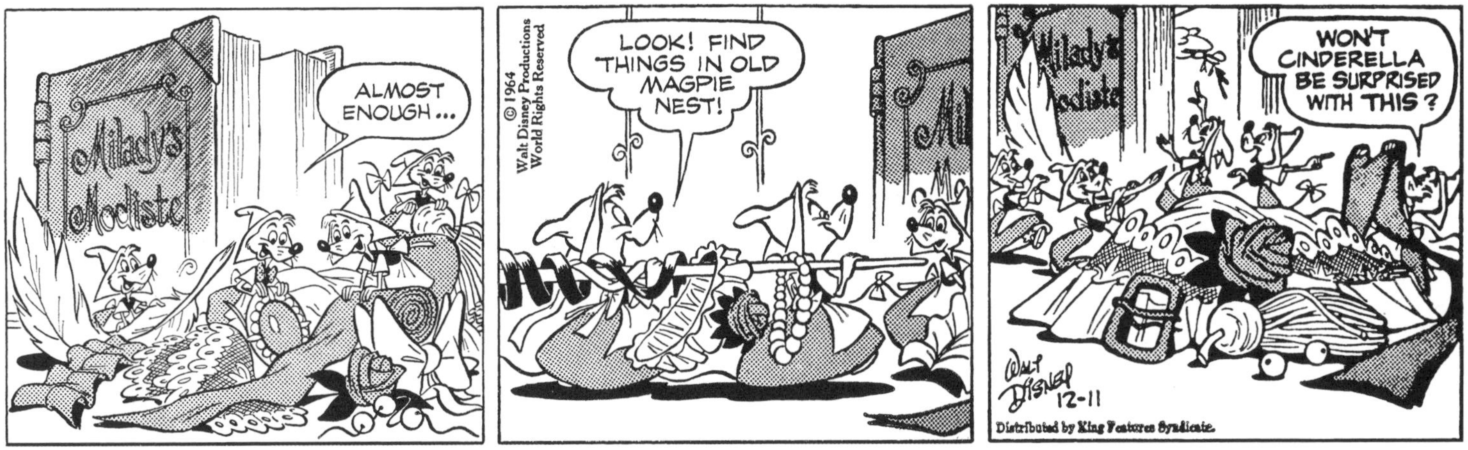
Milady's Modiste
ALMOST ENOUGH ...
© 1964 Walt Disney Productions World Rights Reserved
LOOK! FIND THINGS IN OLD MAGPIE NEST!
WON'T CINDERELLA BE SURPRISED WITH THIS ?
WALT DISNEY
12-11
Distributed by King Features Syndicate.

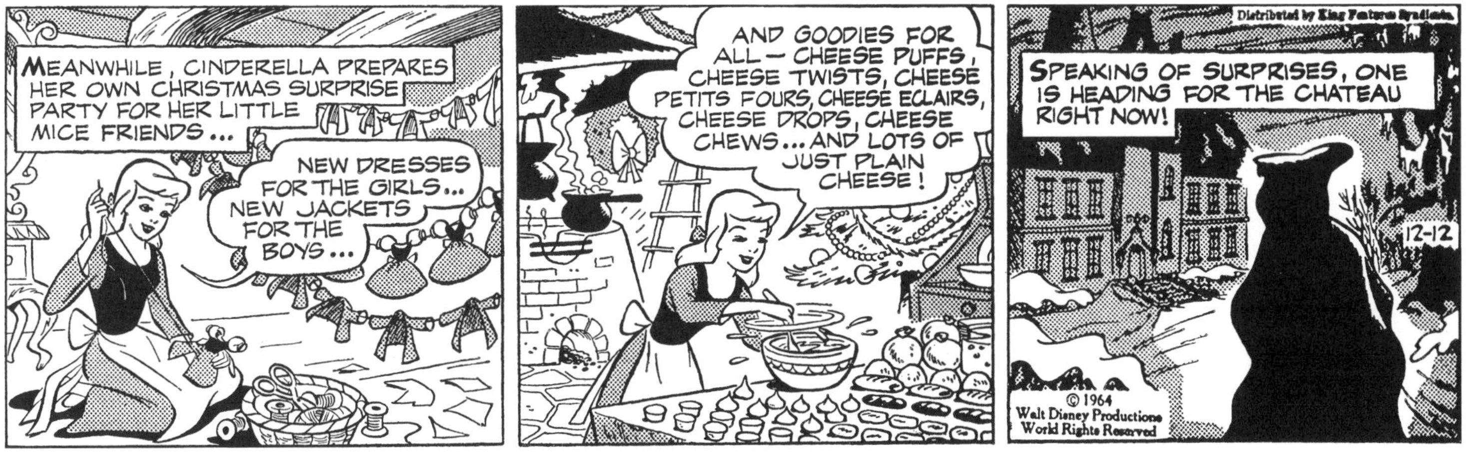
MEANWHILE, CINDERELLA PREPARES HER OWN CHRISTMAS SURPRISE PARTY FOR HER LITTLE MICE FRIENDS ...
NEW DRESSES FOR THE GIRLS ... NEW JACKETS FOR THE BOYS ...
AND GOODIES FOR ALL — CHEESE PUFFS, CHEESE TWISTS, CHEESE PETITS FOURS, CHEESE ECLAIRS, CHEESE DROPS, CHEESE CHEWS ... AND LOTS OF JUST PLAIN CHEESE !
Distributed by King Features Syndicate.
SPEAKING OF SURPRISES, ONE IS HEADING FOR THE CHATEAU RIGHT NOW!
12-12
© 1964 Walt Disney Productions World Rights Reserved

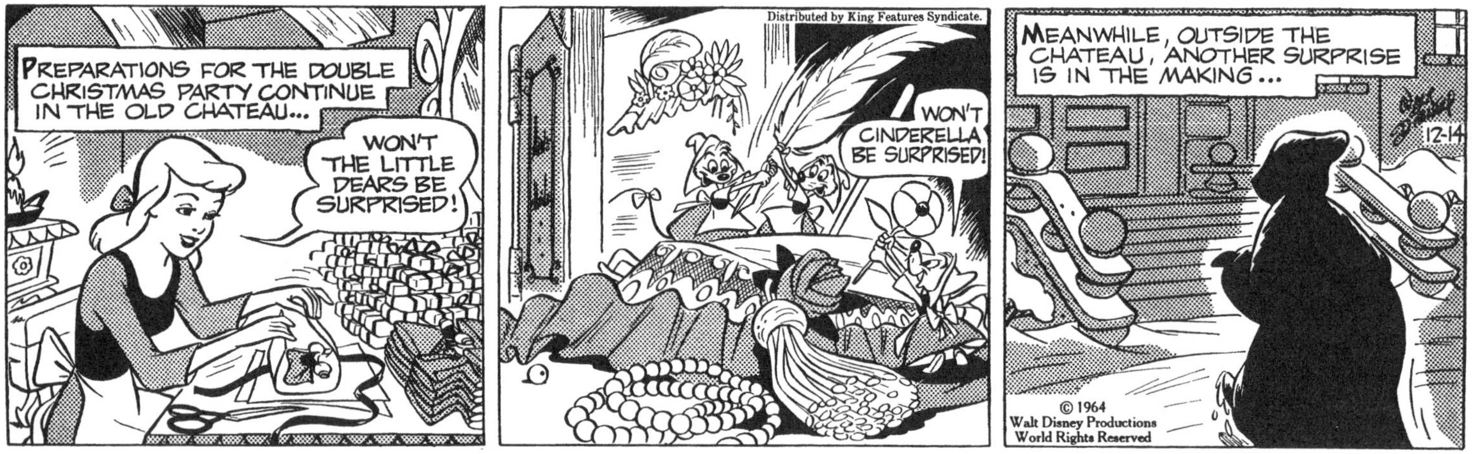
PREPARATIONS FOR THE DOUBLE CHRISTMAS PARTY CONTINUE IN THE OLD CHATEAU...
WON'T THE LITTLE DEARS BE SURPRISED!
Distributed by King Features Syndicate.
WON'T CINDERELLA BE SURPRISED!
MEANWHILE, OUTSIDE THE CHATEAU, ANOTHER SURPRISE IS IN THE MAKING...
12-14
© 1964 Walt Disney Productions World Rights Reserved

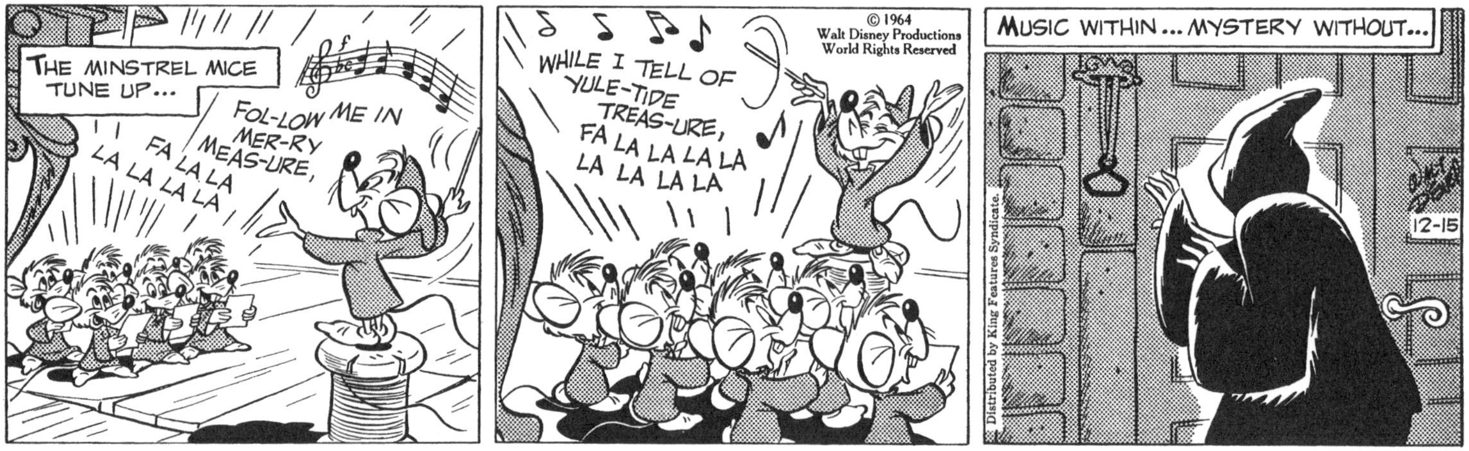
THE MINSTREL MICE TUNE UP...
FOL-LOW ME IN MER-RY MEAS-URE, FA LA LA LA LA LA LA LA
© 1964 Walt Disney Productions World Rights Reserved
WHILE I TELL OF YULE-TIDE TREAS-URE, FA LA LA LA LA LA LA LA LA
MUSIC WITHIN... MYSTERY WITHOUT...
Distributed by King Features Syndicate.
12-15

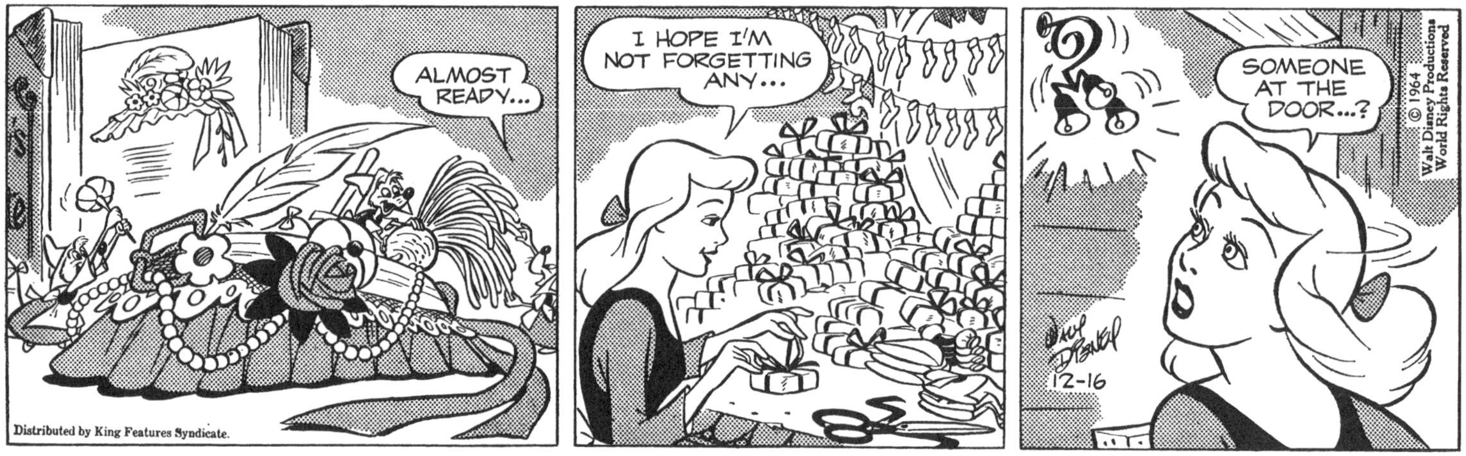
ALMOST READY...
Distributed by King Features Syndicate.
I HOPE I'M NOT FORGETTING ANY...
SOMEONE AT THE DOOR...?
© 1964 Walt Disney Productions World Rights Reserved
12-16

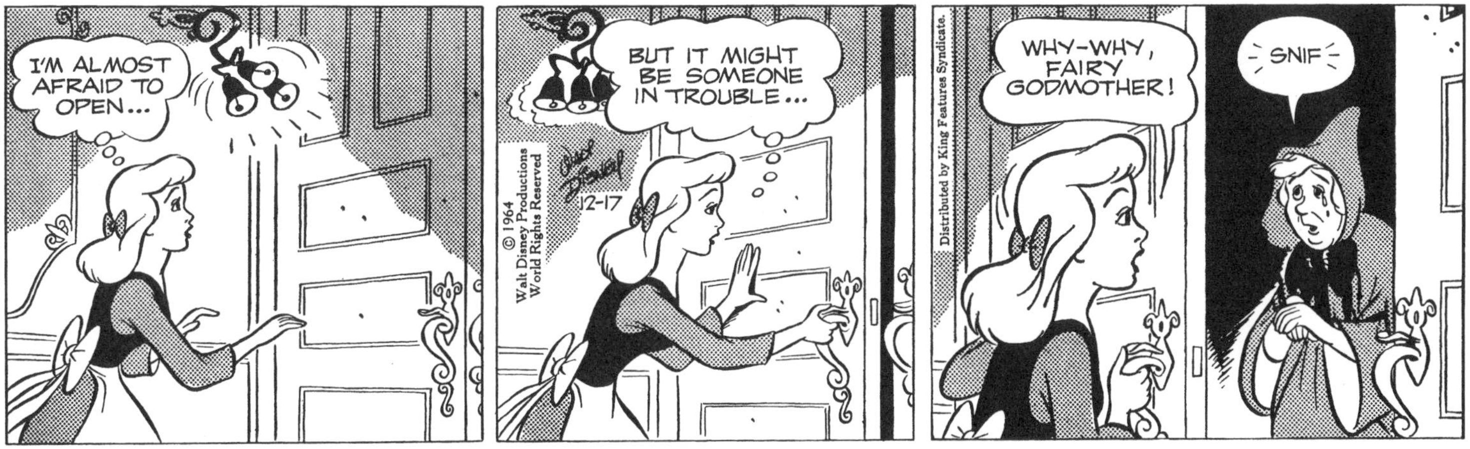
I'M ALMOST AFRAID TO OPEN...
BUT IT MIGHT BE SOMEONE IN TROUBLE...
© 1964 Walt Disney Productions World Rights Reserved
WALT DISNEY 12-17
Distributed by King Features Syndicate.
WHY-WHY, FAIRY GODMOTHER!
SNIF

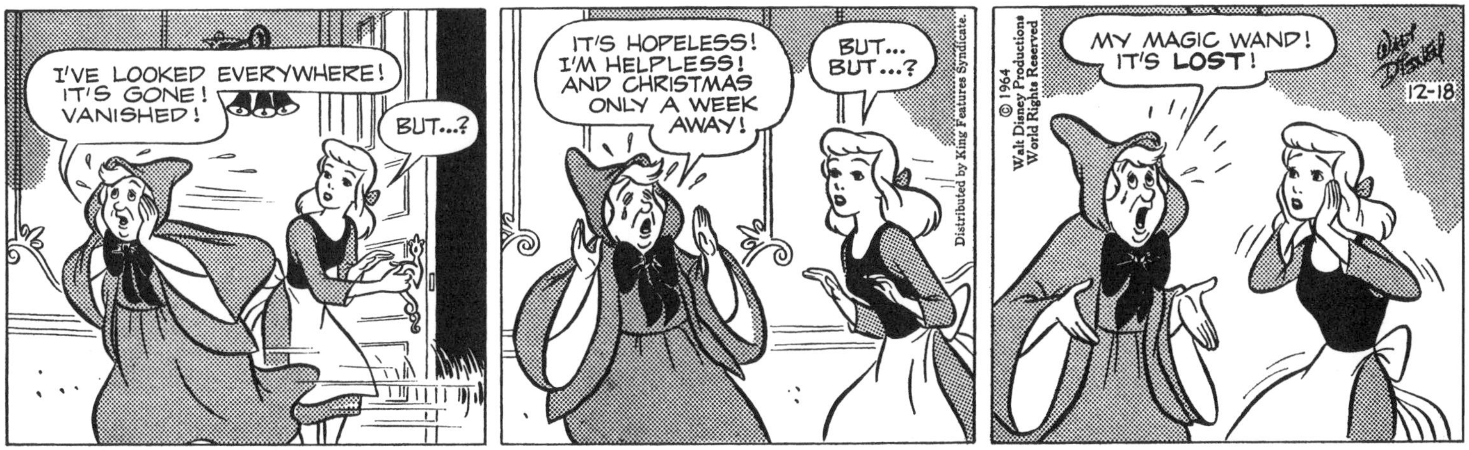
I'VE LOOKED EVERYWHERE! IT'S GONE! VANISHED!
BUT...?
IT'S HOPELESS! I'M HELPLESS! AND CHRISTMAS ONLY A WEEK AWAY!
BUT... BUT...?
Distributed by King Features Syndicate.
© 1964 Walt Disney Productions World Rights Reserved
MY MAGIC WAND! IT'S **LOST**!
WALT DISNEY 12-18

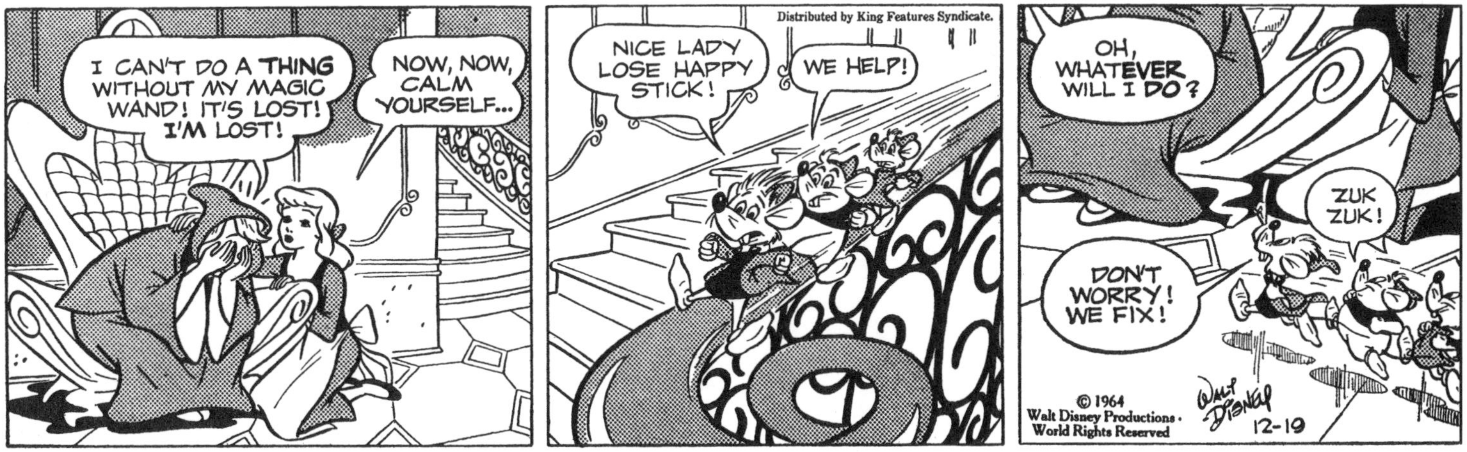
I CAN'T DO A **THING** WITHOUT MY MAGIC WAND! IT'S LOST! **I'M** LOST!
NOW, NOW, CALM YOURSELF...
Distributed by King Features Syndicate.
NICE LADY LOSE HAPPY STICK!
WE HELP!
OH, WHAT**EVER** WILL I **DO**?
ZUK ZUK!
DON'T WORRY! WE FIX!
© 1964 Walt Disney Productions • World Rights Reserved
WALT DISNEY 12-19

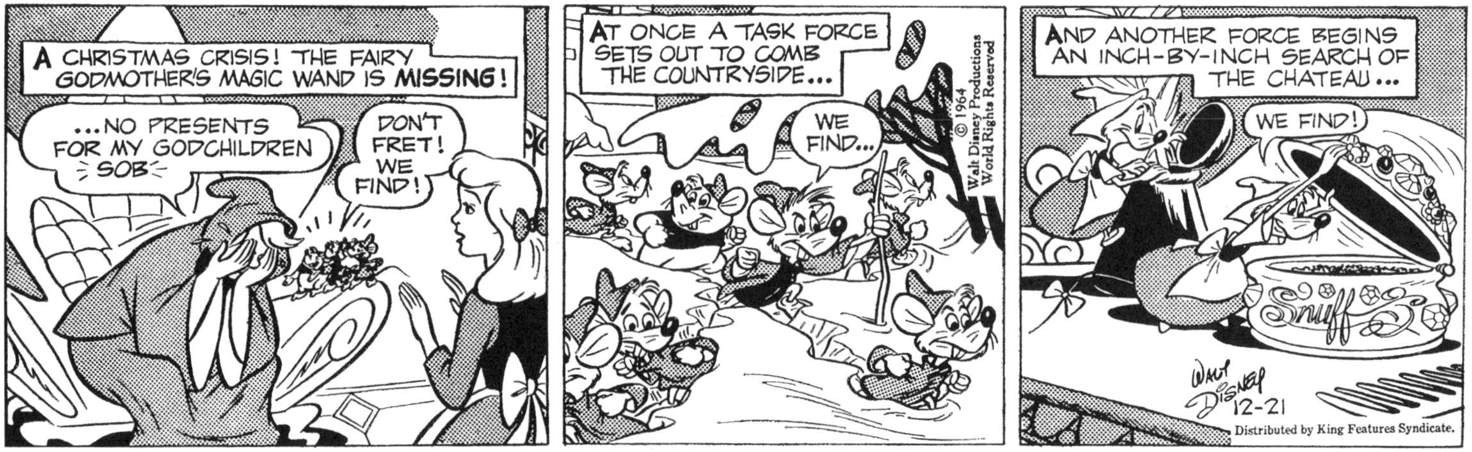
A CHRISTMAS CRISIS! THE FAIRY GODMOTHER'S MAGIC WAND IS MISSING!
...NO PRESENTS FOR MY GODCHILDREN SOB
DON'T FRET! WE FIND!
AT ONCE A TASK FORCE SETS OUT TO COMB THE COUNTRYSIDE...
WE FIND...
© 1964 Walt Disney Productions World Rights Reserved
AND ANOTHER FORCE BEGINS AN INCH-BY-INCH SEARCH OF THE CHATEAU...
WE FIND!
Snuff
WALT DISNEY 12-21
Distributed by King Features Syndicate.

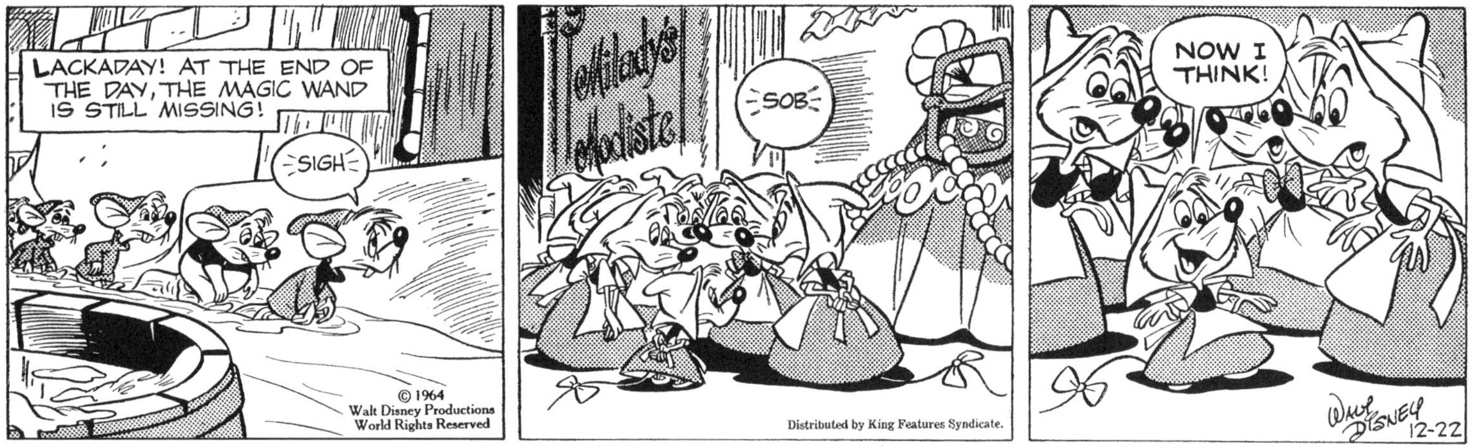
LACKADAY! AT THE END OF THE DAY, THE MAGIC WAND IS STILL MISSING!
SIGH
© 1964 Walt Disney Productions World Rights Reserved
Milady's Modiste
SOB
Distributed by King Features Syndicate.
NOW I THINK!
WALT DISNEY 12-22

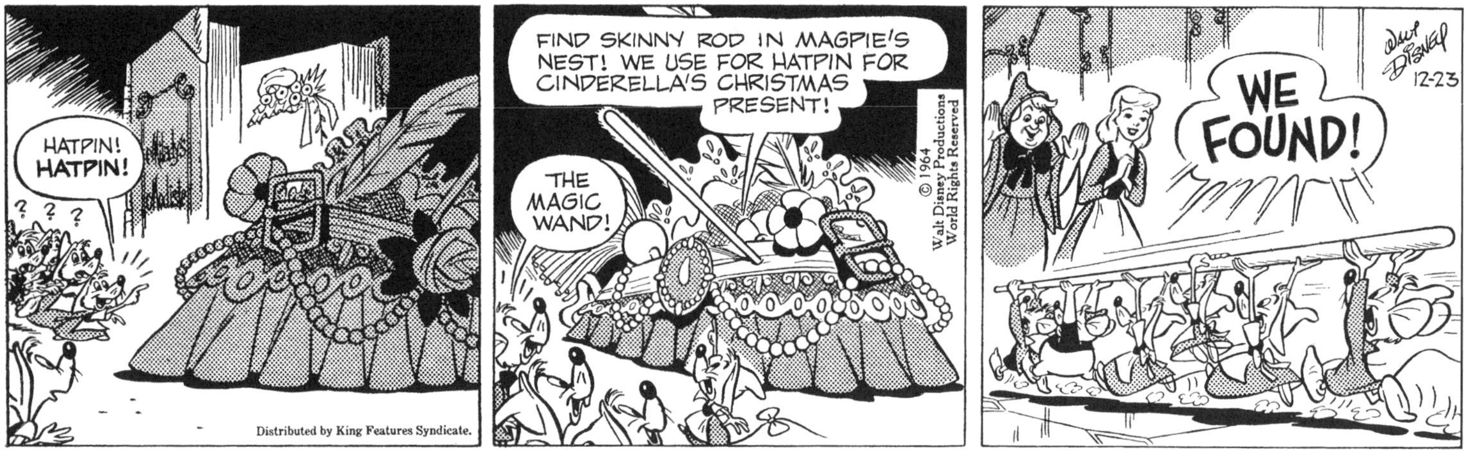
HATPIN! HATPIN!
? ? ?
Distributed by King Features Syndicate.
FIND SKINNY ROD IN MAGPIE'S NEST! WE USE FOR HATPIN FOR CINDERELLA'S CHRISTMAS PRESENT!
THE MAGIC WAND!
© 1964 Walt Disney Productions World Rights Reserved
WALT DISNEY 12-23
WE FOUND!

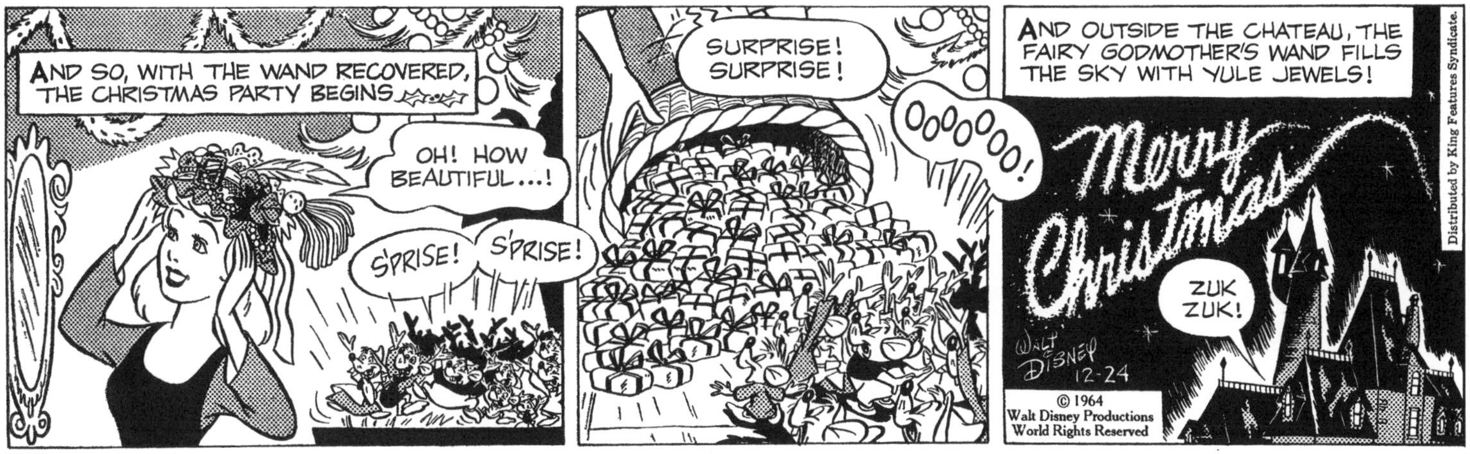
AND SO, WITH THE WAND RECOVERED, THE CHRISTMAS PARTY BEGINS
OH! HOW BEAUTIFUL...!
S'PRISE!
S'PRISE!
SURPRISE! SURPRISE!
OOOOOOO!
AND OUTSIDE THE CHATEAU, THE FAIRY GODMOTHER'S WAND FILLS THE SKY WITH YULE JEWELS!
Merry Christmas
ZUK ZUK!
WALT DISNEY 12-24
© 1964 Walt Disney Productions World Rights Reserved
Distributed by King Features Syndicate.

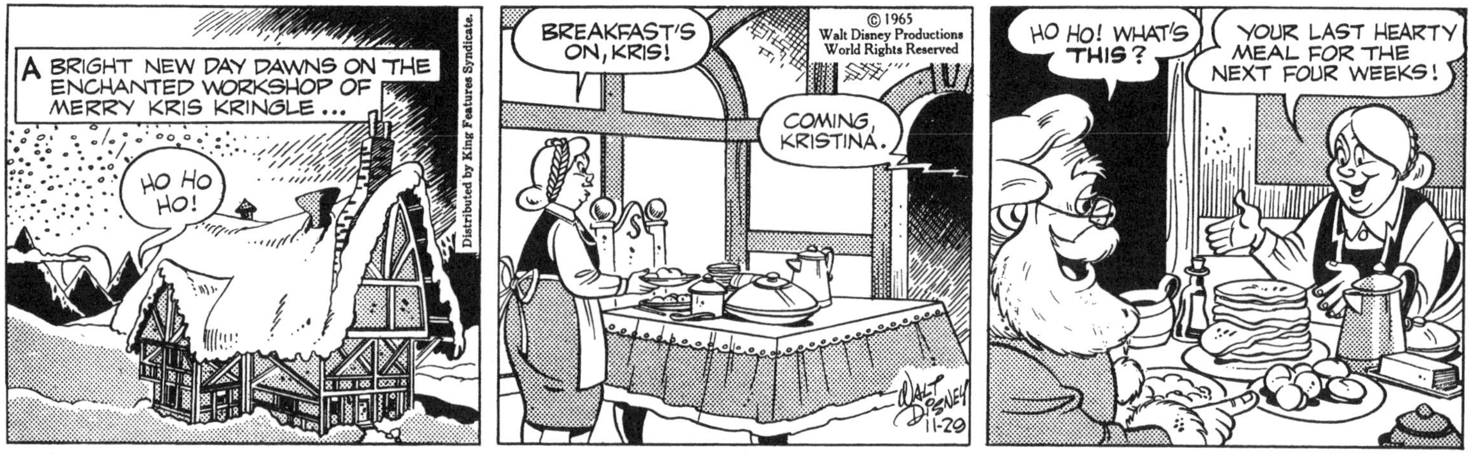
A BRIGHT NEW DAY DAWNS ON THE ENCHANTED WORKSHOP OF MERRY KRIS KRINGLE...
HO HO HO!
Distributed by King Features Syndicate.
BREAKFAST'S ON, KRIS!
© 1965 Walt Disney Productions World Rights Reserved
COMING, KRISTINA.
WALT DISNEY 11-29
HO HO! WHAT'S THIS?
YOUR LAST HEARTY MEAL FOR THE NEXT FOUR WEEKS!

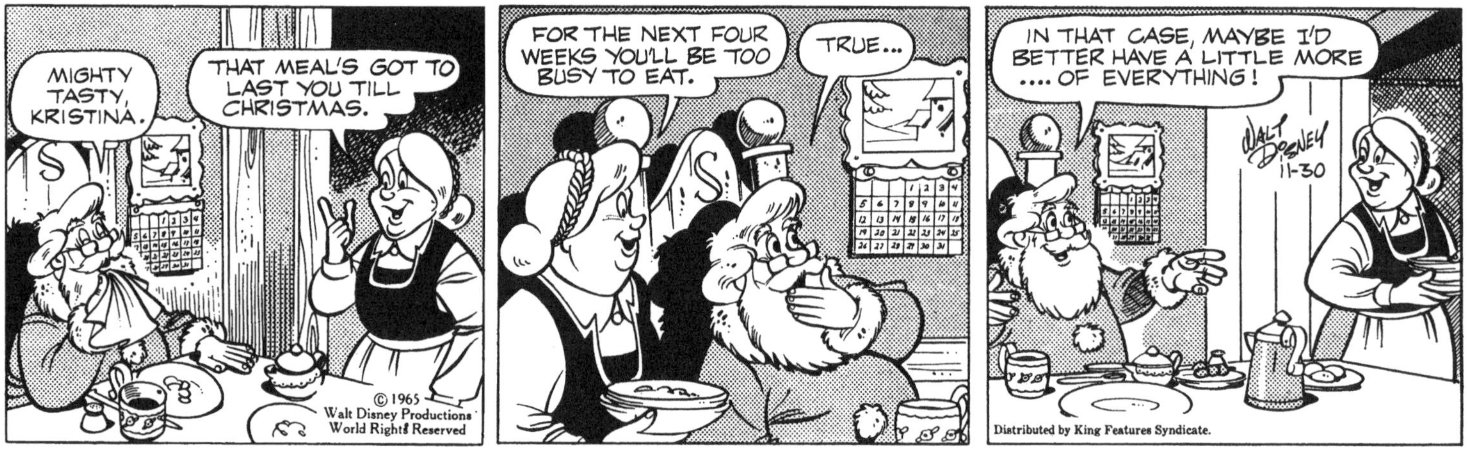
MIGHTY TASTY, KRISTINA.
THAT MEAL'S GOT TO LAST YOU TILL CHRISTMAS.
© 1965 Walt Disney Productions World Rights Reserved
FOR THE NEXT FOUR WEEKS YOU'LL BE TOO BUSY TO EAT.
TRUE...
IN THAT CASE, MAYBE I'D BETTER HAVE A LITTLE MORE .... OF EVERYTHING!
WALT DISNEY 11-30
Distributed by King Features Syndicate.

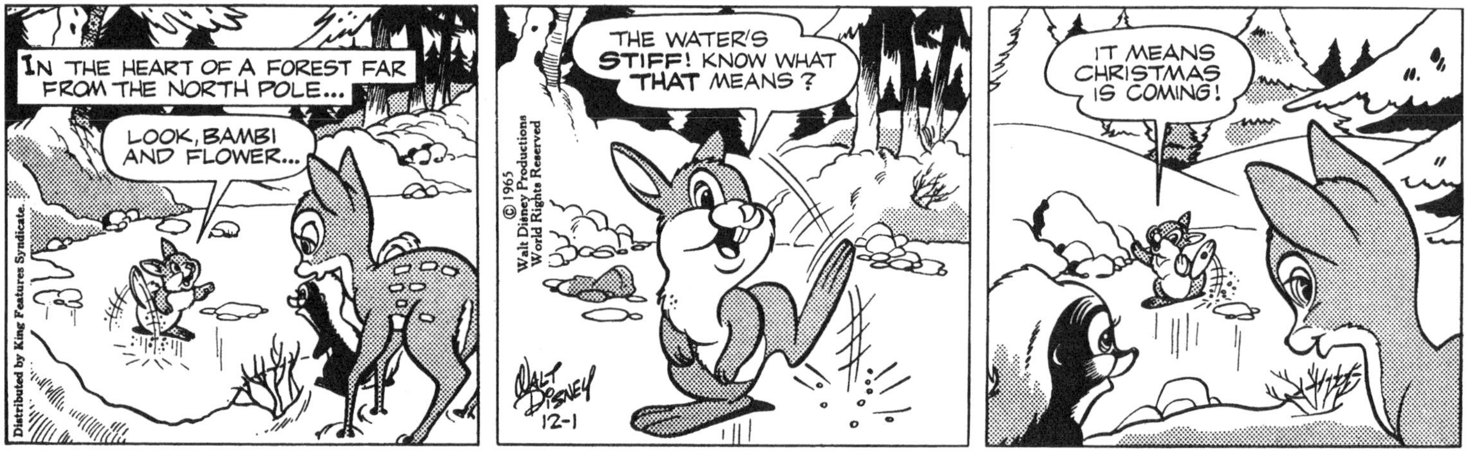
IN THE HEART OF A FOREST FAR FROM THE NORTH POLE...
LOOK, BAMBI AND FLOWER...
Distributed by King Features Syndicate.
THE WATER'S STIFF! KNOW WHAT THAT MEANS?
© 1965 Walt Disney Productions World Rights Reserved
WALT DISNEY 12-1
IT MEANS CHRISTMAS IS COMING!

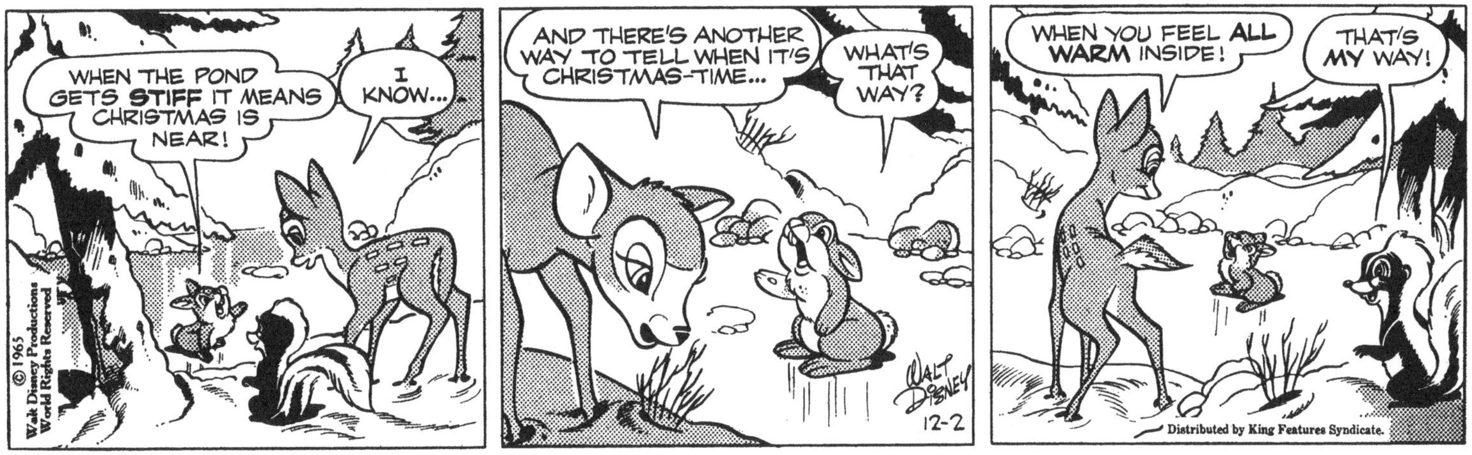
WHEN THE POND GETS STIFF IT MEANS CHRISTMAS IS NEAR!
I KNOW...
© 1965 Walt Disney Productions World Rights Reserved
AND THERE'S ANOTHER WAY TO TELL WHEN IT'S CHRISTMAS-TIME...
WHAT'S THAT WAY?
WALT DISNEY
12-2
WHEN YOU FEEL ALL WARM INSIDE!
THAT'S MY WAY!
Distributed by King Features Syndicate.

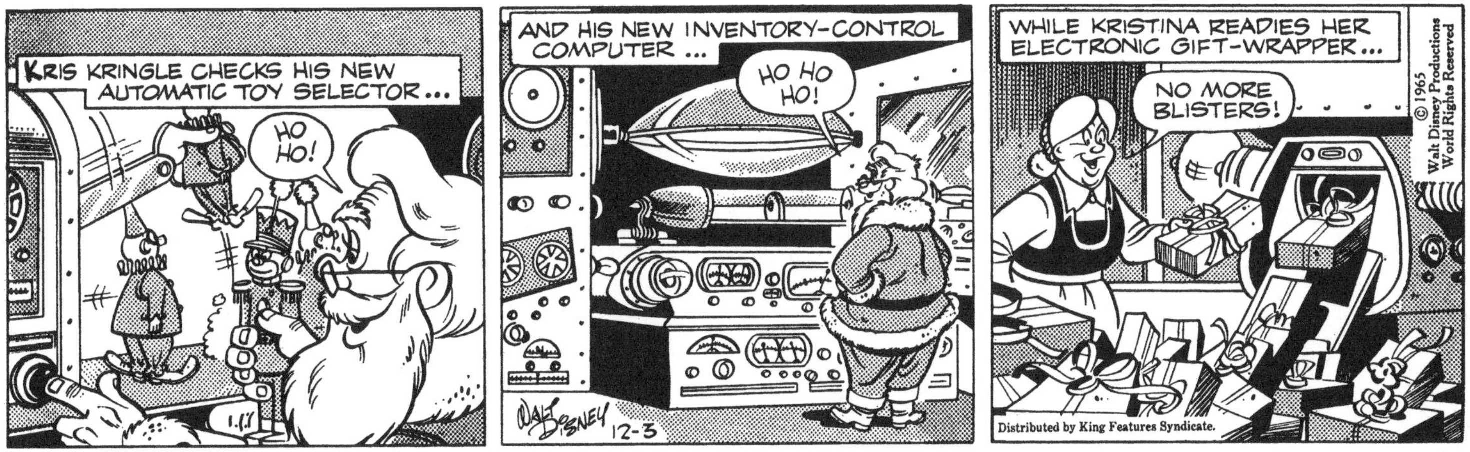
KRIS KRINGLE CHECKS HIS NEW AUTOMATIC TOY SELECTOR...
HO HO!
AND HIS NEW INVENTORY-CONTROL COMPUTER...
HO HO HO!
WALT DISNEY
12-3
WHILE KRISTINA READIES HER ELECTRONIC GIFT-WRAPPER...
NO MORE BLISTERS!
© 1965 Walt Disney Productions World Rights Reserved
Distributed by King Features Syndicate.

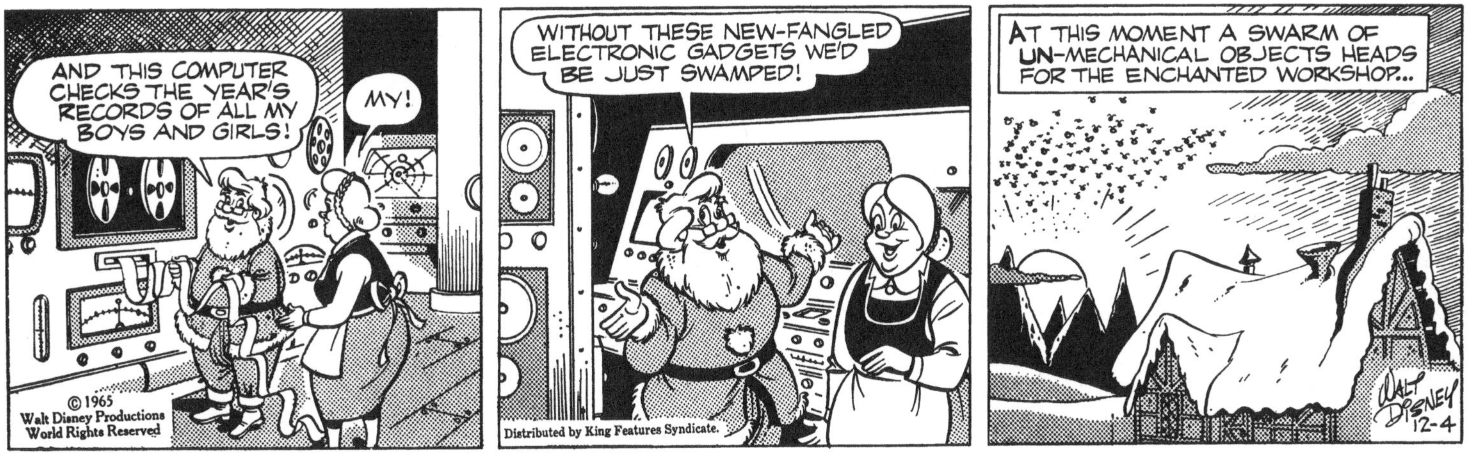
AND THIS COMPUTER CHECKS THE YEAR'S RECORDS OF ALL MY BOYS AND GIRLS!
MY!
© 1965 Walt Disney Productions World Rights Reserved
WITHOUT THESE NEW-FANGLED ELECTRONIC GADGETS WE'D BE JUST SWAMPED!
Distributed by King Features Syndicate.
AT THIS MOMENT A SWARM OF UN-MECHANICAL OBJECTS HEADS FOR THE ENCHANTED WORKSHOP...
WALT DISNEY
12-4

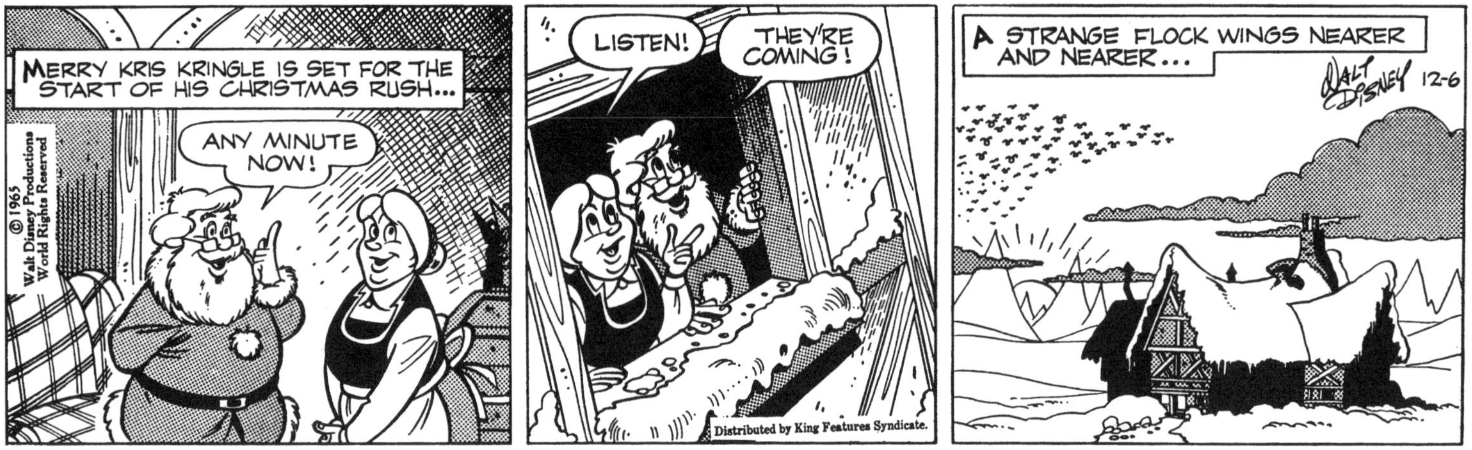
MERRY KRIS KRINGLE IS SET FOR THE START OF HIS CHRISTMAS RUSH...
ANY MINUTE NOW!
© 1965 Walt Disney Productions World Rights Reserved
LISTEN!
THEY'RE COMING!
Distributed by King Features Syndicate.
A STRANGE FLOCK WINGS NEARER AND NEARER...
WALT DISNEY 12-6

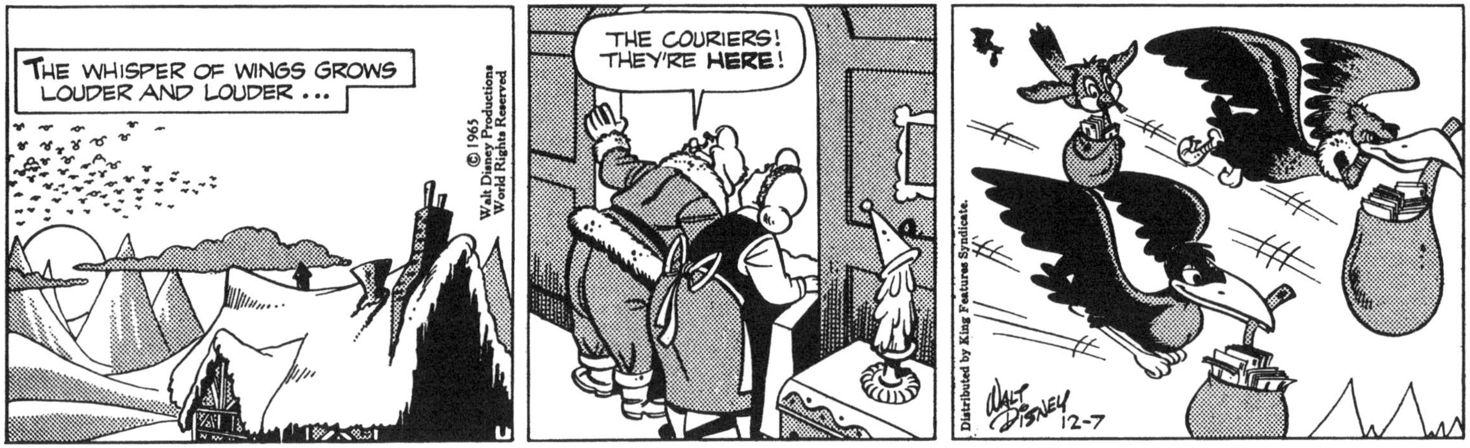
THE WHISPER OF WINGS GROWS LOUDER AND LOUDER...
© 1965 Walt Disney Productions World Rights Reserved
THE COURIERS! THEY'RE HERE!
Distributed by King Features Syndicate.
WALT DISNEY 12-7

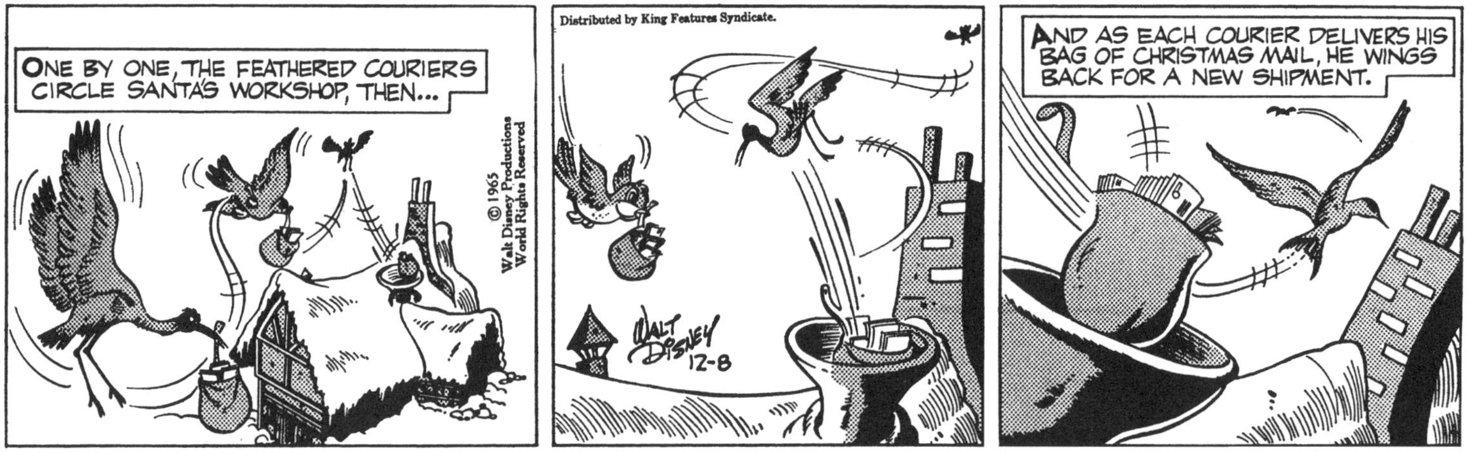
ONE BY ONE, THE FEATHERED COURIERS CIRCLE SANTA'S WORKSHOP, THEN...
© 1965 Walt Disney Productions World Rights Reserved
Distributed by King Features Syndicate.
WALT DISNEY 12-8
AND AS EACH COURIER DELIVERS HIS BAG OF CHRISTMAS MAIL, HE WINGS BACK FOR A NEW SHIPMENT.

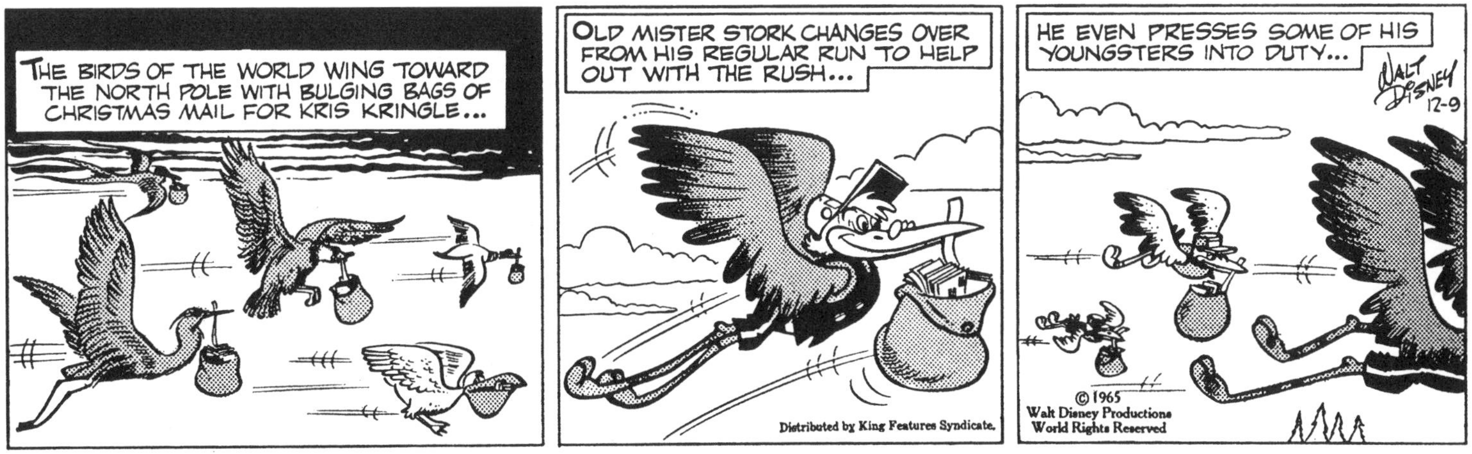
THE BIRDS OF THE WORLD WING TOWARD THE NORTH POLE WITH BULGING BAGS OF CHRISTMAS MAIL FOR KRIS KRINGLE...
OLD MISTER STORK CHANGES OVER FROM HIS REGULAR RUN TO HELP OUT WITH THE RUSH...
Distributed by King Features Syndicate.
HE EVEN PRESSES SOME OF HIS YOUNGSTERS INTO DUTY...
WALT DISNEY 12-9
© 1965 Walt Disney Productions World Rights Reserved

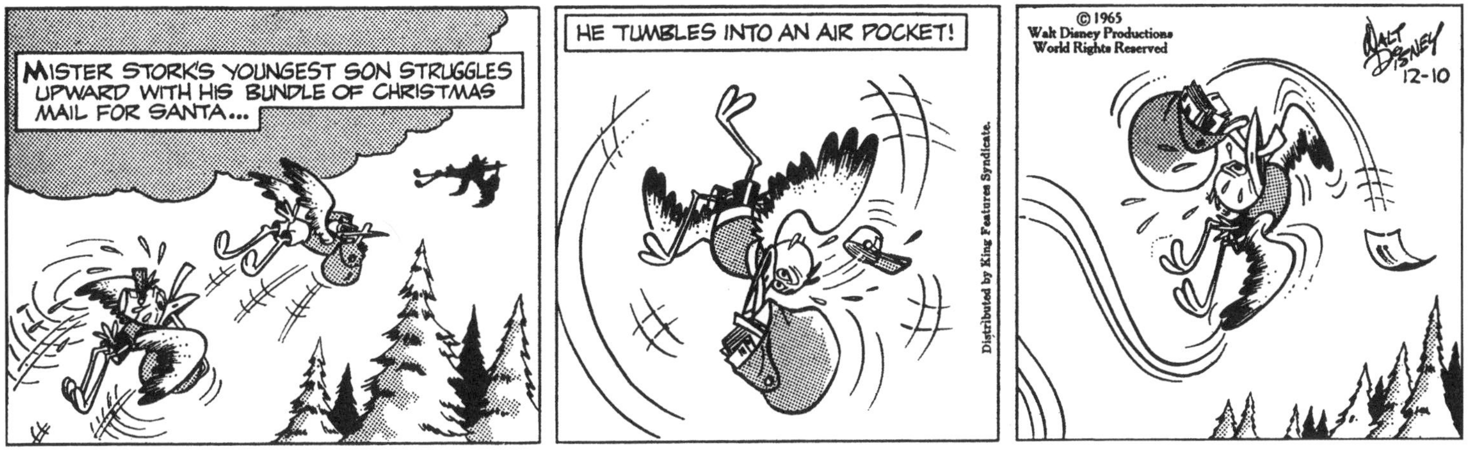
MISTER STORK'S YOUNGEST SON STRUGGLES UPWARD WITH HIS BUNDLE OF CHRISTMAS MAIL FOR SANTA...
HE TUMBLES INTO AN AIR POCKET!
Distributed by King Features Syndicate.
© 1965 Walt Disney Productions World Rights Reserved
WALT DISNEY 12-10

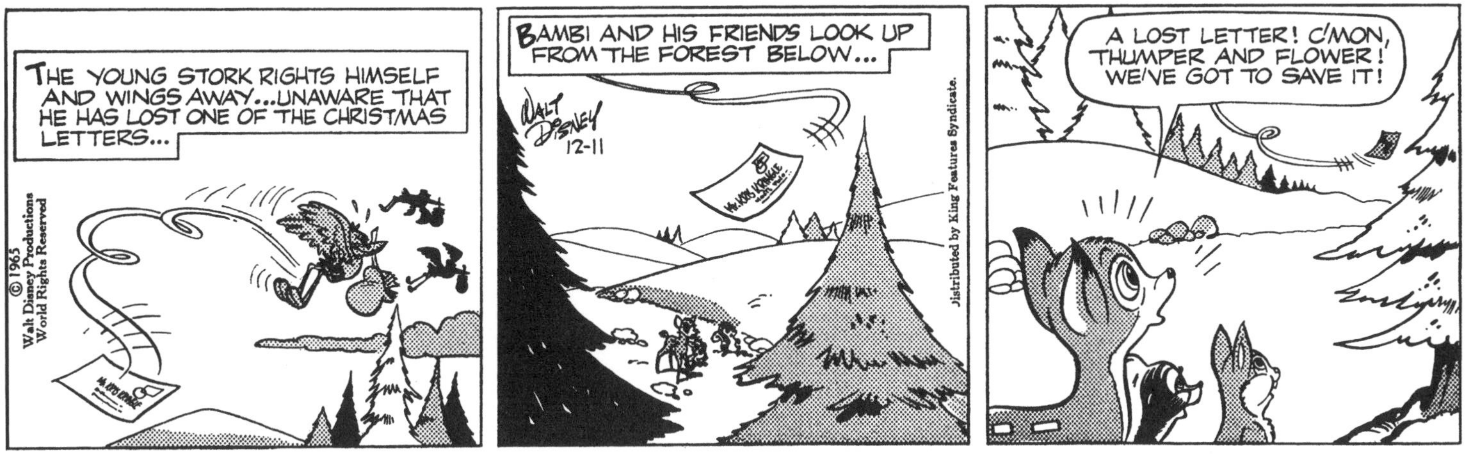
THE YOUNG STORK RIGHTS HIMSELF AND WINGS AWAY...UNAWARE THAT HE HAS LOST ONE OF THE CHRISTMAS LETTERS...
© 1965 Walt Disney Productions World Rights Reserved
BAMBI AND HIS FRIENDS LOOK UP FROM THE FOREST BELOW...
WALT DISNEY 12-11
Distributed by King Features Syndicate.
A LOST LETTER! C'MON, THUMPER AND FLOWER! WE'VE GOT TO SAVE IT!

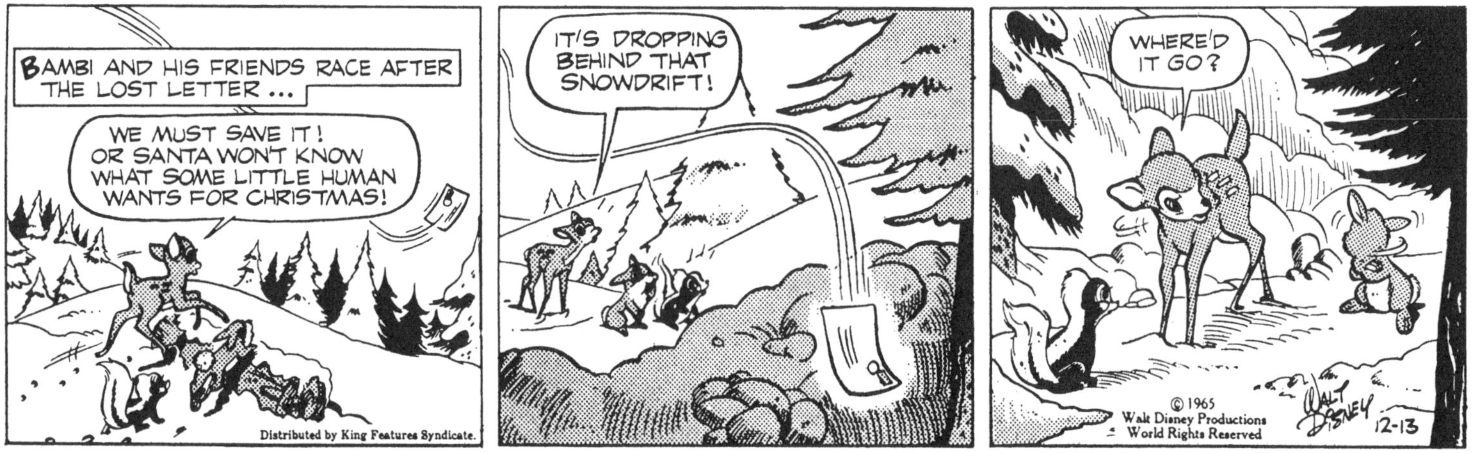
BAMBI AND HIS FRIENDS RACE AFTER THE LOST LETTER ...
WE MUST SAVE IT! OR SANTA WON'T KNOW WHAT SOME LITTLE HUMAN WANTS FOR CHRISTMAS!
Distributed by King Features Syndicate.
IT'S DROPPING BEHIND THAT SNOWDRIFT!
WHERE'D IT GO?
© 1965 Walt Disney Productions World Rights Reserved
WALT DISNEY 12-13

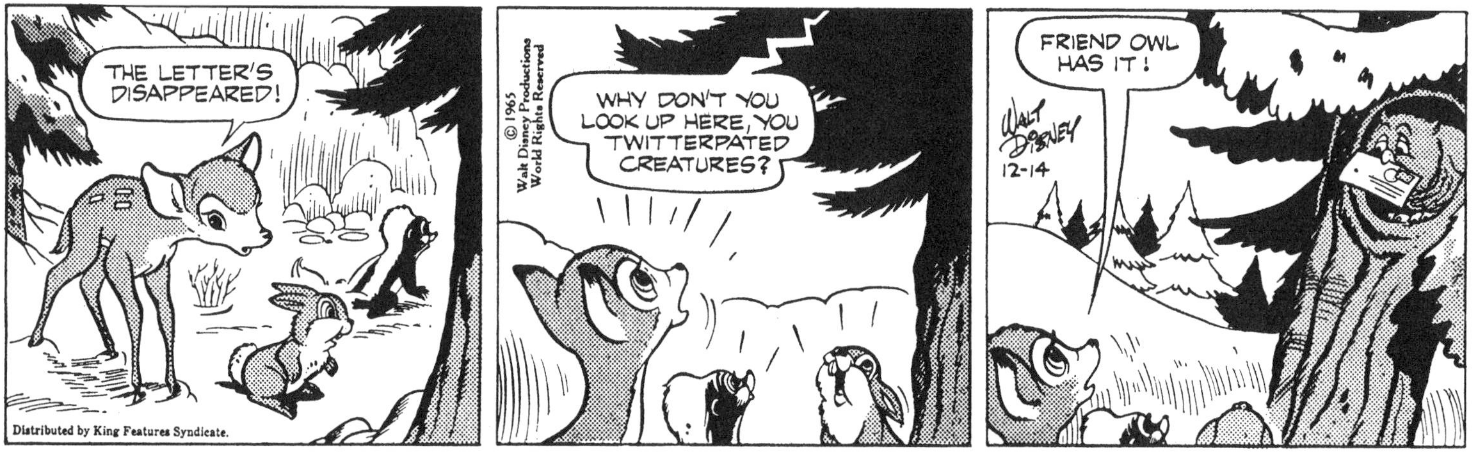
THE LETTER'S DISAPPEARED!
Distributed by King Features Syndicate.
© 1965 Walt Disney Productions World Rights Reserved
WHY DON'T YOU LOOK UP HERE, YOU TWITTERPATED CREATURES?
FRIEND OWL HAS IT!
WALT DISNEY 12-14

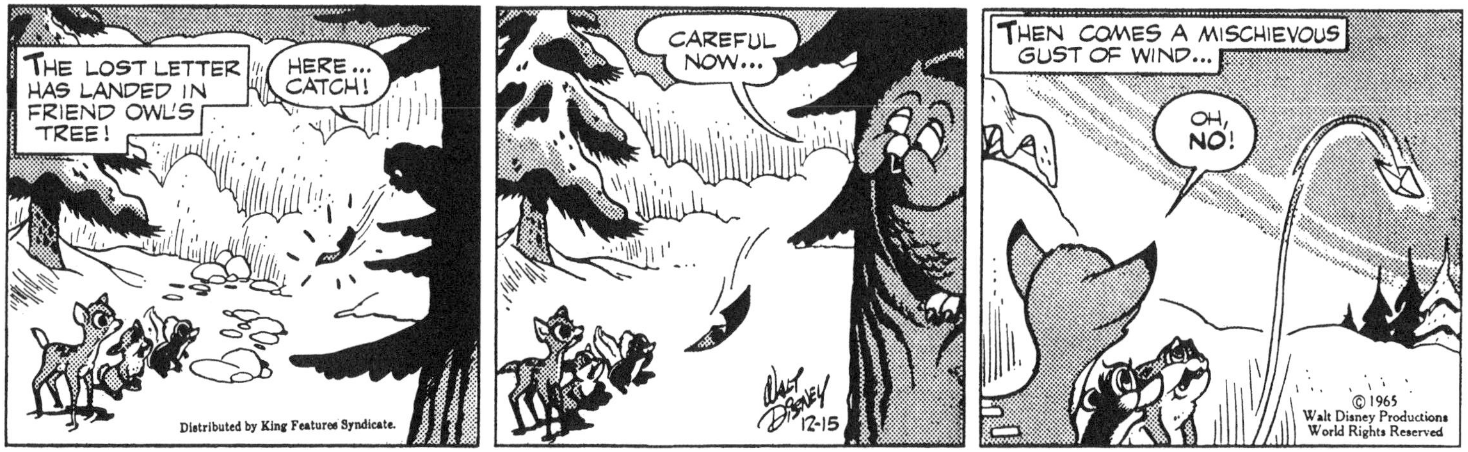
THE LOST LETTER HAS LANDED IN FRIEND OWL'S TREE!
HERE... CATCH!
Distributed by King Features Syndicate.
CAREFUL NOW...
WALT DISNEY 12-15
THEN COMES A MISCHIEVOUS GUST OF WIND...
OH, NO!
© 1965 Walt Disney Productions World Rights Reserved

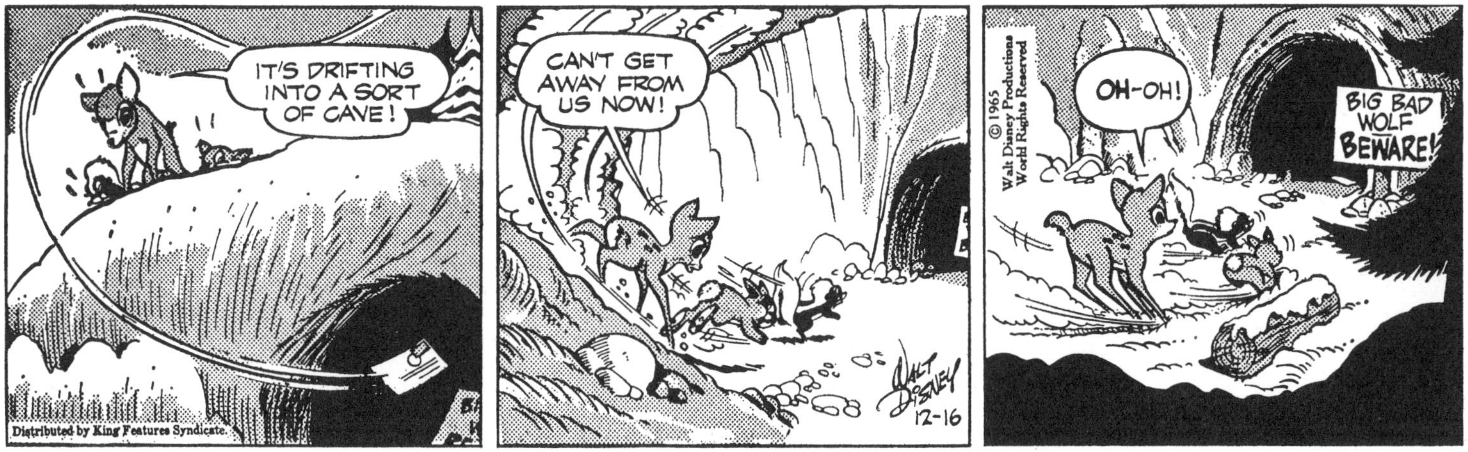
IT'S DRIFTING INTO A SORT OF CAVE!
Distributed by King Features Syndicate.
CAN'T GET AWAY FROM US NOW!
WALT DISNEY 12-16
© 1965 Walt Disney Productions World Rights Reserved
OH-OH!
BIG BAD WOLF BEWARE!

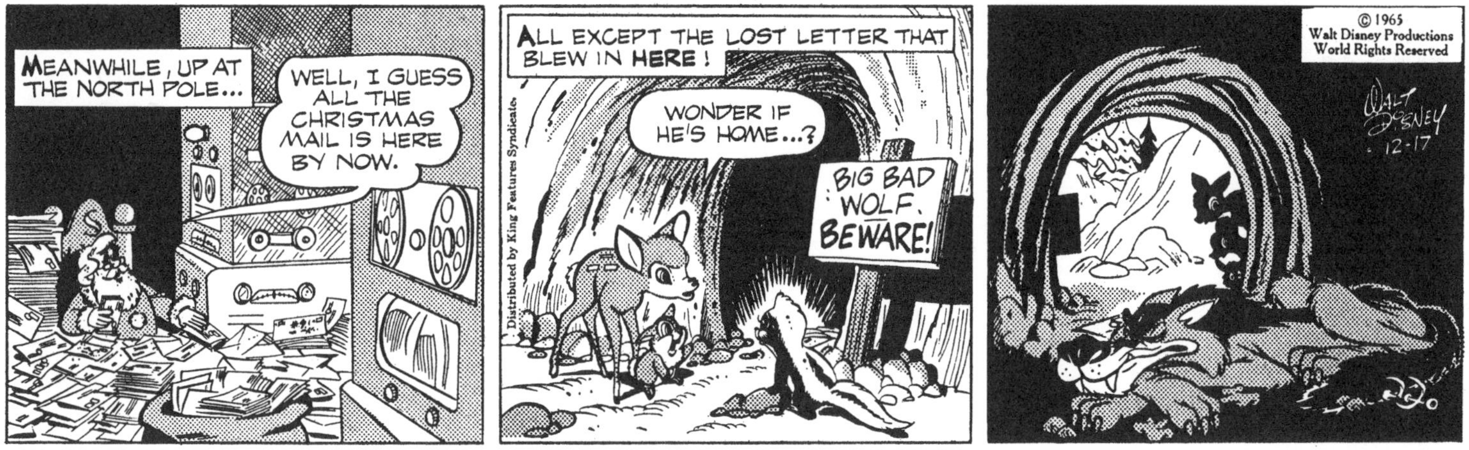
MEANWHILE, UP AT THE NORTH POLE...
WELL, I GUESS ALL THE CHRISTMAS MAIL IS HERE BY NOW.
ALL EXCEPT THE LOST LETTER THAT BLEW IN HERE!
Distributed by King Features Syndicate.
WONDER IF HE'S HOME...?
BIG BAD WOLF BEWARE!
© 1965 Walt Disney Productions World Rights Reserved
WALT DISNEY 12-17

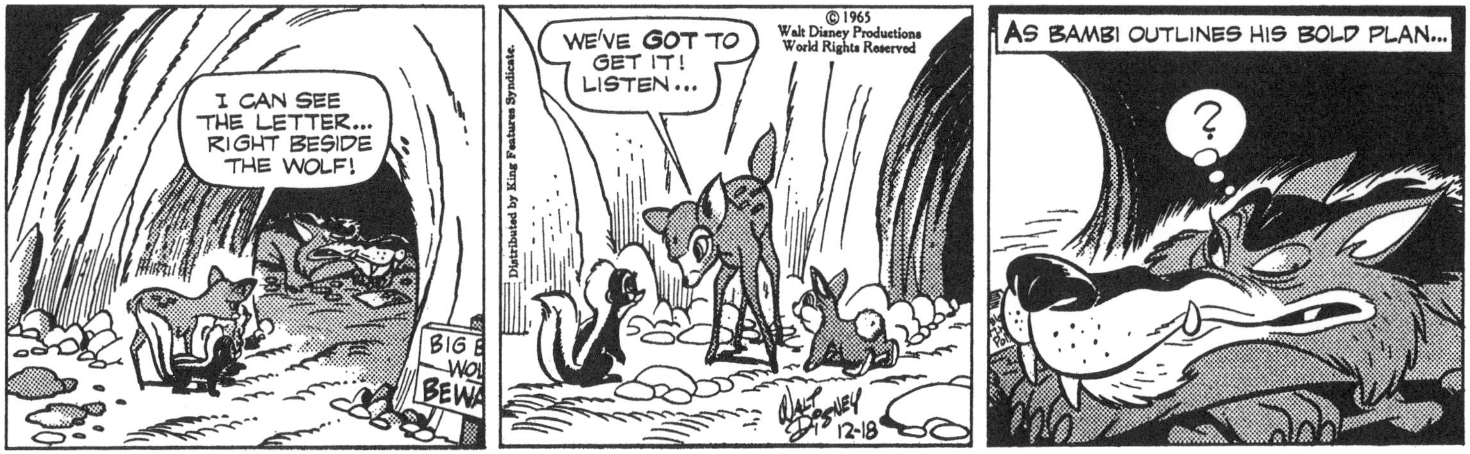
I CAN SEE THE LETTER... RIGHT BESIDE THE WOLF!
Distributed by King Features Syndicate.
© 1965 Walt Disney Productions World Rights Reserved
WE'VE GOT TO GET IT! LISTEN...
WALT DISNEY 12-18
AS BAMBI OUTLINES HIS BOLD PLAN...
?

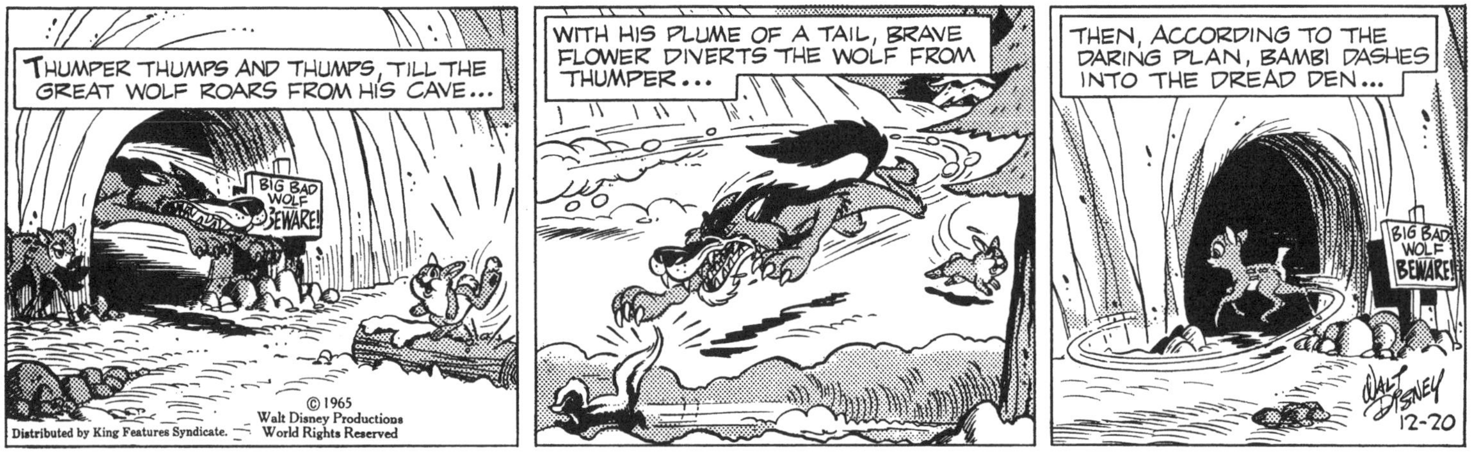
THUMPER THUMPS AND THUMPS, TILL THE GREAT WOLF ROARS FROM HIS CAVE...
BIG BAD WOLF BEWARE!
© 1965 Walt Disney Productions World Rights Reserved
Distributed by King Features Syndicate.
WITH HIS PLUME OF A TAIL, BRAVE FLOWER DIVERTS THE WOLF FROM THUMPER...
THEN, ACCORDING TO THE DARING PLAN, BAMBI DASHES INTO THE DREAD DEN...
BIG BAD WOLF BEWARE!
WALT DISNEY
12-20

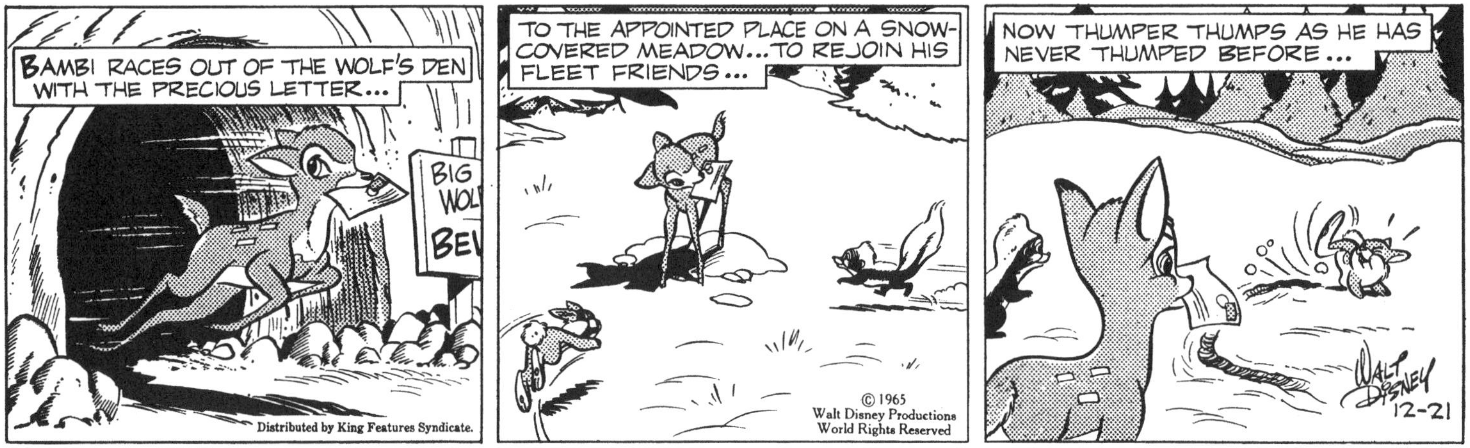
BAMBI RACES OUT OF THE WOLF'S DEN WITH THE PRECIOUS LETTER...
BIG WOL BE
Distributed by King Features Syndicate.
TO THE APPOINTED PLACE ON A SNOW-COVERED MEADOW...TO REJOIN HIS FLEET FRIENDS...
© 1965 Walt Disney Productions World Rights Reserved
NOW THUMPER THUMPS AS HE HAS NEVER THUMPED BEFORE...
WALT DISNEY
12-21

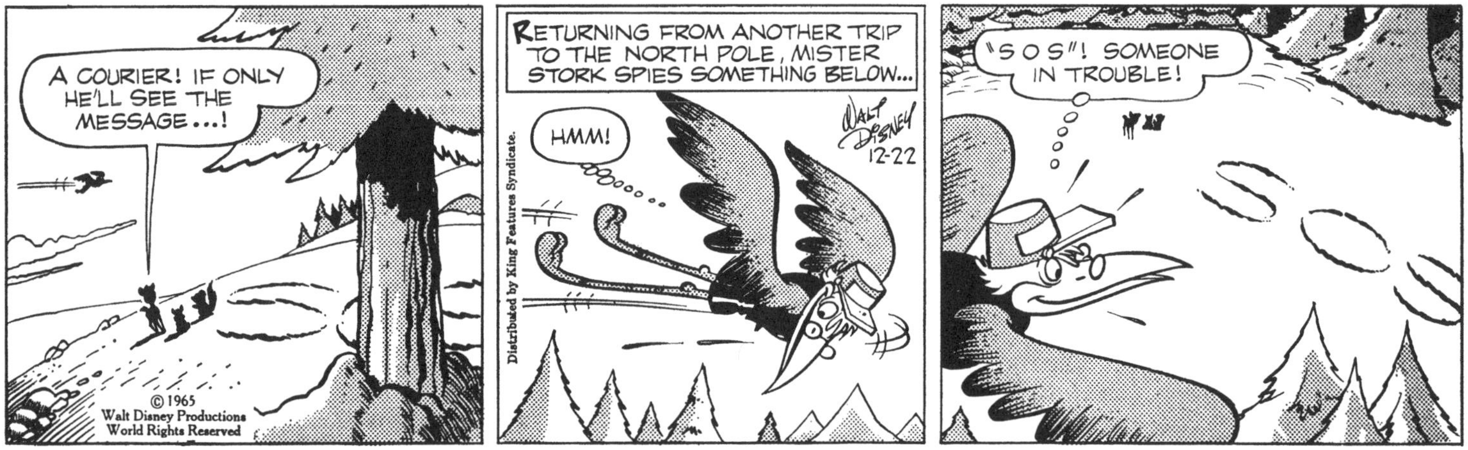
A COURIER! IF ONLY HE'LL SEE THE MESSAGE...!
© 1965 Walt Disney Productions World Rights Reserved
RETURNING FROM ANOTHER TRIP TO THE NORTH POLE, MISTER STORK SPIES SOMETHING BELOW...
HMM!
WALT DISNEY
12-22
Distributed by King Features Syndicate.
"S O S"! SOMEONE IN TROUBLE!

EMERGENCY! A LOST LETTER!
WALT DISNEY 12 23
© 1965 Walt Disney Productions World Rights Reserved
UNLESS SANTA GETS THIS RIGHT AWAY, SOME LITTLE HUMAN WON'T HAVE ANY CHRISTMAS!
GOSH!
AND AWAY WINGS MISTER STORK IN A RACE AGAINST TIME!
Distributed by King Features Syndicate.

MISTER STORK WINS THE RACE!
HO HO HO! JUST IN THE NICK OF TIME!
© 1965 Walt Disney Productions World Rights Reserved
WALT DISNEY 12-24
AND OFF ZOOMS KRIS KRINGLE WITH A LAST-MINUTE BUNDLE FOR THE WRITER OF THE LOST LETTER!
Distributed by King Features Syndicate.
WHO WAS THE WRITER OF THE LOST LETTER?
ONLY KRIS KRINGLE KNOWS.
MAYBE IT WAS YOU!
MERRY CHRISTMAS TO ALL!

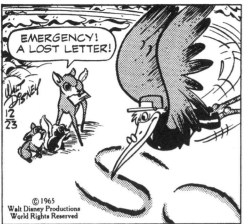

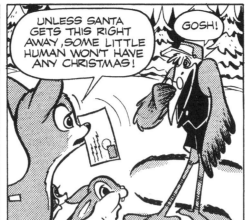

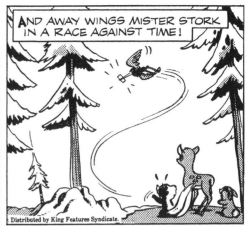

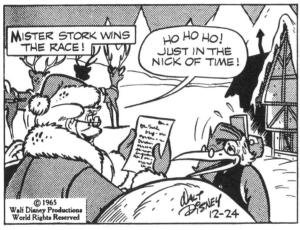

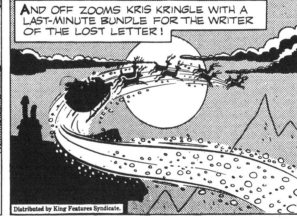

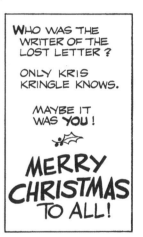

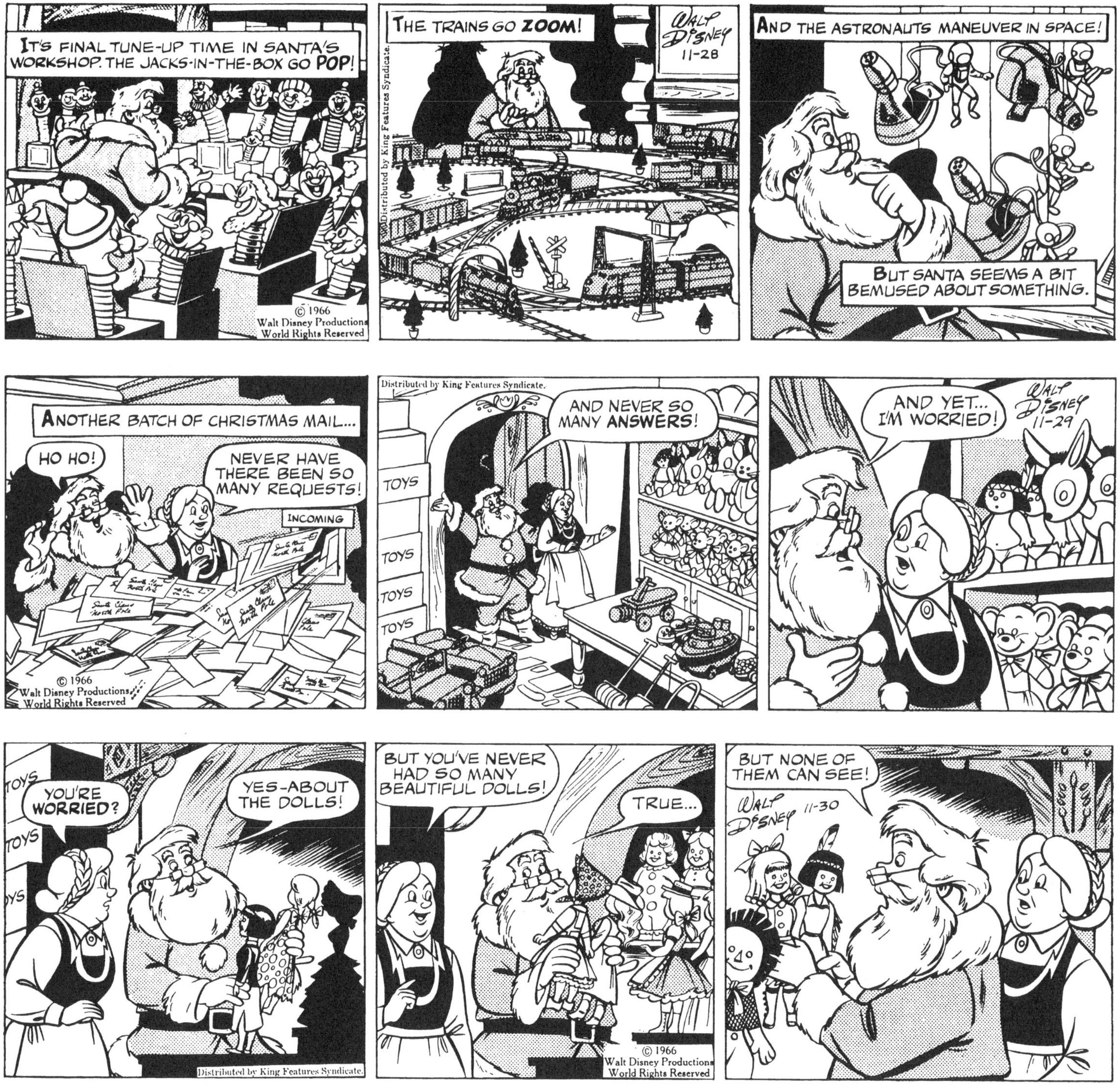
IT'S FINAL TUNE-UP TIME IN SANTA'S WORKSHOP. THE JACKS-IN-THE-BOX GO POP!
© 1966 Walt Disney Productions World Rights Reserved
THE TRAINS GO ZOOM!
Distributed by King Features Syndicate.
WALT DISNEY 11-28
AND THE ASTRONAUTS MANEUVER IN SPACE!
BUT SANTA SEEMS A BIT BEMUSED ABOUT SOMETHING.
ANOTHER BATCH OF CHRISTMAS MAIL...
HO HO!
NEVER HAVE THERE BEEN SO MANY REQUESTS!
INCOMING
© 1966 Walt Disney Productions World Rights Reserved
Distributed by King Features Syndicate.
AND NEVER SO MANY ANSWERS!
TOYS
TOYS
TOYS
TOYS
AND YET... I'M WORRIED!
WALT DISNEY 11-29
YOU'RE WORRIED?
YES-ABOUT THE DOLLS!
Distributed by King Features Syndicate.
BUT YOU'VE NEVER HAD SO MANY BEAUTIFUL DOLLS!
TRUE...
© 1966 Walt Disney Productions World Rights Reserved
BUT NONE OF THEM CAN SEE!
WALT DISNEY 11-30

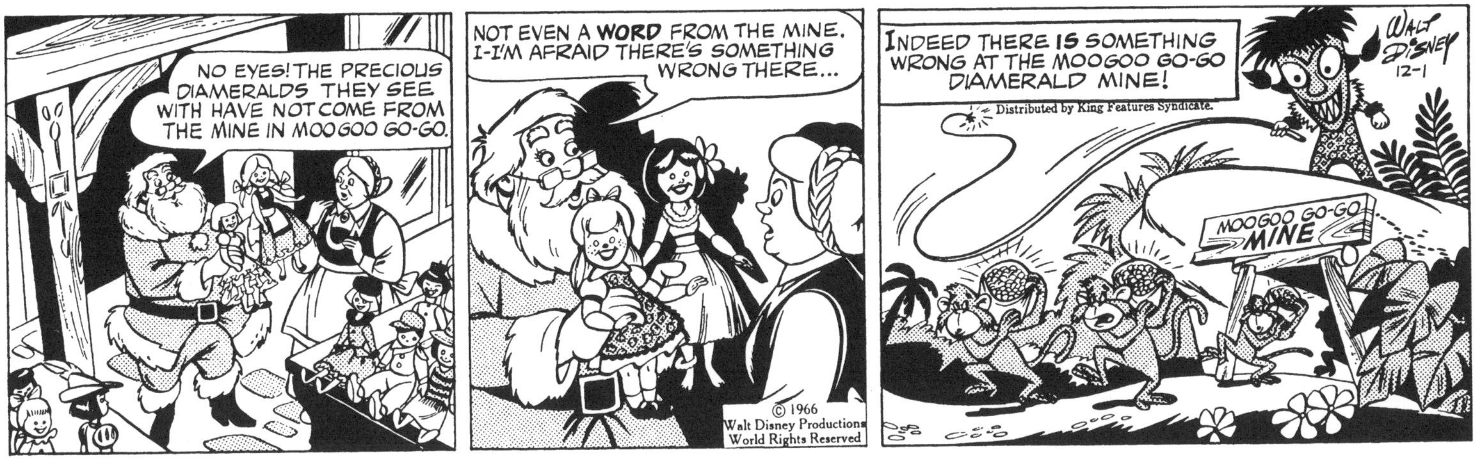
NO EYES! THE PRECIOUS DIAMERALDS THEY SEE WITH HAVE NOT COME FROM THE MINE IN MOOGOO GO-GO.
NOT EVEN A **WORD** FROM THE MINE. I-I'M AFRAID THERE'S SOMETHING WRONG THERE...
© 1966 Walt Disney Productions World Rights Reserved
INDEED THERE **IS** SOMETHING WRONG AT THE MOOGOO GO-GO DIAMERALD MINE!
WALT DISNEY 12-1
Distributed by King Features Syndicate.
MOOGOO GO-GO MINE

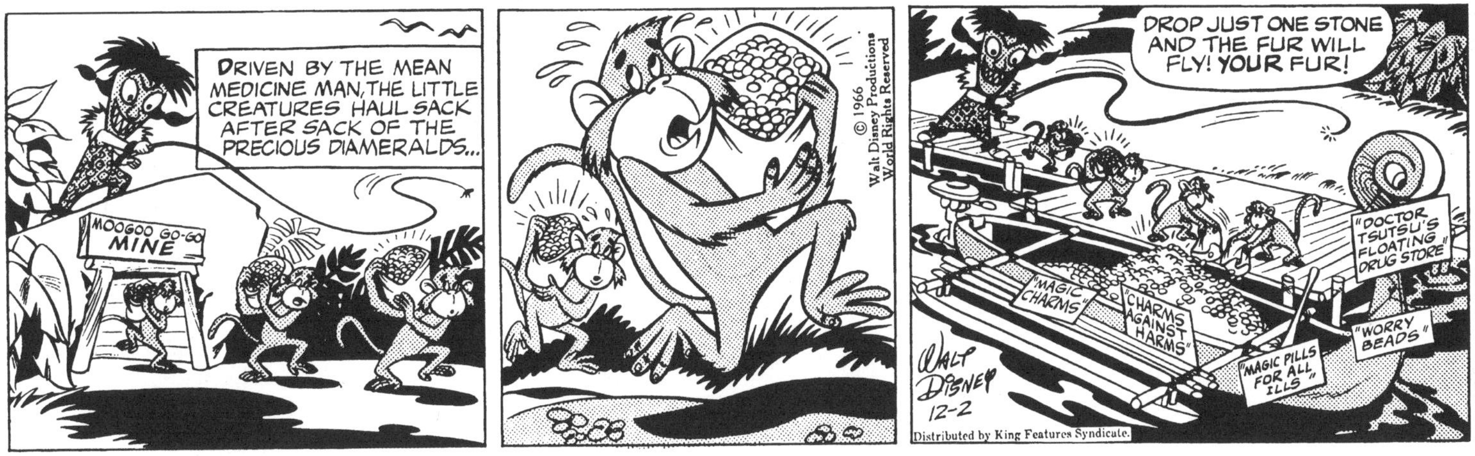
DRIVEN BY THE MEAN MEDICINE MAN, THE LITTLE CREATURES HAUL SACK AFTER SACK OF THE PRECIOUS DIAMERALDS...
MOOGOO GO-GO MINE
© 1966 Walt Disney Productions World Rights Reserved
DROP JUST ONE STONE AND THE FUR WILL FLY! **YOUR** FUR!
"DOCTOR TSUTSU'S FLOATING DRUG STORE"
"MAGIC CHARMS"
"CHARMS AGAINST HARMS"
"WORRY BEADS"
"MAGIC PILLS FOR ALL ILLS"
WALT DISNEY 12-2
Distributed by King Features Syndicate.

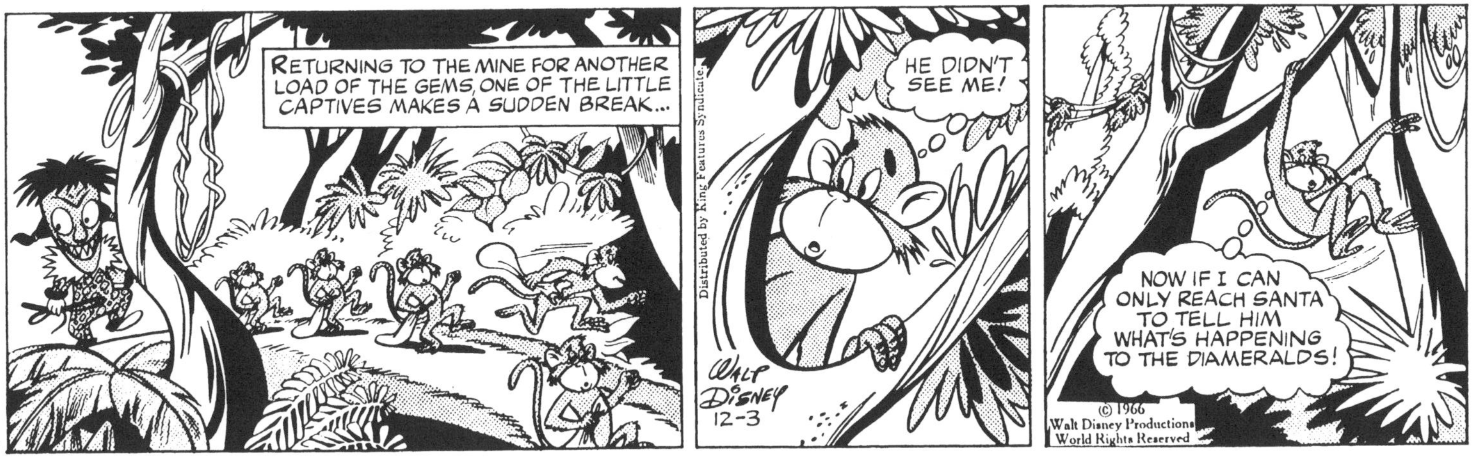
RETURNING TO THE MINE FOR ANOTHER LOAD OF THE GEMS, ONE OF THE LITTLE CAPTIVES MAKES A SUDDEN BREAK...
Distributed by King Features Syndicate.
HE DIDN'T SEE ME!
WALT DISNEY 12-3
NOW IF I CAN ONLY REACH SANTA TO TELL HIM WHAT'S HAPPENING TO THE DIAMERALDS!
© 1966 Walt Disney Productions World Rights Reserved

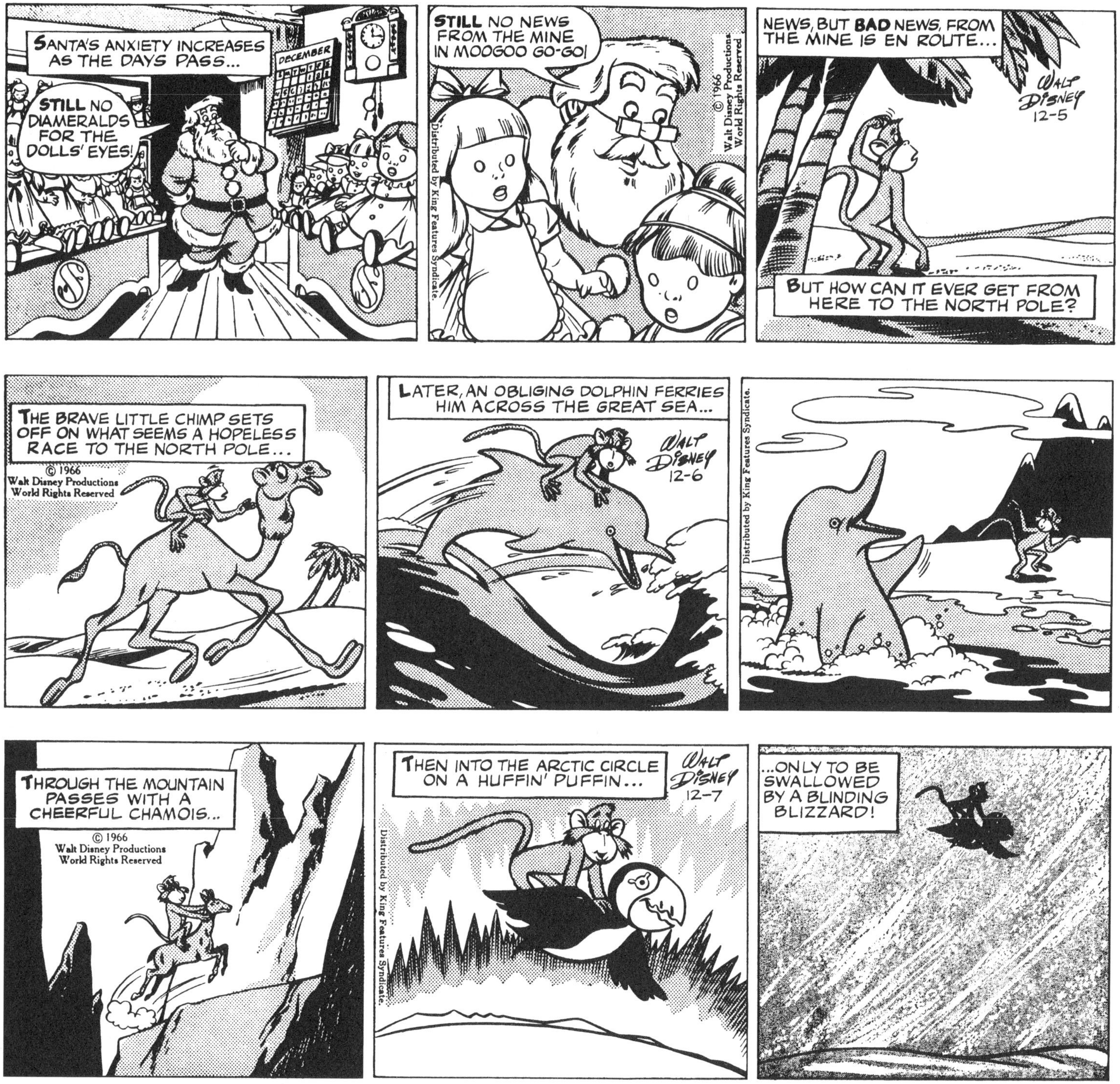
SANTA'S ANXIETY INCREASES AS THE DAYS PASS...
DECEMBER
STILL NO DIAMERALDS FOR THE DOLLS' EYES!
STILL NO NEWS FROM THE MINE IN MOOGOO GO-GO!
© 1966 Walt Disney Productions World Rights Reserved
Distributed by King Features Syndicate.
NEWS, BUT BAD NEWS, FROM THE MINE IS EN ROUTE...
WALT DISNEY 12-5
BUT HOW CAN IT EVER GET FROM HERE TO THE NORTH POLE?
THE BRAVE LITTLE CHIMP SETS OFF ON WHAT SEEMS A HOPELESS RACE TO THE NORTH POLE...
© 1966 Walt Disney Productions World Rights Reserved
LATER, AN OBLIGING DOLPHIN FERRIES HIM ACROSS THE GREAT SEA...
WALT DISNEY 12-6
Distributed by King Features Syndicate.
THROUGH THE MOUNTAIN PASSES WITH A CHEERFUL CHAMOIS...
© 1966 Walt Disney Productions World Rights Reserved
THEN INTO THE ARCTIC CIRCLE ON A HUFFIN' PUFFIN...
WALT DISNEY 12-7
Distributed by King Features Syndicate.
...ONLY TO BE SWALLOWED BY A BLINDING BLIZZARD!

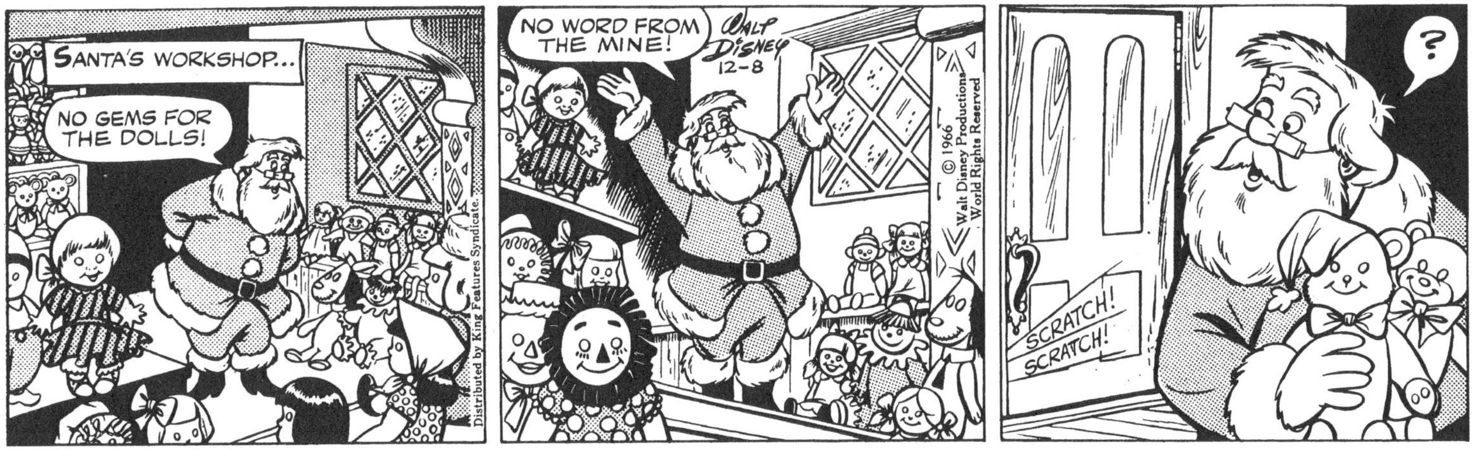
SANTA'S WORKSHOP...
NO GEMS FOR THE DOLLS!
Distributed by King Features Syndicate.
NO WORD FROM THE MINE!
WALT DISNEY 12-8
© 1966 Walt Disney Productions World Rights Reserved
SCRATCH! SCRATCH!
?

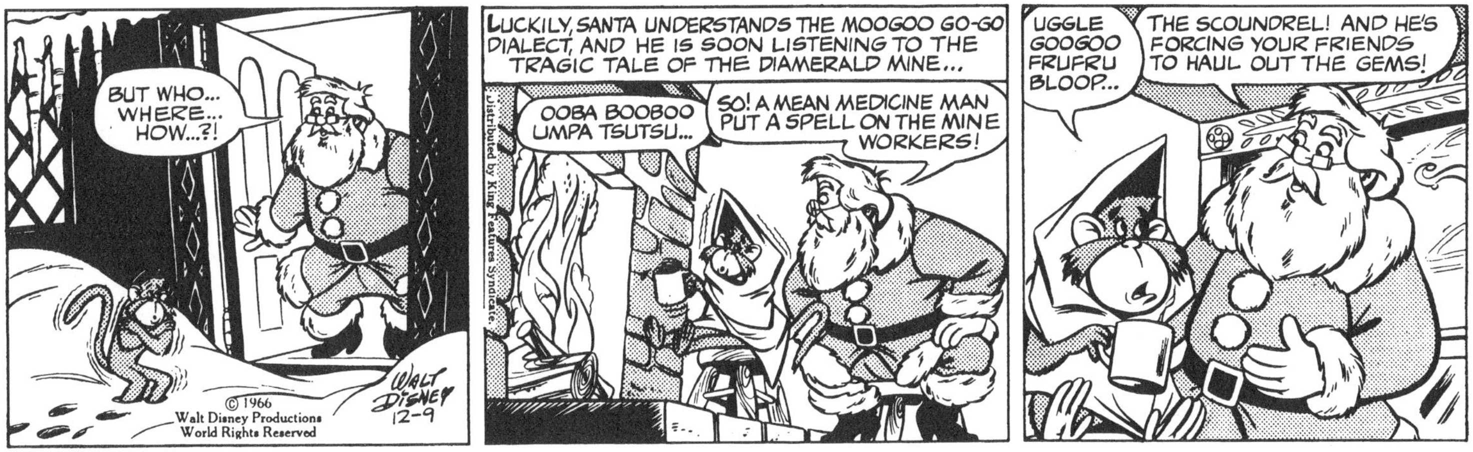
BUT WHO... WHERE... HOW...?!
© 1966 Walt Disney Productions World Rights Reserved
WALT DISNEY 12-9
LUCKILY, SANTA UNDERSTANDS THE MOOGOO GO-GO DIALECT, AND HE IS SOON LISTENING TO THE TRAGIC TALE OF THE DIAMERALD MINE...
Distributed by King Features Syndicate.
OOBA BOOBOO UMPA TSUTSU...
SO! A MEAN MEDICINE MAN PUT A SPELL ON THE MINE WORKERS!
UGGLE GOOGOO FRUFRU BLOOP...
THE SCOUNDREL! AND HE'S FORCING YOUR FRIENDS TO HAUL OUT THE GEMS!

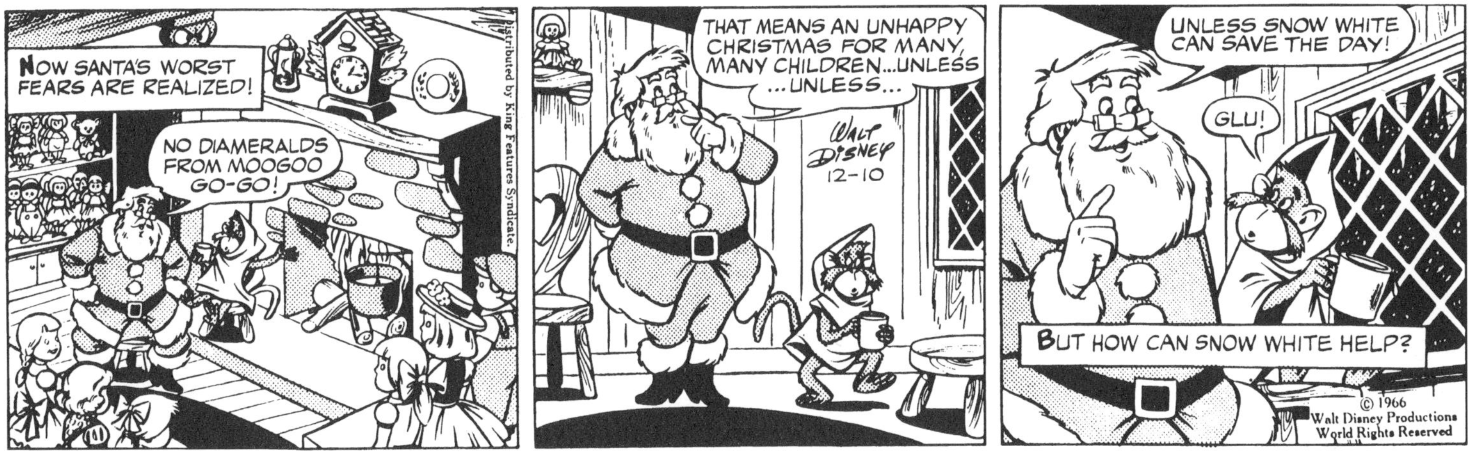
NOW SANTA'S WORST FEARS ARE REALIZED!
NO DIAMERALDS FROM MOOGOO GO-GO!
Distributed by King Features Syndicate.
THAT MEANS AN UNHAPPY CHRISTMAS FOR MANY, MANY CHILDREN...UNLESS ...UNLESS...
WALT DISNEY 12-10
UNLESS SNOW WHITE CAN SAVE THE DAY!
GLU!
BUT HOW CAN SNOW WHITE HELP?
© 1966 Walt Disney Productions World Rights Reserved

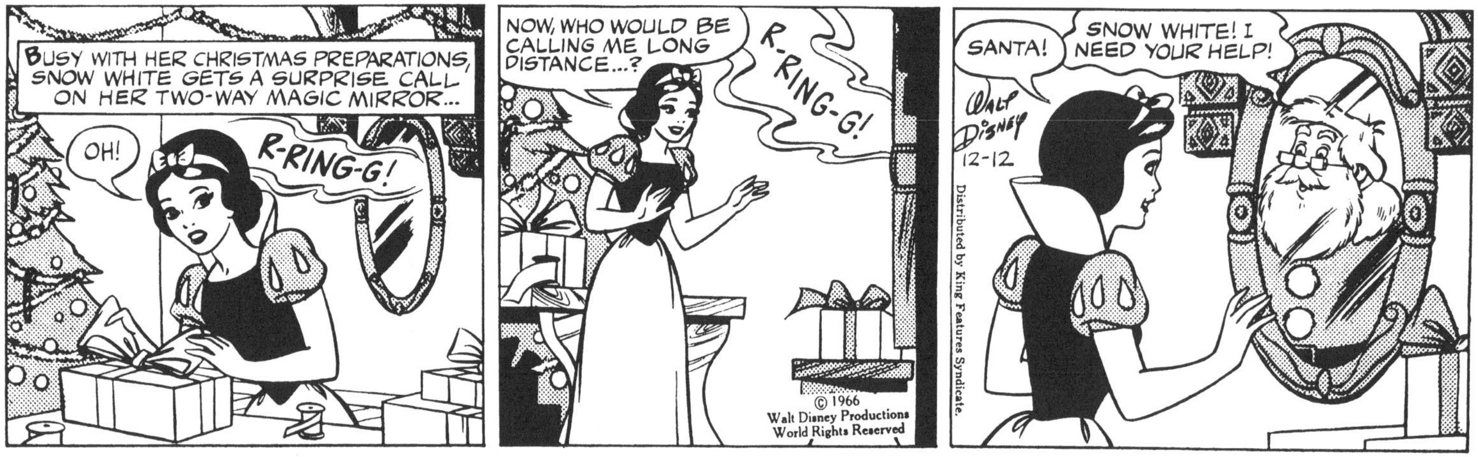
BUSY WITH HER CHRISTMAS PREPARATIONS, SNOW WHITE GETS A SURPRISE CALL ON HER TWO-WAY MAGIC MIRROR...
OH!
R-RING-G!
NOW, WHO WOULD BE CALLING ME LONG DISTANCE...?
R-RING-G!
© 1966 Walt Disney Productions World Rights Reserved
SANTA!
SNOW WHITE! I NEED YOUR HELP!
WALT DISNEY 12-12
Distributed by King Features Syndicate.

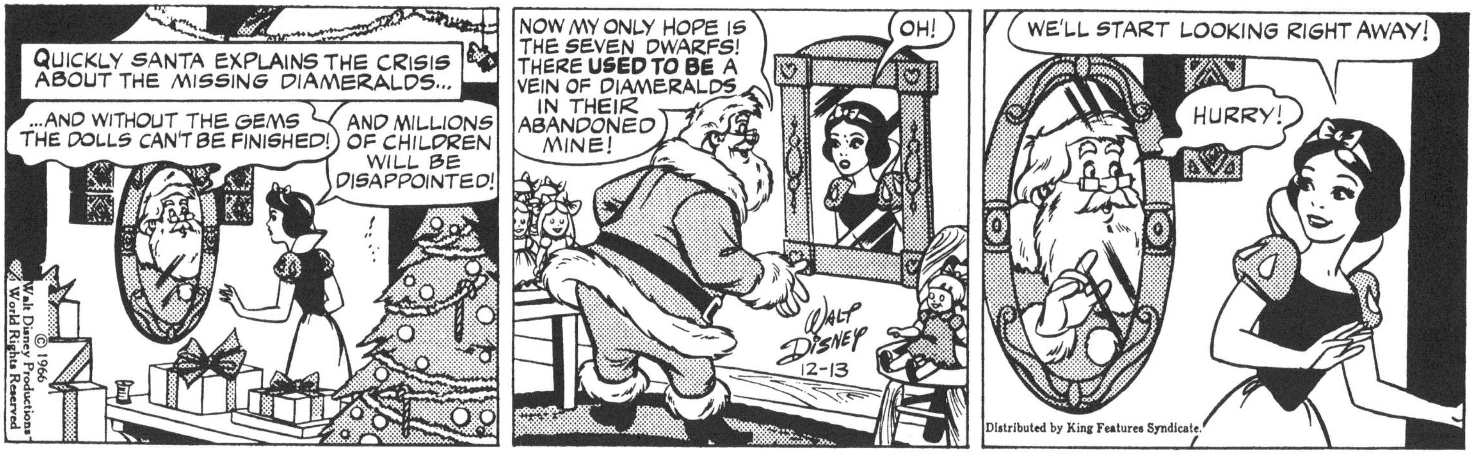
QUICKLY SANTA EXPLAINS THE CRISIS ABOUT THE MISSING DIAMERALDS...
...AND WITHOUT THE GEMS THE DOLLS CAN'T BE FINISHED!
AND MILLIONS OF CHILDREN WILL BE DISAPPOINTED!
© 1966 Walt Disney Productions World Rights Reserved
NOW MY ONLY HOPE IS THE SEVEN DWARFS! THERE USED TO BE A VEIN OF DIAMERALDS IN THEIR ABANDONED MINE!
OH!
WALT DISNEY 12-13
WE'LL START LOOKING RIGHT AWAY!
HURRY!
Distributed by King Features Syndicate.

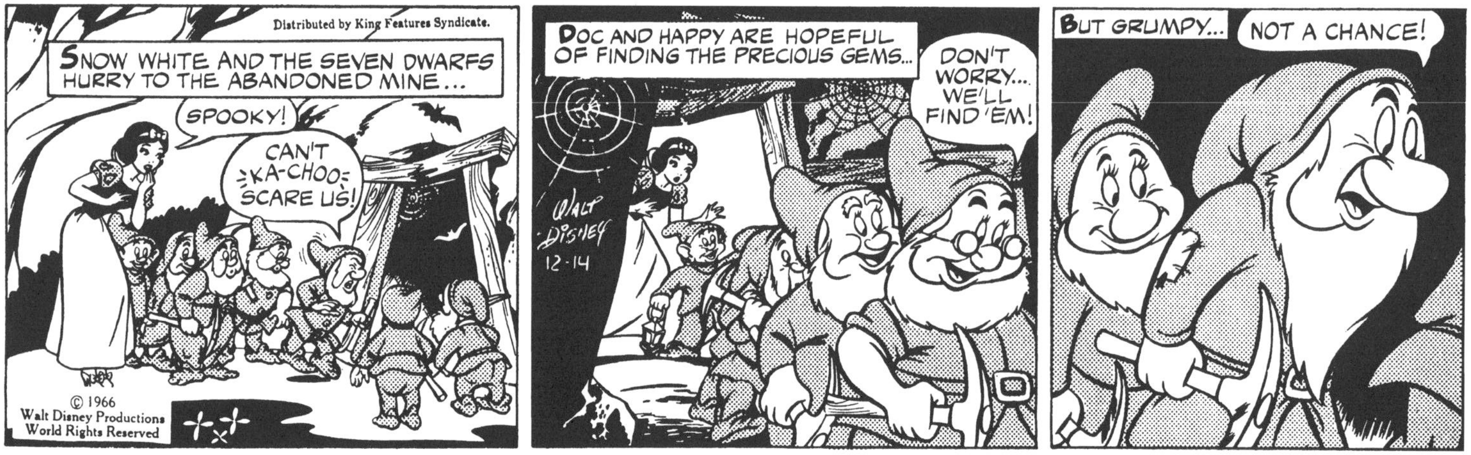
Distributed by King Features Syndicate.
SNOW WHITE AND THE SEVEN DWARFS HURRY TO THE ABANDONED MINE...
SPOOKY!
CAN'T KA-CHOO SCARE US!
© 1966 Walt Disney Productions World Rights Reserved
DOC AND HAPPY ARE HOPEFUL OF FINDING THE PRECIOUS GEMS...
DON'T WORRY... WE'LL FIND 'EM!
WALT DISNEY 12-14
BUT GRUMPY...
NOT A CHANCE!

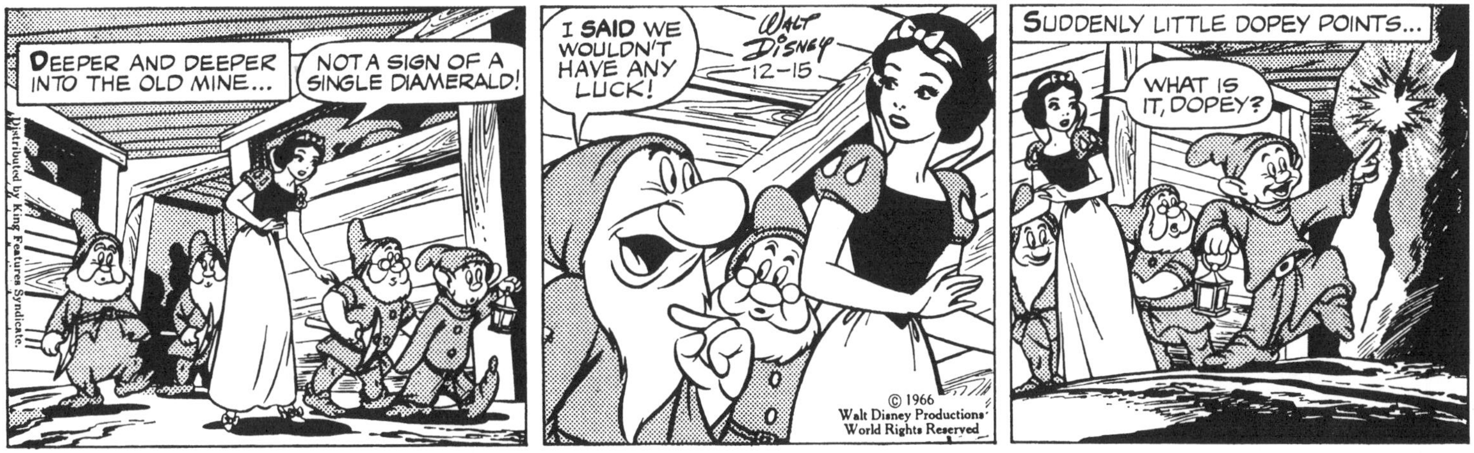
DEEPER AND DEEPER INTO THE OLD MINE...
NOT A SIGN OF A SINGLE DIAMERALD!
Distributed by King Features Syndicate.
I SAID WE WOULDN'T HAVE ANY LUCK!
WALT DISNEY 12-15
© 1966 Walt Disney Productions World Rights Reserved
SUDDENLY LITTLE DOPEY POINTS...
WHAT IS IT, DOPEY?

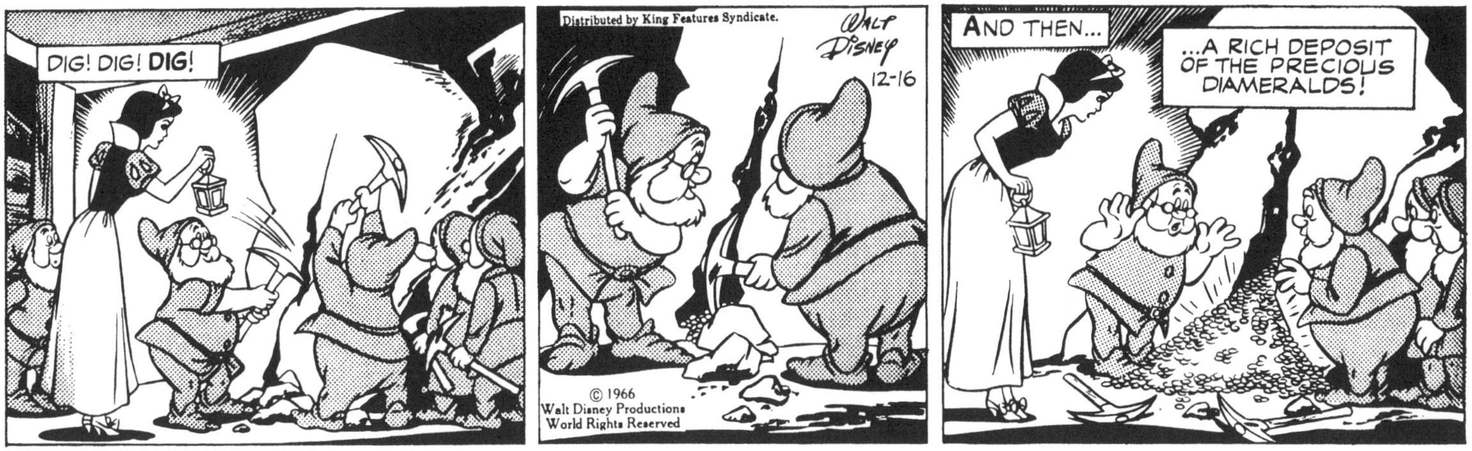
DIG! DIG! DIG!
Distributed by King Features Syndicate.
WALT DISNEY 12-16
© 1966 Walt Disney Productions World Rights Reserved
AND THEN...
...A RICH DEPOSIT OF THE PRECIOUS DIAMERALDS!

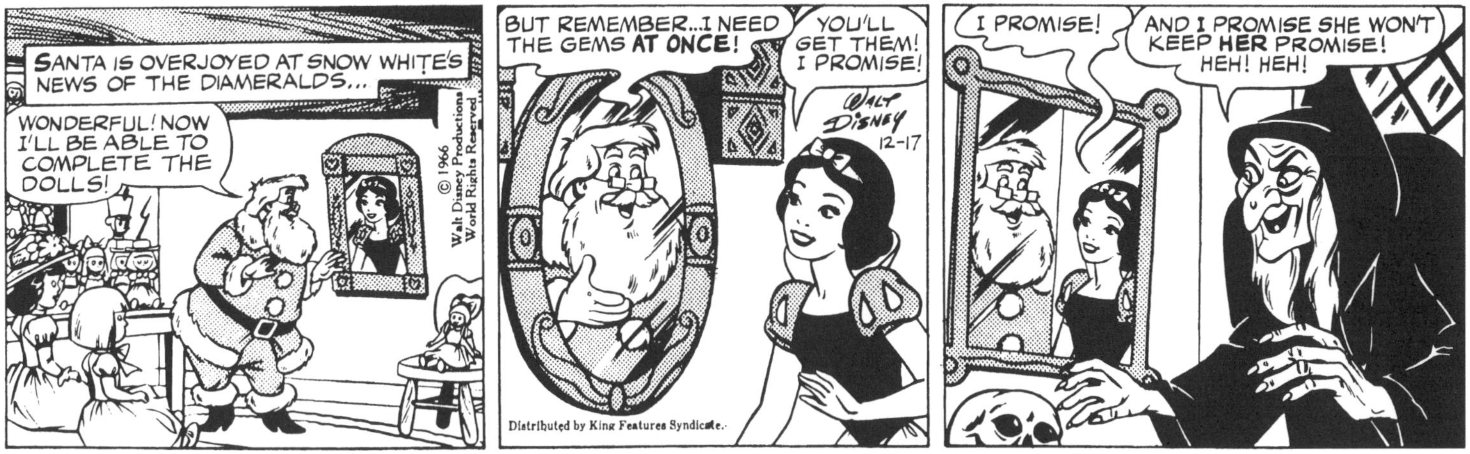
SANTA IS OVERJOYED AT SNOW WHITE'S NEWS OF THE DIAMERALDS...
WONDERFUL! NOW I'LL BE ABLE TO COMPLETE THE DOLLS!
© 1966 Walt Disney Productions World Rights Reserved
BUT REMEMBER...I NEED THE GEMS AT ONCE!
YOU'LL GET THEM! I PROMISE!
WALT DISNEY 12-17
Distributed by King Features Syndicate.
I PROMISE!
AND I PROMISE SHE WON'T KEEP HER PROMISE! HEH! HEH!

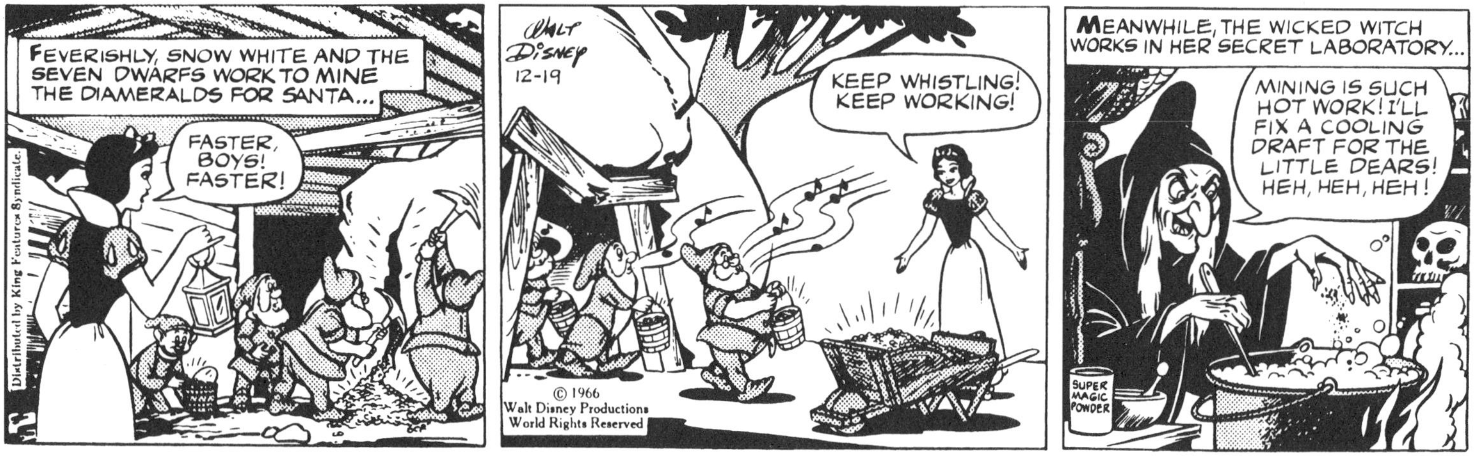
FEVERISHLY, SNOW WHITE AND THE SEVEN DWARFS WORK TO MINE THE DIAMERALDS FOR SANTA...
FASTER, BOYS! FASTER!
Distributed by King Features Syndicate.
WALT DISNEY
12-19
KEEP WHISTLING! KEEP WORKING!
© 1966
Walt Disney Productions
World Rights Reserved
MEANWHILE, THE WICKED WITCH WORKS IN HER SECRET LABORATORY...
MINING IS SUCH HOT WORK! I'LL FIX A COOLING DRAFT FOR THE LITTLE DEARS! HEH, HEH, HEH!
SUPER MAGIC POWDER

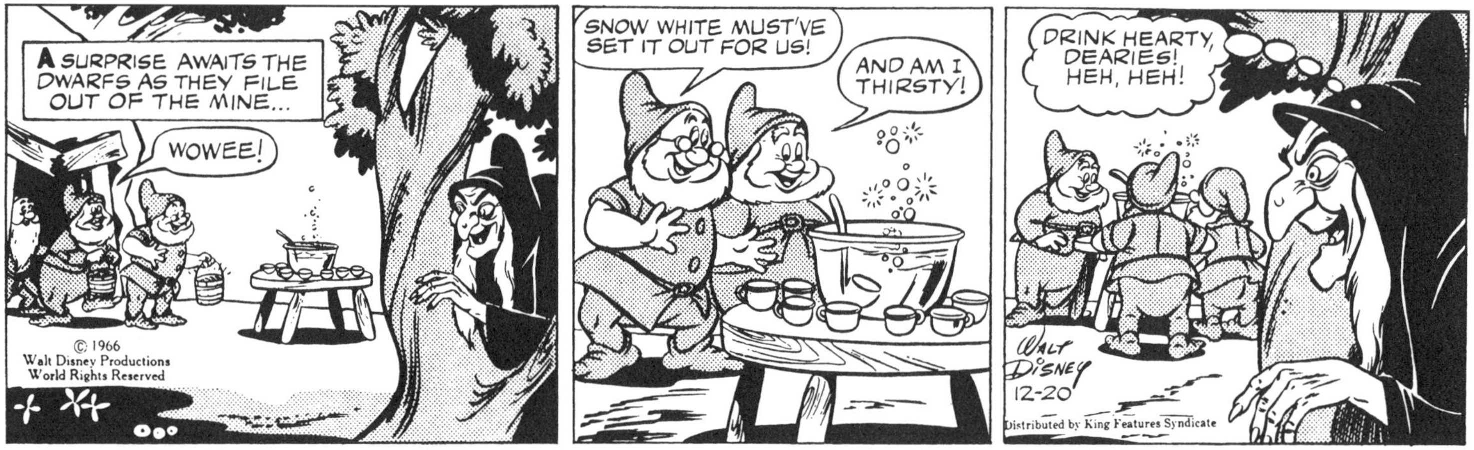
A SURPRISE AWAITS THE DWARFS AS THEY FILE OUT OF THE MINE...
WOWEE!
© 1966
Walt Disney Productions
World Rights Reserved
SNOW WHITE MUST'VE SET IT OUT FOR US!
AND AM I THIRSTY!
DRINK HEARTY, DEARIES! HEH, HEH!
WALT DISNEY
12-20
Distributed by King Features Syndicate

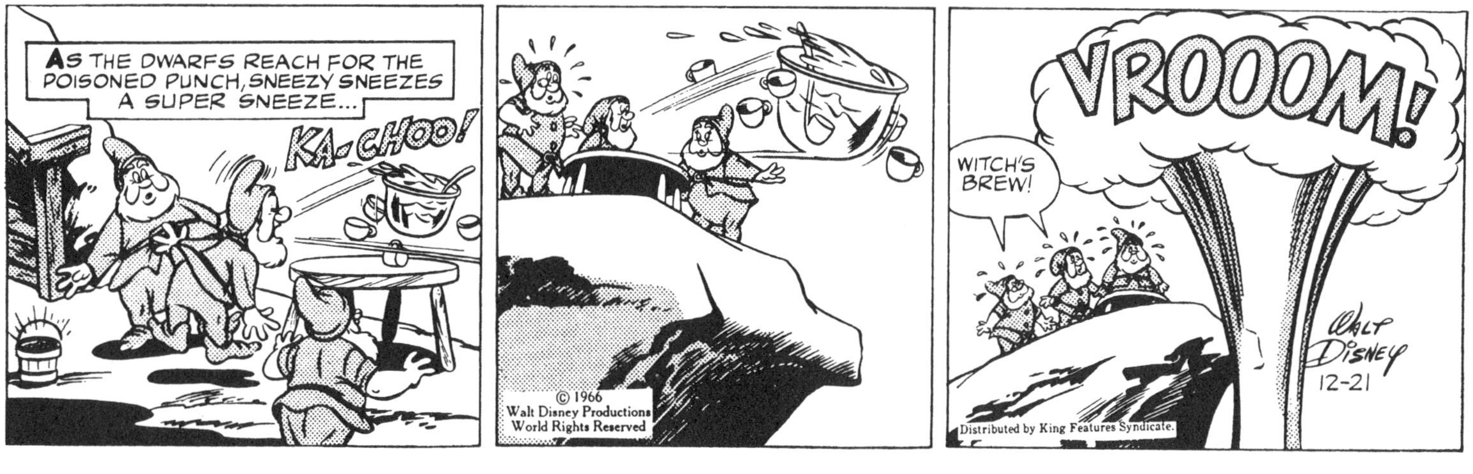
AS THE DWARFS REACH FOR THE POISONED PUNCH, SNEEZY SNEEZES A SUPER SNEEZE...
KA-CHOO!
© 1966
Walt Disney Productions
World Rights Reserved
VROOOM!
WITCH'S BREW!
WALT DISNEY
12-21
Distributed by King Features Syndicate.

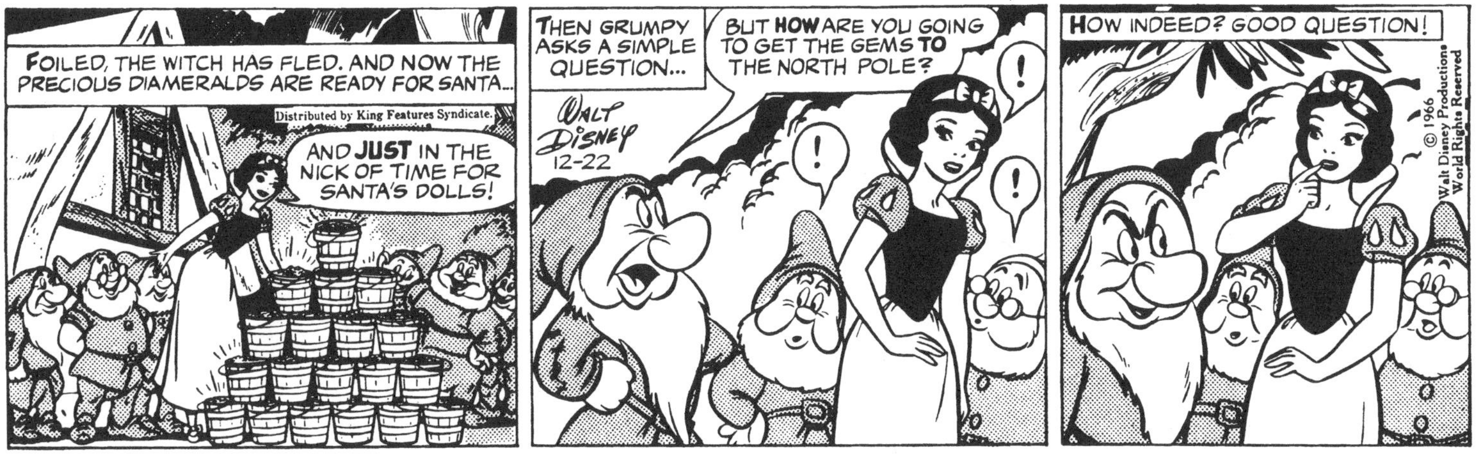
FOILED, THE WITCH HAS FLED. AND NOW THE PRECIOUS DIAMERALDS ARE READY FOR SANTA...
Distributed by King Features Syndicate.
AND JUST IN THE NICK OF TIME FOR SANTA'S DOLLS!
THEN GRUMPY ASKS A SIMPLE QUESTION...
BUT HOW ARE YOU GOING TO GET THE GEMS TO THE NORTH POLE?
WALT DISNEY 12-22
!
!
!
HOW INDEED? GOOD QUESTION!
© 1966 Walt Disney Productions World Rights Reserved

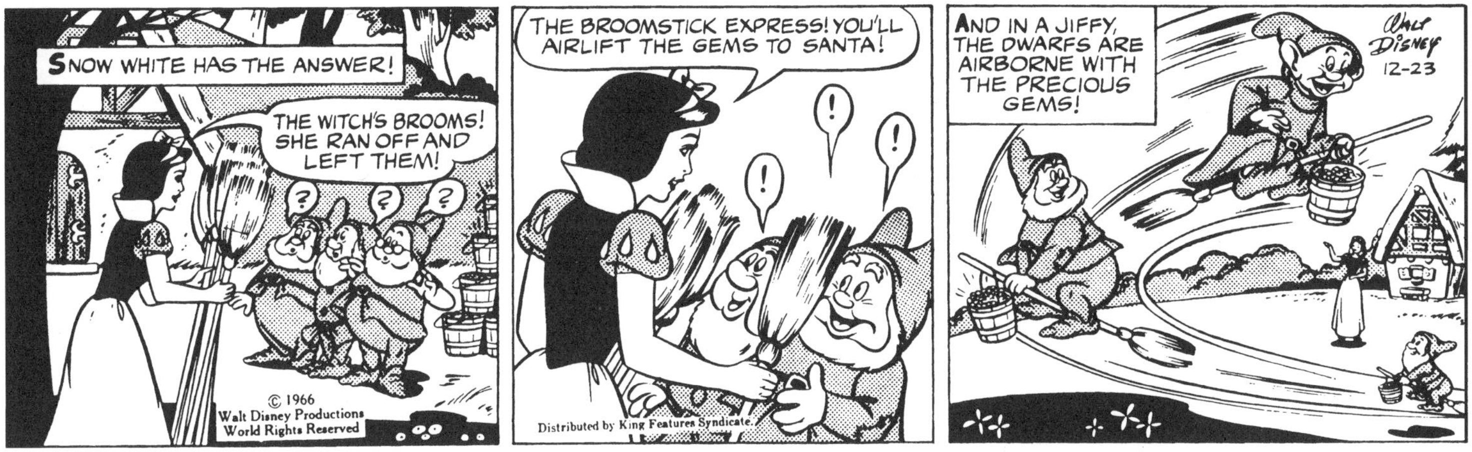
SNOW WHITE HAS THE ANSWER!
THE WITCH'S BROOMS! SHE RAN OFF AND LEFT THEM!
?
?
?
© 1966 Walt Disney Productions World Rights Reserved
THE BROOMSTICK EXPRESS! YOU'LL AIRLIFT THE GEMS TO SANTA!
!
!
!
Distributed by King Features Syndicate.
AND IN A JIFFY, THE DWARFS ARE AIRBORNE WITH THE PRECIOUS GEMS!
WALT DISNEY 12-23

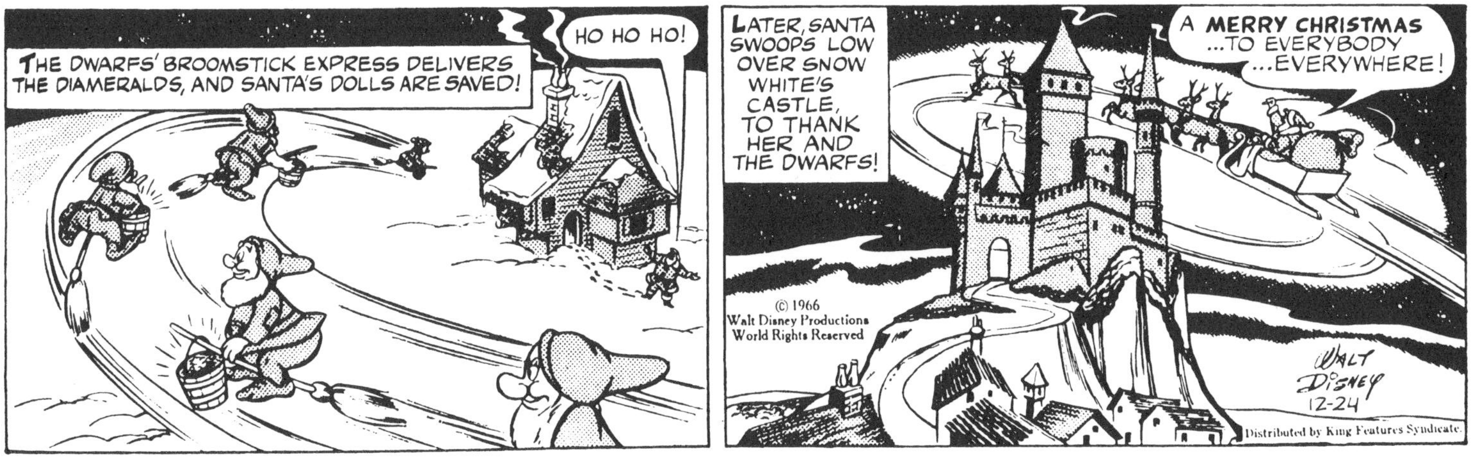
THE DWARFS' BROOMSTICK EXPRESS DELIVERS THE DIAMERALDS, AND SANTA'S DOLLS ARE SAVED!
HO HO HO!
LATER, SANTA SWOOPS LOW OVER SNOW WHITE'S CASTLE, TO THANK HER AND THE DWARFS!
A MERRY CHRISTMAS ...TO EVERYBODY ...EVERYWHERE!
© 1966 Walt Disney Productions World Rights Reserved
WALT DISNEY 12-24
Distributed by King Features Syndicate.

1967

DUMBO AND THE CHRISTMAS MYSTERY

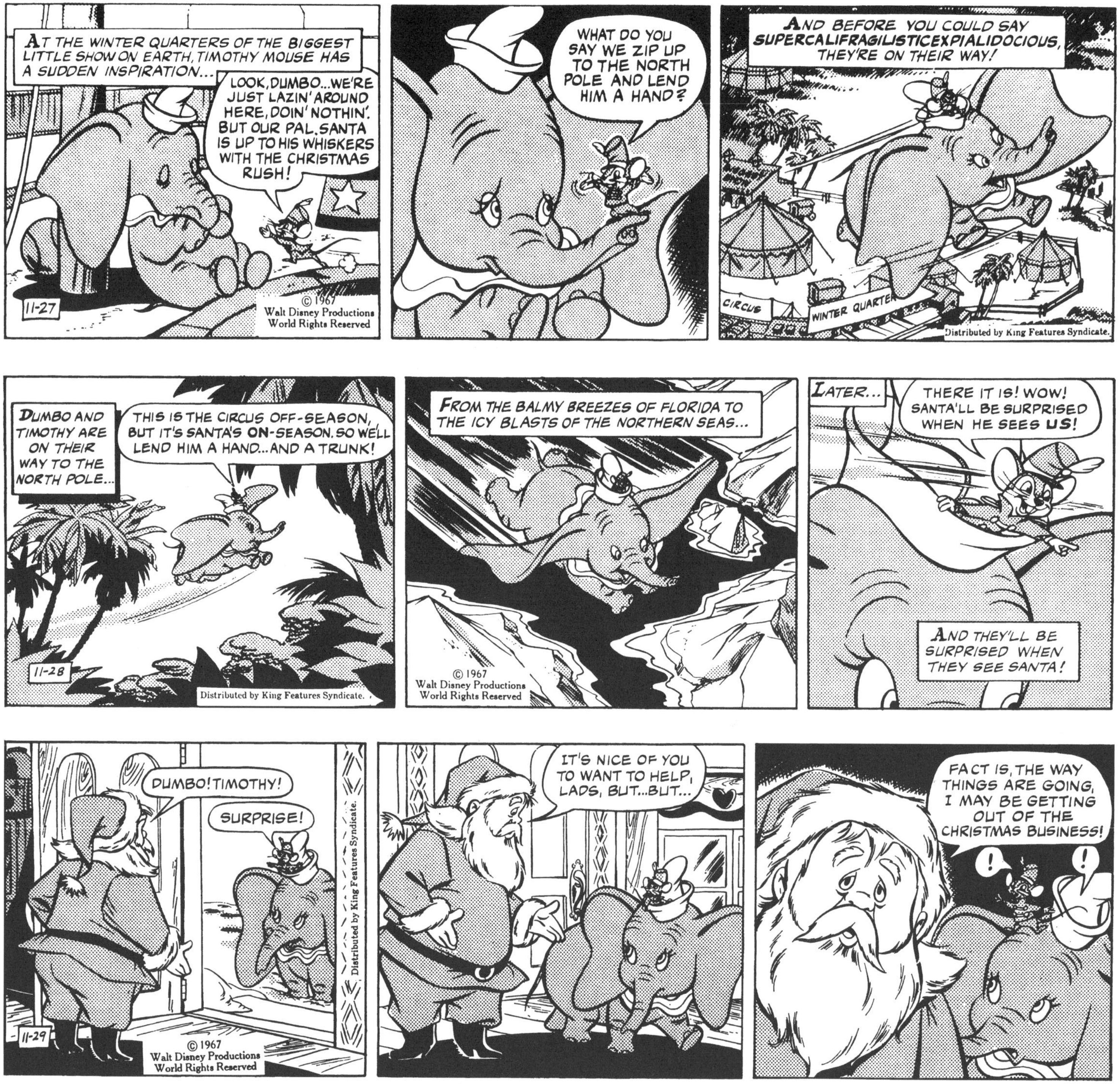
AT THE WINTER QUARTERS OF THE BIGGEST LITTLE SHOW ON EARTH, TIMOTHY MOUSE HAS A SUDDEN INSPIRATION...
LOOK, DUMBO...WE'RE JUST LAZIN' AROUND HERE, DOIN' NOTHIN'. BUT OUR PAL, SANTA IS UP TO HIS WHISKERS WITH THE CHRISTMAS RUSH!
11-27
© 1967 Walt Disney Productions World Rights Reserved
WHAT DO YOU SAY WE ZIP UP TO THE NORTH POLE AND LEND HIM A HAND?
AND BEFORE YOU COULD SAY SUPERCALIFRAGILISTICEXPIALIDOCIOUS, THEY'RE ON THEIR WAY!
CIRCUS
WINTER QUARTE
Distributed by King Features Syndicate.
DUMBO AND TIMOTHY ARE ON THEIR WAY TO THE NORTH POLE...
THIS IS THE CIRCUS OFF-SEASON, BUT IT'S SANTA'S ON-SEASON. SO WE'LL LEND HIM A HAND...AND A TRUNK!
11-28
Distributed by King Features Syndicate.
FROM THE BALMY BREEZES OF FLORIDA TO THE ICY BLASTS OF THE NORTHERN SEAS...
© 1967 Walt Disney Productions World Rights Reserved
LATER...
THERE IT IS! WOW! SANTA'LL BE SURPRISED WHEN HE SEES US!
AND THEY'LL BE SURPRISED WHEN THEY SEE SANTA!
DUMBO! TIMOTHY!
SURPRISE!
Distributed by King Features Syndicate.
11-29
© 1967 Walt Disney Productions World Rights Reserved
IT'S NICE OF YOU TO WANT TO HELP, LADS, BUT...BUT...
FACT IS, THE WAY THINGS ARE GOING, I MAY BE GETTING OUT OF THE CHRISTMAS BUSINESS!
!
!

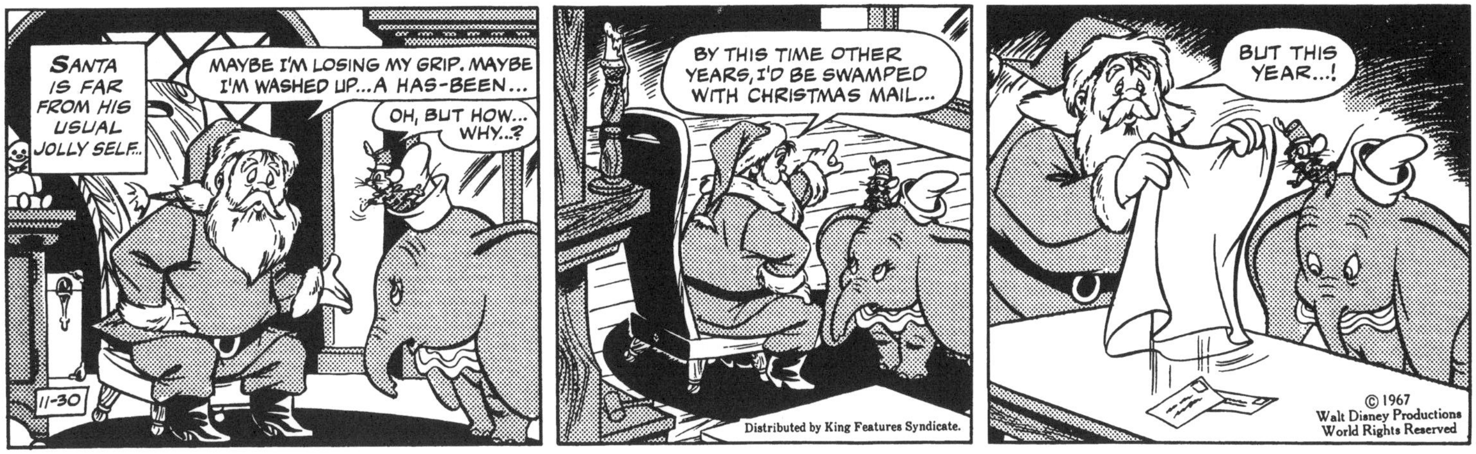
SANTA IS FAR FROM HIS USUAL JOLLY SELF..
MAYBE I'M LOSING MY GRIP. MAYBE I'M WASHED UP...A HAS-BEEN...
OH, BUT HOW... WHY..?
11-30
BY THIS TIME OTHER YEARS, I'D BE SWAMPED WITH CHRISTMAS MAIL...
Distributed by King Features Syndicate.
BUT THIS YEAR...!
© 1967 Walt Disney Productions World Rights Reserved

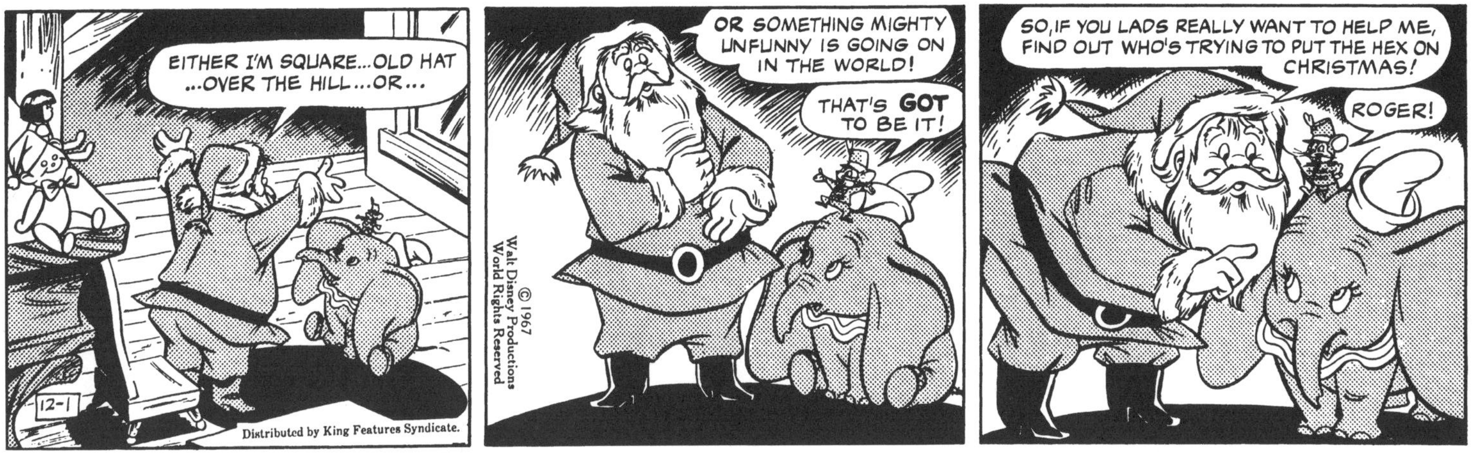
EITHER I'M SQUARE...OLD HAT ...OVER THE HILL...OR...
12-1
Distributed by King Features Syndicate.
OR SOMETHING MIGHTY UNFUNNY IS GOING ON IN THE WORLD!
THAT'S GOT TO BE IT!
© 1967 Walt Disney Productions World Rights Reserved
SO, IF YOU LADS REALLY WANT TO HELP ME, FIND OUT WHO'S TRYING TO PUT THE HEX ON CHRISTMAS!
ROGER!

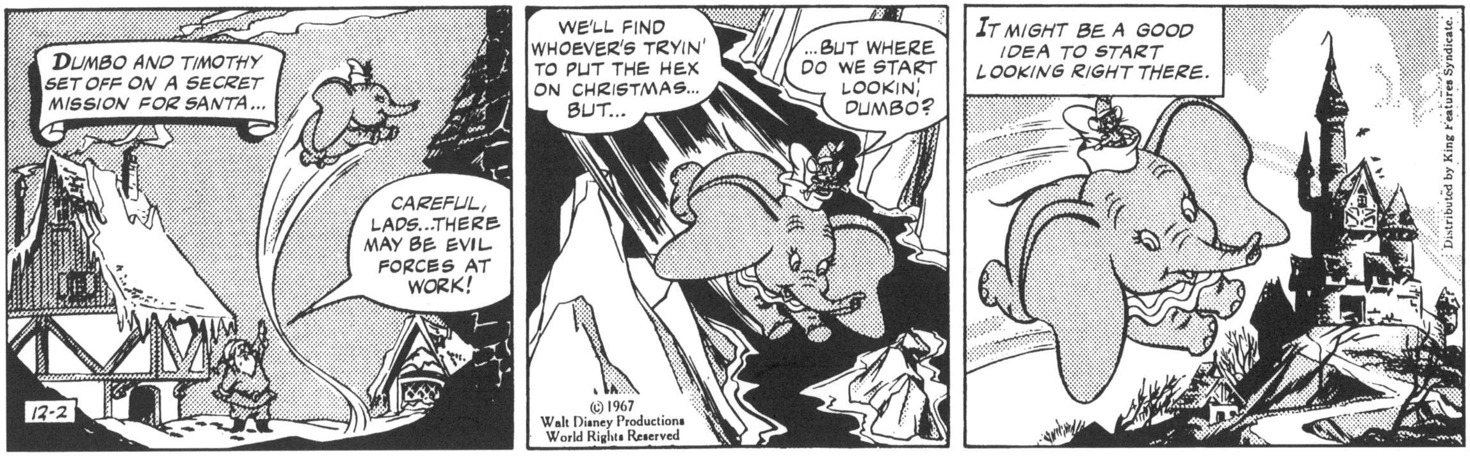
DUMBO AND TIMOTHY SET OFF ON A SECRET MISSION FOR SANTA...
CAREFUL, LADS...THERE MAY BE EVIL FORCES AT WORK!
12-2
WE'LL FIND WHOEVER'S TRYIN' TO PUT THE HEX ON CHRISTMAS... BUT...
...BUT WHERE DO WE START LOOKIN', DUMBO?
© 1967 Walt Disney Productions World Rights Reserved
IT MIGHT BE A GOOD IDEA TO START LOOKING RIGHT THERE.
Distributed by King Features Syndicate.

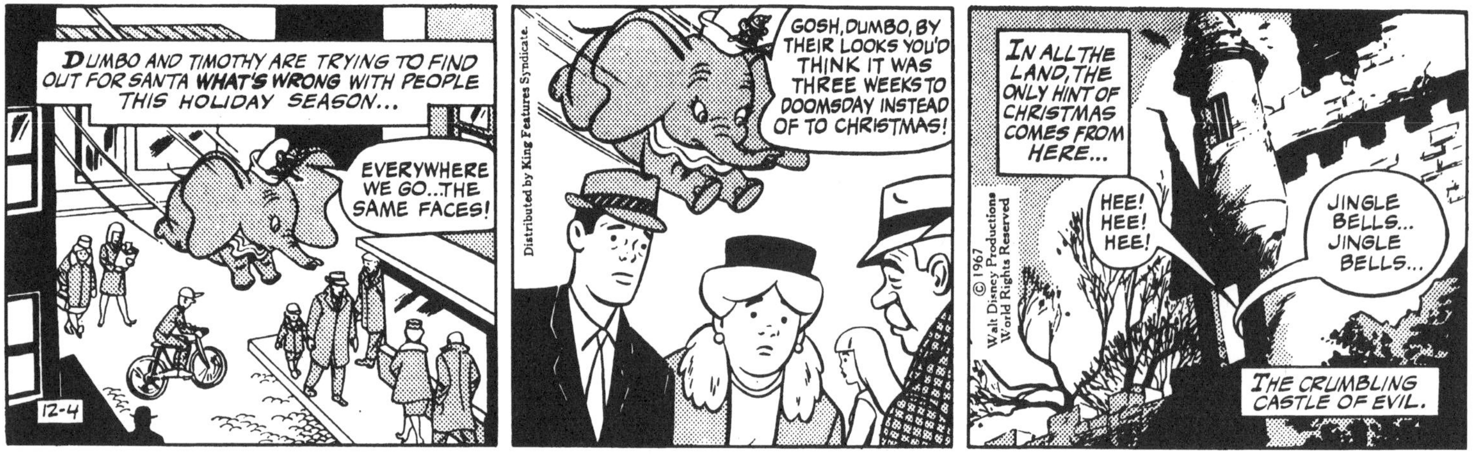
DUMBO AND TIMOTHY ARE TRYING TO FIND OUT FOR SANTA WHAT'S WRONG WITH PEOPLE THIS HOLIDAY SEASON...
EVERYWHERE WE GO..THE SAME FACES!
12-4
Distributed by King Features Syndicate.
GOSH, DUMBO, BY THEIR LOOKS YOU'D THINK IT WAS THREE WEEKS TO DOOMSDAY INSTEAD OF TO CHRISTMAS!
IN ALL THE LAND, THE ONLY HINT OF CHRISTMAS COMES FROM HERE...
© 1967 Walt Disney Productions World Rights Reserved
HEE! HEE! HEE!
JINGLE BELLS... JINGLE BELLS...
THE CRUMBLING CASTLE OF EVIL.

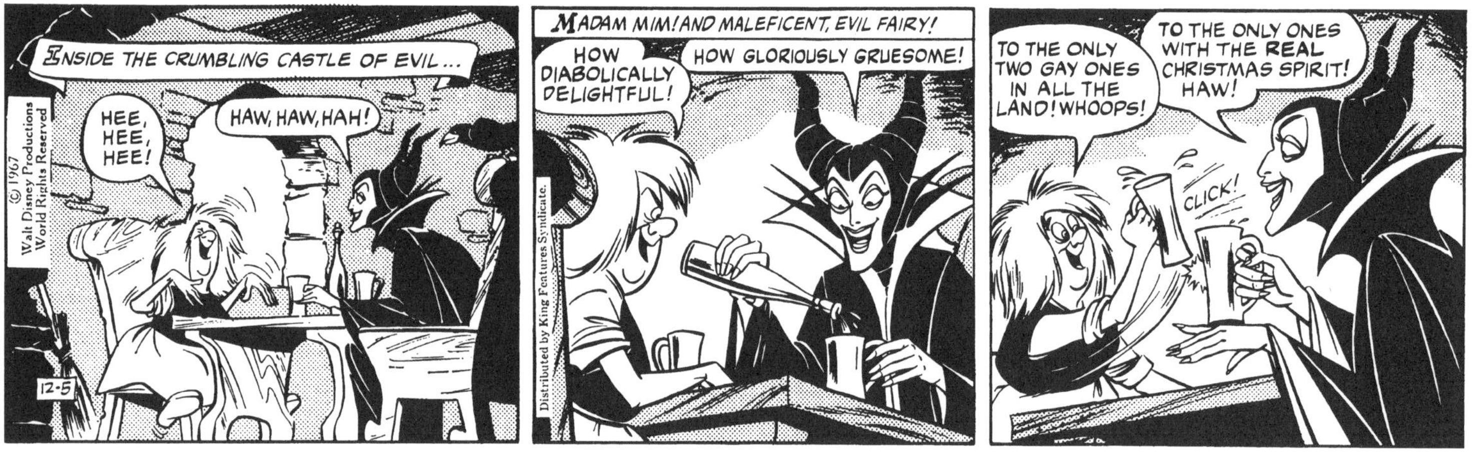
INSIDE THE CRUMBLING CASTLE OF EVIL...
© 1967 Walt Disney Productions World Rights Reserved
HEE, HEE, HEE!
HAW, HAW, HAH!
12-5
MADAM MIM! AND MALEFICENT, EVIL FAIRY!
HOW DIABOLICALLY DELIGHTFUL!
HOW GLORIOUSLY GRUESOME!
Distributed by King Features Syndicate.
TO THE ONLY TWO GAY ONES IN ALL THE LAND! WHOOPS!
TO THE ONLY ONES WITH THE REAL CHRISTMAS SPIRIT! HAW!
CLICK!

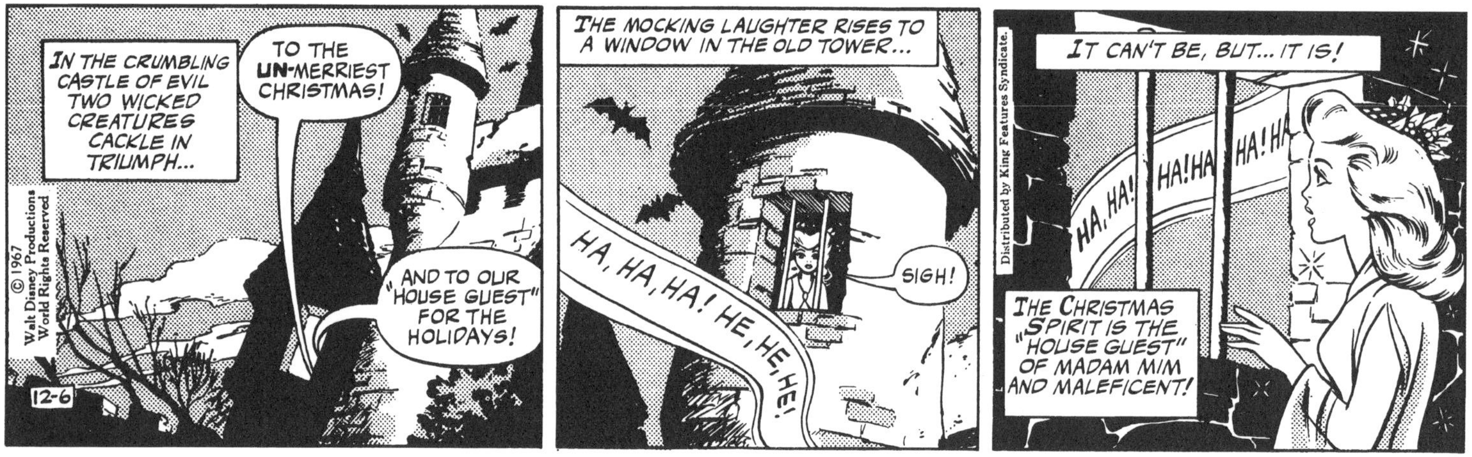
IN THE CRUMBLING CASTLE OF EVIL TWO WICKED CREATURES CACKLE IN TRIUMPH...
TO THE UN-MERRIEST CHRISTMAS!
© 1967 Walt Disney Productions World Rights Reserved
"AND TO OUR "HOUSE GUEST" FOR THE HOLIDAYS!
12-6
THE MOCKING LAUGHTER RISES TO A WINDOW IN THE OLD TOWER...
HA, HA, HA! HE, HE, HE!
SIGH!
Distributed by King Features Syndicate.
IT CAN'T BE, BUT... IT IS!
HA, HA! HA! HA HA! HA
THE CHRISTMAS "SPIRIT IS THE "HOUSE GUEST" OF MADAM MIM AND MALEFICENT!

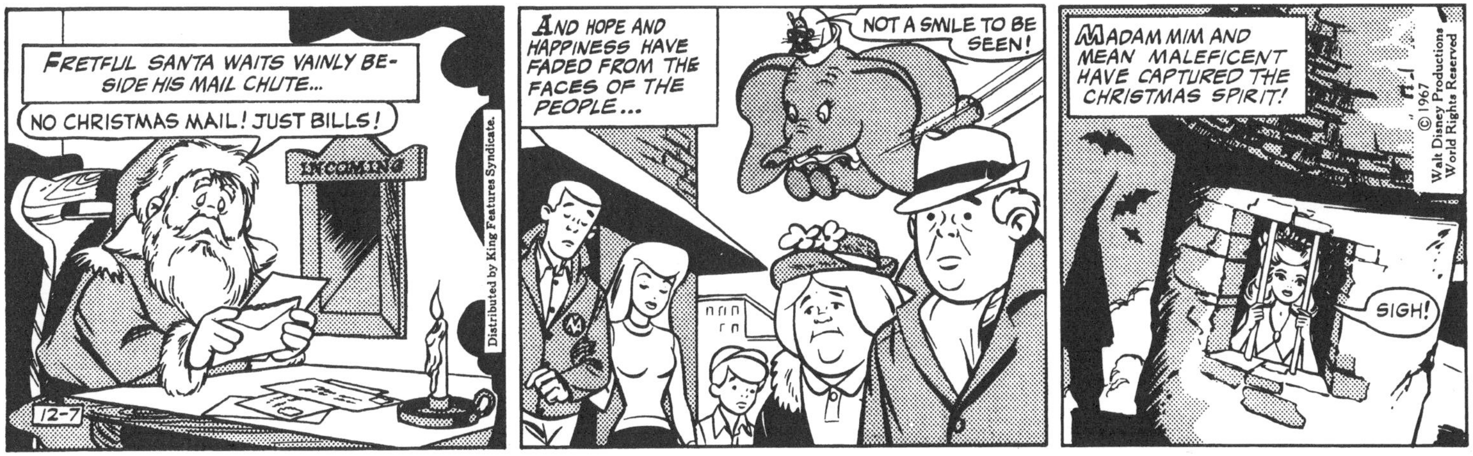
FRETFUL SANTA WAITS VAINLY BESIDE HIS MAIL CHUTE...
NO CHRISTMAS MAIL! JUST BILLS!
INCOMING
12-7
Distributed by King Features Syndicate.
AND HOPE AND HAPPINESS HAVE FADED FROM THE FACES OF THE PEOPLE...
NOT A SMILE TO BE SEEN!
MADAM MIM AND MEAN MALEFICENT HAVE CAPTURED THE CHRISTMAS SPIRIT!
SIGH!
© 1967 Walt Disney Productions World Rights Reserved

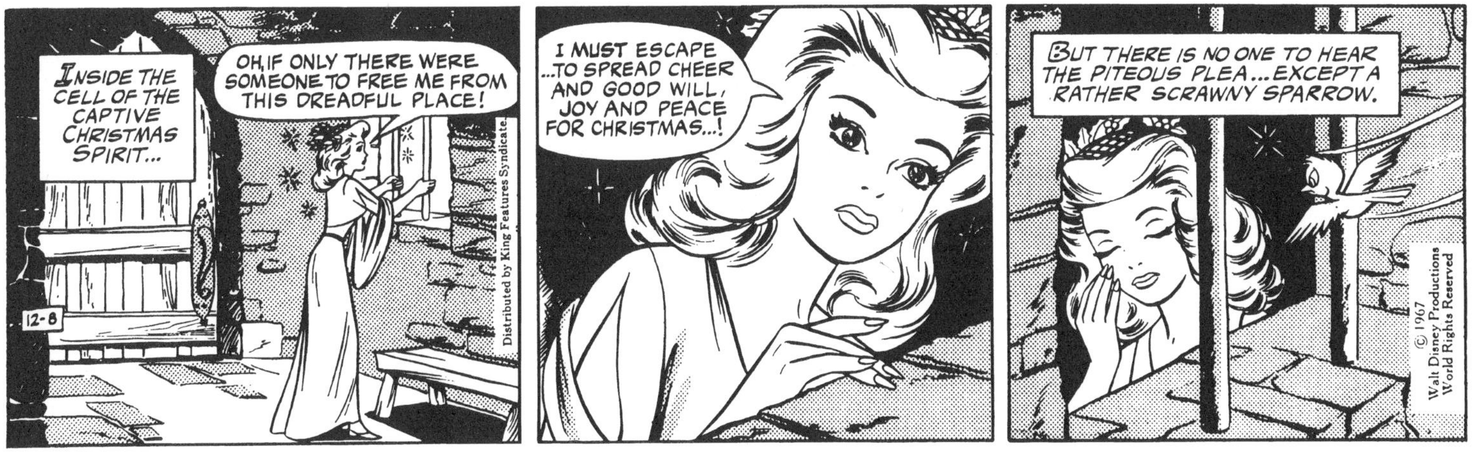
INSIDE THE CELL OF THE CAPTIVE CHRISTMAS SPIRIT...
OH, IF ONLY THERE WERE SOMEONE TO FREE ME FROM THIS DREADFUL PLACE!
12-8
Distributed by King Features Syndicate.
I MUST ESCAPE ...TO SPREAD CHEER AND GOOD WILL, JOY AND PEACE FOR CHRISTMAS...!
BUT THERE IS NO ONE TO HEAR THE PITEOUS PLEA...EXCEPT A RATHER SCRAWNY SPARROW.
© 1967 Walt Disney Productions World Rights Reserved

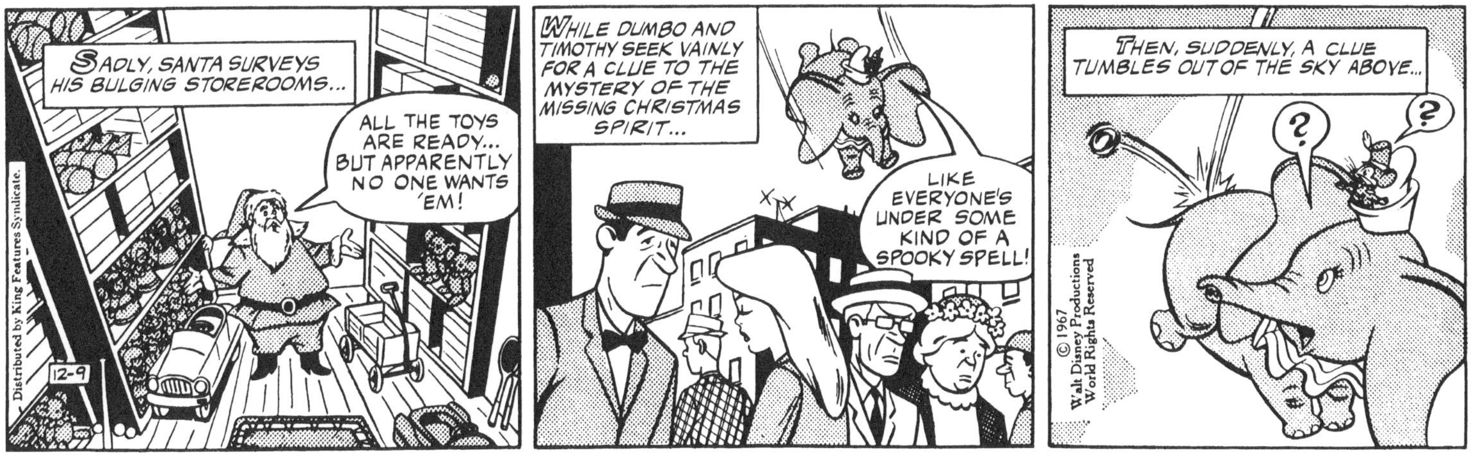
SADLY, SANTA SURVEYS HIS BULGING STOREROOMS...
ALL THE TOYS ARE READY... BUT APPARENTLY NO ONE WANTS 'EM!
12-9
Distributed by King Features Syndicate.
WHILE DUMBO AND TIMOTHY SEEK VAINLY FOR A CLUE TO THE MYSTERY OF THE MISSING CHRISTMAS SPIRIT...
LIKE EVERYONE'S UNDER SOME KIND OF A SPOOKY SPELL!
© 1967 Walt Disney Productions World Rights Reserved
THEN, SUDDENLY, A CLUE TUMBLES OUT OF THE SKY ABOVE...
?
?

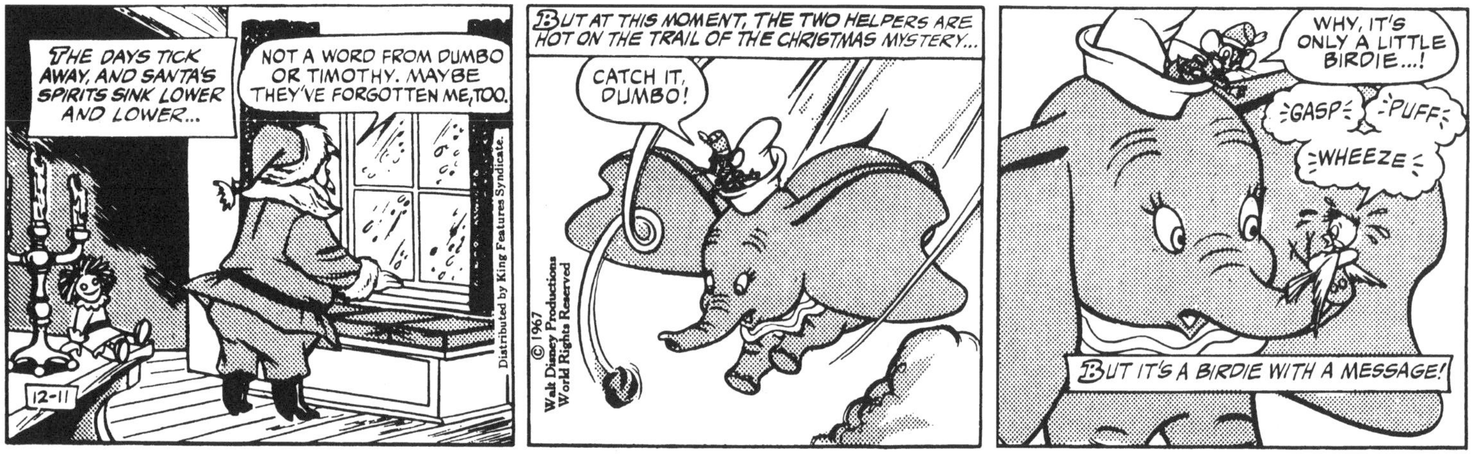
THE DAYS TICK AWAY, AND SANTA'S SPIRITS SINK LOWER AND LOWER...
NOT A WORD FROM DUMBO OR TIMOTHY. MAYBE THEY'VE FORGOTTEN ME, TOO.
12-11
Distributed by King Features Syndicate.
BUT AT THIS MOMENT, THE TWO HELPERS ARE HOT ON THE TRAIL OF THE CHRISTMAS MYSTERY...
CATCH IT, DUMBO!
© 1967 Walt Disney Productions World Rights Reserved
WHY, IT'S ONLY A LITTLE BIRDIE...!
GASP
PUFF
WHEEZE
BUT IT'S A BIRDIE WITH A MESSAGE!

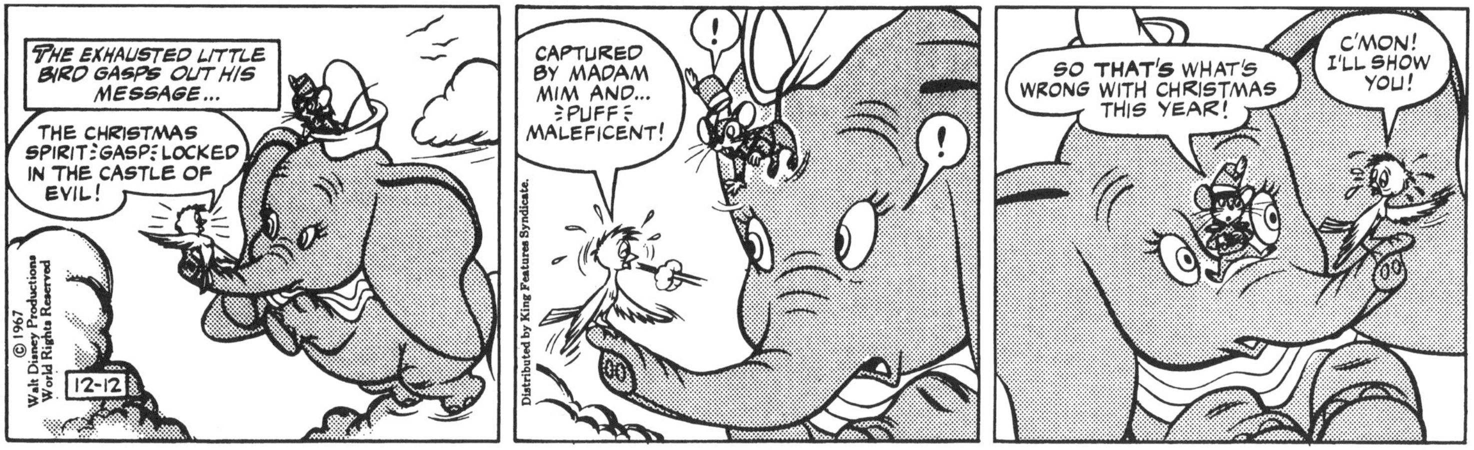
THE EXHAUSTED LITTLE BIRD GASPS OUT HIS MESSAGE...
THE CHRISTMAS SPIRIT GASP LOCKED IN THE CASTLE OF EVIL!
© 1967 Walt Disney Productions World Rights Reserved
12-12
CAPTURED BY MADAM MIM AND... PUFF MALEFICENT!
!
!
Distributed by King Features Syndicate.
SO THAT'S WHAT'S WRONG WITH CHRISTMAS THIS YEAR!
C'MON! I'LL SHOW YOU!

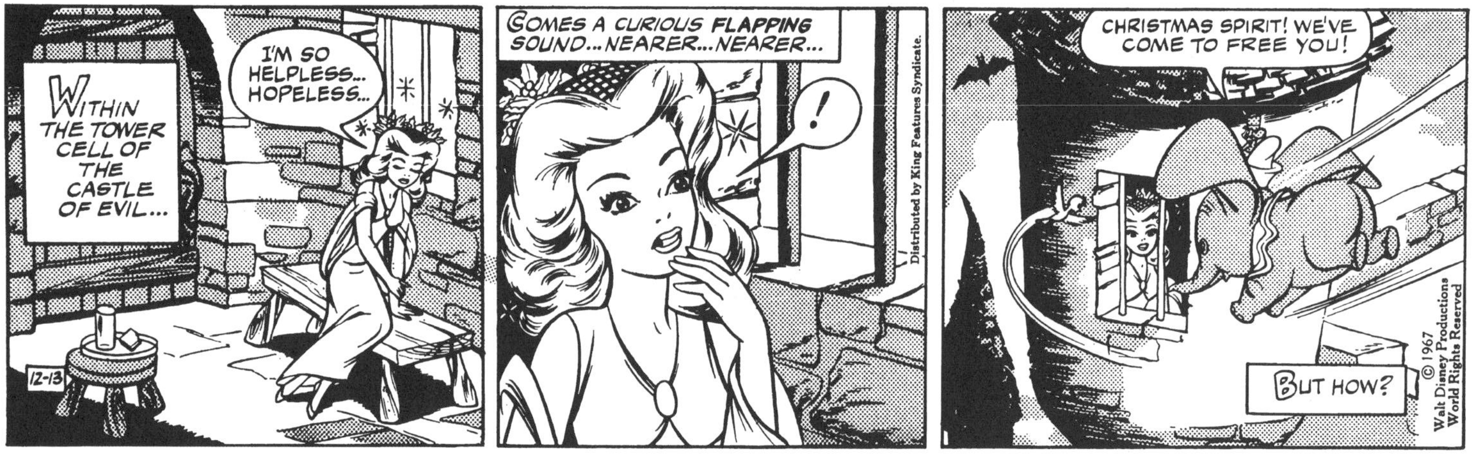
WITHIN THE TOWER CELL OF THE CASTLE OF EVIL...
I'M SO HELPLESS... HOPELESS...
12-13
COMES A CURIOUS FLAPPING SOUND...NEARER...NEARER...
!
Distributed by King Features Syndicate.
CHRISTMAS SPIRIT! WE'VE COME TO FREE YOU!
BUT HOW?
© 1967 Walt Disney Productions World Rights Reserved

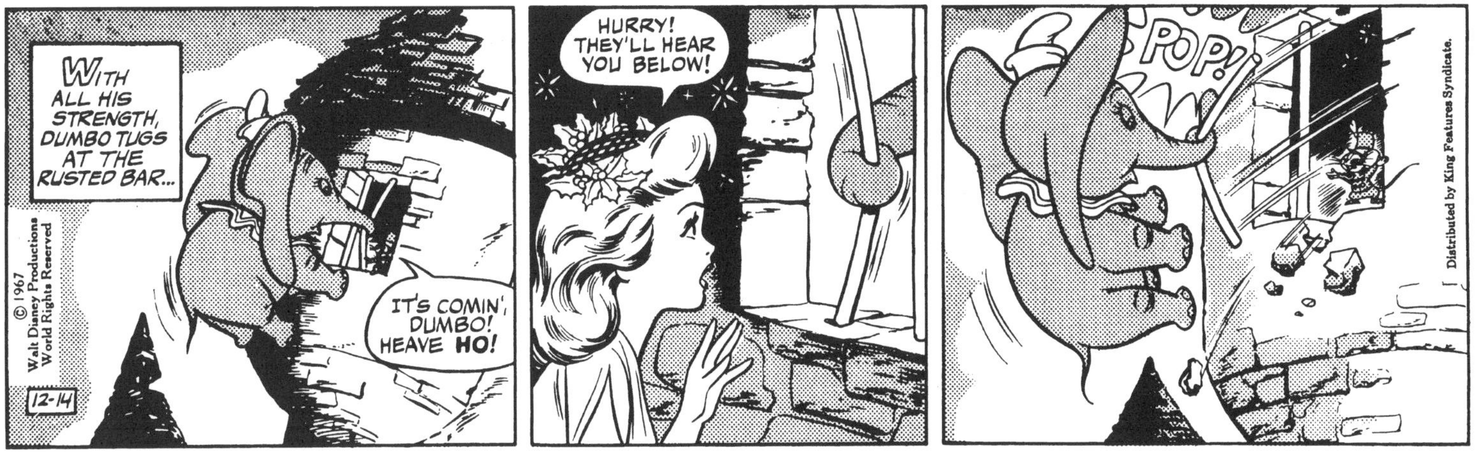
WITH ALL HIS STRENGTH, DUMBO TUGS AT THE RUSTED BAR...
IT'S COMIN', DUMBO! HEAVE HO!
© 1967 Walt Disney Productions World Rights Reserved
12-14
HURRY! THEY'LL HEAR YOU BELOW!
POP!
Distributed by King Features Syndicate.

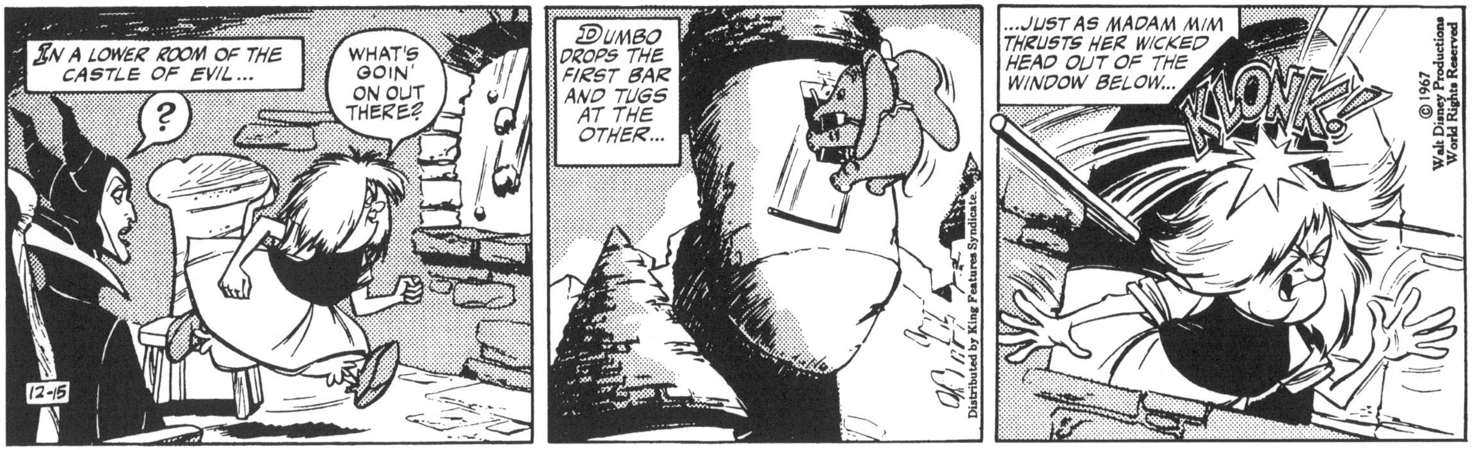
IN A LOWER ROOM OF THE CASTLE OF EVIL...
?
WHAT'S GOIN' ON OUT THERE?
12-15
DUMBO DROPS THE FIRST BAR AND TUGS AT THE OTHER...
Distributed by King Features Syndicate.
...JUST AS MADAM MIM THRUSTS HER WICKED HEAD OUT OF THE WINDOW BELOW...
KLONK!!
© 1967 Walt Disney Productions World Rights Reserved

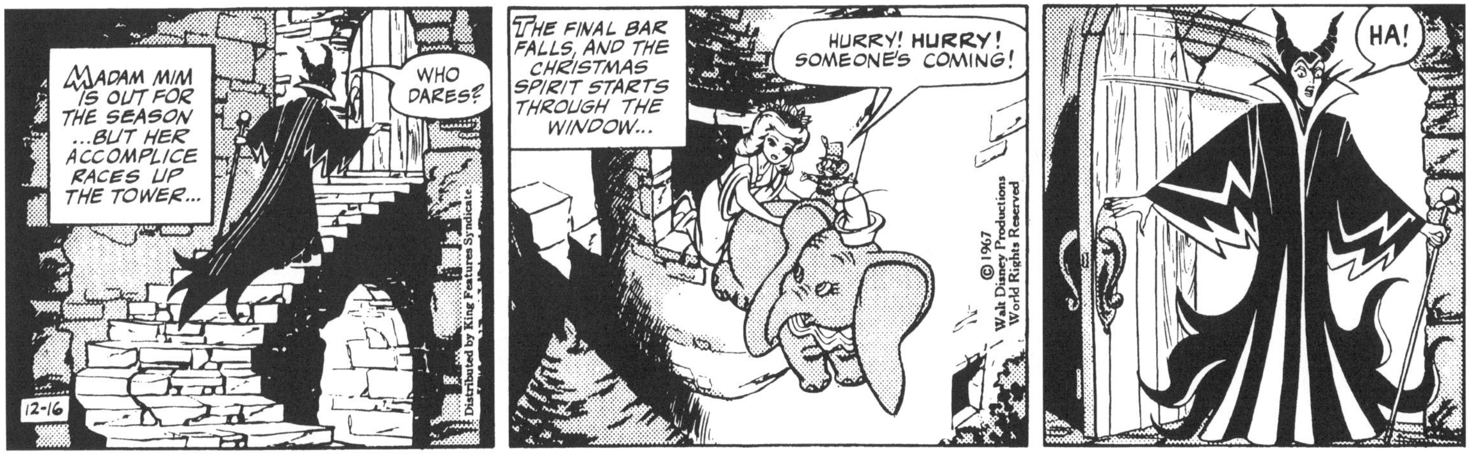
MADAM MIM IS OUT FOR THE SEASON ...BUT HER ACCOMPLICE RACES UP THE TOWER...
WHO DARES?
12-16
Distributed by King Features Syndicate.
THE FINAL BAR FALLS, AND THE CHRISTMAS SPIRIT STARTS THROUGH THE WINDOW...
HURRY! HURRY! SOMEONE'S COMING!
© 1967 Walt Disney Productions World Rights Reserved
HA!

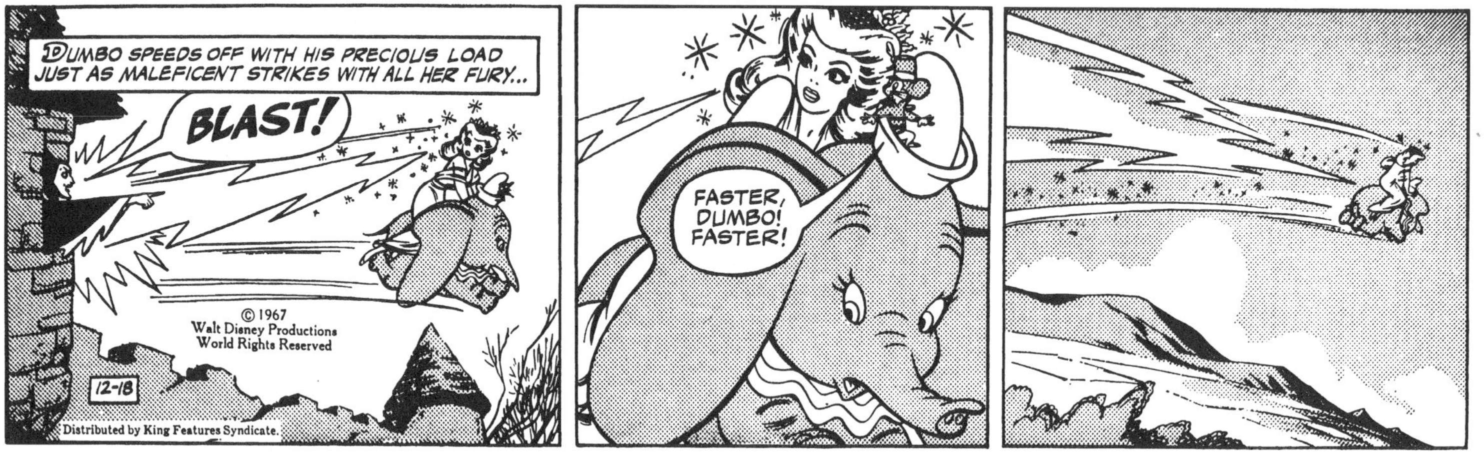
DUMBO SPEEDS OFF WITH HIS PRECIOUS LOAD JUST AS MALEFICENT STRIKES WITH ALL HER FURY...
BLAST!
© 1967 Walt Disney Productions World Rights Reserved
12-18
Distributed by King Features Syndicate.
FASTER, DUMBO! FASTER!

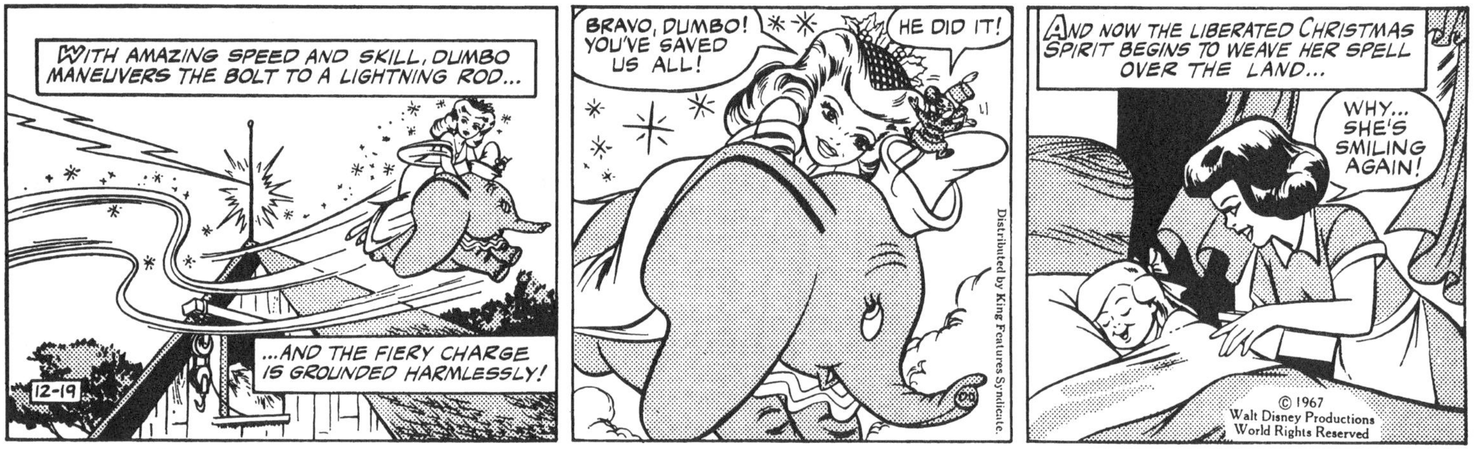
WITH AMAZING SPEED AND SKILL, DUMBO MANEUVERS THE BOLT TO A LIGHTNING ROD...
...AND THE FIERY CHARGE IS GROUNDED HARMLESSLY!
12-19
BRAVO, DUMBO! YOU'VE SAVED US ALL!
HE DID IT!
Distributed by King Features Syndicate.
AND NOW THE LIBERATED CHRISTMAS SPIRIT BEGINS TO WEAVE HER SPELL OVER THE LAND...
WHY... SHE'S SMILING AGAIN!
© 1967 Walt Disney Productions World Rights Reserved

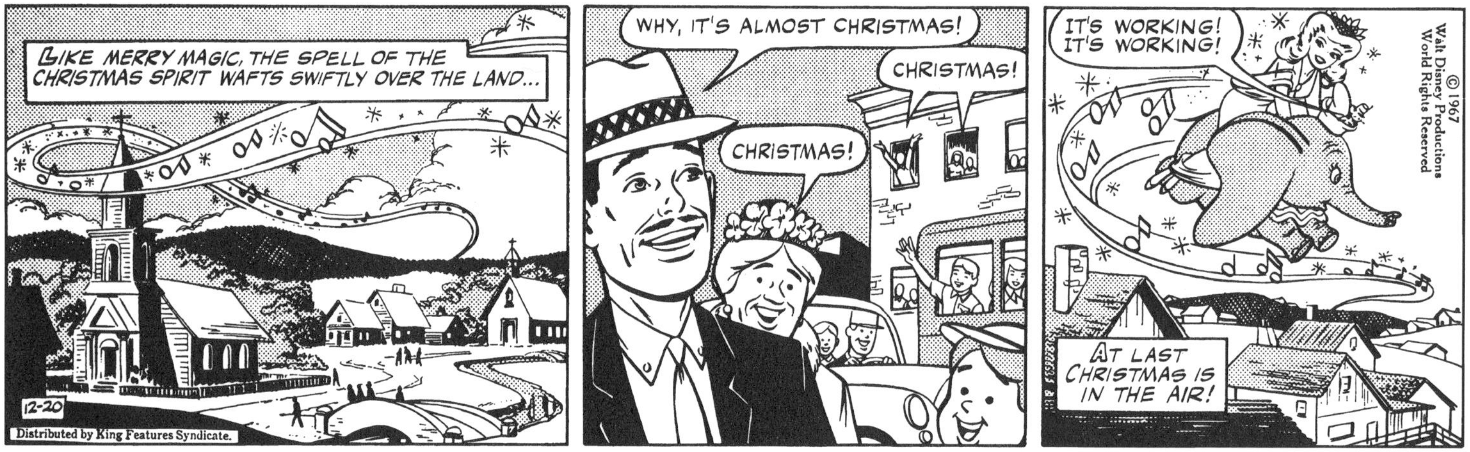
LIKE MERRY MAGIC, THE SPELL OF THE CHRISTMAS SPIRIT WAFTS SWIFTLY OVER THE LAND...
12-20
Distributed by King Features Syndicate.
WHY, IT'S ALMOST CHRISTMAS!
CHRISTMAS!
CHRISTMAS!
IT'S WORKING! IT'S WORKING!
© 1967 Walt Disney Productions World Rights Reserved
AT LAST CHRISTMAS IS IN THE AIR!

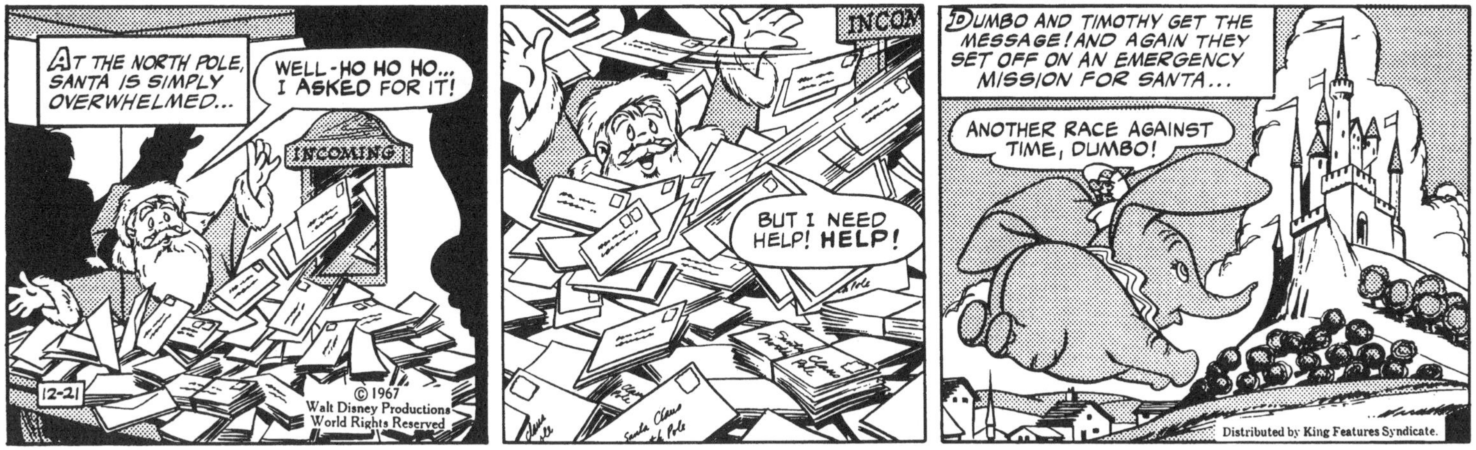
AT THE NORTH POLE, SANTA IS SIMPLY OVERWHELMED...
WELL-HO HO HO... I ASKED FOR IT!
INCOMING
12-21
© 1967 Walt Disney Productions World Rights Reserved
INCOM
BUT I NEED HELP! HELP!
DUMBO AND TIMOTHY GET THE MESSAGE! AND AGAIN THEY SET OFF ON AN EMERGENCY MISSION FOR SANTA...
ANOTHER RACE AGAINST TIME, DUMBO!
Distributed by King Features Syndicate.

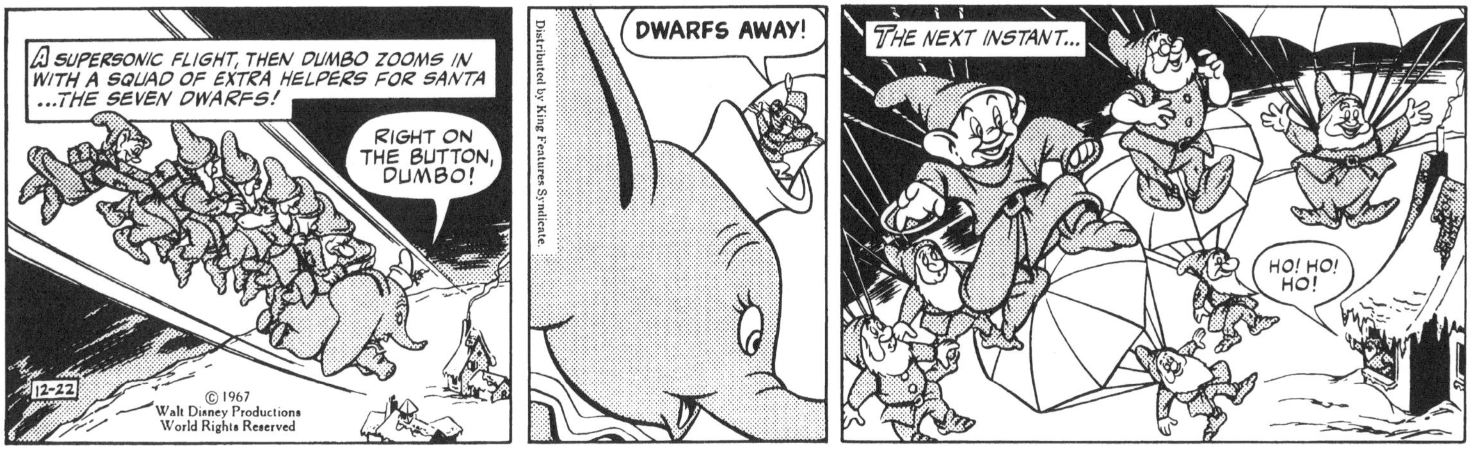
A SUPERSONIC FLIGHT, THEN DUMBO ZOOMS IN WITH A SQUAD OF EXTRA HELPERS FOR SANTA ...THE SEVEN DWARFS!
RIGHT ON THE BUTTON, DUMBO!
12-22
© 1967 Walt Disney Productions World Rights Reserved
Distributed by King Features Syndicate.
DWARFS AWAY!
THE NEXT INSTANT...
HO! HO! HO!

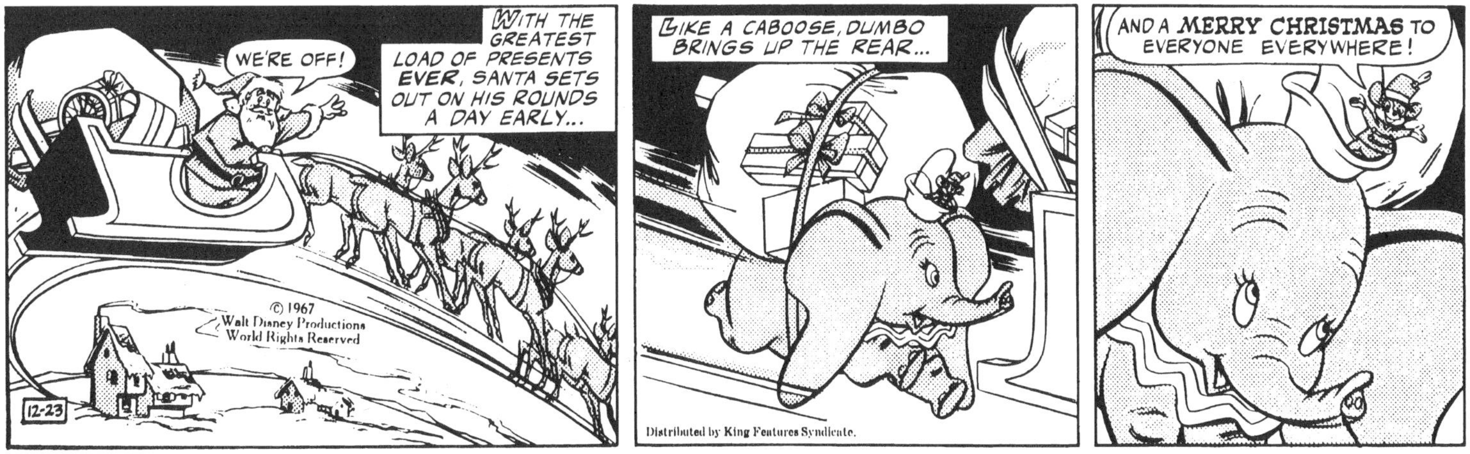
WE'RE OFF!
WITH THE GREATEST LOAD OF PRESENTS EVER, SANTA SETS OUT ON HIS ROUNDS A DAY EARLY...
© 1967 Walt Disney Productions World Rights Reserved
12-23
LIKE A CABOOSE, DUMBO BRINGS UP THE REAR...
Distributed by King Features Syndicate.
AND A MERRY CHRISTMAS TO EVERYONE EVERYWHERE!

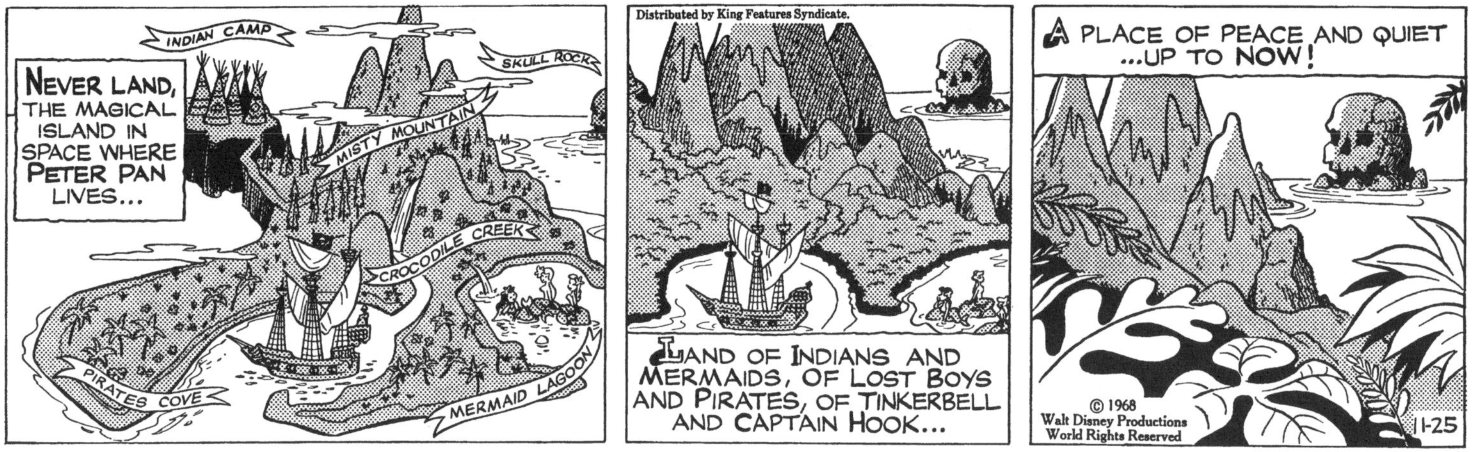
NEVER LAND, THE MAGICAL ISLAND IN SPACE WHERE PETER PAN LIVES...
INDIAN CAMP
SKULL ROCK
MISTY MOUNTAIN
CROCODILE CREEK
PIRATES COVE
MERMAID LAGOON
Distributed by King Features Syndicate.
LAND OF INDIANS AND MERMAIDS, OF LOST BOYS AND PIRATES, OF TINKERBELL AND CAPTAIN HOOK...
A PLACE OF PEACE AND QUIET ...UP TO NOW!
© 1968 Walt Disney Productions World Rights Reserved
11-25

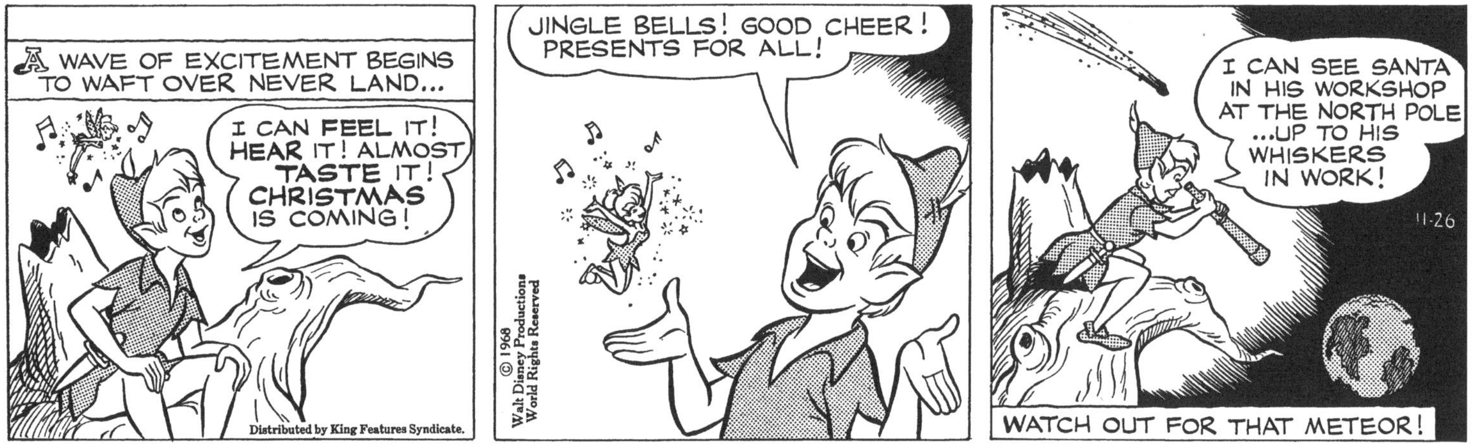
A WAVE OF EXCITEMENT BEGINS TO WAFT OVER NEVER LAND...
I CAN FEEL IT! HEAR IT! ALMOST TASTE IT! CHRISTMAS IS COMING!
Distributed by King Features Syndicate.
JINGLE BELLS! GOOD CHEER! PRESENTS FOR ALL!
© 1968 Walt Disney Productions World Rights Reserved
I CAN SEE SANTA IN HIS WORKSHOP AT THE NORTH POLE ...UP TO HIS WHISKERS IN WORK!
11-26
WATCH OUT FOR THAT METEOR!

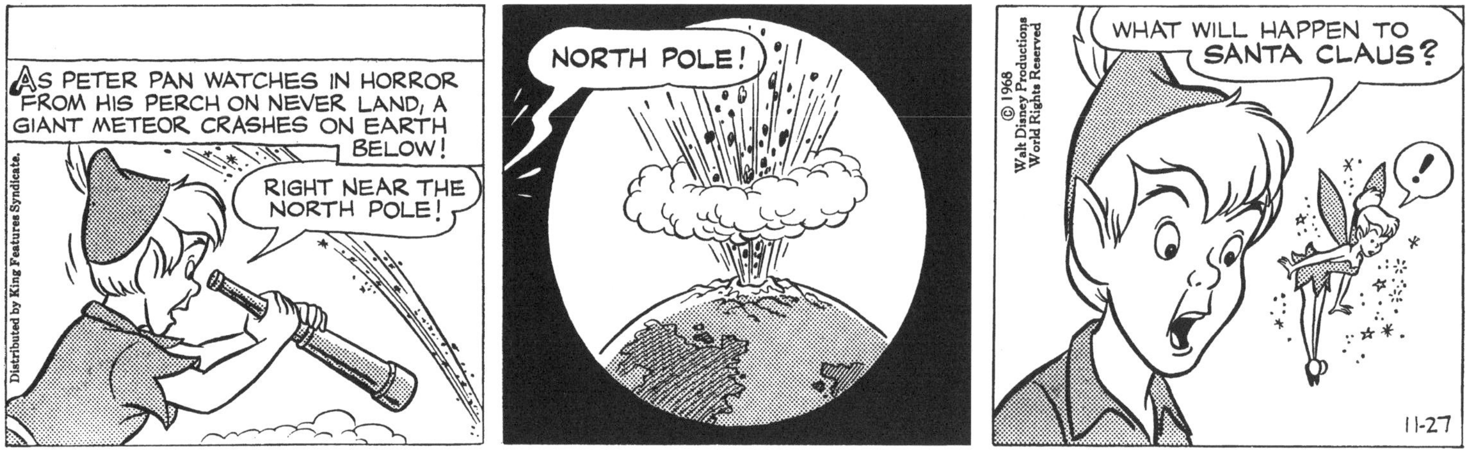
AS PETER PAN WATCHES IN HORROR FROM HIS PERCH ON NEVER LAND, A GIANT METEOR CRASHES ON EARTH BELOW!
RIGHT NEAR THE NORTH POLE!
Distributed by King Features Syndicate.
NORTH POLE!
© 1968 Walt Disney Productions World Rights Reserved
WHAT WILL HAPPEN TO SANTA CLAUS?
!
11-27

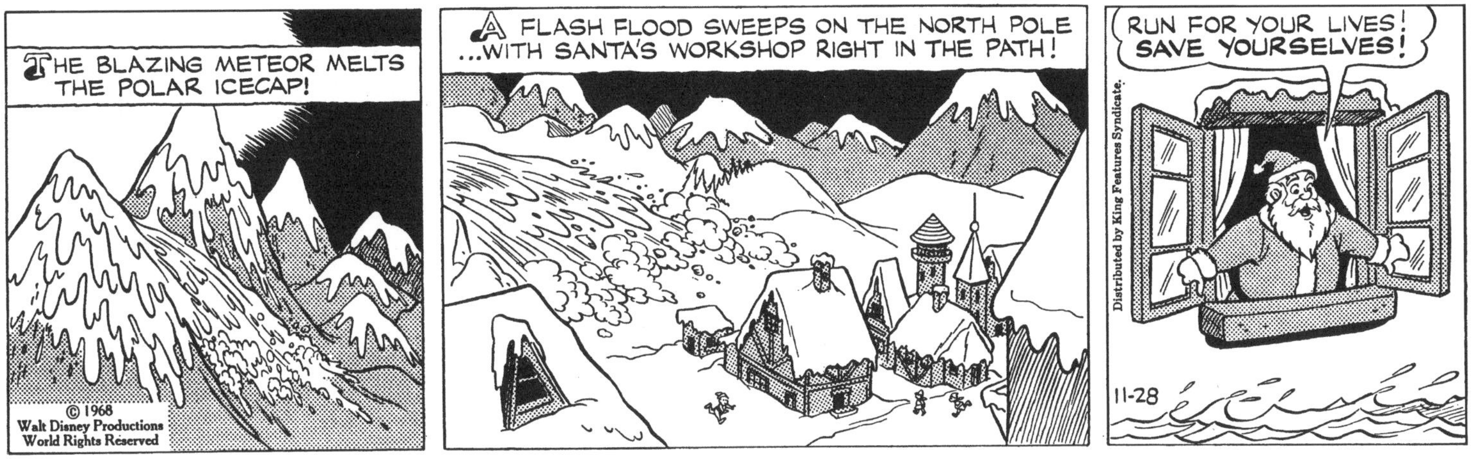
THE BLAZING METEOR MELTS THE POLAR ICECAP!
© 1968 Walt Disney Productions World Rights Reserved
A FLASH FLOOD SWEEPS ON THE NORTH POLE ...WITH SANTA'S WORKSHOP RIGHT IN THE PATH!
RUN FOR YOUR LIVES! SAVE YOURSELVES!
Distributed by King Features Syndicate.
11-28

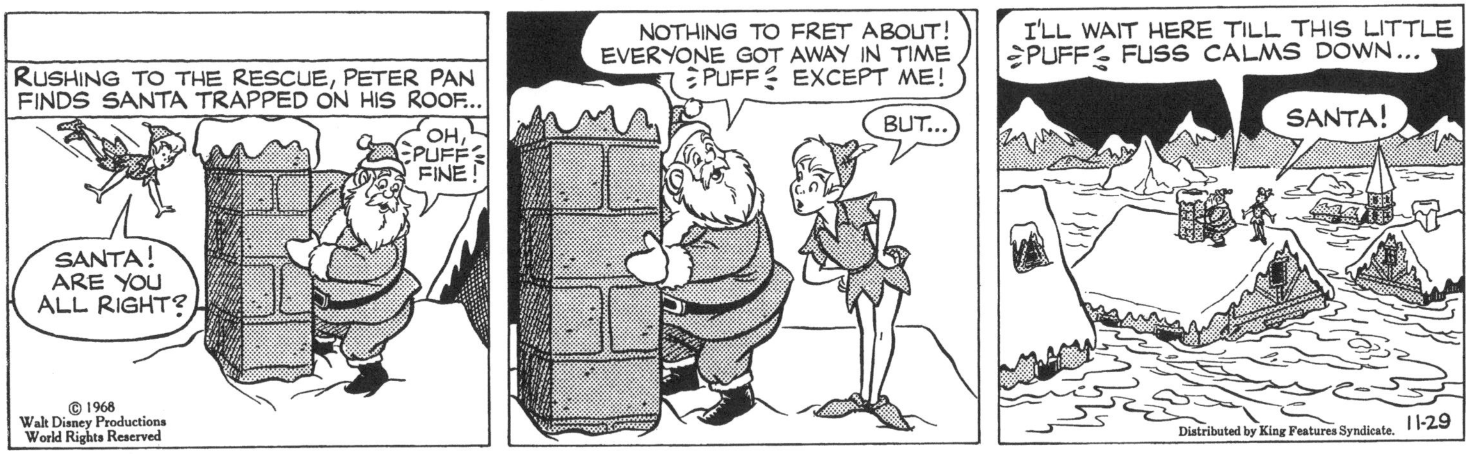
RUSHING TO THE RESCUE, PETER PAN FINDS SANTA TRAPPED ON HIS ROOF...
SANTA! ARE YOU ALL RIGHT?
OH, PUFF FINE!
© 1968 Walt Disney Productions World Rights Reserved
NOTHING TO FRET ABOUT! EVERYONE GOT AWAY IN TIME PUFF EXCEPT ME!
BUT...
I'LL WAIT HERE TILL THIS LITTLE PUFF FUSS CALMS DOWN...
SANTA!
Distributed by King Features Syndicate.
11-29

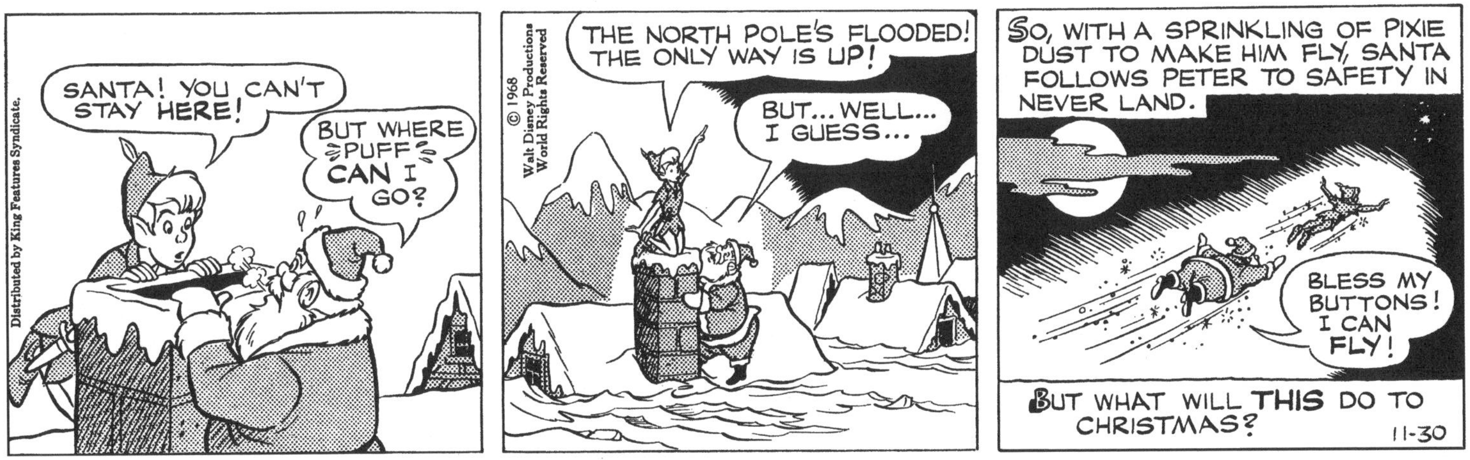
Distributed by King Features Syndicate.
SANTA! YOU CAN'T STAY HERE!
BUT WHERE PUFF CAN I GO?
© 1968 Walt Disney Productions World Rights Reserved
THE NORTH POLE'S FLOODED! THE ONLY WAY IS UP!
BUT...WELL... I GUESS...
SO, WITH A SPRINKLING OF PIXIE DUST TO MAKE HIM FLY, SANTA FOLLOWS PETER TO SAFETY IN NEVER LAND.
BLESS MY BUTTONS! I CAN FLY!
BUT WHAT WILL THIS DO TO CHRISTMAS?
11-30

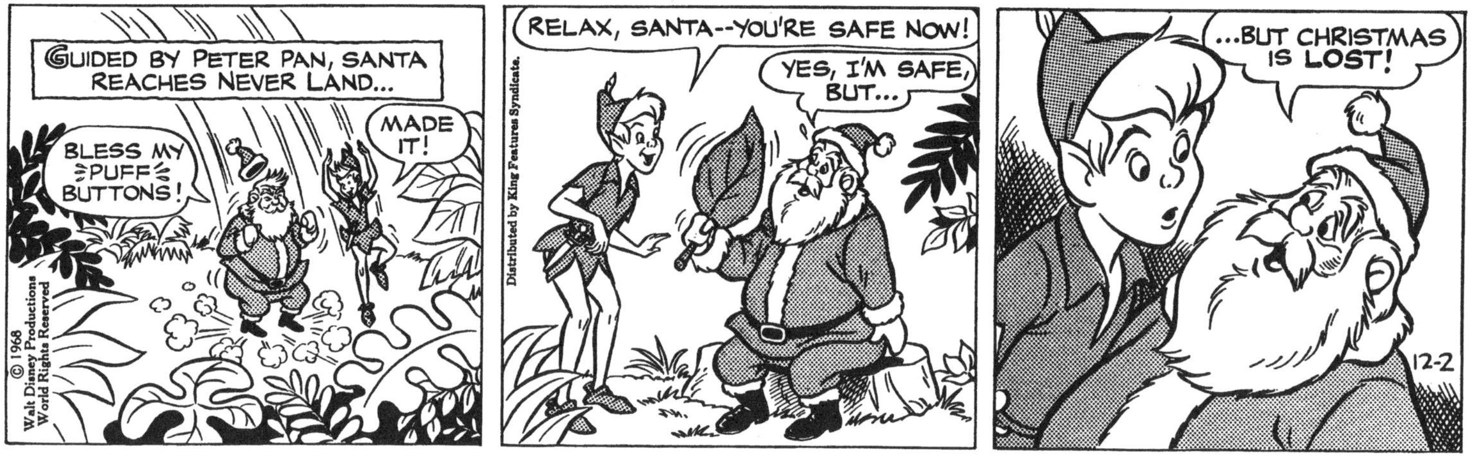
GUIDED BY PETER PAN, SANTA REACHES NEVER LAND...
BLESS MY PUFF BUTTONS!
MADE IT!
© 1968 Walt Disney Productions World Rights Reserved
RELAX, SANTA--YOU'RE SAFE NOW!
YES, I'M SAFE, BUT...
Distributed by King Features Syndicate.
...BUT CHRISTMAS IS LOST!
12-2

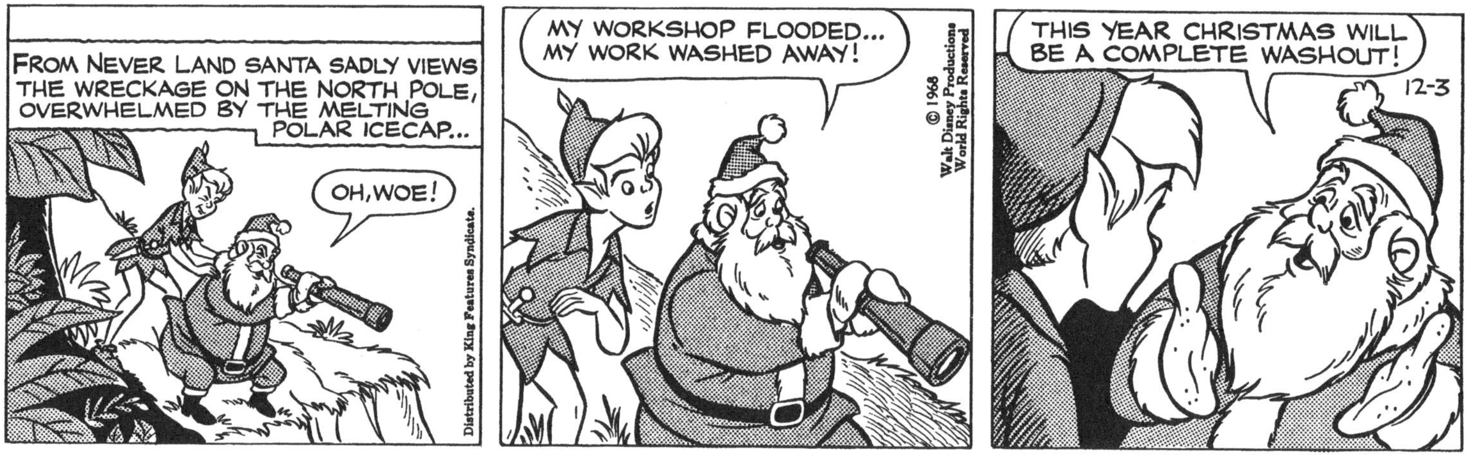
FROM NEVER LAND SANTA SADLY VIEWS THE WRECKAGE ON THE NORTH POLE, OVERWHELMED BY THE MELTING POLAR ICECAP...
OH, WOE!
Distributed by King Features Syndicate.
MY WORKSHOP FLOODED... MY WORK WASHED AWAY!
© 1968 Walt Disney Productions World Rights Reserved
THIS YEAR CHRISTMAS WILL BE A COMPLETE WASHOUT!
12-3

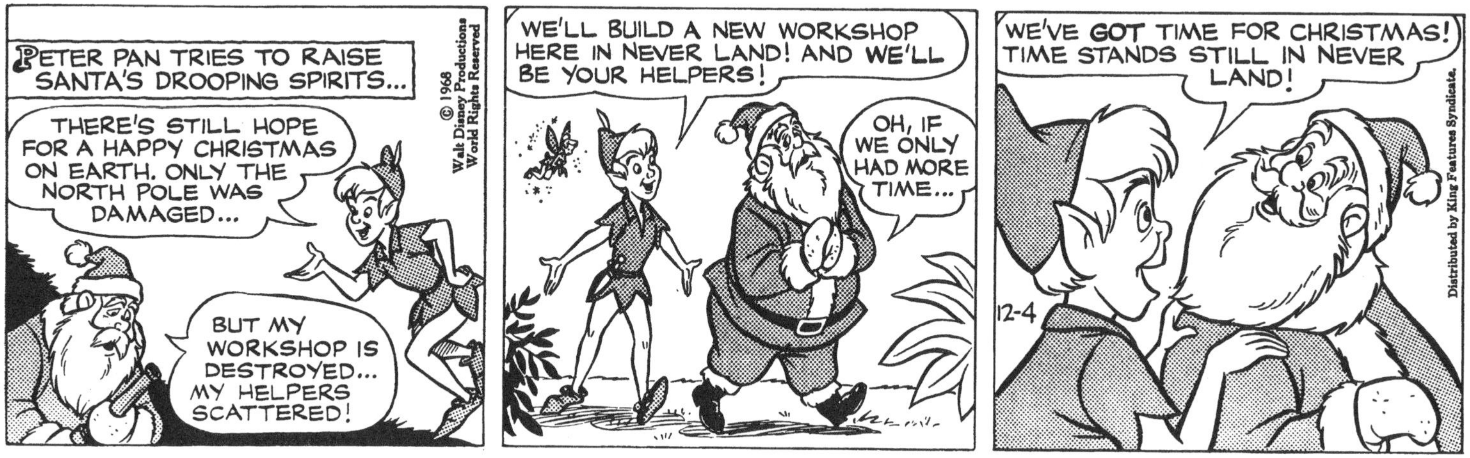
PETER PAN TRIES TO RAISE SANTA'S DROOPING SPIRITS...
THERE'S STILL HOPE FOR A HAPPY CHRISTMAS ON EARTH. ONLY THE NORTH POLE WAS DAMAGED...
BUT MY WORKSHOP IS DESTROYED... MY HELPERS SCATTERED!
© 1968 Walt Disney Productions World Rights Reserved
WE'LL BUILD A NEW WORKSHOP HERE IN NEVER LAND! AND WE'LL BE YOUR HELPERS!
OH, IF WE ONLY HAD MORE TIME...
WE'VE GOT TIME FOR CHRISTMAS! TIME STANDS STILL IN NEVER LAND!
12-4
Distributed by King Features Syndicate.

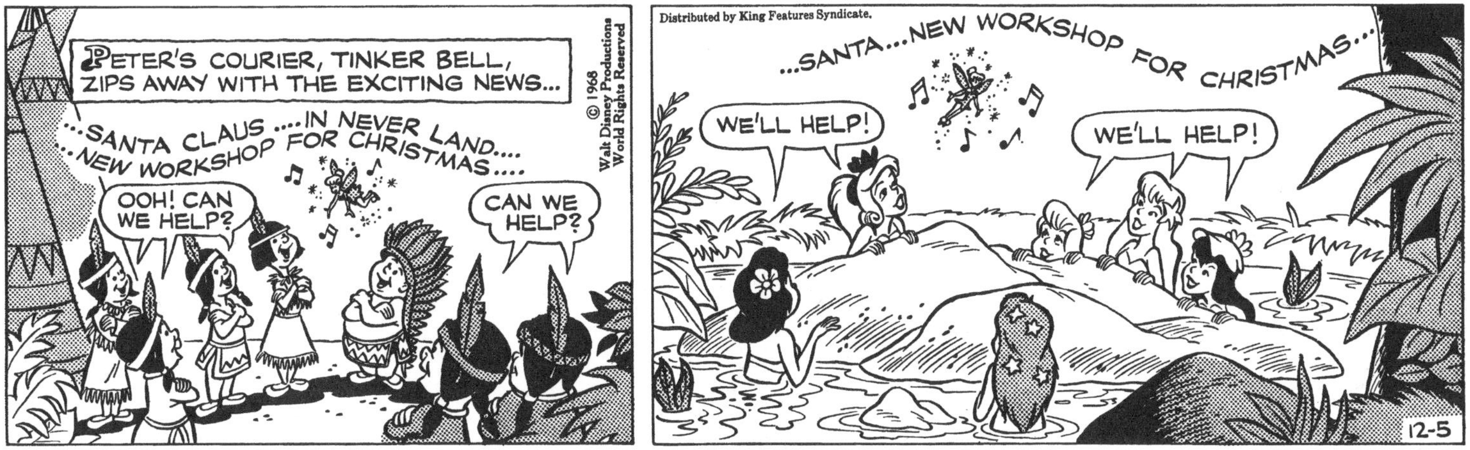
PETER'S COURIER, TINKER BELL, ZIPS AWAY WITH THE EXCITING NEWS...
...SANTA CLAUS ....IN NEVER LAND.... ...NEW WORKSHOP FOR CHRISTMAS....
OOH! CAN WE HELP?
CAN WE HELP?
© 1968 Walt Disney Productions World Rights Reserved
Distributed by King Features Syndicate.
...SANTA...NEW WORKSHOP FOR CHRISTMAS...
WE'LL HELP!
WE'LL HELP!
12-5

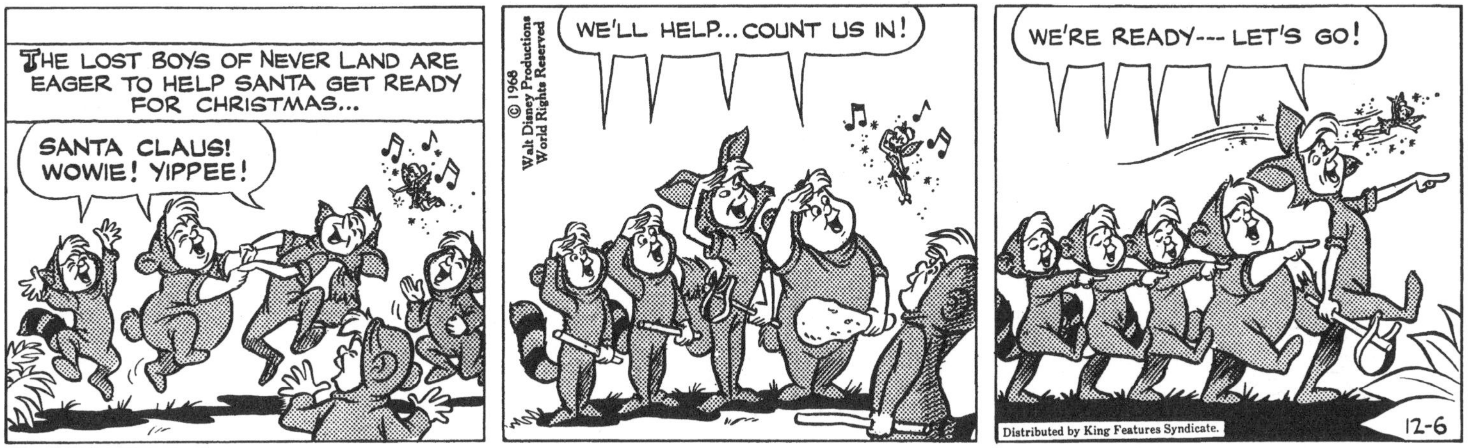
THE LOST BOYS OF NEVER LAND ARE EAGER TO HELP SANTA GET READY FOR CHRISTMAS...
SANTA CLAUS! WOWIE! YIPPEE!
© 1968 Walt Disney Productions World Rights Reserved
WE'LL HELP... COUNT US IN!
WE'RE READY--- LET'S GO!
Distributed by King Features Syndicate.
12-6

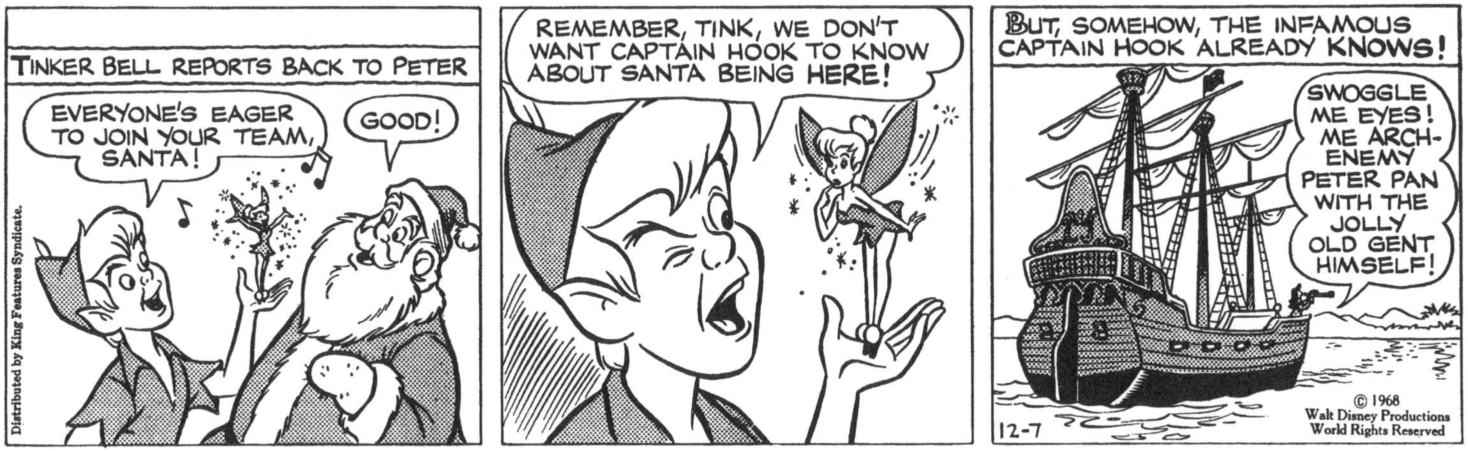
TINKER BELL REPORTS BACK TO PETER
EVERYONE'S EAGER TO JOIN YOUR TEAM, SANTA!
GOOD!
Distributed by King Features Syndicate.
REMEMBER, TINK, WE DON'T WANT CAPTAIN HOOK TO KNOW ABOUT SANTA BEING HERE!
BUT, SOMEHOW, THE INFAMOUS CAPTAIN HOOK ALREADY KNOWS!
SWOGGLE ME EYES! ME ARCH-ENEMY PETER PAN WITH THE JOLLY OLD GENT HIMSELF!
12-7
© 1968 Walt Disney Productions World Rights Reserved

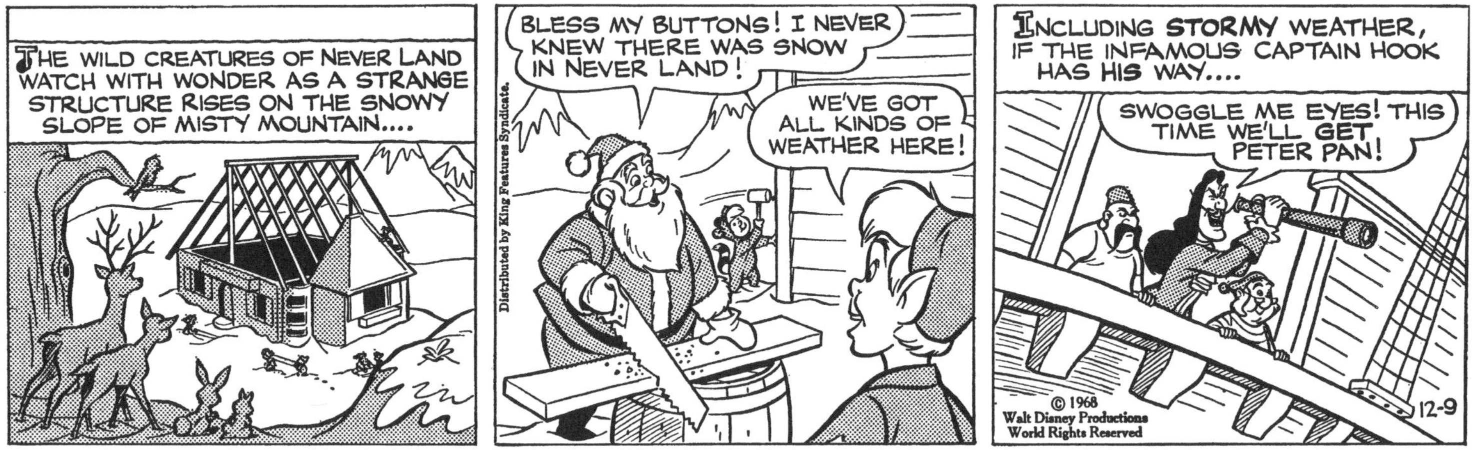
THE WILD CREATURES OF NEVER LAND WATCH WITH WONDER AS A STRANGE STRUCTURE RISES ON THE SNOWY SLOPE OF MISTY MOUNTAIN....
Distributed by King Features Syndicate.
BLESS MY BUTTONS! I NEVER KNEW THERE WAS SNOW IN NEVER LAND!
WE'VE GOT ALL KINDS OF WEATHER HERE!
INCLUDING STORMY WEATHER, IF THE INFAMOUS CAPTAIN HOOK HAS HIS WAY....
SWOGGLE ME EYES! THIS TIME WE'LL GET PETER PAN!
© 1968 Walt Disney Productions World Rights Reserved
12-9

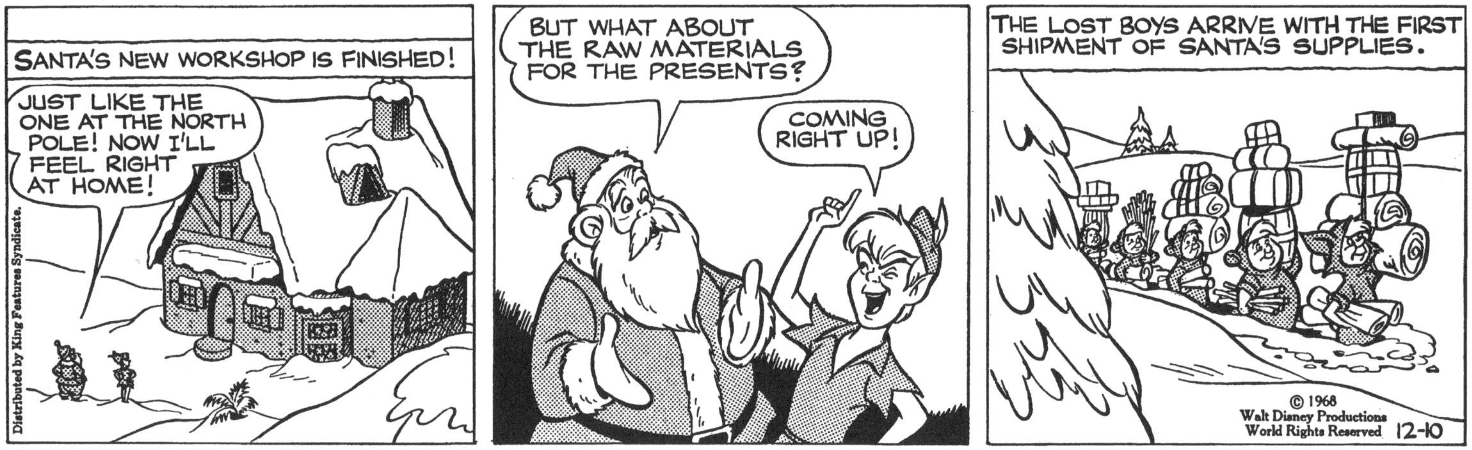
SANTA'S NEW WORKSHOP IS FINISHED!
JUST LIKE THE ONE AT THE NORTH POLE! NOW I'LL FEEL RIGHT AT HOME!
Distributed by King Features Syndicate.
BUT WHAT ABOUT THE RAW MATERIALS FOR THE PRESENTS?
COMING RIGHT UP!
THE LOST BOYS ARRIVE WITH THE FIRST SHIPMENT OF SANTA'S SUPPLIES.
© 1968 Walt Disney Productions World Rights Reserved
12-10

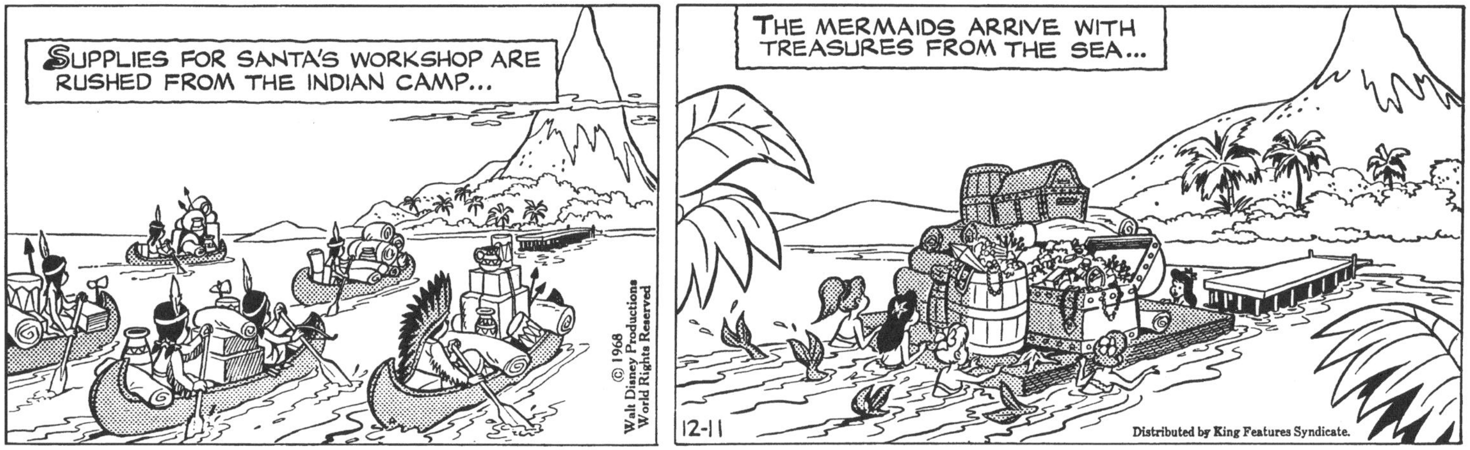
SUPPLIES FOR SANTA'S WORKSHOP ARE RUSHED FROM THE INDIAN CAMP...
© 1968 Walt Disney Productions World Rights Reserved
12-11
THE MERMAIDS ARRIVE WITH TREASURES FROM THE SEA...
Distributed by King Features Syndicate.

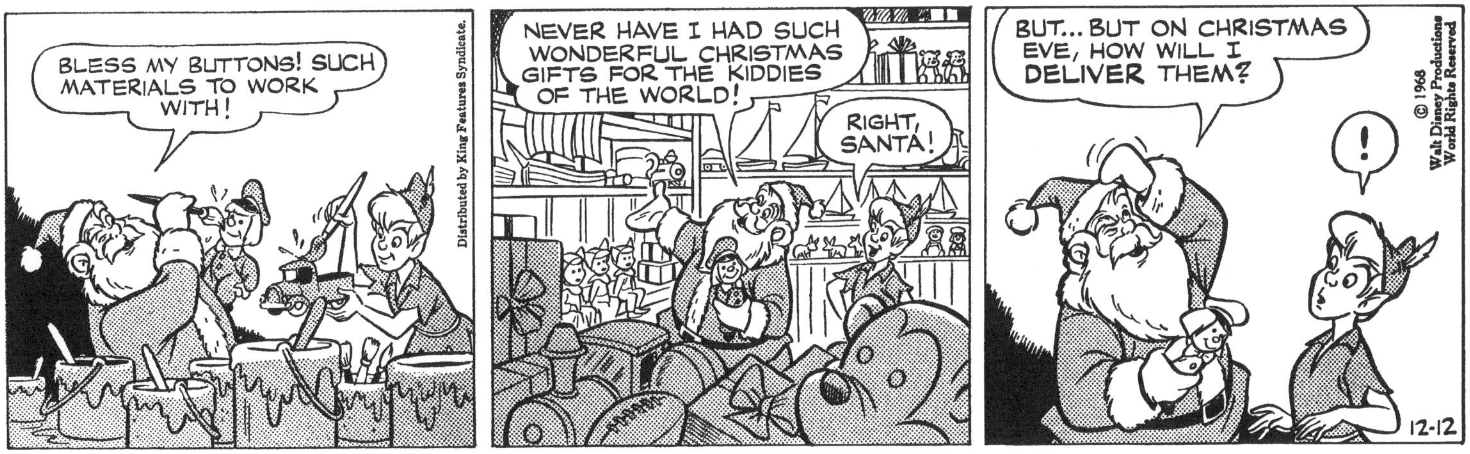
BLESS MY BUTTONS! SUCH MATERIALS TO WORK WITH!
Distributed by King Features Syndicate.
NEVER HAVE I HAD SUCH WONDERFUL CHRISTMAS GIFTS FOR THE KIDDIES OF THE WORLD!
RIGHT, SANTA!
BUT... BUT ON CHRISTMAS EVE, HOW WILL I DELIVER THEM?
!
© 1968 Walt Disney Productions World Rights Reserved
12-12

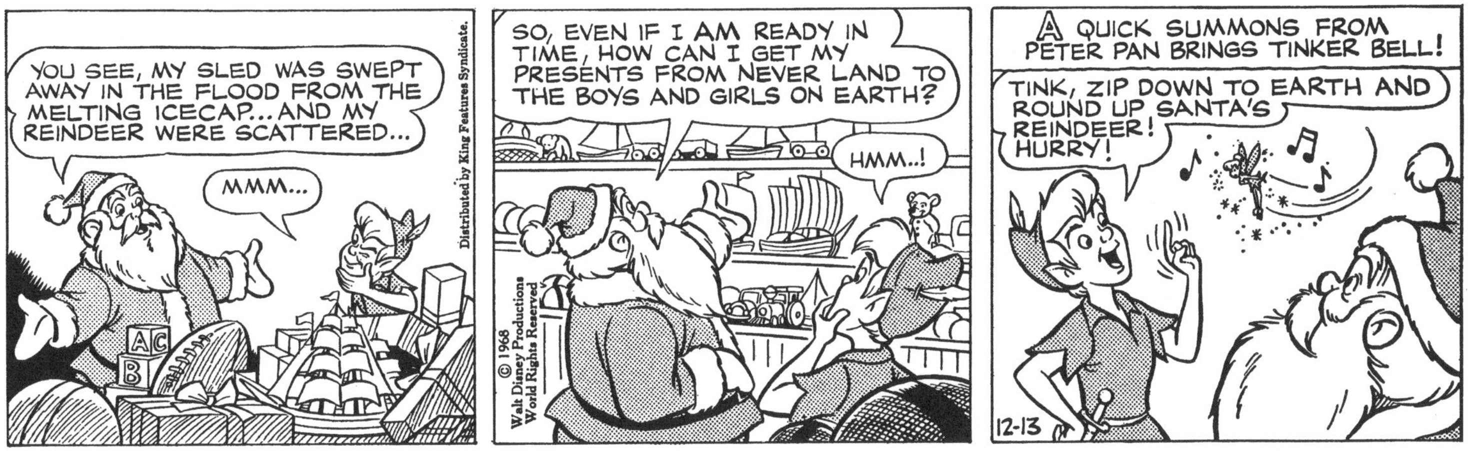
YOU SEE, MY SLED WAS SWEPT AWAY IN THE FLOOD FROM THE MELTING ICECAP... AND MY REINDEER WERE SCATTERED...
MMM...
Distributed by King Features Syndicate.
SO, EVEN IF I AM READY IN TIME, HOW CAN I GET MY PRESENTS FROM NEVER LAND TO THE BOYS AND GIRLS ON EARTH?
HMM..!
© 1968 Walt Disney Productions World Rights Reserved
A QUICK SUMMONS FROM PETER PAN BRINGS TINKER BELL!
TINK, ZIP DOWN TO EARTH AND ROUND UP SANTA'S REINDEER! HURRY!
12-13

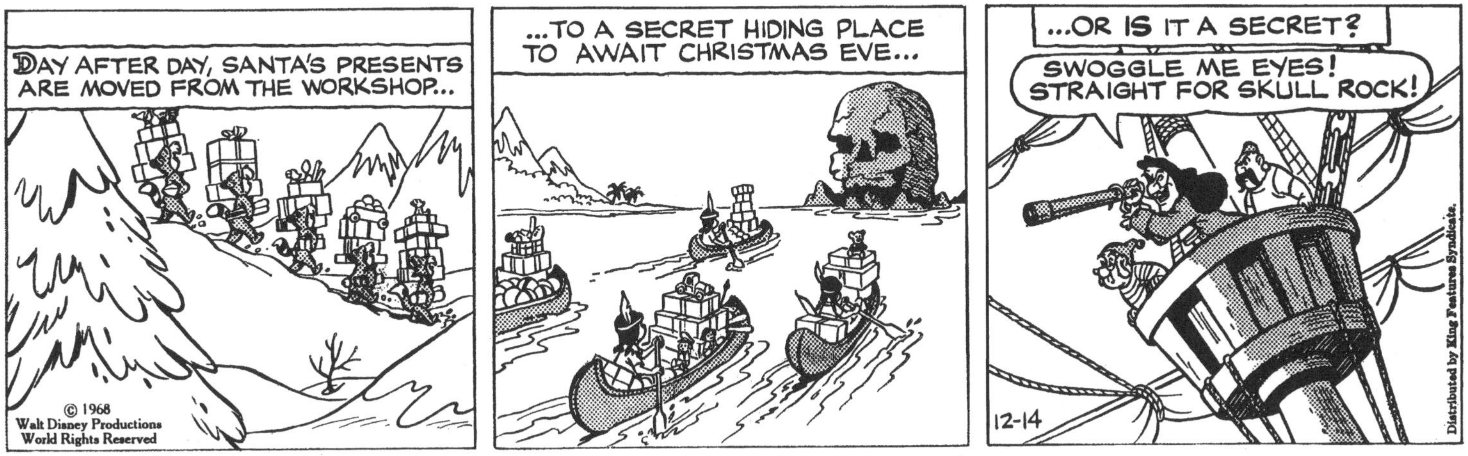
DAY AFTER DAY, SANTA'S PRESENTS ARE MOVED FROM THE WORKSHOP...
© 1968 Walt Disney Productions World Rights Reserved
...TO A SECRET HIDING PLACE TO AWAIT CHRISTMAS EVE...
...OR IS IT A SECRET?
SWOGGLE ME EYES! STRAIGHT FOR SKULL ROCK!
12-14
Distributed by King Features Syndicate.

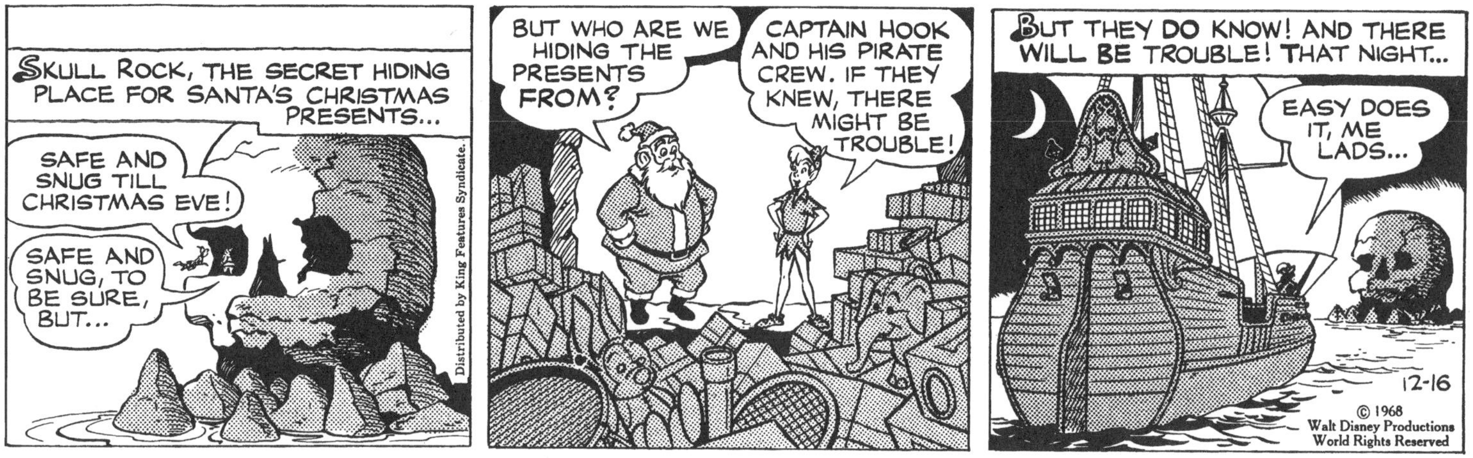
SKULL ROCK, THE SECRET HIDING PLACE FOR SANTA'S CHRISTMAS PRESENTS...
SAFE AND SNUG TILL CHRISTMAS EVE!
SAFE AND SNUG, TO BE SURE, BUT...
Distributed by King Features Syndicate.
BUT WHO ARE WE HIDING THE PRESENTS FROM?
CAPTAIN HOOK AND HIS PIRATE CREW. IF THEY KNEW, THERE MIGHT BE TROUBLE!
BUT THEY DO KNOW! AND THERE WILL BE TROUBLE! THAT NIGHT...
EASY DOES IT, ME LADS...
12-16
© 1968 Walt Disney Productions World Rights Reserved

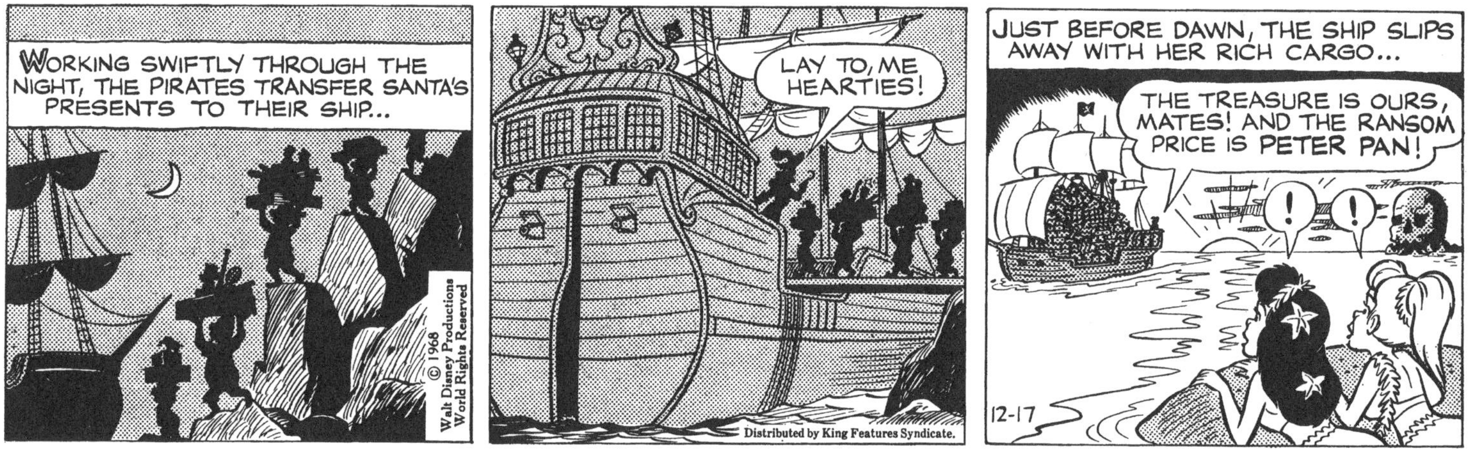
WORKING SWIFTLY THROUGH THE NIGHT, THE PIRATES TRANSFER SANTA'S PRESENTS TO THEIR SHIP...
© 1968 Walt Disney Productions World Rights Reserved
LAY TO, ME HEARTIES!
Distributed by King Features Syndicate.
JUST BEFORE DAWN, THE SHIP SLIPS AWAY WITH HER RICH CARGO...
THE TREASURE IS OURS, MATES! AND THE RANSOM PRICE IS PETER PAN!
!
!
12-17

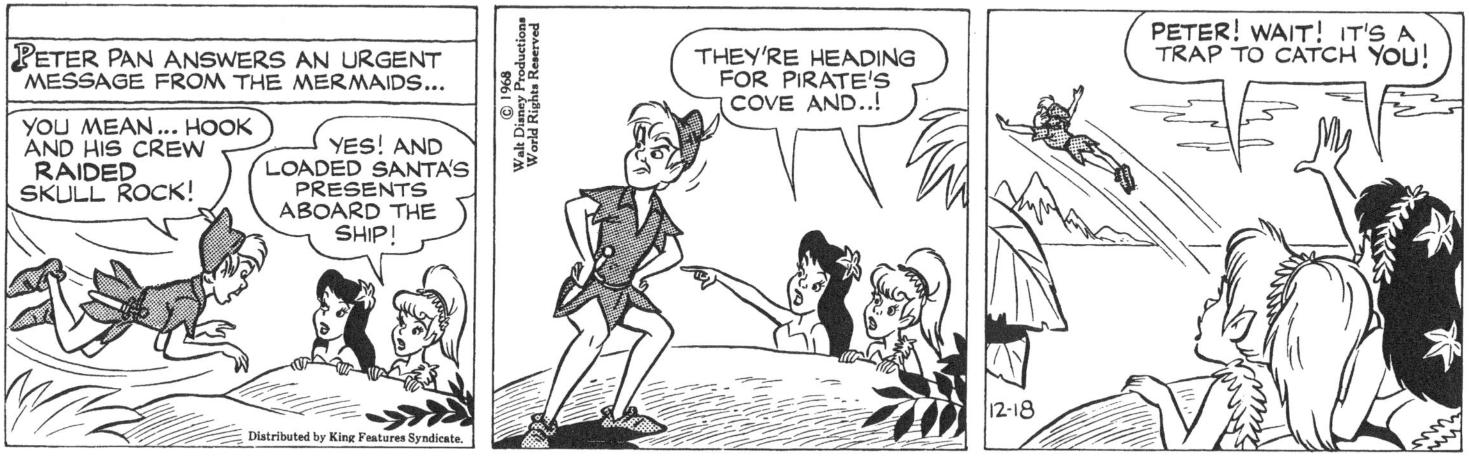
PETER PAN ANSWERS AN URGENT MESSAGE FROM THE MERMAIDS...
YOU MEAN... HOOK AND HIS CREW RAIDED SKULL ROCK!
YES! AND LOADED SANTA'S PRESENTS ABOARD THE SHIP!
Distributed by King Features Syndicate.
© 1968 Walt Disney Productions World Rights Reserved
THEY'RE HEADING FOR PIRATE'S COVE AND...!
PETER! WAIT! IT'S A TRAP TO CATCH YOU!
12-18

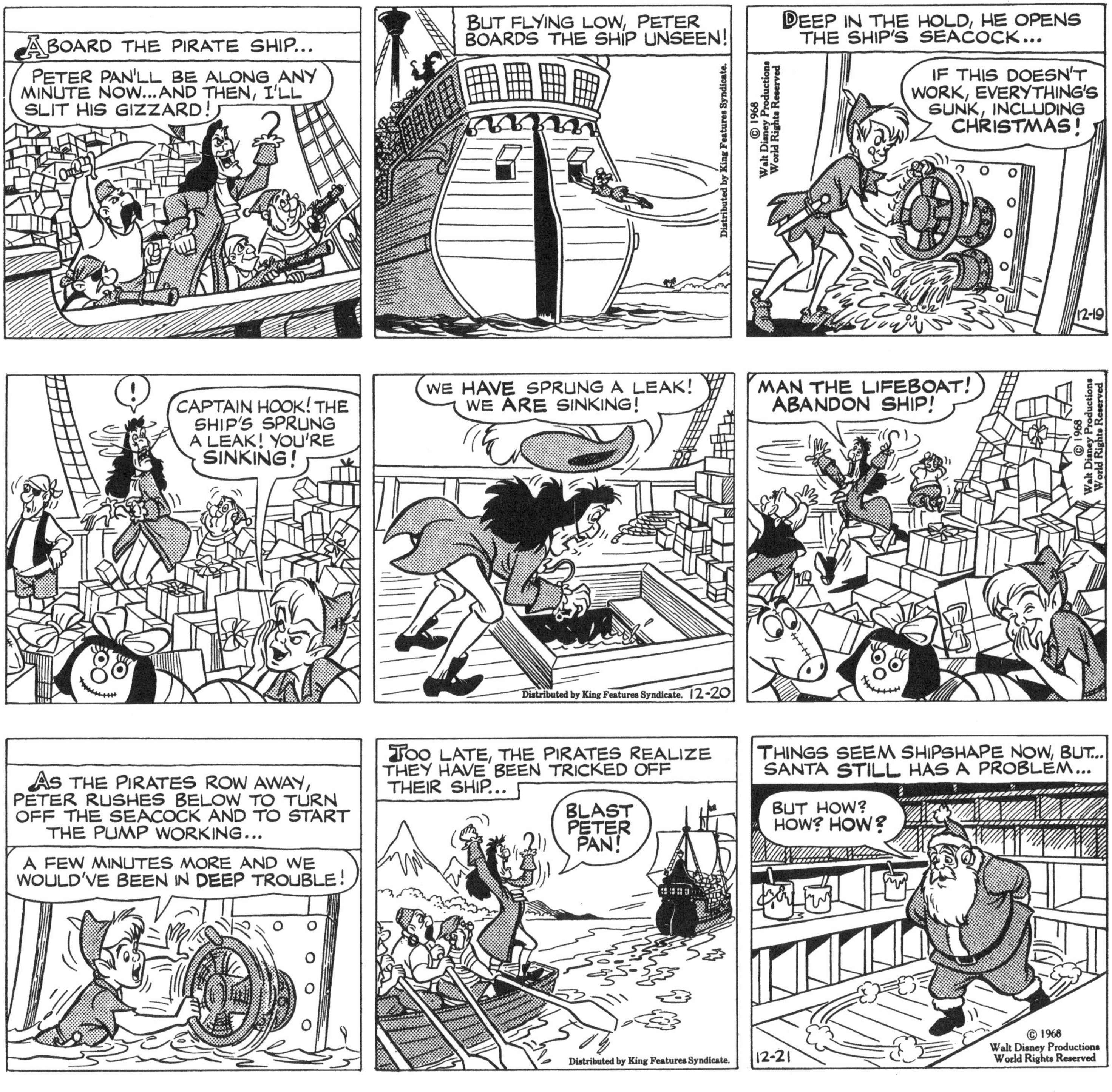
ABOARD THE PIRATE SHIP...
PETER PAN'LL BE ALONG ANY MINUTE NOW...AND THEN, I'LL SLIT HIS GIZZARD!
BUT FLYING LOW, PETER BOARDS THE SHIP UNSEEN!
Distributed by King Features Syndicate.
DEEP IN THE HOLD, HE OPENS THE SHIP'S SEACOCK...
© 1968 Walt Disney Productions World Rights Reserved
IF THIS DOESN'T WORK, EVERYTHING'S SUNK, INCLUDING CHRISTMAS!
12-19
!
CAPTAIN HOOK! THE SHIP'S SPRUNG A LEAK! YOU'RE SINKING!
WE HAVE SPRUNG A LEAK! WE ARE SINKING!
Distributed by King Features Syndicate. 12-20
MAN THE LIFEBOAT! ABANDON SHIP!
© 1968 Walt Disney Productions World Rights Reserved
AS THE PIRATES ROW AWAY, PETER RUSHES BELOW TO TURN OFF THE SEACOCK AND TO START THE PUMP WORKING...
A FEW MINUTES MORE AND WE WOULD'VE BEEN IN DEEP TROUBLE!
TOO LATE, THE PIRATES REALIZE THEY HAVE BEEN TRICKED OFF THEIR SHIP...
BLAST PETER PAN!
Distributed by King Features Syndicate.
THINGS SEEM SHIPSHAPE NOW, BUT... SANTA STILL HAS A PROBLEM...
BUT HOW? HOW? HOW?
12-21
© 1968 Walt Disney Productions World Rights Reserved

Distributed by King Features Syndicate.
AS SANTA BOARDS THE SHIP, TINKER BELL ARRIVES WITH THE LOST REINDEER...
BLESS MY BUTTONS!
© 1968 Walt Disney Productions World Rights Reserved
BUT... BUT WHAT'LL I CARRY THE PRESENTS IN?
YOU'RE STANDING ON IT-- THIS SHIP!
12-23
JUST SPRINKLE HER WITH PIXIE DUST... AND SHE'LL FLY-FLY-FLY!

TRANSFORMED BY PIXIE DUST INTO A GOLDEN SPACE SHIP, THE PIRATE CRAFT IS READY FOR ITS CHRISTMAS CRUISE...
THANKS, PETER AND EVERYBODY, FOR EVERYTHING!
Distributed by King Features Syndicate.
AND AWAY HE GOES!
AND A MERRY CHRISTMAS TO EVERYONE EVERYWHERE!
© 1968 Walt Disney Productions World Rights Reserved
12-24

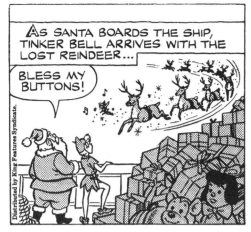

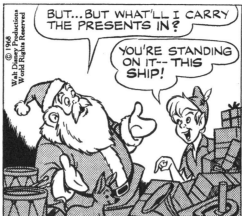

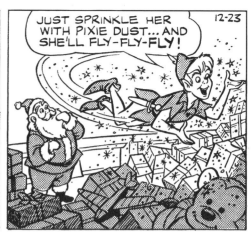

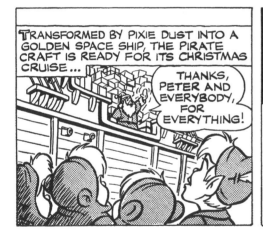

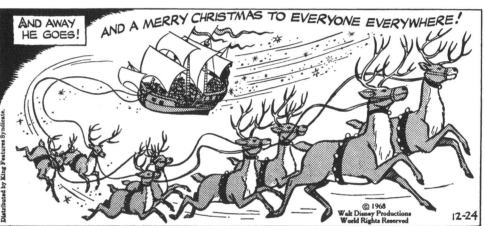

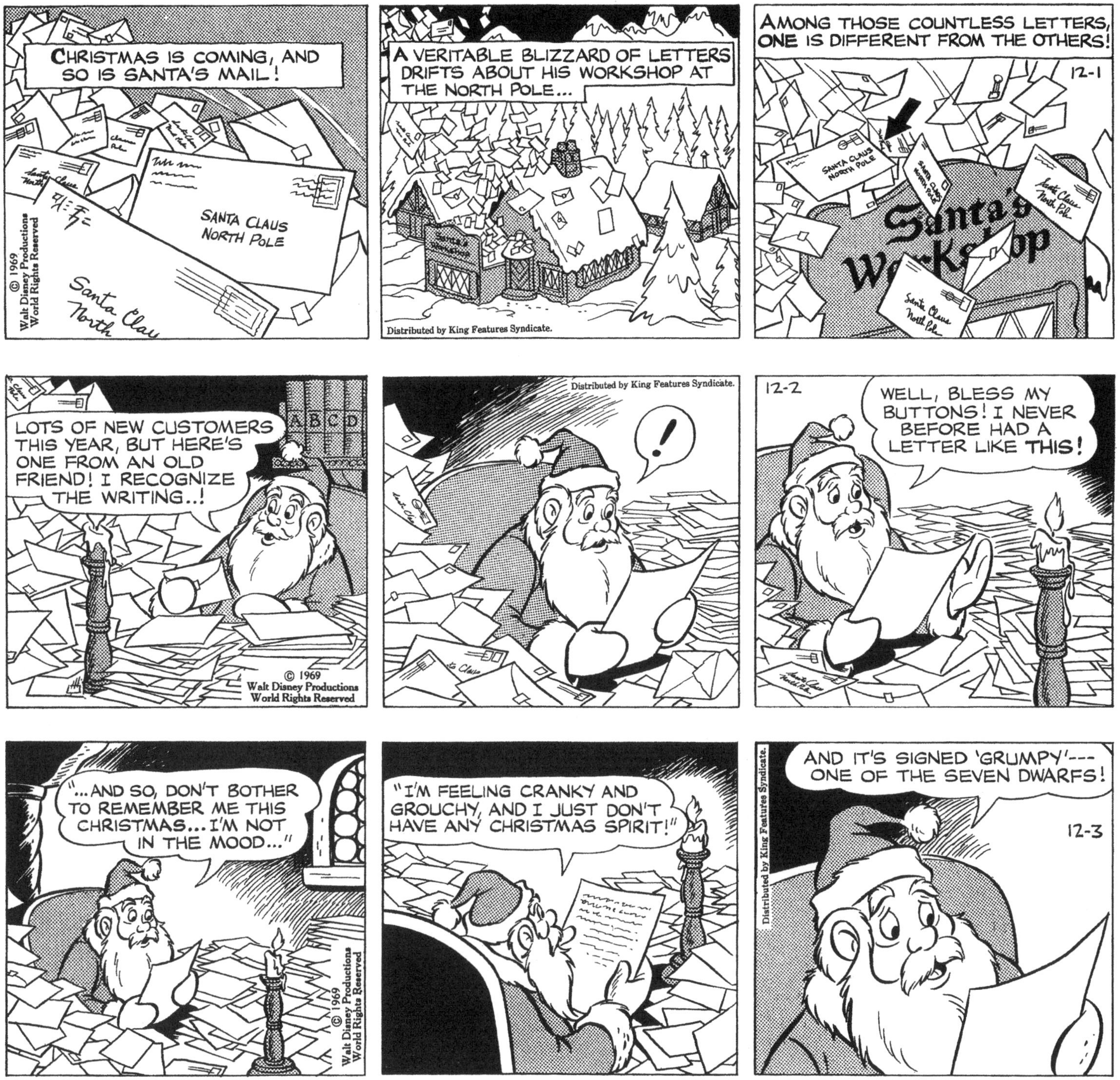
CHRISTMAS IS COMING, AND SO IS SANTA'S MAIL!
SANTA CLAUS NORTH POLE
© 1969 Walt Disney Productions World Rights Reserved
A VERITABLE BLIZZARD OF LETTERS DRIFTS ABOUT HIS WORKSHOP AT THE NORTH POLE...
Distributed by King Features Syndicate.
AMONG THOSE COUNTLESS LETTERS, ONE IS DIFFERENT FROM THE OTHERS!
12-1
SANTA CLAUS NORTH POLE
Santa's Workshop
LOTS OF NEW CUSTOMERS THIS YEAR, BUT HERE'S ONE FROM AN OLD FRIEND! I RECOGNIZE THE WRITING..!
A B C D
© 1969 Walt Disney Productions World Rights Reserved
Distributed by King Features Syndicate.
!
12-2
WELL, BLESS MY BUTTONS! I NEVER BEFORE HAD A LETTER LIKE THIS!
"...AND SO, DON'T BOTHER TO REMEMBER ME THIS CHRISTMAS... I'M NOT IN THE MOOD..."
© 1969 Walt Disney Productions World Rights Reserved
"I'M FEELING CRANKY AND GROUCHY, AND I JUST DON'T HAVE ANY CHRISTMAS SPIRIT!"
Distributed by King Features Syndicate.
AND IT'S SIGNED 'GRUMPY'--- ONE OF THE SEVEN DWARFS!
12-3

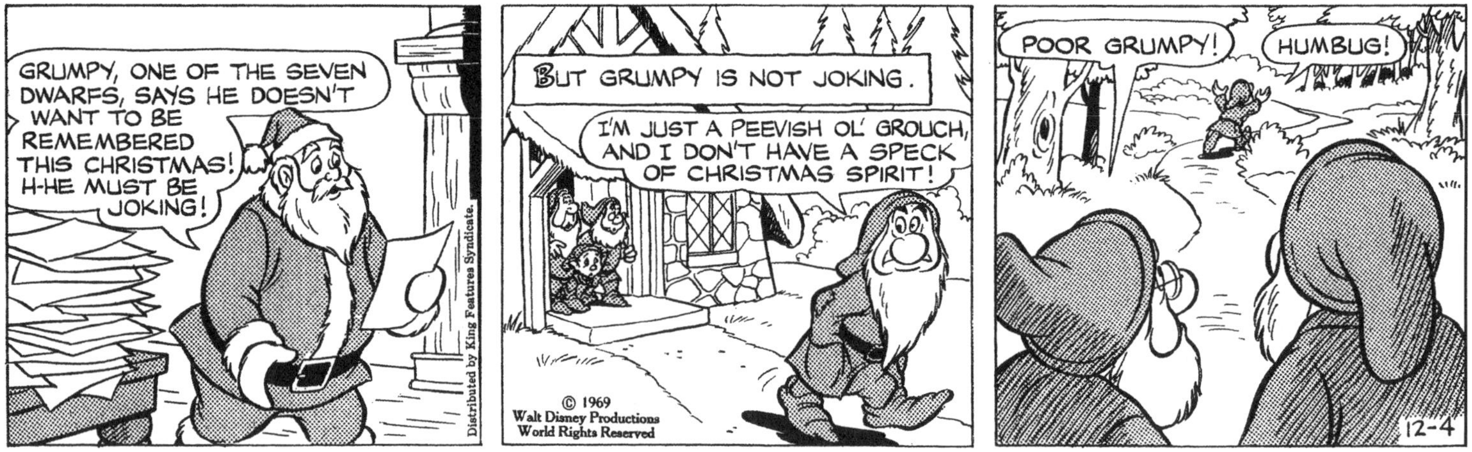
GRUMPY, ONE OF THE SEVEN DWARFS, SAYS HE DOESN'T WANT TO BE REMEMBERED THIS CHRISTMAS! H-HE MUST BE JOKING!
Distributed by King Features Syndicate.
BUT GRUMPY IS NOT JOKING.
I'M JUST A PEEVISH OL' GROUCH, AND I DON'T HAVE A SPECK OF CHRISTMAS SPIRIT!
© 1969
Walt Disney Productions
World Rights Reserved
POOR GRUMPY!
HUMBUG!
12-4

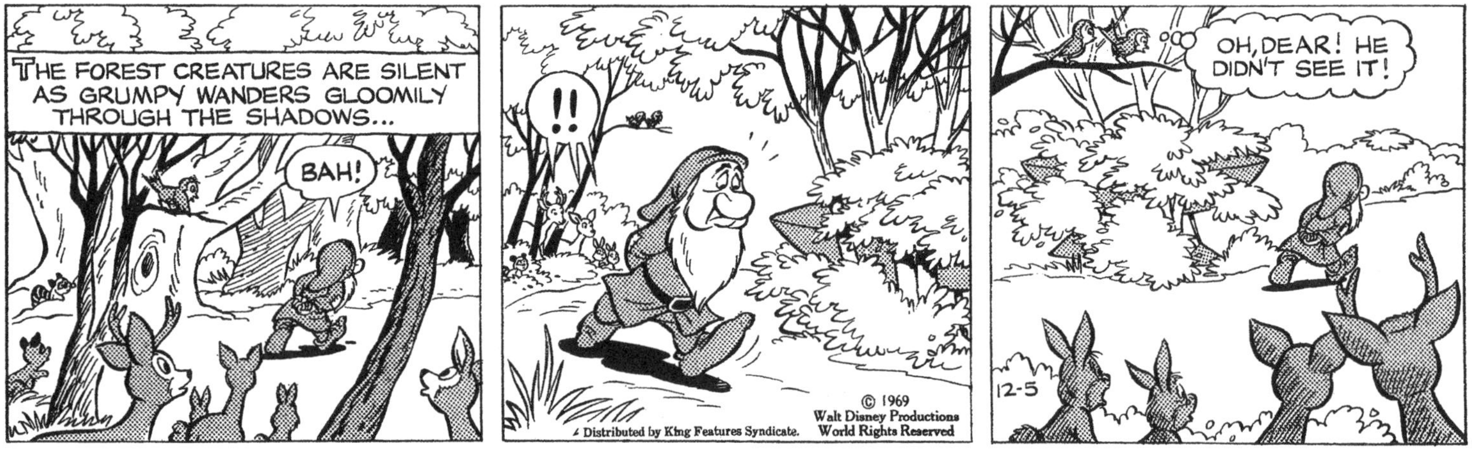
THE FOREST CREATURES ARE SILENT AS GRUMPY WANDERS GLOOMILY THROUGH THE SHADOWS...
BAH!
!!
© 1969
Walt Disney Productions
World Rights Reserved
Distributed by King Features Syndicate.
OH, DEAR! HE DIDN'T SEE IT!
12-5

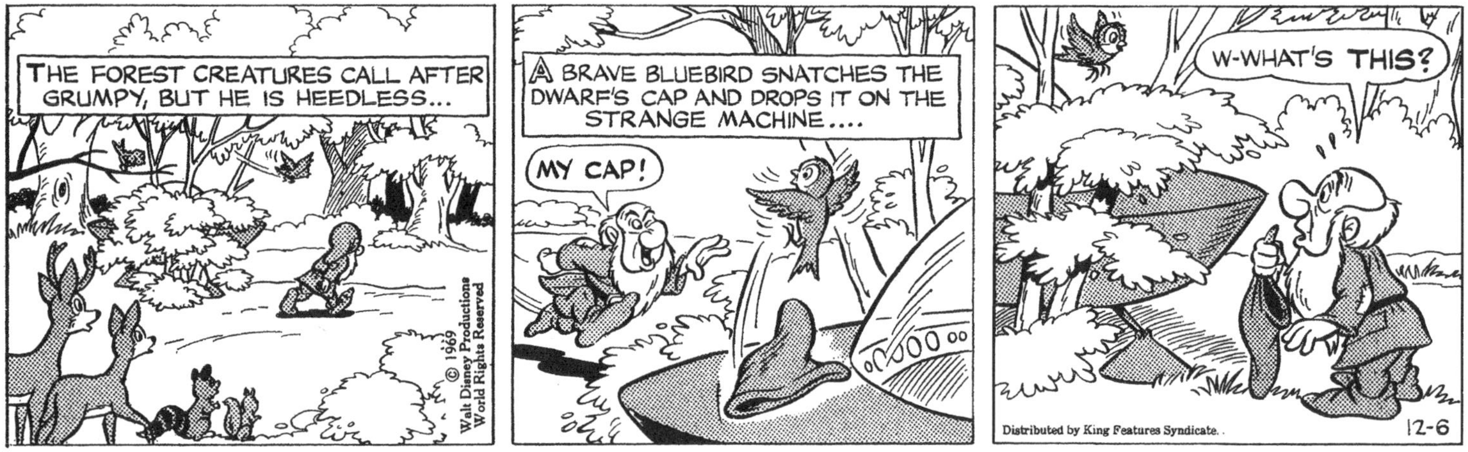
THE FOREST CREATURES CALL AFTER GRUMPY, BUT HE IS HEEDLESS...
© 1969
Walt Disney Productions
World Rights Reserved
A BRAVE BLUEBIRD SNATCHES THE DWARF'S CAP AND DROPS IT ON THE STRANGE MACHINE....
MY CAP!
W-WHAT'S THIS?
Distributed by King Features Syndicate.
12-6

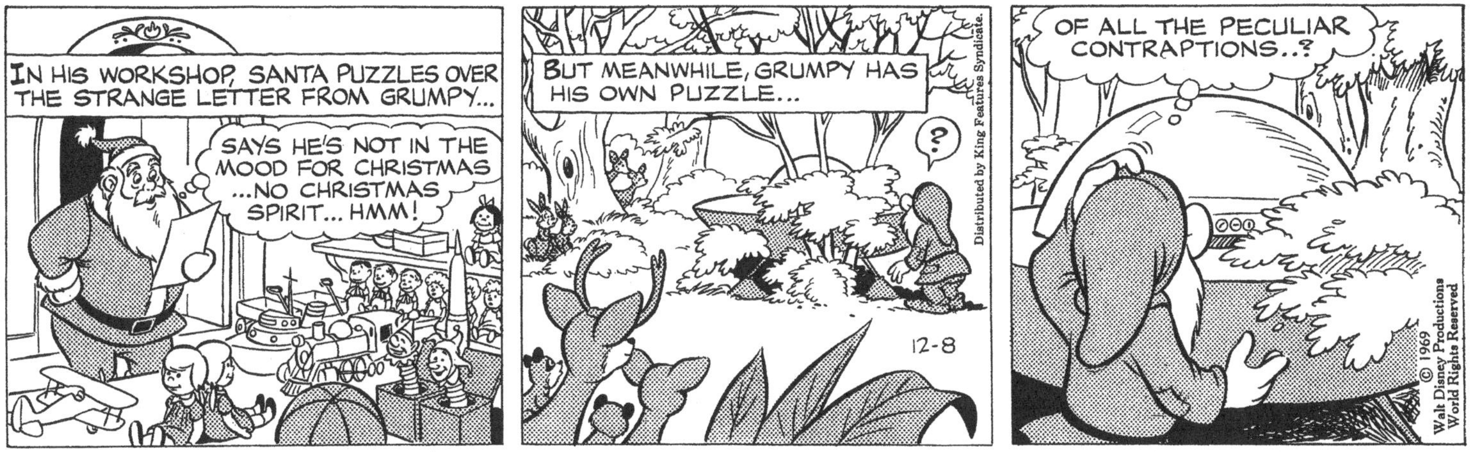
IN HIS WORKSHOP, SANTA PUZZLES OVER THE STRANGE LETTER FROM GRUMPY...
SAYS HE'S NOT IN THE MOOD FOR CHRISTMAS ...NO CHRISTMAS SPIRIT... HMM!
BUT MEANWHILE, GRUMPY HAS HIS OWN PUZZLE...
?
Distributed by King Features Syndicate.
12-8
OF ALL THE PECULIAR CONTRAPTIONS..?
© 1969 Walt Disney Productions World Rights Reserved

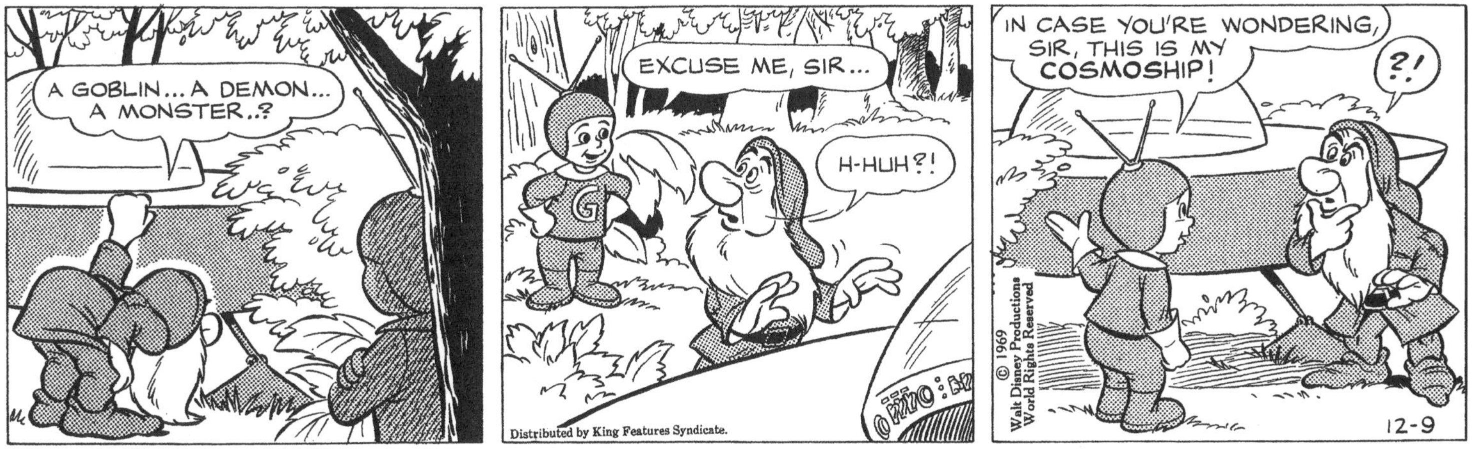
A GOBLIN... A DEMON... A MONSTER..?
EXCUSE ME, SIR...
H-HUH?!
Distributed by King Features Syndicate.
IN CASE YOU'RE WONDERING, SIR, THIS IS MY COSMOSHIP!
?!
© 1969 Walt Disney Productions World Rights Reserved
12-9

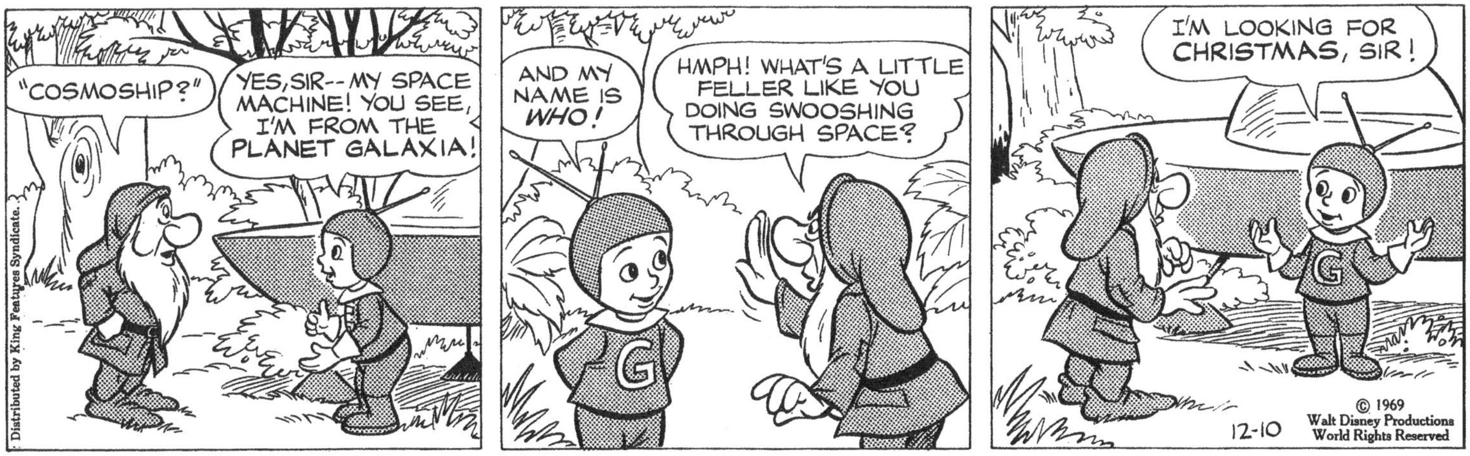
"COSMOSHIP?"
YES, SIR-- MY SPACE MACHINE! YOU SEE, I'M FROM THE PLANET GALAXIA!
Distributed by King Features Syndicate.
AND MY NAME IS WHO!
HMPH! WHAT'S A LITTLE FELLER LIKE YOU DOING SWOOSHING THROUGH SPACE?
I'M LOOKING FOR CHRISTMAS, SIR!
© 1969 Walt Disney Productions World Rights Reserved
12-10

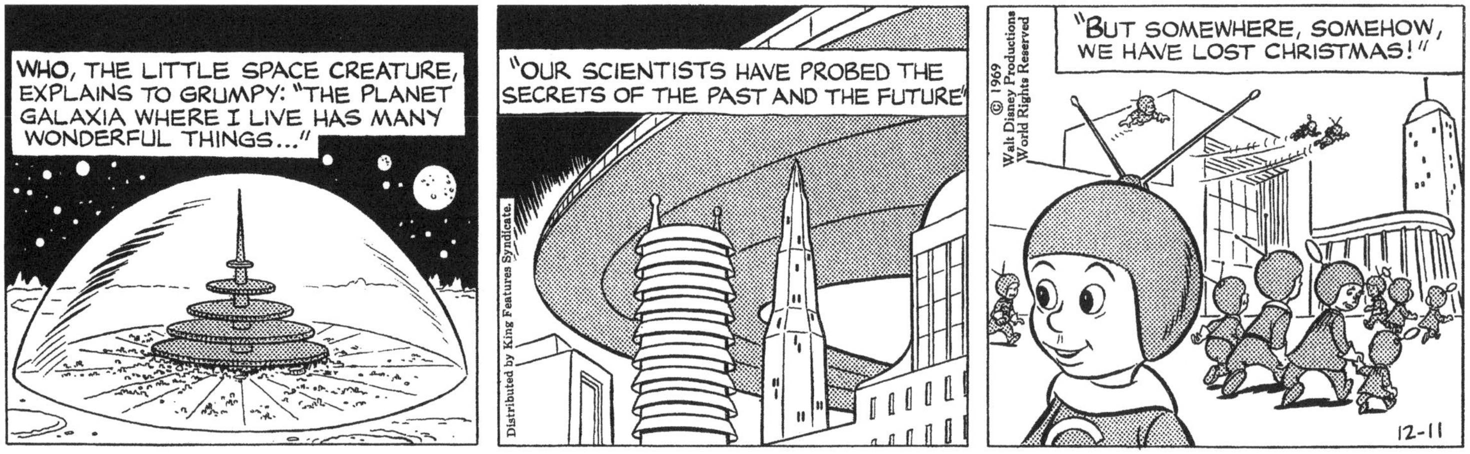
WHO, THE LITTLE SPACE CREATURE, EXPLAINS TO GRUMPY: "THE PLANET GALAXIA WHERE I LIVE HAS MANY WONDERFUL THINGS..."
"OUR SCIENTISTS HAVE PROBED THE SECRETS OF THE PAST AND THE FUTURE"
Distributed by King Features Syndicate.
"BUT SOMEWHERE, SOMEHOW, WE HAVE LOST CHRISTMAS!"
© 1969 Walt Disney Productions World Rights Reserved
12-11

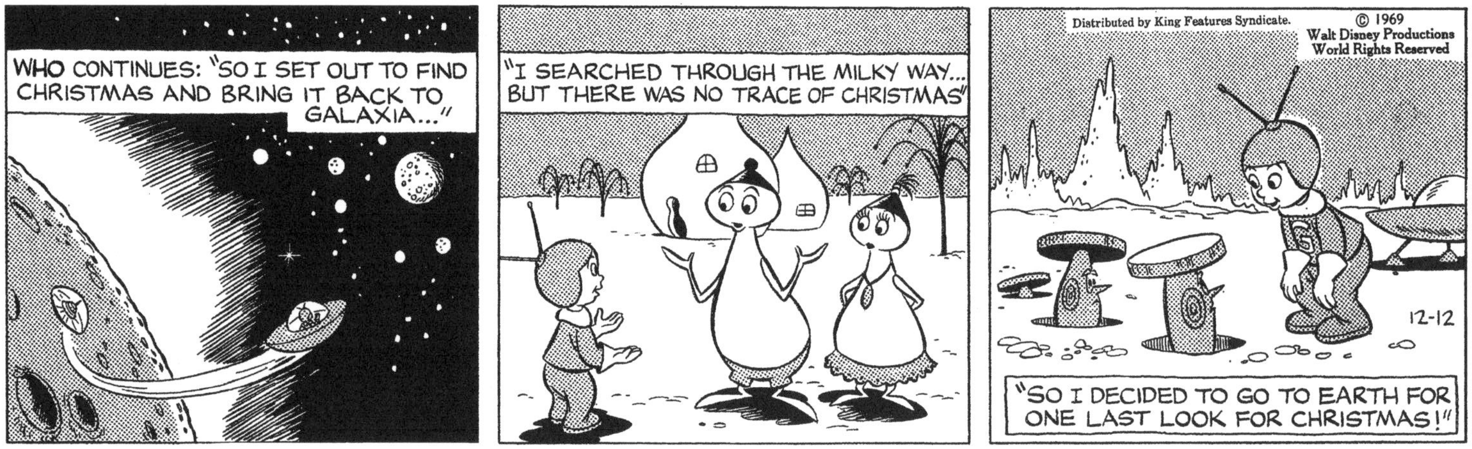
WHO CONTINUES: "SO I SET OUT TO FIND CHRISTMAS AND BRING IT BACK TO GALAXIA..."
"I SEARCHED THROUGH THE MILKY WAY... BUT THERE WAS NO TRACE OF CHRISTMAS"
Distributed by King Features Syndicate.
© 1969 Walt Disney Productions World Rights Reserved
12-12
"SO I DECIDED TO GO TO EARTH FOR ONE LAST LOOK FOR CHRISTMAS!"

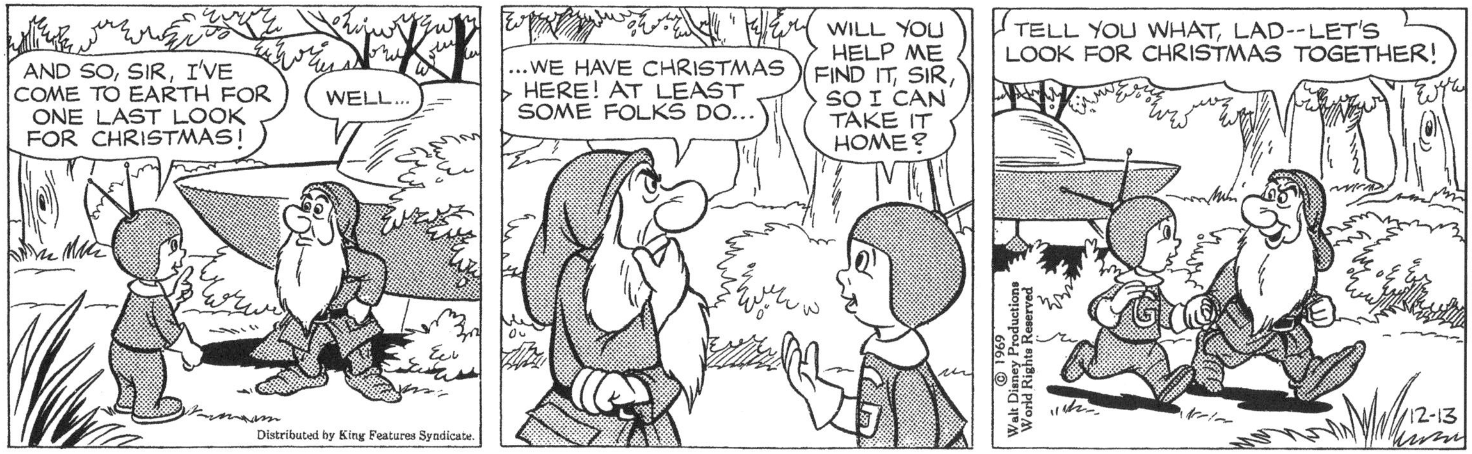
AND SO, SIR, I'VE COME TO EARTH FOR ONE LAST LOOK FOR CHRISTMAS!
WELL...
Distributed by King Features Syndicate.
...WE HAVE CHRISTMAS HERE! AT LEAST SOME FOLKS DO...
WILL YOU HELP ME FIND IT, SIR, SO I CAN TAKE IT HOME?
TELL YOU WHAT, LAD--LET'S LOOK FOR CHRISTMAS TOGETHER!
© 1969 Walt Disney Productions World Rights Reserved
12-13

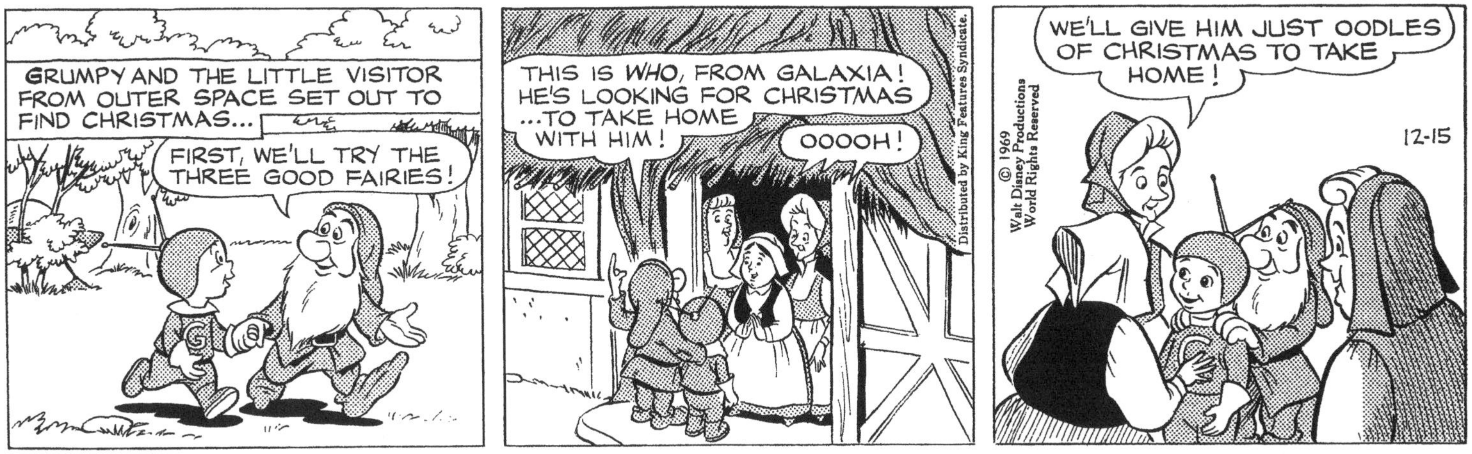
GRUMPY AND THE LITTLE VISITOR FROM OUTER SPACE SET OUT TO FIND CHRISTMAS...
FIRST, WE'LL TRY THE THREE GOOD FAIRIES!
THIS IS *WHO*, FROM GALAXIA! HE'S LOOKING FOR CHRISTMAS ...TO TAKE HOME WITH HIM!
OOOOH!
Distributed by King Features Syndicate.
WE'LL GIVE HIM JUST OODLES OF CHRISTMAS TO TAKE HOME!
© 1969 Walt Disney Productions World Rights Reserved
12-15

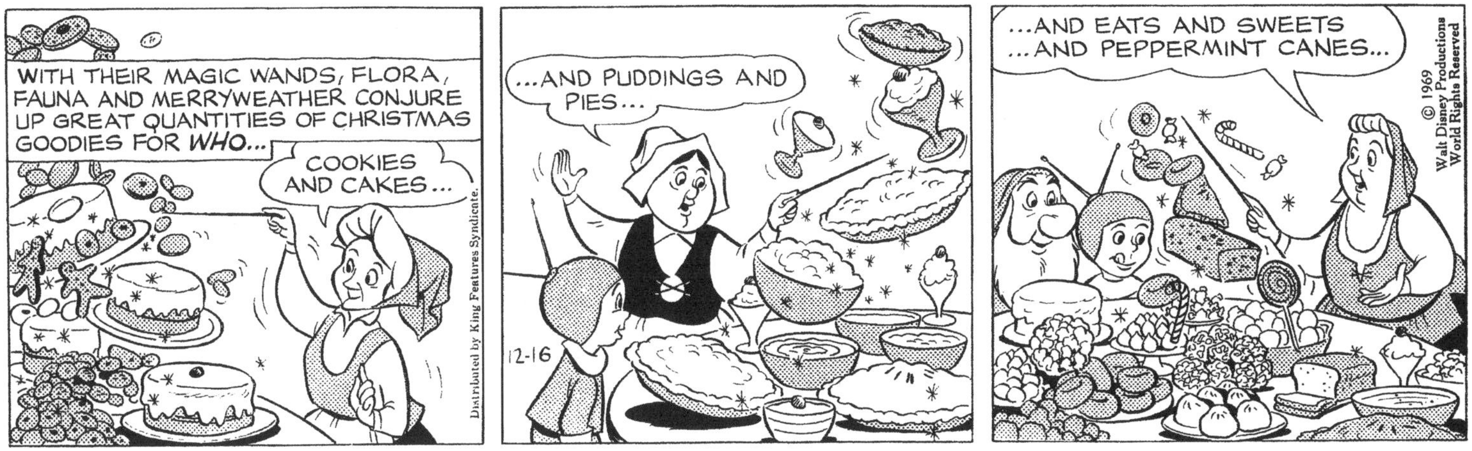
WITH THEIR MAGIC WANDS, FLORA, FAUNA AND MERRYWEATHER CONJURE UP GREAT QUANTITIES OF CHRISTMAS GOODIES FOR *WHO*...
COOKIES AND CAKES...
Distributed by King Features Syndicate.
...AND PUDDINGS AND PIES...
12-16
...AND EATS AND SWEETS ...AND PEPPERMINT CANES...
© 1969 Walt Disney Productions World Rights Reserved

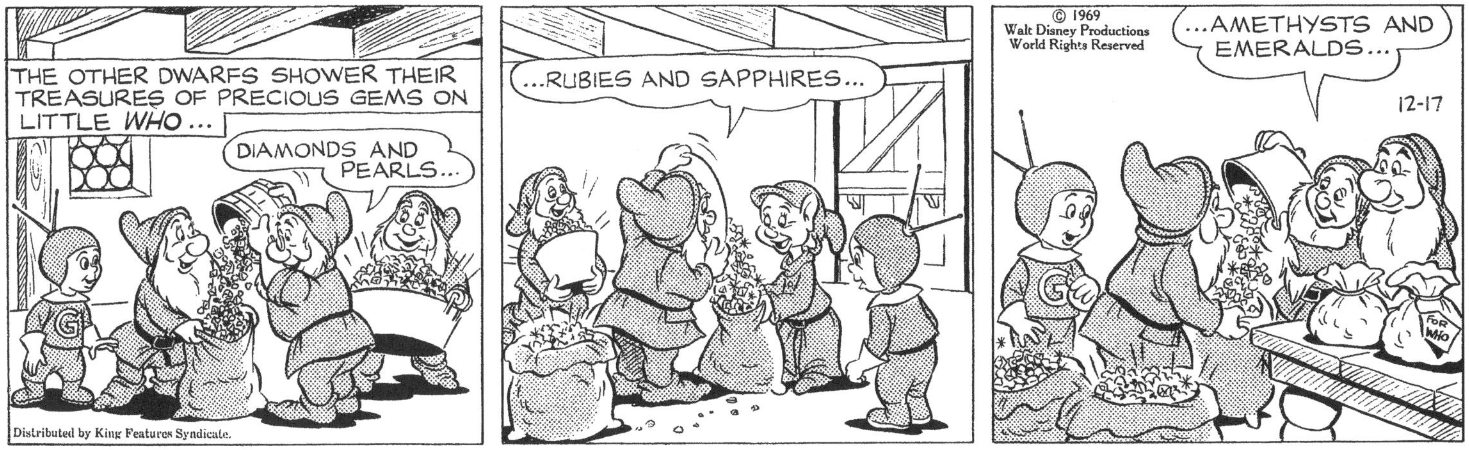
THE OTHER DWARFS SHOWER THEIR TREASURES OF PRECIOUS GEMS ON LITTLE *WHO*...
DIAMONDS AND PEARLS...
Distributed by King Features Syndicate.
...RUBIES AND SAPPHIRES...
© 1969 Walt Disney Productions World Rights Reserved
...AMETHYSTS AND EMERALDS...
12-17
FOR WHO

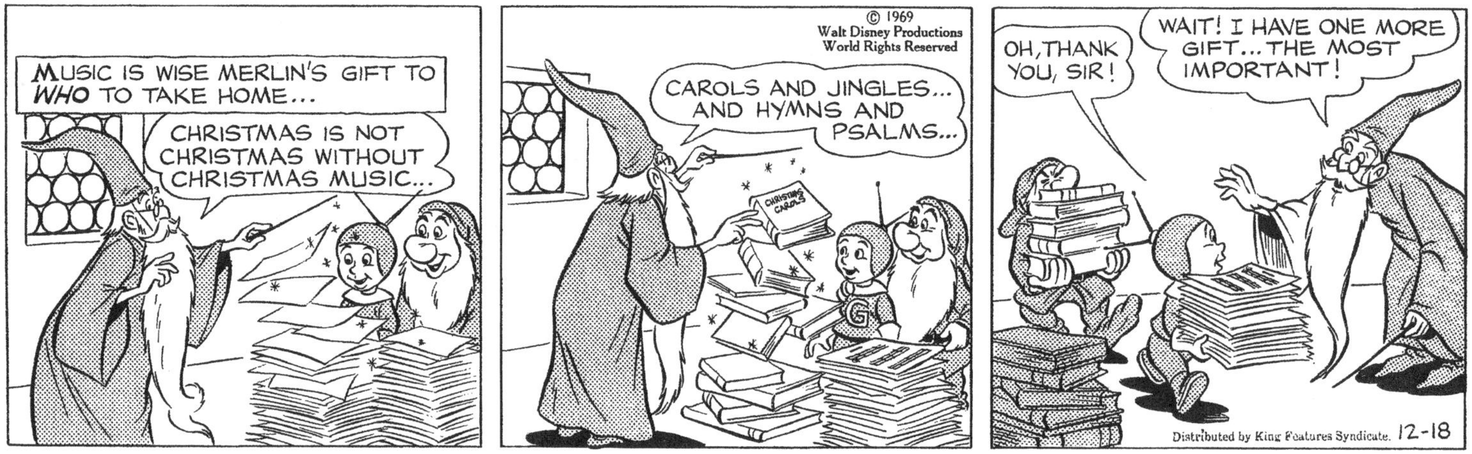
MUSIC IS WISE MERLIN'S GIFT TO *WHO* TO TAKE HOME...
CHRISTMAS IS NOT CHRISTMAS WITHOUT CHRISTMAS MUSIC...
© 1969 Walt Disney Productions World Rights Reserved
CAROLS AND JINGLES... AND HYMNS AND PSALMS...
CHRISTMAS CAROLS
OH, THANK YOU, SIR!
WAIT! I HAVE ONE MORE GIFT... THE MOST IMPORTANT!
Distributed by King Features Syndicate. 12-18

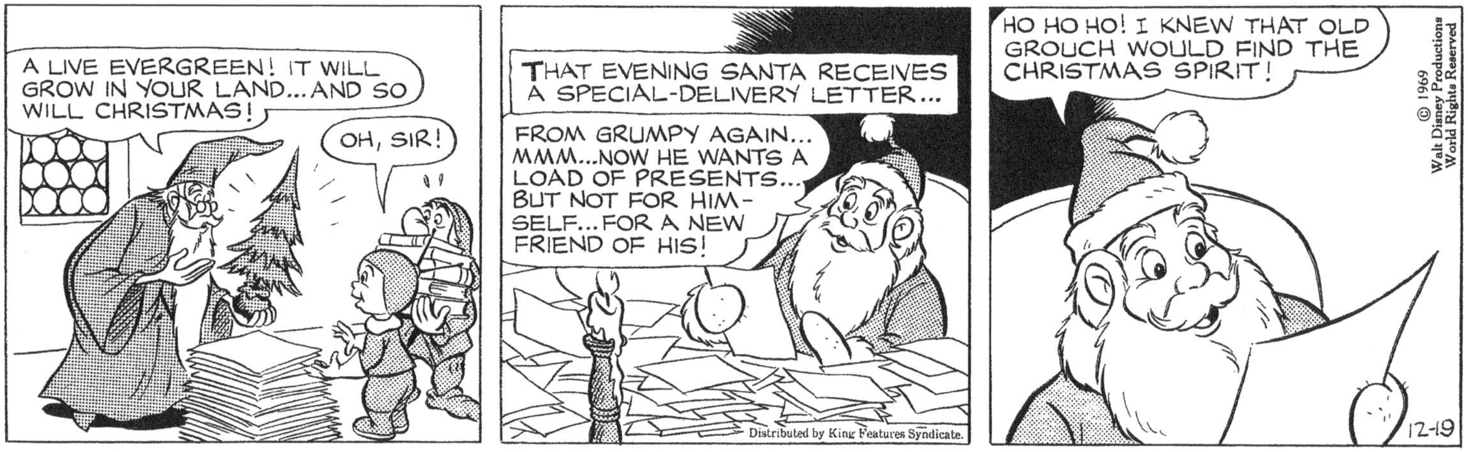
A LIVE EVERGREEN! IT WILL GROW IN YOUR LAND...AND SO WILL CHRISTMAS!
OH, SIR!
THAT EVENING SANTA RECEIVES A SPECIAL-DELIVERY LETTER...
FROM GRUMPY AGAIN... MMM...NOW HE WANTS A LOAD OF PRESENTS... BUT NOT FOR HIMSELF...FOR A NEW FRIEND OF HIS!
Distributed by King Features Syndicate.
HO HO HO! I KNEW THAT OLD GROUCH WOULD FIND THE CHRISTMAS SPIRIT!
© 1969 Walt Disney Productions World Rights Reserved
12-19

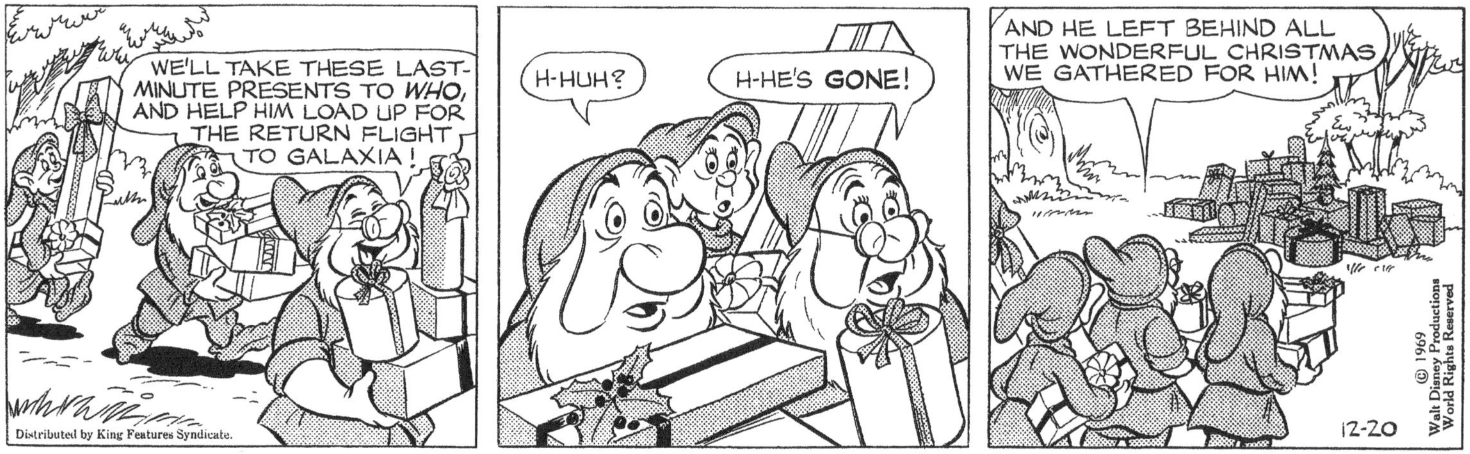
WE'LL TAKE THESE LAST-MINUTE PRESENTS TO *WHO*, AND HELP HIM LOAD UP FOR THE RETURN FLIGHT TO GALAXIA!
Distributed by King Features Syndicate.
H-HUH?
H-HE'S **GONE**!
AND HE LEFT BEHIND ALL THE WONDERFUL CHRISTMAS WE GATHERED FOR HIM!
© 1969 Walt Disney Productions World Rights Reserved
12-20

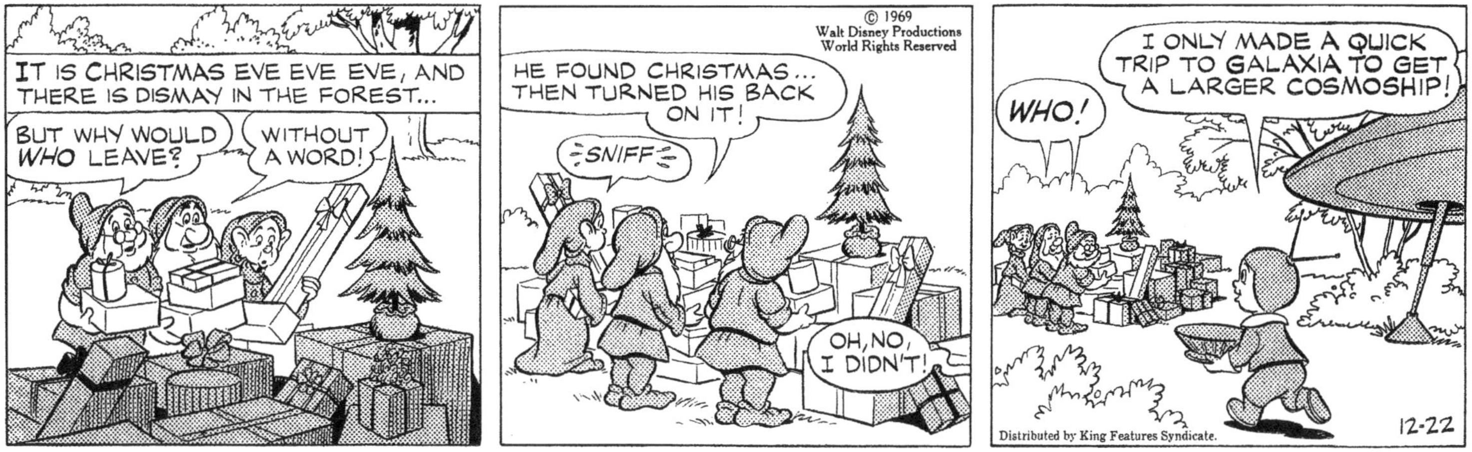
IT IS CHRISTMAS EVE EVE EVE, AND THERE IS DISMAY IN THE FOREST...
BUT WHY WOULD WHO LEAVE?
WITHOUT A WORD!
© 1969 Walt Disney Productions World Rights Reserved
HE FOUND CHRISTMAS... THEN TURNED HIS BACK ON IT!
SNIFF
OH, NO, I DIDN'T!
I ONLY MADE A QUICK TRIP TO GALAXIA TO GET A LARGER COSMOSHIP!
WHO!
Distributed by King Features Syndicate.
12-22

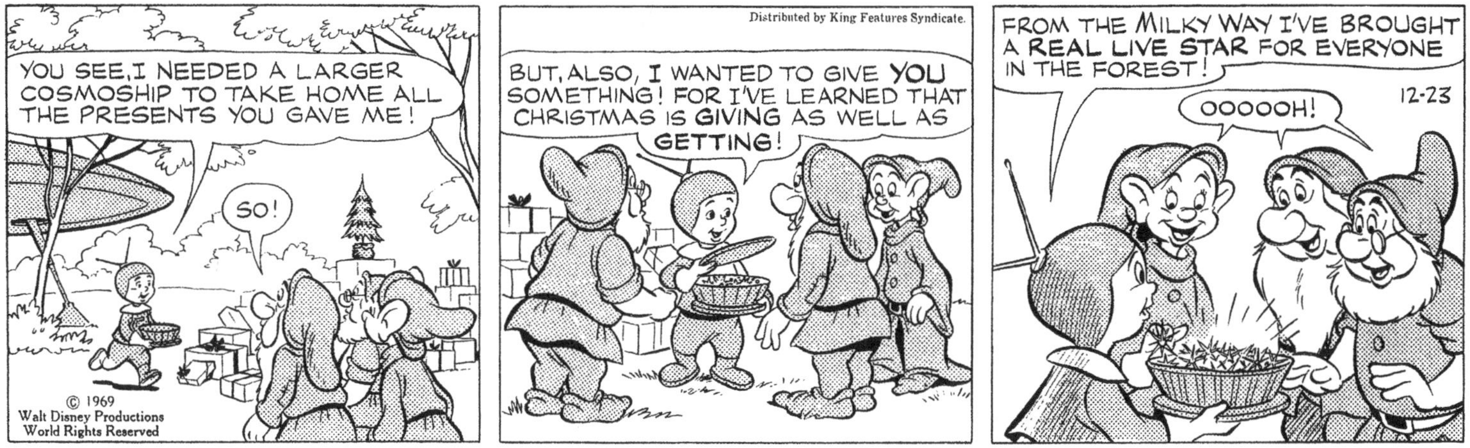
YOU SEE, I NEEDED A LARGER COSMOSHIP TO TAKE HOME ALL THE PRESENTS YOU GAVE ME!
SO!
© 1969 Walt Disney Productions World Rights Reserved
Distributed by King Features Syndicate.
BUT, ALSO, I WANTED TO GIVE YOU SOMETHING! FOR I'VE LEARNED THAT CHRISTMAS IS GIVING AS WELL AS GETTING!
FROM THE MILKY WAY I'VE BROUGHT A REAL LIVE STAR FOR EVERYONE IN THE FOREST!
OOOOOH!
12-23

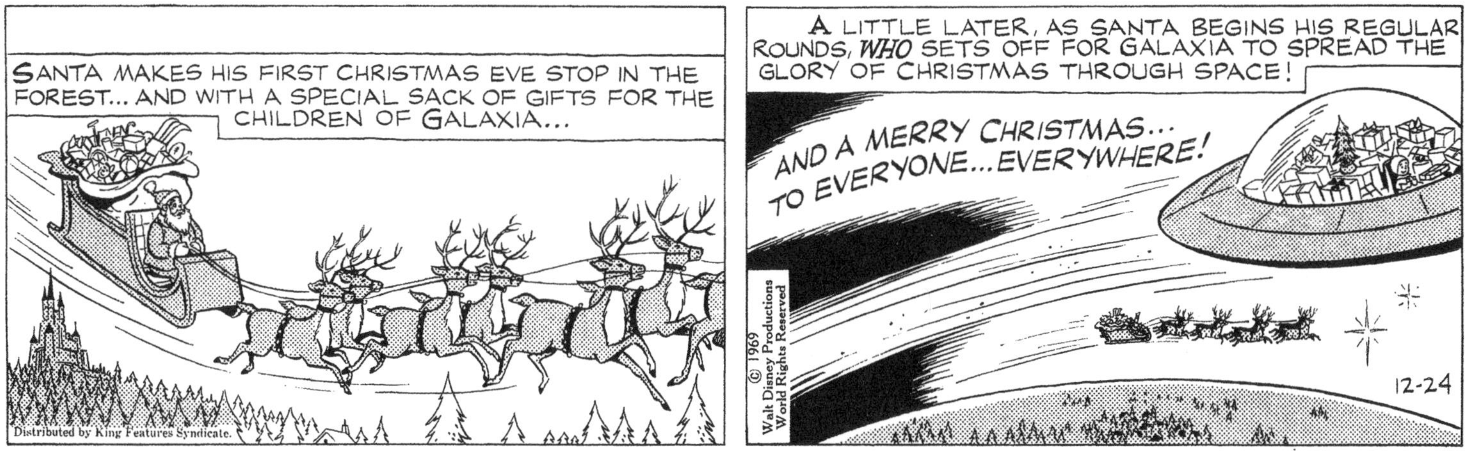
SANTA MAKES HIS FIRST CHRISTMAS EVE STOP IN THE FOREST... AND WITH A SPECIAL SACK OF GIFTS FOR THE CHILDREN OF GALAXIA...
Distributed by King Features Syndicate.
A LITTLE LATER, AS SANTA BEGINS HIS REGULAR ROUNDS, WHO SETS OFF FOR GALAXIA TO SPREAD THE GLORY OF CHRISTMAS THROUGH SPACE!
AND A MERRY CHRISTMAS... TO EVERYONE... EVERYWHERE!
© 1969 Walt Disney Productions World Rights Reserved
12-24

1970

SANTA'S CHRISTMAS CRISIS

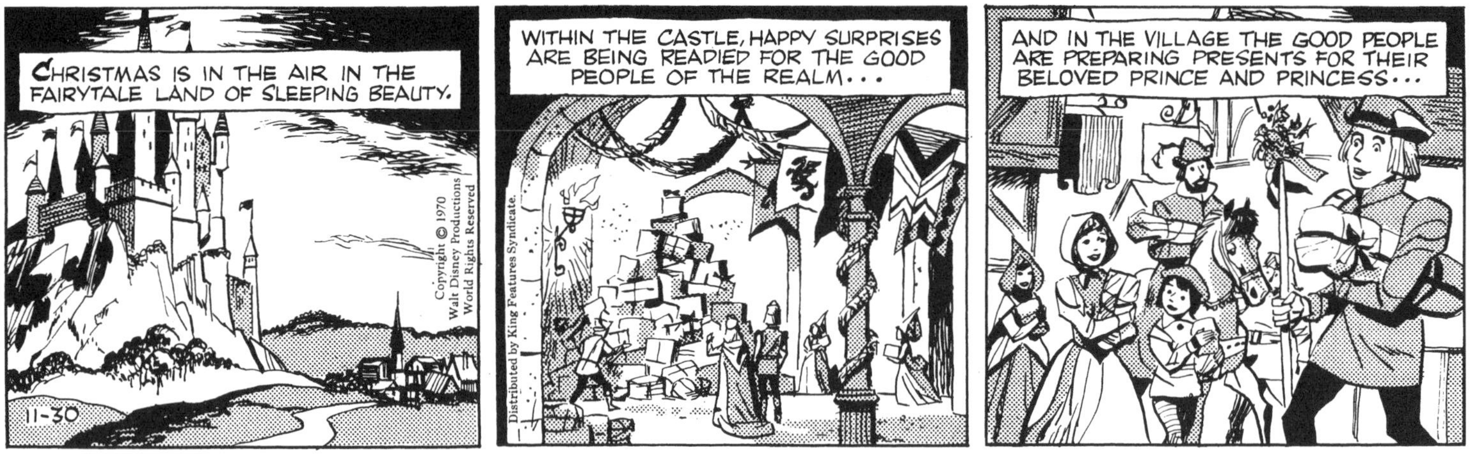
CHRISTMAS IS IN THE AIR IN THE FAIRYTALE LAND OF SLEEPING BEAUTY.
Copyright © 1970 Walt Disney Productions World Rights Reserved
11-30
WITHIN THE CASTLE, HAPPY SURPRISES ARE BEING READIED FOR THE GOOD PEOPLE OF THE REALM...
Distributed by King Features Syndicate.
AND IN THE VILLAGE THE GOOD PEOPLE ARE PREPARING PRESENTS FOR THEIR BELOVED PRINCE AND PRINCESS...

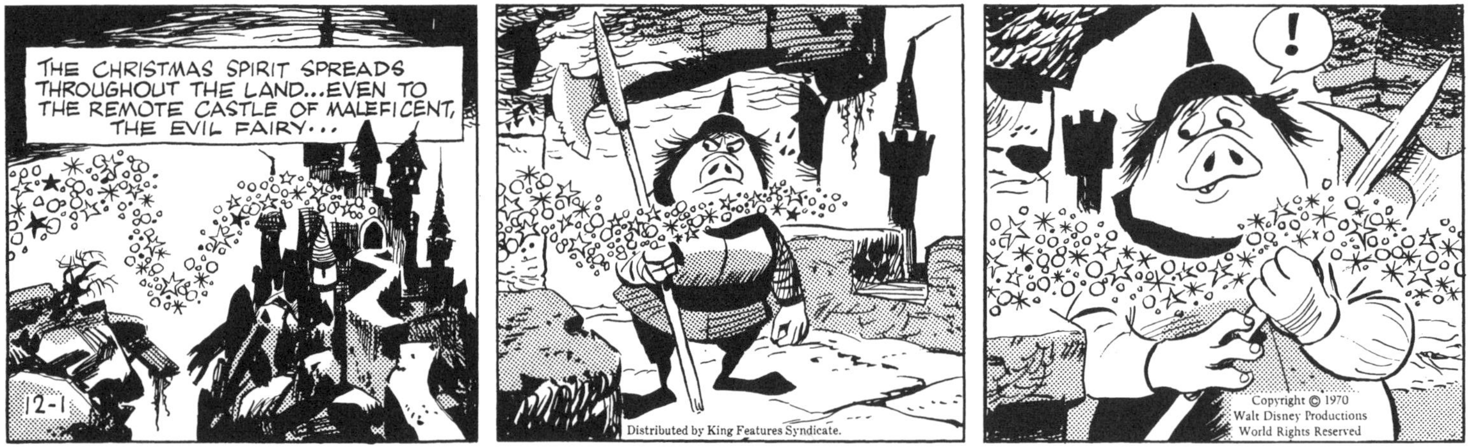
THE CHRISTMAS SPIRIT SPREADS THROUGHOUT THE LAND...EVEN TO THE REMOTE CASTLE OF MALEFICENT, THE EVIL FAIRY...
12-1
Distributed by King Features Syndicate.
!
Copyright © 1970 Walt Disney Productions World Rights Reserved

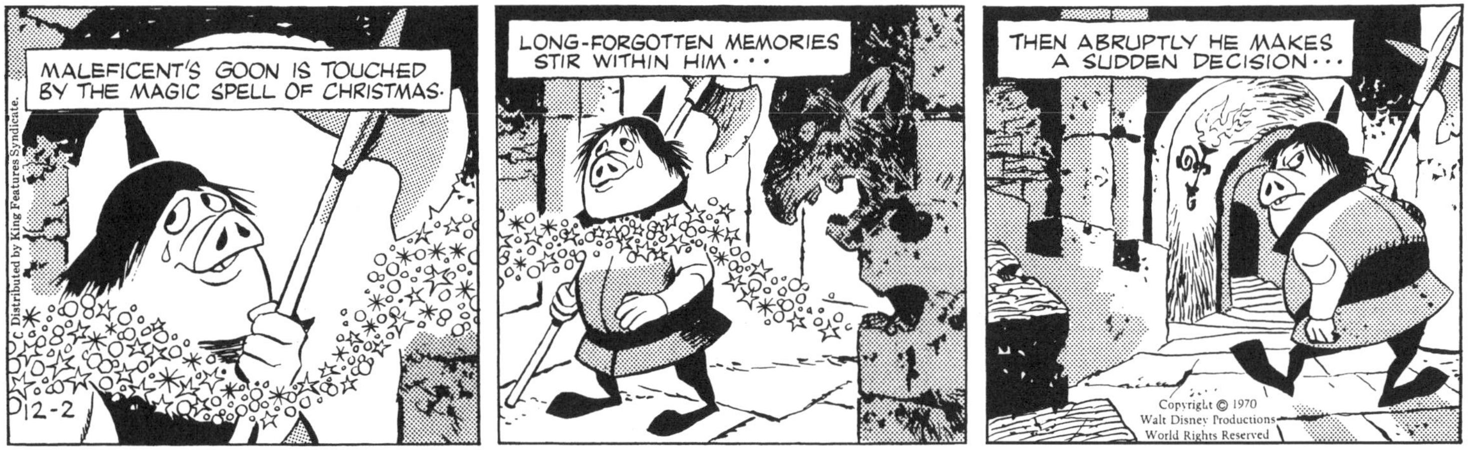
MALEFICENT'S GOON IS TOUCHED BY THE MAGIC SPELL OF CHRISTMAS.
c. Distributed by King Features Syndicate.
12-2
LONG-FORGOTTEN MEMORIES STIR WITHIN HIM...
THEN ABRUPTLY HE MAKES A SUDDEN DECISION...
Copyright © 1970 Walt Disney Productions World Rights Reserved

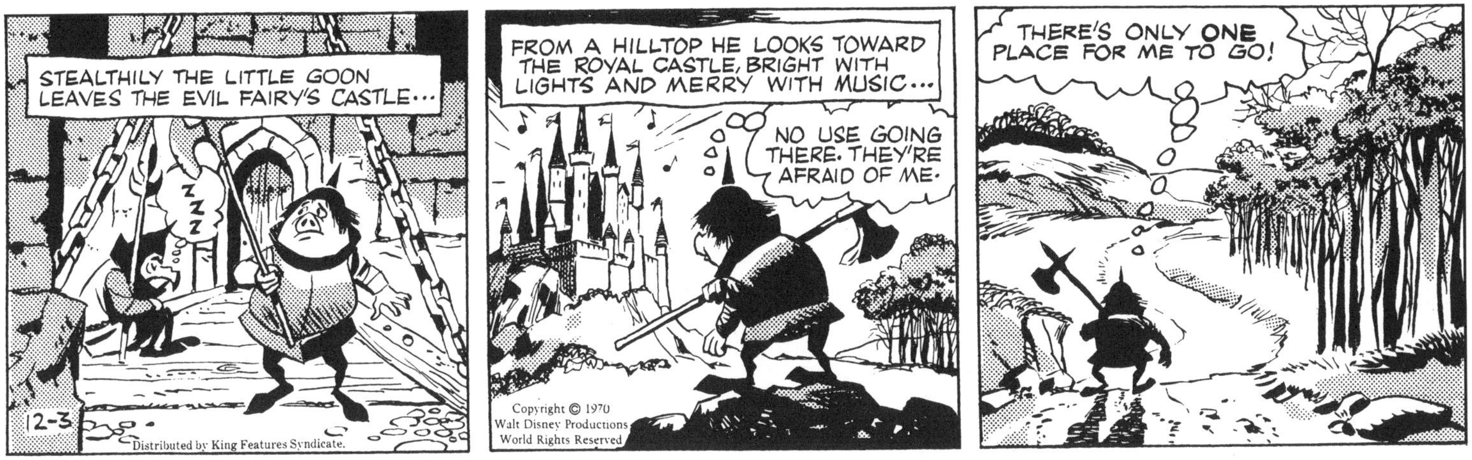

STEALTHILY THE LITTLE GOON LEAVES THE EVIL FAIRY'S CASTLE...
ZZZ
12-3
Distributed by King Features Syndicate.
FROM A HILLTOP HE LOOKS TOWARD THE ROYAL CASTLE, BRIGHT WITH LIGHTS AND MERRY WITH MUSIC...
NO USE GOING THERE. THEY'RE AFRAID OF ME.
Copyright © 1970 Walt Disney Productions World Rights Reserved
THERE'S ONLY ONE PLACE FOR ME TO GO!

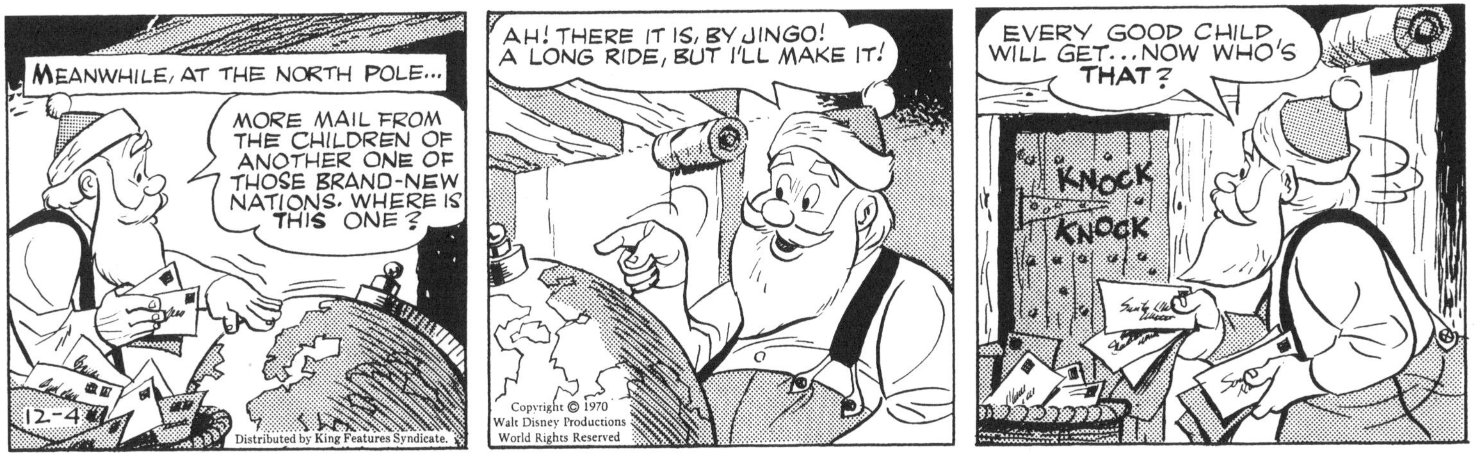

MEANWHILE, AT THE NORTH POLE...
MORE MAIL FROM THE CHILDREN OF ANOTHER ONE OF THOSE BRAND-NEW NATIONS. WHERE IS THIS ONE?
12-4
Distributed by King Features Syndicate.
AH! THERE IT IS, BY JINGO! A LONG RIDE, BUT I'LL MAKE IT!
Copyright © 1970 Walt Disney Productions World Rights Reserved
EVERY GOOD CHILD WILL GET...NOW WHO'S THAT?
KNOCK KNOCK

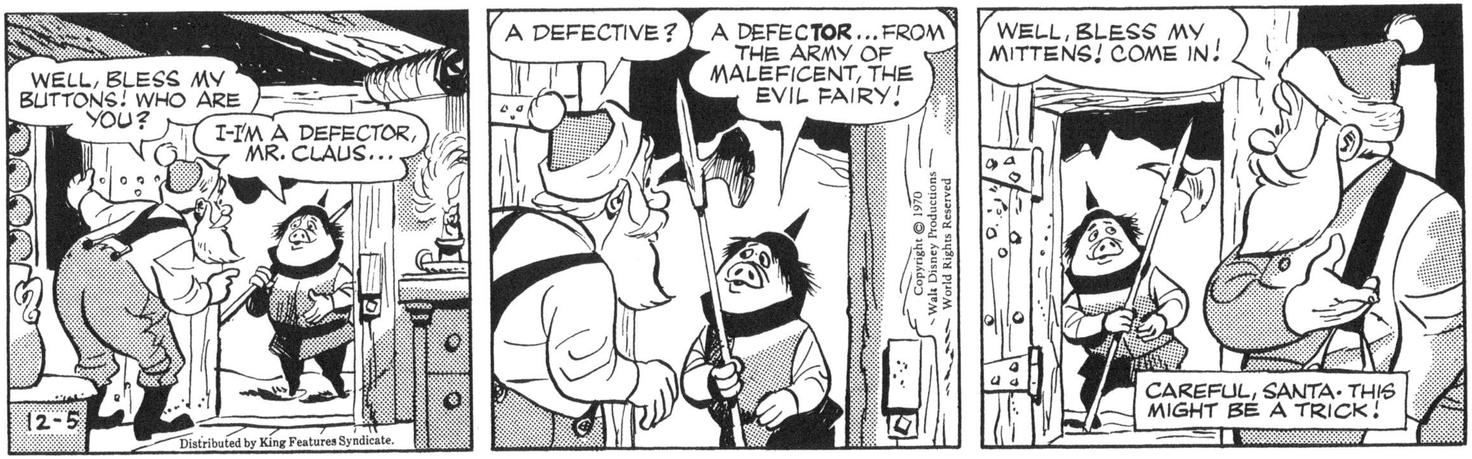

WELL, BLESS MY BUTTONS! WHO ARE YOU?
I-I'M A DEFECTOR, MR. CLAUS...
12-5
Distributed by King Features Syndicate.
A DEFECTIVE?
A DEFECTOR...FROM THE ARMY OF MALEFICENT, THE EVIL FAIRY!
Copyright © 1970 Walt Disney Productions World Rights Reserved
WELL, BLESS MY MITTENS! COME IN!
CAREFUL, SANTA. THIS MIGHT BE A TRICK!

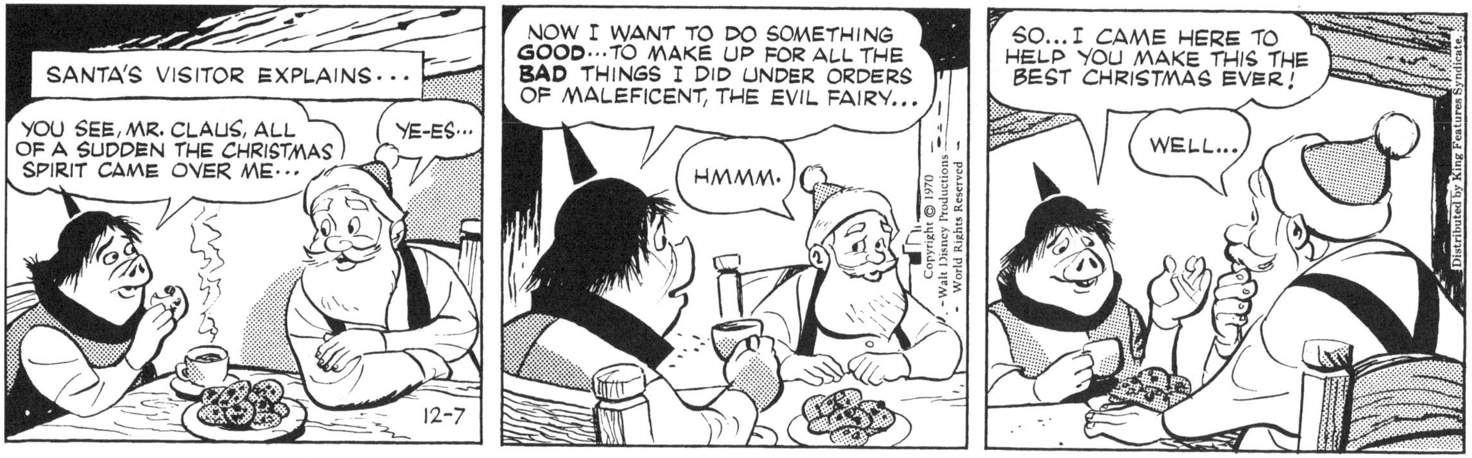
SANTA'S VISITOR EXPLAINS...
YOU SEE, MR. CLAUS, ALL OF A SUDDEN THE CHRISTMAS SPIRIT CAME OVER ME...
YE-ES...
12-7
NOW I WANT TO DO SOMETHING GOOD...TO MAKE UP FOR ALL THE BAD THINGS I DID UNDER ORDERS OF MALEFICENT, THE EVIL FAIRY...
HMMM.
Copyright © 1970 Walt Disney Productions World Rights Reserved
SO...I CAME HERE TO HELP YOU MAKE THIS THE BEST CHRISTMAS EVER!
WELL...
Distributed by King Features Syndicate.

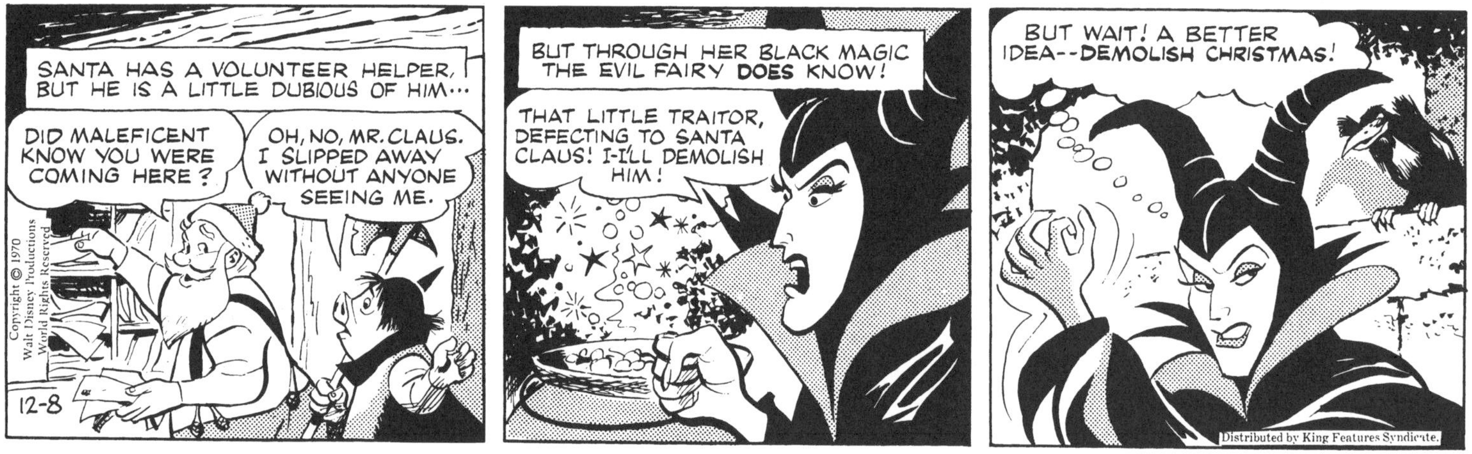
SANTA HAS A VOLUNTEER HELPER, BUT HE IS A LITTLE DUBIOUS OF HIM...
DID MALEFICENT KNOW YOU WERE COMING HERE?
OH, NO, MR. CLAUS. I SLIPPED AWAY WITHOUT ANYONE SEEING ME.
Copyright © 1970 Walt Disney Productions World Rights Reserved
12-8
BUT THROUGH HER BLACK MAGIC THE EVIL FAIRY DOES KNOW!
THAT LITTLE TRAITOR, DEFECTING TO SANTA CLAUS! I-I'LL DEMOLISH HIM!
BUT WAIT! A BETTER IDEA--DEMOLISH CHRISTMAS!
Distributed by King Features Syndicate.

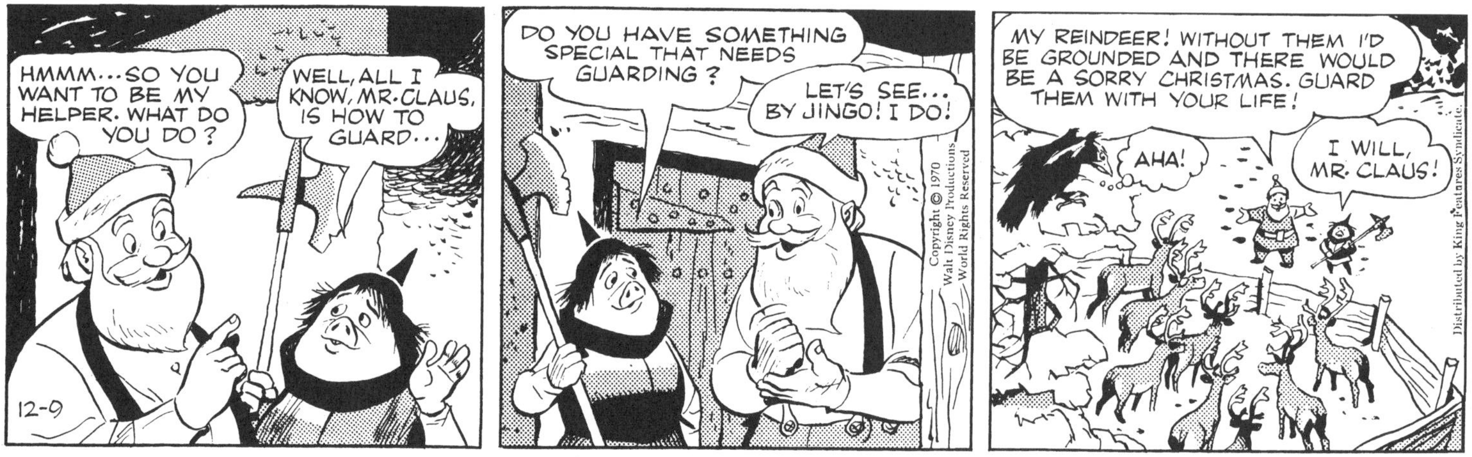
HMMM...SO YOU WANT TO BE MY HELPER. WHAT DO YOU DO?
WELL, ALL I KNOW, MR. CLAUS, IS HOW TO GUARD...
12-9
DO YOU HAVE SOMETHING SPECIAL THAT NEEDS GUARDING?
LET'S SEE... BY JINGO! I DO!
Copyright © 1970 Walt Disney Productions World Rights Reserved
MY REINDEER! WITHOUT THEM I'D BE GROUNDED AND THERE WOULD BE A SORRY CHRISTMAS. GUARD THEM WITH YOUR LIFE!
AHA!
I WILL, MR. CLAUS!
Distributed by King Features Syndicate.

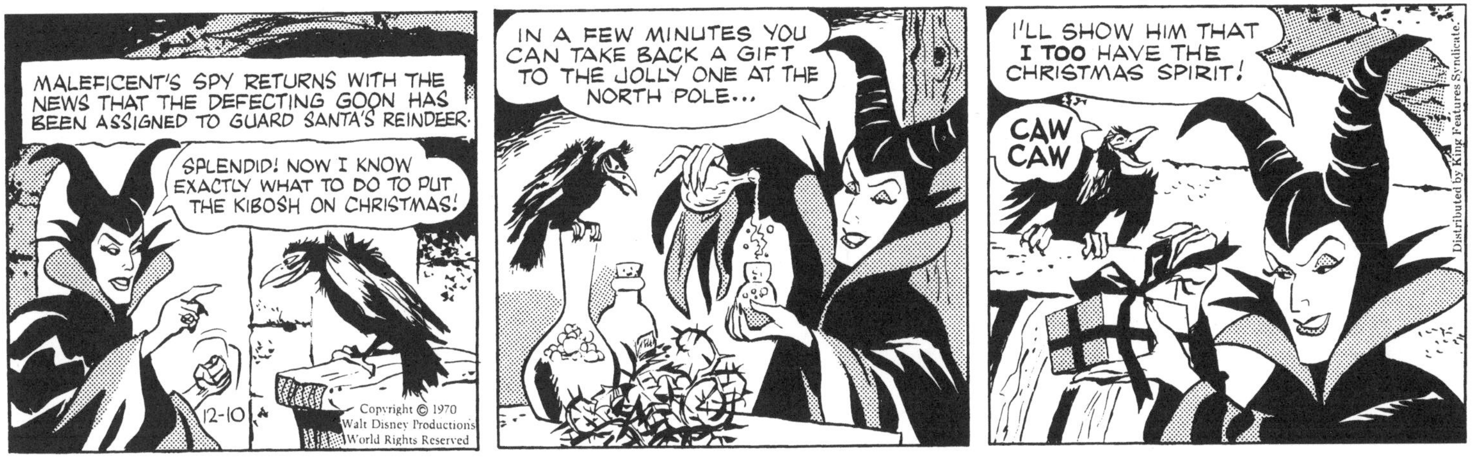
MALEFICENT'S SPY RETURNS WITH THE NEWS THAT THE DEFECTING GOON HAS BEEN ASSIGNED TO GUARD SANTA'S REINDEER.
SPLENDID! NOW I KNOW EXACTLY WHAT TO DO TO PUT THE KIBOSH ON CHRISTMAS!
12-10
Copyright © 1970 Walt Disney Productions World Rights Reserved
IN A FEW MINUTES YOU CAN TAKE BACK A GIFT TO THE JOLLY ONE AT THE NORTH POLE...
I'LL SHOW HIM THAT I TOO HAVE THE CHRISTMAS SPIRIT!
CAW CAW
Distributed by King Features Syndicate.

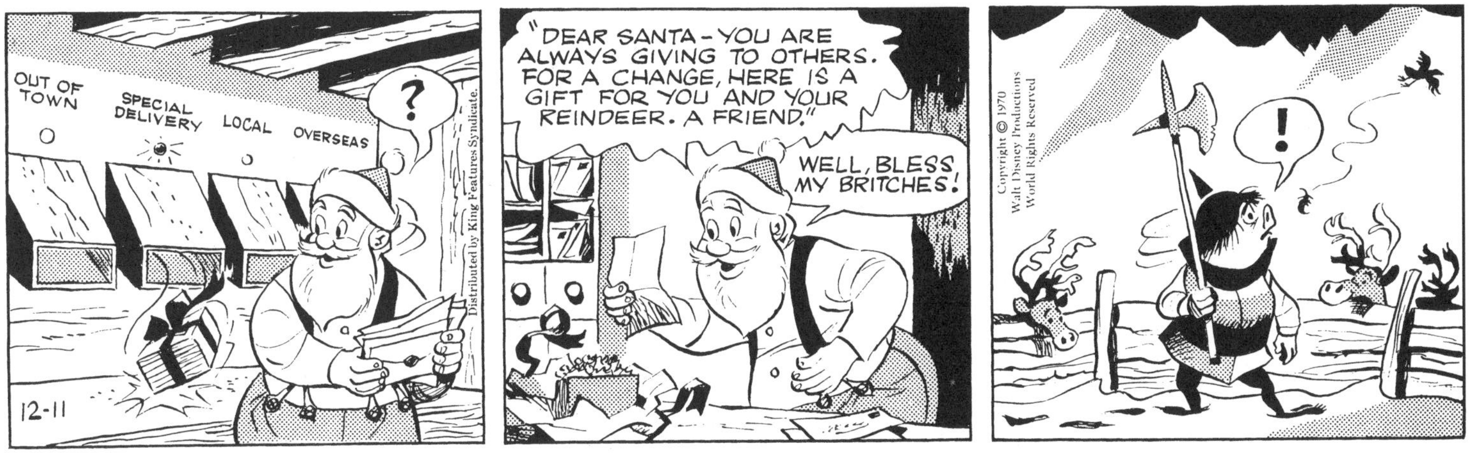
OUT OF TOWN
SPECIAL DELIVERY
LOCAL
OVERSEAS
?
12-11
Distributed by King Features Syndicate.
"DEAR SANTA - YOU ARE ALWAYS GIVING TO OTHERS. FOR A CHANGE, HERE IS A GIFT FOR YOU AND YOUR REINDEER. A FRIEND."
WELL, BLESS MY BRITCHES!
Copyright © 1970 Walt Disney Productions World Rights Reserved
!

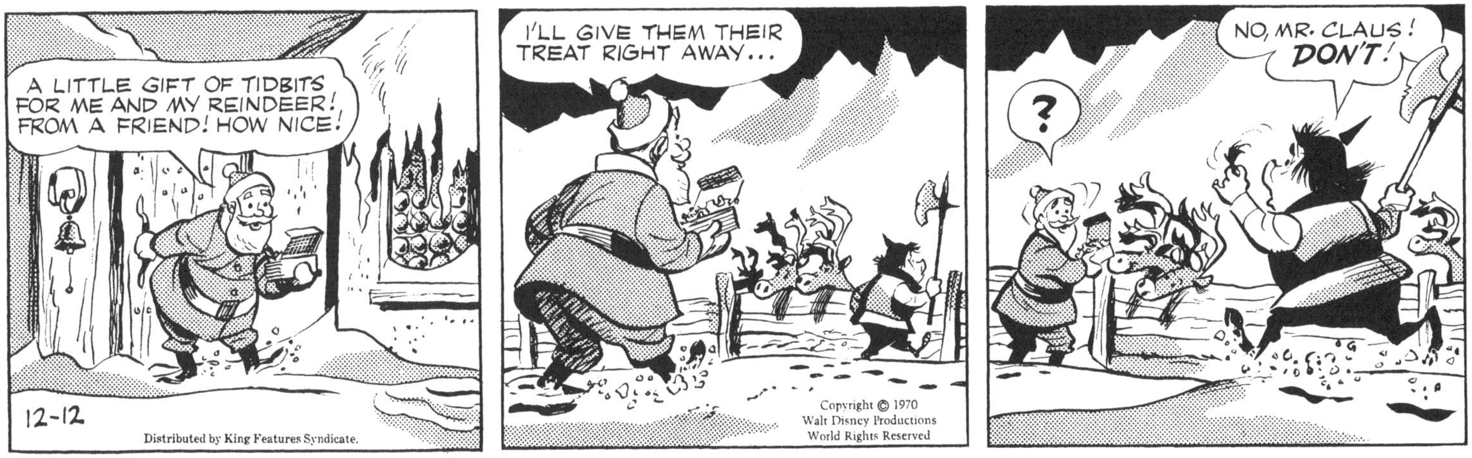
A LITTLE GIFT OF TIDBITS FOR ME AND MY REINDEER! FROM A FRIEND! HOW NICE!
12-12
Distributed by King Features Syndicate.
I'LL GIVE THEM THEIR TREAT RIGHT AWAY...
Copyright © 1970 Walt Disney Productions World Rights Reserved
?
NO, MR. CLAUS! DON'T!

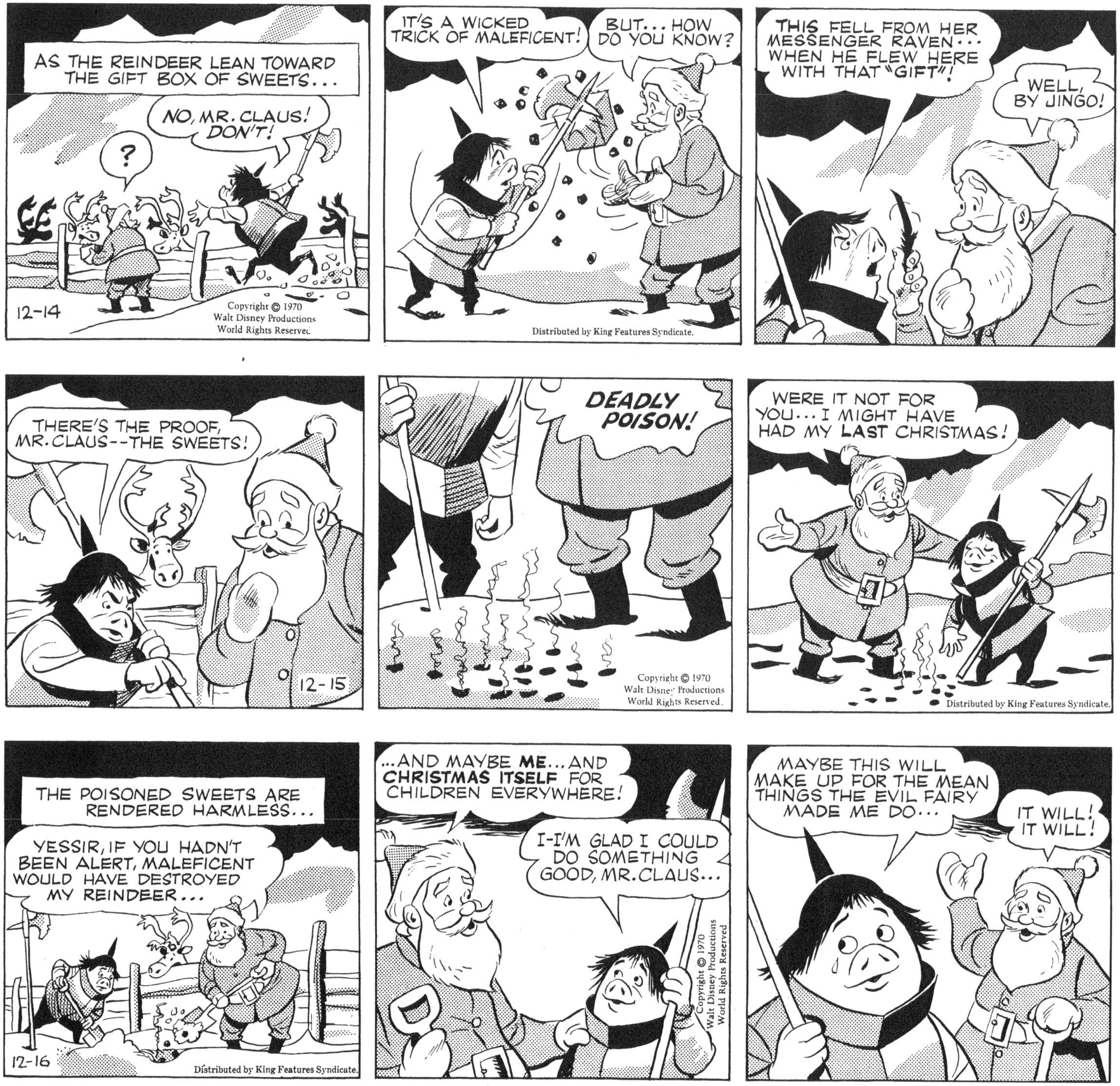
AS THE REINDEER LEAN TOWARD THE GIFT BOX OF SWEETS...
?
NO, MR. CLAUS! DON'T!
12-14
Copyright © 1970 Walt Disney Productions World Rights Reserved
IT'S A WICKED TRICK OF MALEFICENT!
BUT... HOW DO YOU KNOW?
Distributed by King Features Syndicate.
THIS FELL FROM HER MESSENGER RAVEN... WHEN HE FLEW HERE WITH THAT "GIFT"!
WELL, BY JINGO!
THERE'S THE PROOF, MR. CLAUS--THE SWEETS!
12-15
DEADLY POISON!
Copyright © 1970 Walt Disney Productions World Rights Reserved.
WERE IT NOT FOR YOU... I MIGHT HAVE HAD MY LAST CHRISTMAS!
Distributed by King Features Syndicate.
THE POISONED SWEETS ARE RENDERED HARMLESS...
YESSIR, IF YOU HADN'T BEEN ALERT, MALEFICENT WOULD HAVE DESTROYED MY REINDEER...
12-16
Distributed by King Features Syndicate.
...AND MAYBE ME... AND CHRISTMAS ITSELF FOR CHILDREN EVERYWHERE!
I-I'M GLAD I COULD DO SOMETHING GOOD, MR. CLAUS...
Copyright © 1970 Walt Disney Productions World Rights Reserved
MAYBE THIS WILL MAKE UP FOR THE MEAN THINGS THE EVIL FAIRY MADE ME DO...
IT WILL! IT WILL!

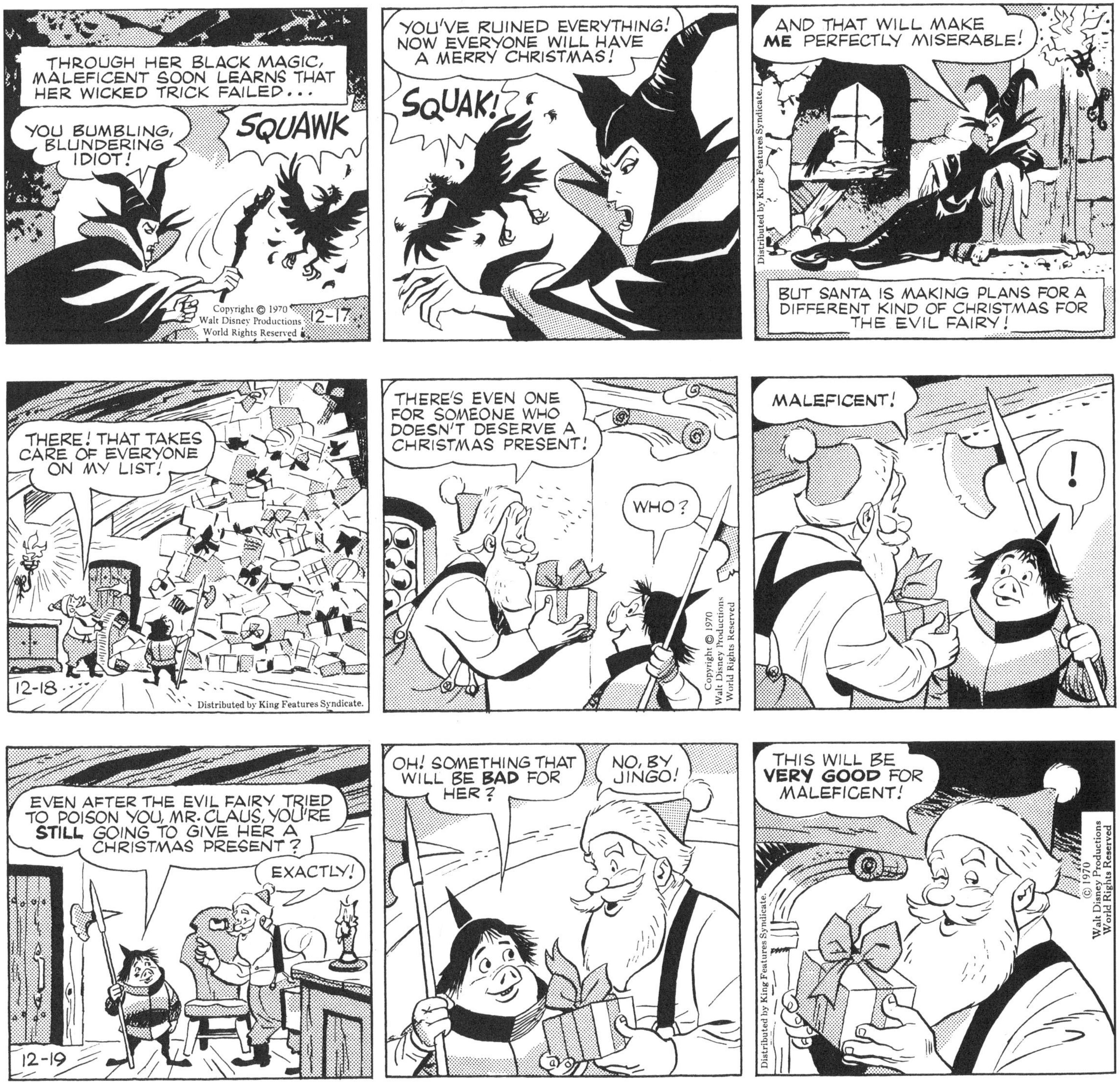
THROUGH HER BLACK MAGIC, MALEFICENT SOON LEARNS THAT HER WICKED TRICK FAILED...
YOU BUMBLING, BLUNDERING IDIOT!
SQUAWK
Copyright © 1970 Walt Disney Productions World Rights Reserved
12-17
YOU'VE RUINED EVERYTHING! NOW EVERYONE WILL HAVE A MERRY CHRISTMAS!
SQUAK!
AND THAT WILL MAKE ME PERFECTLY MISERABLE!
Distributed by King Features Syndicate.
BUT SANTA IS MAKING PLANS FOR A DIFFERENT KIND OF CHRISTMAS FOR THE EVIL FAIRY!
THERE! THAT TAKES CARE OF EVERYONE ON MY LIST!
12-18
Distributed by King Features Syndicate.
THERE'S EVEN ONE FOR SOMEONE WHO DOESN'T DESERVE A CHRISTMAS PRESENT!
WHO?
Copyright © 1970 Walt Disney Productions World Rights Reserved
MALEFICENT!
!
EVEN AFTER THE EVIL FAIRY TRIED TO POISON YOU, MR. CLAUS, YOU'RE STILL GOING TO GIVE HER A CHRISTMAS PRESENT?
EXACTLY!
12-19
OH! SOMETHING THAT WILL BE BAD FOR HER?
NO, BY JINGO!
THIS WILL BE VERY GOOD FOR MALEFICENT!
Distributed by King Features Syndicate.
© 1970 Walt Disney Productions World Rights Reserved

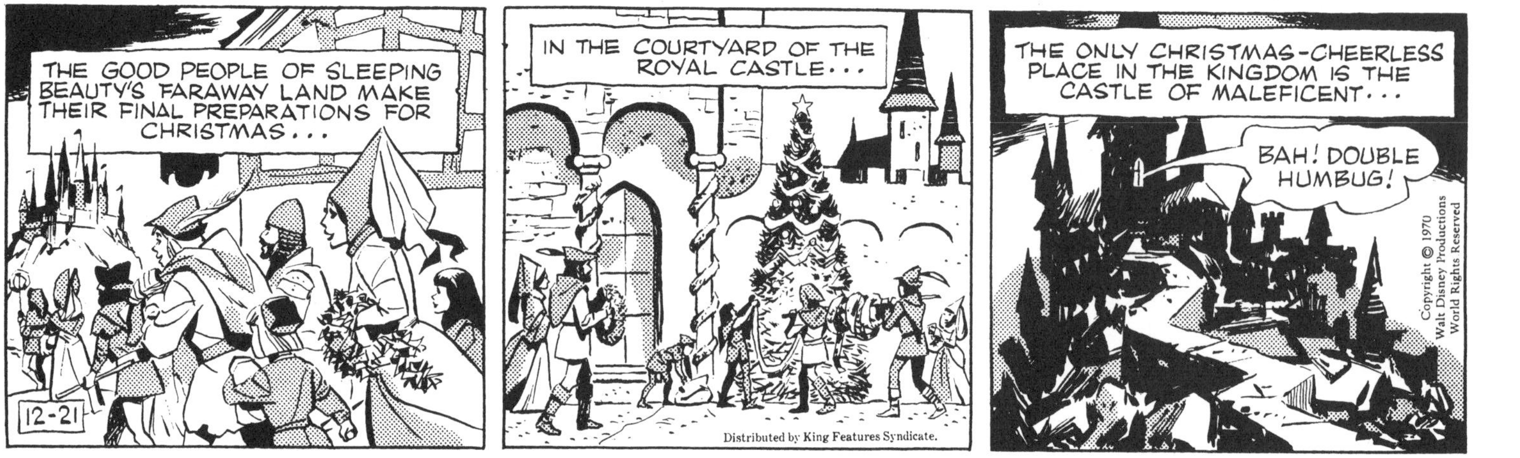
THE GOOD PEOPLE OF SLEEPING BEAUTY'S FARAWAY LAND MAKE THEIR FINAL PREPARATIONS FOR CHRISTMAS...
12-21
IN THE COURTYARD OF THE ROYAL CASTLE...
Distributed by King Features Syndicate.
THE ONLY CHRISTMAS-CHEERLESS PLACE IN THE KINGDOM IS THE CASTLE OF MALEFICENT...
BAH! DOUBLE HUMBUG!
Copyright © 1970 Walt Disney Productions World Rights Reserved

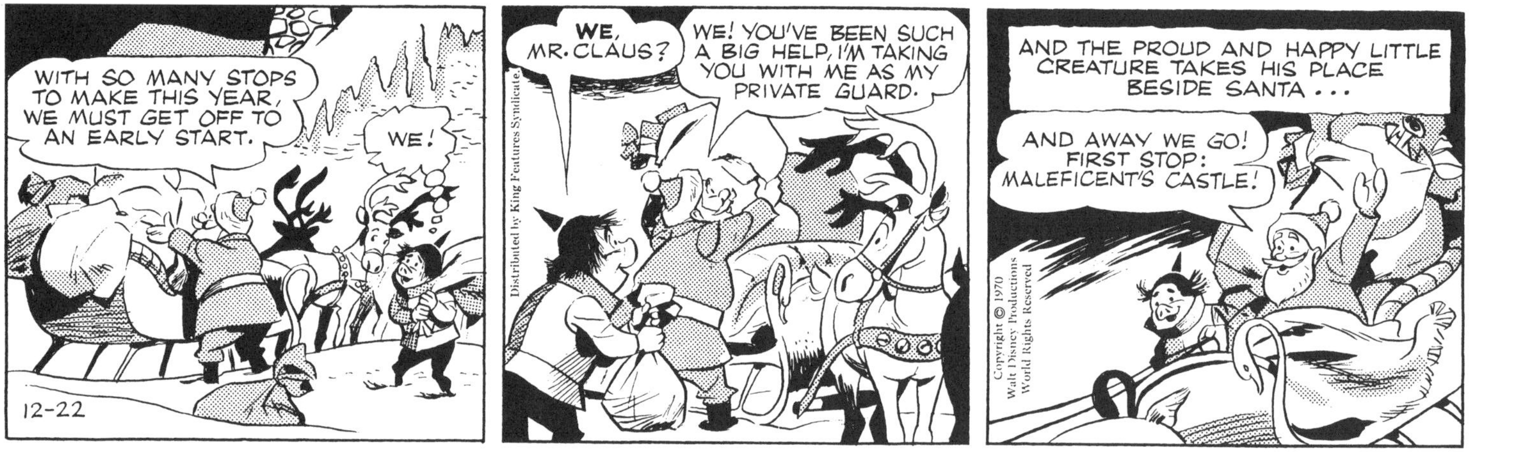
WITH SO MANY STOPS TO MAKE THIS YEAR, WE MUST GET OFF TO AN EARLY START.
WE!
12-22
WE, MR. CLAUS?
WE! YOU'VE BEEN SUCH A BIG HELP, I'M TAKING YOU WITH ME AS MY PRIVATE GUARD.
Distributed by King Features Syndicate.
Copyright © 1970 Walt Disney Productions World Rights Reserved
AND THE PROUD AND HAPPY LITTLE CREATURE TAKES HIS PLACE BESIDE SANTA...
AND AWAY WE GO! FIRST STOP: MALEFICENT'S CASTLE!

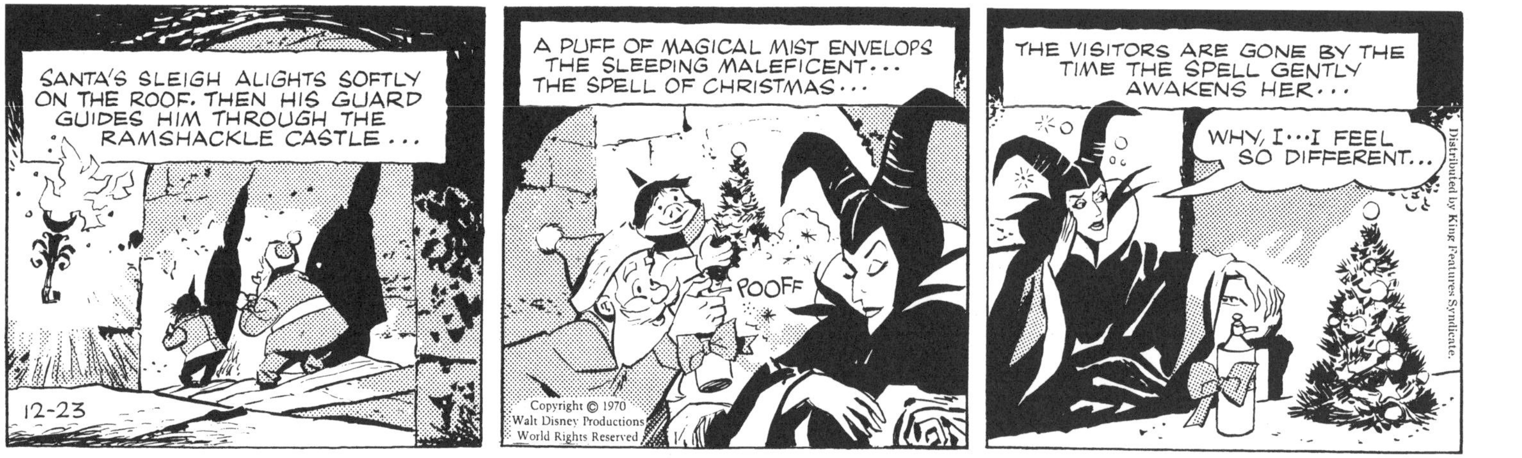
SANTA'S SLEIGH ALIGHTS SOFTLY ON THE ROOF. THEN HIS GUARD GUIDES HIM THROUGH THE RAMSHACKLE CASTLE...
12-23
A PUFF OF MAGICAL MIST ENVELOPS THE SLEEPING MALEFICENT... THE SPELL OF CHRISTMAS...
POOFF
Copyright © 1970 Walt Disney Productions World Rights Reserved
THE VISITORS ARE GONE BY THE TIME THE SPELL GENTLY AWAKENS HER...
WHY, I...I FEEL SO DIFFERENT...
Distributed by King Features Syndicate.

Distributed by King Features Syndicate.
UNDER THE SPELL OF CHRISTMAS MALEFICENT'S MALICE MELTS AWAY...
MERRY CHRISTMAS! MERRY CHRISTMAS!
12-24
HAVING RETURNED GOOD FOR EVIL, SANTA WHIRLS AWAY ON HIS HAPPY JOURNEY...
MERRY CHRISTMAS
EVERYONE... EVERYWHERE
Copyright © 1970
Walt Disney Productions
World Rights Reserved

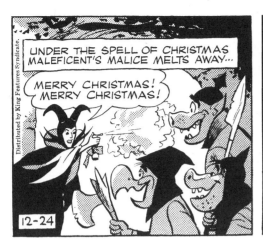

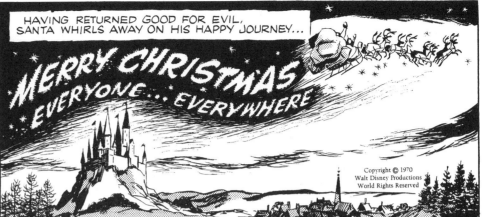

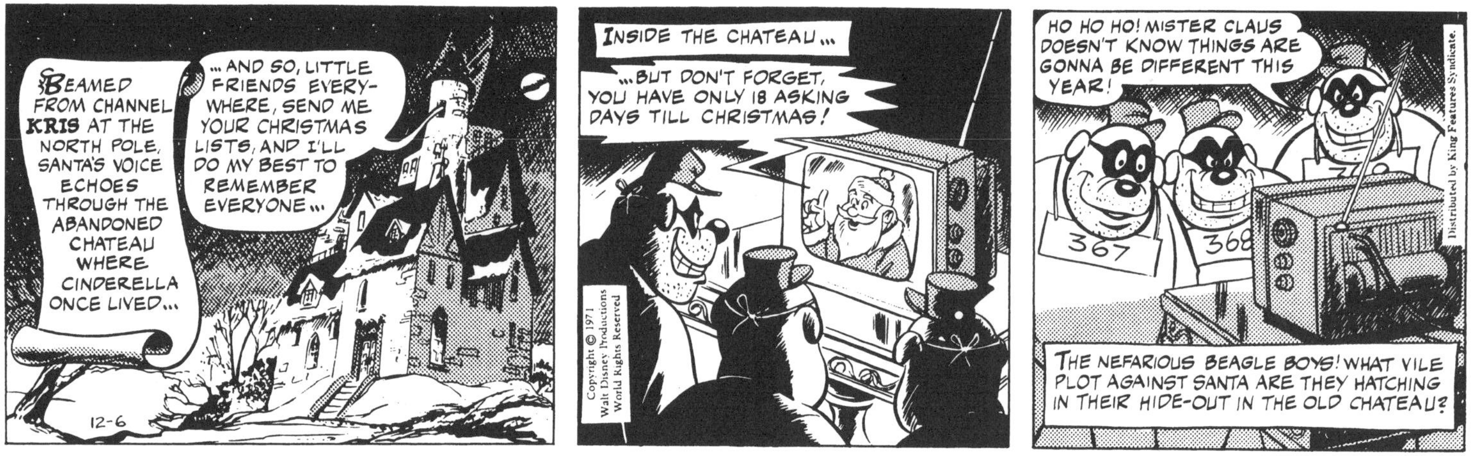
BEAMED FROM CHANNEL KRIS AT THE NORTH POLE, SANTA'S VOICE ECHOES THROUGH THE ABANDONED CHATEAU WHERE CINDERELLA ONCE LIVED...
...AND SO, LITTLE FRIENDS EVERYWHERE, SEND ME YOUR CHRISTMAS LISTS, AND I'LL DO MY BEST TO REMEMBER EVERYONE...
12-6
INSIDE THE CHATEAU...
...BUT DON'T FORGET, YOU HAVE ONLY 18 ASKING DAYS TILL CHRISTMAS!
Copyright © 1971 Walt Disney Productions World Rights Reserved
HO HO HO! MISTER CLAUS DOESN'T KNOW THINGS ARE GONNA BE DIFFERENT THIS YEAR!
367
368
Distributed by King Features Syndicate.
THE NEFARIOUS BEAGLE BOYS! WHAT VILE PLOT AGAINST SANTA ARE THEY HATCHING IN THEIR HIDE-OUT IN THE OLD CHATEAU?

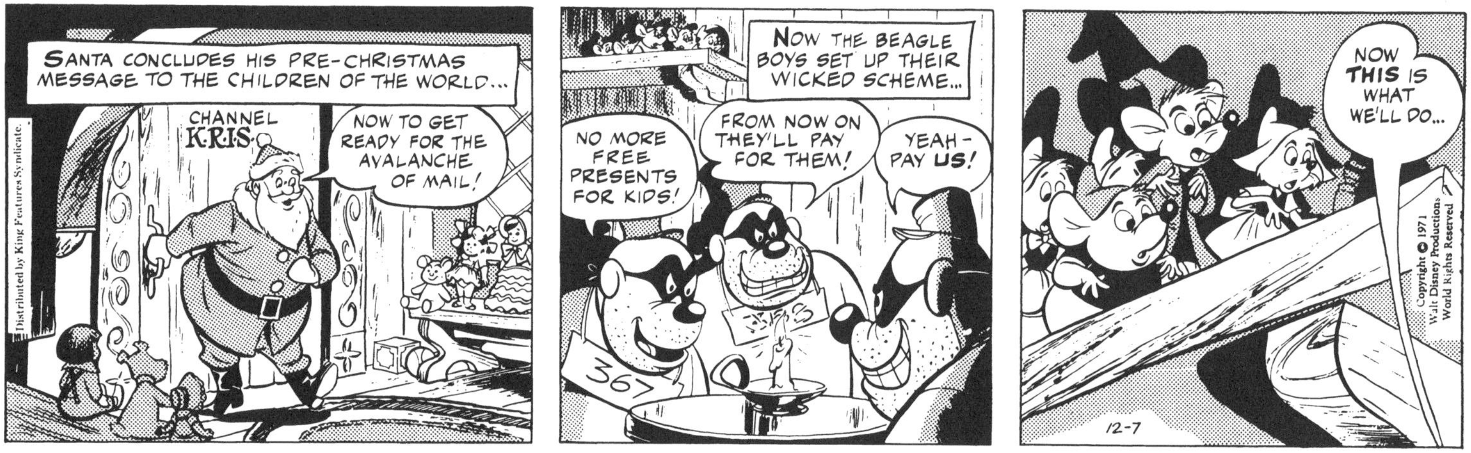
SANTA CONCLUDES HIS PRE-CHRISTMAS MESSAGE TO THE CHILDREN OF THE WORLD...
CHANNEL K·R·I·S
NOW TO GET READY FOR THE AVALANCHE OF MAIL!
Distributed by King Features Syndicate.
NOW THE BEAGLE BOYS SET UP THEIR WICKED SCHEME...
NO MORE FREE PRESENTS FOR KIDS!
FROM NOW ON THEY'LL PAY FOR THEM!
YEAH-PAY US!
367
NOW THIS IS WHAT WE'LL DO...
Copyright © 1971 Walt Disney Productions World Rights Reserved
12-7

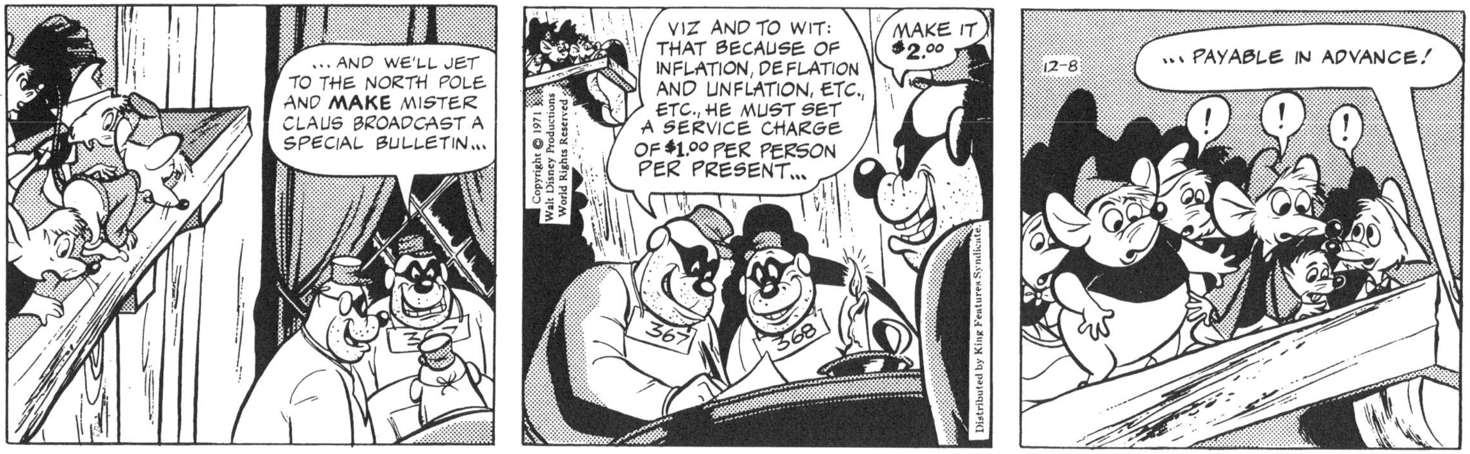
...AND WE'LL JET TO THE NORTH POLE AND MAKE MISTER CLAUS BROADCAST A SPECIAL BULLETIN...
Copyright © 1971 Walt Disney Productions World Rights Reserved
VIZ AND TO WIT: THAT BECAUSE OF INFLATION, DEFLATION AND UNFLATION, ETC., ETC., HE MUST SET A SERVICE CHARGE OF $1.00 PER PERSON PER PRESENT...
MAKE IT $2.00
367
368
Distributed by King Features Syndicate.
12-8
...PAYABLE IN ADVANCE!
!
!
!

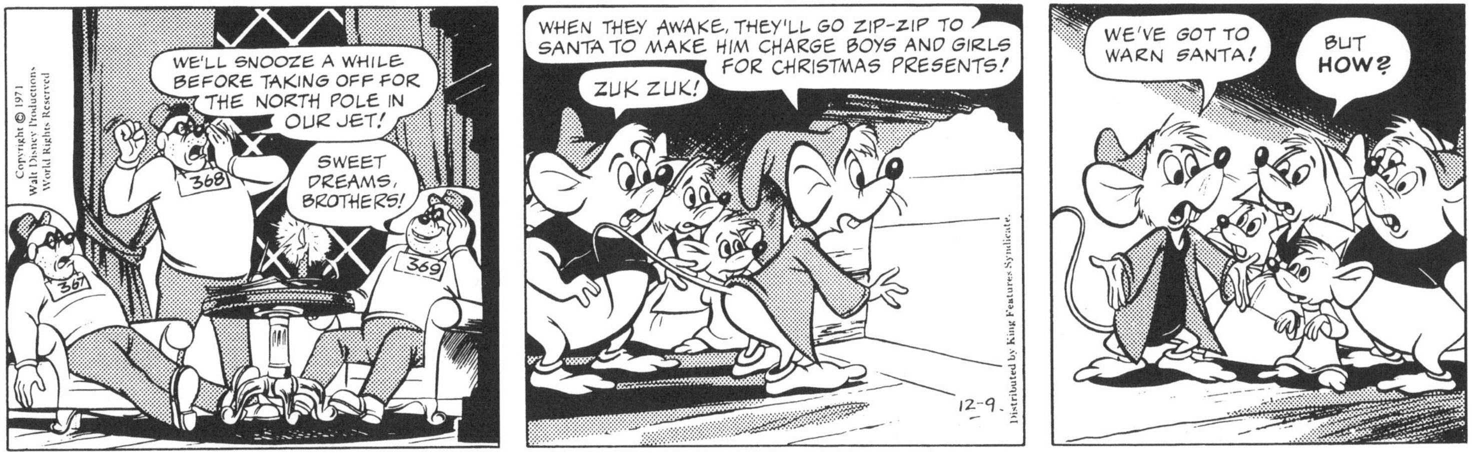
Copyright © 1971 Walt Disney Productions World Rights Reserved
WE'LL SNOOZE A WHILE BEFORE TAKING OFF FOR THE NORTH POLE IN OUR JET!
SWEET DREAMS, BROTHERS!
367
368
369
WHEN THEY AWAKE, THEY'LL GO ZIP-ZIP TO SANTA TO MAKE HIM CHARGE BOYS AND GIRLS FOR CHRISTMAS PRESENTS!
ZUK ZUK!
12-9
Distributed by King Features Syndicate.
WE'VE GOT TO WARN SANTA!
BUT HOW?

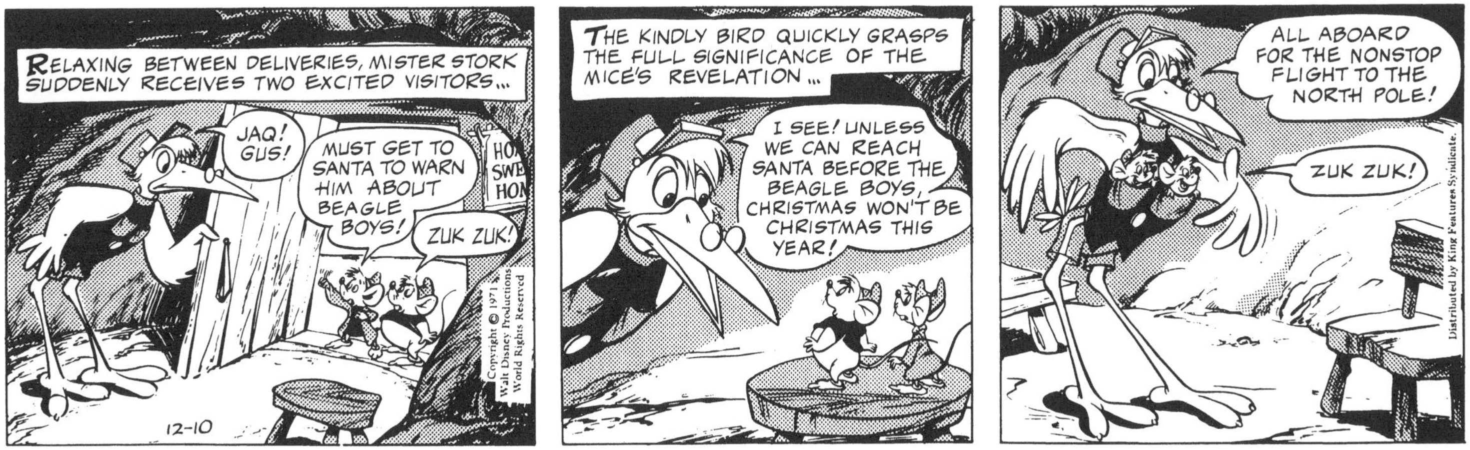
RELAXING BETWEEN DELIVERIES, MISTER STORK SUDDENLY RECEIVES TWO EXCITED VISITORS...
JAQ! GUS!
MUST GET TO SANTA TO WARN HIM ABOUT BEAGLE BOYS!
ZUK ZUK!
Copyright © 1971 Walt Disney Productions World Rights Reserved
12-10
THE KINDLY BIRD QUICKLY GRASPS THE FULL SIGNIFICANCE OF THE MICE'S REVELATION...
I SEE! UNLESS WE CAN REACH SANTA BEFORE THE BEAGLE BOYS, CHRISTMAS WON'T BE CHRISTMAS THIS YEAR!
ALL ABOARD FOR THE NONSTOP FLIGHT TO THE NORTH POLE!
ZUK ZUK!
Distributed by King Features Syndicate.

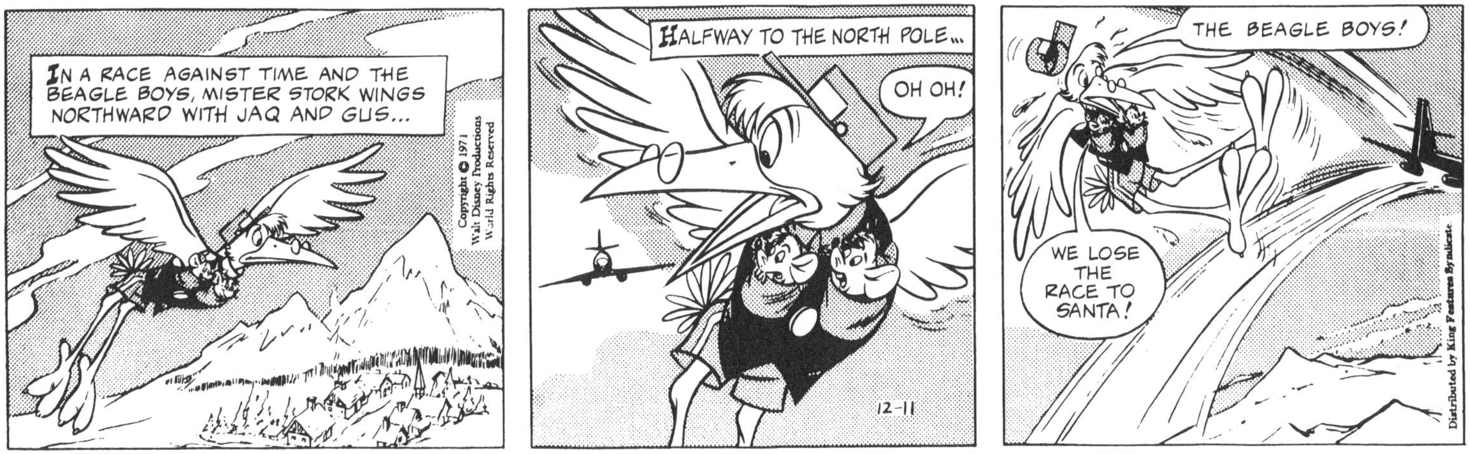
IN A RACE AGAINST TIME AND THE BEAGLE BOYS, MISTER STORK WINGS NORTHWARD WITH JAQ AND GUS...
Copyright © 1971 Walt Disney Productions World Rights Reserved
HALFWAY TO THE NORTH POLE...
OH OH!
12-11
THE BEAGLE BOYS!
WE LOSE THE RACE TO SANTA!
Distributed by King Features Syndicate

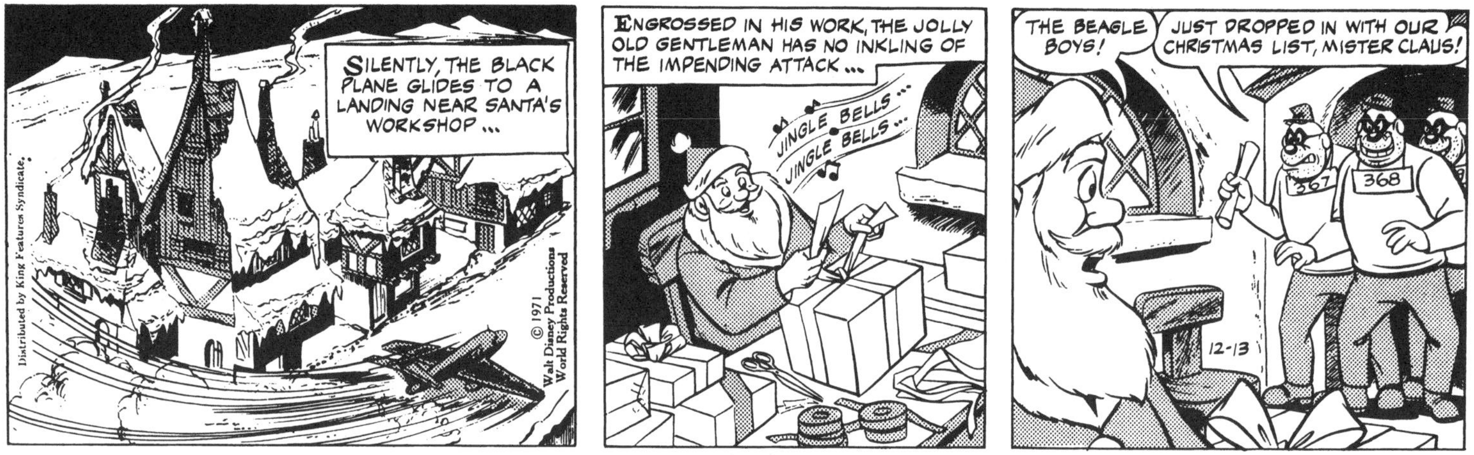
SILENTLY, THE BLACK PLANE GLIDES TO A LANDING NEAR SANTA'S WORKSHOP ...
Distributed by King Features Syndicate.
© 1971 Walt Disney Productions World Rights Reserved
ENGROSSED IN HIS WORK, THE JOLLY OLD GENTLEMAN HAS NO INKLING OF THE IMPENDING ATTACK ...
JINGLE BELLS ... JINGLE BELLS ...
THE BEAGLE BOYS!
JUST DROPPED IN WITH OUR CHRISTMAS LIST, MISTER CLAUS!
367
368
12-13

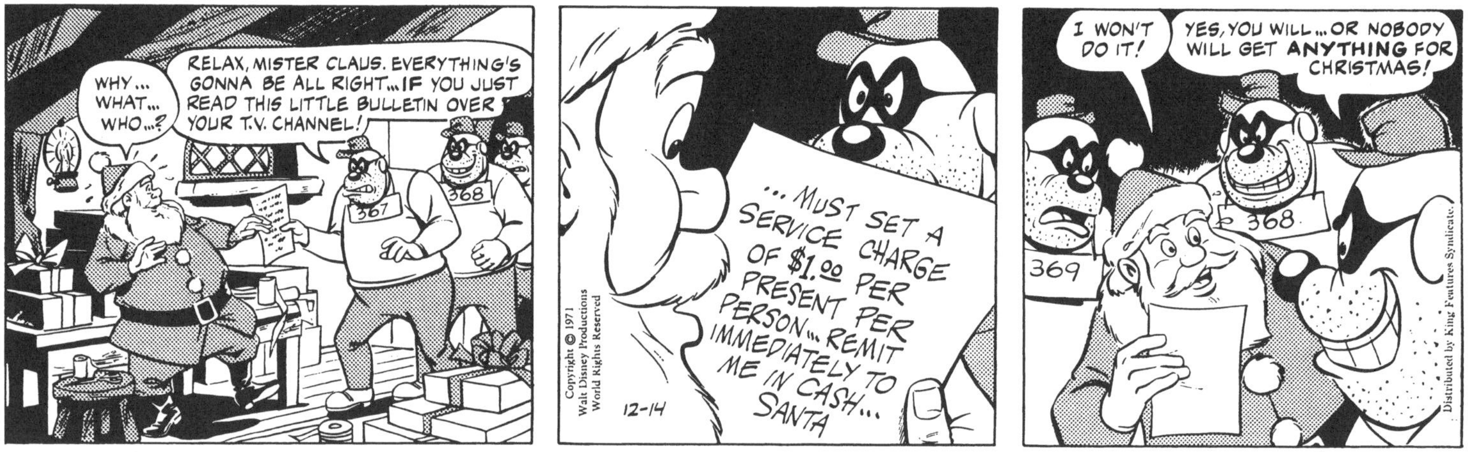
WHY ... WHAT ... WHO ...?
RELAX, MISTER CLAUS. EVERYTHING'S GONNA BE ALL RIGHT ... IF YOU JUST READ THIS LITTLE BULLETIN OVER YOUR T.V. CHANNEL!
367
368
Copyright © 1971 Walt Disney Productions World Rights Reserved
... MUST SET A SERVICE CHARGE OF $1.00 PER PRESENT PER PERSON ... REMIT IMMEDIATELY TO ME IN CASH ... SANTA
12-14
I WON'T DO IT!
YES, YOU WILL ... OR NOBODY WILL GET ANYTHING FOR CHRISTMAS!
369
368
Distributed by King Features Syndicate.

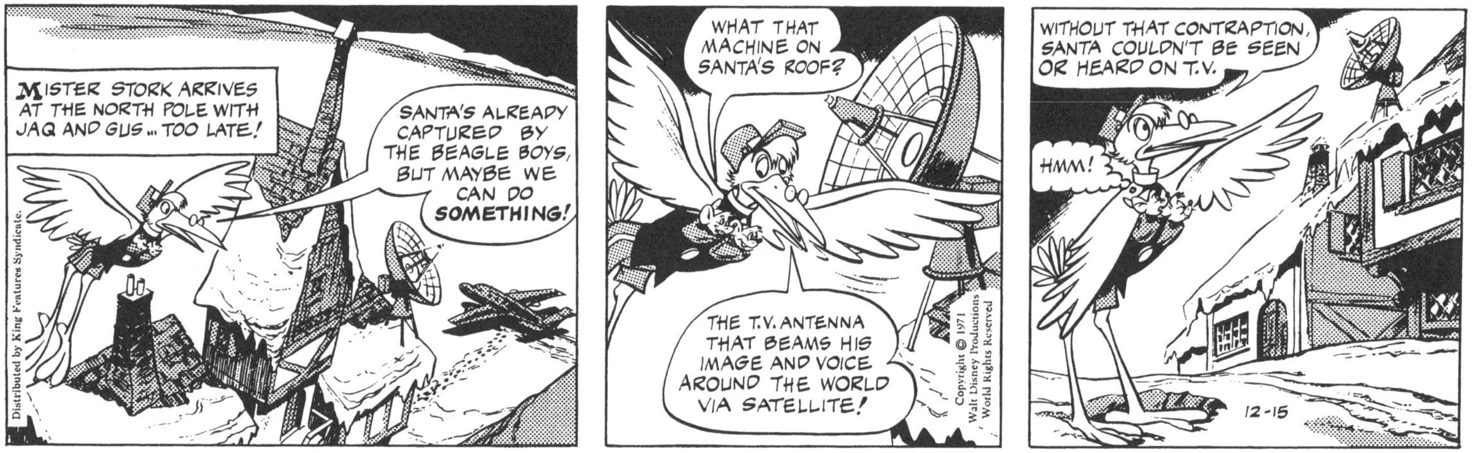
MISTER STORK ARRIVES AT THE NORTH POLE WITH JAQ AND GUS ... TOO LATE!
SANTA'S ALREADY CAPTURED BY THE BEAGLE BOYS, BUT MAYBE WE CAN DO SOMETHING!
Distributed by King Features Syndicate.
WHAT THAT MACHINE ON SANTA'S ROOF?
THE T.V. ANTENNA THAT BEAMS HIS IMAGE AND VOICE AROUND THE WORLD VIA SATELLITE!
Copyright © 1971 Walt Disney Productions World Rights Reserved
WITHOUT THAT CONTRAPTION, SANTA COULDN'T BE SEEN OR HEARD ON T.V.
HMM!
12-15

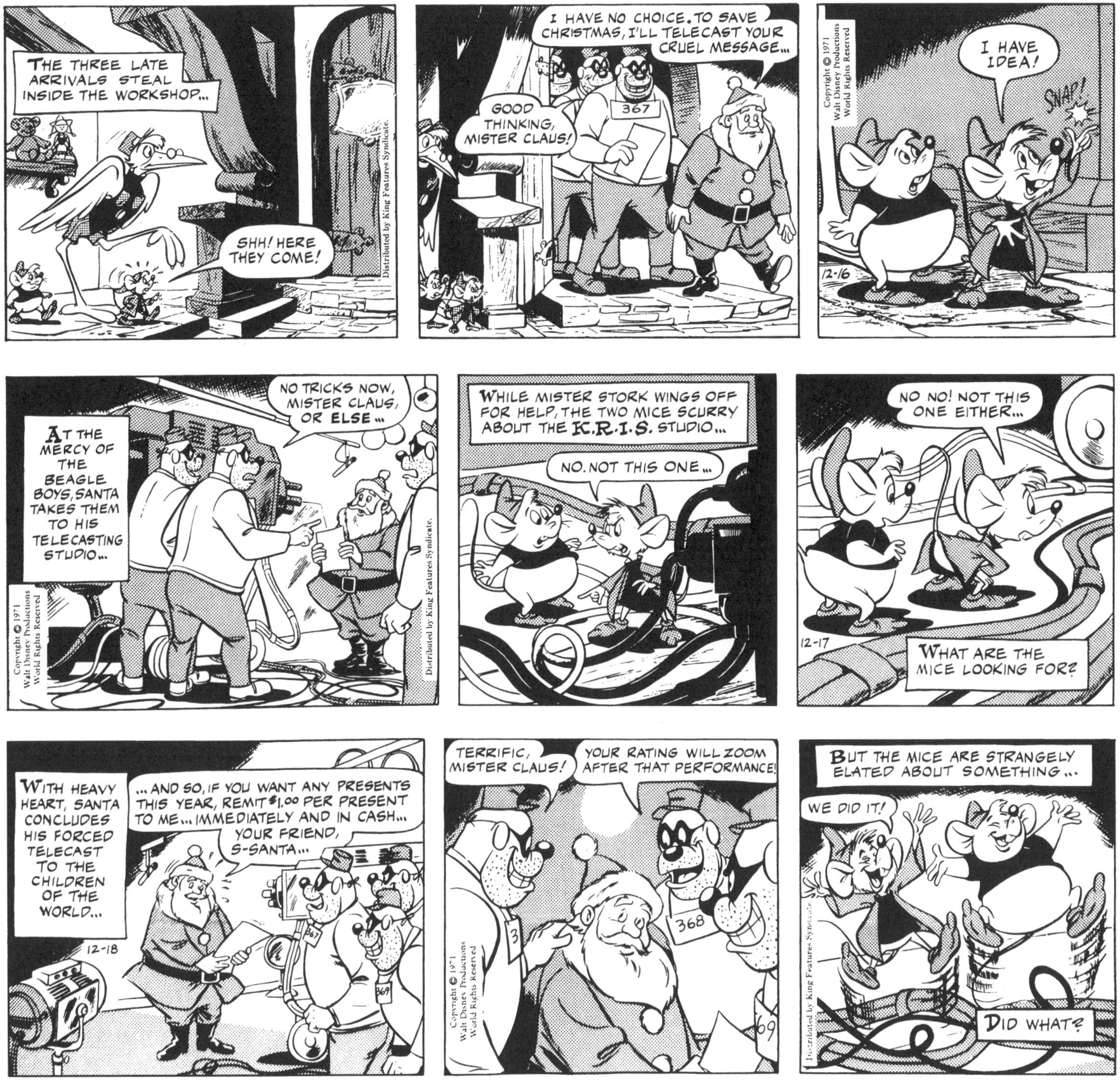
THE THREE LATE ARRIVALS STEAL INSIDE THE WORKSHOP...
SHH! HERE THEY COME!
Distributed by King Features Syndicate.
I HAVE NO CHOICE. TO SAVE CHRISTMAS, I'LL TELECAST YOUR CRUEL MESSAGE...
GOOD THINKING, MISTER CLAUS!
367
Copyright © 1971 Walt Disney Productions World Rights Reserved
I HAVE IDEA!
SNAP!
12-16
AT THE MERCY OF THE BEAGLE BOYS, SANTA TAKES THEM TO HIS TELECASTING STUDIO...
NO TRICKS NOW, MISTER CLAUS, OR ELSE...
Copyright © 1971 Walt Disney Productions World Rights Reserved
Distributed by King Features Syndicate.
WHILE MISTER STORK WINGS OFF FOR HELP, THE TWO MICE SCURRY ABOUT THE K.R.I.S. STUDIO...
NO. NOT THIS ONE...
NO NO! NOT THIS ONE EITHER...
12-17
WHAT ARE THE MICE LOOKING FOR?
WITH HEAVY HEART, SANTA CONCLUDES HIS FORCED TELECAST TO THE CHILDREN OF THE WORLD...
...AND SO, IF YOU WANT ANY PRESENTS THIS YEAR, REMIT $1.00 PER PRESENT TO ME... IMMEDIATELY AND IN CASH... YOUR FRIEND, S-SANTA...
367
369
12-18
TERRIFIC, MISTER CLAUS!
YOUR RATING WILL ZOOM AFTER THAT PERFORMANCE!
Copyright © 1971 Walt Disney Productions World Rights Reserved
368
BUT THE MICE ARE STRANGELY ELATED ABOUT SOMETHING...
WE DID IT!
Distributed by King Features Syndicate.
DID WHAT?

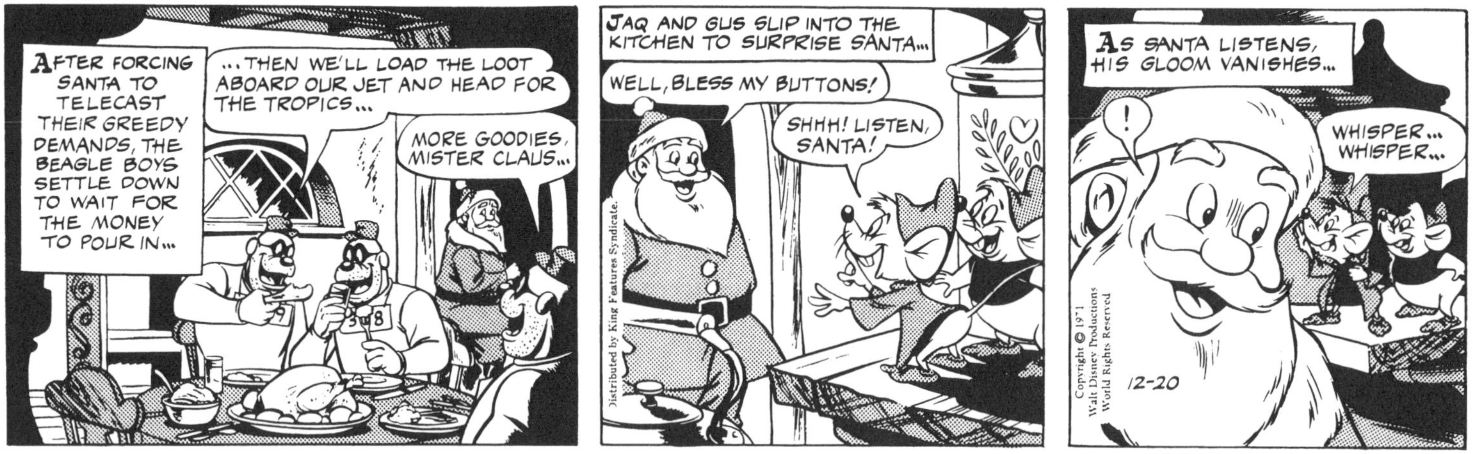
AFTER FORCING SANTA TO TELECAST THEIR GREEDY DEMANDS, THE BEAGLE BOYS SETTLE DOWN TO WAIT FOR THE MONEY TO POUR IN...
...THEN WE'LL LOAD THE LOOT ABOARD OUR JET AND HEAD FOR THE TROPICS...
MORE GOODIES, MISTER CLAUS...
JAQ AND GUS SLIP INTO THE KITCHEN TO SURPRISE SANTA...
WELL, BLESS MY BUTTONS!
SHHH! LISTEN, SANTA!
Distributed by King Features Syndicate.
AS SANTA LISTENS, HIS GLOOM VANISHES...
!
WHISPER... WHISPER...
Copyright © 1971 Walt Disney Productions World Rights Reserved
12-20

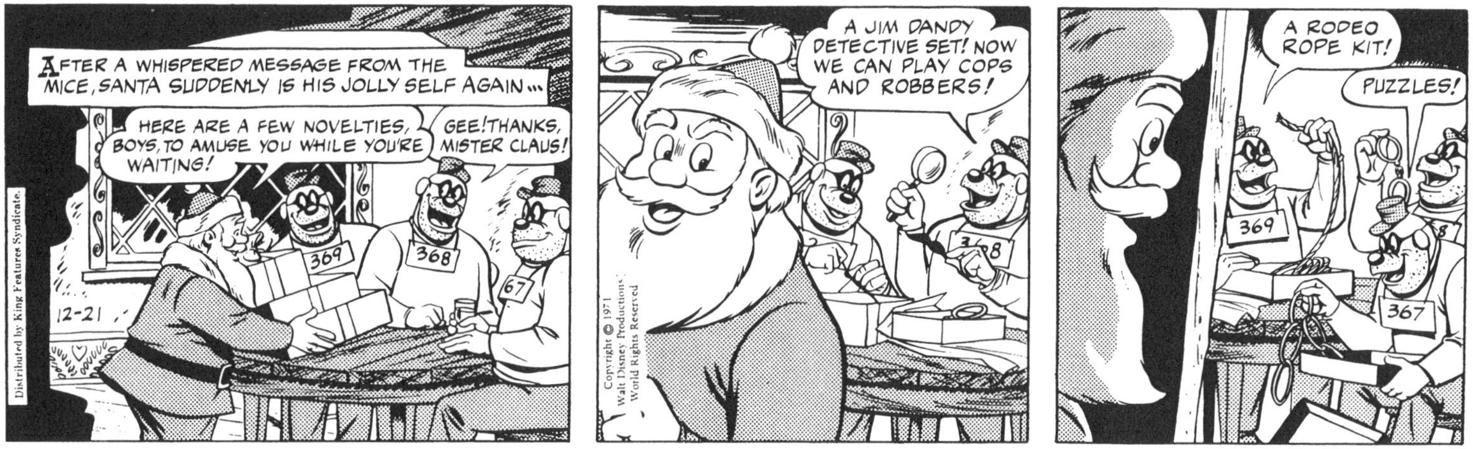
AFTER A WHISPERED MESSAGE FROM THE MICE, SANTA SUDDENLY IS HIS JOLLY SELF AGAIN...
HERE ARE A FEW NOVELTIES, BOYS, TO AMUSE YOU WHILE YOU'RE WAITING!
GEE! THANKS, MISTER CLAUS!
Distributed by King Features Syndicate.
12-21
A JIM DANDY DETECTIVE SET! NOW WE CAN PLAY COPS AND ROBBERS!
Copyright © 1971 Walt Disney Productions World Rights Reserved
A RODEO ROPE KIT!
PUZZLES!

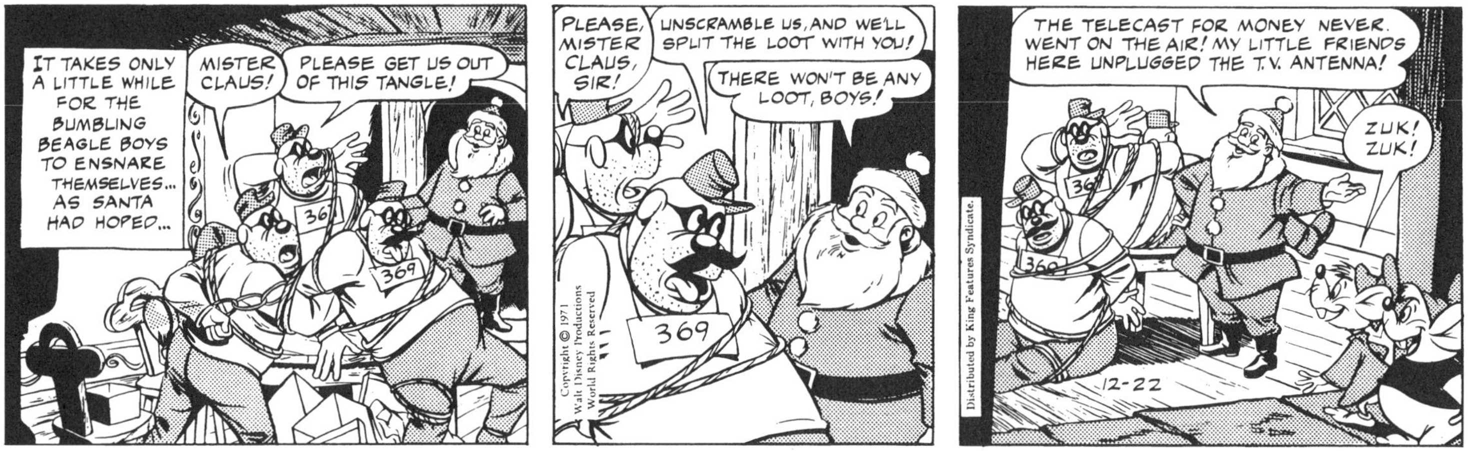
IT TAKES ONLY A LITTLE WHILE FOR THE BUMBLING BEAGLE BOYS TO ENSNARE THEMSELVES... AS SANTA HAD HOPED...
MISTER CLAUS!
PLEASE GET US OUT OF THIS TANGLE!
PLEASE, MISTER CLAUS, SIR!
UNSCRAMBLE US, AND WE'LL SPLIT THE LOOT WITH YOU!
THERE WON'T BE ANY LOOT, BOYS!
Copyright © 1971 Walt Disney Productions World Rights Reserved
THE TELECAST FOR MONEY NEVER WENT ON THE AIR! MY LITTLE FRIENDS HERE UNPLUGGED THE T.V. ANTENNA!
ZUK! ZUK!
Distributed by King Features Syndicate.
12-22

MISTER STORK RETURNS WITH A NORTH POLE PATROL COPTER...
EVERYTHING UNDER CONTROL. THE BEAGLE BOYS CAUGHT THEMSELVES!
AT PATROL HEADQUARTERS...
SORRY WE CAN'T GIVE YOU SEPARATE CELLS... UNTIL WE PRY YOU APART!
36
369
Distributed by King Features Syndicate.
12-23
SANTA SAYS TO TELL YOU "NO HARD FEELINGS ...AND MERRY CHRISTMAS."
Copyright © 1971
Walt Disney Productions
World Rights Reserved

FIRST STOP ON SANTA'S ANNUAL WHIRL AROUND THE WORLD IS THE OLD CHATEAU...
THANKS FOR THE RIDE, SANTA!
THANK YOU THREE HEROES FOR FOILING THE BEAGLE BOYS! YOU SAVED THE DAY— CHRISTMAS DAY!
ZUK! ZUK!
'RAY FOR JAQ AND GUS! 'RAY FOR MISTER STORK!
RAY FOR SANTA CLAUS!
Distributed by King Features Syndicate.
AND SO, THE JOLLY JOURNEY BEGINS...
a Merry Christmas
to Everyone ... Everywhere...
Copyright © 1971
Walt Disney Productions
World Rights Reserved
12-24

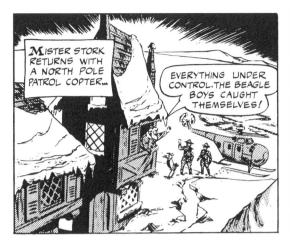

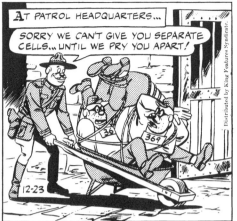

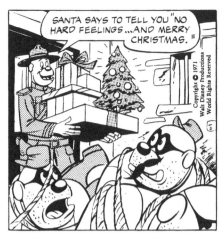

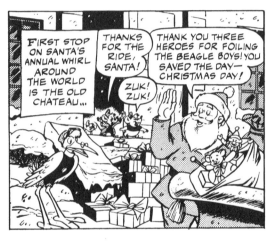

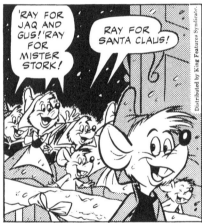

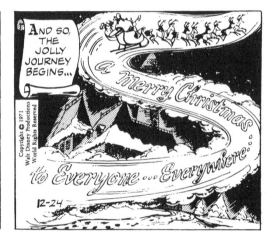

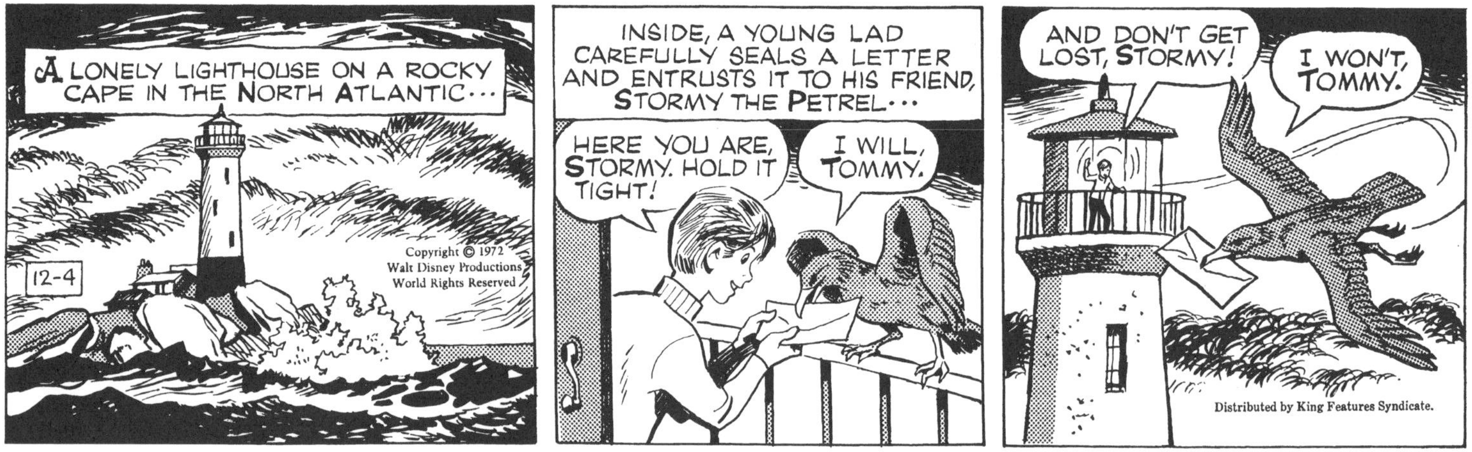
A LONELY LIGHTHOUSE ON A ROCKY CAPE IN THE NORTH ATLANTIC...
Copyright © 1972 Walt Disney Productions World Rights Reserved
12-4
INSIDE, A YOUNG LAD CAREFULLY SEALS A LETTER AND ENTRUSTS IT TO HIS FRIEND, STORMY THE PETREL...
HERE YOU ARE, STORMY. HOLD IT TIGHT!
I WILL, TOMMY.
AND DON'T GET LOST, STORMY!
I WON'T, TOMMY.
Distributed by King Features Syndicate.

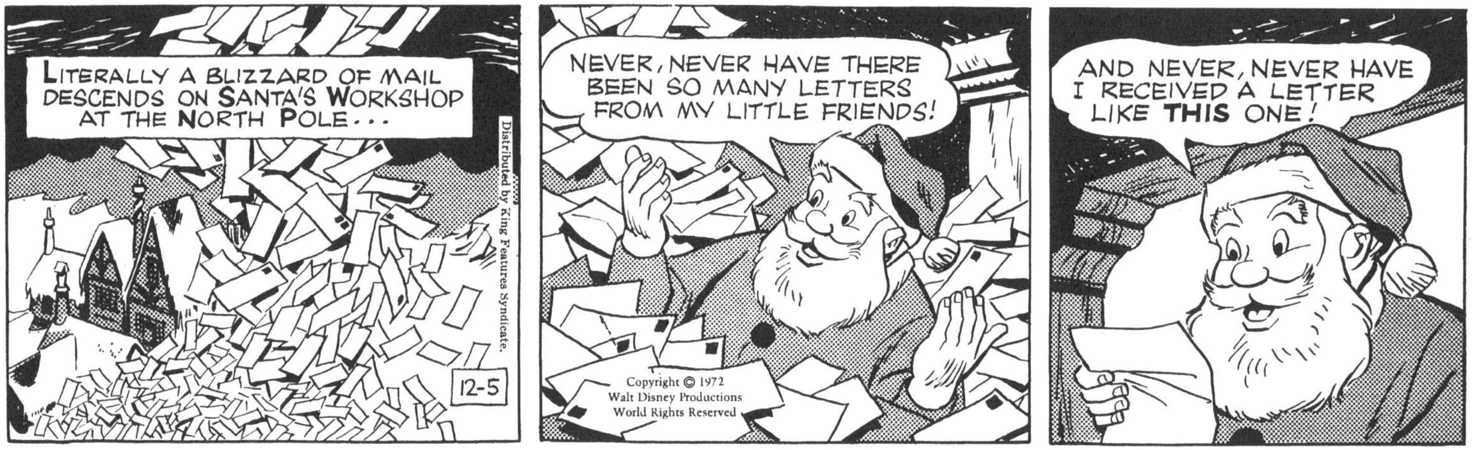
LITERALLY A BLIZZARD OF MAIL DESCENDS ON SANTA'S WORKSHOP AT THE NORTH POLE...
Distributed by King Features Syndicate.
12-5
NEVER, NEVER HAVE THERE BEEN SO MANY LETTERS FROM MY LITTLE FRIENDS!
Copyright © 1972 Walt Disney Productions World Rights Reserved
AND NEVER, NEVER HAVE I RECEIVED A LETTER LIKE THIS ONE!

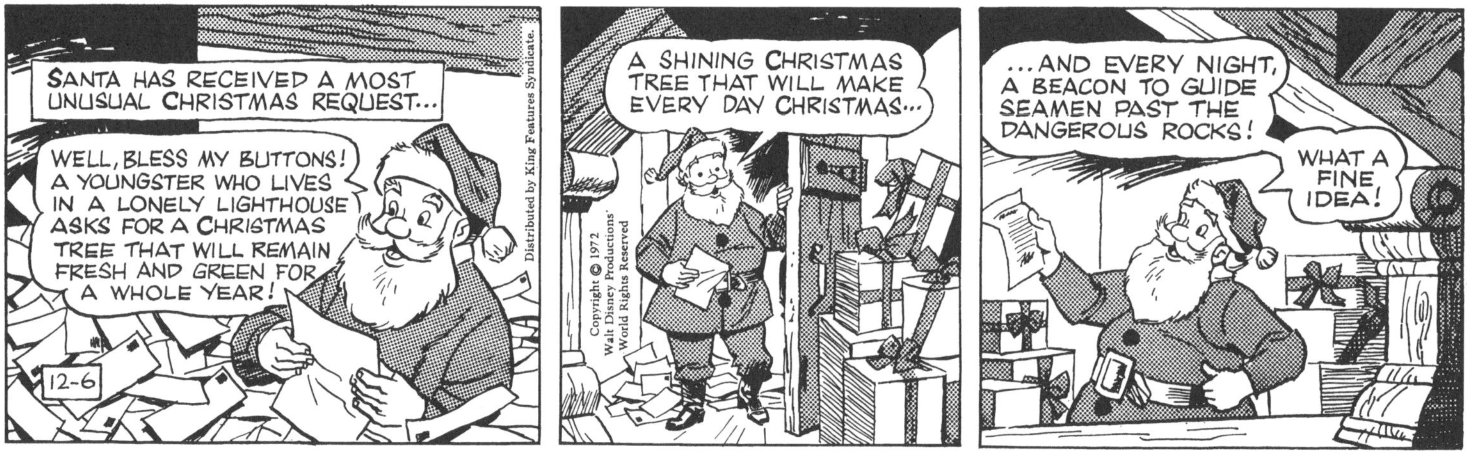
SANTA HAS RECEIVED A MOST UNUSUAL CHRISTMAS REQUEST...
WELL, BLESS MY BUTTONS! A YOUNGSTER WHO LIVES IN A LONELY LIGHTHOUSE ASKS FOR A CHRISTMAS TREE THAT WILL REMAIN FRESH AND GREEN FOR A WHOLE YEAR!
Distributed by King Features Syndicate.
12-6
A SHINING CHRISTMAS TREE THAT WILL MAKE EVERY DAY CHRISTMAS...
Copyright © 1972 Walt Disney Productions World Rights Reserved
...AND EVERY NIGHT, A BEACON TO GUIDE SEAMEN PAST THE DANGEROUS ROCKS!
WHAT A FINE IDEA!

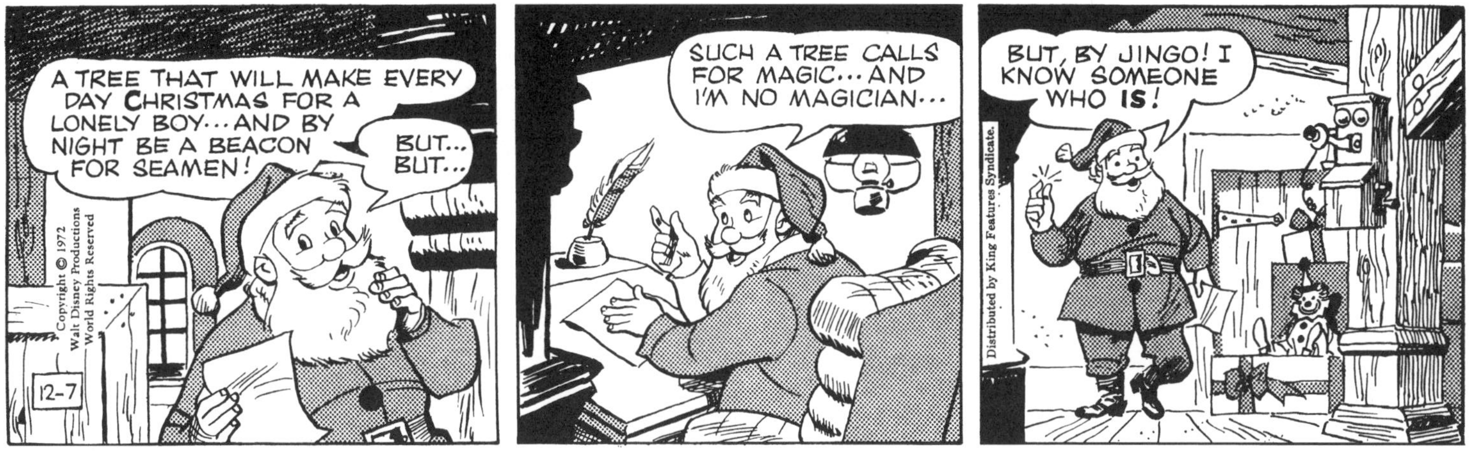
A TREE THAT WILL MAKE EVERY DAY CHRISTMAS FOR A LONELY BOY... AND BY NIGHT BE A BEACON FOR SEAMEN!
BUT... BUT...
Copyright © 1972 Walt Disney Productions World Rights Reserved
12-7
SUCH A TREE CALLS FOR MAGIC... AND I'M NO MAGICIAN...
BUT, BY JINGO! I KNOW SOMEONE WHO IS!
Distributed by King Features Syndicate.

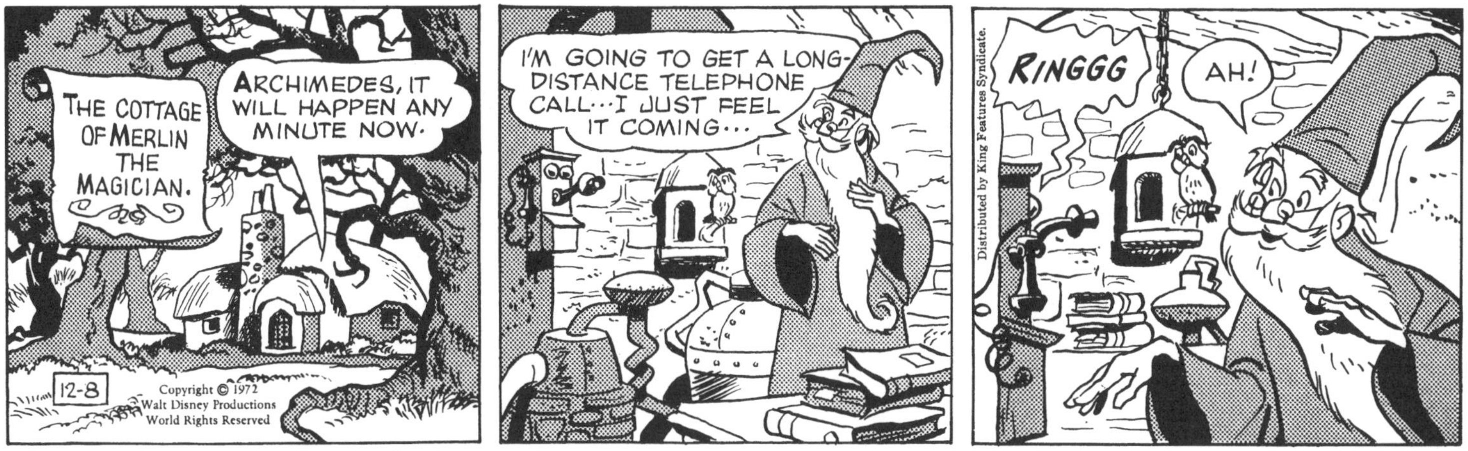
THE COTTAGE OF MERLIN THE MAGICIAN.
ARCHIMEDES, IT WILL HAPPEN ANY MINUTE NOW.
12-8
Copyright © 1972 Walt Disney Productions World Rights Reserved
I'M GOING TO GET A LONG-DISTANCE TELEPHONE CALL... I JUST FEEL IT COMING...
Distributed by King Features Syndicate.
RINGGG
AH!

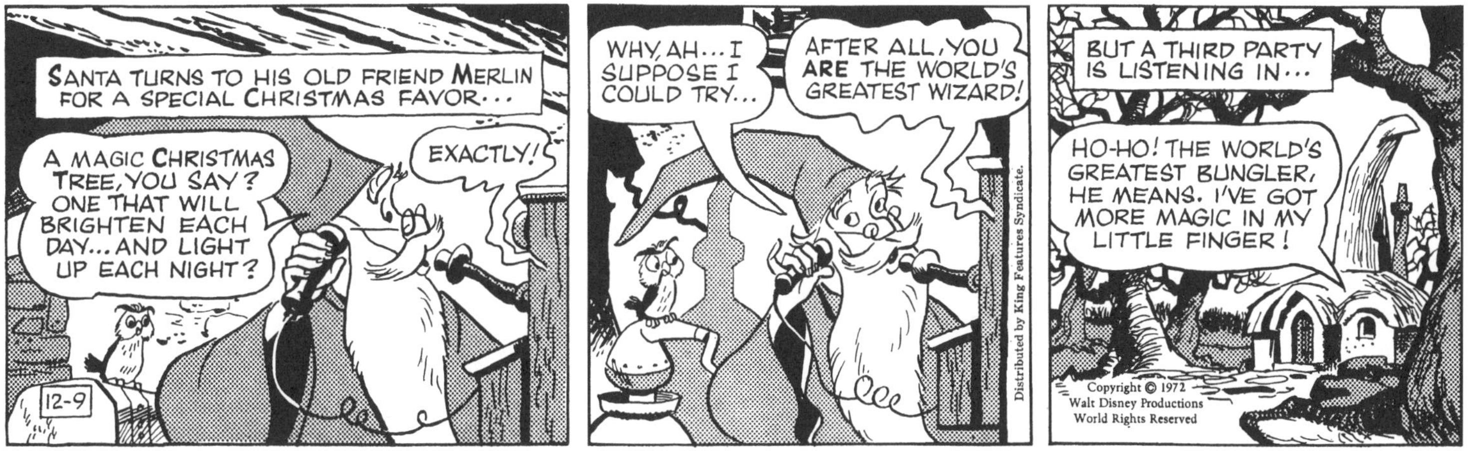
SANTA TURNS TO HIS OLD FRIEND MERLIN FOR A SPECIAL CHRISTMAS FAVOR...
A MAGIC CHRISTMAS TREE, YOU SAY? ONE THAT WILL BRIGHTEN EACH DAY... AND LIGHT UP EACH NIGHT?
EXACTLY!
12-9
WHY, AH... I SUPPOSE I COULD TRY...
AFTER ALL, YOU ARE THE WORLD'S GREATEST WIZARD!
Distributed by King Features Syndicate.
BUT A THIRD PARTY IS LISTENING IN...
HO-HO! THE WORLD'S GREATEST BUNGLER, HE MEANS. I'VE GOT MORE MAGIC IN MY LITTLE FINGER!
Copyright © 1972 Walt Disney Productions World Rights Reserved

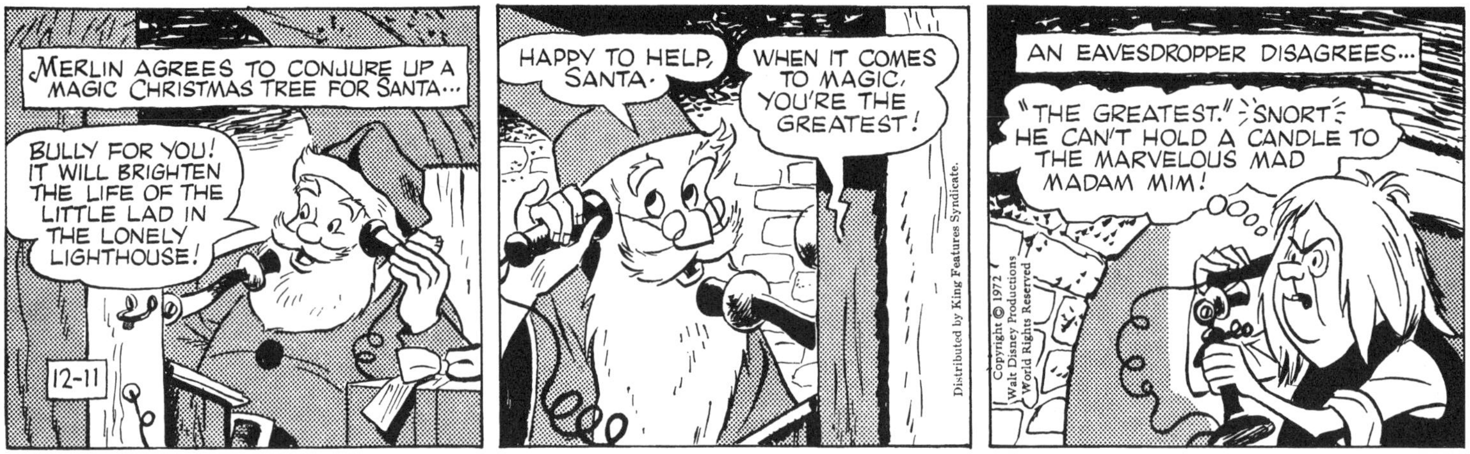
MERLIN AGREES TO CONJURE UP A MAGIC CHRISTMAS TREE FOR SANTA...
BULLY FOR YOU! IT WILL BRIGHTEN THE LIFE OF THE LITTLE LAD IN THE LONELY LIGHTHOUSE!
12-11
HAPPY TO HELP, SANTA.
WHEN IT COMES TO MAGIC, YOU'RE THE GREATEST!
Distributed by King Features Syndicate.
AN EAVESDROPPER DISAGREES...
"THE GREATEST." SNORT HE CAN'T HOLD A CANDLE TO THE MARVELOUS MAD MADAM MIM!
Copyright © 1972 Walt Disney Productions World Rights Reserved

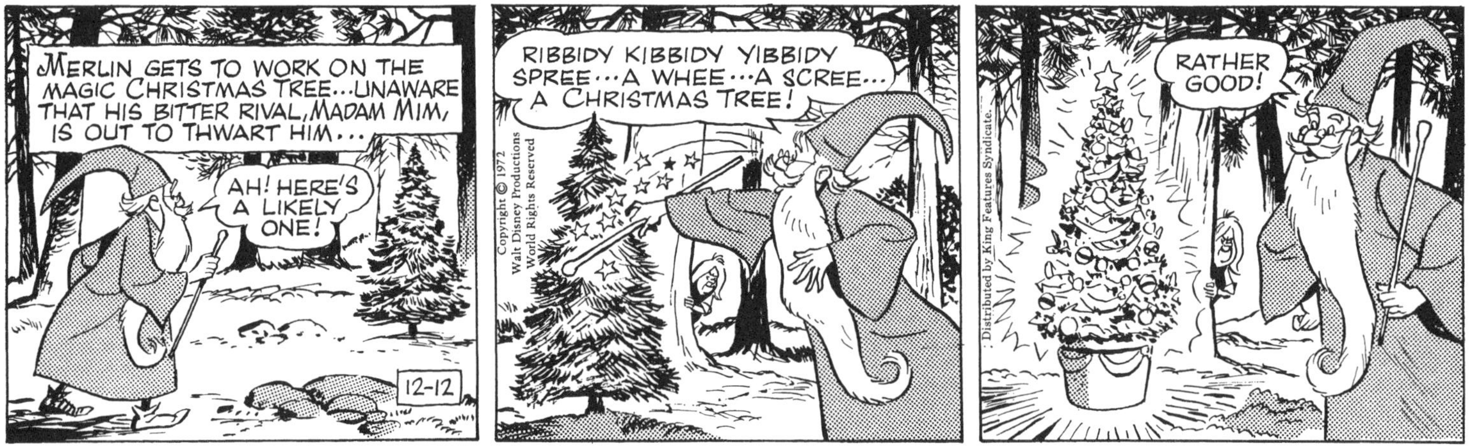
MERLIN GETS TO WORK ON THE MAGIC CHRISTMAS TREE...UNAWARE THAT HIS BITTER RIVAL, MADAM MIM, IS OUT TO THWART HIM...
AH! HERE'S A LIKELY ONE!
12-12
RIBBIDY KIBBIDY YIBBIDY SPREE...A WHEE...A SCREE... A CHRISTMAS TREE!
Copyright © 1972 Walt Disney Productions World Rights Reserved
RATHER GOOD!
Distributed by King Features Syndicate.

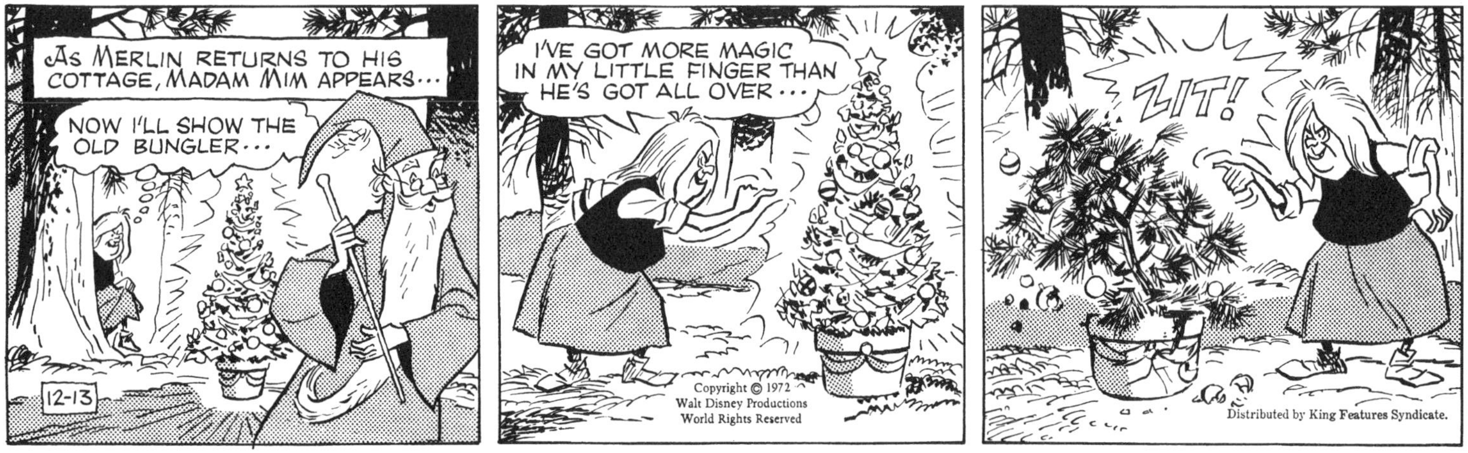
AS MERLIN RETURNS TO HIS COTTAGE, MADAM MIM APPEARS...
NOW I'LL SHOW THE OLD BUNGLER...
12-13
I'VE GOT MORE MAGIC IN MY LITTLE FINGER THAN HE'S GOT ALL OVER...
Copyright © 1972 Walt Disney Productions World Rights Reserved
ZIT!
Distributed by King Features Syndicate.

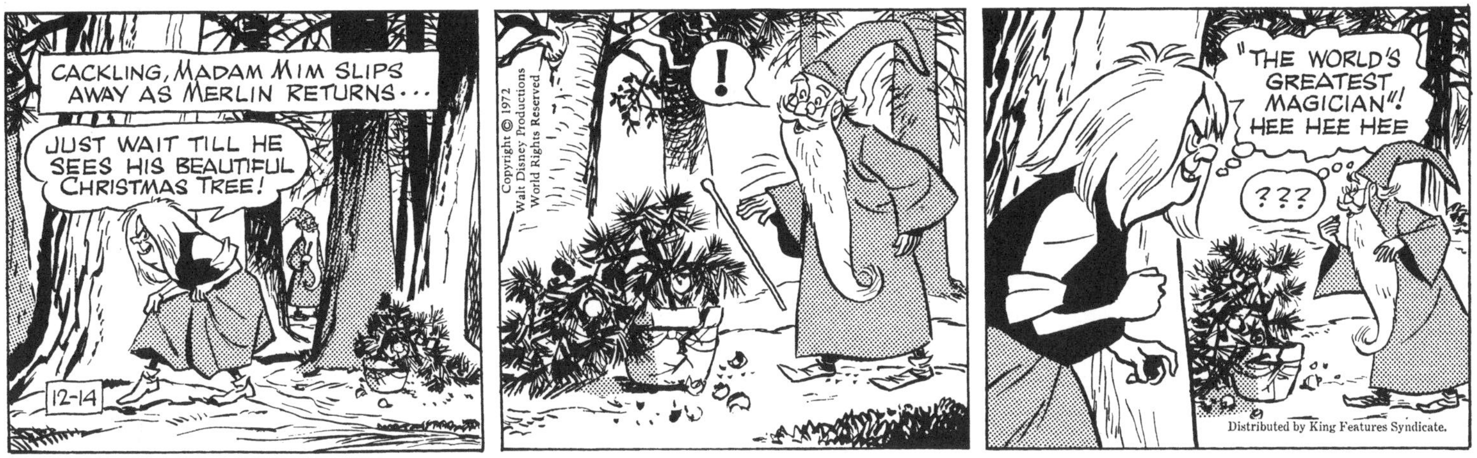
CACKLING, MADAM MIM SLIPS AWAY AS MERLIN RETURNS...
JUST WAIT TILL HE SEES HIS BEAUTIFUL CHRISTMAS TREE!
12-14
!
Copyright © 1972 Walt Disney Productions World Rights Reserved
"THE WORLD'S GREATEST MAGICIAN"! HEE HEE HEE
???
Distributed by King Features Syndicate.

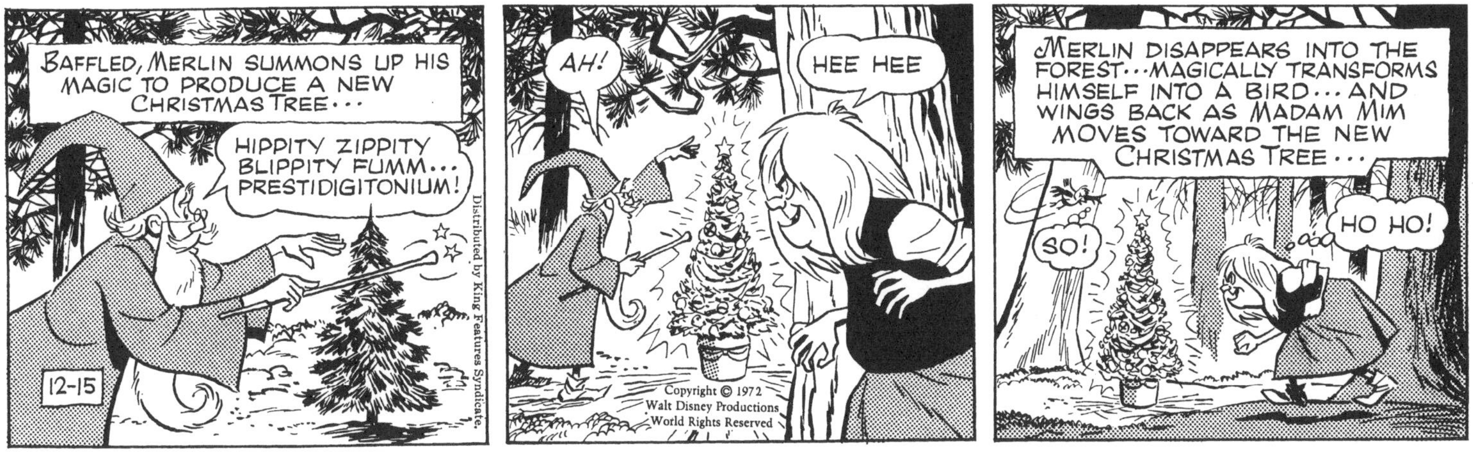
BAFFLED, MERLIN SUMMONS UP HIS MAGIC TO PRODUCE A NEW CHRISTMAS TREE...
HIPPITY ZIPPITY BLIPPITY FUMM... PRESTIDIGITONIUM!
12-15
Distributed by King Features Syndicate.
AH!
HEE HEE
Copyright © 1972 Walt Disney Productions World Rights Reserved
MERLIN DISAPPEARS INTO THE FOREST... MAGICALLY TRANSFORMS HIMSELF INTO A BIRD... AND WINGS BACK AS MADAM MIM MOVES TOWARD THE NEW CHRISTMAS TREE...
SO!
HO HO!

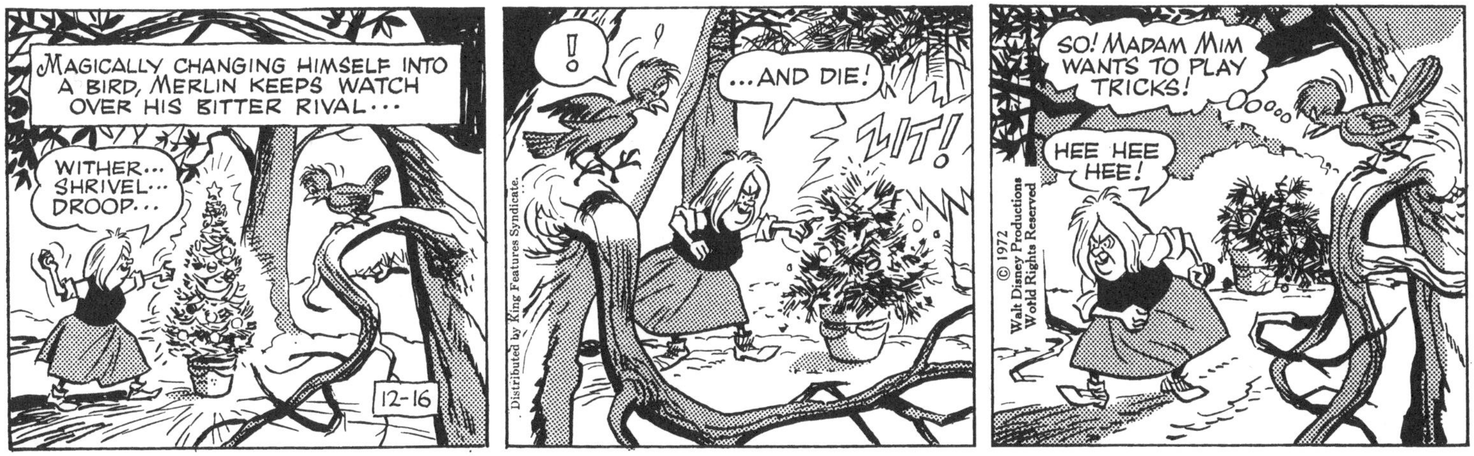
MAGICALLY CHANGING HIMSELF INTO A BIRD, MERLIN KEEPS WATCH OVER HIS BITTER RIVAL...
WITHER... SHRIVEL... DROOP...
12-16
!
...AND DIE!
ZIT!
Distributed by King Features Syndicate.
SO! MADAM MIM WANTS TO PLAY TRICKS!
HEE HEE HEE!
© 1972 Walt Disney Productions World Rights Reserved

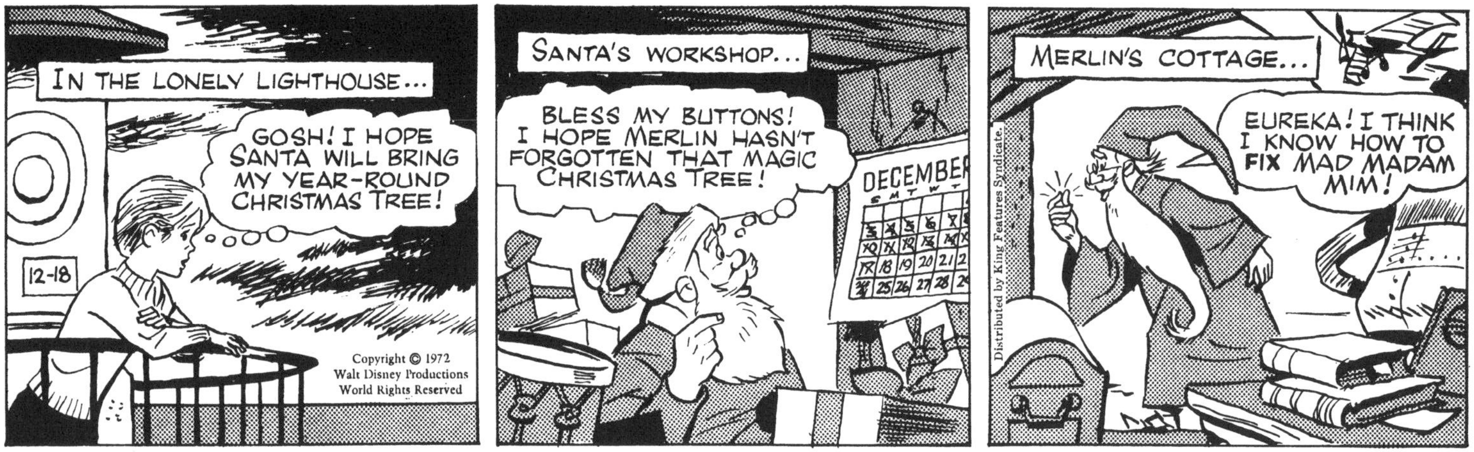
IN THE LONELY LIGHTHOUSE...
GOSH! I HOPE SANTA WILL BRING MY YEAR-ROUND CHRISTMAS TREE!
12-18
Copyright © 1972 Walt Disney Productions World Rights Reserved
SANTA'S WORKSHOP...
BLESS MY BUTTONS! I HOPE MERLIN HASN'T FORGOTTEN THAT MAGIC CHRISTMAS TREE!
DECEMBER
Distributed by King Features Syndicate.
MERLIN'S COTTAGE...
EUREKA! I THINK I KNOW HOW TO **FIX** MAD MADAM MIM!

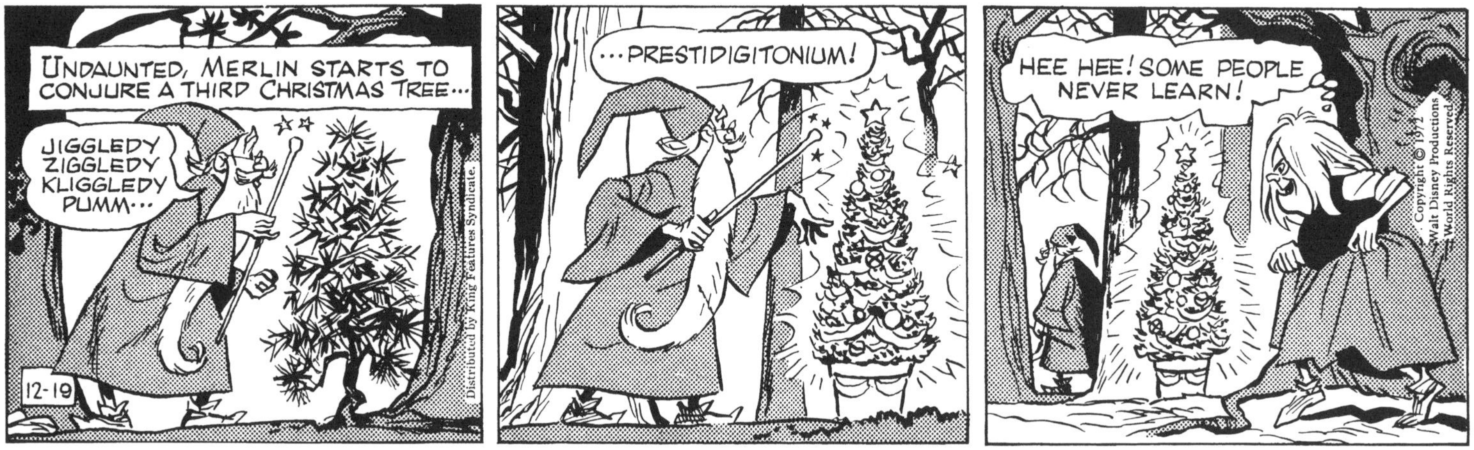
UNDAUNTED, MERLIN STARTS TO CONJURE A THIRD CHRISTMAS TREE...
JIGGLEDY ZIGGLEDY KLIGGLEDY PUMM...
12-19
Distributed by King Features Syndicate.
...PRESTIDIGITONIUM!
HEE HEE! SOME PEOPLE NEVER LEARN!
Copyright © 1972 Walt Disney Productions World Rights Reserved

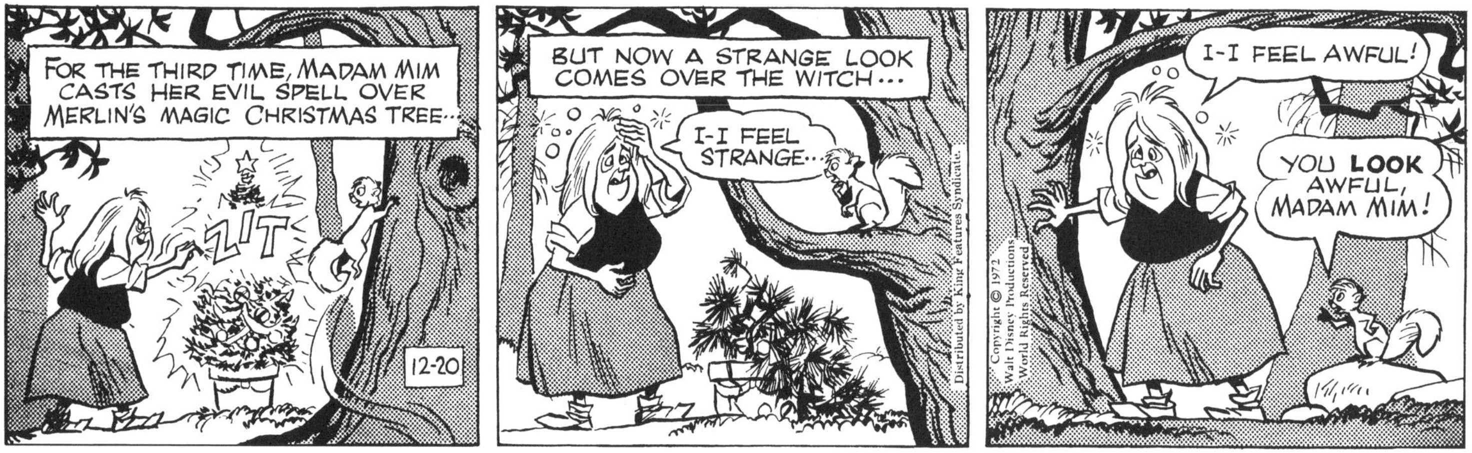
FOR THE THIRD TIME, MADAM MIM CASTS HER EVIL SPELL OVER MERLIN'S MAGIC CHRISTMAS TREE...
ZIT
12-20
BUT NOW A STRANGE LOOK COMES OVER THE WITCH...
I-I FEEL STRANGE...
Distributed by King Features Syndicate.
I-I FEEL AWFUL!
YOU **LOOK** AWFUL, MADAM MIM!
Copyright © 1972 Walt Disney Productions World Rights Reserved

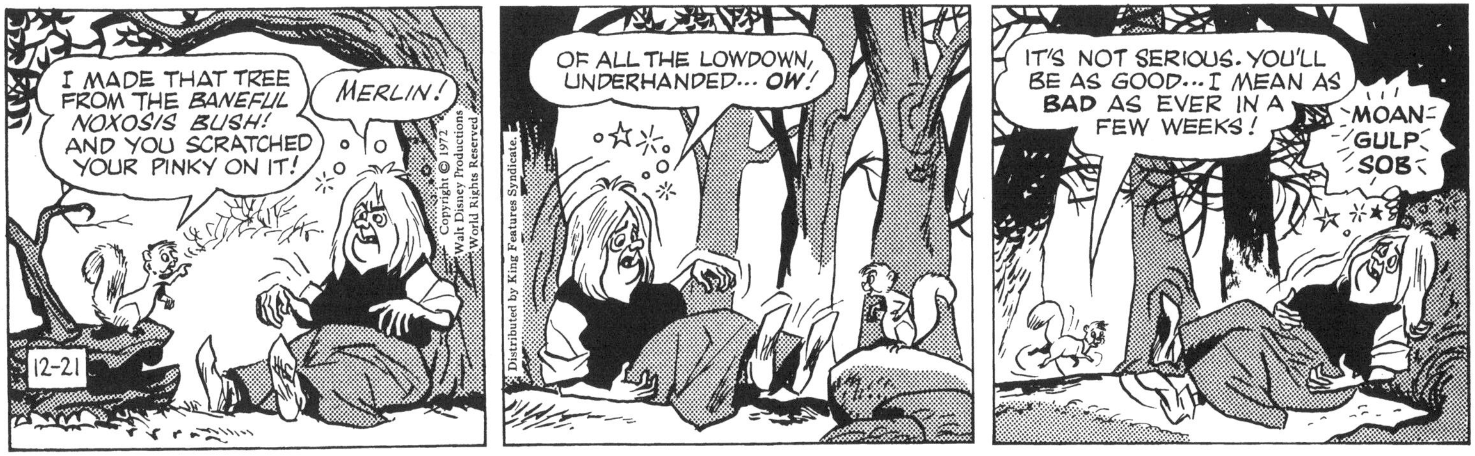
I MADE THAT TREE FROM THE BANEFUL NOXOSIS BUSH! AND YOU SCRATCHED YOUR PINKY ON IT!
MERLIN!
12-21
Copyright © 1972 Walt Disney Productions World Rights Reserved
Distributed by King Features Syndicate.
OF ALL THE LOWDOWN, UNDERHANDED... OW!
IT'S NOT SERIOUS. YOU'LL BE AS GOOD... I MEAN AS BAD AS EVER IN A FEW WEEKS!
MOAN GULP SOB
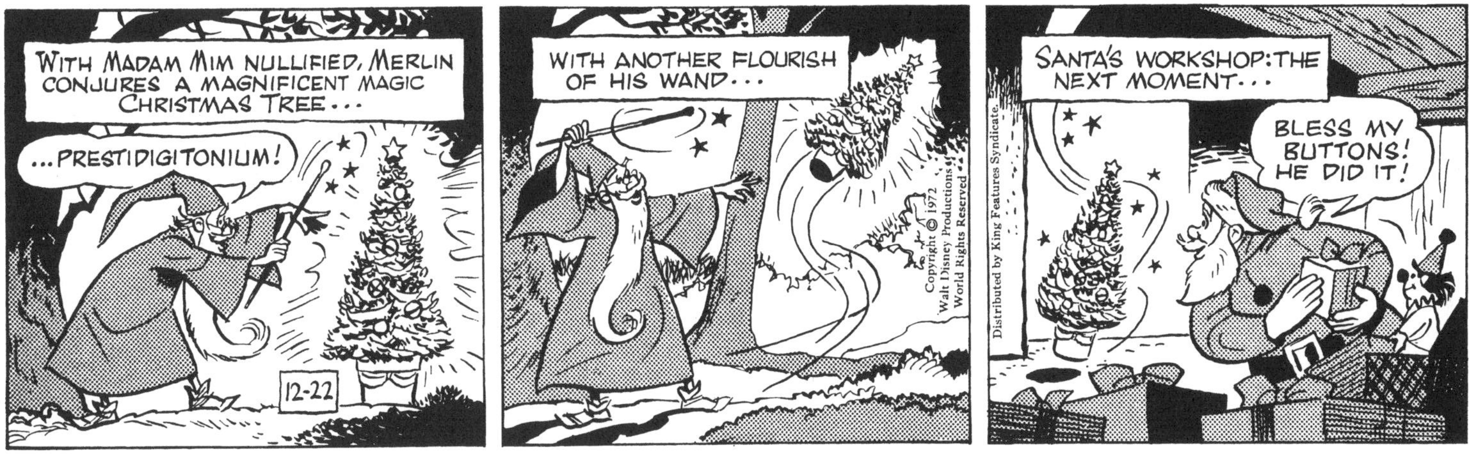
WITH MADAM MIM NULLIFIED, MERLIN CONJURES A MAGNIFICENT MAGIC CHRISTMAS TREE...
...PRESTIDIGITONIUM!
12-22
WITH ANOTHER FLOURISH OF HIS WAND...
Copyright © 1972 Walt Disney Productions World Rights Reserved
Distributed by King Features Syndicate.
SANTA'S WORKSHOP: THE NEXT MOMENT...
BLESS MY BUTTONS! HE DID IT!
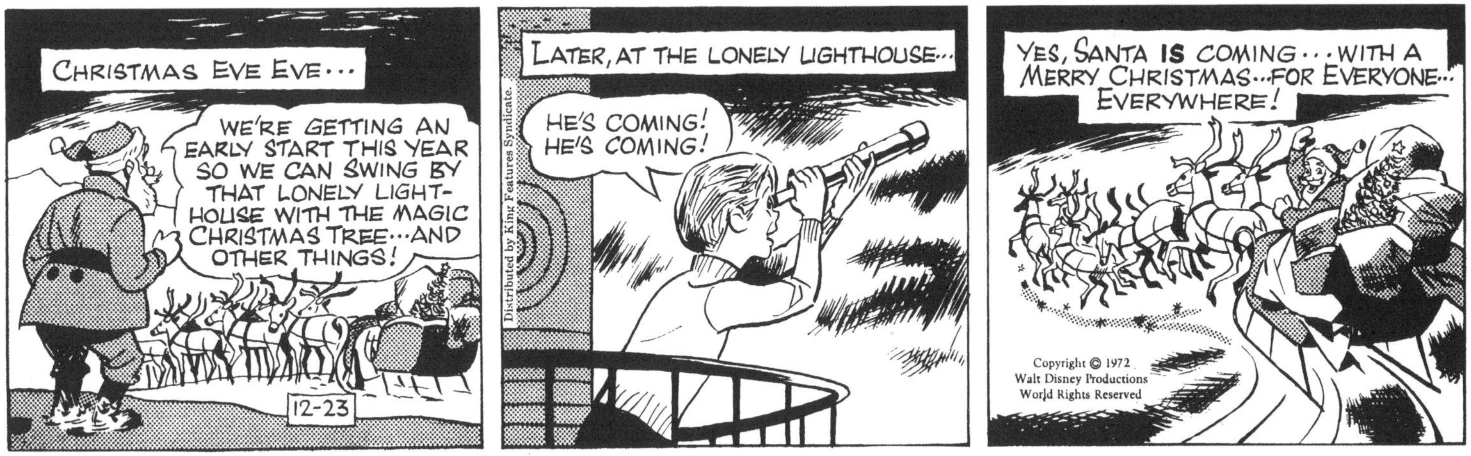
CHRISTMAS EVE EVE...
WE'RE GETTING AN EARLY START THIS YEAR SO WE CAN SWING BY THAT LONELY LIGHTHOUSE WITH THE MAGIC CHRISTMAS TREE...AND OTHER THINGS!
12-23
Distributed by King Features Syndicate.
LATER, AT THE LONELY LIGHTHOUSE...
HE'S COMING! HE'S COMING!
YES, SANTA IS COMING...WITH A MERRY CHRISTMAS...FOR EVERYONE... EVERYWHERE!
Copyright © 1972 Walt Disney Productions World Rights Reserved

1973

A CASTLE FOR CHRISTMAS

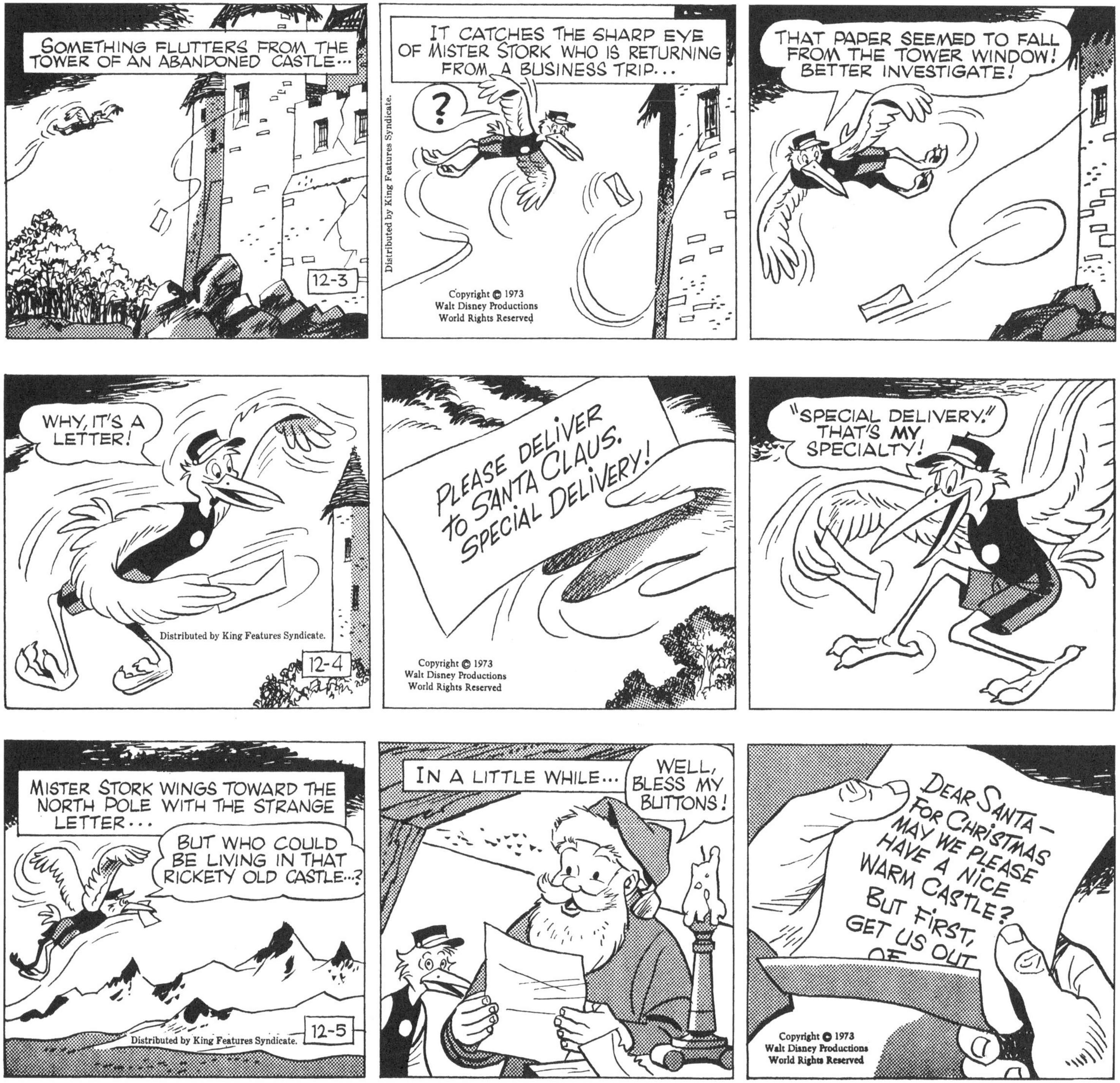
SOMETHING FLUTTERS FROM THE TOWER OF AN ABANDONED CASTLE...
12-3
IT CATCHES THE SHARP EYE OF MISTER STORK WHO IS RETURNING FROM A BUSINESS TRIP...
?
Distributed by King Features Syndicate.
Copyright © 1973
Walt Disney Productions
World Rights Reserved
THAT PAPER SEEMED TO FALL FROM THE TOWER WINDOW! BETTER INVESTIGATE!
WHY, IT'S A LETTER!
Distributed by King Features Syndicate.
12-4
PLEASE DELIVER TO SANTA CLAUS. SPECIAL DELIVERY!
Copyright © 1973
Walt Disney Productions
World Rights Reserved
"SPECIAL DELIVERY!" THAT'S **MY** SPECIALTY!
MISTER STORK WINGS TOWARD THE NORTH POLE WITH THE STRANGE LETTER...
BUT WHO COULD BE LIVING IN THAT RICKETY OLD CASTLE...?
Distributed by King Features Syndicate.
12-5
IN A LITTLE WHILE...
WELL, BLESS MY BUTTONS!
DEAR SANTA— FOR CHRISTMAS MAY WE PLEASE HAVE A NICE WARM CASTLE? BUT FIRST, GET US OUT OF
Copyright © 1973
Walt Disney Productions
World Rights Reserved

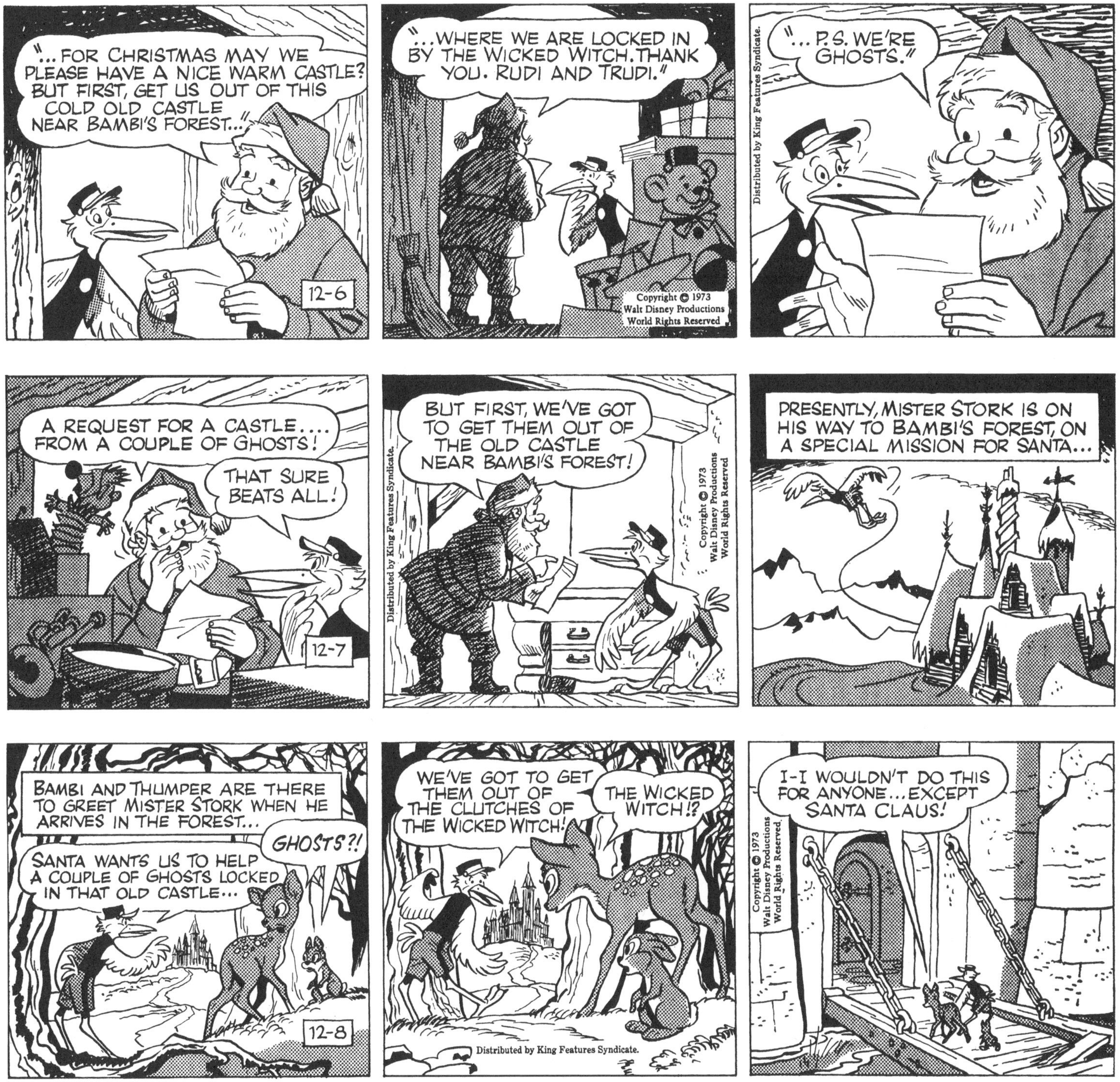
"...FOR CHRISTMAS MAY WE PLEASE HAVE A NICE WARM CASTLE? BUT FIRST, GET US OUT OF THIS COLD OLD CASTLE NEAR BAMBI'S FOREST..."
12-6
"...WHERE WE ARE LOCKED IN BY THE WICKED WITCH. THANK YOU. RUDI AND TRUDI."
Copyright © 1973 Walt Disney Productions World Rights Reserved
Distributed by King Features Syndicate.
"...P.S. WE'RE GHOSTS."
A REQUEST FOR A CASTLE.... FROM A COUPLE OF GHOSTS!
THAT SURE BEATS ALL!
12-7
Distributed by King Features Syndicate.
BUT FIRST, WE'VE GOT TO GET THEM OUT OF THE OLD CASTLE NEAR BAMBI'S FOREST!
Copyright © 1973 Walt Disney Productions World Rights Reserved
PRESENTLY, MISTER STORK IS ON HIS WAY TO BAMBI'S FOREST, ON A SPECIAL MISSION FOR SANTA...
BAMBI AND THUMPER ARE THERE TO GREET MISTER STORK WHEN HE ARRIVES IN THE FOREST...
SANTA WANTS US TO HELP A COUPLE OF GHOSTS LOCKED IN THAT OLD CASTLE...
GHOSTS?!
12-8
WE'VE GOT TO GET THEM OUT OF THE CLUTCHES OF THE WICKED WITCH!
THE WICKED WITCH!?
Distributed by King Features Syndicate.
Copyright © 1973 Walt Disney Productions World Rights Reserved.
I-I WOULDN'T DO THIS FOR ANYONE...EXCEPT SANTA CLAUS!

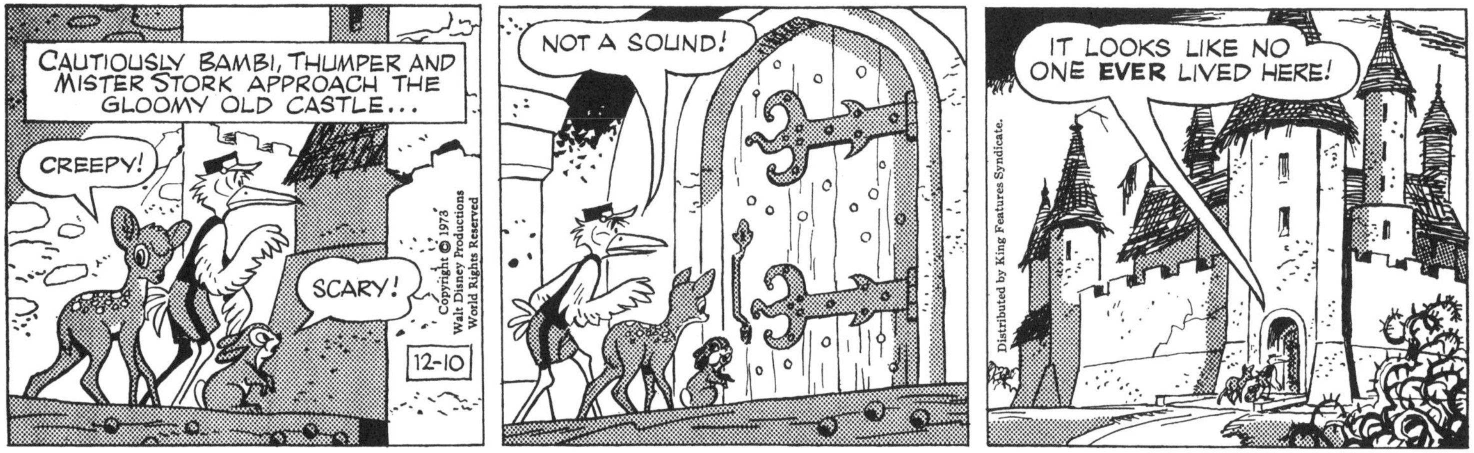
CAUTIOUSLY BAMBI, THUMPER AND MISTER STORK APPROACH THE GLOOMY OLD CASTLE...
CREEPY!
SCARY!
Copyright © 1973 Walt Disney Productions World Rights Reserved
12-10
NOT A SOUND!
IT LOOKS LIKE NO ONE **EVER** LIVED HERE!
Distributed by King Features Syndicate.

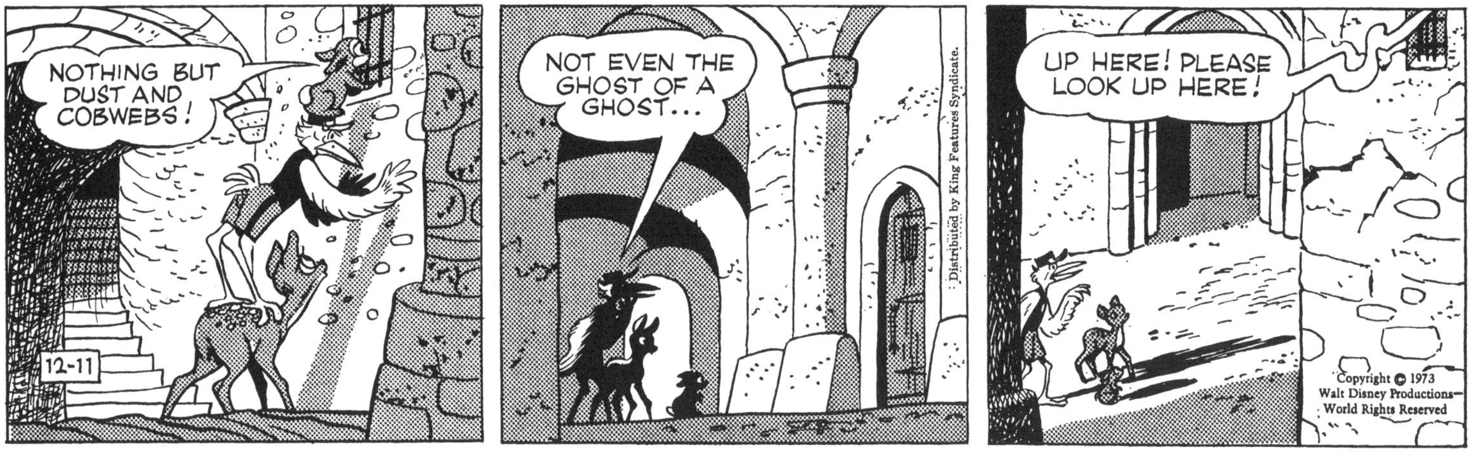
NOTHING BUT DUST AND COBWEBS!
12-11
NOT EVEN THE GHOST OF A GHOST...
Distributed by King Features Syndicate.
UP HERE! PLEASE LOOK UP HERE!
Copyright © 1973 Walt Disney Productions World Rights Reserved

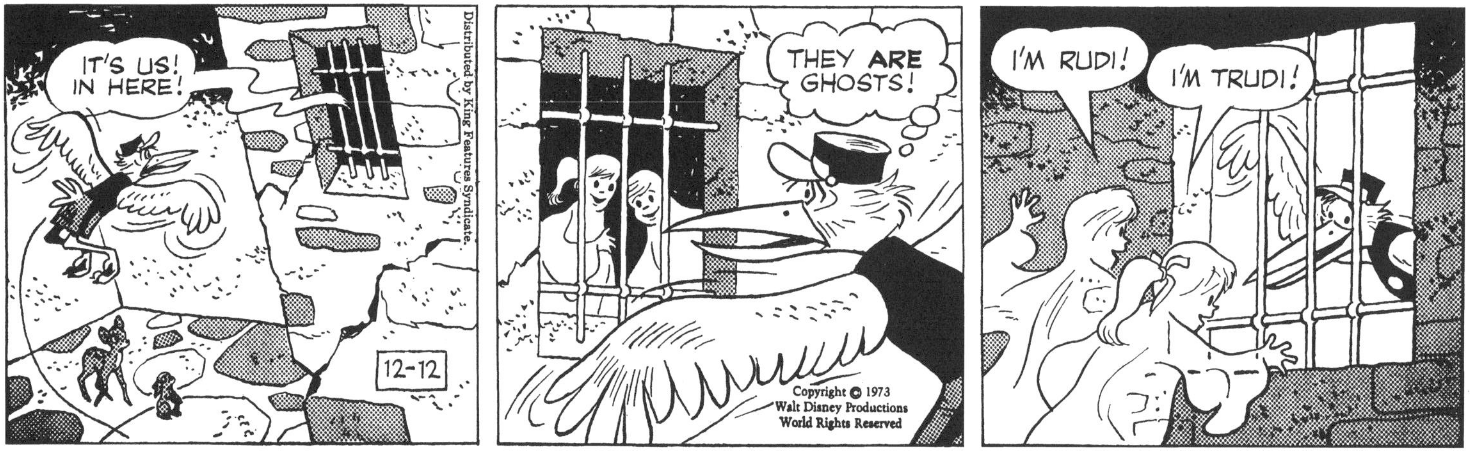
IT'S US! IN HERE!
Distributed by King Features Syndicate.
12-12
THEY **ARE** GHOSTS!
Copyright © 1973 Walt Disney Productions World Rights Reserved
I'M RUDI!
I'M TRUDI!

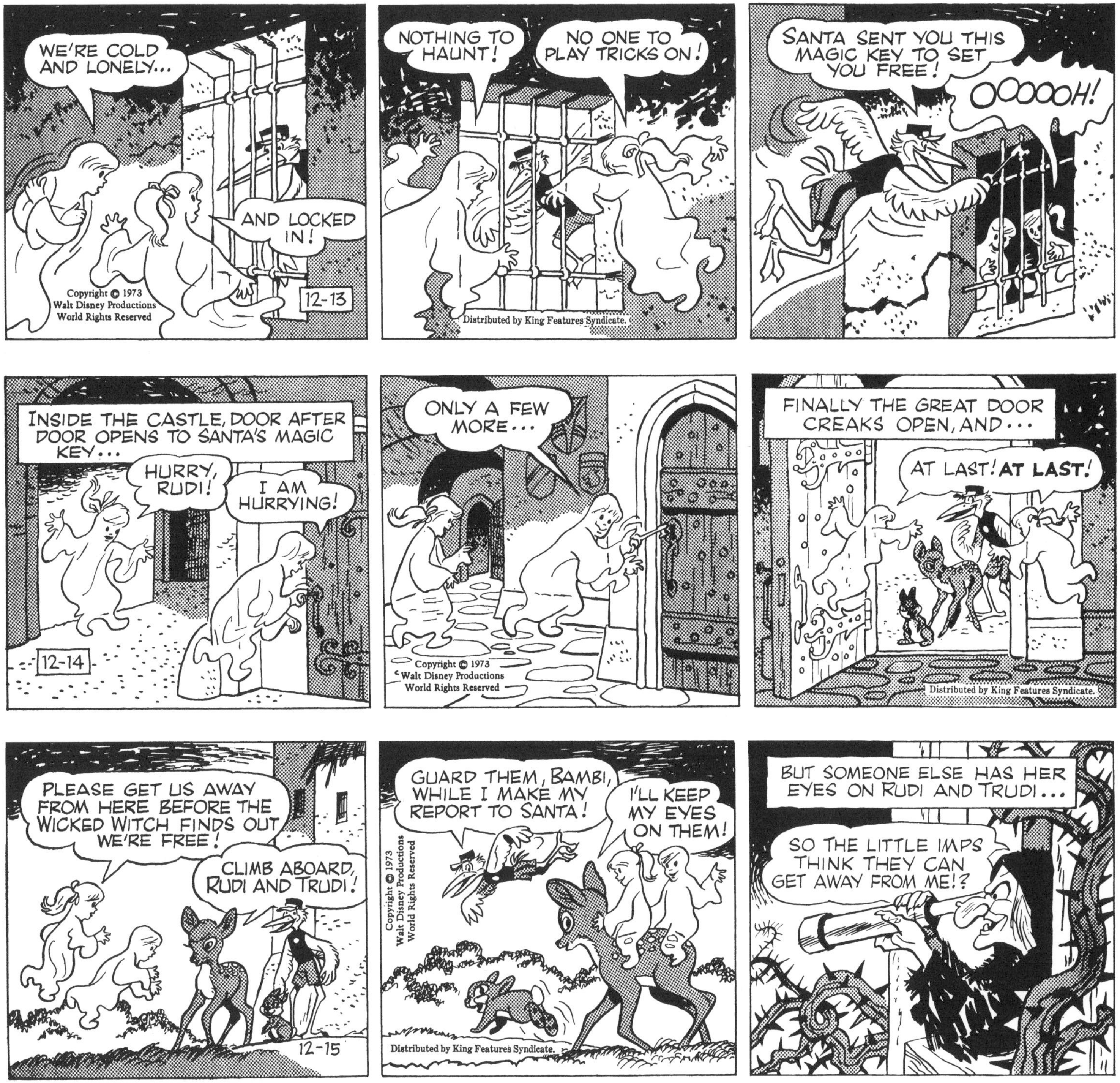
WE'RE COLD AND LONELY...
AND LOCKED IN!
Copyright © 1973
Walt Disney Productions
World Rights Reserved
12-13
NOTHING TO HAUNT!
NO ONE TO PLAY TRICKS ON!
Distributed by King Features Syndicate.
SANTA SENT YOU THIS MAGIC KEY TO SET YOU FREE!
OOOOOH!
INSIDE THE CASTLE, DOOR AFTER DOOR OPENS TO SANTA'S MAGIC KEY...
HURRY, RUDI!
I AM HURRYING!
12-14
ONLY A FEW MORE...
Copyright © 1973
Walt Disney Productions
World Rights Reserved
FINALLY THE GREAT DOOR CREAKS OPEN, AND...
AT LAST! AT LAST!
Distributed by King Features Syndicate.
PLEASE GET US AWAY FROM HERE BEFORE THE WICKED WITCH FINDS OUT WE'RE FREE!
CLIMB ABOARD, RUDI AND TRUDI!
12-15
GUARD THEM, BAMBI, WHILE I MAKE MY REPORT TO SANTA!
I'LL KEEP MY EYES ON THEM!
Copyright © 1973
Walt Disney Productions
World Rights Reserved
Distributed by King Features Syndicate.
BUT SOMEONE ELSE HAS HER EYES ON RUDI AND TRUDI...
SO THE LITTLE IMPS THINK THEY CAN GET AWAY FROM ME!?

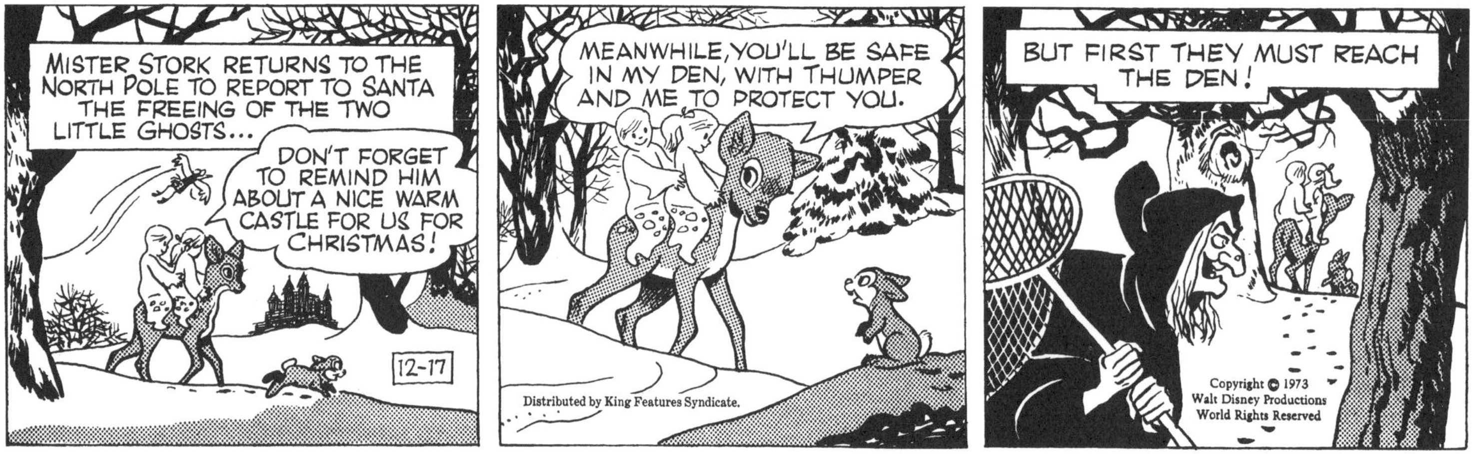
MISTER STORK RETURNS TO THE NORTH POLE TO REPORT TO SANTA THE FREEING OF THE TWO LITTLE GHOSTS...
DON'T FORGET TO REMIND HIM ABOUT A NICE WARM CASTLE FOR US FOR CHRISTMAS!
12-17
MEANWHILE, YOU'LL BE SAFE IN MY DEN, WITH THUMPER AND ME TO PROTECT YOU.
Distributed by King Features Syndicate.
BUT FIRST THEY MUST REACH THE DEN!
Copyright © 1973 Walt Disney Productions World Rights Reserved

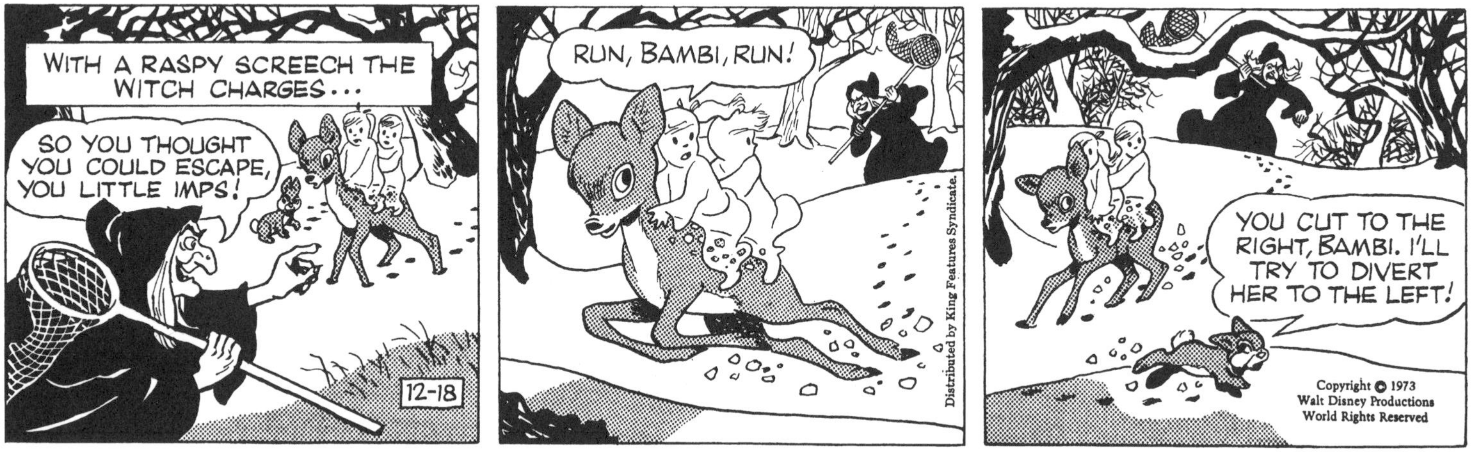
WITH A RASPY SCREECH THE WITCH CHARGES...
SO YOU THOUGHT YOU COULD ESCAPE, YOU LITTLE IMPS!
12-18
RUN, BAMBI, RUN!
Distributed by King Features Syndicate.
YOU CUT TO THE RIGHT, BAMBI. I'LL TRY TO DIVERT HER TO THE LEFT!
Copyright © 1973 Walt Disney Productions World Rights Reserved

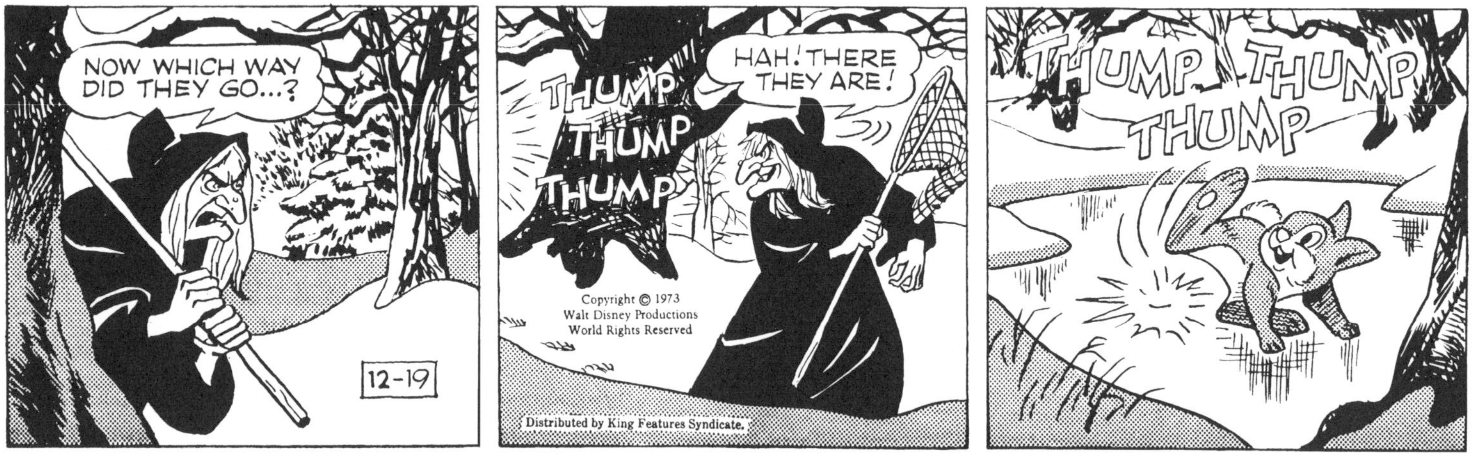
NOW WHICH WAY DID THEY GO...?
12-19
THUMP THUMP THUMP
HAH! THERE THEY ARE!
Copyright © 1973 Walt Disney Productions World Rights Reserved
Distributed by King Features Syndicate.
THUMP THUMP THUMP

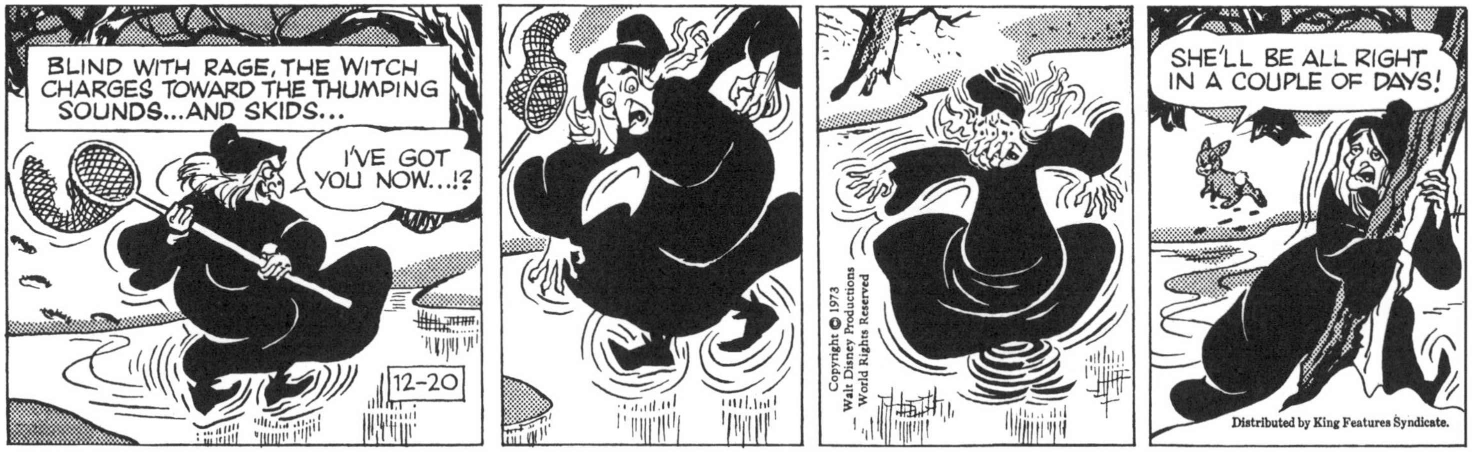
BLIND WITH RAGE, THE WITCH CHARGES TOWARD THE THUMPING SOUNDS...AND SKIDS...
I'VE GOT YOU NOW...!?
12-20
Copyright © 1973
Walt Disney Productions
World Rights Reserved
SHE'LL BE ALL RIGHT IN A COUPLE OF DAYS!
Distributed by King Features Syndicate.

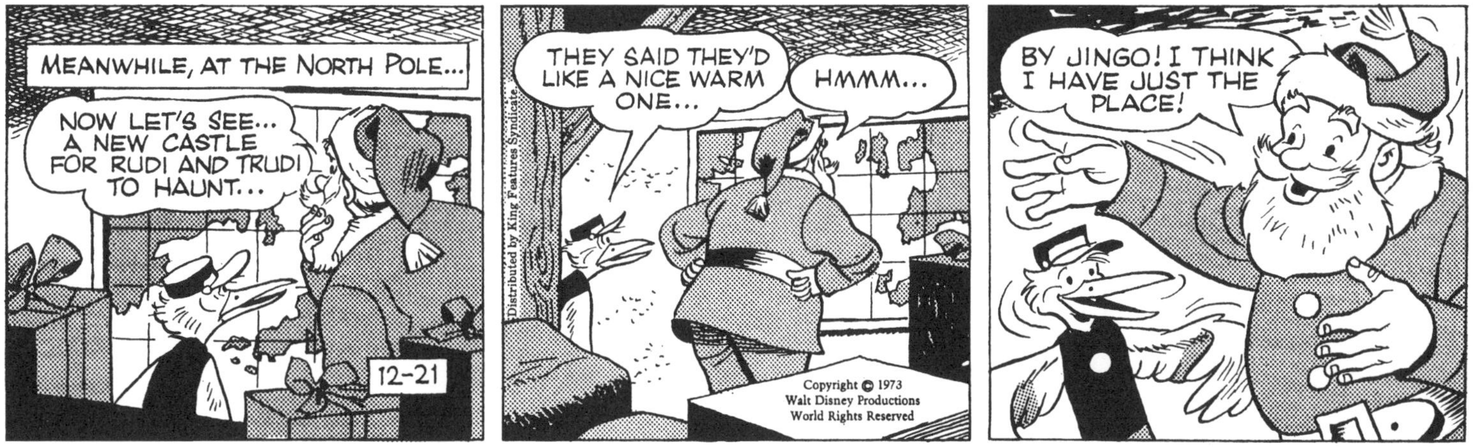
MEANWHILE, AT THE NORTH POLE...
NOW LET'S SEE... A NEW CASTLE FOR RUDI AND TRUDI TO HAUNT...
12-21
Distributed by King Features Syndicate.
THEY SAID THEY'D LIKE A NICE WARM ONE...
HMMM...
Copyright © 1973
Walt Disney Productions
World Rights Reserved
BY JINGO! I THINK I HAVE JUST THE PLACE!

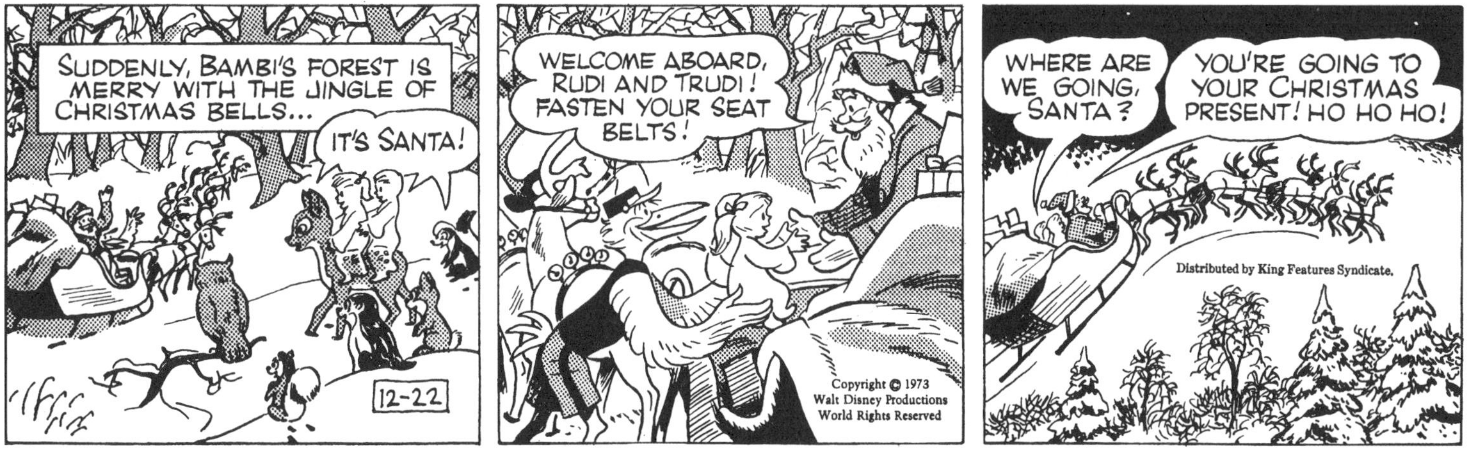
SUDDENLY, BAMBI'S FOREST IS MERRY WITH THE JINGLE OF CHRISTMAS BELLS...
IT'S SANTA!
12-22
WELCOME ABOARD, RUDI AND TRUDI! FASTEN YOUR SEAT BELTS!
Copyright © 1973
Walt Disney Productions
World Rights Reserved
WHERE ARE WE GOING, SANTA?
YOU'RE GOING TO YOUR CHRISTMAS PRESENT! HO HO HO!
Distributed by King Features Syndicate.

A CASTLE IN SUNNY SPAIN...
YOUR NEW HOME, RUDI AND TRUDI! HAPPY HAUNTING!
OOOOH!
WHEEEE!
12-24
IN A FEW MINUTES THEY ARE HAPPILY SETTLED...
GRACIAS, SANTA!
ADIOS, SANTA!
Distributed by King Features Syndicate.
Copyright © 1973 Walt Disney Productions World Rights Reserved
THEN, AWAY SANTA WHIRLS ON HIS REGULAR ROUNDS...
A MERRY CHRISTMAS TO EVERYONE... EVERYWHERE!

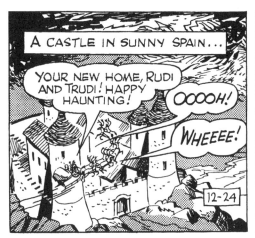

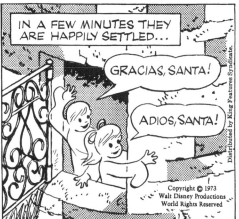

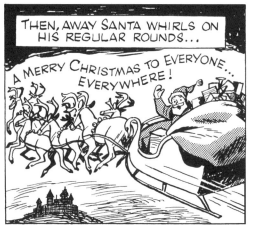

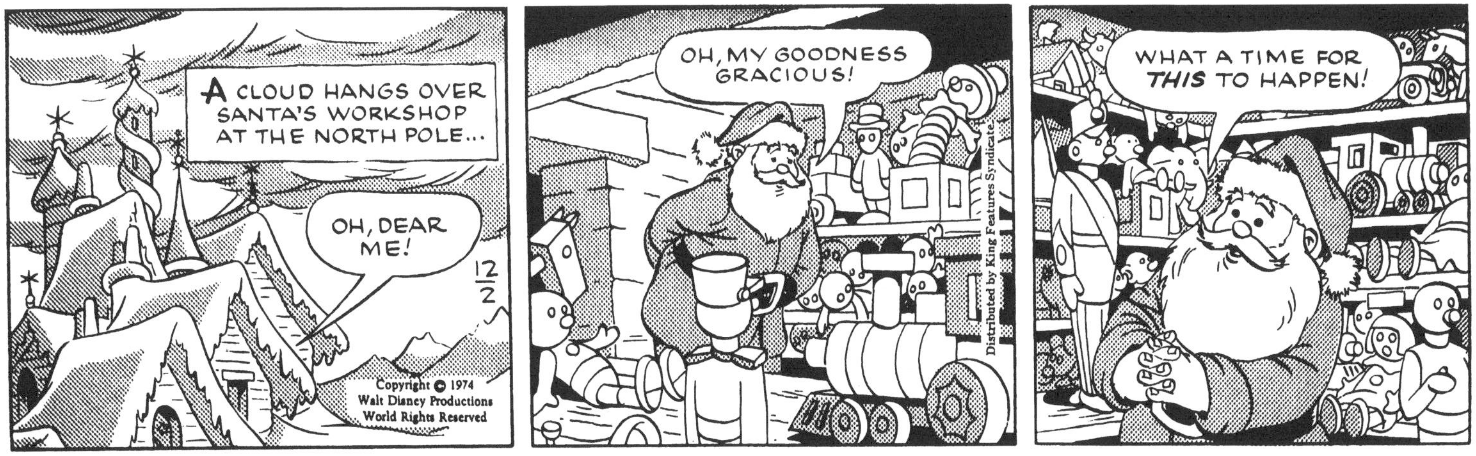
A CLOUD HANGS OVER SANTA'S WORKSHOP AT THE NORTH POLE...
OH, DEAR ME!
12/2
Copyright © 1974 Walt Disney Productions World Rights Reserved
OH, MY GOODNESS GRACIOUS!
Distributed by King Features Syndicate.
WHAT A TIME FOR *THIS* TO HAPPEN!

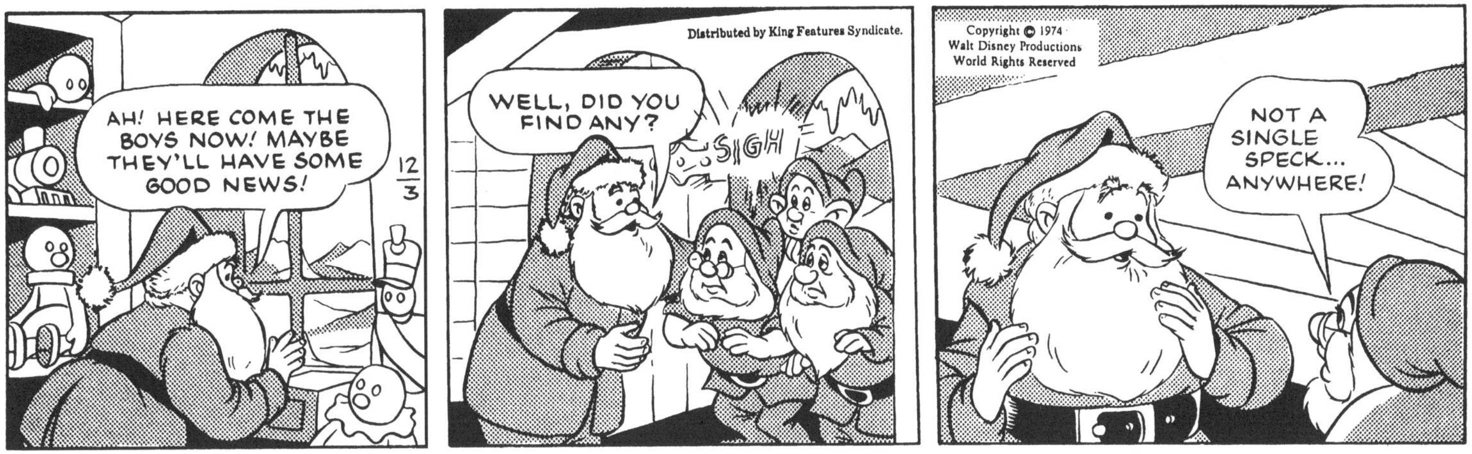
AH! HERE COME THE BOYS NOW! MAYBE THEY'LL HAVE SOME GOOD NEWS!
12/3
Distributed by King Features Syndicate.
WELL, DID YOU FIND ANY?
SIGH
Copyright © 1974 Walt Disney Productions World Rights Reserved
NOT A SINGLE SPECK... ANYWHERE!

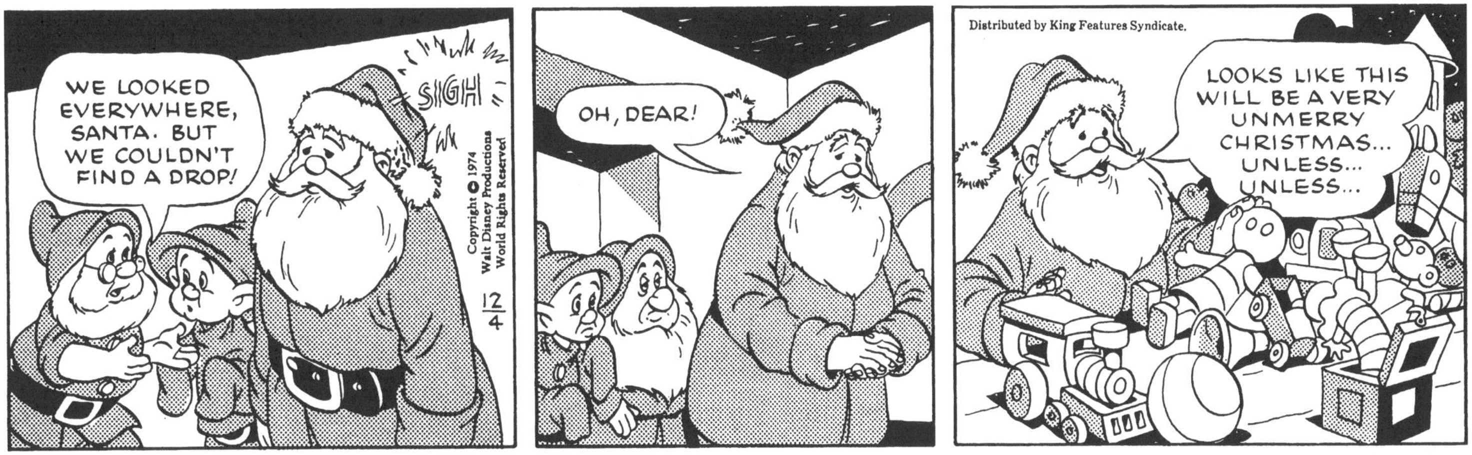
WE LOOKED EVERYWHERE, SANTA. BUT WE COULDN'T FIND A DROP!
SIGH
Copyright © 1974 Walt Disney Productions World Rights Reserved
12/4
OH, DEAR!
Distributed by King Features Syndicate.
LOOKS LIKE THIS WILL BE A VERY UNMERRY CHRISTMAS... UNLESS... UNLESS...

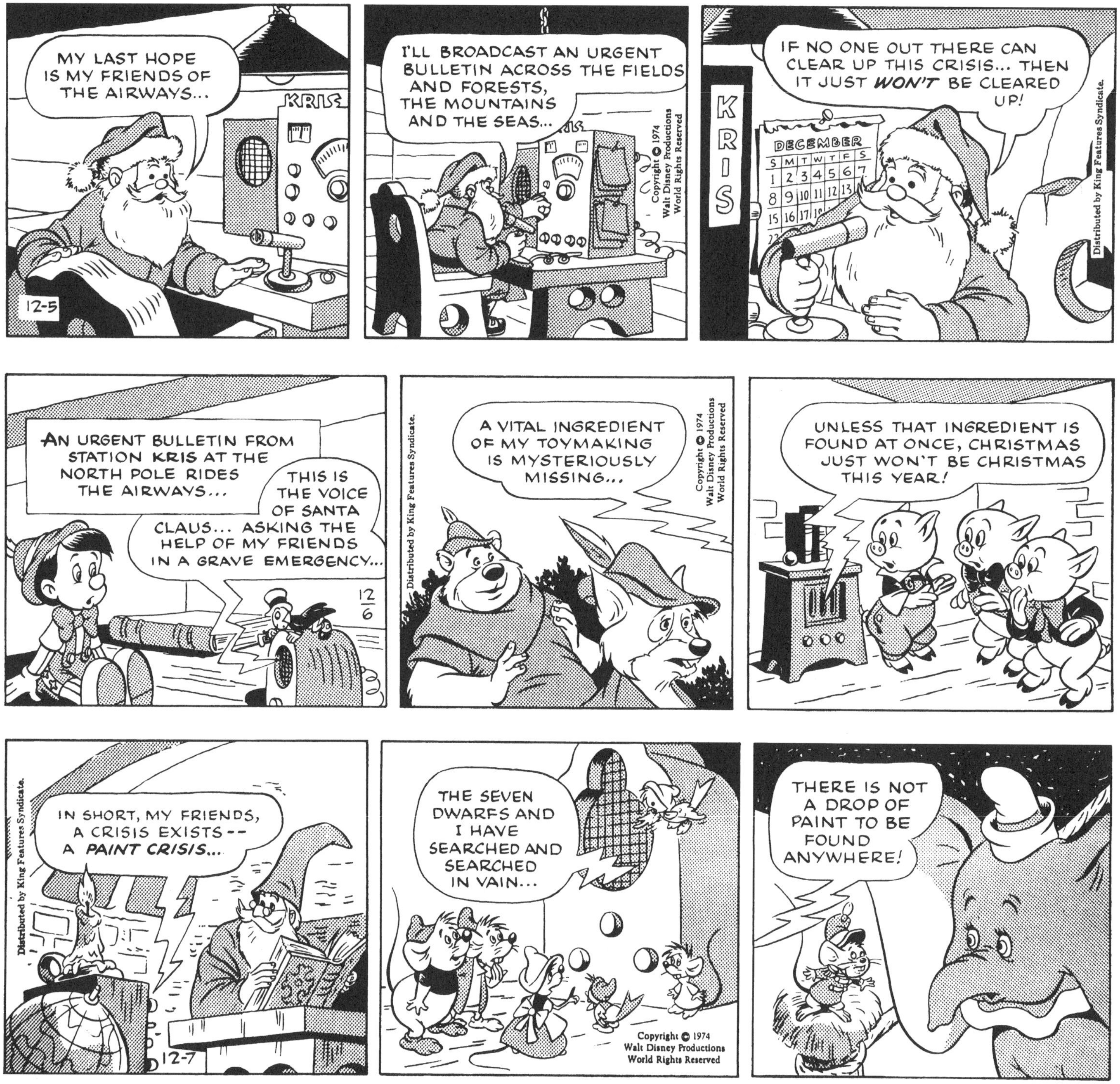
MY LAST HOPE IS MY FRIENDS OF THE AIRWAYS...
KRIS
12-5
I'LL BROADCAST AN URGENT BULLETIN ACROSS THE FIELDS AND FORESTS, THE MOUNTAINS AND THE SEAS...
Copyright © 1974 Walt Disney Productions World Rights Reserved
IF NO ONE OUT THERE CAN CLEAR UP THIS CRISIS... THEN IT JUST ***WON'T*** BE CLEARED UP!
KRIS
DECEMBER
Distributed by King Features Syndicate.
AN URGENT BULLETIN FROM STATION **KRIS** AT THE NORTH POLE RIDES THE AIRWAYS...
THIS IS THE VOICE OF SANTA CLAUS... ASKING THE HELP OF MY FRIENDS IN A GRAVE EMERGENCY...
12 6
Distributed by King Features Syndicate.
A VITAL INGREDIENT OF MY TOYMAKING IS MYSTERIOUSLY MISSING...
Copyright © 1974 Walt Disney Productions World Rights Reserved
UNLESS THAT INGREDIENT IS FOUND AT ONCE, CHRISTMAS JUST WON'T BE CHRISTMAS THIS YEAR!
Distributed by King Features Syndicate.
IN SHORT, MY FRIENDS, A CRISIS EXISTS -- A ***PAINT CRISIS...***
12-7
THE SEVEN DWARFS AND I HAVE SEARCHED AND SEARCHED IN VAIN...
Copyright © 1974 Walt Disney Productions World Rights Reserved
THERE IS NOT A DROP OF PAINT TO BE FOUND ANYWHERE!

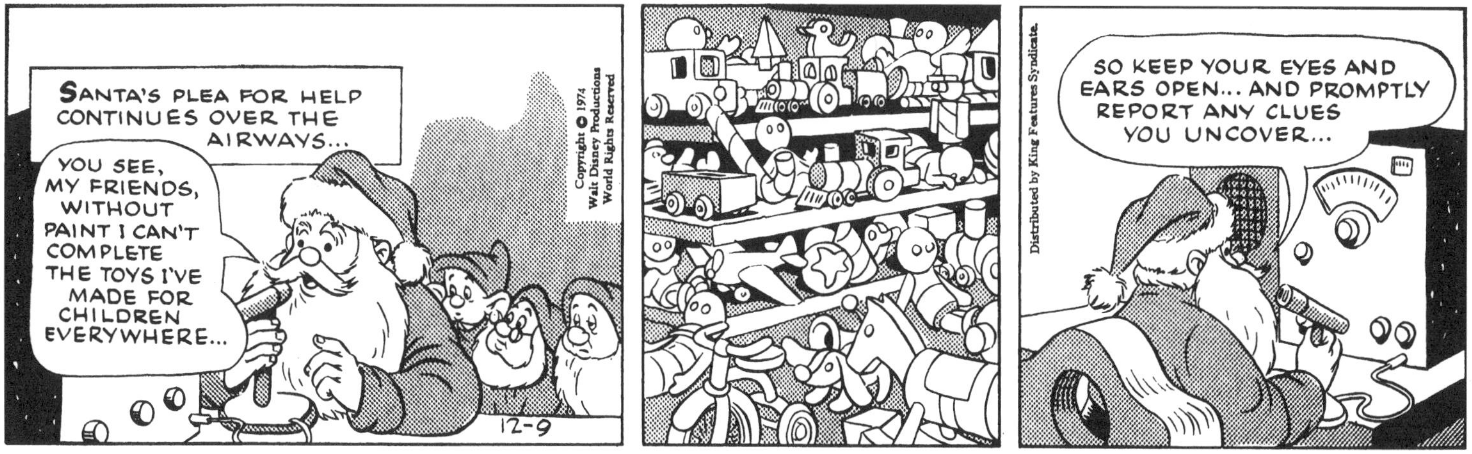
SANTA'S PLEA FOR HELP CONTINUES OVER THE AIRWAYS...
YOU SEE, MY FRIENDS, WITHOUT PAINT I CAN'T COMPLETE THE TOYS I'VE MADE FOR CHILDREN EVERYWHERE...
Copyright © 1974 Walt Disney Productions World Rights Reserved
12-9
Distributed by King Features Syndicate.
SO KEEP YOUR EYES AND EARS OPEN... AND PROMPTLY REPORT ANY CLUES YOU UNCOVER...

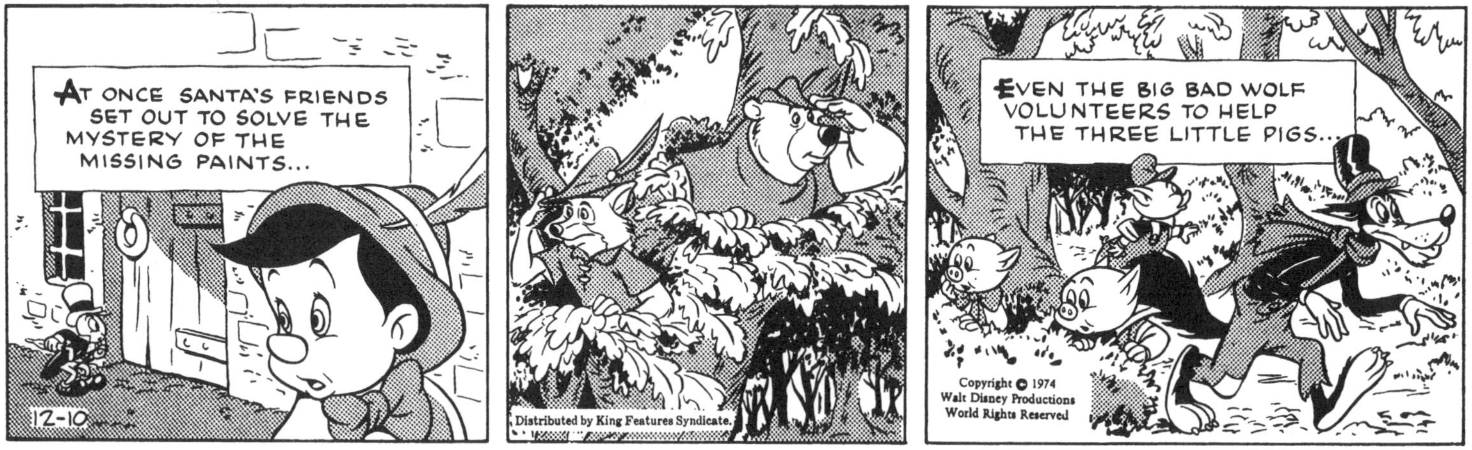
AT ONCE SANTA'S FRIENDS SET OUT TO SOLVE THE MYSTERY OF THE MISSING PAINTS...
12-10
Distributed by King Features Syndicate.
EVEN THE BIG BAD WOLF VOLUNTEERS TO HELP THE THREE LITTLE PIGS...
Copyright © 1974 Walt Disney Productions World Rights Reserved

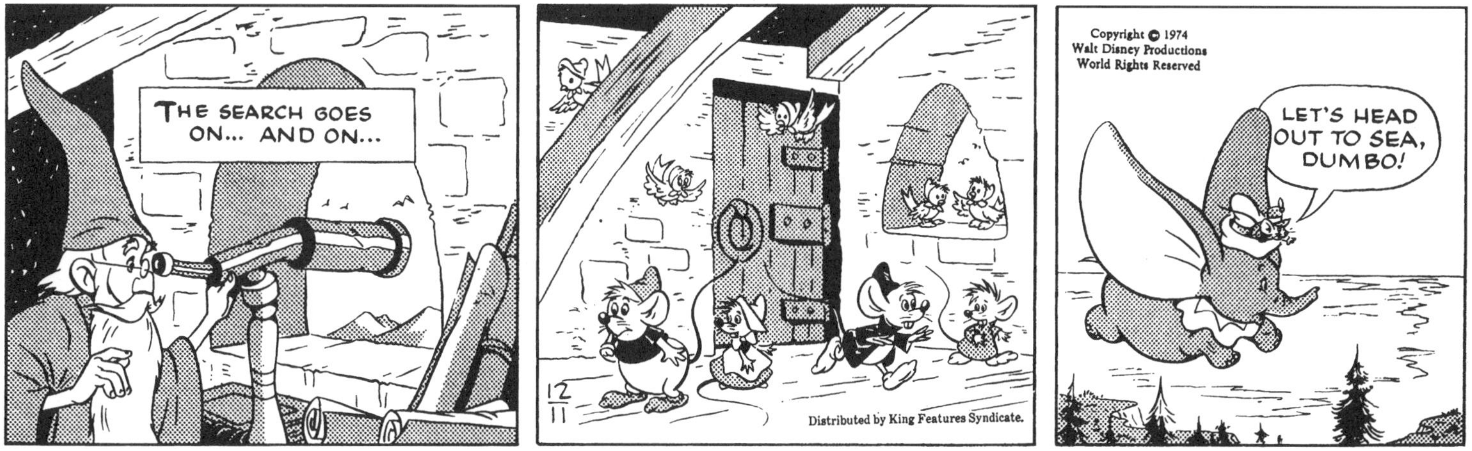
THE SEARCH GOES ON... AND ON...
12 11
Distributed by King Features Syndicate.
Copyright © 1974 Walt Disney Productions World Rights Reserved
LET'S HEAD OUT TO SEA, DUMBO!

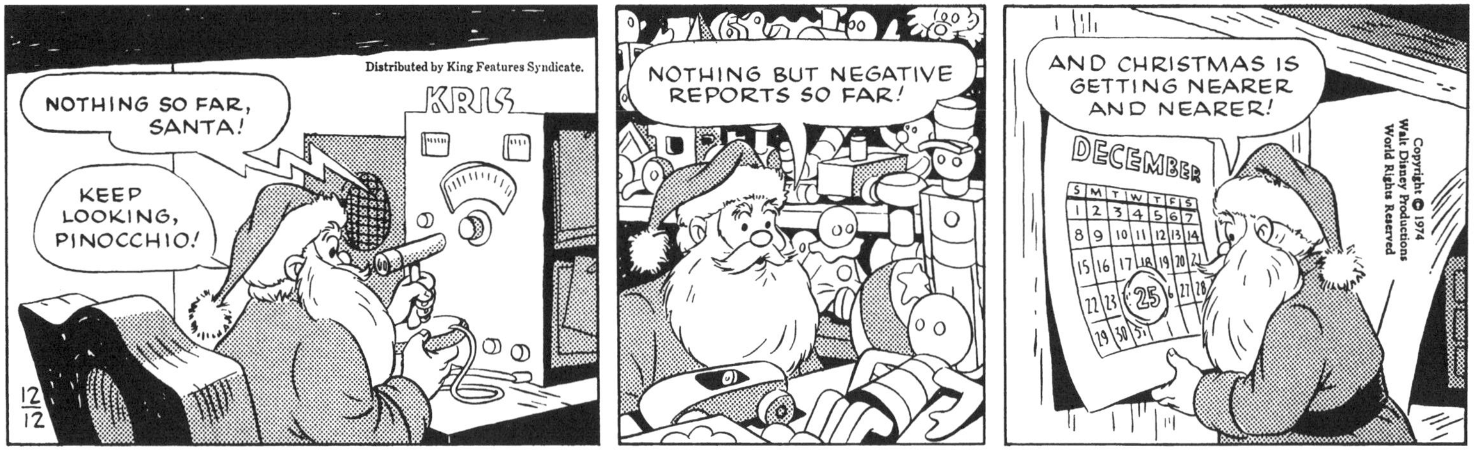
Distributed by King Features Syndicate.
KRIS
NOTHING SO FAR, SANTA!
KEEP LOOKING, PINOCCHIO!
12/12
NOTHING BUT NEGATIVE REPORTS SO FAR!
AND CHRISTMAS IS GETTING NEARER AND NEARER!
DECEMBER
Copyright © 1974 Walt Disney Productions World Rights Reserved

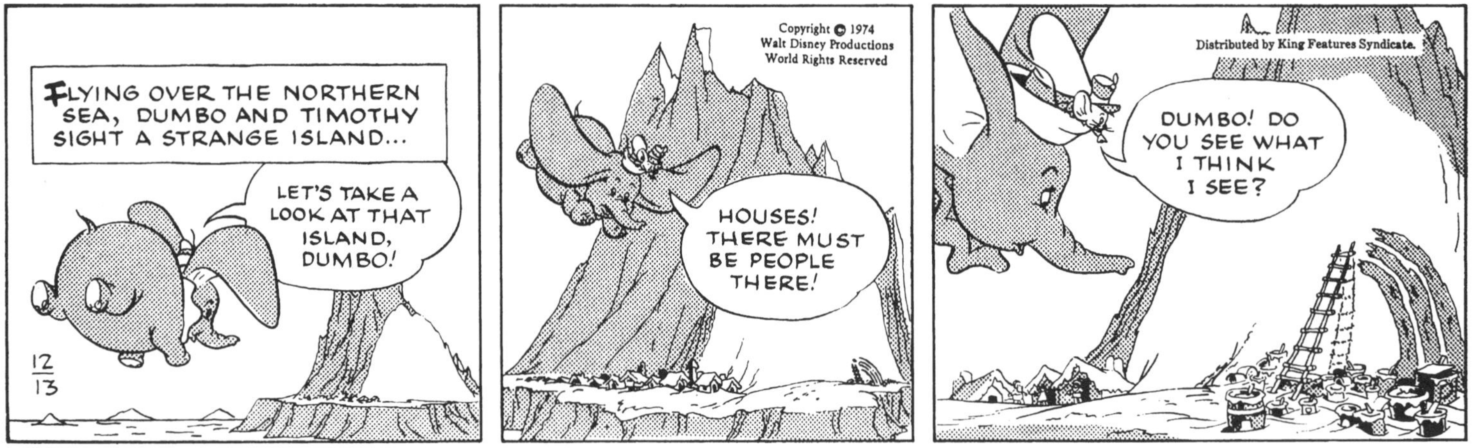
FLYING OVER THE NORTHERN SEA, DUMBO AND TIMOTHY SIGHT A STRANGE ISLAND...
LET'S TAKE A LOOK AT THAT ISLAND, DUMBO!
12/13
Copyright © 1974 Walt Disney Productions World Rights Reserved
HOUSES! THERE MUST BE PEOPLE THERE!
Distributed by King Features Syndicate.
DUMBO! DO YOU SEE WHAT I THINK I SEE?

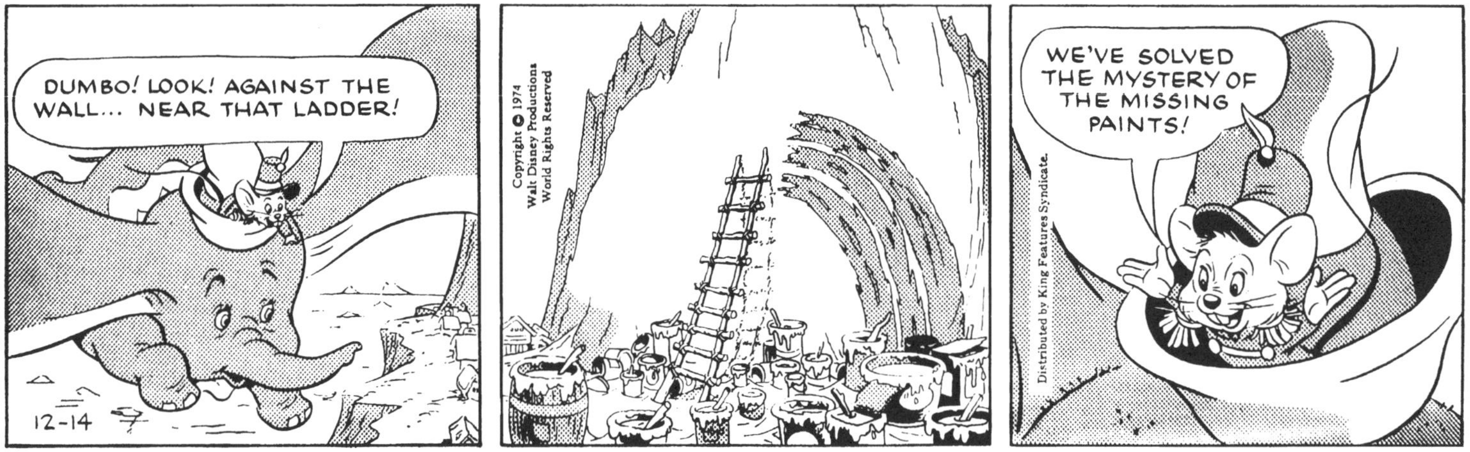
DUMBO! LOOK! AGAINST THE WALL... NEAR THAT LADDER!
12-14
Copyright © 1974 Walt Disney Productions World Rights Reserved
Distributed by King Features Syndicate.
WE'VE SOLVED THE MYSTERY OF THE MISSING PAINTS!

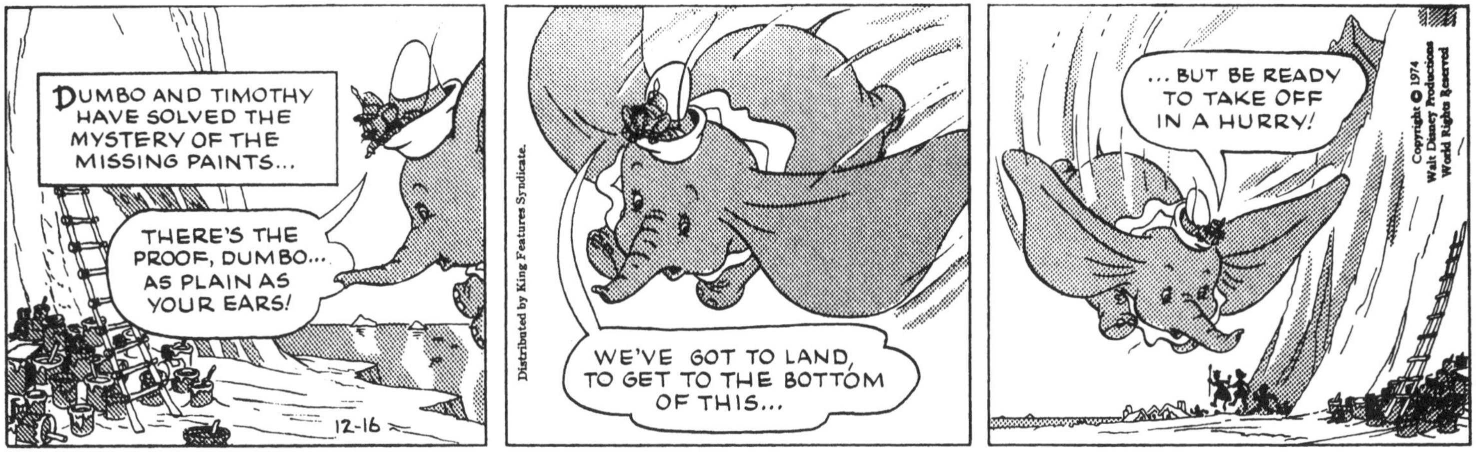
DUMBO AND TIMOTHY HAVE SOLVED THE MYSTERY OF THE MISSING PAINTS...
THERE'S THE PROOF, DUMBO... AS PLAIN AS YOUR EARS!
12-16
Distributed by King Features Syndicate.
WE'VE GOT TO LAND, TO GET TO THE BOTTOM OF THIS...
...BUT BE READY TO TAKE OFF IN A HURRY!
Copyright © 1974 Walt Disney Productions World Rights Reserved

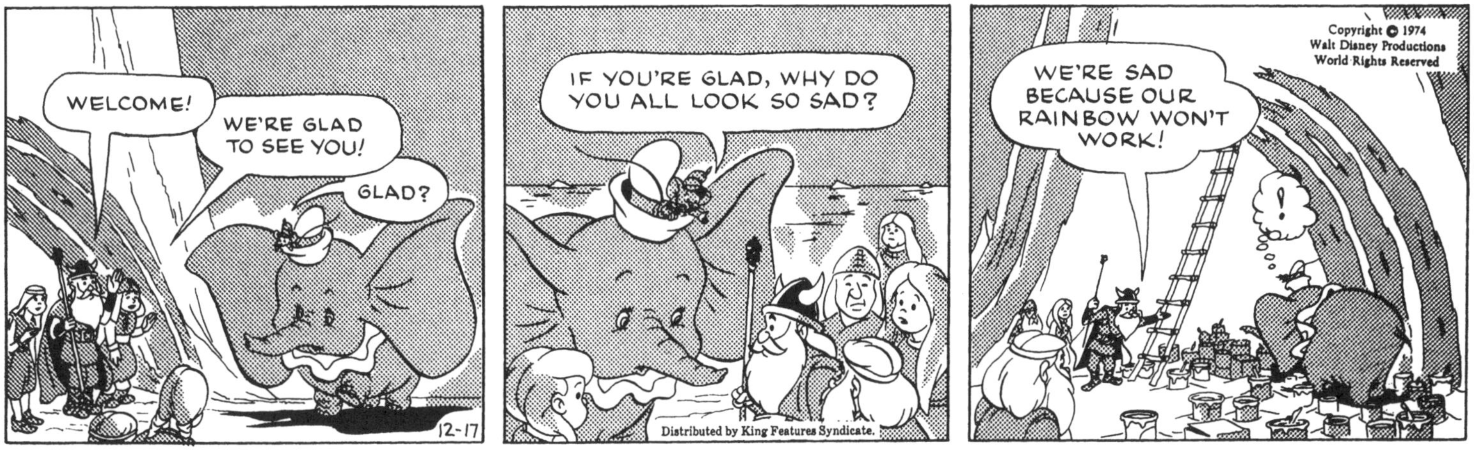
WELCOME!
WE'RE GLAD TO SEE YOU!
GLAD?
12-17
IF YOU'RE GLAD, WHY DO YOU ALL LOOK SO SAD?
Distributed by King Features Syndicate.
Copyright © 1974 Walt Disney Productions World Rights Reserved
WE'RE SAD BECAUSE OUR RAINBOW WON'T WORK!
!

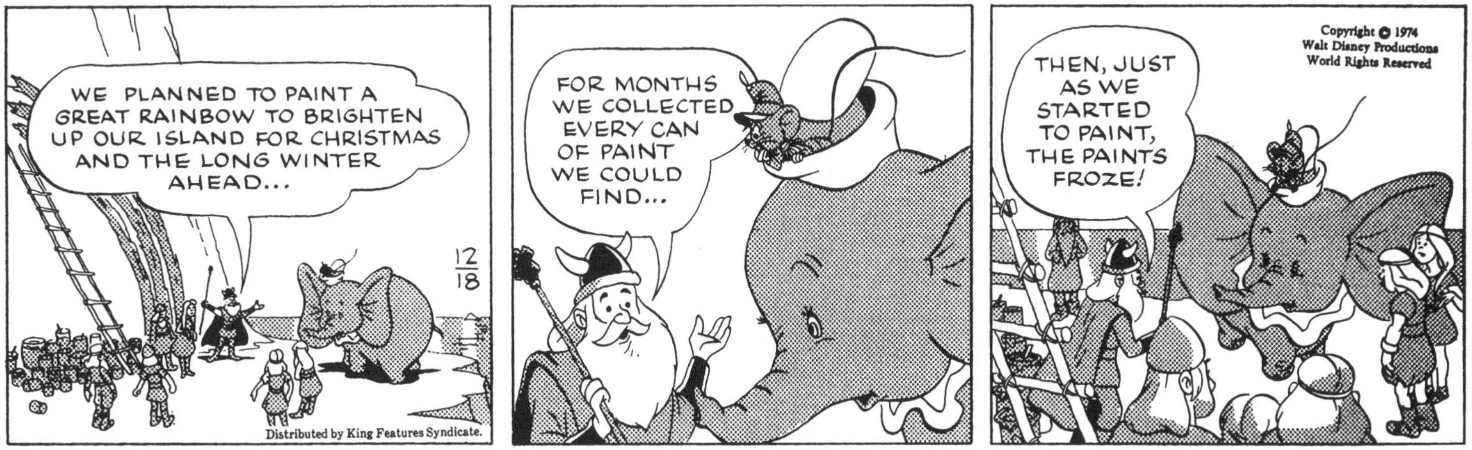
WE PLANNED TO PAINT A GREAT RAINBOW TO BRIGHTEN UP OUR ISLAND FOR CHRISTMAS AND THE LONG WINTER AHEAD...
12/18
Distributed by King Features Syndicate.
FOR MONTHS WE COLLECTED EVERY CAN OF PAINT WE COULD FIND...
Copyright © 1974 Walt Disney Productions World Rights Reserved
THEN, JUST AS WE STARTED TO PAINT, THE PAINTS FROZE!

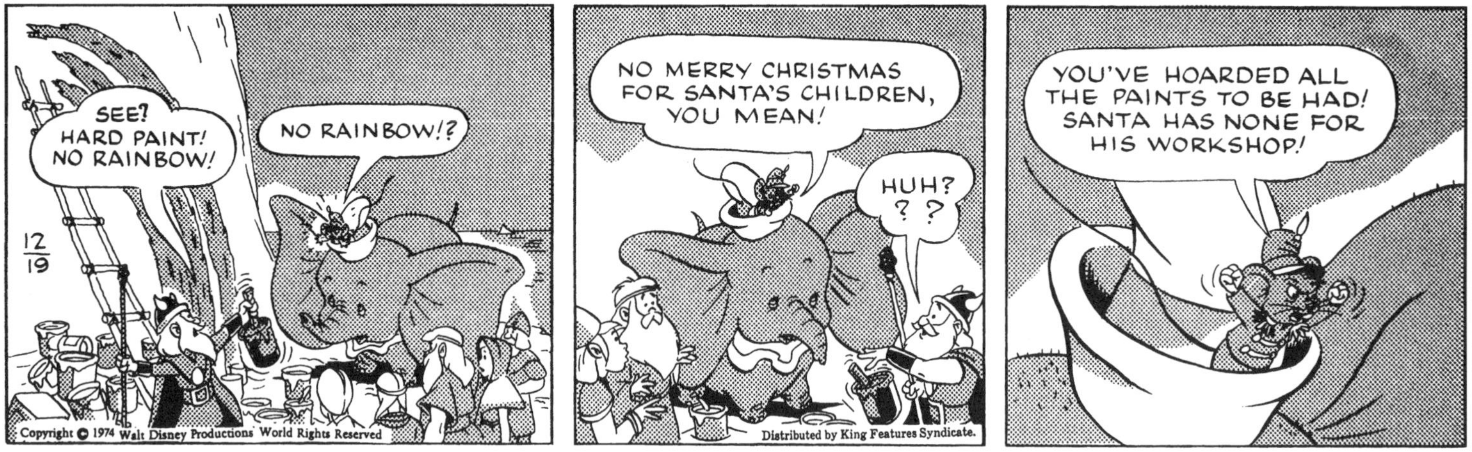

SEE? HARD PAINT! NO RAINBOW!
NO RAINBOW!?
12/19
Copyright © 1974 Walt Disney Productions World Rights Reserved
NO MERRY CHRISTMAS FOR SANTA'S CHILDREN, YOU MEAN!
HUH? ? ?
Distributed by King Features Syndicate.
YOU'VE HOARDED ALL THE PAINTS TO BE HAD! SANTA HAS NONE FOR HIS WORKSHOP!

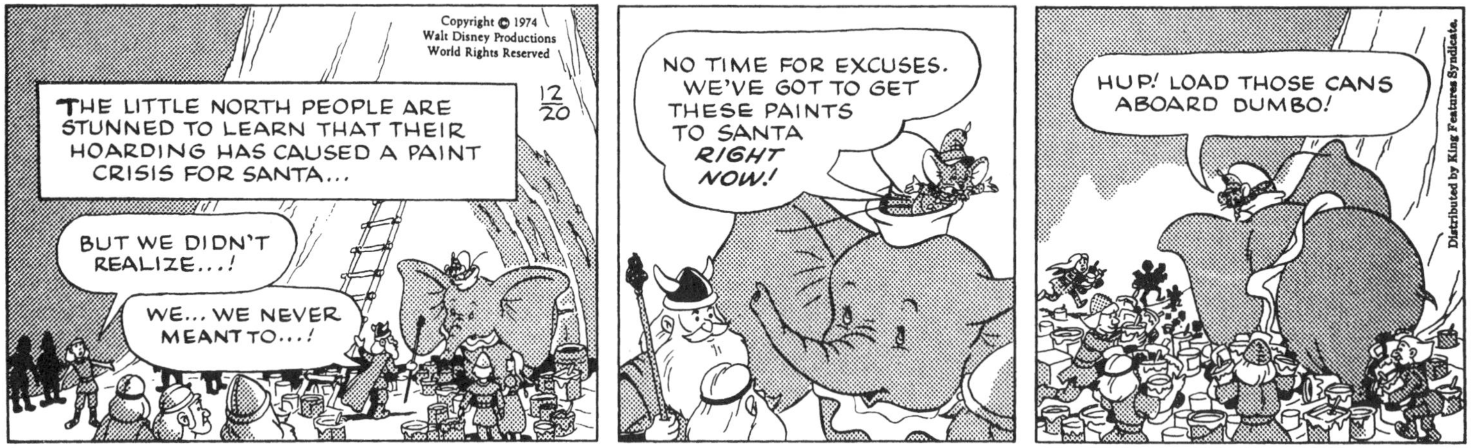

Copyright © 1974 Walt Disney Productions World Rights Reserved
THE LITTLE NORTH PEOPLE ARE STUNNED TO LEARN THAT THEIR HOARDING HAS CAUSED A PAINT CRISIS FOR SANTA...
12/20
BUT WE DIDN'T REALIZE...!
WE... WE NEVER MEANT TO...!
NO TIME FOR EXCUSES. WE'VE GOT TO GET THESE PAINTS TO SANTA *RIGHT NOW!*
HUP! LOAD THOSE CANS ABOARD DUMBO!
Distributed by King Features Syndicate.

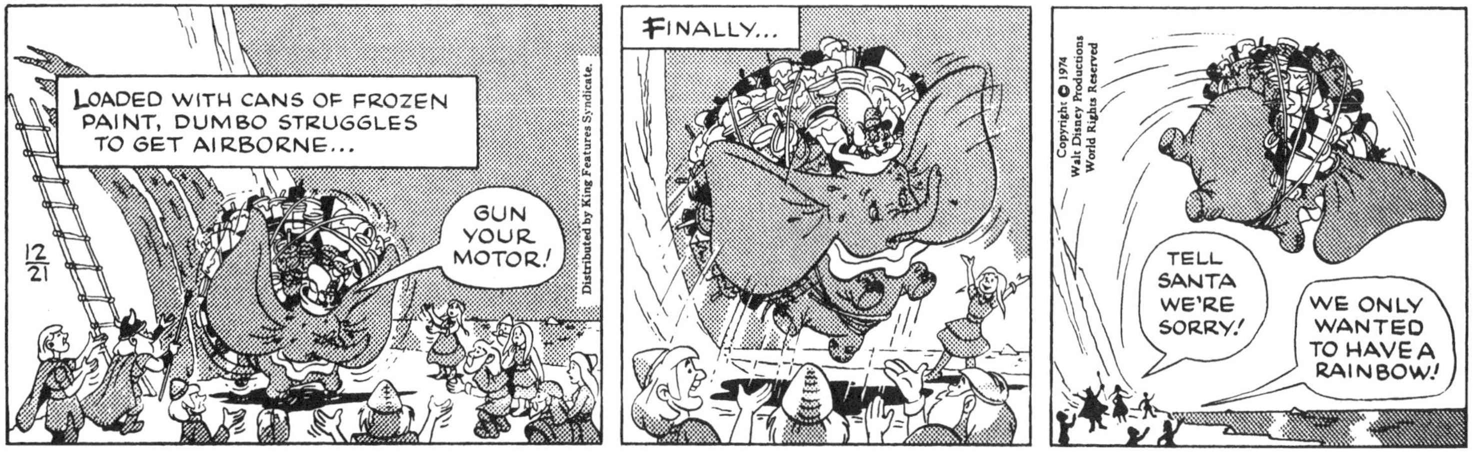

LOADED WITH CANS OF FROZEN PAINT, DUMBO STRUGGLES TO GET AIRBORNE...
12/21
GUN YOUR MOTOR!
Distributed by King Features Syndicate.
FINALLY...
Copyright © 1974 Walt Disney Productions World Rights Reserved
TELL SANTA WE'RE SORRY!
WE ONLY WANTED TO HAVE A RAINBOW!

WITH THE PAINTS THAWED OUT, SANTA AND HIS HELPERS WORK FURIOUSLY OVER THE WEEKEND...
LOOKS LIKE WE'LL *PUFF* MAKE IT AFTER ALL!
SANTA, DON'T FORGET ABOUT THOSE LITTLE NORTH PEOPLE AND THE RAINBOW THEY WANTED!
Distributed by King Features Syndicate.
I'VE ARRANGED WITH MY WIZARD FRIEND, MERLIN, TO GIVE THEM SOMETHING *BETTER* THAN A RAINBOW!
12/23
Copyright © 1974 Walt Disney Productions World Rights Reserved

IT'S CHRISTMAS EVE AS SANTA SETS OUT FROM THE NORTH POLE...
WHAT'S THAT BELOW?
12-24
THE AURORA BOREALIS! MY CHRISTMAS GIFT TO THE LITTLE NORTH PEOPLE!
Copyright © 1974 Walt Disney Productions World Rights Reserved
AND SANTA GOES HIS MERRY WAY...
WITH A MERRY CHRISTMAS TO EVERYONE... EVERYWHERE!
Distributed by King Features Syndicate.

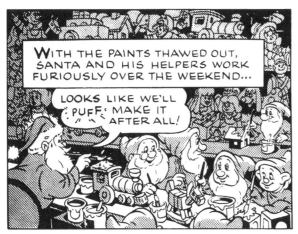

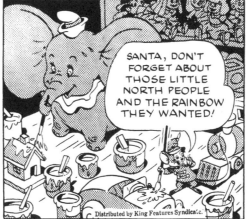

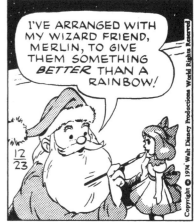

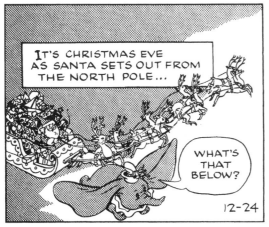

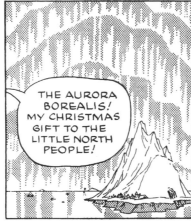

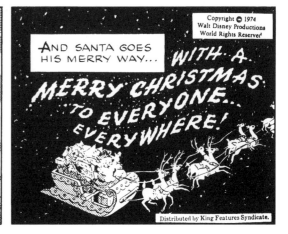

1975

SANTA AND THE PIRATES

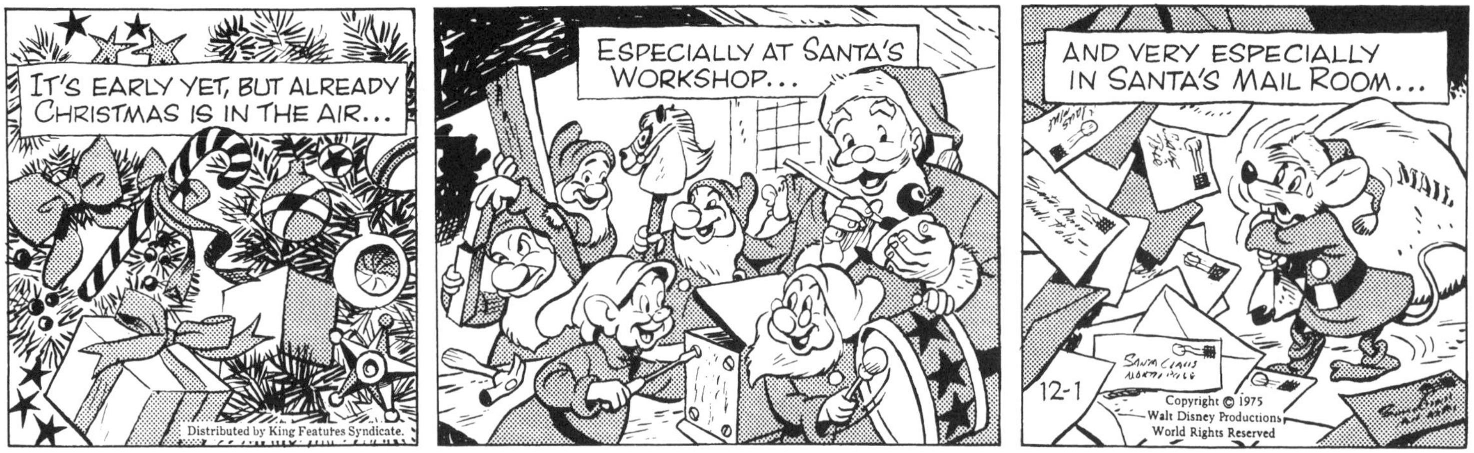
IT'S EARLY YET, BUT ALREADY CHRISTMAS IS IN THE AIR...
Distributed by King Features Syndicate.
ESPECIALLY AT SANTA'S WORKSHOP...
AND VERY ESPECIALLY IN SANTA'S MAIL ROOM...
MAIL
12-1
Copyright © 1975 Walt Disney Productions World Rights Reserved

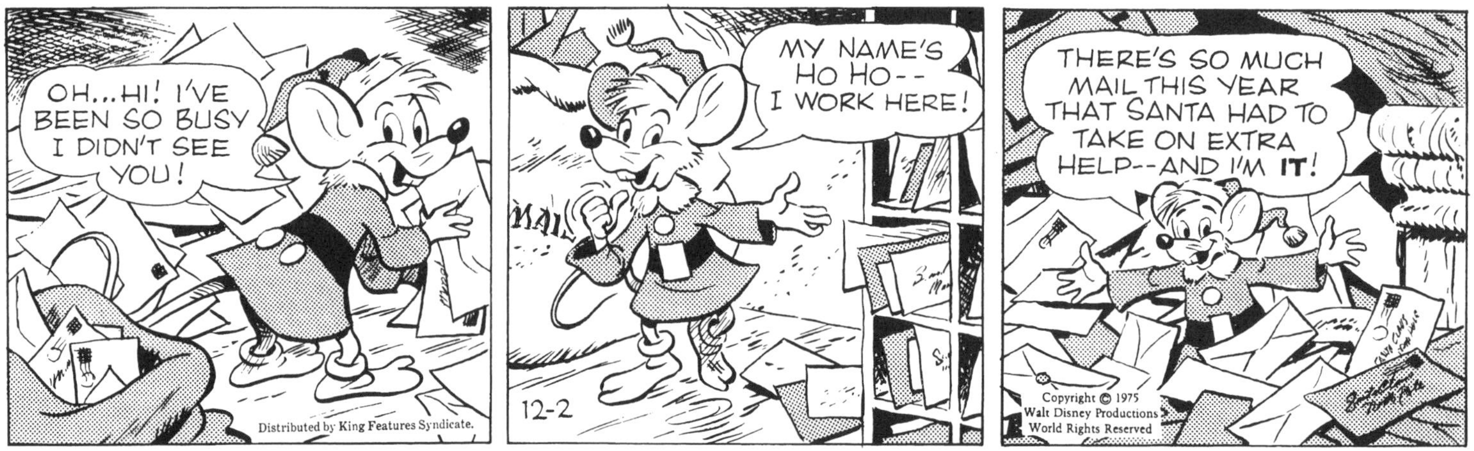
OH...HI! I'VE BEEN SO BUSY I DIDN'T SEE YOU!
Distributed by King Features Syndicate.
MY NAME'S HO HO-- I WORK HERE!
MAIL
12-2
THERE'S SO MUCH MAIL THIS YEAR THAT SANTA HAD TO TAKE ON EXTRA HELP--AND I'M **IT**!
Copyright © 1975 Walt Disney Productions World Rights Reserved

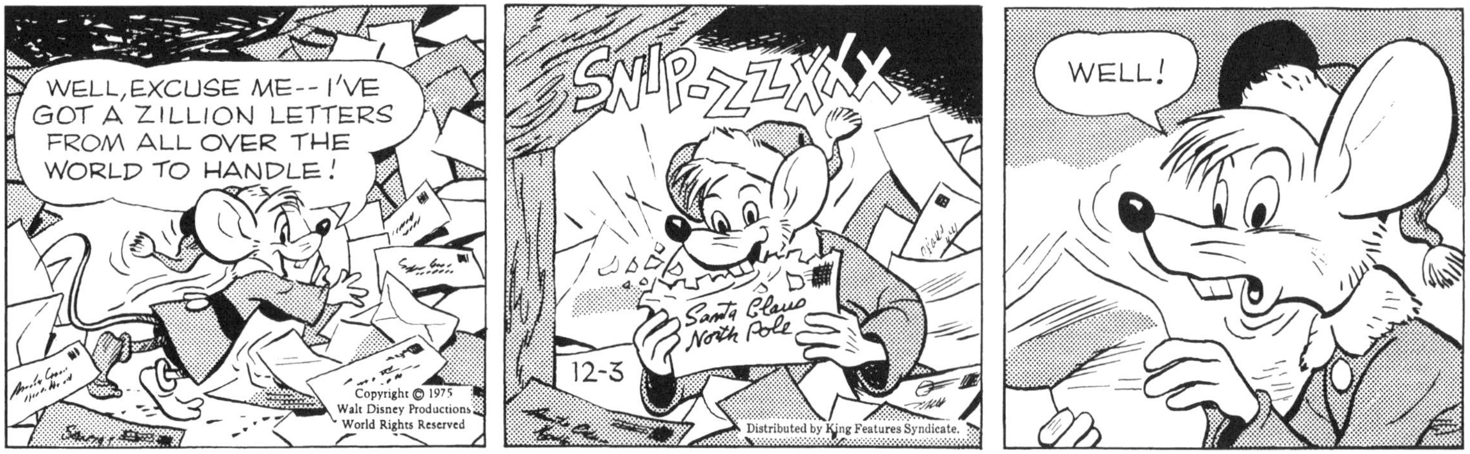
WELL, EXCUSE ME-- I'VE GOT A ZILLION LETTERS FROM ALL OVER THE WORLD TO HANDLE!
Copyright © 1975 Walt Disney Productions World Rights Reserved
SNIP-ZZXXX
Santa Claus North Pole
12-3
Distributed by King Features Syndicate.
WELL!

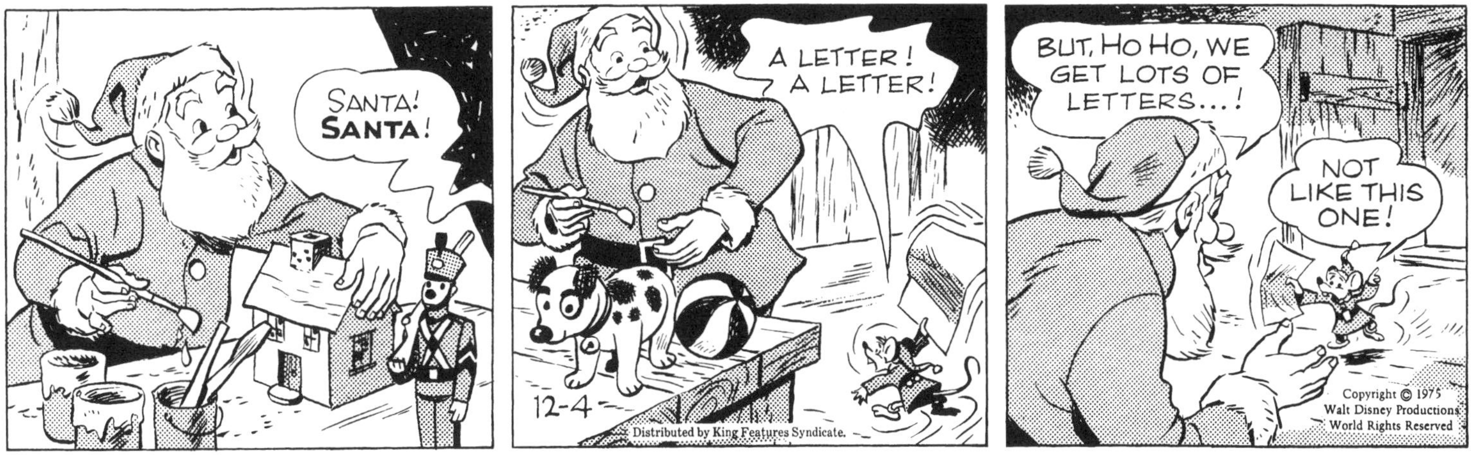
SANTA! SANTA!
A LETTER! A LETTER!
12-4
Distributed by King Features Syndicate.
BUT, HO HO, WE GET LOTS OF LETTERS...!
NOT LIKE THIS ONE!
Copyright © 1975 Walt Disney Productions World Rights Reserved

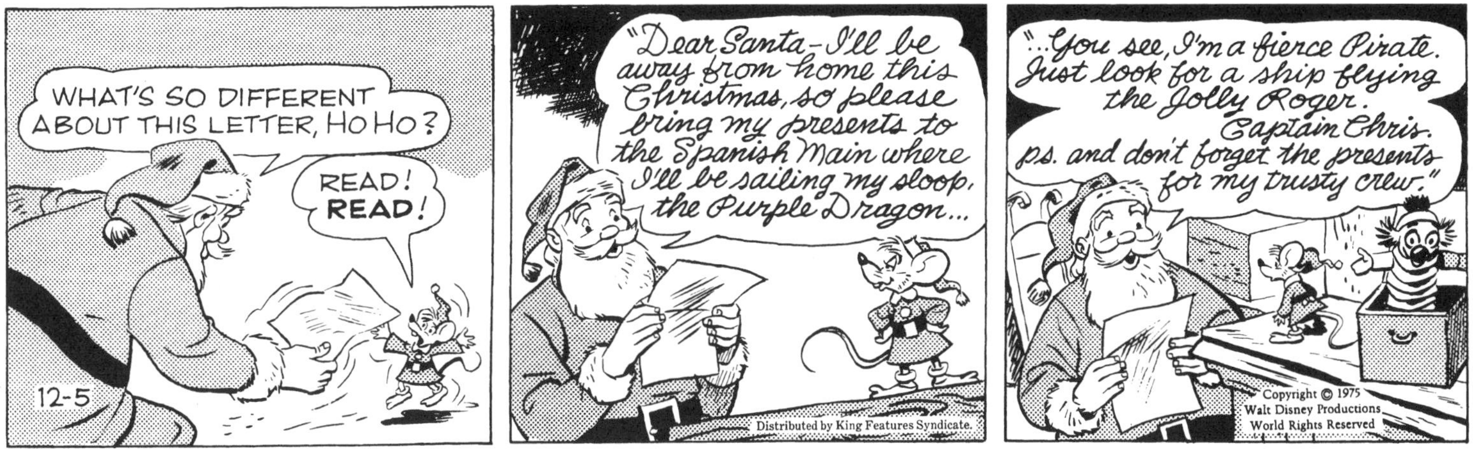
WHAT'S SO DIFFERENT ABOUT THIS LETTER, HO HO?
READ! READ!
12-5
"Dear Santa-I'll be away from home this Christmas, so please bring my presents to the Spanish Main where I'll be sailing my sloop, the Purple Dragon...
Distributed by King Features Syndicate.
"...You see, I'm a fierce Pirate. Just look for a ship flying the Jolly Roger. Captain Chris. ps. and don't forget the presents for my trusty crew."
Copyright © 1975 Walt Disney Productions World Rights Reserved

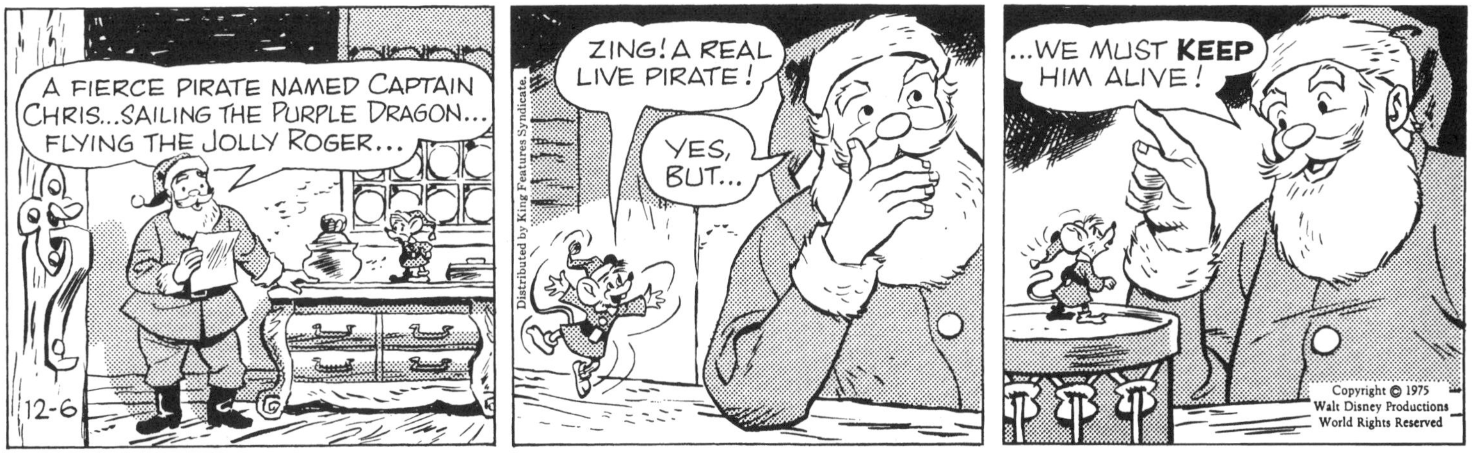
A FIERCE PIRATE NAMED CAPTAIN CHRIS...SAILING THE PURPLE DRAGON... FLYING THE JOLLY ROGER...
12-6
Distributed by King Features Syndicate.
ZING! A REAL LIVE PIRATE!
YES, BUT...
...WE MUST KEEP HIM ALIVE!
Copyright © 1975 Walt Disney Productions World Rights Reserved

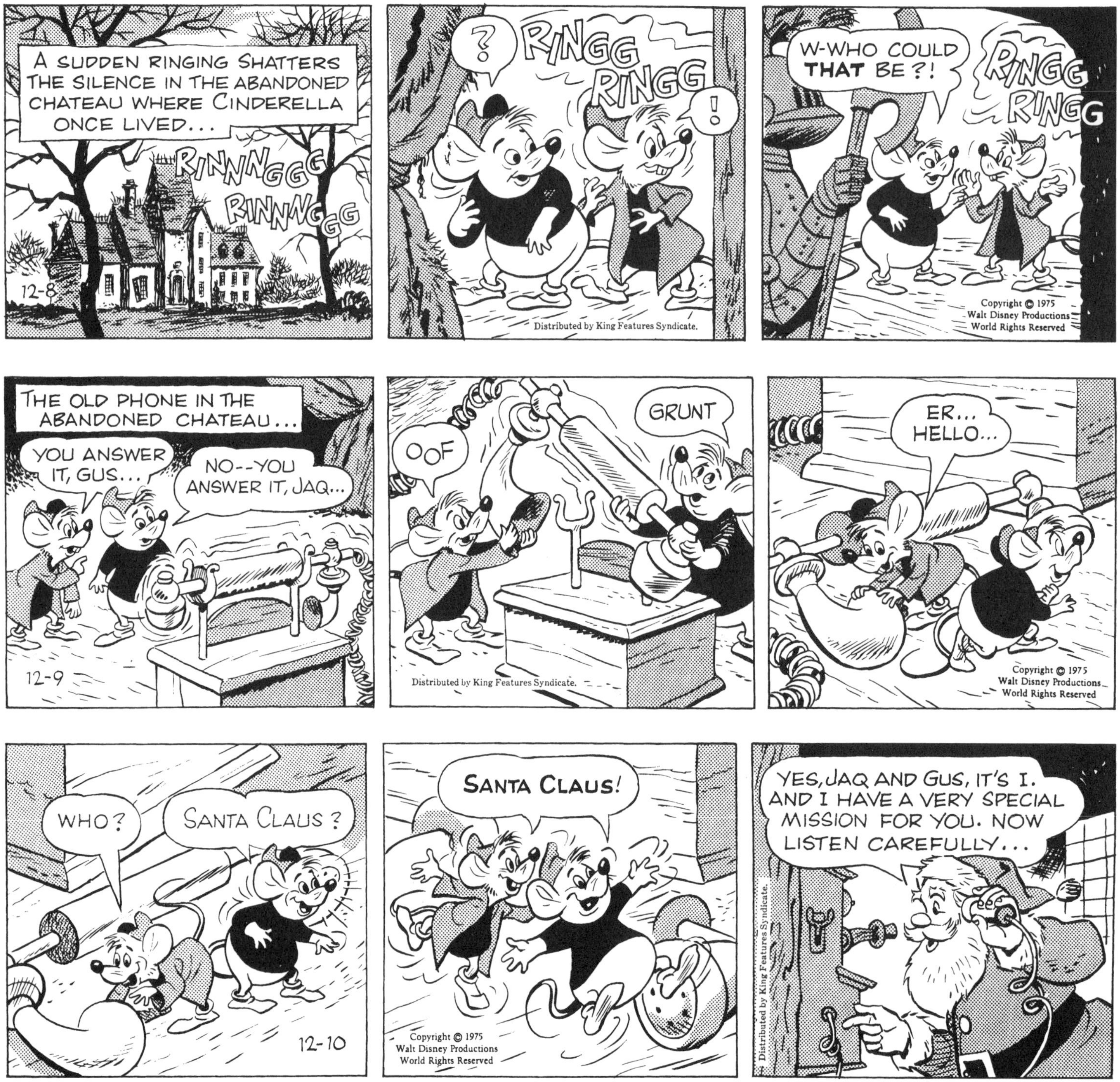
A SUDDEN RINGING SHATTERS THE SILENCE IN THE ABANDONED CHATEAU WHERE CINDERELLA ONCE LIVED...
RINNNGGG
RINNNGGG
12-8
?
RINGG
RINGG
!
Distributed by King Features Syndicate.
W-WHO COULD THAT BE?!
RINGG
RINGG
Copyright © 1975 Walt Disney Productions World Rights Reserved
THE OLD PHONE IN THE ABANDONED CHATEAU...
YOU ANSWER IT, GUS...
NO--YOU ANSWER IT, JAQ...
12-9
OOF
GRUNT
Distributed by King Features Syndicate.
ER... HELLO...
Copyright © 1975 Walt Disney Productions World Rights Reserved
WHO?
SANTA CLAUS?
12-10
SANTA CLAUS!
Copyright © 1975 Walt Disney Productions World Rights Reserved
YES, JAQ AND GUS, IT'S I. AND I HAVE A VERY SPECIAL MISSION FOR YOU. NOW LISTEN CAREFULLY...
Distributed by King Features Syndicate.

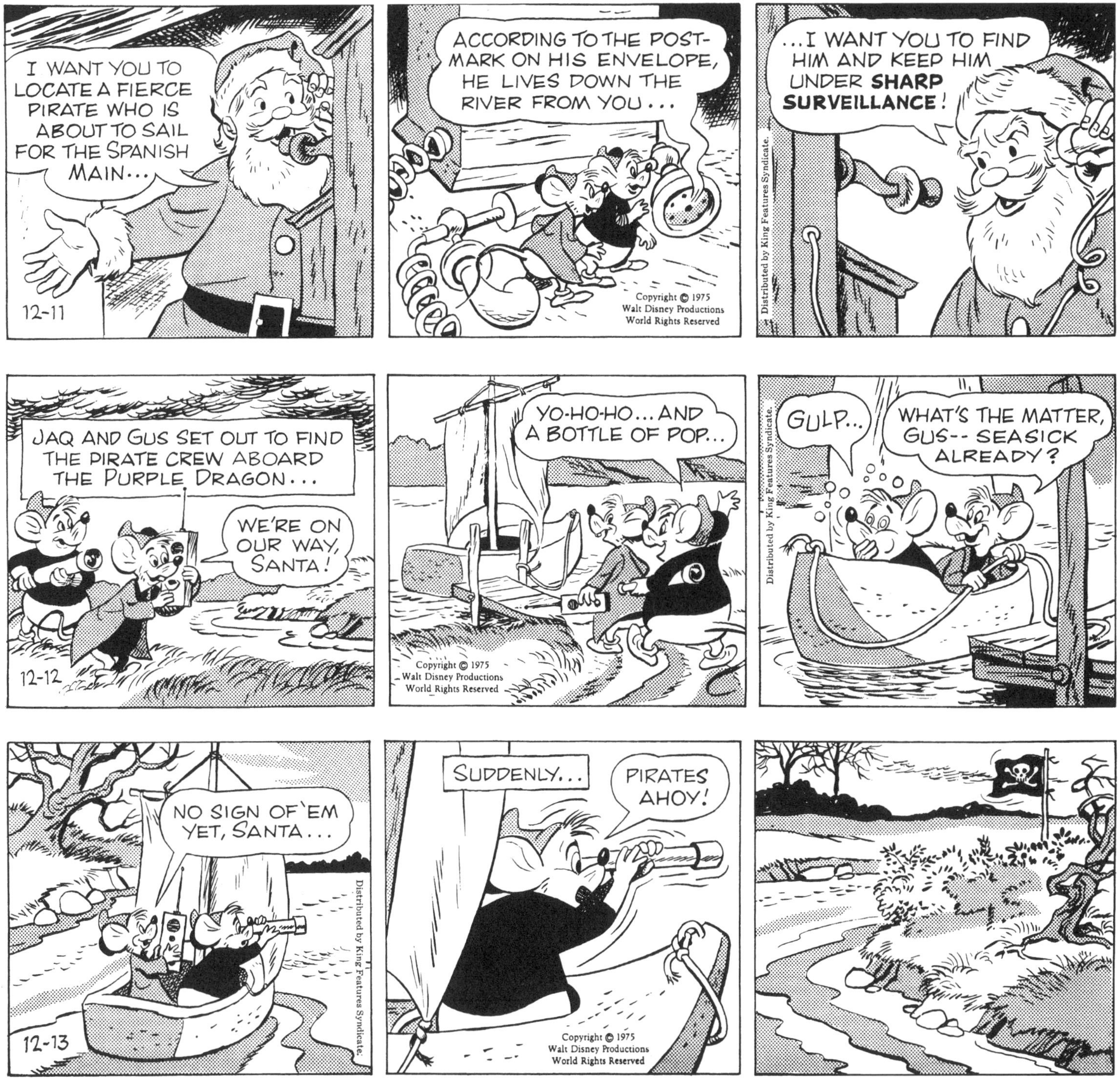
I WANT YOU TO LOCATE A FIERCE PIRATE WHO IS ABOUT TO SAIL FOR THE SPANISH MAIN...
12-11
ACCORDING TO THE POST-MARK ON HIS ENVELOPE, HE LIVES DOWN THE RIVER FROM YOU...
Copyright © 1975 Walt Disney Productions World Rights Reserved
...I WANT YOU TO FIND HIM AND KEEP HIM UNDER **SHARP SURVEILLANCE**!
Distributed by King Features Syndicate.
JAQ AND GUS SET OUT TO FIND THE PIRATE CREW ABOARD THE PURPLE DRAGON...
WE'RE ON OUR WAY, SANTA!
12-12
YO-HO-HO... AND A BOTTLE OF POP...
Copyright © 1975 Walt Disney Productions World Rights Reserved
GULP...
WHAT'S THE MATTER, GUS-- SEASICK ALREADY?
Distributed by King Features Syndicate.
NO SIGN OF 'EM YET, SANTA...
12-13
Distributed by King Features Syndicate.
SUDDENLY...
PIRATES AHOY!
Copyright © 1975 Walt Disney Productions World Rights Reserved

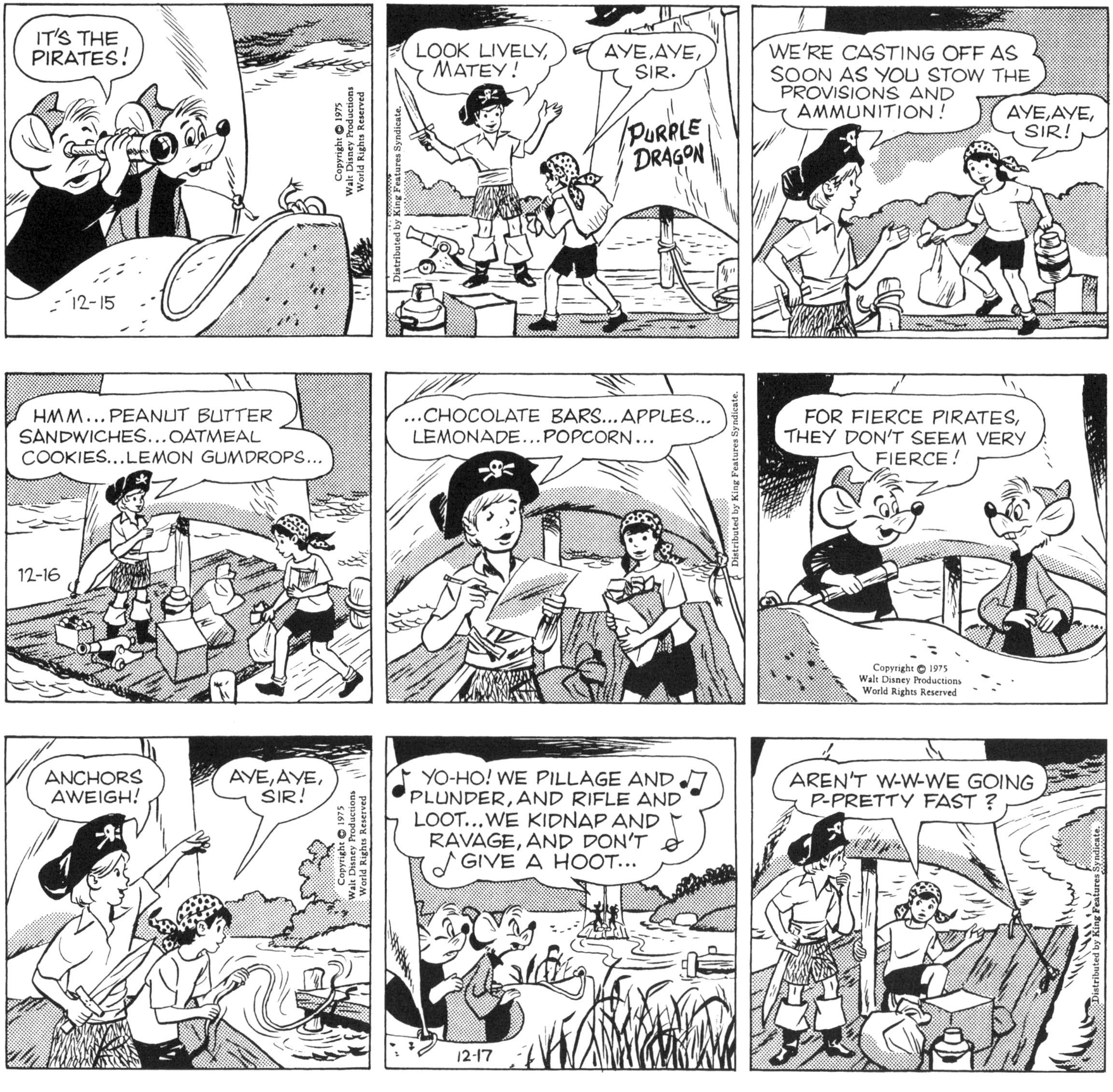
IT'S THE PIRATES!
12-15
Copyright © 1975 Walt Disney Productions World Rights Reserved
Distributed by King Features Syndicate.
LOOK LIVELY, MATEY!
AYE, AYE, SIR.
PURPLE DRAGON
WE'RE CASTING OFF AS SOON AS YOU STOW THE PROVISIONS AND AMMUNITION!
AYE, AYE, SIR!
HMM... PEANUT BUTTER SANDWICHES... OATMEAL COOKIES... LEMON GUMDROPS...
12-16
...CHOCOLATE BARS... APPLES... LEMONADE... POPCORN...
Distributed by King Features Syndicate.
FOR FIERCE PIRATES, THEY DON'T SEEM VERY FIERCE!
Copyright © 1975 Walt Disney Productions World Rights Reserved
ANCHORS AWEIGH!
AYE, AYE, SIR!
Copyright © 1975 Walt Disney Productions World Rights Reserved
YO-HO! WE PILLAGE AND PLUNDER, AND RIFLE AND LOOT... WE KIDNAP AND RAVAGE, AND DON'T GIVE A HOOT...
12-17
AREN'T W-W-WE GOING P-PRETTY FAST?
Distributed by King Features Syndicate.

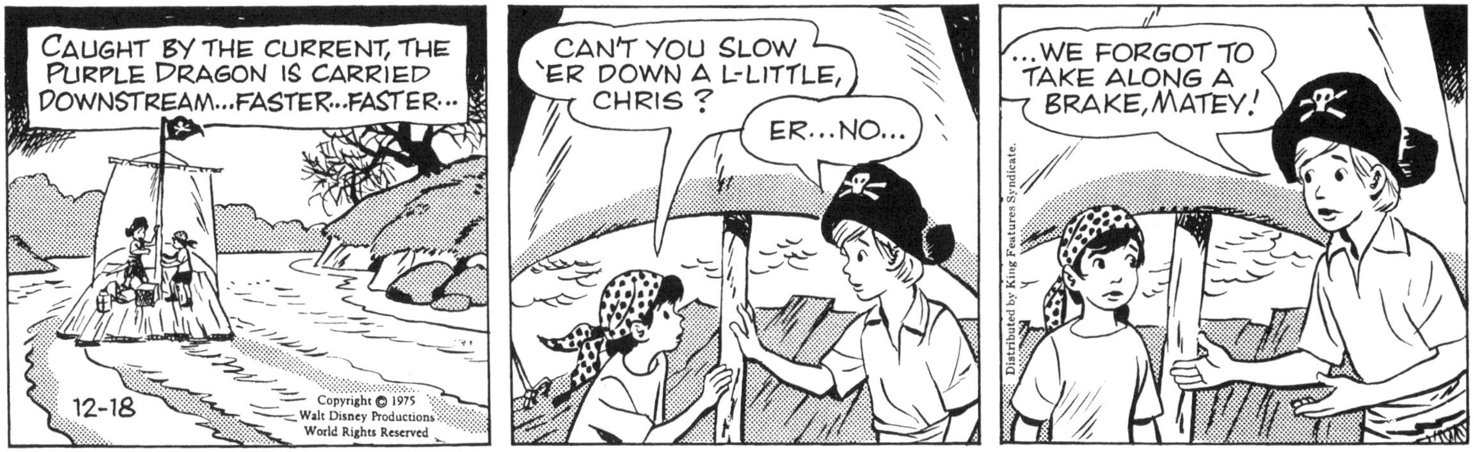
CAUGHT BY THE CURRENT, THE PURPLE DRAGON IS CARRIED DOWNSTREAM...FASTER..FASTER...
12-18
Copyright © 1975 Walt Disney Productions World Rights Reserved
CAN'T YOU SLOW 'ER DOWN A L-LITTLE, CHRIS?
ER...NO...
...WE FORGOT TO TAKE ALONG A BRAKE, MATEY!
Distributed by King Features Syndicate.

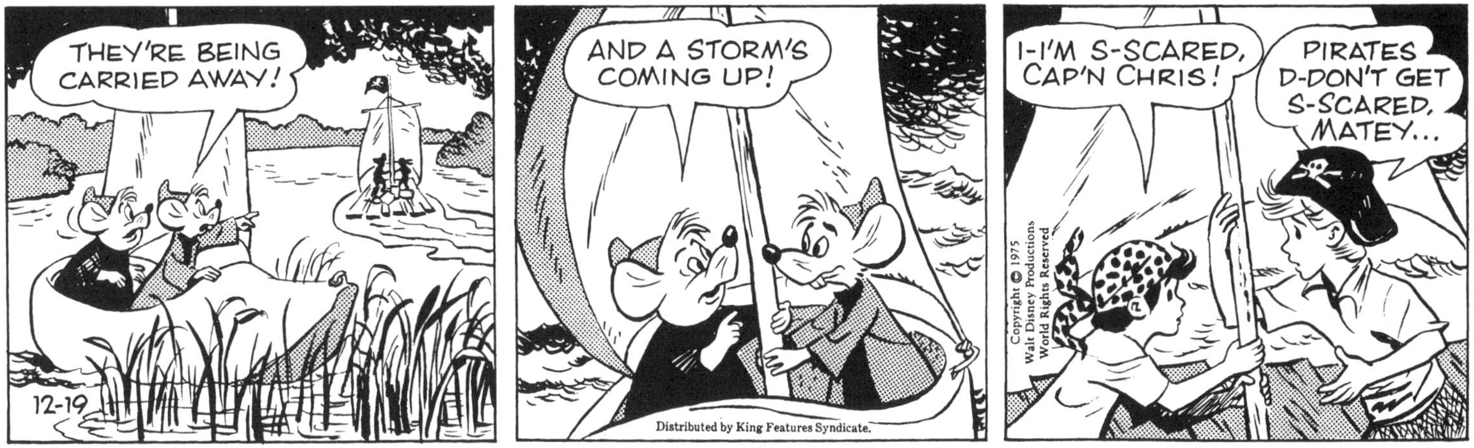
THEY'RE BEING CARRIED AWAY!
12-19
AND A STORM'S COMING UP!
Distributed by King Features Syndicate.
I-I'M S-SCARED, CAP'N CHRIS!
PIRATES D-DON'T GET S-SCARED, MATEY...
Copyright © 1975 Walt Disney Productions World Rights Reserved

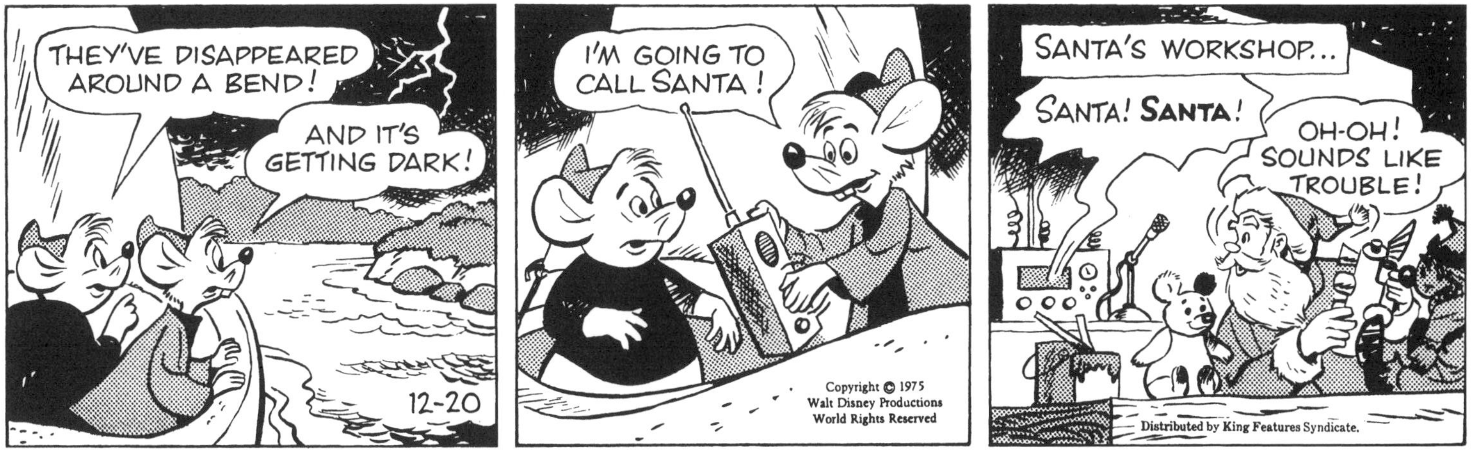
THEY'VE DISAPPEARED AROUND A BEND!
AND IT'S GETTING DARK!
12-20
I'M GOING TO CALL SANTA!
Copyright © 1975 Walt Disney Productions World Rights Reserved
SANTA'S WORKSHOP...
SANTA! **SANTA**!
OH-OH! SOUNDS LIKE TROUBLE!
Distributed by King Features Syndicate.

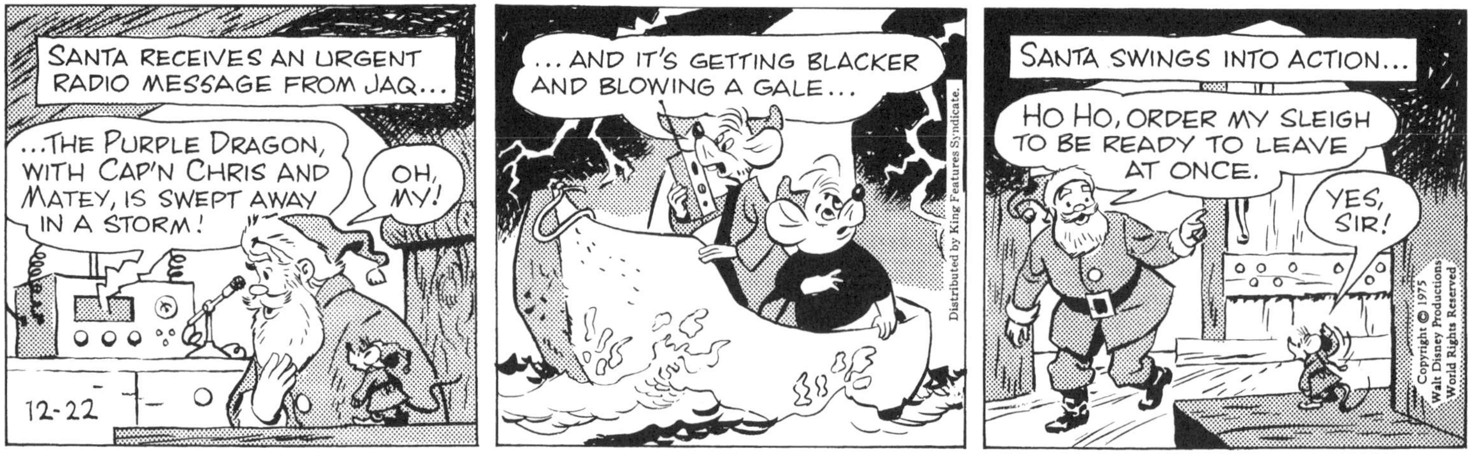
SANTA RECEIVES AN URGENT RADIO MESSAGE FROM JAQ...
...THE PURPLE DRAGON, WITH CAP'N CHRIS AND MATEY, IS SWEPT AWAY IN A STORM!
OH, MY!
12-22
...AND IT'S GETTING BLACKER AND BLOWING A GALE...
Distributed by King Features Syndicate.
SANTA SWINGS INTO ACTION...
HO HO, ORDER MY SLEIGH TO BE READY TO LEAVE AT ONCE.
YES, SIR!
Copyright © 1975 Walt Disney Productions World Rights Reserved

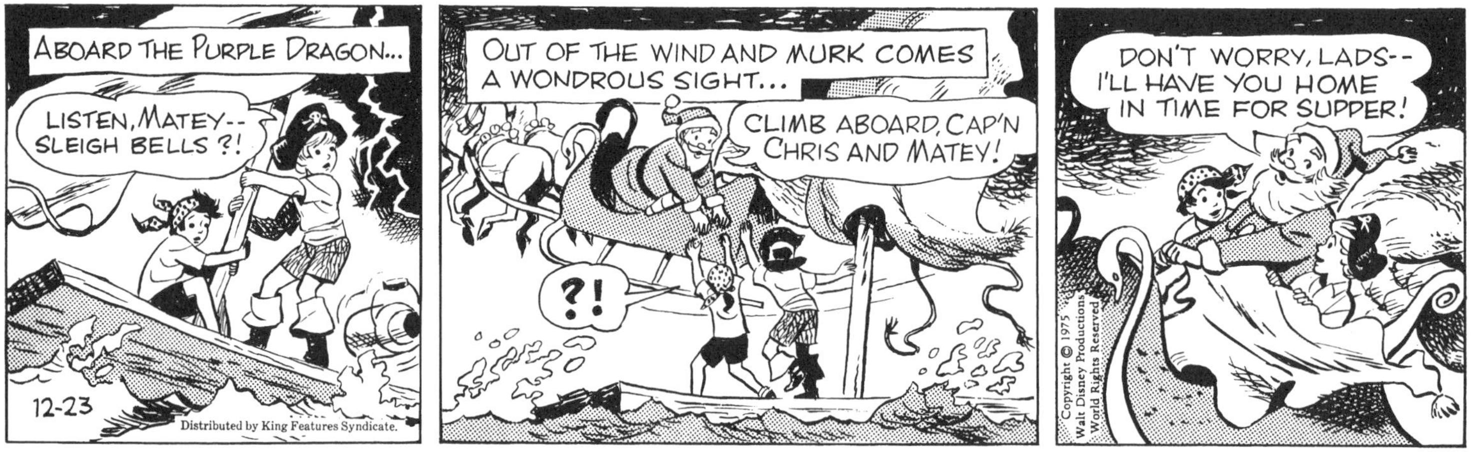
ABOARD THE PURPLE DRAGON...
LISTEN, MATEY-- SLEIGH BELLS ?!
12-23
Distributed by King Features Syndicate.
OUT OF THE WIND AND MURK COMES A WONDROUS SIGHT...
CLIMB ABOARD, CAP'N CHRIS AND MATEY!
?!
DON'T WORRY, LADS-- I'LL HAVE YOU HOME IN TIME FOR SUPPER!
Copyright © 1975 Walt Disney Productions World Rights Reserved

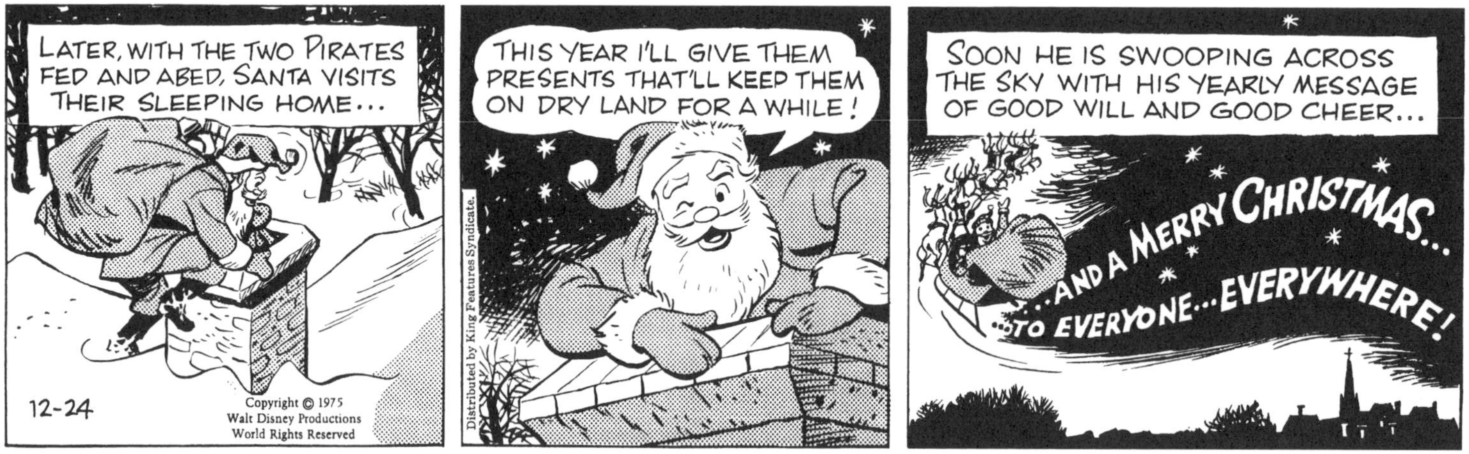
LATER, WITH THE TWO PIRATES FED AND ABED, SANTA VISITS THEIR SLEEPING HOME...
12-24
Copyright © 1975 Walt Disney Productions World Rights Reserved
THIS YEAR I'LL GIVE THEM PRESENTS THAT'LL KEEP THEM ON DRY LAND FOR A WHILE!
Distributed by King Features Syndicate.
SOON HE IS SWOOPING ACROSS THE SKY WITH HIS YEARLY MESSAGE OF GOOD WILL AND GOOD CHEER...
...AND A MERRY CHRISTMAS...
...TO EVERYONE...EVERYWHERE!

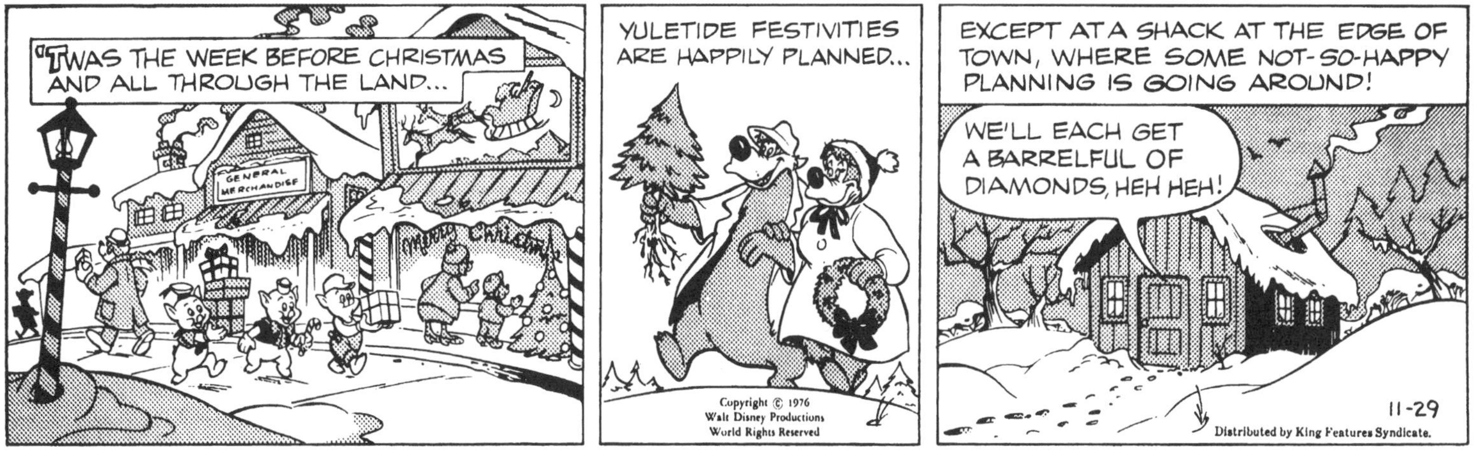
'TWAS THE WEEK BEFORE CHRISTMAS AND ALL THROUGH THE LAND...
GENERAL MERCHANDISE
YULETIDE FESTIVITIES ARE HAPPILY PLANNED...
Copyright © 1976 Walt Disney Productions World Rights Reserved
EXCEPT AT A SHACK AT THE EDGE OF TOWN, WHERE SOME NOT-SO-HAPPY PLANNING IS GOING AROUND!
WE'LL EACH GET A BARRELFUL OF DIAMONDS, HEH HEH!
11-29
Distributed by King Features Syndicate.

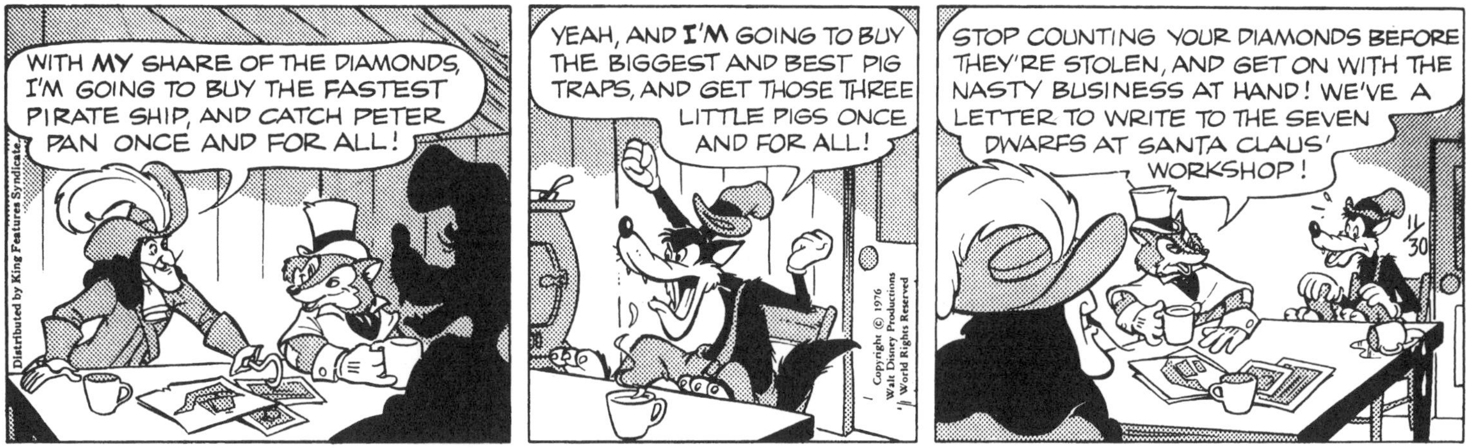
WITH MY SHARE OF THE DIAMONDS, I'M GOING TO BUY THE FASTEST PIRATE SHIP, AND CATCH PETER PAN ONCE AND FOR ALL!
Distributed by King Features Syndicate.
YEAH, AND I'M GOING TO BUY THE BIGGEST AND BEST PIG TRAPS, AND GET THOSE THREE LITTLE PIGS ONCE AND FOR ALL!
Copyright © 1976 Walt Disney Productions World Rights Reserved
STOP COUNTING YOUR DIAMONDS BEFORE THEY'RE STOLEN, AND GET ON WITH THE NASTY BUSINESS AT HAND! WE'VE A LETTER TO WRITE TO THE SEVEN DWARFS AT SANTA CLAUS' WORKSHOP!
11/30

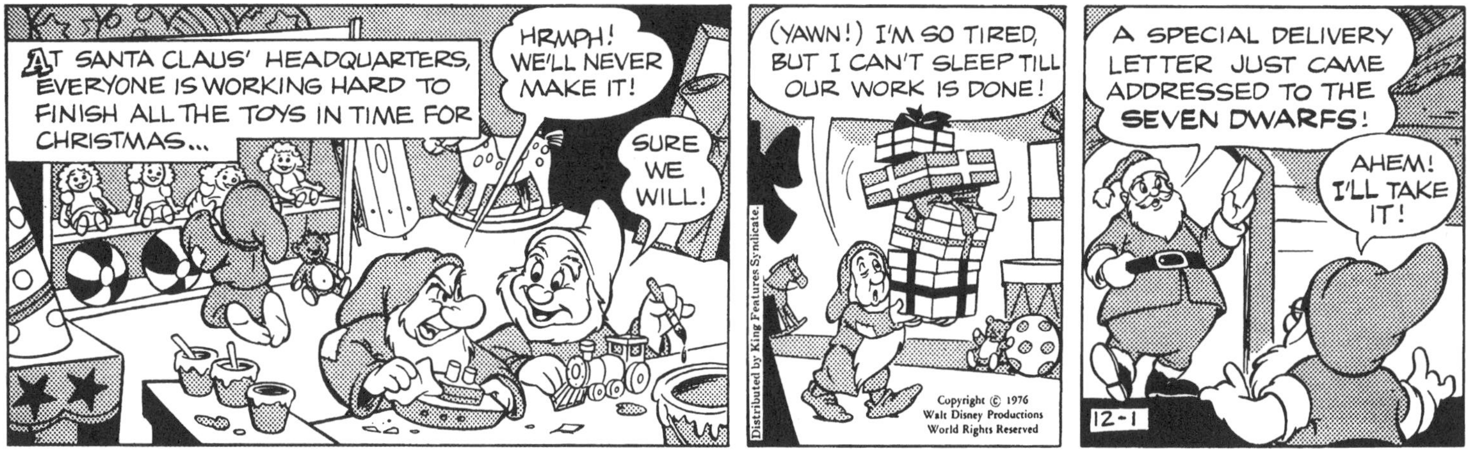
AT SANTA CLAUS' HEADQUARTERS, EVERYONE IS WORKING HARD TO FINISH ALL THE TOYS IN TIME FOR CHRISTMAS...
HRMPH! WE'LL NEVER MAKE IT!
SURE WE WILL!
Distributed by King Features Syndicate.
(YAWN!) I'M SO TIRED, BUT I CAN'T SLEEP TILL OUR WORK IS DONE!
Copyright © 1976 Walt Disney Productions World Rights Reserved
A SPECIAL DELIVERY LETTER JUST CAME ADDRESSED TO THE SEVEN DWARFS!
AHEM! I'LL TAKE IT!
12-1

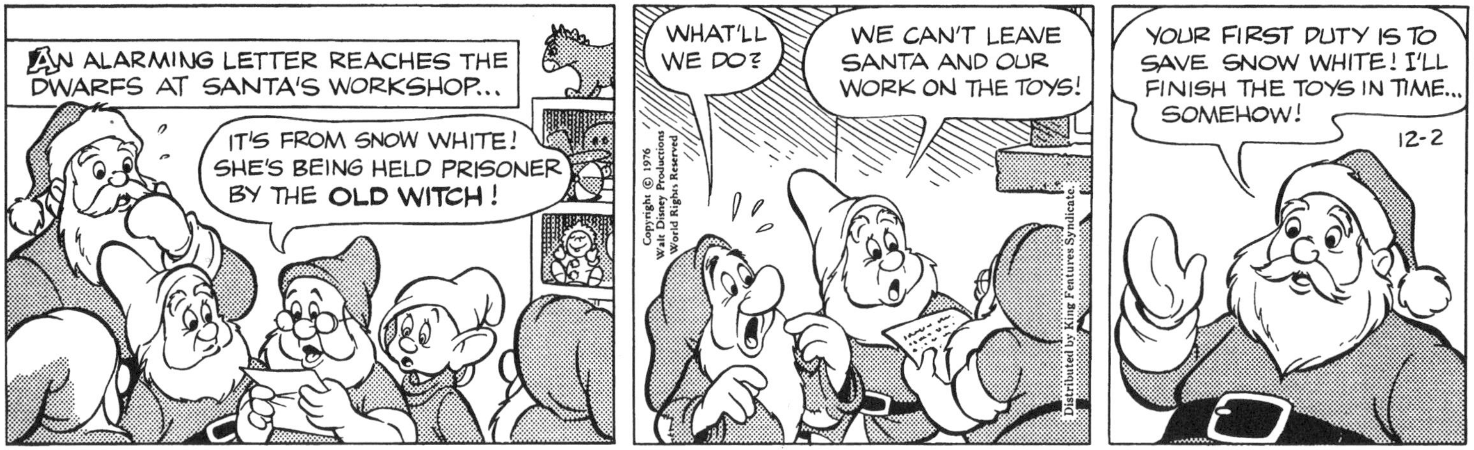
AN ALARMING LETTER REACHES THE DWARFS AT SANTA'S WORKSHOP...
IT'S FROM SNOW WHITE! SHE'S BEING HELD PRISONER BY THE OLD WITCH!
Copyright © 1976 Walt Disney Productions World Rights Reserved
WHAT'LL WE DO?
WE CAN'T LEAVE SANTA AND OUR WORK ON THE TOYS!
Distributed by King Features Syndicate.
YOUR FIRST DUTY IS TO SAVE SNOW WHITE! I'LL FINISH THE TOYS IN TIME... SOMEHOW!
12-2

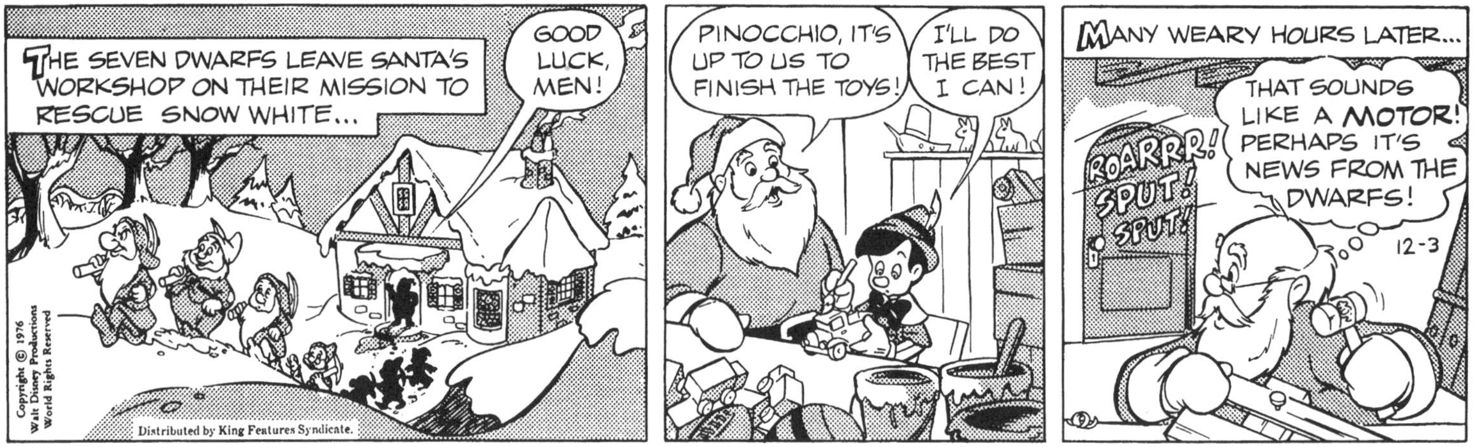
THE SEVEN DWARFS LEAVE SANTA'S WORKSHOP ON THEIR MISSION TO RESCUE SNOW WHITE...
GOOD LUCK, MEN!
Copyright © 1976 Walt Disney Productions World Rights Reserved
Distributed by King Features Syndicate.
PINOCCHIO, IT'S UP TO US TO FINISH THE TOYS!
I'LL DO THE BEST I CAN!
MANY WEARY HOURS LATER...
ROARRR! SPUT! SPUT!
THAT SOUNDS LIKE A MOTOR! PERHAPS IT'S NEWS FROM THE DWARFS!
12-3

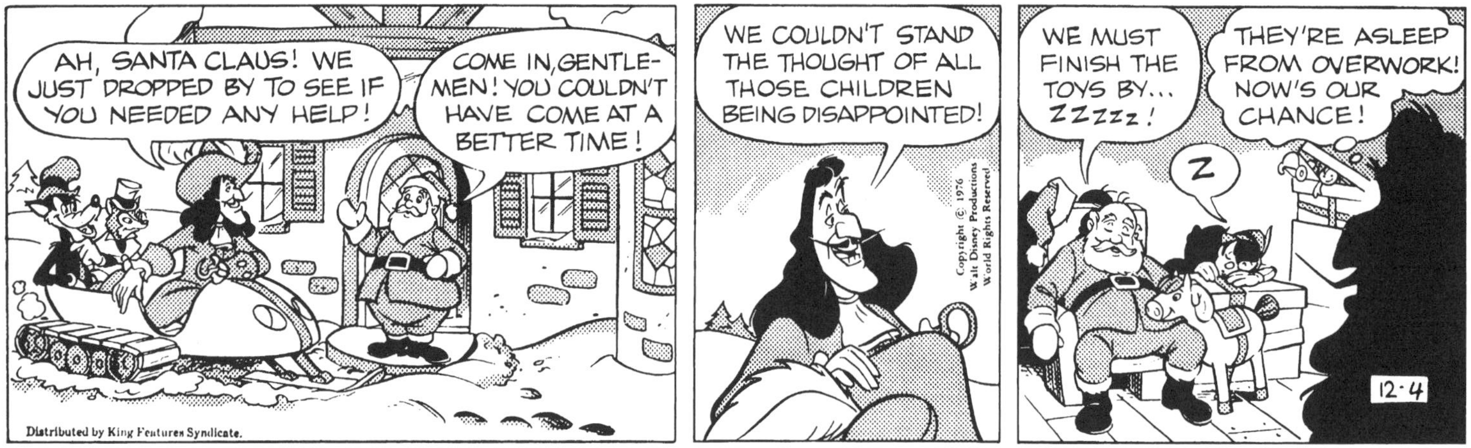
AH, SANTA CLAUS! WE JUST DROPPED BY TO SEE IF YOU NEEDED ANY HELP!
COME IN, GENTLEMEN! YOU COULDN'T HAVE COME AT A BETTER TIME!
Distributed by King Features Syndicate.
WE COULDN'T STAND THE THOUGHT OF ALL THOSE CHILDREN BEING DISAPPOINTED!
Copyright © 1976 Walt Disney Productions World Rights Reserved
WE MUST FINISH THE TOYS BY... ZZzzz!
Z
THEY'RE ASLEEP FROM OVERWORK! NOW'S OUR CHANCE!
12-4

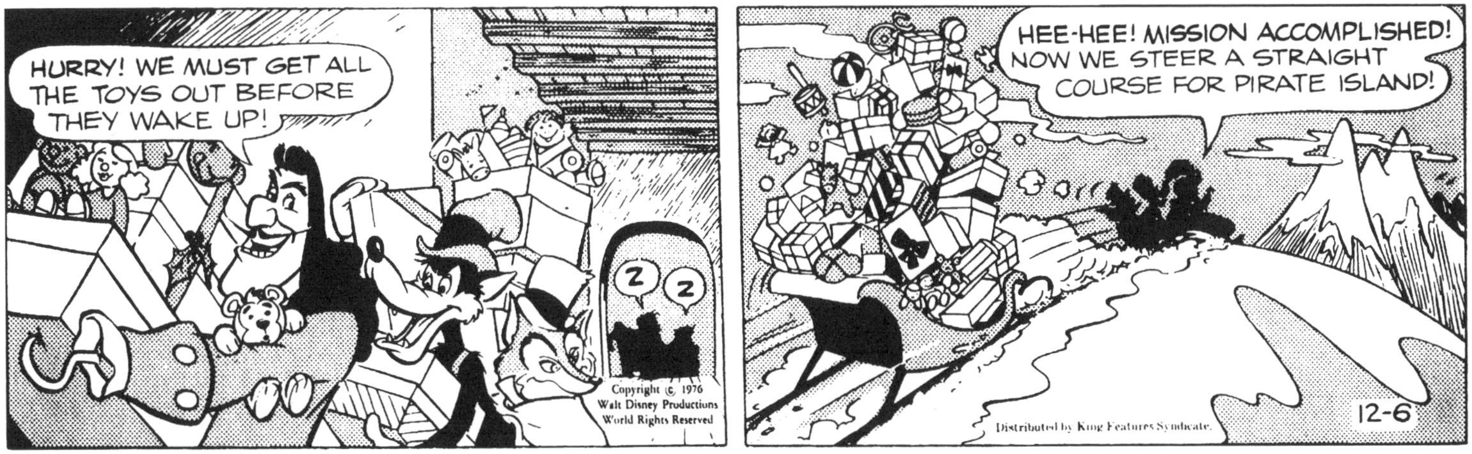
HURRY! WE MUST GET ALL THE TOYS OUT BEFORE THEY WAKE UP!
Z Z
Copyright © 1976 Walt Disney Productions World Rights Reserved
HEE-HEE! MISSION ACCOMPLISHED! NOW WE STEER A STRAIGHT COURSE FOR PIRATE ISLAND!
Distributed by King Features Syndicate.
12-6

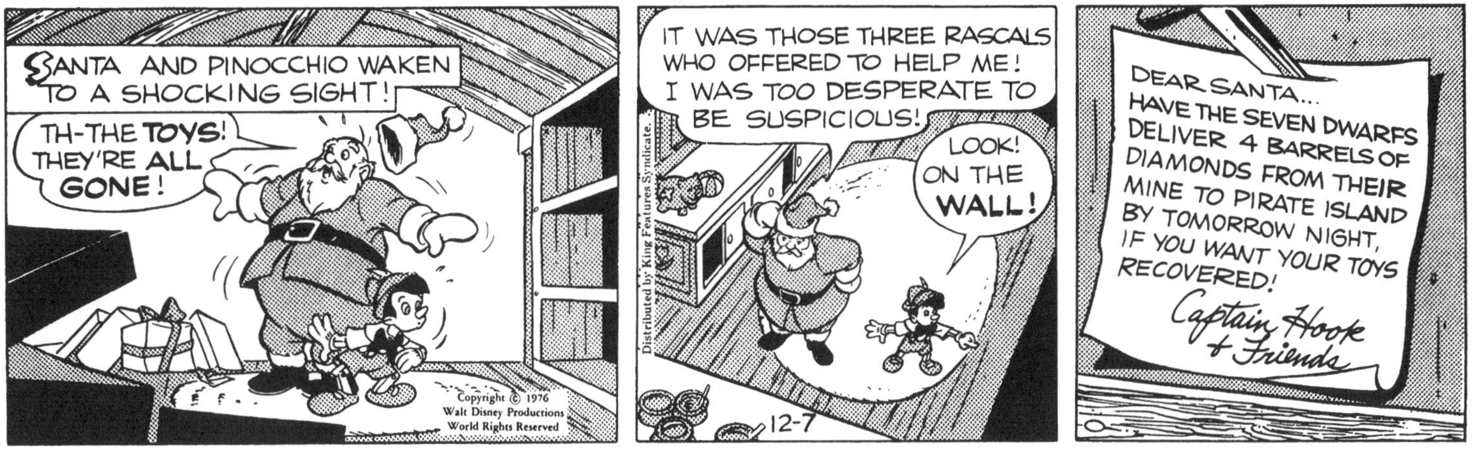
SANTA AND PINOCCHIO WAKEN TO A SHOCKING SIGHT!
TH-THE TOYS! THEY'RE ALL GONE!
Copyright © 1976 Walt Disney Productions World Rights Reserved
IT WAS THOSE THREE RASCALS WHO OFFERED TO HELP ME! I WAS TOO DESPERATE TO BE SUSPICIOUS!
LOOK! ON THE WALL!
Distributed by King Features Syndicate.
12-7
DEAR SANTA... HAVE THE SEVEN DWARFS DELIVER 4 BARRELS OF DIAMONDS FROM THEIR MINE TO PIRATE ISLAND BY TOMORROW NIGHT, IF YOU WANT YOUR TOYS RECOVERED!
Captain Hook + Friends

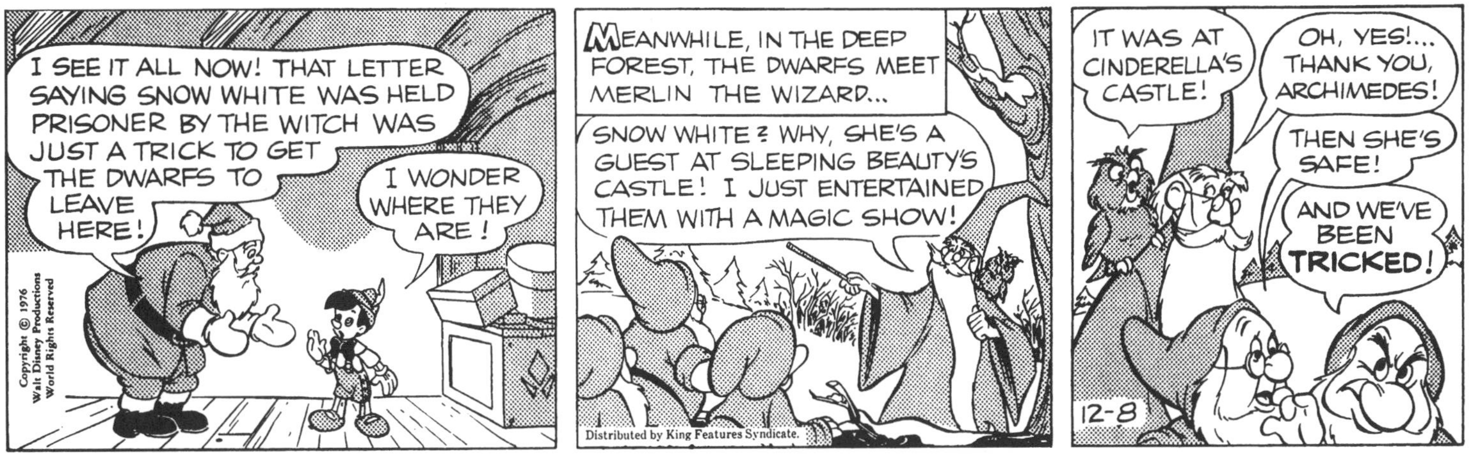
I SEE IT ALL NOW! THAT LETTER SAYING SNOW WHITE WAS HELD PRISONER BY THE WITCH WAS JUST A TRICK TO GET THE DWARFS TO LEAVE HERE!
I WONDER WHERE THEY ARE!
Copyright © 1976 Walt Disney Productions World Rights Reserved
MEANWHILE, IN THE DEEP FOREST, THE DWARFS MEET MERLIN THE WIZARD...
SNOW WHITE? WHY, SHE'S A GUEST AT SLEEPING BEAUTY'S CASTLE! I JUST ENTERTAINED THEM WITH A MAGIC SHOW!
Distributed by King Features Syndicate.
IT WAS AT CINDERELLA'S CASTLE!
OH, YES!... THANK YOU, ARCHIMEDES!
THEN SHE'S SAFE!
AND WE'VE BEEN TRICKED!
12-8

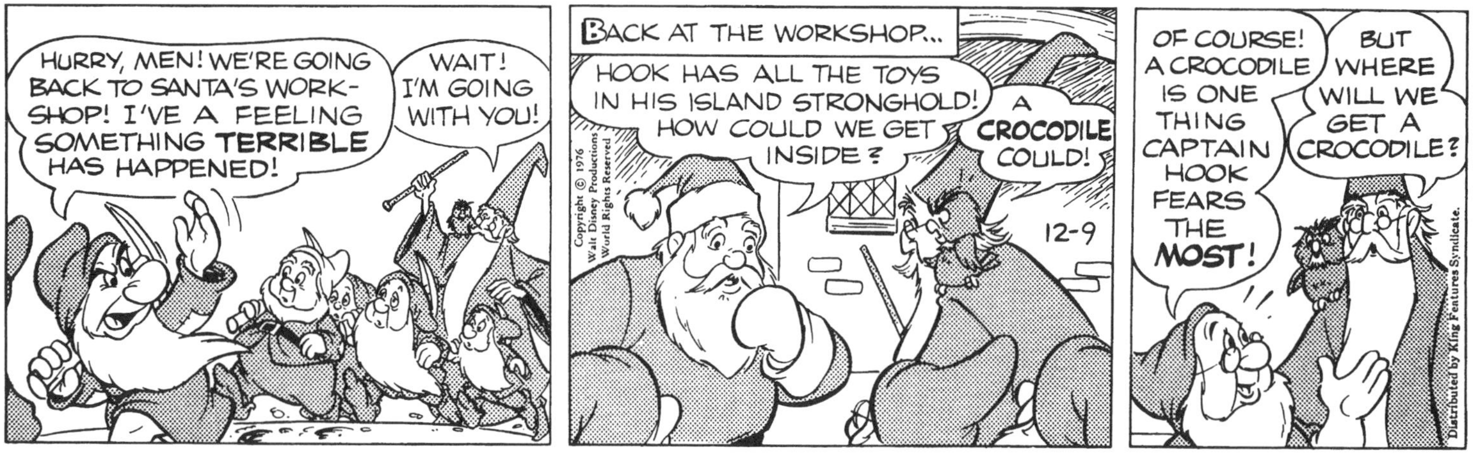
HURRY, MEN! WE'RE GOING BACK TO SANTA'S WORK-SHOP! I'VE A FEELING SOMETHING TERRIBLE HAS HAPPENED!
WAIT! I'M GOING WITH YOU!
BACK AT THE WORKSHOP...
HOOK HAS ALL THE TOYS IN HIS ISLAND STRONGHOLD! HOW COULD WE GET INSIDE?
A CROCODILE COULD!
Copyright © 1976 Walt Disney Productions World Rights Reserved
12-9
OF COURSE! A CROCODILE IS ONE THING CAPTAIN HOOK FEARS THE MOST!
BUT WHERE WILL WE GET A CROCODILE?
Distributed by King Features Syndicate.

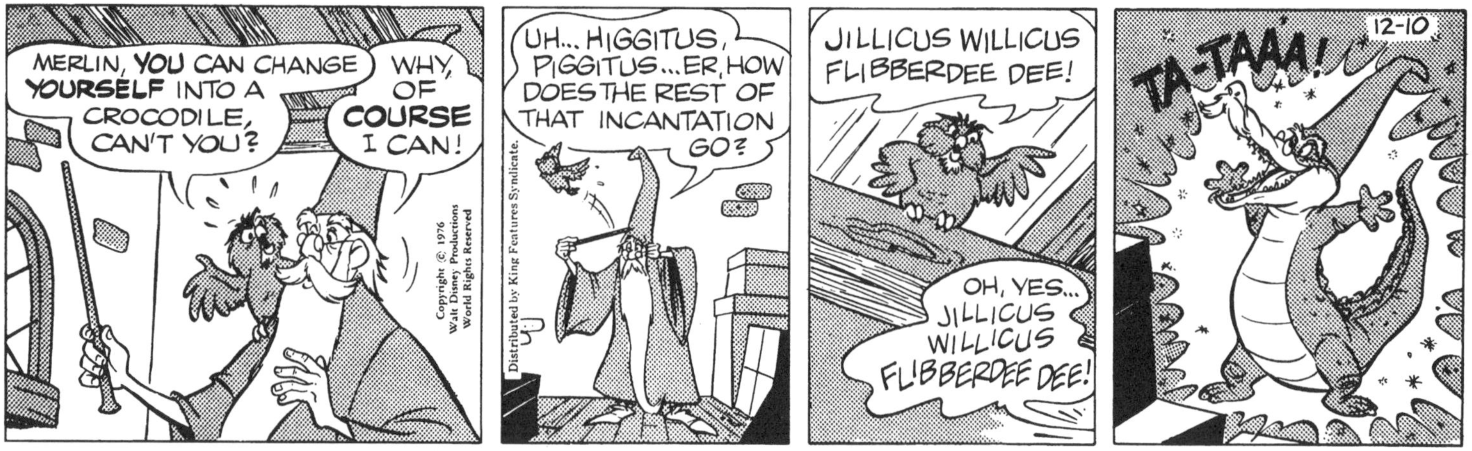
MERLIN, YOU CAN CHANGE YOURSELF INTO A CROCODILE, CAN'T YOU?
WHY, OF COURSE I CAN!
Copyright © 1976 Walt Disney Productions World Rights Reserved
UH... HIGGITUS, PIGGITUS...ER, HOW DOES THE REST OF THAT INCANTATION GO?
Distributed by King Features Syndicate.
JILLICUS WILLICUS FLIBBERDEE DEE!
OH, YES... JILLICUS WILLICUS FLIBBERDEE DEE!
12-10
TA-TAAA!

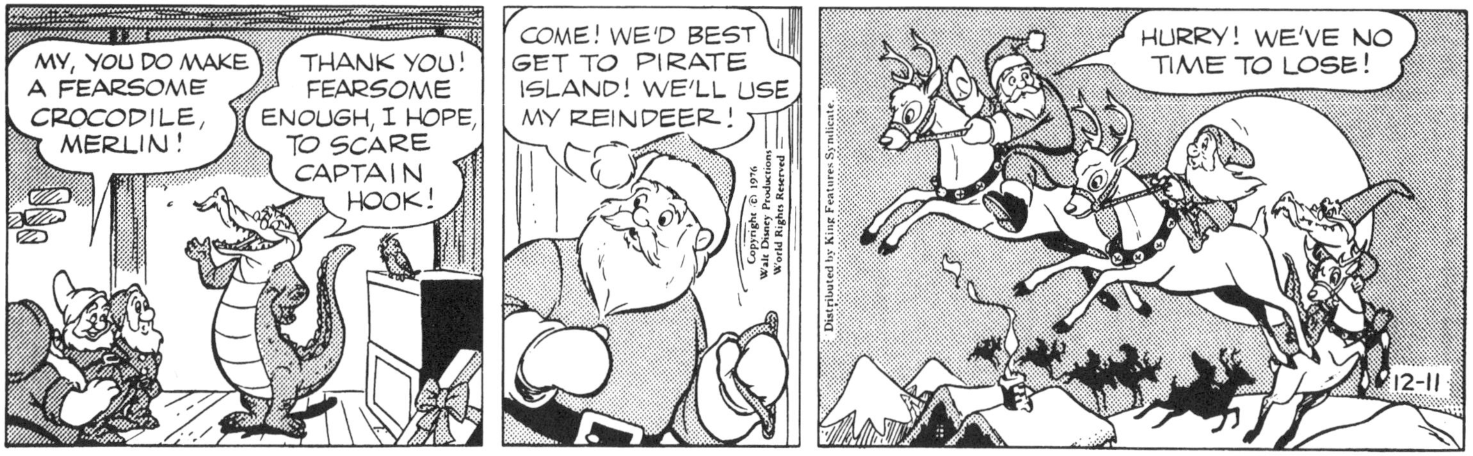
MY, YOU DO MAKE A FEARSOME CROCODILE, MERLIN!
THANK YOU! FEARSOME ENOUGH, I HOPE, TO SCARE CAPTAIN HOOK!
COME! WE'D BEST GET TO PIRATE ISLAND! WE'LL USE MY REINDEER!
Copyright © 1976 Walt Disney Productions World Rights Reserved
HURRY! WE'VE NO TIME TO LOSE!
Distributed by King Features Syndicate.
12-11

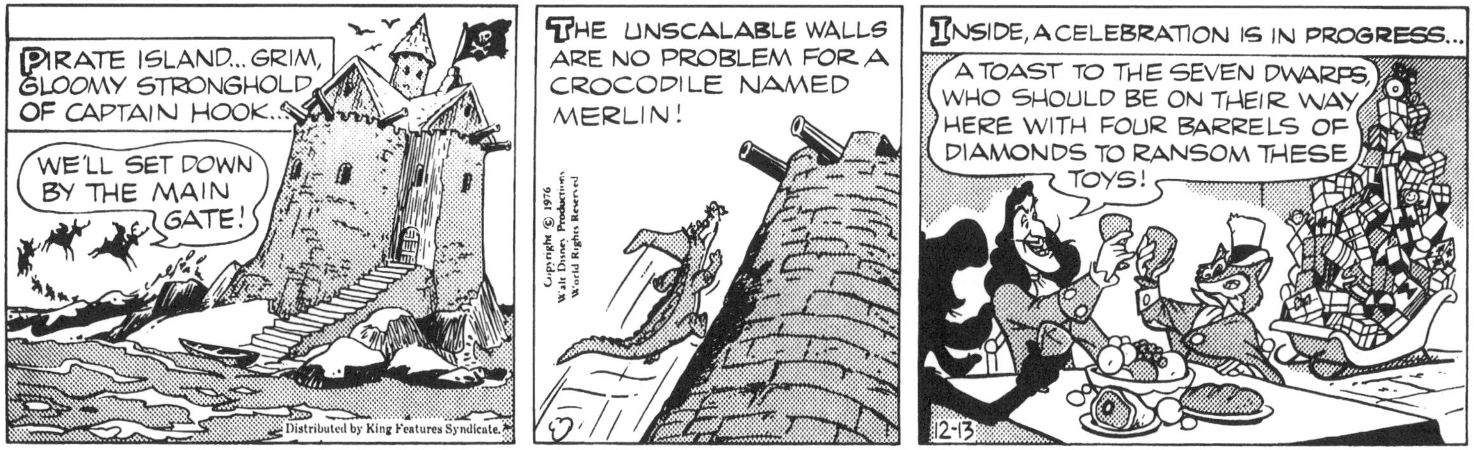
PIRATE ISLAND... GRIM, GLOOMY STRONGHOLD OF CAPTAIN HOOK...
WE'LL SET DOWN BY THE MAIN GATE!
Distributed by King Features Syndicate.
THE UNSCALABLE WALLS ARE NO PROBLEM FOR A CROCODILE NAMED MERLIN!
Copyright © 1976 Walt Disney Productions World Rights Reserved
INSIDE, A CELEBRATION IS IN PROGRESS...
A TOAST TO THE SEVEN DWARFS, WHO SHOULD BE ON THEIR WAY HERE WITH FOUR BARRELS OF DIAMONDS TO RANSOM THESE TOYS!
12-13

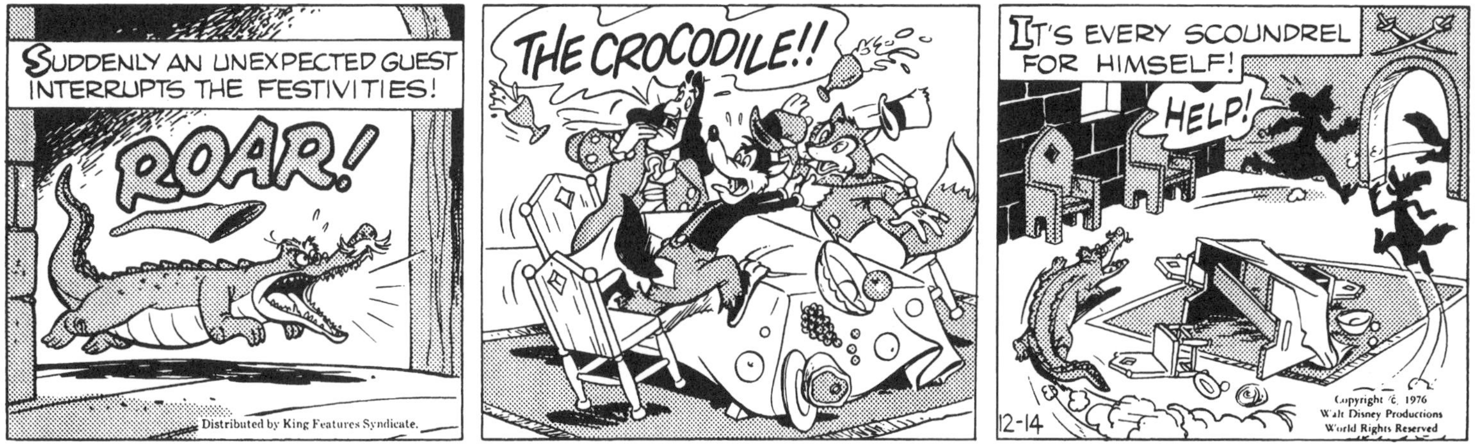
SUDDENLY AN UNEXPECTED GUEST INTERRUPTS THE FESTIVITIES!
ROAR!
Distributed by King Features Syndicate.
THE CROCODILE!!
IT'S EVERY SCOUNDREL FOR HIMSELF!
HELP!
12-14
Copyright © 1976 Walt Disney Productions World Rights Reserved

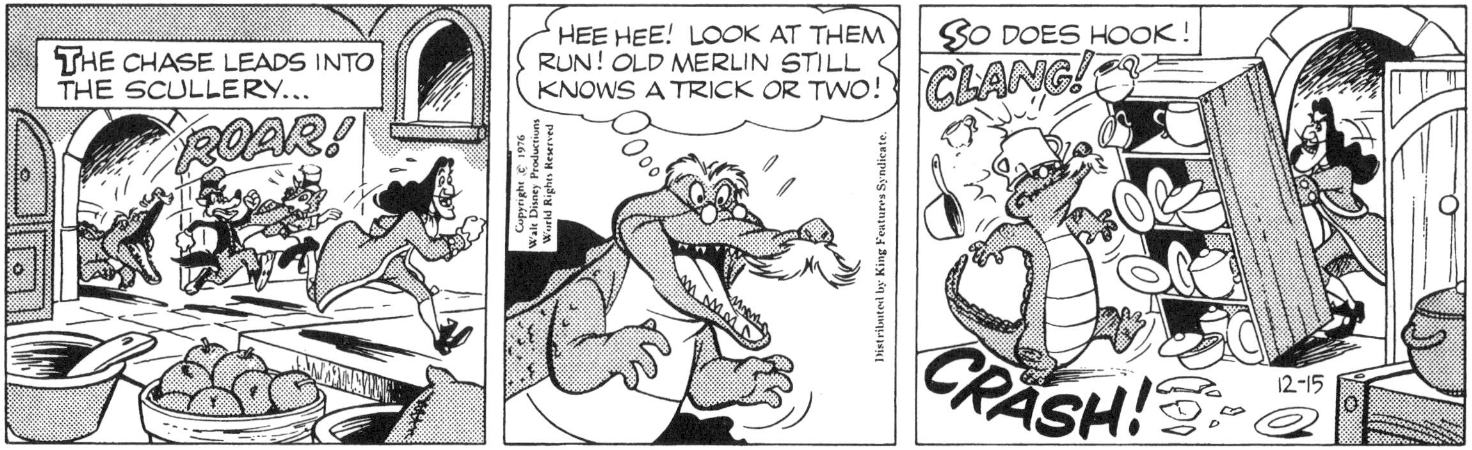
THE CHASE LEADS INTO THE SCULLERY...
ROAR!
HEE HEE! LOOK AT THEM RUN! OLD MERLIN STILL KNOWS A TRICK OR TWO!
Copyright © 1976 Walt Disney Productions World Rights Reserved
Distributed by King Features Syndicate.
SO DOES HOOK!
CLANG!
CRASH!
12-15

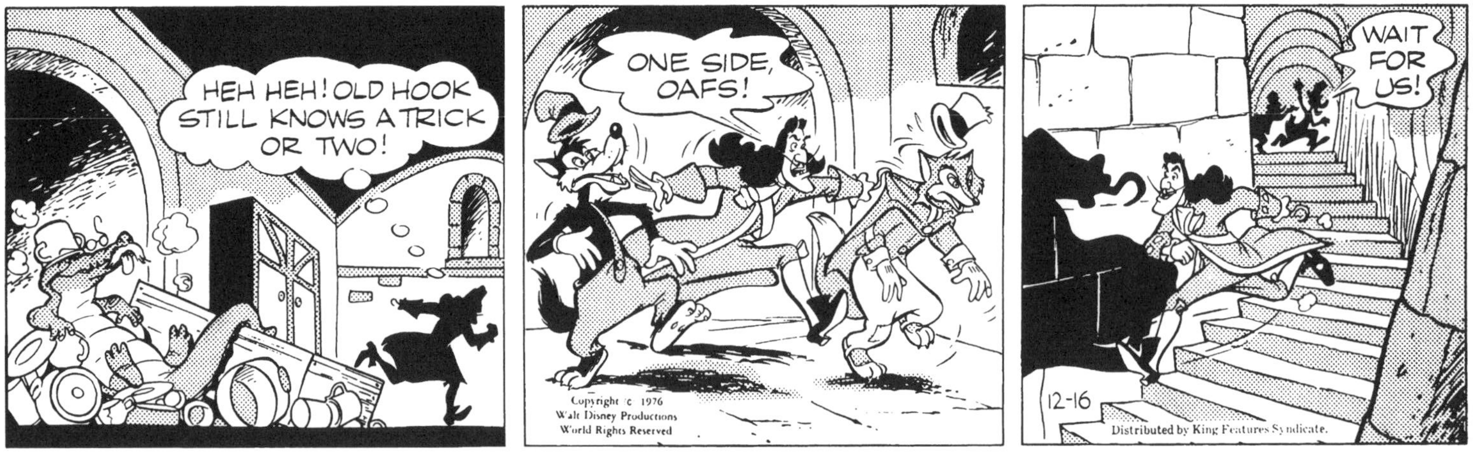
HEH HEH! OLD HOOK STILL KNOWS A TRICK OR TWO!
ONE SIDE, OAFS!
Copyright (c) 1976 Walt Disney Productions World Rights Reserved
WAIT FOR US!
12-16
Distributed by King Features Syndicate.

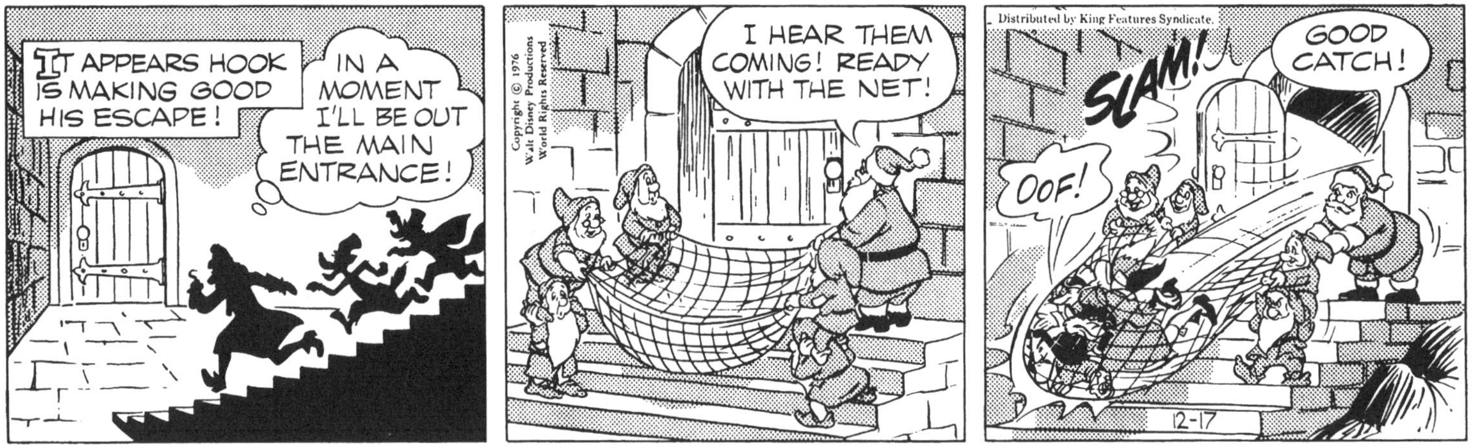
IT APPEARS HOOK IS MAKING GOOD HIS ESCAPE!
IN A MOMENT I'LL BE OUT THE MAIN ENTRANCE!
Copyright © 1976 Walt Disney Productions World Rights Reserved
I HEAR THEM COMING! READY WITH THE NET!
Distributed by King Features Syndicate.
SLAM!
GOOD CATCH!
OOF!
12-17

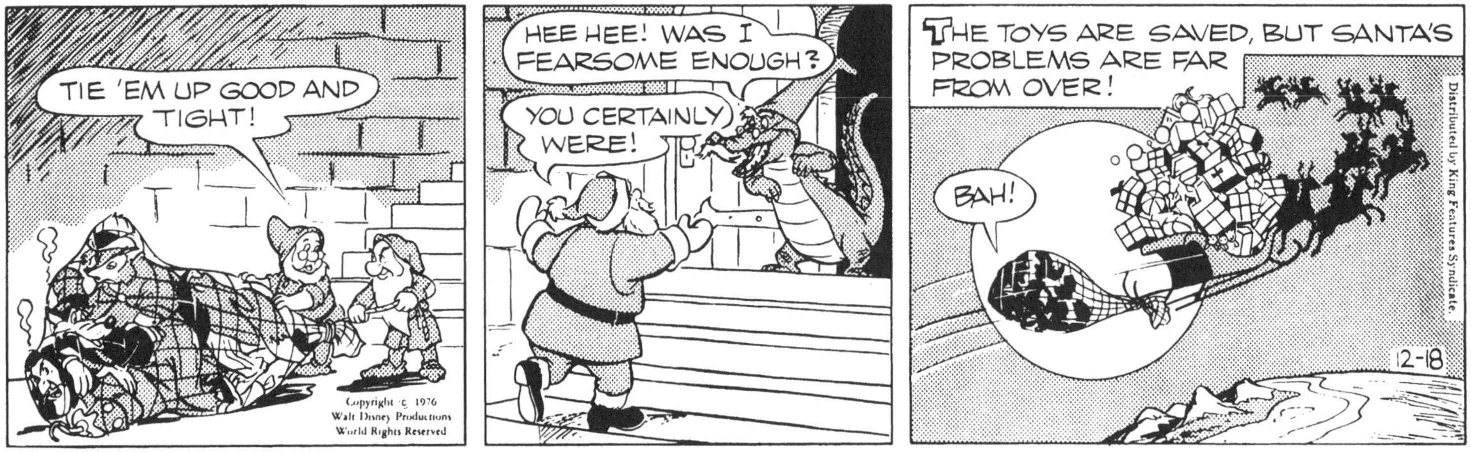
TIE 'EM UP GOOD AND TIGHT!
Copyright (c) 1976 Walt Disney Productions World Rights Reserved
HEE HEE! WAS I FEARSOME ENOUGH?
YOU CERTAINLY WERE!
THE TOYS ARE SAVED, BUT SANTA'S PROBLEMS ARE FAR FROM OVER!
BAH!
Distributed by King Features Syndicate.
12-18

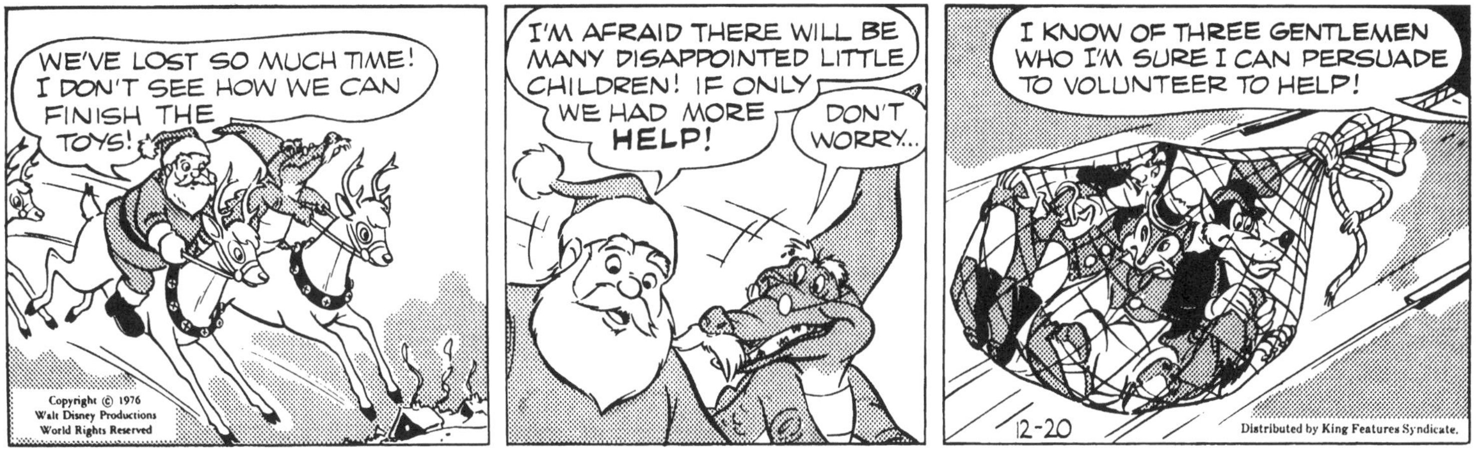
WE'VE LOST SO MUCH TIME! I DON'T SEE HOW WE CAN FINISH THE TOYS!
Copyright © 1976 Walt Disney Productions World Rights Reserved
I'M AFRAID THERE WILL BE MANY DISAPPOINTED LITTLE CHILDREN! IF ONLY WE HAD MORE **HELP!**
DON'T WORRY...
I KNOW OF THREE GENTLEMEN WHO I'M SURE I CAN PERSUADE TO VOLUNTEER TO HELP!
12-20
Distributed by King Features Syndicate.

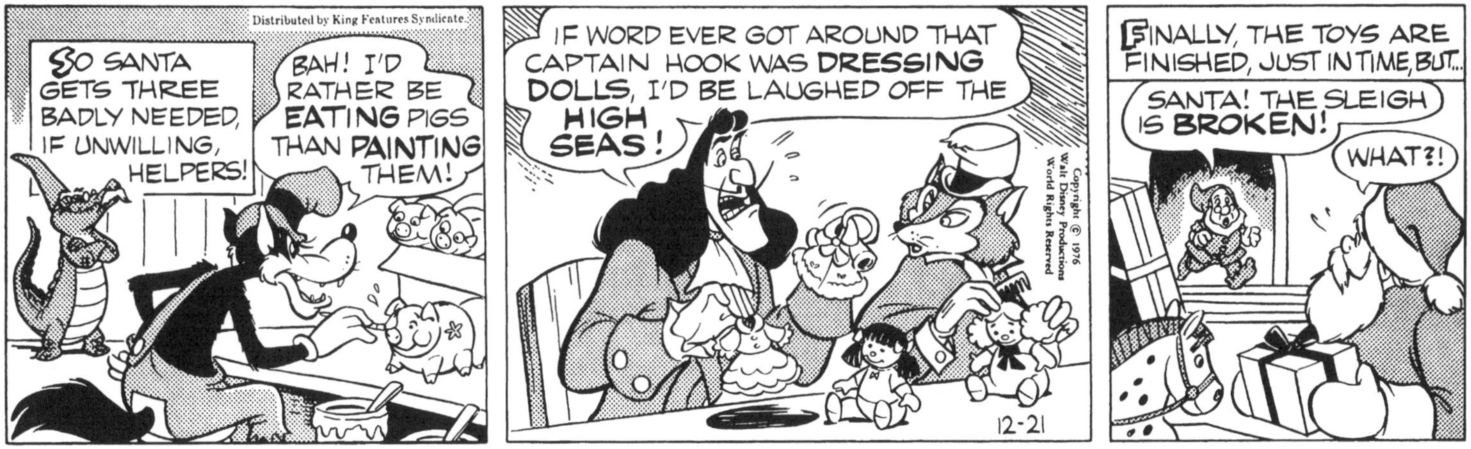
Distributed by King Features Syndicate.
SO SANTA GETS THREE BADLY NEEDED, IF UNWILLING, HELPERS!
BAH! I'D RATHER BE **EATING** PIGS THAN **PAINTING** THEM!
IF WORD EVER GOT AROUND THAT CAPTAIN HOOK WAS **DRESSING DOLLS**, I'D BE LAUGHED OFF THE **HIGH SEAS**!
Copyright © 1976 Walt Disney Productions World Rights Reserved
12-21
FINALLY, THE TOYS ARE FINISHED, JUST IN TIME, BUT...
SANTA! THE SLEIGH IS **BROKEN!**
WHAT?!

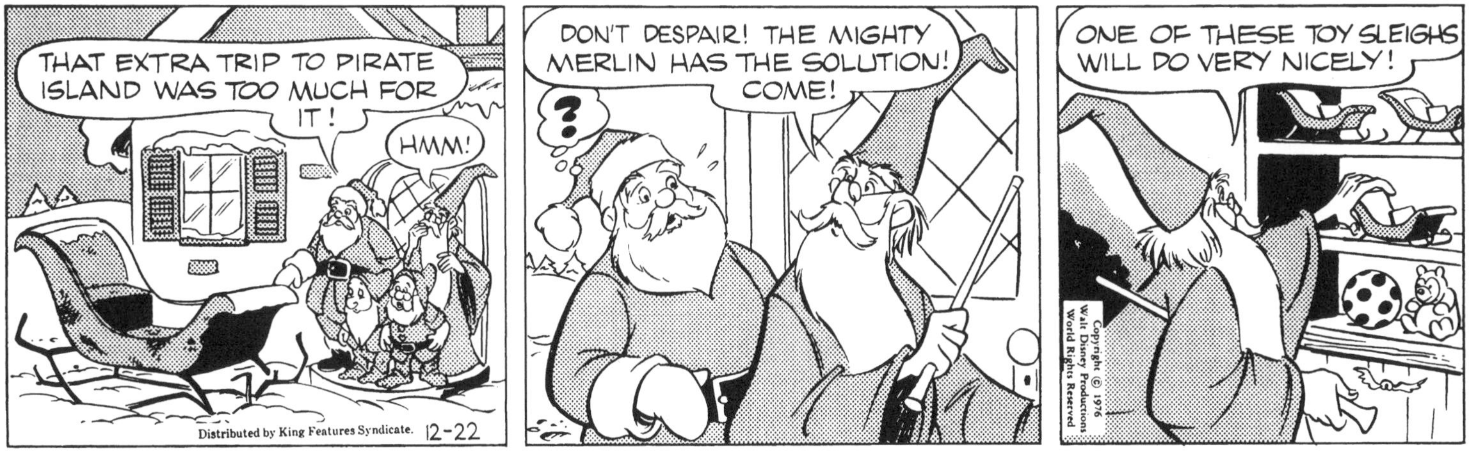
THAT EXTRA TRIP TO PIRATE ISLAND WAS TOO MUCH FOR IT!
HMM!
Distributed by King Features Syndicate.
12-22
?
DON'T DESPAIR! THE MIGHTY MERLIN HAS THE SOLUTION! COME!
ONE OF THESE TOY SLEIGHS WILL DO VERY NICELY!
Copyright © 1976 Walt Disney Productions World Rights Reserved

B-BUT THAT TINY SLEIGH CAN'T POSSIBLY HOLD ALL THE GIFTS!
WE'LL SEE...
Distributed by King Features Syndicate.
12-23
HIGGITUS, PIGGITUS... HMM! HOW DOES THAT INCANTATION GO?
JILLICUS! WILLICUS! FLIBBERDEE DEE!
Copyright © 1976 Walt Disney Productions World Rights Reserved
OF COURSE! JILLICUS WILLICUS FLIBBERDEE DEE!

TA-TAAA!!
12-24
SO...
A MERRY CHRISTMAS TO EVERYONE... AND I DO MEAN EVERYONE!
NOW, DON'T YOU FEEL GOOD ABOUT HELPING OUT?
OH, BAH!
Copyright © 1976 Walt Disney Productions World Rights Reserved
Distributed by King Features Syndicate.

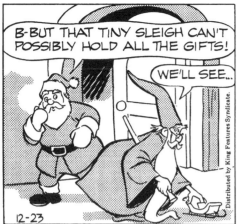

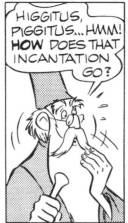

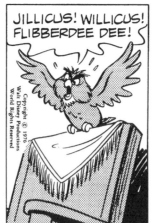

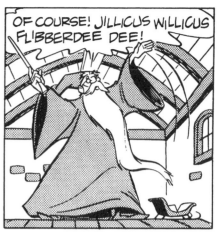

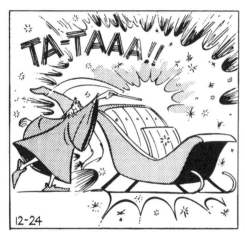

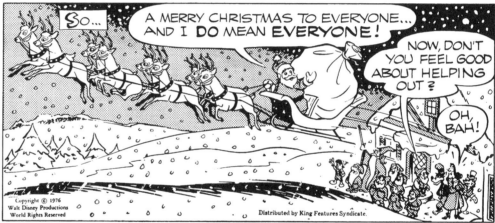

1977

NO PUPPETS FOR CHRISTMAS

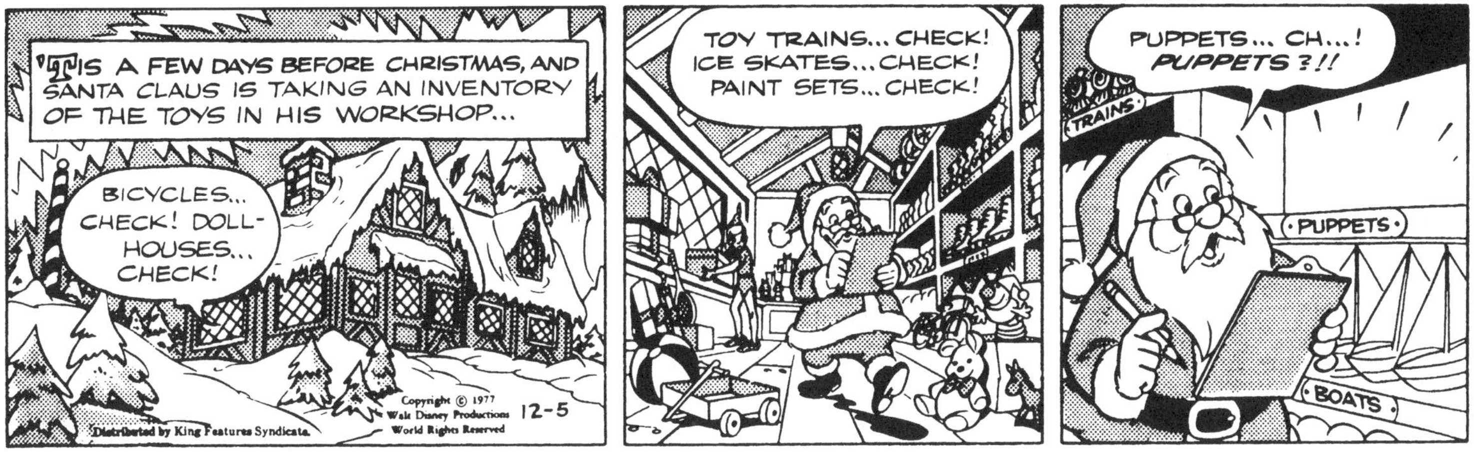
'TIS A FEW DAYS BEFORE CHRISTMAS, AND SANTA CLAUS IS TAKING AN INVENTORY OF THE TOYS IN HIS WORKSHOP...
BICYCLES... CHECK! DOLL-HOUSES... CHECK!
Copyright © 1977 Walt Disney Productions World Rights Reserved
12-5
Distributed by King Features Syndicate.
TOY TRAINS... CHECK! ICE SKATES... CHECK! PAINT SETS... CHECK!
PUPPETS... CH...! PUPPETS ?!!
TRAINS
PUPPETS
BOATS

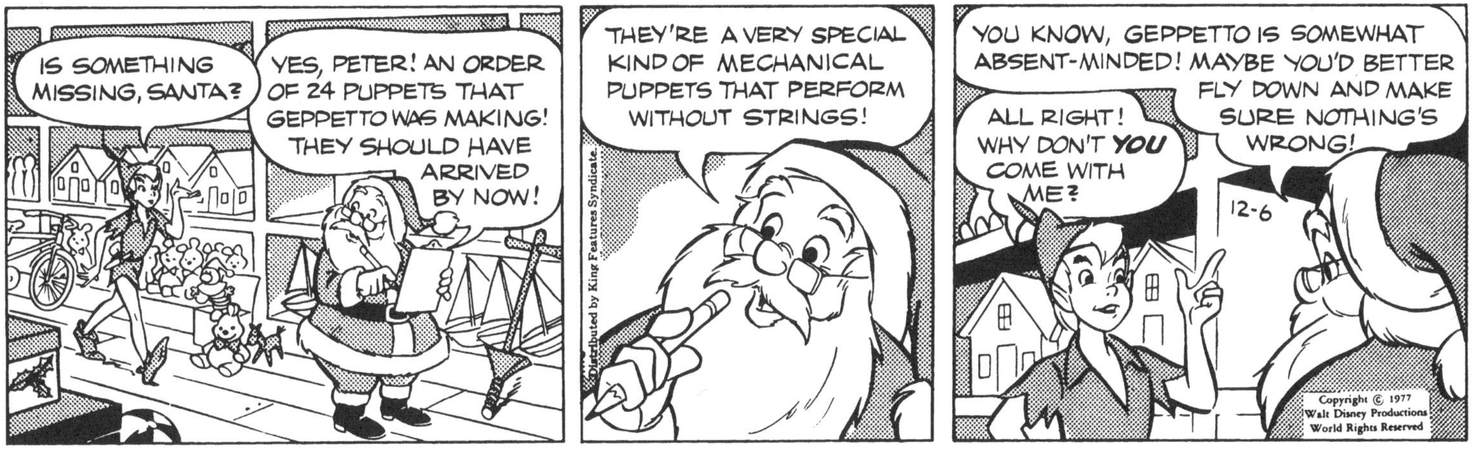
IS SOMETHING MISSING, SANTA?
YES, PETER! AN ORDER OF 24 PUPPETS THAT GEPPETTO WAS MAKING! THEY SHOULD HAVE ARRIVED BY NOW!
Distributed by King Features Syndicate.
THEY'RE A VERY SPECIAL KIND OF MECHANICAL PUPPETS THAT PERFORM WITHOUT STRINGS!
YOU KNOW, GEPPETTO IS SOMEWHAT ABSENT-MINDED! MAYBE YOU'D BETTER FLY DOWN AND MAKE SURE NOTHING'S WRONG!
ALL RIGHT! WHY DON'T YOU COME WITH ME?
12-6
Copyright © 1977 Walt Disney Productions World Rights Reserved

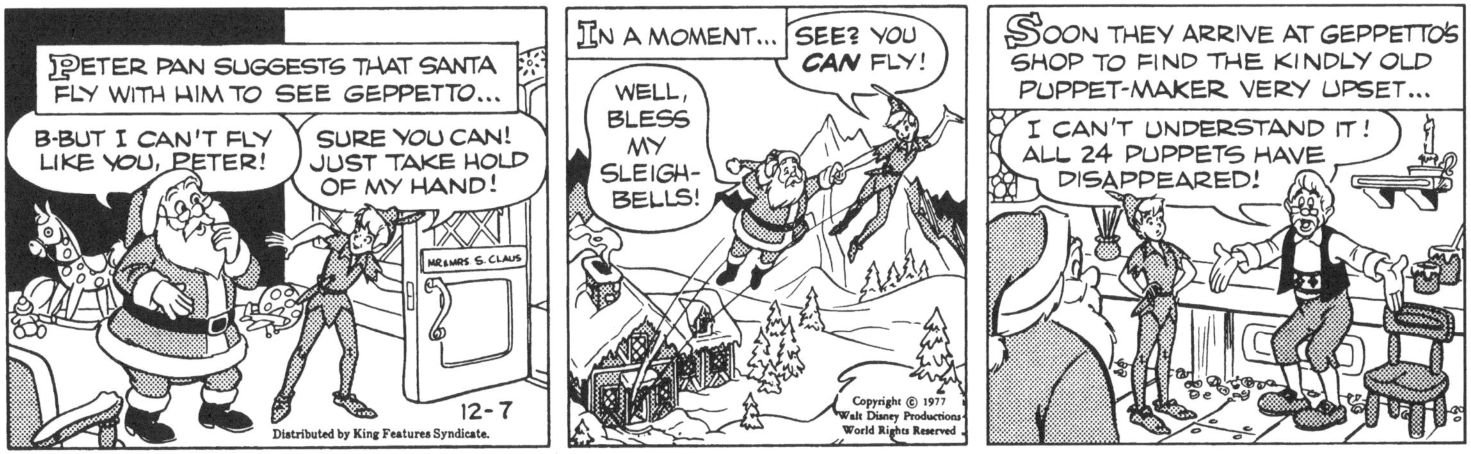
PETER PAN SUGGESTS THAT SANTA FLY WITH HIM TO SEE GEPPETTO...
B-BUT I CAN'T FLY LIKE YOU, PETER!
SURE YOU CAN! JUST TAKE HOLD OF MY HAND!
MR.&MRS. S. CLAUS
12-7
Distributed by King Features Syndicate.
IN A MOMENT...
SEE? YOU CAN FLY!
WELL, BLESS MY SLEIGH-BELLS!
Copyright © 1977 Walt Disney Productions World Rights Reserved
SOON THEY ARRIVE AT GEPPETTO'S SHOP TO FIND THE KINDLY OLD PUPPET-MAKER VERY UPSET...
I CAN'T UNDERSTAND IT! ALL 24 PUPPETS HAVE DISAPPEARED!

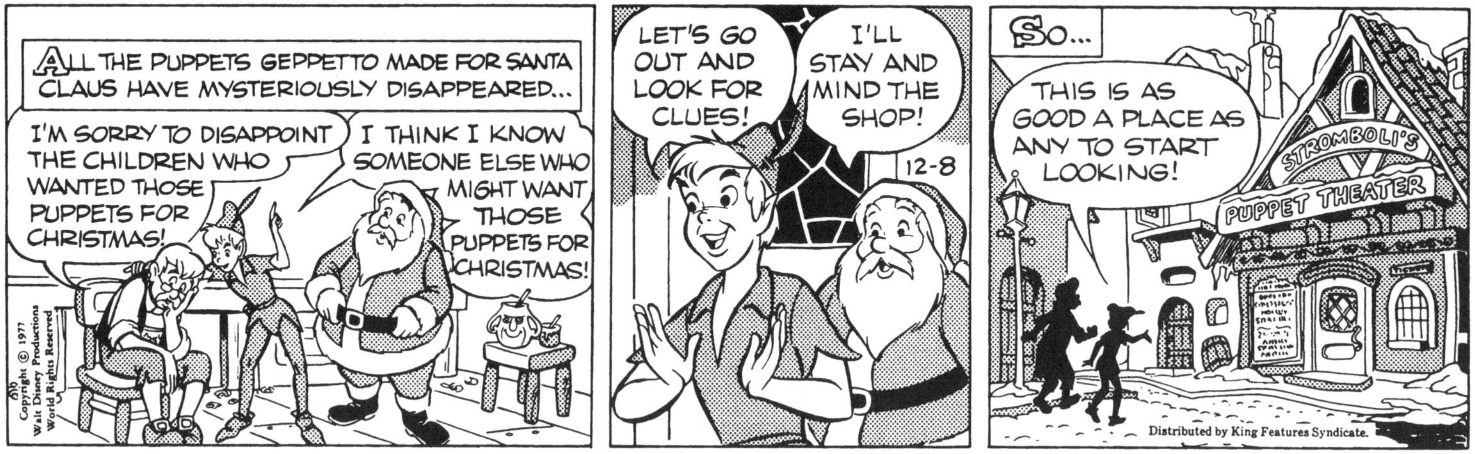
ALL THE PUPPETS GEPPETTO MADE FOR SANTA CLAUS HAVE MYSTERIOUSLY DISAPPEARED...
I'M SORRY TO DISAPPOINT THE CHILDREN WHO WANTED THOSE PUPPETS FOR CHRISTMAS!
I THINK I KNOW SOMEONE ELSE WHO MIGHT WANT THOSE PUPPETS FOR CHRISTMAS!
Copyright © 1977 Walt Disney Productions World Rights Reserved
LET'S GO OUT AND LOOK FOR CLUES!
I'LL STAY AND MIND THE SHOP!
12-8
SO...
THIS IS AS GOOD A PLACE AS ANY TO START LOOKING!
STROMBOLI'S
PUPPET THEATER
Distributed by King Features Syndicate.

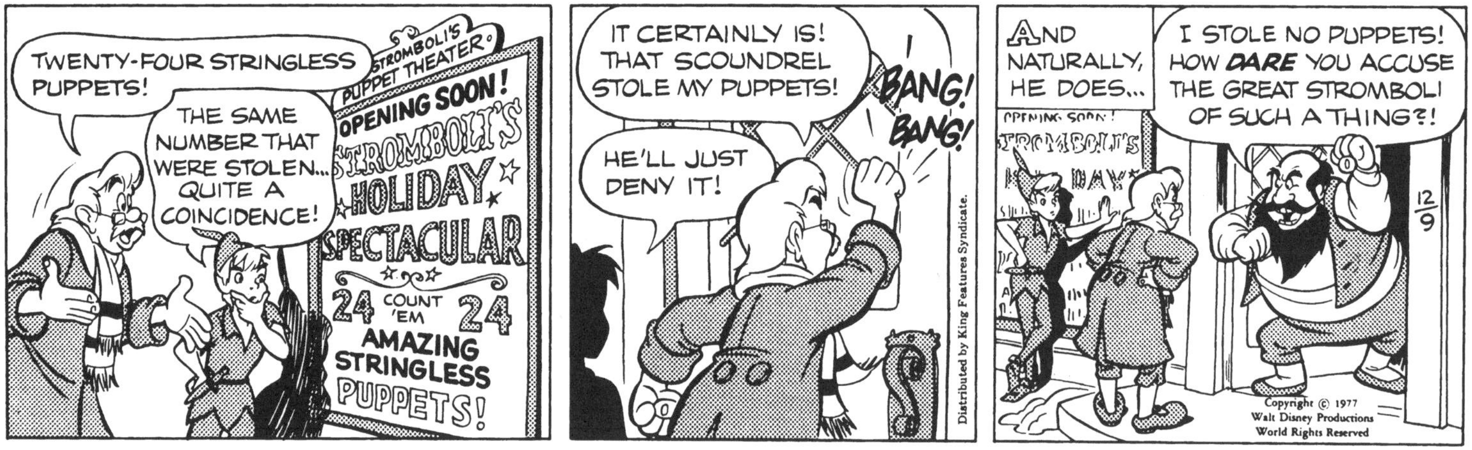
TWENTY-FOUR STRINGLESS PUPPETS!
THE SAME NUMBER THAT WERE STOLEN... QUITE A COINCIDENCE!
STROMBOLI'S PUPPET THEATER
OPENING SOON!
STROMBOLI'S HOLIDAY SPECTACULAR
24 COUNT 'EM 24
AMAZING STRINGLESS PUPPETS!
IT CERTAINLY IS! THAT SCOUNDREL STOLE MY PUPPETS!
BANG! BANG!
HE'LL JUST DENY IT!
Distributed by King Features Syndicate.
AND NATURALLY, HE DOES...
I STOLE NO PUPPETS! HOW DARE YOU ACCUSE THE GREAT STROMBOLI OF SUCH A THING?!
12/9
Copyright © 1977 Walt Disney Productions World Rights Reserved

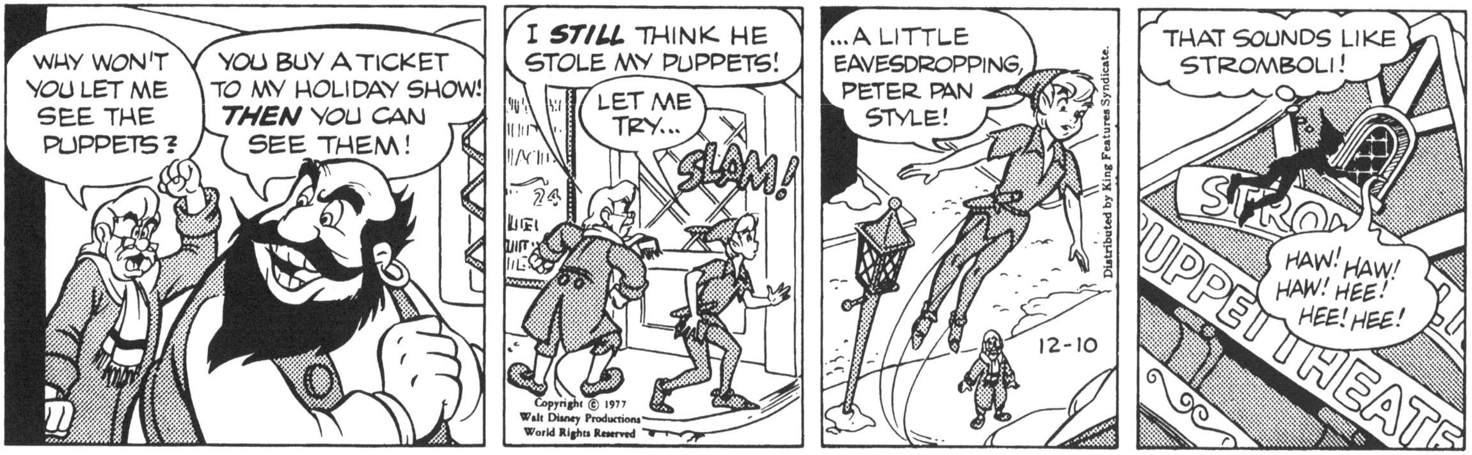
WHY WON'T YOU LET ME SEE THE PUPPETS?
YOU BUY A TICKET TO MY HOLIDAY SHOW! THEN YOU CAN SEE THEM!
I STILL THINK HE STOLE MY PUPPETS!
LET ME TRY...
SLAM!
Copyright © 1977 Walt Disney Productions World Rights Reserved
...A LITTLE EAVESDROPPING, PETER PAN STYLE!
Distributed by King Features Syndicate.
12-10
THAT SOUNDS LIKE STROMBOLI!
HAW! HAW! HAW! HEE! HEE! HEE! HEE!
PUPPET THEATE

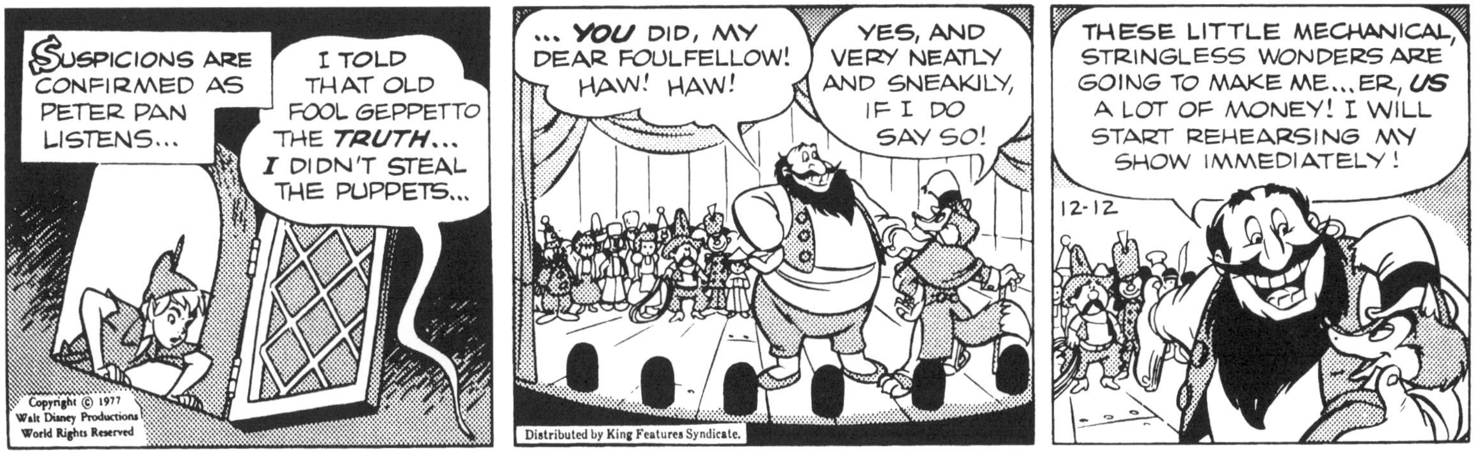

SUSPICIONS ARE CONFIRMED AS PETER PAN LISTENS...
I TOLD THAT OLD FOOL GEPPETTO THE *TRUTH*... *I* DIDN'T STEAL THE PUPPETS...
Copyright © 1977 Walt Disney Productions World Rights Reserved
... *YOU* DID, MY DEAR FOULFELLOW! HAW! HAW!
YES, AND VERY NEATLY AND SNEAKILY, IF I DO SAY SO!
Distributed by King Features Syndicate.
THESE LITTLE MECHANICAL, STRINGLESS WONDERS ARE GOING TO MAKE ME... ER, *US* A LOT OF MONEY! I WILL START REHEARSING MY SHOW IMMEDIATELY!
12-12

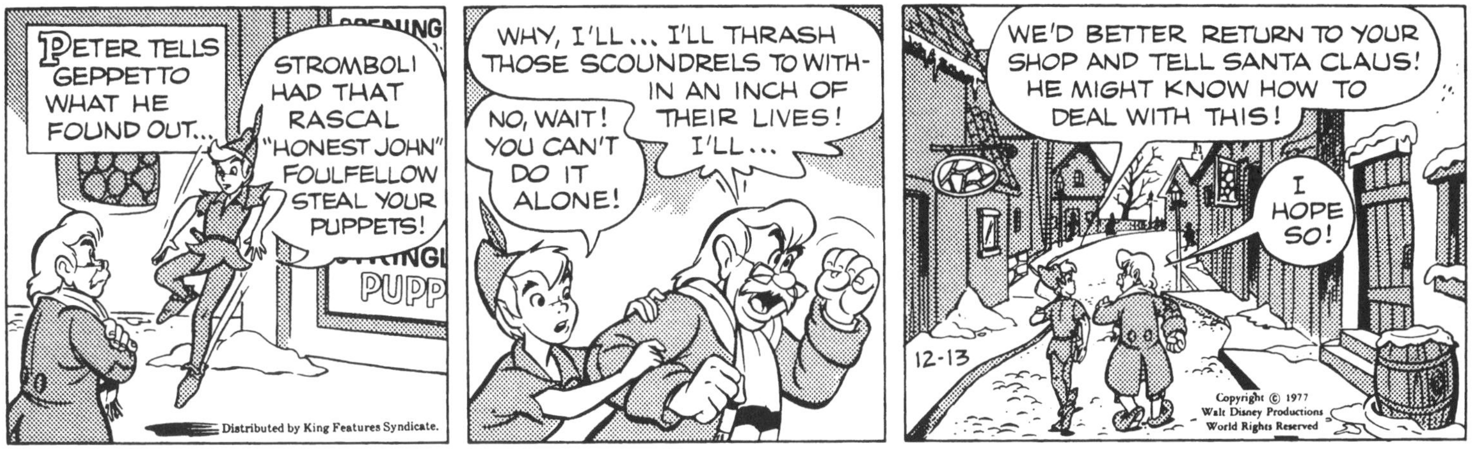

PETER TELLS GEPPETTO WHAT HE FOUND OUT...
STROMBOLI HAD THAT RASCAL "HONEST JOHN" FOULFELLOW STEAL YOUR PUPPETS!
Distributed by King Features Syndicate.
WHY, I'LL... I'LL THRASH THOSE SCOUNDRELS TO WITHIN AN INCH OF THEIR LIVES! I'LL...
NO, WAIT! YOU CAN'T DO IT ALONE!
WE'D BETTER RETURN TO YOUR SHOP AND TELL SANTA CLAUS! HE MIGHT KNOW HOW TO DEAL WITH THIS!
I HOPE SO!
12-13
Copyright © 1977 Walt Disney Productions World Rights Reserved

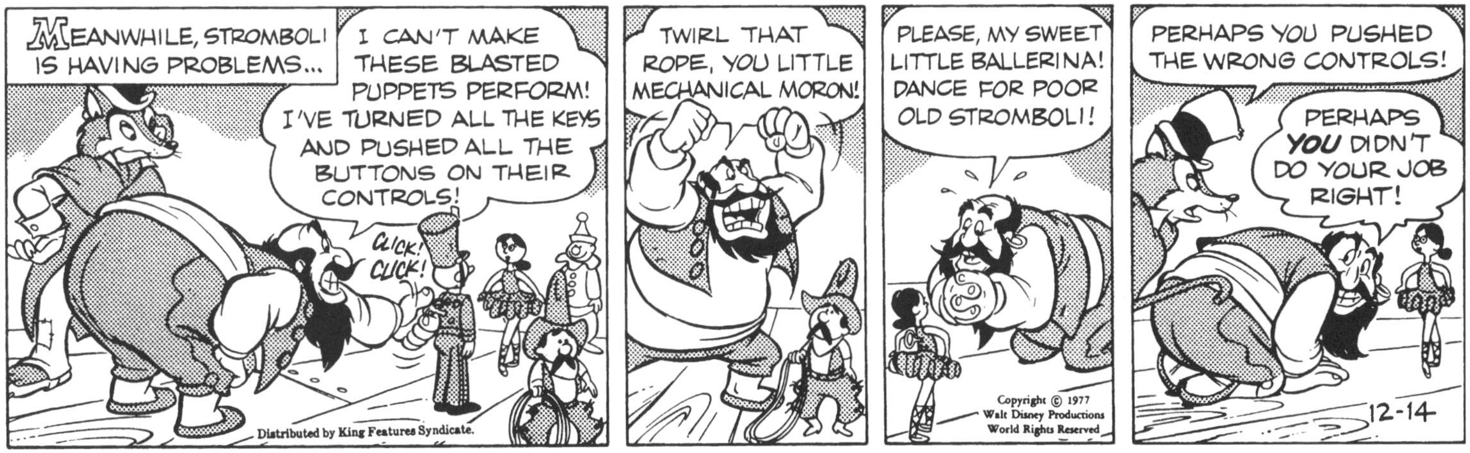

MEANWHILE, STROMBOLI IS HAVING PROBLEMS...
I CAN'T MAKE THESE BLASTED PUPPETS PERFORM! I'VE TURNED ALL THE KEYS AND PUSHED ALL THE BUTTONS ON THEIR CONTROLS!
CLICK! CLICK!
Distributed by King Features Syndicate.
TWIRL THAT ROPE, YOU LITTLE MECHANICAL MORON!
PLEASE, MY SWEET LITTLE BALLERINA! DANCE FOR POOR OLD STROMBOLI!
Copyright © 1977 Walt Disney Productions World Rights Reserved
PERHAPS YOU PUSHED THE WRONG CONTROLS!
PERHAPS *YOU* DIDN'T DO YOUR JOB RIGHT!
12-14

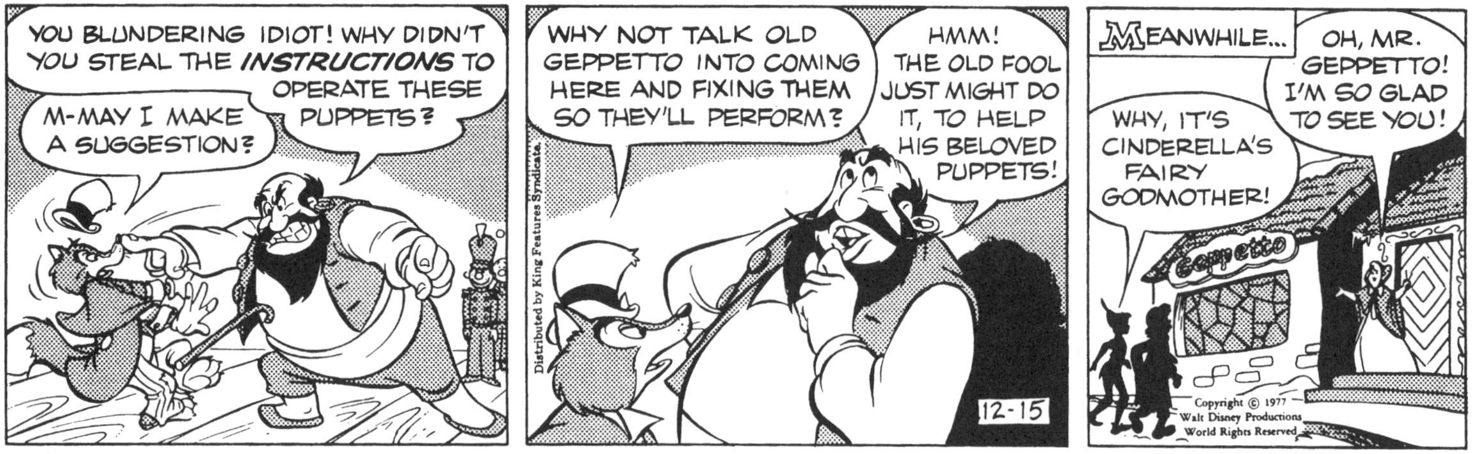
YOU BLUNDERING IDIOT! WHY DIDN'T YOU STEAL THE *INSTRUCTIONS* TO OPERATE THESE PUPPETS?
M-MAY I MAKE A SUGGESTION?
Distributed by King Features Syndicate.
WHY NOT TALK OLD GEPPETTO INTO COMING HERE AND FIXING THEM SO THEY'LL PERFORM?
HMM! THE OLD FOOL JUST MIGHT DO IT, TO HELP HIS BELOVED PUPPETS!
12-15
MEANWHILE...
OH, MR. GEPPETTO! I'M SO GLAD TO SEE YOU!
WHY, IT'S CINDERELLA'S FAIRY GODMOTHER!
Geppetto
Copyright © 1977 Walt Disney Productions World Rights Reserved

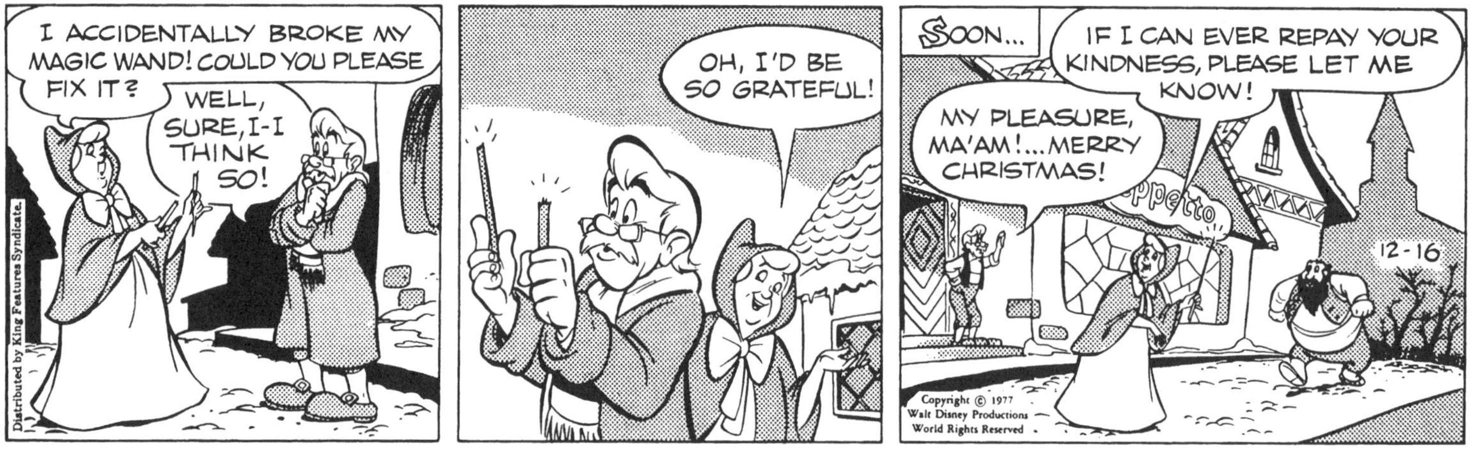
I ACCIDENTALLY BROKE MY MAGIC WAND! COULD YOU PLEASE FIX IT?
WELL, SURE, I-I THINK SO!
Distributed by King Features Syndicate.
OH, I'D BE SO GRATEFUL!
SOON...
IF I CAN EVER REPAY YOUR KINDNESS, PLEASE LET ME KNOW!
MY PLEASURE, MA'AM!...MERRY CHRISTMAS!
12-16
Copyright © 1977 Walt Disney Productions World Rights Reserved

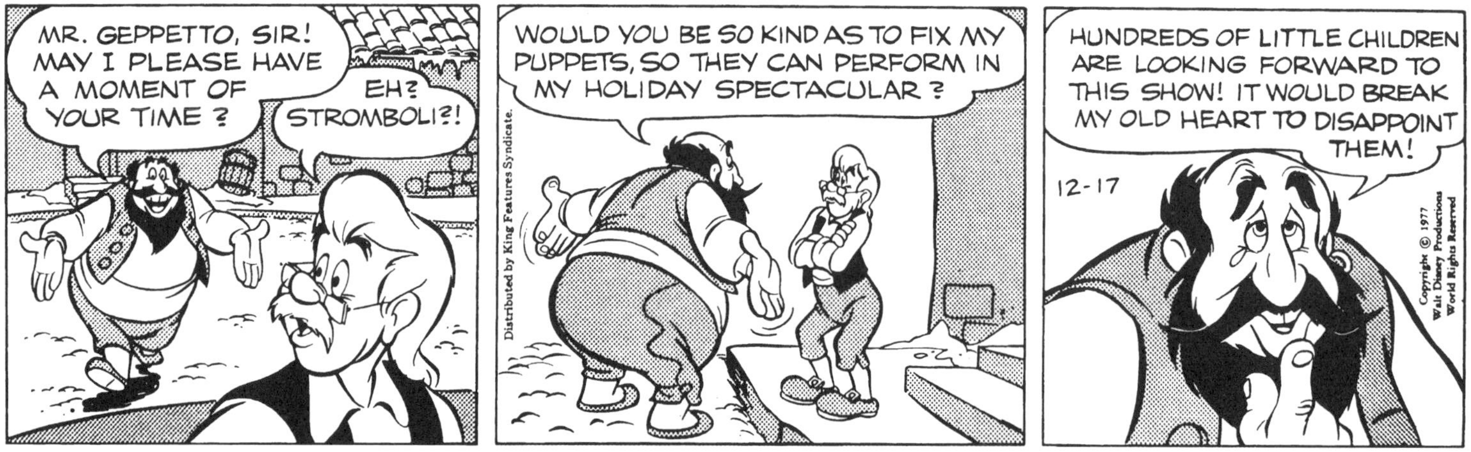
MR. GEPPETTO, SIR! MAY I PLEASE HAVE A MOMENT OF YOUR TIME?
EH? STROMBOLI?!
Distributed by King Features Syndicate.
WOULD YOU BE SO KIND AS TO FIX MY PUPPETS, SO THEY CAN PERFORM IN MY HOLIDAY SPECTACULAR?
HUNDREDS OF LITTLE CHILDREN ARE LOOKING FORWARD TO THIS SHOW! IT WOULD BREAK MY OLD HEART TO DISAPPOINT THEM!
12-17
Copyright © 1977 Walt Disney Productions World Rights Reserved

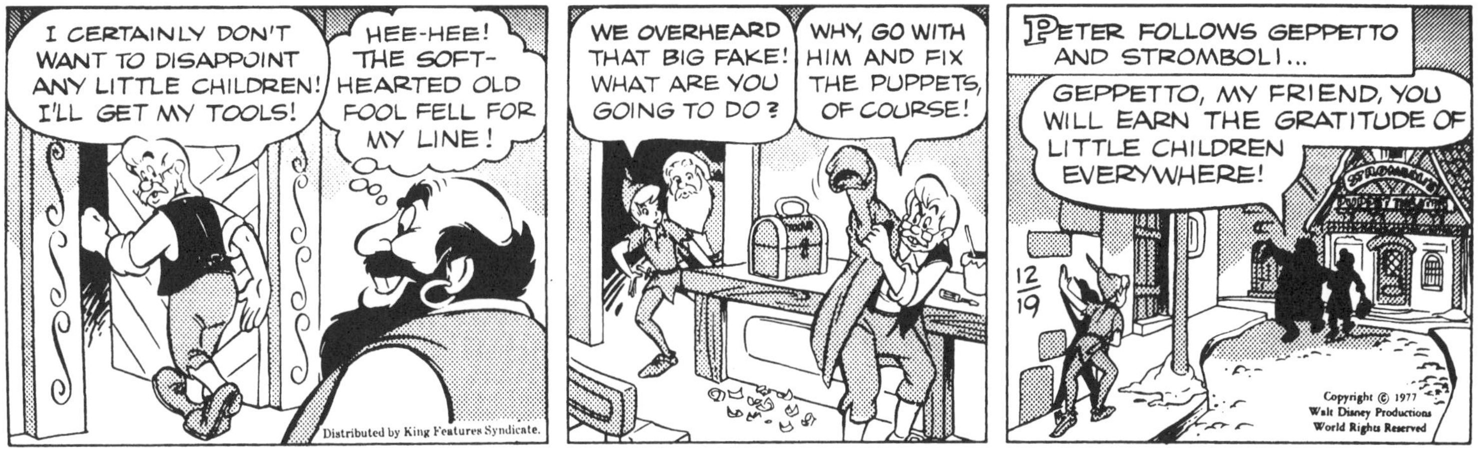
I CERTAINLY DON'T WANT TO DISAPPOINT ANY LITTLE CHILDREN! I'LL GET MY TOOLS!
HEE-HEE! THE SOFT-HEARTED OLD FOOL FELL FOR MY LINE!
Distributed by King Features Syndicate.
WE OVERHEARD THAT BIG FAKE! WHAT ARE YOU GOING TO DO?
WHY, GO WITH HIM AND FIX THE PUPPETS, OF COURSE!
PETER FOLLOWS GEPPETTO AND STROMBOLI...
GEPPETTO, MY FRIEND, YOU WILL EARN THE GRATITUDE OF LITTLE CHILDREN EVERYWHERE!
12/19
Copyright © 1977 Walt Disney Productions World Rights Reserved

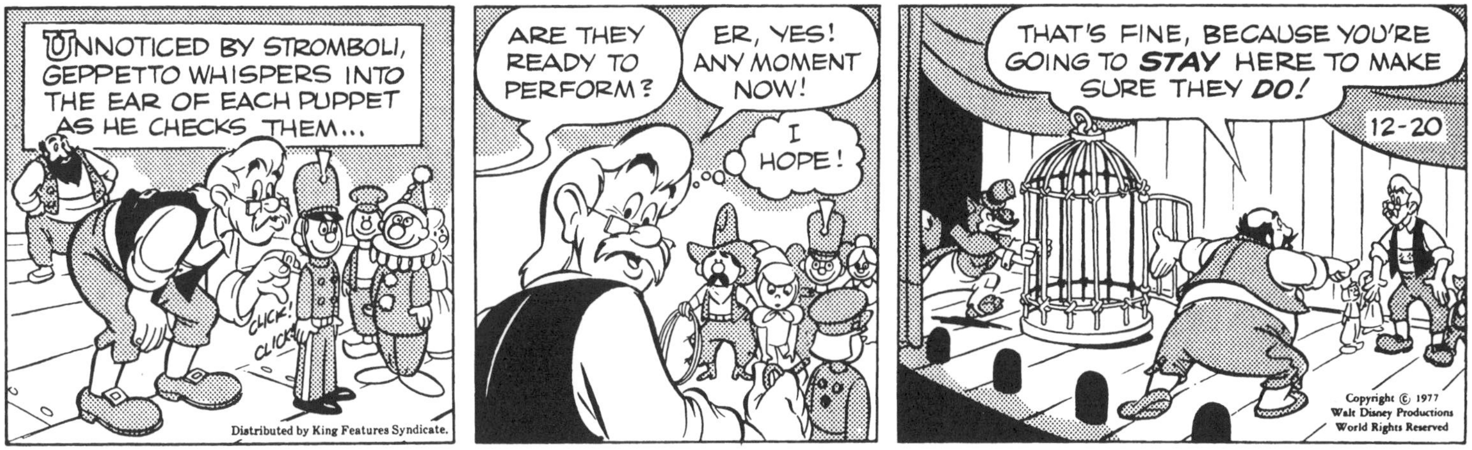
UNNOTICED BY STROMBOLI, GEPPETTO WHISPERS INTO THE EAR OF EACH PUPPET AS HE CHECKS THEM...
CLICK! CLICK!
Distributed by King Features Syndicate.
ARE THEY READY TO PERFORM?
ER, YES! ANY MOMENT NOW!
I HOPE!
THAT'S FINE, BECAUSE YOU'RE GOING TO STAY HERE TO MAKE SURE THEY DO!
12-20
Copyright © 1977 Walt Disney Productions World Rights Reserved

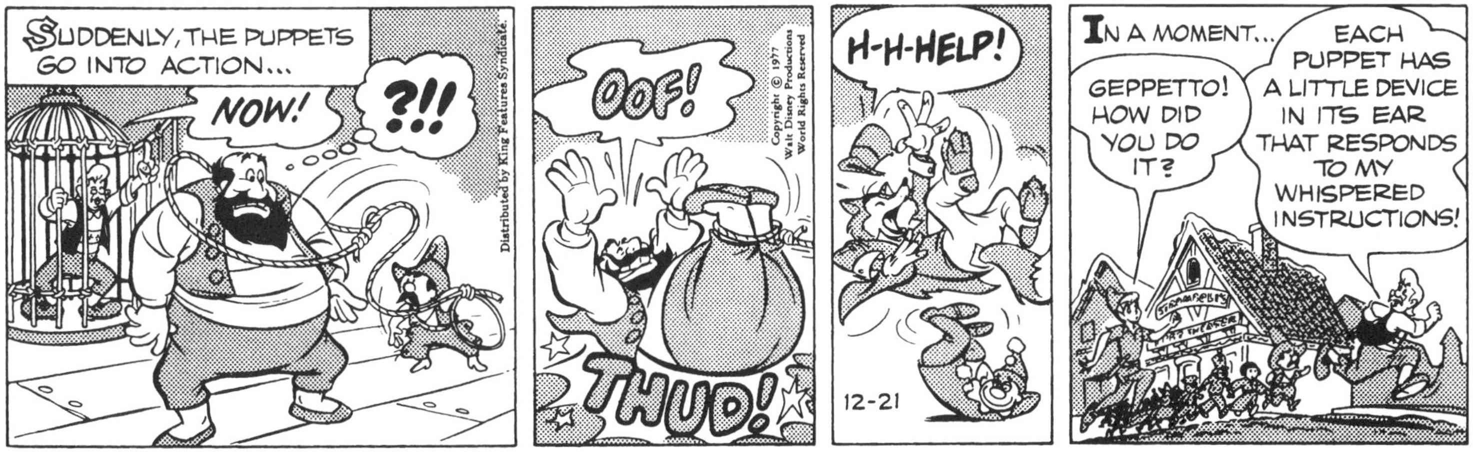
SUDDENLY, THE PUPPETS GO INTO ACTION...
NOW!
?!!
Distributed by King Features Syndicate.
OOF!
Copyright © 1977 Walt Disney Productions World Rights Reserved
THUD!
H-H-HELP!
12-21
IN A MOMENT...
GEPPETTO! HOW DID YOU DO IT?
EACH PUPPET HAS A LITTLE DEVICE IN ITS EAR THAT RESPONDS TO MY WHISPERED INSTRUCTIONS!

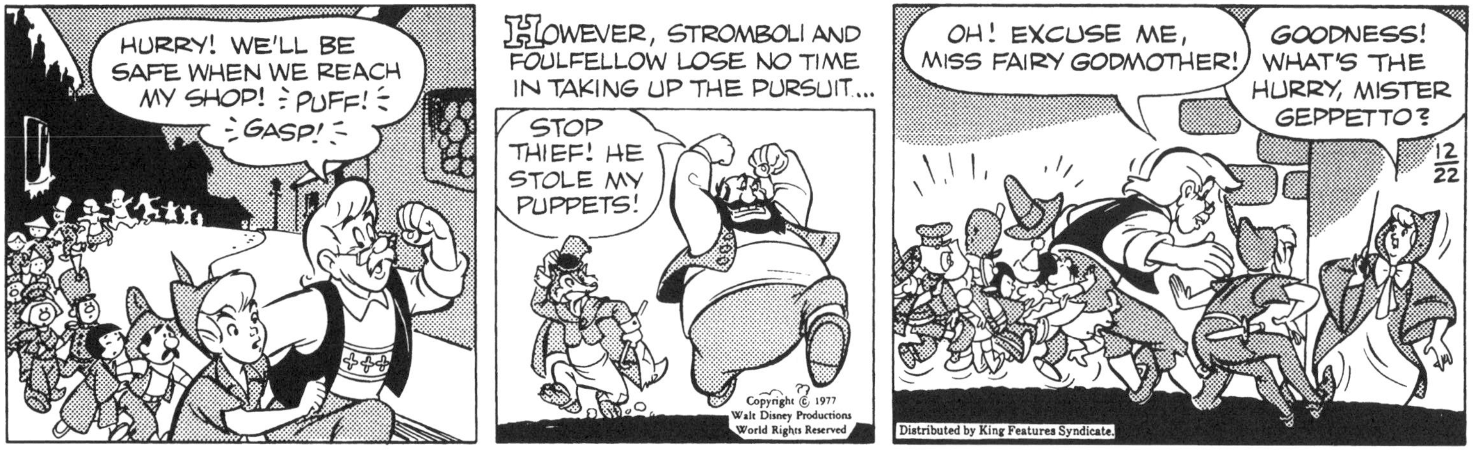
HURRY! WE'LL BE SAFE WHEN WE REACH MY SHOP! PUFF! GASP!
HOWEVER, STROMBOLI AND FOULFELLOW LOSE NO TIME IN TAKING UP THE PURSUIT...
STOP THIEF! HE STOLE MY PUPPETS!
Copyright © 1977 Walt Disney Productions World Rights Reserved
OH! EXCUSE ME, MISS FAIRY GODMOTHER!
GOODNESS! WHAT'S THE HURRY, MISTER GEPPETTO?
12/22
Distributed by King Features Syndicate.

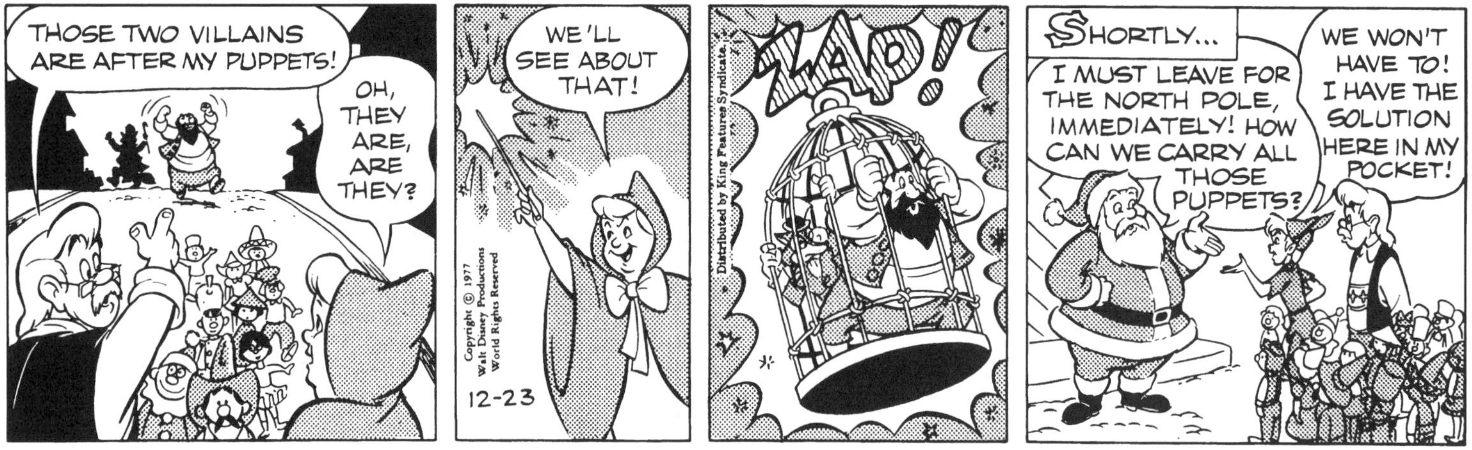
THOSE TWO VILLAINS ARE AFTER MY PUPPETS!
OH, THEY ARE, ARE THEY?
WE'LL SEE ABOUT THAT!
Copyright © 1977 Walt Disney Productions World Rights Reserved
12-23
ZAP!
Distributed by King Features Syndicate.
SHORTLY...
I MUST LEAVE FOR THE NORTH POLE, IMMEDIATELY! HOW CAN WE CARRY ALL THOSE PUPPETS?
WE WON'T HAVE TO! I HAVE THE SOLUTION HERE IN MY POCKET!

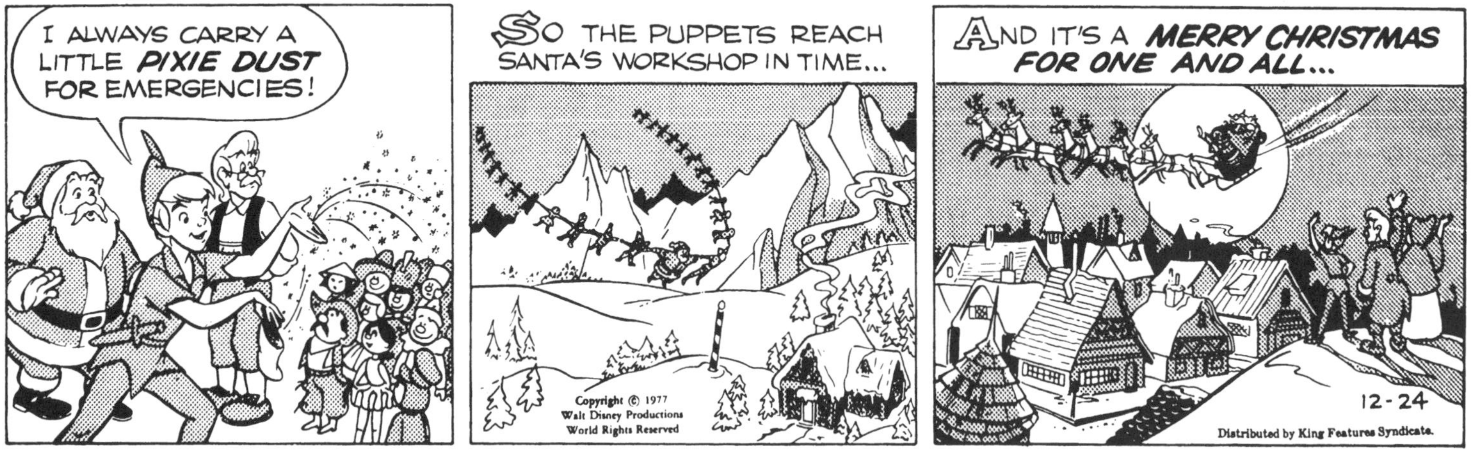
I ALWAYS CARRY A LITTLE PIXIE DUST FOR EMERGENCIES!
SO THE PUPPETS REACH SANTA'S WORKSHOP IN TIME...
Copyright © 1977 Walt Disney Productions World Rights Reserved
AND IT'S A MERRY CHRISTMAS FOR ONE AND ALL...
12-24
Distributed by King Features Syndicate.

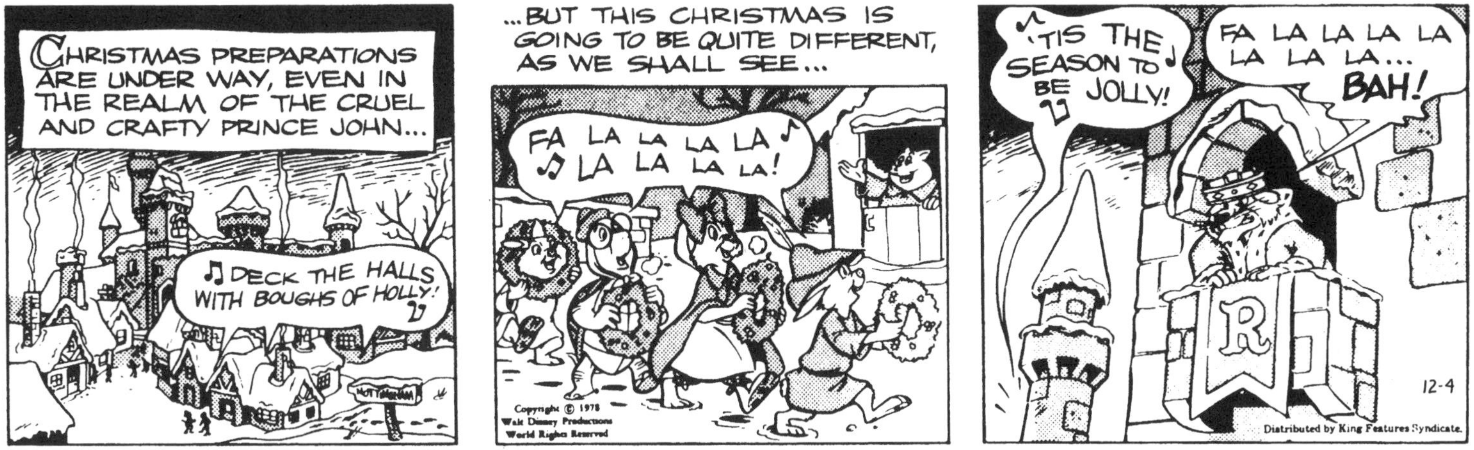
CHRISTMAS PREPARATIONS ARE UNDER WAY, EVEN IN THE REALM OF THE CRUEL AND CRAFTY PRINCE JOHN...
♫ DECK THE HALLS WITH BOUGHS OF HOLLY!
...BUT THIS CHRISTMAS IS GOING TO BE QUITE DIFFERENT, AS WE SHALL SEE...
FA LA LA LA LA ♪ ♫ LA LA LA LA!
Copyright © 1978 Walt Disney Productions World Rights Reserved
♪ 'TIS THE SEASON TO BE JOLLY!
FA LA LA LA LA LA LA LA... BAH!
R
12-4
Distributed by King Features Syndicate.

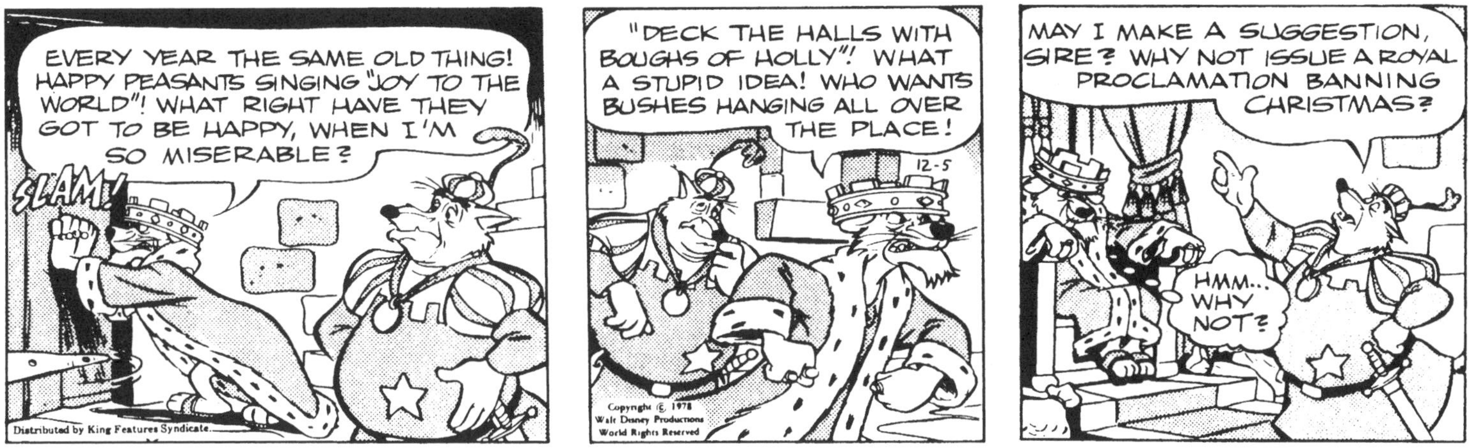
EVERY YEAR THE SAME OLD THING! HAPPY PEASANTS SINGING "JOY TO THE WORLD"! WHAT RIGHT HAVE THEY GOT TO BE HAPPY, WHEN I'M SO MISERABLE?
SLAM!
Distributed by King Features Syndicate.
"DECK THE HALLS WITH BOUGHS OF HOLLY"! WHAT A STUPID IDEA! WHO WANTS BUSHES HANGING ALL OVER THE PLACE!
12-5
Copyright © 1978 Walt Disney Productions World Rights Reserved
MAY I MAKE A SUGGESTION, SIRE? WHY NOT ISSUE A ROYAL PROCLAMATION BANNING CHRISTMAS?
HMM... WHY NOT?

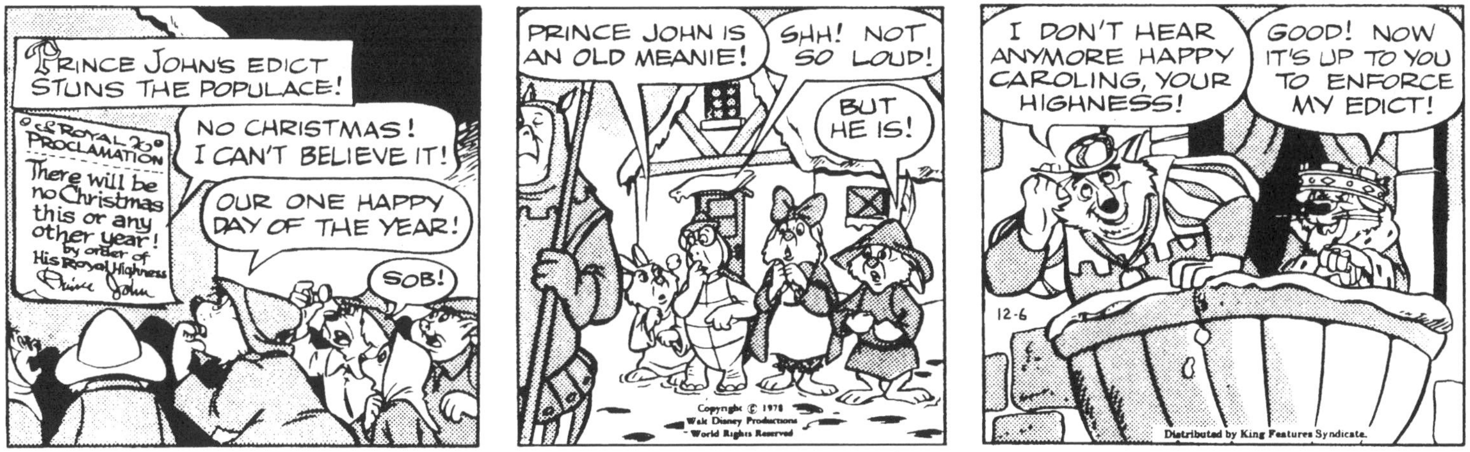
PRINCE JOHN'S EDICT STUNS THE POPULACE!
ROYAL PROCLAMATION
There will be no Christmas this or any other year! by order of His Royal Highness Prince John
NO CHRISTMAS! I CAN'T BELIEVE IT!
OUR ONE HAPPY DAY OF THE YEAR!
SOB!
PRINCE JOHN IS AN OLD MEANIE!
SHH! NOT SO LOUD!
BUT HE IS!
Copyright © 1978 Walt Disney Productions World Rights Reserved
I DON'T HEAR ANYMORE HAPPY CAROLING, YOUR HIGHNESS!
GOOD! NOW IT'S UP TO YOU TO ENFORCE MY EDICT!
12-6
Distributed by King Features Syndicate.

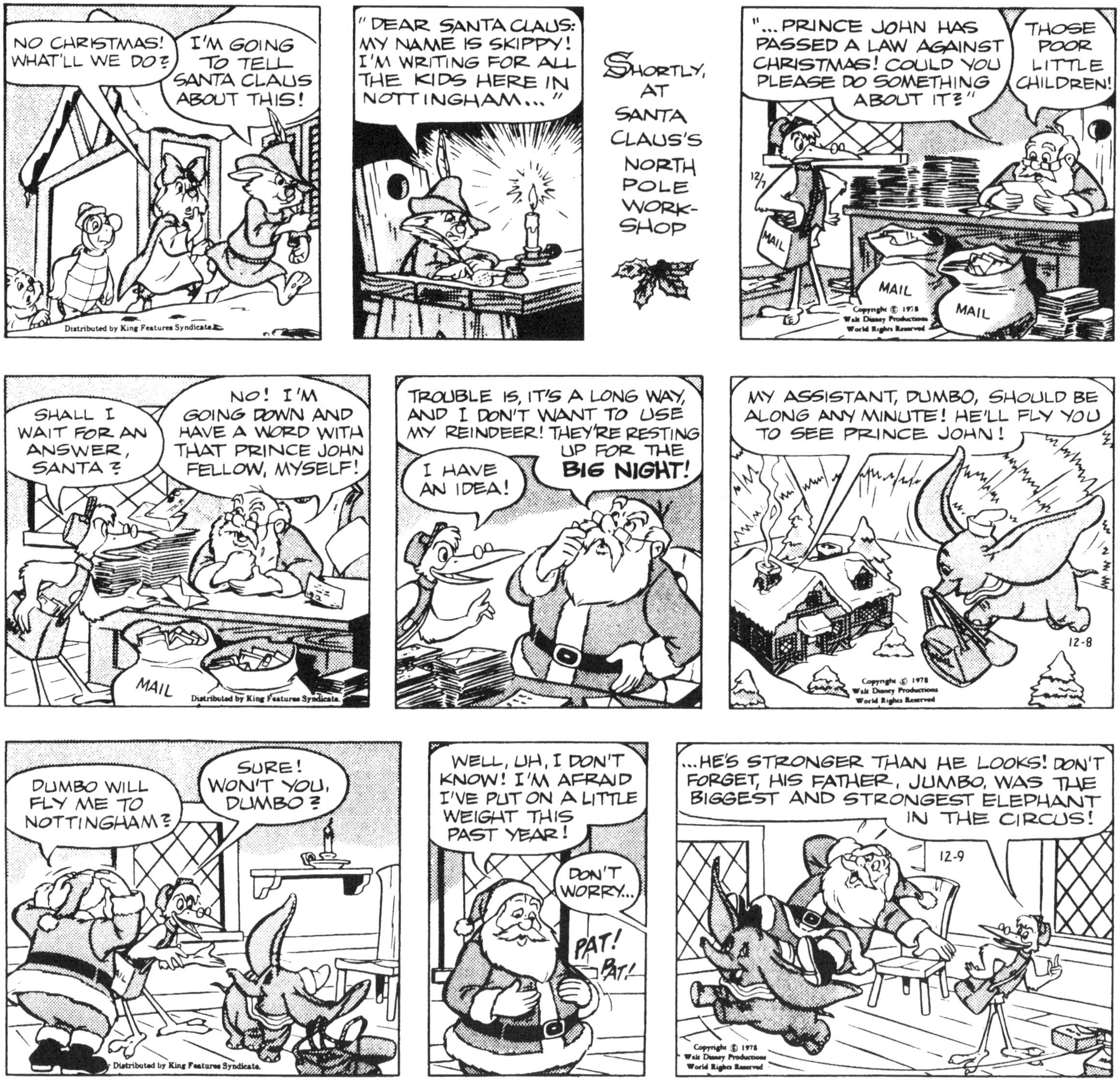
NO CHRISTMAS! WHAT'LL WE DO?
I'M GOING TO TELL SANTA CLAUS ABOUT THIS!
Distributed by King Features Syndicate.
"DEAR SANTA CLAUS: MY NAME IS SKIPPY! I'M WRITING FOR ALL THE KIDS HERE IN NOTTINGHAM..."
SHORTLY, AT SANTA CLAUS'S NORTH POLE WORK-SHOP
"...PRINCE JOHN HAS PASSED A LAW AGAINST CHRISTMAS! COULD YOU PLEASE DO SOMETHING ABOUT IT?"
THOSE POOR LITTLE CHILDREN!
12/7
MAIL
MAIL
MAIL
Copyright © 1978 Walt Disney Productions World Rights Reserved
SHALL I WAIT FOR AN ANSWER, SANTA?
NO! I'M GOING DOWN AND HAVE A WORD WITH THAT PRINCE JOHN FELLOW, MYSELF!
MAIL
Distributed by King Features Syndicate.
TROUBLE IS, IT'S A LONG WAY, AND I DON'T WANT TO USE MY REINDEER! THEY'RE RESTING UP FOR THE **BIG NIGHT!**
I HAVE AN IDEA!
MY ASSISTANT, DUMBO, SHOULD BE ALONG ANY MINUTE! HE'LL FLY YOU TO SEE PRINCE JOHN!
12-8
Copyright © 1978 Walt Disney Productions World Rights Reserved
DUMBO WILL FLY ME TO NOTTINGHAM?
SURE! WON'T YOU, DUMBO?
Distributed by King Features Syndicate.
WELL, UH, I DON'T KNOW! I'M AFRAID I'VE PUT ON A LITTLE WEIGHT THIS PAST YEAR!
DON'T WORRY...
PAT! PAT!
...HE'S STRONGER THAN HE LOOKS! DON'T FORGET, HIS FATHER, JUMBO, WAS THE BIGGEST AND STRONGEST ELEPHANT IN THE CIRCUS!
12-9
Copyright © 1978 Walt Disney Productions World Rights Reserved

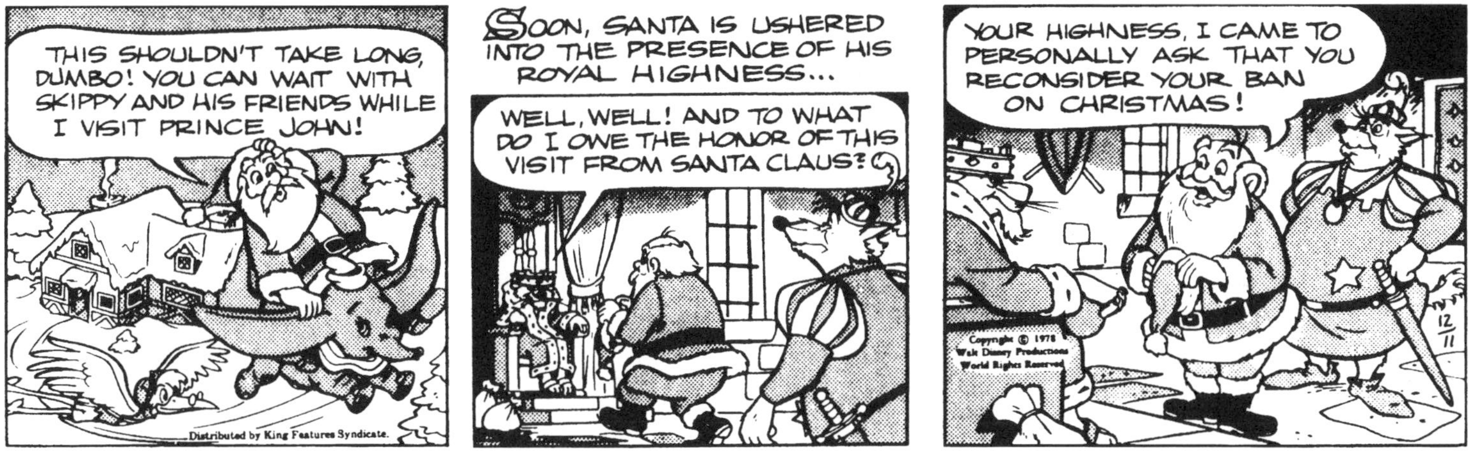
THIS SHOULDN'T TAKE LONG, DUMBO! YOU CAN WAIT WITH SKIPPY AND HIS FRIENDS WHILE I VISIT PRINCE JOHN!
Distributed by King Features Syndicate.
SOON, SANTA IS USHERED INTO THE PRESENCE OF HIS ROYAL HIGHNESS...
WELL, WELL! AND TO WHAT DO I OWE THE HONOR OF THIS VISIT FROM SANTA CLAUS?
YOUR HIGHNESS, I CAME TO PERSONALLY ASK THAT YOU RECONSIDER YOUR BAN ON CHRISTMAS!
Copyright © 1978 Walt Disney Productions World Rights Reserved
12/11

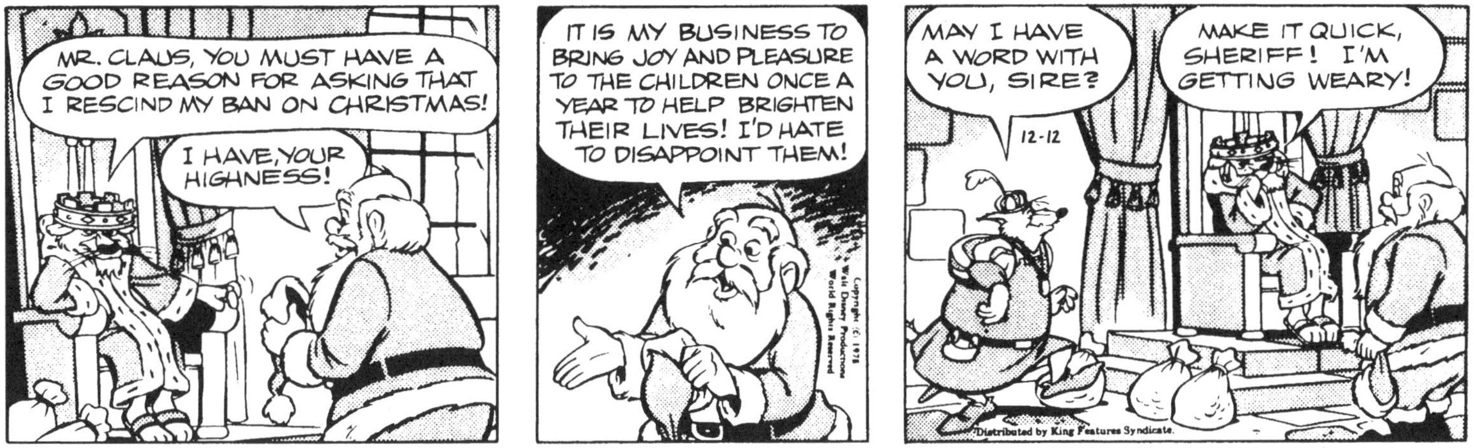
MR. CLAUS, YOU MUST HAVE A GOOD REASON FOR ASKING THAT I RESCIND MY BAN ON CHRISTMAS!
I HAVE, YOUR HIGHNESS!
IT IS MY BUSINESS TO BRING JOY AND PLEASURE TO THE CHILDREN ONCE A YEAR TO HELP BRIGHTEN THEIR LIVES! I'D HATE TO DISAPPOINT THEM!
Copyright © 1978 Walt Disney Productions World Rights Reserved
MAY I HAVE A WORD WITH YOU, SIRE?
MAKE IT QUICK, SHERIFF! I'M GETTING WEARY!
12-12
Distributed by King Features Syndicate.

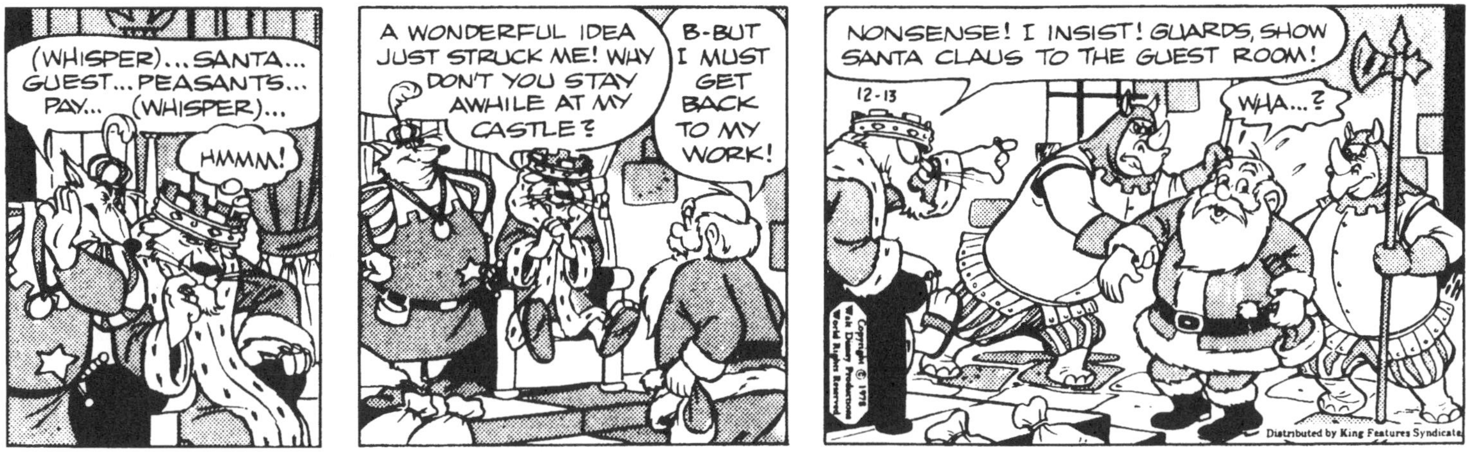
(WHISPER)...SANTA... GUEST...PEASANTS... PAY... (WHISPER)...
HMMM!
A WONDERFUL IDEA JUST STRUCK ME! WHY DON'T YOU STAY AWHILE AT MY CASTLE?
B-BUT I MUST GET BACK TO MY WORK!
NONSENSE! I INSIST! GUARDS, SHOW SANTA CLAUS TO THE GUEST ROOM!
12-13
WHA...?
Copyright © 1978 Walt Disney Productions World Rights Reserved
Distributed by King Features Syndicate.

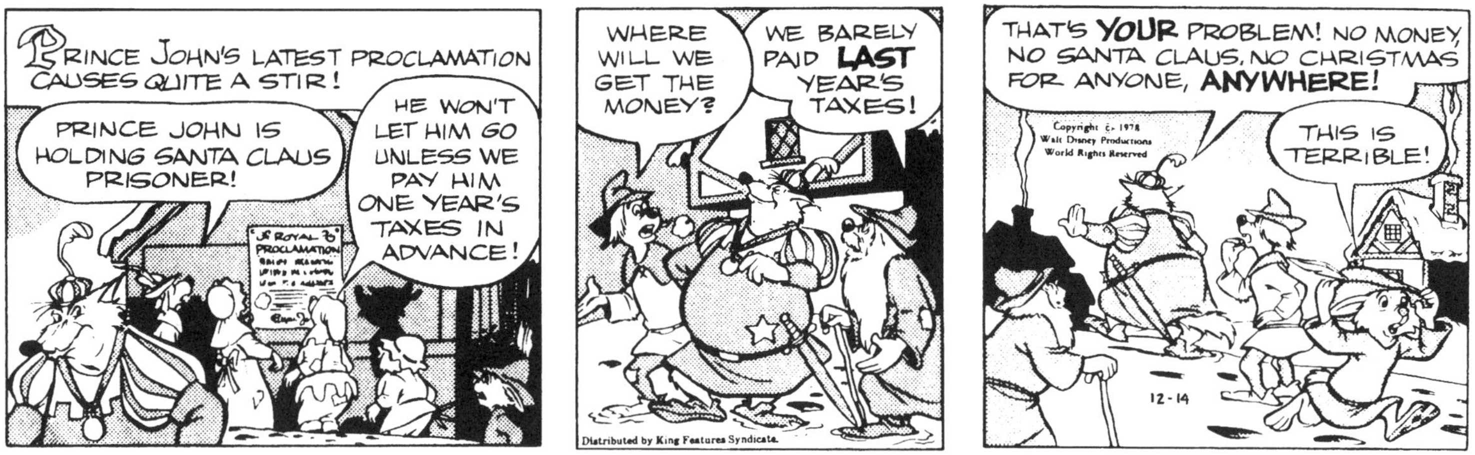
PRINCE JOHN'S LATEST PROCLAMATION CAUSES QUITE A STIR!
PRINCE JOHN IS HOLDING SANTA CLAUS PRISONER!
HE WON'T LET HIM GO UNLESS WE PAY HIM ONE YEAR'S TAXES IN ADVANCE!
ROYAL PROCLAMATION
WHERE WILL WE GET THE MONEY?
WE BARELY PAID LAST YEAR'S TAXES!
Distributed by King Features Syndicate.
THAT'S YOUR PROBLEM! NO MONEY, NO SANTA CLAUS, NO CHRISTMAS FOR ANYONE, ANYWHERE!
Copyright © 1978 Walt Disney Productions World Rights Reserved
THIS IS TERRIBLE!
12-14

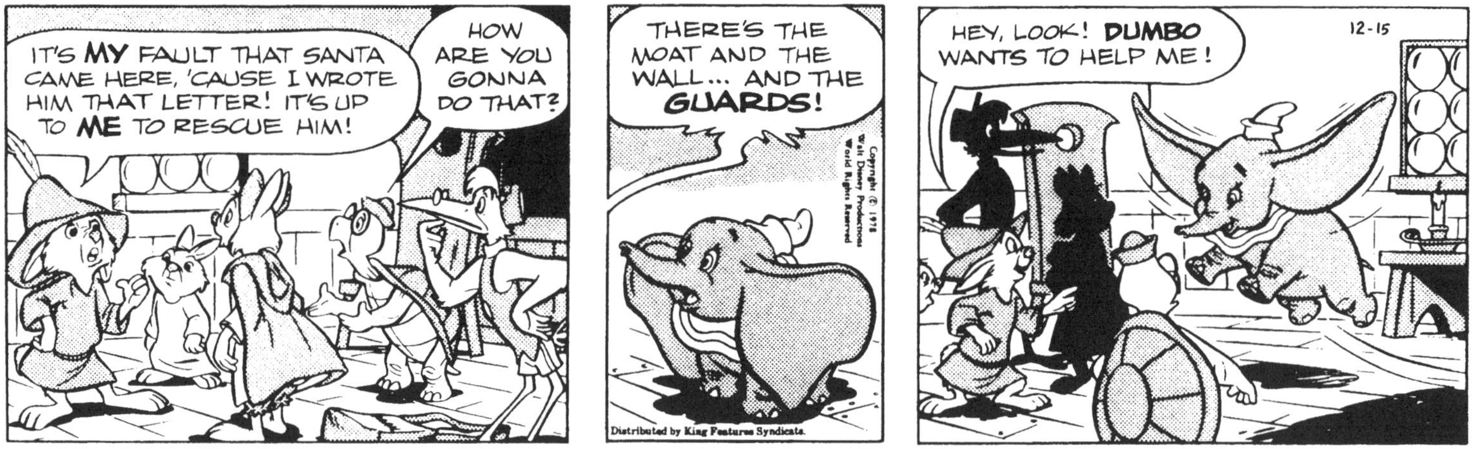
IT'S MY FAULT THAT SANTA CAME HERE, 'CAUSE I WROTE HIM THAT LETTER! IT'S UP TO ME TO RESCUE HIM!
HOW ARE YOU GONNA DO THAT?
THERE'S THE MOAT AND THE WALL... AND THE GUARDS!
Copyright © 1978 Walt Disney Productions World Rights Reserved
Distributed by King Features Syndicate.
HEY, LOOK! DUMBO WANTS TO HELP ME!
12-15

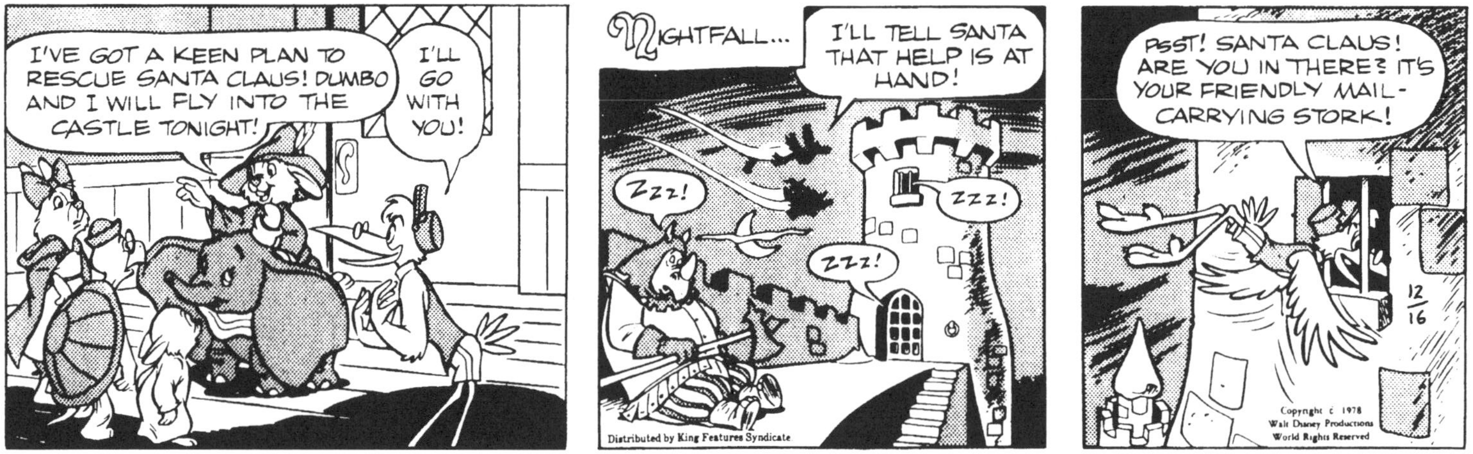
I'VE GOT A KEEN PLAN TO RESCUE SANTA CLAUS! DUMBO AND I WILL FLY INTO THE CASTLE TONIGHT!
I'LL GO WITH YOU!
NIGHTFALL...
I'LL TELL SANTA THAT HELP IS AT HAND!
ZZZ!
ZZZ!
ZZZ!
Distributed by King Features Syndicate
PSST! SANTA CLAUS! ARE YOU IN THERE? IT'S YOUR FRIENDLY MAIL-CARRYING STORK!
12/16
Copyright © 1978 Walt Disney Productions World Rights Reserved

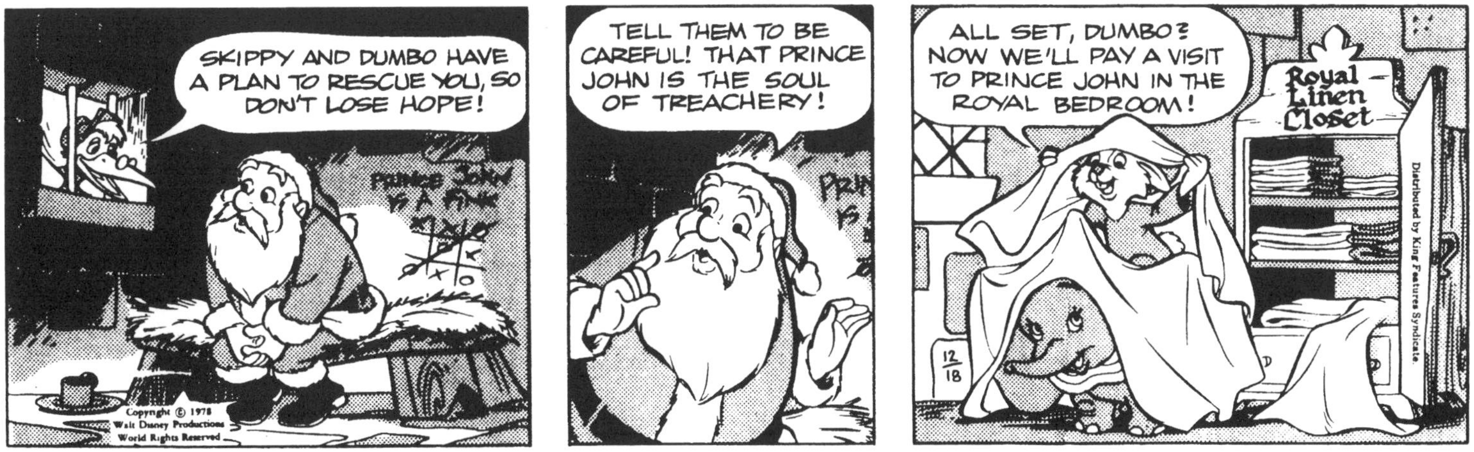
SKIPPY AND DUMBO HAVE A PLAN TO RESCUE YOU, SO DON'T LOSE HOPE!
Copyright © 1978 Walt Disney Productions World Rights Reserved
TELL THEM TO BE CAREFUL! THAT PRINCE JOHN IS THE SOUL OF TREACHERY!
ALL SET, DUMBO? NOW WE'LL PAY A VISIT TO PRINCE JOHN IN THE ROYAL BEDROOM!
Royal Linen Closet
Distributed by King Features Syndicate
12/18

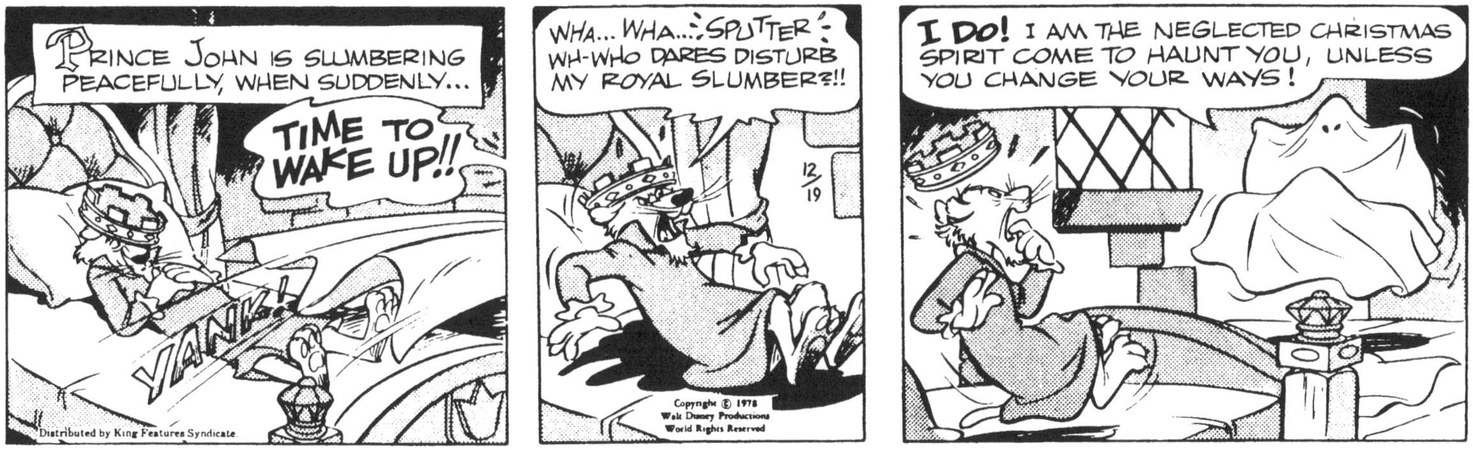
PRINCE JOHN IS SLUMBERING PEACEFULLY, WHEN SUDDENLY...
TIME TO WAKE UP!!
YANK!
Distributed by King Features Syndicate
WHA... WHA... SPUTTER WH-WHO DARES DISTURB MY ROYAL SLUMBER?!!
12/19
Copyright © 1978 Walt Disney Productions World Rights Reserved
I DO! I AM THE NEGLECTED CHRISTMAS SPIRIT COME TO HAUNT YOU, UNLESS YOU CHANGE YOUR WAYS!

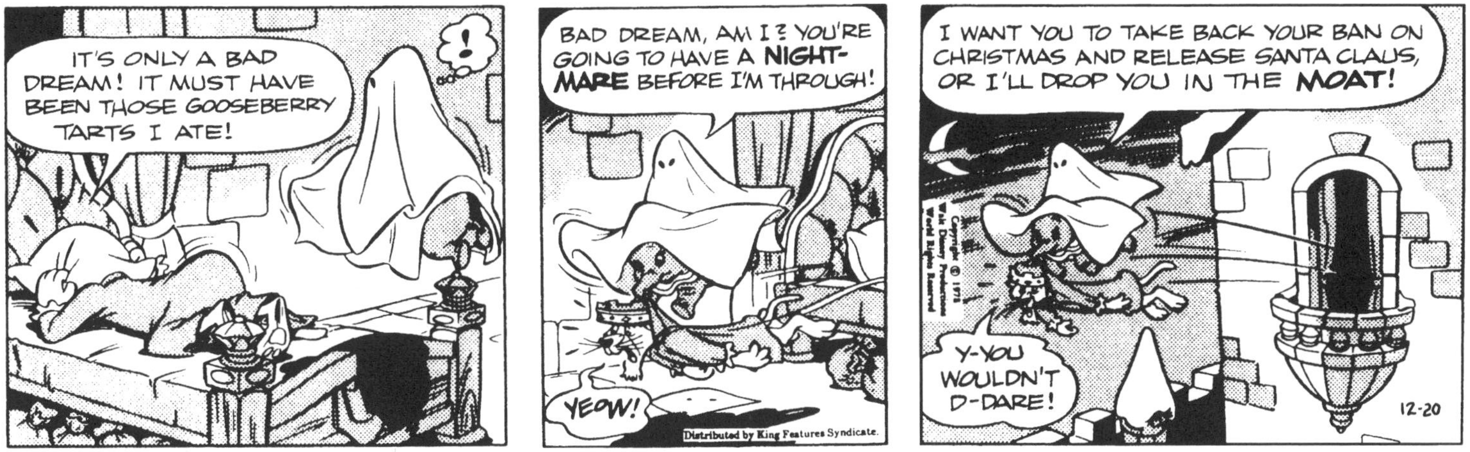
IT'S ONLY A BAD DREAM! IT MUST HAVE BEEN THOSE GOOSEBERRY TARTS I ATE!
!
BAD DREAM, AM I? YOU'RE GOING TO HAVE A NIGHT-MARE BEFORE I'M THROUGH!
YEOW!
Distributed by King Features Syndicate.
I WANT YOU TO TAKE BACK YOUR BAN ON CHRISTMAS AND RELEASE SANTA CLAUS, OR I'LL DROP YOU IN THE MOAT!
Copyright © 1978 Walt Disney Productions World Rights Reserved
Y-YOU WOULDN'T D-DARE!
12-20

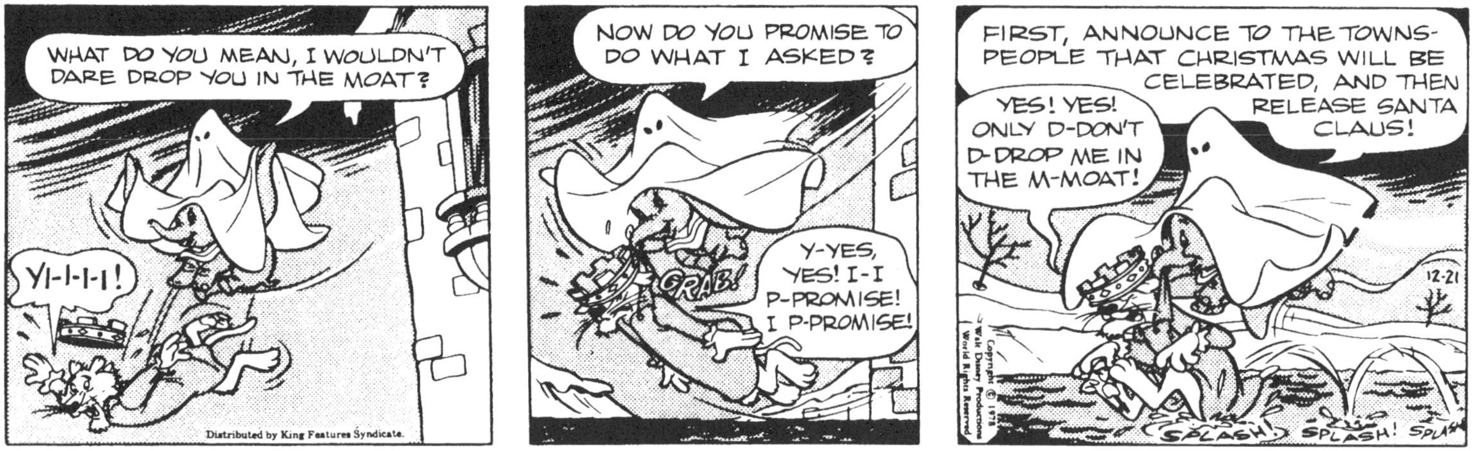
WHAT DO YOU MEAN, I WOULDN'T DARE DROP YOU IN THE MOAT?
YI-I-I-I!
Distributed by King Features Syndicate.
NOW DO YOU PROMISE TO DO WHAT I ASKED?
GRAB!
Y-YES, YES! I-I P-PROMISE! I P-PROMISE!
FIRST, ANNOUNCE TO THE TOWNSPEOPLE THAT CHRISTMAS WILL BE CELEBRATED, AND THEN RELEASE SANTA CLAUS!
YES! YES! ONLY D-DON'T D-DROP ME IN THE M-MOAT!
12-21
Copyright © 1978 Walt Disney Productions World Rights Reserved
SPLASH! SPLASH! SPLASH

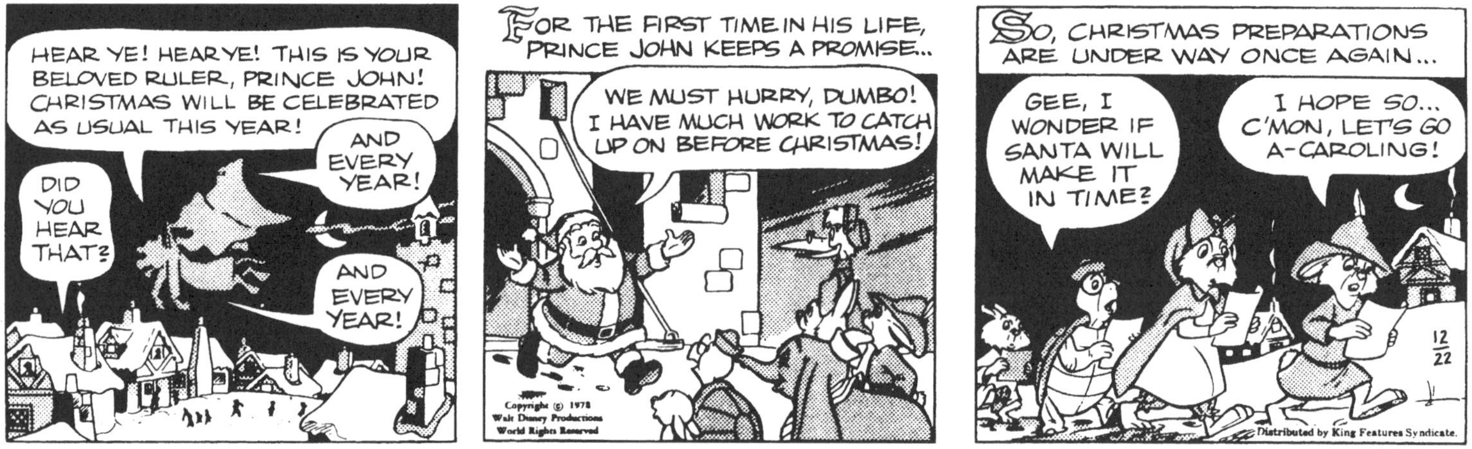
HEAR YE! HEAR YE! THIS IS YOUR BELOVED RULER, PRINCE JOHN! CHRISTMAS WILL BE CELEBRATED AS USUAL THIS YEAR!
AND EVERY YEAR!
DID YOU HEAR THAT?
AND EVERY YEAR!
FOR THE FIRST TIME IN HIS LIFE, PRINCE JOHN KEEPS A PROMISE...
WE MUST HURRY, DUMBO! I HAVE MUCH WORK TO CATCH UP ON BEFORE CHRISTMAS!
Copyright © 1978 Walt Disney Productions World Rights Reserved
SO, CHRISTMAS PREPARATIONS ARE UNDER WAY ONCE AGAIN...
GEE, I WONDER IF SANTA WILL MAKE IT IN TIME?
I HOPE SO... C'MON, LET'S GO A-CAROLING!
12/22
Distributed by King Features Syndicate.

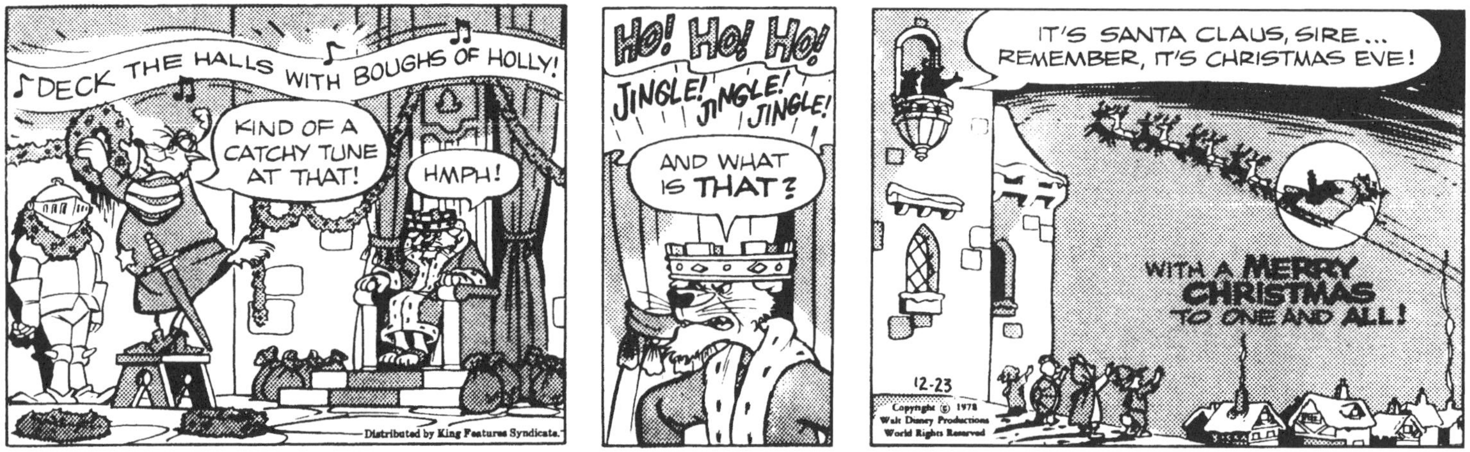
♪DECK THE HALLS WITH BOUGHS OF HOLLY!
KIND OF A CATCHY TUNE AT THAT!
HMPH!
Distributed by King Features Syndicate.
HO! HO! HO!
JINGLE! JINGLE! JINGLE!
AND WHAT IS THAT?
IT'S SANTA CLAUS, SIRE... REMEMBER, IT'S CHRISTMAS EVE!
WITH A MERRY CHRISTMAS TO ONE AND ALL!
12-23
Copyright © 1978 Walt Disney Productions World Rights Reserved

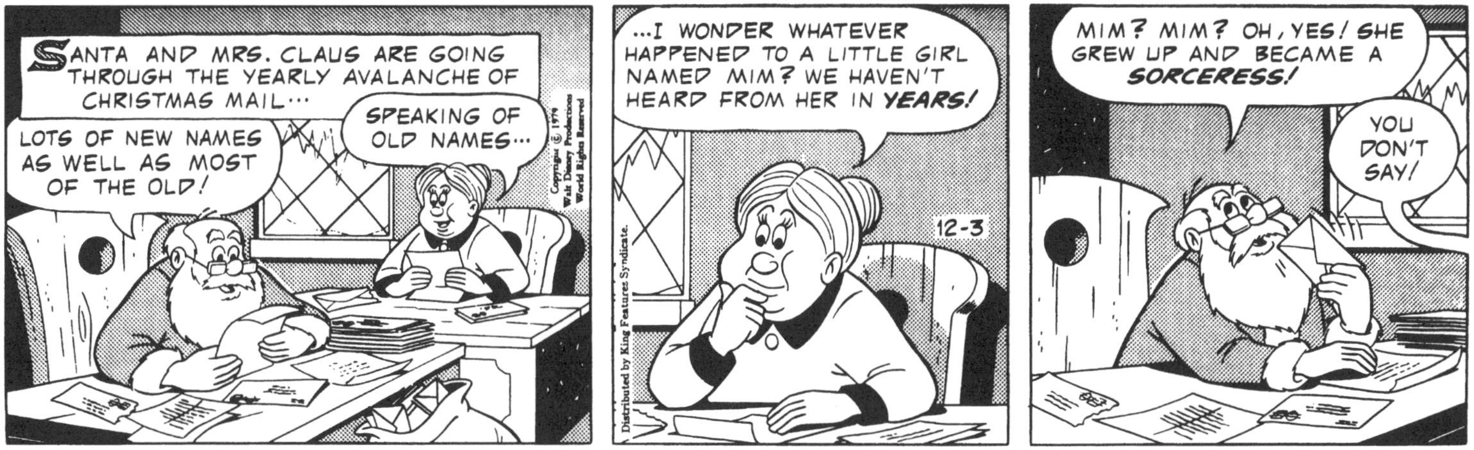
SANTA AND MRS. CLAUS ARE GOING THROUGH THE YEARLY AVALANCHE OF CHRISTMAS MAIL...
LOTS OF NEW NAMES AS WELL AS MOST OF THE OLD!
SPEAKING OF OLD NAMES...
Copyright © 1979 Walt Disney Productions World Rights Reserved
...I WONDER WHATEVER HAPPENED TO A LITTLE GIRL NAMED MIM? WE HAVEN'T HEARD FROM HER IN YEARS!
12-3
Distributed by King Features Syndicate.
MIM? MIM? OH, YES! SHE GREW UP AND BECAME A SORCERESS!
YOU DON'T SAY!

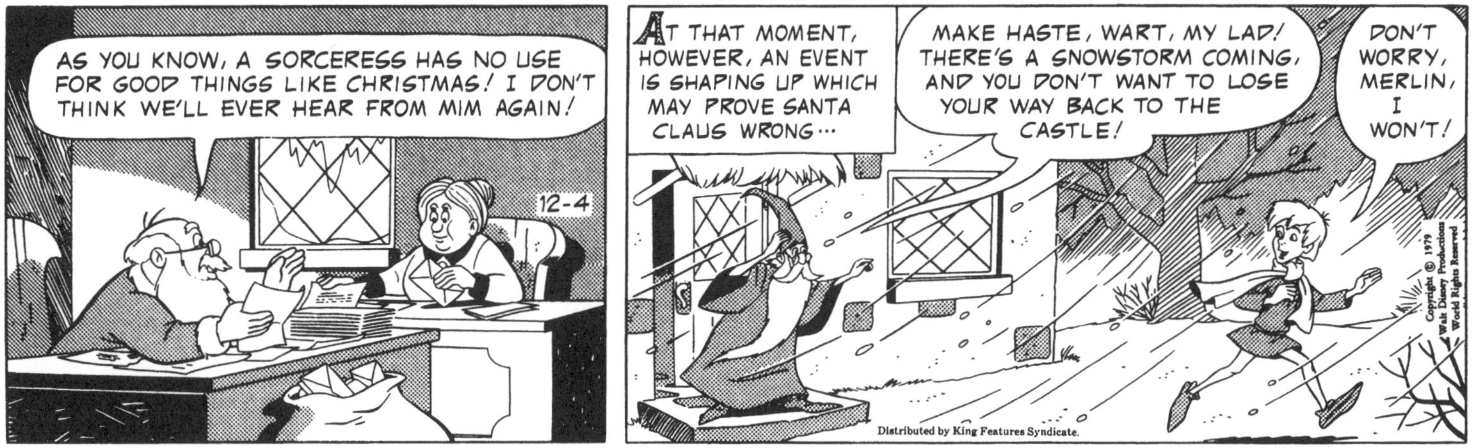
AS YOU KNOW, A SORCERESS HAS NO USE FOR GOOD THINGS LIKE CHRISTMAS! I DON'T THINK WE'LL EVER HEAR FROM MIM AGAIN!
12-4
AT THAT MOMENT, HOWEVER, AN EVENT IS SHAPING UP WHICH MAY PROVE SANTA CLAUS WRONG...
MAKE HASTE, WART, MY LAD! THERE'S A SNOWSTORM COMING, AND YOU DON'T WANT TO LOSE YOUR WAY BACK TO THE CASTLE!
DON'T WORRY, MERLIN, I WON'T!
Copyright © 1979 Walt Disney Productions World Rights Reserved
Distributed by King Features Syndicate.

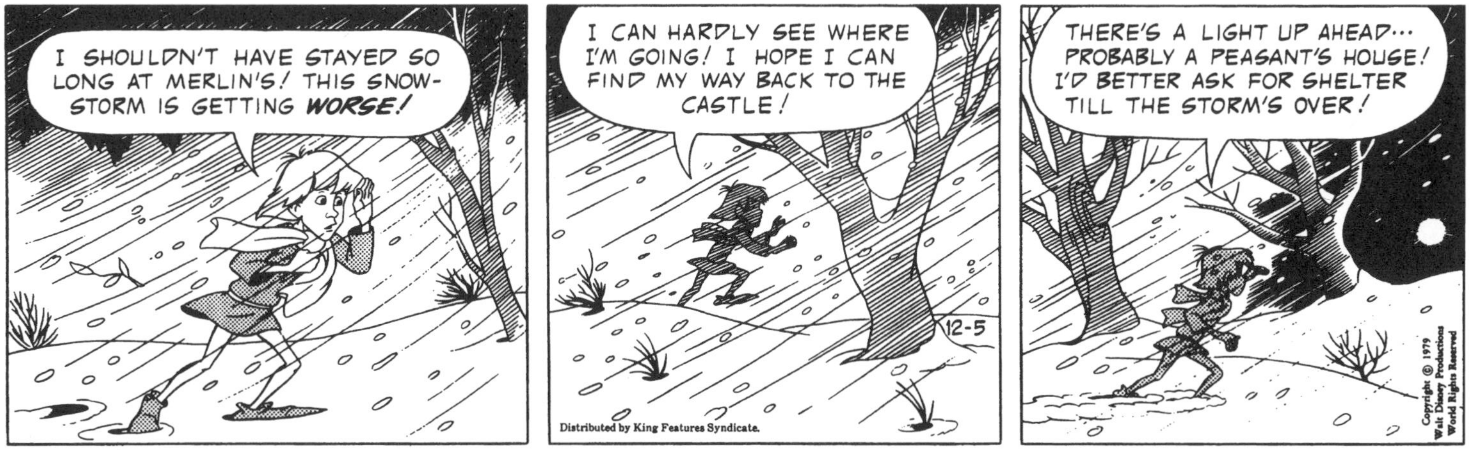
I SHOULDN'T HAVE STAYED SO LONG AT MERLIN'S! THIS SNOW-STORM IS GETTING WORSE!
I CAN HARDLY SEE WHERE I'M GOING! I HOPE I CAN FIND MY WAY BACK TO THE CASTLE!
12-5
Distributed by King Features Syndicate.
THERE'S A LIGHT UP AHEAD... PROBABLY A PEASANT'S HOUSE! I'D BETTER ASK FOR SHELTER TILL THE STORM'S OVER!
Copyright © 1979 Walt Disney Productions World Rights Reserved

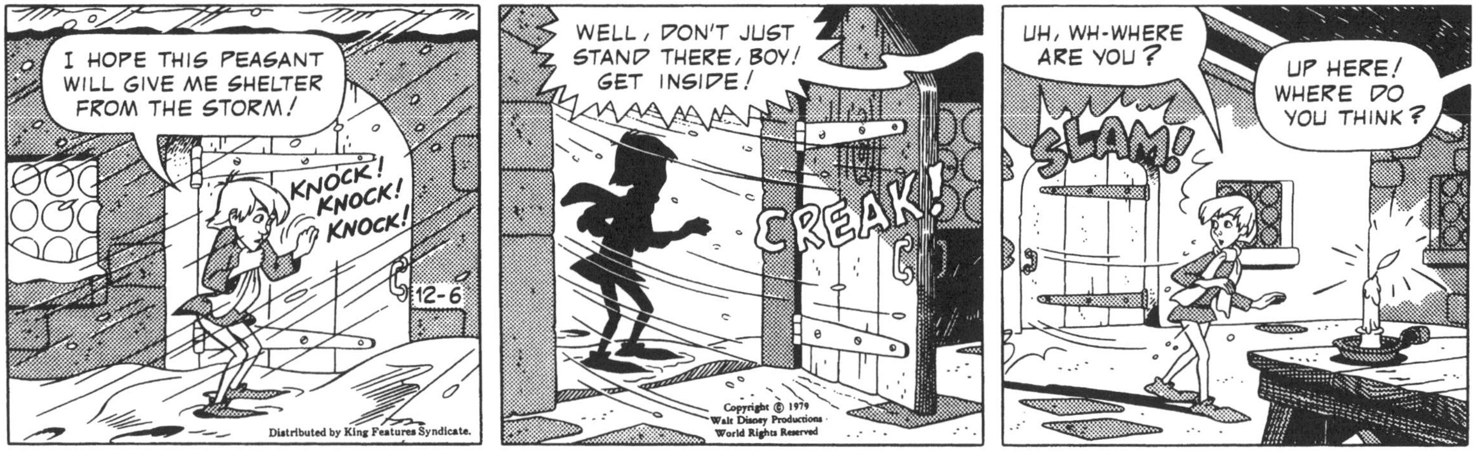
I HOPE THIS PEASANT WILL GIVE ME SHELTER FROM THE STORM!
KNOCK! KNOCK! KNOCK!
12-6
Distributed by King Features Syndicate.
WELL, DON'T JUST STAND THERE, BOY! GET INSIDE!
CREAK!
Copyright © 1979 Walt Disney Productions World Rights Reserved
SLAM!
UH, WH-WHERE ARE YOU?
UP HERE! WHERE DO YOU THINK?

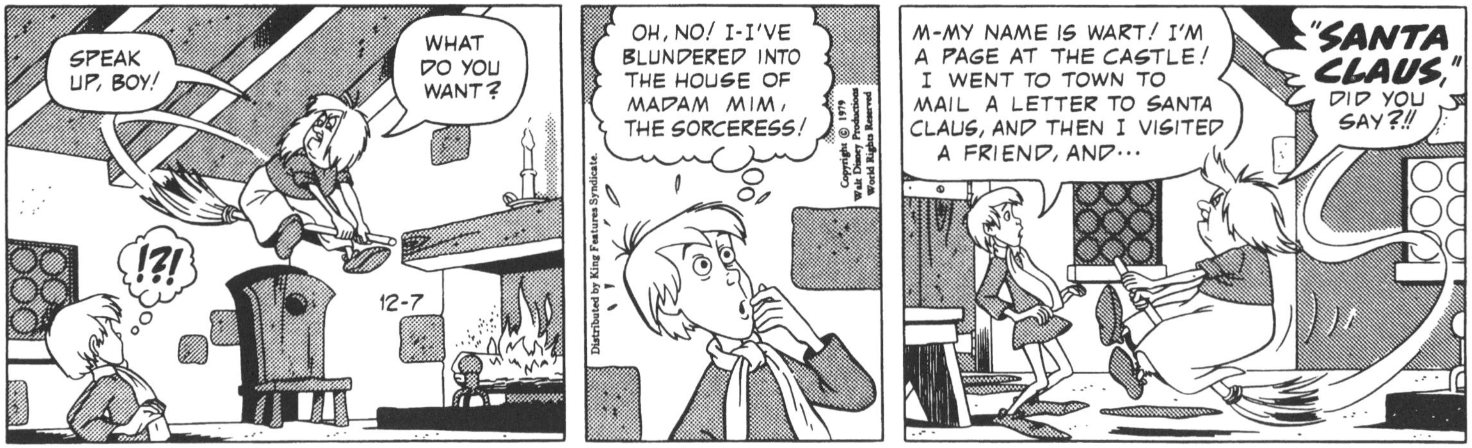
SPEAK UP, BOY!
WHAT DO YOU WANT?
!?!
12-7
Distributed by King Features Syndicate.
OH, NO! I-I'VE BLUNDERED INTO THE HOUSE OF MADAM MIM, THE SORCERESS!
Copyright © 1979 Walt Disney Productions World Rights Reserved
M-MY NAME IS WART! I'M A PAGE AT THE CASTLE! I WENT TO TOWN TO MAIL A LETTER TO SANTA CLAUS, AND THEN I VISITED A FRIEND, AND...
"SANTA CLAUS," DID YOU SAY?!!

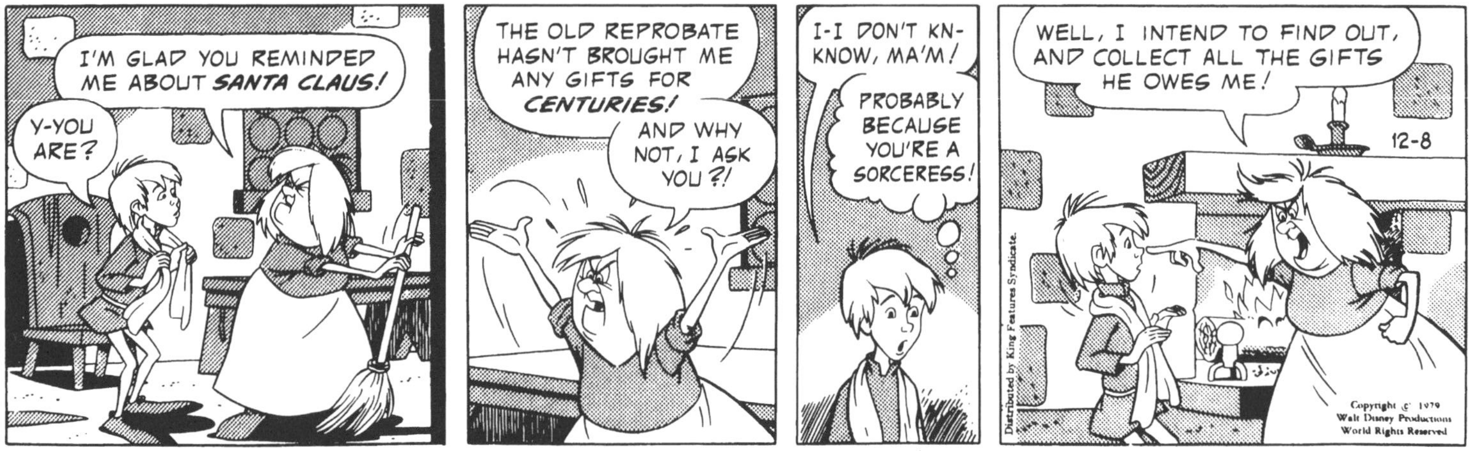
I'M GLAD YOU REMINDED ME ABOUT SANTA CLAUS!
Y-YOU ARE?
THE OLD REPROBATE HASN'T BROUGHT ME ANY GIFTS FOR CENTURIES!
AND WHY NOT, I ASK YOU?!
I-I DON'T KN-KNOW, MA'M!
PROBABLY BECAUSE YOU'RE A SORCERESS!
Distributed by King Features Syndicate.
WELL, I INTEND TO FIND OUT, AND COLLECT ALL THE GIFTS HE OWES ME!
12-8
Copyright © 1979 Walt Disney Productions World Rights Reserved

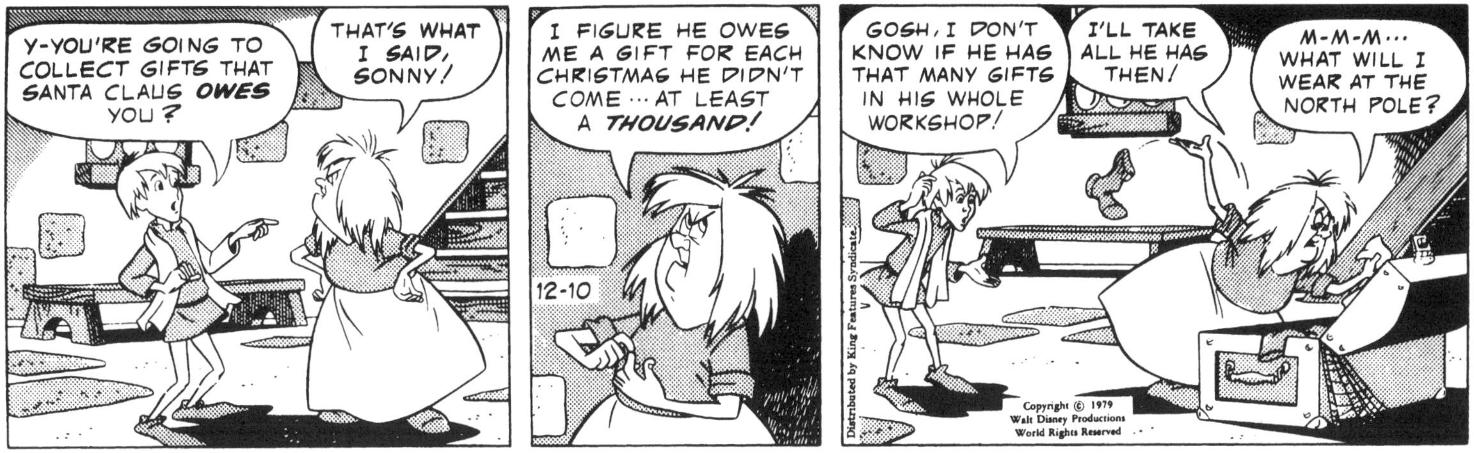
Y-YOU'RE GOING TO COLLECT GIFTS THAT SANTA CLAUS **OWES** YOU?
THAT'S WHAT I **SAID,** SONNY!
I FIGURE HE OWES ME A GIFT FOR EACH CHRISTMAS HE DIDN'T COME ... AT LEAST A ***THOUSAND!***
12-10
GOSH, I DON'T KNOW IF HE HAS THAT MANY GIFTS IN HIS WHOLE WORKSHOP!
I'LL TAKE ALL HE HAS THEN!
M-M-M... WHAT WILL I WEAR AT THE NORTH POLE?
Distributed by King Features Syndicate.
Copyright © 1979 Walt Disney Productions World Rights Reserved

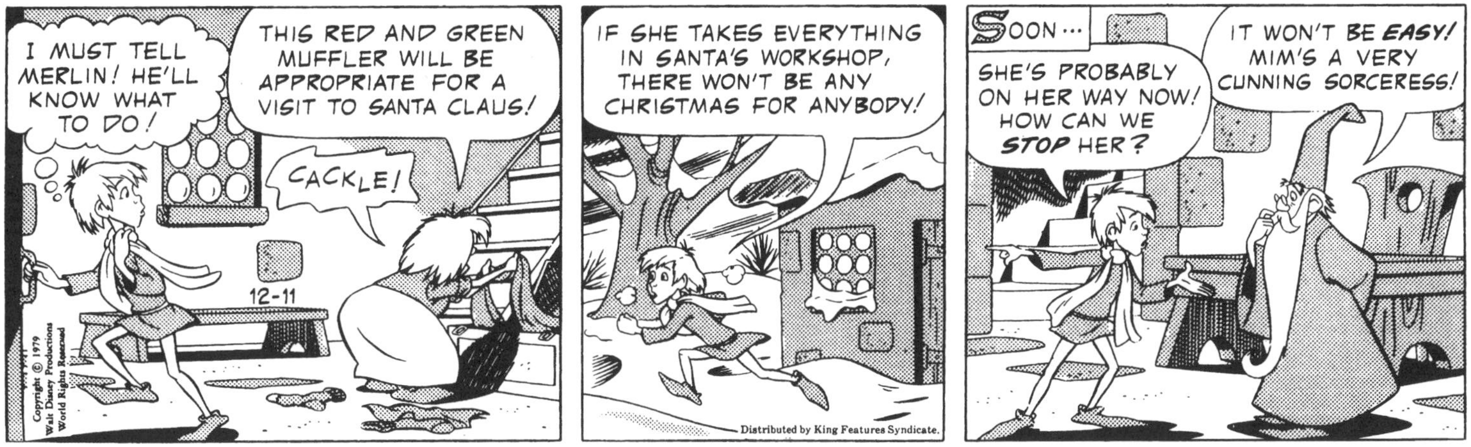
I MUST TELL MERLIN! HE'LL KNOW WHAT TO DO!
THIS RED AND GREEN MUFFLER WILL BE APPROPRIATE FOR A VISIT TO SANTA CLAUS!
CACKLE!
12-11
Copyright © 1979 Walt Disney Productions World Rights Reserved
IF SHE TAKES EVERYTHING IN SANTA'S WORKSHOP, THERE WON'T BE ANY CHRISTMAS FOR ANYBODY!
Distributed by King Features Syndicate.
SOON...
SHE'S PROBABLY ON HER WAY NOW! HOW CAN WE **STOP** HER?
IT WON'T BE ***EASY!*** MIM'S A VERY CUNNING SORCERESS!

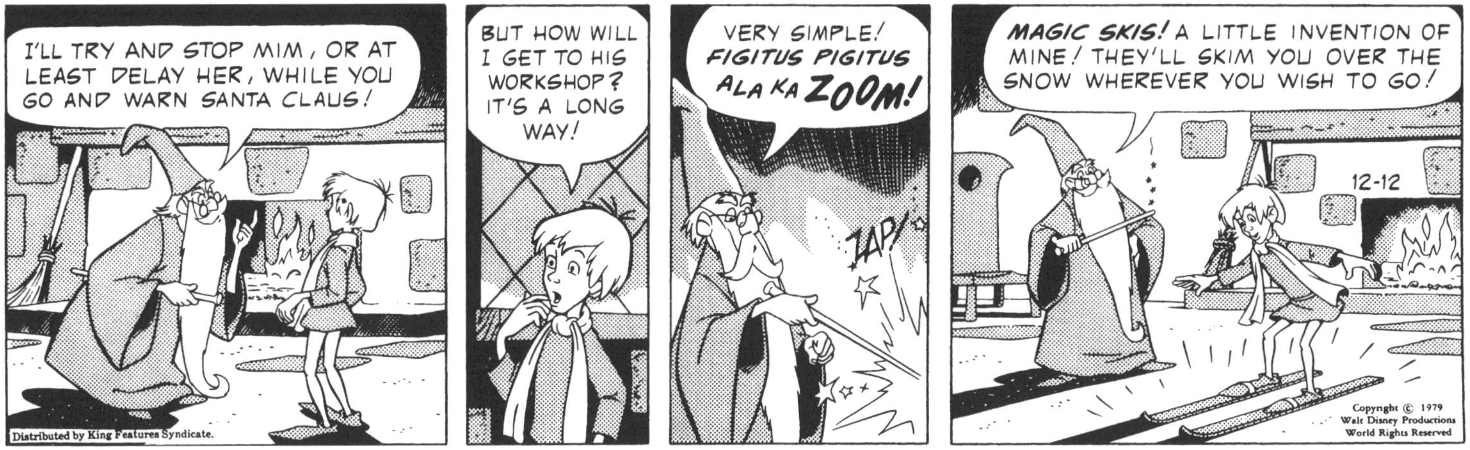
I'LL TRY AND STOP MIM, OR AT LEAST DELAY HER, WHILE YOU GO AND WARN SANTA CLAUS!
Distributed by King Features Syndicate.
BUT HOW WILL I GET TO HIS WORKSHOP? IT'S A LONG WAY!
VERY SIMPLE! ***FIGITUS PIGITUS ALA KA ZOOM!***
ZAP!
MAGIC SKIS! A LITTLE INVENTION OF MINE! THEY'LL SKIM YOU OVER THE SNOW WHEREVER YOU WISH TO GO!
12-12
Copyright © 1979 Walt Disney Productions World Rights Reserved

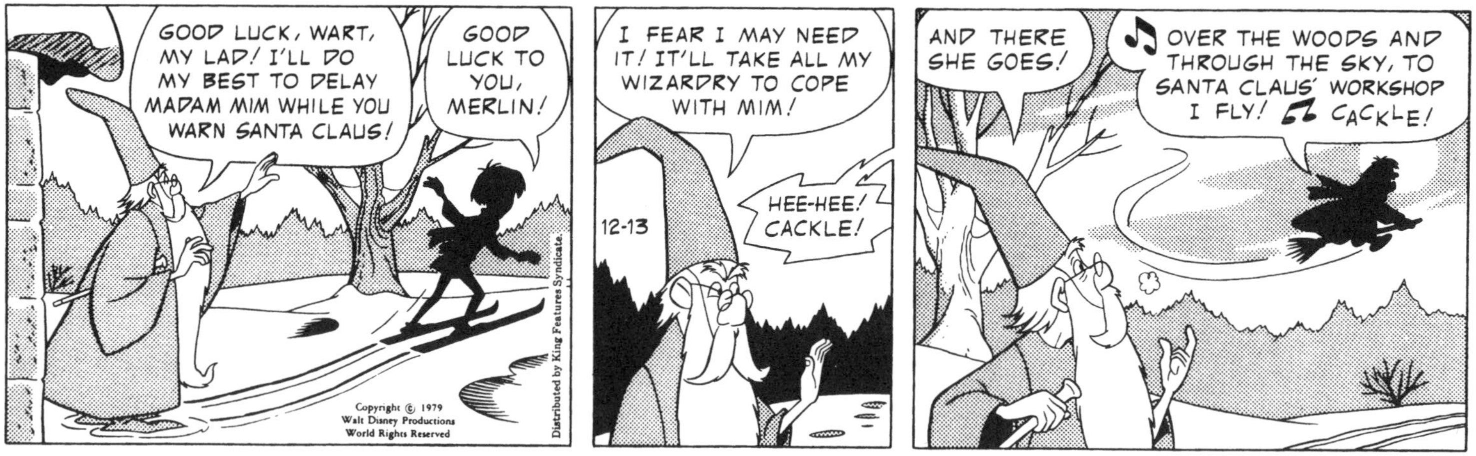
GOOD LUCK, WART, MY LAD! I'LL DO MY BEST TO DELAY MADAM MIM WHILE YOU WARN SANTA CLAUS!
GOOD LUCK TO YOU, MERLIN!
Copyright © 1979 Walt Disney Productions World Rights Reserved
Distributed by King Features Syndicate.
12-13
I FEAR I MAY NEED IT! IT'LL TAKE ALL MY WIZARDRY TO COPE WITH MIM!
HEE-HEE! CACKLE!
AND THERE SHE GOES!
♫ OVER THE WOODS AND THROUGH THE SKY, TO SANTA CLAUS' WORKSHOP I FLY! ♫ CACKLE!

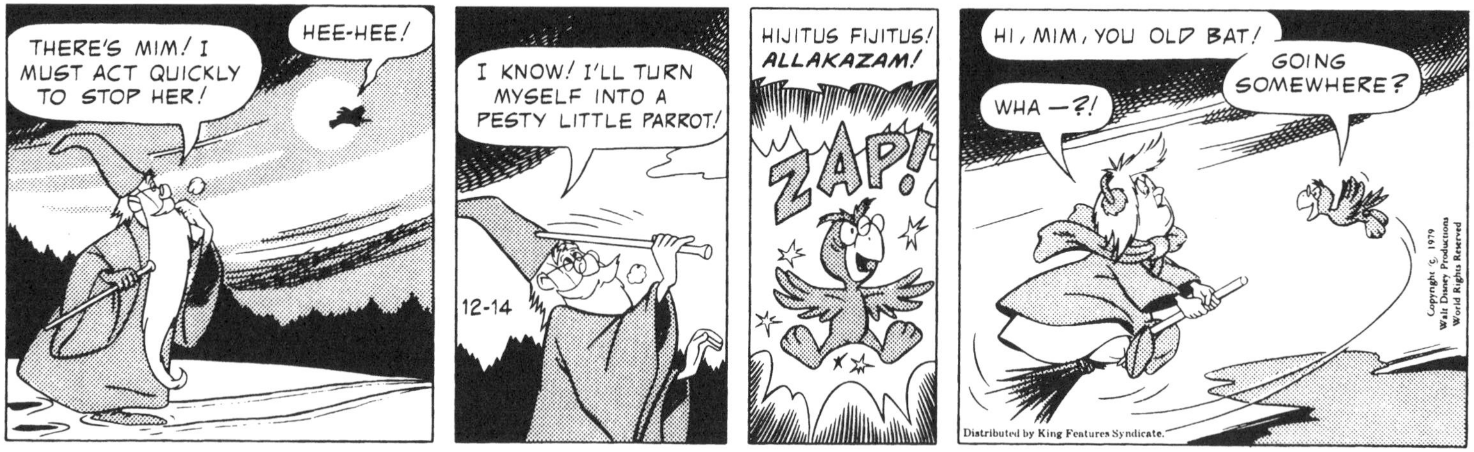
THERE'S MIM! I MUST ACT QUICKLY TO STOP HER!
HEE-HEE!
12-14
I KNOW! I'LL TURN MYSELF INTO A PESTY LITTLE PARROT!
HIJITUS FIJITUS! ALLAKAZAM!
ZAP!
HI, MIM, YOU OLD BAT!
GOING SOMEWHERE?
WHA —?!
Copyright © 1979 Walt Disney Productions World Rights Reserved
Distributed by King Features Syndicate.

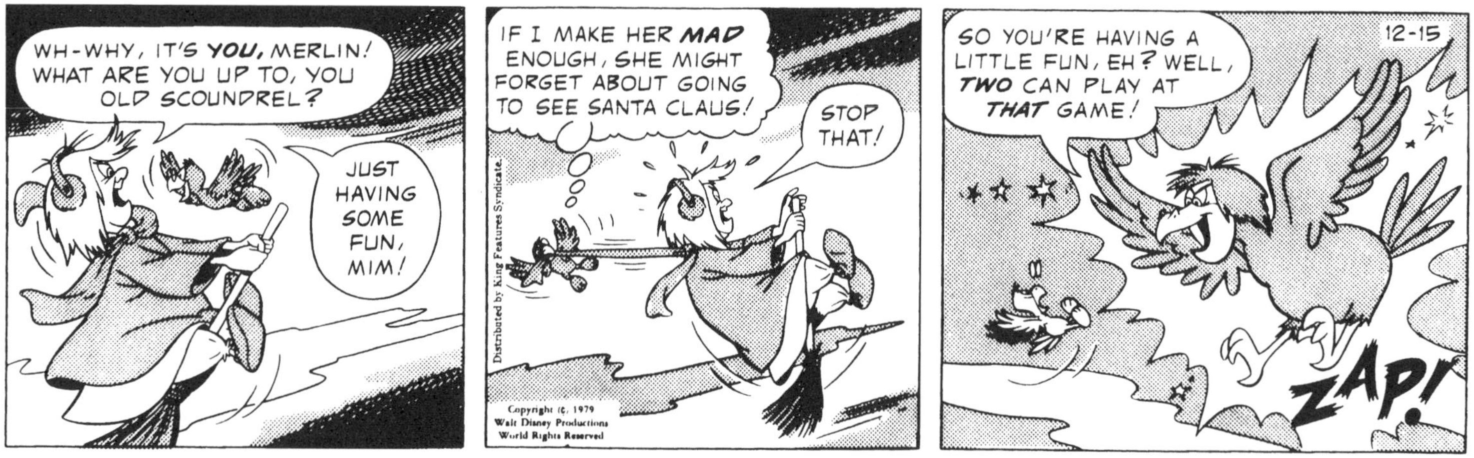
WH-WHY, IT'S YOU, MERLIN! WHAT ARE YOU UP TO, YOU OLD SCOUNDREL?
JUST HAVING SOME FUN, MIM!
IF I MAKE HER MAD ENOUGH, SHE MIGHT FORGET ABOUT GOING TO SEE SANTA CLAUS!
STOP THAT!
Distributed by King Features Syndicate.
Copyright © 1979 Walt Disney Productions World Rights Reserved
12-15
SO YOU'RE HAVING A LITTLE FUN, EH? WELL, TWO CAN PLAY AT THAT GAME!
ZAP!

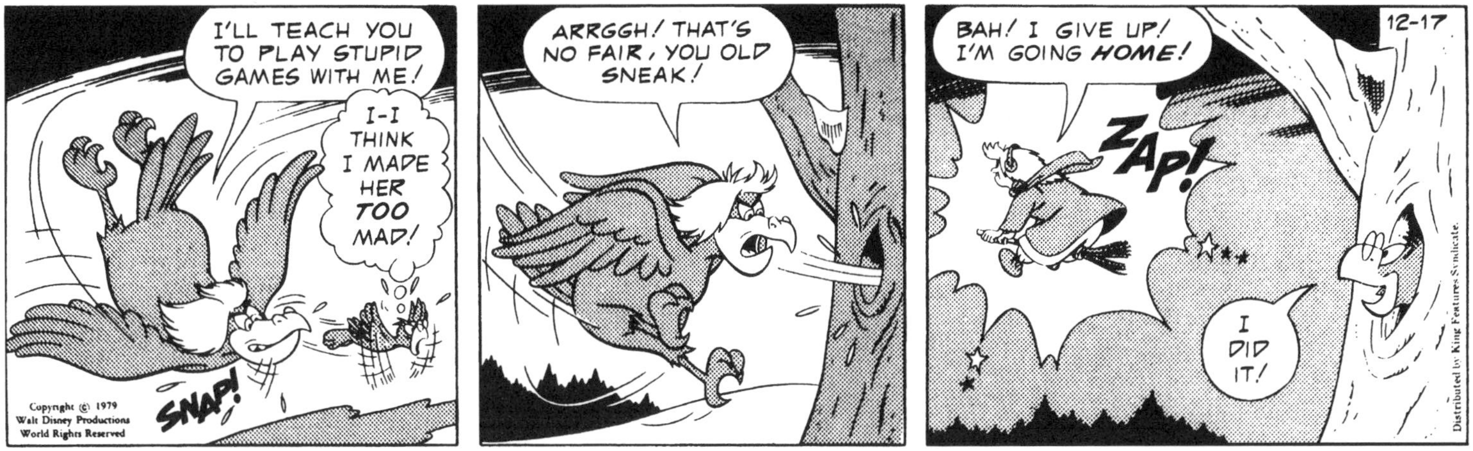
I'LL TEACH YOU TO PLAY STUPID GAMES WITH ME!
I-I THINK I MADE HER TOO MAD!
SNAP!
Copyright © 1979 Walt Disney Productions World Rights Reserved
ARRGGH! THAT'S NO FAIR, YOU OLD SNEAK!
12-17
BAH! I GIVE UP! I'M GOING HOME!
ZAP!
I DID IT!
Distributed by King Features Syndicate.

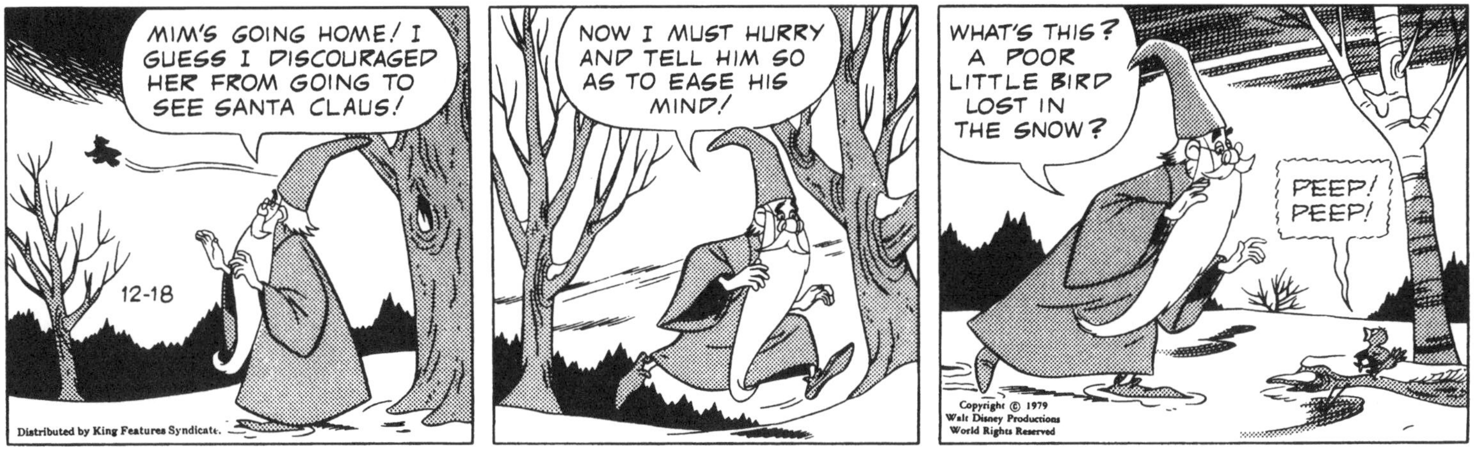
MIM'S GOING HOME! I GUESS I DISCOURAGED HER FROM GOING TO SEE SANTA CLAUS!
12-18
Distributed by King Features Syndicate.
NOW I MUST HURRY AND TELL HIM SO AS TO EASE HIS MIND!
WHAT'S THIS? A POOR LITTLE BIRD LOST IN THE SNOW?
PEEP! PEEP!
Copyright © 1979 Walt Disney Productions World Rights Reserved

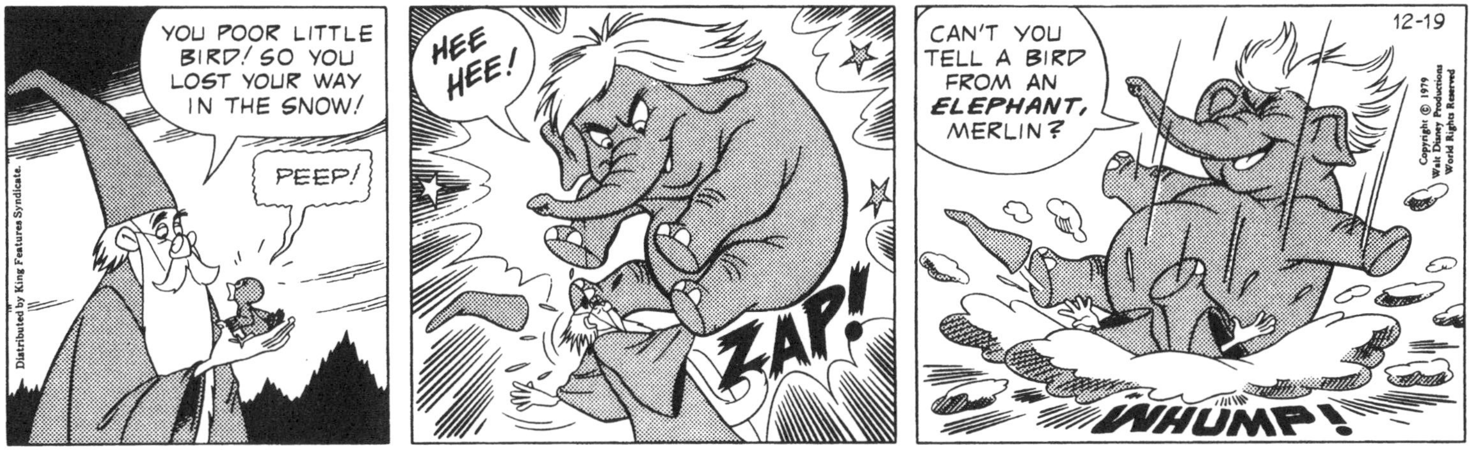
YOU POOR LITTLE BIRD! SO YOU LOST YOUR WAY IN THE SNOW!
PEEP!
Distributed by King Features Syndicate.
HEE HEE!
ZAP!
12-19
CAN'T YOU TELL A BIRD FROM AN ELEPHANT, MERLIN?
WHUMP!
Copyright © 1979 Walt Disney Productions World Rights Reserved

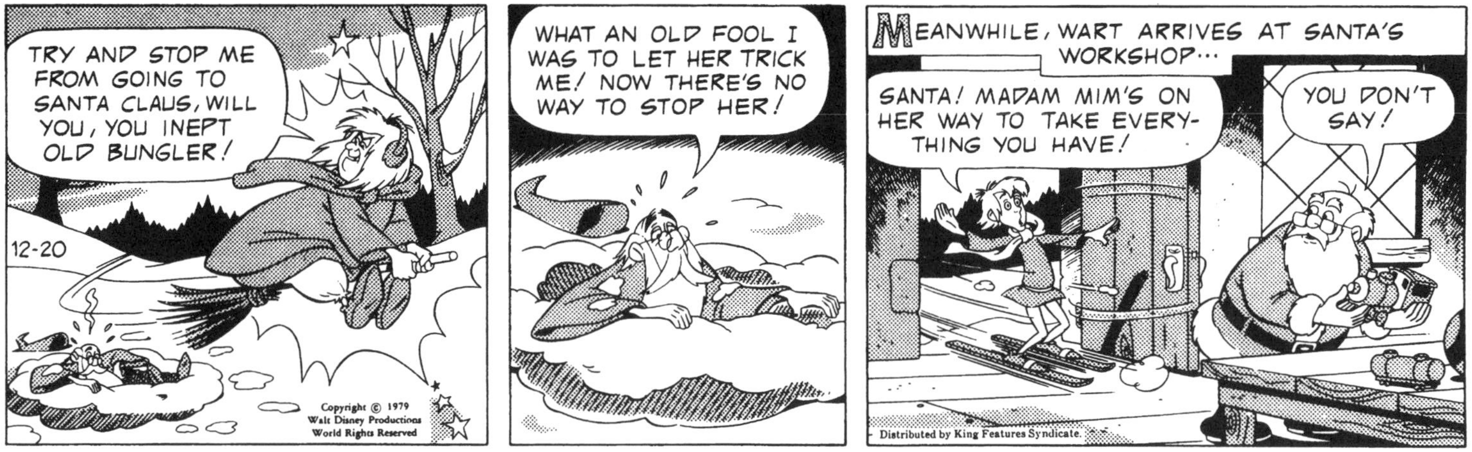
TRY AND STOP ME FROM GOING TO SANTA CLAUS, WILL YOU, YOU INEPT OLD BUNGLER!
12-20
Copyright © 1979 Walt Disney Productions World Rights Reserved
WHAT AN OLD FOOL I WAS TO LET HER TRICK ME! NOW THERE'S NO WAY TO STOP HER!
MEANWHILE, WART ARRIVES AT SANTA'S WORKSHOP...
SANTA! MADAM MIM'S ON HER WAY TO TAKE EVERYTHING YOU HAVE!
YOU DON'T SAY!
Distributed by King Features Syndicate.

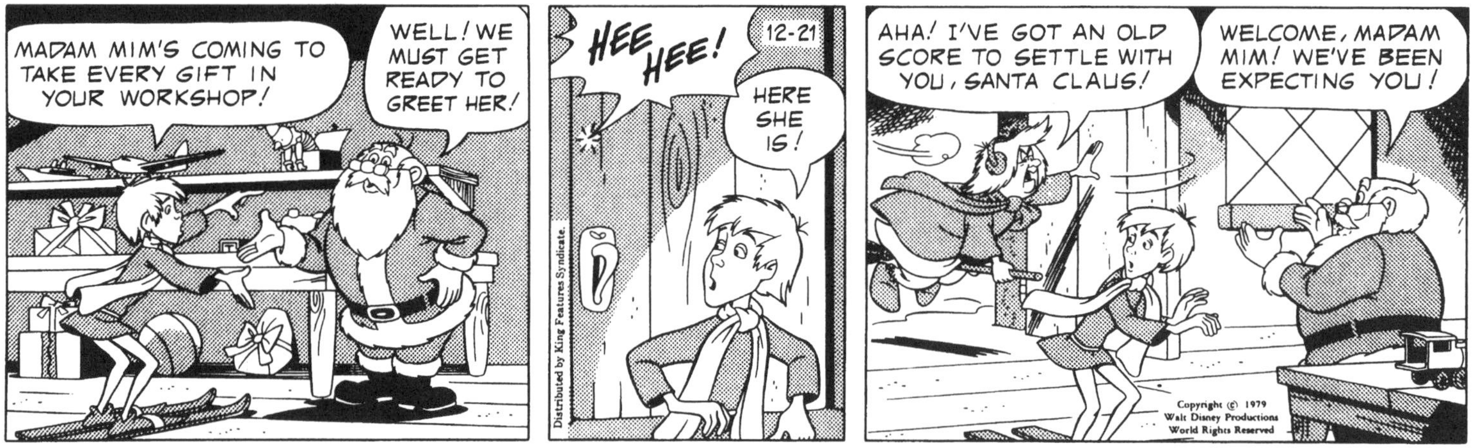
MADAM MIM'S COMING TO TAKE EVERY GIFT IN YOUR WORKSHOP!
WELL! WE MUST GET READY TO GREET HER!
HEE HEE!
12-21
HERE SHE IS!
Distributed by King Features Syndicate.
AHA! I'VE GOT AN OLD SCORE TO SETTLE WITH YOU, SANTA CLAUS!
WELCOME, MADAM MIM! WE'VE BEEN EXPECTING YOU!
Copyright © 1979 Walt Disney Productions World Rights Reserved

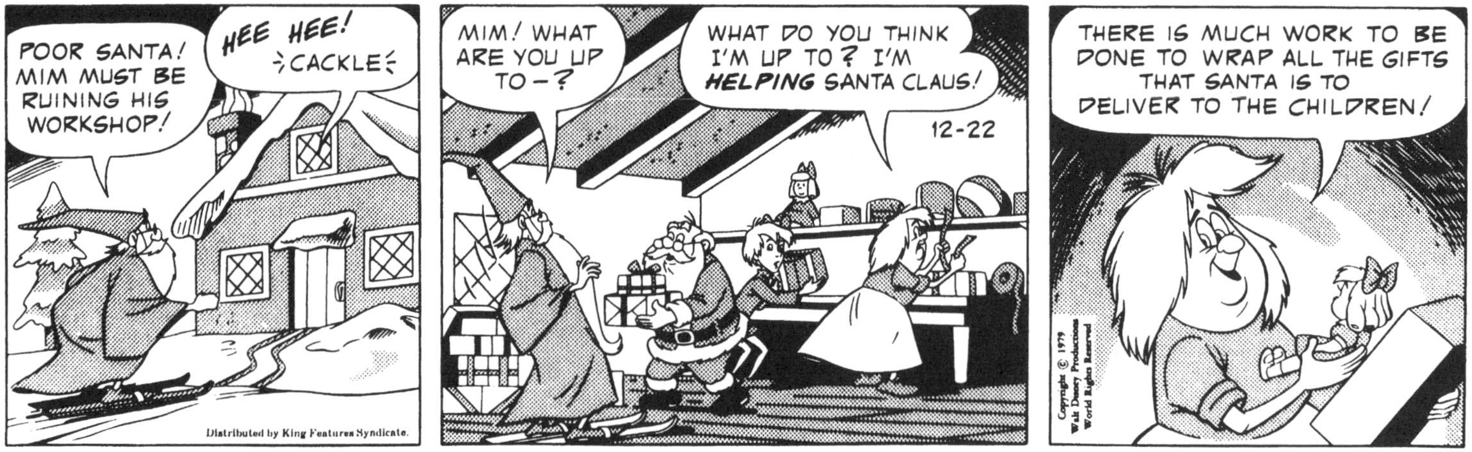
POOR SANTA! MIM MUST BE RUINING HIS WORKSHOP!
HEE HEE! CACKLE
Distributed by King Features Syndicate.
MIM! WHAT ARE YOU UP TO–?
WHAT DO YOU THINK I'M UP TO? I'M HELPING SANTA CLAUS!
12-22
THERE IS MUCH WORK TO BE DONE TO WRAP ALL THE GIFTS THAT SANTA IS TO DELIVER TO THE CHILDREN!
Copyright © 1979 Walt Disney Productions World Rights Reserved

WH-WHAT DID YOU DO TO HER?
NOTHING REALLY!
TRA LA LA LA LAAA LA LA LA LAAA!
MIM'S MAGIC JUST CAN'T COMPETE WITH THE MAGIC OF CHRISTMAS!
12-24
...AND A MERRY CHRISTMAS TO EVERYONE... EVERYWHERE!!
Copyright © 1979 Walt Disney Productions World Rights Reserved
Distributed by King Features Syndicate.

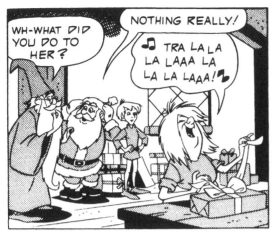

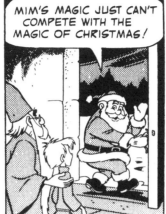

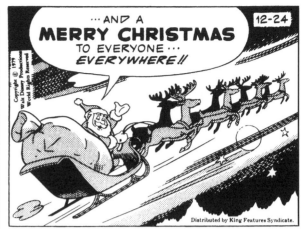

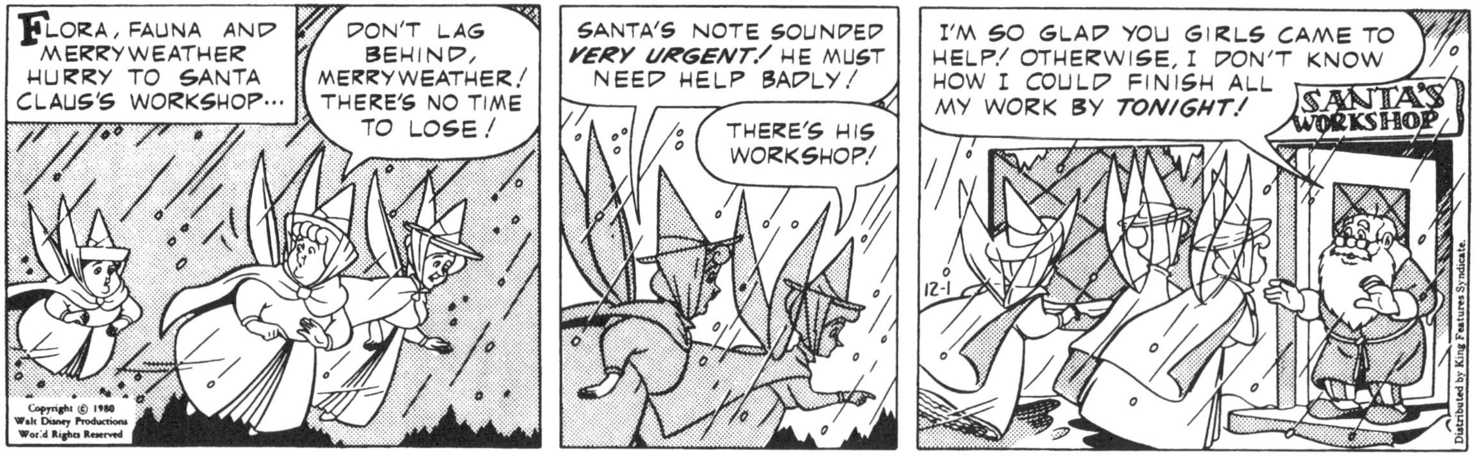
FLORA, FAUNA AND MERRYWEATHER HURRY TO SANTA CLAUS'S WORKSHOP...
DON'T LAG BEHIND, MERRYWEATHER! THERE'S NO TIME TO LOSE!
Copyright © 1980 Walt Disney Productions World Rights Reserved
SANTA'S NOTE SOUNDED VERY URGENT! HE MUST NEED HELP BADLY!
THERE'S HIS WORKSHOP!
I'M SO GLAD YOU GIRLS CAME TO HELP! OTHERWISE, I DON'T KNOW HOW I COULD FINISH ALL MY WORK BY TONIGHT!
SANTA'S WORKSHOP
12-1
Distributed by King Features Syndicate.

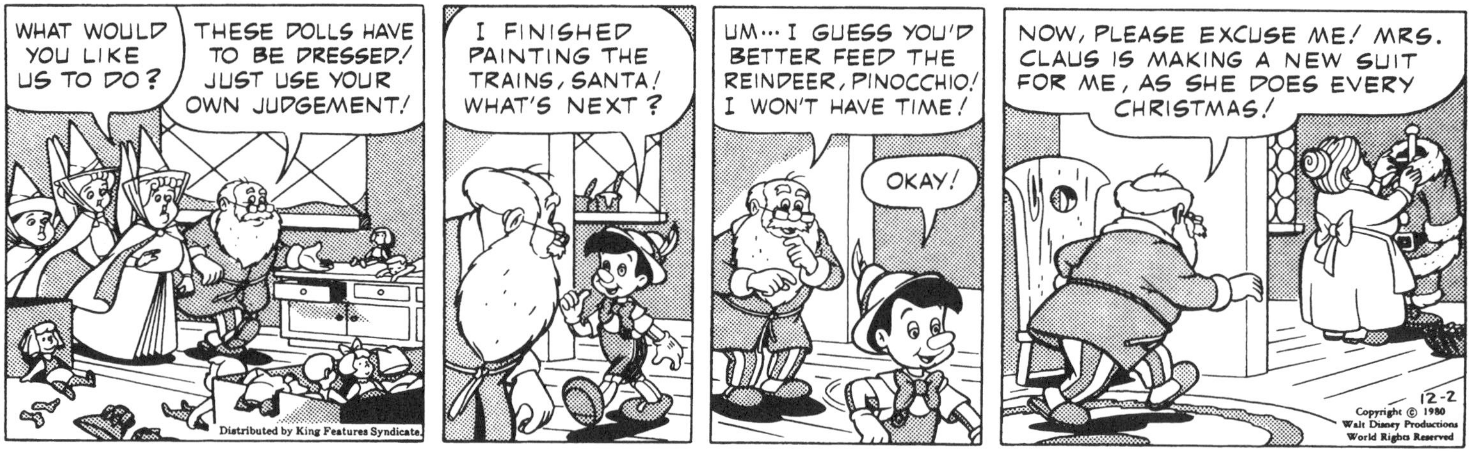
WHAT WOULD YOU LIKE US TO DO?
THESE DOLLS HAVE TO BE DRESSED! JUST USE YOUR OWN JUDGEMENT!
Distributed by King Features Syndicate.
I FINISHED PAINTING THE TRAINS, SANTA! WHAT'S NEXT?
UM... I GUESS YOU'D BETTER FEED THE REINDEER, PINOCCHIO! I WON'T HAVE TIME!
OKAY!
NOW, PLEASE EXCUSE ME! MRS. CLAUS IS MAKING A NEW SUIT FOR ME, AS SHE DOES EVERY CHRISTMAS!
12-2
Copyright © 1980 Walt Disney Productions World Rights Reserved

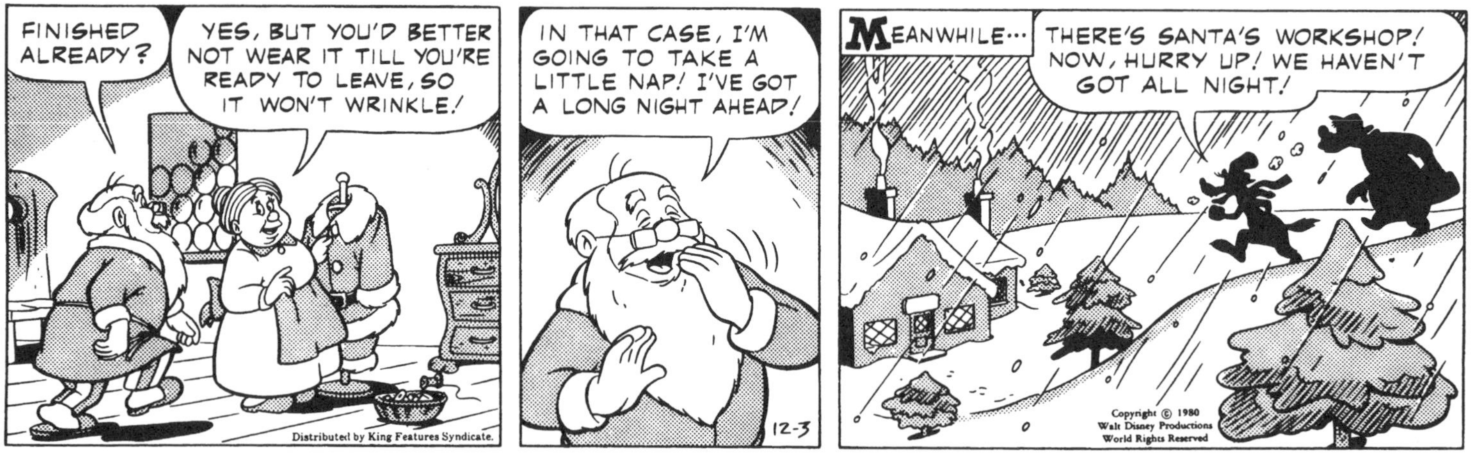
FINISHED ALREADY?
YES, BUT YOU'D BETTER NOT WEAR IT TILL YOU'RE READY TO LEAVE, SO IT WON'T WRINKLE!
Distributed by King Features Syndicate.
IN THAT CASE, I'M GOING TO TAKE A LITTLE NAP! I'VE GOT A LONG NIGHT AHEAD!
12-3
MEANWHILE...
THERE'S SANTA'S WORKSHOP! NOW, HURRY UP! WE HAVEN'T GOT ALL NIGHT!
Copyright © 1980 Walt Disney Productions World Rights Reserved

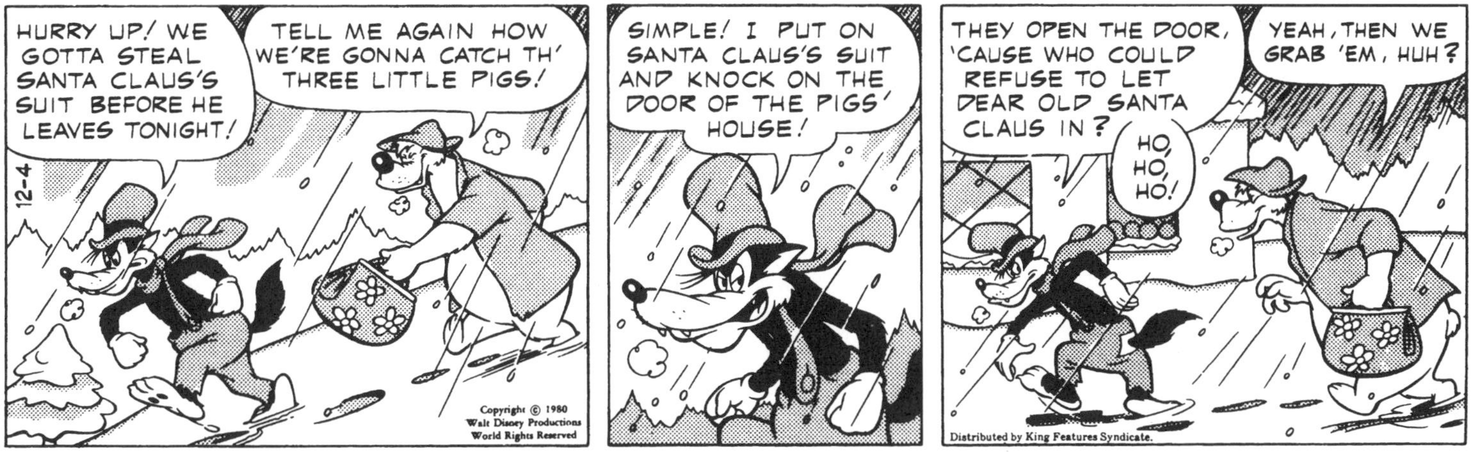
HURRY UP! WE GOTTA STEAL SANTA CLAUS'S SUIT BEFORE HE LEAVES TONIGHT!
TELL ME AGAIN HOW WE'RE GONNA CATCH TH' THREE LITTLE PIGS!
12-4
Copyright © 1980 Walt Disney Productions World Rights Reserved
SIMPLE! I PUT ON SANTA CLAUS'S SUIT AND KNOCK ON THE DOOR OF THE PIGS' HOUSE!
THEY OPEN THE DOOR, 'CAUSE WHO COULD REFUSE TO LET DEAR OLD SANTA CLAUS IN?
YEAH, THEN WE GRAB 'EM, HUH?
HO, HO, HO!
Distributed by King Features Syndicate.

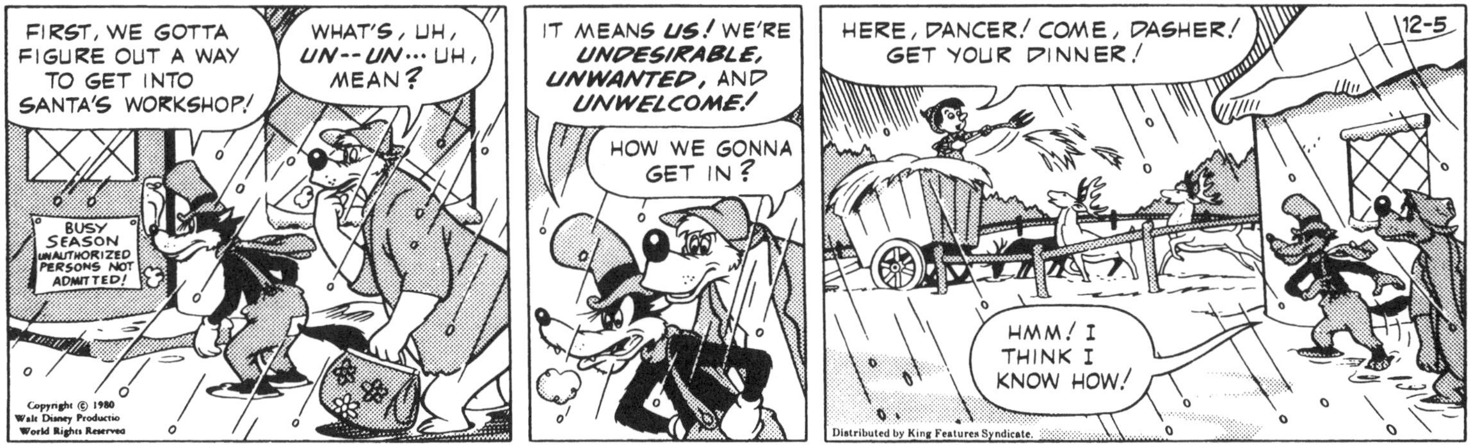
FIRST, WE GOTTA FIGURE OUT A WAY TO GET INTO SANTA'S WORKSHOP!
WHAT'S, UH, UN--UN... UH, MEAN?
BUSY SEASON UNAUTHORIZED PERSONS NOT ADMITTED!
Copyright © 1980 Walt Disney Productio World Rights Reservea
IT MEANS US! WE'RE UNDESIRABLE, UNWANTED, AND UNWELCOME!
HOW WE GONNA GET IN?
12-5
HERE, DANCER! COME, DASHER! GET YOUR DINNER!
HMM! I THINK I KNOW HOW!
Distributed by King Features Syndicate.

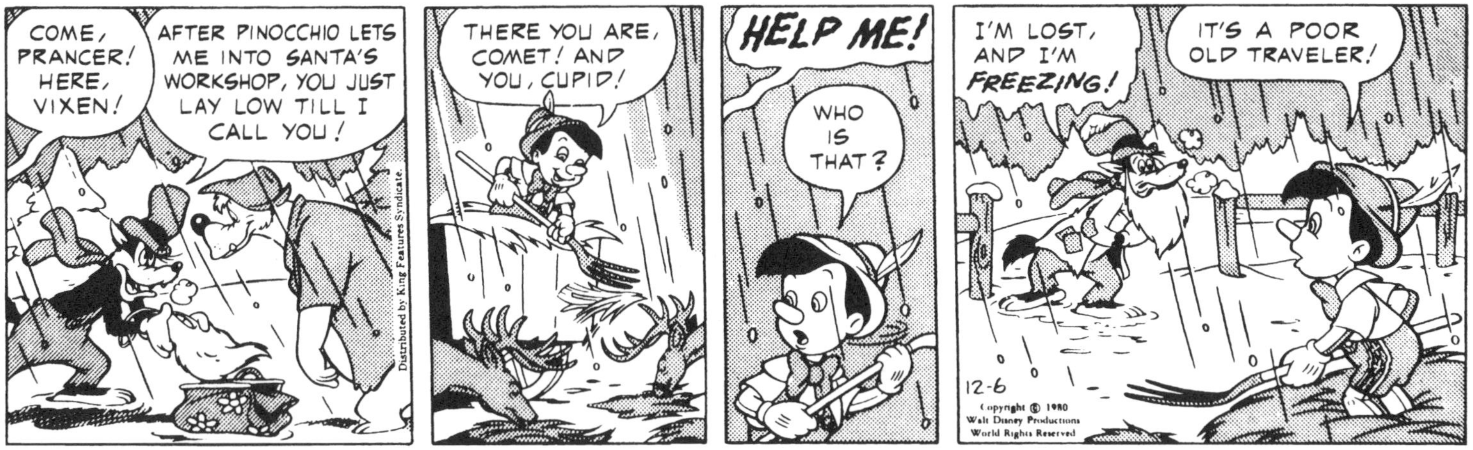
COME, PRANCER! HERE, VIXEN!
AFTER PINOCCHIO LETS ME INTO SANTA'S WORKSHOP, YOU JUST LAY LOW TILL I CALL YOU!
Distributed by King Features Syndicate.
THERE YOU ARE, COMET! AND YOU, CUPID!
HELP ME!
WHO IS THAT?
I'M LOST, AND I'M FREEZING!
IT'S A POOR OLD TRAVELER!
12-6
Copyright © 1980 Walt Disney Productions World Rights Reserved

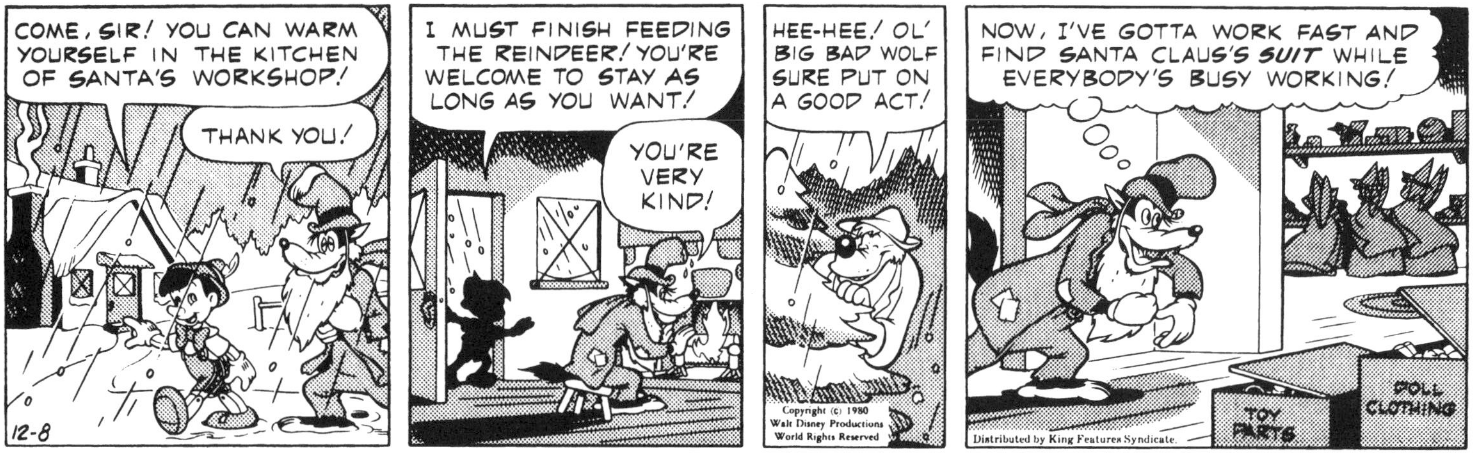
COME, SIR! YOU CAN WARM YOURSELF IN THE KITCHEN OF SANTA'S WORKSHOP!
THANK YOU!
12-8
I MUST FINISH FEEDING THE REINDEER! YOU'RE WELCOME TO STAY AS LONG AS YOU WANT!
YOU'RE VERY KIND!
HEE-HEE! OL' BIG BAD WOLF SURE PUT ON A GOOD ACT!
Copyright (c) 1980 Walt Disney Productions World Rights Reserved
NOW, I'VE GOTTA WORK FAST AND FIND SANTA CLAUS'S SUIT WHILE EVERYBODY'S BUSY WORKING!
TOY PARTS
DOLL CLOTHING
Distributed by King Features Syndicate.

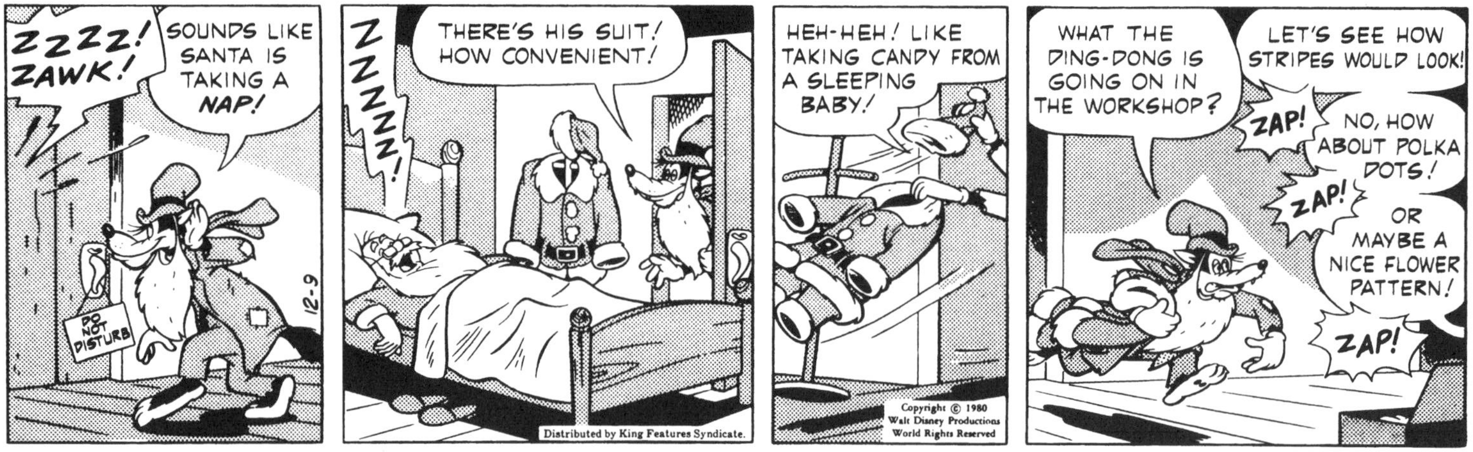
ZZZZ! ZAWK!
SOUNDS LIKE SANTA IS TAKING A NAP!
DO NOT DISTURB
12-9
ZZZZZ!
THERE'S HIS SUIT! HOW CONVENIENT!
Distributed by King Features Syndicate.
HEH-HEH! LIKE TAKING CANDY FROM A SLEEPING BABY!
Copyright © 1980 Walt Disney Productions World Rights Reserved
WHAT THE DING-DONG IS GOING ON IN THE WORKSHOP?
LET'S SEE HOW STRIPES WOULD LOOK!
ZAP!
NO, HOW ABOUT POLKA DOTS!
ZAP!
OR MAYBE A NICE FLOWER PATTERN!
ZAP!

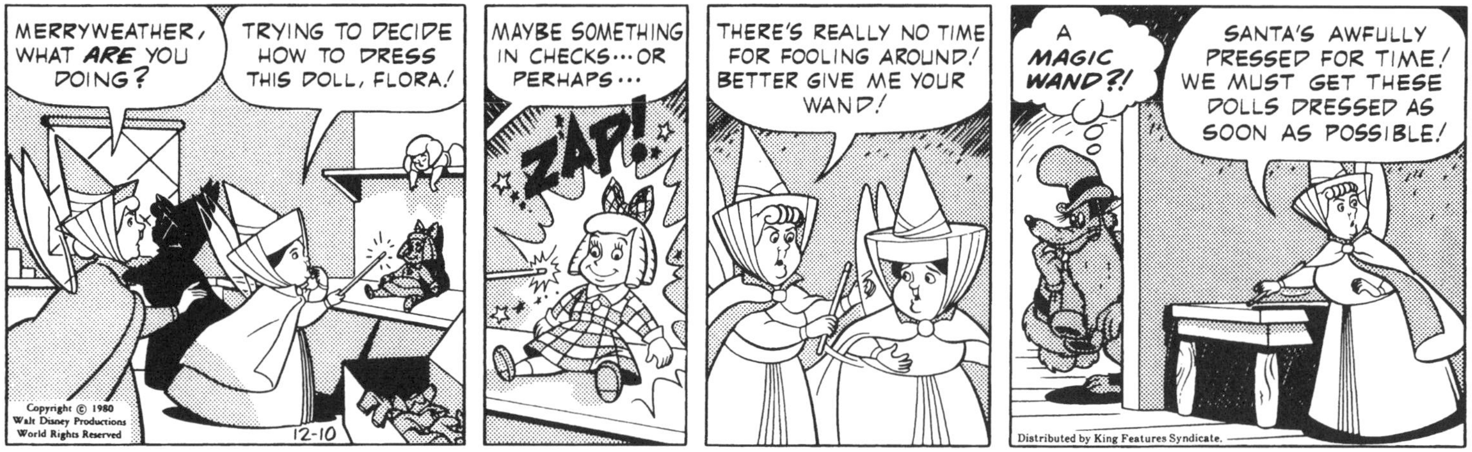
MERRYWEATHER, WHAT ARE YOU DOING?
TRYING TO DECIDE HOW TO DRESS THIS DOLL, FLORA!
Copyright © 1980 Walt Disney Productions World Rights Reserved
12-10
MAYBE SOMETHING IN CHECKS···OR PERHAPS···
ZAP!
THERE'S REALLY NO TIME FOR FOOLING AROUND! BETTER GIVE ME YOUR WAND!
A MAGIC WAND?!
SANTA'S AWFULLY PRESSED FOR TIME! WE MUST GET THESE DOLLS DRESSED AS SOON AS POSSIBLE!
Distributed by King Features Syndicate.

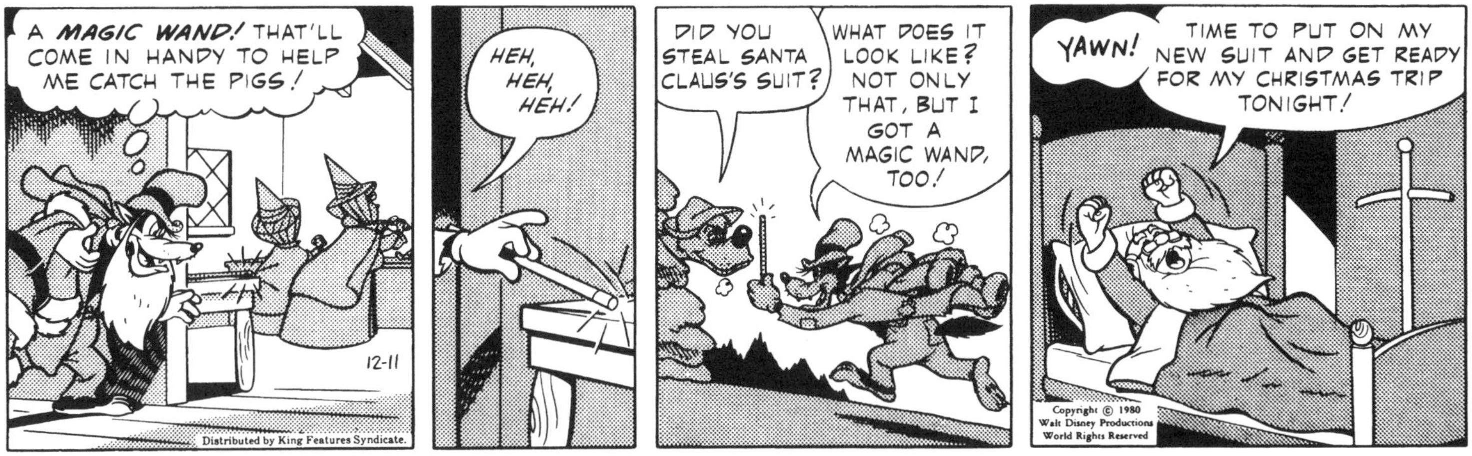
A MAGIC WAND! THAT'LL COME IN HANDY TO HELP ME CATCH THE PIGS!
12-11
Distributed by King Features Syndicate.
HEH, HEH, HEH!
DID YOU STEAL SANTA CLAUS'S SUIT?
WHAT DOES IT LOOK LIKE? NOT ONLY THAT, BUT I GOT A MAGIC WAND, TOO!
YAWN!
TIME TO PUT ON MY NEW SUIT AND GET READY FOR MY CHRISTMAS TRIP TONIGHT!
Copyright © 1980 Walt Disney Productions World Rights Reserved

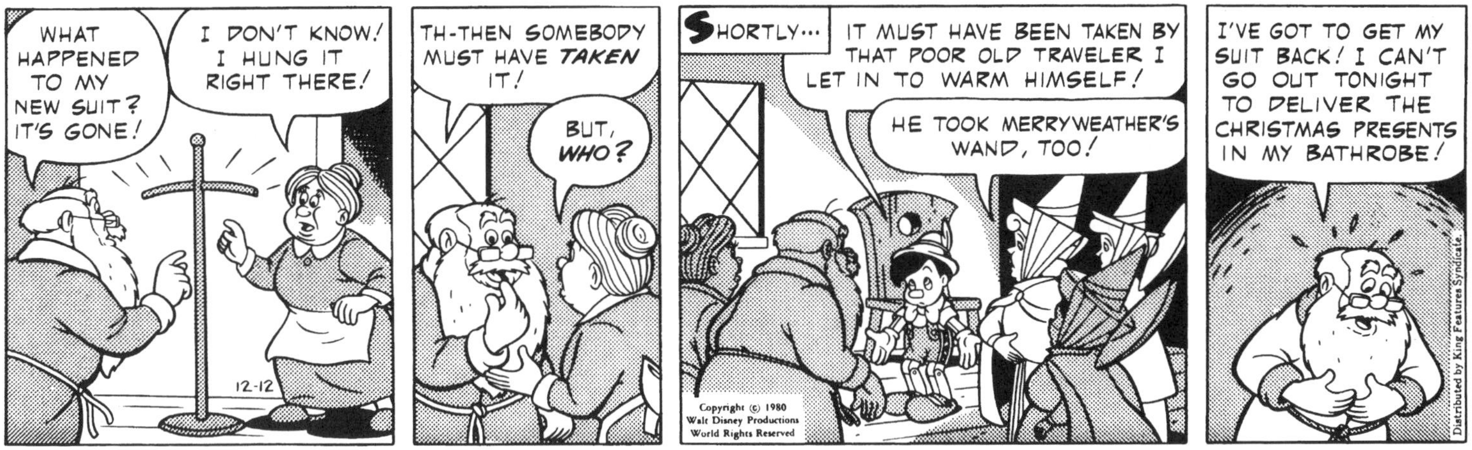
WHAT HAPPENED TO MY NEW SUIT? IT'S GONE!
I DON'T KNOW! I HUNG IT RIGHT THERE!
12-12
TH-THEN SOMEBODY MUST HAVE TAKEN IT!
BUT, WHO?
SHORTLY...
IT MUST HAVE BEEN TAKEN BY THAT POOR OLD TRAVELER I LET IN TO WARM HIMSELF!
HE TOOK MERRYWEATHER'S WAND, TOO!
Copyright (c) 1980 Walt Disney Productions World Rights Reserved
I'VE GOT TO GET MY SUIT BACK! I CAN'T GO OUT TONIGHT TO DELIVER THE CHRISTMAS PRESENTS IN MY BATHROBE!
Distributed by King Features Syndicate.

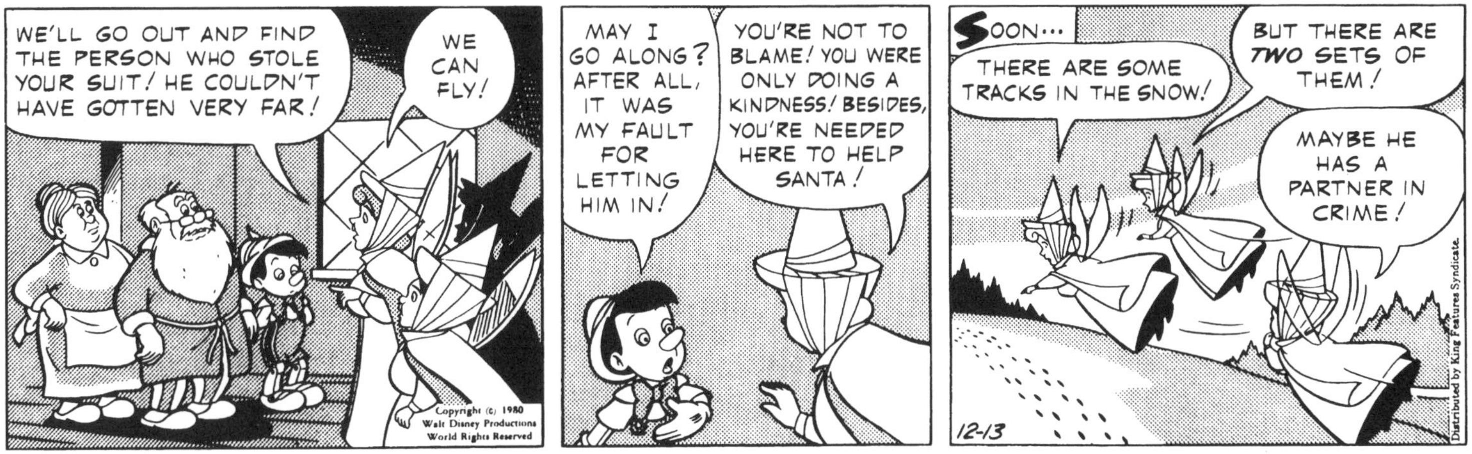
WE'LL GO OUT AND FIND THE PERSON WHO STOLE YOUR SUIT! HE COULDN'T HAVE GOTTEN VERY FAR!
WE CAN FLY!
Copyright (c) 1980 Walt Disney Productions World Rights Reserved
MAY I GO ALONG? AFTER ALL, IT WAS MY FAULT FOR LETTING HIM IN!
YOU'RE NOT TO BLAME! YOU WERE ONLY DOING A KINDNESS! BESIDES, YOU'RE NEEDED HERE TO HELP SANTA!
SOON...
THERE ARE SOME TRACKS IN THE SNOW!
BUT THERE ARE TWO SETS OF THEM!
MAYBE HE HAS A PARTNER IN CRIME!
12-13
Distributed by King Features Syndicate.

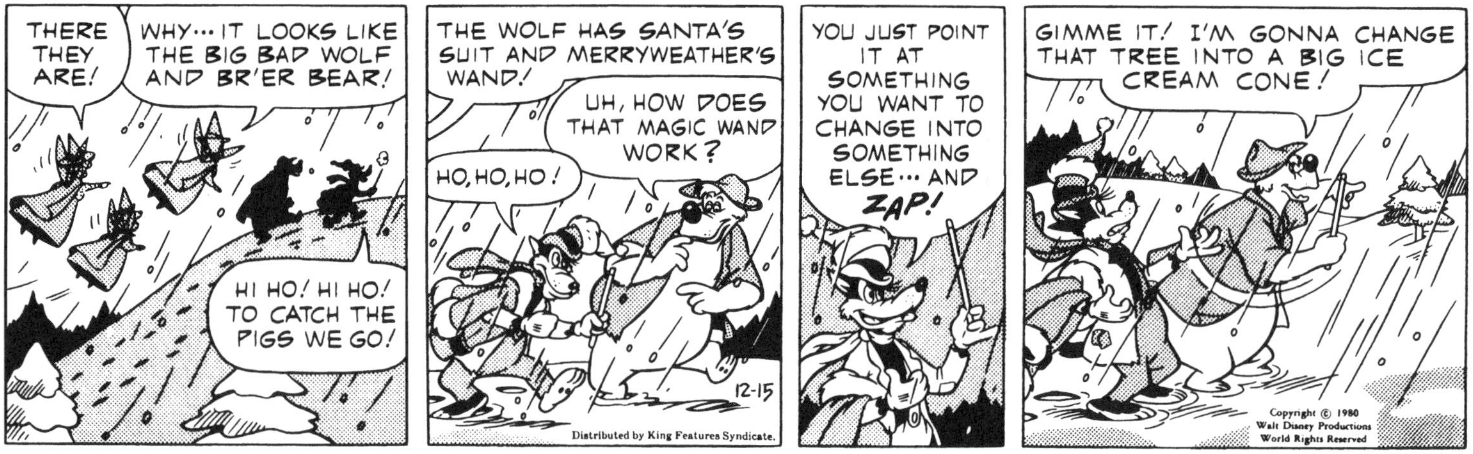
THERE THEY ARE!
WHY... IT LOOKS LIKE THE BIG BAD WOLF AND BR'ER BEAR!
HI HO! HI HO! TO CATCH THE PIGS WE GO!
THE WOLF HAS SANTA'S SUIT AND MERRYWEATHER'S WAND!
UH, HOW DOES THAT MAGIC WAND WORK?
HO, HO, HO!
12-15
Distributed by King Features Syndicate.
YOU JUST POINT IT AT SOMETHING YOU WANT TO CHANGE INTO SOMETHING ELSE... AND ZAP!
GIMME IT! I'M GONNA CHANGE THAT TREE INTO A BIG ICE CREAM CONE!
Copyright © 1980 Walt Disney Productions World Rights Reserved

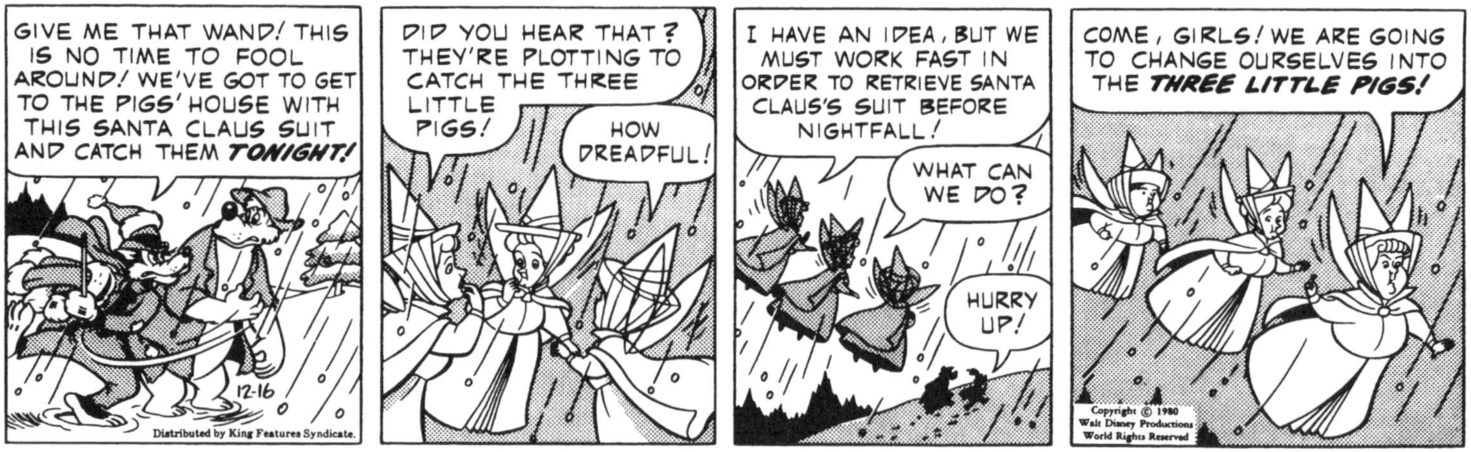
GIVE ME THAT WAND! THIS IS NO TIME TO FOOL AROUND! WE'VE GOT TO GET TO THE PIGS' HOUSE WITH THIS SANTA CLAUS SUIT AND CATCH THEM TONIGHT!
12-16
Distributed by King Features Syndicate.
DID YOU HEAR THAT? THEY'RE PLOTTING TO CATCH THE THREE LITTLE PIGS!
HOW DREADFUL!
I HAVE AN IDEA, BUT WE MUST WORK FAST IN ORDER TO RETRIEVE SANTA CLAUS'S SUIT BEFORE NIGHTFALL!
WHAT CAN WE DO?
HURRY UP!
COME, GIRLS! WE ARE GOING TO CHANGE OURSELVES INTO THE THREE LITTLE PIGS!
Copyright © 1980 Walt Disney Productions World Rights Reserved

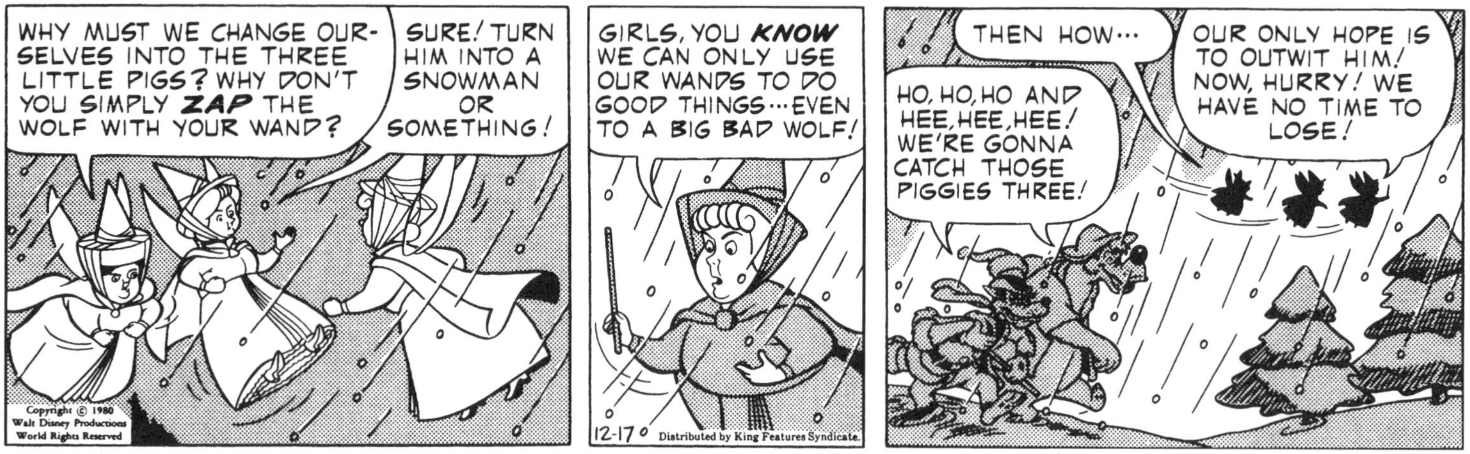
WHY MUST WE CHANGE OURSELVES INTO THE THREE LITTLE PIGS? WHY DON'T YOU SIMPLY ZAP THE WOLF WITH YOUR WAND?
SURE! TURN HIM INTO A SNOWMAN OR SOMETHING!
Copyright © 1980 Walt Disney Productions World Rights Reserved
GIRLS, YOU KNOW WE CAN ONLY USE OUR WANDS TO DO GOOD THINGS... EVEN TO A BIG BAD WOLF!
12-17
Distributed by King Features Syndicate.
THEN HOW...
OUR ONLY HOPE IS TO OUTWIT HIM! NOW, HURRY! WE HAVE NO TIME TO LOSE!
HO, HO, HO AND HEE, HEE, HEE! WE'RE GONNA CATCH THOSE PIGGIES THREE!

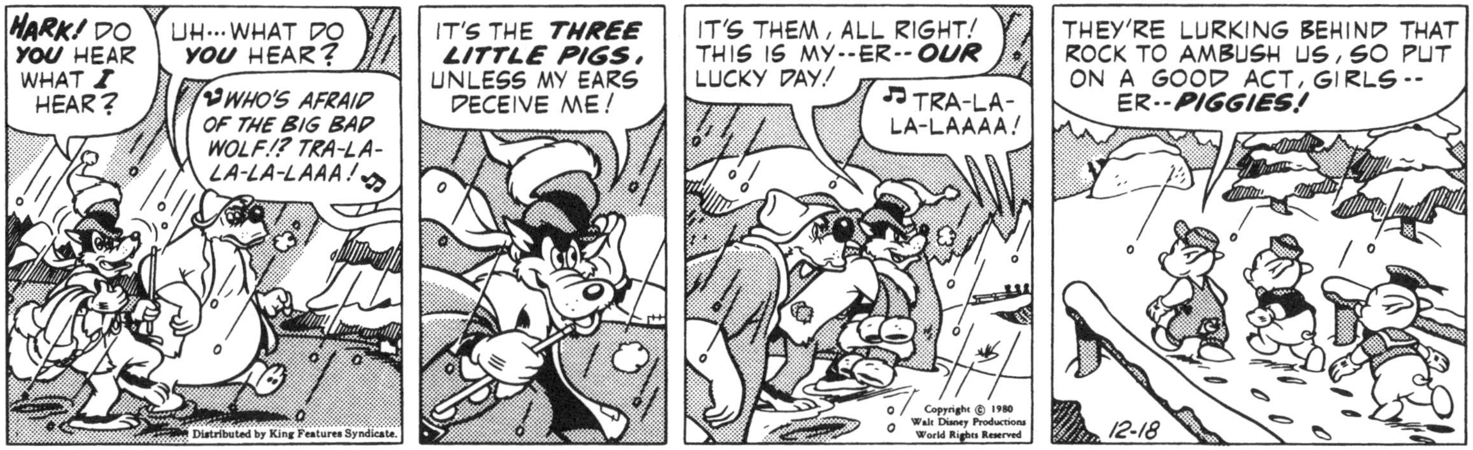
HARK! DO YOU HEAR WHAT I HEAR?
UH...WHAT DO YOU HEAR?
WHO'S AFRAID OF THE BIG BAD WOLF!? TRA-LA-LA-LA-LAAA!
IT'S THE THREE LITTLE PIGS, UNLESS MY EARS DECEIVE ME!
IT'S THEM, ALL RIGHT! THIS IS MY--ER--OUR LUCKY DAY!
TRA-LA-LA-LAAAA!
THEY'RE LURKING BEHIND THAT ROCK TO AMBUSH US, SO PUT ON A GOOD ACT, GIRLS--ER--PIGGIES!
12-18
Distributed by King Features Syndicate.
Copyright © 1980 Walt Disney Productions World Rights Reserved

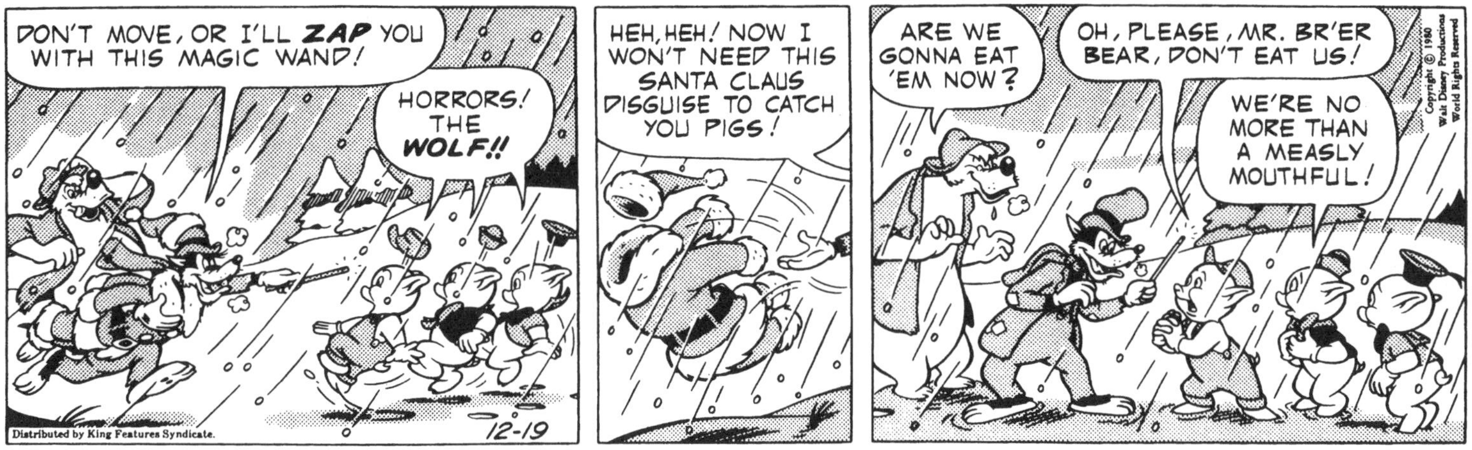
DON'T MOVE, OR I'LL ZAP YOU WITH THIS MAGIC WAND!
HORRORS! THE WOLF!!
HEH, HEH! NOW I WON'T NEED THIS SANTA CLAUS DISGUISE TO CATCH YOU PIGS!
ARE WE GONNA EAT 'EM NOW?
OH, PLEASE, MR. BR'ER BEAR, DON'T EAT US!
WE'RE NO MORE THAN A MEASLY MOUTHFUL!
12-19
Distributed by King Features Syndicate.
Copyright © 1980 Walt Disney Productions World Rights Reserved

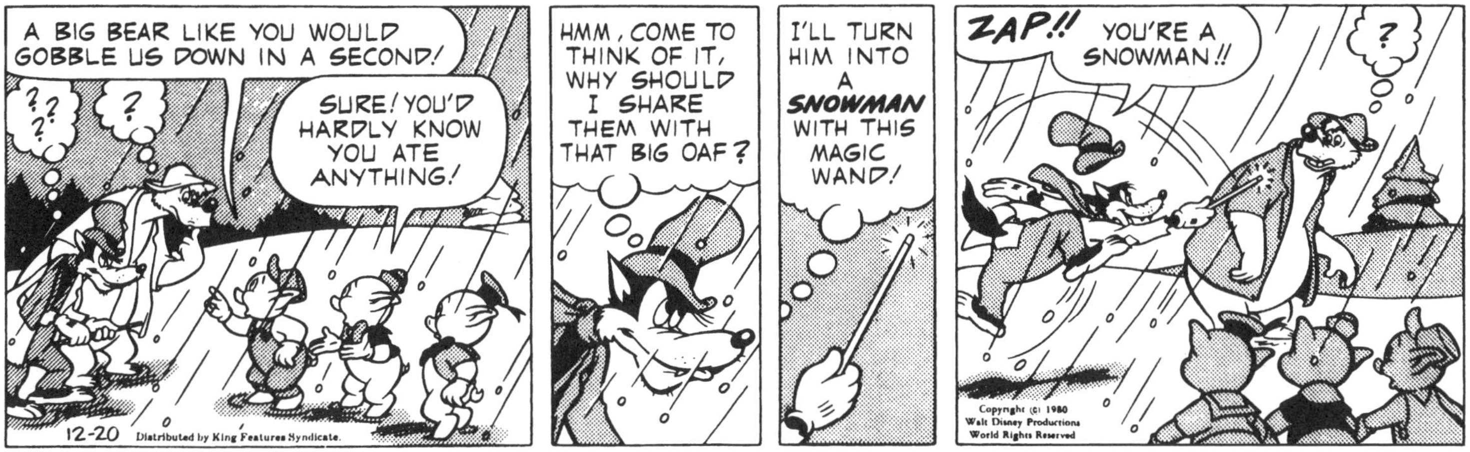
A BIG BEAR LIKE YOU WOULD GOBBLE US DOWN IN A SECOND!
SURE! YOU'D HARDLY KNOW YOU ATE ANYTHING!
HMM, COME TO THINK OF IT, WHY SHOULD I SHARE THEM WITH THAT BIG OAF?
I'LL TURN HIM INTO A SNOWMAN WITH THIS MAGIC WAND!
ZAP!!
YOU'RE A SNOWMAN!!
12-20
Distributed by King Features Syndicate.
Copyright © 1980 Walt Disney Productions World Rights Reserved

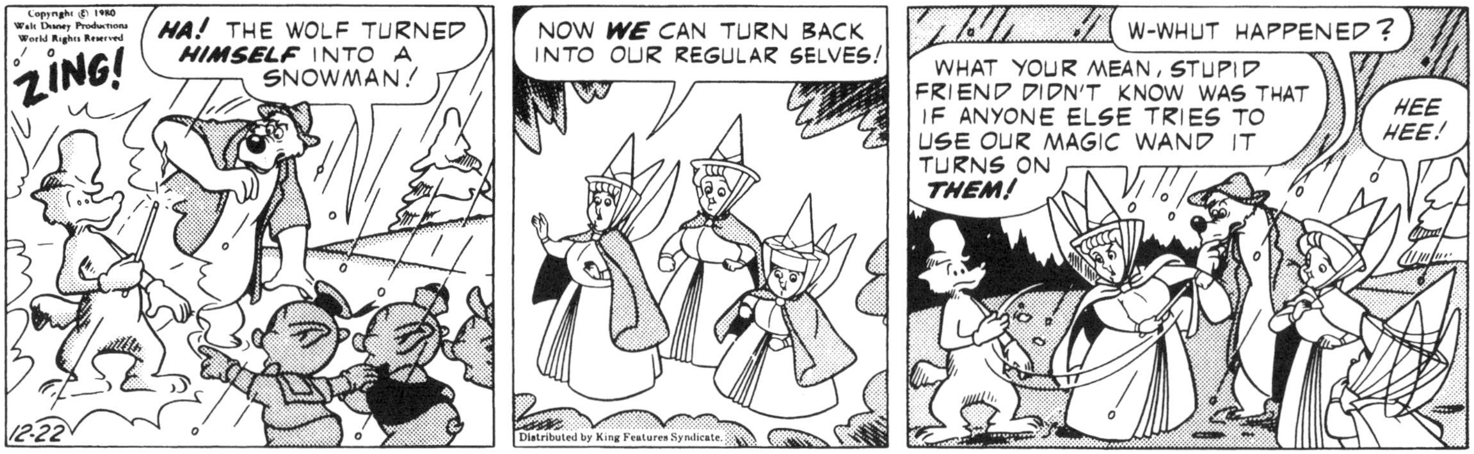
Copyright © 1980 Walt Disney Productions World Rights Reserved
ZING!
HA! THE WOLF TURNED HIMSELF INTO A SNOWMAN!
12-22
NOW WE CAN TURN BACK INTO OUR REGULAR SELVES!
Distributed by King Features Syndicate.
W-WHUT HAPPENED?
WHAT YOUR MEAN, STUPID FRIEND DIDN'T KNOW WAS THAT IF ANYONE ELSE TRIES TO USE OUR MAGIC WAND IT TURNS ON THEM!
HEE HEE!

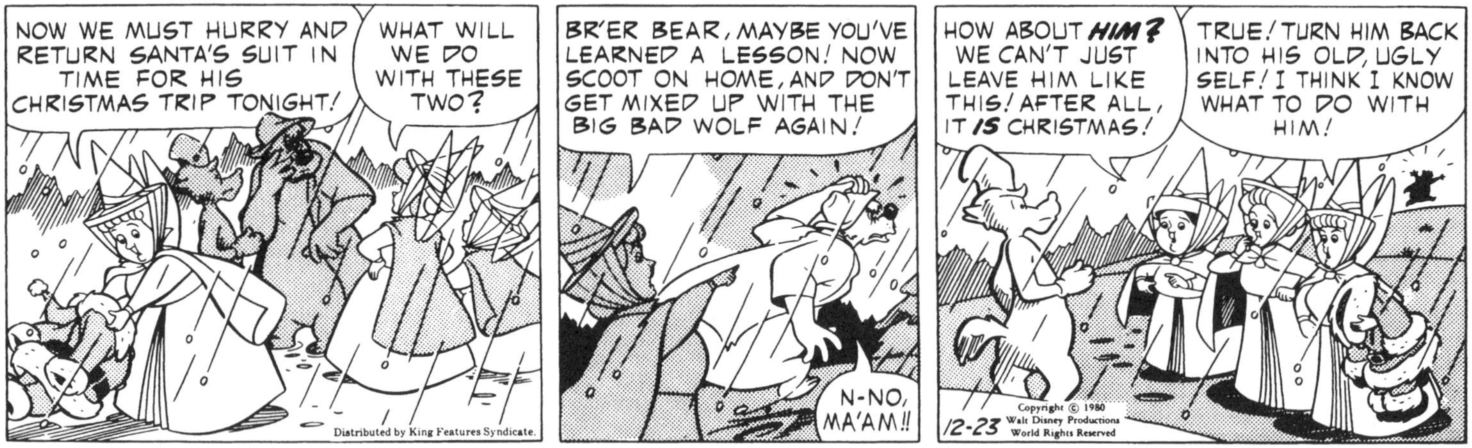
NOW WE MUST HURRY AND RETURN SANTA'S SUIT IN TIME FOR HIS CHRISTMAS TRIP TONIGHT!
WHAT WILL WE DO WITH THESE TWO?
Distributed by King Features Syndicate.
BR'ER BEAR, MAYBE YOU'VE LEARNED A LESSON! NOW SCOOT ON HOME, AND DON'T GET MIXED UP WITH THE BIG BAD WOLF AGAIN!
N-NO, MA'AM!!
HOW ABOUT HIM? WE CAN'T JUST LEAVE HIM LIKE THIS! AFTER ALL, IT IS CHRISTMAS!
TRUE! TURN HIM BACK INTO HIS OLD, UGLY SELF! I THINK I KNOW WHAT TO DO WITH HIM!
12-23
Copyright © 1980 Walt Disney Productions World Rights Reserved

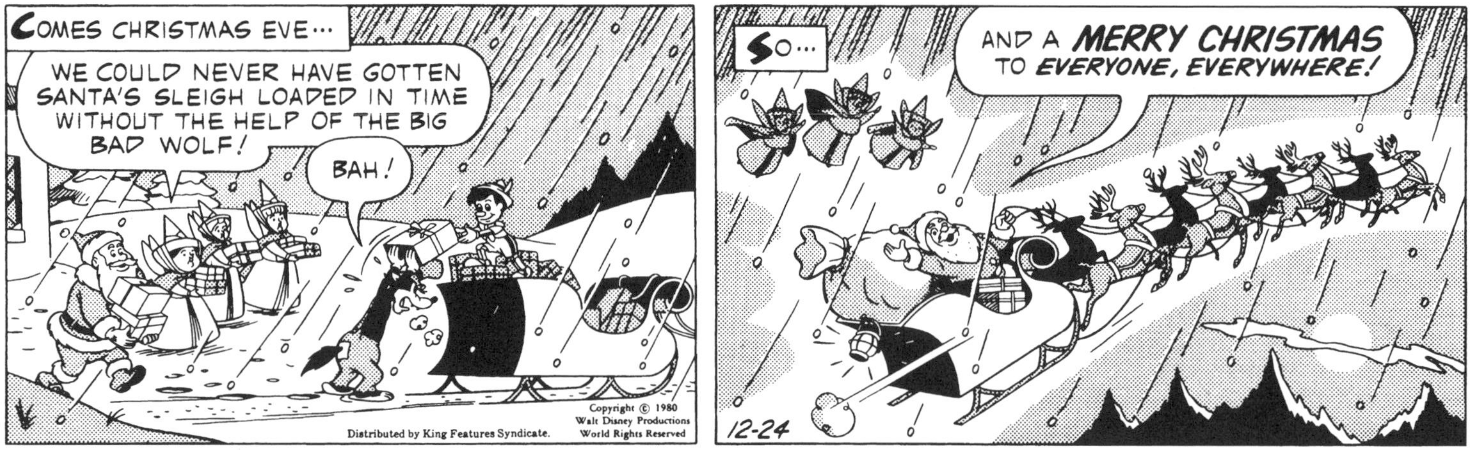
COMES CHRISTMAS EVE...
WE COULD NEVER HAVE GOTTEN SANTA'S SLEIGH LOADED IN TIME WITHOUT THE HELP OF THE BIG BAD WOLF!
BAH!
Distributed by King Features Syndicate.
Copyright © 1980 Walt Disney Productions World Rights Reserved
SO...
AND A MERRY CHRISTMAS TO EVERYONE, EVERYWHERE!
12-24

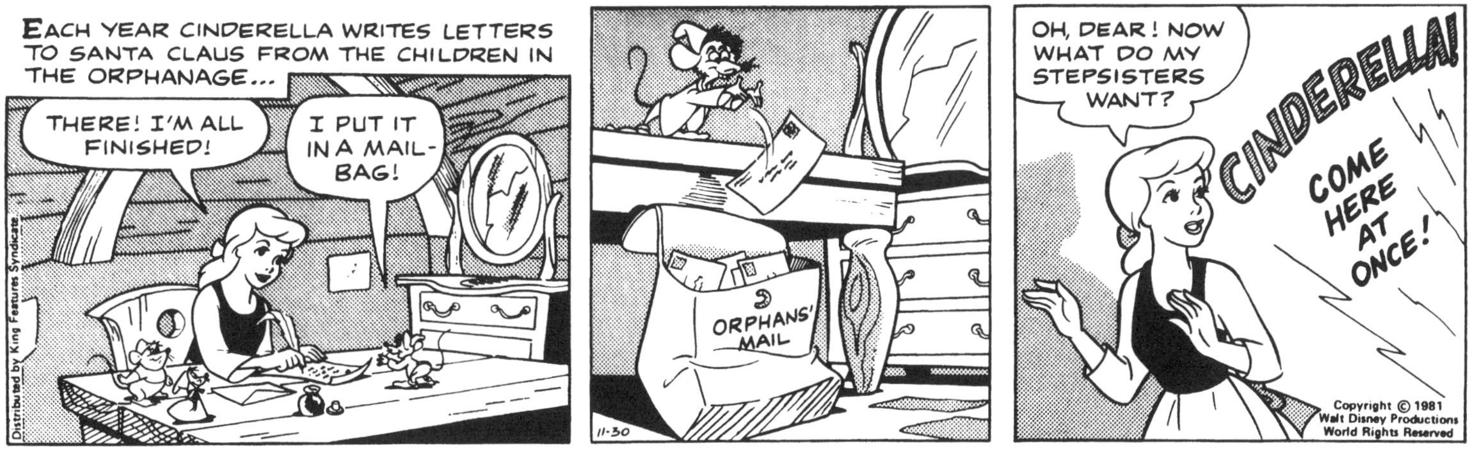
EACH YEAR CINDERELLA WRITES LETTERS TO SANTA CLAUS FROM THE CHILDREN IN THE ORPHANAGE...
THERE! I'M ALL FINISHED!
I PUT IT IN A MAIL-BAG!
ORPHANS' MAIL
OH, DEAR! NOW WHAT DO MY STEPSISTERS WANT?
CINDERELLA!
COME HERE AT ONCE!
Distributed by King Features Syndicate.
11-30
Copyright © 1981 Walt Disney Productions World Rights Reserved

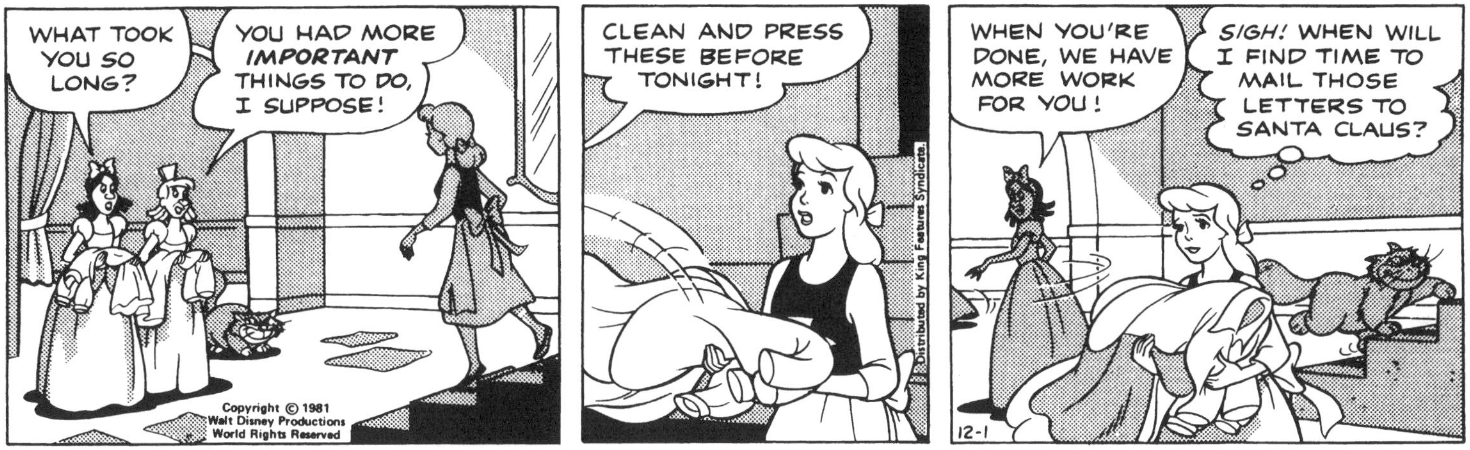
WHAT TOOK YOU SO LONG?
YOU HAD MORE IMPORTANT THINGS TO DO, I SUPPOSE!
Copyright © 1981 Walt Disney Productions World Rights Reserved
CLEAN AND PRESS THESE BEFORE TONIGHT!
Distributed by King Features Syndicate.
WHEN YOU'RE DONE, WE HAVE MORE WORK FOR YOU!
SIGH! WHEN WILL I FIND TIME TO MAIL THOSE LETTERS TO SANTA CLAUS?
12-1

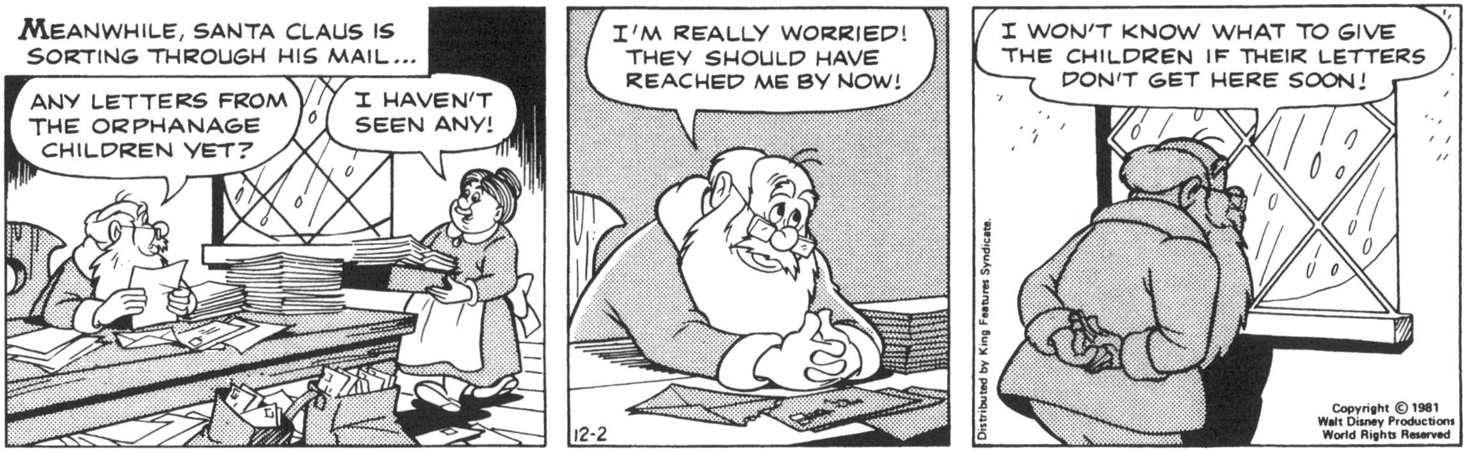
MEANWHILE, SANTA CLAUS IS SORTING THROUGH HIS MAIL...
ANY LETTERS FROM THE ORPHANAGE CHILDREN YET?
I HAVEN'T SEEN ANY!
I'M REALLY WORRIED! THEY SHOULD HAVE REACHED ME BY NOW!
12-2
Distributed by King Features Syndicate.
I WON'T KNOW WHAT TO GIVE THE CHILDREN IF THEIR LETTERS DON'T GET HERE SOON!
Copyright © 1981 Walt Disney Productions World Rights Reserved

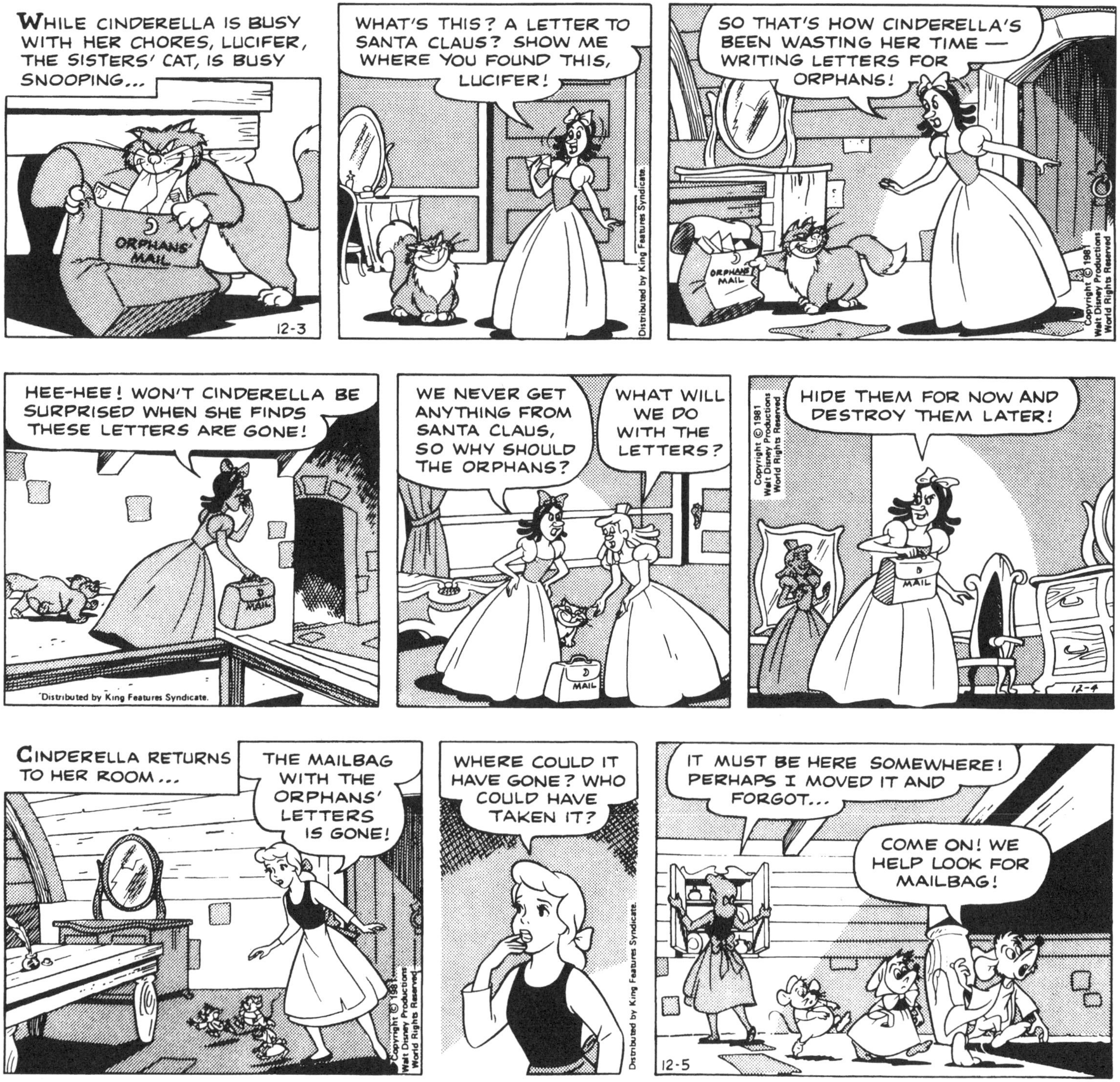

WHILE CINDERELLA IS BUSY WITH HER CHORES, LUCIFER, THE SISTERS' CAT, IS BUSY SNOOPING...
ORPHANS' MAIL
12-3
WHAT'S THIS? A LETTER TO SANTA CLAUS? SHOW ME WHERE YOU FOUND THIS, LUCIFER!
Distributed by King Features Syndicate.
SO THAT'S HOW CINDERELLA'S BEEN WASTING HER TIME — WRITING LETTERS FOR ORPHANS!
ORPHANS' MAIL
Copyright © 1981 Walt Disney Productions World Rights Reserved
HEE-HEE! WON'T CINDERELLA BE SURPRISED WHEN SHE FINDS THESE LETTERS ARE GONE!
MAIL
Distributed by King Features Syndicate.
WE NEVER GET ANYTHING FROM SANTA CLAUS, SO WHY SHOULD THE ORPHANS?
WHAT WILL WE DO WITH THE LETTERS?
MAIL
Copyright © 1981 Walt Disney Productions World Rights Reserved
HIDE THEM FOR NOW AND DESTROY THEM LATER!
MAIL
12-4
CINDERELLA RETURNS TO HER ROOM...
THE MAILBAG WITH THE ORPHANS' LETTERS IS GONE!
Copyright © 1981 Walt Disney Productions World Rights Reserved
WHERE COULD IT HAVE GONE? WHO COULD HAVE TAKEN IT?
Distributed by King Features Syndicate.
IT MUST BE HERE SOMEWHERE! PERHAPS I MOVED IT AND FORGOT...
COME ON! WE HELP LOOK FOR MAILBAG!
12-5

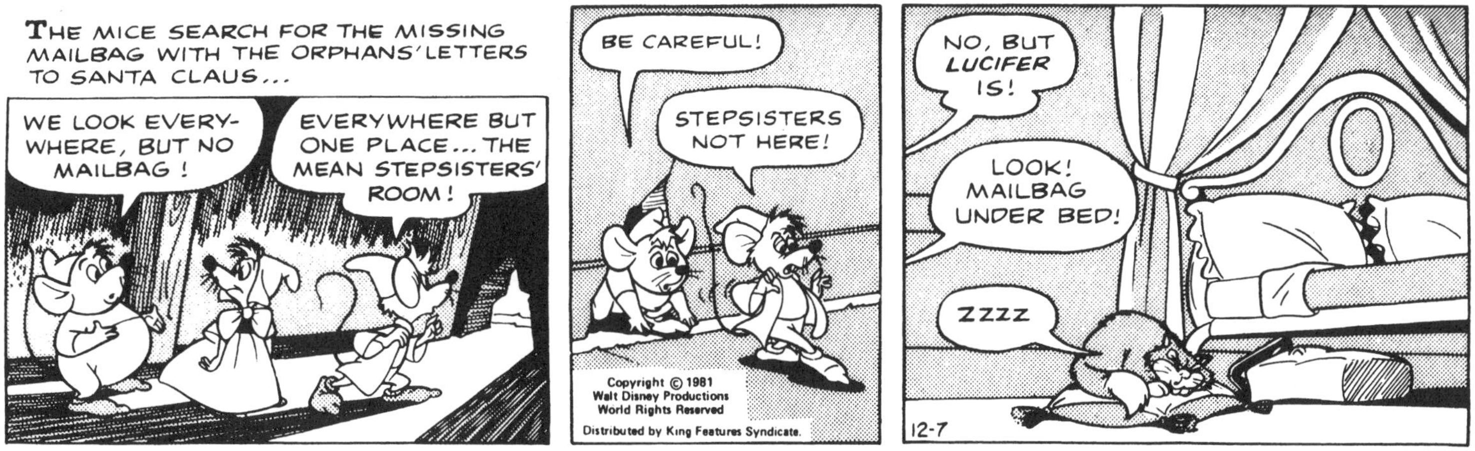
THE MICE SEARCH FOR THE MISSING MAILBAG WITH THE ORPHANS' LETTERS TO SANTA CLAUS...
WE LOOK EVERYWHERE, BUT NO MAILBAG !
EVERYWHERE BUT ONE PLACE... THE MEAN STEPSISTERS' ROOM !
BE CAREFUL!
STEPSISTERS NOT HERE!
Copyright © 1981 Walt Disney Productions World Rights Reserved
Distributed by King Features Syndicate.
NO, BUT LUCIFER IS!
LOOK! MAILBAG UNDER BED!
ZZZZ
12-7

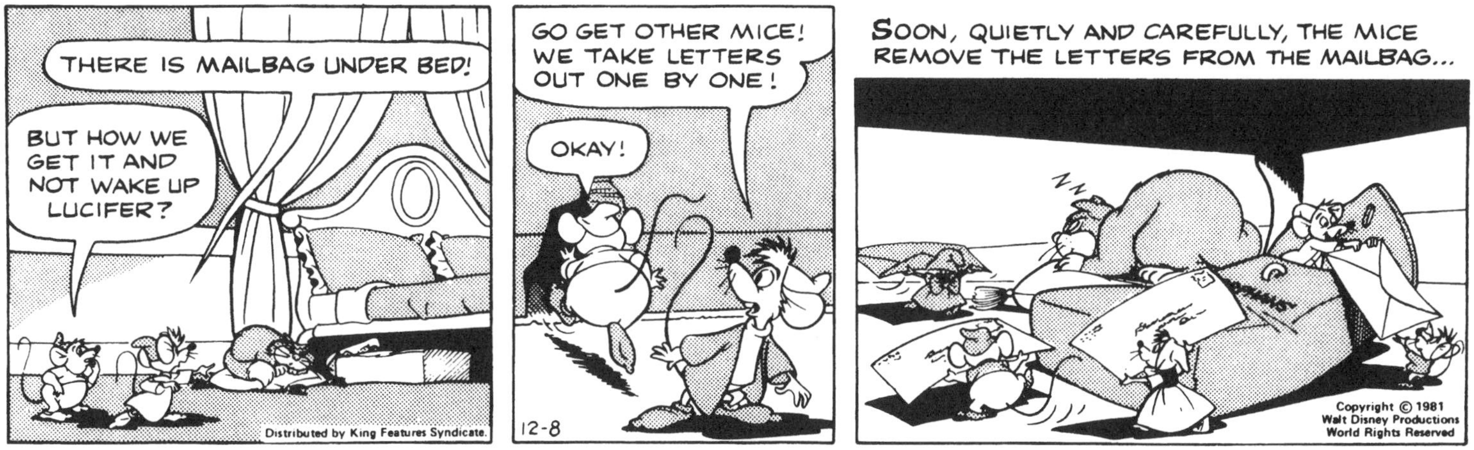
THERE IS MAILBAG UNDER BED!
BUT HOW WE GET IT AND NOT WAKE UP LUCIFER?
Distributed by King Features Syndicate.
GO GET OTHER MICE! WE TAKE LETTERS OUT ONE BY ONE!
OKAY!
12-8
SOON, QUIETLY AND CAREFULLY, THE MICE REMOVE THE LETTERS FROM THE MAILBAG...
Copyright © 1981 Walt Disney Productions World Rights Reserved

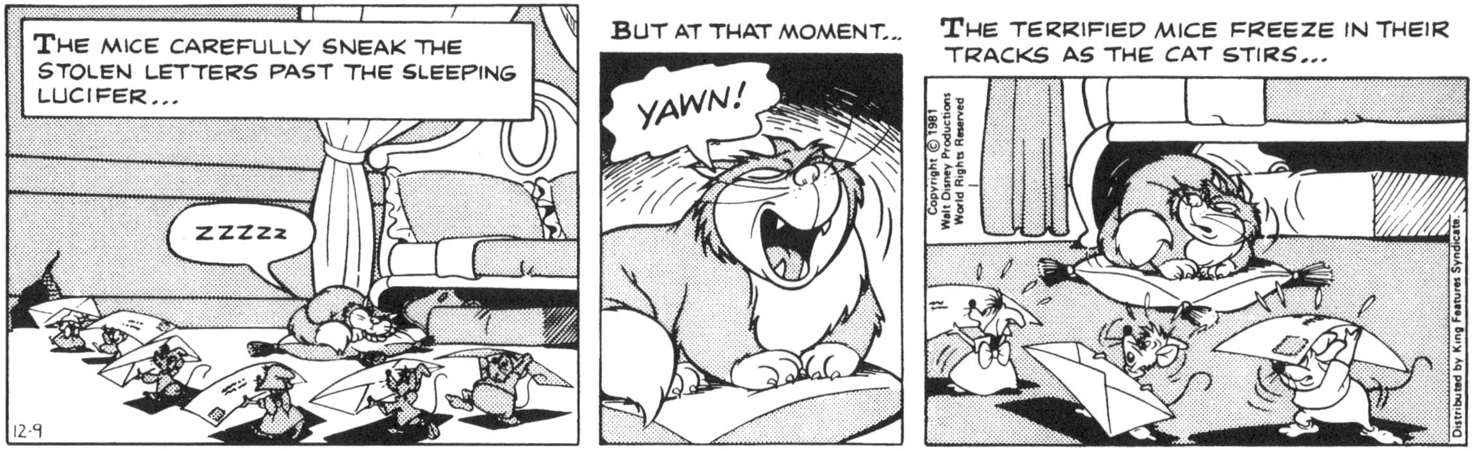
THE MICE CAREFULLY SNEAK THE STOLEN LETTERS PAST THE SLEEPING LUCIFER...
ZZZZz
12-9
BUT AT THAT MOMENT...
YAWN!
THE TERRIFIED MICE FREEZE IN THEIR TRACKS AS THE CAT STIRS...
Copyright © 1981 Walt Disney Productions World Rights Reserved
Distributed by King Features Syndicate.

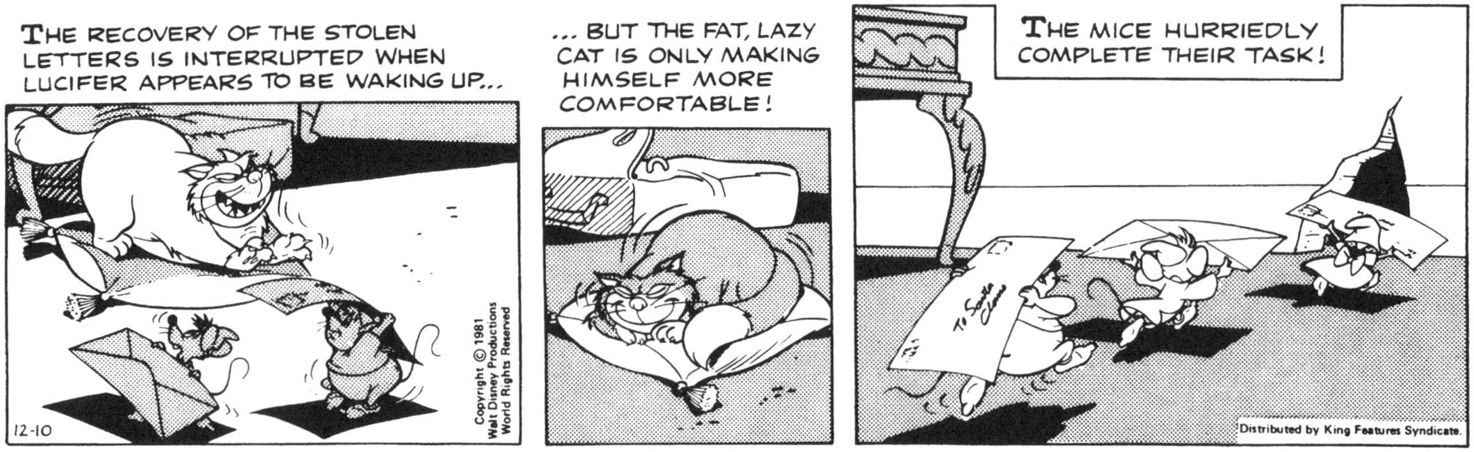
THE RECOVERY OF THE STOLEN LETTERS IS INTERRUPTED WHEN LUCIFER APPEARS TO BE WAKING UP...
... BUT THE FAT, LAZY CAT IS ONLY MAKING HIMSELF MORE COMFORTABLE!
THE MICE HURRIEDLY COMPLETE THEIR TASK!
To Santa Claus
12-10
Copyright © 1981 Walt Disney Productions World Rights Reserved
Distributed by King Features Syndicate.

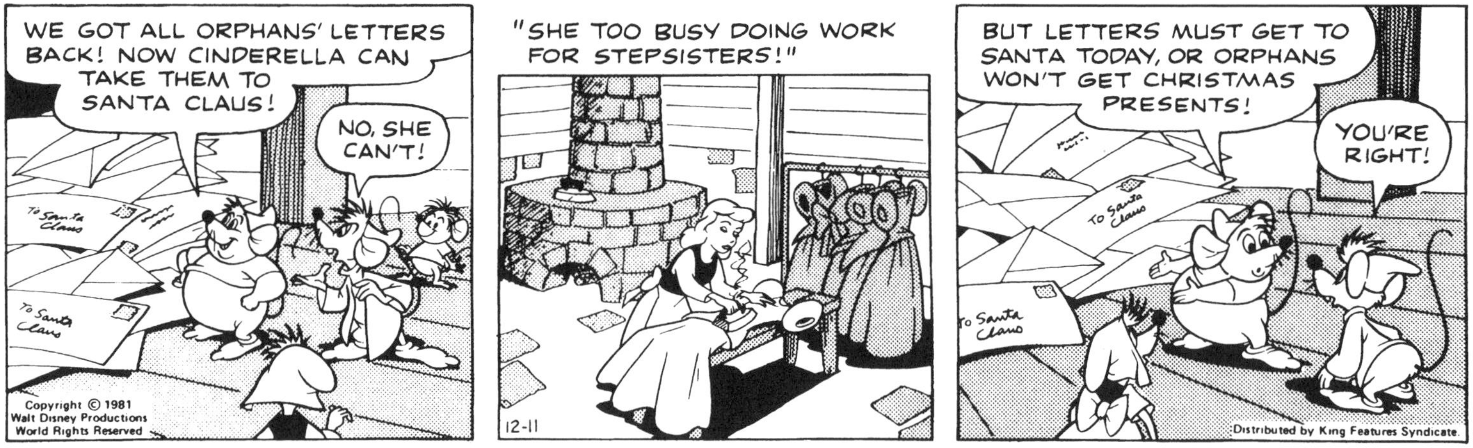
WE GOT ALL ORPHANS' LETTERS BACK! NOW CINDERELLA CAN TAKE THEM TO SANTA CLAUS!
NO, SHE CAN'T!
To Santa Claus
To Santa Claus
"SHE TOO BUSY DOING WORK FOR STEPSISTERS!"
BUT LETTERS MUST GET TO SANTA TODAY, OR ORPHANS WON'T GET CHRISTMAS PRESENTS!
YOU'RE RIGHT!
To Santa Claus
To Santa Claus
Copyright © 1981 Walt Disney Productions World Rights Reserved
12-11
Distributed by King Features Syndicate.

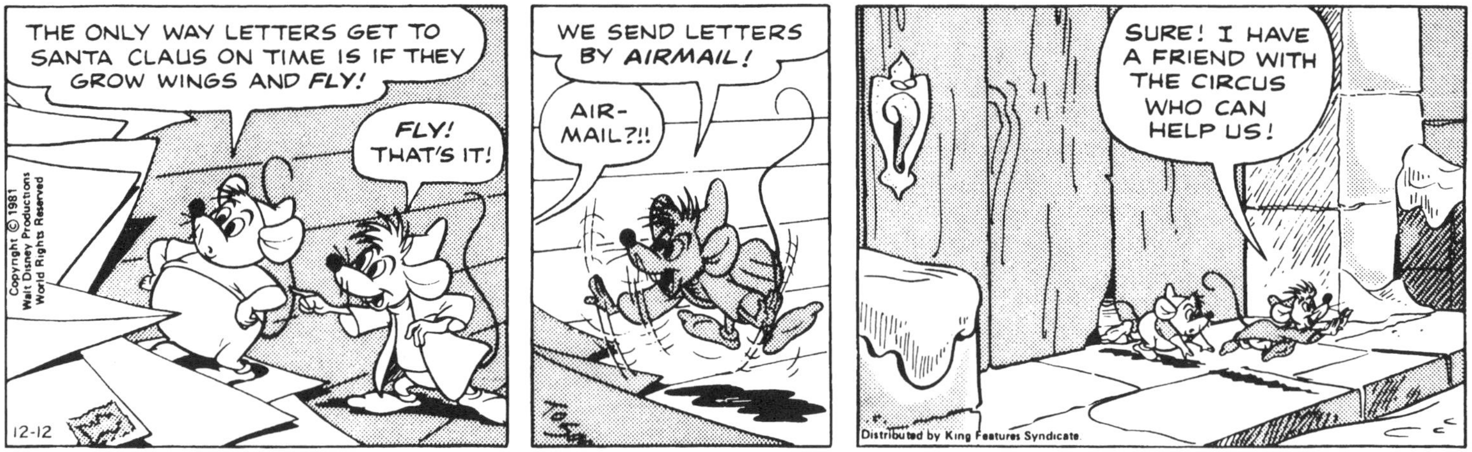
THE ONLY WAY LETTERS GET TO SANTA CLAUS ON TIME IS IF THEY GROW WINGS AND FLY!
FLY! THAT'S IT!
WE SEND LETTERS BY AIRMAIL!
AIR-MAIL?!!
SURE! I HAVE A FRIEND WITH THE CIRCUS WHO CAN HELP US!
Copyright © 1981 Walt Disney Productions World Rights Reserved
12-12
Distributed by King Features Syndicate.

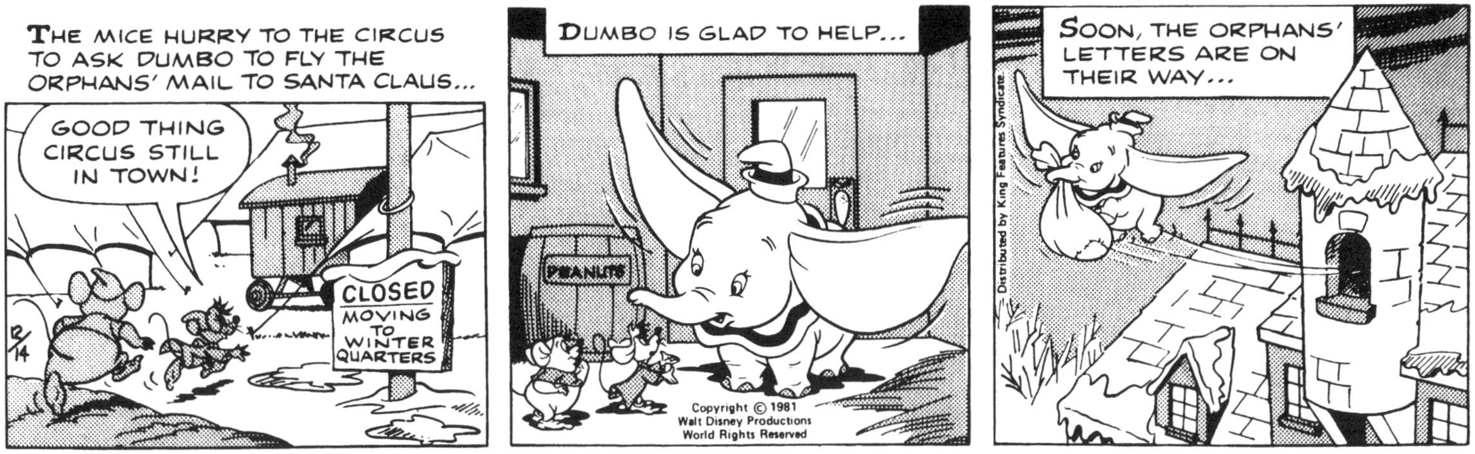
THE MICE HURRY TO THE CIRCUS TO ASK DUMBO TO FLY THE ORPHANS' MAIL TO SANTA CLAUS...
GOOD THING CIRCUS STILL IN TOWN!
CLOSED
MOVING TO WINTER QUARTERS
12/14
DUMBO IS GLAD TO HELP...
PEANUTS
Copyright © 1981
Walt Disney Productions
World Rights Reserved
SOON, THE ORPHANS' LETTERS ARE ON THEIR WAY...
Distributed by King Features Syndicate.

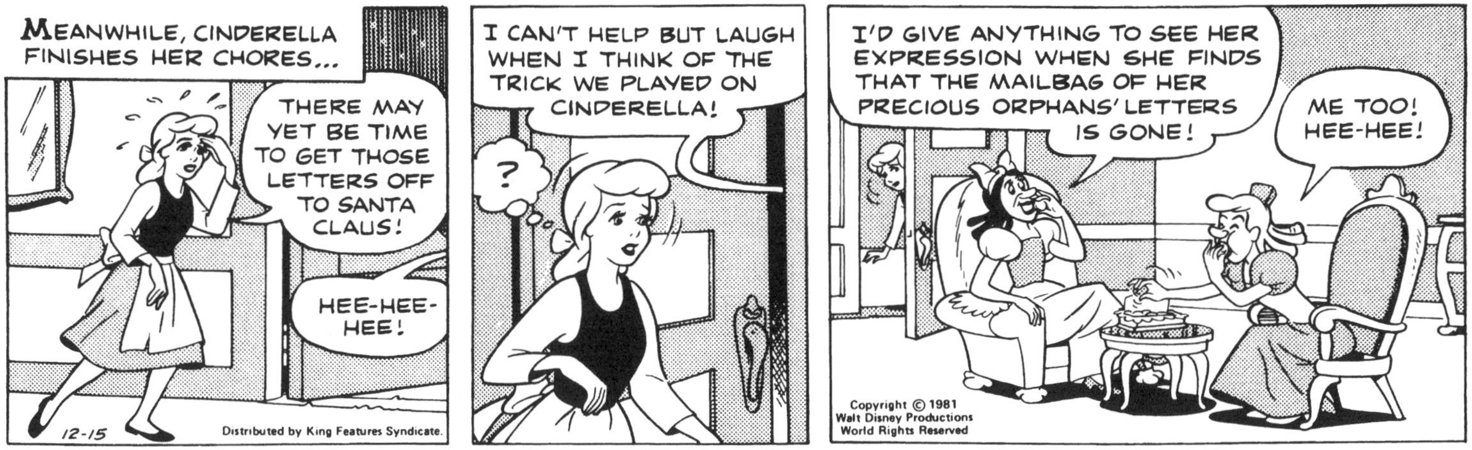
MEANWHILE, CINDERELLA FINISHES HER CHORES...
THERE MAY YET BE TIME TO GET THOSE LETTERS OFF TO SANTA CLAUS!
HEE-HEE-HEE!
12-15
Distributed by King Features Syndicate.
I CAN'T HELP BUT LAUGH WHEN I THINK OF THE TRICK WE PLAYED ON CINDERELLA!
?
I'D GIVE ANYTHING TO SEE HER EXPRESSION WHEN SHE FINDS THAT THE MAILBAG OF HER PRECIOUS ORPHANS' LETTERS IS GONE!
ME TOO! HEE-HEE!
Copyright © 1981
Walt Disney Productions
World Rights Reserved

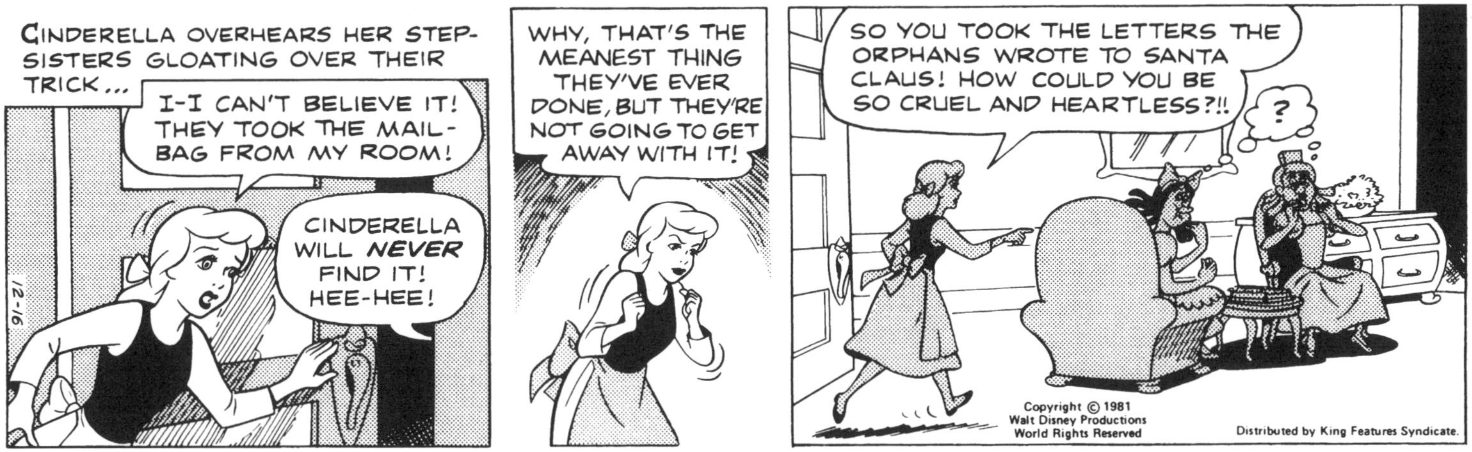
CINDERELLA OVERHEARS HER STEP-SISTERS GLOATING OVER THEIR TRICK...
I-I CAN'T BELIEVE IT! THEY TOOK THE MAIL-BAG FROM MY ROOM!
CINDERELLA WILL NEVER FIND IT! HEE-HEE!
12-16
WHY, THAT'S THE MEANEST THING THEY'VE EVER DONE, BUT THEY'RE NOT GOING TO GET AWAY WITH IT!
SO YOU TOOK THE LETTERS THE ORPHANS WROTE TO SANTA CLAUS! HOW COULD YOU BE SO CRUEL AND HEARTLESS?!!
?
Copyright © 1981
Walt Disney Productions
World Rights Reserved
Distributed by King Features Syndicate.

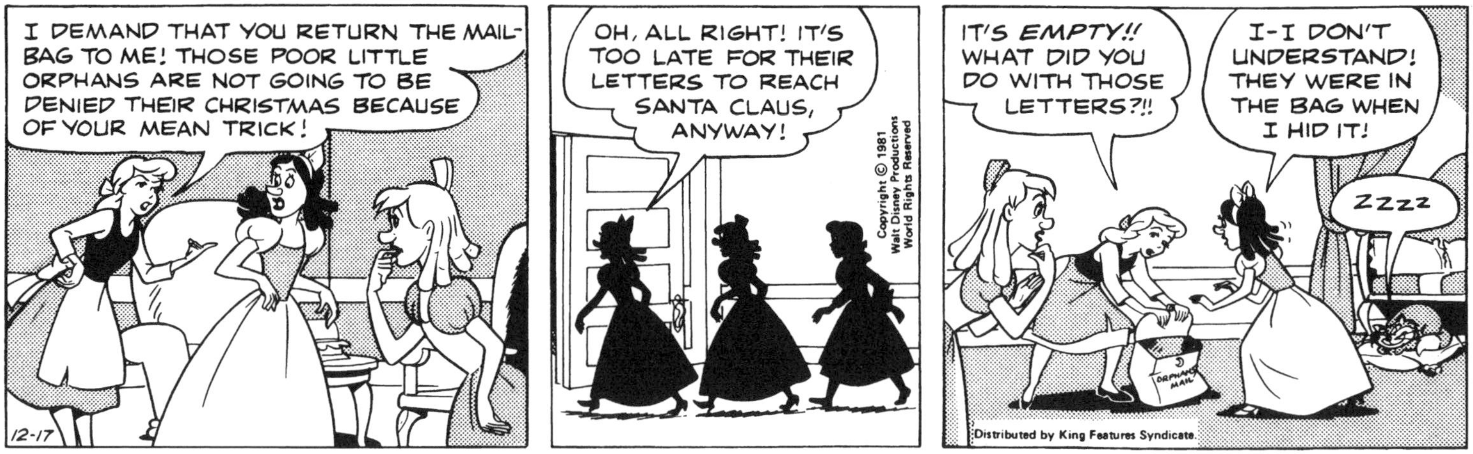
I DEMAND THAT YOU RETURN THE MAIL-BAG TO ME! THOSE POOR LITTLE ORPHANS ARE NOT GOING TO BE DENIED THEIR CHRISTMAS BECAUSE OF YOUR MEAN TRICK!
12-17
OH, ALL RIGHT! IT'S TOO LATE FOR THEIR LETTERS TO REACH SANTA CLAUS, ANYWAY!
Copyright © 1981 Walt Disney Productions World Rights Reserved
IT'S EMPTY!! WHAT DID YOU DO WITH THOSE LETTERS?!!
I-I DON'T UNDERSTAND! THEY WERE IN THE BAG WHEN I HID IT!
ZZZZ
ORPHANS MAIL
Distributed by King Features Syndicate.

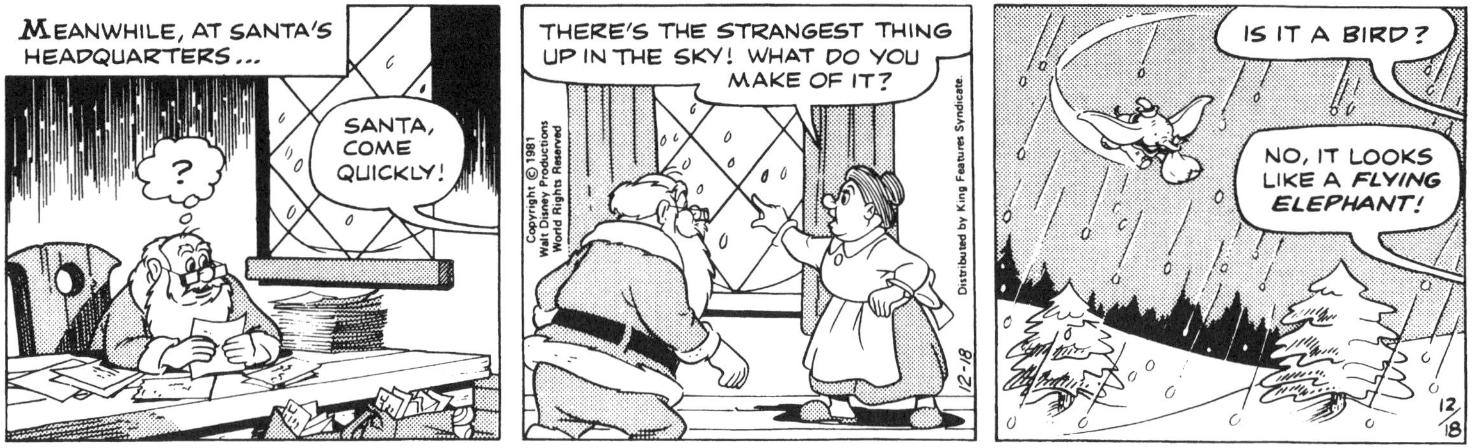
MEANWHILE, AT SANTA'S HEADQUARTERS...
?
SANTA, COME QUICKLY!
Copyright © 1981 Walt Disney Productions World Rights Reserved
THERE'S THE STRANGEST THING UP IN THE SKY! WHAT DO YOU MAKE OF IT?
Distributed by King Features Syndicate.
12-18
IS IT A BIRD?
NO, IT LOOKS LIKE A FLYING ELEPHANT!
12/18

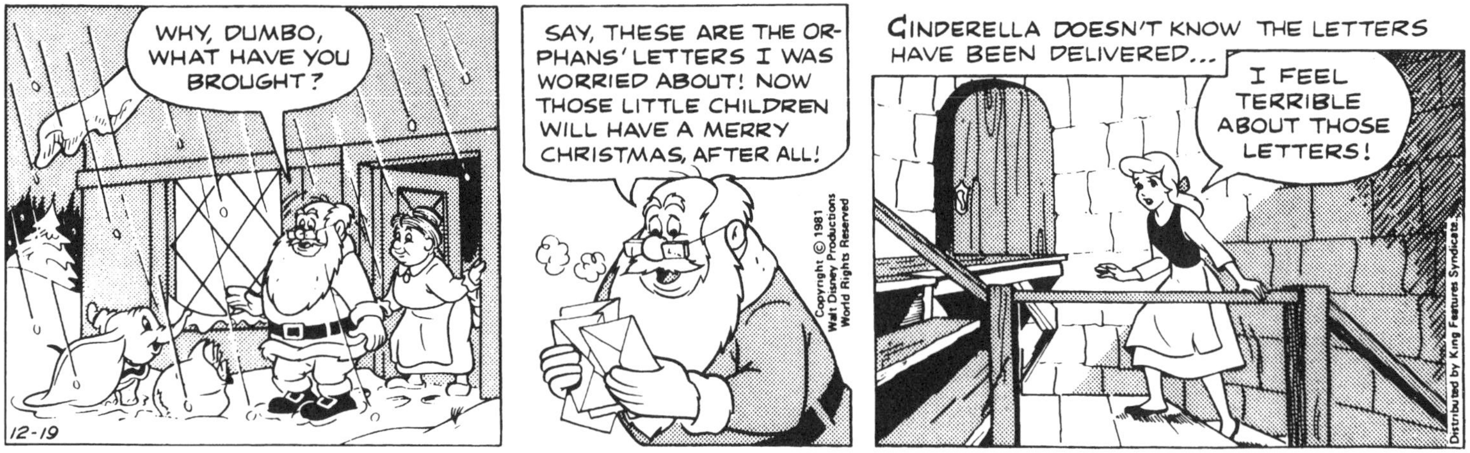
WHY, DUMBO, WHAT HAVE YOU BROUGHT?
12-19
SAY, THESE ARE THE ORPHANS' LETTERS I WAS WORRIED ABOUT! NOW THOSE LITTLE CHILDREN WILL HAVE A MERRY CHRISTMAS, AFTER ALL!
Copyright © 1981 Walt Disney Productions World Rights Reserved
CINDERELLA DOESN'T KNOW THE LETTERS HAVE BEEN DELIVERED...
I FEEL TERRIBLE ABOUT THOSE LETTERS!
Distributed by King Features Syndicate.

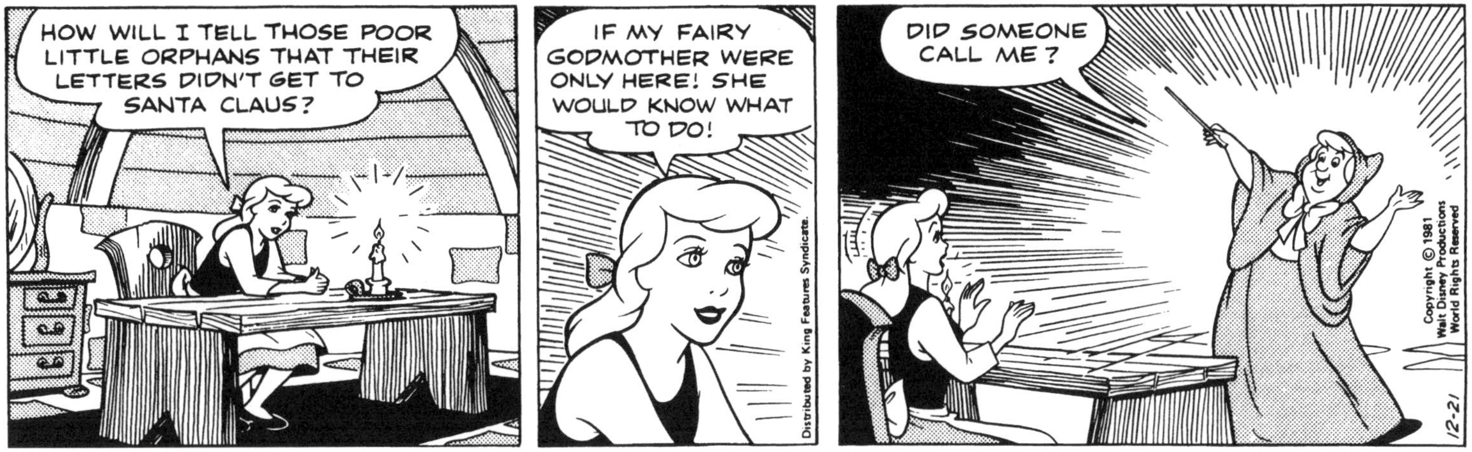
HOW WILL I TELL THOSE POOR LITTLE ORPHANS THAT THEIR LETTERS DIDN'T GET TO SANTA CLAUS?
IF MY FAIRY GODMOTHER WERE ONLY HERE! SHE WOULD KNOW WHAT TO DO!
Distributed by King Features Syndicate.
DID SOMEONE CALL ME?
Copyright © 1981 Walt Disney Productions World Rights Reserved
12-21

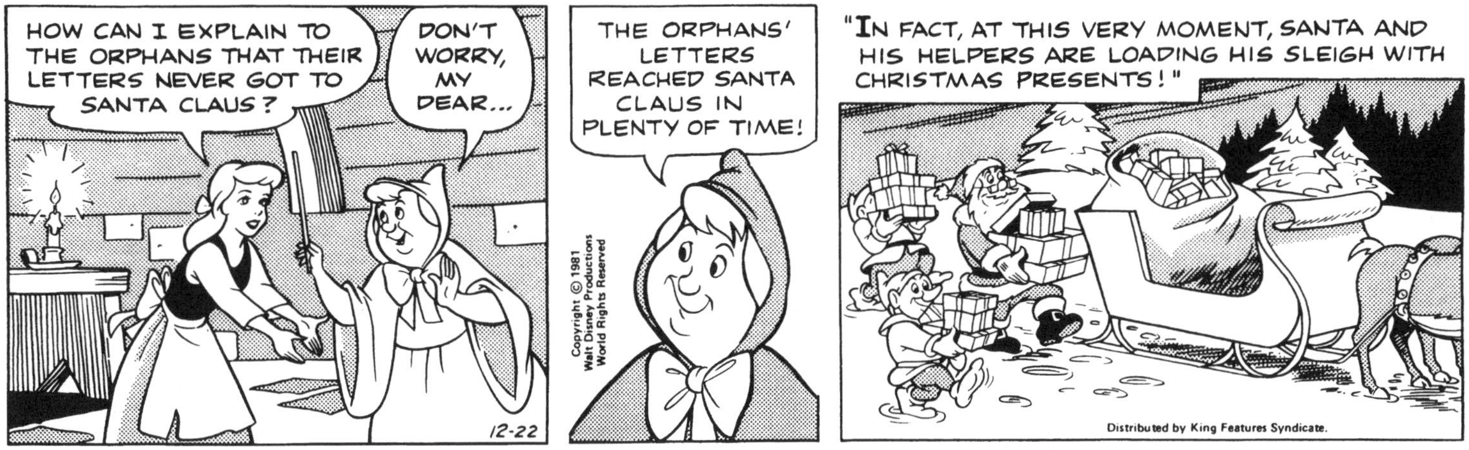
HOW CAN I EXPLAIN TO THE ORPHANS THAT THEIR LETTERS NEVER GOT TO SANTA CLAUS?
DON'T WORRY, MY DEAR...
12-22
THE ORPHANS' LETTERS REACHED SANTA CLAUS IN PLENTY OF TIME!
Copyright © 1981 Walt Disney Productions World Rights Reserved
"IN FACT, AT THIS VERY MOMENT, SANTA AND HIS HELPERS ARE LOADING HIS SLEIGH WITH CHRISTMAS PRESENTS!"
Distributed by King Features Syndicate.

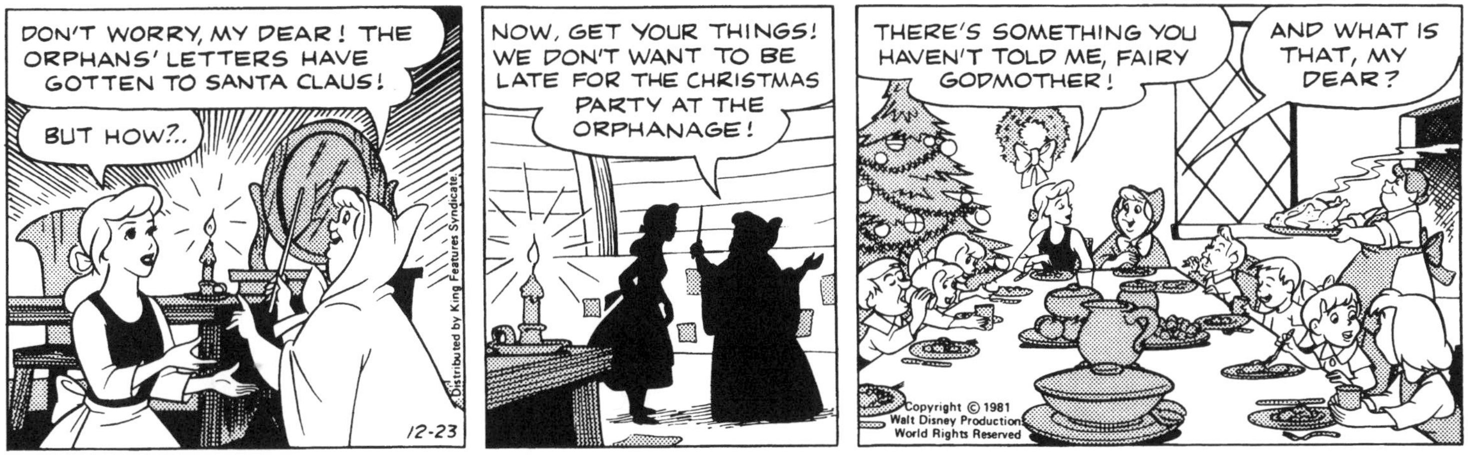
DON'T WORRY, MY DEAR! THE ORPHANS' LETTERS HAVE GOTTEN TO SANTA CLAUS!
BUT HOW?..
Distributed by King Features Syndicate.
12-23
NOW, GET YOUR THINGS! WE DON'T WANT TO BE LATE FOR THE CHRISTMAS PARTY AT THE ORPHANAGE!
THERE'S SOMETHING YOU HAVEN'T TOLD ME, FAIRY GODMOTHER!
AND WHAT IS THAT, MY DEAR?
Copyright © 1981 Walt Disney Productions World Rights Reserved

Distributed by King Features Syndicate.
HOW DID YOU KNOW THAT THE ORPHANS' LETTERS REACHED SANTA CLAUS?
WELL, LET'S JUST SAY...
...A *LITTLE MOUSE* TOLD ME!
12-24
Copyright © 1981 Walt Disney Productions World Rights Reserved
AND SO... A MERRY CHRISTMAS TO ALL!

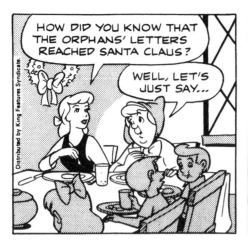

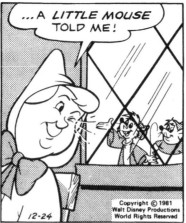

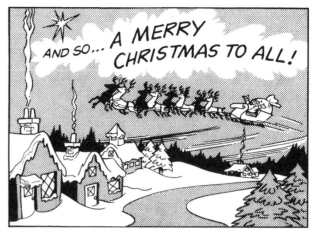

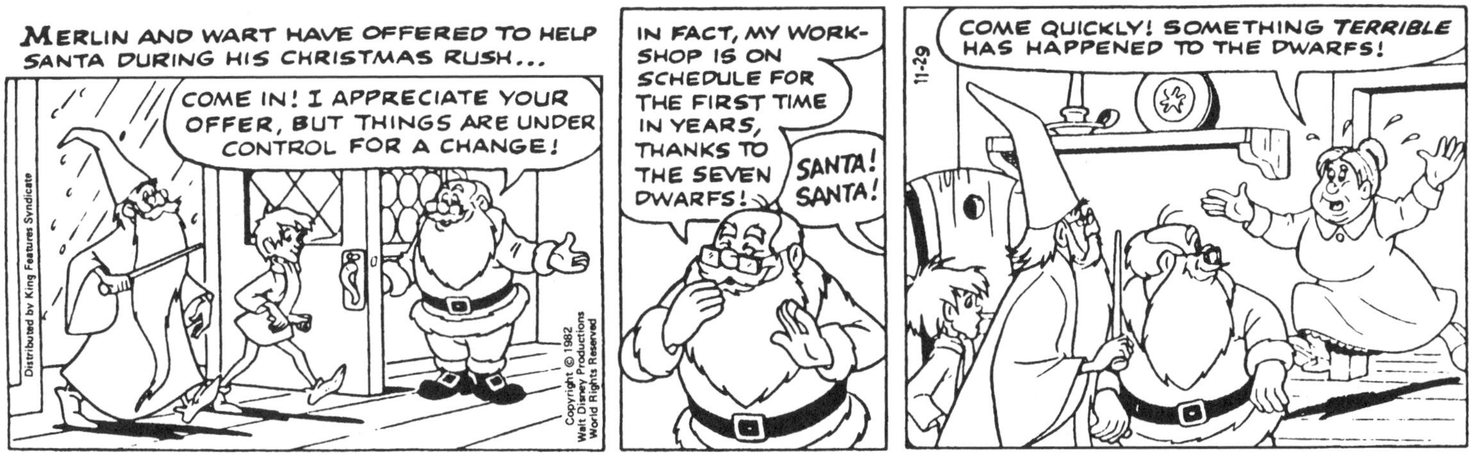
MERLIN AND WART HAVE OFFERED TO HELP SANTA DURING HIS CHRISTMAS RUSH...
COME IN! I APPRECIATE YOUR OFFER, BUT THINGS ARE UNDER CONTROL FOR A CHANGE!
Distributed by King Features Syndicate
Copyright © 1982 Walt Disney Productions World Rights Reserved
IN FACT, MY WORK-SHOP IS ON SCHEDULE FOR THE FIRST TIME IN YEARS, THANKS TO THE SEVEN DWARFS!
SANTA! SANTA!
11-29
COME QUICKLY! SOMETHING TERRIBLE HAS HAPPENED TO THE DWARFS!

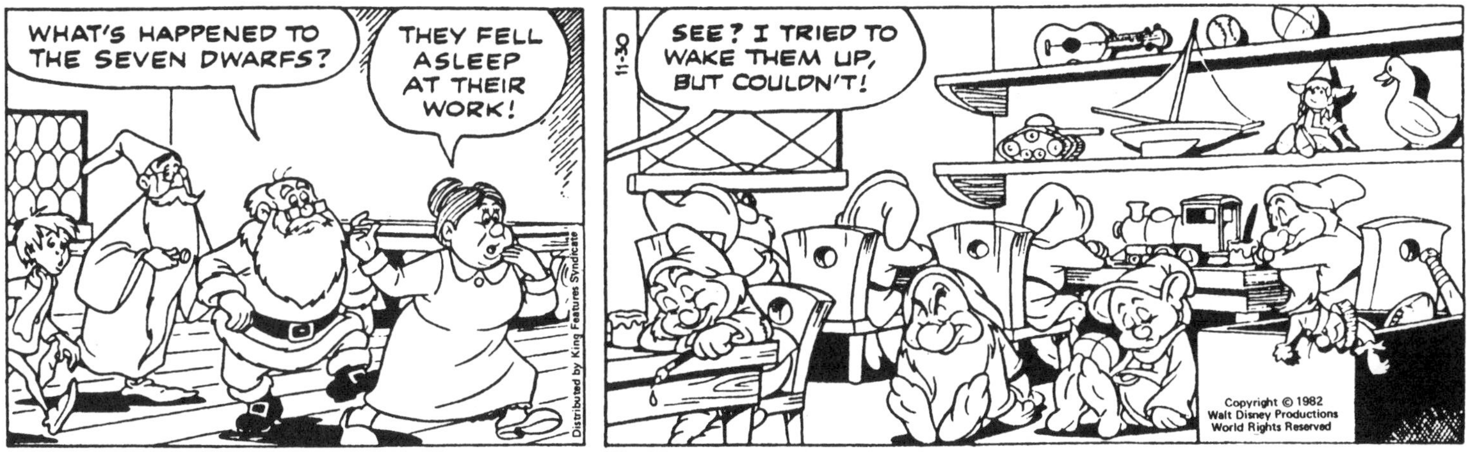
WHAT'S HAPPENED TO THE SEVEN DWARFS?
THEY FELL ASLEEP AT THEIR WORK!
Distributed by King Features Syndicate
11-30
SEE? I TRIED TO WAKE THEM UP, BUT COULDN'T!
Copyright © 1982 Walt Disney Productions World Rights Reserved

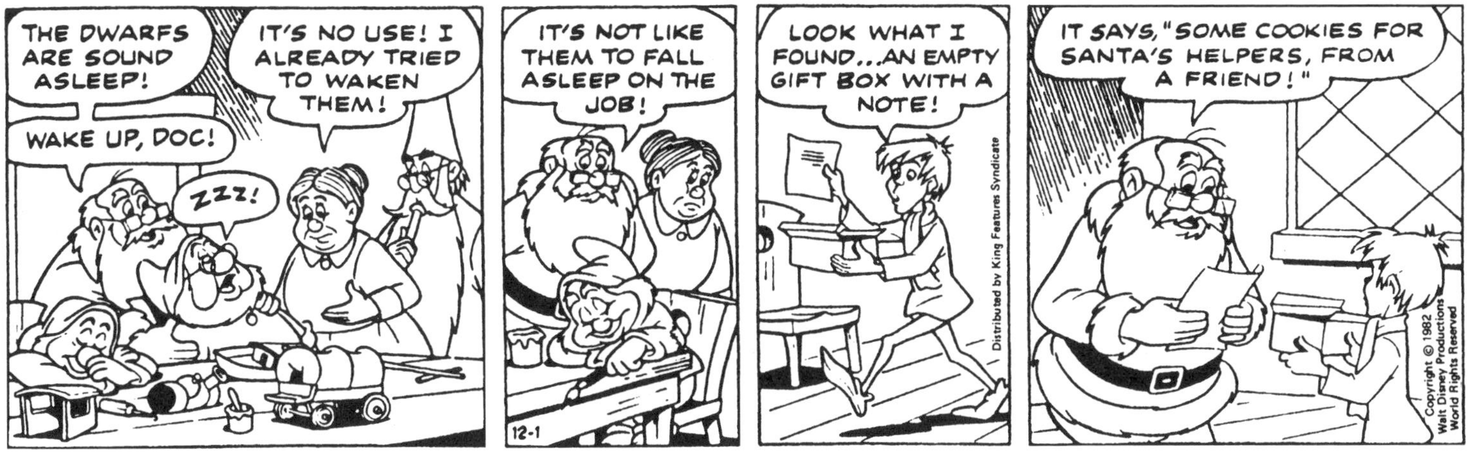
THE DWARFS ARE SOUND ASLEEP!
IT'S NO USE! I ALREADY TRIED TO WAKEN THEM!
WAKE UP, DOC!
ZZZ!
IT'S NOT LIKE THEM TO FALL ASLEEP ON THE JOB!
12-1
LOOK WHAT I FOUND...AN EMPTY GIFT BOX WITH A NOTE!
Distributed by King Features Syndicate
IT SAYS, "SOME COOKIES FOR SANTA'S HELPERS, FROM A FRIEND!"
Copyright © 1982 Walt Disney Productions World Rights Reserved

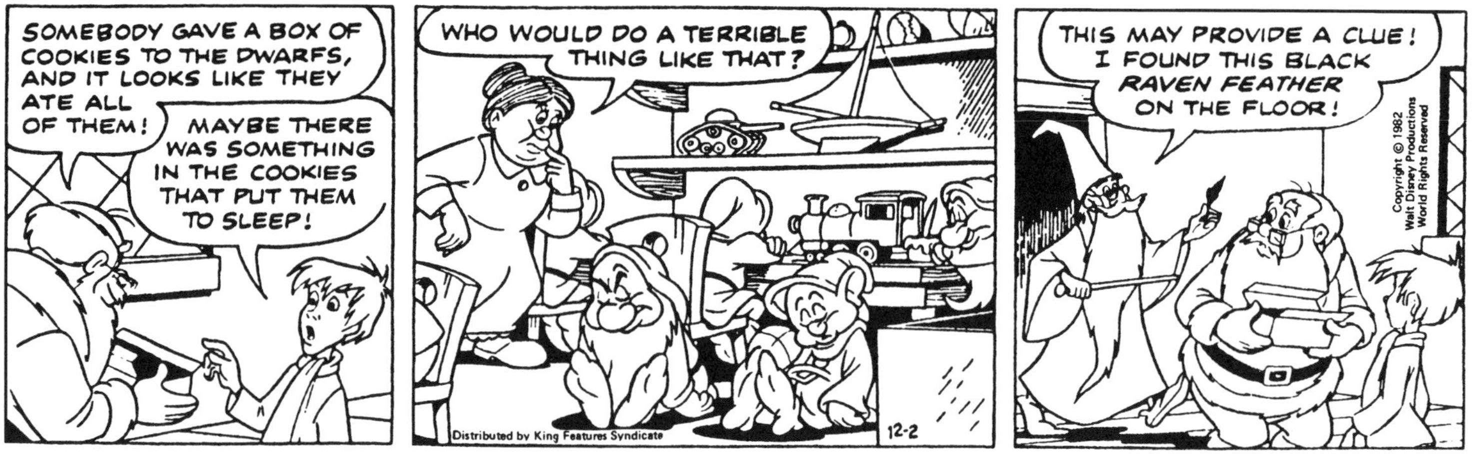
SOMEBODY GAVE A BOX OF COOKIES TO THE DWARFS, AND IT LOOKS LIKE THEY ATE ALL OF THEM!
MAYBE THERE WAS SOMETHING IN THE COOKIES THAT PUT THEM TO SLEEP!
WHO WOULD DO A TERRIBLE THING LIKE THAT?
Distributed by King Features Syndicate
12-2
THIS MAY PROVIDE A CLUE! I FOUND THIS BLACK *RAVEN FEATHER* ON THE FLOOR!
Copyright © 1982 Walt Disney Productions World Rights Reserved

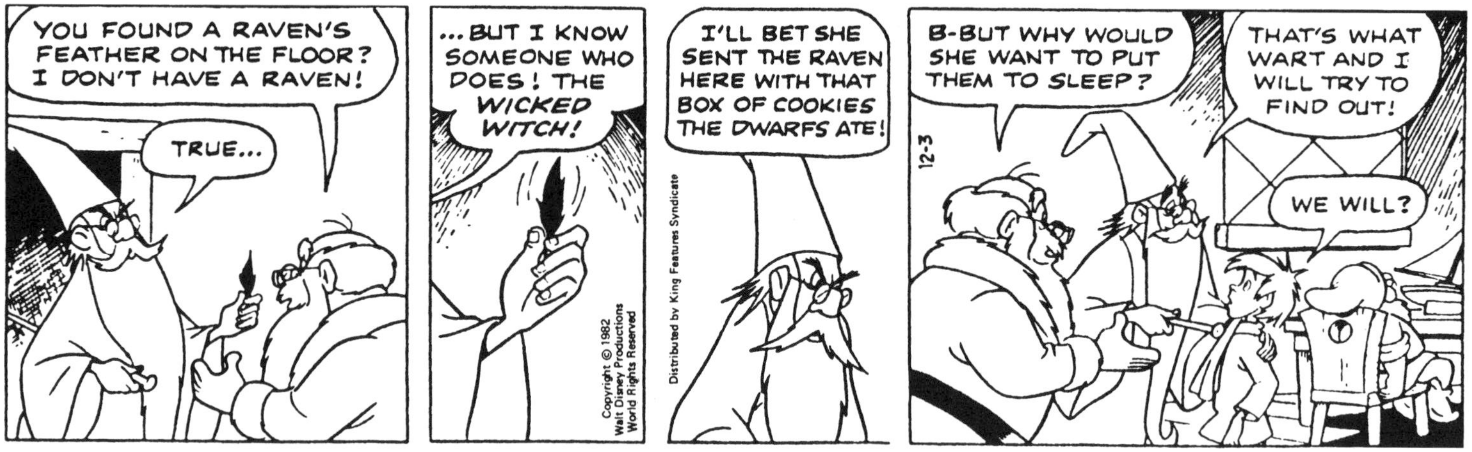
YOU FOUND A RAVEN'S FEATHER ON THE FLOOR? I DON'T HAVE A RAVEN!
TRUE...
...BUT I KNOW SOMEONE WHO DOES! THE *WICKED WITCH!*
Copyright © 1982 Walt Disney Productions World Rights Reserved
I'LL BET SHE SENT THE RAVEN HERE WITH THAT BOX OF COOKIES THE DWARFS ATE!
Distributed by King Features Syndicate
12-3
B-BUT WHY WOULD SHE WANT TO PUT THEM TO SLEEP?
THAT'S WHAT WART AND I WILL TRY TO FIND OUT!
WE WILL?

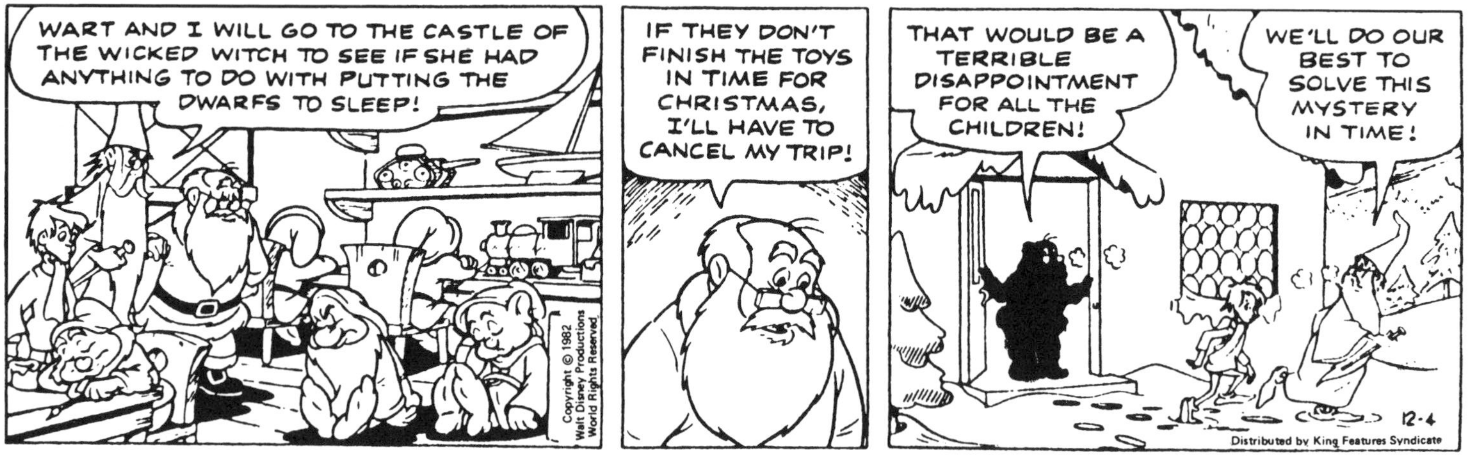
WART AND I WILL GO TO THE CASTLE OF THE WICKED WITCH TO SEE IF SHE HAD ANYTHING TO DO WITH PUTTING THE DWARFS TO SLEEP!
Copyright © 1982 Walt Disney Productions World Rights Reserved
IF THEY DON'T FINISH THE TOYS IN TIME FOR CHRISTMAS, I'LL HAVE TO CANCEL MY TRIP!
THAT WOULD BE A TERRIBLE DISAPPOINTMENT FOR ALL THE CHILDREN!
WE'LL DO OUR BEST TO SOLVE THIS MYSTERY IN TIME!
12-4
Distributed by King Features Syndicate

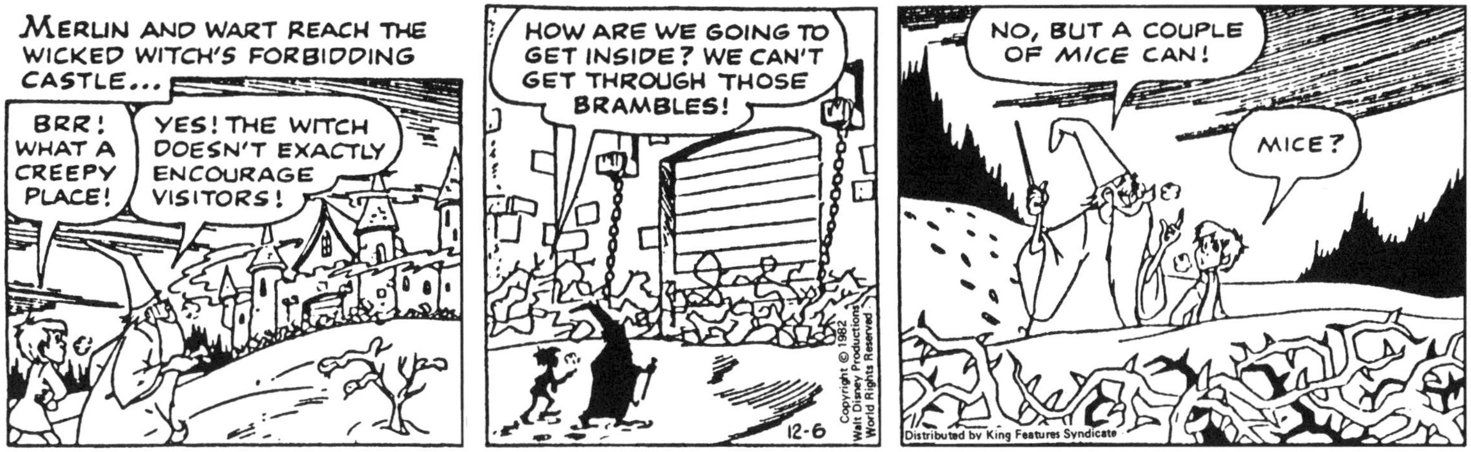
MERLIN AND WART REACH THE WICKED WITCH'S FORBIDDING CASTLE...
BRR! WHAT A CREEPY PLACE!
YES! THE WITCH DOESN'T EXACTLY ENCOURAGE VISITORS!
HOW ARE WE GOING TO GET INSIDE? WE CAN'T GET THROUGH THOSE BRAMBLES!
12-6
Copyright © 1982 Walt Disney Productions World Rights Reserved
NO, BUT A COUPLE OF MICE CAN!
MICE?
Distributed by King Features Syndicate

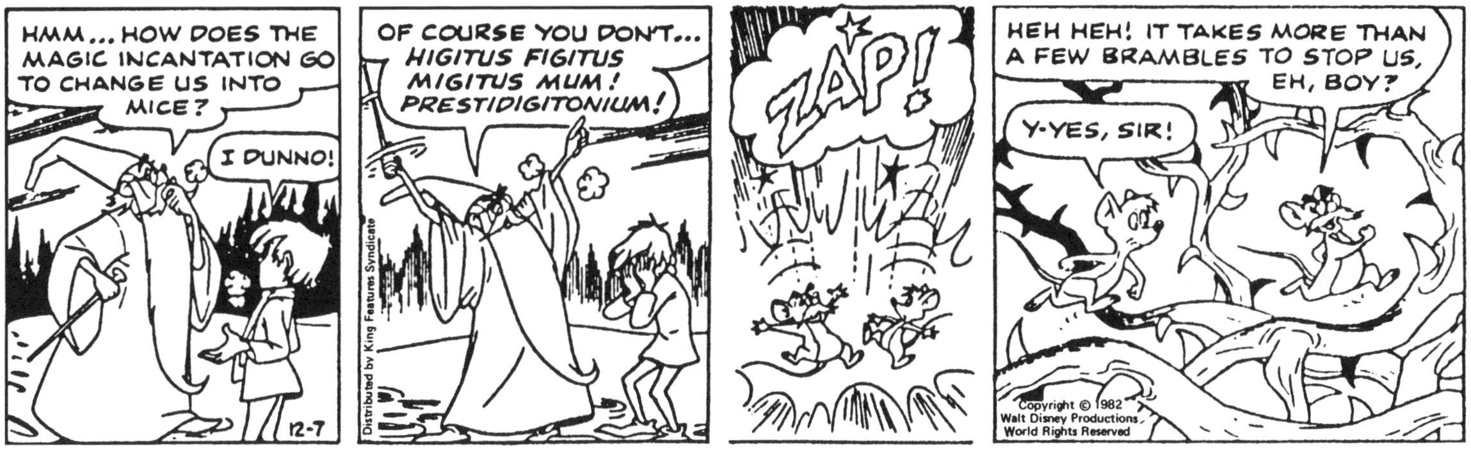
HMM... HOW DOES THE MAGIC INCANTATION GO TO CHANGE US INTO MICE?
I DUNNO!
12-7
OF COURSE YOU DON'T... HIGITUS FIGITUS MIGITUS MUM! PRESTIDIGITONIUM!
Distributed by King Features Syndicate
ZAP!
HEH HEH! IT TAKES MORE THAN A FEW BRAMBLES TO STOP US, EH, BOY?
Y-YES, SIR!
Copyright © 1982 Walt Disney Productions World Rights Reserved

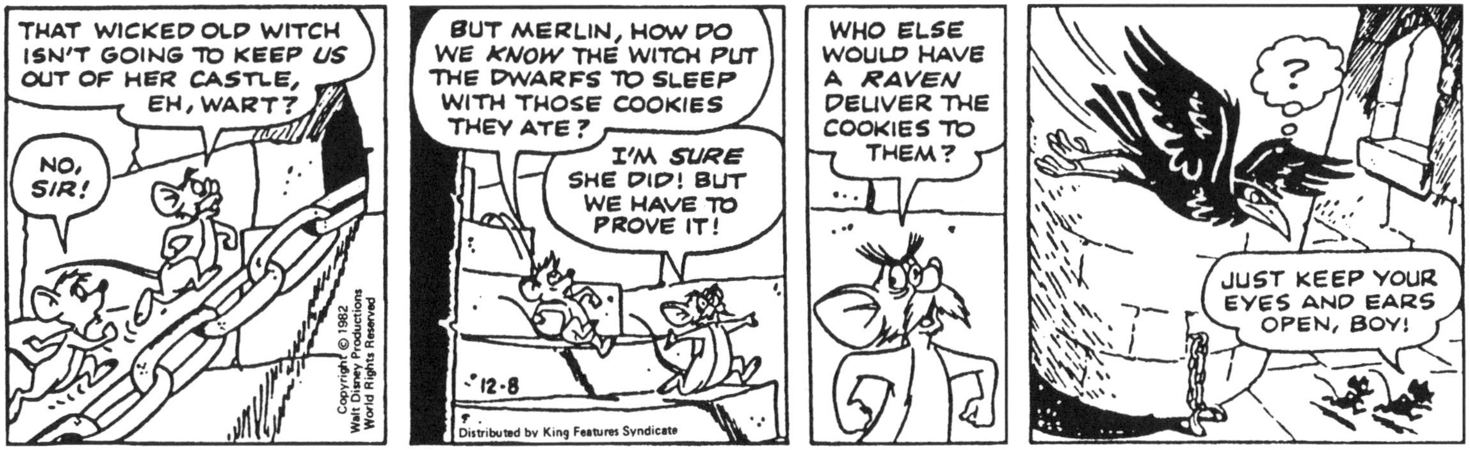
THAT WICKED OLD WITCH ISN'T GOING TO KEEP US OUT OF HER CASTLE, EH, WART?
NO, SIR!
Copyright © 1982 Walt Disney Productions World Rights Reserved
BUT MERLIN, HOW DO WE KNOW THE WITCH PUT THE DWARFS TO SLEEP WITH THOSE COOKIES THEY ATE?
I'M SURE SHE DID! BUT WE HAVE TO PROVE IT!
12-8
Distributed by King Features Syndicate
WHO ELSE WOULD HAVE A RAVEN DELIVER THE COOKIES TO THEM?
?
JUST KEEP YOUR EYES AND EARS OPEN, BOY!

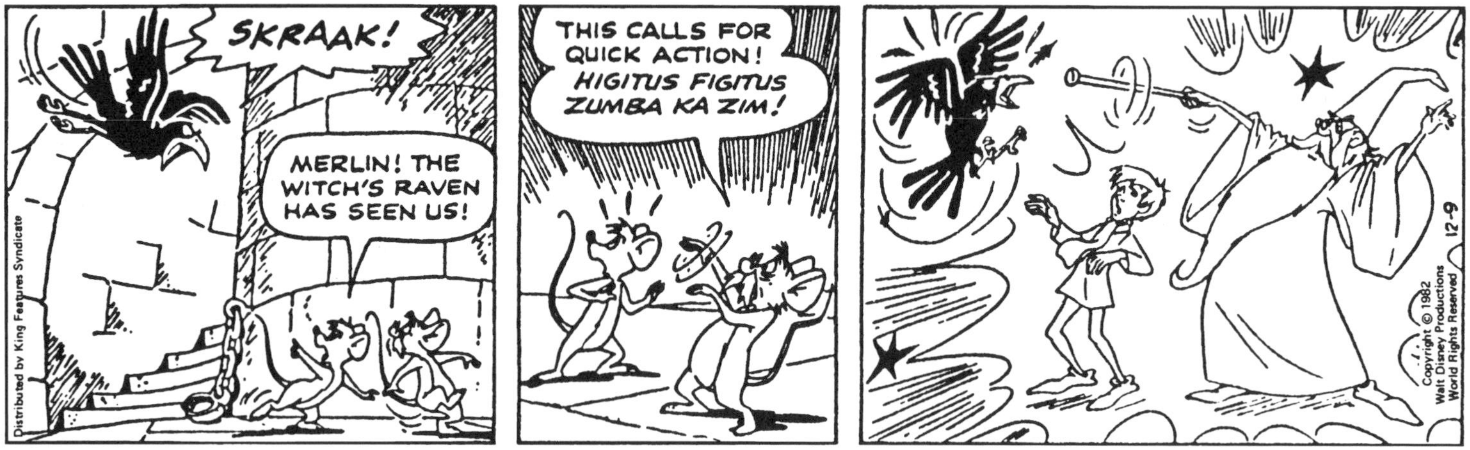
SKRAAK!
MERLIN! THE WITCH'S RAVEN HAS SEEN US!
Distributed by King Features Syndicate
THIS CALLS FOR QUICK ACTION! *HIGITUS FIGITUS ZUMBA KA ZIM!*
12-9
Copyright © 1982 Walt Disney Productions World Rights Reserved

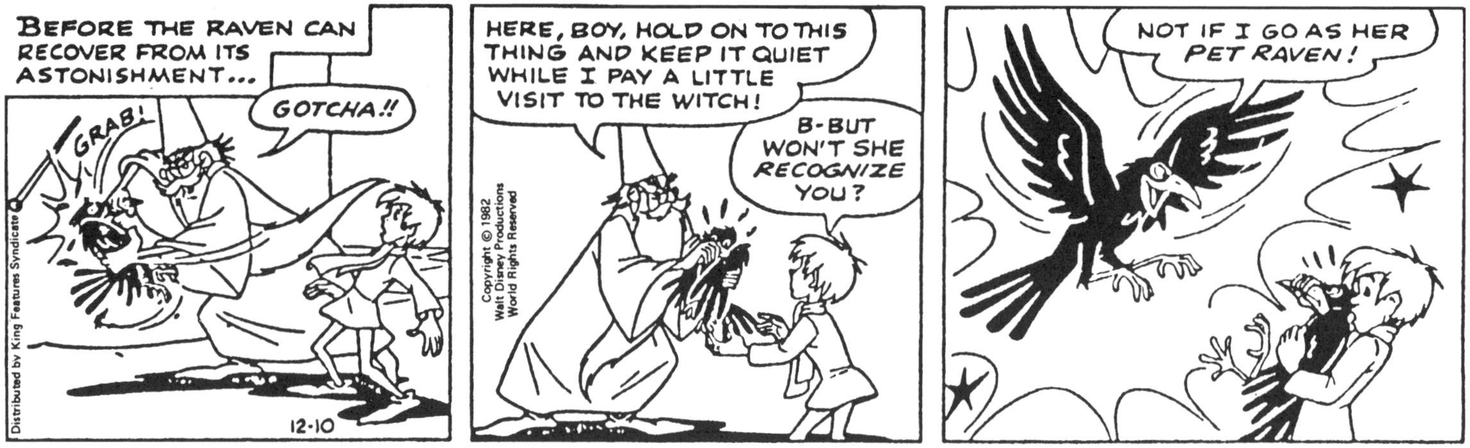
BEFORE THE RAVEN CAN RECOVER FROM ITS ASTONISHMENT...
GOTCHA!!
GRAB!
Distributed by King Features Syndicate
12-10
HERE, BOY, HOLD ON TO THIS THING AND KEEP IT QUIET WHILE I PAY A LITTLE VISIT TO THE WITCH!
B-BUT WON'T SHE *RECOGNIZE* YOU?
Copyright © 1982 Walt Disney Productions World Rights Reserved
NOT IF I GO AS HER *PET RAVEN!*

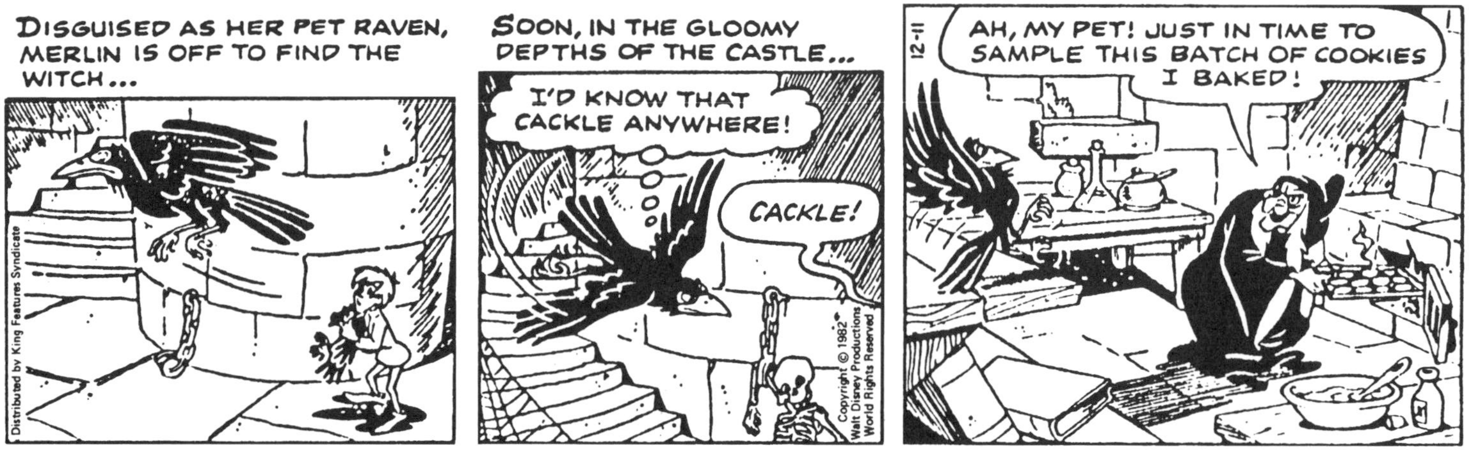
DISGUISED AS HER PET RAVEN, MERLIN IS OFF TO FIND THE WITCH...
Distributed by King Features Syndicate
SOON, IN THE GLOOMY DEPTHS OF THE CASTLE...
I'D KNOW THAT CACKLE ANYWHERE!
CACKLE!
Copyright © 1982 Walt Disney Productions World Rights Reserved
12-11
AH, MY PET! JUST IN TIME TO SAMPLE THIS BATCH OF COOKIES I BAKED!

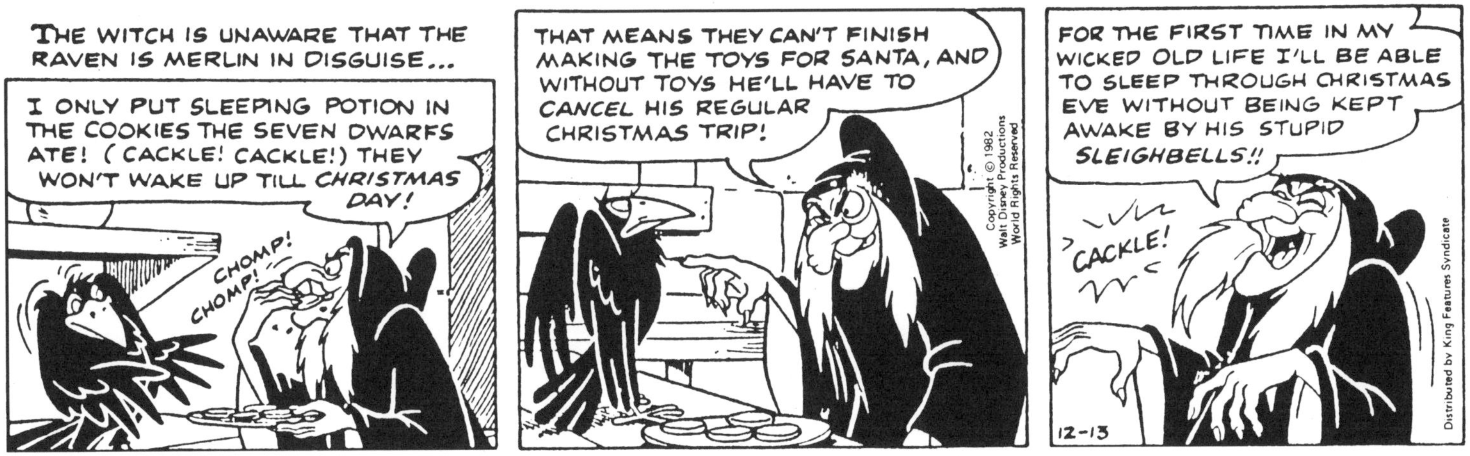
THE WITCH IS UNAWARE THAT THE RAVEN IS MERLIN IN DISGUISE...
I ONLY PUT SLEEPING POTION IN THE COOKIES THE SEVEN DWARFS ATE! (CACKLE! CACKLE!) THEY WON'T WAKE UP TILL *CHRISTMAS DAY!*
CHOMP! CHOMP!
THAT MEANS THEY CAN'T FINISH MAKING THE TOYS FOR SANTA, AND WITHOUT TOYS HE'LL HAVE TO *CANCEL* HIS REGULAR CHRISTMAS TRIP!
Copyright © 1982 Walt Disney Productions World Rights Reserved
FOR THE FIRST TIME IN MY WICKED OLD LIFE I'LL BE ABLE TO SLEEP THROUGH CHRISTMAS EVE WITHOUT BEING KEPT AWAKE BY HIS STUPID *SLEIGHBELLS!!*
CACKLE!
12-13
Distributed by King Features Syndicate

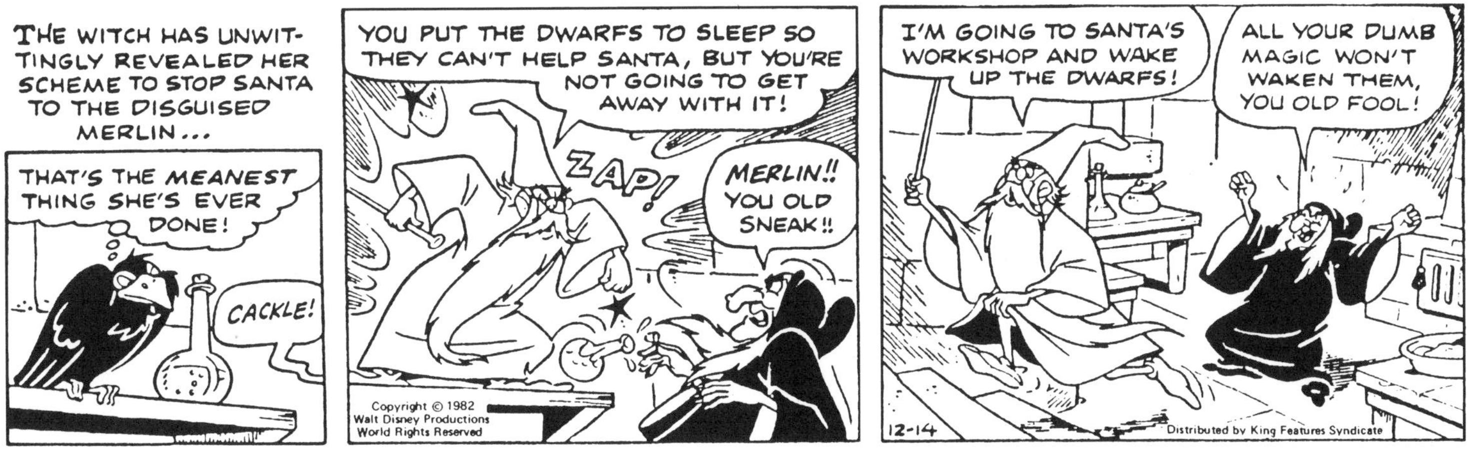
THE WITCH HAS UNWITTINGLY REVEALED HER SCHEME TO STOP SANTA TO THE DISGUISED MERLIN...
THAT'S THE *MEANEST* THING SHE'S EVER DONE!
CACKLE!
YOU PUT THE DWARFS TO SLEEP SO THEY CAN'T HELP SANTA, BUT YOU'RE NOT GOING TO GET AWAY WITH IT!
ZAP!
MERLIN!! YOU OLD SNEAK!!
Copyright © 1982 Walt Disney Productions World Rights Reserved
I'M GOING TO SANTA'S WORKSHOP AND WAKE UP THE DWARFS!
ALL YOUR DUMB MAGIC WON'T WAKEN THEM, YOU OLD FOOL!
12-14
Distributed by King Features Syndicate

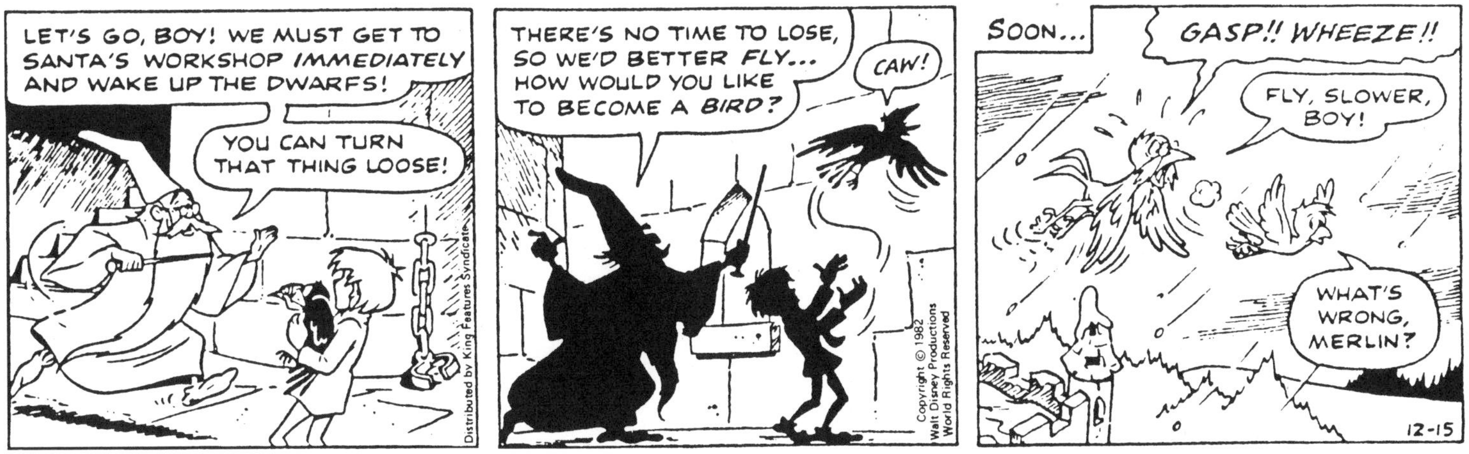
LET'S GO, BOY! WE MUST GET TO SANTA'S WORKSHOP *IMMEDIATELY* AND WAKE UP THE DWARFS!
YOU CAN TURN THAT THING LOOSE!
Distributed by King Features Syndicate
THERE'S NO TIME TO LOSE, SO WE'D BETTER *FLY*... HOW WOULD YOU LIKE TO BECOME A *BIRD?*
CAW!
Copyright © 1982 Walt Disney Productions World Rights Reserved
SOON...
GASP!! WHEEZE!!
FLY, SLOWER, BOY!
WHAT'S WRONG, MERLIN?
12-15

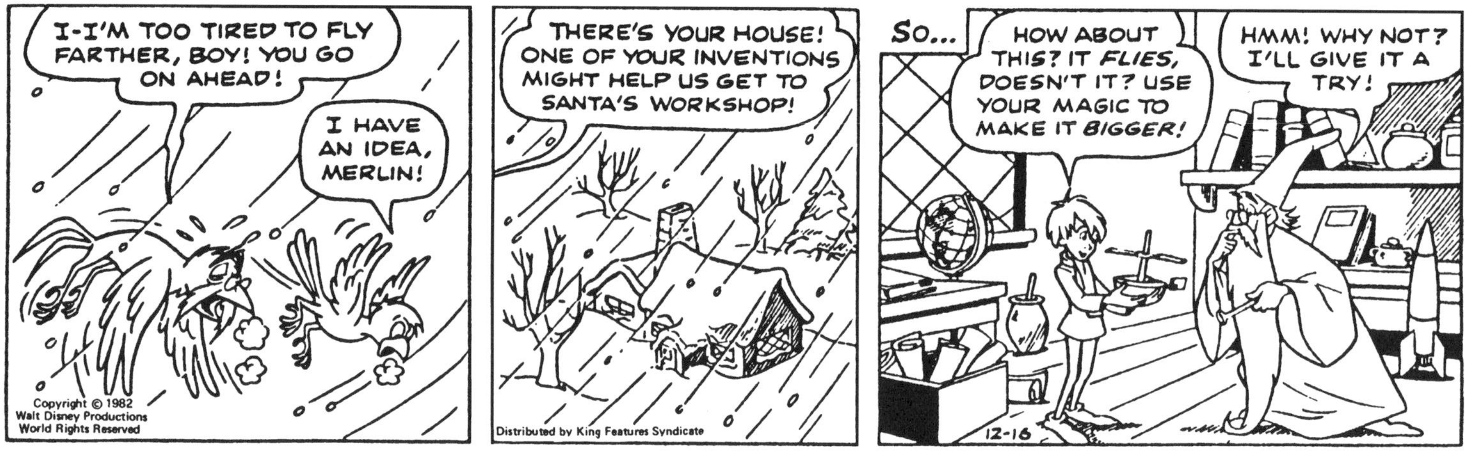
I-I'M TOO TIRED TO FLY FARTHER, BOY! YOU GO ON AHEAD!
I HAVE AN IDEA, MERLIN!
Copyright © 1982 Walt Disney Productions World Rights Reserved
THERE'S YOUR HOUSE! ONE OF YOUR INVENTIONS MIGHT HELP US GET TO SANTA'S WORKSHOP!
Distributed by King Features Syndicate
SO...
HOW ABOUT THIS? IT FLIES, DOESN'T IT? USE YOUR MAGIC TO MAKE IT BIGGER!
HMM! WHY NOT? I'LL GIVE IT A TRY!
12-16

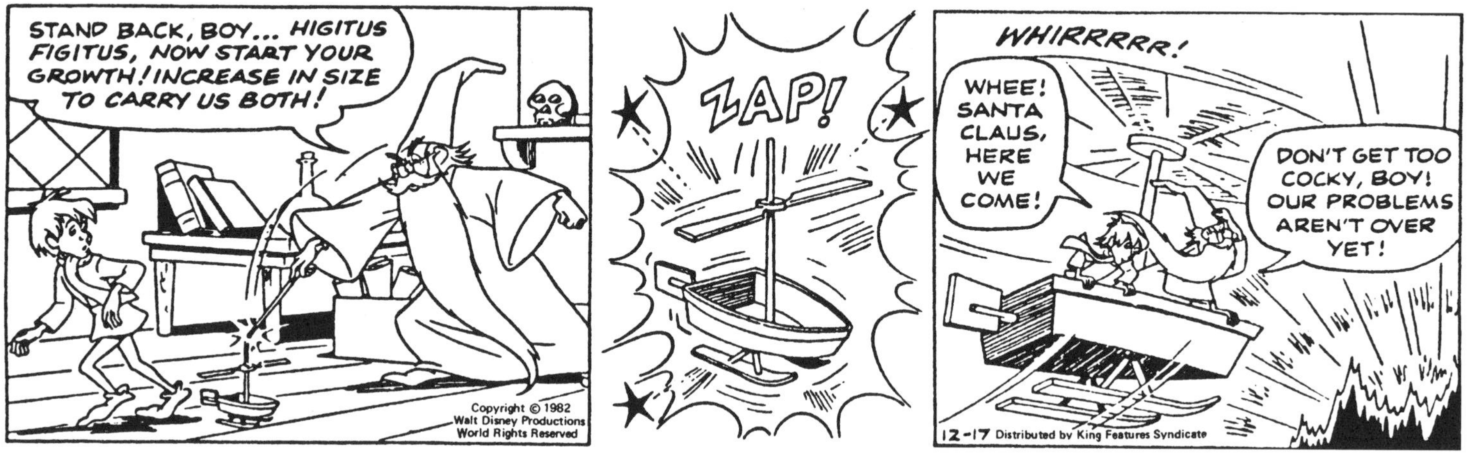
STAND BACK, BOY... HIGITUS FIGITUS, NOW START YOUR GROWTH! INCREASE IN SIZE TO CARRY US BOTH!
Copyright © 1982 Walt Disney Productions World Rights Reserved
ZAP!
WHIRRRRR!
WHEE! SANTA CLAUS, HERE WE COME!
DON'T GET TOO COCKY, BOY! OUR PROBLEMS AREN'T OVER YET!
12-17 Distributed by King Features Syndicate

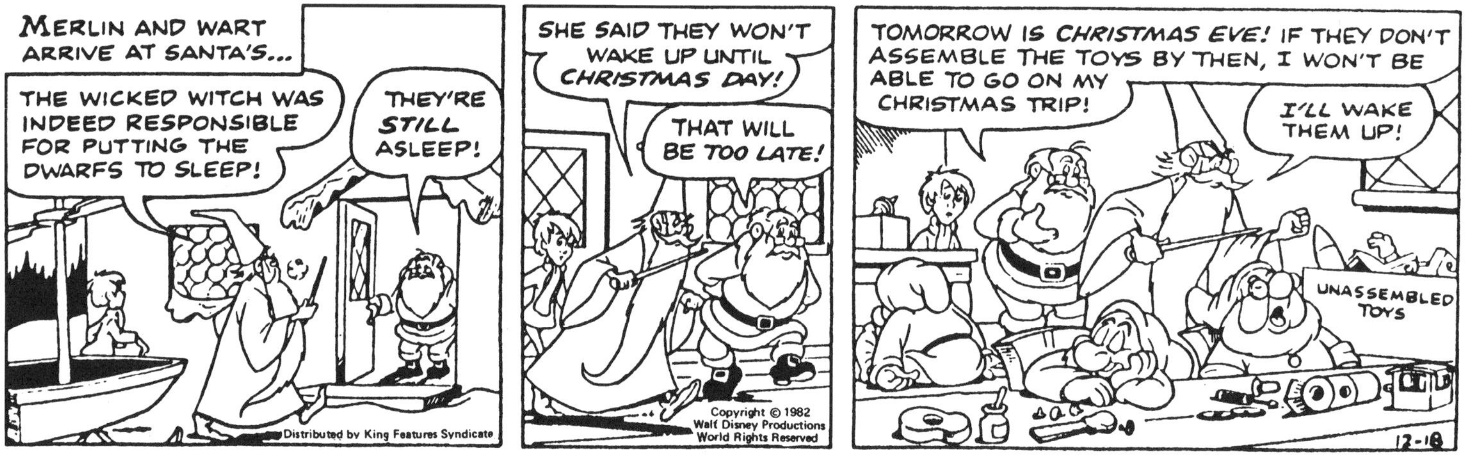
MERLIN AND WART ARRIVE AT SANTA'S...
THE WICKED WITCH WAS INDEED RESPONSIBLE FOR PUTTING THE DWARFS TO SLEEP!
THEY'RE STILL ASLEEP!
Distributed by King Features Syndicate
SHE SAID THEY WON'T WAKE UP UNTIL CHRISTMAS DAY!
THAT WILL BE TOO LATE!
Copyright © 1982 Walt Disney Productions World Rights Reserved
TOMORROW IS CHRISTMAS EVE! IF THEY DON'T ASSEMBLE THE TOYS BY THEN, I WON'T BE ABLE TO GO ON MY CHRISTMAS TRIP!
I'LL WAKE THEM UP!
UNASSEMBLED TOYS
12-18

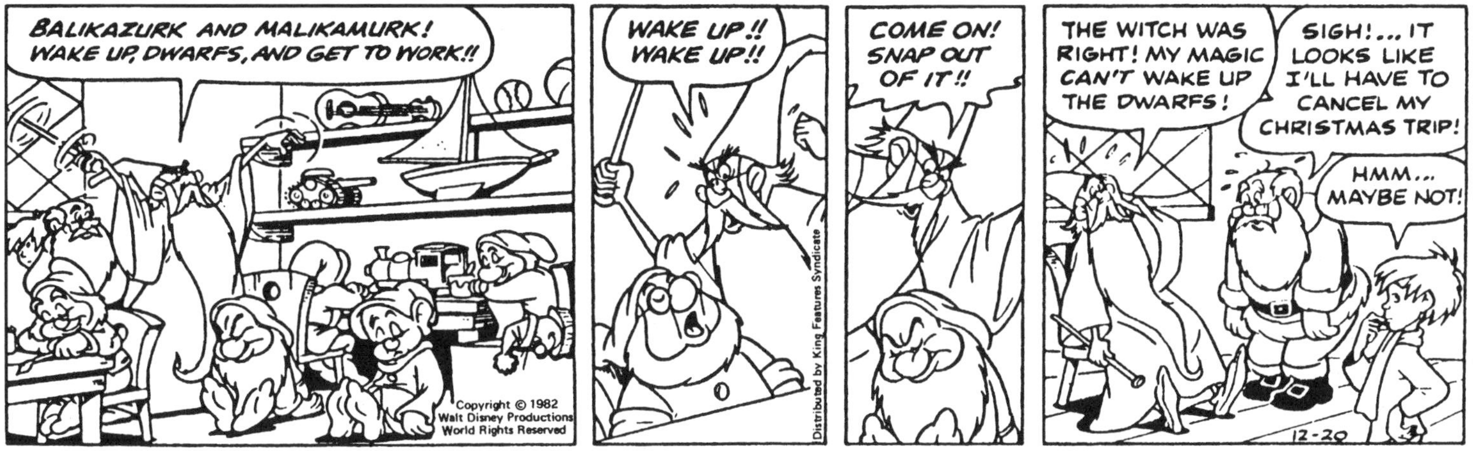
BALIKAZURK AND MALIKAMURK! WAKE UP, DWARFS, AND GET TO WORK!!
Copyright © 1982 Walt Disney Productions World Rights Reserved
WAKE UP!! WAKE UP!!
Distributed by King Features Syndicate
COME ON! SNAP OUT OF IT!!
THE WITCH WAS RIGHT! MY MAGIC CAN'T WAKE UP THE DWARFS!
SIGH!... IT LOOKS LIKE I'LL HAVE TO CANCEL MY CHRISTMAS TRIP!
HMM... MAYBE NOT!
12-20

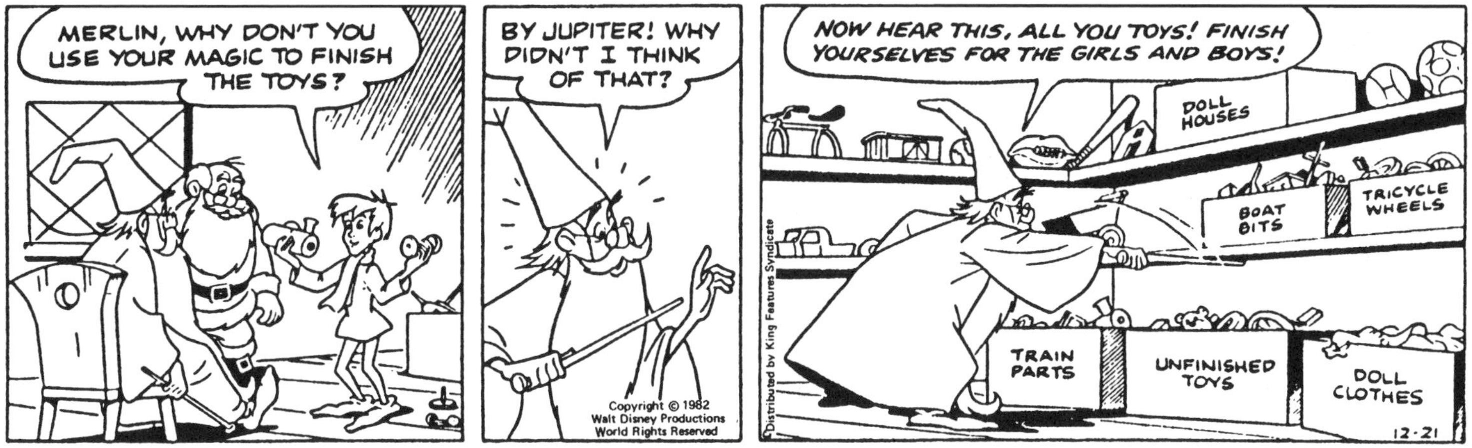
MERLIN, WHY DON'T YOU USE YOUR MAGIC TO FINISH THE TOYS?
BY JUPITER! WHY DIDN'T I THINK OF THAT?
Copyright © 1982 Walt Disney Productions World Rights Reserved
NOW HEAR THIS, ALL YOU TOYS! FINISH YOURSELVES FOR THE GIRLS AND BOYS!
DOLL HOUSES
BOAT BITS
TRICYCLE WHEELS
TRAIN PARTS
UNFINISHED TOYS
DOLL CLOTHES
Distributed by King Features Syndicate
12-21

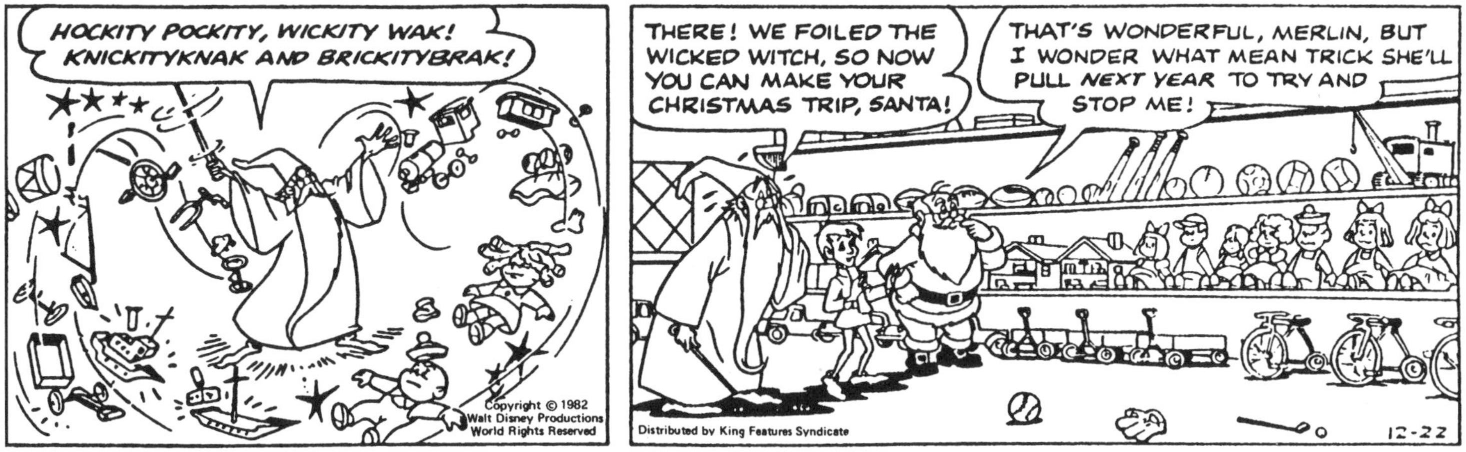
HOCKITY POCKITY, WICKITY WAK! KNICKITYKNAK AND BRICKITYBRAK!
Copyright © 1982 Walt Disney Productions World Rights Reserved
THERE! WE FOILED THE WICKED WITCH, SO NOW YOU CAN MAKE YOUR CHRISTMAS TRIP, SANTA!
THAT'S WONDERFUL, MERLIN, BUT I WONDER WHAT MEAN TRICK SHE'LL PULL NEXT YEAR TO TRY AND STOP ME!
Distributed by King Features Syndicate
12-22

THE WITCH TRIED TO STOP YOU FROM MAKING YOUR CHRISTMAS TRIP SO SHE WOULDN'T BE KEPT AWAKE BY YOUR SLEIGHBELLS... RIGHT?
THAT'S RIGHT!
Distributed by King Features Syndicate
SO WHY DON'T WE FIX IT SO SHE DOESN'T HEAR THE BELLS?
SURELY YOU DON'T THINK I SHOULD MUFFLE MY SLEIGHBELLS?
NO, NO! OF COURSE NOT! I HAVE IN MIND GIVING HER A LITTLE PRESENT TO BE OPENED BEFORE CHRISTMAS!
POOF!
Copyright © 1982 Walt Disney Productions World Rights Reserved
12-23

A PRESENT FROM SANTA? SOUND-PROOF EAR MUFFS!
TO BE OPENED BEFORE CHRISTMAS
COMES CHRISTMAS EVE, AND THE WICKED WITCH SLEEPS BLISSFULLY THROUGH THE NIGHT!
ZZAWP! ZZZZZ!!
JINGLE! JINGLE! JINGLE!
Copyright © 1982 Walt Disney Productions World Rights Reserved
TO BE OPENED BEFORE CHRISTMAS
AND SO, A MERRY CHRISTMAS TO EVERYONE!
Distributed by King Features Syndicate
12-24

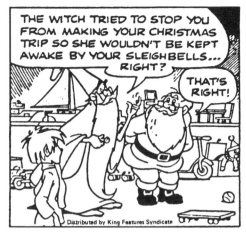

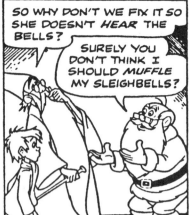

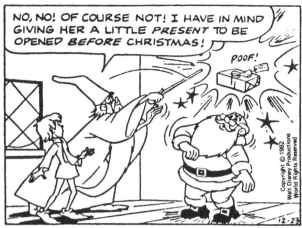

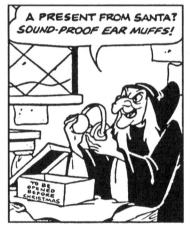

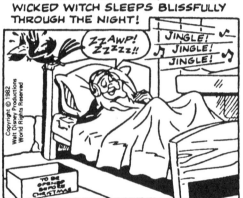

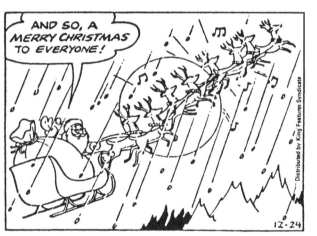

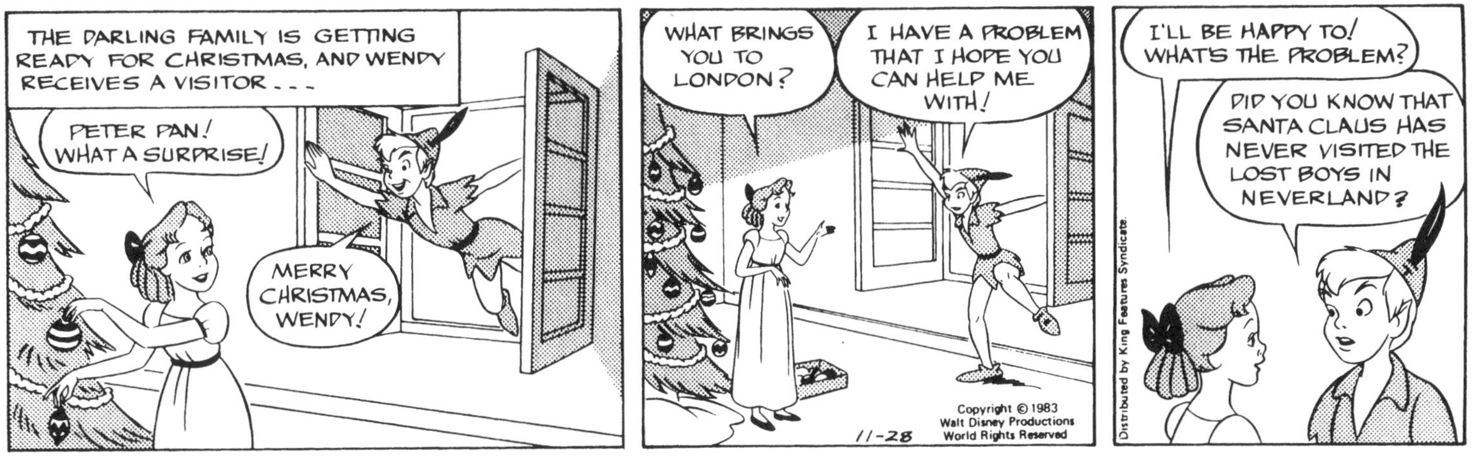
THE DARLING FAMILY IS GETTING READY FOR CHRISTMAS, AND WENDY RECEIVES A VISITOR - - -
PETER PAN! WHAT A SURPRISE!
MERRY CHRISTMAS, WENDY!
WHAT BRINGS YOU TO LONDON?
I HAVE A PROBLEM THAT I HOPE YOU CAN HELP ME WITH!
Copyright © 1983 Walt Disney Productions World Rights Reserved
11-28
I'LL BE HAPPY TO! WHAT'S THE PROBLEM?
DID YOU KNOW THAT SANTA CLAUS HAS NEVER VISITED THE LOST BOYS IN NEVERLAND?
Distributed by King Features Syndicate.

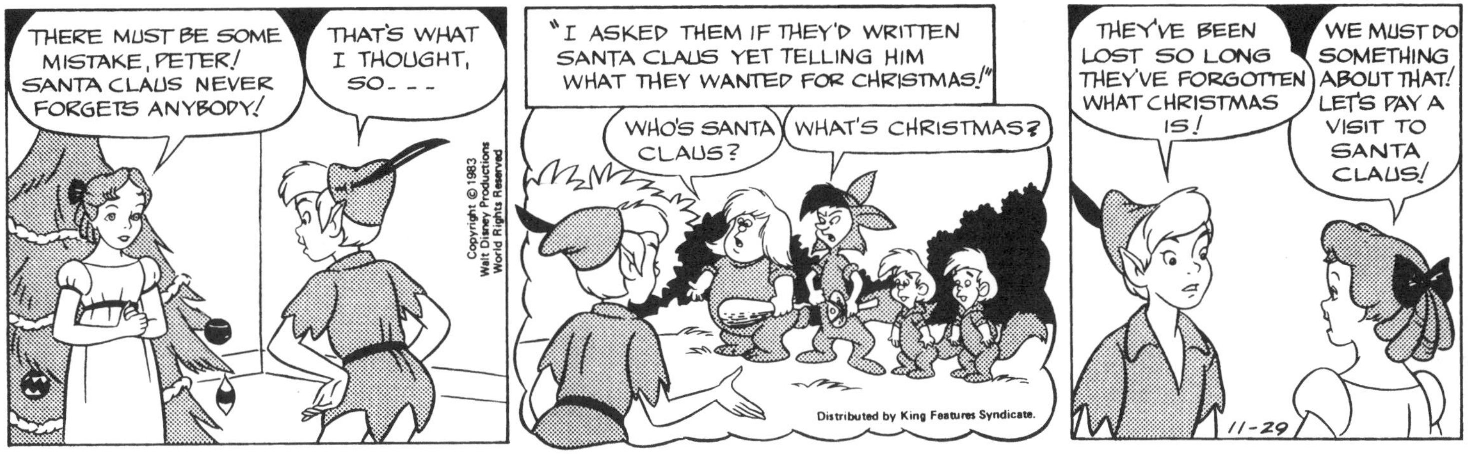
THERE MUST BE SOME MISTAKE, PETER! SANTA CLAUS NEVER FORGETS ANYBODY!
THAT'S WHAT I THOUGHT, SO- - -
Copyright © 1983 Walt Disney Productions World Rights Reserved
"I ASKED THEM IF THEY'D WRITTEN SANTA CLAUS YET TELLING HIM WHAT THEY WANTED FOR CHRISTMAS!"
WHO'S SANTA CLAUS?
WHAT'S CHRISTMAS?
Distributed by King Features Syndicate.
THEY'VE BEEN LOST SO LONG THEY'VE FORGOTTEN WHAT CHRISTMAS IS!
WE MUST DO SOMETHING ABOUT THAT! LET'S PAY A VISIT TO SANTA CLAUS!
11-29

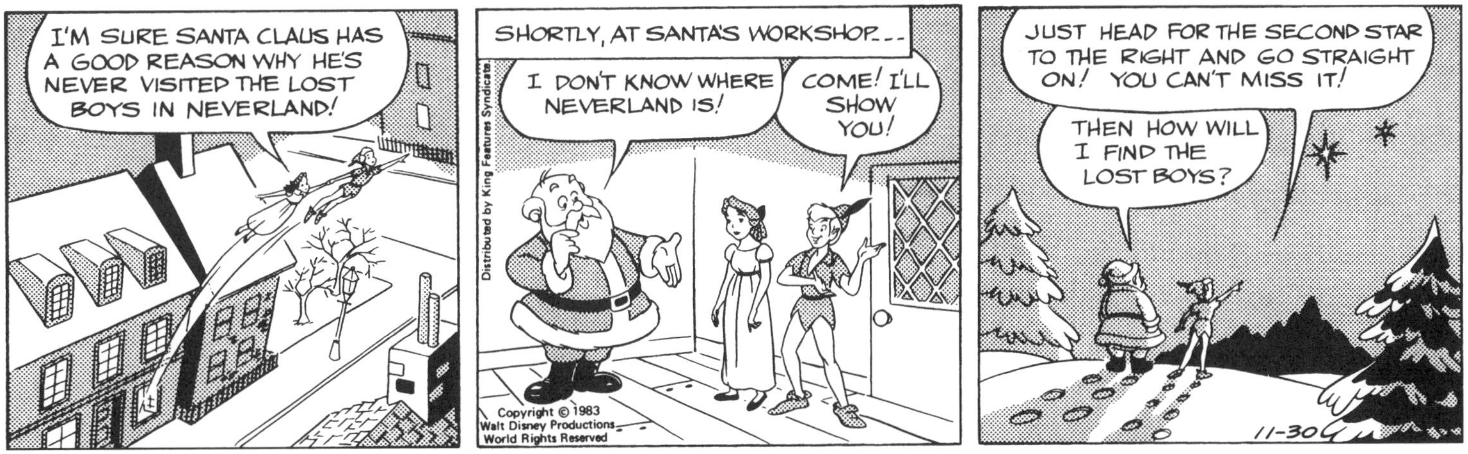
I'M SURE SANTA CLAUS HAS A GOOD REASON WHY HE'S NEVER VISITED THE LOST BOYS IN NEVERLAND!
SHORTLY, AT SANTA'S WORKSHOP- - -
Distributed by King Features Syndicate.
I DON'T KNOW WHERE NEVERLAND IS!
COME! I'LL SHOW YOU!
Copyright © 1983 Walt Disney Productions World Rights Reserved
JUST HEAD FOR THE SECOND STAR TO THE RIGHT AND GO STRAIGHT ON! YOU CAN'T MISS IT!
THEN HOW WILL I FIND THE LOST BOYS?
11-30

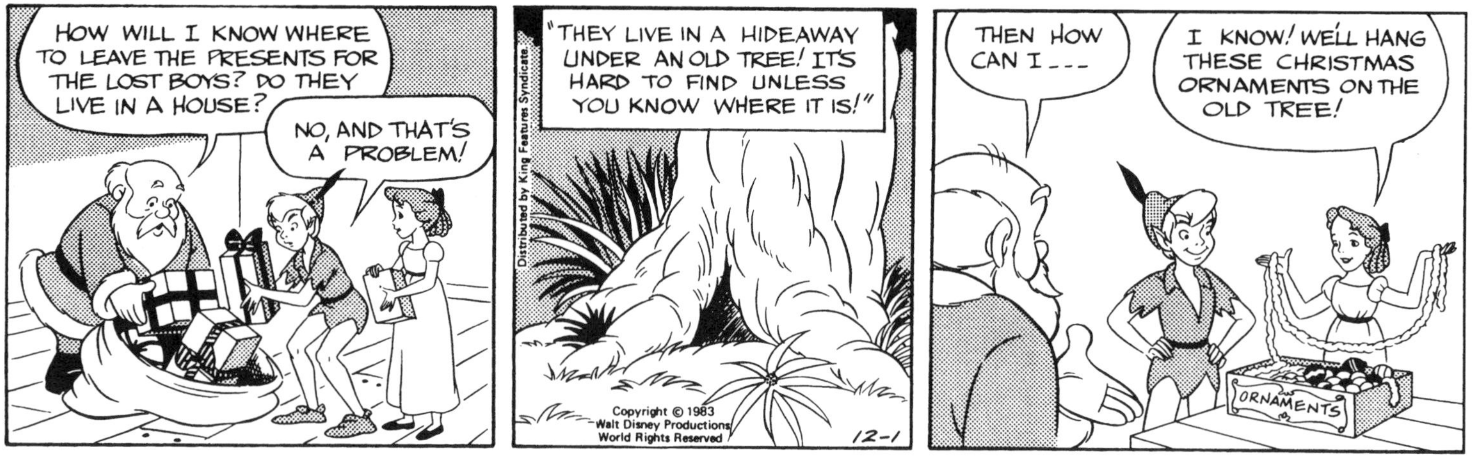
HOW WILL I KNOW WHERE TO LEAVE THE PRESENTS FOR THE LOST BOYS? DO THEY LIVE IN A HOUSE?
NO, AND THAT'S A PROBLEM!
Distributed by King Features Syndicate
"THEY LIVE IN A HIDEAWAY UNDER AN OLD TREE! IT'S HARD TO FIND UNLESS YOU KNOW WHERE IT IS!"
Copyright © 1983 Walt Disney Productions World Rights Reserved
12-1
THEN HOW CAN I ---
I KNOW! WE'LL HANG THESE CHRISTMAS ORNAMENTS ON THE OLD TREE!
ORNAMENTS

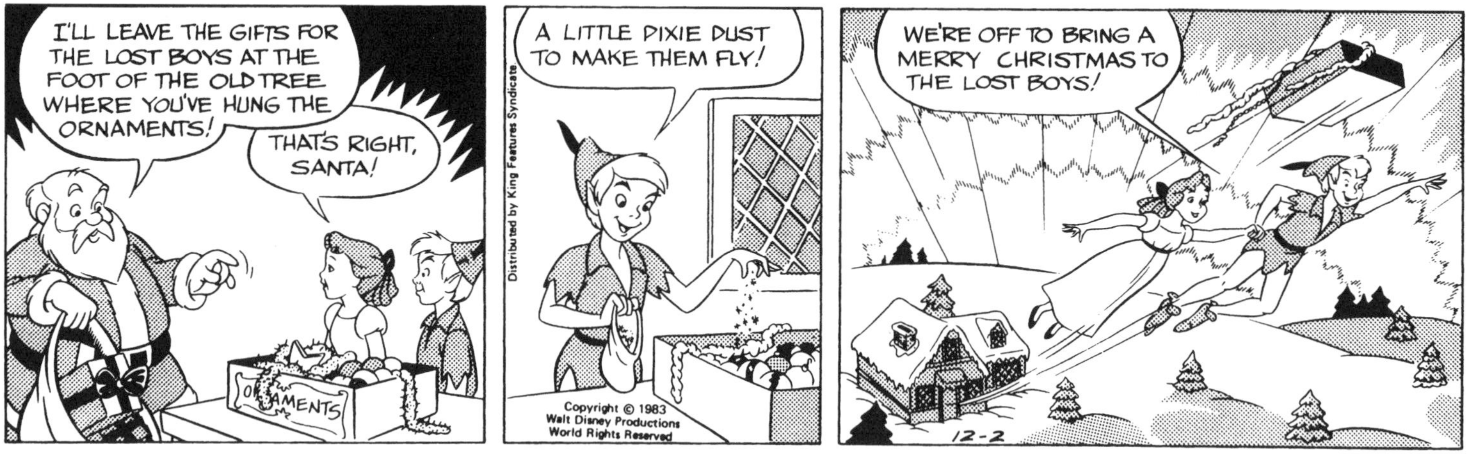
I'LL LEAVE THE GIFTS FOR THE LOST BOYS AT THE FOOT OF THE OLD TREE WHERE YOU'VE HUNG THE ORNAMENTS!
THAT'S RIGHT, SANTA!
ORNAMENTS
Distributed by King Features Syndicate
A LITTLE PIXIE DUST TO MAKE THEM FLY!
Copyright © 1983 Walt Disney Productions World Rights Reserved
WE'RE OFF TO BRING A MERRY CHRISTMAS TO THE LOST BOYS!
12-2

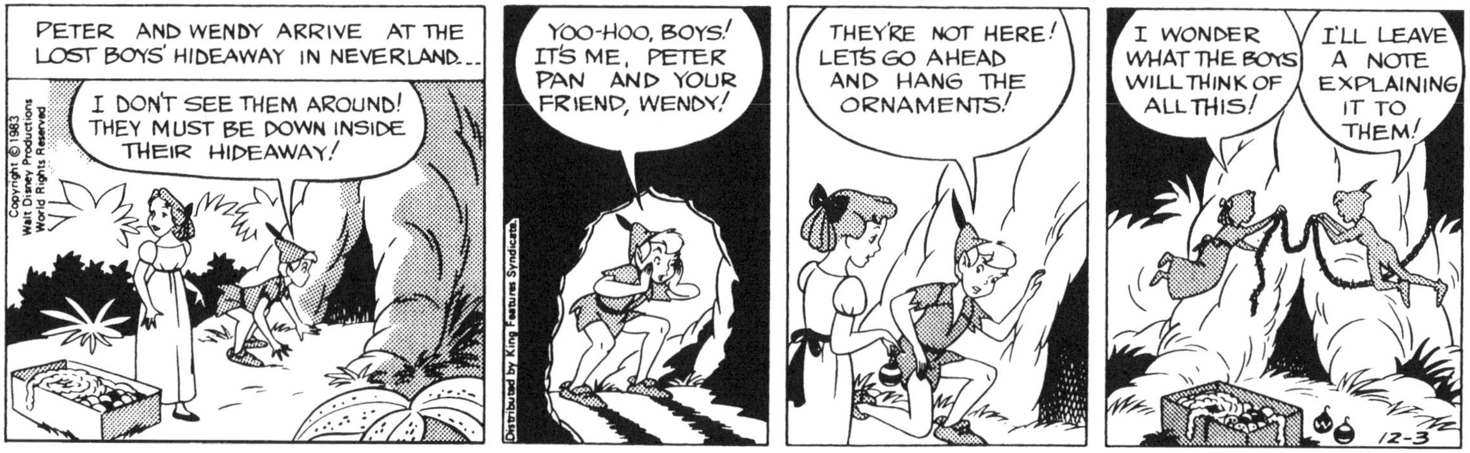
PETER AND WENDY ARRIVE AT THE LOST BOYS' HIDEAWAY IN NEVERLAND...
Copyright © 1983 Walt Disney Productions World Rights Reserved
I DON'T SEE THEM AROUND! THEY MUST BE DOWN INSIDE THEIR HIDEAWAY!
Distributed by King Features Syndicate
YOO-HOO, BOYS! IT'S ME, PETER PAN AND YOUR FRIEND, WENDY!
THEY'RE NOT HERE! LET'S GO AHEAD AND HANG THE ORNAMENTS!
I WONDER WHAT THE BOYS WILL THINK OF ALL THIS!
I'LL LEAVE A NOTE EXPLAINING IT TO THEM!
12-3

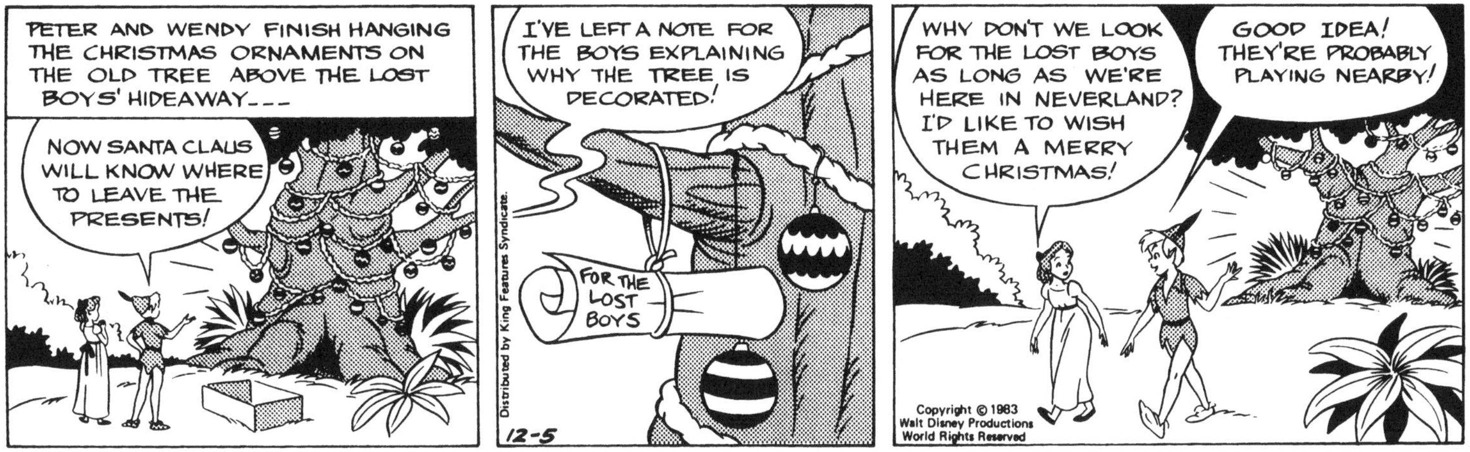
PETER AND WENDY FINISH HANGING THE CHRISTMAS ORNAMENTS ON THE OLD TREE ABOVE THE LOST BOYS' HIDEAWAY---
NOW SANTA CLAUS WILL KNOW WHERE TO LEAVE THE PRESENTS!
I'VE LEFT A NOTE FOR THE BOYS EXPLAINING WHY THE TREE IS DECORATED!
FOR THE LOST BOYS
Distributed by King Features Syndicate.
12-5
WHY DON'T WE LOOK FOR THE LOST BOYS AS LONG AS WE'RE HERE IN NEVERLAND? I'D LIKE TO WISH THEM A MERRY CHRISTMAS!
GOOD IDEA! THEY'RE PROBABLY PLAYING NEARBY!
Copyright © 1983 Walt Disney Productions World Rights Reserved

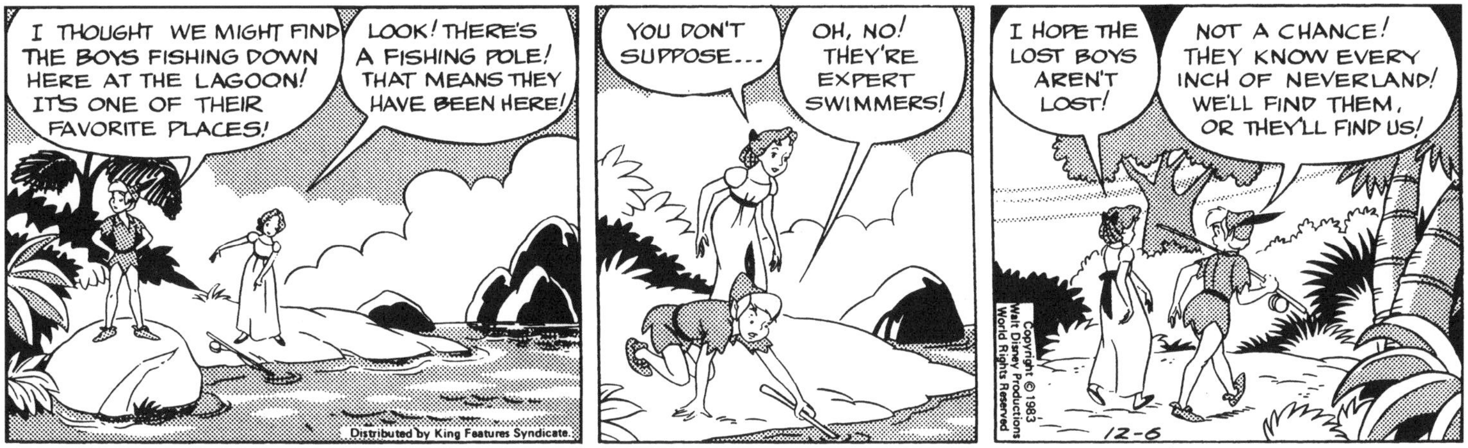
I THOUGHT WE MIGHT FIND THE BOYS FISHING DOWN HERE AT THE LAGOON! IT'S ONE OF THEIR FAVORITE PLACES!
LOOK! THERE'S A FISHING POLE! THAT MEANS THEY HAVE BEEN HERE!
Distributed by King Features Syndicate.
YOU DON'T SUPPOSE---
OH, NO! THEY'RE EXPERT SWIMMERS!
I HOPE THE LOST BOYS AREN'T LOST!
NOT A CHANCE! THEY KNOW EVERY INCH OF NEVERLAND! WE'LL FIND THEM, OR THEY'LL FIND US!
Copyright © 1983 Walt Disney Productions World Rights Reserved
12-6

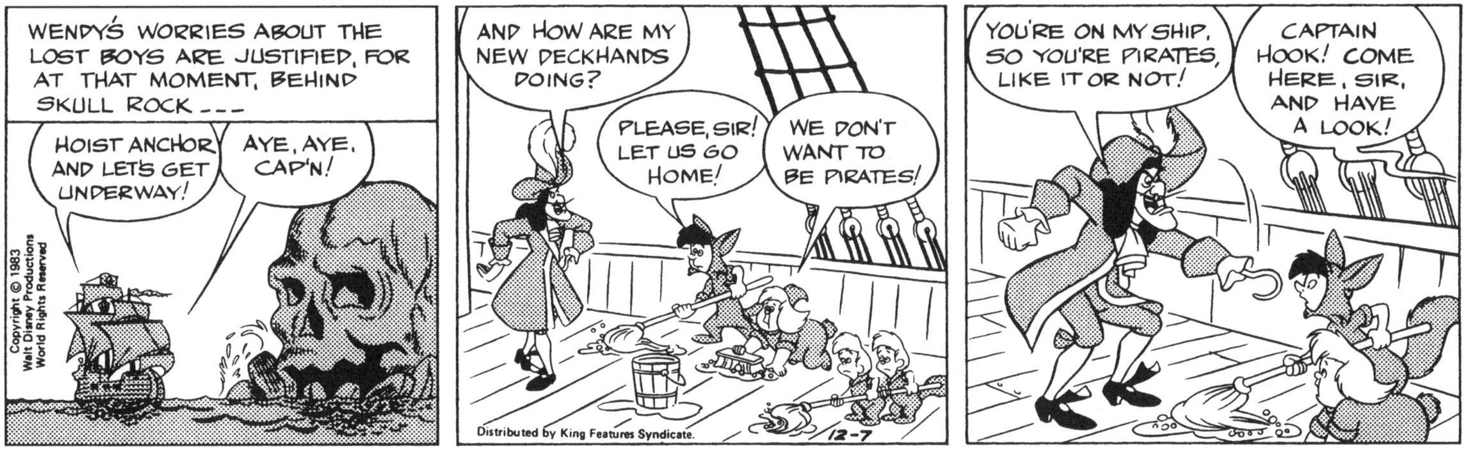
WENDY'S WORRIES ABOUT THE LOST BOYS ARE JUSTIFIED, FOR AT THAT MOMENT, BEHIND SKULL ROCK---
HOIST ANCHOR AND LET'S GET UNDERWAY!
AYE, AYE, CAP'N!
Copyright © 1983 Walt Disney Productions World Rights Reserved
AND HOW ARE MY NEW DECKHANDS DOING?
PLEASE, SIR! LET US GO HOME!
WE DON'T WANT TO BE PIRATES!
Distributed by King Features Syndicate.
12-7
YOU'RE ON MY SHIP, SO YOU'RE PIRATES, LIKE IT OR NOT!
CAPTAIN HOOK! COME HERE, SIR, AND HAVE A LOOK!

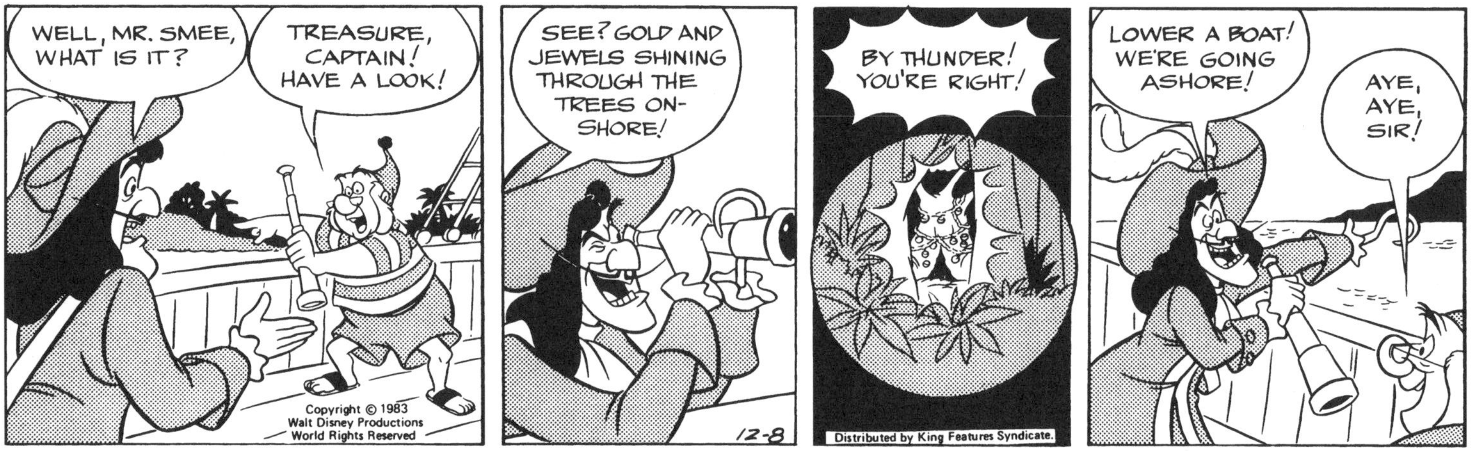
WELL, MR. SMEE, WHAT IS IT?
TREASURE, CAPTAIN! HAVE A LOOK!
Copyright © 1983 Walt Disney Productions World Rights Reserved
SEE? GOLD AND JEWELS SHINING THROUGH THE TREES ON-SHORE!
12-8
BY THUNDER! YOU'RE RIGHT!
Distributed by King Features Syndicate.
LOWER A BOAT! WE'RE GOING ASHORE!
AYE, AYE, SIR!

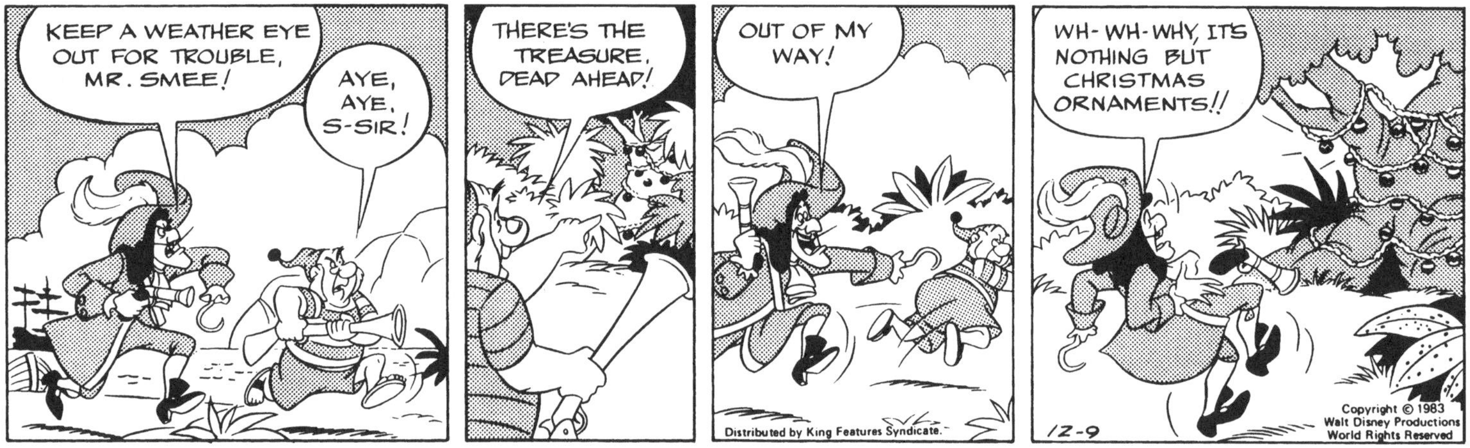
KEEP A WEATHER EYE OUT FOR TROUBLE, MR. SMEE!
AYE, AYE, S-SIR!
THERE'S THE TREASURE, DEAD AHEAD!
OUT OF MY WAY!
Distributed by King Features Syndicate.
WH-WH-WHY, IT'S NOTHING BUT CHRISTMAS ORNAMENTS!!
12-9
Copyright © 1983 Walt Disney Productions World Rights Reserved

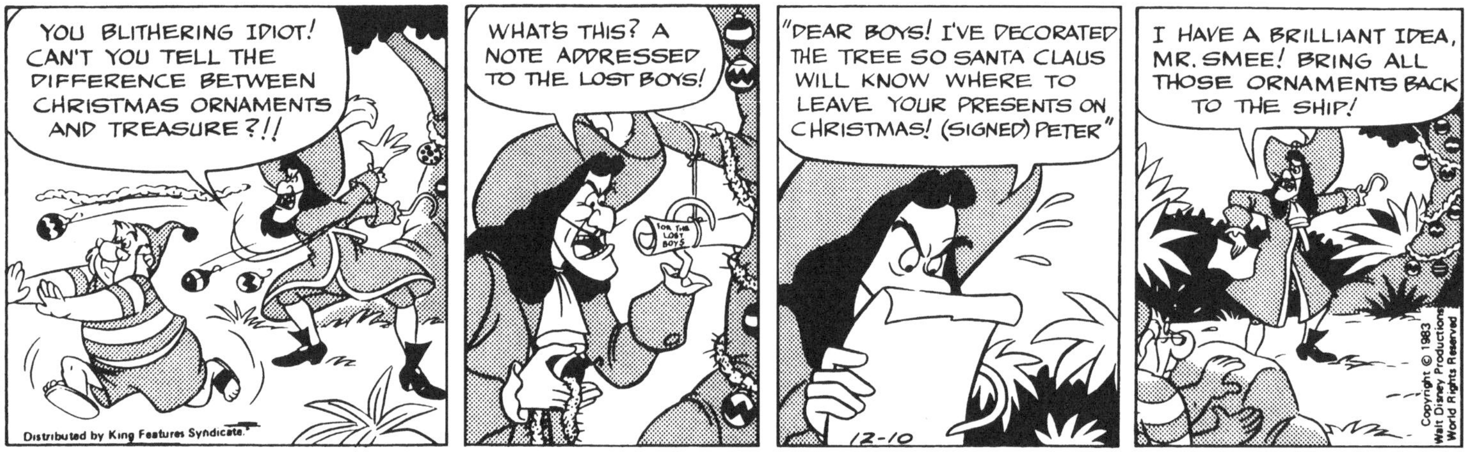
YOU BLITHERING IDIOT! CAN'T YOU TELL THE DIFFERENCE BETWEEN CHRISTMAS ORNAMENTS AND TREASURE?!!
Distributed by King Features Syndicate.
WHAT'S THIS? A NOTE ADDRESSED TO THE LOST BOYS!
"DEAR BOYS! I'VE DECORATED THE TREE SO SANTA CLAUS WILL KNOW WHERE TO LEAVE YOUR PRESENTS ON CHRISTMAS! (SIGNED) PETER"
12-10
I HAVE A BRILLIANT IDEA, MR. SMEE! BRING ALL THOSE ORNAMENTS BACK TO THE SHIP!
Copyright © 1983 Walt Disney Productions World Rights Reserved

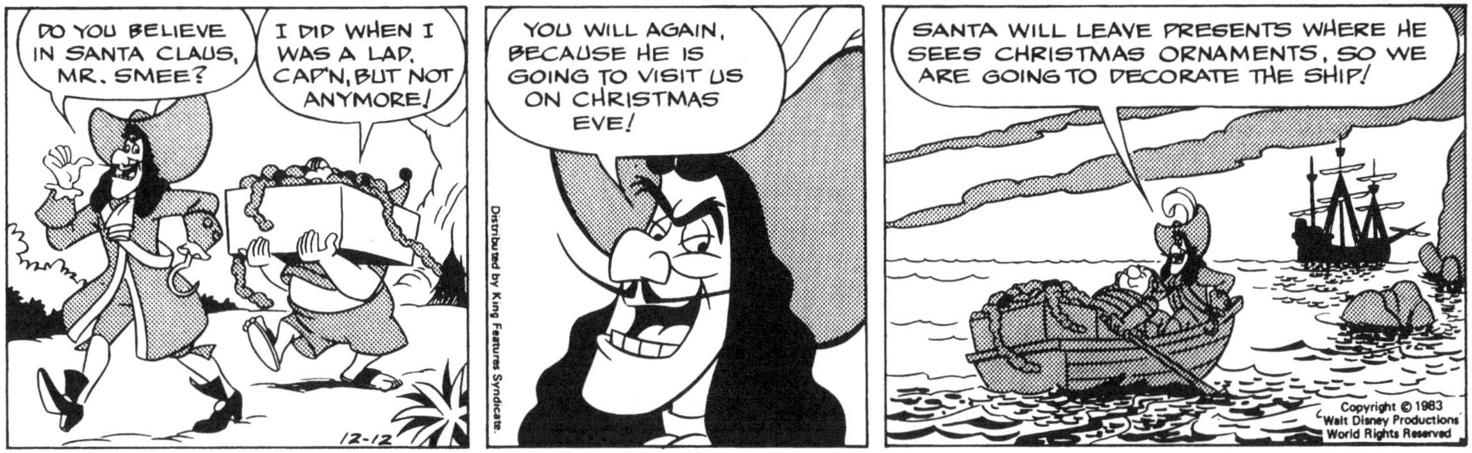
DO YOU BELIEVE IN SANTA CLAUS, MR. SMEE?
I DID WHEN I WAS A LAD, CAP'N, BUT NOT ANYMORE!
12-12
Distributed by King Features Syndicate.
YOU WILL AGAIN, BECAUSE HE IS GOING TO VISIT US ON CHRISTMAS EVE!
SANTA WILL LEAVE PRESENTS WHERE HE SEES CHRISTMAS ORNAMENTS, SO WE ARE GOING TO DECORATE THE SHIP!
Copyright © 1983 Walt Disney Productions World Rights Reserved

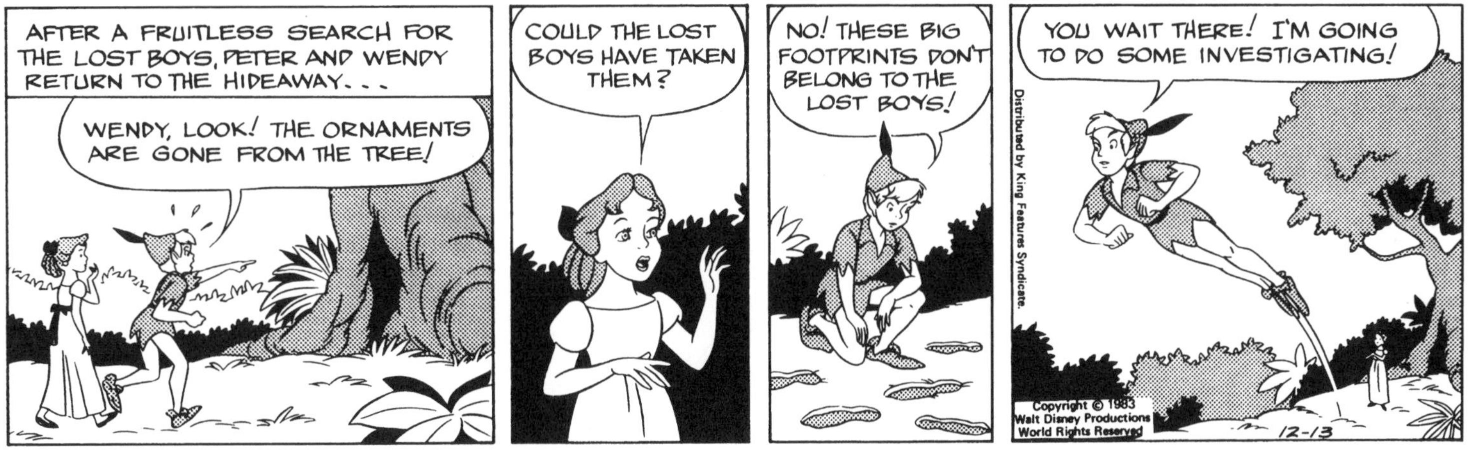
AFTER A FRUITLESS SEARCH FOR THE LOST BOYS, PETER AND WENDY RETURN TO THE HIDEAWAY...
WENDY, LOOK! THE ORNAMENTS ARE GONE FROM THE TREE!
COULD THE LOST BOYS HAVE TAKEN THEM?
NO! THESE BIG FOOTPRINTS DON'T BELONG TO THE LOST BOYS!
Distributed by King Features Syndicate.
YOU WAIT THERE! I'M GOING TO DO SOME INVESTIGATING!
Copyright © 1983 Walt Disney Productions World Rights Reserved
12-13

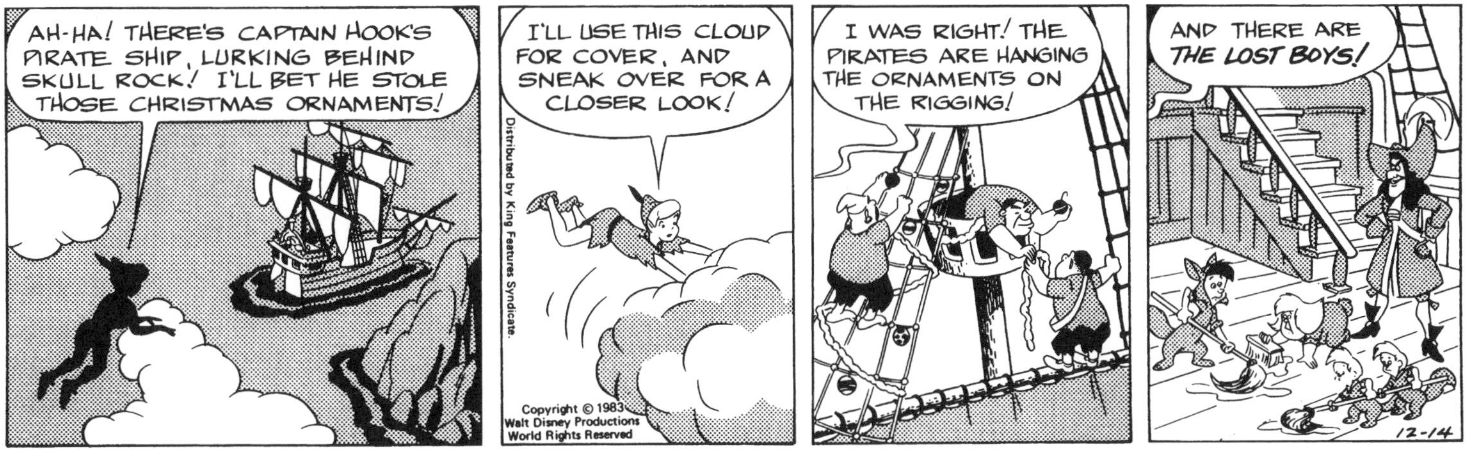
AH-HA! THERE'S CAPTAIN HOOK'S PIRATE SHIP, LURKING BEHIND SKULL ROCK! I'LL BET HE STOLE THOSE CHRISTMAS ORNAMENTS!
Distributed by King Features Syndicate.
I'LL USE THIS CLOUD FOR COVER, AND SNEAK OVER FOR A CLOSER LOOK!
Copyright © 1983 Walt Disney Productions World Rights Reserved
I WAS RIGHT! THE PIRATES ARE HANGING THE ORNAMENTS ON THE RIGGING!
AND THERE ARE *THE LOST BOYS!*
12-14

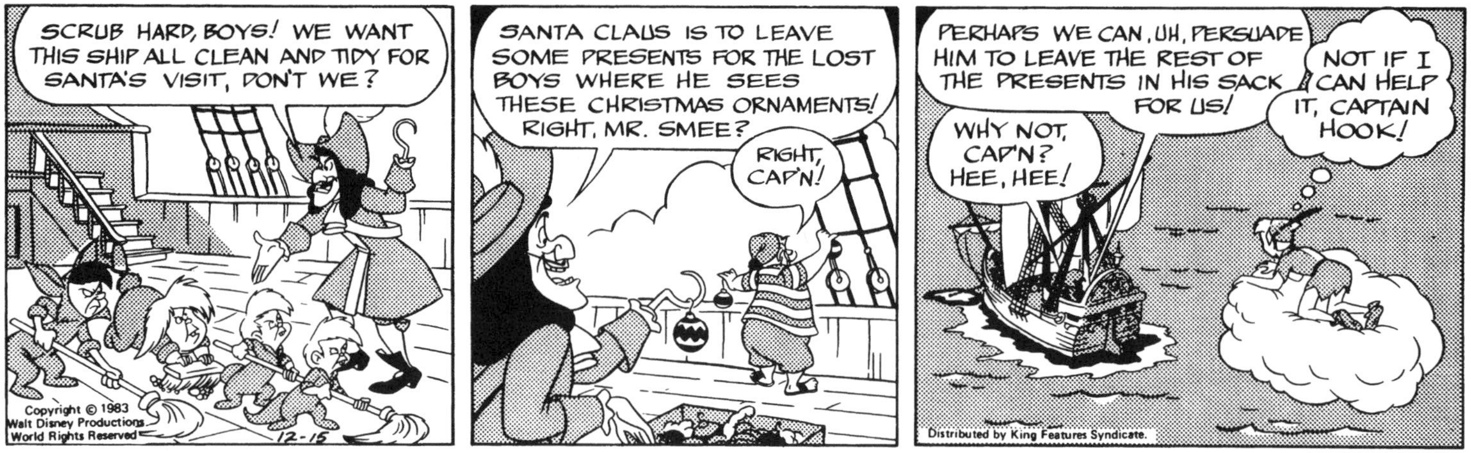
SCRUB HARD, BOYS! WE WANT THIS SHIP ALL CLEAN AND TIDY FOR SANTA'S VISIT, DON'T WE?
Copyright © 1983 Walt Disney Productions World Rights Reserved
12-15
SANTA CLAUS IS TO LEAVE SOME PRESENTS FOR THE LOST BOYS WHERE HE SEES THESE CHRISTMAS ORNAMENTS! RIGHT, MR. SMEE?
RIGHT, CAP'N!
PERHAPS WE CAN, UH, PERSUADE HIM TO LEAVE THE REST OF THE PRESENTS IN HIS SACK FOR US!
WHY NOT, CAP'N? HEE, HEE!
NOT IF I CAN HELP IT, CAPTAIN HOOK!
Distributed by King Features Syndicate.

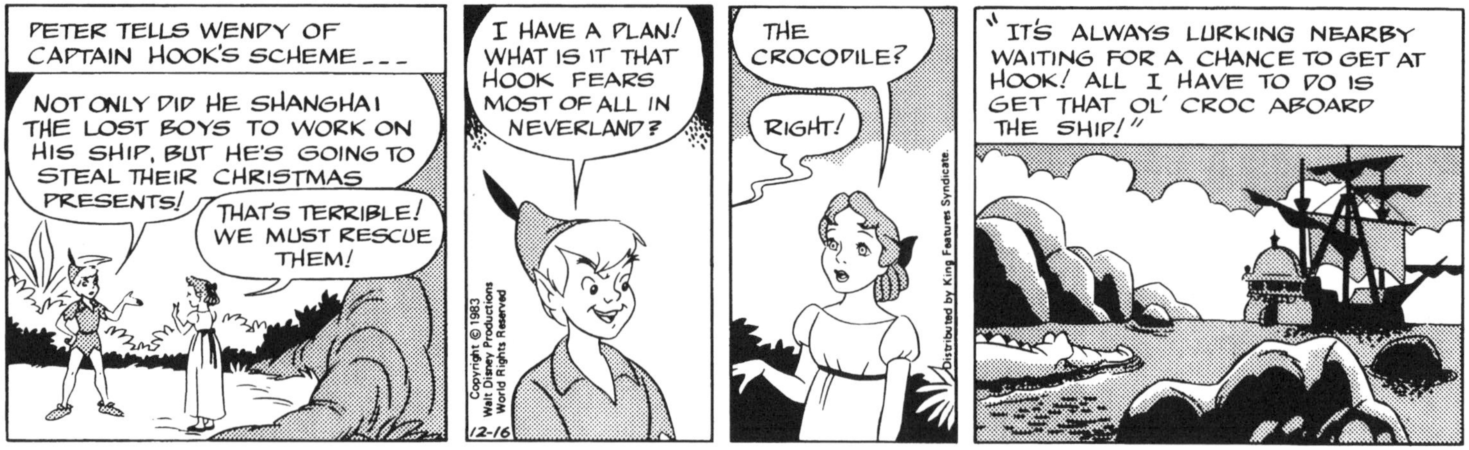
PETER TELLS WENDY OF CAPTAIN HOOK'S SCHEME---
NOT ONLY DID HE SHANGHAI THE LOST BOYS TO WORK ON HIS SHIP, BUT HE'S GOING TO STEAL THEIR CHRISTMAS PRESENTS!
THAT'S TERRIBLE! WE MUST RESCUE THEM!
I HAVE A PLAN! WHAT IS IT THAT HOOK FEARS MOST OF ALL IN NEVERLAND?
Copyright © 1983 Walt Disney Productions World Rights Reserved
12-16
THE CROCODILE?
RIGHT!
Distributed by King Features Syndicate.
"IT'S ALWAYS LURKING NEARBY WAITING FOR A CHANCE TO GET AT HOOK! ALL I HAVE TO DO IS GET THAT OL' CROC ABOARD THE SHIP!"

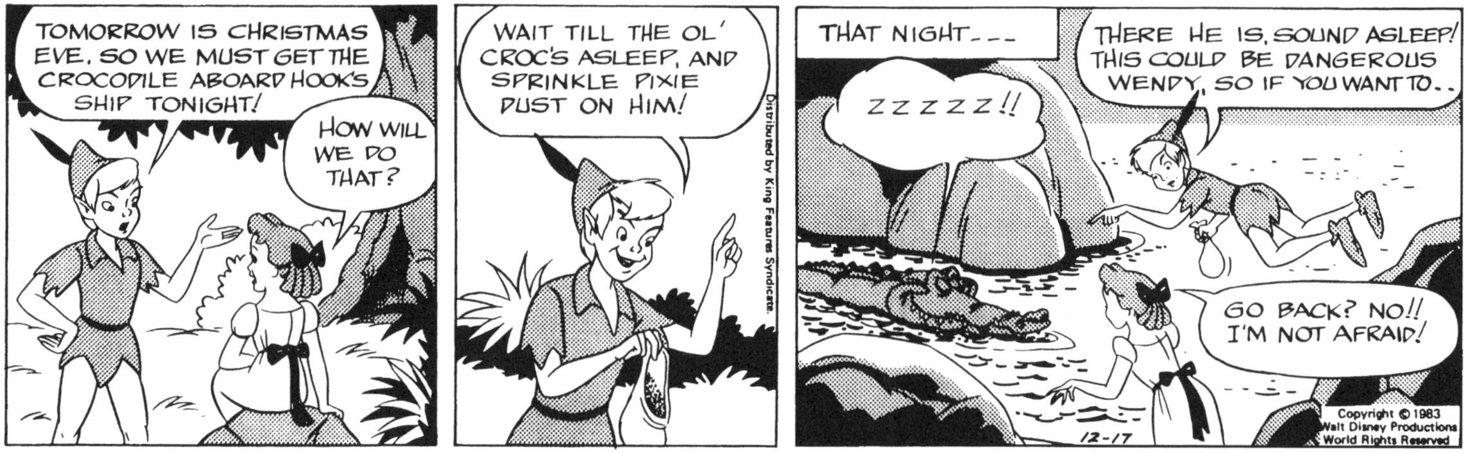
TOMORROW IS CHRISTMAS EVE, SO WE MUST GET THE CROCODILE ABOARD HOOK'S SHIP TONIGHT!
HOW WILL WE DO THAT?
WAIT TILL THE OL' CROC'S ASLEEP, AND SPRINKLE PIXIE DUST ON HIM!
Distributed by King Features Syndicate.
THAT NIGHT---
ZZZZZ!!
THERE HE IS, SOUND ASLEEP! THIS COULD BE DANGEROUS WENDY, SO IF YOU WANT TO..
GO BACK? NO!! I'M NOT AFRAID!
Copyright © 1983 Walt Disney Productions World Rights Reserved
12-17

PETER SPRINKLES PIXIE DUST ON THE SLEEPING CROCODILE FROM HEAD TO TAIL - - -

THAT SHOULD BE ENOUGH TO MAKE HIM AS LIGHT AS A FEATHER!

UPSY-DAISY!

ZZZ!

12-19

CAPTAIN HOOK IS GOING TO FIND AN UNWELCOME PASSENGER ABOARD HIS SHIP IN THE MORNING!

ZZZ!

THE CROCODILE IS LOWERED GENTLY TO THE DECK OF HOOK'S SHIP WHILE THE PIRATES SLEEP...

ZZZZZ!

Copyright © 1983 Walt Disney Productions World Rights Reserved

12-20

THE LOST BOYS ARE LOCKED UP BELOW! THEY'RE SAFE TILL WE CAN FREE THEM!

Distributed by King Features Syndicate.

EARLY THE NEXT MORNING...

MISTER SMEE! WHERE'RE MY TEA AND BISCUITS?

COMING, CAPTAIN! COMING!!

SMEE DOESN'T WATCH HIS STEP!

OOF!!

!?!

CRASH!!

ROAR!!

Distributed by King Features Syndicate.

Copyright © 1983 Walt Disney Productions World Rights Reserved

WHAT'S ALL THE COMMO...

YEEOWW!

ABANDON SHIP!

12-21

193 • December 19-21, 1983

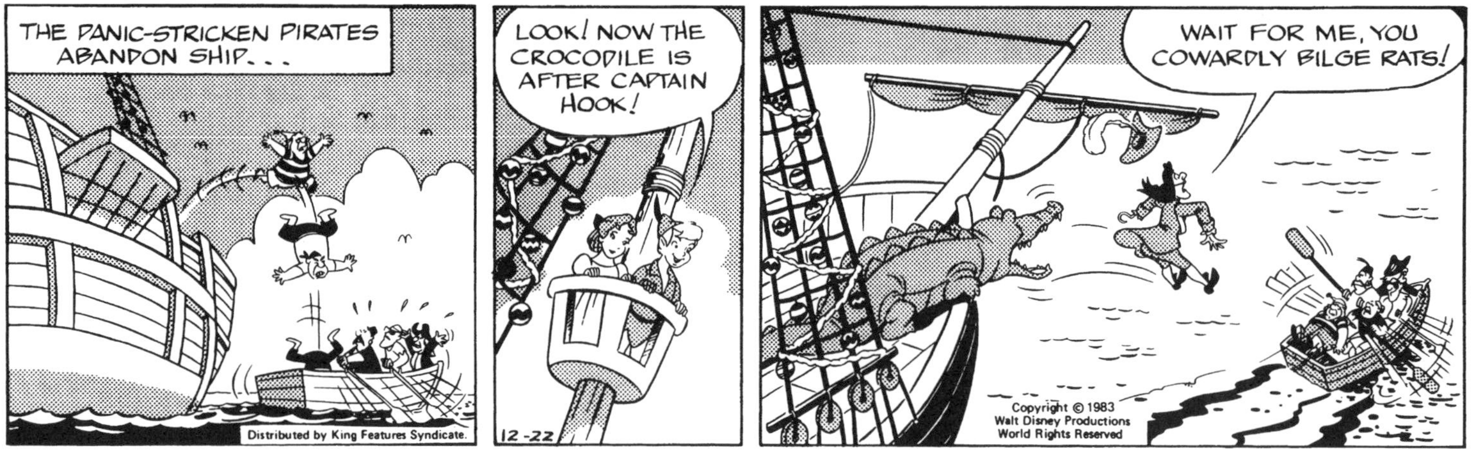
THE PANIC-STRICKEN PIRATES ABANDON SHIP...
Distributed by King Features Syndicate.
LOOK! NOW THE CROCODILE IS AFTER CAPTAIN HOOK!
12-22
WAIT FOR ME, YOU COWARDLY BILGE RATS!
Copyright © 1983 Walt Disney Productions World Rights Reserved

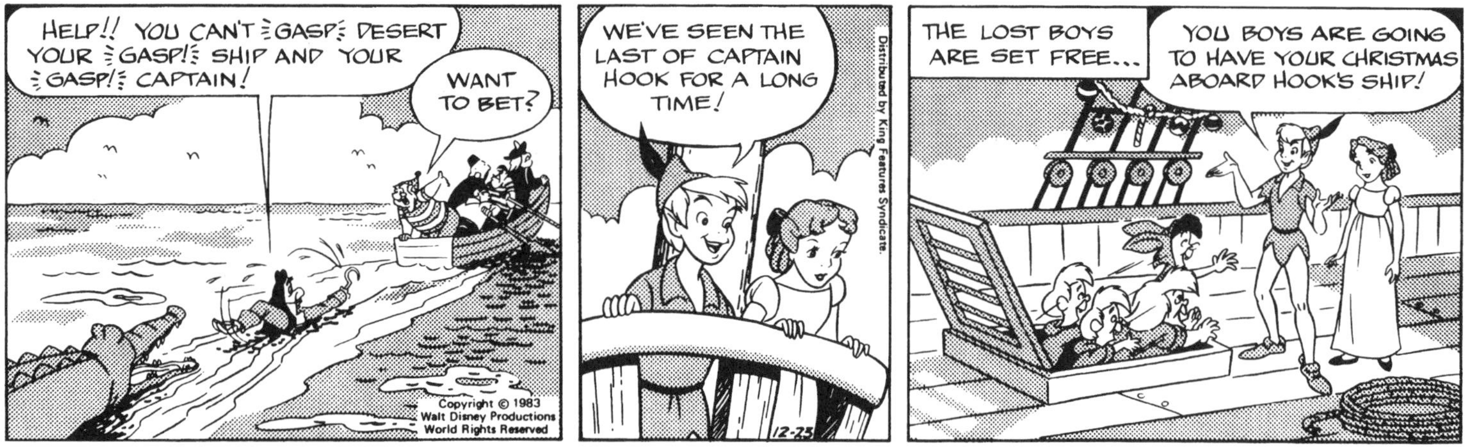
HELP!! YOU CAN'T GASP! DESERT YOUR GASP! SHIP AND YOUR GASP! CAPTAIN!
WANT TO BET?
Copyright © 1983 Walt Disney Productions World Rights Reserved
WE'VE SEEN THE LAST OF CAPTAIN HOOK FOR A LONG TIME!
Distributed by King Features Syndicate.
12-23
THE LOST BOYS ARE SET FREE...
YOU BOYS ARE GOING TO HAVE YOUR CHRISTMAS ABOARD HOOK'S SHIP!

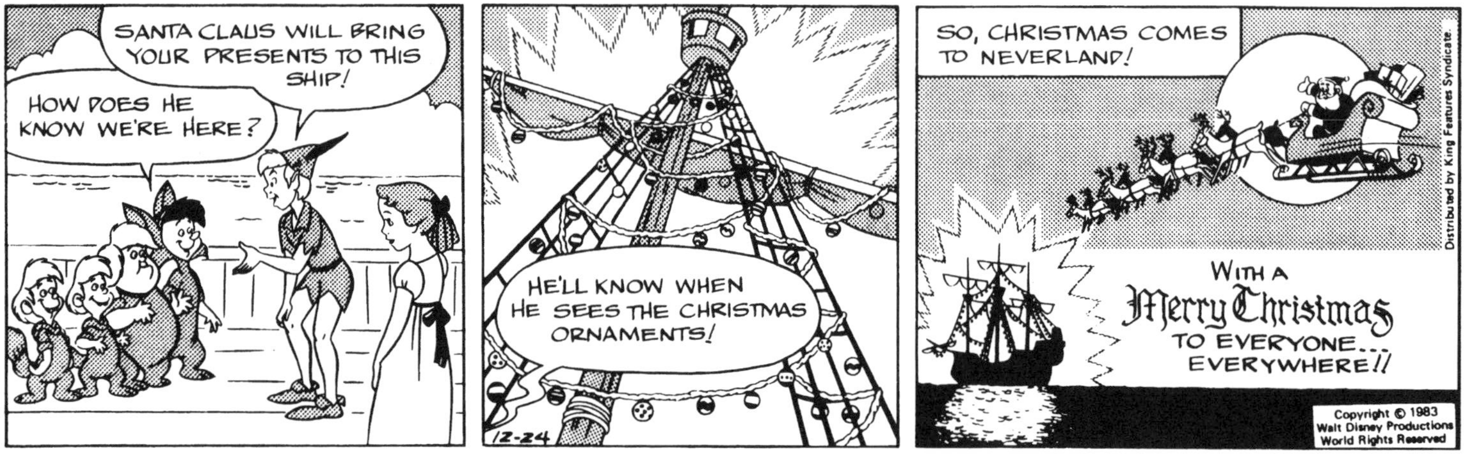
SANTA CLAUS WILL BRING YOUR PRESENTS TO THIS SHIP!
HOW DOES HE KNOW WE'RE HERE?
HE'LL KNOW WHEN HE SEES THE CHRISTMAS ORNAMENTS!
12-24
SO, CHRISTMAS COMES TO NEVERLAND!
Distributed by King Features Syndicate.
WITH A Merry Christmas TO EVERYONE... EVERYWHERE!!
Copyright © 1983 Walt Disney Productions World Rights Reserved

1984

A CHRISTMAS PRESENT FOR MR. TOAD

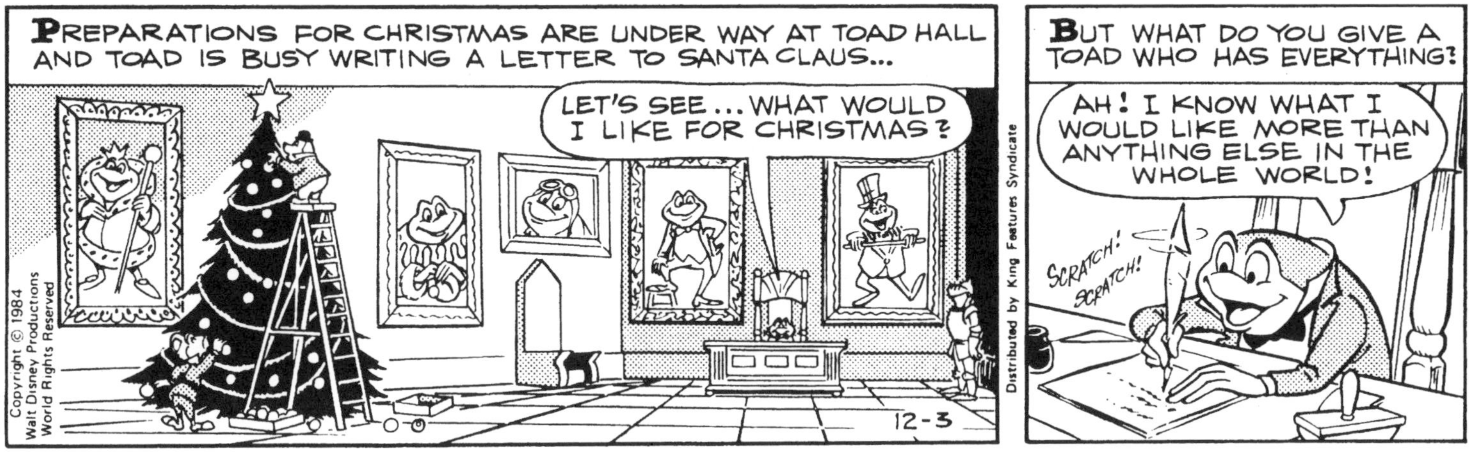
PREPARATIONS FOR CHRISTMAS ARE UNDER WAY AT TOAD HALL AND TOAD IS BUSY WRITING A LETTER TO SANTA CLAUS...
LET'S SEE... WHAT WOULD I LIKE FOR CHRISTMAS?
Copyright © 1984 Walt Disney Productions World Rights Reserved
12-3
Distributed by King Features Syndicate
BUT WHAT DO YOU GIVE A TOAD WHO HAS EVERYTHING?
AH! I KNOW WHAT I WOULD LIKE MORE THAN ANYTHING ELSE IN THE WHOLE WORLD!
SCRATCH! SCRATCH!

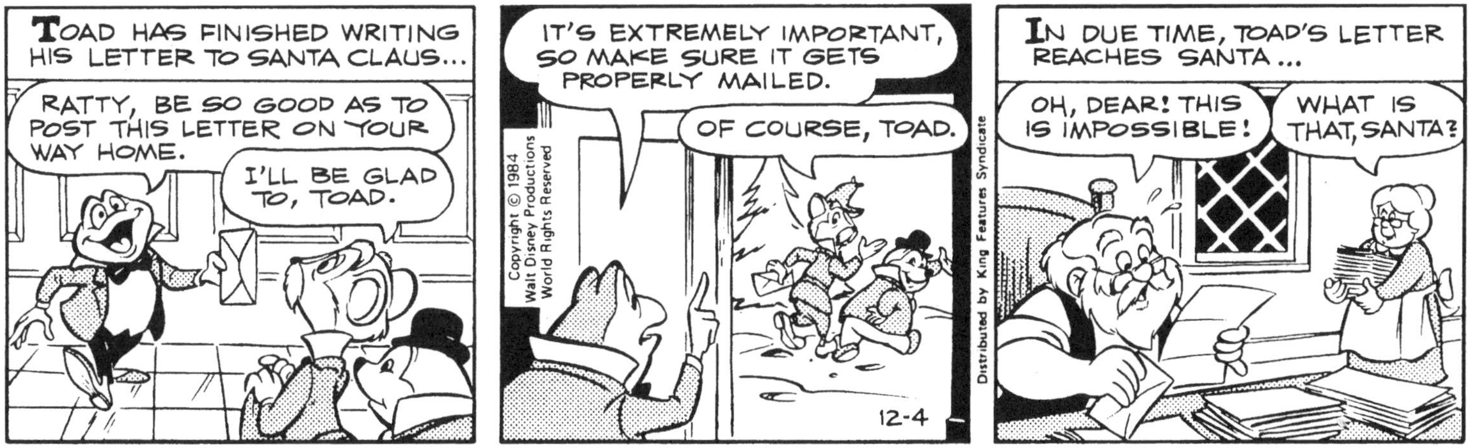
TOAD HAS FINISHED WRITING HIS LETTER TO SANTA CLAUS...
RATTY, BE SO GOOD AS TO POST THIS LETTER ON YOUR WAY HOME.
I'LL BE GLAD TO, TOAD.
Copyright © 1984 Walt Disney Productions World Rights Reserved
IT'S EXTREMELY IMPORTANT, SO MAKE SURE IT GETS PROPERLY MAILED.
OF COURSE, TOAD.
12-4
Distributed by King Features Syndicate
IN DUE TIME, TOAD'S LETTER REACHES SANTA...
OH, DEAR! THIS IS IMPOSSIBLE!
WHAT IS THAT, SANTA?

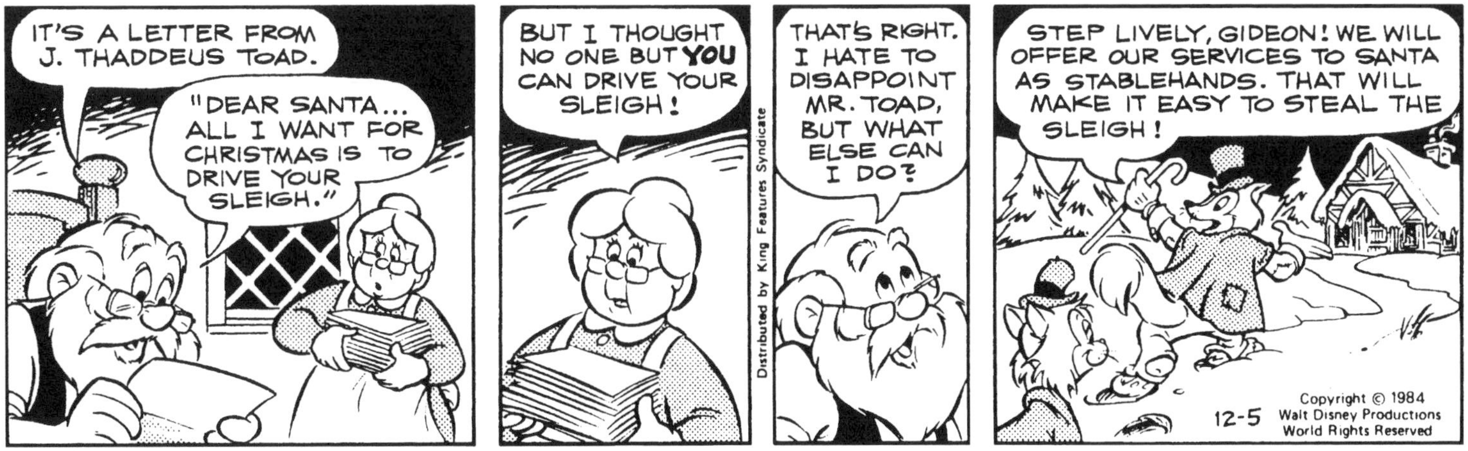
IT'S A LETTER FROM J. THADDEUS TOAD.
"DEAR SANTA... ALL I WANT FOR CHRISTMAS IS TO DRIVE YOUR SLEIGH."
BUT I THOUGHT NO ONE BUT YOU CAN DRIVE YOUR SLEIGH!
Distributed by King Features Syndicate
THAT'S RIGHT. I HATE TO DISAPPOINT MR. TOAD, BUT WHAT ELSE CAN I DO?
STEP LIVELY, GIDEON! WE WILL OFFER OUR SERVICES TO SANTA AS STABLEHANDS. THAT WILL MAKE IT EASY TO STEAL THE SLEIGH!
12-5
Copyright © 1984 Walt Disney Productions World Rights Reserved

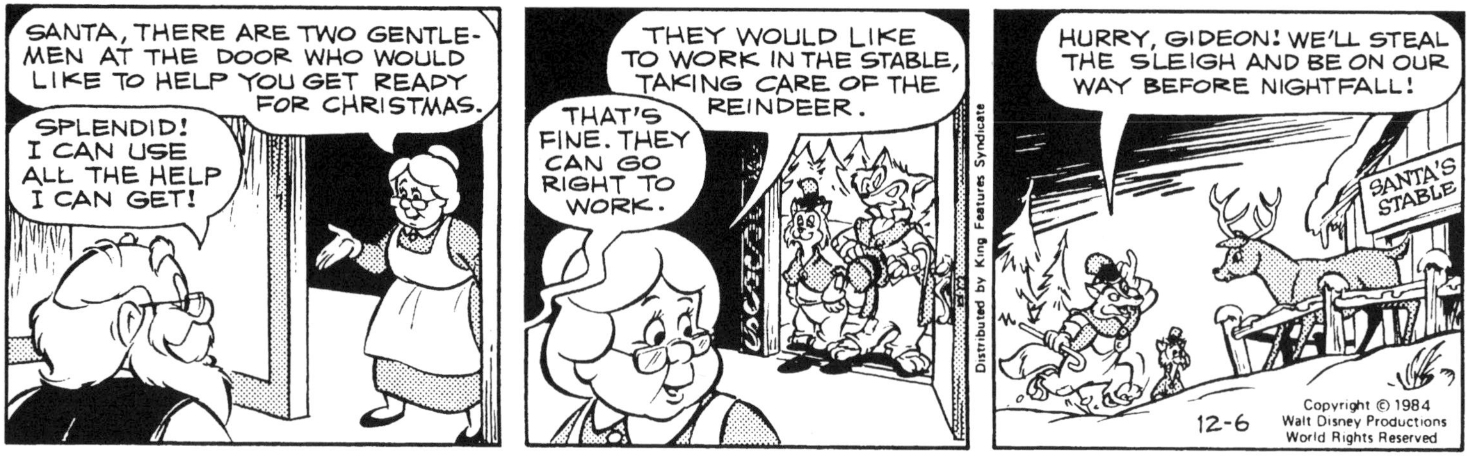
SANTA, THERE ARE TWO GENTLEMEN AT THE DOOR WHO WOULD LIKE TO HELP YOU GET READY FOR CHRISTMAS.
SPLENDID! I CAN USE ALL THE HELP I CAN GET!
THEY WOULD LIKE TO WORK IN THE STABLE, TAKING CARE OF THE REINDEER.
THAT'S FINE. THEY CAN GO RIGHT TO WORK.
Distributed by King Features Syndicate
HURRY, GIDEON! WE'LL STEAL THE SLEIGH AND BE ON OUR WAY BEFORE NIGHTFALL!
SANTA'S STABLE
12-6
Copyright © 1984 Walt Disney Productions World Rights Reserved

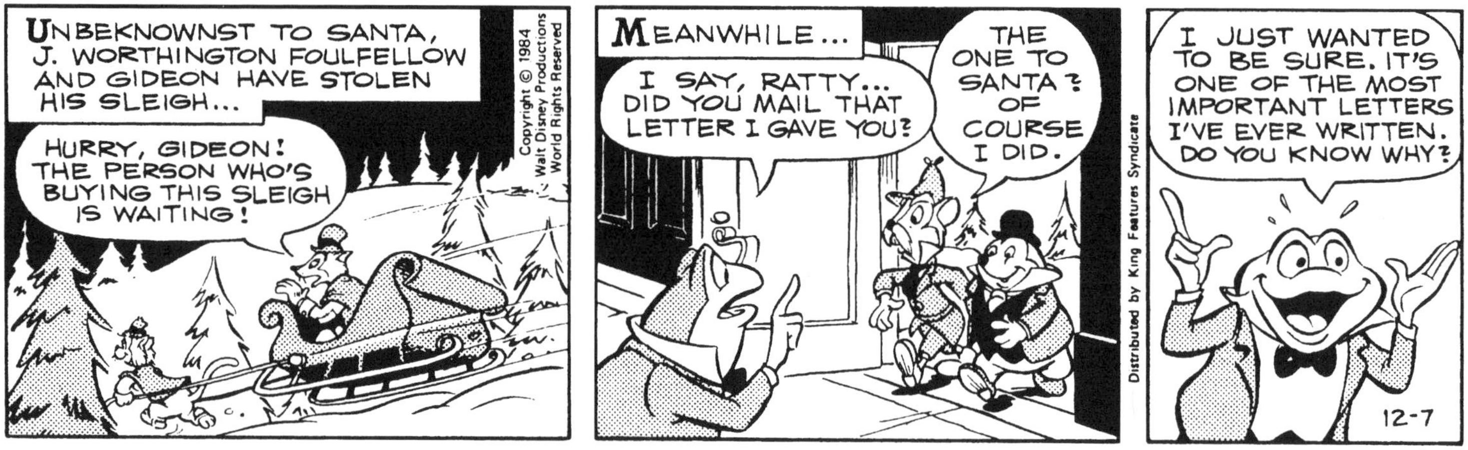
UNBEKNOWNST TO SANTA, J. WORTHINGTON FOULFELLOW AND GIDEON HAVE STOLEN HIS SLEIGH...
HURRY, GIDEON! THE PERSON WHO'S BUYING THIS SLEIGH IS WAITING!
Copyright © 1984 Walt Disney Productions World Rights Reserved
MEANWHILE...
I SAY, RATTY... DID YOU MAIL THAT LETTER I GAVE YOU?
THE ONE TO SANTA? OF COURSE I DID.
Distributed by King Features Syndicate
I JUST WANTED TO BE SURE. IT'S ONE OF THE MOST IMPORTANT LETTERS I'VE EVER WRITTEN. DO YOU KNOW WHY?
12-7

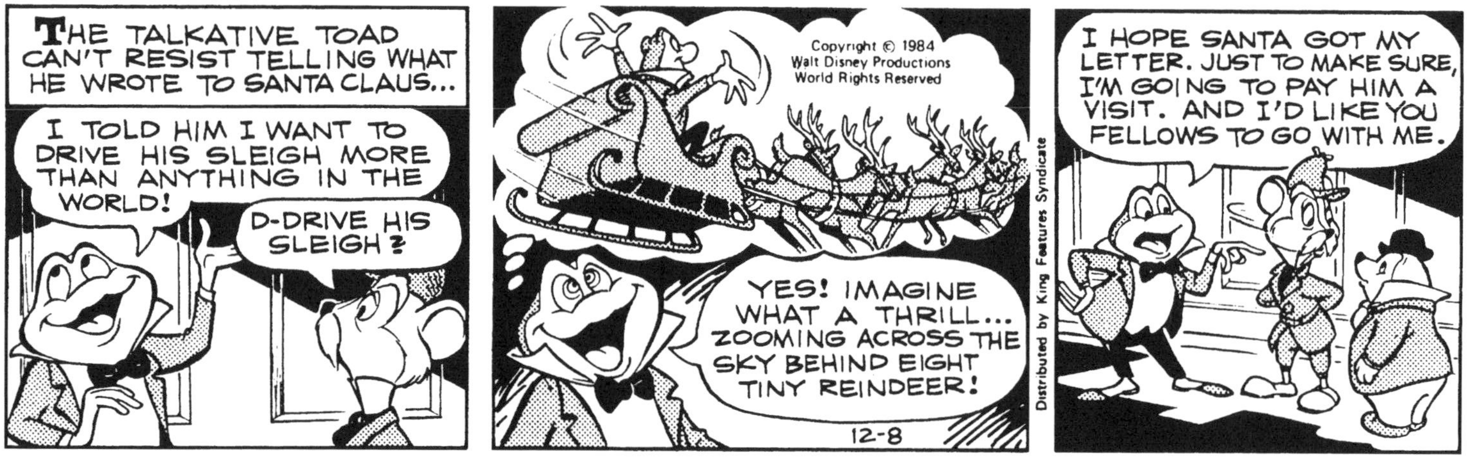
THE TALKATIVE TOAD CAN'T RESIST TELLING WHAT HE WROTE TO SANTA CLAUS...
I TOLD HIM I WANT TO DRIVE HIS SLEIGH MORE THAN ANYTHING IN THE WORLD!
D-DRIVE HIS SLEIGH?
Copyright © 1984 Walt Disney Productions World Rights Reserved
YES! IMAGINE WHAT A THRILL... ZOOMING ACROSS THE SKY BEHIND EIGHT TINY REINDEER!
12-8
Distributed by King Features Syndicate
I HOPE SANTA GOT MY LETTER. JUST TO MAKE SURE, I'M GOING TO PAY HIM A VISIT. AND I'D LIKE YOU FELLOWS TO GO WITH ME.

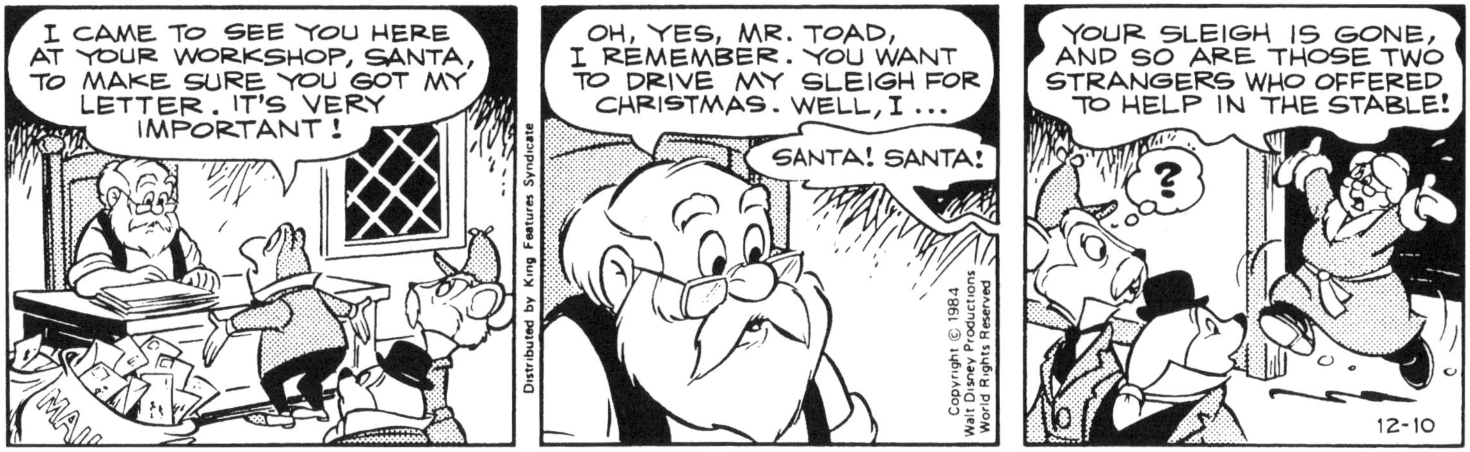
I CAME TO SEE YOU HERE AT YOUR WORKSHOP, SANTA, TO MAKE SURE YOU GOT MY LETTER. IT'S VERY IMPORTANT!
MAIL
Distributed by King Features Syndicate
OH, YES, MR. TOAD, I REMEMBER. YOU WANT TO DRIVE MY SLEIGH FOR CHRISTMAS. WELL, I ...
SANTA! SANTA!
Copyright © 1984 Walt Disney Productions World Rights Reserved
YOUR SLEIGH IS GONE, AND SO ARE THOSE TWO STRANGERS WHO OFFERED TO HELP IN THE STABLE!
?
12-10

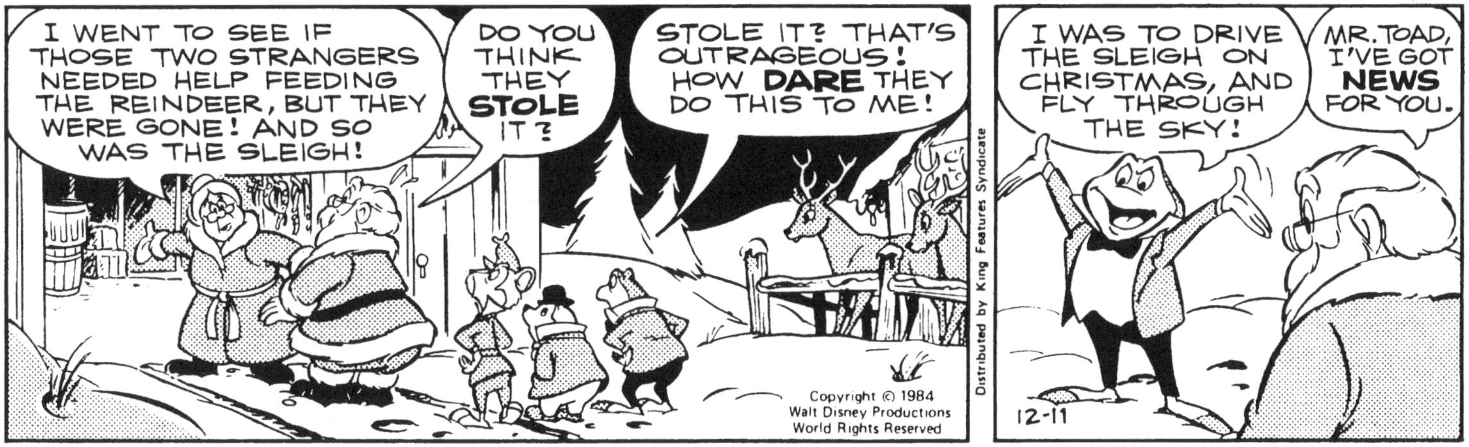
I WENT TO SEE IF THOSE TWO STRANGERS NEEDED HELP FEEDING THE REINDEER, BUT THEY WERE GONE! AND SO WAS THE SLEIGH!
DO YOU THINK THEY STOLE IT?
STOLE IT? THAT'S OUTRAGEOUS! HOW DARE THEY DO THIS TO ME!
Copyright © 1984 Walt Disney Productions World Rights Reserved
Distributed by King Features Syndicate
I WAS TO DRIVE THE SLEIGH ON CHRISTMAS, AND FLY THROUGH THE SKY!
MR. TOAD, I'VE GOT NEWS FOR YOU.
12-11

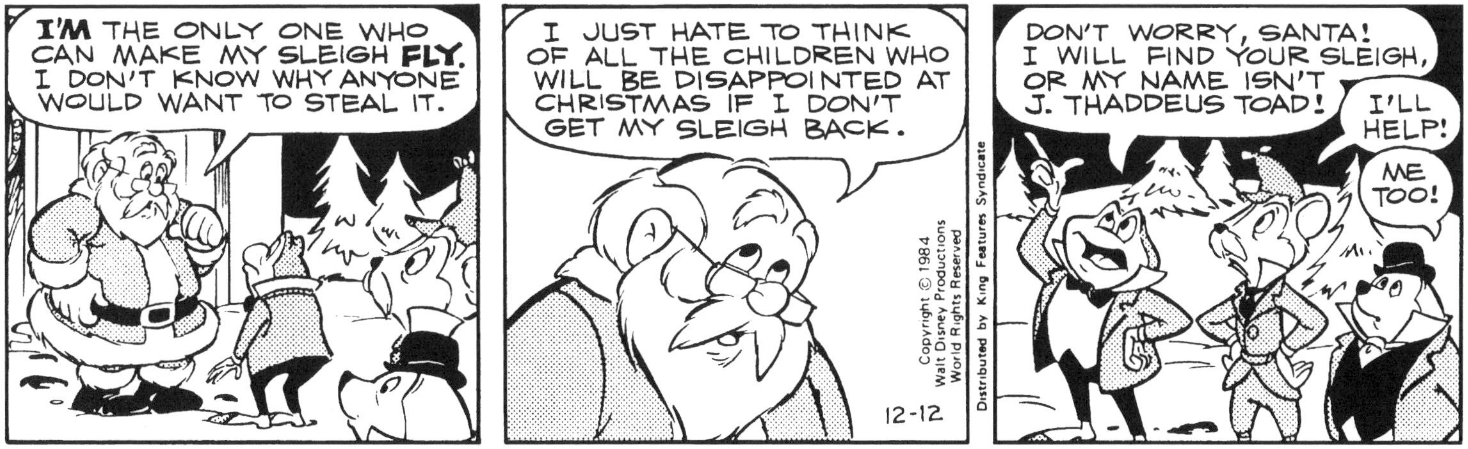
I'M THE ONLY ONE WHO CAN MAKE MY SLEIGH FLY. I DON'T KNOW WHY ANYONE WOULD WANT TO STEAL IT.
I JUST HATE TO THINK OF ALL THE CHILDREN WHO WILL BE DISAPPOINTED AT CHRISTMAS IF I DON'T GET MY SLEIGH BACK.
Copyright © 1984 Walt Disney Productions World Rights Reserved
12-12
Distributed by King Features Syndicate
DON'T WORRY, SANTA! I WILL FIND YOUR SLEIGH, OR MY NAME ISN'T J. THADDEUS TOAD!
I'LL HELP!
ME TOO!

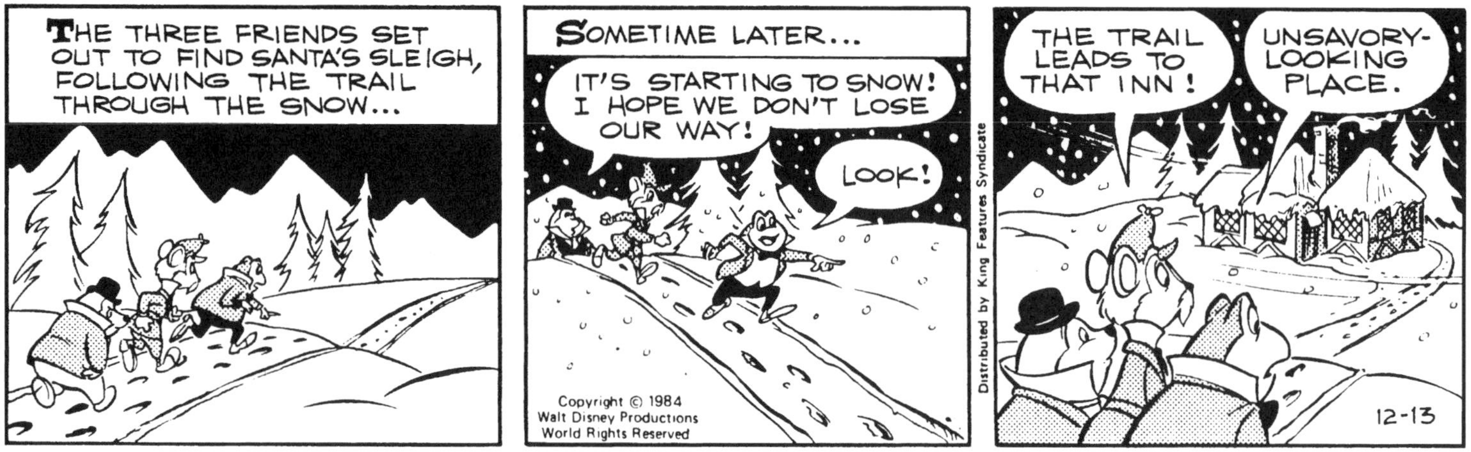
THE THREE FRIENDS SET OUT TO FIND SANTA'S SLEIGH, FOLLOWING THE TRAIL THROUGH THE SNOW...
SOMETIME LATER...
IT'S STARTING TO SNOW! I HOPE WE DON'T LOSE OUR WAY!
LOOK!
Copyright © 1984
Walt Disney Productions
World Rights Reserved
Distributed by King Features Syndicate
THE TRAIL LEADS TO THAT INN!
UNSAVORY-LOOKING PLACE.
12-13

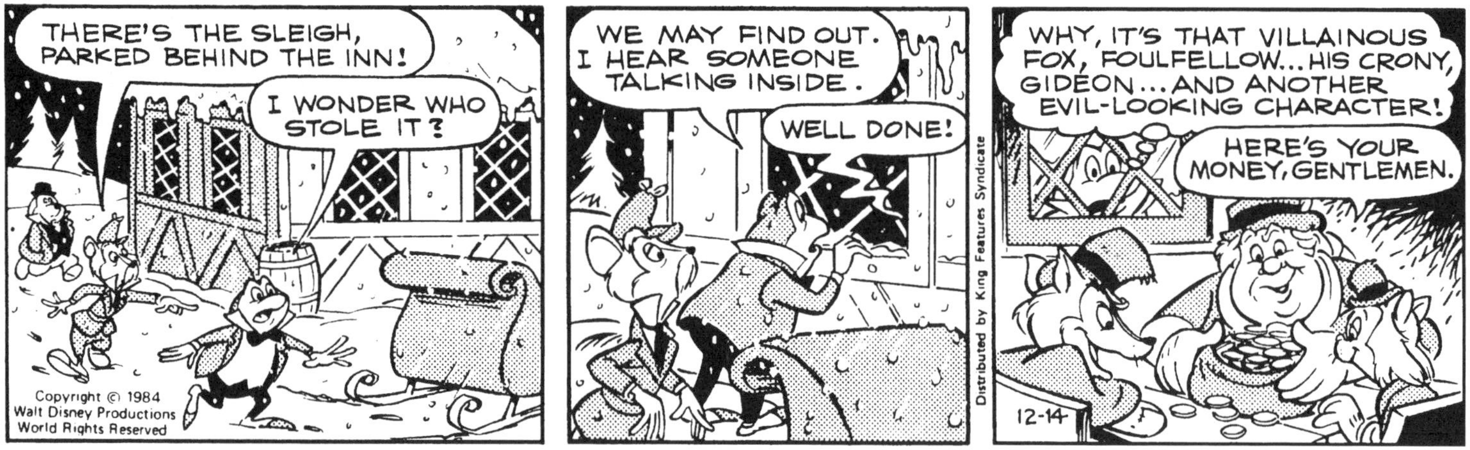
THERE'S THE SLEIGH, PARKED BEHIND THE INN!
I WONDER WHO STOLE IT?
Copyright © 1984
Walt Disney Productions
World Rights Reserved
WE MAY FIND OUT. I HEAR SOMEONE TALKING INSIDE.
WELL DONE!
Distributed by King Features Syndicate
WHY, IT'S THAT VILLAINOUS FOX, FOULFELLOW...HIS CRONY, GIDEON...AND ANOTHER EVIL-LOOKING CHARACTER!
HERE'S YOUR MONEY, GENTLEMEN.
12-14

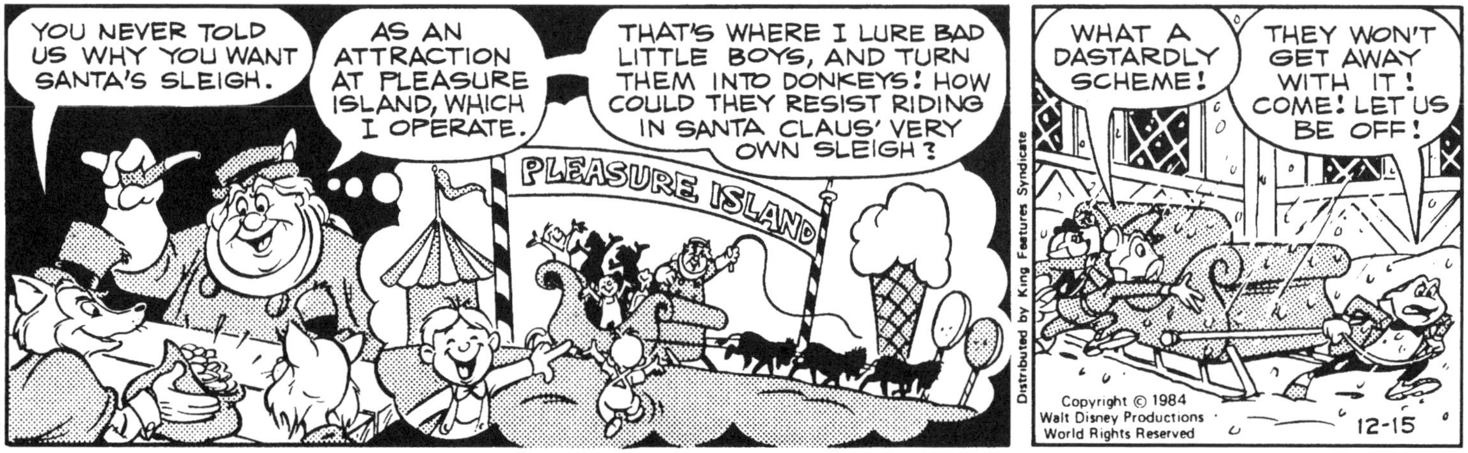
YOU NEVER TOLD US WHY YOU WANT SANTA'S SLEIGH.
AS AN ATTRACTION AT PLEASURE ISLAND, WHICH I OPERATE.
THAT'S WHERE I LURE BAD LITTLE BOYS, AND TURN THEM INTO DONKEYS! HOW COULD THEY RESIST RIDING IN SANTA CLAUS' VERY OWN SLEIGH?
PLEASURE ISLAND
Distributed by King Features Syndicate
WHAT A DASTARDLY SCHEME!
THEY WON'T GET AWAY WITH IT! COME! LET US BE OFF!
Copyright © 1984
Walt Disney Productions
World Rights Reserved
12-15

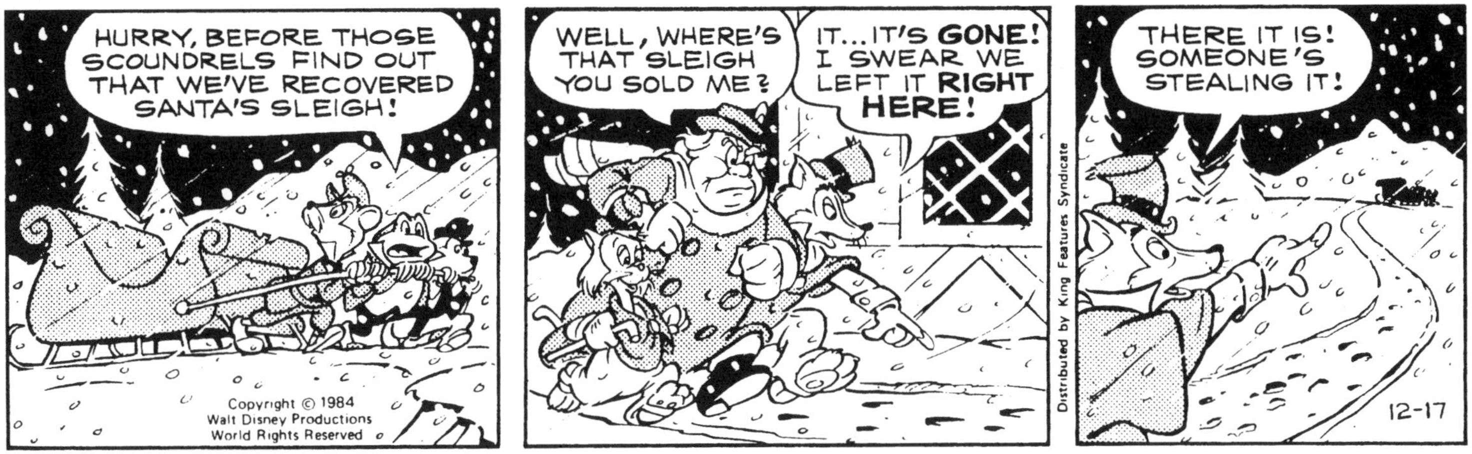
HURRY, BEFORE THOSE SCOUNDRELS FIND OUT THAT WE'VE RECOVERED SANTA'S SLEIGH!
Copyright © 1984 Walt Disney Productions World Rights Reserved
WELL, WHERE'S THAT SLEIGH YOU SOLD ME?
IT... IT'S **GONE!** I SWEAR WE LEFT IT **RIGHT HERE!**
Distributed by King Features Syndicate
THERE IT IS! SOMEONE'S STEALING IT!
12-17

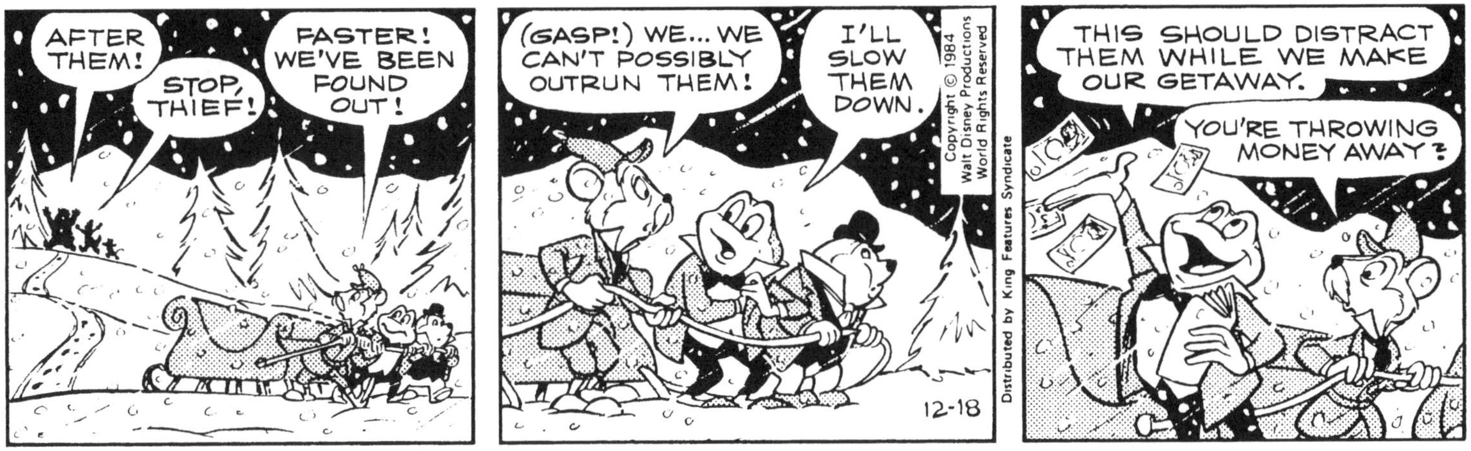
AFTER THEM!
STOP, THIEF!
FASTER! WE'VE BEEN FOUND OUT!
(GASP!) WE... WE CAN'T POSSIBLY OUTRUN THEM!
I'LL SLOW THEM DOWN.
Copyright © 1984 Walt Disney Productions World Rights Reserved
12-18
Distributed by King Features Syndicate
THIS SHOULD DISTRACT THEM WHILE WE MAKE OUR GETAWAY.
YOU'RE THROWING MONEY AWAY?

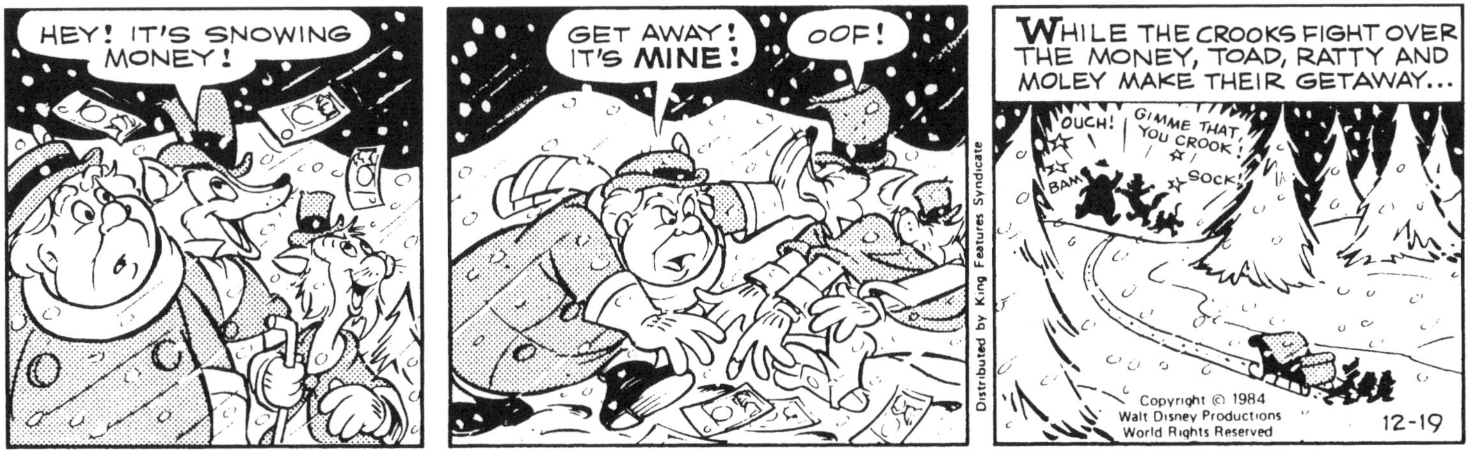
HEY! IT'S SNOWING MONEY!
GET AWAY! IT'S **MINE!**
OOF!
Distributed by King Features Syndicate
WHILE THE CROOKS FIGHT OVER THE MONEY, TOAD, RATTY AND MOLEY MAKE THEIR GETAWAY...
OUCH!
GIMME THAT, YOU CROOK!
BAM
SOCK!
Copyright © 1984 Walt Disney Productions World Rights Reserved
12-19

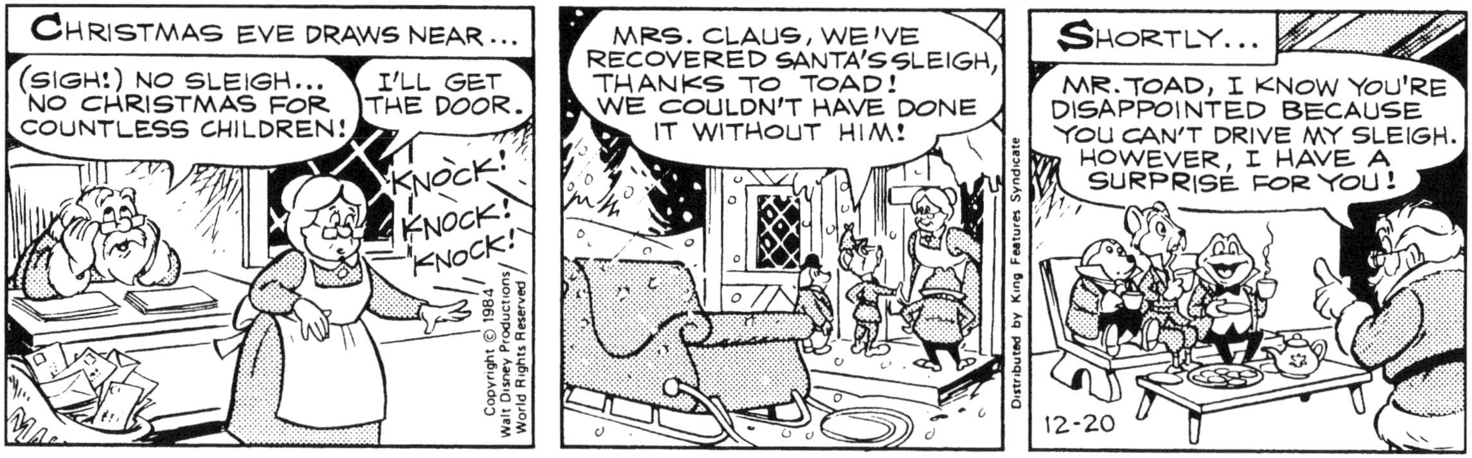
CHRISTMAS EVE DRAWS NEAR...
(SIGH!) NO SLEIGH... NO CHRISTMAS FOR COUNTLESS CHILDREN!
I'LL GET THE DOOR.
KNOCK! KNOCK! KNOCK!
Copyright © 1984 Walt Disney Productions World Rights Reserved
MRS. CLAUS, WE'VE RECOVERED SANTA'S SLEIGH, THANKS TO TOAD! WE COULDN'T HAVE DONE IT WITHOUT HIM!
Distributed by King Features Syndicate
SHORTLY...
MR. TOAD, I KNOW YOU'RE DISAPPOINTED BECAUSE YOU CAN'T DRIVE MY SLEIGH. HOWEVER, I HAVE A SURPRISE FOR YOU!
12-20

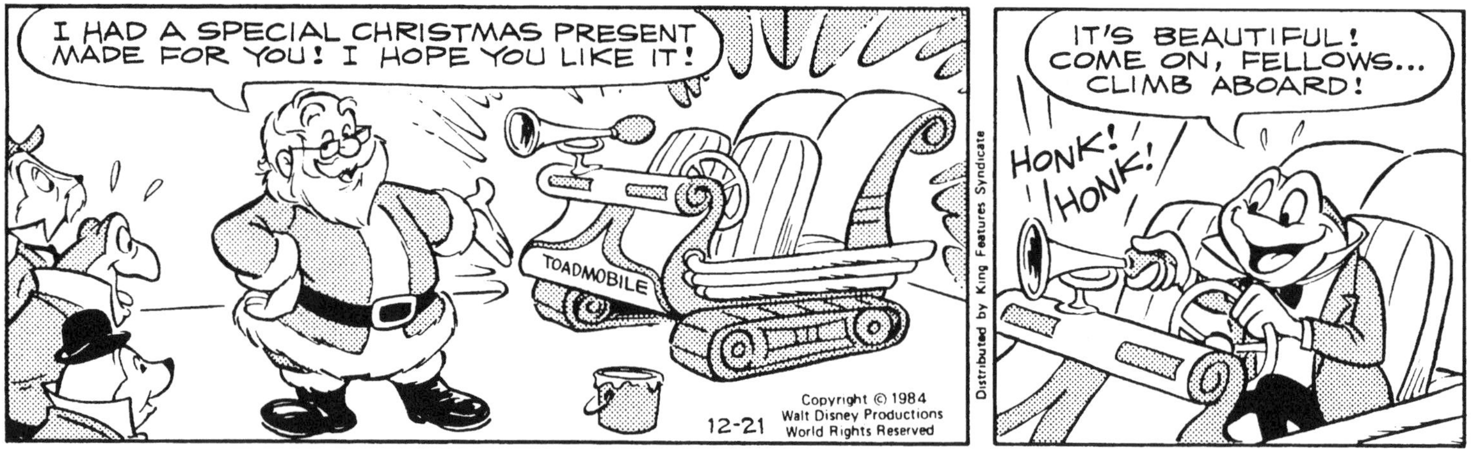
I HAD A SPECIAL CHRISTMAS PRESENT MADE FOR YOU! I HOPE YOU LIKE IT!
TOADMOBILE
12-21
Copyright © 1984 Walt Disney Productions World Rights Reserved
Distributed by King Features Syndicate
IT'S BEAUTIFUL! COME ON, FELLOWS... CLIMB ABOARD!
HONK! HONK!

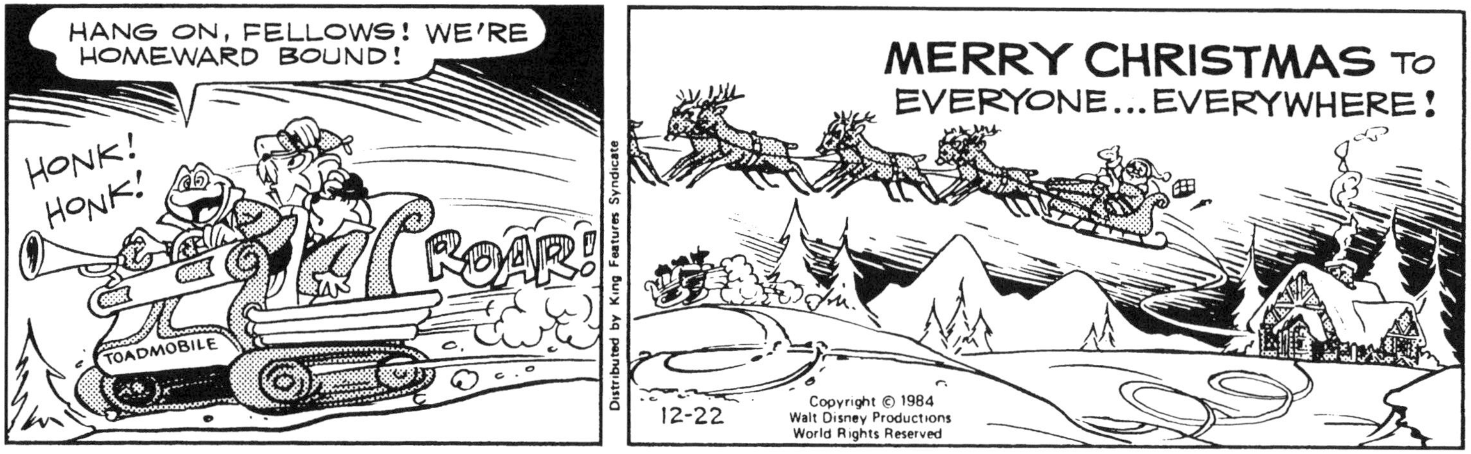
HANG ON, FELLOWS! WE'RE HOMEWARD BOUND!
HONK! HONK!
ROAR!
TOADMOBILE
Distributed by King Features Syndicate
MERRY CHRISTMAS TO EVERYONE...EVERYWHERE!
12-22
Copyright © 1984 Walt Disney Productions World Rights Reserved

1985

CRUELLA'S VERY FURRY CHRISTMAS

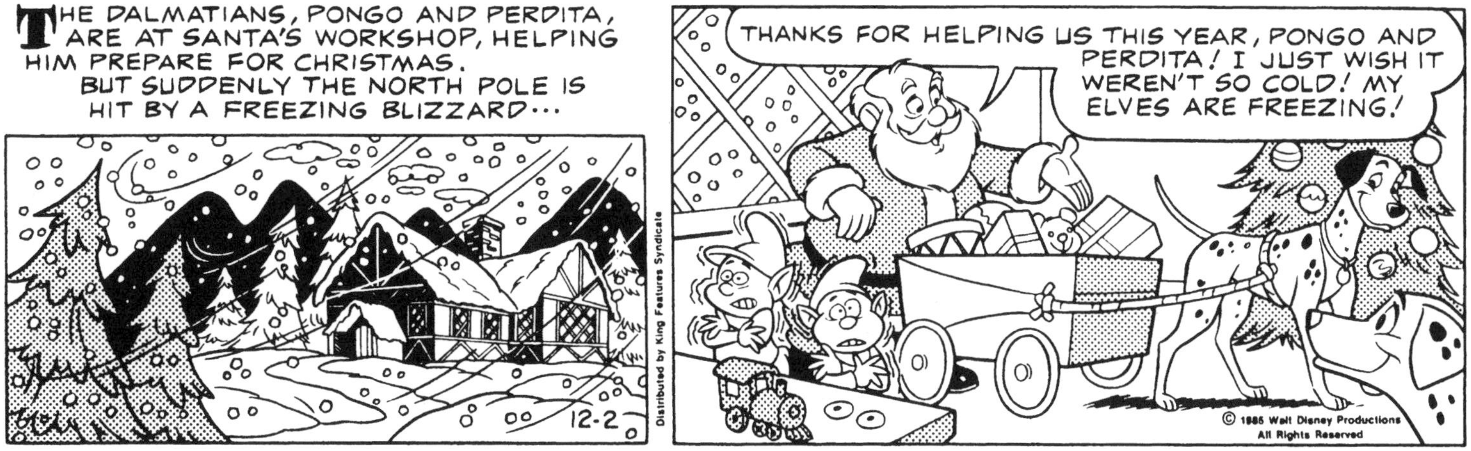
THE DALMATIANS, PONGO AND PERDITA, ARE AT SANTA'S WORKSHOP, HELPING HIM PREPARE FOR CHRISTMAS.
BUT SUDDENLY THE NORTH POLE IS HIT BY A FREEZING BLIZZARD...
12-2
Distributed by King Features Syndicate
THANKS FOR HELPING US THIS YEAR, PONGO AND PERDITA! I JUST WISH IT WEREN'T SO COLD! MY ELVES ARE FREEZING!
© 1985 Walt Disney Productions
All Rights Reserved

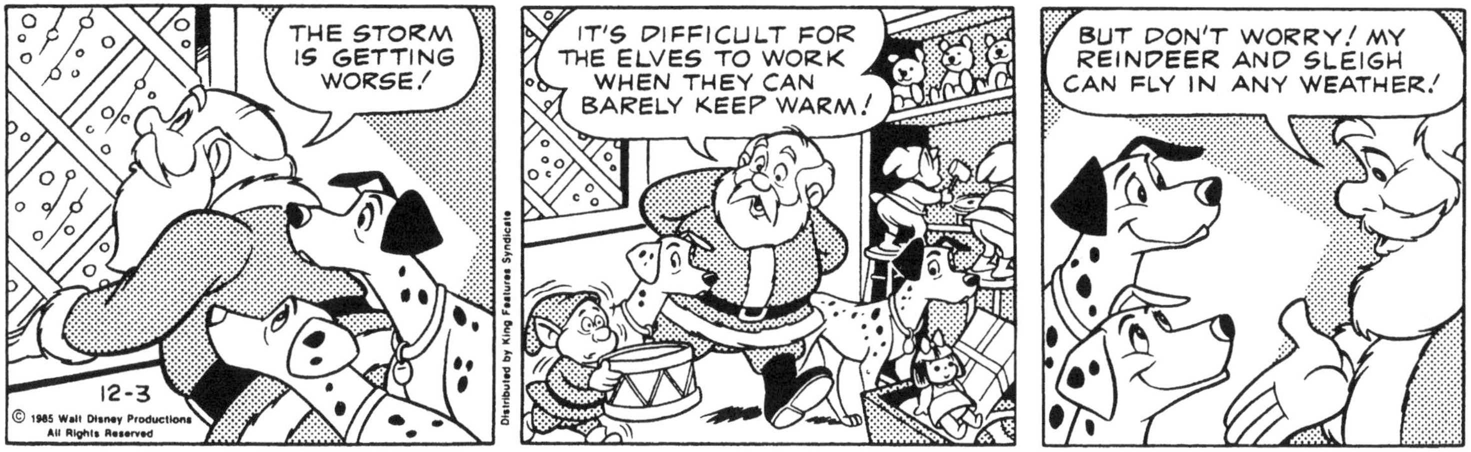
THE STORM IS GETTING WORSE!
12-3
© 1985 Walt Disney Productions
All Rights Reserved
Distributed by King Features Syndicate
IT'S DIFFICULT FOR THE ELVES TO WORK WHEN THEY CAN BARELY KEEP WARM!
BUT DON'T WORRY! MY REINDEER AND SLEIGH CAN FLY IN ANY WEATHER!

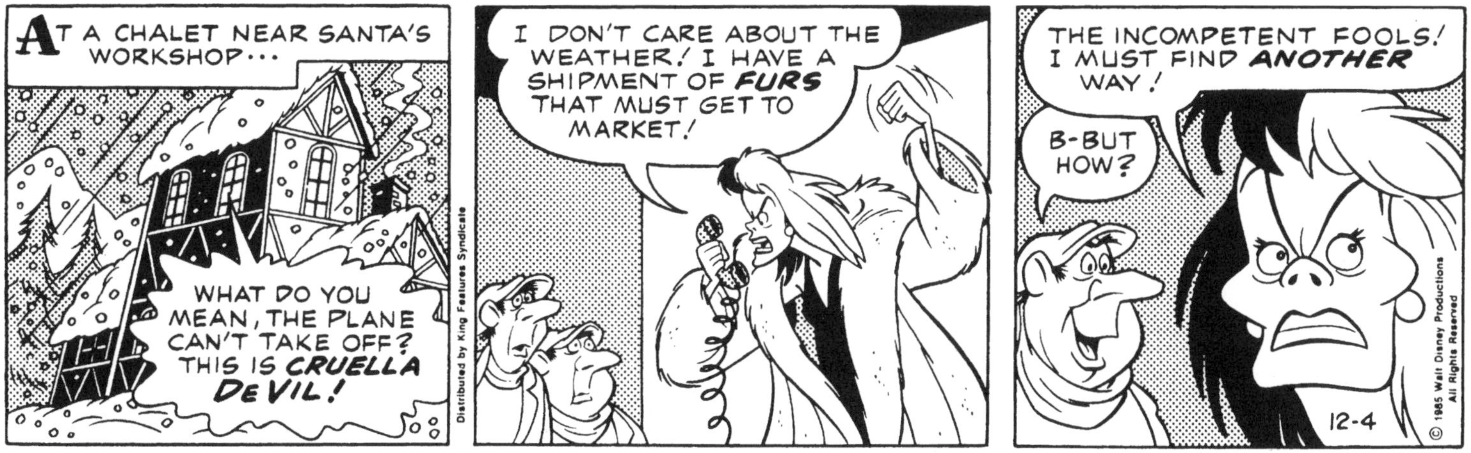
AT A CHALET NEAR SANTA'S WORKSHOP...
WHAT DO YOU MEAN, THE PLANE CAN'T TAKE OFF? THIS IS CRUELLA DeVIL!
Distributed by King Features Syndicate
I DON'T CARE ABOUT THE WEATHER! I HAVE A SHIPMENT OF FURS THAT MUST GET TO MARKET!
THE INCOMPETENT FOOLS! I MUST FIND ANOTHER WAY!
B-BUT HOW?
12-4
© 1985 Walt Disney Productions
All Rights Reserved

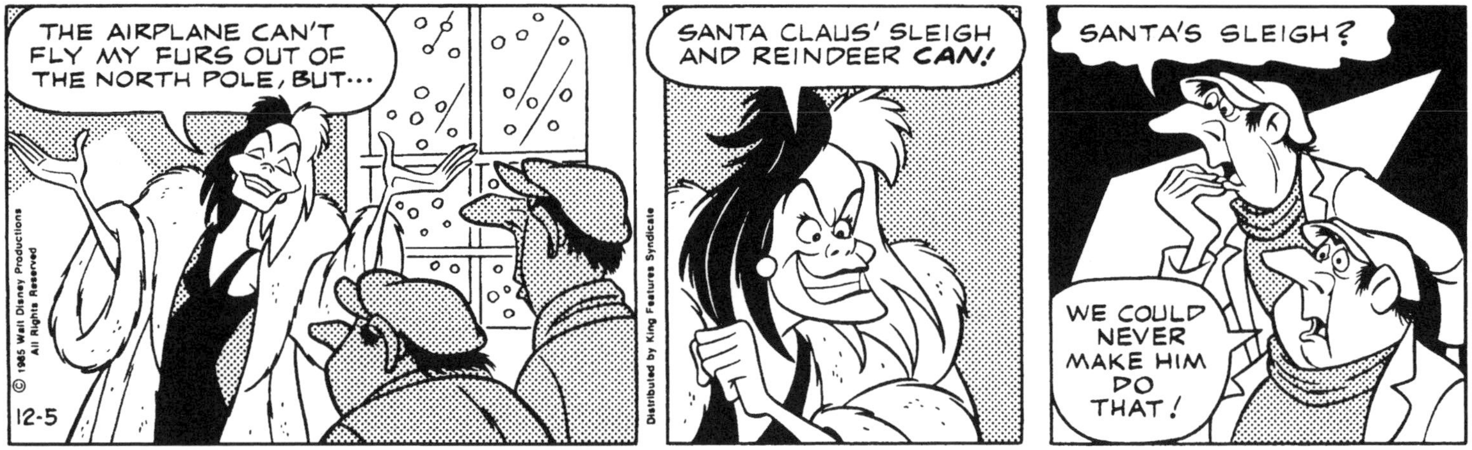
THE AIRPLANE CAN'T FLY MY FURS OUT OF THE NORTH POLE, BUT...
© 1985 Walt Disney Productions All Rights Reserved
12-5
SANTA CLAUS' SLEIGH AND REINDEER CAN!
Distributed by King Features Syndicate
SANTA'S SLEIGH?
WE COULD NEVER MAKE HIM DO THAT!

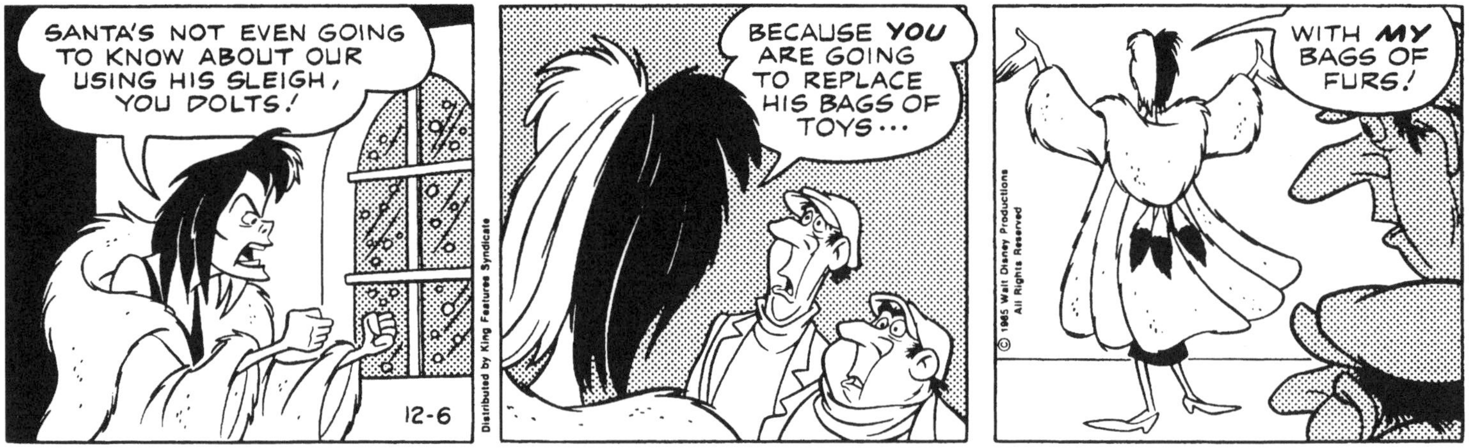
SANTA'S NOT EVEN GOING TO KNOW ABOUT OUR USING HIS SLEIGH, YOU DOLTS!
12-6
Distributed by King Features Syndicate
BECAUSE YOU ARE GOING TO REPLACE HIS BAGS OF TOYS...
WITH MY BAGS OF FURS!
© 1985 Walt Disney Productions All Rights Reserved

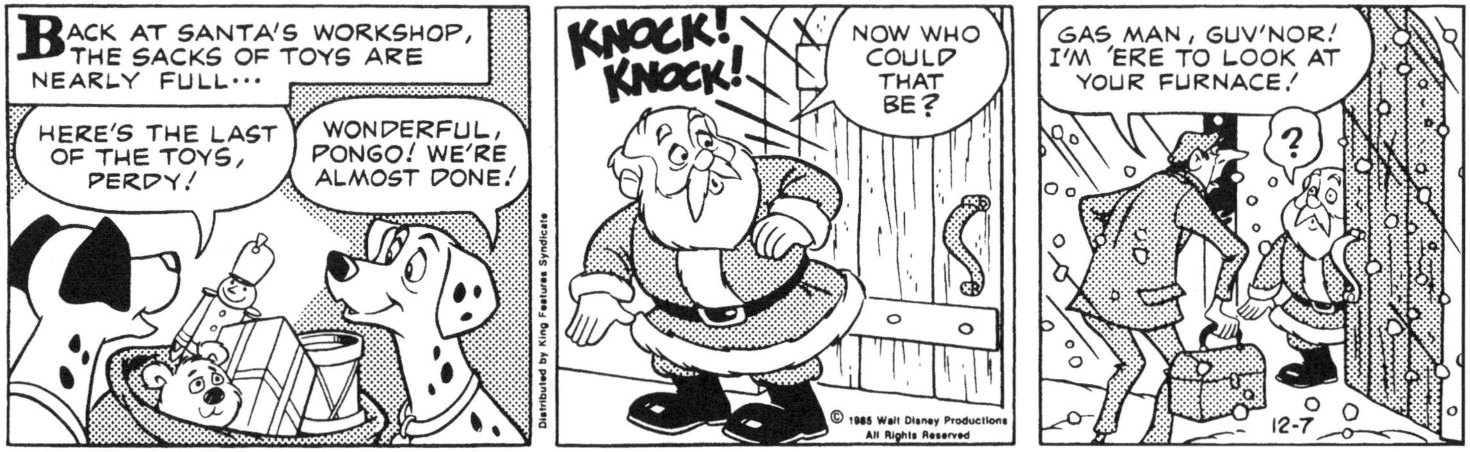
BACK AT SANTA'S WORKSHOP, THE SACKS OF TOYS ARE NEARLY FULL...
HERE'S THE LAST OF THE TOYS, PERDY!
WONDERFUL, PONGO! WE'RE ALMOST DONE!
Distributed by King Features Syndicate
KNOCK! KNOCK!
NOW WHO COULD THAT BE?
© 1985 Walt Disney Productions All Rights Reserved
GAS MAN, GUV'NOR! I'M 'ERE TO LOOK AT YOUR FURNACE!
?
12-7

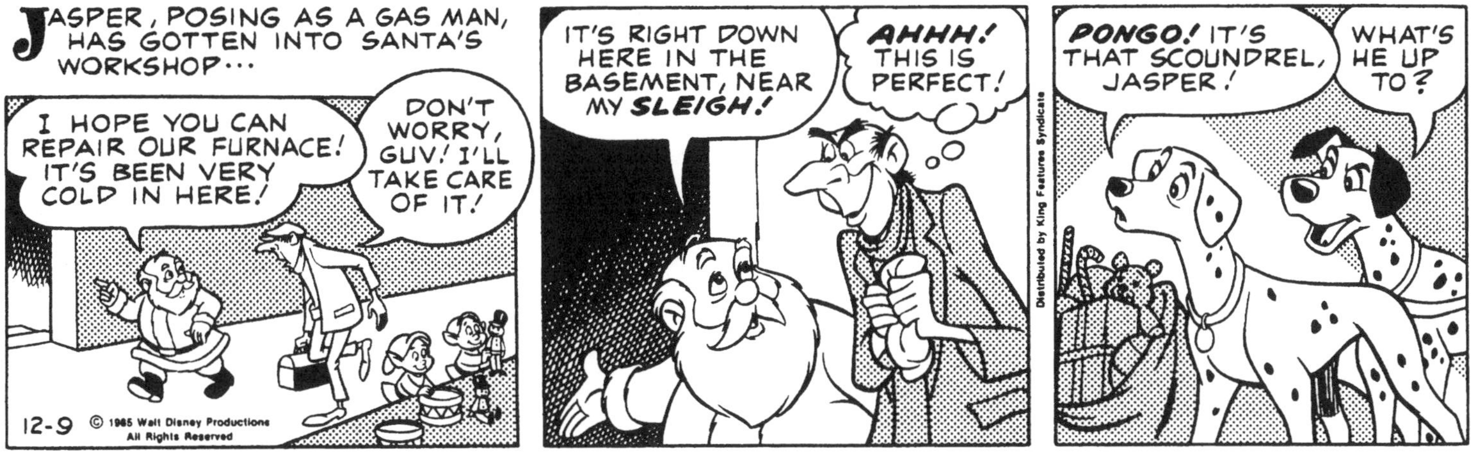
JASPER, POSING AS A GAS MAN, HAS GOTTEN INTO SANTA'S WORKSHOP···
I HOPE YOU CAN REPAIR OUR FURNACE! IT'S BEEN VERY COLD IN HERE!
DON'T WORRY, GUV! I'LL TAKE CARE OF IT!
12-9
© 1985 Walt Disney Productions All Rights Reserved
IT'S RIGHT DOWN HERE IN THE BASEMENT, NEAR MY SLEIGH!
AHHH! THIS IS PERFECT!
Distributed by King Features Syndicate
PONGO! IT'S THAT SCOUNDREL, JASPER!
WHAT'S HE UP TO?

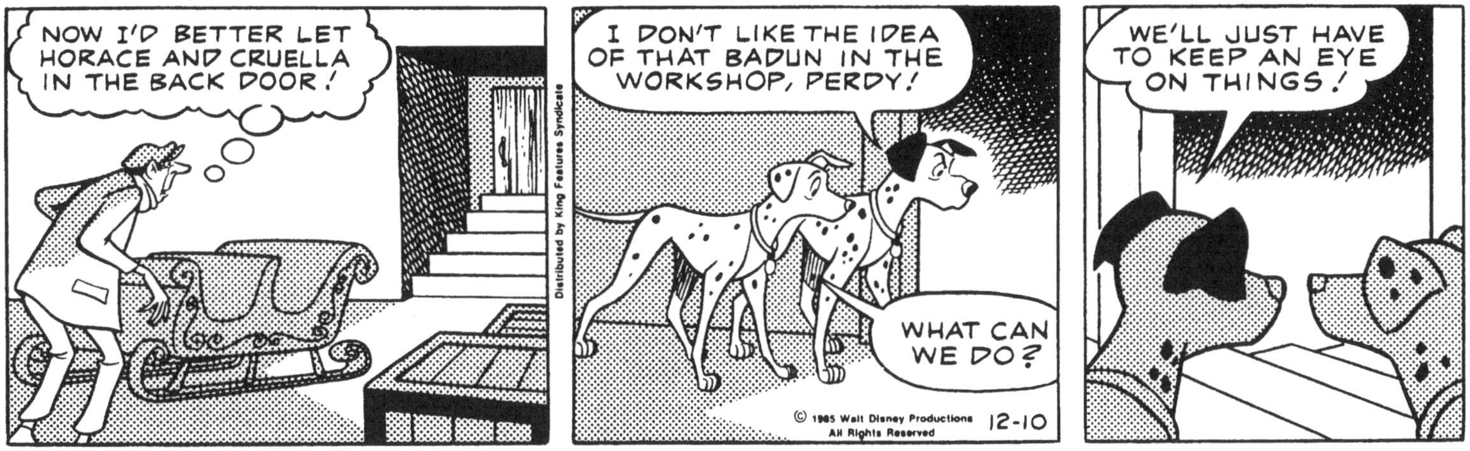
NOW I'D BETTER LET HORACE AND CRUELLA IN THE BACK DOOR!
Distributed by King Features Syndicate
I DON'T LIKE THE IDEA OF THAT BADUN IN THE WORKSHOP, PERDY!
WHAT CAN WE DO?
© 1985 Walt Disney Productions All Rights Reserved
12-10
WE'LL JUST HAVE TO KEEP AN EYE ON THINGS!

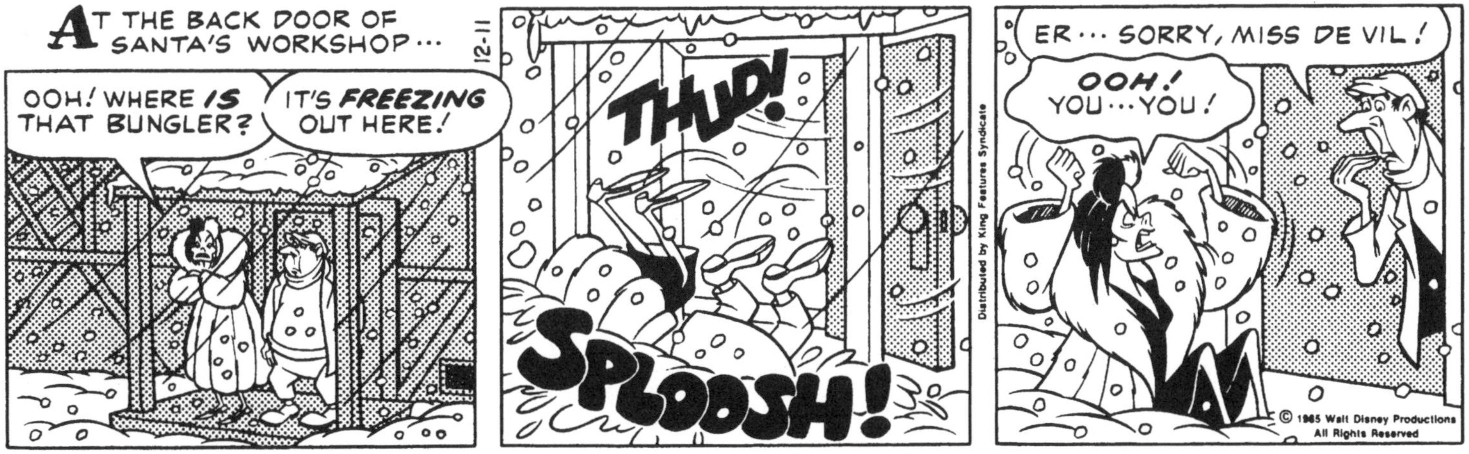
AT THE BACK DOOR OF SANTA'S WORKSHOP···
12-11
OOH! WHERE IS THAT BUNGLER?
IT'S FREEZING OUT HERE!
THUD!
SPLOOSH!
Distributed by King Features Syndicate
ER··· SORRY, MISS DE VIL!
OOH! YOU···YOU!
© 1985 Walt Disney Productions All Rights Reserved

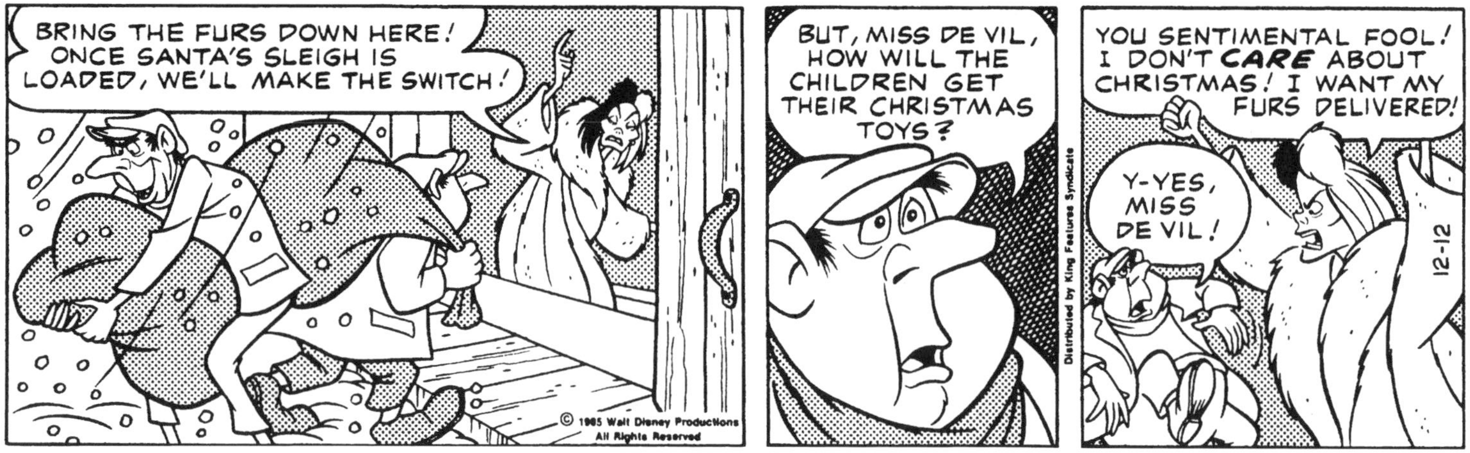
BRING THE FURS DOWN HERE! ONCE SANTA'S SLEIGH IS LOADED, WE'LL MAKE THE SWITCH!
© 1985 Walt Disney Productions All Rights Reserved
BUT, MISS DE VIL, HOW WILL THE CHILDREN GET THEIR CHRISTMAS TOYS?
Distributed by King Features Syndicate
YOU SENTIMENTAL FOOL! I DON'T CARE ABOUT CHRISTMAS! I WANT MY FURS DELIVERED!
Y-YES, MISS DE VIL!
12-12

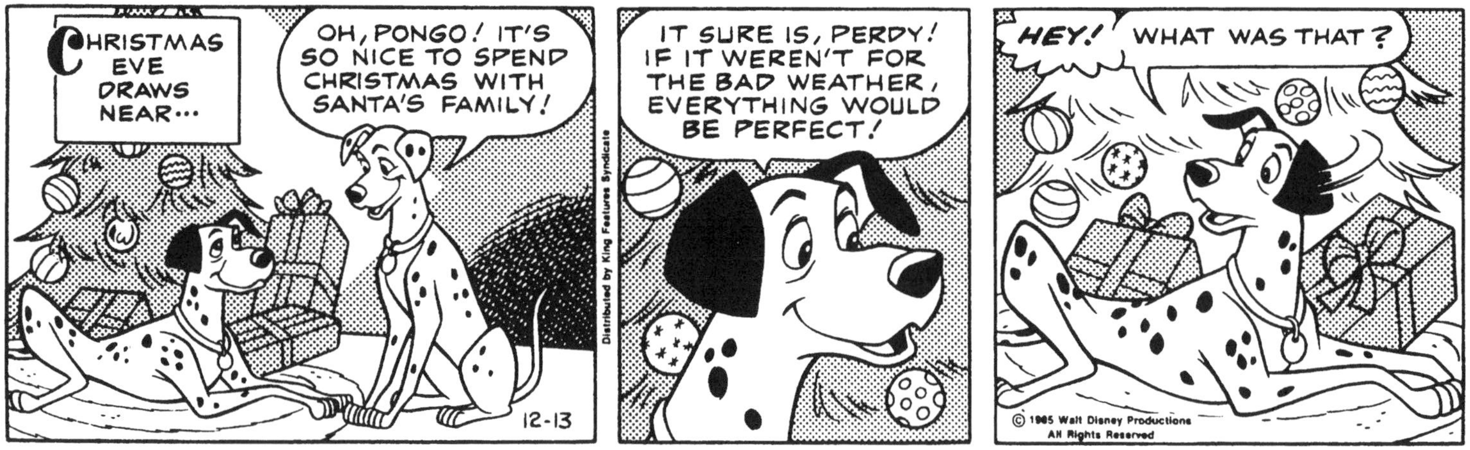
CHRISTMAS EVE DRAWS NEAR...
OH, PONGO! IT'S SO NICE TO SPEND CHRISTMAS WITH SANTA'S FAMILY!
12-13
Distributed by King Features Syndicate
IT SURE IS, PERDY! IF IT WEREN'T FOR THE BAD WEATHER, EVERYTHING WOULD BE PERFECT!
HEY!
WHAT WAS THAT?
© 1985 Walt Disney Productions All Rights Reserved

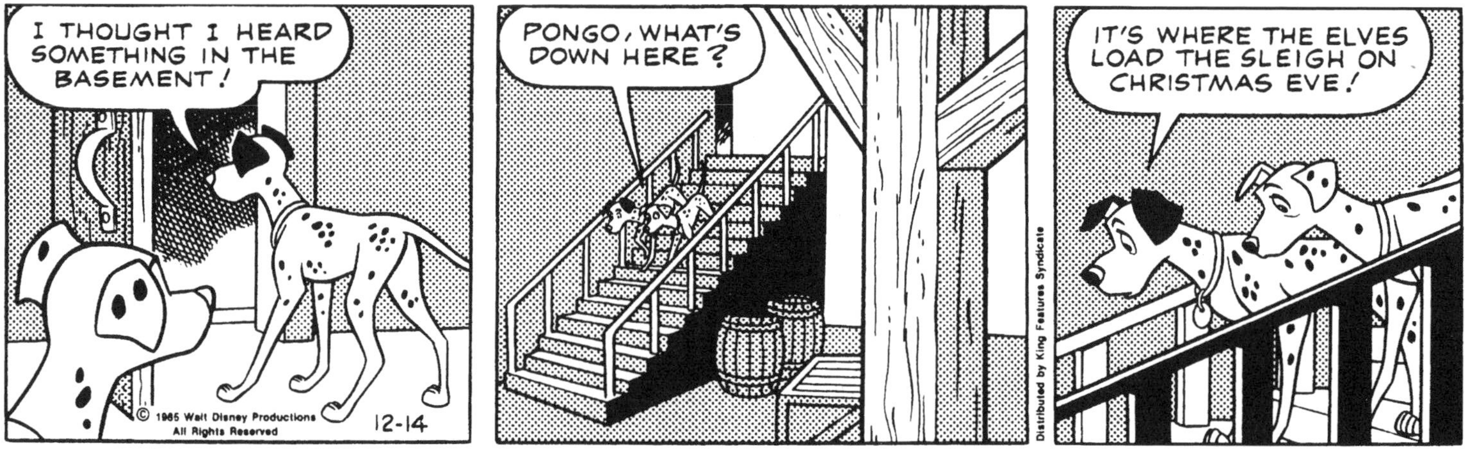
I THOUGHT I HEARD SOMETHING IN THE BASEMENT!
© 1985 Walt Disney Productions All Rights Reserved
12-14
PONGO, WHAT'S DOWN HERE?
Distributed by King Features Syndicate
IT'S WHERE THE ELVES LOAD THE SLEIGH ON CHRISTMAS EVE!

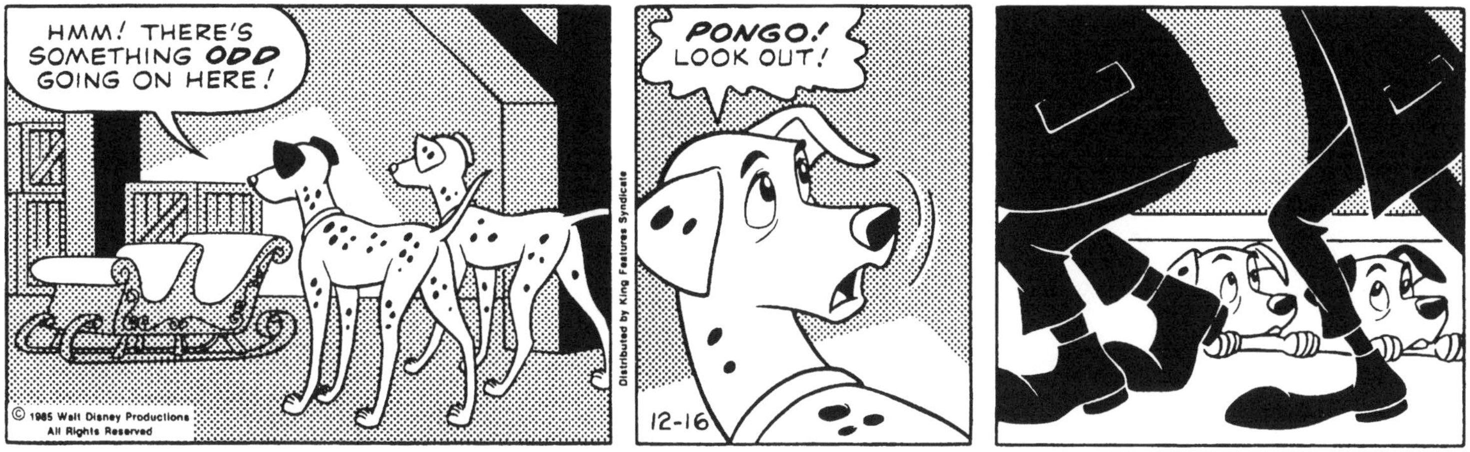
HMM! THERE'S SOMETHING ODD GOING ON HERE!
© 1985 Walt Disney Productions All Rights Reserved
Distributed by King Features Syndicate
PONGO! LOOK OUT!
12-16

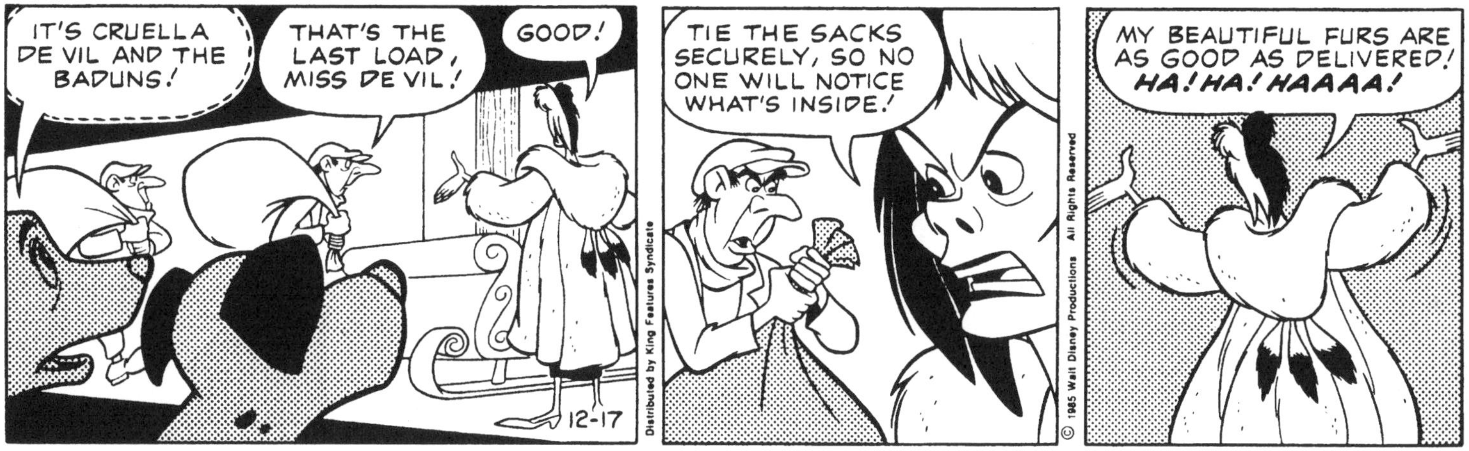
IT'S CRUELLA DE VIL AND THE BADUNS!
THAT'S THE LAST LOAD, MISS DE VIL!
GOOD!
12-17
Distributed by King Features Syndicate
TIE THE SACKS SECURELY, SO NO ONE WILL NOTICE WHAT'S INSIDE!
© 1985 Walt Disney Productions All Rights Reserved
MY BEAUTIFUL FURS ARE AS GOOD AS DELIVERED! HA! HA! HAAAA!

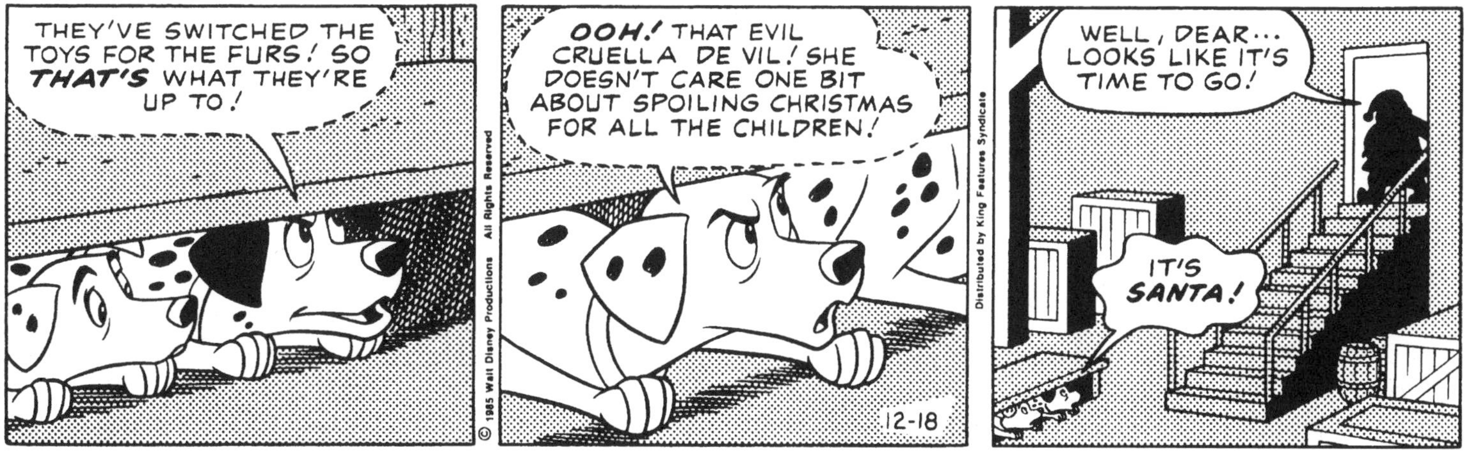
THEY'VE SWITCHED THE TOYS FOR THE FURS! SO THAT'S WHAT THEY'RE UP TO!
© 1985 Walt Disney Productions All Rights Reserved
OOH! THAT EVIL CRUELLA DE VIL! SHE DOESN'T CARE ONE BIT ABOUT SPOILING CHRISTMAS FOR ALL THE CHILDREN!
12-18
Distributed by King Features Syndicate
WELL, DEAR... LOOKS LIKE IT'S TIME TO GO!
IT'S SANTA!

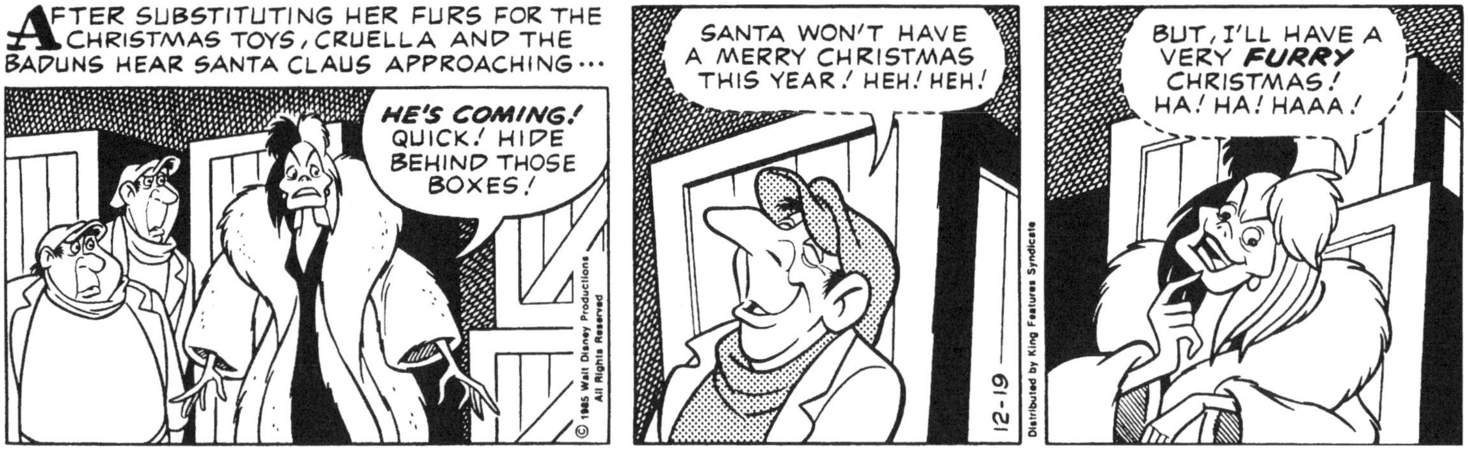
AFTER SUBSTITUTING HER FURS FOR THE CHRISTMAS TOYS, CRUELLA AND THE BADUNS HEAR SANTA CLAUS APPROACHING...
HE'S COMING! QUICK! HIDE BEHIND THOSE BOXES!
© 1985 Walt Disney Productions All Rights Reserved
SANTA WON'T HAVE A MERRY CHRISTMAS THIS YEAR! HEH! HEH!
12-19
Distributed by King Features Syndicate
BUT, I'LL HAVE A VERY FURRY CHRISTMAS! HA! HA! HAAA!

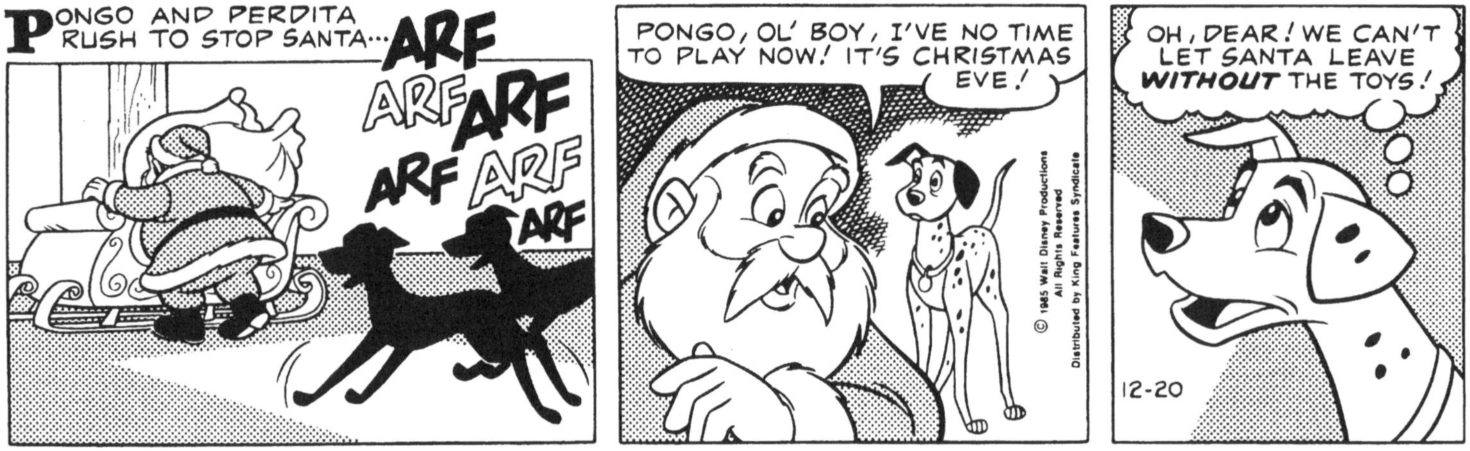
PONGO AND PERDITA RUSH TO STOP SANTA...
ARF
ARF ARF
ARF ARF
ARF
PONGO, OL' BOY, I'VE NO TIME TO PLAY NOW! IT'S CHRISTMAS EVE!
© 1985 Walt Disney Productions All Rights Reserved
Distributed by King Features Syndicate
OH, DEAR! WE CAN'T LET SANTA LEAVE WITHOUT THE TOYS!
12-20

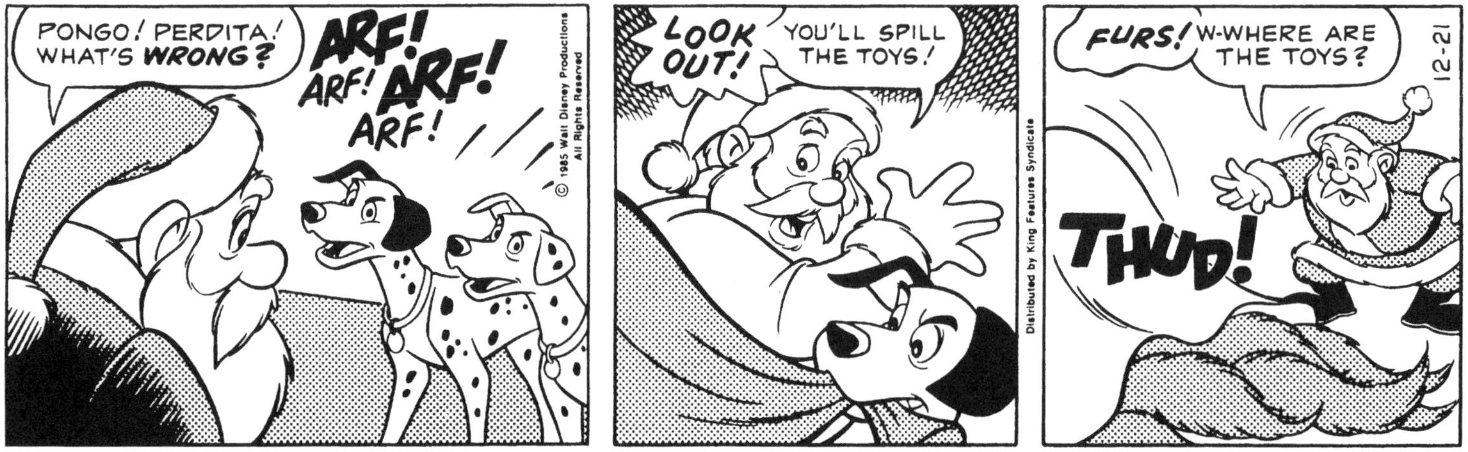
PONGO! PERDITA! WHAT'S WRONG?
ARF! ARF! ARF! ARF!
© 1985 Walt Disney Productions All Rights Reserved
LOOK OUT!
YOU'LL SPILL THE TOYS!
Distributed by King Features Syndicate
FURS! W-WHERE ARE THE TOYS?
12-21
THUD!

I'VE GOT A SLEIGHFUL OF FURS··· BUT WHAT HAPPENED TO THE TOYS?
Distributed by King Features Syndicate
AHA! NOW I KNOW! THANKS, PONGO!
IT WAS CRUELLA!
SHE MADE US DO IT!
12-23
WELL, I'VE GOT A CHRISTMAS SURPRISE FOR ALL THREE OF YOU!
© 1985 Walt Disney Productions All Rights Reserved

I'VE NEVER BEEN SO HUMILIATED! MAKING FUR COATS FOR ELVES! BAH!
PASS THE THREAD, PLEASE!
AHHH! NICE AND WARM!
12-24
Distributed by King Features Syndicate
MERRY CHRISTMAS
TO EVERYONE EVERYWHERE!
© 1985 Walt Disney Productions All Rights Reserved

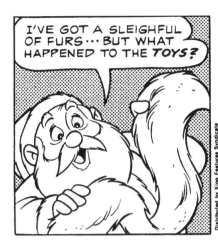

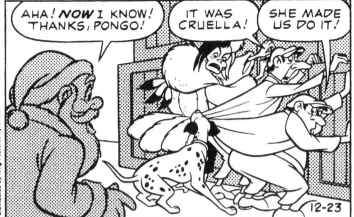

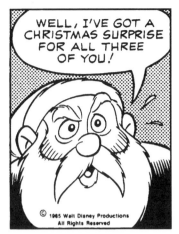

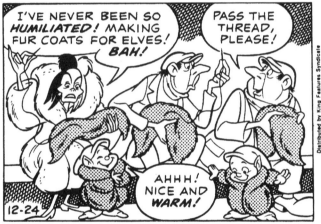

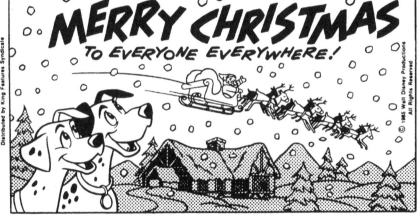

1987

SNOW WHITE'S SINISTER CHRISTMAS GIFT

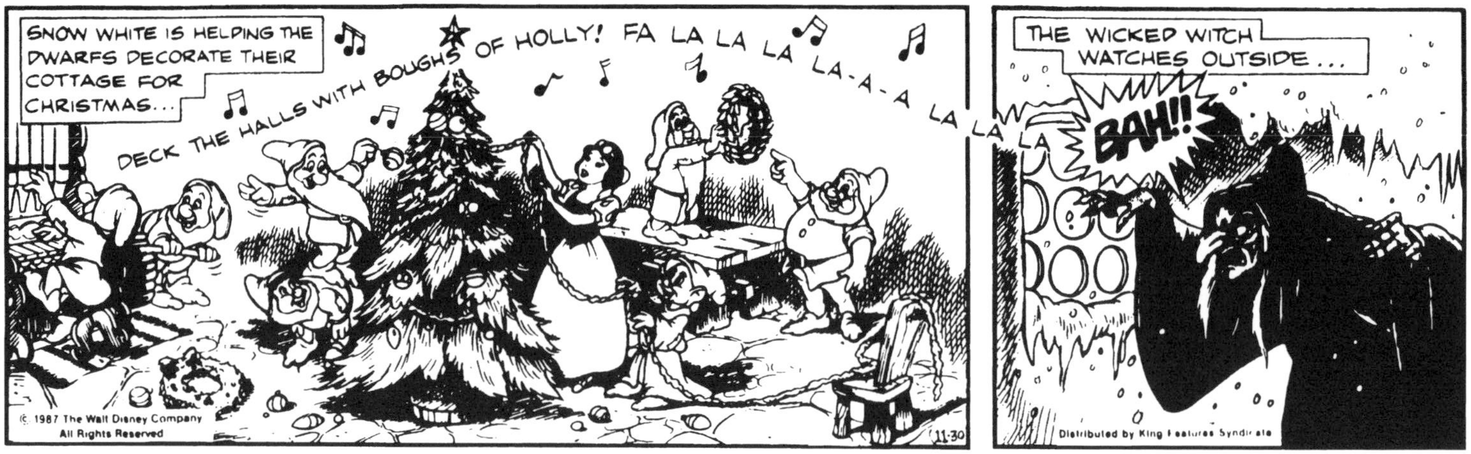
SNOW WHITE IS HELPING THE DWARFS DECORATE THEIR COTTAGE FOR CHRISTMAS...
DECK THE HALLS WITH BOUGHS OF HOLLY! FA LA LA LA LA-A-A LA LA LA LA
THE WICKED WITCH WATCHES OUTSIDE...
BAH!!
© 1987 The Walt Disney Company All Rights Reserved
11-30
Distributed by King Features Syndicate

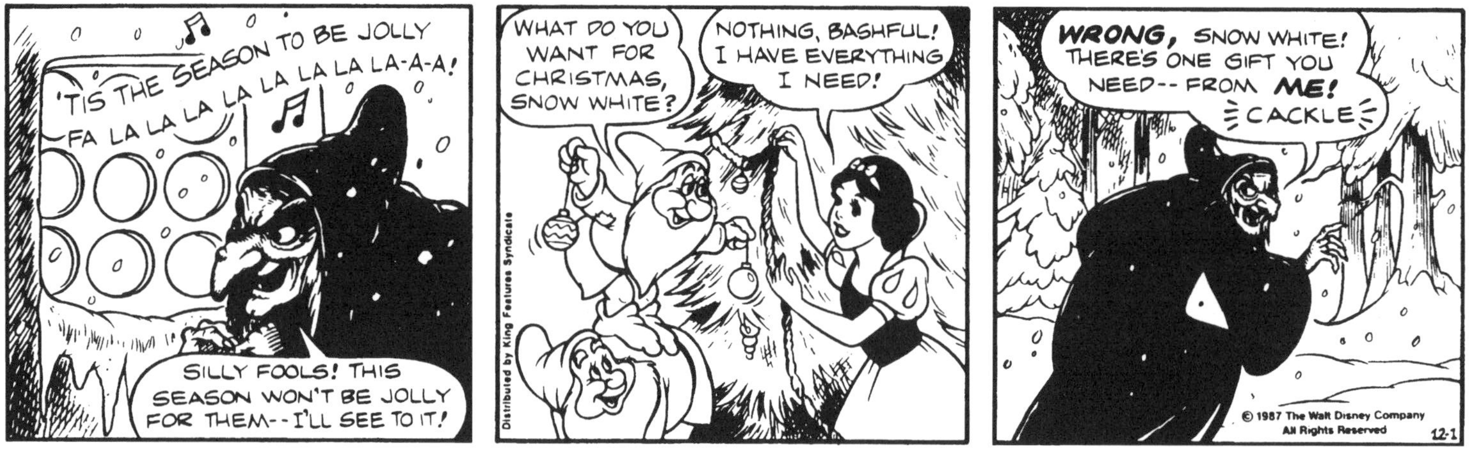
'TIS THE SEASON TO BE JOLLY FA LA LA LA LA LA LA LA LA-A-A!
SILLY FOOLS! THIS SEASON WON'T BE JOLLY FOR THEM--I'LL SEE TO IT!
WHAT DO YOU WANT FOR CHRISTMAS, SNOW WHITE?
NOTHING, BASHFUL! I HAVE EVERYTHING I NEED!
Distributed by King Features Syndicate
WRONG, SNOW WHITE! THERE'S ONE GIFT YOU NEED--FROM ME!
CACKLE
© 1987 The Walt Disney Company All Rights Reserved
12-1

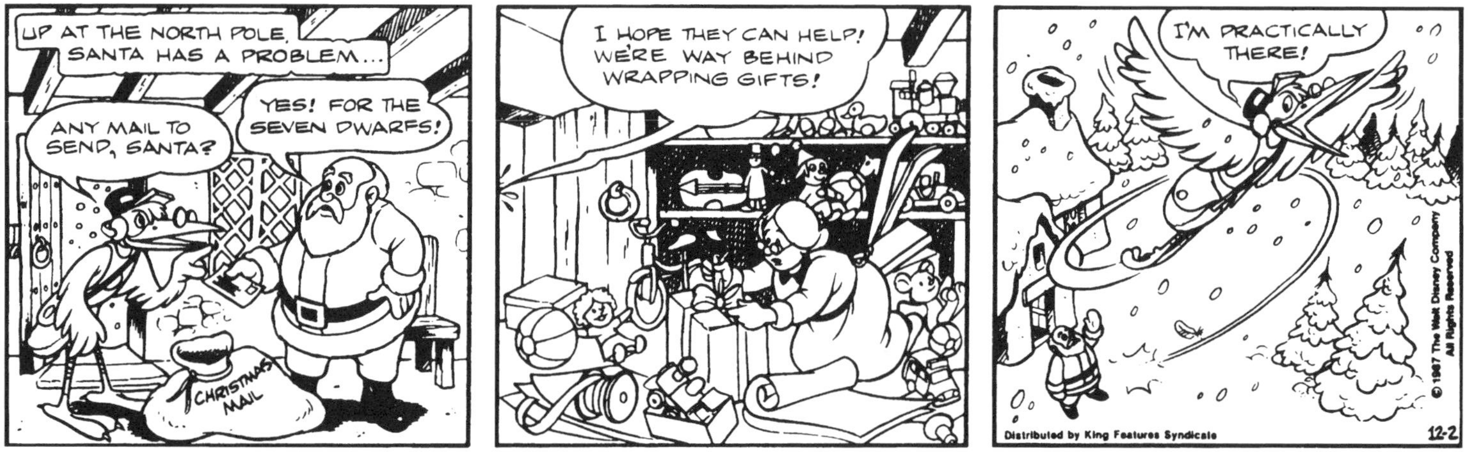
UP AT THE NORTH POLE, SANTA HAS A PROBLEM...
ANY MAIL TO SEND, SANTA?
YES! FOR THE SEVEN DWARFS!
CHRISTMAS MAIL
I HOPE THEY CAN HELP! WE'RE WAY BEHIND WRAPPING GIFTS!
I'M PRACTICALLY THERE!
© 1987 The Walt Disney Company All Rights Reserved
Distributed by King Features Syndicate
12-2

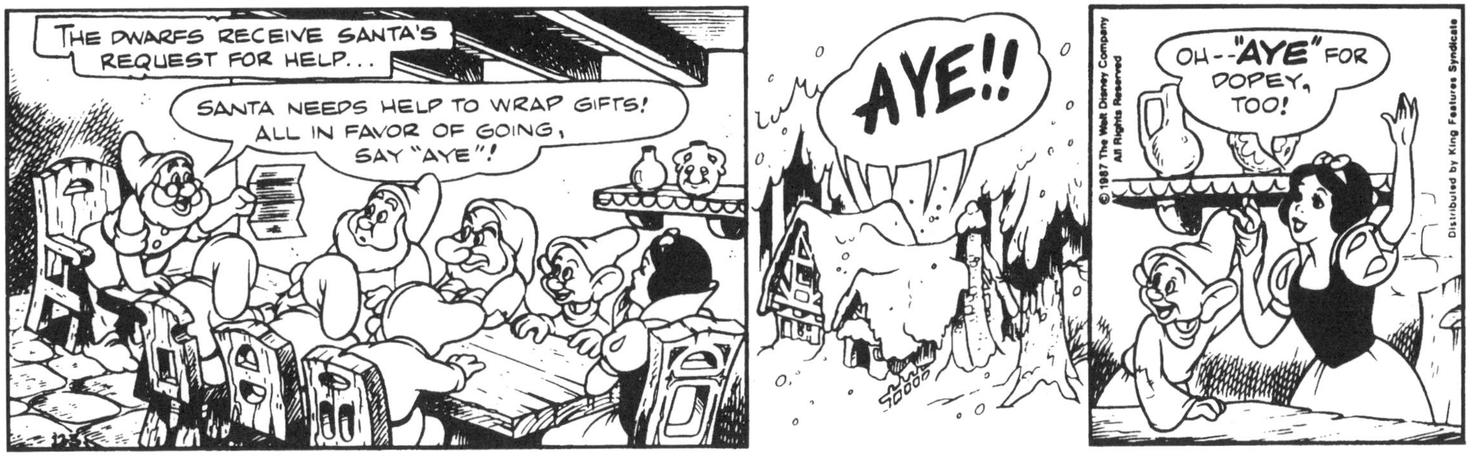
THE DWARFS RECEIVE SANTA'S REQUEST FOR HELP...
SANTA NEEDS HELP TO WRAP GIFTS! ALL IN FAVOR OF GOING, SAY "AYE"!
AYE!!
OH--"AYE" FOR DOPEY, TOO!
© 1987 The Walt Disney Company All Rights Reserved
Distributed by King Features Syndicate

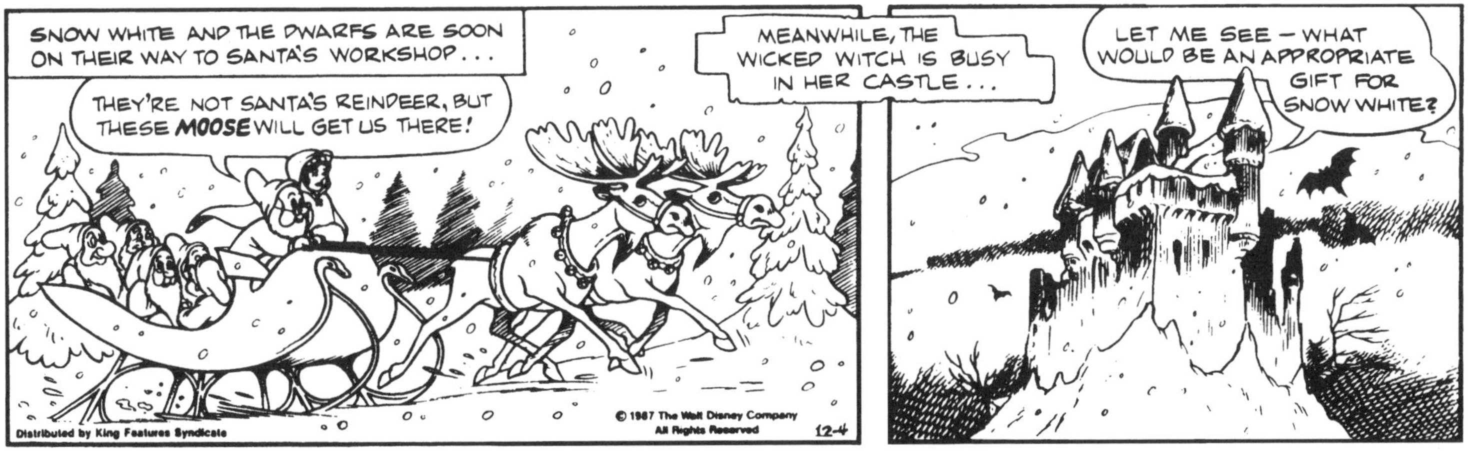
SNOW WHITE AND THE DWARFS ARE SOON ON THEIR WAY TO SANTA'S WORKSHOP...
THEY'RE NOT SANTA'S REINDEER, BUT THESE MOOSE WILL GET US THERE!
Distributed by King Features Syndicate
© 1987 The Walt Disney Company All Rights Reserved
12-4
MEANWHILE, THE WICKED WITCH IS BUSY IN HER CASTLE...
LET ME SEE — WHAT WOULD BE AN APPROPRIATE GIFT FOR SNOW WHITE?

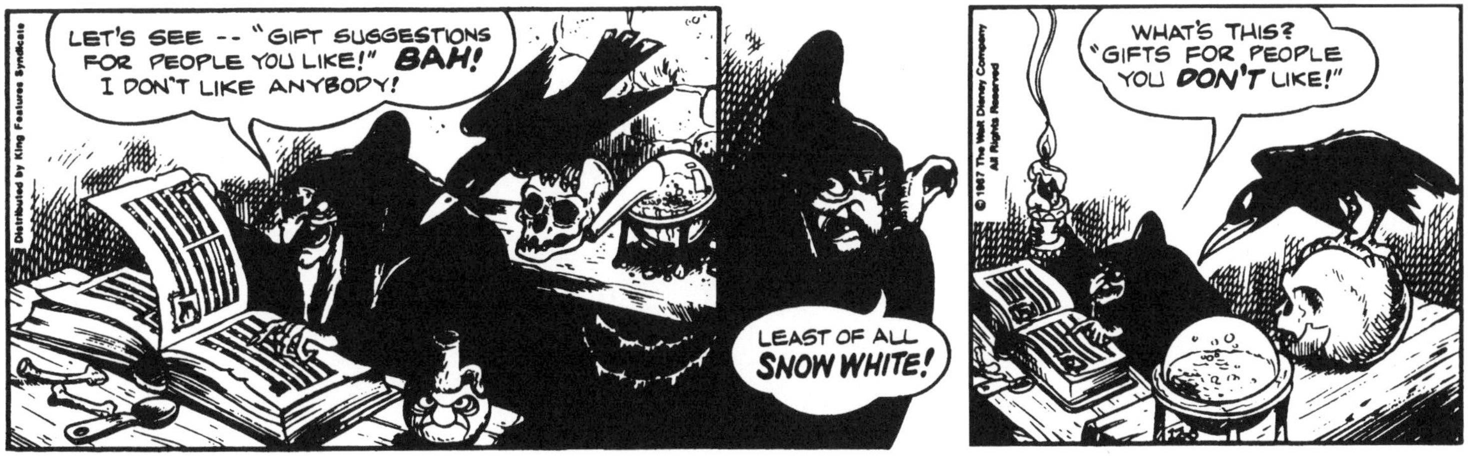
Distributed by King Features Syndicate
LET'S SEE -- "GIFT SUGGESTIONS FOR PEOPLE YOU LIKE!" BAH! I DON'T LIKE ANYBODY!
LEAST OF ALL SNOW WHITE!
© 1987 The Walt Disney Company All Rights Reserved
WHAT'S THIS? "GIFTS FOR PEOPLE YOU DON'T LIKE!"

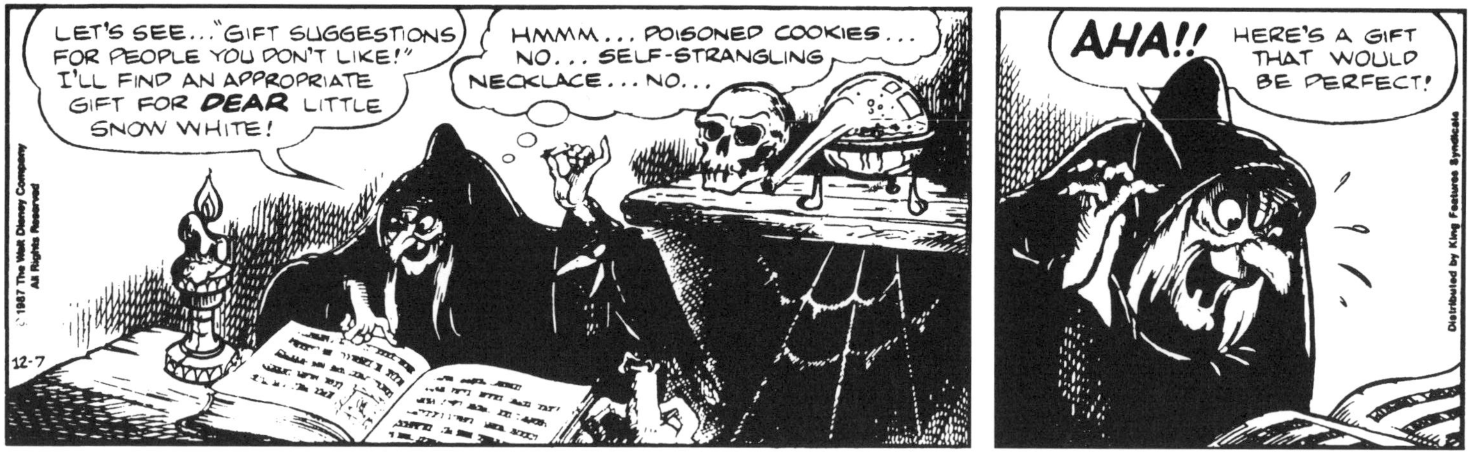
LET'S SEE... "GIFT SUGGESTIONS FOR PEOPLE YOU DON'T LIKE!" I'LL FIND AN APPROPRIATE GIFT FOR **DEAR** LITTLE SNOW WHITE!
HMMM... POISONED COOKIES... NO... SELF-STRANGLING NECKLACE... NO...
© 1987 The Walt Disney Company All Rights Reserved
12-7
AHA!! HERE'S A GIFT THAT WOULD BE PERFECT!
Distributed by King Features Syndicate

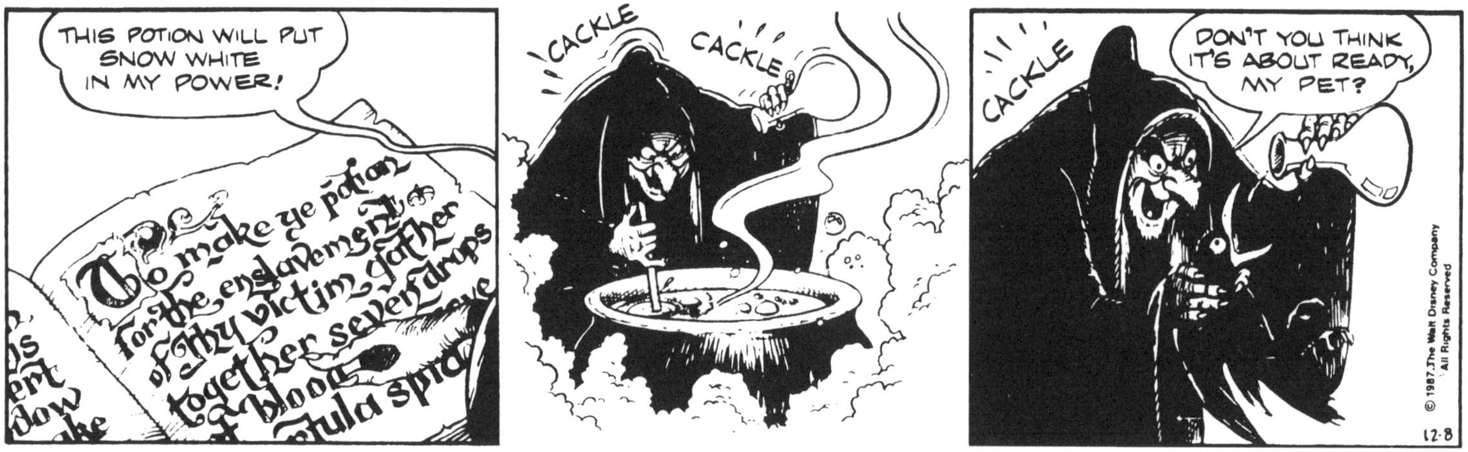
THIS POTION WILL PUT SNOW WHITE IN MY POWER!
To make ye potion
for the enslavement
of thy victim gather
together seven drops
CACKLE
CACKLE
CACKLE
DON'T YOU THINK IT'S ABOUT READY, MY PET?
© 1987 The Walt Disney Company All Rights Reserved
12-8

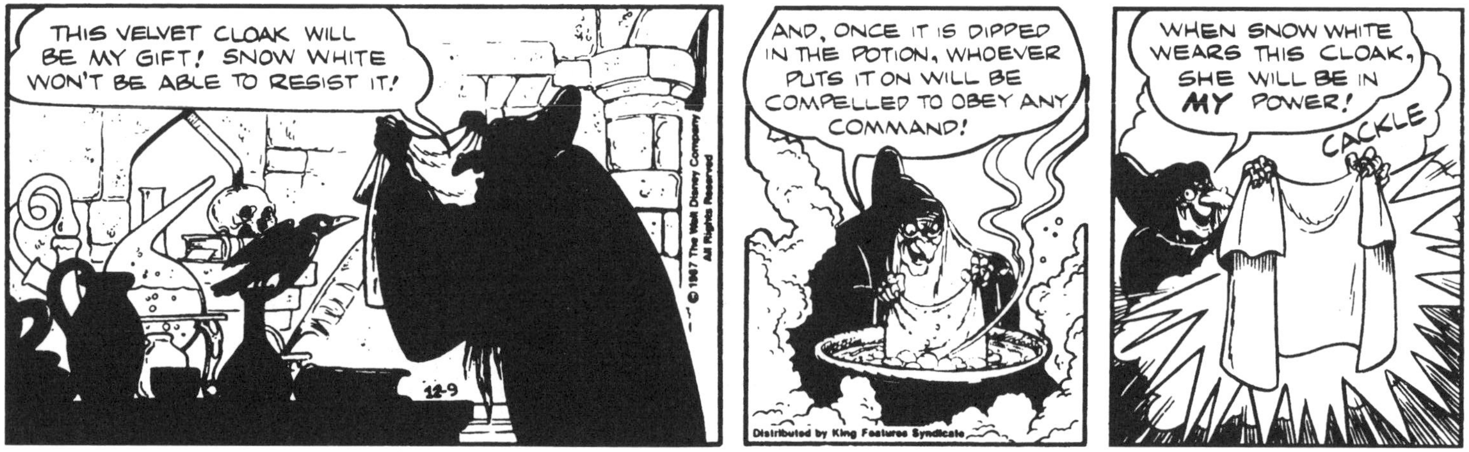
THIS VELVET CLOAK WILL BE MY GIFT! SNOW WHITE WON'T BE ABLE TO RESIST IT!
© 1987 The Walt Disney Company All Rights Reserved
12-9
AND, ONCE IT IS DIPPED IN THE POTION, WHOEVER PUTS IT ON WILL BE COMPELLED TO OBEY ANY COMMAND!
Distributed by King Features Syndicate
WHEN SNOW WHITE WEARS THIS CLOAK, SHE WILL BE IN **MY** POWER!
CACKLE

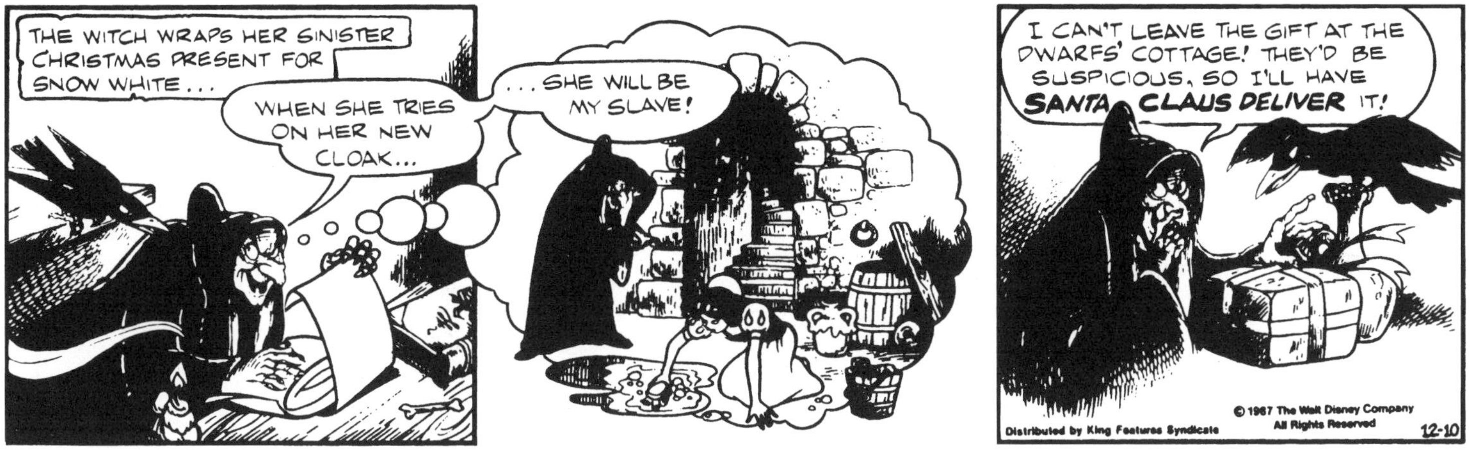
THE WITCH WRAPS HER SINISTER CHRISTMAS PRESENT FOR SNOW WHITE...
WHEN SHE TRIES ON HER NEW CLOAK...
...SHE WILL BE MY SLAVE!
I CAN'T LEAVE THE GIFT AT THE DWARFS' COTTAGE! THEY'D BE SUSPICIOUS, SO I'LL HAVE **SANTA CLAUS DELIVER** IT!
© 1987 The Walt Disney Company All Rights Reserved
Distributed by King Features Syndicate
12-10

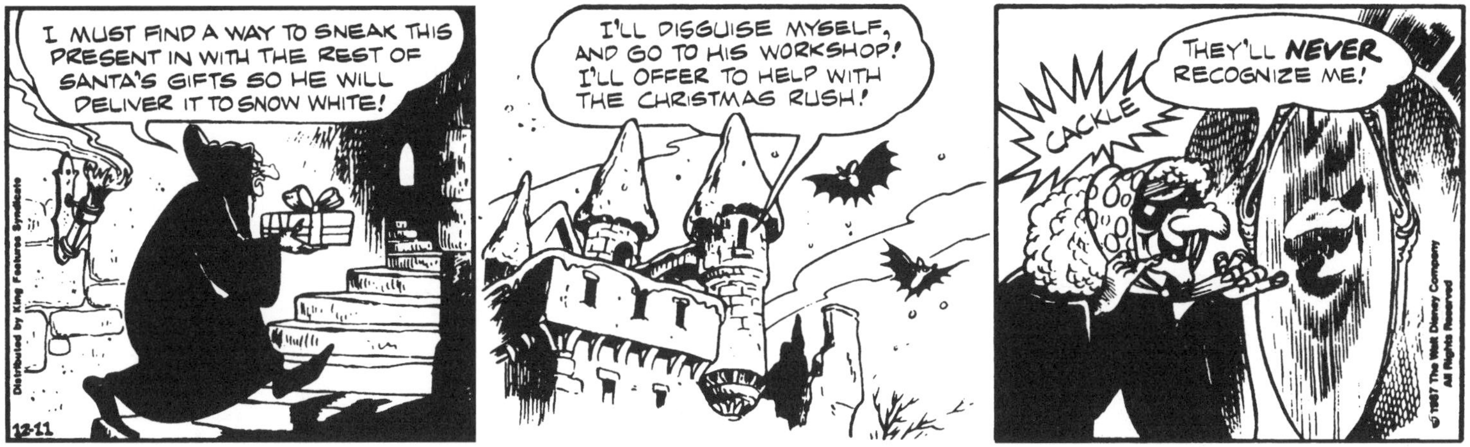
I MUST FIND A WAY TO SNEAK THIS PRESENT IN WITH THE REST OF SANTA'S GIFTS SO HE WILL DELIVER IT TO SNOW WHITE!
Distributed by King Features Syndicate
12-11
I'LL DISGUISE MYSELF, AND GO TO HIS WORKSHOP! I'LL OFFER TO HELP WITH THE CHRISTMAS RUSH!
CACKLE
THEY'LL **NEVER** RECOGNIZE ME!
© 1987 The Walt Disney Company All Rights Reserved

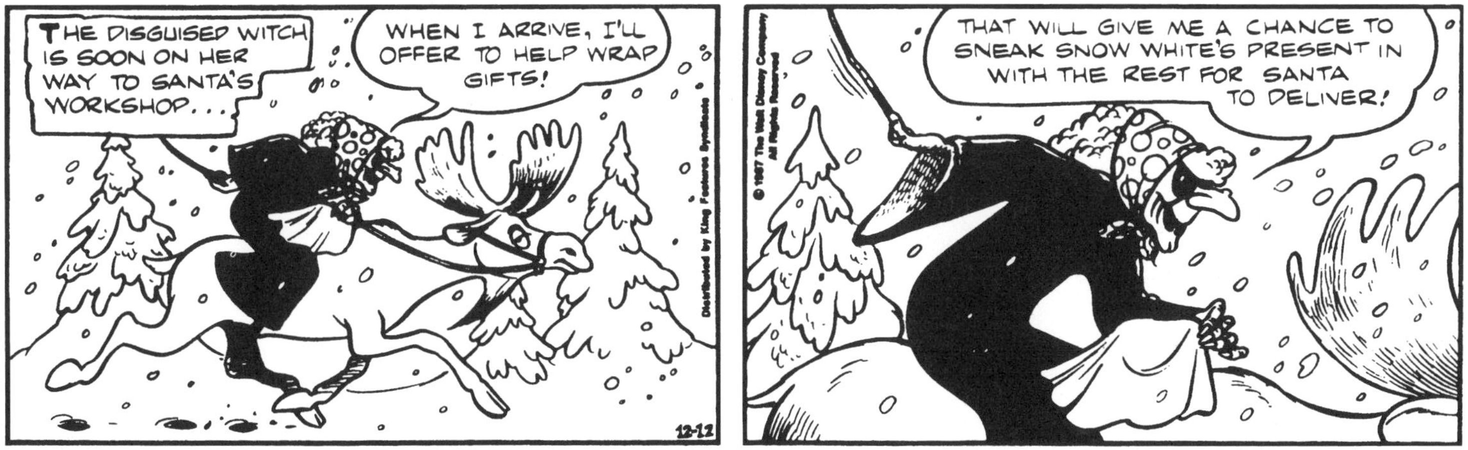
THE DISGUISED WITCH IS SOON ON HER WAY TO SANTA'S WORKSHOP...
WHEN I ARRIVE, I'LL OFFER TO HELP WRAP GIFTS!
Distributed by King Features Syndicate
12-12
© 1987 The Walt Disney Company All Rights Reserved
THAT WILL GIVE ME A CHANCE TO SNEAK SNOW WHITE'S PRESENT IN WITH THE REST FOR SANTA TO DELIVER!

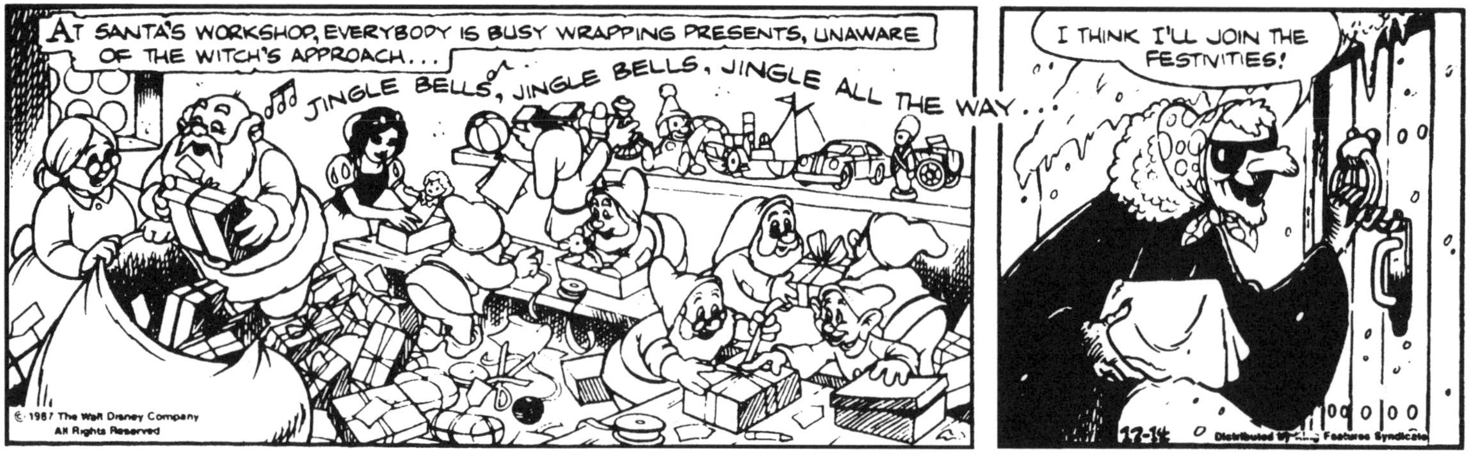
AT SANTA'S WORKSHOP, EVERYBODY IS BUSY WRAPPING PRESENTS, UNAWARE OF THE WITCH'S APPROACH...
JINGLE BELLS, JINGLE BELLS, JINGLE ALL THE WAY...
© 1987 The Walt Disney Company
All Rights Reserved
I THINK I'LL JOIN THE FESTIVITIES!
12-14
Distributed by King Features Syndicate

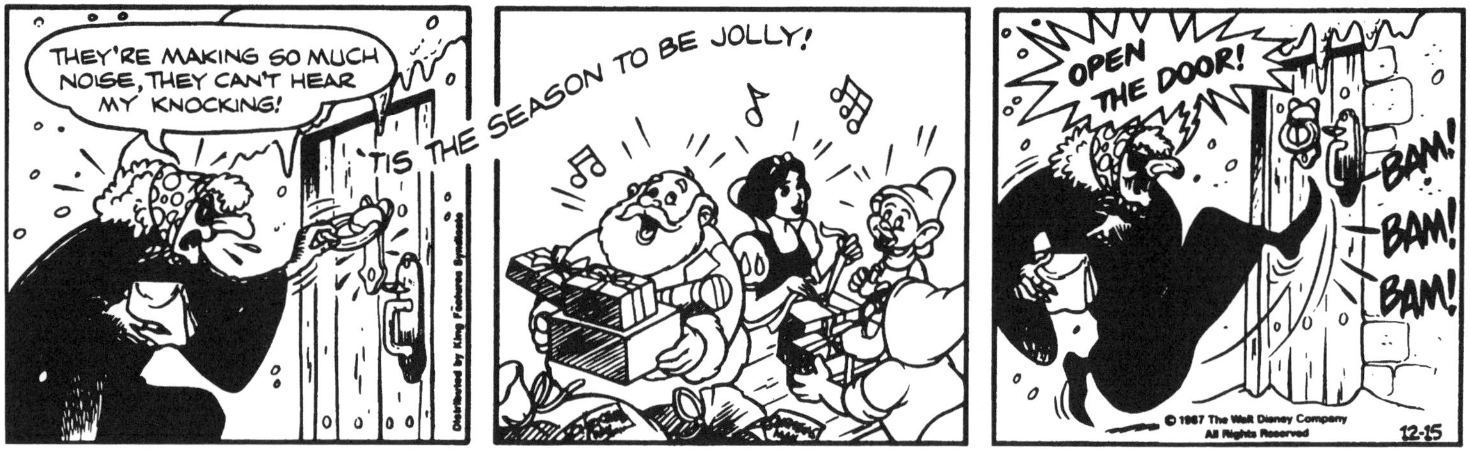
THEY'RE MAKING SO MUCH NOISE, THEY CAN'T HEAR MY KNOCKING!
Distributed by King Features Syndicate
'TIS THE SEASON TO BE JOLLY!
OPEN THE DOOR!
BAM!
BAM!
BAM!
© 1987 The Walt Disney Company
All Rights Reserved
12-15

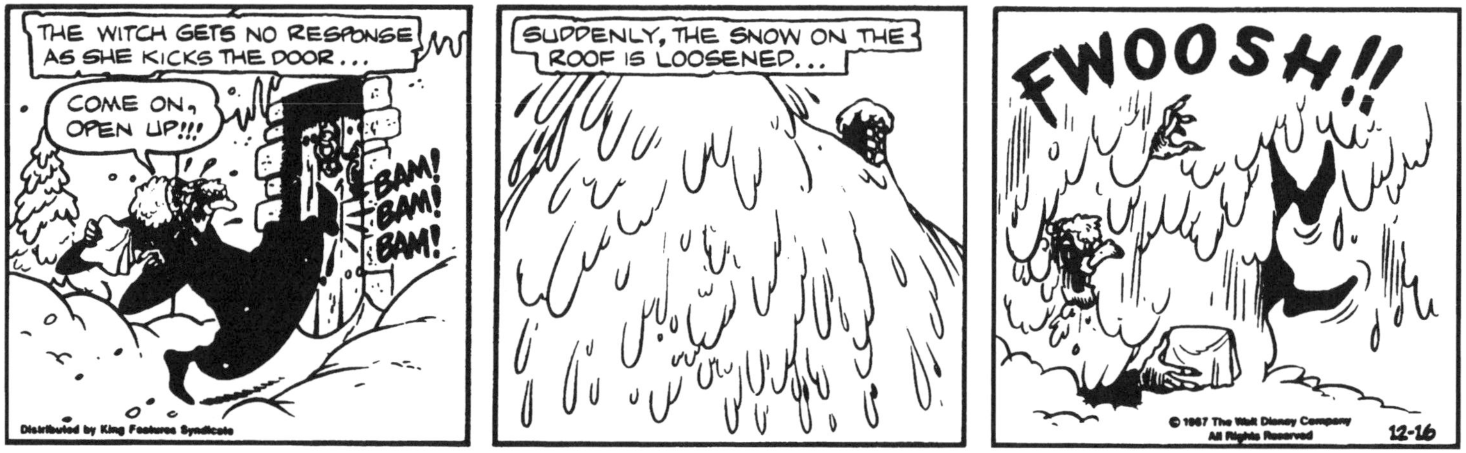
THE WITCH GETS NO RESPONSE AS SHE KICKS THE DOOR...
COME ON, OPEN UP!!!
BAM!
BAM!
BAM!
Distributed by King Features Syndicate
SUDDENLY, THE SNOW ON THE ROOF IS LOOSENED...
FWOOSH!!
© 1987 The Walt Disney Company
All Rights Reserved
12-16

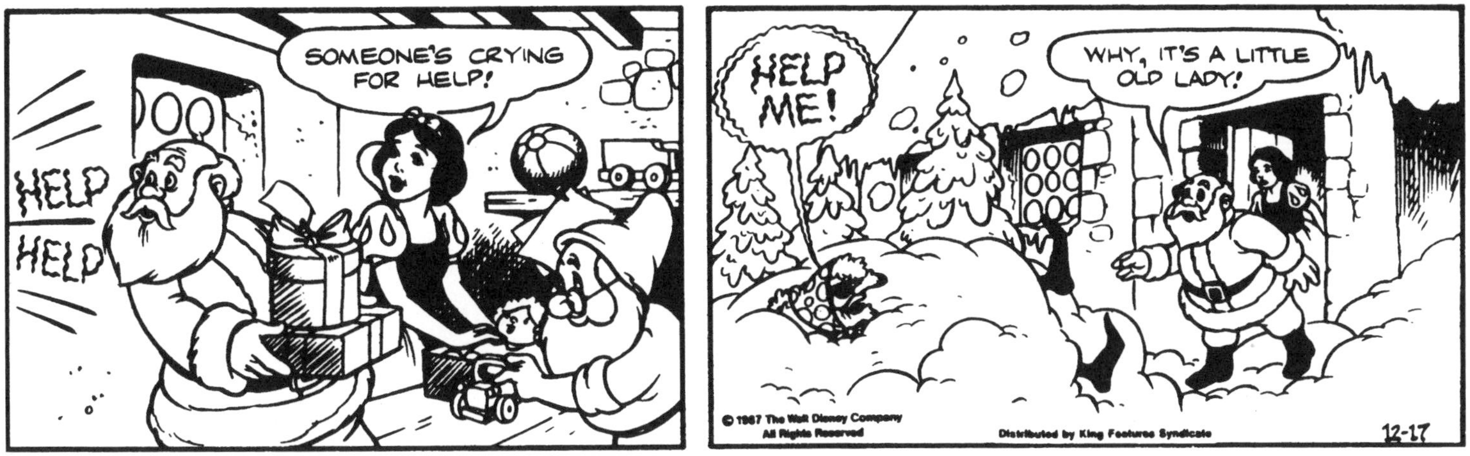
SOMEONE'S CRYING FOR HELP!
HELP
HELP
HELP ME!
WHY, IT'S A LITTLE OLD LADY!
© 1987 The Walt Disney Company All Rights Reserved
Distributed by King Features Syndicate
12-17

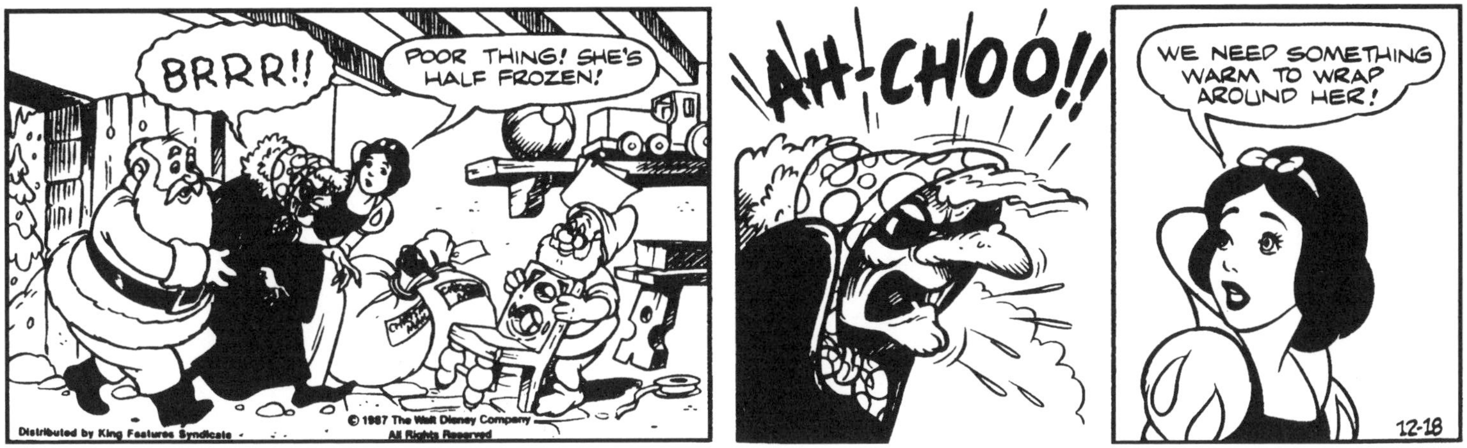
BRRRR!!
POOR THING! SHE'S HALF FROZEN!
Distributed by King Features Syndicate
© 1987 The Walt Disney Company All Rights Reserved
AH-CHOO!!
WE NEED SOMETHING WARM TO WRAP AROUND HER!
12-18

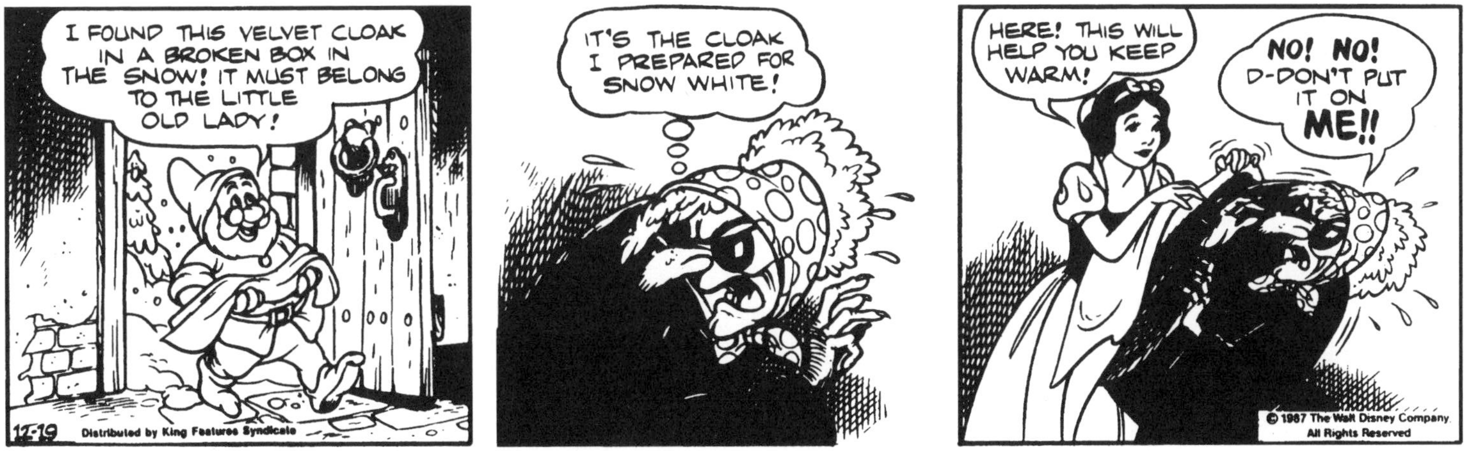
I FOUND THIS VELVET CLOAK IN A BROKEN BOX IN THE SNOW! IT MUST BELONG TO THE LITTLE OLD LADY!
12-19
Distributed by King Features Syndicate
IT'S THE CLOAK I PREPARED FOR SNOW WHITE!
HERE! THIS WILL HELP YOU KEEP WARM!
NO! NO! D-DON'T PUT IT ON ME!!
© 1987 The Walt Disney Company All Rights Reserved

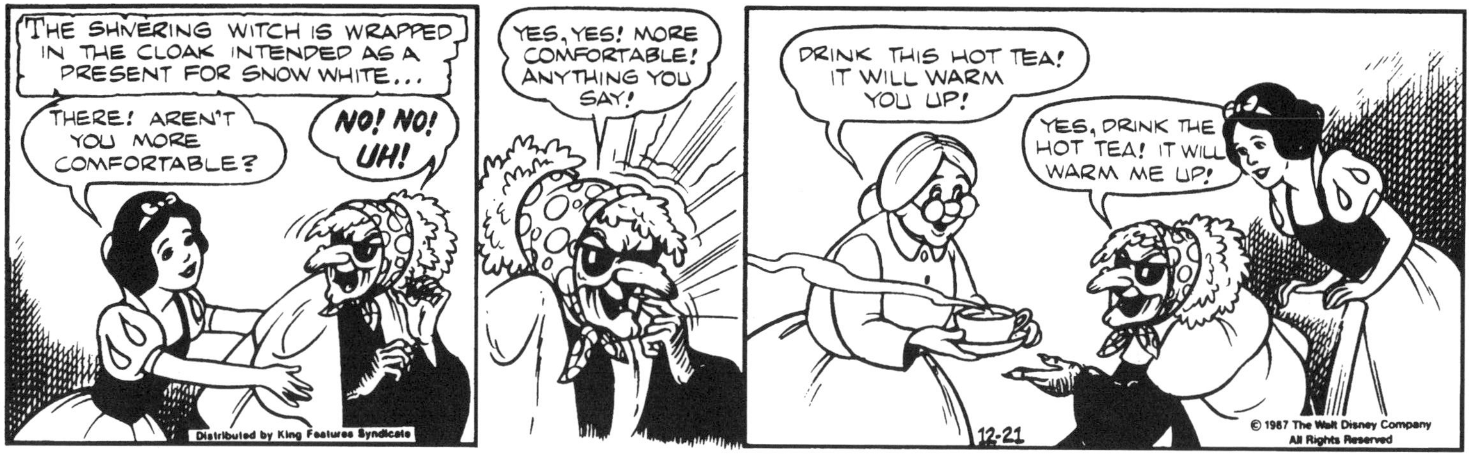
THE SHIVERING WITCH IS WRAPPED IN THE CLOAK INTENDED AS A PRESENT FOR SNOW WHITE...
THERE! AREN'T YOU MORE COMFORTABLE?
NO! NO! UH!
Distributed by King Features Syndicate
YES, YES! MORE COMFORTABLE! ANYTHING YOU SAY!
DRINK THIS HOT TEA! IT WILL WARM YOU UP!
YES, DRINK THE HOT TEA! IT WILL WARM ME UP!
12-21
© 1987 The Walt Disney Company All Rights Reserved

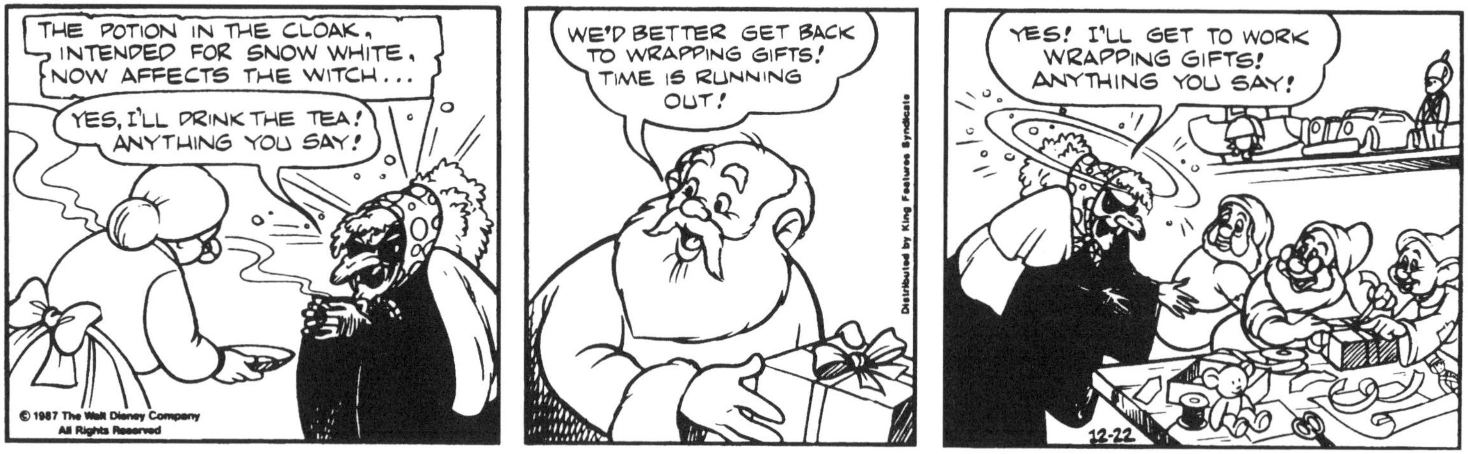
THE POTION IN THE CLOAK, INTENDED FOR SNOW WHITE, NOW AFFECTS THE WITCH...
YES, I'LL DRINK THE TEA! ANYTHING YOU SAY!
© 1987 The Walt Disney Company All Rights Reserved
WE'D BETTER GET BACK TO WRAPPING GIFTS! TIME IS RUNNING OUT!
Distributed by King Features Syndicate
YES! I'LL GET TO WORK WRAPPING GIFTS! ANYTHING YOU SAY!
12-22

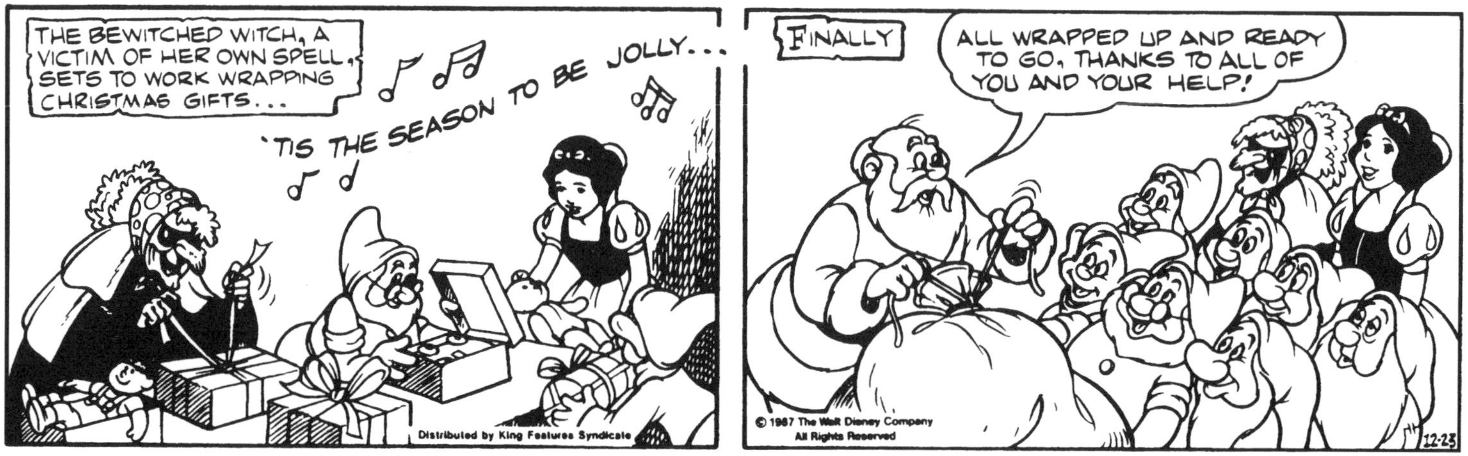
THE BEWITCHED WITCH, A VICTIM OF HER OWN SPELL, SETS TO WORK WRAPPING CHRISTMAS GIFTS...
'TIS THE SEASON TO BE JOLLY...
Distributed by King Features Syndicate
FINALLY
ALL WRAPPED UP AND READY TO GO, THANKS TO ALL OF YOU AND YOUR HELP!
© 1987 The Walt Disney Company All Rights Reserved
12-23

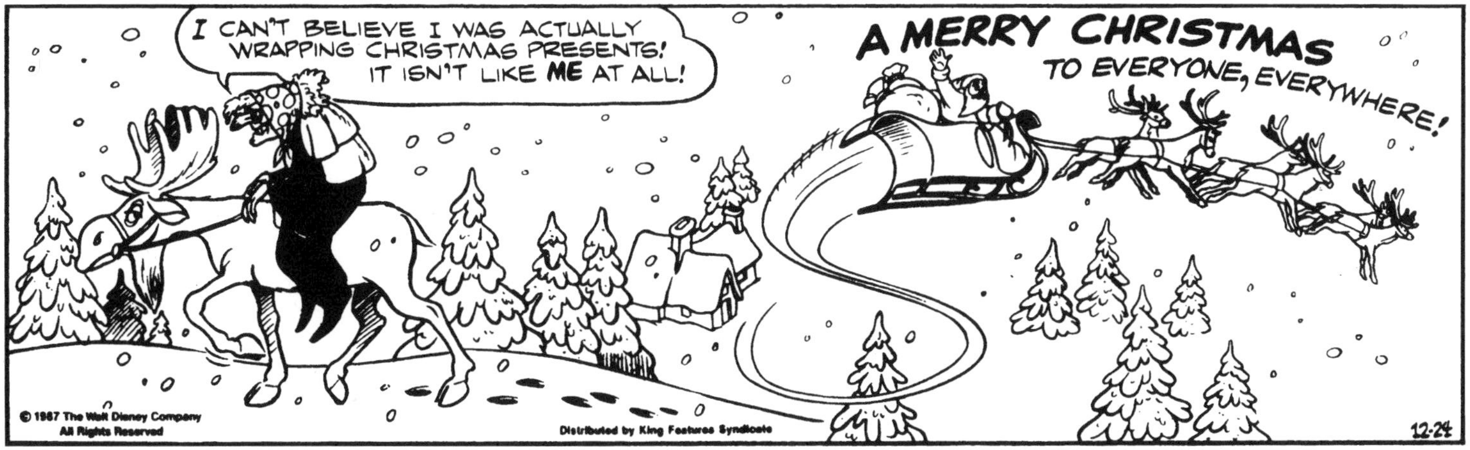
I CAN'T BELIEVE I WAS ACTUALLY WRAPPING CHRISTMAS PRESENTS! IT ISN'T LIKE ME AT ALL!
A MERRY CHRISTMAS
TO EVERYONE, EVERYWHERE!
© 1987 The Walt Disney Company All Rights Reserved
Distributed by King Features Syndicate
12-24

1992

BEAUTY AND THE BEAST

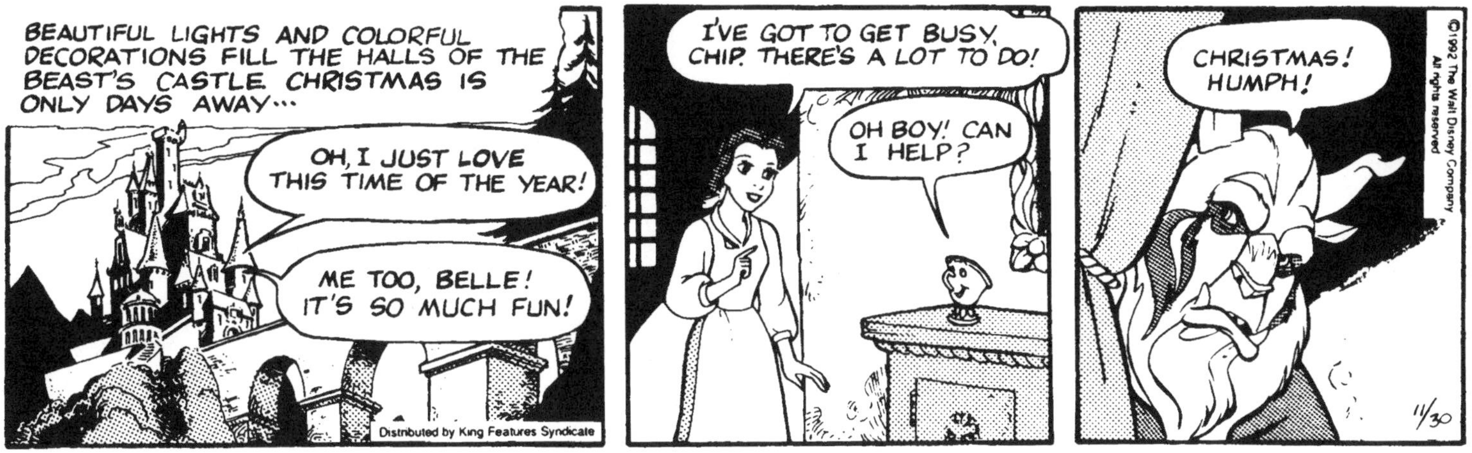

BEAUTIFUL LIGHTS AND COLORFUL DECORATIONS FILL THE HALLS OF THE BEAST'S CASTLE. CHRISTMAS IS ONLY DAYS AWAY...
OH, I JUST LOVE THIS TIME OF THE YEAR!
ME TOO, BELLE! IT'S SO MUCH FUN!
Distributed by King Features Syndicate
I'VE GOT TO GET BUSY, CHIP. THERE'S A LOT TO DO!
OH BOY! CAN I HELP?
CHRISTMAS! HUMPH!
©1992 The Walt Disney Company All rights reserved
11/30

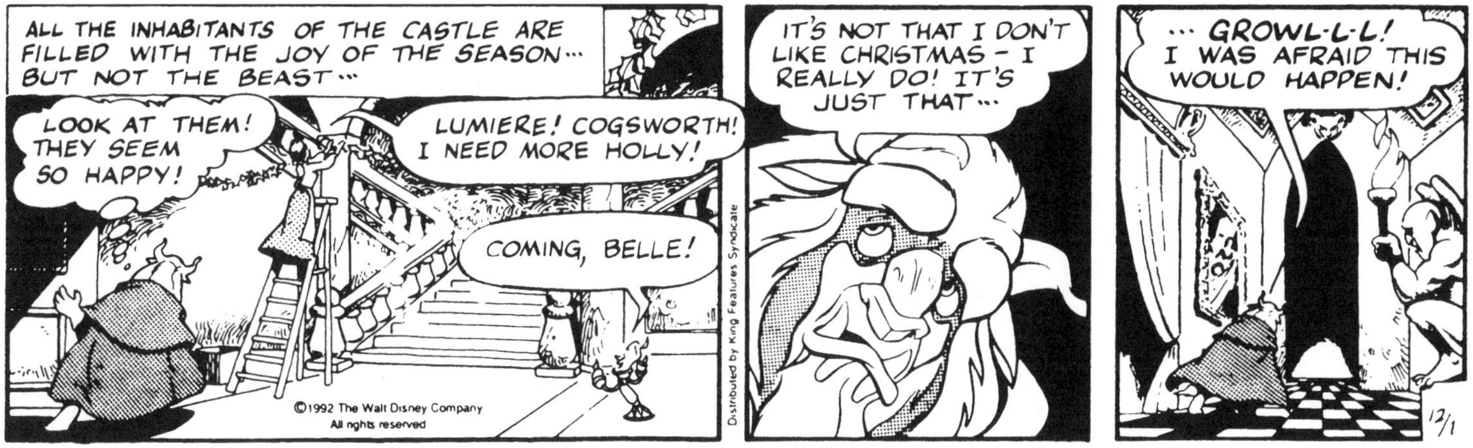

ALL THE INHABITANTS OF THE CASTLE ARE FILLED WITH THE JOY OF THE SEASON... BUT NOT THE BEAST...
LOOK AT THEM! THEY SEEM SO HAPPY!
LUMIERE! COGSWORTH! I NEED MORE HOLLY!
COMING, BELLE!
©1992 The Walt Disney Company All rights reserved
Distributed by King Features Syndicate
IT'S NOT THAT I DON'T LIKE CHRISTMAS – I REALLY DO! IT'S JUST THAT...
... GROWL-L-L! I WAS AFRAID THIS WOULD HAPPEN!
12/1

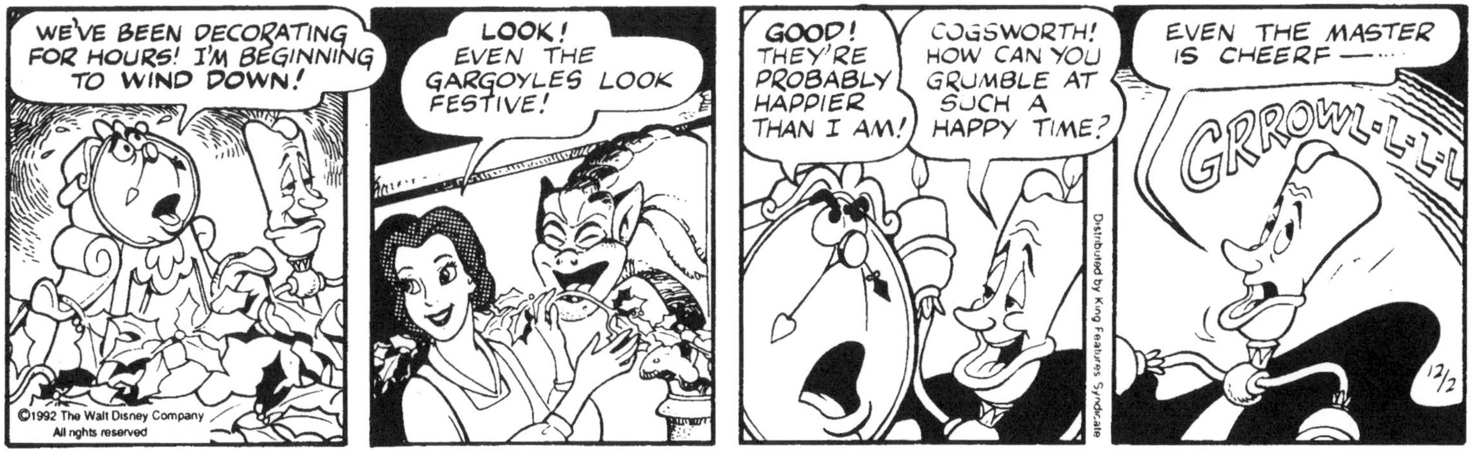

WE'VE BEEN DECORATING FOR HOURS! I'M BEGINNING TO WIND DOWN!
©1992 The Walt Disney Company All rights reserved
LOOK! EVEN THE GARGOYLES LOOK FESTIVE!
GOOD! THEY'RE PROBABLY HAPPIER THAN I AM!
COGSWORTH! HOW CAN YOU GRUMBLE AT SUCH A HAPPY TIME?
Distributed by King Features Syndicate
EVEN THE MASTER IS CHEERF —...
GRROWL-L-L-L
12/2

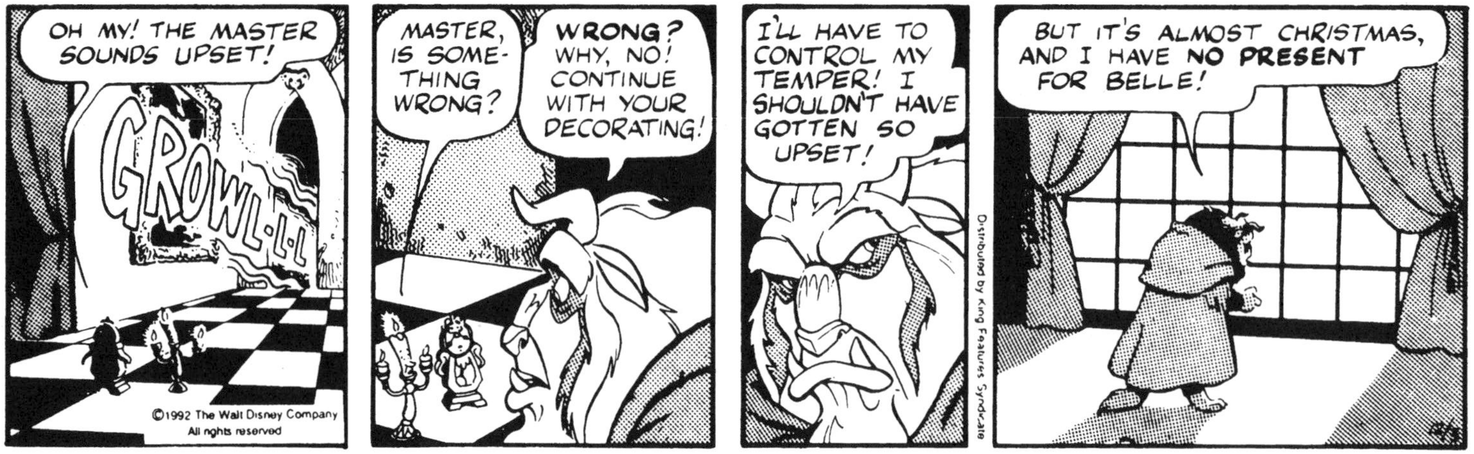
OH MY! THE MASTER SOUNDS UPSET!
GROWL-L-L
©1992 The Walt Disney Company All rights reserved
MASTER, IS SOME-THING WRONG?
WRONG? WHY, NO! CONTINUE WITH YOUR DECORATING!
I'LL HAVE TO CONTROL MY TEMPER! I SHOULDN'T HAVE GOTTEN SO UPSET!
Distributed by King Features Syndicate
BUT IT'S ALMOST CHRISTMAS, AND I HAVE NO PRESENT FOR BELLE!

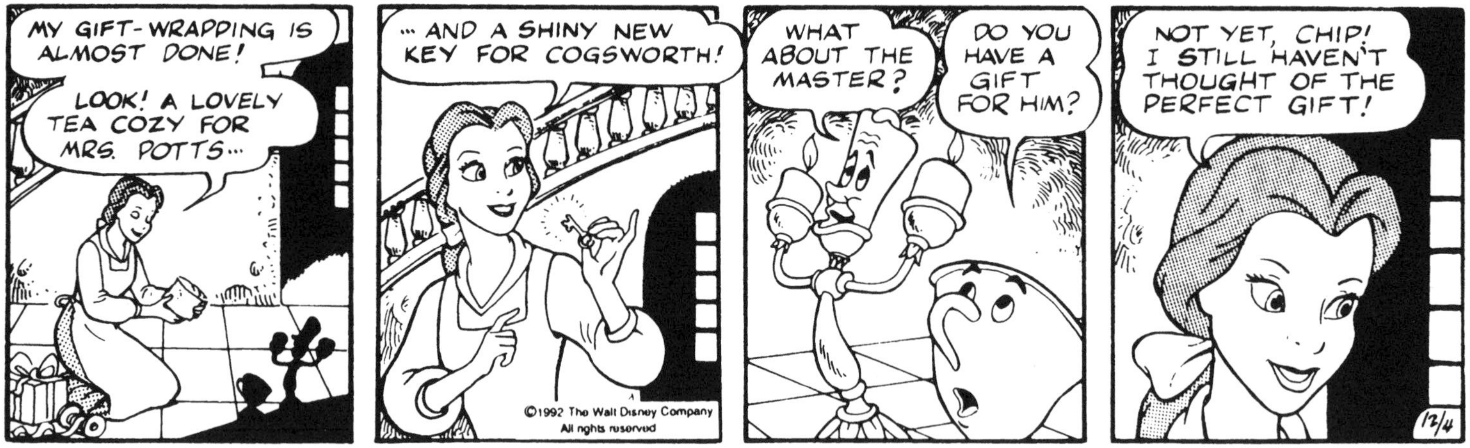
MY GIFT-WRAPPING IS ALMOST DONE!
LOOK! A LOVELY TEA COZY FOR MRS. POTTS...
... AND A SHINY NEW KEY FOR COGSWORTH!
©1992 The Walt Disney Company All rights reserved
WHAT ABOUT THE MASTER?
DO YOU HAVE A GIFT FOR HIM?
NOT YET, CHIP! I STILL HAVEN'T THOUGHT OF THE PERFECT GIFT!
12/4

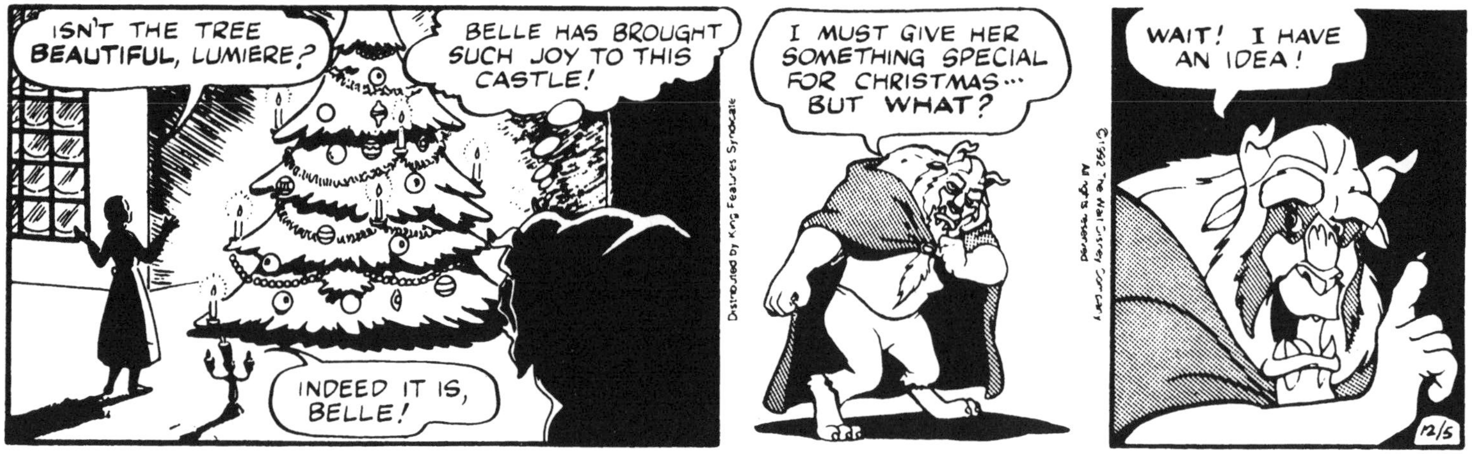
ISN'T THE TREE BEAUTIFUL, LUMIERE?
BELLE HAS BROUGHT SUCH JOY TO THIS CASTLE!
INDEED IT IS, BELLE!
Distributed by King Features Syndicate
I MUST GIVE HER SOMETHING SPECIAL FOR CHRISTMAS... BUT WHAT?
WAIT! I HAVE AN IDEA!
12/5

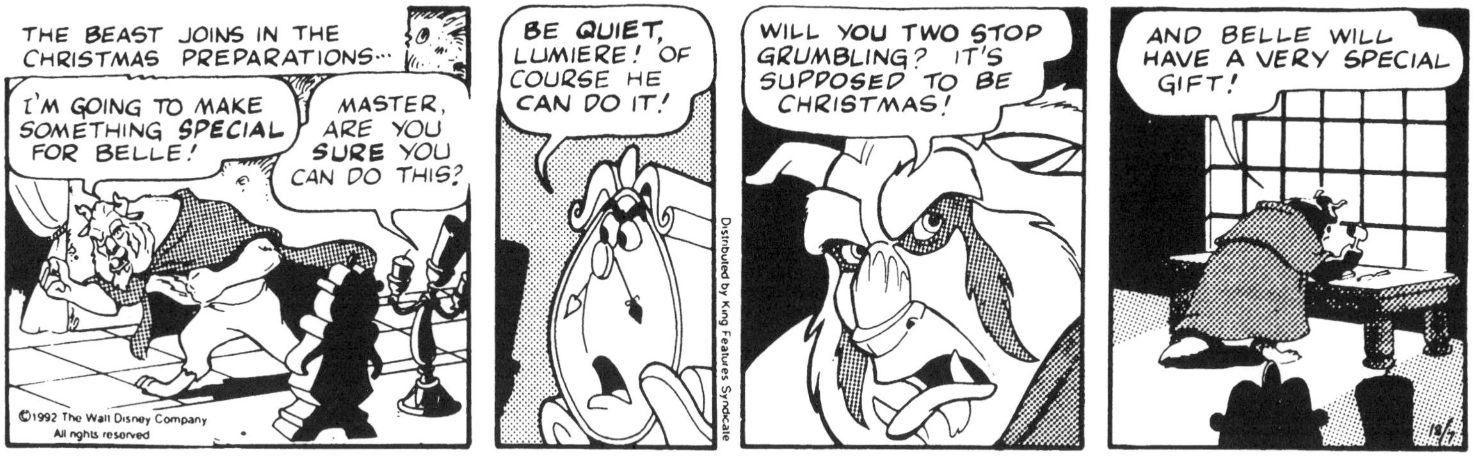
THE BEAST JOINS IN THE CHRISTMAS PREPARATIONS···
I'M GOING TO MAKE SOMETHING SPECIAL FOR BELLE!
MASTER, ARE YOU SURE YOU CAN DO THIS?
BE QUIET, LUMIERE! OF COURSE HE CAN DO IT!
WILL YOU TWO STOP GRUMBLING? IT'S SUPPOSED TO BE CHRISTMAS!
AND BELLE WILL HAVE A VERY SPECIAL GIFT!
©1992 The Walt Disney Company All rights reserved
Distributed by King Features Syndicate
12/7

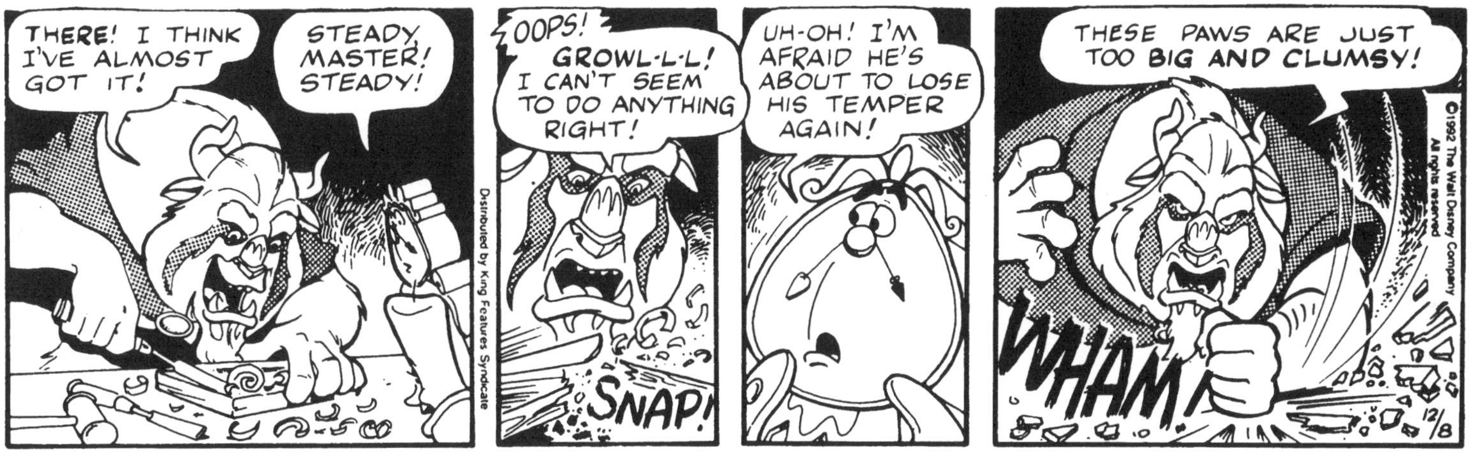
THERE! I THINK I'VE ALMOST GOT IT!
STEADY, MASTER! STEADY!
Distributed by King Features Syndicate
OOPS!
GROWL-L-L! I CAN'T SEEM TO DO ANYTHING RIGHT!
SNAP!
UH-OH! I'M AFRAID HE'S ABOUT TO LOSE HIS TEMPER AGAIN!
THESE PAWS ARE JUST TOO BIG AND CLUMSY!
WHAM!
©1992 The Walt Disney Company All rights reserved
12/8

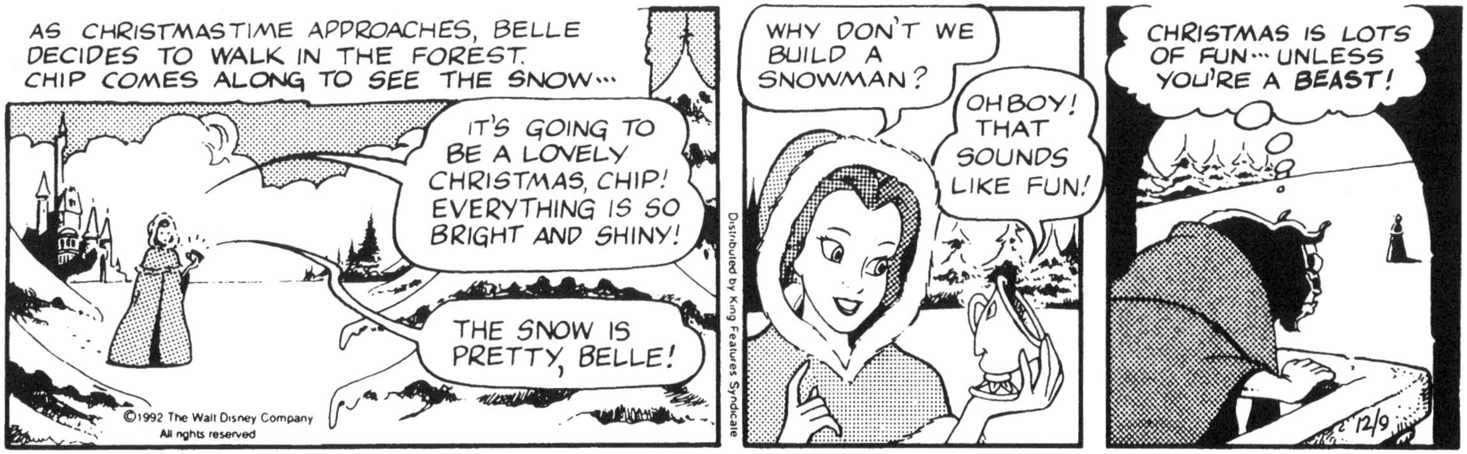
AS CHRISTMASTIME APPROACHES, BELLE DECIDES TO WALK IN THE FOREST. CHIP COMES ALONG TO SEE THE SNOW···
IT'S GOING TO BE A LOVELY CHRISTMAS, CHIP! EVERYTHING IS SO BRIGHT AND SHINY!
THE SNOW IS PRETTY, BELLE!
©1992 The Walt Disney Company All rights reserved
Distributed by King Features Syndicate
WHY DON'T WE BUILD A SNOWMAN?
OH BOY! THAT SOUNDS LIKE FUN!
CHRISTMAS IS LOTS OF FUN··· UNLESS YOU'RE A BEAST!
12/9

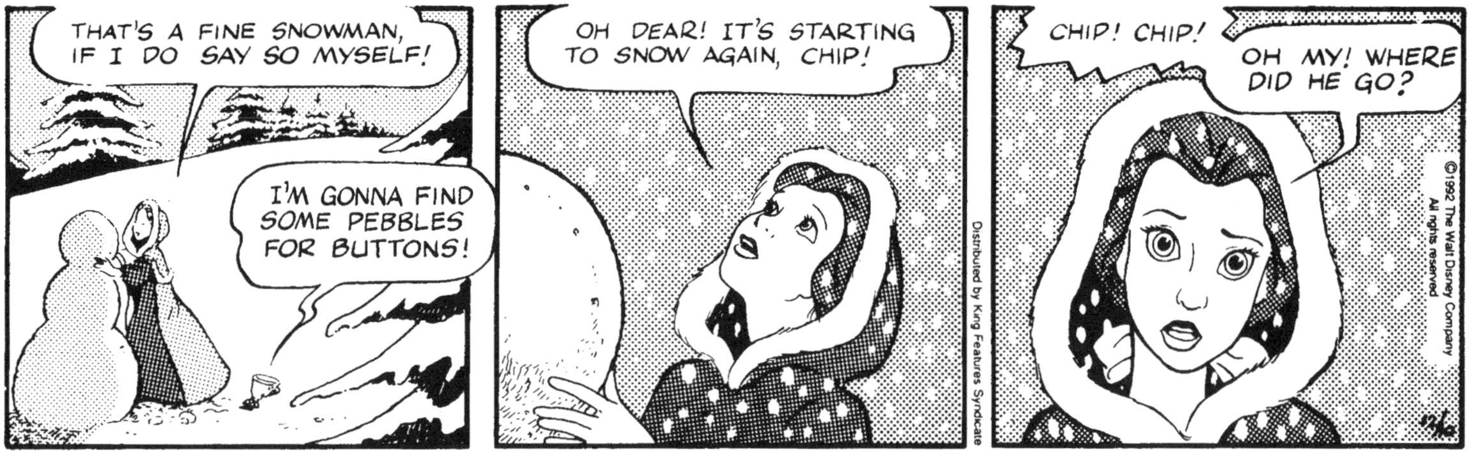
THAT'S A FINE SNOWMAN, IF I DO SAY SO MYSELF!
I'M GONNA FIND SOME PEBBLES FOR BUTTONS!
OH DEAR! IT'S STARTING TO SNOW AGAIN, CHIP!
Distributed by King Features Syndicate
CHIP! CHIP!
OH MY! WHERE DID HE GO?
©1992 The Walt Disney Company All rights reserved

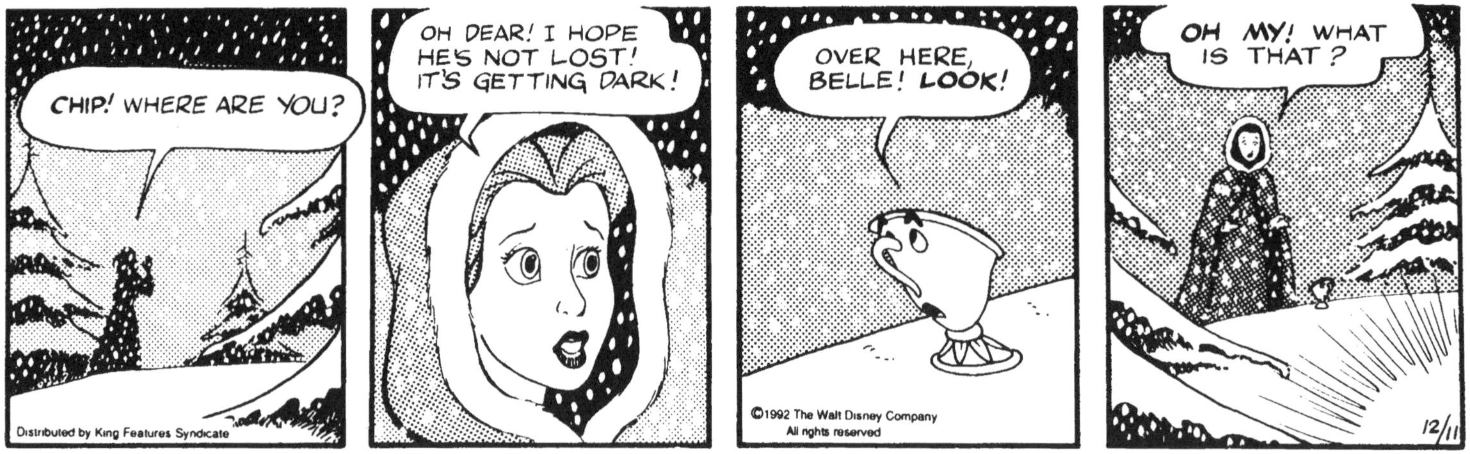
CHIP! WHERE ARE YOU?
Distributed by King Features Syndicate
OH DEAR! I HOPE HE'S NOT LOST! IT'S GETTING DARK!
OVER HERE, BELLE! LOOK!
©1992 The Walt Disney Company All rights reserved
OH MY! WHAT IS THAT?
12/11

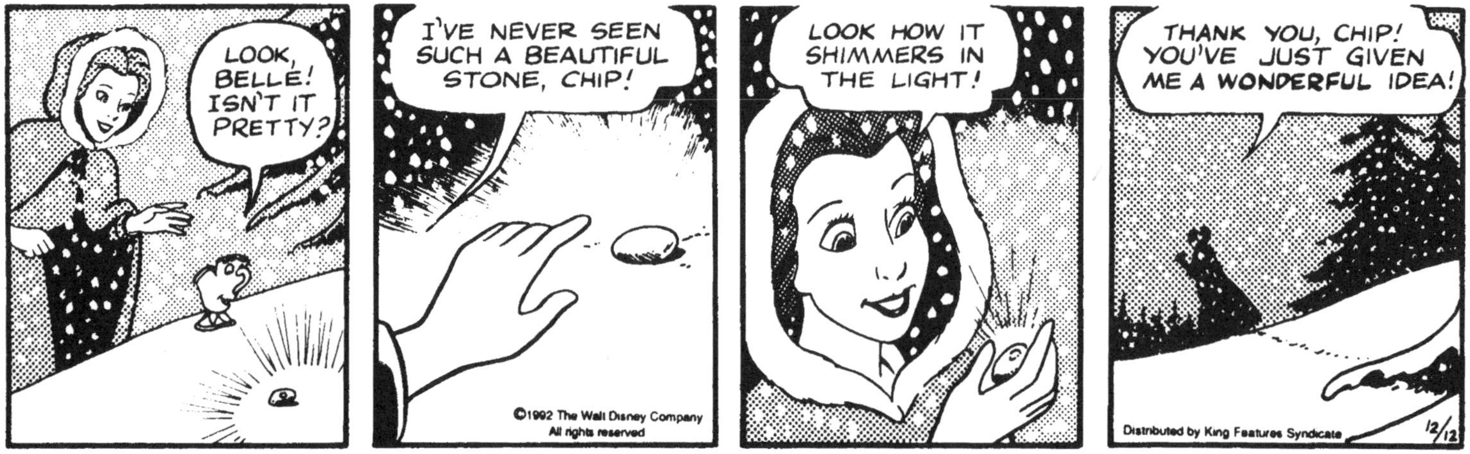
LOOK, BELLE! ISN'T IT PRETTY?
I'VE NEVER SEEN SUCH A BEAUTIFUL STONE, CHIP!
©1992 The Walt Disney Company All rights reserved
LOOK HOW IT SHIMMERS IN THE LIGHT!
THANK YOU, CHIP! YOU'VE JUST GIVEN ME A WONDERFUL IDEA!
Distributed by King Features Syndicate
12/12

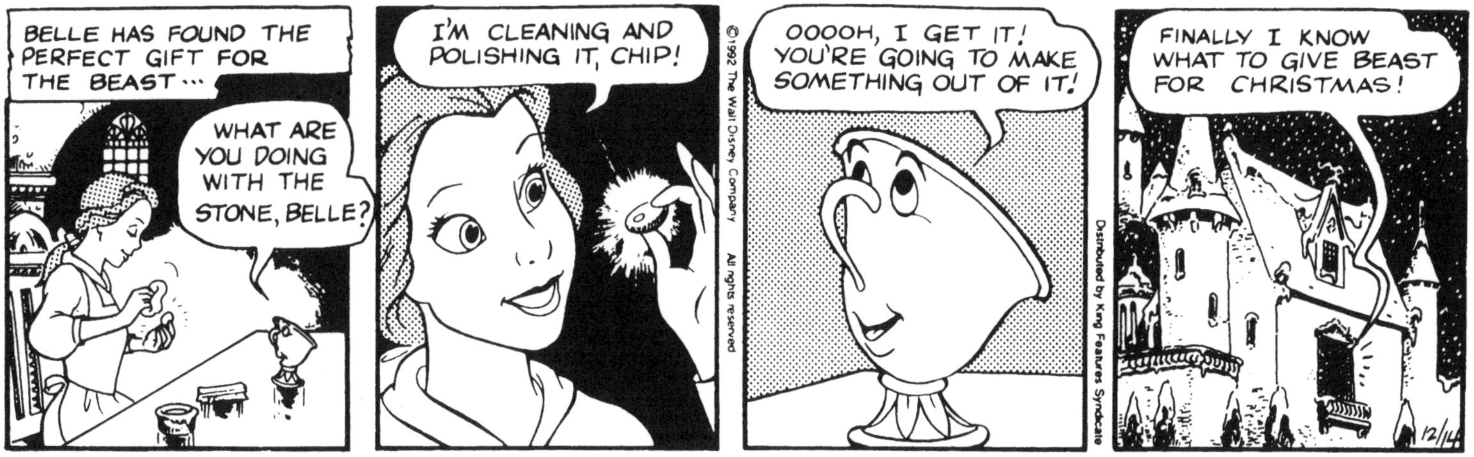
BELLE HAS FOUND THE PERFECT GIFT FOR THE BEAST...
WHAT ARE YOU DOING WITH THE STONE, BELLE?
I'M CLEANING AND POLISHING IT, CHIP!
©1992 The Walt Disney Company All rights reserved
OOOOH, I GET IT! YOU'RE GOING TO MAKE SOMETHING OUT OF IT!
Distributed by King Features Syndicate
FINALLY I KNOW WHAT TO GIVE BEAST FOR CHRISTMAS!
12/14

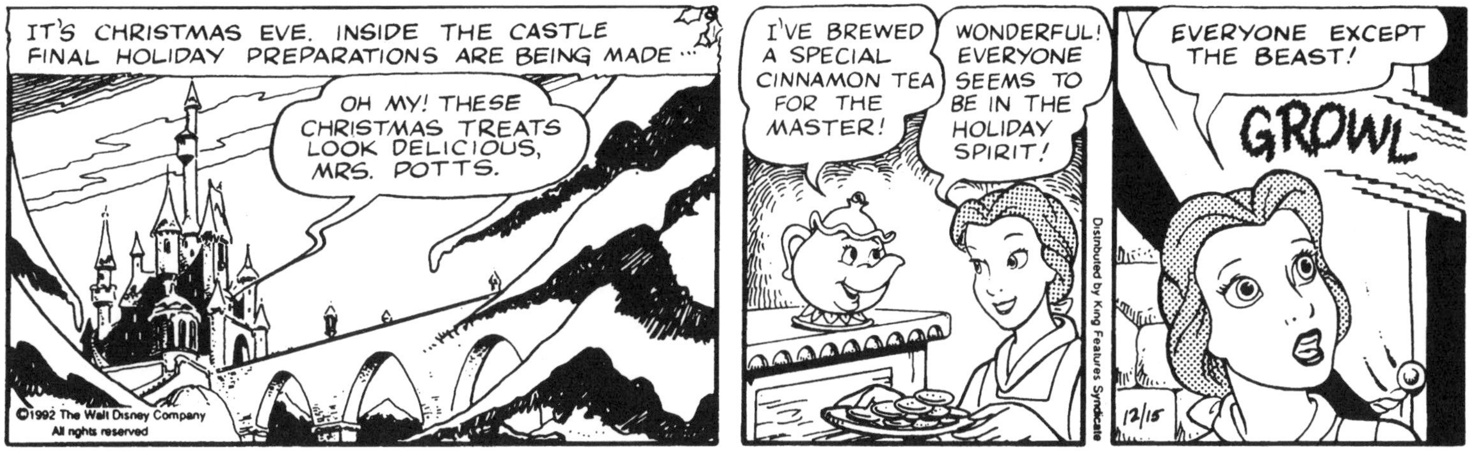
IT'S CHRISTMAS EVE. INSIDE THE CASTLE FINAL HOLIDAY PREPARATIONS ARE BEING MADE...
OH MY! THESE CHRISTMAS TREATS LOOK DELICIOUS, MRS. POTTS.
©1992 The Walt Disney Company All rights reserved
I'VE BREWED A SPECIAL CINNAMON TEA FOR THE MASTER!
WONDERFUL! EVERYONE SEEMS TO BE IN THE HOLIDAY SPIRIT!
Distributed by King Features Syndicate
EVERYONE EXCEPT THE BEAST!
GROWL
12/15

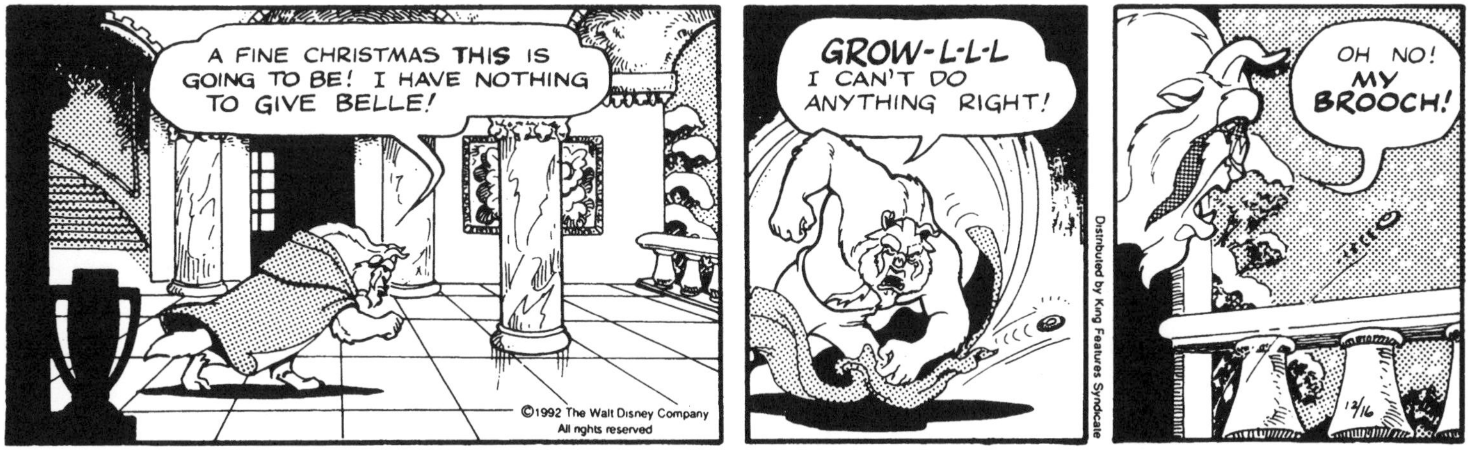
A FINE CHRISTMAS THIS IS GOING TO BE! I HAVE NOTHING TO GIVE BELLE!
©1992 The Walt Disney Company All rights reserved
GROW-L-L-L I CAN'T DO ANYTHING RIGHT!
Distributed by King Features Syndicate
OH NO! MY BROOCH!
12/16

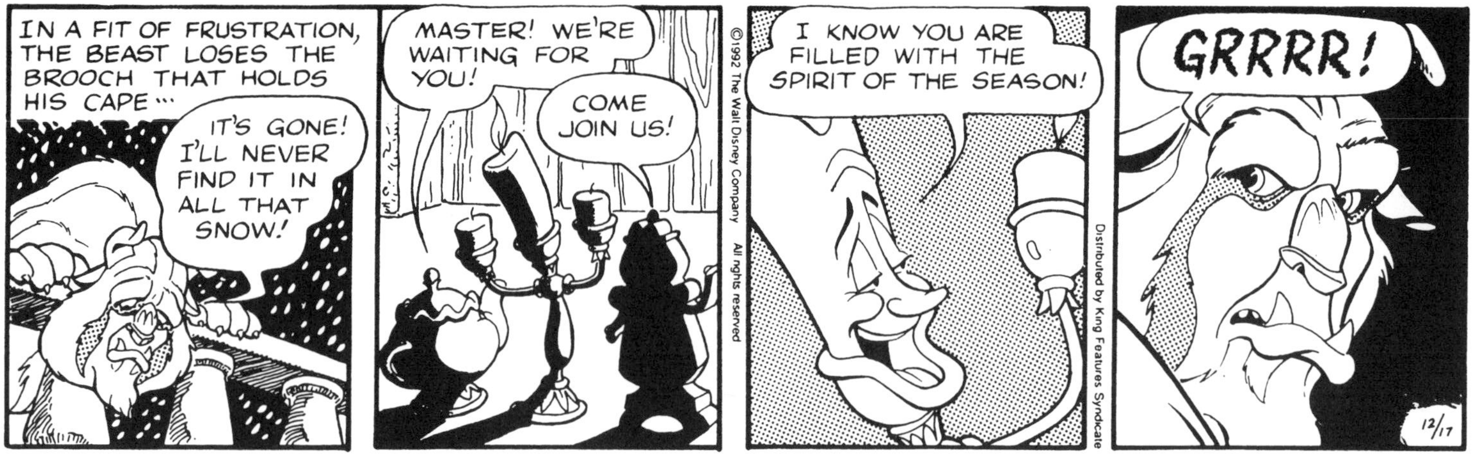
IN A FIT OF FRUSTRATION, THE BEAST LOSES THE BROOCH THAT HOLDS HIS CAPE...
IT'S GONE! I'LL NEVER FIND IT IN ALL THAT SNOW!
MASTER! WE'RE WAITING FOR YOU!
COME JOIN US!
©1992 The Walt Disney Company All rights reserved
I KNOW YOU ARE FILLED WITH THE SPIRIT OF THE SEASON!
Distributed by King Features Syndicate
GRRRR!
12/17

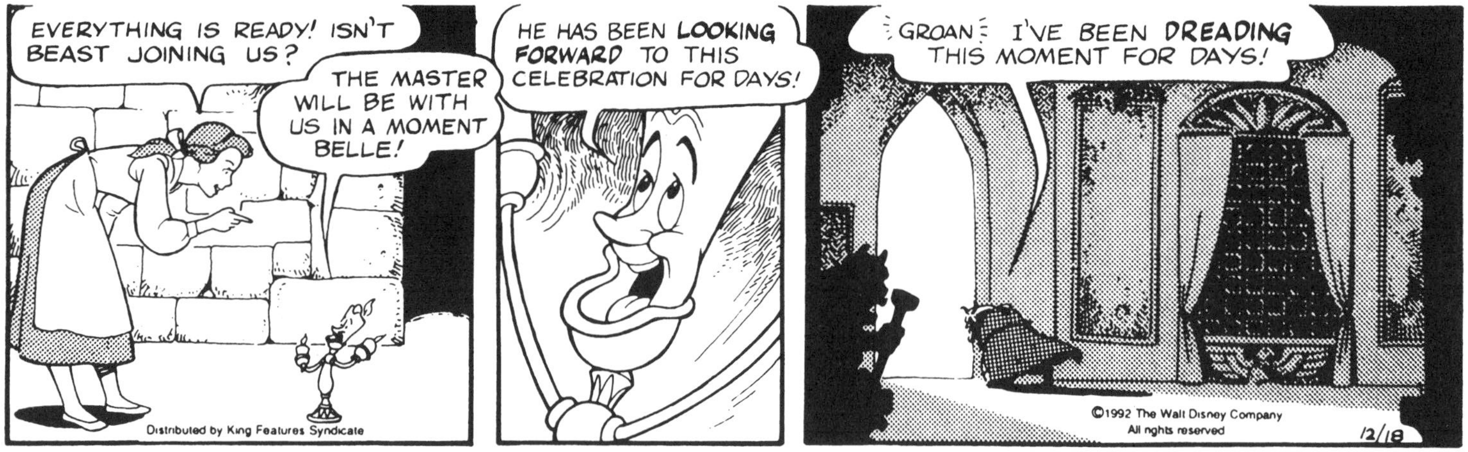
EVERYTHING IS READY! ISN'T BEAST JOINING US?
THE MASTER WILL BE WITH US IN A MOMENT BELLE!
Distributed by King Features Syndicate
HE HAS BEEN **LOOKING FORWARD** TO THIS CELEBRATION FOR DAYS!
GROAN I'VE BEEN **DREADING** THIS MOMENT FOR DAYS!
©1992 The Walt Disney Company All rights reserved
12/18

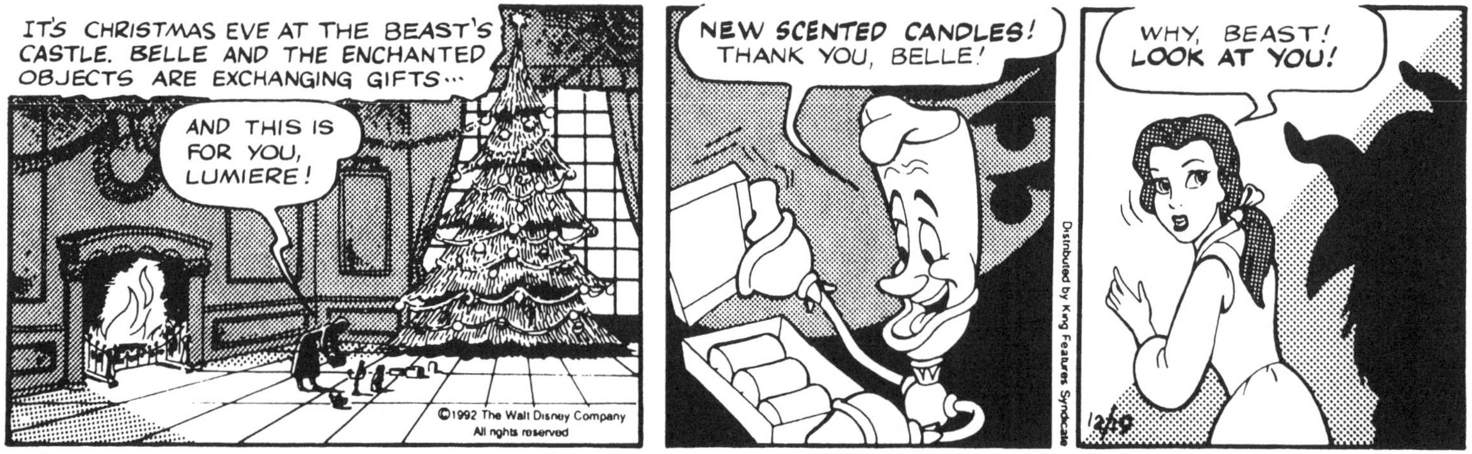
IT'S CHRISTMAS EVE AT THE BEAST'S CASTLE. BELLE AND THE ENCHANTED OBJECTS ARE EXCHANGING GIFTS...
AND THIS IS FOR YOU, LUMIERE!
©1992 The Walt Disney Company All rights reserved
NEW SCENTED CANDLES! THANK YOU, BELLE!
Distributed by King Features Syndicate
WHY, BEAST! **LOOK AT YOU!**
12/19

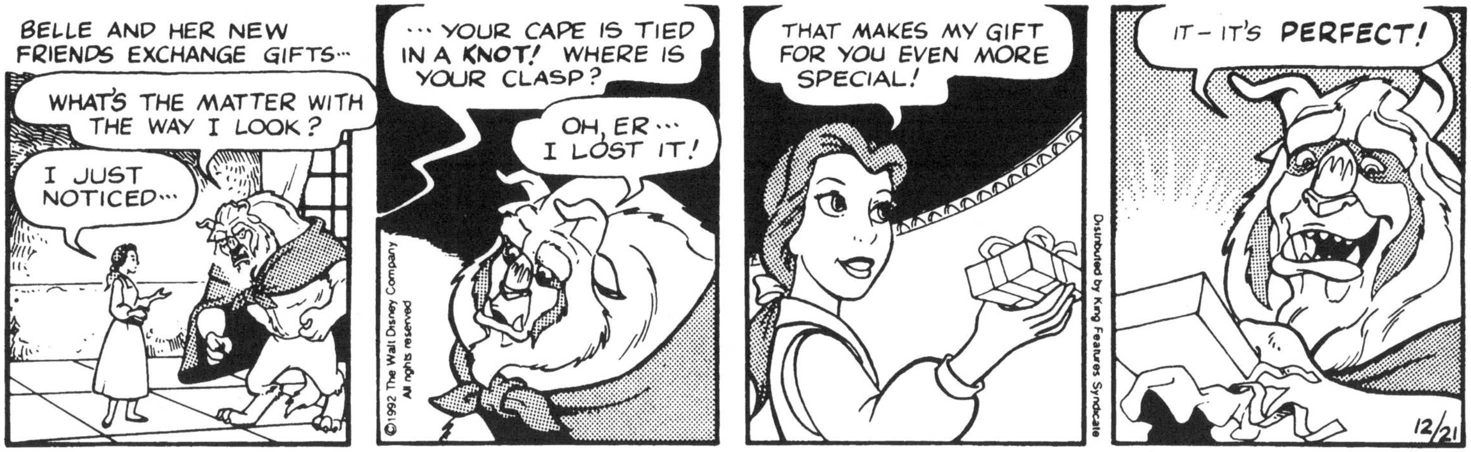
BELLE AND HER NEW FRIENDS EXCHANGE GIFTS···
WHAT'S THE MATTER WITH THE WAY I LOOK?
I JUST NOTICED···
··· YOUR CAPE IS TIED IN A KNOT! WHERE IS YOUR CLASP?
OH, ER ··· I LOST IT!
© 1992 The Walt Disney Company All rights reserved
THAT MAKES MY GIFT FOR YOU EVEN MORE SPECIAL!
Distributed by King Features Syndicate
IT – IT'S PERFECT!
12/21

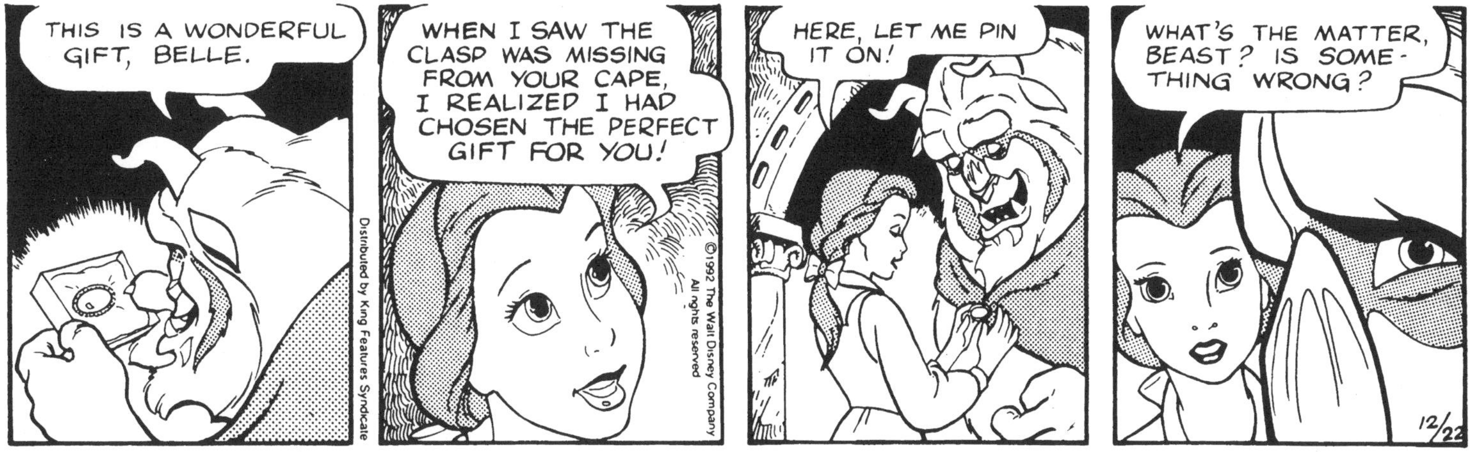
THIS IS A WONDERFUL GIFT, BELLE.
Distributed by King Features Syndicate
WHEN I SAW THE CLASP WAS MISSING FROM YOUR CAPE, I REALIZED I HAD CHOSEN THE PERFECT GIFT FOR YOU!
© 1992 The Walt Disney Company All rights reserved
HERE, LET ME PIN IT ON!
WHAT'S THE MATTER, BEAST? IS SOME-THING WRONG?
12/22

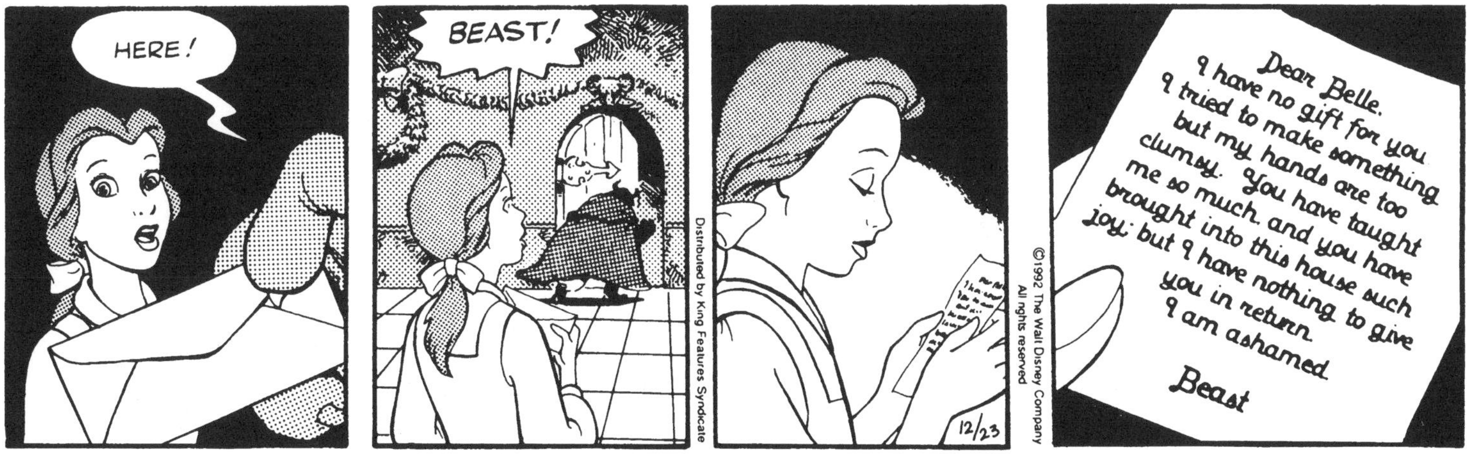
HERE!
BEAST!
Distributed by King Features Syndicate
12/23
© 1992 The Walt Disney Company All rights reserved
Dear Belle.
I have no gift for you
I tried to make something
but my hands are too
clumsy. You have taught
me so much. and you have
brought into this house such
joy; but I have nothing to give
you in return
I am ashamed
Beast

BEAST! COME BACK!
WHERE ARE YOU?
©1992 The Walt Disney Company All rights reserved
THERE YOU ARE!
Distributed by King Features Syndicate
PLEASE, BELLE! GO AWAY!

YOU HAVE GIVEN ME SO MUCH, AND I... I HAVE NOTHING FOR YOU.
THAT'S NOT TRUE! DEAR, SWEET BEAST! YOU HAVE GIVEN ME THE GIFT OF YOUR HEART!
DON'T YOU SEE? THERE IS NO GREATER GIFT IN THE ENTIRE WORLD!
Distributed by King Features Syndicate
©1992 The Walt Disney Company All rights reserved
MERRY CHRISTMAS, BELLE!
MERRY CHRISTMAS, DEAR BEAST!
The END
12/25

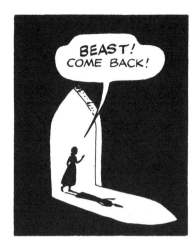

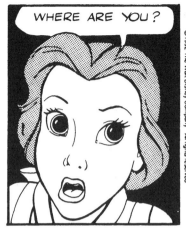

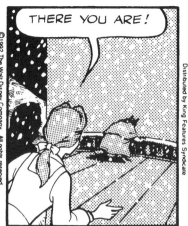

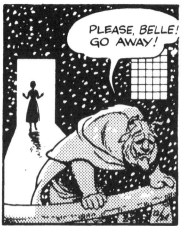

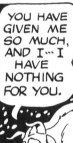

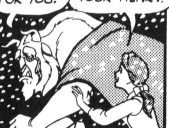

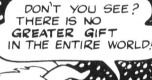

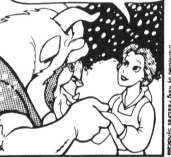

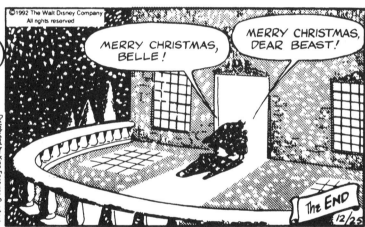

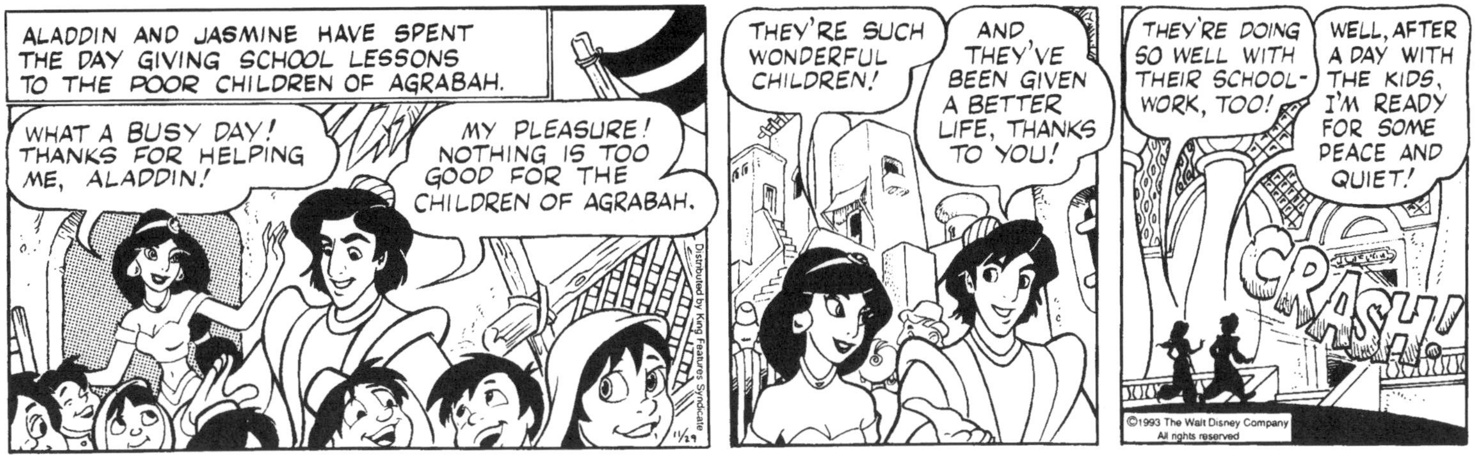
ALADDIN AND JASMINE HAVE SPENT THE DAY GIVING SCHOOL LESSONS TO THE POOR CHILDREN OF AGRABAH.
WHAT A BUSY DAY! THANKS FOR HELPING ME, ALADDIN!
MY PLEASURE! NOTHING IS TOO GOOD FOR THE CHILDREN OF AGRABAH.
Distributed by King Features Syndicate
11/29
THEY'RE SUCH WONDERFUL CHILDREN!
AND THEY'VE BEEN GIVEN A BETTER LIFE, THANKS TO YOU!
THEY'RE DOING SO WELL WITH THEIR SCHOOL-WORK, TOO!
WELL, AFTER A DAY WITH THE KIDS, I'M READY FOR SOME PEACE AND QUIET!
CRASH!
©1993 The Walt Disney Company All rights reserved

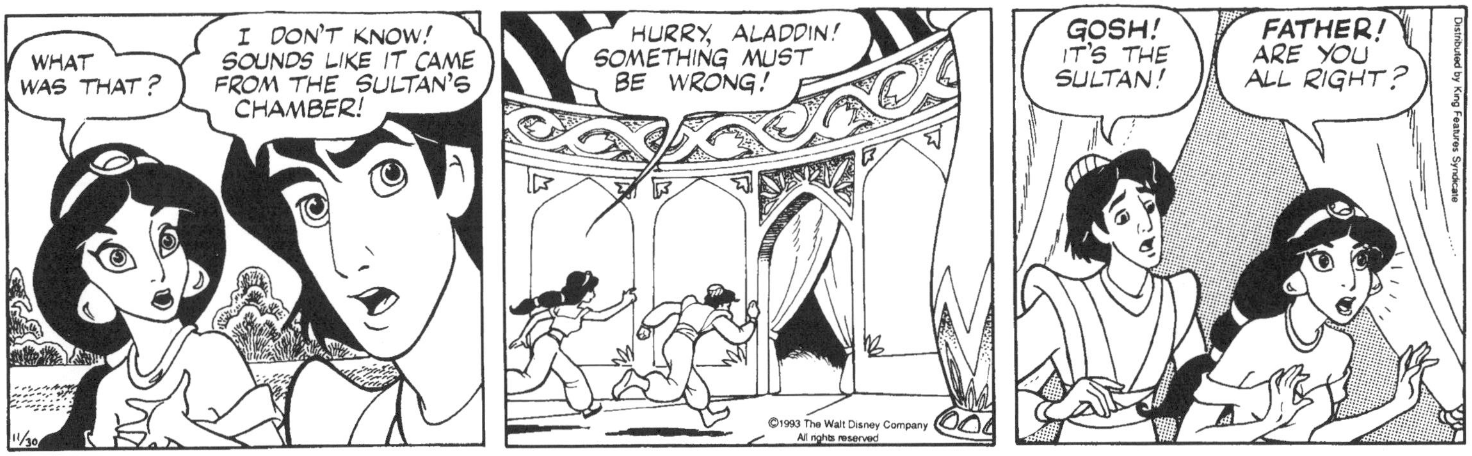
WHAT WAS THAT?
I DON'T KNOW! SOUNDS LIKE IT CAME FROM THE SULTAN'S CHAMBER!
11/30
HURRY, ALADDIN! SOMETHING MUST BE WRONG!
©1993 The Walt Disney Company All rights reserved
GOSH! IT'S THE SULTAN!
FATHER! ARE YOU ALL RIGHT?
Distributed by King Features Syndicate

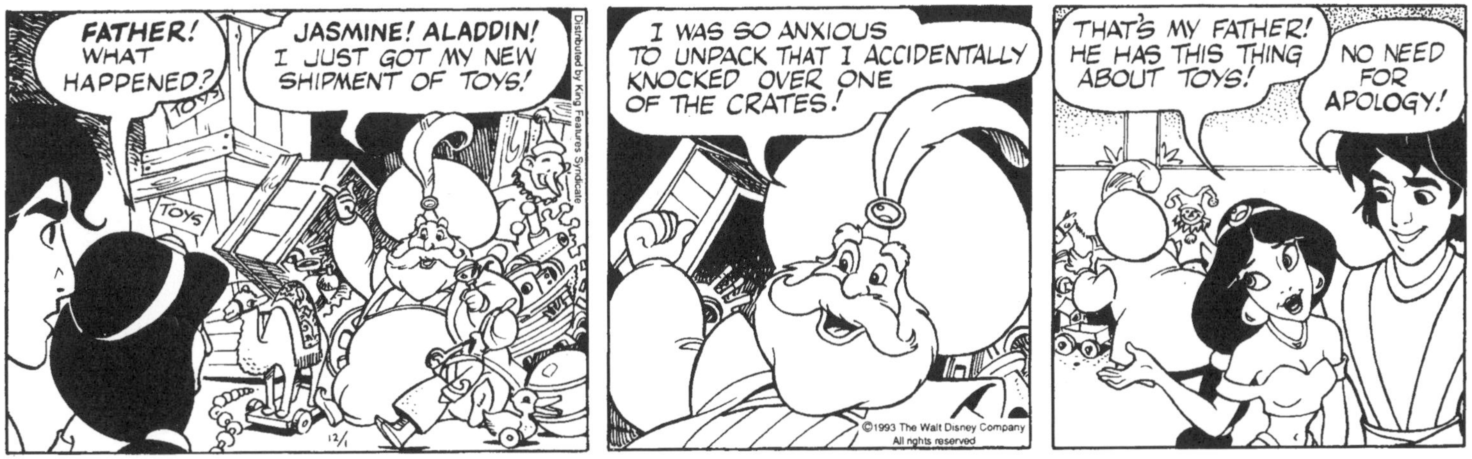
FATHER! WHAT HAPPENED?
JASMINE! ALADDIN! I JUST GOT MY NEW SHIPMENT OF TOYS!
TOYS
TOYS
Distributed by King Features Syndicate
12/1
I WAS SO ANXIOUS TO UNPACK THAT I ACCIDENTALLY KNOCKED OVER ONE OF THE CRATES!
©1993 The Walt Disney Company All rights reserved
THAT'S MY FATHER! HE HAS THIS THING ABOUT TOYS!
NO NEED FOR APOLOGY!

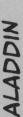

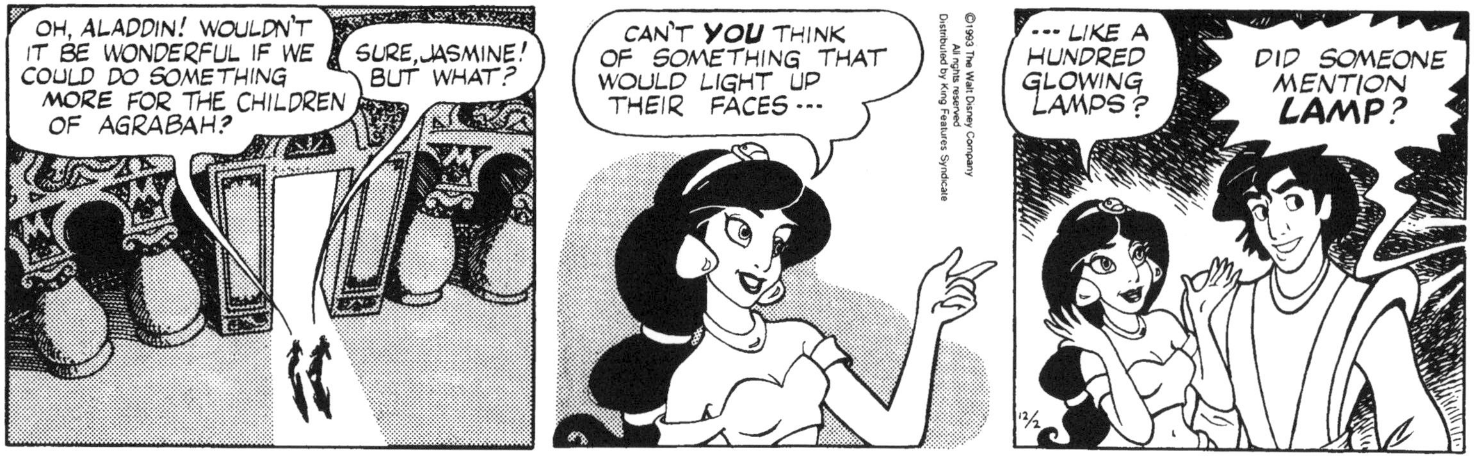
OH, ALADDIN! WOULDN'T IT BE WONDERFUL IF WE COULD DO SOMETHING MORE FOR THE CHILDREN OF AGRABAH?
SURE, JASMINE! BUT WHAT?
CAN'T YOU THINK OF SOMETHING THAT WOULD LIGHT UP THEIR FACES ---
©1993 The Walt Disney Company All rights reserved Distributed by King Features Syndicate
--- LIKE A HUNDRED GLOWING LAMPS?
DID SOMEONE MENTION LAMP?
12/2

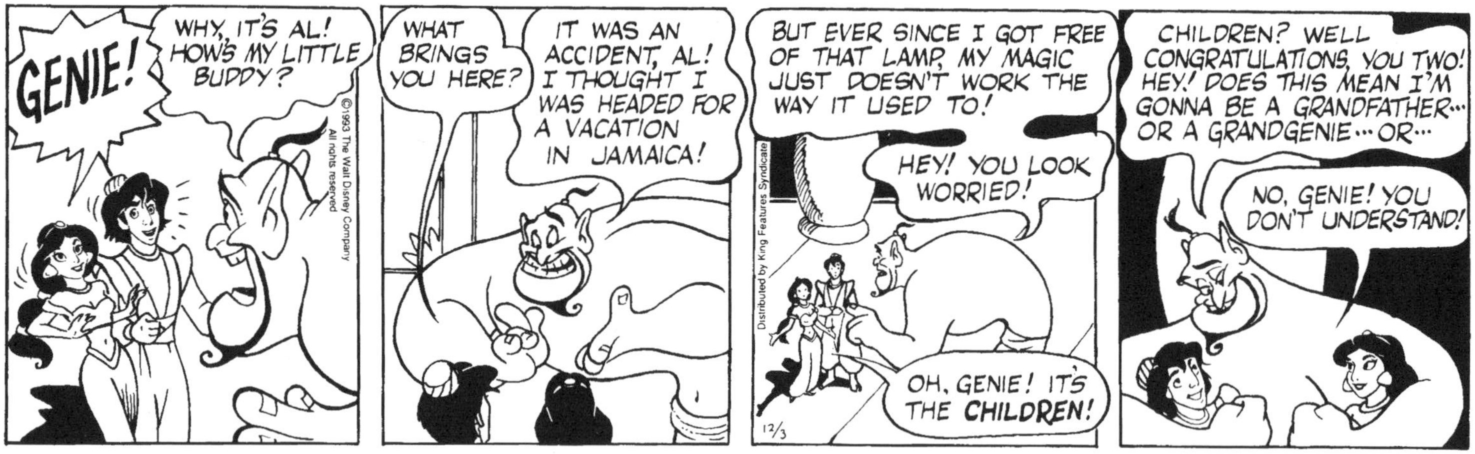
GENIE!
WHY, IT'S AL! HOW'S MY LITTLE BUDDY?
©1993 The Walt Disney Company All rights reserved
WHAT BRINGS YOU HERE?
IT WAS AN ACCIDENT, AL! I THOUGHT I WAS HEADED FOR A VACATION IN JAMAICA!
BUT EVER SINCE I GOT FREE OF THAT LAMP, MY MAGIC JUST DOESN'T WORK THE WAY IT USED TO!
HEY! YOU LOOK WORRIED!
OH, GENIE! IT'S THE CHILDREN!
Distributed by King Features Syndicate
12/3
CHILDREN? WELL CONGRATULATIONS, YOU TWO! HEY! DOES THIS MEAN I'M GONNA BE A GRANDFATHER... OR A GRANDGENIE... OR...
NO, GENIE! YOU DON'T UNDERSTAND!

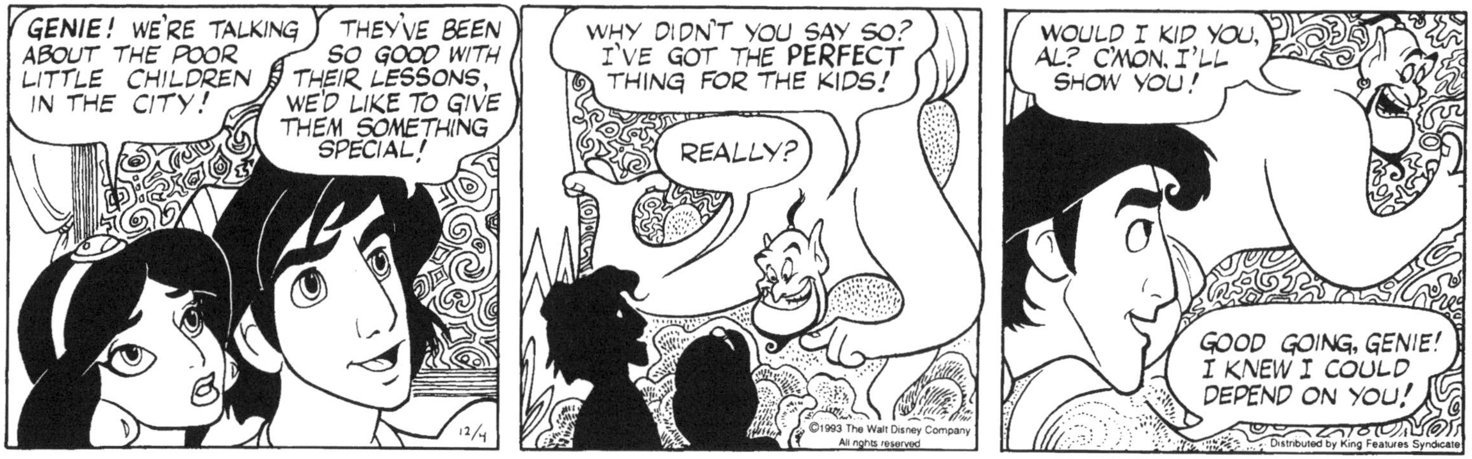
GENIE! WE'RE TALKING ABOUT THE POOR LITTLE CHILDREN IN THE CITY!
THEY'VE BEEN SO GOOD WITH THEIR LESSONS, WE'D LIKE TO GIVE THEM SOMETHING SPECIAL!
12/4
WHY DIDN'T YOU SAY SO? I'VE GOT THE PERFECT THING FOR THE KIDS!
REALLY?
©1993 The Walt Disney Company All rights reserved
WOULD I KID YOU, AL? C'MON, I'LL SHOW YOU!
GOOD GOING, GENIE! I KNEW I COULD DEPEND ON YOU!
Distributed by King Features Syndicate

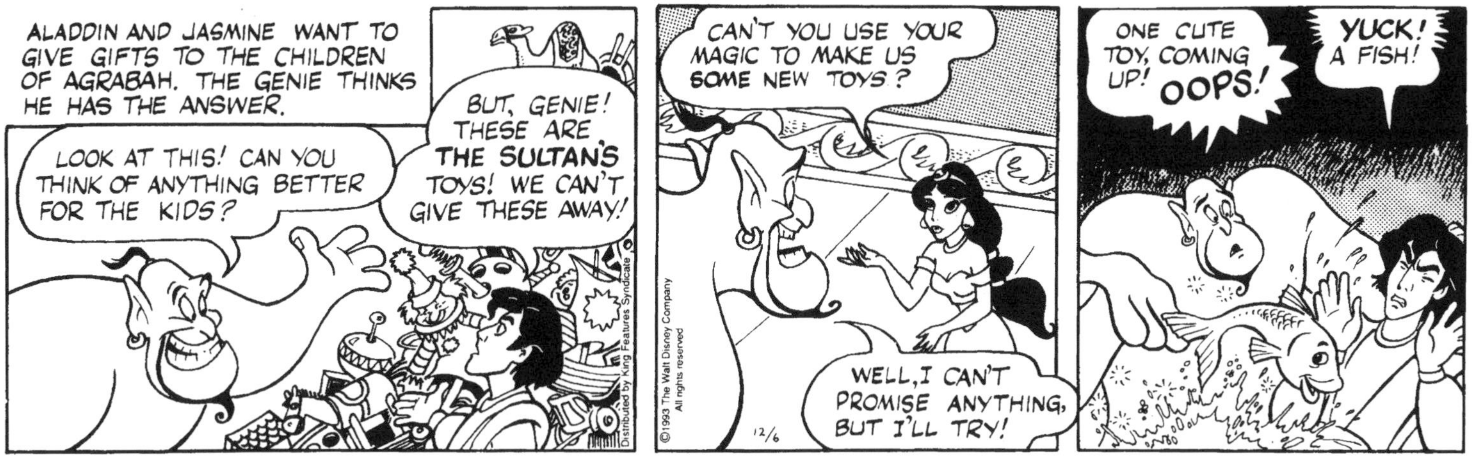
ALADDIN AND JASMINE WANT TO GIVE GIFTS TO THE CHILDREN OF AGRABAH. THE GENIE THINKS HE HAS THE ANSWER.
LOOK AT THIS! CAN YOU THINK OF ANYTHING BETTER FOR THE KIDS?
BUT, GENIE! THESE ARE **THE SULTAN'S** TOYS! WE CAN'T GIVE THESE AWAY!
Distributed by King Features Syndicate
CAN'T YOU USE YOUR MAGIC TO MAKE US **SOME** NEW TOYS?
WELL, I CAN'T PROMISE ANYTHING, BUT I'LL TRY!
©1993 The Walt Disney Company All rights reserved
12/6
ONE CUTE TOY, COMING UP! **OOPS!**
YUCK! A FISH!

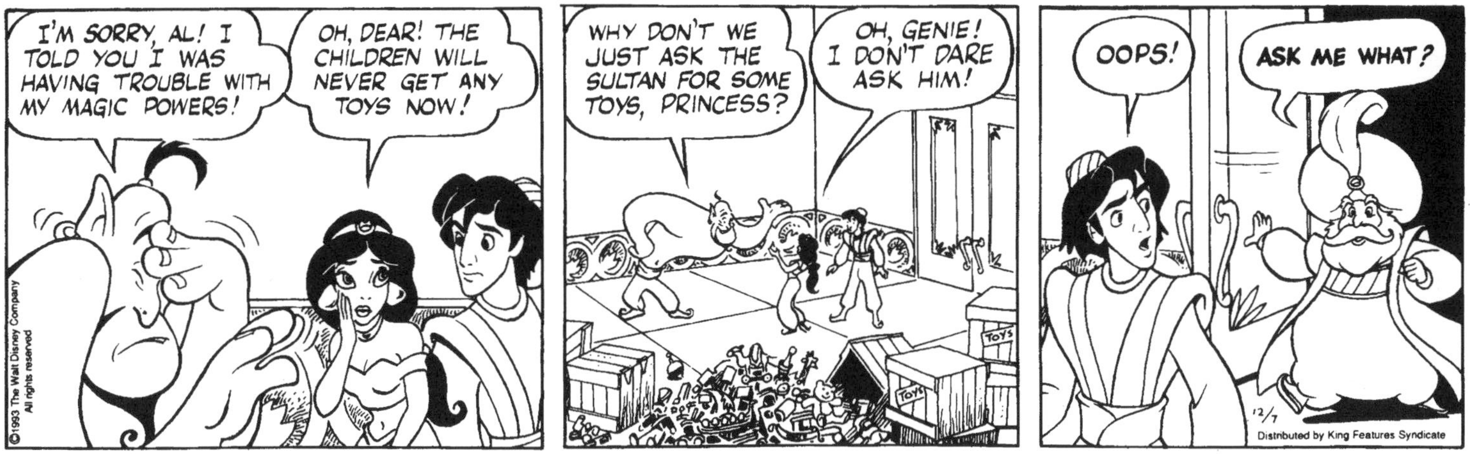
I'M SORRY, AL! I TOLD YOU I WAS HAVING TROUBLE WITH MY MAGIC POWERS!
OH, DEAR! THE CHILDREN WILL NEVER GET ANY TOYS NOW!
©1993 The Walt Disney Company All rights reserved
WHY DON'T WE JUST ASK THE SULTAN FOR SOME TOYS, PRINCESS?
OH, GENIE! I DON'T DARE ASK HIM!
TOYS
TOYS
OOPS!
ASK ME WHAT?
12/7
Distributed by King Features Syndicate

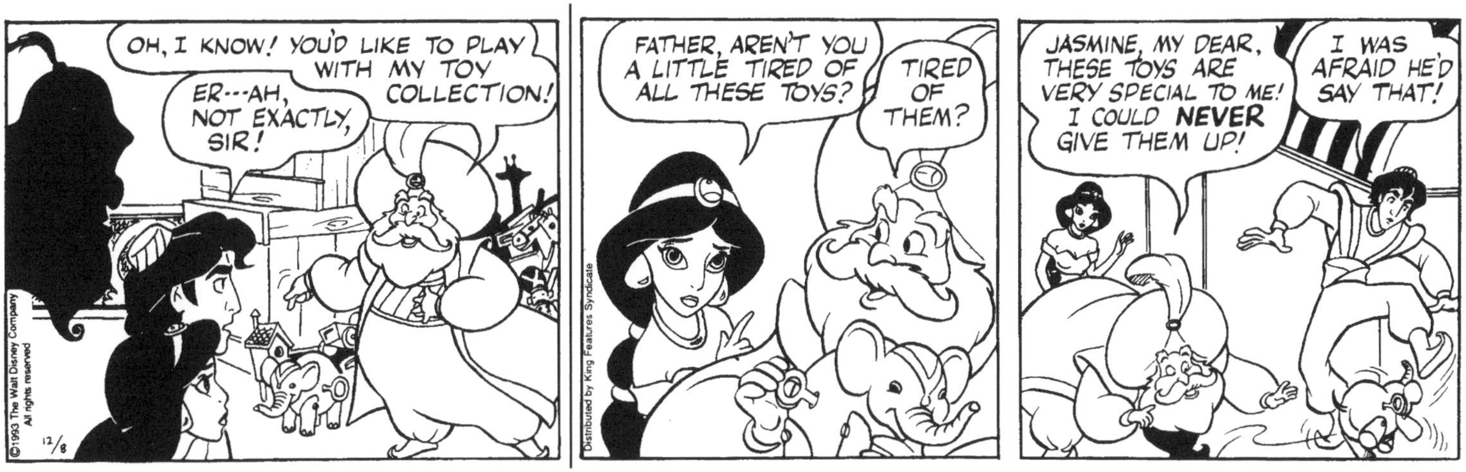
OH, I KNOW! YOU'D LIKE TO PLAY WITH MY TOY COLLECTION!
ER---AH, NOT EXACTLY, SIR!
©1993 The Walt Disney Company All rights reserved
12/8
FATHER, AREN'T YOU A LITTLE TIRED OF ALL THESE TOYS?
TIRED OF THEM?
Distributed by King Features Syndicate
JASMINE, MY DEAR, THESE TOYS ARE VERY SPECIAL TO ME! I COULD **NEVER** GIVE THEM UP!
I WAS AFRAID HE'D SAY THAT!

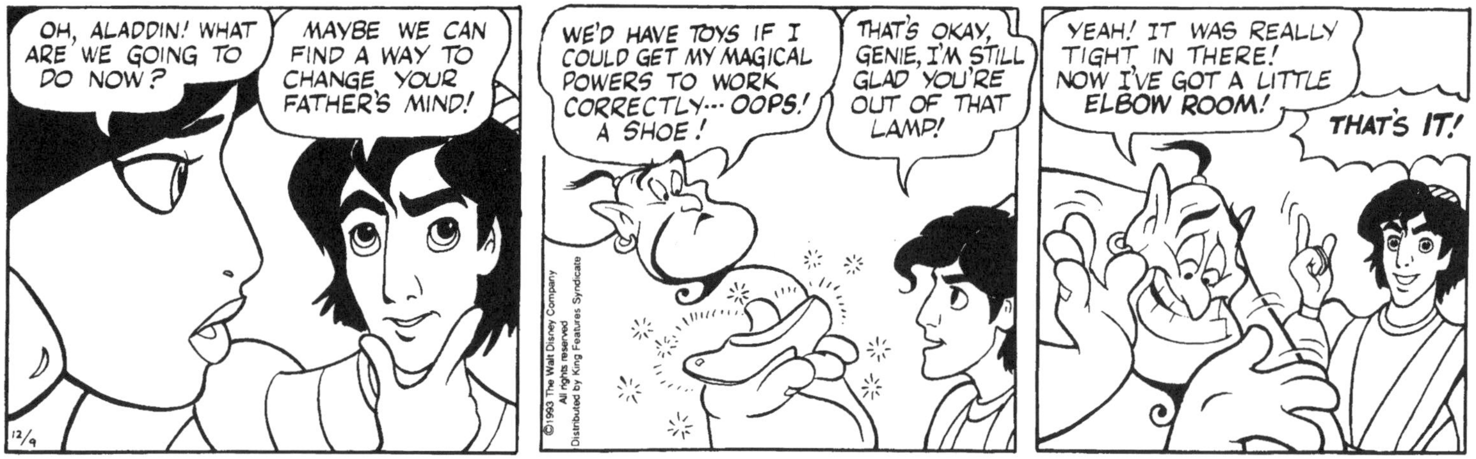
OH, ALADDIN! WHAT ARE WE GOING TO DO NOW?
MAYBE WE CAN FIND A WAY TO CHANGE YOUR FATHER'S MIND!
12/9
WE'D HAVE TOYS IF I COULD GET MY MAGICAL POWERS TO WORK CORRECTLY... OOPS! A SHOE!
THAT'S OKAY, GENIE, I'M STILL GLAD YOU'RE OUT OF THAT LAMP!
©1993 The Walt Disney Company All rights reserved Distributed by King Features Syndicate
YEAH! IT WAS REALLY TIGHT IN THERE! NOW I'VE GOT A LITTLE ELBOW ROOM!
THAT'S IT!

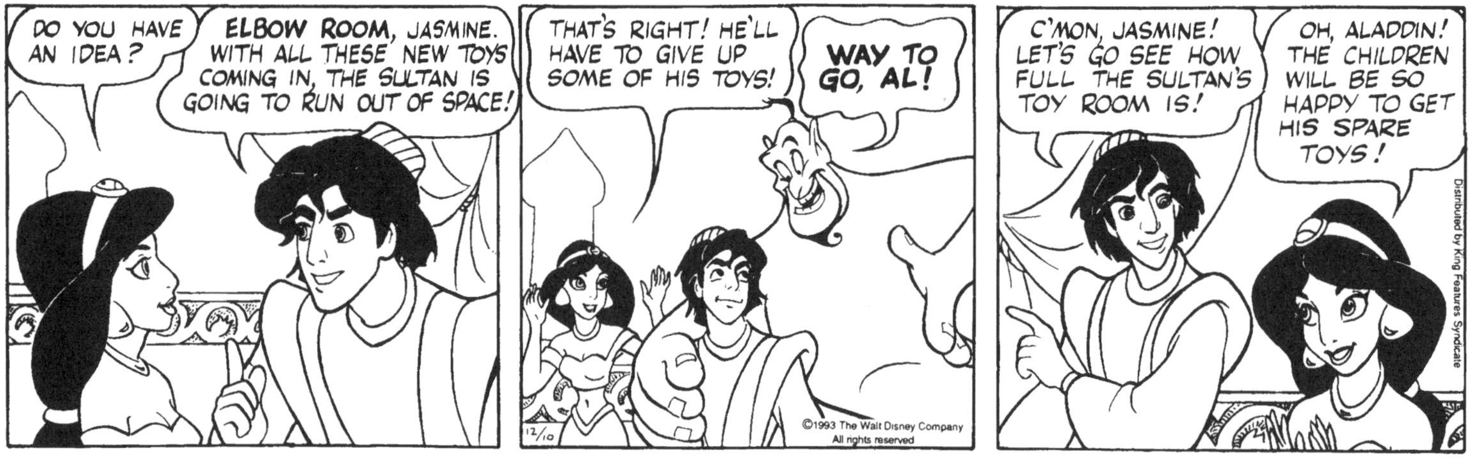
DO YOU HAVE AN IDEA?
ELBOW ROOM, JASMINE. WITH ALL THESE NEW TOYS COMING IN, THE SULTAN IS GOING TO RUN OUT OF SPACE!
THAT'S RIGHT! HE'LL HAVE TO GIVE UP SOME OF HIS TOYS!
WAY TO GO, AL!
12/10
©1993 The Walt Disney Company All rights reserved
C'MON, JASMINE! LET'S GO SEE HOW FULL THE SULTAN'S TOY ROOM IS!
OH, ALADDIN! THE CHILDREN WILL BE SO HAPPY TO GET HIS SPARE TOYS!
Distributed by King Features Syndicate

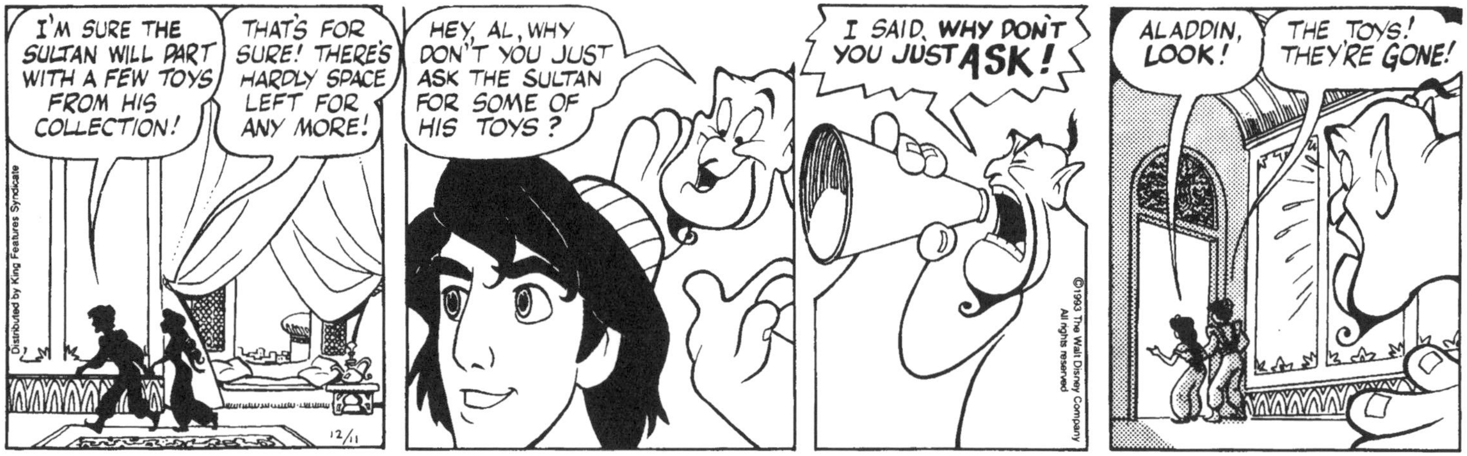
I'M SURE THE SULTAN WILL PART WITH A FEW TOYS FROM HIS COLLECTION!
THAT'S FOR SURE! THERE'S HARDLY SPACE LEFT FOR ANY MORE!
Distributed by King Features Syndicate
12/11
HEY, AL, WHY DON'T YOU JUST ASK THE SULTAN FOR SOME OF HIS TOYS?
I SAID, WHY DON'T YOU JUST ASK!
©1993 The Walt Disney Company All rights reserved
ALADDIN, LOOK!
THE TOYS! THEY'RE GONE!

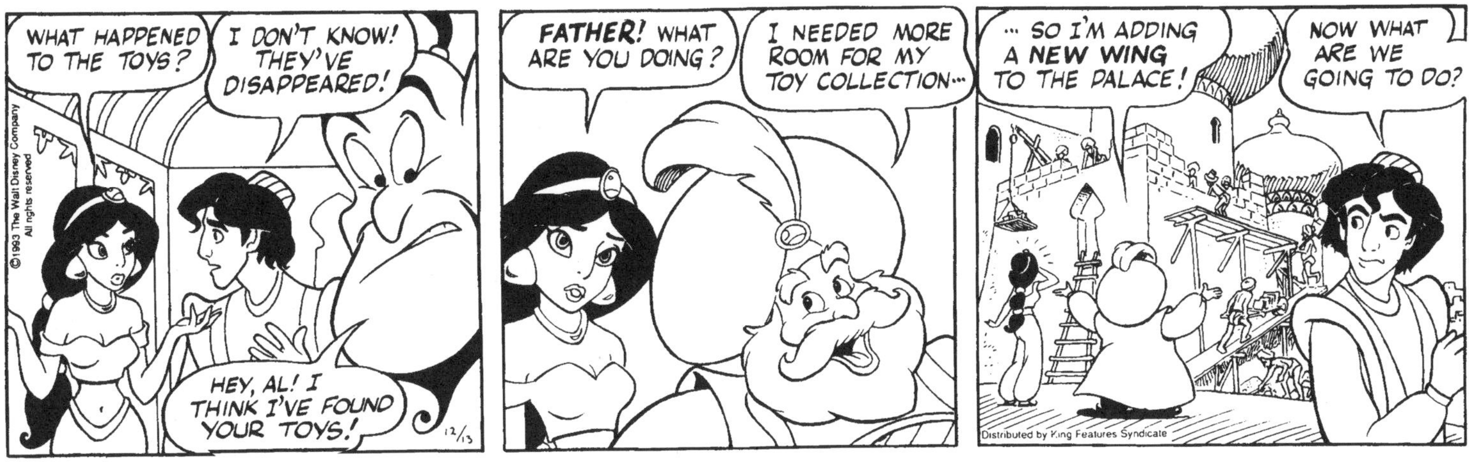
WHAT HAPPENED TO THE TOYS?
I DON'T KNOW! THEY'VE DISAPPEARED!
HEY, AL! I THINK I'VE FOUND YOUR TOYS!
©1993 The Walt Disney Company All rights reserved
12/13
FATHER! WHAT ARE YOU DOING?
I NEEDED MORE ROOM FOR MY TOY COLLECTION...
... SO I'M ADDING A NEW WING TO THE PALACE!
NOW WHAT ARE WE GOING TO DO?
Distributed by King Features Syndicate

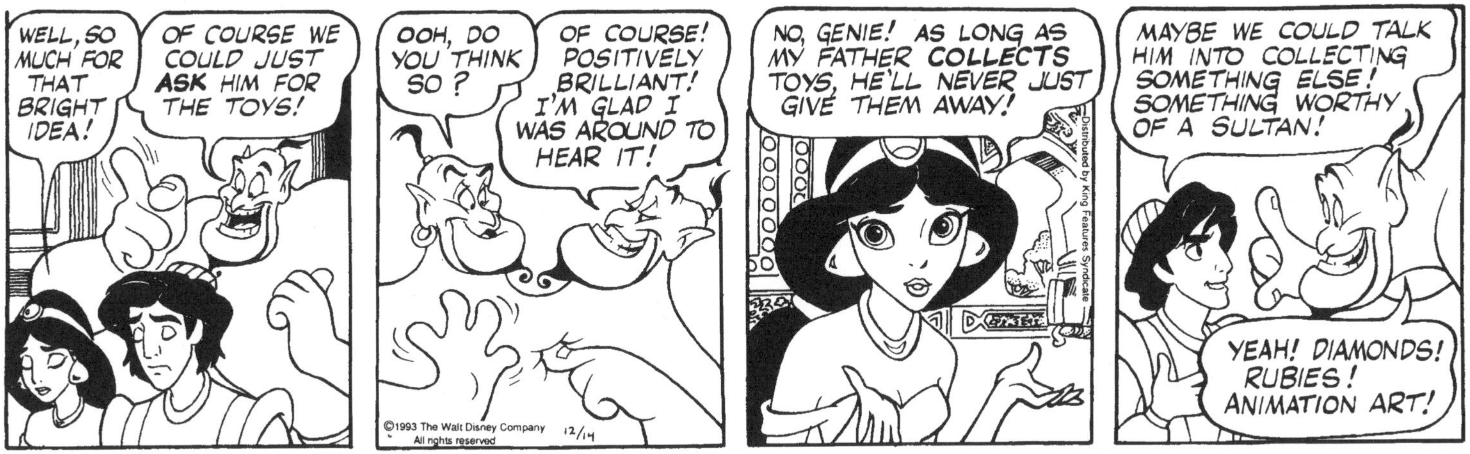
WELL, SO MUCH FOR THAT BRIGHT IDEA!
OF COURSE WE COULD JUST ASK HIM FOR THE TOYS!
OOH, DO YOU THINK SO?
OF COURSE! POSITIVELY BRILLIANT! I'M GLAD I WAS AROUND TO HEAR IT!
©1993 The Walt Disney Company All rights reserved
12/14
NO, GENIE! AS LONG AS MY FATHER COLLECTS TOYS, HE'LL NEVER JUST GIVE THEM AWAY!
Distributed by King Features Syndicate
MAYBE WE COULD TALK HIM INTO COLLECTING SOMETHING ELSE! SOMETHING WORTHY OF A SULTAN!
YEAH! DIAMONDS! RUBIES! ANIMATION ART!

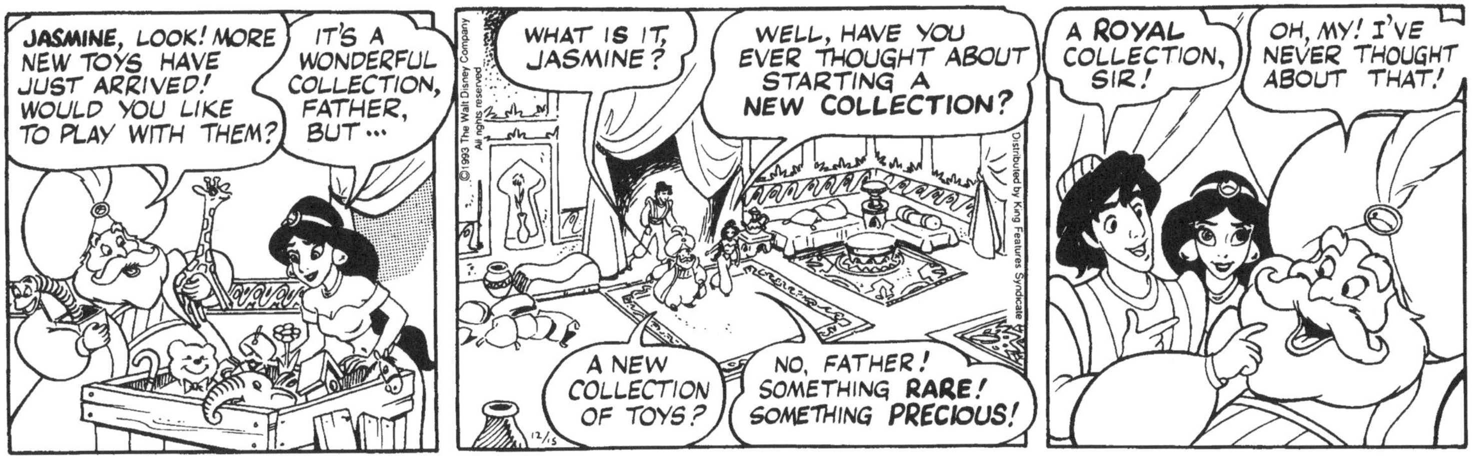
JASMINE, LOOK! MORE NEW TOYS HAVE JUST ARRIVED! WOULD YOU LIKE TO PLAY WITH THEM?
IT'S A WONDERFUL COLLECTION, FATHER, BUT...
©1993 The Walt Disney Company All rights reserved
WHAT IS IT, JASMINE?
WELL, HAVE YOU EVER THOUGHT ABOUT STARTING A NEW COLLECTION?
A NEW COLLECTION OF TOYS?
NO, FATHER! SOMETHING RARE! SOMETHING PRECIOUS!
Distributed by King Features Syndicate
12/15
A ROYAL COLLECTION, SIR!
OH, MY! I'VE NEVER THOUGHT ABOUT THAT!

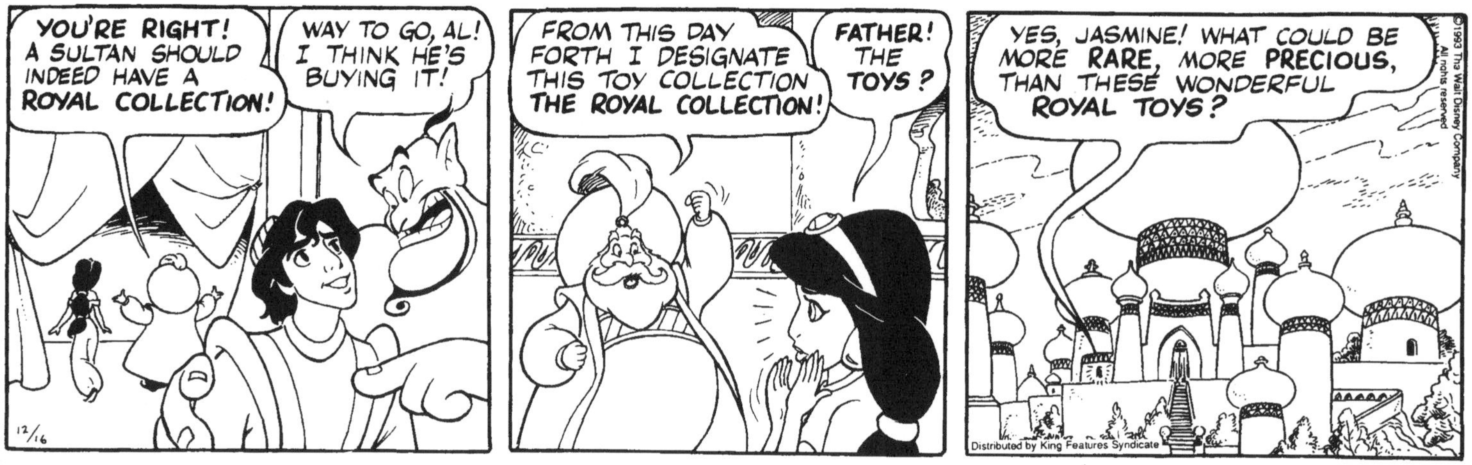
YOU'RE RIGHT! A SULTAN SHOULD INDEED HAVE A ROYAL COLLECTION!
WAY TO GO, AL! I THINK HE'S BUYING IT!
12/16
FROM THIS DAY FORTH I DESIGNATE THIS TOY COLLECTION THE ROYAL COLLECTION!
FATHER! THE TOYS?
YES, JASMINE! WHAT COULD BE MORE RARE, MORE PRECIOUS, THAN THESE WONDERFUL ROYAL TOYS?
©1993 The Walt Disney Company All rights reserved
Distributed by King Features Syndicate

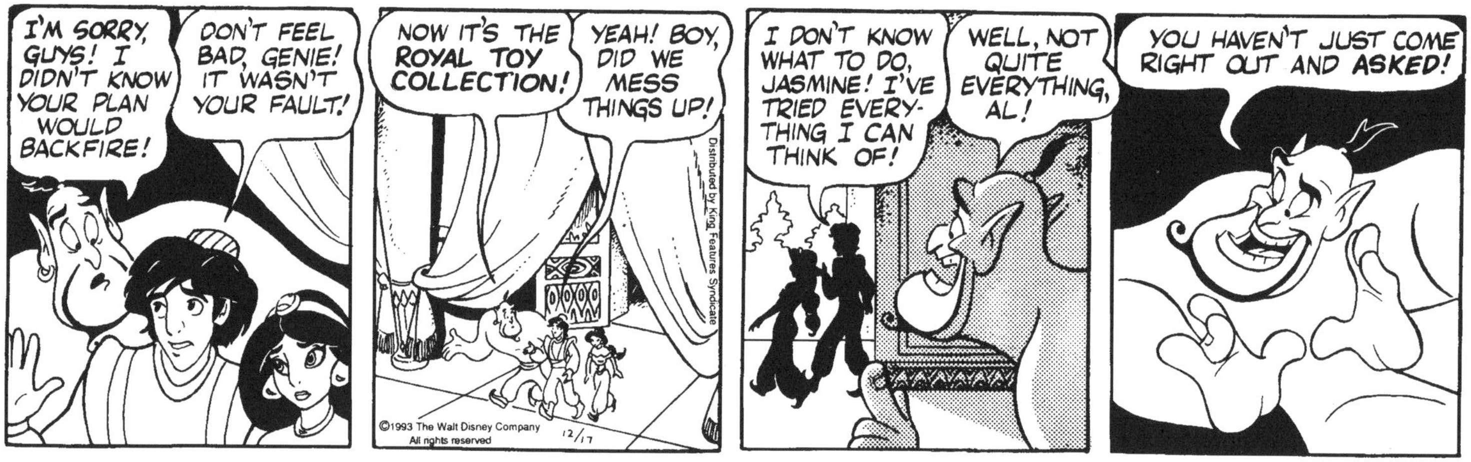
I'M SORRY, GUYS! I DIDN'T KNOW YOUR PLAN WOULD BACKFIRE!
DON'T FEEL BAD, GENIE! IT WASN'T YOUR FAULT!
NOW IT'S THE ROYAL TOY COLLECTION!
YEAH! BOY, DID WE MESS THINGS UP!
Distributed by King Features Syndicate
©1993 The Walt Disney Company All rights reserved
12/17
I DON'T KNOW WHAT TO DO, JASMINE! I'VE TRIED EVERYTHING I CAN THINK OF!
WELL, NOT QUITE EVERYTHING, AL!
YOU HAVEN'T JUST COME RIGHT OUT AND ASKED!

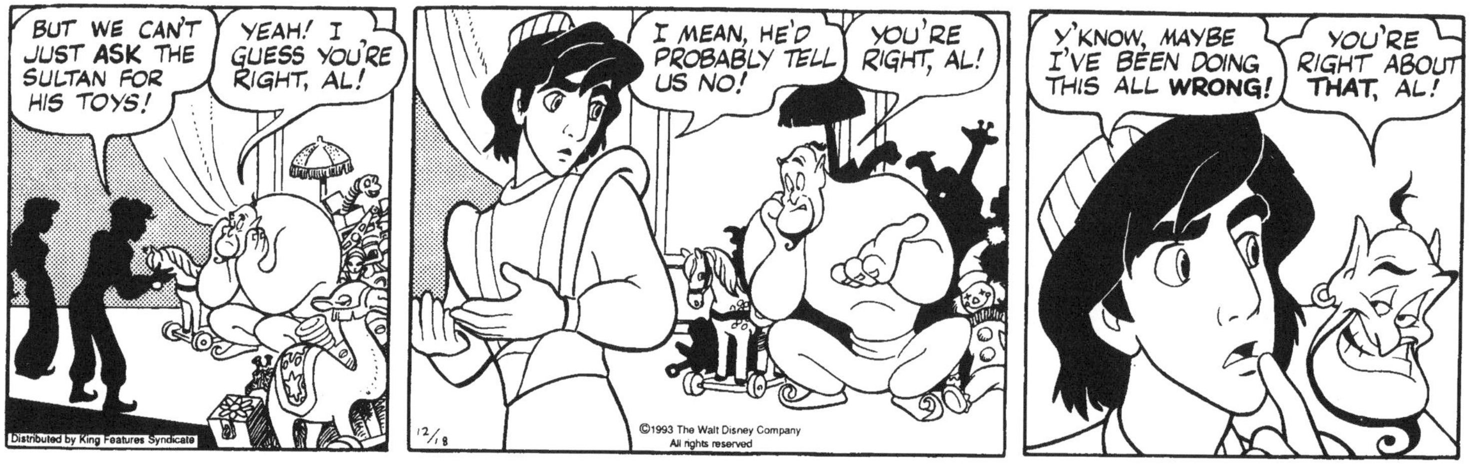
BUT WE CAN'T JUST ASK THE SULTAN FOR HIS TOYS!
YEAH! I GUESS YOU'RE RIGHT, AL!
Distributed by King Features Syndicate
I MEAN, HE'D PROBABLY TELL US NO!
YOU'RE RIGHT, AL!
12/18
©1993 The Walt Disney Company All rights reserved
Y'KNOW, MAYBE I'VE BEEN DOING THIS ALL WRONG!
YOU'RE RIGHT ABOUT THAT, AL!

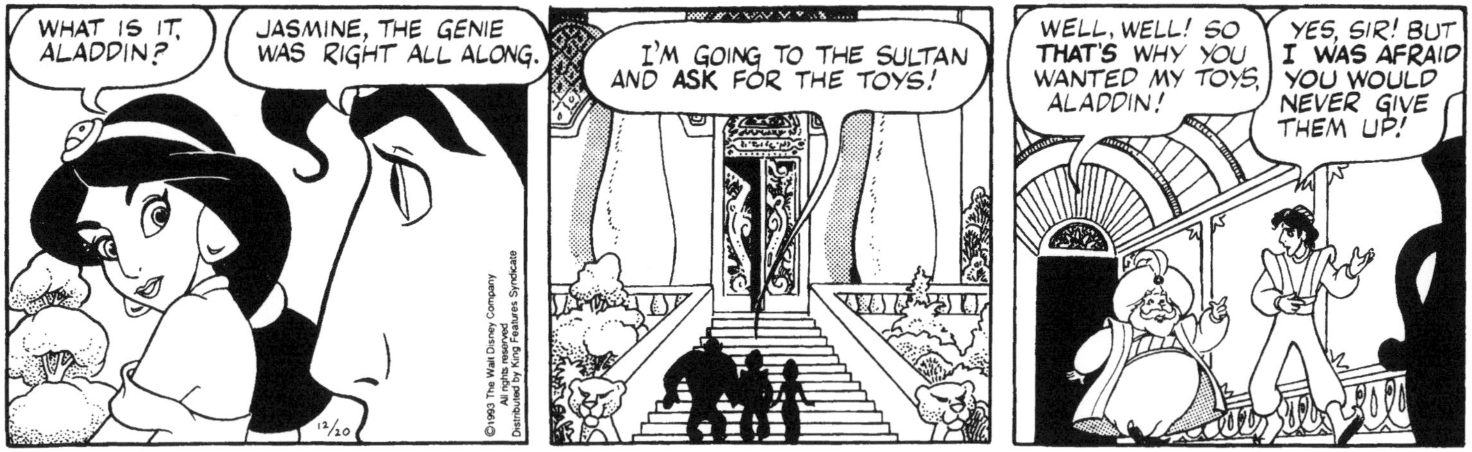
WHAT IS IT, ALADDIN?
JASMINE, THE GENIE WAS RIGHT ALL ALONG.
12/20
©1993 The Walt Disney Company
All rights reserved
Distributed by King Features Syndicate
I'M GOING TO THE SULTAN AND ASK FOR THE TOYS!
WELL, WELL! SO THAT'S WHY YOU WANTED MY TOYS, ALADDIN!
YES, SIR! BUT I WAS AFRAID YOU WOULD NEVER GIVE THEM UP!

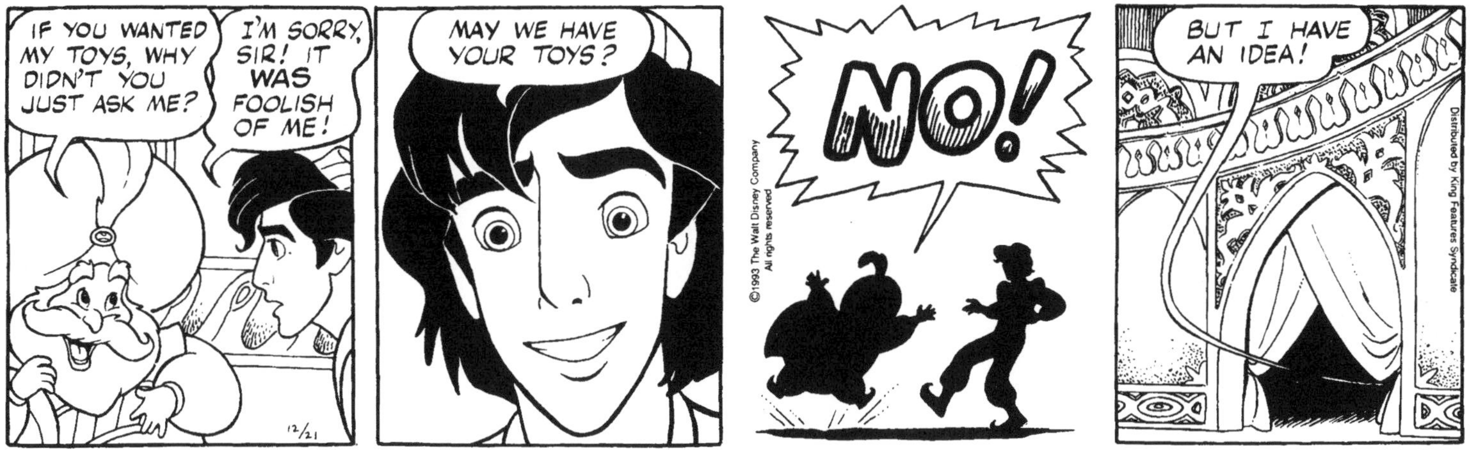
IF YOU WANTED MY TOYS, WHY DIDN'T YOU JUST ASK ME?
I'M SORRY, SIR! IT WAS FOOLISH OF ME!
12/21
MAY WE HAVE YOUR TOYS?
©1993 The Walt Disney Company
All rights reserved
NO!
BUT I HAVE AN IDEA!
Distributed by King Features Syndicate

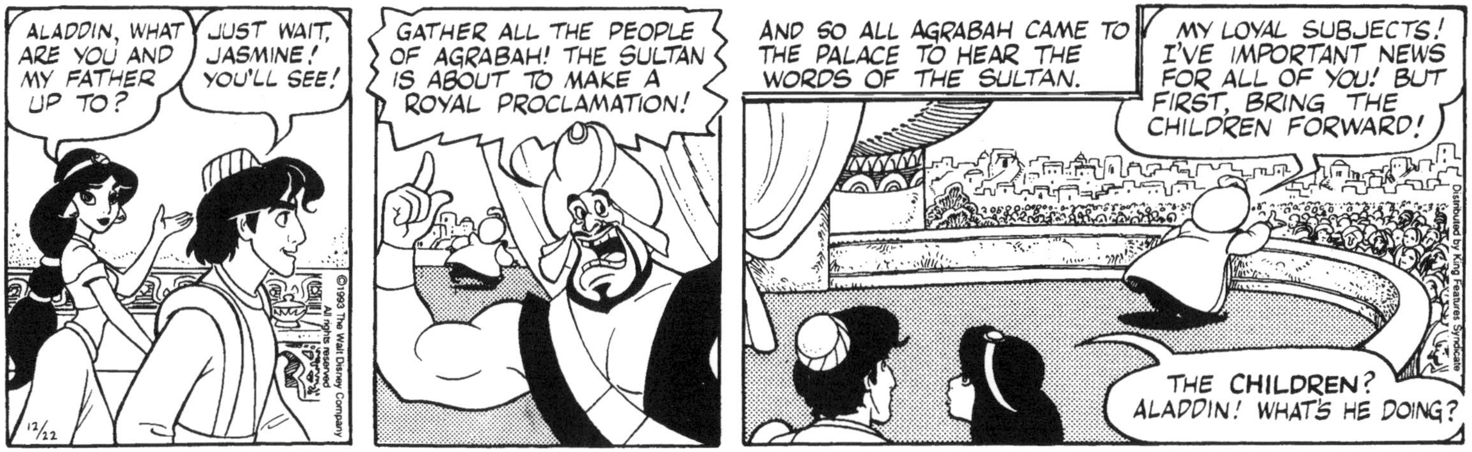
ALADDIN, WHAT ARE YOU AND MY FATHER UP TO?
JUST WAIT, JASMINE! YOU'LL SEE!
12/22
©1993 The Walt Disney Company
All rights reserved
GATHER ALL THE PEOPLE OF AGRABAH! THE SULTAN IS ABOUT TO MAKE A ROYAL PROCLAMATION!
AND SO ALL AGRABAH CAME TO THE PALACE TO HEAR THE WORDS OF THE SULTAN.
MY LOYAL SUBJECTS! I'VE IMPORTANT NEWS FOR ALL OF YOU! BUT FIRST, BRING THE CHILDREN FORWARD!
THE CHILDREN? ALADDIN! WHAT'S HE DOING?
Distributed by King Features Syndicate

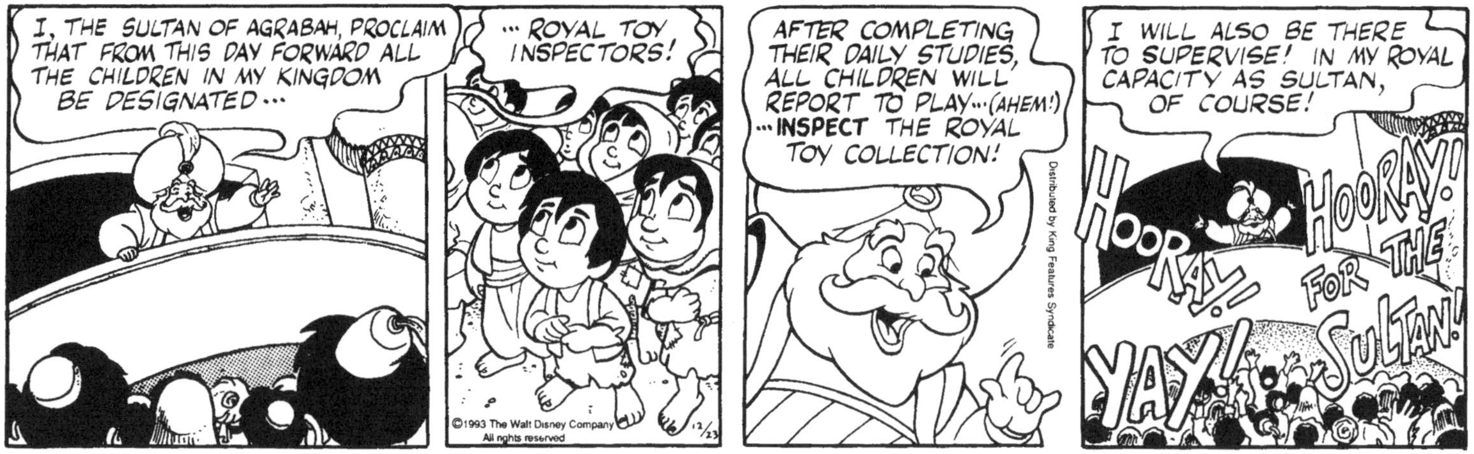
I, THE SULTAN OF AGRABAH, PROCLAIM THAT FROM THIS DAY FORWARD ALL THE CHILDREN IN MY KINGDOM BE DESIGNATED...
...ROYAL TOY INSPECTORS!
©1993 The Walt Disney Company All rights reserved
12/23
AFTER COMPLETING THEIR DAILY STUDIES, ALL CHILDREN WILL REPORT TO PLAY...(AHEM!) ...INSPECT THE ROYAL TOY COLLECTION!
Distributed by King Features Syndicate
I WILL ALSO BE THERE TO SUPERVISE! IN MY ROYAL CAPACITY AS SULTAN, OF COURSE!
HOORAY!
HOORAY! FOR THE SULTAN!
YAY!

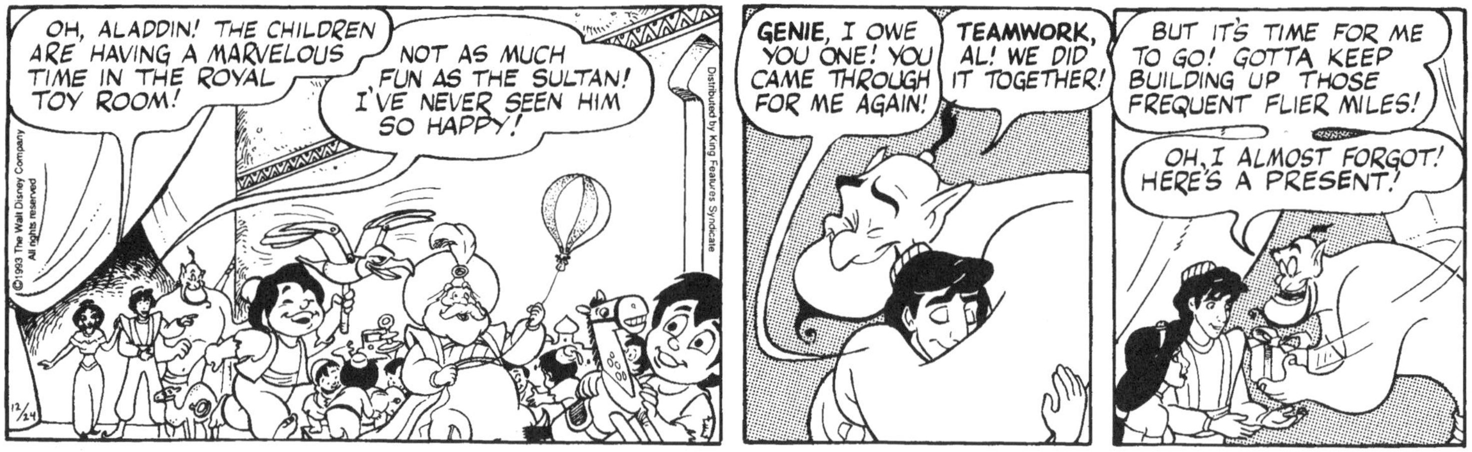
OH, ALADDIN! THE CHILDREN ARE HAVING A MARVELOUS TIME IN THE ROYAL TOY ROOM!
NOT AS MUCH FUN AS THE SULTAN! I'VE NEVER SEEN HIM SO HAPPY!
©1993 The Walt Disney Company All rights reserved
Distributed by King Features Syndicate
12/24
GENIE, I OWE YOU ONE! YOU CAME THROUGH FOR ME AGAIN!
TEAMWORK, AL! WE DID IT TOGETHER!
BUT IT'S TIME FOR ME TO GO! GOTTA KEEP BUILDING UP THOSE FREQUENT FLIER MILES!
OH, I ALMOST FORGOT! HERE'S A PRESENT!

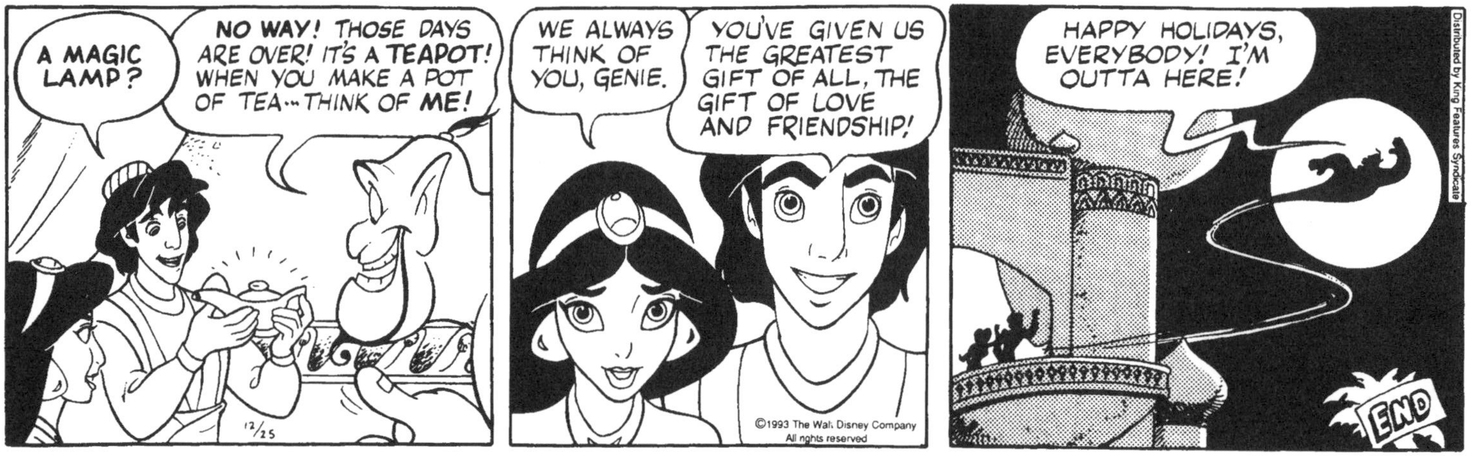
A MAGIC LAMP?
NO WAY! THOSE DAYS ARE OVER! IT'S A TEAPOT! WHEN YOU MAKE A POT OF TEA...THINK OF ME!
12/25
WE ALWAYS THINK OF YOU, GENIE.
YOU'VE GIVEN US THE GREATEST GIFT OF ALL, THE GIFT OF LOVE AND FRIENDSHIP!
©1993 The Walt Disney Company All rights reserved
HAPPY HOLIDAYS, EVERYBODY! I'M OUTTA HERE!
Distributed by King Features Syndicate
END

1994

THE LION KING

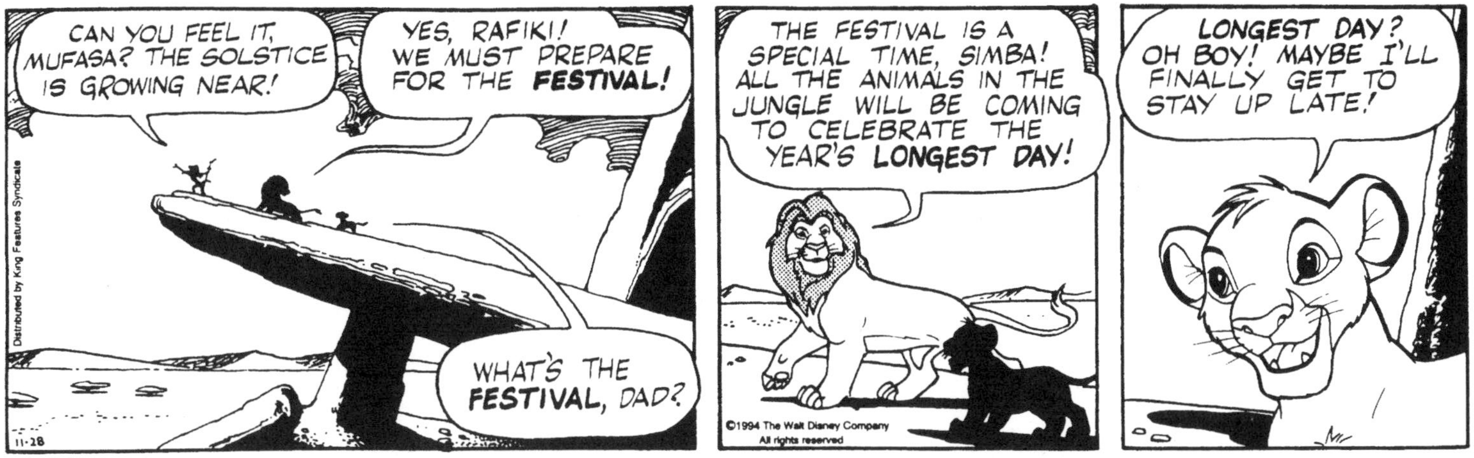
CAN YOU FEEL IT, MUFASA? THE SOLSTICE IS GROWING NEAR!
YES, RAFIKI! WE MUST PREPARE FOR THE **FESTIVAL!**
WHAT'S THE **FESTIVAL**, DAD?
THE FESTIVAL IS A SPECIAL TIME, SIMBA! ALL THE ANIMALS IN THE JUNGLE WILL BE COMING TO CELEBRATE THE YEAR'S **LONGEST DAY!**
LONGEST DAY? OH BOY! MAYBE I'LL FINALLY GET TO STAY UP LATE!
Distributed by King Features Syndicate
11-28
©1994 The Walt Disney Company All rights reserved

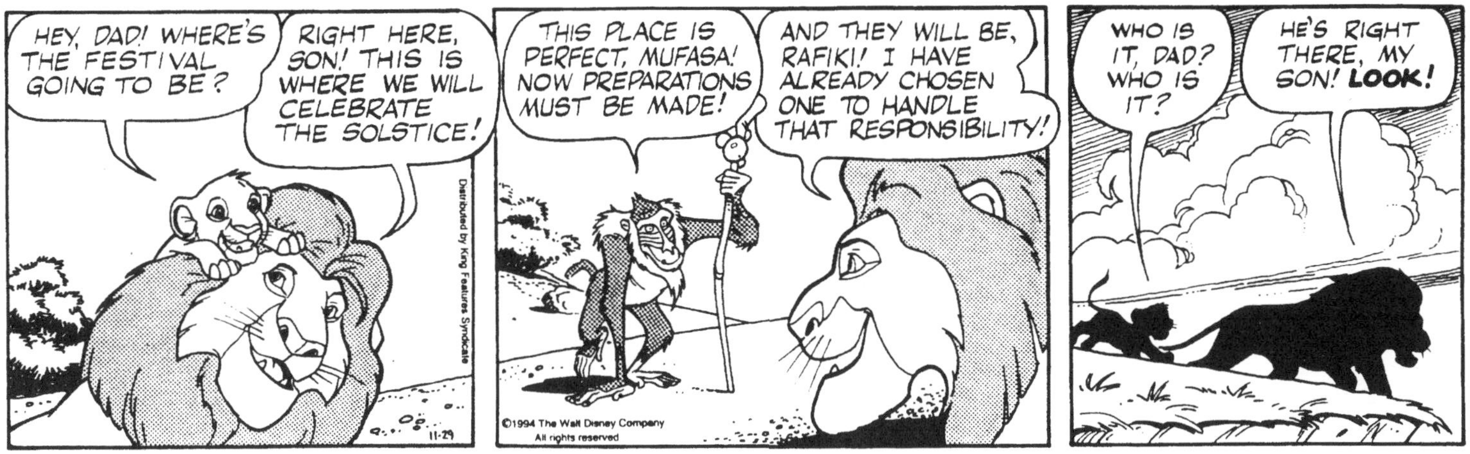
HEY, DAD! WHERE'S THE FESTIVAL GOING TO BE?
RIGHT HERE, SON! THIS IS WHERE WE WILL CELEBRATE THE SOLSTICE!
Distributed by King Features Syndicate
11-29
THIS PLACE IS PERFECT, MUFASA! NOW PREPARATIONS MUST BE MADE!
AND THEY WILL BE, RAFIKI! I HAVE ALREADY CHOSEN ONE TO HANDLE THAT RESPONSIBILITY!
©1994 The Walt Disney Company All rights reserved
WHO IS IT, DAD? WHO IS IT?
HE'S RIGHT THERE, MY SON! **LOOK!**

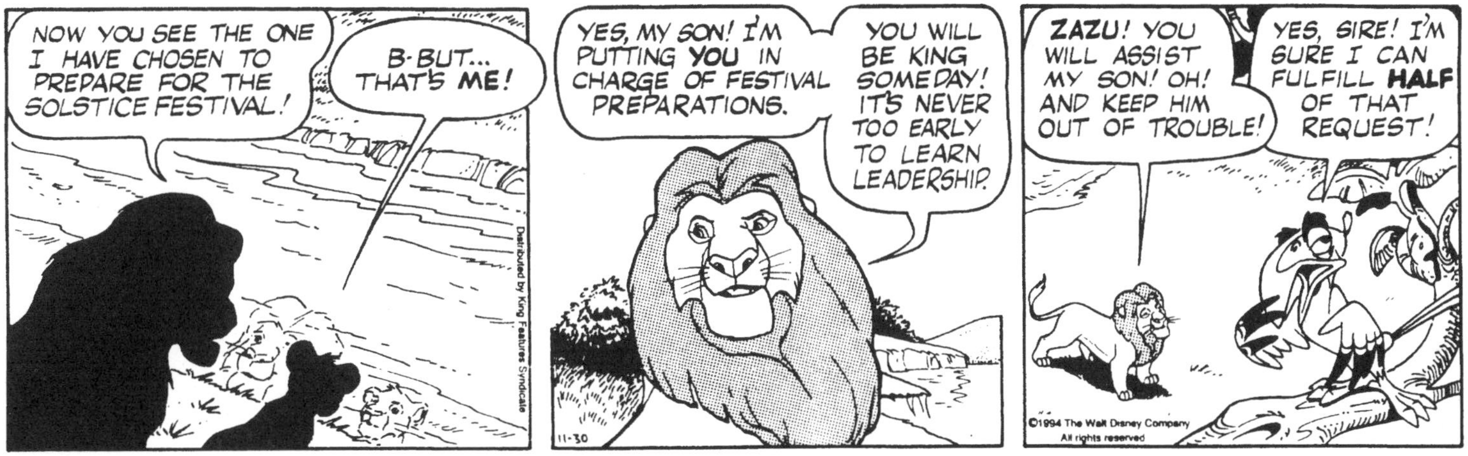
NOW YOU SEE THE ONE I HAVE CHOSEN TO PREPARE FOR THE SOLSTICE FESTIVAL!
B-BUT... THAT'S **ME!**
Distributed by King Features Syndicate
YES, MY SON! I'M PUTTING **YOU** IN CHARGE OF FESTIVAL PREPARATIONS.
YOU WILL BE KING SOMEDAY! IT'S NEVER TOO EARLY TO LEARN LEADERSHIP!
11-30
ZAZU! YOU WILL ASSIST MY SON! OH! AND KEEP HIM OUT OF TROUBLE!
YES, SIRE! I'M SURE I CAN FULFILL **HALF** OF THAT REQUEST!
©1994 The Walt Disney Company All rights reserved

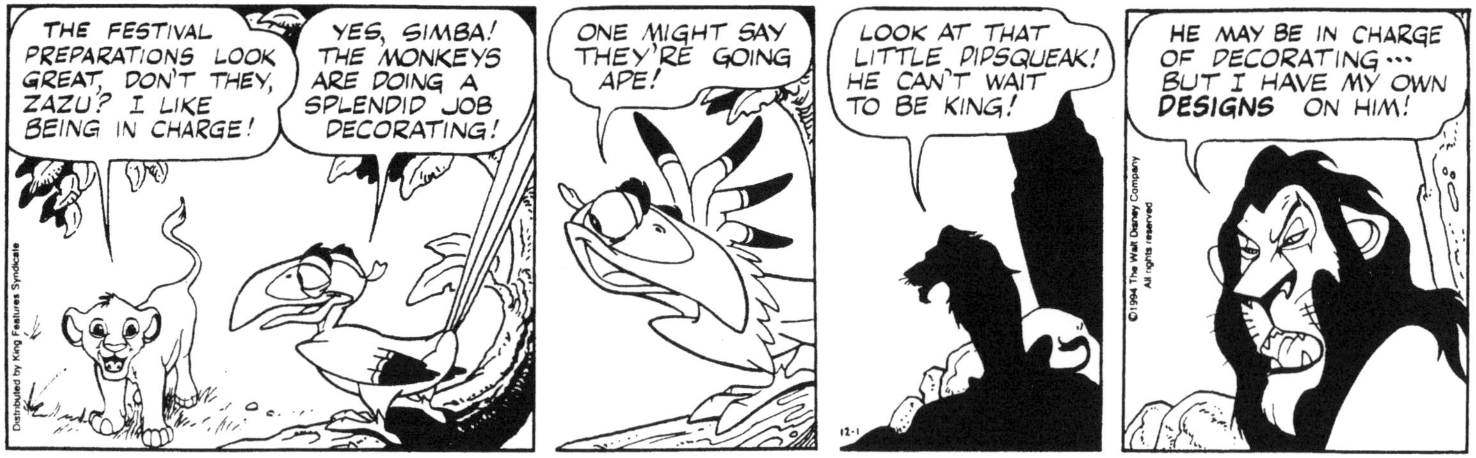
THE FESTIVAL PREPARATIONS LOOK GREAT, DON'T THEY, ZAZU? I LIKE BEING IN CHARGE!
YES, SIMBA! THE MONKEYS ARE DOING A SPLENDID JOB DECORATING!
Distributed by King Features Syndicate
ONE MIGHT SAY THEY'RE GOING APE!
LOOK AT THAT LITTLE PIPSQUEAK! HE CAN'T WAIT TO BE KING!
12-1
HE MAY BE IN CHARGE OF DECORATING... BUT I HAVE MY OWN **DESIGNS** ON HIM!
©1994 The Walt Disney Company All rights reserved

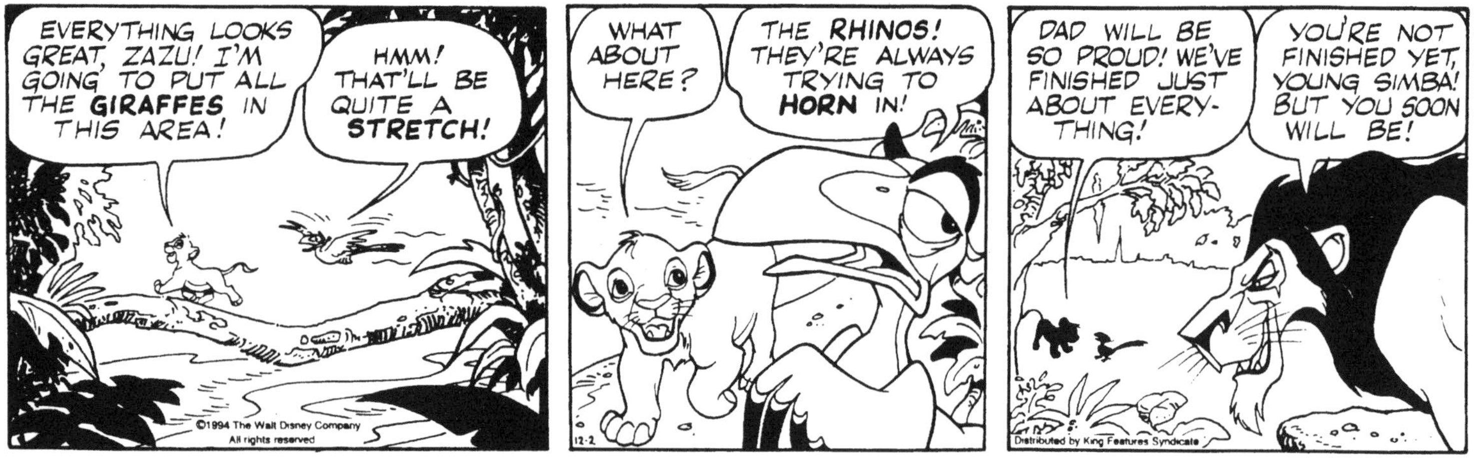
EVERYTHING LOOKS GREAT, ZAZU! I'M GOING TO PUT ALL THE **GIRAFFES** IN THIS AREA!
HMM! THAT'LL BE QUITE A **STRETCH**!
©1994 The Walt Disney Company All rights reserved
WHAT ABOUT HERE?
THE **RHINOS**! THEY'RE ALWAYS TRYING TO **HORN** IN!
12-2
DAD WILL BE SO PROUD! WE'VE FINISHED JUST ABOUT EVERYTHING!
YOU'RE NOT FINISHED YET, YOUNG SIMBA! BUT YOU SOON WILL BE!
Distributed by King Features Syndicate

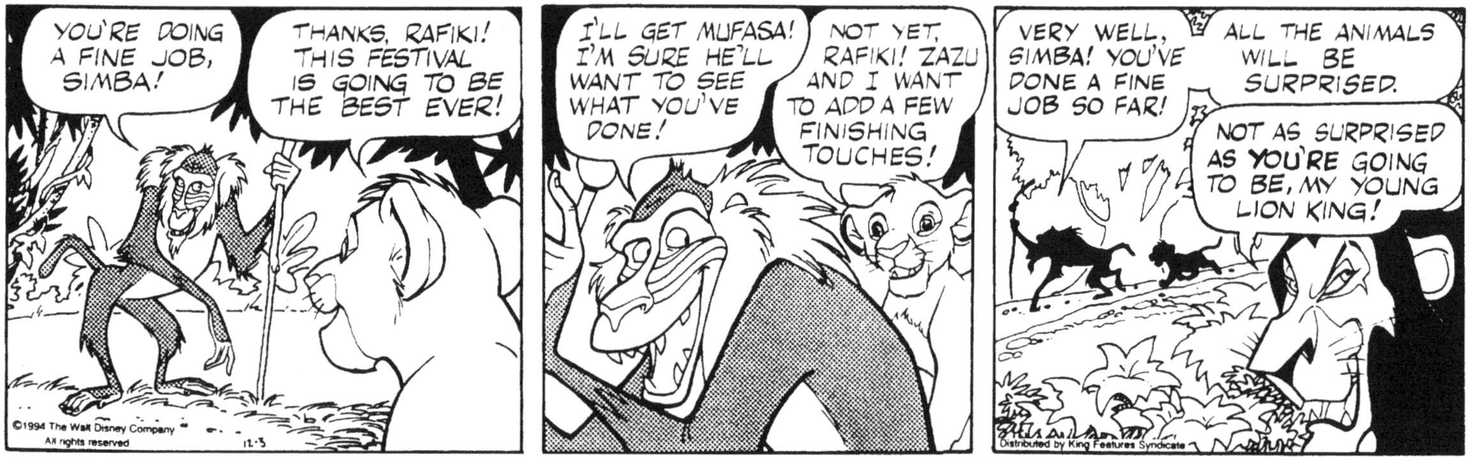
YOU'RE DOING A FINE JOB, SIMBA!
THANKS, RAFIKI! THIS FESTIVAL IS GOING TO BE THE BEST EVER!
©1994 The Walt Disney Company All rights reserved
12-3
I'LL GET MUFASA! I'M SURE HE'LL WANT TO SEE WHAT YOU'VE DONE!
NOT YET, RAFIKI! ZAZU AND I WANT TO ADD A FEW FINISHING TOUCHES!
VERY WELL, SIMBA! YOU'VE DONE A FINE JOB SO FAR!
ALL THE ANIMALS WILL BE SURPRISED.
NOT AS SURPRISED AS **YOU'RE** GOING TO BE, MY YOUNG LION KING!
Distributed by King Features Syndicate

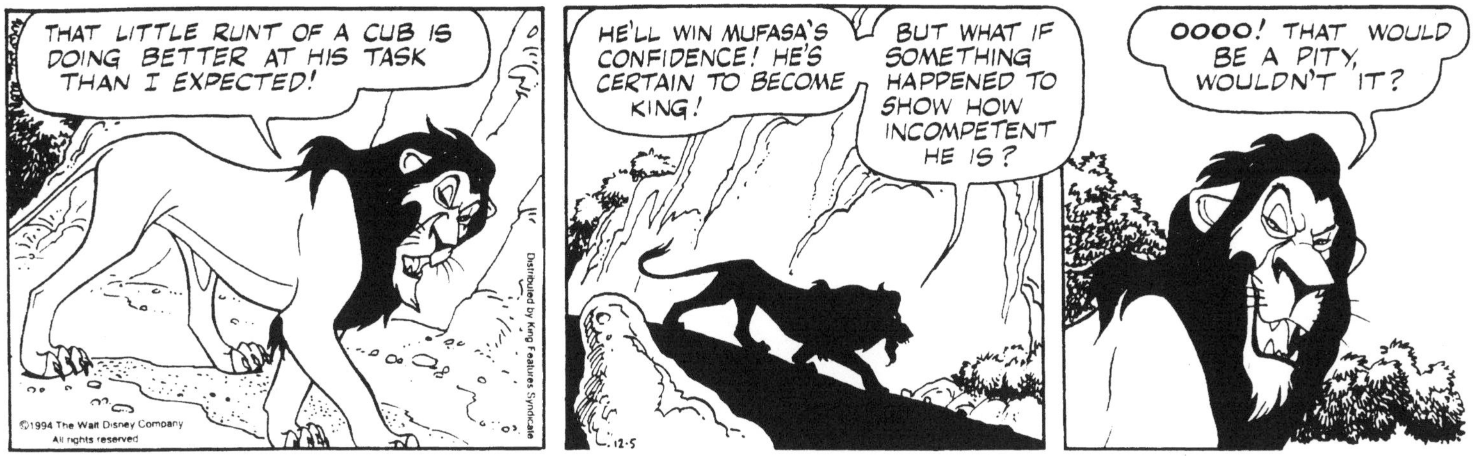
THAT LITTLE RUNT OF A CUB IS DOING BETTER AT HIS TASK THAN I EXPECTED!
©1994 The Walt Disney Company All rights reserved
Distributed by King Features Syndicate
HE'LL WIN MUFASA'S CONFIDENCE! HE'S CERTAIN TO BECOME KING!
BUT WHAT IF SOMETHING HAPPENED TO SHOW HOW INCOMPETENT HE IS?
12-5
OOOO! THAT WOULD BE A PITY, WOULDN'T IT?

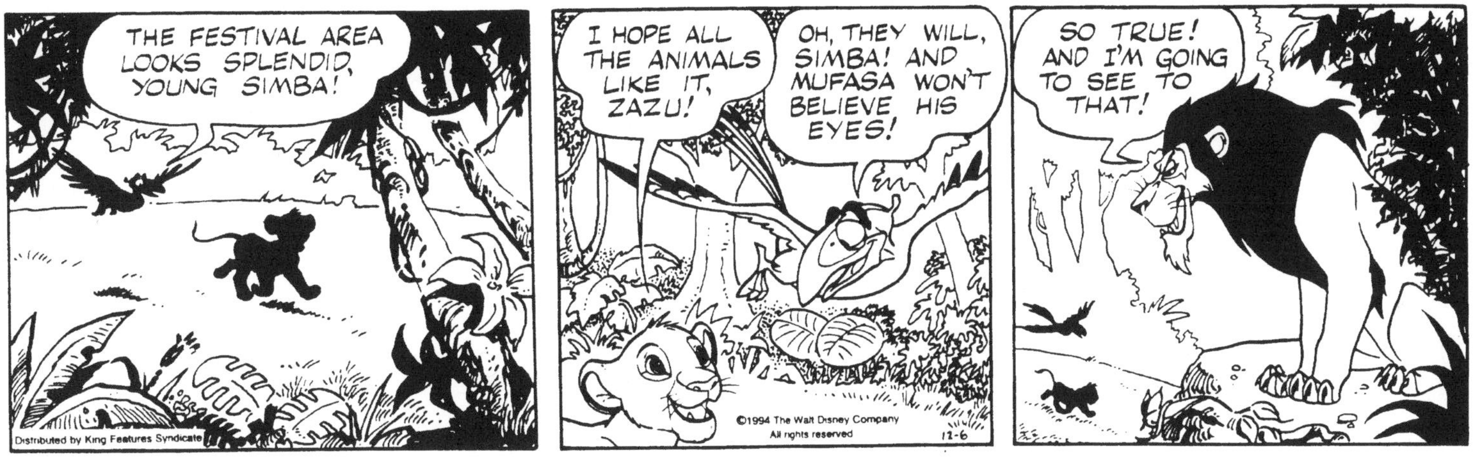
THE FESTIVAL AREA LOOKS SPLENDID, YOUNG SIMBA!
Distributed by King Features Syndicate
I HOPE ALL THE ANIMALS LIKE IT, ZAZU!
OH, THEY WILL, SIMBA! AND MUFASA WON'T BELIEVE HIS EYES!
©1994 The Walt Disney Company All rights reserved
12-6
SO TRUE! AND I'M GOING TO SEE TO THAT!

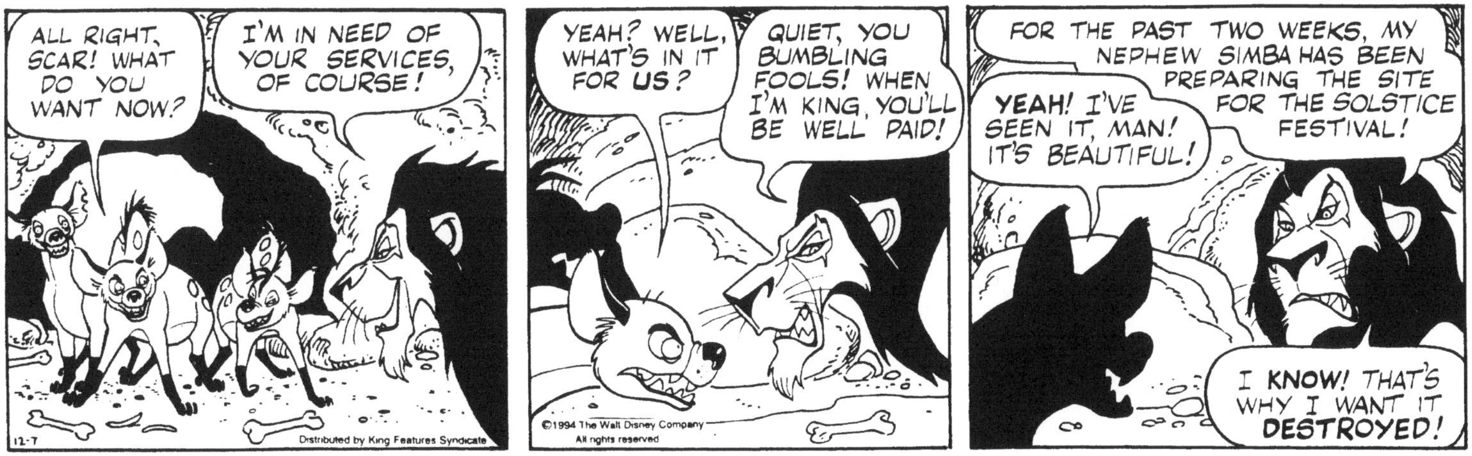
ALL RIGHT, SCAR! WHAT DO YOU WANT NOW?
I'M IN NEED OF YOUR SERVICES, OF COURSE!
12-7
Distributed by King Features Syndicate
YEAH? WELL, WHAT'S IN IT FOR **US**?
QUIET, YOU BUMBLING FOOLS! WHEN I'M KING, YOU'LL BE WELL PAID!
©1994 The Walt Disney Company All rights reserved
FOR THE PAST TWO WEEKS, MY NEPHEW SIMBA HAS BEEN PREPARING THE SITE FOR THE SOLSTICE FESTIVAL!
YEAH! I'VE SEEN IT, MAN! IT'S BEAUTIFUL!
I **KNOW!** THAT'S WHY I WANT IT **DESTROYED!**

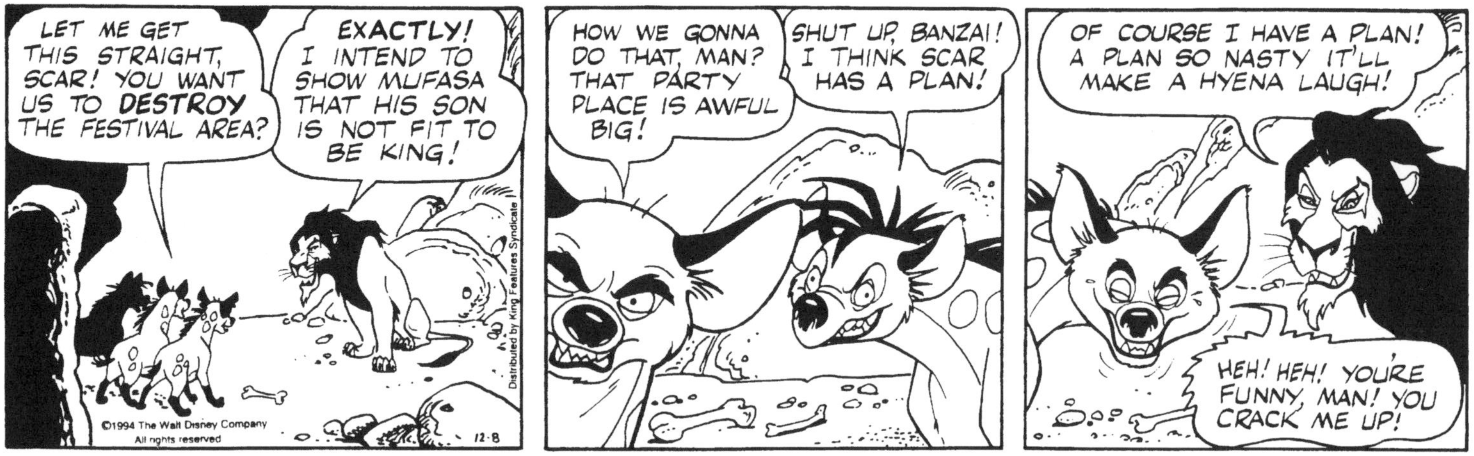
LET ME GET THIS STRAIGHT, SCAR! YOU WANT US TO **DESTROY** THE FESTIVAL AREA?
EXACTLY! I INTEND TO SHOW MUFASA THAT HIS SON IS NOT FIT TO BE KING!
©1994 The Walt Disney Company All rights reserved
Distributed by King Features Syndicate
12-8
HOW WE GONNA DO THAT, MAN? THAT PARTY PLACE IS AWFUL BIG!
SHUT UP, BANZAI! I THINK SCAR HAS A PLAN!
OF COURSE I HAVE A PLAN! A PLAN SO NASTY IT'LL MAKE A HYENA LAUGH!
HEH! HEH! YOU'RE FUNNY, MAN! YOU CRACK ME UP!

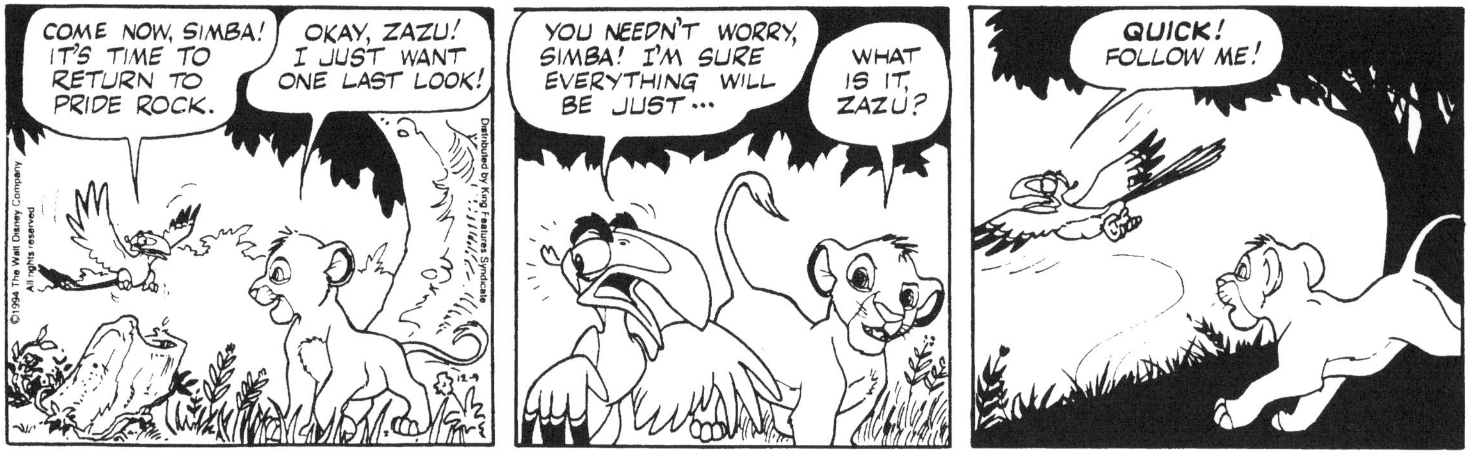
COME NOW, SIMBA! IT'S TIME TO RETURN TO PRIDE ROCK.
OKAY, ZAZU! I JUST WANT ONE LAST LOOK!
©1994 The Walt Disney Company All rights reserved
Distributed by King Features Syndicate
12-9
YOU NEEDN'T WORRY, SIMBA! I'M SURE EVERYTHING WILL BE JUST...
WHAT IS IT, ZAZU?
QUICK! FOLLOW ME!

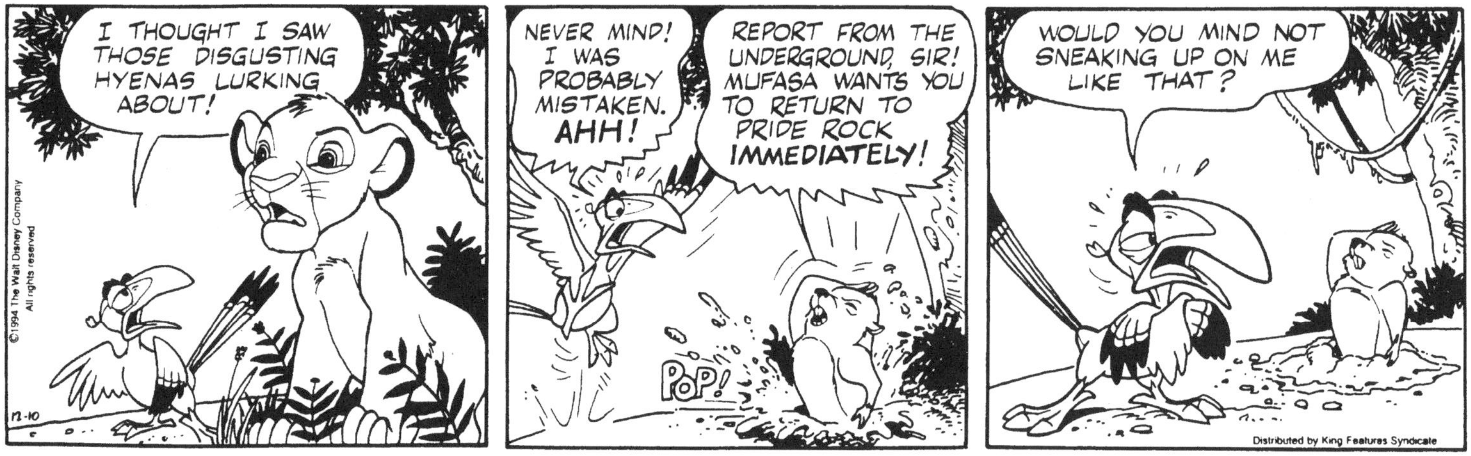
I THOUGHT I SAW THOSE DISGUSTING HYENAS LURKING ABOUT!
©1994 The Walt Disney Company All rights reserved
12-10
NEVER MIND! I WAS PROBABLY MISTAKEN. **AHH!**
REPORT FROM THE UNDERGROUND, SIR! MUFASA WANTS YOU TO RETURN TO PRIDE ROCK **IMMEDIATELY!**
POP!
WOULD YOU MIND NOT SNEAKING UP ON ME LIKE THAT?
Distributed by King Features Syndicate

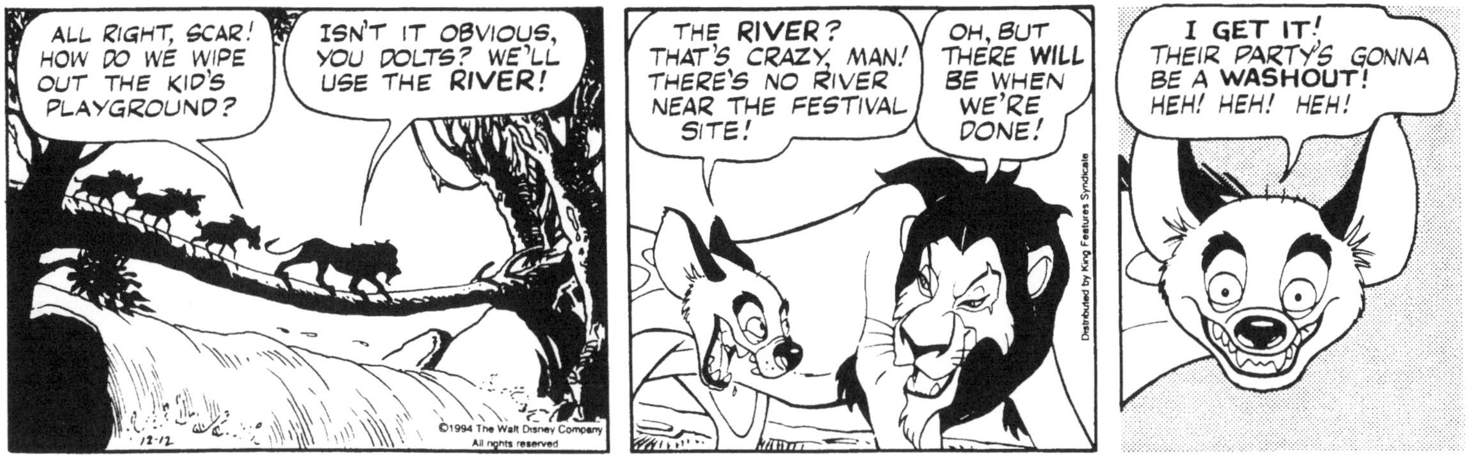
ALL RIGHT, SCAR! HOW DO WE WIPE OUT THE KID'S PLAYGROUND?
ISN'T IT OBVIOUS, YOU DOLTS? WE'LL USE THE RIVER!
12-12
©1994 The Walt Disney Company All rights reserved
THE RIVER? THAT'S CRAZY, MAN! THERE'S NO RIVER NEAR THE FESTIVAL SITE!
OH, BUT THERE WILL BE WHEN WE'RE DONE!
Distributed by King Features Syndicate
I GET IT! THEIR PARTY'S GONNA BE A WASHOUT! HEH! HEH! HEH!

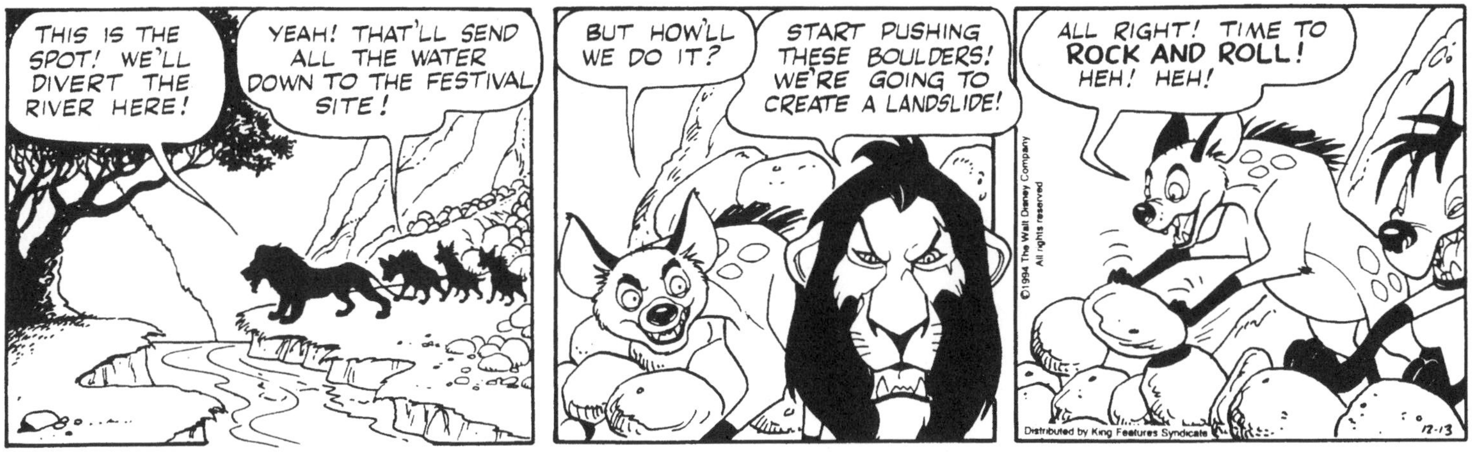
THIS IS THE SPOT! WE'LL DIVERT THE RIVER HERE!
YEAH! THAT'LL SEND ALL THE WATER DOWN TO THE FESTIVAL SITE!
BUT HOW'LL WE DO IT?
START PUSHING THESE BOULDERS! WE'RE GOING TO CREATE A LANDSLIDE!
©1994 The Walt Disney Company All rights reserved
ALL RIGHT! TIME TO ROCK AND ROLL! HEH! HEH!
Distributed by King Features Syndicate
12-13

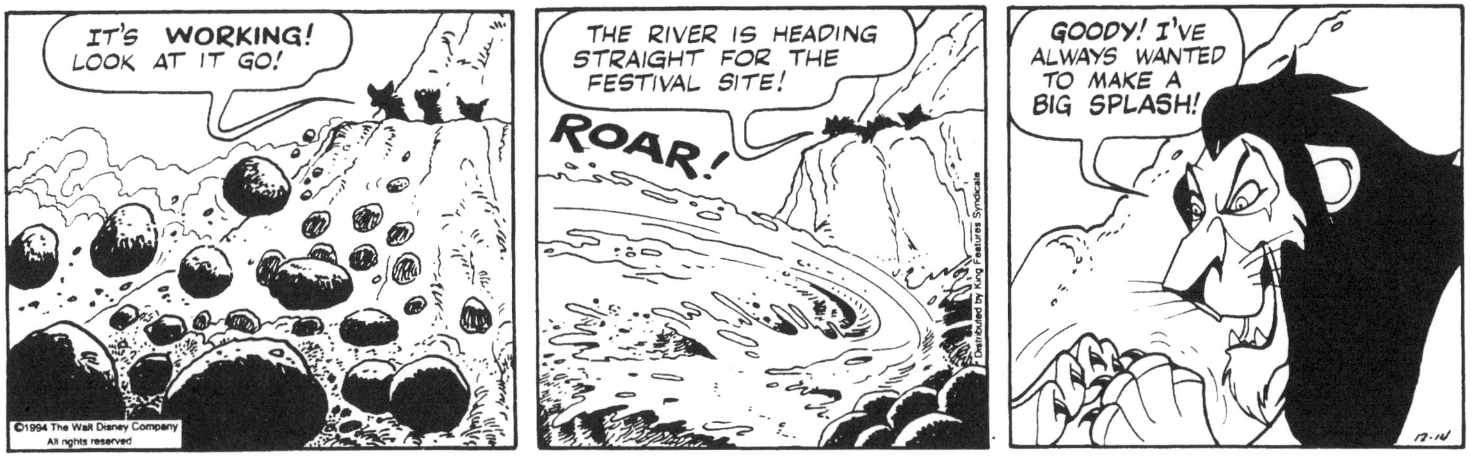
IT'S WORKING! LOOK AT IT GO!
©1994 The Walt Disney Company All rights reserved
THE RIVER IS HEADING STRAIGHT FOR THE FESTIVAL SITE!
ROAR!
Distributed by King Features Syndicate
GOODY! I'VE ALWAYS WANTED TO MAKE A BIG SPLASH!
12-14

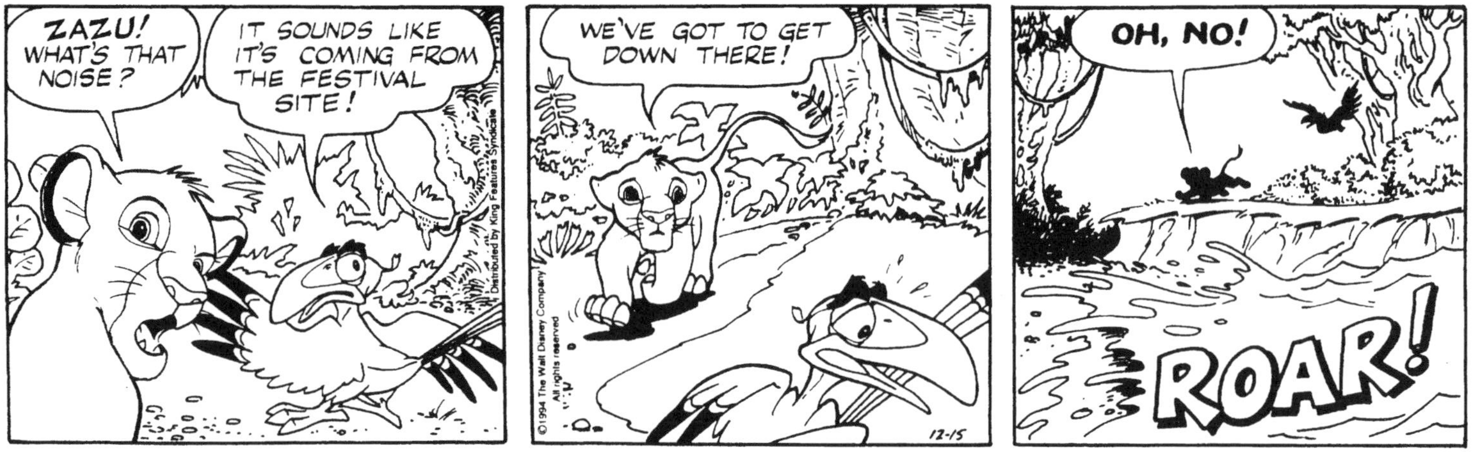
ZAZU! WHAT'S THAT NOISE?
IT'S COMING FROM THE FESTIVAL SITE!
Distributed by King Features Syndicate
WE'VE GOT TO GET DOWN THERE!
©1994 The Walt Disney Company All rights reserved
12-15
OH, NO!
ROAR!

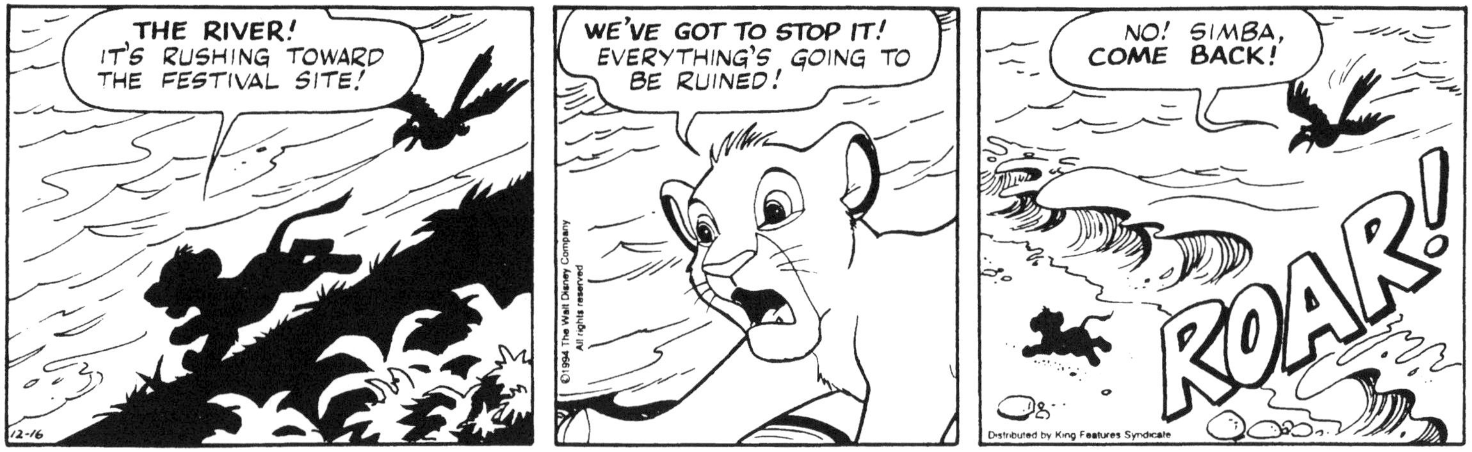
THE RIVER! IT'S RUSHING TOWARD THE FESTIVAL SITE!
12-16
WE'VE GOT TO STOP IT! EVERYTHING'S GOING TO BE RUINED!
©1994 The Walt Disney Company All rights reserved
NO! SIMBA, COME BACK!
ROAR!
Distributed by King Features Syndicate

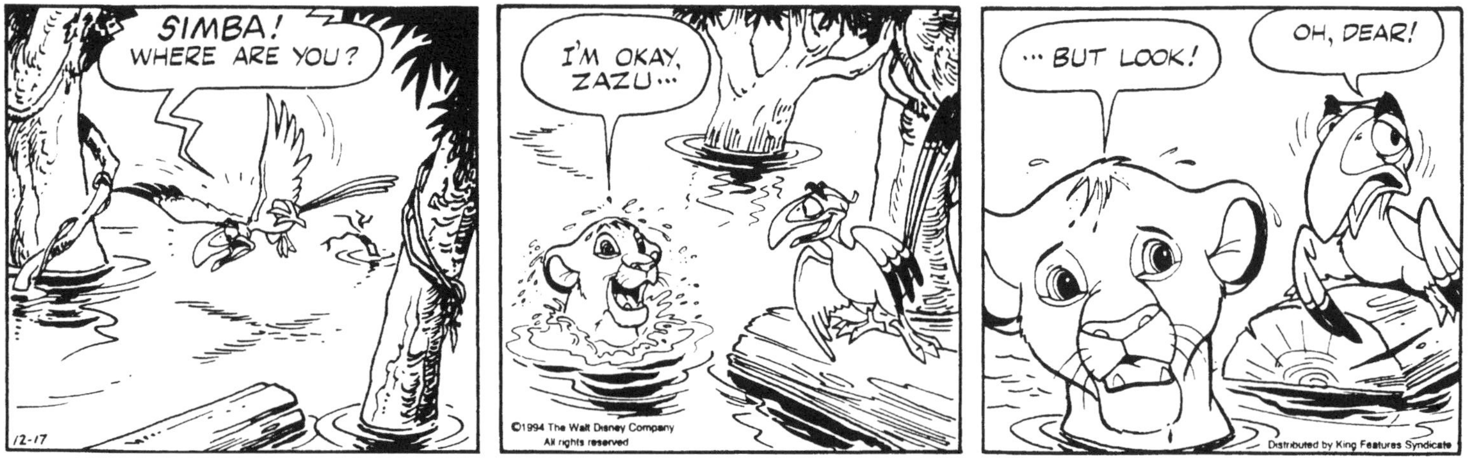
SIMBA! WHERE ARE YOU?
12-17
I'M OKAY, ZAZU...
©1994 The Walt Disney Company All rights reserved
...BUT LOOK!
OH, DEAR!
Distributed by King Features Syndicate

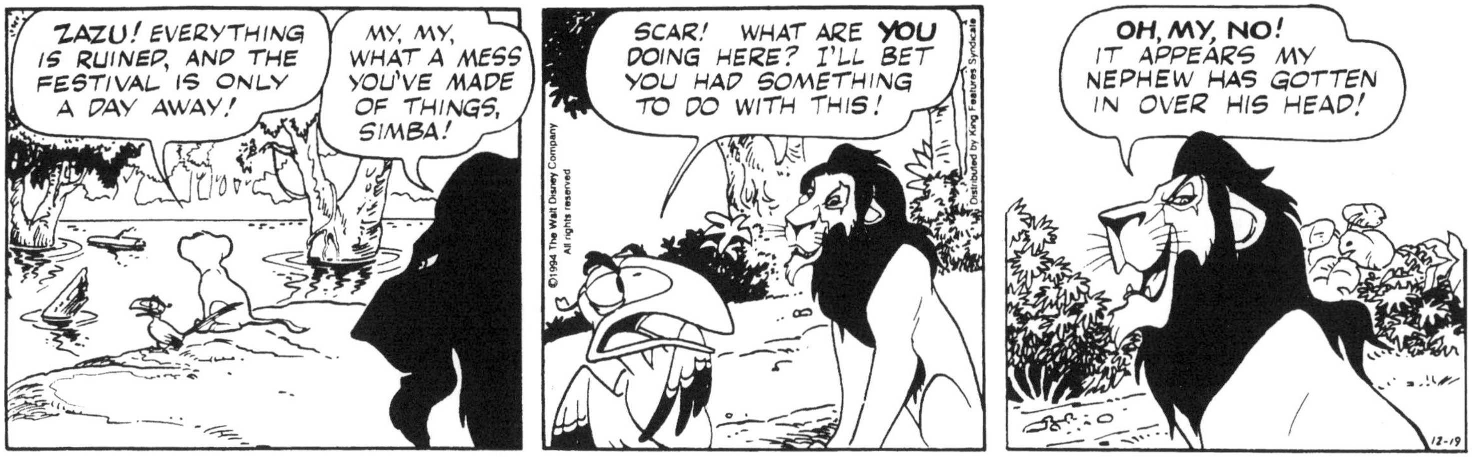
ZAZU! EVERYTHING IS RUINED, AND THE FESTIVAL IS ONLY A DAY AWAY!
MY, MY, WHAT A MESS YOU'VE MADE OF THINGS, SIMBA!
SCAR! WHAT ARE YOU DOING HERE? I'LL BET YOU HAD SOMETHING TO DO WITH THIS!
©1994 The Walt Disney Company All rights reserved
Distributed by King Features Syndicate
OH, MY, NO! IT APPEARS MY NEPHEW HAS GOTTEN IN OVER HIS HEAD!
12-19

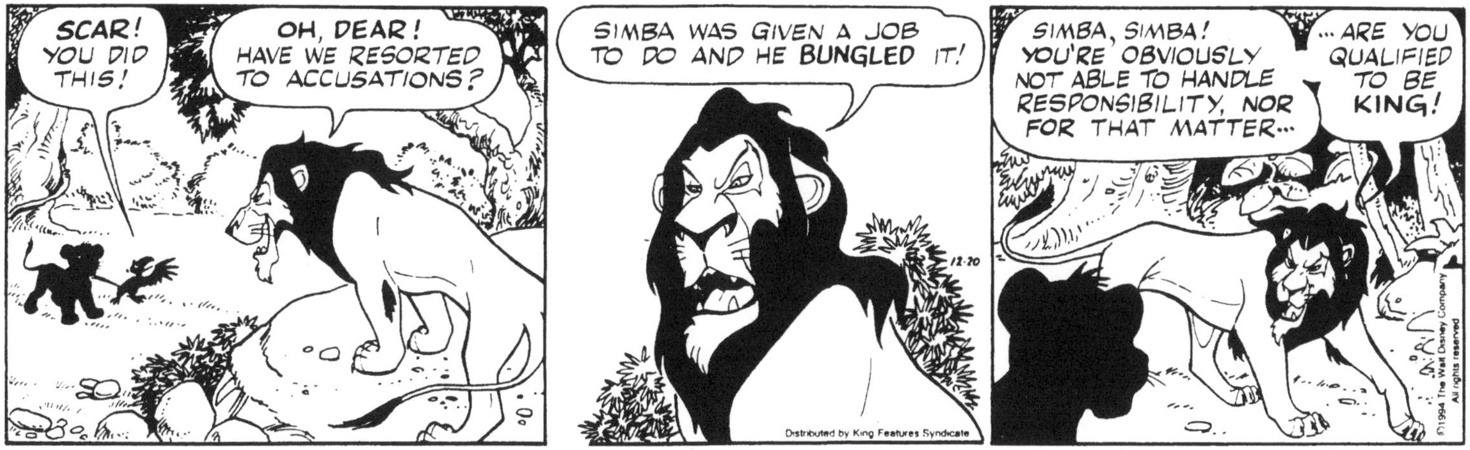
SCAR! YOU DID THIS!
OH, DEAR! HAVE WE RESORTED TO ACCUSATIONS?
SIMBA WAS GIVEN A JOB TO DO AND HE BUNGLED IT!
12-20
Distributed by King Features Syndicate
SIMBA, SIMBA! YOU'RE OBVIOUSLY NOT ABLE TO HANDLE RESPONSIBILITY, NOR FOR THAT MATTER...
...ARE YOU QUALIFIED TO BE KING!
©1994 The Walt Disney Company All rights reserved

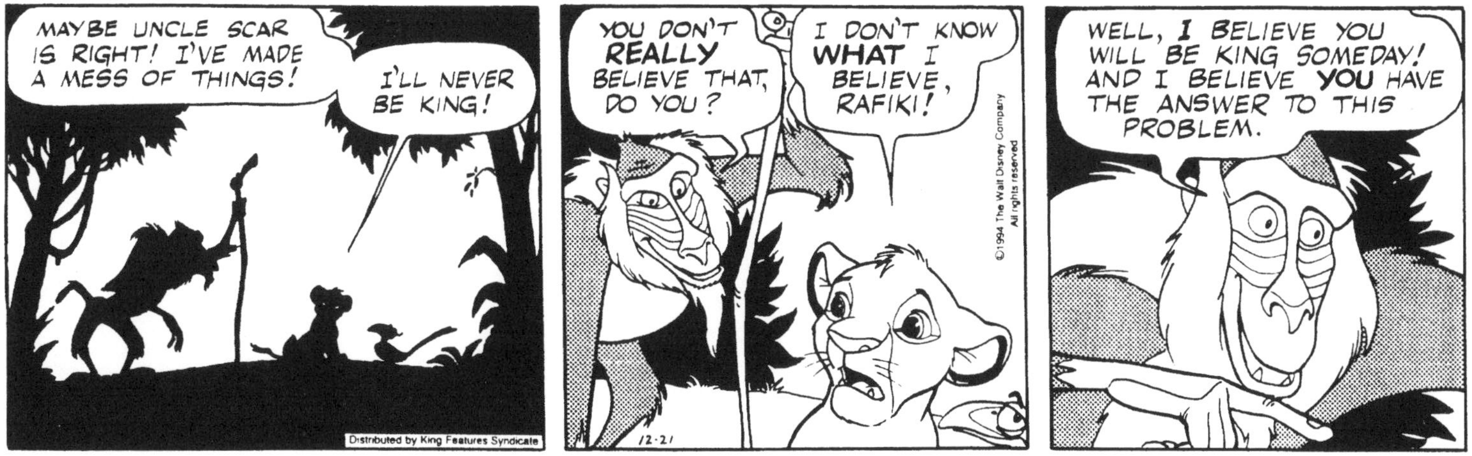
MAYBE UNCLE SCAR IS RIGHT! I'VE MADE A MESS OF THINGS!
I'LL NEVER BE KING!
Distributed by King Features Syndicate
YOU DON'T REALLY BELIEVE THAT, DO YOU?
I DON'T KNOW WHAT I BELIEVE, RAFIKI!
©1994 The Walt Disney Company All rights reserved
12-21
WELL, I BELIEVE YOU WILL BE KING SOMEDAY! AND I BELIEVE YOU HAVE THE ANSWER TO THIS PROBLEM.

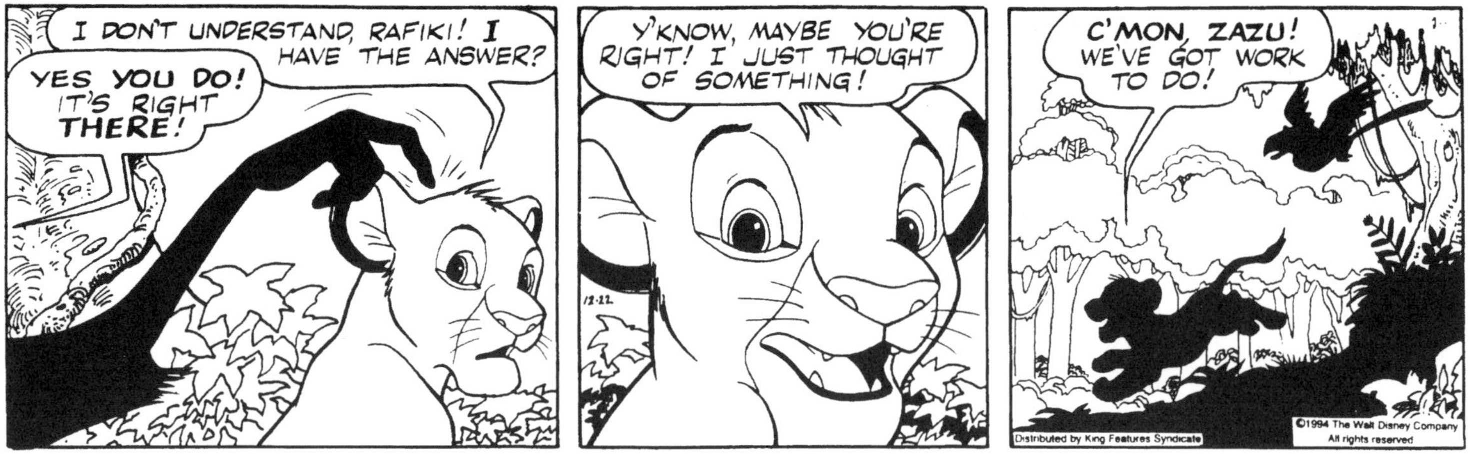
I DON'T UNDERSTAND, RAFIKI! I HAVE THE ANSWER?
YES YOU DO! IT'S RIGHT THERE!
12-22
Y'KNOW, MAYBE YOU'RE RIGHT! I JUST THOUGHT OF SOMETHING!
C'MON, ZAZU! WE'VE GOT WORK TO DO!
Distributed by King Features Syndicate
©1994 The Walt Disney Company All rights reserved

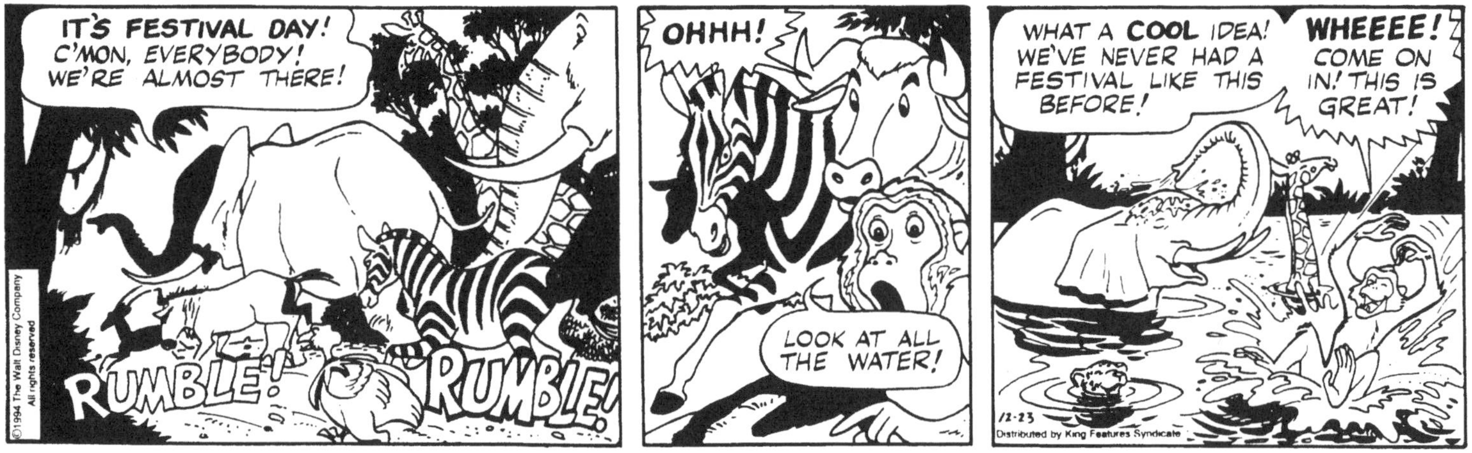
IT'S FESTIVAL DAY! C'MON, EVERYBODY! WE'RE ALMOST THERE!
RUMBLE! RUMBLE!
©1994 The Walt Disney Company All rights reserved
OHHH!
LOOK AT ALL THE WATER!
WHAT A COOL IDEA! WE'VE NEVER HAD A FESTIVAL LIKE THIS BEFORE!
WHEEEE! COME ON IN! THIS IS GREAT!
12-23
Distributed by King Features Syndicate

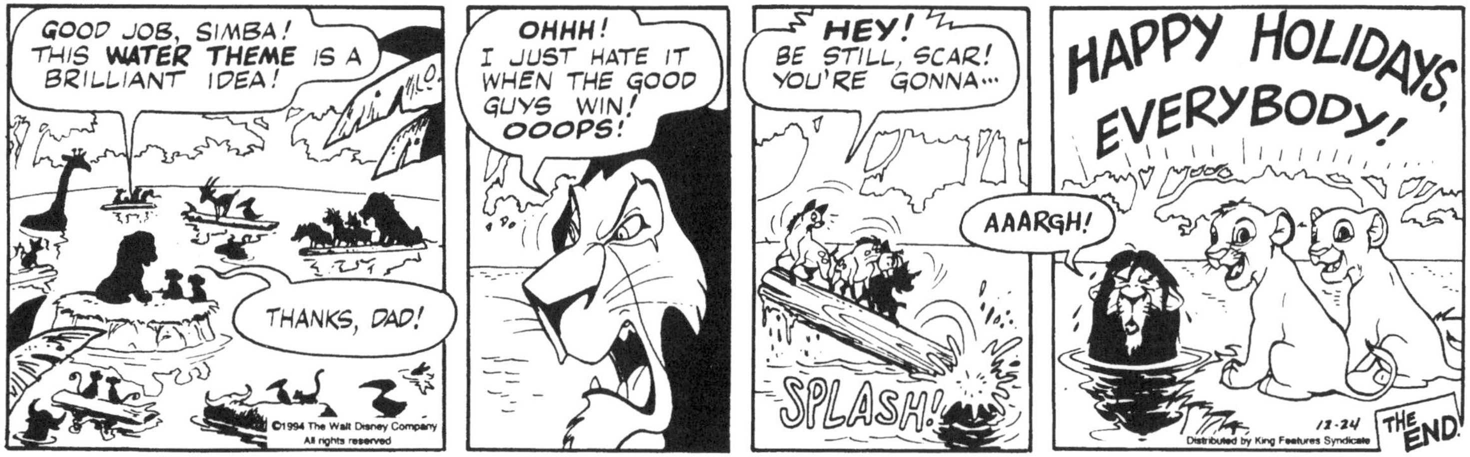
GOOD JOB, SIMBA! THIS WATER THEME IS A BRILLIANT IDEA!
THANKS, DAD!
©1994 The Walt Disney Company All rights reserved
OHHH! I JUST HATE IT WHEN THE GOOD GUYS WIN! OOOPS!
HEY! BE STILL, SCAR! YOU'RE GONNA...
SPLASH!
HAPPY HOLIDAYS, EVERYBODY!
AAARGH!
12-24
Distributed by King Features Syndicate
THE END.

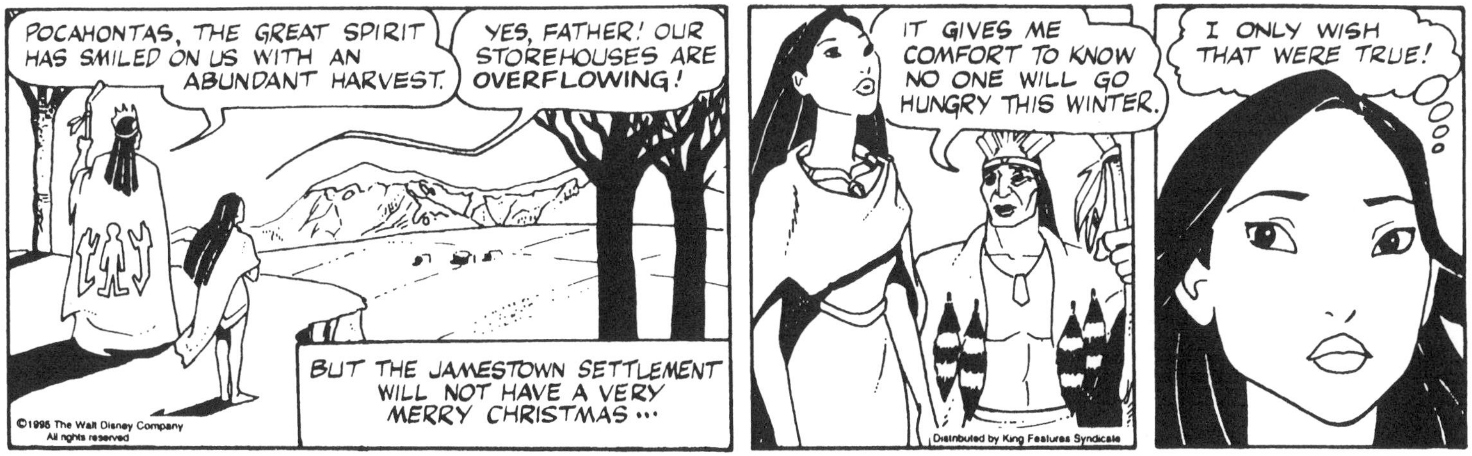
POCAHONTAS, THE GREAT SPIRIT HAS SMILED ON US WITH AN ABUNDANT HARVEST.
YES, FATHER! OUR STOREHOUSES ARE OVERFLOWING!
BUT THE JAMESTOWN SETTLEMENT WILL NOT HAVE A VERY MERRY CHRISTMAS...
©1995 The Walt Disney Company All rights reserved
IT GIVES ME COMFORT TO KNOW NO ONE WILL GO HUNGRY THIS WINTER.
Distributed by King Features Syndicate
I ONLY WISH THAT WERE TRUE!

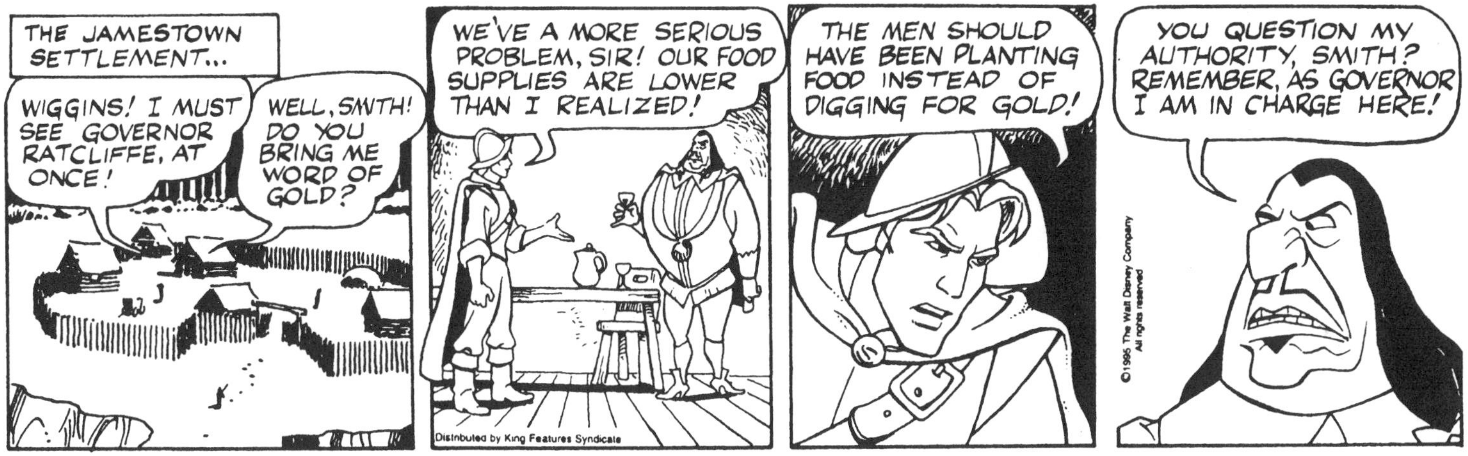
THE JAMESTOWN SETTLEMENT...
WIGGINS! I MUST SEE GOVERNOR RATCLIFFE, AT ONCE!
WELL, SMITH! DO YOU BRING ME WORD OF GOLD?
WE'VE A MORE SERIOUS PROBLEM, SIR! OUR FOOD SUPPLIES ARE LOWER THAN I REALIZED!
Distributed by King Features Syndicate
THE MEN SHOULD HAVE BEEN PLANTING FOOD INSTEAD OF DIGGING FOR GOLD!
©1995 The Walt Disney Company All rights reserved
YOU QUESTION MY AUTHORITY, SMITH? REMEMBER, AS GOVERNOR I AM IN CHARGE HERE!

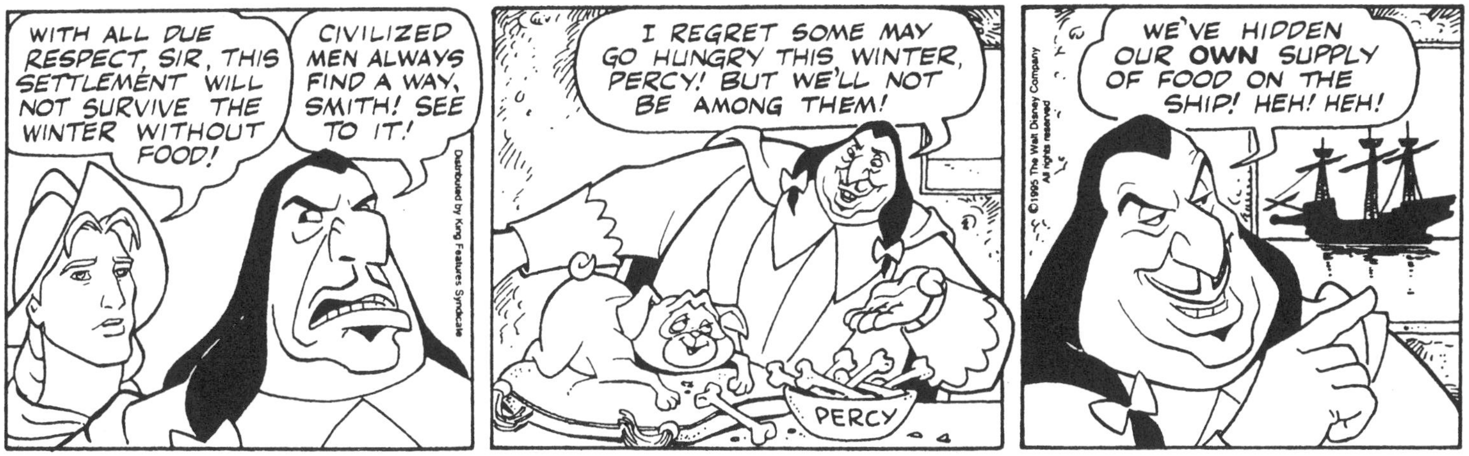
WITH ALL DUE RESPECT, SIR, THIS SETTLEMENT WILL NOT SURVIVE THE WINTER WITHOUT FOOD!
CIVILIZED MEN ALWAYS FIND A WAY, SMITH! SEE TO IT!
Distributed by King Features Syndicate
I REGRET SOME MAY GO HUNGRY THIS WINTER, PERCY! BUT WE'LL NOT BE AMONG THEM!
PERCY
©1995 The Walt Disney Company All rights reserved
WE'VE HIDDEN OUR OWN SUPPLY OF FOOD ON THE SHIP! HEH! HEH!

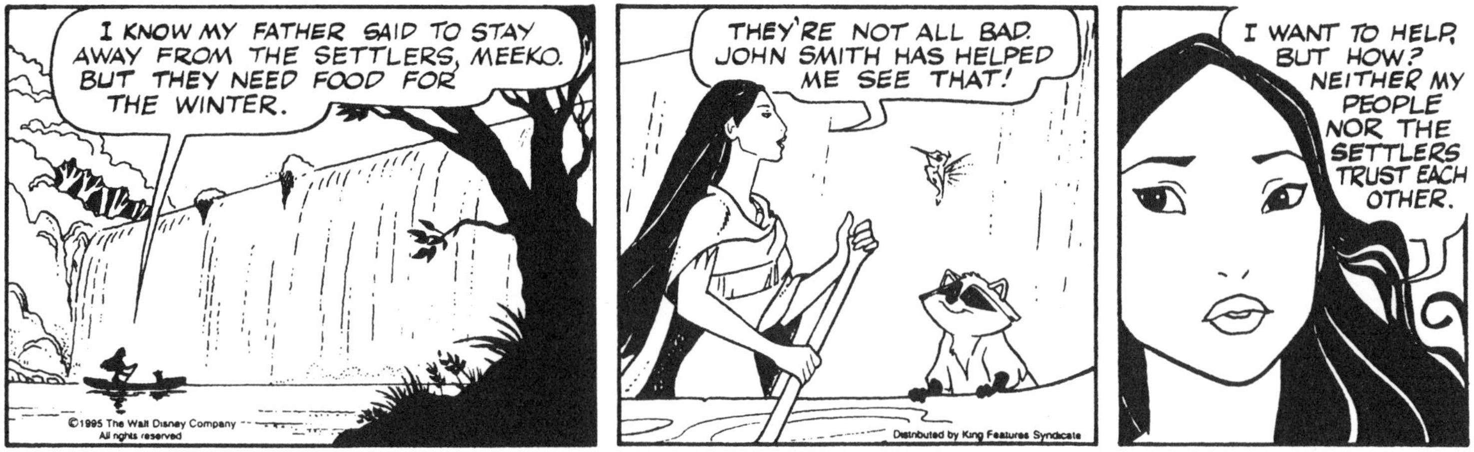
I KNOW MY FATHER SAID TO STAY AWAY FROM THE SETTLERS, MEEKO. BUT THEY NEED FOOD FOR THE WINTER.
©1995 The Walt Disney Company All rights reserved
THEY'RE NOT ALL BAD. JOHN SMITH HAS HELPED ME SEE THAT!
Distributed by King Features Syndicate
I WANT TO HELP, BUT HOW? NEITHER MY PEOPLE NOR THE SETTLERS TRUST EACH OTHER.

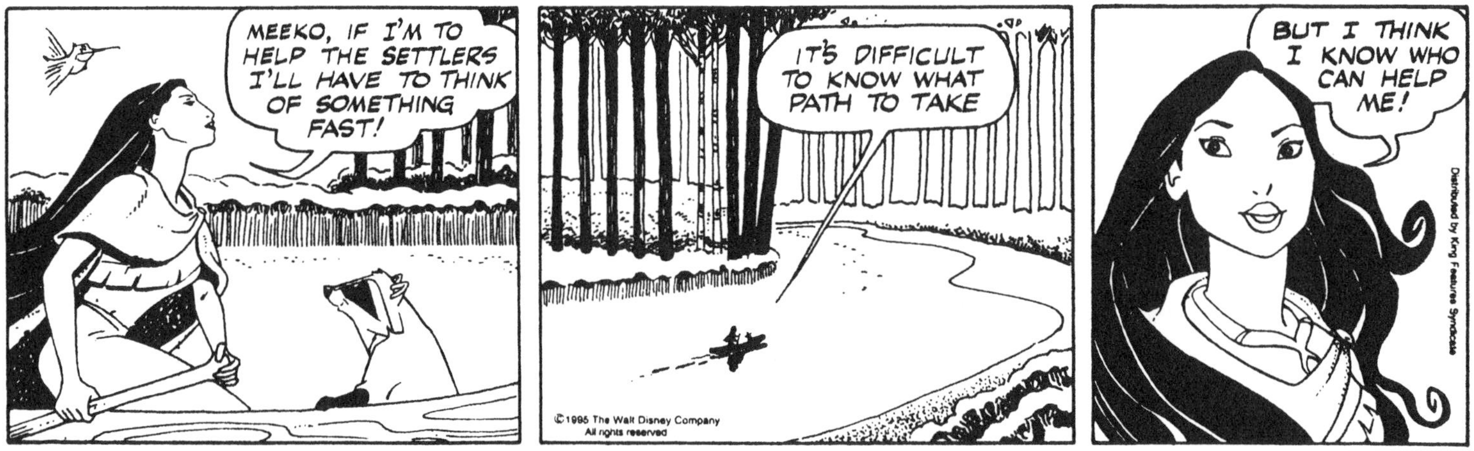
MEEKO, IF I'M TO HELP THE SETTLERS I'LL HAVE TO THINK OF SOMETHING FAST!
IT'S DIFFICULT TO KNOW WHAT PATH TO TAKE
©1995 The Walt Disney Company All rights reserved
BUT I THINK I KNOW WHO CAN HELP ME!
Distributed by King Features Syndicate

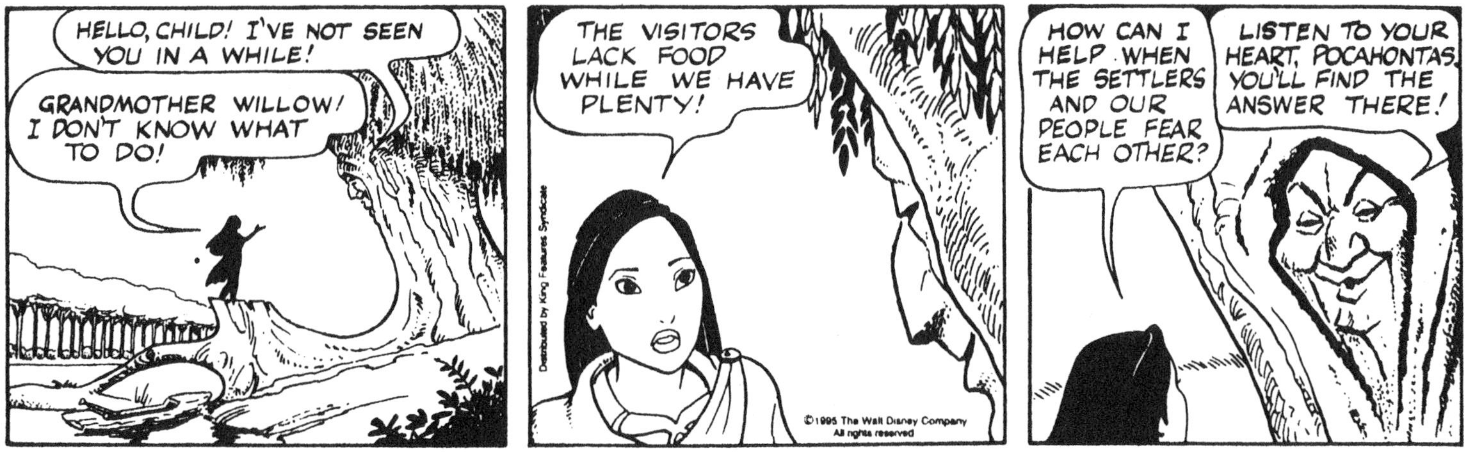
HELLO, CHILD! I'VE NOT SEEN YOU IN A WHILE!
GRANDMOTHER WILLOW! I DON'T KNOW WHAT TO DO!
Distributed by King Features Syndicate
THE VISITORS LACK FOOD WHILE WE HAVE PLENTY!
©1995 The Walt Disney Company All rights reserved
HOW CAN I HELP WHEN THE SETTLERS AND OUR PEOPLE FEAR EACH OTHER?
LISTEN TO YOUR HEART, POCAHONTAS. YOU'LL FIND THE ANSWER THERE!

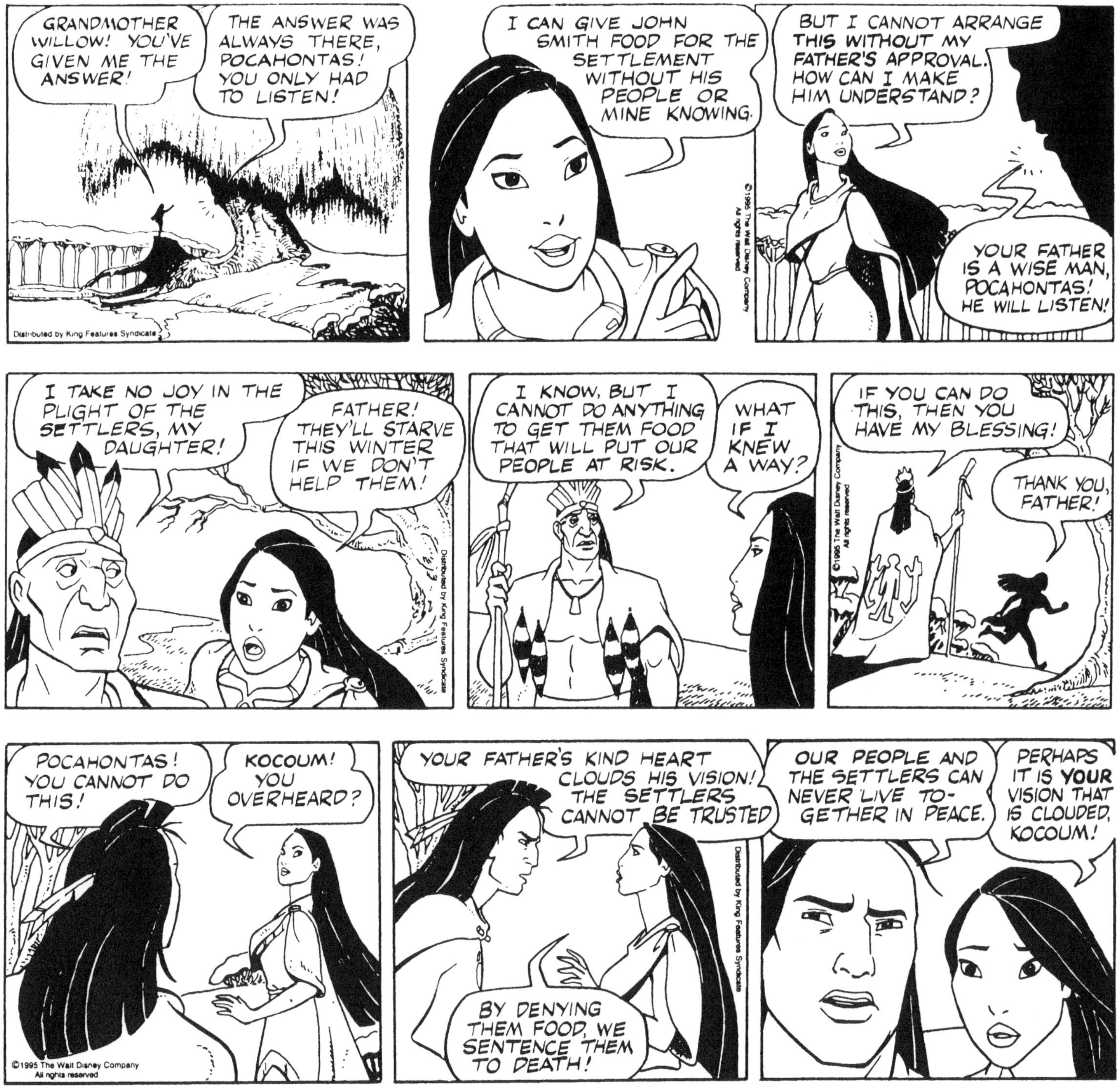

GRANDMOTHER WILLOW! YOU'VE GIVEN ME THE ANSWER!
THE ANSWER WAS ALWAYS THERE, POCAHONTAS! YOU ONLY HAD TO LISTEN!
Distributed by King Features Syndicate
I CAN GIVE JOHN SMITH FOOD FOR THE SETTLEMENT WITHOUT HIS PEOPLE OR MINE KNOWING.
©1995 The Walt Disney Company All rights reserved
BUT I CANNOT ARRANGE THIS WITHOUT MY FATHER'S APPROVAL. HOW CAN I MAKE HIM UNDERSTAND?
YOUR FATHER IS A WISE MAN, POCAHONTAS! HE WILL LISTEN!
I TAKE NO JOY IN THE PLIGHT OF THE SETTLERS, MY DAUGHTER!
FATHER! THEY'LL STARVE THIS WINTER IF WE DON'T HELP THEM!
Distributed by King Features Syndicate
I KNOW, BUT I CANNOT DO ANYTHING TO GET THEM FOOD THAT WILL PUT OUR PEOPLE AT RISK.
WHAT IF I KNEW A WAY?
IF YOU CAN DO THIS, THEN YOU HAVE MY BLESSING!
THANK YOU, FATHER!
©1995 The Walt Disney Company All rights reserved
POCAHONTAS! YOU CANNOT DO THIS!
KOCOUM! YOU OVERHEARD?
©1995 The Walt Disney Company All rights reserved
YOUR FATHER'S KIND HEART CLOUDS HIS VISION! THE SETTLERS CANNOT BE TRUSTED
BY DENYING THEM FOOD, WE SENTENCE THEM TO DEATH!
Distributed by King Features Syndicate
OUR PEOPLE AND THE SETTLERS CAN NEVER LIVE TOGETHER IN PEACE.
PERHAPS IT IS YOUR VISION THAT IS CLOUDED, KOCOUM!

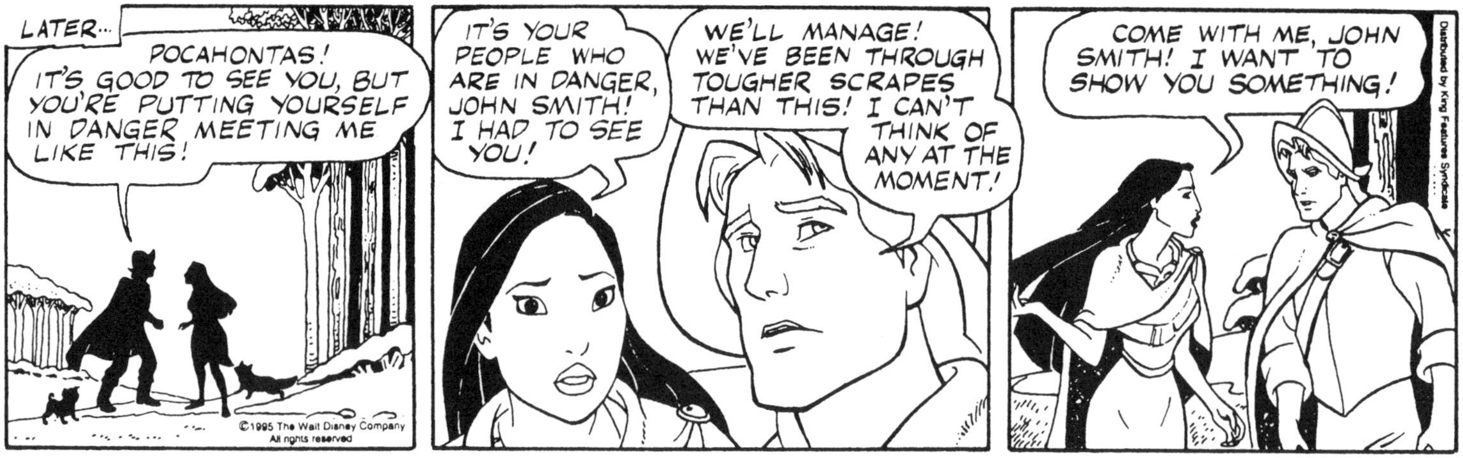
LATER...
POCAHONTAS! IT'S GOOD TO SEE YOU, BUT YOU'RE PUTTING YOURSELF IN DANGER MEETING ME LIKE THIS!
©1995 The Walt Disney Company All rights reserved
IT'S YOUR PEOPLE WHO ARE IN DANGER, JOHN SMITH! I HAD TO SEE YOU!
WE'LL MANAGE! WE'VE BEEN THROUGH TOUGHER SCRAPES THAN THIS! I CAN'T THINK OF ANY AT THE MOMENT!
COME WITH ME, JOHN SMITH! I WANT TO SHOW YOU SOMETHING!
Distributed by King Features Syndicate

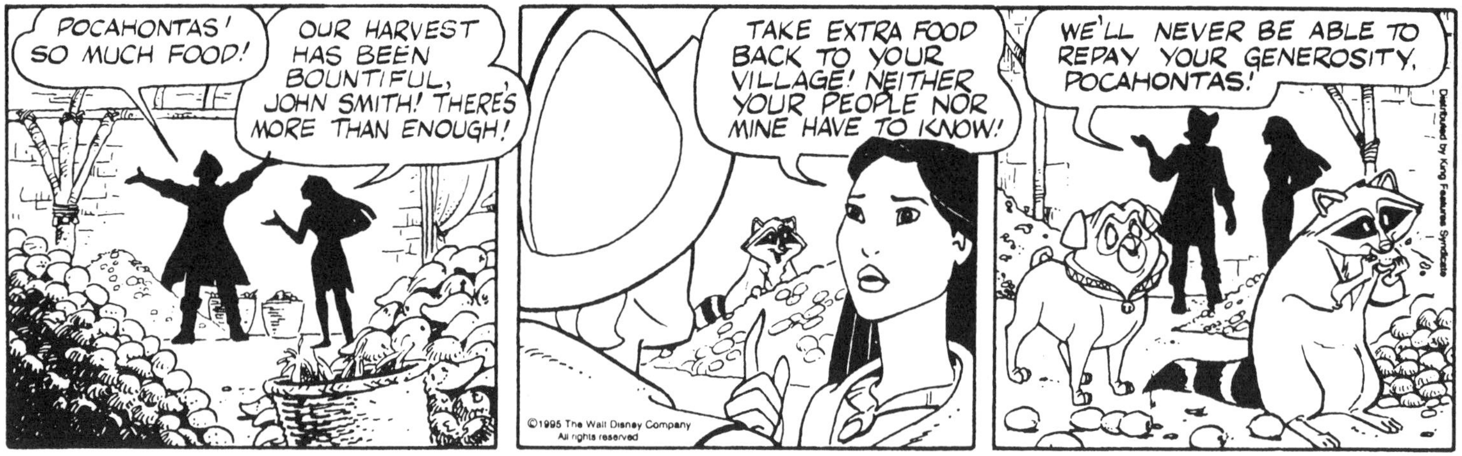
POCAHONTAS! SO MUCH FOOD!
OUR HARVEST HAS BEEN BOUNTIFUL, JOHN SMITH! THERE'S MORE THAN ENOUGH!
TAKE EXTRA FOOD BACK TO YOUR VILLAGE! NEITHER YOUR PEOPLE NOR MINE HAVE TO KNOW!
©1995 The Walt Disney Company All rights reserved
WE'LL NEVER BE ABLE TO REPAY YOUR GENEROSITY, POCAHONTAS!
Distributed by King Features Syndicate

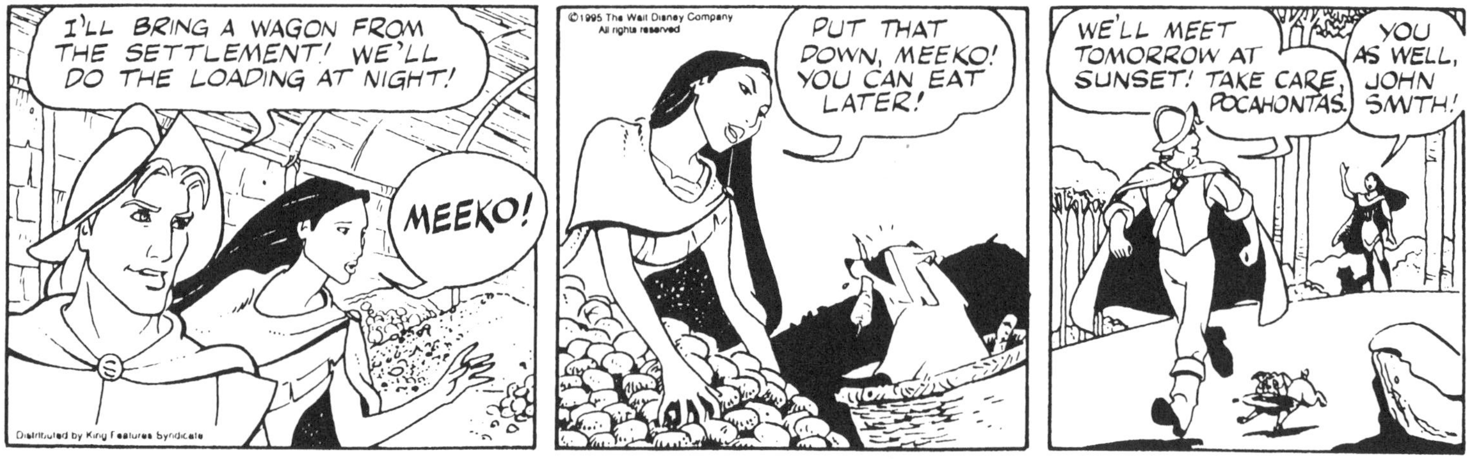
I'LL BRING A WAGON FROM THE SETTLEMENT! WE'LL DO THE LOADING AT NIGHT!
MEEKO!
Distributed by King Features Syndicate
©1995 The Walt Disney Company All rights reserved
PUT THAT DOWN, MEEKO! YOU CAN EAT LATER!
WE'LL MEET TOMORROW AT SUNSET! TAKE CARE, POCAHONTAS.
YOU AS WELL, JOHN SMITH!

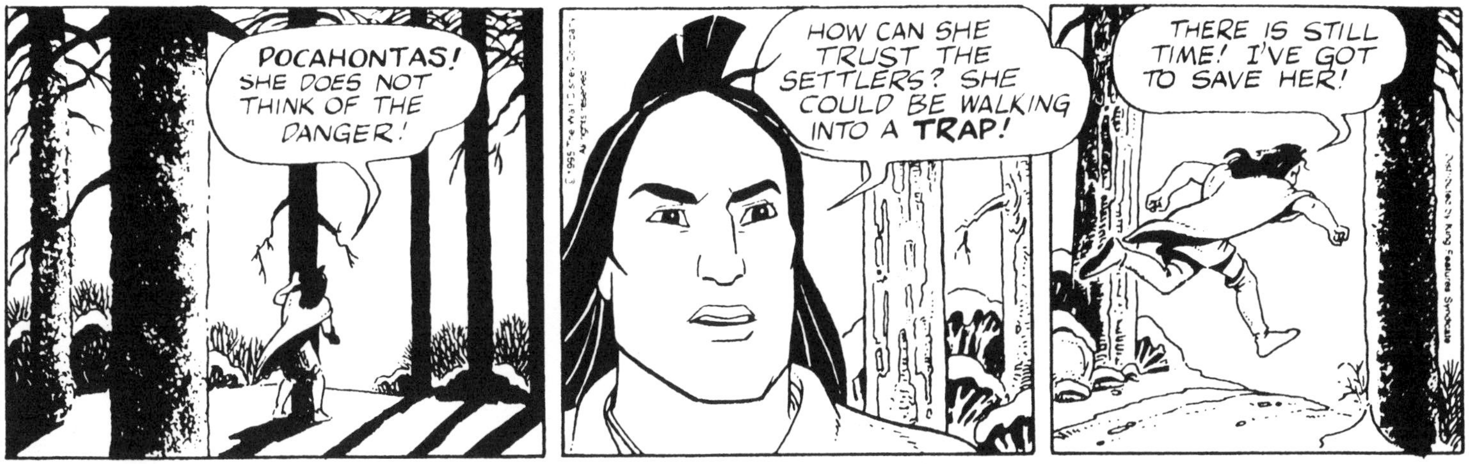
POCAHONTAS! SHE DOES NOT THINK OF THE DANGER!
HOW CAN SHE TRUST THE SETTLERS? SHE COULD BE WALKING INTO A TRAP!
THERE IS STILL TIME! I'VE GOT TO SAVE HER!
Distributed by King Features Syndicate

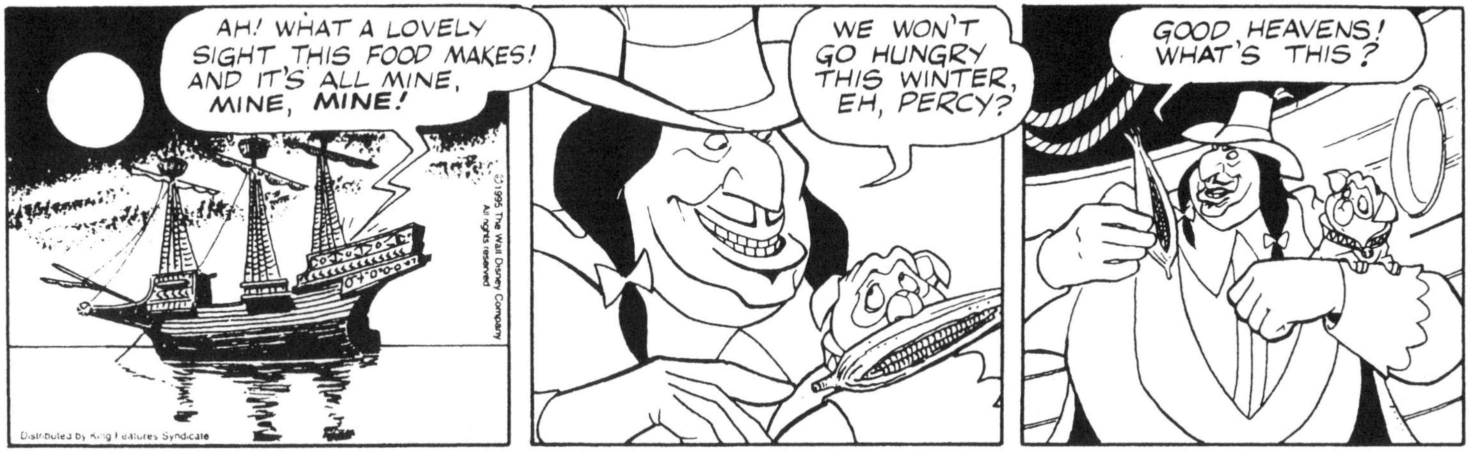
AH! WHAT A LOVELY SIGHT THIS FOOD MAKES! AND IT'S ALL MINE, MINE, MINE!
©1995 The Walt Disney Company All rights reserved
Distributed by King Features Syndicate
WE WON'T GO HUNGRY THIS WINTER, EH, PERCY?
GOOD HEAVENS! WHAT'S THIS?

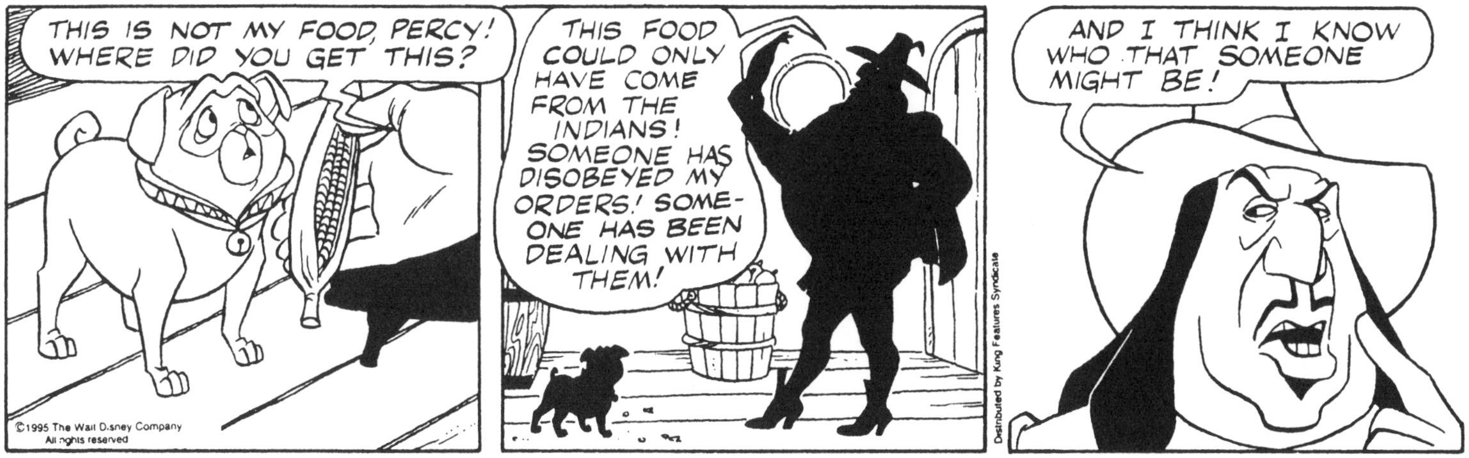
THIS IS NOT MY FOOD, PERCY! WHERE DID YOU GET THIS?
©1995 The Walt Disney Company All rights reserved
THIS FOOD COULD ONLY HAVE COME FROM THE INDIANS! SOMEONE HAS DISOBEYED MY ORDERS! SOMEONE HAS BEEN DEALING WITH THEM!
Distributed by King Features Syndicate
AND I THINK I KNOW WHO THAT SOMEONE MIGHT BE!

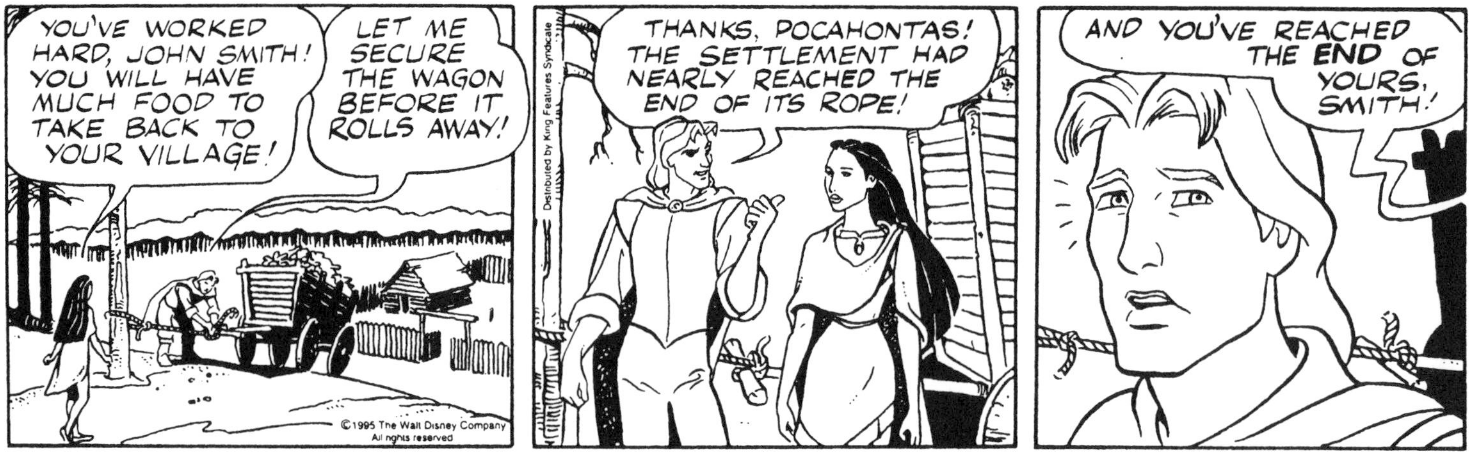
YOU'VE WORKED HARD, JOHN SMITH! YOU WILL HAVE MUCH FOOD TO TAKE BACK TO YOUR VILLAGE!
LET ME SECURE THE WAGON BEFORE IT ROLLS AWAY!
©1995 The Walt Disney Company All rights reserved
Distributed by King Features Syndicate
THANKS, POCAHONTAS! THE SETTLEMENT HAD NEARLY REACHED THE END OF ITS ROPE!
AND YOU'VE REACHED THE **END** OF YOURS, SMITH!

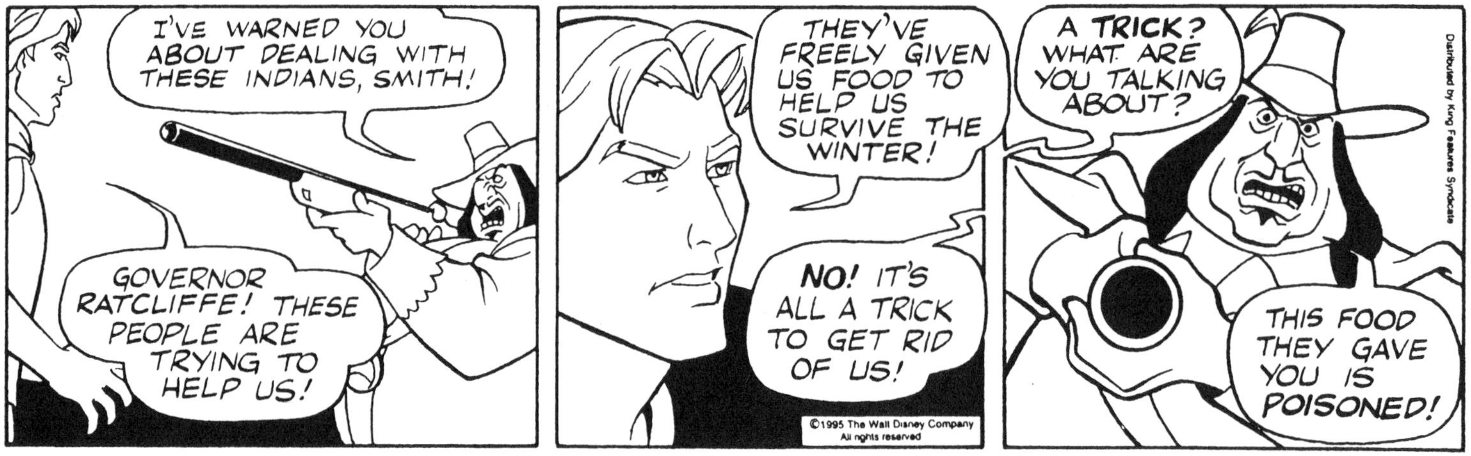
I'VE WARNED YOU ABOUT DEALING WITH THESE INDIANS, SMITH!
GOVERNOR RATCLIFFE! THESE PEOPLE ARE TRYING TO HELP US!
THEY'VE FREELY GIVEN US FOOD TO HELP US SURVIVE THE WINTER!
NO! IT'S ALL A TRICK TO GET RID OF US!
©1995 The Walt Disney Company All rights reserved
A **TRICK**? WHAT ARE YOU TALKING ABOUT?
THIS FOOD THEY GAVE YOU IS **POISONED!**
Distributed by King Features Syndicate

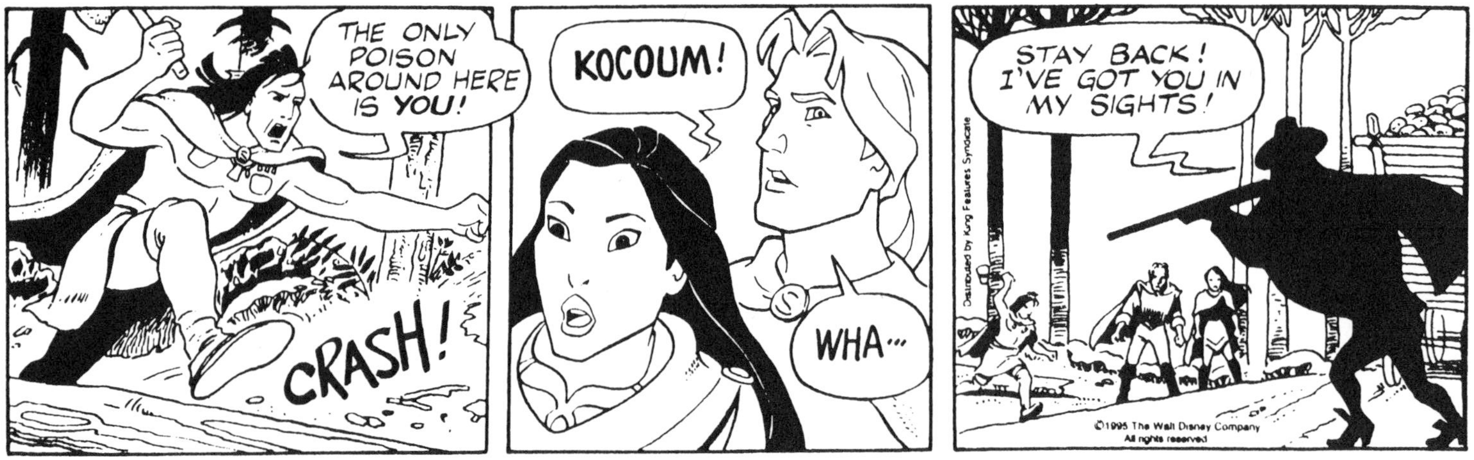
THE ONLY POISON AROUND HERE IS **YOU!**
CRASH!
KOCOUM!
WHA...
Distributed by King Features Syndicate
STAY BACK! I'VE GOT YOU IN MY SIGHTS!
©1995 The Walt Disney Company All rights reserved

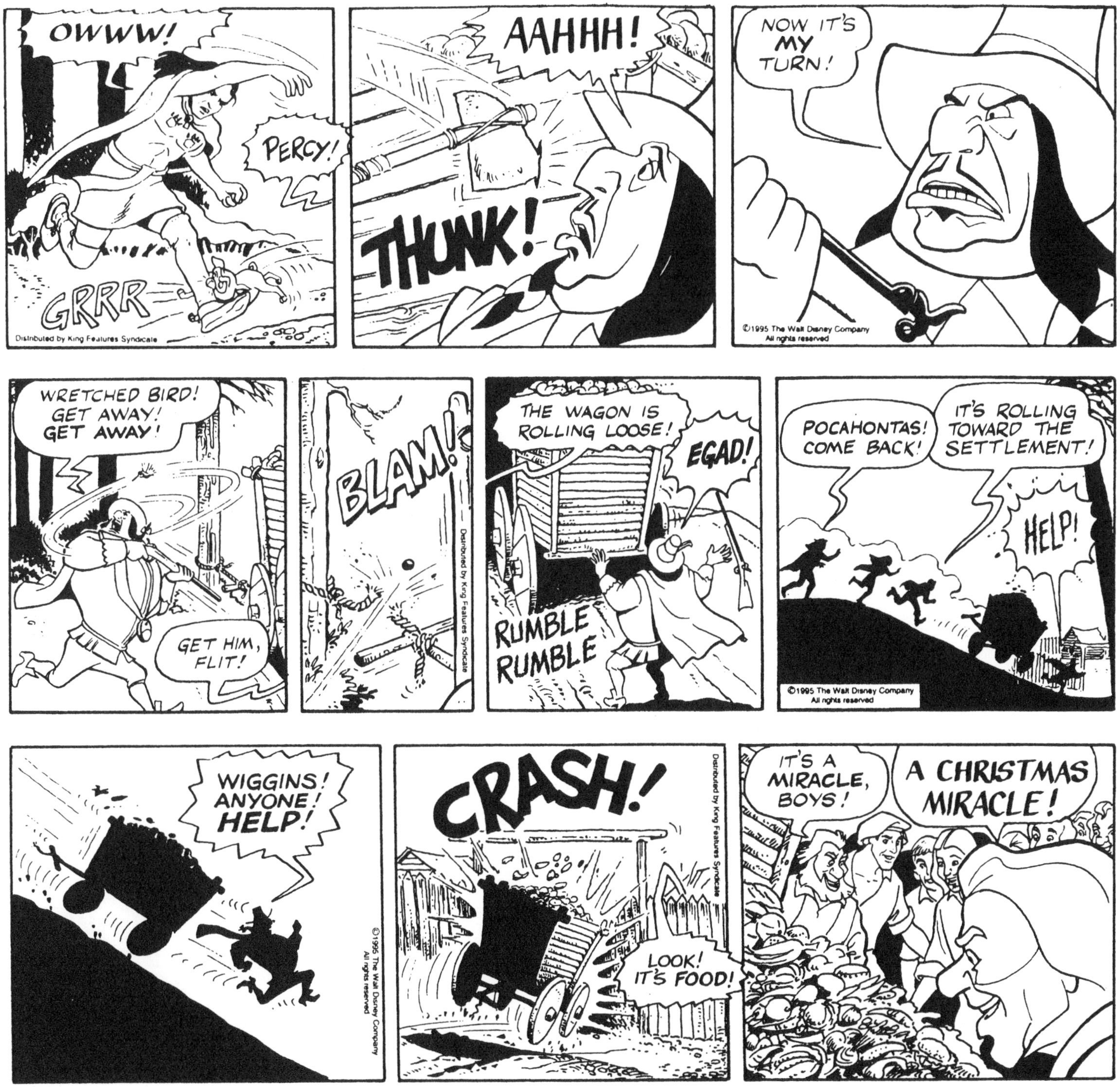
OWWW!
PERCY!
GRRR
Distributed by King Features Syndicate
AAHHH!
THUNK!
NOW IT'S MY TURN!
©1995 The Walt Disney Company All rights reserved
WRETCHED BIRD! GET AWAY! GET AWAY!
GET HIM, FLIT!
BLAM!
Distributed by King Features Syndicate
THE WAGON IS ROLLING LOOSE!
EGAD!
RUMBLE RUMBLE
POCAHONTAS! COME BACK!
IT'S ROLLING TOWARD THE SETTLEMENT!
HELP!
©1995 The Walt Disney Company All rights reserved
WIGGINS! ANYONE! HELP!
©1995 The Walt Disney Company All rights reserved
CRASH!
Distributed by King Features Syndicate
LOOK! IT'S FOOD!
IT'S A MIRACLE, BOYS!
A CHRISTMAS MIRACLE!

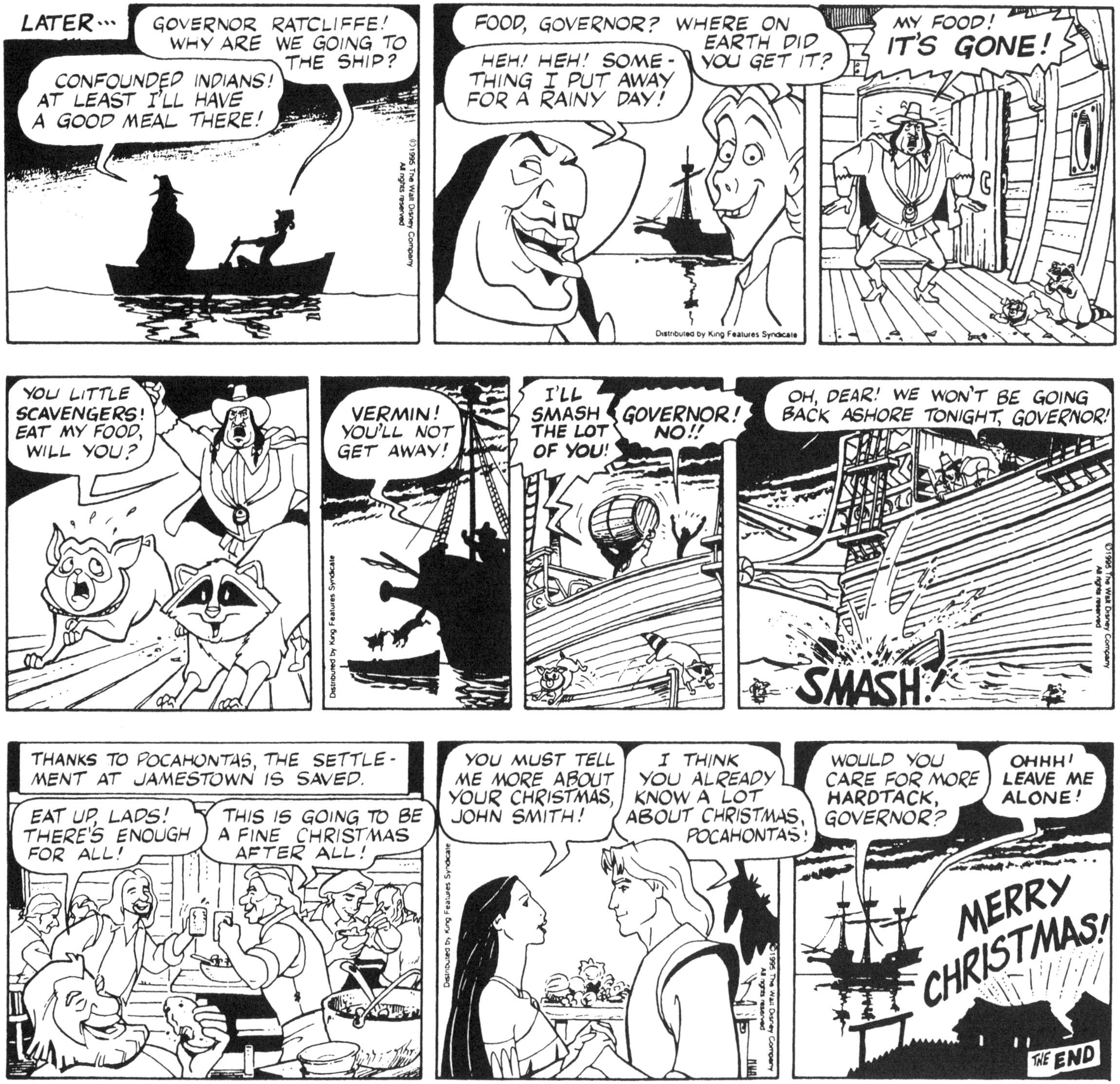
LATER...
GOVERNOR RATCLIFFE! WHY ARE WE GOING TO THE SHIP?
CONFOUNDED INDIANS! AT LEAST I'LL HAVE A GOOD MEAL THERE!
© 1995 The Walt Disney Company All rights reserved
FOOD, GOVERNOR? WHERE ON EARTH DID YOU GET IT?
HEH! HEH! SOMETHING I PUT AWAY FOR A RAINY DAY!
Distributed by King Features Syndicate
MY FOOD! IT'S GONE!
YOU LITTLE SCAVENGERS! EAT MY FOOD, WILL YOU?
VERMIN! YOU'LL NOT GET AWAY!
Distributed by King Features Syndicate
I'LL SMASH THE LOT OF YOU!
GOVERNOR! NO!!
OH, DEAR! WE WON'T BE GOING BACK ASHORE TONIGHT, GOVERNOR!
SMASH!
© 1995 The Walt Disney Company All rights reserved
THANKS TO POCAHONTAS, THE SETTLEMENT AT JAMESTOWN IS SAVED.
EAT UP, LADS! THERE'S ENOUGH FOR ALL!
THIS IS GOING TO BE A FINE CHRISTMAS AFTER ALL!
Distributed by King Features Syndicate
YOU MUST TELL ME MORE ABOUT YOUR CHRISTMAS, JOHN SMITH!
I THINK YOU ALREADY KNOW A LOT ABOUT CHRISTMAS, POCAHONTAS!
© 1995 The Walt Disney Company All rights reserved
WOULD YOU CARE FOR MORE HARDTACK, GOVERNOR?
OHHH! LEAVE ME ALONE!
MERRY CHRISTMAS!
THE END

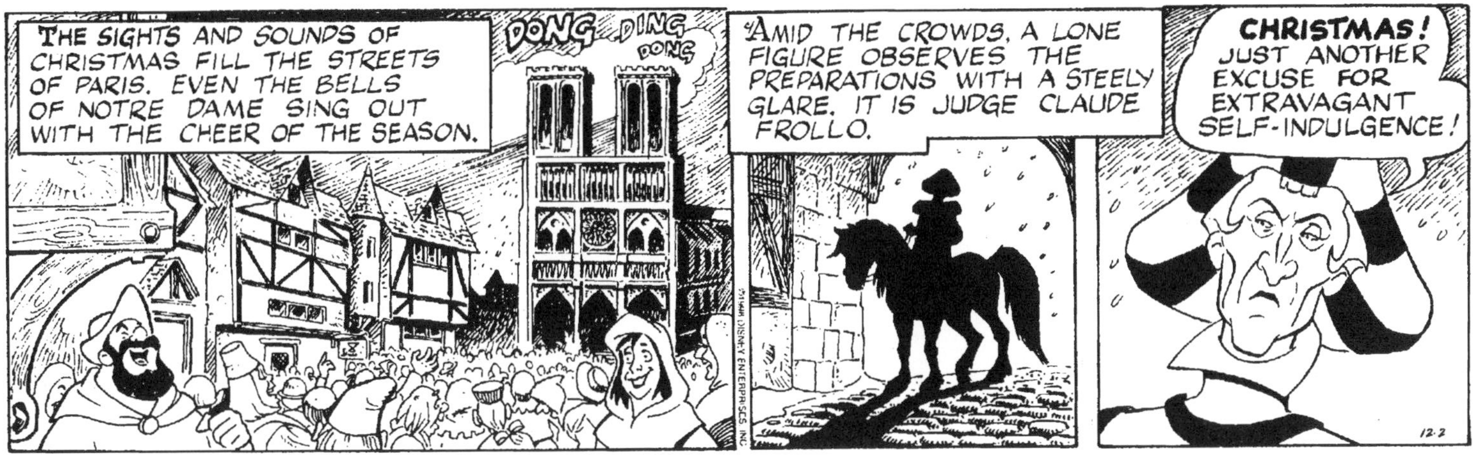
THE SIGHTS AND SOUNDS OF CHRISTMAS FILL THE STREETS OF PARIS. EVEN THE BELLS OF NOTRE DAME SING OUT WITH THE CHEER OF THE SEASON.
DONG DING DONG
AMID THE CROWDS, A LONE FIGURE OBSERVES THE PREPARATIONS WITH A STEELY GLARE. IT IS JUDGE CLAUDE FROLLO.
CHRISTMAS! JUST ANOTHER EXCUSE FOR EXTRAVAGANT SELF-INDULGENCE!
12-2

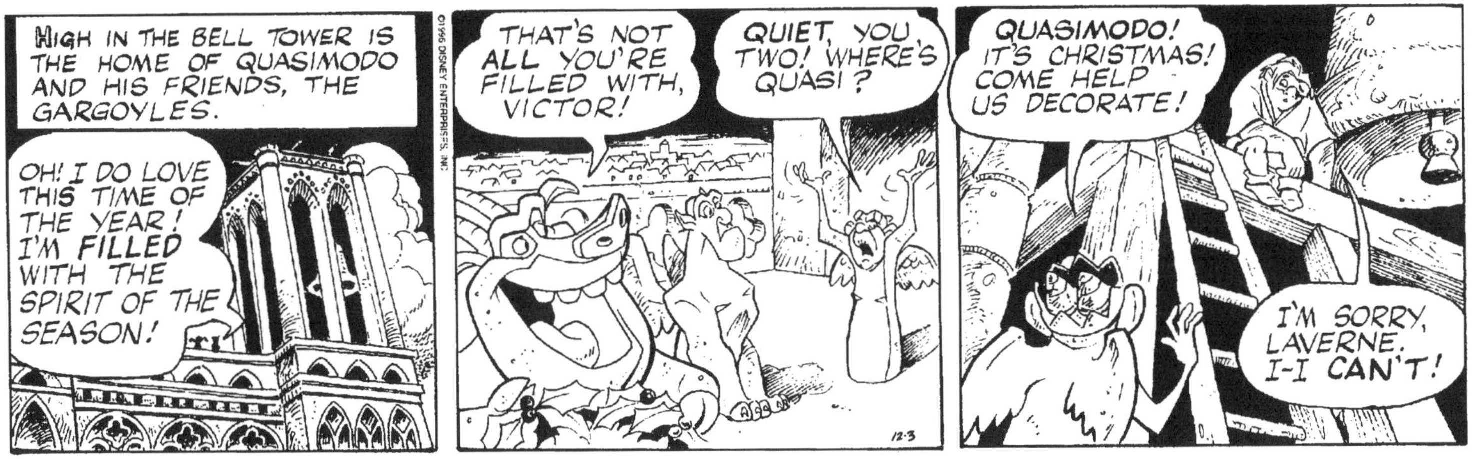
HIGH IN THE BELL TOWER IS THE HOME OF QUASIMODO AND HIS FRIENDS, THE GARGOYLES.
OH! I DO LOVE THIS TIME OF THE YEAR! I'M FILLED WITH THE SPIRIT OF THE SEASON!
©1996 DISNEY ENTERPRISES, INC.
THAT'S NOT ALL YOU'RE FILLED WITH, VICTOR!
QUIET, YOU TWO! WHERE'S QUASI?
12-3
QUASIMODO! IT'S CHRISTMAS! COME HELP US DECORATE!
I'M SORRY, LAVERNE. I-I CAN'T!

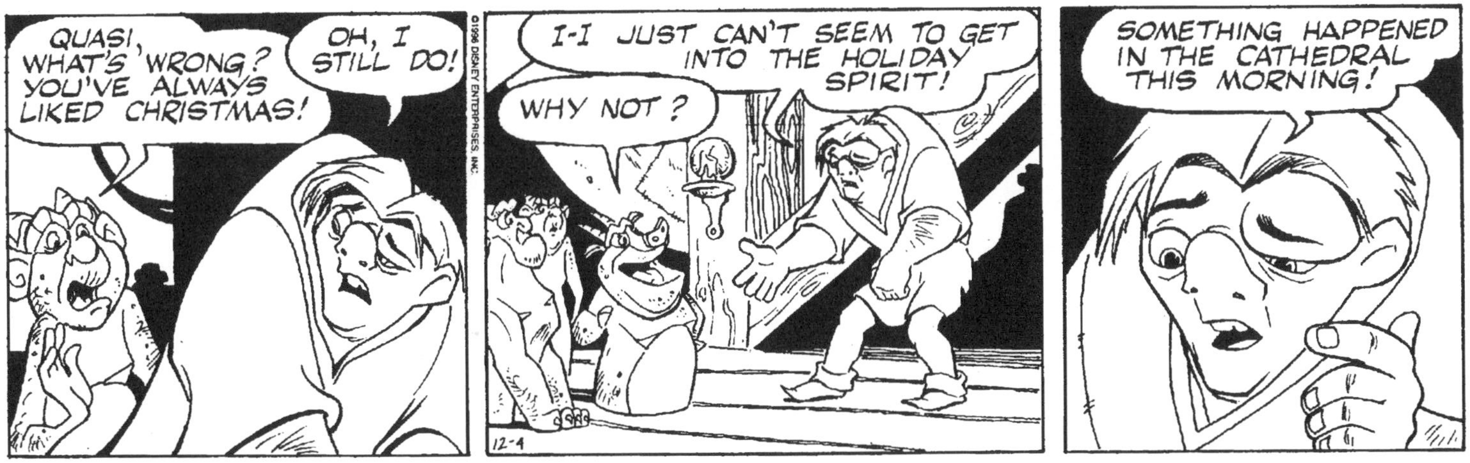
QUASI, WHAT'S WRONG? YOU'VE ALWAYS LIKED CHRISTMAS!
OH, I STILL DO!
©1996 DISNEY ENTERPRISES, INC.
I-I JUST CAN'T SEEM TO GET INTO THE HOLIDAY SPIRIT!
WHY NOT?
12-4
SOMETHING HAPPENED IN THE CATHEDRAL THIS MORNING!

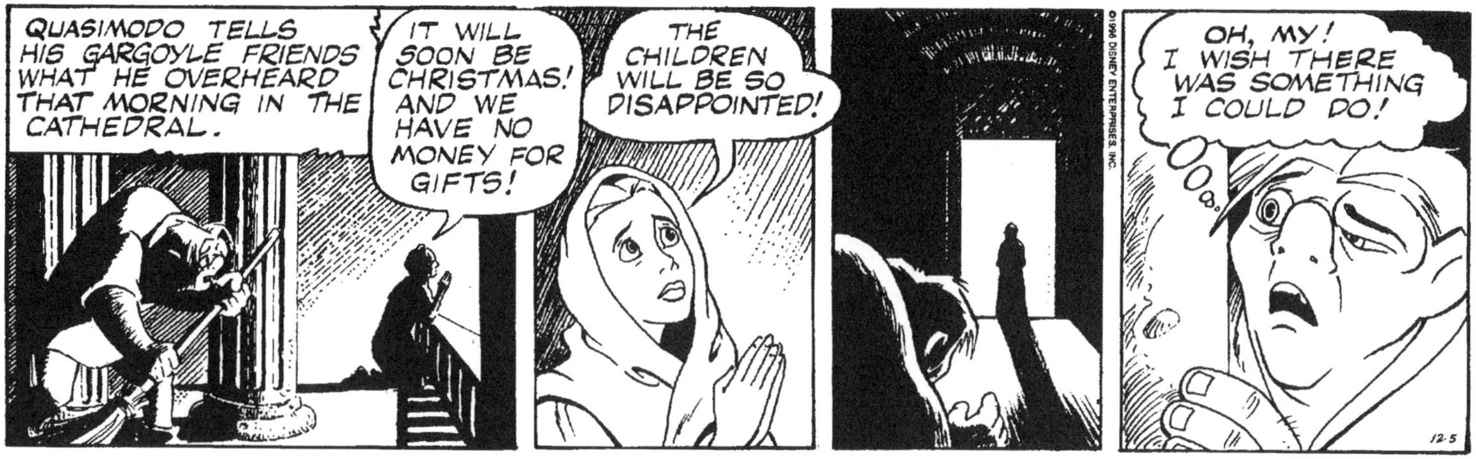
QUASIMODO TELLS HIS GARGOYLE FRIENDS WHAT HE OVERHEARD THAT MORNING IN THE CATHEDRAL.
IT WILL SOON BE CHRISTMAS! AND WE HAVE NO MONEY FOR GIFTS!
THE CHILDREN WILL BE SO DISAPPOINTED!
©1996 DISNEY ENTERPRISES, INC.
OH, MY! I WISH THERE WAS SOMETHING I COULD DO!
12-5

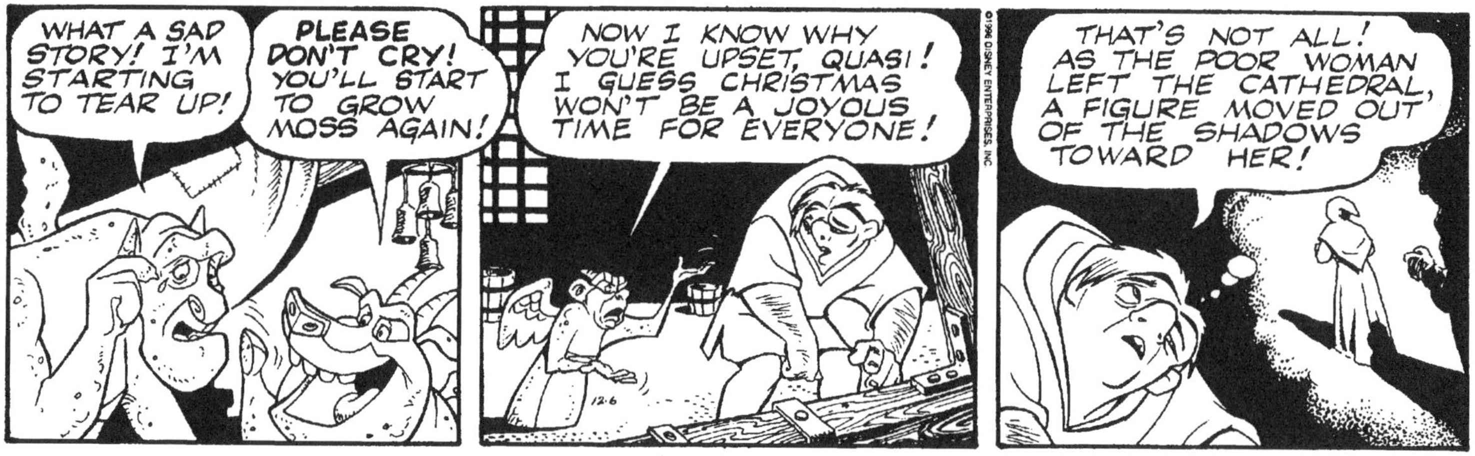
WHAT A SAD STORY! I'M STARTING TO TEAR UP!
PLEASE DON'T CRY! YOU'LL START TO GROW MOSS AGAIN!
NOW I KNOW WHY YOU'RE UPSET, QUASI! I GUESS CHRISTMAS WON'T BE A JOYOUS TIME FOR EVERYONE!
12-6
©1996 DISNEY ENTERPRISES, INC.
THAT'S NOT ALL! AS THE POOR WOMAN LEFT THE CATHEDRAL, A FIGURE MOVED OUT OF THE SHADOWS TOWARD HER!

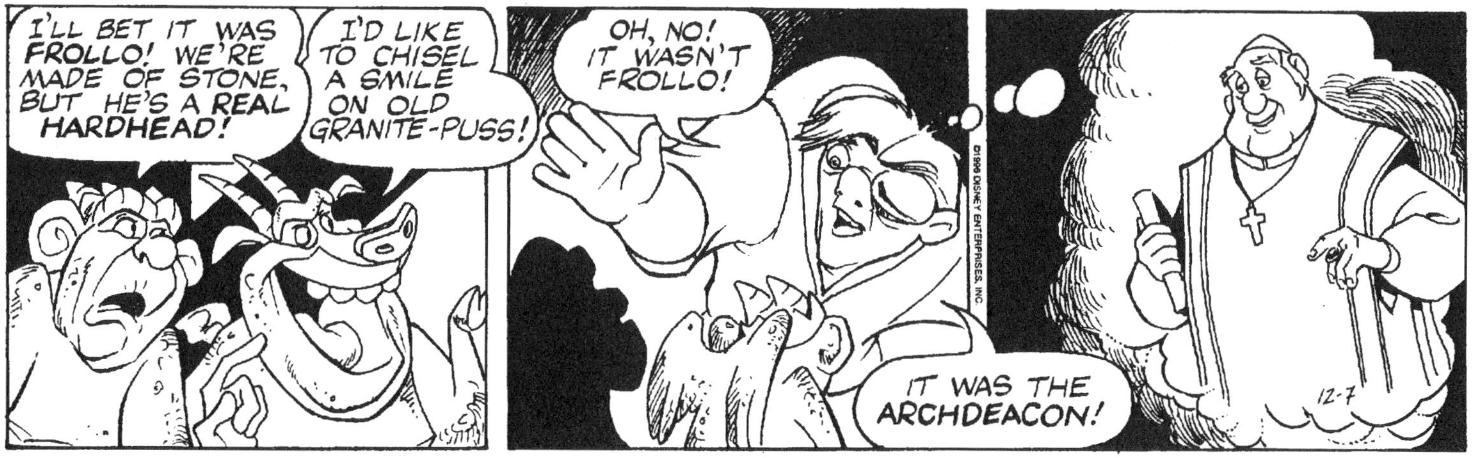
I'LL BET IT WAS FROLLO! WE'RE MADE OF STONE, BUT HE'S A REAL HARDHEAD!
I'D LIKE TO CHISEL A SMILE ON OLD GRANITE-PUSS!
OH, NO! IT WASN'T FROLLO!
©1996 DISNEY ENTERPRISES, INC.
IT WAS THE ARCHDEACON!
12-7

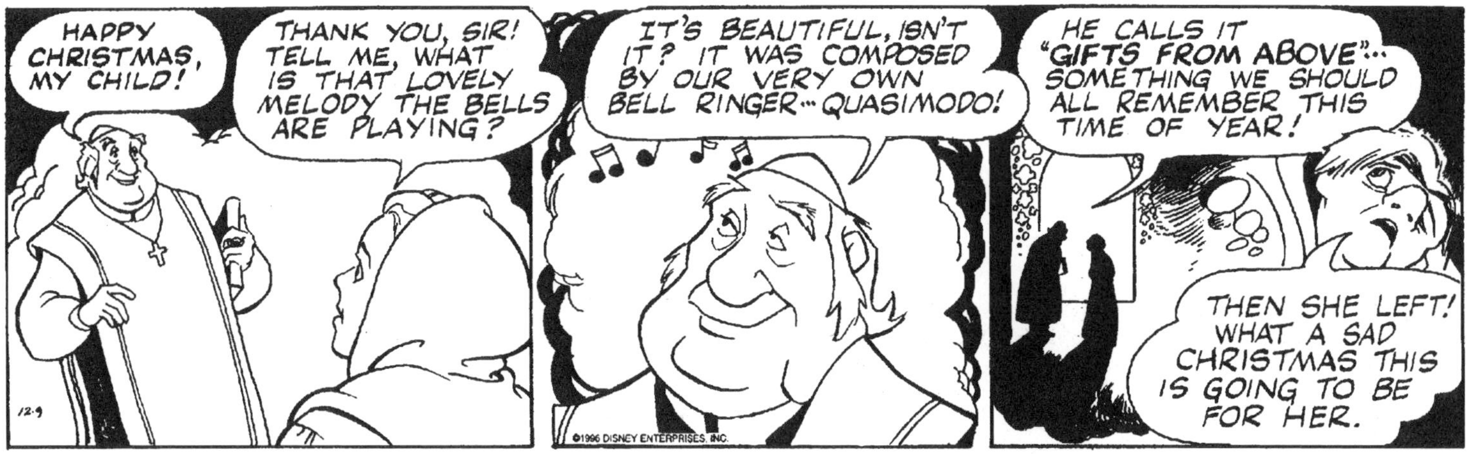
HAPPY CHRISTMAS, MY CHILD!
THANK YOU, SIR! TELL ME, WHAT IS THAT LOVELY MELODY THE BELLS ARE PLAYING?
IT'S BEAUTIFUL, ISN'T IT? IT WAS COMPOSED BY OUR VERY OWN BELL RINGER··· QUASIMODO!
HE CALLS IT "GIFTS FROM ABOVE"... SOMETHING WE SHOULD ALL REMEMBER THIS TIME OF YEAR!
THEN SHE LEFT! WHAT A SAD CHRISTMAS THIS IS GOING TO BE FOR HER.
12·9
©1996 DISNEY ENTERPRISES, INC.

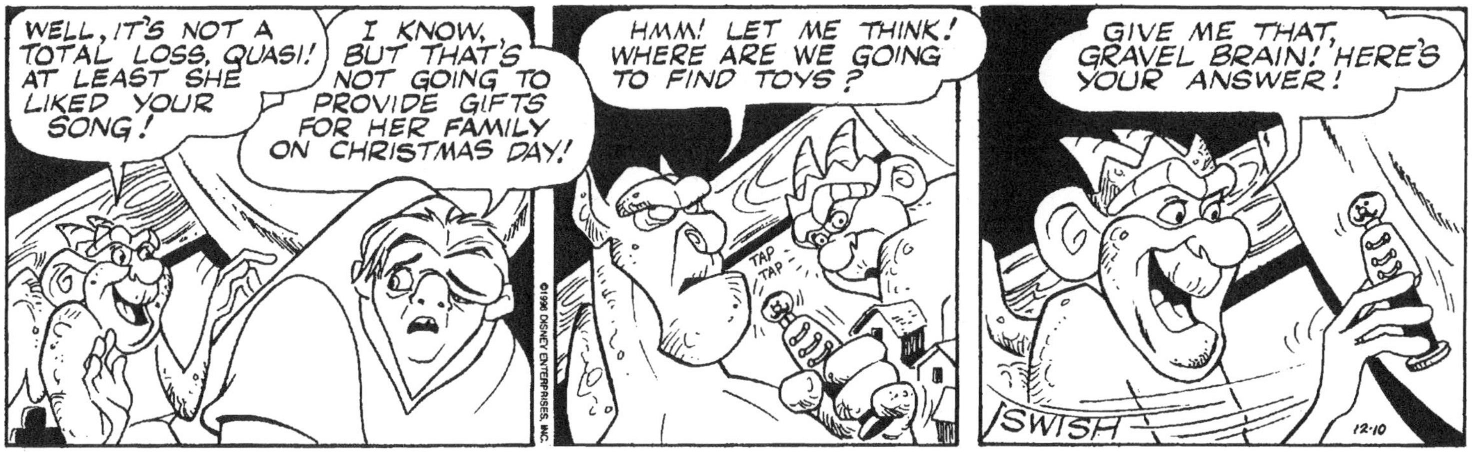
WELL, IT'S NOT A TOTAL LOSS, QUASI! AT LEAST SHE LIKED YOUR SONG!
I KNOW, BUT THAT'S NOT GOING TO PROVIDE GIFTS FOR HER FAMILY ON CHRISTMAS DAY!
HMM! LET ME THINK! WHERE ARE WE GOING TO FIND TOYS?
TAP TAP
GIVE ME THAT, GRAVEL BRAIN! HERE'S YOUR ANSWER!
SWISH
12·10
©1996 DISNEY ENTERPRISES, INC.

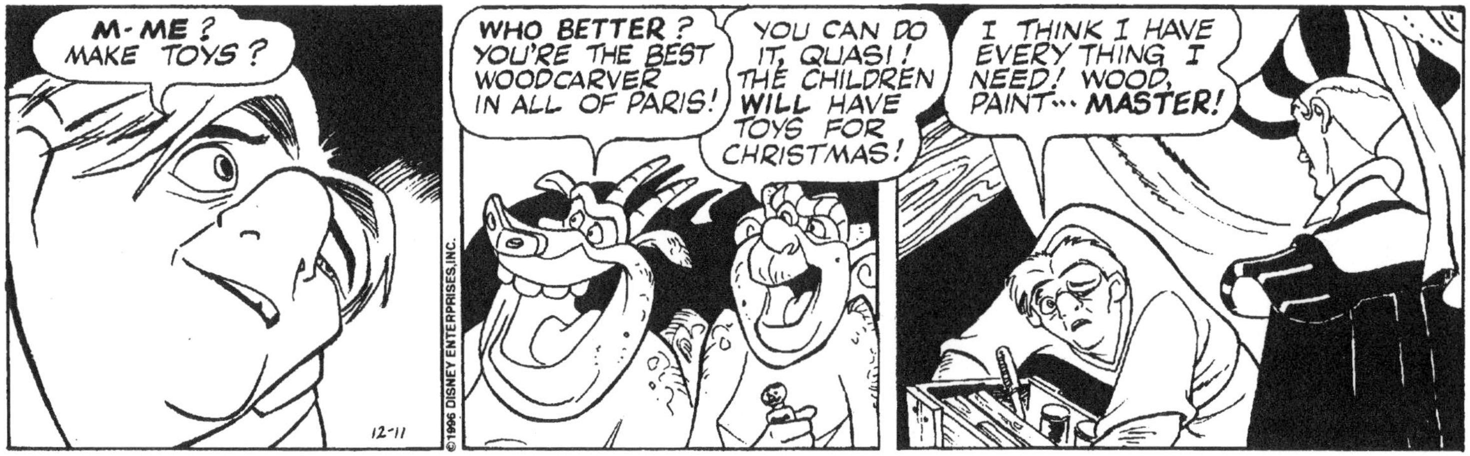
M-ME? MAKE TOYS?
WHO BETTER? YOU'RE THE BEST WOODCARVER IN ALL OF PARIS!
YOU CAN DO IT, QUASI! THE CHILDREN WILL HAVE TOYS FOR CHRISTMAS!
I THINK I HAVE EVERYTHING I NEED! WOOD, PAINT··· MASTER!
12·11
©1996 DISNEY ENTERPRISES, INC.

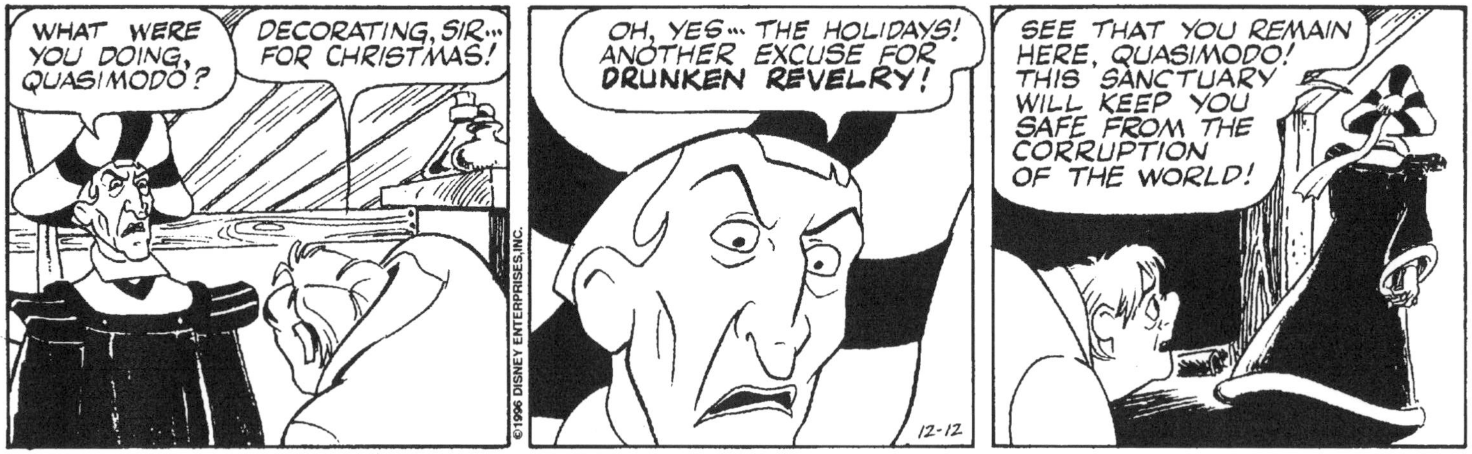
WHAT WERE YOU DOING, QUASIMODO?
DECORATING, SIR... FOR CHRISTMAS!
©1996 DISNEY ENTERPRISES, INC.
OH, YES... THE HOLIDAYS! ANOTHER EXCUSE FOR **DRUNKEN REVELRY**!
12-12
SEE THAT YOU REMAIN HERE, QUASIMODO! THIS SANCTUARY WILL KEEP YOU SAFE FROM THE CORRUPTION OF THE WORLD!

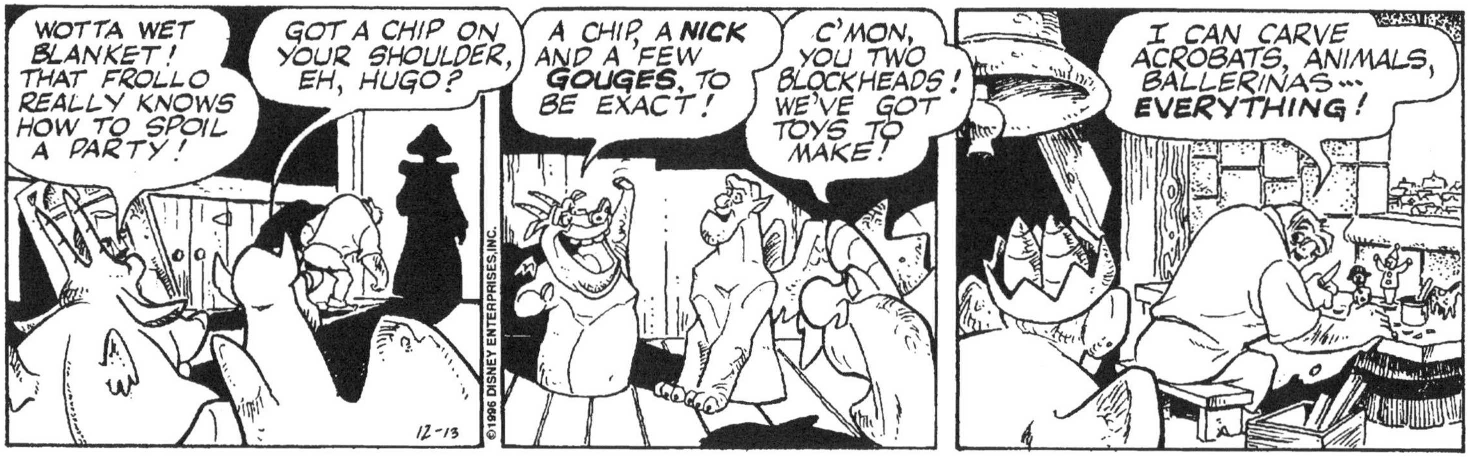
WOTTA WET BLANKET! THAT FROLLO REALLY KNOWS HOW TO SPOIL A PARTY!
GOT A CHIP ON YOUR SHOULDER, EH, HUGO?
12-13
©1996 DISNEY ENTERPRISES, INC.
A CHIP, A **NICK** AND A FEW **GOUGES**, TO BE EXACT!
C'MON, YOU TWO BLOCKHEADS! WE'VE GOT TOYS TO MAKE!
I CAN CARVE ACROBATS, ANIMALS, BALLERINAS... **EVERYTHING**!

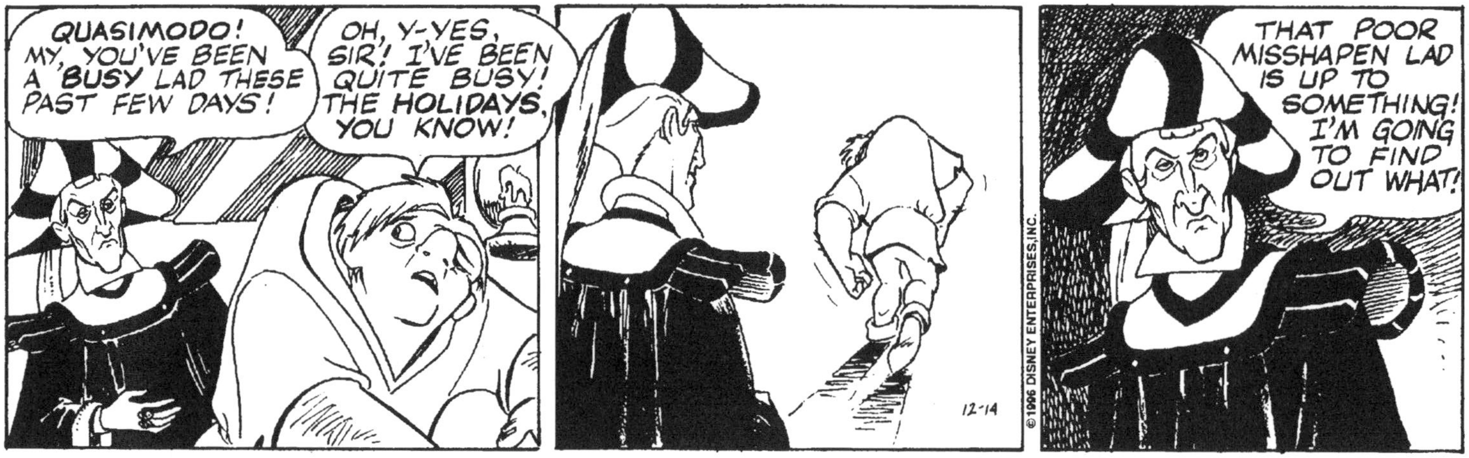
QUASIMODO! MY, YOU'VE BEEN A **BUSY** LAD THESE PAST FEW DAYS!
OH, Y-YES, SIR! I'VE BEEN QUITE BUSY! THE **HOLIDAYS**, YOU KNOW!
12-14
©1996 DISNEY ENTERPRISES, INC.
THAT POOR MISSHAPEN LAD IS UP TO SOMETHING! I'M GOING TO FIND OUT WHAT!

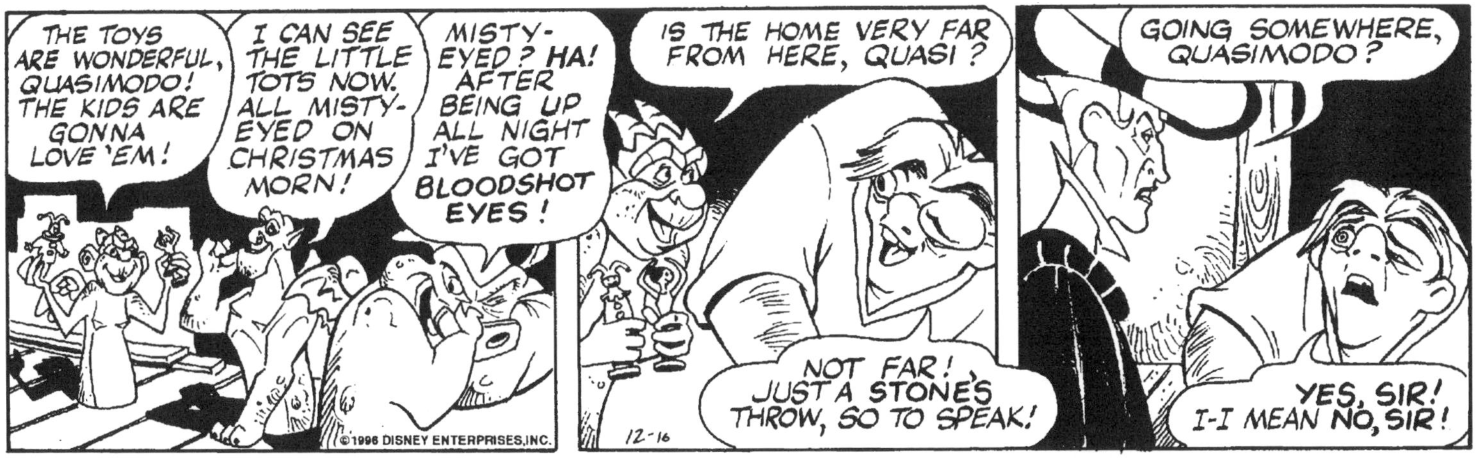
THE TOYS ARE WONDERFUL, QUASIMODO! THE KIDS ARE GONNA LOVE 'EM!
I CAN SEE THE LITTLE TOTS NOW. ALL MISTY-EYED ON CHRISTMAS MORN!
MISTY-EYED? HA! AFTER BEING UP ALL NIGHT I'VE GOT BLOODSHOT EYES!
©1996 DISNEY ENTERPRISES, INC.
IS THE HOME VERY FAR FROM HERE, QUASI?
NOT FAR! JUST A STONE'S THROW, SO TO SPEAK!
12-16
GOING SOMEWHERE, QUASIMODO?
YES, SIR! I-I MEAN NO, SIR!

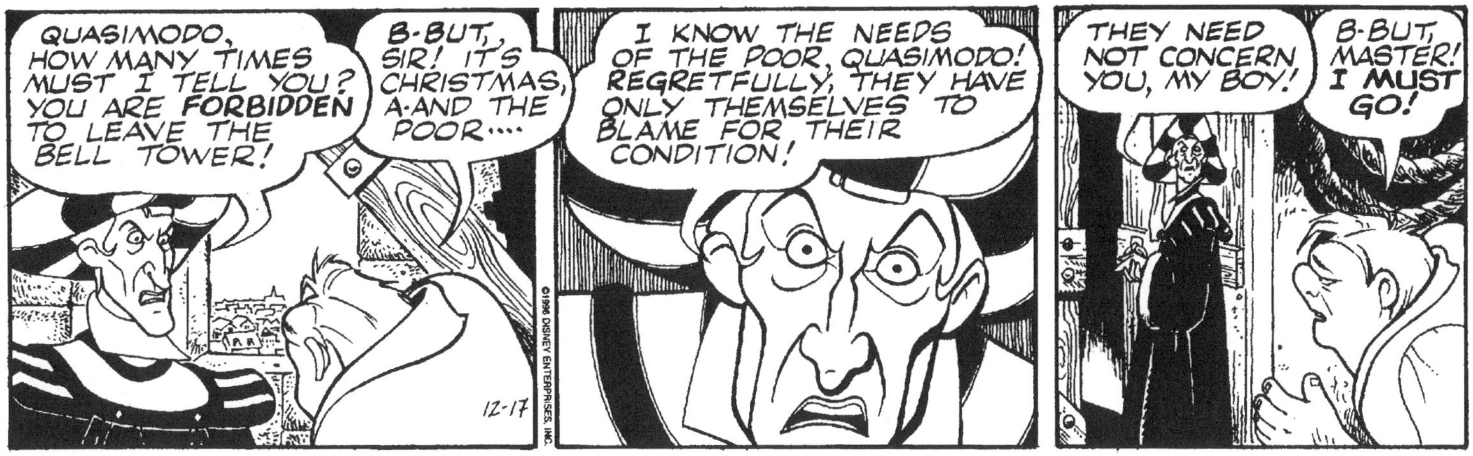
QUASIMODO, HOW MANY TIMES MUST I TELL YOU? YOU ARE FORBIDDEN TO LEAVE THE BELL TOWER!
B-BUT, SIR! IT'S CHRISTMAS, A-AND THE POOR....
12-17
©1996 DISNEY ENTERPRISES, INC.
I KNOW THE NEEDS OF THE POOR, QUASIMODO! REGRETFULLY, THEY HAVE ONLY THEMSELVES TO BLAME FOR THEIR CONDITION!
THEY NEED NOT CONCERN YOU, MY BOY!
B-BUT, MASTER! I MUST GO!

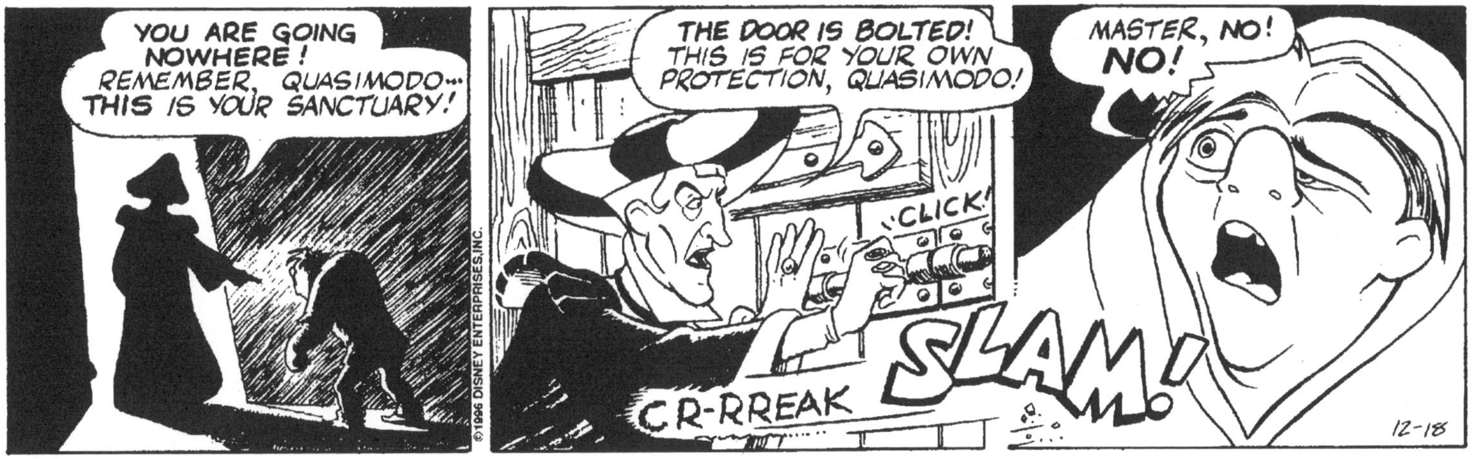
YOU ARE GOING NOWHERE! REMEMBER, QUASIMODO... THIS IS YOUR SANCTUARY!
©1996 DISNEY ENTERPRISES, INC.
THE DOOR IS BOLTED! THIS IS FOR YOUR OWN PROTECTION, QUASIMODO!
CLICK!
CR-RREAK
SLAM!
MASTER, NO! NO!
12-18

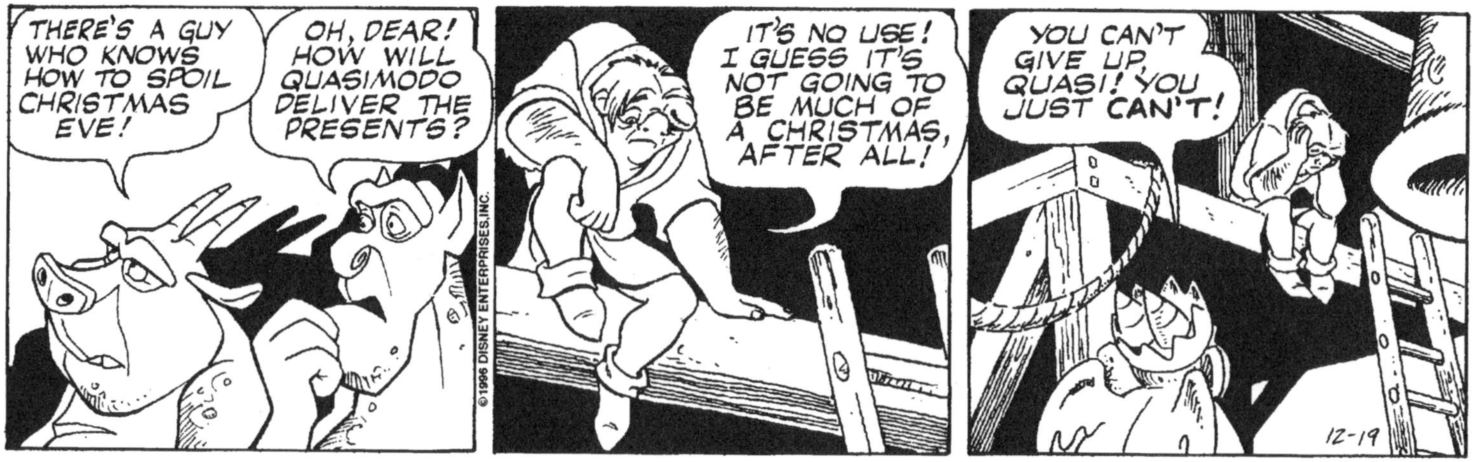
THERE'S A GUY WHO KNOWS HOW TO SPOIL CHRISTMAS EVE!
OH, DEAR! HOW WILL QUASIMODO DELIVER THE PRESENTS?
©1996 DISNEY ENTERPRISES, INC.
IT'S NO USE! I GUESS IT'S NOT GOING TO BE MUCH OF A CHRISTMAS, AFTER ALL!
YOU CAN'T GIVE UP, QUASI! YOU JUST CAN'T!
12-19

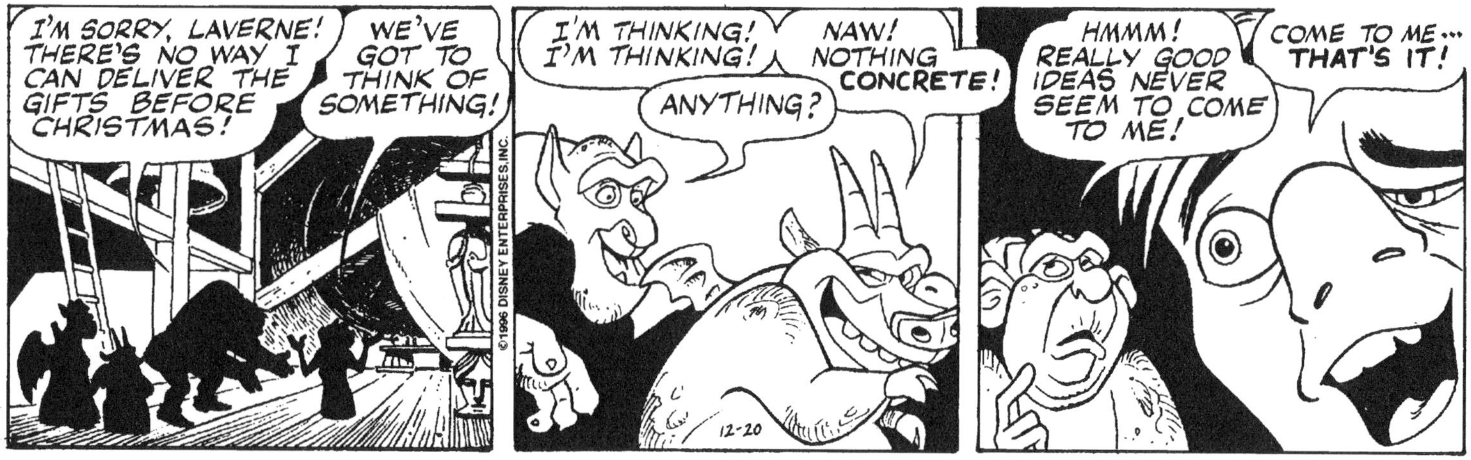
I'M SORRY, LAVERNE! THERE'S NO WAY I CAN DELIVER THE GIFTS BEFORE CHRISTMAS!
WE'VE GOT TO THINK OF SOMETHING!
©1996 DISNEY ENTERPRISES, INC.
I'M THINKING! I'M THINKING!
ANYTHING?
NAW! NOTHING CONCRETE!
12-20
HMMM! REALLY GOOD IDEAS NEVER SEEM TO COME TO ME!
COME TO ME... THAT'S IT!

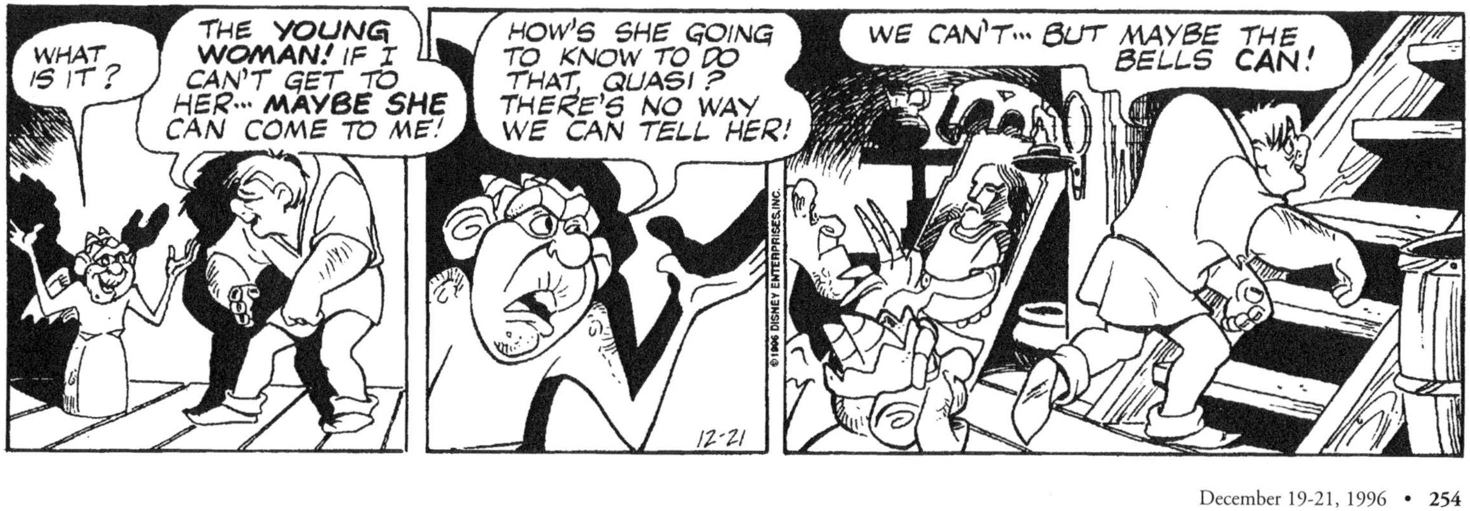
WHAT IS IT?
THE YOUNG WOMAN! IF I CAN'T GET TO HER... MAYBE SHE CAN COME TO ME!
HOW'S SHE GOING TO KNOW TO DO THAT, QUASI? THERE'S NO WAY WE CAN TELL HER!
12-21
©1996 DISNEY ENTERPRISES, INC.
WE CAN'T... BUT MAYBE THE BELLS CAN!

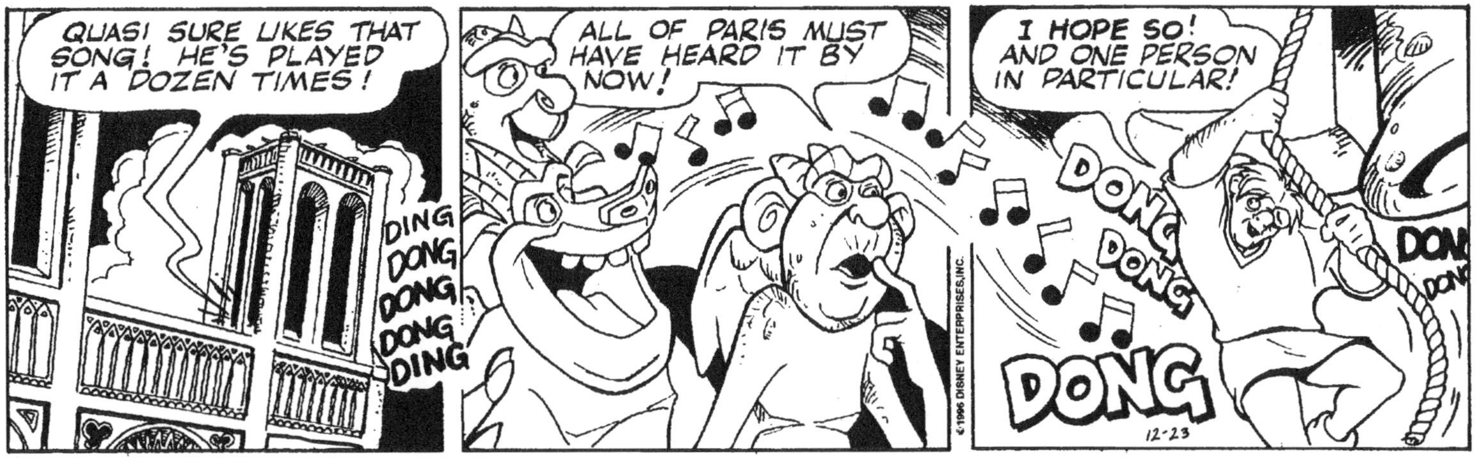
QUASI SURE LIKES THAT SONG! HE'S PLAYED IT A DOZEN TIMES!
DING DONG DONG DONG DONG DING
ALL OF PARIS MUST HAVE HEARD IT BY NOW!
©1996 DISNEY ENTERPRISES, INC.
I HOPE SO! AND ONE PERSON IN PARTICULAR!
DONG DONG
DONG
DONG DONG
12-23
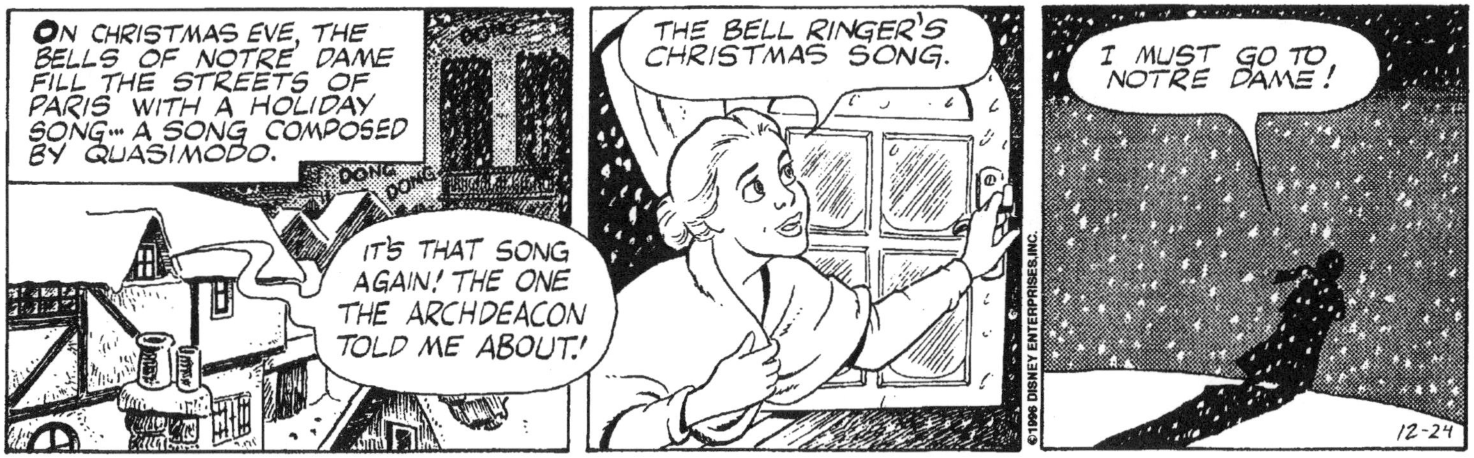
ON CHRISTMAS EVE, THE BELLS OF NOTRE DAME FILL THE STREETS OF PARIS WITH A HOLIDAY SONG... A SONG COMPOSED BY QUASIMODO.
DONG DONG
IT'S THAT SONG AGAIN! THE ONE THE ARCHDEACON TOLD ME ABOUT!
THE BELL RINGER'S CHRISTMAS SONG.
©1996 DISNEY ENTERPRISES, INC.
I MUST GO TO NOTRE DAME!
12-24
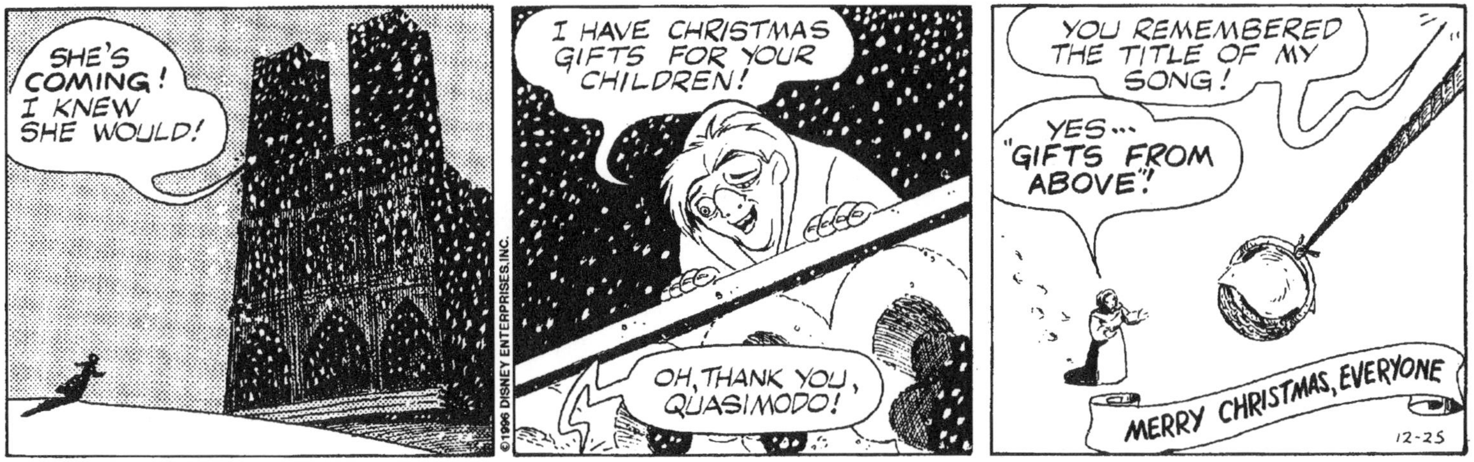
SHE'S COMING! I KNEW SHE WOULD!
©1996 DISNEY ENTERPRISES, INC.
I HAVE CHRISTMAS GIFTS FOR YOUR CHILDREN!
OH, THANK YOU, QUASIMODO!
YOU REMEMBERED THE TITLE OF MY SONG!
YES... "GIFTS FROM ABOVE"!
MERRY CHRISTMAS, EVERYONE
12-25

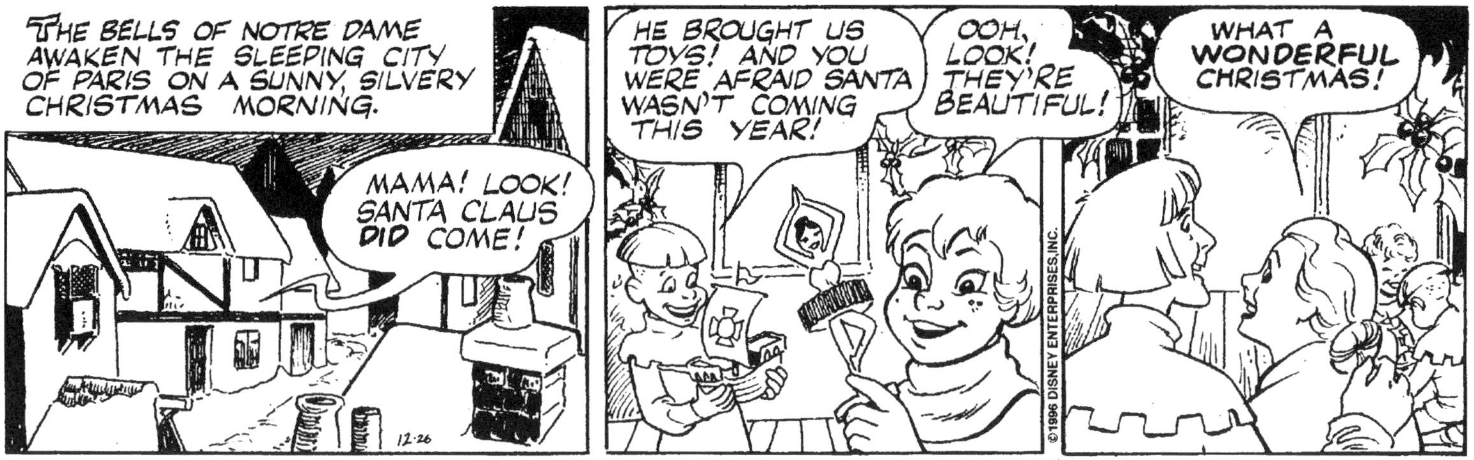
THE BELLS OF NOTRE DAME AWAKEN THE SLEEPING CITY OF PARIS ON A SUNNY, SILVERY CHRISTMAS MORNING.
MAMA! LOOK! SANTA CLAUS DID COME!
12-26
HE BROUGHT US TOYS! AND YOU WERE AFRAID SANTA WASN'T COMING THIS YEAR!
OOH, LOOK! THEY'RE BEAUTIFUL!
©1996 DISNEY ENTERPRISES, INC.
WHAT A WONDERFUL CHRISTMAS!

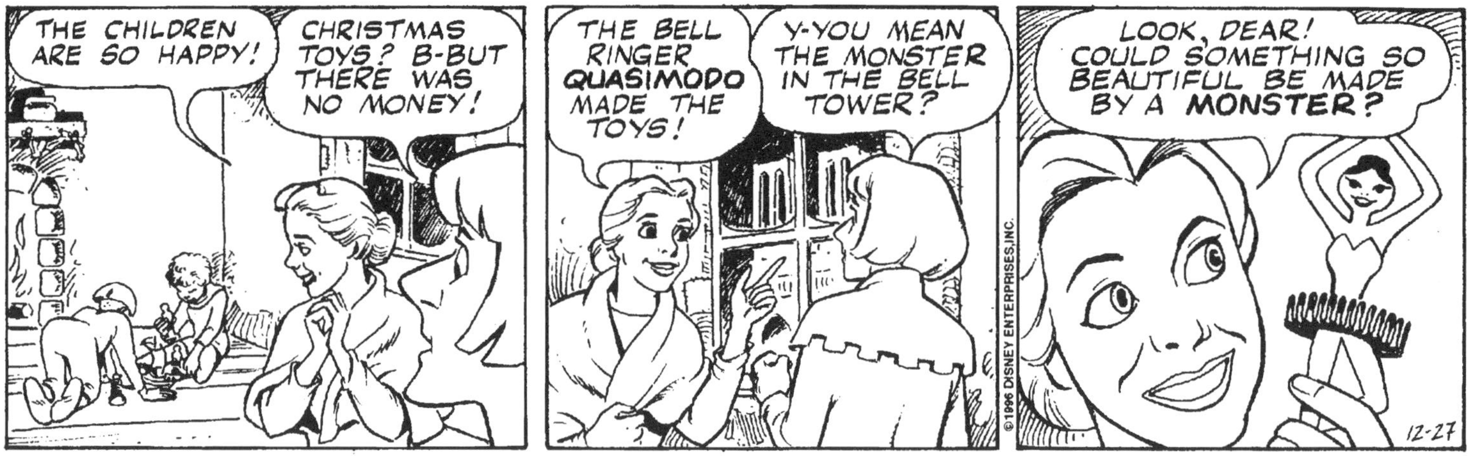
THE CHILDREN ARE SO HAPPY!
CHRISTMAS TOYS? B-BUT THERE WAS NO MONEY!
THE BELL RINGER QUASIMODO MADE THE TOYS!
Y-YOU MEAN THE MONSTER IN THE BELL TOWER?
©1996 DISNEY ENTERPRISES, INC.
LOOK, DEAR! COULD SOMETHING SO BEAUTIFUL BE MADE BY A MONSTER?
12-27

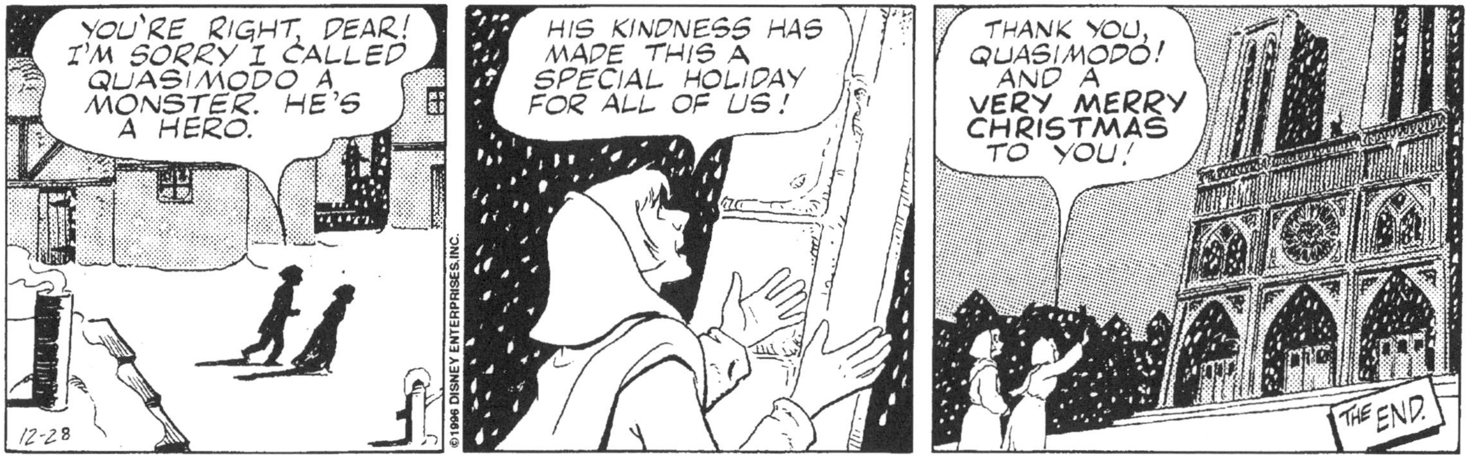
YOU'RE RIGHT, DEAR! I'M SORRY I CALLED QUASIMODO A MONSTER. HE'S A HERO.
12-28
©1996 DISNEY ENTERPRISES, INC.
HIS KINDNESS HAS MADE THIS A SPECIAL HOLIDAY FOR ALL OF US!
THANK YOU, QUASIMODO! AND A VERY MERRY CHRISTMAS TO YOU!
THE END.

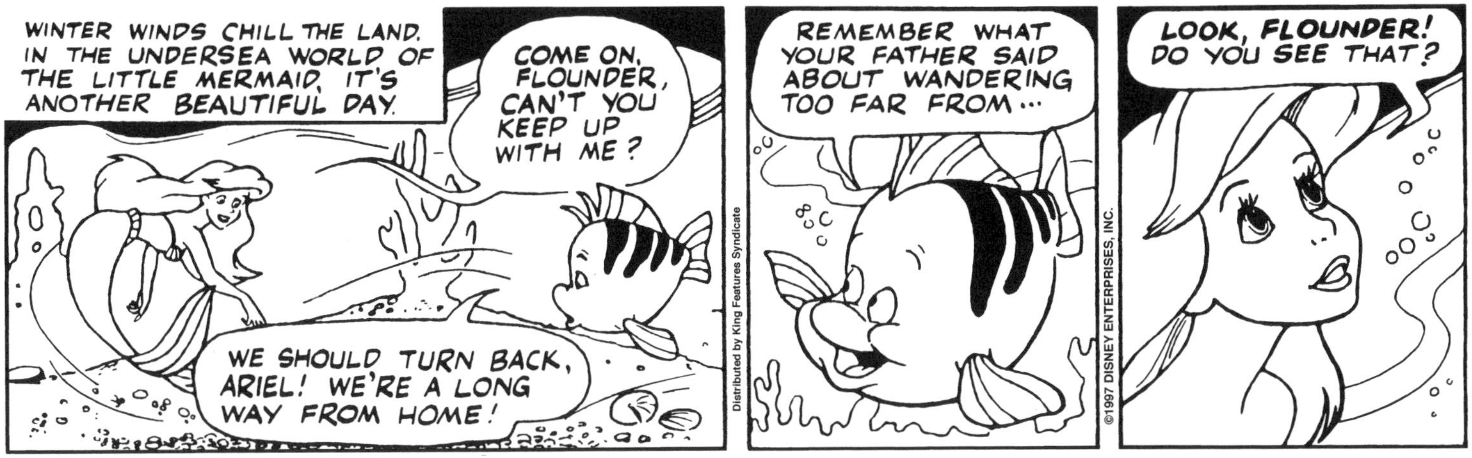
WINTER WINDS CHILL THE LAND. IN THE UNDERSEA WORLD OF THE LITTLE MERMAID, IT'S ANOTHER BEAUTIFUL DAY.
COME ON, FLOUNDER, CAN'T YOU KEEP UP WITH ME?
WE SHOULD TURN BACK, ARIEL! WE'RE A LONG WAY FROM HOME!
Distributed by King Features Syndicate
REMEMBER WHAT YOUR FATHER SAID ABOUT WANDERING TOO FAR FROM...
©1997 DISNEY ENTERPRISES, INC.
LOOK, FLOUNDER! DO YOU SEE THAT?

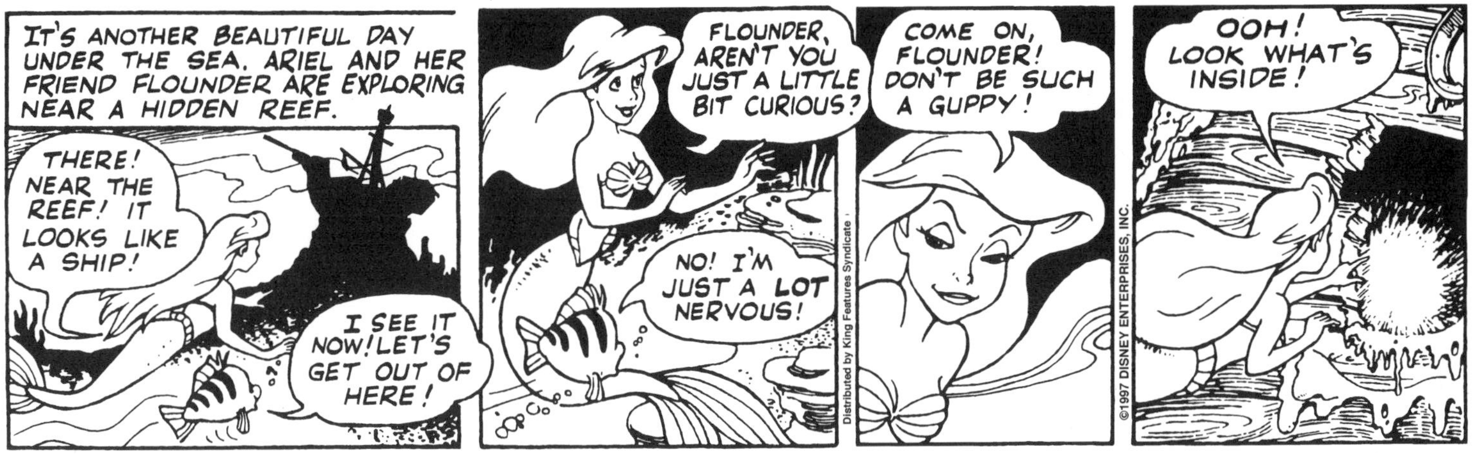
IT'S ANOTHER BEAUTIFUL DAY UNDER THE SEA. ARIEL AND HER FRIEND FLOUNDER ARE EXPLORING NEAR A HIDDEN REEF.
THERE! NEAR THE REEF! IT LOOKS LIKE A SHIP!
I SEE IT NOW! LET'S GET OUT OF HERE!
FLOUNDER, AREN'T YOU JUST A LITTLE BIT CURIOUS?
NO! I'M JUST A LOT NERVOUS!
Distributed by King Features Syndicate
COME ON, FLOUNDER! DON'T BE SUCH A GUPPY!
©1997 DISNEY ENTERPRISES, INC.
OOH! LOOK WHAT'S INSIDE!

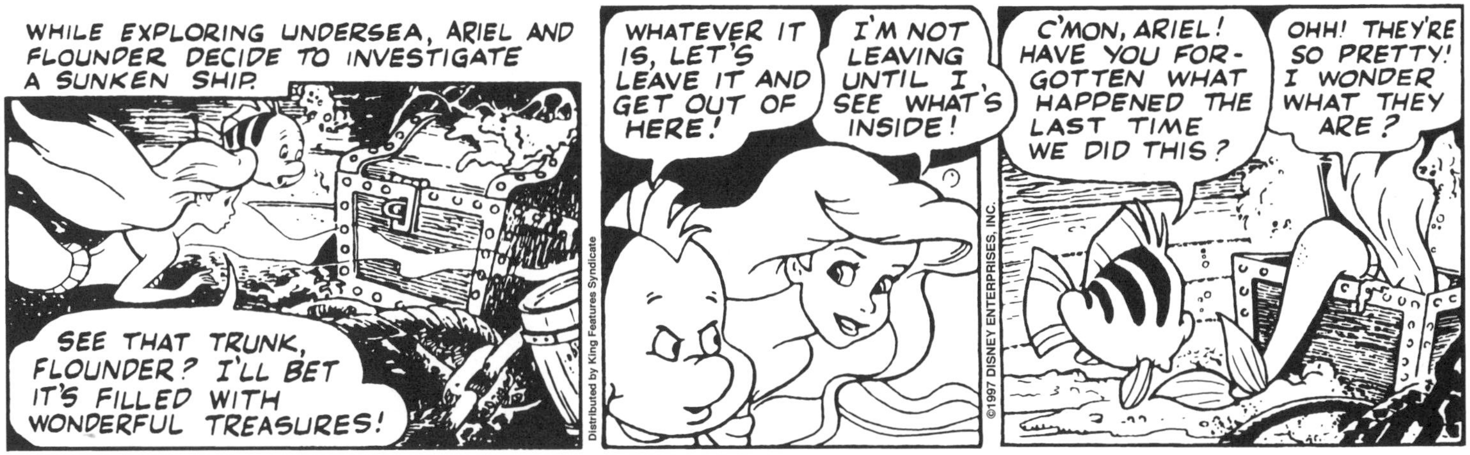
WHILE EXPLORING UNDERSEA, ARIEL AND FLOUNDER DECIDE TO INVESTIGATE A SUNKEN SHIP.
SEE THAT TRUNK, FLOUNDER? I'LL BET IT'S FILLED WITH WONDERFUL TREASURES!
Distributed by King Features Syndicate
WHATEVER IT IS, LET'S LEAVE IT AND GET OUT OF HERE!
I'M NOT LEAVING UNTIL I SEE WHAT'S INSIDE!
©1997 DISNEY ENTERPRISES, INC.
C'MON, ARIEL! HAVE YOU FORGOTTEN WHAT HAPPENED THE LAST TIME WE DID THIS?
OHH! THEY'RE SO PRETTY! I WONDER WHAT THEY ARE?

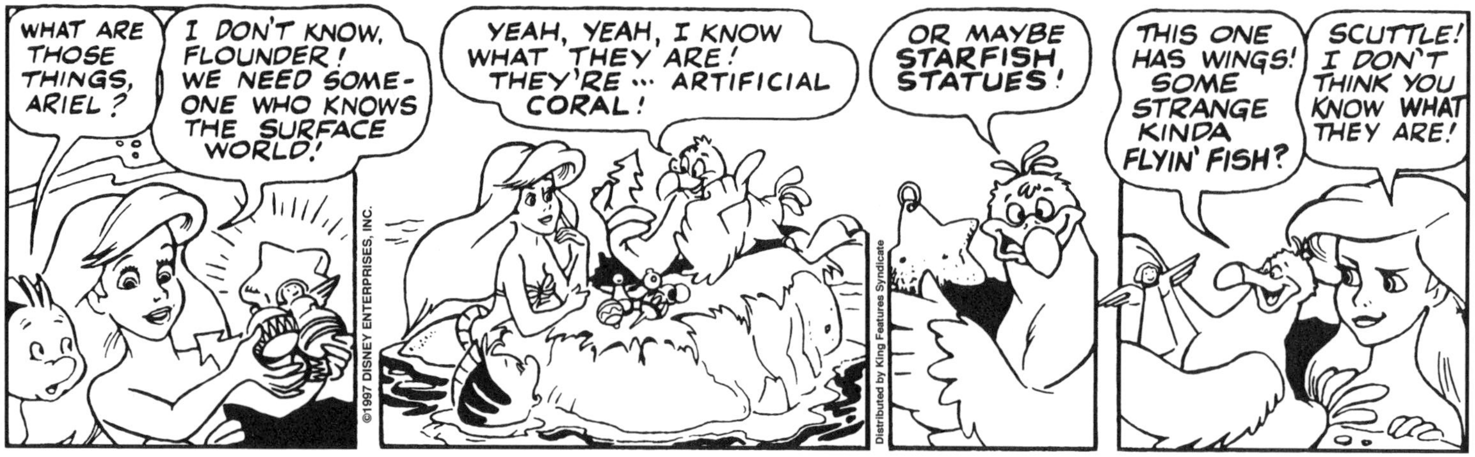
WHAT ARE THOSE THINGS, ARIEL?
I DON'T KNOW, FLOUNDER! WE NEED SOME-ONE WHO KNOWS THE SURFACE WORLD!
©1997 DISNEY ENTERPRISES, INC.
YEAH, YEAH, I KNOW WHAT THEY ARE! THEY'RE ... ARTIFICIAL CORAL!
Distributed by King Features Syndicate
OR MAYBE STARFISH STATUES!
THIS ONE HAS WINGS! SOME STRANGE KINDA FLYIN' FISH?
SCUTTLE! I DON'T THINK YOU KNOW WHAT THEY ARE!

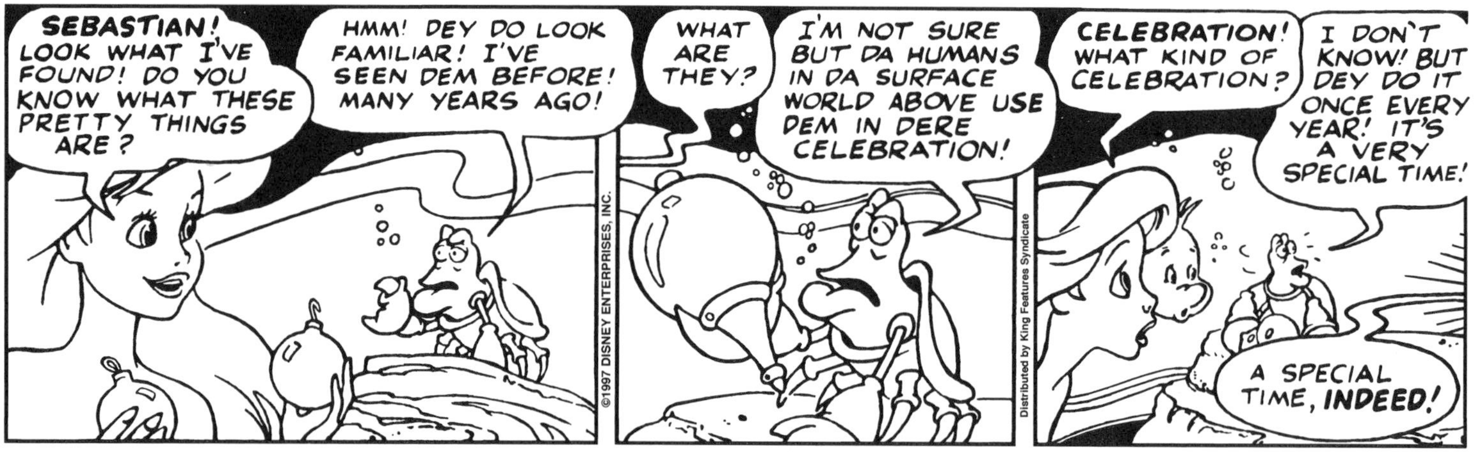
SEBASTIAN! LOOK WHAT I'VE FOUND! DO YOU KNOW WHAT THESE PRETTY THINGS ARE?
HMM! DEY DO LOOK FAMILIAR! I'VE SEEN DEM BEFORE! MANY YEARS AGO!
©1997 DISNEY ENTERPRISES, INC.
WHAT ARE THEY?
I'M NOT SURE BUT DA HUMANS IN DA SURFACE WORLD ABOVE USE DEM IN DERE CELEBRATION!
Distributed by King Features Syndicate
CELEBRATION! WHAT KIND OF CELEBRATION?
I DON'T KNOW! BUT DEY DO IT ONCE EVERY YEAR! IT'S A VERY SPECIAL TIME!
A SPECIAL TIME, INDEED!

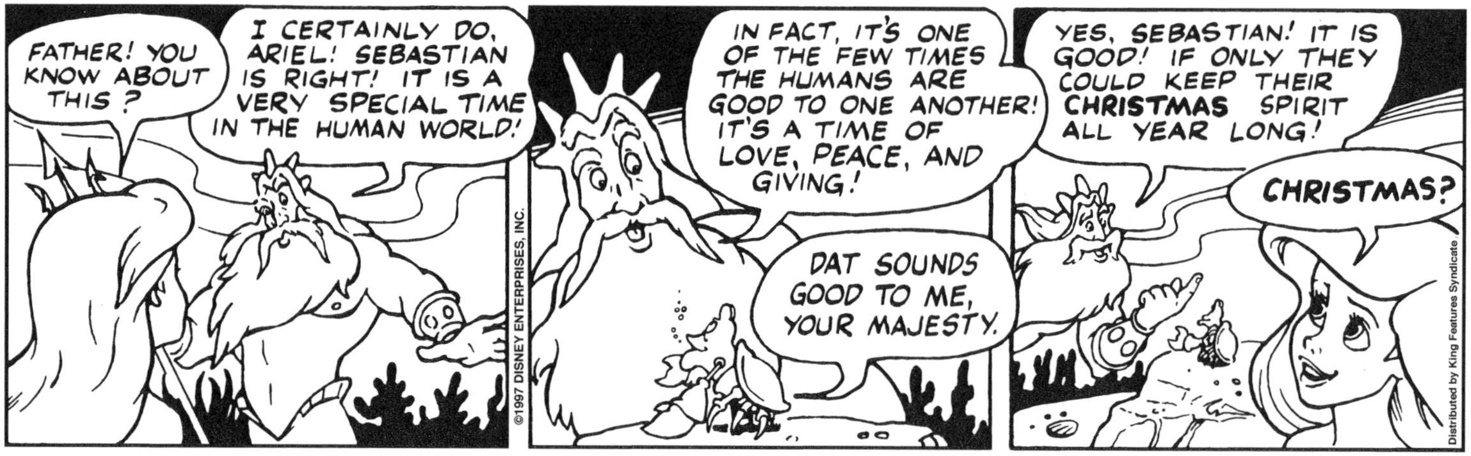
FATHER! YOU KNOW ABOUT THIS?
I CERTAINLY DO, ARIEL! SEBASTIAN IS RIGHT! IT IS A VERY SPECIAL TIME IN THE HUMAN WORLD!
©1997 DISNEY ENTERPRISES, INC.
IN FACT, IT'S ONE OF THE FEW TIMES THE HUMANS ARE GOOD TO ONE ANOTHER! IT'S A TIME OF LOVE, PEACE, AND GIVING!
DAT SOUNDS GOOD TO ME, YOUR MAJESTY.
YES, SEBASTIAN! IT IS GOOD! IF ONLY THEY COULD KEEP THEIR CHRISTMAS SPIRIT ALL YEAR LONG!
CHRISTMAS?
Distributed by King Features Syndicate

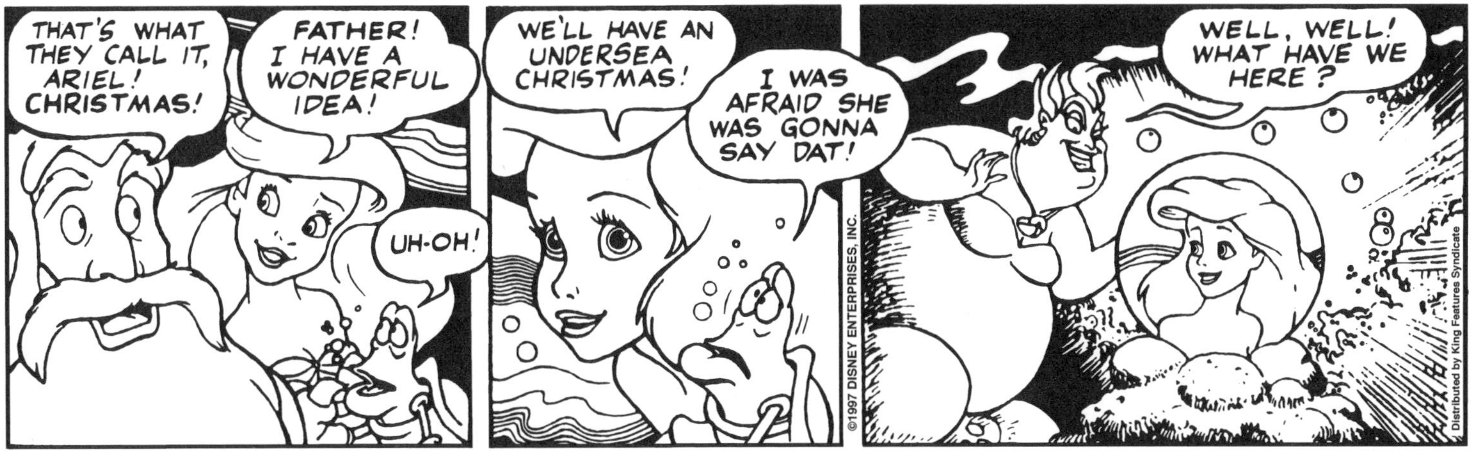
THAT'S WHAT THEY CALL IT, ARIEL! CHRISTMAS!
FATHER! I HAVE A WONDERFUL IDEA!
UH-OH!
WE'LL HAVE AN UNDERSEA CHRISTMAS!
I WAS AFRAID SHE WAS GONNA SAY DAT!
©1997 DISNEY ENTERPRISES, INC.
WELL, WELL! WHAT HAVE WE HERE?
Distributed by King Features Syndicate

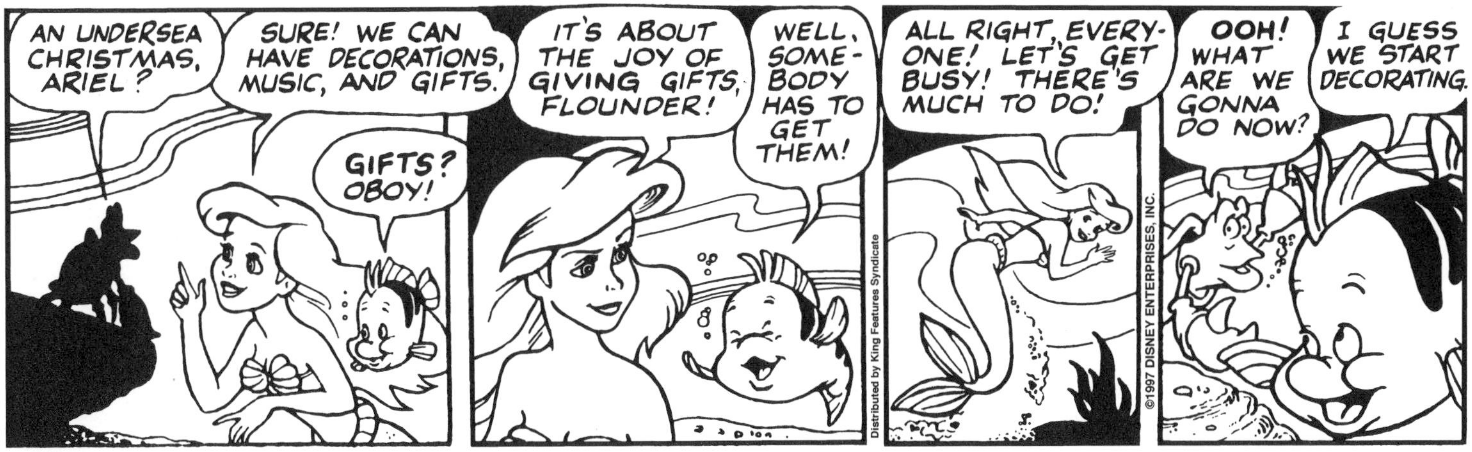
AN UNDERSEA CHRISTMAS, ARIEL?
SURE! WE CAN HAVE DECORATIONS, MUSIC, AND GIFTS.
GIFTS? OBOY!
IT'S ABOUT THE JOY OF GIVING GIFTS, FLOUNDER!
WELL, SOME-BODY HAS TO GET THEM!
Distributed by King Features Syndicate
ALL RIGHT, EVERY-ONE! LET'S GET BUSY! THERE'S MUCH TO DO!
©1997 DISNEY ENTERPRISES, INC.
OOH! WHAT ARE WE GONNA DO NOW?
I GUESS WE START DECORATING.

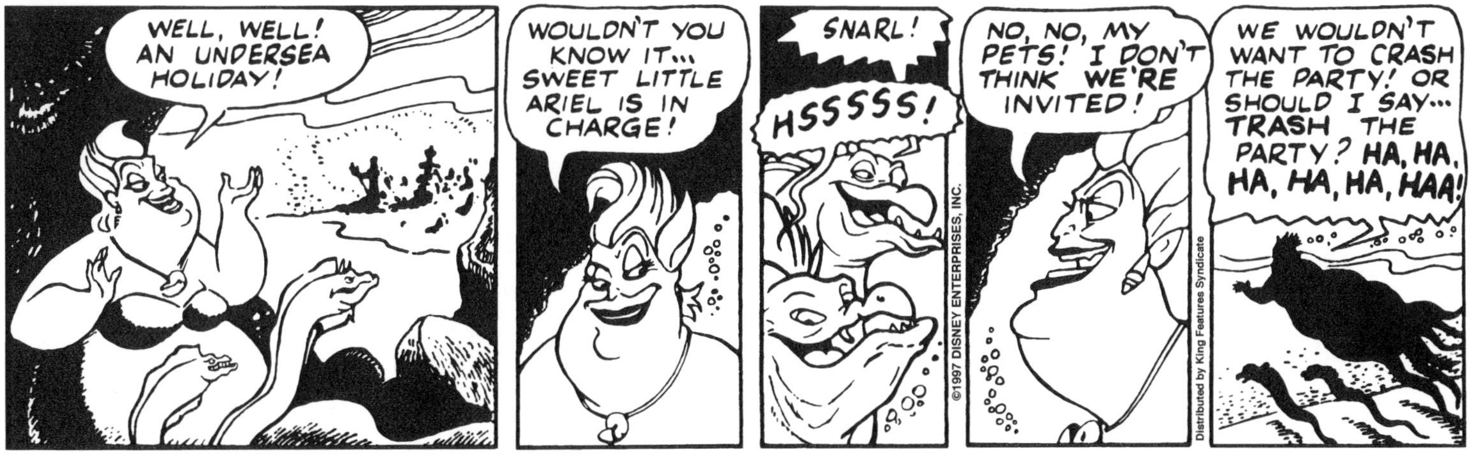
WELL, WELL! AN UNDERSEA HOLIDAY!
WOULDN'T YOU KNOW IT... SWEET LITTLE ARIEL IS IN CHARGE!
SNARL!
HSSSSS!
©1997 DISNEY ENTERPRISES, INC.
NO, NO, MY PETS! I DON'T THINK WE'RE INVITED!
Distributed by King Features Syndicate
WE WOULDN'T WANT TO CRASH THE PARTY! OR SHOULD I SAY... TRASH THE PARTY? HA, HA, HA, HA, HA, HAA!

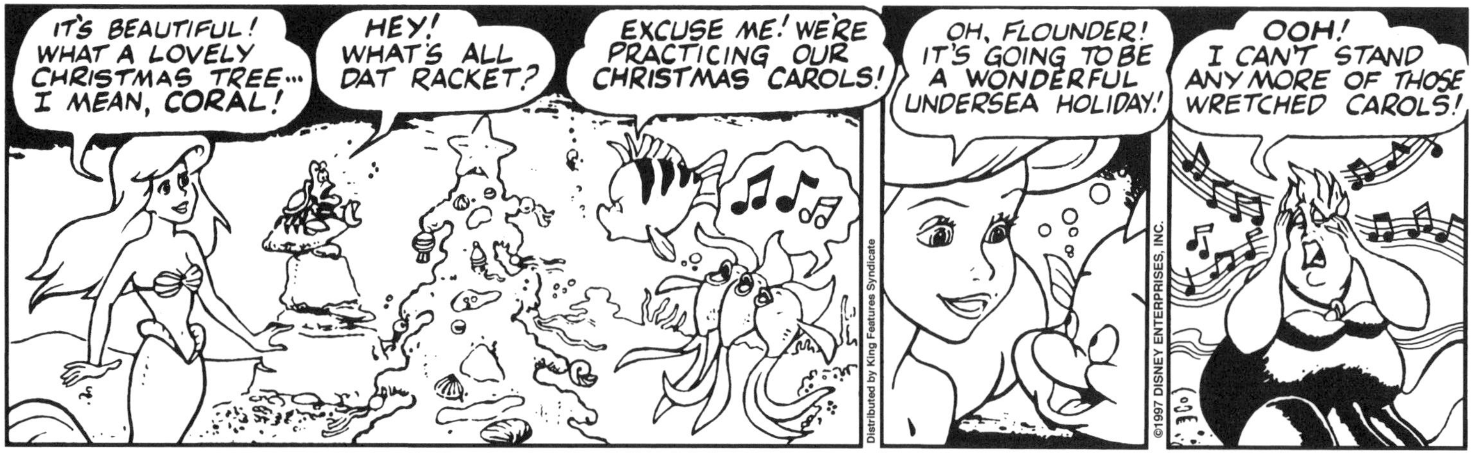
IT'S BEAUTIFUL! WHAT A LOVELY CHRISTMAS TREE... I MEAN, CORAL!
HEY! WHAT'S ALL DAT RACKET?
EXCUSE ME! WE'RE PRACTICING OUR CHRISTMAS CAROLS!
Distributed by King Features Syndicate
OH, FLOUNDER! IT'S GOING TO BE A WONDERFUL UNDERSEA HOLIDAY!
©1997 DISNEY ENTERPRISES, INC.
OOH! I CAN'T STAND ANYMORE OF THOSE WRETCHED CAROLS!

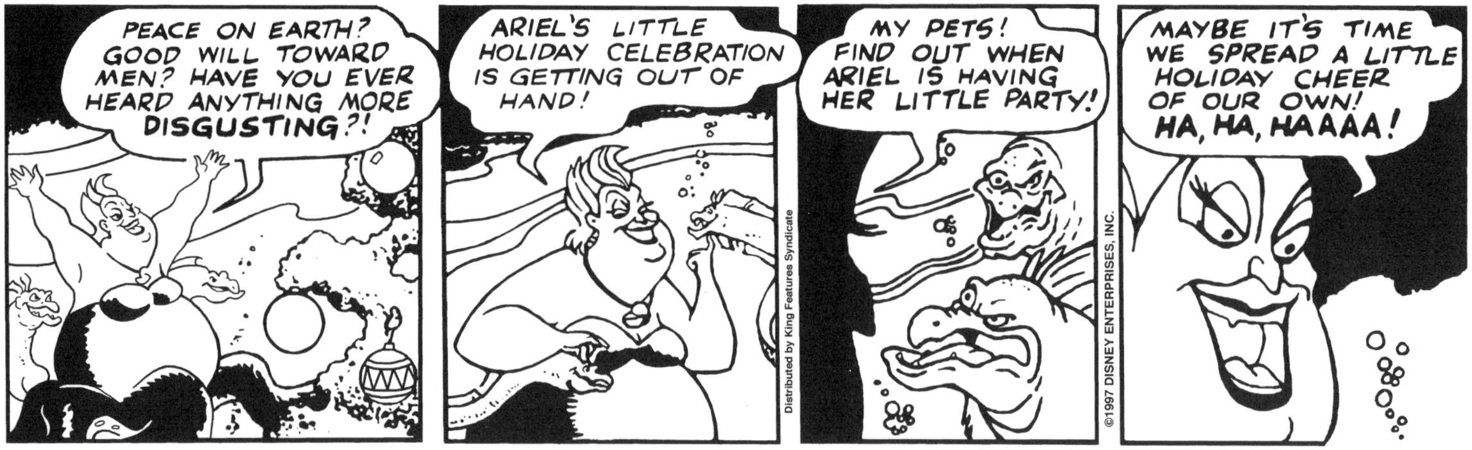
PEACE ON EARTH? GOOD WILL TOWARD MEN? HAVE YOU EVER HEARD ANYTHING MORE DISGUSTING?!
ARIEL'S LITTLE HOLIDAY CELEBRATION IS GETTING OUT OF HAND!
Distributed by King Features Syndicate
MY PETS! FIND OUT WHEN ARIEL IS HAVING HER LITTLE PARTY!
©1997 DISNEY ENTERPRISES, INC.
MAYBE IT'S TIME WE SPREAD A LITTLE HOLIDAY CHEER OF OUR OWN! HA, HA, HAAAA!

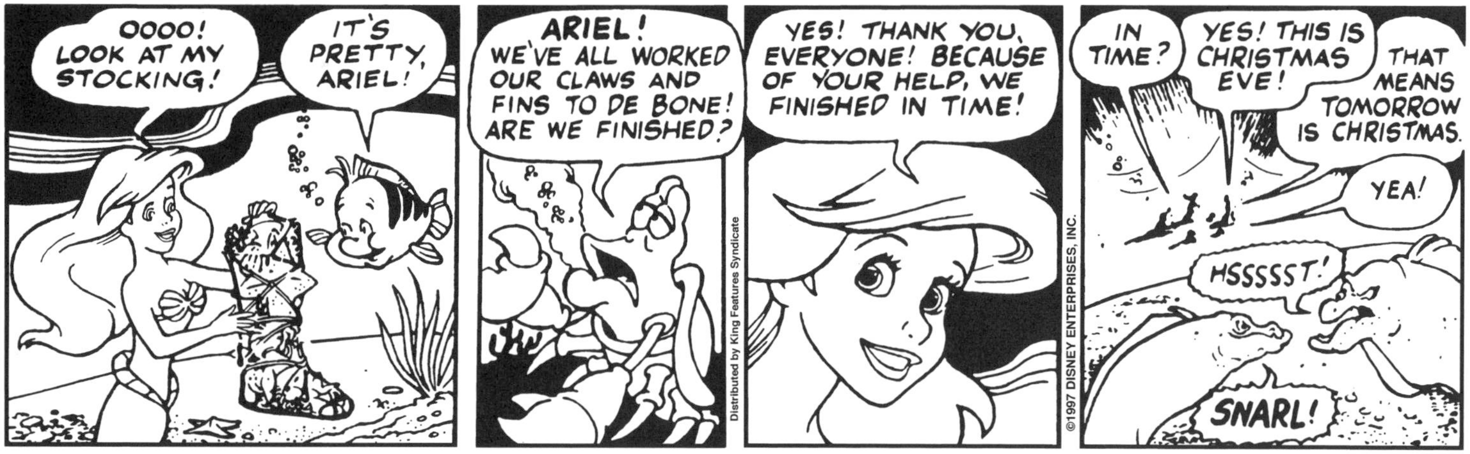
OOOO! LOOK AT MY STOCKING!
IT'S PRETTY, ARIEL!
ARIEL! WE'VE ALL WORKED OUR CLAWS AND FINS TO DE BONE! ARE WE FINISHED?
Distributed by King Features Syndicate
YES! THANK YOU, EVERYONE! BECAUSE OF YOUR HELP, WE FINISHED IN TIME!
©1997 DISNEY ENTERPRISES, INC.
IN TIME?
YES! THIS IS CHRISTMAS EVE!
THAT MEANS TOMORROW IS CHRISTMAS.
YEA!
HSSSSST!
SNARL!

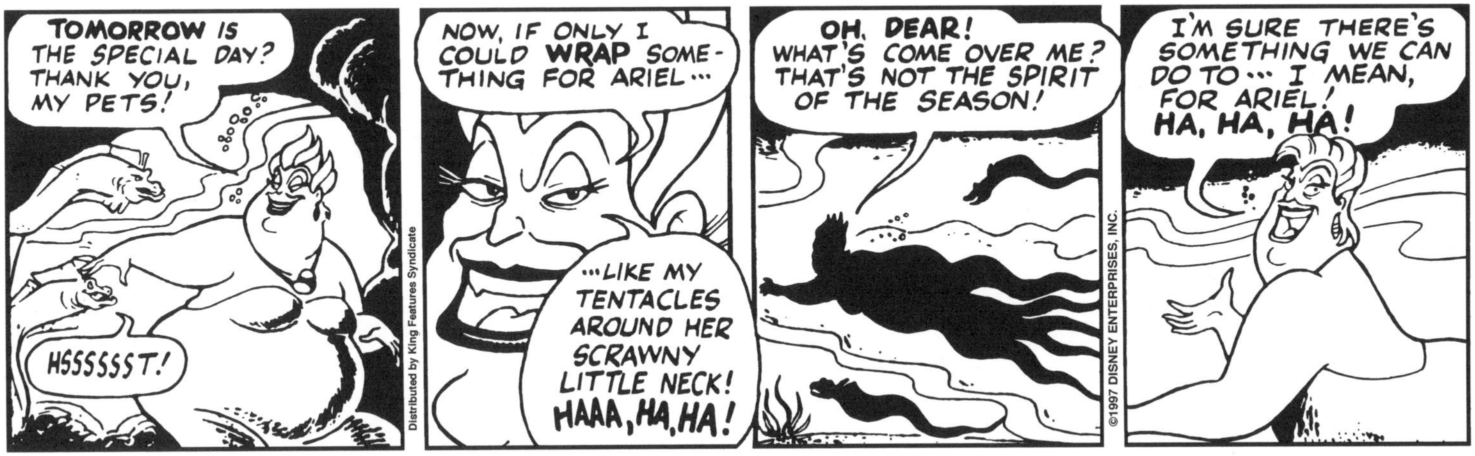
TOMORROW IS THE SPECIAL DAY? THANK YOU, MY PETS!
HSSSSSST!
NOW, IF ONLY I COULD WRAP SOME-THING FOR ARIEL...
...LIKE MY TENTACLES AROUND HER SCRAWNY LITTLE NECK! HAAA, HA, HA!
Distributed by King Features Syndicate
OH, DEAR! WHAT'S COME OVER ME? THAT'S NOT THE SPIRIT OF THE SEASON!
©1997 DISNEY ENTERPRISES, INC.
I'M SURE THERE'S SOMETHING WE CAN DO TO... I MEAN, FOR ARIEL! HA, HA, HA!

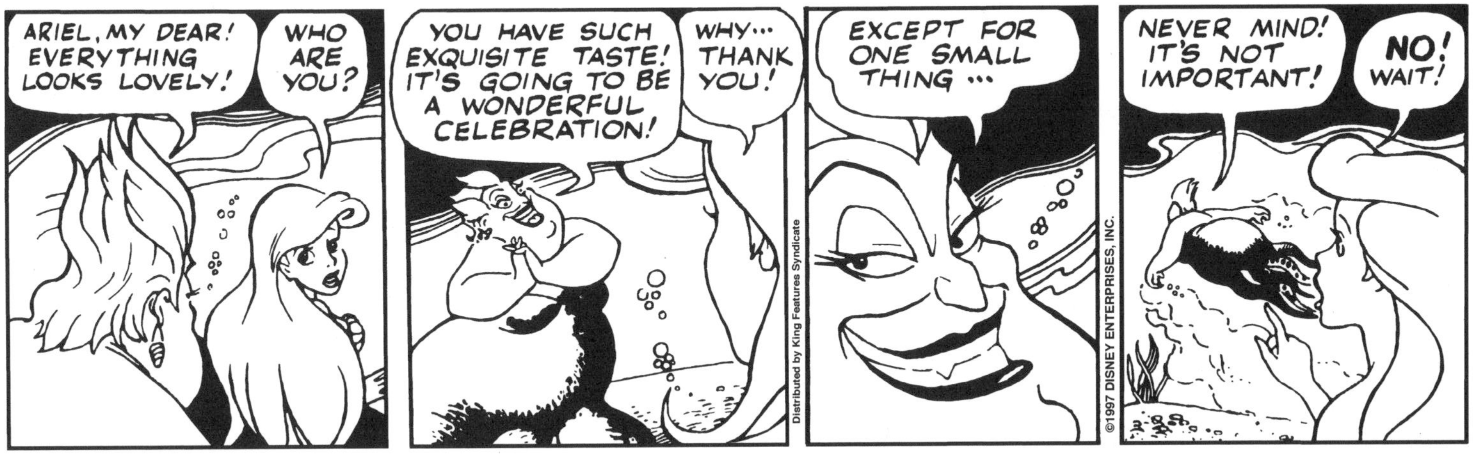
ARIEL, MY DEAR! EVERYTHING LOOKS LOVELY!
WHO ARE YOU?
YOU HAVE SUCH EXQUISITE TASTE! IT'S GOING TO BE A WONDERFUL CELEBRATION!
WHY... THANK YOU!
Distributed by King Features Syndicate
EXCEPT FOR ONE SMALL THING...
©1997 DISNEY ENTERPRISES, INC.
NEVER MIND! IT'S NOT IMPORTANT!
NO! WAIT!

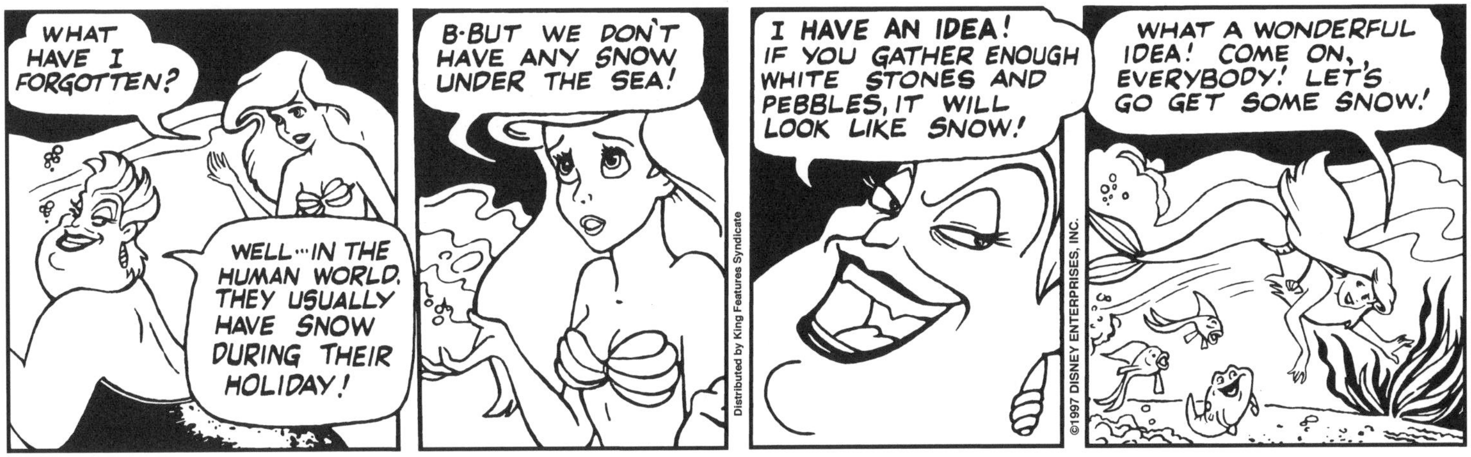
WHAT HAVE I FORGOTTEN?
WELL... IN THE HUMAN WORLD, THEY USUALLY HAVE SNOW DURING THEIR HOLIDAY!
B-BUT WE DON'T HAVE ANY SNOW UNDER THE SEA!
Distributed by King Features Syndicate
I HAVE AN IDEA! IF YOU GATHER ENOUGH WHITE STONES AND PEBBLES, IT WILL LOOK LIKE SNOW!
©1997 DISNEY ENTERPRISES, INC.
WHAT A WONDERFUL IDEA! COME ON, EVERYBODY! LET'S GO GET SOME SNOW!

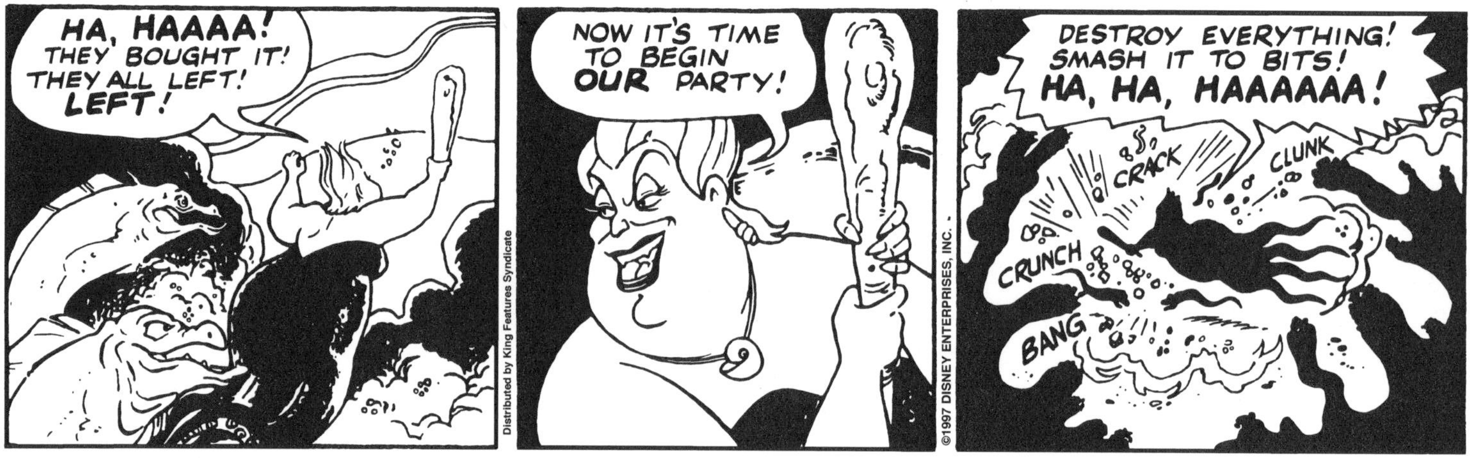
HA, HAAAA! THEY BOUGHT IT! THEY ALL LEFT! LEFT!
Distributed by King Features Syndicate
NOW IT'S TIME TO BEGIN OUR PARTY!
©1997 DISNEY ENTERPRISES, INC.
DESTROY EVERYTHING! SMASH IT TO BITS! HA, HA, HAAAAAA!
CRACK
CLUNK
CRUNCH
BANG

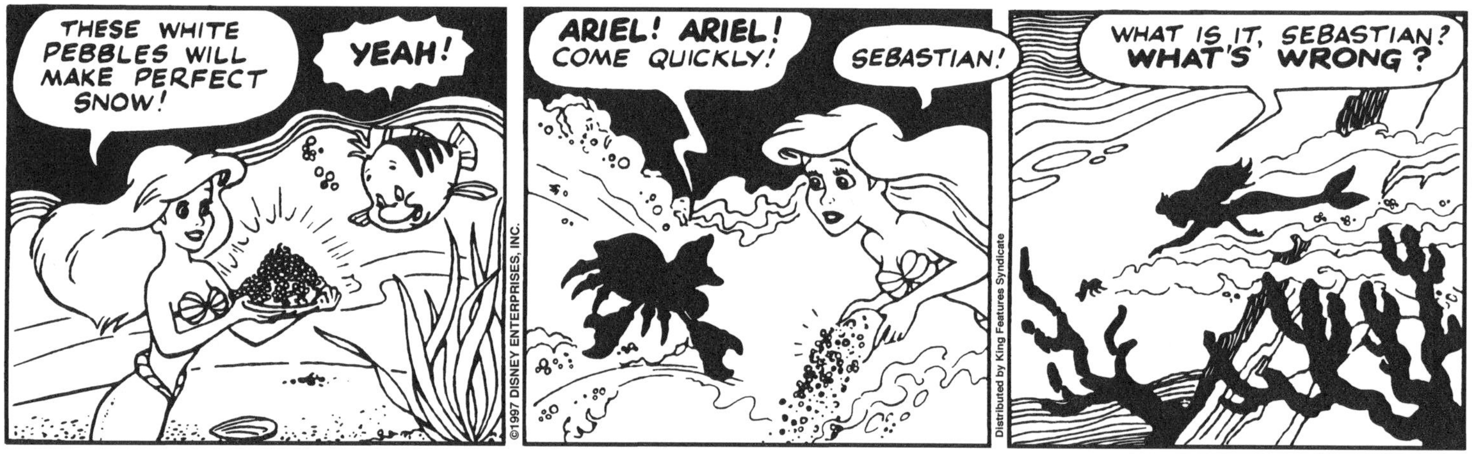
THESE WHITE PEBBLES WILL MAKE PERFECT SNOW!
YEAH!
©1997 DISNEY ENTERPRISES, INC.
ARIEL! ARIEL! COME QUICKLY!
SEBASTIAN!
Distributed by King Features Syndicate
WHAT IS IT, SEBASTIAN? WHAT'S WRONG?

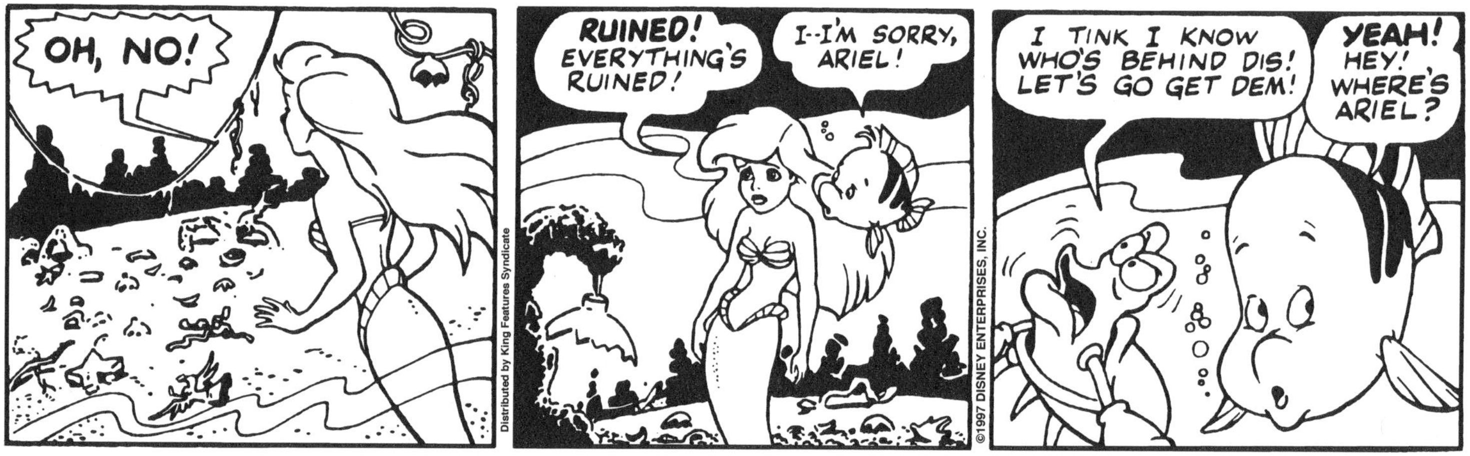
OH, NO!
Distributed by King Features Syndicate
RUINED! EVERYTHING'S RUINED!
I-I'M SORRY, ARIEL!
©1997 DISNEY ENTERPRISES, INC.
I TINK I KNOW WHO'S BEHIND DIS! LET'S GO GET DEM!
YEAH! HEY! WHERE'S ARIEL?

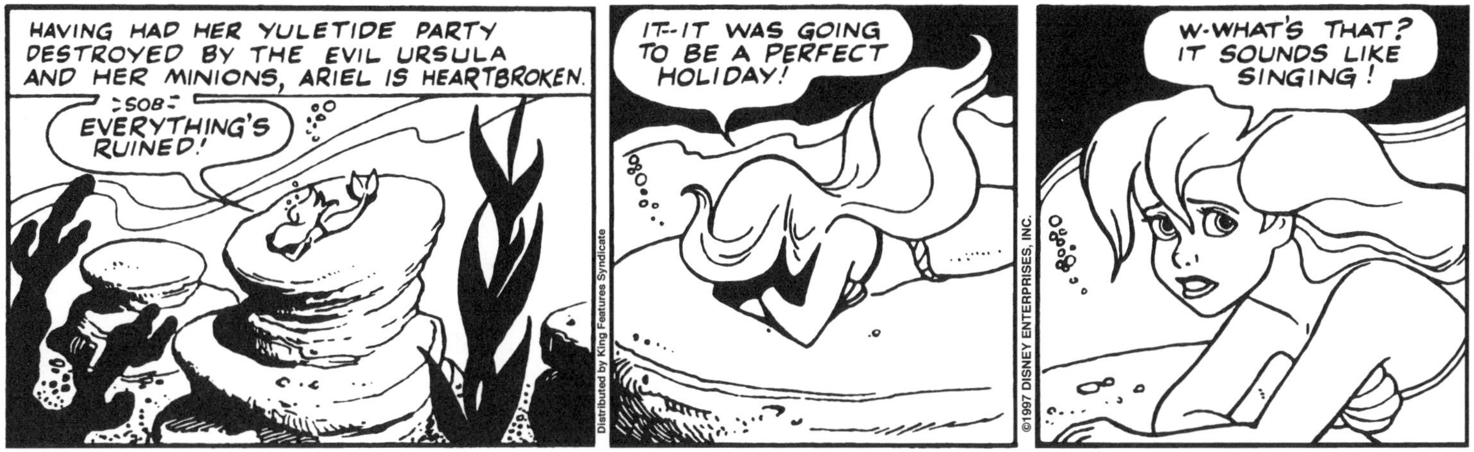
HAVING HAD HER YULETIDE PARTY DESTROYED BY THE EVIL URSULA AND HER MINIONS, ARIEL IS HEARTBROKEN.
-SOB- EVERYTHING'S RUINED!
Distributed by King Features Syndicate
IT-IT WAS GOING TO BE A PERFECT HOLIDAY!
©1997 DISNEY ENTERPRISES, INC.
W-WHAT'S THAT? IT SOUNDS LIKE SINGING!

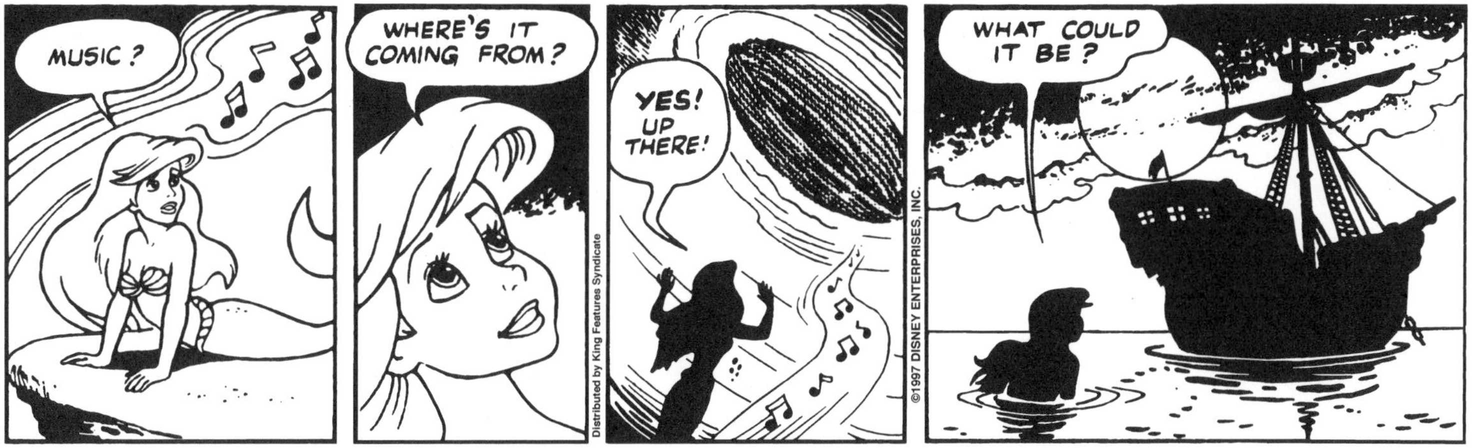
MUSIC?
WHERE'S IT COMING FROM?
Distributed by King Features Syndicate
YES! UP THERE!
©1997 DISNEY ENTERPRISES, INC.
WHAT COULD IT BE?

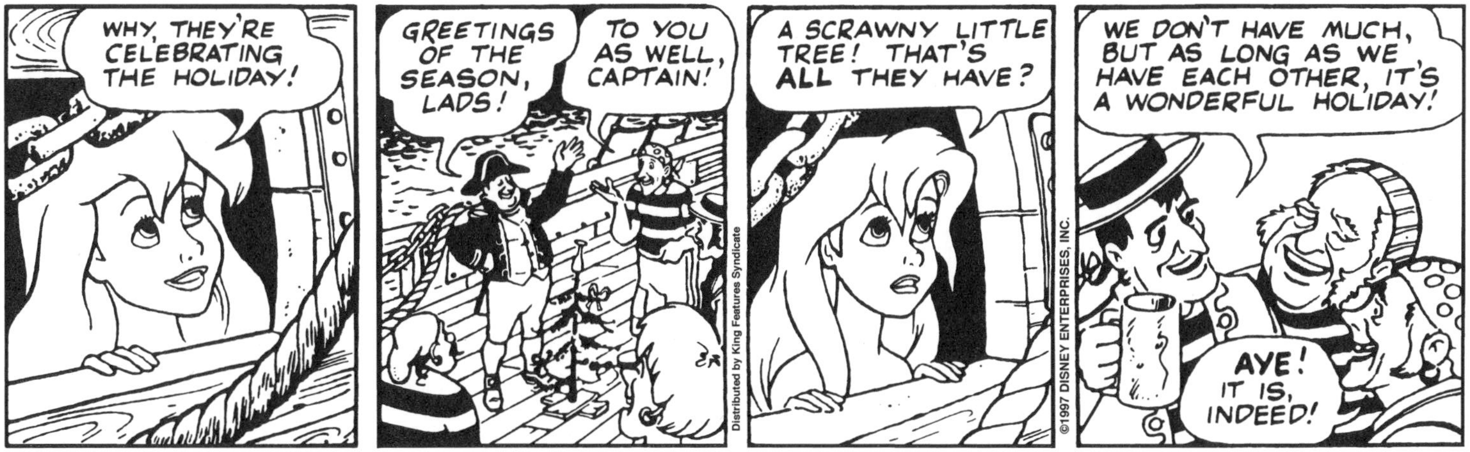
WHY, THEY'RE CELEBRATING THE HOLIDAY!
GREETINGS OF THE SEASON, LADS!
TO YOU AS WELL, CAPTAIN!
Distributed by King Features Syndicate
A SCRAWNY LITTLE TREE! THAT'S ALL THEY HAVE?
©1997 DISNEY ENTERPRISES, INC.
WE DON'T HAVE MUCH, BUT AS LONG AS WE HAVE EACH OTHER, IT'S A WONDERFUL HOLIDAY!
AYE! IT IS, INDEED!

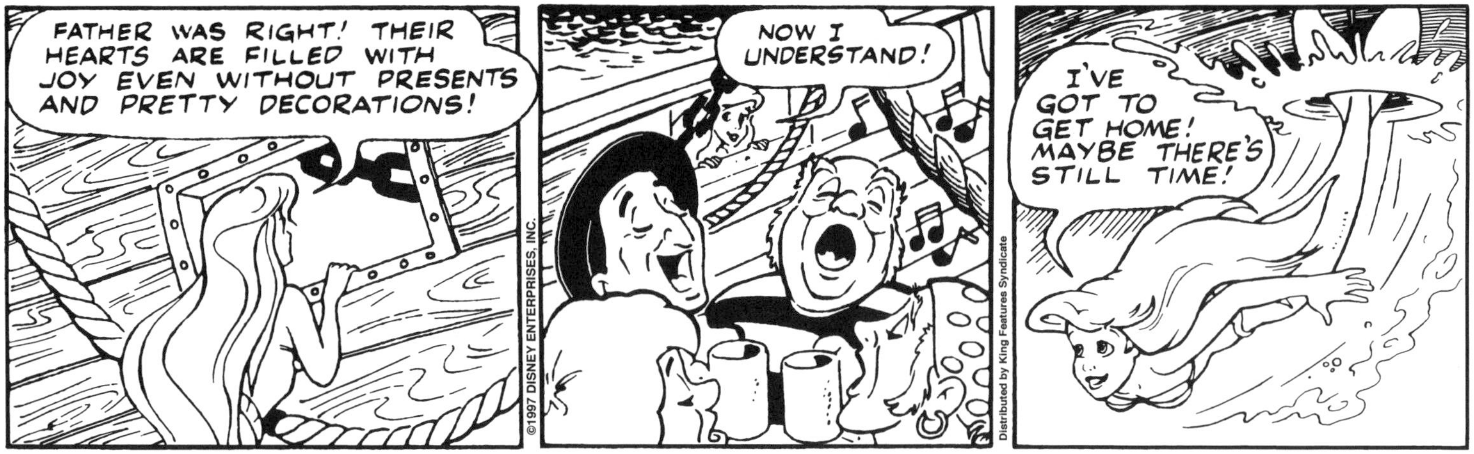
FATHER WAS RIGHT! THEIR HEARTS ARE FILLED WITH JOY EVEN WITHOUT PRESENTS AND PRETTY DECORATIONS!
©1997 DISNEY ENTERPRISES, INC.
NOW I UNDERSTAND!
Distributed by King Features Syndicate
I'VE GOT TO GET HOME! MAYBE THERE'S STILL TIME!

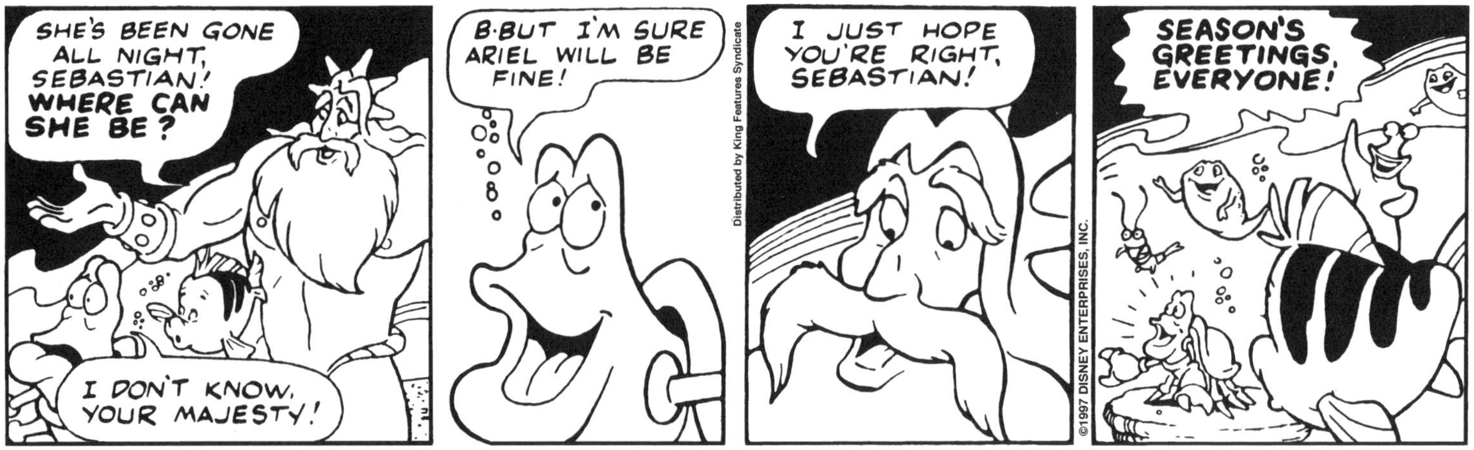
SHE'S BEEN GONE ALL NIGHT, SEBASTIAN! **WHERE CAN SHE BE?**
I DON'T KNOW, YOUR MAJESTY!
B-BUT I'M SURE ARIEL WILL BE FINE!
Distributed by King Features Syndicate
I JUST HOPE YOU'RE RIGHT, SEBASTIAN!
©1997 DISNEY ENTERPRISES, INC.
SEASON'S GREETINGS, EVERYONE!

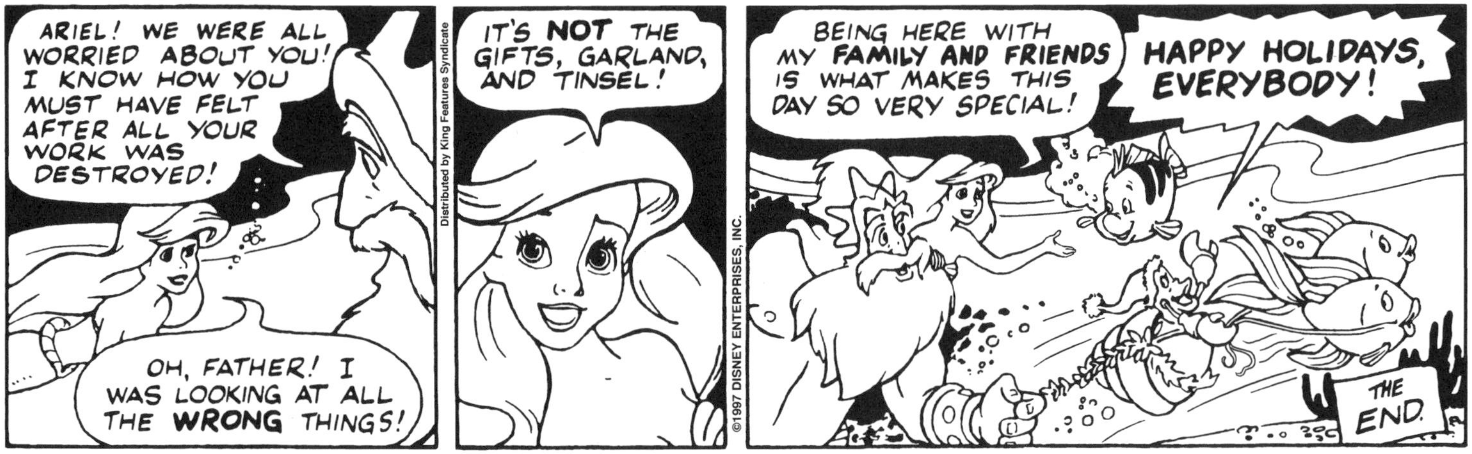
ARIEL! WE WERE ALL WORRIED ABOUT YOU! I KNOW HOW YOU MUST HAVE FELT AFTER ALL YOUR WORK WAS DESTROYED!
OH, FATHER! I WAS LOOKING AT ALL THE **WRONG** THINGS!
Distributed by King Features Syndicate
IT'S **NOT** THE GIFTS, GARLAND, AND TINSEL!
©1997 DISNEY ENTERPRISES, INC.
BEING HERE WITH MY **FAMILY AND FRIENDS** IS WHAT MAKES THIS DAY SO VERY SPECIAL!
HAPPY HOLIDAYS, EVERYBODY!
THE END.